The Boundless Sea

The Two Italies
Frederick II: A Medieval Emperor
A Mediterranean Emporium
The Western Mediterranean Kingdoms
The Discovery of Mankind: Atlantic Encounters
in the Age of Columbus
The Great Sea: A Human History of the Mediterranean

DAVID ABULAFIA

The Boundless Sea

A Human History of the Oceans

ALLEN LANE

an imprint of

PENGUIN BOOKS

ALLEN LANE

UK | USA | Canada | Ireland | Australia
India | New Zealand | South Africa

Allen Lane is part of the Penguin Random House group of companies
whose addresses can be found at global.penguinrandomhouse.com.

First published in the United States of America by Oxford University Press 2019
First published in Great Britain by Allen Lane 2019
001

Set in 10.2/13.5 pt Sabon LT Std
Typeset by Jouve (UK), Milton Keynes
Printed and bound in Great Britain by Clays Ltd, Elcograf S.p.A.

A CIP catalogue record for this book is available from the British Library

ISBN: 978-1-846-14508-7

My bounty is as boundless as the sea
(Shakespeare)

Praeceptoribus Paulinis

PNB CED TEBH AHM JRMS PFT

necnon INRD

Contents

PART FOUR
Oceans in Conversation, AD 1492–1900

PART FIVE
The Oceans Contained, AD 1850–2000

List of Illustrations

Every effort has been made to contact all copyright holders. The publishers will be pleased to amend in future editions any errors or omissions brought to their attention.

1. *Tepuke*, a modern canoe based on ancient Polynesian design, built by the Vaka Taumako Project. (Photo: Wade Fairley, 2008)
2. Rock carving of a boat with a claw sail, possibly dating back to the early settlements, Olowalu, Maui. (Photo: Bill Brooks/Alamy)
3. Relief carving of the Egyptian fleet during the expedition to the Land of Punt, 18th Dynasty. Funerary temple of Hatshepsut, Deir El-Bahri, Egypt. (Photo: Prisma Archivo/Alamy)
4. Drawing of relief carving of the Egyptian fleet in the expedition to the Land of Punt. (Photo: Interfoto/Alamy)
5. Seal depicting four gazelles, Dilmun (Bahrain), late third millennium BC. National Museum, Bahrain. (Photo: by kind courtesy Harriet E. W. Crawford, author of *Early Dilmun Seals from Saar: Art and Commerce in Bronze Age Bahrain*)
6. Seal showing a sewn-plank ship, India (probably Bengal or Andhra Pradesh), 4th–5th century AD, found in Thailand. National Museum, Bangkok. (Photo: Thierry Ollivier)
7. Coin of the Emperor Victorinus, minted in Cologne, c.AD 270, found in Thailand. National Museum, U Thong, Suphanburi, Thailand, bequeathed by Air Vice Marshal Montri Haanawichai. (Photo: Thierry Ollivier)
8. Terracotta head of a Persian or Arab merchant, Western Thailand, 7th or 8th century AD. National Museum, Bangkok. (Photo: Thierry Ollivier)
9. Porcelain ewer, China (possibly Guangdong), c.AD 1000. British Museum, London. (Photo: © The Trustees of the British Museum)
10. Three Intaglios, Oc-èo site, My Lam Village, An Giang Provence, Fu Nan Period 6th century. Museum of Vietnamese History, Ho Chi Min City. (Photo: © Kaz Tsuruta)
11. 19th-century copy of an original copper plate from Kollam, south India, AD 849. Cambridge University Library, MS Oo.1.14. (Photo: By kind permission of the Syndics of Cambridge University Library)

Preface

In the making of connections between human societies, the role of the sea is particularly fascinating. Connections across large open spaces have brought together peoples, religions and civilizations in stimulating ways. Sometimes this has been through individual encounters, as travellers, including pilgrims and merchants, found themselves visiting alien environments; sometimes it has been the result of mass migrations that have changed the character of regions; sometimes it has been the result as much of the movement of goods as of people, when the inhabitants of distant lands saw, admired, and imported or copied the art works of another culture, or read its literature, or were taken aback by some rare and precious item that opened their eyes to its existence. Such contacts were made overland and up and down river systems, as well as by sea; but overland they were mediated by the cultures that lay along the routes being followed, whereas links across the sea could tie together very different worlds, as far apart as Portugal and Japan or Sweden and China.

This book is intended to sit alongside my earlier book, *The Great Sea: A Human History of the Mediterranean,* first published in 2011. Like that book, it is a human rather than a natural history, emphasizing the role of often adventurous traders in making and maintaining contact. Whereas the Mediterranean accounts for 0.8 per cent of the maritime surface of the globe, seas as a whole account for about 70 per cent of the world's surface, and most of this watery space consists of the vast open areas we call oceans. From outer space, the Earth is mainly blue. The oceans have distinct but gigantic wind systems, generated by the movement of air over vast masses of both warm and cold water: one has only to think of the seasonal monsoons in the Indian Ocean. The Roaring Forties that would helpfully sweep sailing vessels from the Atlantic into the Indian Ocean were the same winds that made entry into the Pacific from the southern Atlantic, around Cape Horn, so frightening. Currents such as the Gulf Stream, which keeps the British Isles relatively warm, or the not dissimilar Kuroshio or Japan current, stretch across thousands of miles.[1] We divide

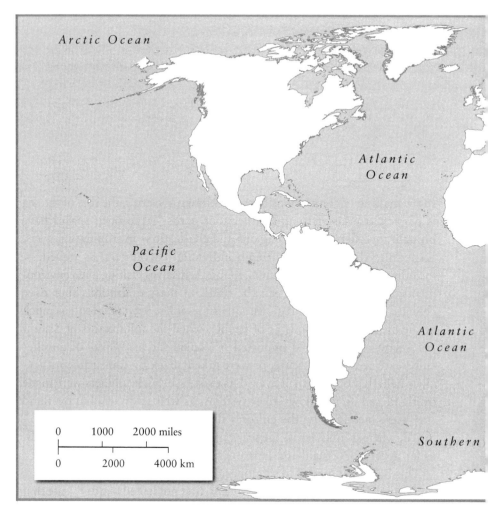

the all-encompassing global sea into the three great oceans; but ancient geographers, with some justice, imagined it to be a single *Okeanos* of intermingled waters, a concept revived in modern use of the term 'World Ocean' to describe all the oceans as a single unit.[2]

The three major oceans have attracted increasing interest as the study of maritime history has expanded beyond what might more properly be called naval history, which concentrates on warfare (or peace-keeping) on the surface of the sea, to greater involvement with the wider questions of how, why and when people crossed large maritime spaces, whether for trade or as migrants, and what sort of interdependence was created between lands far apart from one another by this movement across the oceans. This has led to debates about the origins of globalization, some

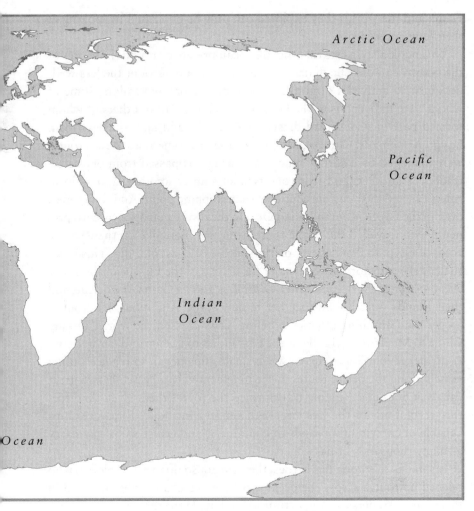

of which have been conducted at cross-purposes, since the concept of 'globalization' is a vague one that can be defined in many ways. A question related to the theme of globalization that has often been raised is why Europeans opened up routes across the world after 1500, in the wake of Columbus and da Gama, while the Chinese, under Zheng He, launched extraordinarily ambitious voyages in the early fifteenth century that came to a sudden stop. This leads into a range of questions about the 'Great Divergence' between Europe and Asia or other continents, although, as with globalization, much depends on the criteria one adopts to measure the process. This book makes plain the dramatic effect of the entry of European traders and conquerors into distant oceans following the voyages of Columbus and da Gama, while also insisting that Columbus, da

Gama and the worlds they explored can only be explained by looking at their long antecedents.

This book also insists that the European presence around the shores of the oceans can only be understood by taking into account the less well-documented activities of non-European merchants and sailors, some of whom were indigenous to the lands in which they lived, others of whom formed part of widespread diasporas – Greeks and later on Jews from Egypt, Armenians, Chinese, Malays, and so on. Sometimes the sea routes were managed by a sort of relay team, as goods passed from one set of traders to another, and from one type of ship to another, and as local rulers exacted their customs duties at each stopping point. And sometimes, even in the Greco-Roman Indian Ocean, they were managed by entrepreneurs who travelled the whole route from, say, Bereniké on the Red Sea coast of Egypt to Pondicherry on the south-east coast of India. This is not to deny the transformative effect of the arrival of the Europeans in nearly every corner of the oceans. After Columbus and da Gama, the oceans and their islands were bound together in new ways. Ambitious new routes, longer than anything attempted before, criss-crossed the world, linking China to Mexico via Manila or the East Indies to Lisbon and Amsterdam. A further revolution occurred when steamships began to replace sailing vessels along the ocean routes in the nineteenth century, while two great canals at Suez and Panama transformed the routes themselves. And further revolutions in the late twentieth century introduced massive ships capable of carrying thousands of containers, and cruise ships that carry as many thousands of passengers.

Insofar as this book has heroes, they are not so often the explorers who opened up routes across the oceans, but the merchants who followed in their wake. Traders saw opportunities and made the tenuous links established by those who found new routes into firm, reliable and regular connections, whether in the era of Greco-Roman commerce across the Indian Ocean or in the aftermath of Columbus's voyages to the Caribbean. They settled down in trading stations that became major ports – Aden, Havana, Macau, Melaka, Quanzhou, to give just a few examples. But right up to the early days of the steamship maritime travel involved risk from shipwreck, piracy, disease, and – not least – rajahs, sultans and other rulers who saw merchants as fair game in their hunt for funds, which they raised from confiscation as well as taxation. The history of long-distance travel across the seas is the history of people willing to take risks, both physical and financial: men (mainly) who gambled on business opportunities in faraway lands, in the search for profit. Using a loose definition, we could call these people capitalists, businessmen reinvesting their resources in the hope of generating greater and greater wealth. Such people are visible at the very start of the history of Indian Ocean trade, in the cities of Bronze Age Mesopotamia, and throughout the centuries that followed.

The history of maritime trade is not all concerned with exotic items such as the spices of the Indies. Increasingly, historians have laid emphasis on humdrum local trade networks bringing primary produce – grain, oil, wine, wool, and so on – towards markets and towns. Yet those looking for really big profits were tempted to stray much further afield, eventually creating links across the oceans that had the power to stimulate economic growth at both ends of lengthy lines of communication: cities in China producing fine porcelain, for instance, and cities in Holland buying large quantities of it. Sometimes trade was masked as the payment and receipt of tribute, particularly in medieval China and Japan. Princely palaces might set the agenda by making clear what exotic objects they craved, but rulers could never prevent their diplomats from trading on the side, and attempts to close ports only generated new unofficial ones, as at Quanzhou in medieval China, which became a meeting point for merchants from Java, Malaya, India, the Arab world, and even Venice and Genoa.

Alongside the peaceful merchants, to be sure, there were plenty of sea raiders, most famously the Vikings; but here too the search for profit made raiders into at least part-time traders. There is undeniable fascination in looking at the exotic objects and foodstuffs that were carried across some-times enormous distances, and in thinking about what these things meant to the people among whom they arrived – whether walrus tusks from Greenland or lacquer boxes from Japan or sacks of cloves and nutmeg from the Moluccas. The eternal appeal of rare and beautiful items from far-off lands, along with curiosity about those lands, prompted merchants and mariners to try out new routes and to chance upon unknown lands (not least the two vast continents of the Americas). But it is also important not to forget the human beings who were themselves treated as disposable cargo – notably the millions of slaves who were carried across the early modern Atlantic. When looking for female travellers across the oceans, it is here that we shall find significant numbers of women. Women also appear among the migrants who arrived in places as diverse as Viking Iceland, Puritan North America and Māori New Zealand – even among the Norse travellers who attempted to settle in North America in the Viking age. Too often, though, the documents are silent about the women's history of the sea, other than legends about sea goddesses.

It is instructive to compare movement across the sea with movement across land. Many of the problems of carrying large quantities of goods and people overland were only resolved when railways were constructed in the nineteenth century, facilitating, for instance, the transfer of vast amounts of tea from remote quarters of India to the Indian Ocean and, ultimately, the teeming tea shops of London. Further back in time, the famous Silk Road that linked China to western Asia and, at some periods, Europe as well, flourished for relatively short periods, notably the ninth century and the late thirteenth to early fourteenth century. Its cultural significance is not in doubt, as the ideas and arts of Buddhism and Islam were carried across the expanse of Eurasia. But the Silk Road carried only a small fraction of the goods that could be and were conveyed by ship from China and south-east Asia by way of Malaya and India towards Egypt and the Mediterranean. This 'Silk Route of the Sea' that crossed the Indian Ocean has an uninterrupted history going back 2,000 years, to the age of Emperor Augustus, and the astonishing quantities of porcelain found on board ships wrecked in the South China Sea makes this point as clearly as anything: the hundreds of thousands of plates and bowls loaded on late medieval junks for transfer to the Red Sea simply could not have been carried overland on the backs of camels – one eleventh-century wreck contains half a million pieces of Chinese porcelain. Chinese porcelain was greatly prized in medieval Egypt, to the point where attempts were made to imitate it: at least 700,000 sherds have been found underneath Fustat, or Old Cairo. These figures are nothing compared to the quantities of porcelain shipped from China to Europe in the eighteenth century.

Historians have debated when and how widely the terms 'Atlantic', 'Pacific' and 'Indian' Ocean came into use, and whether they are appropriate. After all, the Indian Ocean bathes east Africa, Arabia and the Malay Peninsula as well as India; and early modern geographers tended to distinguish the northern Atlantic from its southern or 'Ethiopic' twin. The central and southern Pacific was often described as the 'South Sea'. Nonetheless, schools of Atlantic, Pacific and Indian Ocean historians have emerged; indeed, a recent survey showed that more publications about Atlantic history have been juddering off the presses than publications about the Mediterranean, which was long the favourite pool of water among historians, beginning with the pioneering writings of Fernand Braudel. 'We are all Atlanticists now,' the eminent Harvard historian David Armitage proclaimed, as he set out different ways of writing Atlantic history, whether comparative, local or transatlantic (that is, about connections across the ocean).[3] But the sense that maritime history is being compartmentalized into four main disconnected chunks, Atlantic, Pacific, Indian Ocean and Mediterranean, has attracted increasing criticism; their interaction with one another must not be ignored. This book is an attempt to write the history of the three great oceans together. That does mean, in the millennia before Columbus, treating them separately, because they constituted three spheres of human movement that were not directly connected to one another by the movement of humans from one ocean to another, even though goods (mainly spices) reached the ports of the medieval Atlantic from as far away as the East Indies, having passed through a non-oceanic sea, the Mediterranean. After 1492, though, I have laid as strong an emphasis as possible on the interconnections between the oceans, so that even chapters about (say) the English and their rivals in the seventeenth-century Caribbean have been written with an eye on the global context. This makes the last five centuries more manageable. But it also represents reality: the oceans had become intimately interconnected, as a quick glance at the Portuguese, Dutch or Danish maritime networks quickly shows. This interconnection of the oceans was the great revolution that followed the discovery of the Americas and of the route from Europe to Asia by way of the southern tip of Africa, and it has received too little attention.

One important theme of this book is the human occupation of previously uninhabited islands, beginning with the extraordinary achievements of Polynesian sailors in settling the scattered islands of the largest ocean of all. Within the Atlantic, Madeira, the Azores, the Cape Verde Islands and St Helena had an importance far greater than their tiny size would suggest. In the Indian Ocean, one very large island, Madagascar, was a miniature continent with its own distinctive wildlife; it was settled by Austronesians from the East Indies during what historians of Europe call the Middle Ages. In some cases humans, and the animals they brought with them, totally transformed these island environments: the most famous example is the extinction of the dodo after humans occupied Mauritius.[4] Inevitably, though, immeasurably more has to be left out than included, and I have not attempted to write what pretends to be a *complete* or *comprehensive* history of the oceans, which would take up many volumes, but a *rounded* history of the oceans that homes in on what I think are the best illustrations of long-distance maritime connections. Some of these, such as the trade in Chinese tea and porcelain, had an enormous cultural and economic impact on places as far from China as Sweden and New England.

Another reservation about the way oceanic history has been written concerns its chronological span. The Atlantic, in particular, has suffered from an assumption that its history only begins with Columbus, allowing for a quick reference to the brief stay of Norse men and women somewhere in North America (though their stay in Greenland was by no means brief,

lasting over 400 years). Quite apart from evidence for trade and migration
in the pre-Columbian Caribbean, going back millennia, we have the rich
evidence for trade in eastern Atlantic waters from Neolithic times onwards,
linking Orkney and Shetland, as well as Denmark, to Atlantic France and
Iberia; much later, we can watch the Hanseatic merchants of the late Middle Ages trading from Danzig to Lisbon. The close relationship between
the Baltic and the North Sea, and then the Atlantic beyond, means that
these seas need to be considered as extensions of the Atlantic. The ancient
and medieval Indian Ocean has attracted much more attention than the
early Atlantic, and it too has extensions. One is the South China Sea, at
the entrance to the Pacific; but the seas all the way up to Korea and Japan
have interacted strongly since ancient times. These seas have looked away
from the Pacific of the Polynesian navigators, which was a separate world
consisting of often tiny islands scattered across a vast and, it must have
seemed, unbounded space. For this reason the maritime history of Japan,
Korea and China before about 1500 will be found in the Indian Ocean
chapters. Another extension is the Red Sea, which gave access to Egypt
and beyond that the Mediterranean; that too receives close attention in
this book.[5] As for the Arctic Ocean, if it can be called an ocean rather
than, as some have argued, a confined and largely frozen 'Mediterranean'
stuck between Eurasia and North America, the history of the human
presence has been told here through the repeated attempts to carve a route
through Arctic ice and water to the Far East by way of the North-West
and North-East Passages – if they existed. And the Southern or Antarctic
Ocean is simply a label for the cold waters at the bottom of our planet,
which are in effect part of the three major oceans, starting somewhere in
the latitude of New Zealand – though the search for the assumed Southern
Continent, which was thought to be much more temperate than Antarctica, does feature here.[6]

There is a great deal that this book is not about. Although it is, as the
subtitle insists, a 'human history', rather than natural history, it is not
concerned with the impact of human beings on the oceanic environment –
what has been described as the 'submarine' history of the oceans. This
book remains on the surface of the sea, with the exception of frequent use
of evidence from shipwrecks, the remains of ships that were after all
intended to stay on the surface. Ocean ecology is an important and urgent
issue in the twenty-first century and has been discussed with passion by
environmental experts.[7] Humans are destroying the oceans by dumping
plastics and effluents, and marine life pays a heavy price. Climate change
may at last render accessible sea routes carrying large quantities of goods
through the Arctic Ocean from Europe to and from the Far East. These

are crucial matters, but this book is concerned instead with contacts between humans across the oceans, linking shores and islands, mostly in epochs when human impact on the seas themselves was limited, even though human impact on mid-sea islands such as Madeira or Hawai'i was massive. I am also not much concerned with fishing, except where it has generated long-distance contacts; so I do have a fair amount to say about herrings and cod in the Atlantic aboard Hanseatic and Dutch vessels, and about English ships that probably ventured close to Newfoundland fishing for cod before John Cabot's arrival there in 1497. Later, American whalers briefly feature, in a discussion of the worldwide trade in whale products, and here one can point to severe ecological damage well before 1900, as whale populations of large areas of sea were hunted almost to extinction.

One very important result of the creation of new contacts between distant landmasses has been the importation and cultivation of alien crops far from their place of origin. The great example is the potato, a South American product that became the staple food of the Irish poor (with tragic consequences); well before that, the Islamic world provided conduits carrying oranges and bananas as far west as Spain, while Asiatic sugar struck roots in the Mediterranean, in Atlantic islands such as Madeira, and eventually in Brazil and the Caribbean. Only part of that story can be told here, the part concerned with the routes these products took. A classic work by Alfred Crosby and a pioneering study of the movement of foodstuffs within Islamic lands by Andrew Watson have looked at the bigger picture.[8] These were developments in which the Mediterranean was heavily involved; but in this book the Mediterranean lurks offstage. As a largely closed inland sea, long and narrow, with constant and intensive contact between its shores, it is as different in character from the open oceans as mountains are from plains. Besides, I have written about it at length in my previous book.

Writing this book has taken me into periods and places that are far removed from the Mediterranean. But the origins of this book lie in an essay simply entitled 'Mediterraneans' that I wrote for a book entitled *Rethinking the Mediterranean*, edited by William Harris of Columbia University, in which I compared the 'classic' Mediterranean with other closed or semi-closed watery spaces such as the Baltic and the Caribbean.[9] This led me deeper into the history of other, much larger seas, as did a book I wrote about a very different aspect of the Atlantic at the end of the Middle Ages entitled *The Discovery of Mankind*, in which I observed the surprise of western Europeans at their first encounters with peoples in the Canaries, the Caribbean and Brazil, peoples whose very existence they had not suspected.[10] Longer ago, I wrote a lengthy chapter about 'Asia, Africa and the Trade of Medieval Europe' for a new edition of part of the *Cambridge Economic History of Europe*, at the invitation of the great economic historian Sir Michael ('Munia') Postan.[11] Over lunch in Peterhouse (where I observed some of its Fellows cruelly baiting the Master, Hugh Trevor-Roper) Postan asked me what I would be saying in my chapter about medieval Malaya. I realized that I knew nothing about it, and started on a trail that led me via the problematic empire of Śri Vijaya in Sumatra to early Singapore and Melaka as they are portrayed in the remarkable *Malay Annals*; this interest in early south-east Asia has never abated.

This book, written mainly in Cambridge and to a lesser extent in Oxford, could not have been written without the facilities and companionship that Gonville and Caius College, Cambridge, supplies. I am particularly grateful to one of the college's generous alumni, Andreas Papathomas, for the foundation of the Papathomas Professorial Fellowship, which it is my privilege to hold; it reflects his own interest, as a prominent shipowner, in maritime affairs. Among the college's many History Fellows, Sujit Sivasundaram and Bronwen Everill have been ready with thoughts and suggestions, and I have benefited also from many conversations with John Casey, Ruth Scurr and K. C. Lin, and with members of the ever-lively Sherrington Society, who listened to an early draft of parts of my Polynesian chapters. Two Oxford colleges have very kindly opened their doors to me, for which I am very grateful: my thanks are due to the Principals (Alan Bowman and John Bowers) and Fellows of Brasenose College, sister college to Caius; and to the Principals (Frances Lannon and Alan Rusbridger) and Fellows of Lady Margaret Hall, not least Anna Sapir Abulafia, Professorial Fellow and President of the Common Room at LMH. I am also very grateful to those who have attended talks based on the book or concerned with my views about how to write maritime history at (among other places) the Legatum Institute and Erasmus Forum in London, the British Academy Soirée, the èStoria Festival in Gorizia, the Perse School, North London Collegiate School, St Paul's School, the Universidade Nova in Lisbon, the University of Greifswald (with warm thanks to Michael North), the University of Rostock, the University of Heidelberg, John Darwin's seminar at Oxford, the Oxford Centre for Hebrew and Jewish Studies, Harvard University, Princeton University, La Trobe University (Melbourne), Nanyang Technological University and the Asiatic Museum, both in Singapore, the College of Europe in Warsaw (with particular thanks to Richard Butterwick-Pawlikowski and Nicolas Nizowicz), and the newly founded University of Gibraltar, with which it is a special pleasure to be closely associated, thanks to Daniella Tilbury, its imaginative and energetic first Vice-Chancellor. On the other side of the strait, I am grateful to the Instituto de Estudios Ceutíes in Ceuta for its hospitality in 2015, during the conference commemorating the Portuguese conquest of the town in 1415. Members of the Algae, a literary circle at the Athenaeum in London, notably Colin Renfrew, Roger Knight, David Cordingly and Felipe Fernández-Armesto, have fruitfully discussed aspects of this book with me as it was being put together. John Guy kindly explained the upbringing of Sir Thomas Gresham. I am also grateful to Arturo Giráldez for advice about the Manila galleons, to Andrew Lambert for his thoughts about the nature of sea power, to Barry Cunliffe for discussing the early Atlantic with me, to Sidney Corcos (Jerusalem) for rich data about the Corcos family, and to Chang Na (Nanjing) for her enthusiastic and invaluable help with the *pinyin* version of Chinese names.

Special thanks are due to those who have been of such enormous help during my travels across the oceans, beginning with a word of praise for the British diplomatic service in several countries. I was seated by chance next to Steven Fisher, formerly British ambassador to the Dominican Republic, at a dinner in Cambridge, and he urged me to visit Santo Domingo, with the largest, oldest and best-preserved colonial quarter anywhere in the Americas; he made contact for me with Chris Campbell, his successor, who introduced me to Thelma de la Rosa García, a counsellor at the embassy, and she provided outstanding support in the Dominican Republic, especially in arranging museum visits and a very valuable meeting with Juan Rodríguez Acosta, director of the Museo del Hombre Dominicano. Steven Fisher also arranged for me to meet His Excellency Bernardo Vega, president of the Academia Dominicana de História, where it was my privilege to lecture; and he introduced me to Esteban Priete Vicioso, architect in charge of the cathedral and other ancient buildings in Santo Domingo, who very kindly took me around all the major sites. To all of these, as well as the delightful staff of the magnificent Nicolás de Ovando hotel in Santo Domingo, based in Ovando's palace dating back to 1502, my immeasurable thanks for their exceptional hospitality. Joe Moshenska in Cambridge provided valuable information on the eve of my visit to Santo Domingo. I also received very generous help during my visit to the Cape Verde Islands, thanks to the enthusiastic support of Marie-Louise Sørensen and Chris Evans, the leaders of the archaeological team from Cambridge that has been excavating the earliest European church in the Tropics at Cidade Velha. José Silva Lima and Jaylson Monteiro, from the Ministry of Culture, very kindly showed me the World Heritage Site at Cidade Velha and the museums in Praia.

On the other side of the world, A. T. H. (Tony) Smith welcomed me to Wellington, New Zealand, and James Kane showed me places I needed to see in Sydney, NSW. Judge William Waung was a delightful host in Hong Kong, showing me the splendid new maritime museum with which he has been closely involved; my warm thanks too to Arun and Christine Nigam, Anthony Phillips, Paul Serfaty and the Royal Geographical Society (Hong Kong). In Singapore, Antony Phillipson, British High Commissioner, directed me to the Fort Cannon excavations; John Miksic enlightened me about his exciting discoveries; Patricia Welch was very hospitable during my two visits to the city-state; Andrea Nanetti was my kind host at Nanyang Technological University. My wife and I benefited from the limitless hospitality of Hiroshi Takayama and his colleagues and students in Tokyo, Kamakura, Kyoto and Nara, including Minoru Ozawa, Keizo Asaji and Noriko Yamabe – it is difficult to express sufficient thanks when the hospitality is so generous and gracious. The same applies to my hosts in Shanghai, Hangzhou and Nanjing: Michelle Garnaut and the staff of the Shanghai Literary Festival; Lu Dapeng from the Social Sciences Academic Press; Dr Jia Min from Fudan University; Prof. Zhu Feng and Dr Chang Na from Nanjing University; and many others.

I am particularly grateful to the Joukowsky Institute, under Peter van Dommelen, and John Carter Brown Library, under Neil Safier, for their welcome to Brown University in Rhode Island during November– December 2017 – for listening to my presentations and also for allowing me to spend an all-too-brief period as a Fellow at the JCB using its superb collection of material from the earliest days of European exploration onwards. I owe my invitation to Brown to two very delightful hosts, Miguel-Ángel Cau Ontiveros and Catalina Mas Florit. David González Cruz of the University of Huelva very amiably guided me and others around the sites connected to Columbus, including Palos and the convent of La Rábida, during a lively conference to mark the 525th anniversary of Columbus's arrival in the New World. Yasir Suleiman and Paul Anderson at the Centre for Islamic Studies in Cambridge arranged a number of visits by a team from Cambridge to universities in the Islamic world; particular thanks go to my fellow travellers Alice Wilson, now at the University of Sussex, in Morocco and the UAE, and Yonatan Mendel, then at the Centre for Jewish–Arab Relations at the Van Leer Institute in Israel and now at the University of the Negev, in the UAE and Qatar. The Lines from Seamus Heaney's translation of *Beowulf* are quoted by permission of Faber and Faber.

None of this would have been possible without the support of my editor at Penguin Books, Stuart Proffitt, and my editor at Oxford University Press

New York, Tim Bent, nor that of my agent, Bill Hamilton of A. M. Heath. Candida Brazil has done superb work on my text, as have my copy-editor, Mark Handsley, and proofreaders, Stephen Ryan and Chris Shaw, my picture researcher, Cecilia Mackay, and Ben Sinyor at Penguin. I could not be in better hands. Nor could I have written the book without the unrivalled facilities of Cambridge University Library, and of Gonville and Caius College Library, where special thanks are due to Mark Statham. Meanwhile Anna has put up with all the maritime museums and book-shops that somehow intruded into our holidays abroad. My thanks to her and my daughters, Bianca and Rosa, are 'as boundless as the sea'.

David Abulafia
Gonville and Caius College, Cambridge
8 May 2019

Note on Transliteration and Dating

The transliteration of the names of people and places is a nightmare in a book that covers such a long period and embraces so many cultures, as well as changes of regime. I have tried to combine authenticity with clarity. With Greek names, I have preferred forms closer to the original Greek sounds than the Latinized forms long in use: *Periplous* for a book in Greek describing maritime routes, rather than the bastardized form *Periplus*; *Herodotos* not *Herodotus*. Old Norse names have been kept as close as possible to what is in the sources (omitting the final -r of the nominative form); and, now that Icelandic crime stories are widely read, I am confident people can cope with Ð and ð (soft 'th' as in 'that') and Þ and þ (hard 'th' as in 'thin'), valuable letters which are a sad loss from the English alphabet. Turkish ı is a short vowel similar to the 'i' in 'sir', c is 'j' and ç is 'ch'. I have rendered Polynesian glottal stops with a ', though I am aware that many transcriptions use ', which I have used for Arabic names to represent the guttural sound known as *'ayin*.

Place names are particularly difficult; some have been officially changed only in recent times, even if they have more ancient origins (*Essaouira* for *Mogador*; *Mumbai* for *Bombay*; *Sri Lanka* for *Ceylon*; *Gdansk* for *Danzig*), and I have sometimes switched back and forth. Where European and indigenous names are very similar I have preferred the indigenous version, if it is in current use: *Melaka* rather than *Malacca*, recognizing that the city originated a hundred years before the Portuguese conquest (but one still talks of the 'Malacca Strait'); *Macau* rather than *Macao*. I have alternated between *New Zealand* and the lovely Māori name *Aotearoa* ('Long White Cloud'). *Guangzhou* became known to westerners as *Canton*, a Portuguese corruption of *Guangdong* (the name of the wider region); but it would be perverse to call ancient Guangzhou 'Canton', so I have used 'Canton' only when writing about the period of intensive European trade up the Pearl River. Generally, I have done my best to use modern *pinyin* spelling of Chinese names, so *Zheng He* instead of *Cheng Ho* for the famous admiral, and *Quanzhou* rather than the older transliteration of *Ch'üan-chou*, even though the 'q' sound in *pinyin* is closer to 'ch' or 'ts' than to 'k'. The Korean pirate Chang Pogo is, however, generally known by the old version of his name, which I have preferred.

Nowadays it is quite common to find BCE and CE being used instead of BC and AD, even though the actual date remains exactly the same. Since, for those who do not want to use a Christian dating system, BC could stand for 'Backward Chronology' just as well as 'Before Christ', and AD could stand for 'Accepted Date' instead of *Anno Domini*, I have retained the traditional forms. BP, on the other hand, signifies 'Before the Present', and is used by archaeologists among others, generally calculating backwards from 1950, so not quite the 'present'.

PART ONE

The Oldest Ocean: The Pacific, *176,000 BC–AD 1350*

I

The Oldest Ocean

I

The Pacific Ocean is far and away the largest ocean, covering a third of the Earth's surface, and the distance from Sumatra to the Ecuadorian shore at the Equator is around 18,000 kilometres. Even if Polynesian sailors may, very occasionally, have landed on the shores of South America, regular contact between the opposing shores was non-existent before the Spaniards launched their Manila galleons linking the Philippines to Mexico in the sixteenth century. In the midst of the sea there lie the hundreds of islands in the dozens of archipelagoes that make up Polynesia, Micronesia and Melanesia, three broadly defined zones whose ethnic distinctiveness from one another was much exaggerated by nineteenth-century anthropologists. Some strings of islands, such as the Solomon Islands, are closely enough packed for the inhabitants to be able to see or in some other way detect the presence of close neighbours. Others, notably Easter Island (Rapa Nui), the Hawai'i islands and New Zealand (Aotea-roa) are well out of sight of the nearest landfall, and in the last two cases some way removed from the main lines of Polynesian navigation.

Within this vast space, however, there are extraordinary signs of unity. Captain Cook and the natural historian Joseph Banks explored immense tracts of the Pacific in the years around 1770, and they were intrigued to find that the languages spoken in Hawai'i, Tahiti and New Zealand were mutually comprehensible and that what are now called 'Oceanic' languages were spoken across the whole north–south span of Polynesia. 'It is extraordinary,' Cook stated, 'that the same Nation each having adopted some peculiar custom or habit etcetera never the less a carefull observer will soon see the Affinity each has to the other.'[1] Indeed, later research showed that these languages were related to the language now spoken in Malaysia and Indonesia, and even to the Malagasy language of Madagas-car, all forming a large 'Austronesian' group of languages. Polynesian *vaka*

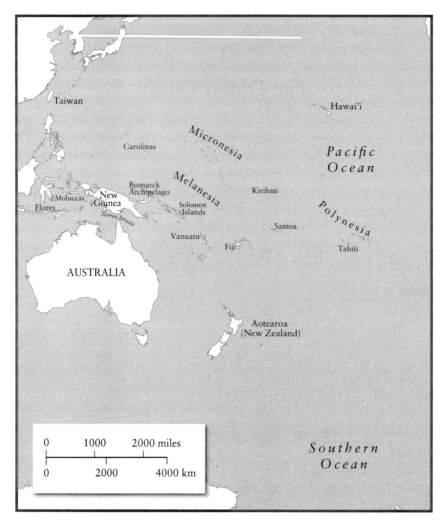

or *waka*, the term for a canoe, matches Malay *wangka*. Reconstruction of the ancestral Austronesian language, based on a remarkably rich common vocabulary concerned with ships and navigation, reveals that the distant ancestors of the Polynesians were maritime folk, who spoke of canoes commanded by captains with outriggers, platforms, masts, sails or paddles, and even carved prows and sterns.[2] That said, the eerily beautiful languages of the Pacific had broken away from those of south-east Asia many millennia ago, suggesting a common linguistic origin among the early settlers in the Pacific. It is important to use the phrase 'linguistic origin', because language and ethnic origins may be at odds with one another.[3]

The Pacific was both the first area far from land to be settled by humans, tens of thousands of years ago, and the last. That statement needs to be qualified: a few small, uninhabited islands in the Atlantic and in the Indian Ocean were settled from the fifteenth century onwards, places such as Madeira, St Helena, Mauritius, that will be seen to have played a role out of all proportion to their size in the maritime networks that came into existence as the Portuguese, the Dutch and other rivals claimed dominion over the sea routes across the world; and Antarctica, with no permanent population, can be left out of account. But the last substantial territory to be colonized by humans was New Zealand, whose settlement is variously dated somewhere between AD 950 and 1350. Even though many of its original inhabitants, who were at first concentrated on the warmer North Island, lived in the interior away from the sea, stories about the arrival of the first canoes abounded; the Māoris and the Hawai'ians had no doubt that they were migrants. Once settled, the Māoris lost interest in large ocean-going seacraft and confined their navigation to boats better suited to coastal waters. They could say little about the place from which they had come, other than that it bore the all-too-common name Hawaiki, a name that conveyed a sense of 'the place where our ancestors lived long ago'. Further north, among the chains of islands, movement across the sea generally remained the norm. These were people who treated the sea with the familiarity that Tuaregs might show to the Sahara desert or Incas to the mountains of the Andes: these were all obstacles that could be overcome, with precise knowledge, determination and confidence.

Over several millennia an extraordinary maritime culture had come into being, out in the middle of the ocean, lacking long shorelines, great ports and access to long rivers bringing produce down from the inner parts of massive continents. Instead, it was a largely interconnected world consisting of atolls, coral reefs and volcanic islands: a very diverse world, offering very different opportunities to those who settled, and thereby providing a great stimulus to local and even long-distance exchange.[4] These Polynesians lacked the elaborate tools available to navigators, most importantly the art of writing. Their knowledge was passed down orally, and yet it was extremely detailed, very accurate and in many respects superior to the instruments of the western navigators, such as Magellan and Cook, for whom the Pacific was a sea of constant surprises and uncertainty. There is a simple point that sums up the mastery over the seas accomplished by the Polynesian navigators: apart from a northern route across the Atlantic, managed for several centuries by the Vikings and their descendants, western European sailors did not venture deep into their neighbourhood ocean until the end of the Middle Ages.

It is difficult to reconstruct the process of settlement. Did it occur from west to east across the islands of the Pacific, or should we think instead of a series of spirals that gradually encompassed the islands, creating several distinct networks of settlement? When did the pioneers arrive? If we cannot even date their arrival in the last territory, New Zealand, with confidence, it is all the more difficult to do so on small islands where archaeological research has been spasmodic, based as much on serendipity as carefully constructed programmes of excavation. What sort of boats did the first navigators employ? Across the Pacific there developed different types of boat, with different shapes of sail (lateen, square, claw and the upside-down triangles known as sprit sails). But the most challenging problem of all is why the navigators went looking for more islands. The question is rendered more difficult by the fact that there were phases of expansion and phases when expansion ceased. It is also complicated by the often fiery disputes between the experts, some of whom have tried to prove their point by getting on board and sailing the seas in reconstructed Polynesian ships.

In this account of the settlement of the Pacific islands some substantial territories are largely missing: Japan, Taiwan, the Philippines, the islands of Indonesia. They maintained a close relationship to the Asian mainland and formed the outer edges of what might be described as little Mediterraneans, the Japan Sea and Yellow Sea in the north, and the South China Sea (which has often been compared to the Mediterranean) in the south. Another territory, the Australian continent, was inhabited by people some of whom used the sea as a source of food, and who greatly respected the sea, but made no known attempts to venture across the waves once they had settled in their arid continent. The main concern here is with the open ocean, with communities scattered over Polynesia, Micronesia and Melanesia who inhabited small islands, New Zealand apart, and whose remoteness was generally no barrier to lively interaction across hundreds and even thousands of miles.

II

The antiquity of navigation across the Pacific is demonstrated by the arrival of humans in Australia. The distances involved were smaller than nowadays, because sea levels were much lower between 140,000 and 18,000 years ago, while much water was locked in northern ice floes and glaciers. At one extreme, the sea level stood 100 metres lower than present levels, but within that time frame it rose and fell, so at some points it was only about twenty metres lower than nowadays.[5] During this era, the Pleistocene, the Australian continent encompassed the whole of New

Guinea and Tasmania; but it remained isolated from continental Asia (which included Java) by stretches of open sea dotted with islands that have been given the name Wallacea, after Darwin's illustrious contemporary. This separation, which took place 40,000,000 years ago, ensured that animal species unique to Australia continued to flourish there, especially marsupial mammals. There was a sort of island bridge linking south-east Asia (named Sunda by the geologists) to Sahul (Australia and New Guinea), and it included the small island of Flores. Here we encounter the first great enigma. In 2003 archaeologists excavating a cave shelter on Flores discovered the remains of several early humans, dating very roughly to the second half of the low-water period and possibly several centuries later; more recent discoveries suggest that other early hominids reached as far as the Philippines.[6] These people were very small, a little over a metre in height, and their brain capacity was no greater than that of a chimpanzee. However, other physical features make it clear that they were an early form of human. Their small size was most probably the result of adaptation to the restricted diet of the island, similar to the dwarfism found in other species across the world that have lived in challenging environments. If that is so (and that is only one if) they probably descended from earlier, taller hominids who had managed to reach Flores before about 100,000 BC; but since then, and ever after, the island has been isolated from 'Sunda' and the Asian mainland by a stretch of sea. Setting aside the speculations of nineteenth-century theorists that the inhabitants of the Pacific were a separate creation of mankind by God, we are left with evidence that early humans crossed the sea, by whatever means we can only guess. It has also been suggested that the Flores humans (unkindly nicknamed 'hobbits' by the press) co-existed with modern humans on the island around 12,000 BC, and that memories of these little people survive in folk tales; but such folk tales are so widespread in every human society that it is hard to believe they are credible. The evidence is further complicated by the contemporary survival on Flores and in parts of the Philippines of stegodons (animals related to elephants) which seem to have reached these places by swimming across the sea. Flores remains a mystery.

That modern humans (*Homo sapiens sapiens*) reached further still more than 60,000 years ago is clear from discoveries right across New Guinea, Australia and Tasmania (then joined to Australia). There are finds of axes from northern New Guinea that can be shown to be 40,000–60,000 years old.[7] In 2017 Australian archaeologists announced the discovery of a rock shelter in northern Australia that contained implements dating back to 65,000 years ago, and wondered whether there was interaction between what seem to be the first Australian members of

Homo sapiens and other types of human who could still be found in east Asia, notably the mysterious Denisovans, who are thought to have been similar to but different from the European Neanderthals.[8] There is therefore no doubt that the original Aborigines (very possibly the ancestors of the modern ones) arrived on the continent more than 60,000 years ago; and they must have done so by crossing spaces of over a hundred miles of open sea, often finding themselves out of sight of land.[9] Archaeologists sometimes express surprise and puzzlement at the idea that early humans of the *sapiens* type could have turned into sailors. But it is not at all surprising; as humans, of various types, moved out of Africa to colonize much of the world by land they had to cross rivers, and used the skills learned on rivers to cross lakes; and having learned about lakes seas were a challenge, but one that could be met. Short sea journeys taken by the first humans to move eastwards on the route out of Africa may well have included a crossing of the Red Sea near Aden and a crossing of the Persian Gulf near Hormuz. These early humans had plenty of mental equipment, which they turned to good use in establishing that extraordinary mastery over nature that the Australian Aborigines still possess. It makes more sense to insist on that ability than to speculate about the types of boats these travellers might have used; bamboo, logs, bark boats, reed boats and much else have been suggested, but no archaeological evidence has been found, which is hardly surprising; if any remains survive from the very earliest journeys they lie on the long-submerged coast of the Sahul continent.[10] So the best answer is that in 65,000 years of travel boat designs must have changed, and that in any case boats would have been adapted to appropriate conditions; sails might have been developed where wind was a vital factor in reaching a place, but not when inter-island navigation was possible in calm waters within sight of land.[11]

When looking at the relationship between the original inhabitants of Australia and the sea several considerations have to be borne in mind. One is that exploitation of the coastline for food, whether that involves fishing from boats or foraging on beaches, does not provide proof of longer-distance travel across the sea and of the making of connections with other communities, either elsewhere in Australia or on islands beyond its shores. Another is that the use of modern evidence, such as Aboriginal opinions about the nature of the sea, though unavoidable, is very problematic. Tribes have moved around; physical conditions have changed; Aboriginal technology has also changed, as the people of the land have adapted themselves to local conditions, and as contact with Europeans has radically (and often disastrously) transformed daily life, inherited knowledge and social attitudes.

At various times the Australian interior was more hospitable to life than it is now, and the earliest settlers headed inland, looking for fresh water; Aboriginal tribes began to colonize the coastlines rather later, about 30,000 years ago at most, judging from current archaeological evidence; no site older than around 33,000 BC has been found on the coast. The continent remained very lightly populated; there was apparently no pressure to occupy coastal land, because food was readily available elsewhere. Shells found at cave sites a little way into the interior show how links were forged between coastal settlements and the population of inner Australia; but these shells almost certainly came as ornaments rather than food, and early sites close to the coast often reveal a diet based as much, or much more, on local fauna such as wallabies, rather than fish.[12] But the interior became increasingly arid, and living on the coast became more attractive; stone fish traps found in the Kimberley region, on the north coast of Western Australia, have been dated to a maximum of 3,500 years ago, but there is every reason to argue that these are the lineal descendants of earlier fish traps that were widely used along the Australian coast.[13]

These fish traps were a common feature of life in the Torres Strait Islands, the chain of islands between Australia and New Guinea. Nowadays it is standard usage in Australia to speak of 'the Aboriginal peoples and the Torres Strait islanders', recognizing the distinct status, origin and culture of the people of these islands, whose technology has long been more advanced than that of the Australian Aborigines: more Neolithic than Old Stone Age. Ethnically, they are closer to the peoples of Papua New Guinea and Melanesia, and in recent times at least cultural influences from New Guinea have been profound, including myths, rituals and technology. In the Torres Strait, groups of people could be found who operated very different economies: some who depended on small-scale agriculture, and others who were 'saltwater people', making extensive use of the sea, including voyages back and forth between islands and to the coasts of both New Guinea and Australia, setting out in dugout canoes with outriggers and sails.[14] Some of these influences from the north were then transmitted along the north-east coast of Australia to Aboriginal peoples living by the sea: masks and headdresses of types familiar from Papua New Guinea were being used along the shoreline when the first Europeans explored what is now known as Queensland, and other borrowings may have included types of harpoon and fish hook. In modern times, fish and sea creatures such as turtles and dugongs completely dominate the diet of the Torres Strait islanders, supplying about two thirds of a kilo per day, on average. Saltwater people using bark boats went out into the open sea to catch pelagic fish, that is, fish that live near the surface of the sea. They developed trading links with their neighbours, which can be traced back with certainty to around AD 1650 when Indonesian merchants from Macassar became regular visitors; however, all the signs are that this was a much more ancient connection, and that as a result of wider contacts some Aboriginal peoples such as the Yolŋu (roughly pronounced *Yol-ngu*) knew a little about the world beyond their coastline.[15]

In the Torres Strait, on the island of Mer – which, according to one legend, was a giant dugong who lay down in the middle of the sea and became land – evidence abounds that this area had become a trading station at the centre of a lively network of maritime trade, certainly 2,000 years ago but almost certainly in the much more distant past as well.[16] The bones of dogs, rats, dugongs, turtles and of many types of fish provide part of the proof that the rich resources of the sea were fully exploited, but a bone pipe dating to around AD 1 indicates wider trading links. The islanders appear to have developed outrigger canoes that made contact across the sea safe and regular. Their style of boat influenced the design of canoes along the coast of Queensland.[17] The islands of the Torres Strait, then, and their sea-based population, formed a sea bridge between the cultures of prehistoric Melanesia and those of northern Australia which, thanks to the sea, were not as isolated from the outside world as is easily assumed. The Torres Strait islanders were venturesome sailors, but others were much more cautious in their dealings with the open sea. One Aboriginal people in Australia insist that the sea is alive and that it has angry moods during which it is likely to kill people: 'when you are on the sea you mustn't say anything bad about it. Not criticise it. Because the sea is alive, like a person. So you must respect it.'[18] On Croker Island, not far from Darwin in the Northern Territory, the Aborigines claim that the great Rainbow Serpent inhabits the seabed and has to be placated through special rituals, because the serpent will use the sea to kill and maim. In the same region, the Yanyuwa people describe themselves as 'people who originate in the sea',[19] and their boats, like the sea, became animate. Humans could impregnate their boats with magical power by singing 'power songs' that would calm the sea and that would stay inside the boat, as if it possessed its own soul.[20]

It was to the north of New Guinea that really striking changes would occur, with the colonization of the Pacific islands. Some islands off the north coast of New Guinea were colonized 35,000 years ago. The Solomon Islands were being visited 29,000 years ago, and raiders from New Guinea remained a threat to Solomon islanders over the centuries.[21] The Admiralty Islands were settled 13,000 years ago, if not earlier, and these involved a sea journey of nearly 100 miles, including navigation out of sight of land.

One site, on Buka in the Solomon Islands, yielded evidence that the diet of the settlers around 26,000 BC included fish and shellfish as well as mammals and lizards.[22] But man cannot live by fish alone, and the availability of one vital necessity was counterbalanced by the lack of other necessities. Sometimes there was no hard stone suitable for cutting. In that case it was necessary to obtain obsidian or another prime cutting stone from further afield. Although the distance is not great, obsidian from New Britain has been found on New Ireland, both in the vicinity of New Guinea, and assigned a date of 20,000 BP ('Before the Present'). There are plenty of doubters, however. It has been suggested that times of low sea levels are precisely the times when there is no incentive to cross the sea, because there is more land to colonize. When the sea level rises, the land shrinks and people go in search of new land.[23] But all this is speculation. We simply do not know.

III

The name given to the culture that spread across vast tracts of the prehistoric Pacific is 'Lapita'. Amid all the speculation it is no surprise to find that this is not the name any people gave to themselves, but the name of the archaeological site where their distinctive culture was first identified. An extraordinary feature of Lapita culture is its spread. No other prehistoric culture embraces such a large geographical area, in this case including both the Solomon Islands, which had been settled very early, and islands as remote as Fiji and Samoa.[24] The vast majority of the islands where Lapita settlers arrived were virgin territory, far beyond the range of the earliest Austronesian navigators. That is not to say that the Lapita navigators were the descendants of the earliest Austronesian settlers who had ventured beyond New Guinea millennia earlier. The genetic identity of the Lapita people remains uncertain, and the best answer is that they consisted of a mix of peoples of various origins who gave rise to the varied populations of Polynesia and much of Melanesia; the uniformity of their culture was not necessarily backed by uniformity in their appearance, and woolly-haired Melanesians and straight-haired Polynesians (those are already generalizations taken too far) participated in a single culture. Rather, this culture seems to have had an initial focal point in the western Pacific, probably in Taiwan, where the language of the indigenous population is related to those spoken across Oceania; and later on it was disseminated outwards from newer focal points deeper in the Pacific, notably Samoa. Taiwan was itself home to a lively prehistoric culture in the third millennium BC, and pottery found in the northern Moluccas is strikingly similar to that of the Polynesian Lapita, suggesting ancestral links to the inhabitants of the islands off the south-east coast of Asia. As speakers of Austronesian languages mixed with the population along and off the coast of New Guinea, an ethnically mixed population came into being, whose varied origins are reflected in their DNA. The route they took, over many centuries, therefore began in the Bismarck archipelago before they spread eastwards through the Solomons.[25]

Lapita represents a change of gear in oceanic expansion. Until about 1500 BC local exchanges between islands are easily provable from fragments of obsidian, the sharp-edged volcanic glass that was traded between islands, in return for what it is hard to say – probably foodstuffs, but even the term 'trade' must be used with caution; people may simply have gone out to volcanic islands to collect the material off the beaches. The Lapita folk brought pottery, which is their distinctive archaeological 'signature', and they brought animals for which there is no earlier evidence in the islands, notably pigs, dogs and domestic birds.[26] They also brought Pacific rats, and the bones of these stowaways can be used to date the arrival of navigators in islands across much of the Pacific; here again the evidence strongly indicates gradual movement from west to east.[27] In broad terms, they were a Neolithic ('New Stone Age') people or group of peoples, familiar with agriculture, stock-rearing and ceramics.[28] Farming transformed the environment of one island after another, as land was cleared for agriculture and as local species of birds were hunted, eaten and driven to extinction; the most famous case, much later, would be the giant *moa* birds of New Zealand, but there were local crocodiles and giant iguanas that proved unable to resist human conquest.

On the other hand, the settlers proved to be experts in agronomy, for they transformed the often limited resources of islands in Remote Oceania (the area around Fiji and Samoa) that were so isolated that they offered few fruits and none of the tubers which provided the staple starch in their diet. Twenty-eight species of plant have been identified that were brought across the ocean by the Lapita people: bananas, breadfruit, sugar cane, yams, coconuts, wild ginger and bamboo were some of the most significant, though different types of island were suited to different types of plant – yams flourished best in Melanesia. (Another arrival was the sweet potato, apparently from South America, which raises the question of whether Polynesian navigators at some stage reached the opposite side of the Pacific.) The proto-Oceanic vocabulary, reconstructed by philologists, offers words for planting, weeding, harvesting and the mounds under which yams were grown, once again suggesting that the horticultural traditions of the Lapita went far back in time to the days when their ancestors lived in Taiwan.[29] The arrival of plants from places further west suggests that the voyages eastwards were indeed colonizing ventures, and were not accidental discoveries by lost navigators stranded on desert islands, a question to which it will be necessary to return. The movement of the Lapita peoples across the ocean may not seem rapid. One estimate for the time taken to reach western Polynesia from the Bismarck archipelago is 500 years. Yet this may only represent twenty generations, which in the larger scheme of things makes this expansion quite fast, even, in the timescale of prehistorians, explosive.

The motives behind this movement of people are hard to fathom. One historian of Polynesian navigation, David Lewis, identified a spirit of adventure – a 'restless urge' – among Polynesians, citing the Raiateans from Tahiti, who would go voyaging for several months, touring the islands of that part of the ocean. They were observed by Joseph Banks, Captain Cook's scientific companion, so the evidence is late and somewhat circumstantial. David Lewis also pointed to the 'proud self-respect' of the navigators, a pride that would prompt sailors to set out to sea in bad weather if, for instance, they saw that the natives of an island they were visiting were taking to the sea, even just to fish. This idea fits well with the concepts of honour and shame of which anthropologists studying these ocean societies have written. Viking-style raids between islands have also been postulated; one could imagine a first phase during which the raiders took away coconuts, obsidian and breadfruit that they found on deserted islands; then, following settlement, inter-island wars were certainly common.[30] But these cases suit a world already partly settled; the question here is how and why the settlement occurred in the first place. Overpopulation might seem the obvious choice, but there is not enough evidence to suggest dense settlement of the western islands and intolerable pressure on resources.[31]

As the settlers moved further eastwards, they left behind diseases brought millennia ago from New Guinea and eastern Asia, such as malaria – unsullied island habitats are often healthy, and offer a long life expectancy. But the longer people live and the healthier they are, the greater number of children they can expect to have, with a better chance of survival to adulthood. In such an environment younger children might take part in migration almost as a matter of course, on the proven assumption that there were plenty of places to settle out in the ocean. The Polynesians set great store by genealogies, emphasizing the rights of eldest children, while sibling rivalry is a constant feature of Polynesian legends, suggesting that younger sons were well advised to keep on the move till they found a new homestead.[32] One idea is that the early Polynesians were primarily dependent on what the sea offered – 'ocean foragers' – and that the search for the produce of the sea brought them further and further out into the ocean, followed by the development of farming settlements as the pioneers bedded down in their new homes. In 'Remote Oceania' their seafood diet included not just oysters, clams and cowries but turtles, eels, parrot fish and sharks; most of this fishy diet came from the edges of the reefs or from even closer to shore. There is no evidence of short-term camps as voyagers squatted in islands; they arrived in new places and they created homes there; and they preferred to live on the shore, carefully choosing sites that offered access to the open sea through gaps in the reefs that surrounded many of the islands. There they built wooden houses on stilts, a type of house widely dispersed throughout the Austronesian world. This was not a sudden invasion of strings of uninhabited islands, but a process of steady expansion eastwards (not necessarily in a straight line).[33]

The pottery evidence is so remarkable because it shows clearly that this was a single culture with regional variations. The pottery was handmade, without the use of a wheel, and without kilns, meaning it was probably fired out in the open. Here we have a common 'dentate' style, where pots were often stamped with a tooth-shaped instrument, and intricate patterns were created with great artistry. These patterns have been seen as a sort of vocabulary, conveying messages now lost; there were also local varia-tions in the pottery styles, and the most striking fragments to have survived show incised human faces, or at least features such as eyes. Possibly these represent gods or ancestors, and the designs may have been similar to those used in tattooing, which was widespread (tattooing instruments have turned up in excavations). The spread of this pottery through 'Remote Oceania' provides vital clues about the arrival of the first humans on islands deep within the Pacific. The inhabitants of the Bismarck archipel-ago were making Lapita-style pots around 1500 BC. Over the next century or so the pottery reached 'Near Oceania' (Vanuatu, Kiribati and neigh-bouring island chains). By 1200 BC it was being produced in Samoa. Interestingly, only the oldest pottery from Fiji shows such concern for intricate decoration. Was this art lost over a generation or two? Did the decoration lose its significance, particularly in new societies which were not yet part of networks of reciprocal exchange? Oddly, as the Lapita people moved still further eastwards they brought their plants and ani-mals, and their knowledge of navigation, but eventually lost interest in pottery entirely.[34]

There was a single culture; but was there a shared culture? Chemical analysis of the clay proves that pots were carried from island to island, though no doubt some were moved around the Pacific simply as utensils containing the food navigators needed; many undecorated pots would have been suitable for use as containers for sago flour, which kept well and provided ideal nutrition for navigators. Care needs to be taken with the assumption that the movement of these goods and other items such as obsidian and chert (the class of rock that includes flint) adds up to 'trade'. Trade might be defined as the systematic exchange of goods, for which a notional though generally variable value is set. In Pacific island societies, as the great ethnographer Bronisław Malinowski showed, the exchange of goods was not simply concerned with commercial acquisition; reciprocal exchange was a means by which individuals established their place in the social and political pecking order, a way of establishing claims to leadership and of emphasizing who was a client to whom.[35] This would be even truer of societies that experienced plenty, as these island communities generally did; and yet there were certainly foodstuffs and tools, most notably cutting implements and adzes, that were not to be found on coral atolls and that needed to be obtained over the water. The closer one looks at this world, the more connected it appears to be.

An example from the western end of the Lapita world provides rich evidence. Talepakemalai lies on the northern edge of the Bismarck archipelago. The history of this village can be traced over five or even seven centuries, beginning halfway through the second millennium BC. At that point, early in Lapita history, obsidian arrived from islands not far away, as well as adzes and chert for making tools, plus pottery from twelve sources, not all identifiable but all distinct in the composition of their clay. Meanwhile the islanders were adept at making fish hooks, and also decorative jewellery consisting of beads, rings and other objects created out of shell. Archaeologists therefore speculate that some sort of exchange network linked Talepakemalai to a series of island communities in western Near Oceania. Yet by the first millennium the early expansion had slowed, a process mirrored in the contraction (or 'regionalization') of this part of the Lapita world. This could reflect a greater degree of autarky, that is to say, less need to rely on neighbours for certain types of goods, which could now be produced locally. The local economy perhaps strengthened, but what the archaeologists tend to see is less evidence for external links, which gives the illusion of Lapita decline. This may have some bearing on a phenomenon to be observed in a moment, the long interval between the Lapita expansion and a new phase of exploration and settlement in the first millennium AD.[36]

We know very little about Lapita boats. One or two rock carvings offer clues to the shape of sails (including an interesting 'claw' shape, with a roughly triangular profile, but with a concave top line); but much depends on the Austronesian words reconstructed by philologists, because nothing of the original boats survives in the archaeological record. Broadly, we can conceive of sailing vessels with outriggers, similar to those used in later centuries; some may have been catamarans, though double canoes of this sort seem to have developed mainly in Remote Oceania, around Fiji. By modern times the variety of boats was considerable, but they conform to a common type: sailing vessels whose builders paid close attention to their stability.[37] It was understood that a single hull did not suit small boats in high seas. Polynesian boats were hard to topple; and those that set out for new lands must have been large enough to carry men, women, supplies of food and water (often stored in bamboo tubes), domestic animals and seeds or tubers ready for planting in new lands. Those heading for familiar territory evidently carried goods to be exchanged, such as ceramics, local produce of the soil, and tools or blocks of stone for making into tools. No doubt there was great variety, though some features, such as the use of vegetable fibres to tie together the components, were probably standard. These bonds, made of coconut fibre, were strong and resilient, and rendered the hull more secure because of the flexibility they offered.

Navigators had to face strong challenges. The most obvious were the easterly winds. Colonization of the Pacific occurred in the face of the wind rather than as a result of happy accidents as sailors were caught in the wind and carried to unknown islands. The trade winds and the currents all point westwards; the trade winds cross the Lapita area of settlement from south-east to north-west, forming a coherent band that matches quite well the Lapita area. The Pacific currents consist of four main trans-Pacific movements: a southern current lying away from all the islands; the South Equatorial Current heading westwards with a slight southward inclination; and above the Equator two contrary currents that separate Hawai'i from the rest of the Polynesian world. Looking at the South Equatorial Current, as with the winds, the broad shape of movement from Samoa westwards very roughly coincides with the zone of Lapita settlement. Evidently, Polynesian navigators perfected the art of sailing against the wind; they needed to ensure that they could return from their explorations, and the best way to do that was to challenge the winds and currents, tacking back and forth, moving slowly but securely.

As they developed these techniques over many centuries, they also learned the art of dead reckoning, judging distance as they sailed to gain some sense of longitude; they appear to have found this easier to do than European sailors, who had to await the invention of the chronometer in the eighteenth century to be sure of their longitude. Tupaia, a Polynesian navigator who accompanied Captain Cook, astonished Cook's companions by his almost instinctive awareness of where the ship stood, without instruments or written records. The Polynesian navigators proved that one can solve some challenging problems without any technology at all, just the super-computer of the human brain.[38] As for latitude, much easier to judge, they observed the stars: 'to travel between the south of the main Solomons and the Santa Cruz group was as simple as following a zenith star path – east or west – with the seasonal winds.'[39] Knowing the stars was the key to successful navigation. This was not casual knowledge but a science learned during a long apprenticeship, through practical experience and by way of an elaborate oral tradition; it was a secret science, intended for carefully chosen initiates who would be able to navigate the boats while the rest of the crew performed more humdrum tasks.

Even in the 1930s these methods were taught to boys, beginning at the age of five, as the story of a celebrated sailor from the Carolinas named Piailug reveals. Once his grandfather decided that the boy should become a navigator, he had to spend his time listening to stories of the sea and acquiring information about the science of navigation. His grandfather assured him that as a navigator he would be better than a chieftain, would eat better food than others and would be respected throughout society. By the age of twelve he was travelling the ocean with his grandfather, and he began to master the secrets of the sea – the movement of birds, the changing map of the stars, but also magical lore. All this was committed to memory, leading to a full initiation around the age of sixteen which involved a month of seclusion during which his teachers bombarded him with the knowledge he needed. He had no use for written texts, but he made models out of sticks and stones that he could memorize and rebuild, when the time came to instruct the next generation in the art of navigation.[40] In the Carolinas, navigators would prepare a sidereal compass, a chart of the key points in the night sky, which in modern times they greatly preferred to a magnetic compass; in other parts of the Pacific similar compass-type charts were constructed out of sticks and stones to show wind direction or the movement of the sun across the sky.[41]

The Polynesians did not necessarily require a compass of any sort. There is the story of a schooner captain who lost his compass overboard and confessed to his Polynesian crew that he was lost. They told him not to worry, and took him where he wanted to go. Puzzled by the ease with which they had achieved this, he asked how they knew where the island was. 'Why,' they replied, 'it has always been there.'[42] The extraordinary confidence Polynesian navigators possessed in their methods can also be judged from an interview with a navigator from the Marshall Islands conducted in 1962: 'we older Marshallese people navigate our boats both by feel and by sight, but I think it is knowing the feel of the vessel that is the most important.' He explained that a practised navigator would have no difficulty sailing in daytime or at night, and that it was important to take proper account of the movement of the waves:

> by the boat motion and the wave pattern a Marshallese sailor who has been trained in this kind of navigation may know if he is thirty miles, twenty or ten, or even closer, to an atoll or island. He also knows if he has lost his way, and by looking for a certain joining of the waves, he will be able to get back on course.[43]

In cloudy weather, any break in the clouds at night-time had to be exploited immediately; but there were other signs, such as the swell of the sea, that a practised navigator could use to identify where the boat was heading. There were plenty of additional signs, various combinations of which made a landfall a certainty. Land could be detected through the flight of birds such as terns coming out to sea to feed. Their range from land was known; the direction they came in the morning and returned at night was the best possible clue to where land lay. Other signs included cloud formations, which might change colour, reflecting the land that lay underneath (coral atolls would cast an opal tinge on the cloud above). Phosphorescent patches in the sea were a further sign that land was near. Increasing amounts of flotsam generally suggested land.[44] The very smell of the sea air would help guide a sailor to a known haven.[45] It was important to compensate for currents and wind, making use of the sun by day and the stars by night to adjust course as appropriate. One of the most extraordinary methods of navigation was what might be called the Polynesian Theory of Relativity, a system known in the Carolina Islands as *etak*. Here, the assumption was that the boat remained still and the rest of the world moved. Judgements therefore had to be made about how the position of the islands altered in relation to the boat – a relationship not just between the boat and its destination, but between the destination and another island in the vicinity; the method depended on placing this third point accurately in relation to the stars. This was not perhaps Einstein; but it involved some powerful mental geometry, not to mention an astonishingly detailed, carefully memorized, mobile map of the heavens.[46]

It is therefore completely wrong to conclude that without writing there can be no exact science, even if the navigational science of the Polynesians had a good share of incantations, magical practices and invocation of the gods. The extraordinary understanding that Polynesian sailors developed of the sea and its whims, and the increasing evidence that they settled the islands in the face of the winds rather than by being blown towards land-falls, has significant implications in explaining the voyages. Much ink has been spilled contesting the apparently plausible views of Andrew Sharp, whose book *Ancient Voyagers in the Pacific*, first presented to the Poly-nesian Society in 1956, insisted that those who found new land by and large did so by accident, when they were blown off course or otherwise lost. Sharp did not challenge the argument that Polynesian sailors were exceptionally skilled, but he did underestimate their remarkable abilities.[47] What Sharp really demonstrated was something else: we still do not really know why the Lapita people and their successors, including the Māoris, settled one territory after another across the vast expanse of ocean. We can say with some confidence how it was done, and more or less at what periods it was done (though, even there, there is forceful disagreement). Why they kept on the move is a topic for speculation.

The period of rapid Lapita expansion reached a climax around 1000 BC when Vanuatu and the Fijian islands were settled. This involved ambi-tious journeys well out of sight of land, particularly to reach Fiji; there were a few more stepping stones on the route eastwards that led the Poly-nesians to Samoa and Tonga. The Lapita had reached the limits of their expansion, and had created a series of networks across about 4,500 kilo-metres of the Pacific, in a great arc from New Guinea to Tonga.[48] Just as great a mystery as the origins of Lapita expansion is its cessation for up to a millennium. Was this because Polynesian boats were unable to venture on to the vast tracts of open ocean separating Lapita lands from Hawai'i, New Zealand and Easter Island? The problem with this argument is that Lapita sailors had already managed to reach Fiji and Samoa, well out in the ocean.[49] These were very skilled and imaginative navigators, and it is hard to believe that they were incapable of adapting their already impres-sively durable boats to face stormier seas. Overpopulation was apparently not a strain on them. A fine ecological balance had been achieved, despite the radical replanting of large tracts of soil on the islands. The problem with materialistic explanations is that migration in many parts of the world has often been stimulated by religious beliefs that are impossible to recover so far back in time. Supposing for the moment that the Polynesian explorers were guided by a religious imperative to seek the rising sun (an argument for which, admittedly, there is hardly even circumstantial evi-dence), then cultural fashions could have changed as religious ideas altered. Once the cult of local ancestors developed strongly, a greater sense of being rooted in the island where one lived would act as a brake on further expansion – though not, as it turned out, indefinitely.

2

Songs of the Navigators

Pacific navigation revived by the fifth century AD. Why this should have happened is as uncertain as why it had ceased in the late Lapita period. A link to the so-called Little Climatic Optimum has been suggested, but this does not quite fit the chronology, which suggests a revival of navigation at least a couple of centuries earlier. Rising sea levels during warmer weather might have made life difficult on low-lying islands with plantations by the shore, stimulating migration.[1] Only in the millennium after about AD 300 did settlement expand north and south, and much further west, into areas of varied climate and resources, as far as Hawai'i in the north and New Zealand in the south. During this phase Tahiti and the Society Islands were one focus of settlement, beginning around AD 600, if evidence from domesticated coconuts on the island of Mo'orea is given full credit; however, the earliest inhabited sites on these islands that have actually been discovered date from somewhere between 800 and 1200, although many earlier sites may be under water as the coastline has altered.[2]

The journey northwards from Tahiti or the Marquesas to Hawai'i may have taken three to four weeks, and winds blowing in various directions had to be managed: first east to west, then west to east, and finally east to west again. Attempts to mimic the Polynesian voyages during the 1970s, led by Ben Finney in the canoe *Hokule'a*, showed that the journey was manageable. Finney, along with the New Zealander Jeff Evans, has been a pioneer in reconstructing traditional boat types and in encouraging the Polynesians to take an interest in their ancient navigational skills, and his experimental voyages are taken seriously.[3] A more difficult question is whether the Hawai'i archipelago was settled immediately after discovery by a group of migrants bringing plants and animals, including pigs and dogs, as in the island chains further south. It cannot be assumed that the settlement of Hawai'i, a whole group of islands, was a single event;

different islands may have been colonized at different times, sometimes from neighbouring islands in the archipelago, and sometimes from the island chains much further south, around Tahiti and Samoa.

The Hawai'ian islands cannot have been discovered by accident; the winds simply do not permit an accidental arrival from, say, Samoa.[4] People had gone in search of new islands, and they now ranged far from those with which they were already familiar. This must have tested their navigational abilities to the limit. They no longer had sight of such night-time star guides as the Southern Cross. Once they were in the northern hemisphere they had entered what was for them a new world. Oral traditions told of discoveries and of journeys back to the starting point to carry the news that there was new land to settle. These oral traditions are full of fascinating information about navigation and even some remembered history, but how well that history was remembered, amid many miraculous accretions, including giant octopuses, is a moot point.

A distinction began to emerge between two basic types of society in Polynesia, the so-called open societies, in which a variety of different groups, including warriors and priests, competed for power and land, and what are called stratified societies, of which early Tahiti and Hawai'i are good examples, where there was much less fluidity and a clearly defined elite emerged, with power concentrated in the hands of hereditary chieftains. On Tahiti and its close neighbours in the Society Islands the chieftains expected tribute payments of food and bark-cloth; they expressed their power through their intimate ties to the war god Oro, a relationship they sealed by acts of human sacrifice.[5] Around AD 1200, the Tahitians began to build terraces and to lay out orchards where they cultivated breadfruit. They built storage pits for the breadfruit. They also constructed stone temples with platforms, or *marae*, that stood right by the ocean and sometimes jutted out into it. War canoes would set out from the *marae*, and a new chieftain would arrive by boat for his installation. These were societies wedded to the sea. Chieftains from some of the less well-endowed islands to the east preyed on the richer central islands, and managed to extract tribute from them. Leadership in war, celebrated in the cult of Oro, consolidated the hold of chieftains from the lesser isles over neighbouring territories. Little maritime empires came into being, and chieftaincies were by no means confined to a single island or part of one. Tension between chieftains, and in particular between their sons, would explain the urge to go and seek new lands, without quite explaining why the new burst of colonization occurred when it did. Arriving in already populated islands could, however, be dangerous: in some places it was apparently the custom to kill newcomers the moment they were found.[6]

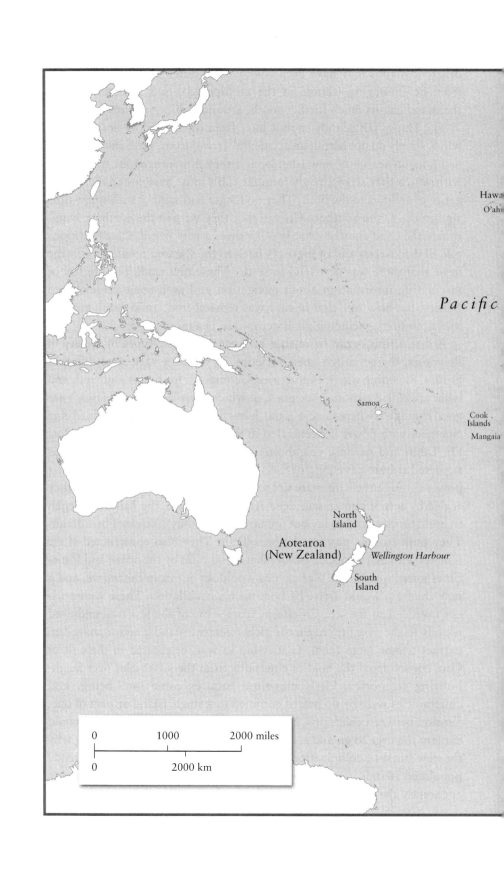

Hawa
O'ah

Pacific

Samoa

Cook
Islands
Mangaia

North
Island

Aotearoa
(New Zealand)   *Wellington Harbour*

South
Island

0	1000	2000 miles

0   2000 km

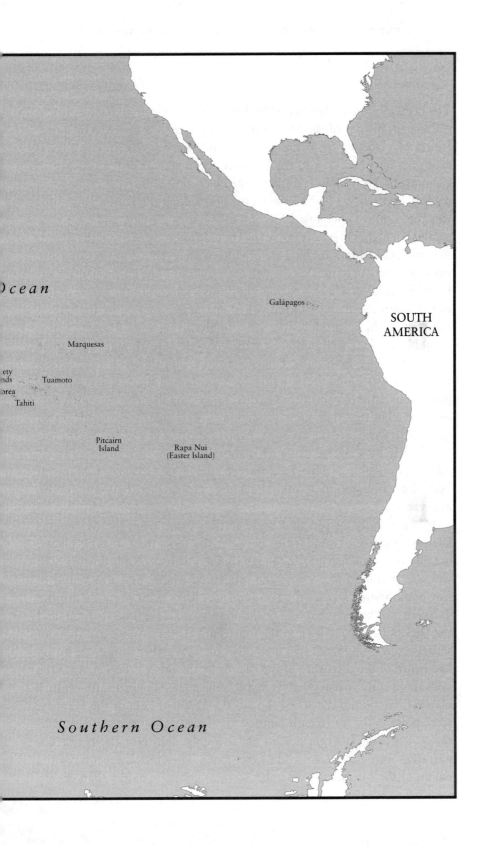

II

The deep interest understandably shown by American archaeologists in the ancient history of the fiftieth state in the Union is matched by a profusion of evidence from the archipelago. There is the archaeological evidence; but there is also the evidence, hard though it is to assess, of elaborate oral traditions recorded in the nineteenth century, at a time when reading and writing had become a passion among the Hawai'ians – this was the result of energetic Christian missionary activity, and for a time resulted in higher literacy than in the United States.[7] Moreover, the islands have attracted attention because organized hierarchical states came into existence without parallel in the Polynesian world.[8] The Polynesian settlers found a paradise: whereas each of the atolls and reefs of the island chains of the south Pacific had an individual character, marked by limitations on what could be produced in often unpromising soils, Hawai'i was a veritable garden, well endowed with volcanic soil, though with some variety between the islands. Evidence from O'ahu shows that settlement was under way along the shoreline by 800, though the first arrivals may have occurred several centuries earlier, suggesting that this was not a one-off settlement that then grew prodigiously. Particularly eloquent, if that is the right word, are the rat bones from O'ahu and elsewhere. Pacific rats could only have arrived in such remote places by travelling as stowaways, or possibly as a live food reserve, on Polynesian canoes. Many rat bones have been found in sinkholes dated to somewhere between AD 900 and 1200.[9]

It is generally agreed that these settlers came from the Marquesas Islands, because of similarities between the tools used in both places, notably adzes and fish hooks, though contacts were probably flowing both ways, so it is hard to be sure who influenced whom, and a new style of fish hook adopted around 1200 indicates links with the area around Tahiti. It will be seen that oral tradition spoke of close links to Tahiti and the Society Islands, at least in the fourteenth century. So we can think of settlers converging from two main directions, whether or not one group had heard of the discovery of the islands by the other group. Among the tales about early voyages that were still being related in nineteenth-century Hawai'i, two stand out, even though the assumed date of the events is some point in the fourteenth century AD. These dates depend on calculations of generations that are, to put it mildly, approximate. Hawai'ian narrators were not interested in exact dates. They measured time by the names of the rulers, and inevitably some reigns were longer than others.

The tales told of voyages across vast swathes of the Pacific, reflecting an era before Hawai'i became closed off from the rest of Oceania.

One story begins on the outer island of O'ahu, where the ruler Muli'eleali tried to divide his section of the island among his three sons, in the same way that he had inherited one third of O'ahu from his own father. But the obvious problem was that generation by generation there was less land on which to subsist. His two youngest sons therefore rebelled and were sent into exile, moving to the larger island of Hawai'i itself. They introduced new methods of irrigation that had been developed on O'ahu in order to cultivate staple root vegetables (notably taro), but a combination of hurricanes and floods wrecked their work, and they decided that they had had enough of the Hawai'ian islands; they would return to the land of their ancestors, a place called Kahiki. If there is any truth in the story, they sailed their double canoe to what is now south-western Tahiti, an area with striking cultural similarities to Hawai'i: the Taputapuatea temple in this part of Tahiti bears an identical name to the Kapukapuakea temple in northern O'ahu, allowing for a sound shift that converted *t* to *k* in the Hawai'ian dialects (so *Kahiki* is a Hawai'ian version of *Tahiti*). One of the brothers then decided he was homesick and returned north, where he made a very successful marriage to a chieftain's daughter and found himself appointed a paramount chief of Kaua'i, an outlying island beyond O'ahu. But his father-in-law had left behind a son from another marriage he had made in Kahiki/Tahiti, and the story tells of journeys back and forth to Kahiki. Another rather gory tale recounts the experiences of Pa'ao around the same time. He originated in the Society Islands. When his son was accused by Pa'ao's brother of stealing breadfruit, Pa'ao cut his son open to show that his stomach was empty, and then rolled his canoe out to sea over the body of his nephew, the child of the brother who had made the accusation. That meant that two lines of succession were obliterated in the feud. He set out for Hawai'i, building temples and generating a new line of descendants, who became an important dynasty of hereditary priests in the Hawai'ian islands. Reduced to essentials, these tales indicate an ease of movement between Hawai'i and Tahiti or the islands around Tonga that persisted into the fourteenth century.

One of the tales preserves a song that is as clear about the memory of at least partly Tahitian origins as one could wish:

> *Eia Hawai'i, he moku, he kanaka,*
> *He kanaka Hawai'i – e,*
> *He kanaka Hawai'i,*
> *He kama na Kahiki . . .*

> Here is Hawai'i, an island, a man,
> Here is Hawai'i – indeed,
> Hawai'i is a man,
> A child of Tahiti . . . [10]

Proof that these stories are not total fantasies has been provided by DNA evidence that links the modern native Hawai'ian population to the population of the Marquesas, in eastern Polynesia, and to the Society Islands a little further west.[11] Archaeological finds have been more reticent about contacts between Hawai'i and the Society Islands. An adze made of stone from Hawai'i fashioned in Tahitian style and found 2,500 miles away on a coral island in the Tuamoto archipelago provides minute but precious evidence of contact. This 'hawaiite' rock could only be traced back to Hawai'i. Around Tuamoto, adzes were produced from stone carried from a wide range of islands around south-eastern Polynesia; to have identified a Hawai'ian example, even just one, indicates lengthy (though not necessarily direct) links far beyond obvious trading neighbours. Alas, it is impossible to date this type of material securely.[12]

The oral traditions about later happenings on Hawai'i have nothing to say about sea journeys after the time of Pa'ao and the men from O'ahu. All the archaeological evidence too indicates a caesura: Hawai'i, for whatever reason, became secluded from the rest of the Polynesian world. Around 1400 a long pause in voyaging out of Hawai'i began, despite the continuing circulation of oral traditions about the inhabitants' arrival across the sea.[13] Yet this did not reflect contraction at home in Hawai'i. The population grew rapidly, reaching about a quarter of a million by the time Captain Cook arrived in the late eighteenth century. Whatever tension this created as the land became ever more densely populated was resolved partly by war and partly by the assertion of strong central authority by the chieftains – a process, in some interpretations, of 'state formation'. As in Tahiti, the war god, here named Kuy, was propitiated by human sacrifice; the stone temple platforms became increasingly elaborate; and in time the chieftains claimed divine descent, thereby marking themselves out clearly from the common people. These ordinary islanders worked on the land controlled by lesser chieftains, offering their labour services and regular tribute. All this was a source of great enrichment to the greater and lesser chieftains, for the growth in population was also addressed: it was reflected in ever greater intensification of agriculture, with organized field systems, fish farms where mullet were encouraged to breed, and irrigation projects, under the patronage of the god of flowing water, Kane. By the sixteenth century something like an organized state had emerged in Hawai'i, a stratified society that might very loosely be described as 'feudal'.[14] The fertility of the land and the efficiency of Hawai'ian agriculture had reduced dependence on the sea, except for local fishing. The islands had never depended on the rest of Polynesia for vital goods – they were too far away. They became little continents, turned away from the sea that had borne their first settlers to their safe havens.

III

Before turning eastwards to Rapa Nui (Easter Island) and southwards to New Zealand, the last part of Oceania to be settled, a question about contacts right across the Pacific needs to be addressed. Since Polynesian navigators reached as far east as Rapa Nui, isolated in vast tracts of open ocean, is it conceivable that some reached further still and arrived in South America? The search to identify the first people to reach America is based on any number of false premises, beginning with the assumption that people would recognize what they discovered as part of two massive continents (something that Columbus, for one, failed to do); they would then deserve to be hailed as the 'true discoverers' of the New World. But the question of links between Polynesia and South America was posed in the reverse form – South Americans reaching and indeed colonizing Polynesia – by the Norwegian explorer and self-publicist Thor Heyerdahl. He became obsessed by the idea that the Polynesians were of American descent, and that they took advantage of the easterly winds to sail their boats deep into the Pacific. He insisted that he could see Native American influence on innumerable Polynesian artefacts. The raft he constructed, *Kon-Tiki*, bore no resemblance to the type of vessel used by Polynesian navigators all the way across Oceania; it was copied from Peruvian sailing rafts deployed after the Spanish conquest of the Inca Empire.[15] Nonetheless, in 1947 he sailed his raft across the open ocean, miraculously survived the experience, and assumed that just because it was possible to land (in his case, crash-land) in Polynesia such voyages must have happened in the past. Evidence from DNA and from the spread of the Austronesian languages unequivocally demonstrates that the Polynesians migrated from west to east and not from east to west; and even if Crick and Watson had yet to identify the structure of DNA when Heyerdahl set sail, the linguistic evidence had long been clear. This did not prevent Heyerdahl being voted the most famous Norwegian of all time (rather than Amundsen or Nansen, just to mention Norwegian explorers), nor did it prevent the construction of a much-visited museum in Oslo where his strange ocean-going craft is displayed.

The diplomatic view of modern Norwegian scholars is that Heyerdahl opened up some important questions. And the question about links between Oceania and South America is a real one. There is evidence for contact in the era of Polynesian navigation, though it is not easy to decipher. Most of the supposed similarities between objects produced in Oceania and along the American coastline have functional explanations; it is not beyond the capacity of human beings to invent the same simple item at different times and in different places. This applies for instance to harpoons, fish hooks manufactured out of shell, and plank-constructed boats of the sort favoured by the Chumash Indians off Santa Barbara, California, and in much of Polynesia.[16] The Chumash Indians are often cited as the sort of people who might have ventured across the sea, since they were busy boat-builders, specializing in journeys between the mainland and the Channel Islands opposite Santa Barbara; they were also one of the most economic-ally sophisticated peoples along that coastline, with a monetary system based on a currency made out of pierced shells (periodically destroyed to prevent rampant inflation). But their boats were hard-pressed to cross the Santa Barbara Channel in rough weather and were far too small and simple to venture out into the open ocean; besides, fish supplies were plentiful in inland waters.[17] As one goes down the American shoreline the impression of societies interested in the sea solely for coastal fishing strengthens: the Kumiai Indians of Baja California loved sardines, sole, tuna (including bonito) and shellfish, but were not navigators; they used small reed boats, often capable of carrying just a couple of people.[18] Nor do these peoples show any sign of receiving goods from distant Polynesia.

Thor Heyerdahl was anxious to show that the Galápagos Islands, with the rich fishing grounds around them, were the first stepping stone into the Pacific for his supposed Amerindian navigators. This, he hoped, would embarrass the often virulent critics of his *Kon-Tiki* expedition.[19] Since the Galápagos lie 600 miles west of Ecuador, reaching them would have been no mean achievement; they were discovered, or maybe rediscovered, by the Spaniards in 1535, and it is no surprise that a fair amount of Spanish pottery was found when Heyerdahl and his companions went to look for evidence of early visits to the islands a few years after the *Kon-Tiki* exped-ition. Although the Norwegians identified dozens of other fragments of pottery as South American, mainly from Ecuador, they had to admit to uncertainty about the dating of much of what they found, which was very simple pottery that could have been made before or after the Spanish con-quest of the Inca Empire. Some more elaborate fragments may simply show that in the sixteenth century native Indian potters perpetuated styles from the Inca era – one would expect nothing less, since the overwhelming majority of the population remained Indian. So we can conclude that South American Indians did venture out on ships at least as far as the Galápagos; the question remains whether these were Spanish galleons or the balsa wood rafts in which Heyerdahl placed his faith, and the most likely explanation is that the pottery arrived aboard galleons. Nonetheless, the Incas did preserve myths about rulers going out to sea on mysterious voyages, and maybe these should not be totally discounted.

The best evidence for pre-Spanish contact is provided by plants that are very unlikely to have travelled such great distances by natural means, surviving winds and seas without being destroyed: bottle gourds and sweet potatoes spread across the Pacific, but originated in South America; in the other direction, coconuts reached Panama. The word used by the Quechua Indians in South America for the sweet potato, *kamote*, has been imaginatively compared to Easter Island *kumara* and Polynesian *kuumala*.[20] Seasonal winds made journeys to South America possible, but there is no evidence for any attempt to settle there and no evidence for active commerce between South America and any part of Polynesia.[21] It might be argued that the sweet potato was diffused by the Spaniards when they gained control over trans-Pacific trade routes in the sixteenth century. However, the places where they were most actively cultivated lay some way from the Spanish trade routes – Hawai'i, New Zealand and Easter Island – and carbonized tubers of sweet potato excavated by archaeologists in New Zealand, Hawai'i and Mangaia can all be dated to the period before the arrival of the Europeans. Mangaia lies in the Cook Islands, part of Remote Oceania situated north-east of New Zealand; its specimens have been carbon-dated to about AD 1000. While it is possible to imagine birds carrying seeds across many thousands of miles, tubers are another story. It is therefore safe to say that Polynesian navigators extended their range right across the Pacific during this extraordinarily ambitious second phase of expansion.

Even more remarkable than possible contact with the admittedly vast landmass of South America, impossible to miss if you go far enough eastwards, is the settlement of Rapa Nui, or Easter Island, in the middle of nowhere. And yet, by contrast with Hawai'i, it at least lies on the plane of Polynesia, and reaching Rapa Nui posed less of a challenge in dealing with the winds. There are probably as many theories about the significance of the island's enigmatic giant statues as there are statues. The question here is, rather, by what means navigators reached Rapa Nui and what sort of outside contacts the islanders maintained after its discovery and settlement. Heyerdahl, naturally, saw Easter Island as one of the first bases of his pioneering Peruvian sailors; the locals obliged him by offering him pieces of South American pottery, but they were just modern Chilean ceramics (the island is governed by Chile) – they wanted to keep the eccentric Norwegian gentleman happy.

The first difficulty is agreeing on a date for settlement. One version of the islanders' own traditions told how the inhabitants were led there by Hotu Matu'a from Hiva, who was seeking the sunrise; his name merely means 'Great Parent'. There are several islands in the Marquesas group, to the north-east of Rapa Nui, that contain the word 'Hiva' in their name, and, as has been seen, the Marquesas may well have been the source of the Hawai'ian population.[22] These traditions also report a six-week voyage inspired by Hoto Matu'a's tattooist, who said he had dreamed of a fine volcanic isle to the east. The striking feature is not so much the detail in the story but the awareness that the islanders had come across the sea, and that the world consisted of more than their own island, a view that, in their extreme isolation, they could easily have held, and that other less isolated island peoples have held.[23]

Counting the fifty-seven generations said to have elapsed between Hotu Matu'a and the recording of the legend one reaches a date of AD 450; but such methods, as will be clear from New Zealand, are without much merit, and some of those working with the same oral material have produced dates in the twelfth or even the sixteenth century. Fortunately modern science resolves the difficulty, up to a point: Carbon 14 dating shows that settlers were already installed on Rapa Nui around the end of the seventh century AD (690±130), a date derived from material found at a temple platform. Yet this too is not a flawless way of establishing dates; an even earlier date of AD 318 came from a grave that also contained a bone dated AD 1629. The language of the islanders, though clearly Polynesian (as seen in the place names especially) has distinctive features that lead linguists who specialize in glottochronology to conclude that it broke away from neighbouring tongues around AD 400; it mixes features from western and eastern Polynesian, and there has been time for a local vocabulary to develop, such as the word *poki* (child). The islanders also developed a very distinctive script, or possibly brought it along from somewhere else that abandoned its use, though that is to assume that the script was not developed after contact with and in imitation of the Europeans. It was a sacred script, almost always inscribed with care on wooden panels; unfortunately no attempt at decipherment has been totally convincing.[24]

Rapa Nui is best known for the remarkable statues and temple platforms that pepper Easter Island. The high period of construction stretched over several hundred years from 1200 to 1600. The statues, which originally looked away from the sea and towards the volcanic interior, apparently represented ancestors, while the often elaborate platforms seem to have been used not just for rituals but as astronomical observatories, so that the loss of interest in navigation was evidently not accompanied by a loss of interest in reading the skies. Local priests saw the night sky as a calendar that they used to fix their festivals.[25] Cut off from the rest of the world, the island tried to survive from its own resources, but, steadily denuded of tree cover by its inhabitants, Rapa Nui became impoverished. Environmental collapse provides the best explanation for the end of the era of prosperity that brought these platforms and statues into being – indeed, over the following centuries statues were cast down, the inhabitants went to war with one another, often living in caves, and competition for scarce resources intensified.

Easter Island may well be the great exception to the general rule that islands were searched out deliberately; whether or not it was found by accident, it remained off the mental map of the Polynesian navigators. Like Hawai'i and New Zealand, it did not feature on the hand-drawn map the Polynesian navigator Tupaia prepared for Captain Cook, which only extended as far east as the Marquesas.[26] Pitcairn Island too was cut off from the rest of Polynesia and was empty when the mutineers from the *Bounty* arrived in 1790; but it had been inhabited in the past, as stone remains were found – clearly there had been an extremely isolated population that had died out or emigrated. And a similar story can be told of Kiritimati (in Kiribati), to which the mutineers eventually moved.[27] Some attempts at colonization were simply not successful, because the fortunes of these island communities depended on their position within still larger communities of islands that interacted across the ocean through trade, warfare and marriage ties.

These most remote islands, then, were the realms of Pluto and the outermost planets, places beyond the outer edge of the interactive world of the Polynesian chiefdoms, who warred with one another, whose people traded with one another, and who preserved over generation after generation their unwritten but detailed and highly effective science of navigation. That still leaves untold the discovery and settlement of what are by far the largest islands in Polynesia, and the most inhospitable climatically: the North and South Islands of New Zealand.

IV

The history of the discovery of New Zealand has always been a tangle. In European accounts, Abel Tasman and Captain Cook appear prominently, as explorers who found the islands and who worked out their shape. That is to ignore the native Māori population of what the descendants of the original settlers still call Aotearoa, a name attributed to Hine-te-aparangi, the wife of Kupe, the first Polynesian navigator to reach North Island – the mountainous, often cold, South Island was visited and was lightly settled over the centuries, but the great majority of Māoris would choose to live in the warmer north. The Māori name of the island means 'Long White Cloud' (*ao* + *tea* + *roa*, 'cloud white long'), because that is what Kupe's wife thought she saw when she first approached its shores, not realizing that this was land. Calculating back the generations, orthodox opinion places the discovery of New Zealand in the middle of the tenth century AD, a date often refined to 925, though more modern research insists that the supposed founder may have arrived as late as the middle of the fourteenth century, assuming that these genealogies have any merit at all and that Kupe really existed, or indeed that he was not more than one person.[28] This was supposedly followed by a second settlement, led by a certain Toi, around 1150, and then the arrival of a whole fleet of canoes in about 1350. That, at least, was the view accepted both by Māoris and by *Pakeha* (white Europeans) who tried to write the very early history of New Zealand in the nineteenth and twentieth centuries. Kupe was enthusiastically described as the 'Columbus, Magellan or Cook' of the Māoris, a historical figure who certainly existed and who was the most eminent representative of hundreds of generations of Polynesian navigators in the Pacific.[29] A Māori song began:

> *Ka tito au, ka tito au,*
> *Ka tito au ki a Kupe,*
> *Te tangata nana i hoehoe te moana,*
> *Te tangata nana i topetope te whenua.*

> I will sing, I will sing,
> I will sing of Kupe,
> The man who paddled the ocean,
> The man who divided up the land.

The difficulty is that all the information we have about Kupe is derived from oral traditions, impressive in their command of the finer details of genealogy, so that even the names of the wives of slaves are given, but packed with legendary materials – sometimes a giant octopus, sometimes tribes of goblins, not to mention canoes that turned into stone and a miraculous belt that churned the surface of the sea. Just because the art of navigation was transmitted orally and was evidently a very exact science, we cannot assume that this genealogical information deserves the same credit; indeed, these genealogies vary from place to place, with generations added and subtracted to accommodate the traditions of local chieftains. History and symbolism were mixed together, and then contaminated by contact with the *Pakeha*.[30] Nor is there a single agreed account of Kupe's career; in one version *Aotearoa* was the name of Kupe's canoe.

These oral traditions themselves were written down, admittedly by Māoris, but under the influence of British missionaries and other modern settlers. In one version Kupe sees his god Io in a dream, and the god says to him: 'Go forth upon the great ocean . . . take and possess yourself of some land which I will show to you.' The strong echoes here of the story of Abraham being led to Canaan by God indicate that this tale tells one more about the impact of Christian missionaries than about Māori traditions. The most vocal critic of attempts to use these tales as history has called them 'modern New Zealand folktales'.[31] That said, they are illuminating both for the stories they tell about the original settlement as the native inhabitants of Aotearoa imagined it and for the information they convey about navigating the open ocean. At their core is the certainty that the settlers came from far across the sea, and that their ancestors lived in a place called Hawaiki. It has been seen that the letter *k* becomes *t* in some Polynesian dialects, and in others a glottal stop is often used instead of either, so Hawaiki is another form of the name Hawai'i; or, rather, Hawai'i took its name from a supposed ancestral home much further to the south, to which the Māoris also attributed their origins.[32] They did not claim to have come from the island group now called Hawai'i. Once again, though, it is important not to be too credulous. The name 'Hawaiki' was a generic term for the place of one's ancestors – 'the old country', as it were, whose name was reused again and again to confer a sense that connections to those ancestors had not been lost by migrants as far away as what we now call Hawai'i. Children in the womb were described as being 'in Hawaiki' before they were born.[33] Hawaiki is portrayed in the Māori legends as the home of a seafaring community that sustained itself by fishing and was riven by conflict between competing chieftains, but there is little information about the shape and size of the island or about what grew there, because it was an idealized place of origin.[34]

There exist many versions of this story, some of which provide plenty of names and details, such as the number of people on board Kupe's boat (one account says thirty). On both the North and the South Islands Kupe was said to have given a name to any number of places along the coast that he supposedly visited; for instance, his point of departure from North Island was and is known as Hokianga nui a Kupe, which means 'Great Returning Place of Kupe'.[35] It was natural that local chieftains sought to increase their prestige by showing that their territory had links to the discoverer of Aotea-roa. The most dramatic version of his story celebrates Kupe's contest with an octopus that led him southwards towards Aotearoa and then along the coasts of North Island, and in some variants South Island too.

The tale begins back in Hawaiki. Muturangi was an inhabitant of Hawaiki who owned a pet octopus – not any ordinary octopus but an enormous one named Te Wheke ('the octopus') with dozens of children. (If the idea of an ocean-going octopus as a pet seems strange, so is the assertion that Kupe's daughters kept an eel and a mullet as pets.) The octopus and her young would follow the boats of Kupe and his compan-ions as they headed out into the open sea searching for deep-sea fish, and they would grab with their tentacles the bait Kupe trailed in the water, making the work of the fishermen impossible and leaving the islanders famished. Muturangi thought this was good sport and refused to rein in his pet octopus, so the only option left was for Kupe and his friends to go and search for Te Wheke and her brood, and kill all of them. This was agreed at a meeting of the village elders, who seem to have been quite unable to restrain Muturangi. So Kupe and his friends went out to sea with a simple but cunning plan: as a rule, the bait that the octopuses ate was trailed in the ocean, and allowed to sink far down, to a point where the fishermen could not detect their presence. This time they paid out shorter fishing lines, so they were able to sense when the octopuses seized the bait, and then they pulled in their lines, bringing up the young octo-puses, which they cut to pieces. All the time, though, the mother octopus watched the massacre of her children without attacking, while keeping her distance from the canoes. Te Wheke planned to wreak revenge in due course. But Kupe and his friends were not content to have destroyed only the young octopuses. They would search out Te Wheke and destroy her as well. Kupe's wife insisted he should not abandon her in Hawaiki and go on such a dangerous mission, so he solved the problem by taking her and his children along on his canoe, plus a crew of sixty, and set off in pursuit of Te Wheke; his companion Ngake, or Ngahue, who had sailed ahead of him, found Te Wheke and together they pursued the octopus further and further southwards, tracing the orange glow of the beast as she swam far beneath the surface of the sea.

They found themselves in increasingly unfamiliar waters where the temperatures were much lower and the nights much longer, but still they refused to abandon their mission. Then Hine-te-aparangi, Kupe's wife, saw the first signs of land and the two canoes were able to replenish sup-plies on the north coast of North Island. Ngahue was given the task of tracking Te Wheke down the east coast, in the hope of trapping her; and

Kupe would explore the west coast, before returning to help Ngahue finish off the troublesome monster. Ngahue did manage to bottle the octopus up in a great cave, from which she could not escape without confronting his fully armed crew; but when Kupe arrived at last and engaged with her he was only able to wound her, and as evening fell she managed to escape in the confusion of battle. She swam south and this drew the two canoes ever further towards the southern tip of North Island, and then into what is now Wellington Harbour, a large volcanic caldera filled with ocean water. Here the crews rested and once again took on supplies. Ngahue set out to explore the South Island that lay on the horizon, but before long the canoes were reunited and tracked down Te Wheke. Their tactics involved a combination of subterfuge and brute strength. They confused Te Wheke by hurling calabashes at her head, and she was convinced these were human heads, so she turned her attention from the canoes to the calabashes and wrapped her already damaged tentacles around them. After this, Kupe launched his adze at the spot between the eyes where an octopus is most vulnerable and the animal was slaughtered.[36]

Kupe sailed back to Hawaiki with the first news of this great land to the south. He was asked if the lands he had discovered were inhabited and gave a non-committal answer: he had seen a wood hen, a bellbird and a fantail; he had found that the soil was rich and that the islands had an abundance of fish. (All the signs are that the island was uninhabited before the arrival of the Māoris, but some oral traditions spoke of goblins or of red-skinned people with flat noses, thin calves and lank hair, for whom there is no archaeological evidence.)[37] So would he go back there? He answered that question with the question: *E hoki Kupe?* 'Will Kupe return?', a phrase that continued to be used in Aotearoa as a polite but firm refusal. Needless to say, the Māoris could point to exact places where a canoe, or an anchor, a mast or even the first dog to reach North Island had turned to stone and could still be seen on the coast of Aotearoa.[38]

Oral histories separated Kupe's discovery from later phases of rediscovery and then of large-scale settlement. An important feature of these stories is the insistence that news of New Zealand was brought back to Polynesia (usually identified simply as 'Hawaiki'). Toi was a chieftain from Hawaiki who is supposed, on the usual calculation of generations, to have lived in the twelfth century. The stories about him vary, and what will be followed here is a so-called 'orthodox' version that has been widely circulated because it is preserved in a nineteenth-century manuscript and goes into some detail; but there is doubt whether it records authentic Māori tradition.[39] In Hawaiki, he and his men were challenged to a canoe race by neighbours from other islands, and sixty canoes entered the contest. Toi himself did not take part but watched the contest from a high point with a great crowd of onlookers; however, his two grandsons, Turahui and Whatonga, did join the tournament. The race took the canoes far out to sea, and for once the learned Polynesian navigators did not read the weather signs with due care and attention; winds and fogs dispersed the canoes and several disappeared entirely. Consultation of the gods produced no clear answers to the fate of Toi's grandsons and the other canoes that had disappeared. Toi himself therefore set out, thinking that he might find the lost canoes far to the south, in lands he had only heard about: 'I will go on to the land discovered by Kupe in the expanse known as *Tiritiri o te moana*, the land that is shrouded by the high mists. I may reach land, but if I do not, I will rest forever in the bosom of the Ocean Maid.'[40]

Whether described as Aotearoa, the long white cloud, or as the land shrouded in mist, this was a place defined in large part by its unattractive weather. Toi reached the isthmus of Auckland and found a dense population, so many people that he compared them to ants. He lived among them and several crew members settled down with local women. (As has been seen, there is no doubt that these earlier settlers were a fantasy of later tellers of tales.)[41] Toi established himself near Whakatane on the north coast of North Island, a particularly well-favoured area with a benign climate. But he was soon drawn into tribal wars, which proves that these accounts of the often difficult relations between those living on the island reflect the violent and destructive conflict that still characterized Māori society at the time of Captain Cook.

Fortunately, Toi's grandsons had survived the storm that had scattered the canoes during the contest back in Hawaiki, and they had indeed made landfall, though not in Aotearoa, but at a place named after its ruler, Rangiatea (this could be a reference to the island of Ra'iatea, a hundred miles from Tahiti). And, at home in Hawaiki, Toi's daughter-in-law did not believe that Toi would find Turahui and Whatonga so easily; she had a much better plan, which was to send the pet green cuckoo owned by Turahui on a mission to find the lost grandsons. She tied a knotted message around the bird, which duly found Turahui on Rangiatea's island, and he had no difficulty deciphering the message: 'Are you alive? At what island are you?' He made a new knotted cord that stated 'We are all alive at Rangiatea', and watched the direction the bird took; then the grandsons and their companions set out in six canoes along the same trajectory and reached Hawaiki safely, where they were rapturously received.[42]

Once again, then, we have a story that not merely commemorates the discovery and settlement of Aotearoa, but one that places the islands of New Zealand amid the great island chains of Polynesia. Other stories confirm this: one account of journeys to and fro between Hawaiki and Aotearoa describes the introduction of sweet potato into Aotearoa. A visitor from Hawaiki had carried with him some dried sweet potato that he carried in his belt; he offered it to his hosts on Aotearoa, reconstituted with water, and they found it delicious. They then sent to Hawaiki for seeds, which duly arrived.[43] But the fascination of the story of Turahui goes further: the use of knotted cords is reminiscent of the Peruvian *quipus*, which were the closest the Incas came to devising writing, and which they used for messages and for keeping accounts; this is not for a moment to suggest that Peruvians radiated as far as New Zealand, but it does serve as a reminder that apparently illiterate peoples have often developed their own mnemonic systems, and that archaeology is good at finding inscriptions on stone but not so good at finding knotted cords.

There is no need here to retell all the details of the story of how Whatonga went in search of Toi, though the most detailed accounts described in great detail a lavishly decorated canoe with places for sixty-six men, including several chieftains; images of three gods were carried on board. Having secured the help of these gods, the canoe was said to have circumnavigated much of North Island, finally reaching Whakatane and the home of Toi, who was now chieftain of a great tribe generated by his followers after they took native women as their brides.[44] There is something in these stories that recalls Telemachos going out to find his father, Odysseus, and though contamination by Greek myths seems unlikely, it cannot be excluded, for all the versions we have were recorded after the arrival of European missionaries and settlers.

Finally, supposedly in the mid-fourteenth century, we hear of a mass movement of people, in stories that tell how all the great lineages of Aotearoa descended from the *heke* or Great Migration of a fleet of canoes from Hawaiki. The canoes, rather than Kupe and Toi, marked the real beginning of time on Aotearoa for the Māori tribes. In the oral accounts they were described in sometimes meticulous detail, including even the exact position where individual sailors sat by the thwarts; later generations knew which canoe had brought their own ancestors. When the gods were brought on board a vessel became taboo (*tapu*) and only fresh food could be eaten; no cooking was allowed. Bags made of seaweed were filled with fresh water and towed behind the boat, keeping the water cool and reducing the weight of the cargo.[45] To calm the waves, the sailors sang magical incantations as they crossed the ocean:

> Fiercely plies the shaft of this my paddle,
> Named *Kautu ki te rangi*.

To the heavens raise it, to the skies uplift it.
It guides to the distant horizon,
To the horizon that seems to draw near,
To the horizon that instils fear,
To the horizon that causes dread,
The horizon of unknown power,
Bounded by sacred restrictions.

All of this reflects the everyday practices of later generations, whose skill in building beautifully carved boats can still be admired in Te Papa, the National Museum of New Zealand at Wellington; such boats could easily measure twenty or even thirty metres in length. The stories of this migration report quarrels over the food tribute paid to chieftains on Hawaiki, so one might like to argue that pressure on food supplies motivated the migrants. They also report the arrival of all the canoes but one on the east coast of North Island, followed by a tour of the coast so that each chieftain could acquire his own patch of territory without getting in the way of his neighbours. Once again, we hear of the introduction of the sweet potato and of ceremonies to dedicate a tuber to one of the patron gods of the migrants; otherwise the migrants seem to have brought few plants or none, and to have been content with what grew in the unfamiliar temperate climate of New Zealand. Dogs, hens and rats (themselves often eaten as food, as a delicacy conserved in fat) are also mentioned in the oral traditions. There is some debate about the Carbon 14 dating of rat bones, some of which appear to be 2,000 years old, but this is far earlier than other evidence for a human presence will allow. Two dogs were sacrificed to the god Maru by the crew of the boat *Aotea* ('White Cloud') that arrived on the west coast.[46]

Hard evidence for the coming of the Māori as far back as the tenth century has not been found. Increasingly, archaeologists have been content to argue from silence and to insist that the date for migration should be pushed later, right into the middle of the fourteenth century, but possibly a little earlier. This does not discount the possibility that people vaguely comparable to Kupe and Toi arrived much earlier, without establishing a settlement. Discovery is not generally a sudden process; awareness of new land spreads thinly but does not necessarily lead to further action, as the example of the Norse arrival in North America shows: the crucial change occurs when this new knowledge takes its place in a wider world view.

Early settlements, which according to tradition were concentrated on the west coast of North Island, would have left few traces, and some material such as stone adzes is hard to date. More suggestive is the discovery of Māori refuse piled up in middens that also included the bones of now extinct flightless birds known as *moa*. On South Island graves were found that included among the burial goods blown *moa* eggs alongside adzes and fish hooks of typical Polynesian design. Did the Māoris hunt these birds to extinction? The name *moa* was simply a Polynesian word for domestic fowl. Arriving in Aotearoa, the settlers transferred the name to several species of flightless bird that had lived in relative peace on an island that lacked mammals which might have preyed on the birds; humans, indeed, were the first mammals to arrive – as a general rule isolated islands do not contain native mammals. In some of the oral traditions there are references to native birds of this sort.[47] Particularly on the cool South Island, where cultivation of the soil posed greater challenges to those used to traditional Polynesian agriculture, the settlers may for a while have relied on the flesh of birds and on fish and seafood for sustenance. But most of this is speculation. It cannot be proved that land clearance was under way before about 1200.[48] The important point is that newly arrived people who settled previously uninhabited islands rapidly changed the ecological balance, whether by clearing the land for crops, by introducing Pacific rats that attacked wildlife, or by themselves throwing off balance the delicate relationship between native flora and fauna and the environment.[49] What was true in Aotearoa was true in virtually every island humans settled, in all the oceans.

In Aotearoa, as in Hawai'i, the population turned its back on the sea, and regular contact with the rest of the Polynesian world ceased. The new territory offered the resources the settlers needed, without the shortages of vital goods that would stimulate trade. For instance, the characteristic green stone out of which implements and adornments were made was plentiful on New Zealand, and so was obsidian, a volcanic product that not surprisingly is abundant on these two islands where volcanic activity has always been lively. The Polynesians had reached the limit of their spread across the Pacific by the middle of the fourteenth century AD. The settlement of the Pacific had, with a significant interruption, taken 3,000 years, but had embraced distances of more than 3,000 miles. We shall return to the open Pacific when European sailors entered its waters – first Magellan, and later the famous Manila galleons linking the Philippines to Central and South America. Yet it has to be admitted that the simple but effective maritime technology of the Polynesians trumped that of European sailors, not to mention the Chinese and the Japanese.

PART TWO

The Middle Ocean: The Indian Ocean and Its Neighbours, 4500 BC–AD 1500

3
The Waters of Paradise

I

Even a cursory look at a map reveals a fundamental difference between the Pacific Ocean and the Indian Ocean. Whereas the Pacific is dotted with islands, especially in the south-west, the human presence in the Indian Ocean is defined by its coasts. The scattered, empty islands of the Pacific meant that it became an ocean of migrants; the settled, connected shores of the Indian Ocean made it into a network of traders. Remote, widely scattered islands such as Mauritius and Réunion were discovered and settled by Europeans and those they brought with them as slaves or indentured servants long after the Polynesians had already set foot on every habitable Pacific island. Besides, the great concentration of Indian Ocean islands only begins beyond the ocean's eastern edge, spilling into the Pacific, in the territories now known as Indonesia and Malaysia. Among other islands, the Andamans were made famous by Marco Polo and other travellers because the inhabitants were said to kill or even eat any visitors; but only one island of any great size stands off Africa, and that place, Madagascar, was partly settled by Malays or Indonesians who had travelled all the way from the edges of the Pacific.

This comparison does, however, leave out of account an area within the Pacific that only gradually became an important area of maritime activity: the South China Sea, stretching from Singapore across to the Philippines and up to Taiwan, and the seas beyond, the Yellow Sea and the Japan Sea, encompassing the coasts of northern China, Korea and the Japanese archipelago. This great arc, unlike the vast tracts of Polynesia, Melanesia and Micronesia, developed close links with the Indian Ocean and can sensibly be treated as an extension of the Indian Ocean world. Nothing symbolizes these links better than the appetite of Chinese and Japanese Buddhists in the first millennium AD for Indian texts, relics and even works of art, so that a fresco painted in the Nara region of Japan in

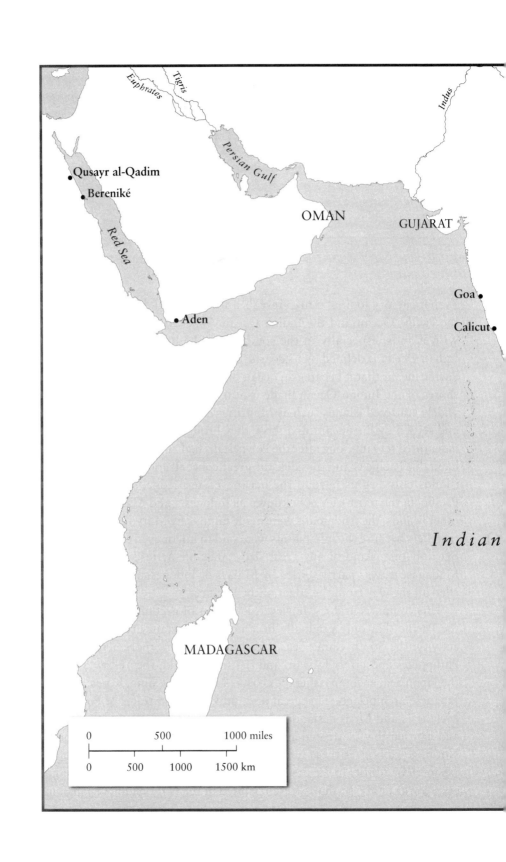

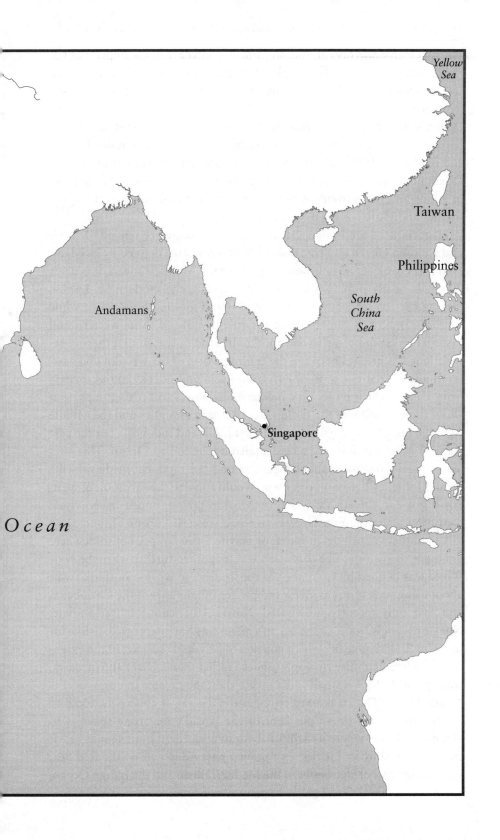

AD 759 clearly portrays an Indian princess, and carries the imprint of the Hellenistic artists who, in the wake of Alexander the Great, brought Greek artistic styles to north-western India.[1] The waters to the east of China remained remarkably quiet for much longer than the waters of the Indian Ocean, whose history as a thoroughfare began, in fits and starts, as Egyptians and Sumerians sent their first trading expeditions down the Red Sea and the Gulf. All this testifies to the extraordinary vitality of the Indian Ocean since antiquity; by the first millennium the only sea where exchanges of goods and the movement of people were more intense was the much smaller and more confined Mediterranean.

Historians of the Indian Ocean have in consequence tended to think of the Indian Ocean as a sort of Mediterranean, a sea defined by its edges, even if there exists no southern edge. Like the Mediterranean, it is a sea that falls neatly into two halves, with Ceylon, the modern Sri Lanka, playing the role of Sicily, a substantial island looking both ways, while southern India has something of the role of Italy, with its western and eastern flanks connected to one another by land or sea, so that these areas functioned as bridges between the trading world of the western and eastern 'Indies'. That is a term drawn from Latin and Greek, and ultimately from Hindi, which by its very indeterminacy says something important about the vast space of the Indian Ocean; for in antiquity and the Middle Ages the term 'Indies' embraced not just India and Indonesia but the east coast of Africa, that is, anywhere lapped by the Indian Ocean. This later led to much confusion about where to find the mythical medieval king Prester John, a Christian prince who would come to the salvation of western Europe in the struggle against Muslim power; and it led to equal confusion when the first Gypsies to reach western Europe around 1400 talked blithely of origins in India, or maybe 'little Egypt', but somewhere out there, at any rate. The confusion was magnified further when the New World was defined by Columbus as the 'Indies', so we do not think twice about using such terms as 'West Indian' for inhabitants of the Caribbean, and have only recently substituted 'Native American' for 'Red Indian'. Not surprisingly, some of the ocean's historians have expressed dislike for the term 'Indian Ocean', which appears to privilege one part of the extensive shoreline, but this is to apply modern rather than ancient and medieval concepts of India – a small India rather than the greater Indies.[2]

The Indian Ocean is hard to measure. To say it covers 75,000,000 square kilometres or 27 per cent of the world's maritime space is to assume we know where its arbitrarily drawn southern limit should lie.[3] It can be defined by its historic exit points: past Aden and up the Red Sea, which acted as a bridge between the Mediterranean and the Indian Ocean;

through the Strait of Malacca past Singapore into the Pacific. To these can be added, much later, with the Portuguese entry into the Indian Ocean in 1497, the Cape of Good Hope, giving access to the Atlantic. Another southern edge, the west coast of Australia, was not of much interest to anyone sailing the seas until the nineteenth century, and even then to a very limited degree. But one of the earliest and most vibrant exit points, even though it leads to rivers rather than the open sea, passes through the waters between Arabia and Iran variously known as the Persian and the Arabian Gulf.[4]

It seems odd to speak of 'the slow creation' of the Indian Ocean, as if this space had not been in existence for millions of years before sea traffic began to pass along its shores and across its open spaces. But from the perspective of maritime history the question is when the Indian Ocean began to function as a unit – in other words, when the coasts of east Africa, Arabia, India and south-east Asia began to interact across the sea, whether through migration or through trade. In addition to breaking down these shores into a series of discrete, and at times quite disconnected, coasts, attention has to focus on the two major gulfs that penetrate deep into the Middle East, the Red Sea and the Persian Gulf, channels that gave access to two of the earliest, richest and most innovative civilizations of the ancient world, those of ancient Egypt and Mesopotamia. To say that they made very profitable use of the sea routes running south-eastwards from their lands is not to say that the pharaohs or the merchants of the Sumerian and Babylonian cities made uninterrupted use of these routes; nor is it to claim that they ventured very far out into the ocean, though, as will be seen, the Sumerians did make contact by sea with another great civilization that lay to the east of Mesopotamia. The beginnings of Indian Ocean trade were jerky; maritime ventures such as the Egyptian expeditions down the Red Sea to the 'land of Punt' were intermittent, and there is no evidence in the earliest documents or in the archaeological records that regular voyages took place around Arabia, linking Egyptian ports on the Red Sea to the Persian Gulf. And yet the produce of the lands along the shores of the Indian Ocean was irresistible: expensive necessities such as copper, luxury materials such as black ebony and white ivory, as well as aromatic resins such as frankincense and myrrh. Egyptians talked of the products of Punt, which they described as 'the god's land', and in early Mesopotamia the route down the Persian Gulf was said to lead to the abode of the Blessed.

The nearer edges of the Indian Ocean and even the Red Sea and the Persian Gulf were vaguely defined, according to mental maps on which place names moved around and seem to have indicated where particular products could be found, rather than where a destination actually lay: the

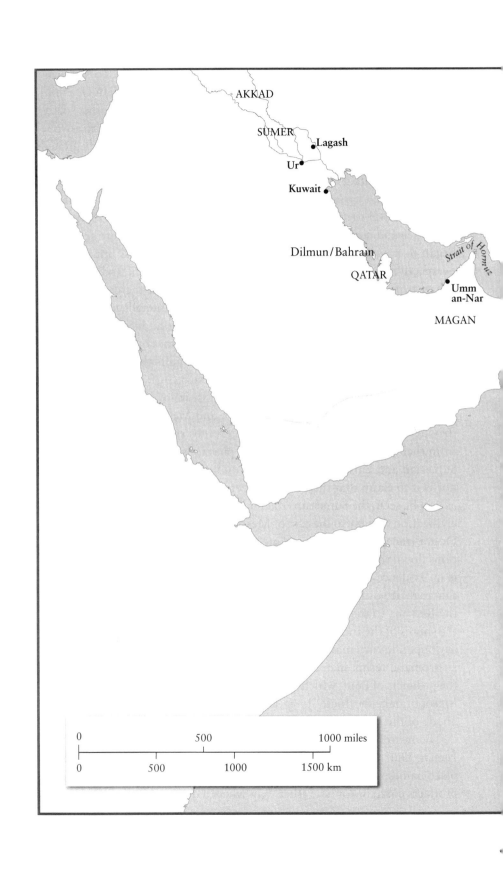

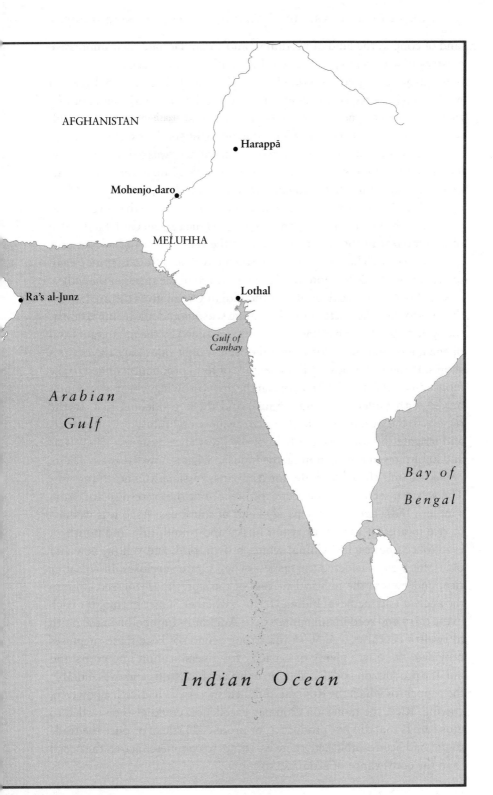

land of copper, the land of perfumes, and so on. Despite their impressive mastery of astronomy, the ancient Babylonians had no sense of the scale of the great ocean that lay beyond the Gulf. A highly schematic Babylonian world map preserved on a cuneiform tablet in the British Museum, dating from 700–500 BC, not surprisingly placed Iraq at the centre of the world, with the Bitter Sea (Persian Gulf) leading off to the south-east and a Salt Sea surrounding the landmass. The aim of the mapmaker was to illustrate Babylonian mythology rather than to guide sailors to a safe haven, and in this sense it is comparable to the equally schematic world maps of medieval Europe such as the Hereford *mappamundi*. But there is a sense that, even 2,000 years after the first regular voyages crept out of the Persian Gulf, knowledge of and interest in the wider expanses of the Indian Ocean had not progressed very far. That would happen when Greek and Roman trade began to penetrate ever deeper into the ocean in search of the spices of the Indies.

One famous physical feature of the Indian Ocean gives the area unity: the monsoons. They determine the sailing seasons and, more importantly, the cycle of production of the foodstuffs consumed by the inhabitants and of the goods that have for millennia been sought out along the ocean's shores. Perhaps the most striking feature of food production linked to the monsoons is the distinction between the areas growing wheat (sometimes mixed with millet or similar grains) and those producing rice. In the regions to the west the best hope was to await winter rains, or to dig canals and irrigate the soil with the help of the great river systems – the Tigris and Euphrates in Mesopotamia, the Indus in what is now Pakistan. There, bread became 'the staff of life' for Arabians, Persians and north Indians. The western sector was the sector of bread. But the eastern sector, from southern India across to the paddy fields of south-east Asia, was wedded to rice in a great variety of types: husky and round, thin and polished, even (once one reached China) white, brown, pink and yellow, new and old – this was considered the tastiest type.[5] Grain surpluses, in wheat or rice, underwrote the political success of the states that emerged close to the ancient and medieval Indian Ocean – whether Sumer in Iraq, far back in the third and second millennia BC, or Angkor in Cambodia in the ninth to twelfth centuries AD. With the strong economic base these surpluses provided, there was plenty of capacity for diversification into crafts and into the production and distribution of luxury foodstuffs and dyes, notably the pepper for which the Romans and their successors had such a powerful craving. Rice, the monsoon crop par excellence, could also be traded to those areas that did not produce it, or produced little of it; once the trade routes had been established, there was more to commerce across the ocean than the conveyance of aromatic spices.

The origin of the monsoons lies in the high air temperatures created in the Asian landmass during the summer; cooler air is drawn north-eastwards across the ocean. And then in winter it is much the opposite, as the landmass cools sharply but the ocean retains its warmth. So between June and October winds blow favourably for shipping bound from the south-west of the ocean towards Indonesia, even if that often means sailing through thick blankets of warm rain. On the other hand, strong winds and tempests at sea made navigation in the western Indian Ocean very hazardous in high summer, interrupting traffic to western India, and sailors had to await the slackening of the winds in late August before essaying this route, although there was a window of opportunity for the Omani dhows that had a good chance of reaching India from Arabia in May, June and July. September to May was the period of the year when sailing from Gujarat in western India to Aden proved most feasible. During the fifteenth century, vessels set out from Calicut in January, bound for Aden, and then returned in late summer or early autumn. Winter was also the ideal time to head down from Aden or Oman to the coast of east Africa, returning in April and May – a slow return, generally, as it involved sailing against the currents. Within the Red Sea one had to know that the safe period for a journey northwards lay in January and February, while those bound southwards would need to take advantage of winds that blew southwards in summer time. So, both in the ocean at large and in its subsidiary seas, it was vital to understand how and when the winds shifted from south to north.

Without knowledge of the winds, medieval Arabic writers insisted, a captain would prove himself 'an ignorant and inexperienced adventurer'. From December onwards the winds come from the north and reach as far as Madagascar. By spring, vast quantities of water have been dumped on India and on the southern tip of Arabia (creating an extraordinarily fertile zone in western Oman). Even so, the changes in the winds were predictable rather than certain, and a wise captain knew that helping winds could blow earlier in the season than expected, or that the monsoons could vary in ferocity from year to year. The captain would also take into account the seasonal changes in the currents, though these were heavily influenced by the monsoon winds: in the Red Sea the summer current ran helpfully from north to south, but in winter the movement of water was more complex, and navigation along this sea, already littered with reefs, could be quite perilous; the Persian Gulf followed a similar pattern in summer but thankfully made an uncomplicated reverse in winter.[6]

These characteristics of the Indian Ocean affected the movement of people and the conduct of trade to a much greater degree than one would find in the narrow space of the Mediterranean, where it was possible to challenge the winds and currents, even out of season. The monsoon cycle imposed on travellers a long stay in port as they awaited the turning of the winds. Differences in the wind direction and currents in the western and eastern sectors of the Indian Ocean meant that sea journeys generally had to be conducted in stages. This was even true in the confined space of the Red Sea, where merchants had to await suitable winds in way stations along the coast such as Bereniké and Qusayr al-Qadim, which developed into quite substantial towns servicing the trade routes in the Roman and medieval periods. It is therefore no surprise that in the medieval period, at any rate, the spice route was cut into segments and different stretches were handled by merchants and sailors of different origins – Malays, Tamils, Gujaratis, Persians, Arabs of Arabia, Jews or Copts or Arabs of Egypt. Southern India was the limit of penetration of so-called Roman merchants, that is, businessmen seeking to pipe spices and perfumes into the Mediterranean via the Red Sea. Only with the coming of the Portuguese did a sailing nation appear that sought to span all the great trade routes of this ocean, but they were as confined by the monsoon season as anyone when trading to and beyond Calicut and Goa.

I I

The Persian or Arabian Gulf is a small area into which many contrasts have been packed: its north-eastern shore leads steeply upwards to the mountains of Persia, offering few good harbours; its south-eastern shores are dry, sandy spaces, mainly flat but afflicted by the intense heat of Arabia and the high humidity of an area close to the warm sea; its northern tip is waterlogged, filled with the silt of the Tigris and Euphrates that has carried the shoreline ever southwards and gives access to lands rich in wheat, themselves contained by desert and upland. After about 4000 BC a relatively benign phase came to an end which had seen moderate rainfall in Arabia, and increasing aridification set in – this, indeed, provided a stimulus to trade, as self-sufficiency broke down. Another major change occurred with a fall in sea levels of about two metres by around 6000 BC, so that archaeological sites that would have been originally on the shoreline now stand a little higher up, a short way inland.[7] Within the Gulf, islands and peninsulas have offered stopping points for travellers, notably at Bahrain, Qatar and Umm an-Nar (near Abu Dhabi); and then, beyond the narrowing of the sea at the Strait of Hormuz, backed by the mountains of Oman, there is access to the ocean itself, and the chance to make

way along the coasts of what are now Iran and Pakistan as far as the
opening of other rivers: the Indus and the many river systems of north-west
India. These different environments were not generally self-sufficient and
depended upon exchange; date palms played a particularly important part
in the networks of maritime trade that emerged as early as the sixth
millennium BC.

At this time a relatively advanced culture developed in southern Iraq
that has been given the name Ubaid; by 4500 BC it came to be characterized by temples, palaces and the beginning of towns.[8] The domestication
of animals and the cultivation of the soil, already under way several thousand years before, produced, in several corners of Asia and the Middle
East, hierarchical and increasingly sophisticated societies, the ancestors
of those that would create the massive cities and spectacular artworks of
Mesopotamia, Egypt, China and (though rather later) the Indus Valley. It
is impossible to underestimate the importance in these societies of the great
rivers, not so much as means of communication, though that came later,
but as sources of fresh water for agriculture. However, knowledge of
Ubaid is still very fragmentary. Over so many centuries there must have
been enormous transformations, and identifying them is rendered no
easier by the sparse and often inconsistent dating that has been suggested
by archaeologists.

The basis of the wealth of the Ubaid culture seems to have been mastery
over agricultural produce and the possession of flocks, used not just as
food but as the foundation of leather and cloth industries, though inevitably the hard evidence consists mainly of Ubaid pottery, with its distinctive
and often elegant linear decoration. Who controlled this proto-urban
society cannot be said with any certainty; but the occasional presence of
traders can be assumed with some confidence. This is because Ubaid pottery turns up regularly on sites away from southern Iraq, in Saudi Arabia,
in Oman and on the other side of the Gulf in Iran.[9] Shards of very early
Ubaid pottery, with a green tinge and purple decoration, are definitely of
Mesopotamian origin. Yet other Ubaid goods, such as the typical southern
Mesopotamian figurines, have not appeared on sites along the Arabian
coast, leading archaeologists to conclude that the pottery fragments are
evidence for occasional visits by merchants from Iraq, but not proof that
a fully fledged trading network had come into existence. The people of
the coast were still limited in their technology to fairly standard stone
tools, and did not have the wherewithal, as far as one can tell, to launch
expeditions across the water; nor were their own settlements long-lasting
towns in germ, but rather villages that came and went off the map.[10] As
early as the late sixth millennium, dates, apparently traded, were arriving

in Kuwait and on the island of Dalma off Abu Dhabi, for their carbonized remains have been identified by archaeologists; then as now the date was an everyday stand-by in the daily diet, a reliable source of energy and a quick stomach-filler.

This was not just a simple route up and down the Gulf, linked to the settlements of Ubaid. Beads of carnelian, a semi-precious stone from Iran or Pakistan, have been found in Qatar, as also in Iraq.[11] Plenty of boats were being built along the shores of the Gulf in the fifth, fourth and third millennia BC. Around 5000 BC, to judge from impressions left in fragments of bitumen found at as-Sabiyah in Kuwait, boats were constructed out of reed bundles covered with tar. There are traces of barnacles, a sign that these boats set out across saltwater.[12] Further evidence survives in the form of a pottery model of a ship and a small painted disc carrying the image of a sailing vessel. Tunny-fishing was certainly one maritime activity of the inhabitants of early Bahrain, to judge from the fish bones found there by archaeologists. The finds of Ubaid pottery are neatly spread out along the Arabian coast, which suggests that boats were jumping from one waterhole to another as they wended their way down the Gulf.[13]

It would be hard to insist that this water traffic had yet become the economic mainstay of Ubaid Iraq, however important it was to the developing communities of Bahrain and other Gulf stopping places. Ubaid enjoyed increasingly intense land traffic towards Syria in the west, Afghanistan in the east and central Asia in the north; southern Arabia would become more and more important in later phases, when the search for metal ores was under way. The maritime inhabitants of the Persian Gulf lagged behind Ubaid in technological sophistication, living in *barasti* huts made of wooden poles and palm leaves, while the Mesopotamians increasingly accustomed themselves to stone-walled houses.[14] Fourth-millennium Ubaidi traders came to collect dates from the Arabian coast and delivered grain or cloth in return as well as acquiring Gulf pearls, in demand in the increasingly sophisticated towns of Iraq. Pearl-fishing has been a mainstay of economic life in the Gulf over many millennia, and references in the earliest cuneiform tablets from Mesopotamia to the importation of 'fish-eyes', meaning pearls, leads one to suspect that this trade goes back very far in time; pearls, given their organic origin, tend to survive much less well on archaeological sites than precious stones made out of minerals.

The traders also brought down the Gulf that upmarket cutting material of volcanic origin, obsidian, which came all the way from Anatolia by way of Mesopotamia. Rather than imagining that somewhere in the Caucasus beside Lake Van a merchant had thought of sending this item to a distant village on a remote sea, we should assume that this was handed from person to person, taking many years or even generations to end up where it did.[15] This may all look rather unpromising. What product or process could create firmer links between the ever more magnificent civilization of ancient Mesopotamia and a sea bordered by sand dunes and rough mountains? One answer is that those mountains contained a particular mineral much in demand in the luxurious cities of early Bronze Age Mesopotamia.

III

The discovery of Sumerian civilization came as a great surprise to the archaeologists who painstakingly excavated and reconstructed the cities of a much more familiar group of civilizations in Mesopotamia that were mentioned in the Bible. It was known that the early Babylonian kings, speakers of the Semitic language known as Akkadian, called themselves 'kings of Sumer and Akkad'. But where and what was Sumer? The unearthing of the lowest levels at Ur and other cities brought, particularly to the British Museum, astonishing treasures 2,000 years older than the enormous Assyrian carvings and reliefs of around 700 BC that were also carted to London. The Assyrians and Babylonians proved to be the heirs to a very much older civilization of the third millennium BC that did not make use of a Semitic language, as they did, but that wrote in a similar cuneiform script; and this could be deciphered once the sound values of the Akkadian of Babylonia were known, as the enormously plentiful Akkadian tablets that still survive helpfully include bilingual texts and dictionaries of Sumerian.[16] Sumerian literature exerted a fascination for Babylonians long after Sumer was buried beneath the rubble, rather as knowledge of ancient Rome and its language has persisted over the centuries in Europe and beyond. Sumerian myths were rewritten for Babylonian audiences, notably the series of tales about Gilgamesh, king of Uruk. Indeed, it was the Sumerians who as far as we know invented the first coherent, standardized system of writing, even if other civilizations such as that of Egypt preferred not to use the clay tablets impressed with a dense mass of often microscopic letters that came to be favoured in Mesopotamia. But these tablets make up in durability (once baked) for their apparent illegibility.

It is extraordinary, at such a remote period in the past, that we can make use of all three building blocks out of which the early history of mankind has to be constructed, rather than just one of them: works of literature; archaeological finds; and the day-to-day documents left by business houses in the third millennium BC. Taken together, they show how the Gulf emerged as one of the great maritime thoroughfares of that millennium, and how it experienced decline. They help us understand not just the economic foundations of the first true civilization in the world, Sumer, in southern Iraq, but its connections to other great civilizations, especially that of the Indus. They provide the first glimpses of communities of merchants and their hangers-on who settled in ports en route from India to Sumer and left behind their detritus – seals, pottery, necklaces. The exotic lands of Dilmun and Meluḫḫa emerge from a fog, and with increasing confidence they can be located on the mental map of the Sumerians. But even citing these names raises problems. Like the term 'Indies', the names Dilmun and Meluḫḫa meant different things at different times, and the assumed location of Meluḫḫa eventually shifted from Asia to east Africa, long after the Sumerians had been conquered by the Babylonians and Assyrians. And as for Dilmun, it entered literature as a never-never land, a paradise where resided Ziusudra, known to the Babylonians as Uti-napishtim; he was the survivor of the Great Deluge that swept away the rest of mankind in a version of the story of the Flood that in many precise details, such as the sending out of birds to test the waters, anticipates the account of Noah in the book of Genesis. In the Sumerian Flood narrative, Ziusudra was sent by the gods to Dilmun, which was to be found 'where the sun rises', and was granted the eternal life that others, such as the hero Gilgamesh, sought but did not find. Bilgames, as the Sumerians called that hero, even sought out Ziusudra in 'the Land of the Living'; but in the end Bilgames too was fated to follow his great friend Enkidu down into the gloomy Netherworld where disconsolate souls flitted about but there was nothing to enjoy.[17]

Dilmun appears again and again in the cuneiform tablets that have been excavated in the Sumerian cities.[18] The one Sumerian word to have reached modern English and many other languages is 'abyss', recalling the Sumerian *abzu*, the great freshwater deeps on which the world was said to float, with the seabed forming a barrier between saltwater and the waters of the *abzu* which welled up and fed the springs of life on earth. The god of the *abzu* was Enki, who was both the patron of the oldest of the Sumerian cities, Eridu, and a frequent visitor to Dilmun. And one can see why he would wish to go there and escape the chatter of humans, which had driven the gods to such distraction that they unleashed the flood waters on the earth, for, as one tablet proclaims:

> The land of Dilmun is holy, the land of Dilmun is pure,
> The land of Dilmun is clean, the land of Dilmun is holy . . .

> In Dilmun the raven utters no cry,
> The wild hen utters not the cry of the wild hen,
> The lion kills not,
> The wolf snatches not the lamb,
> Unknown is the kid-devouring wild dog,
> Unknown is the grain-devouring boar.[19]

There, there is neither sickness nor old age. Indeed, such is the store of plenty that Dilmun has become the 'house of the docks and quays of the land', in other words a rich centre of trade.[20] Dilmun slid from being an Eden on earth to a real place with ships, merchants and treasures piled up in its storehouses. The god Enki blessed Dilmun and listed the places with which it would trade in luxury products: gold from a place called Harali, lapis lazuli from Tukrish (presumably Afghanistan, the great source of the vivid blue mineral), carnelian and fine wood from Meluḫḫa, copper from Magan, ebony from the 'Sea Land', but also grain, sesame oil, fine garments from Ur in Mesopotamia, handled by skilled Sumerian sailors:

> May the wide sea bring you its abundance.
> The city – its dwellings are good dwellings,
> Dilmun – its dwellings are good dwellings,
> Its barley is very small barley,
> Its dates are very large dates.[21]

If, as will be seen, Meluḫḫa was a major neighbouring civilization and Magan was a land rich in copper, then what was being portrayed here was a great trading city blessed by a great god that lay somewhere towards or within the Indian Ocean, an entrepôt intermediate between Sumer, Magan and Meluḫḫa; the task is to see if anything in the archaeological record proves Dilmun was not simply a fantasy of Sumerian poets.

The clay tablets are the place to begin. Official documents – religious litanies, royal inscriptions, and so on – enumerated products such as black wood from Meluḫḫa, presumably ebony, and a table and chair from Magan, so the places mentioned by the Sumerian poets were real ones. There are several references to boats of Dilmun, Magan and Meluḫḫa; they are known to have reached Akkad in the reign of King Sargon the Great, who was probably the most dynamic ruler of Sumer and Akkad, and who lived in the twenty-third or twenty-second century BC: 'at the wharf of Agade he made moor ships from Meluḫḫa, ships from Magan and ships from Dilmun . . . 5,400 soldiers ate daily in his palace'.[22] This hardly comes as a surprise: supposedly the son of a gardener who became royal cupbearer and eventually usurped the throne, Sargon, like many a usurper, assumed that magnificence and luxury would cast a veil over his controversial origins and path to power. After Sargon's reign, there was an interruption in ties to Magan, for some mysterious reason, and one of his successors, Ur-Nammu (2112–2095 BC) displayed special pride in restoring this contact, for he had four cones made out of clay and inscribed with the same inscription in honour of the god Nanna:

> For Nanna, the chief son of Enlil, his lord, Ur-Nammu, the mighty male, the king of Ur, the king of Sumer and Akkad, the king who built the temple of Nanna, caused the former state of affairs to reappear, at the edge of the sea in the customs house trade was [*gap in the inscriptions*] . . . Ur-Nammu restored the Magan trade [*literally*: boat] into Nanna's hands.[23]

These expeditions into the still uncertain waters of the Persian Gulf were, then, dedicated to the gods, whose protection was sought and whose temples benefited from the copper and luxury goods brought from Dilmun, Magan and beyond.

The best evidence for the reality of Dilmun lies in what would be regarded as quite humdrum documents about merchants and their import–export businesses, were they not so exceptionally old. Lu-Enlilla, for instance, was a *garaša-abba* or seafaring merchant from Ur, one of the greatest Sumerian cities, who traded on behalf of the Temple of Nanna and was commissioned by its administrator, a certain Daia, to take fine cloths and wool on a trading expedition; he was to exchange these goods for copper of Magan. Copper was the great desideratum: Sumer had emerged at a time when copper and, subsequently, copper smelted with tin to make bronze, was required in ever vaster quantities not just to forge strong weapons and tools but to create beautiful objects – figurines, panels, bowls. Sumer was rich in the produce of the soil and of its flocks of sheep and cattle, but poor in metals, robust timber and good quality stone. The copper-bearing mountains of Oman were the place to which to turn for metal, and there is no doubt that Magan corresponds to what is now the Omani peninsula (now partly under the rule of the sultan of Oman and partly under the rule of the sheikhs of the UAE).[24] Proof that the copper came from there lies in the small natural nickel content of Omani copper, which is closer to the nickel content found in copper objects from Sumer than it is to the copper of lands to the north. Copper from the mountains to the north of Mesopotamia was also more expensive and, given the vast quantities that were traded, was more difficult to transport than the seaborne copper of Magan. Oddly, Magan bought barley from Ur but provided Lu-Enlilla with onions, which were plentiful enough in

Mesopotamia, so maybe the sailors on board a ship bound from there had overstocked their larder with them and Lu-Enlilla simply had to put up with that.[25] Meanwhile life in Magan improved; settlements became more permanent, stone towers were built, as well as monumental tombs. This was still a dispersed society, and nothing remotely comparable to the great cities of Sumer emerged, but merchants in search of copper (of which fragments survive in local graves) had given a stimulus to an area that in earlier centuries had been a deserted backwater.[26]

The sea was becoming more important as Ur and its neighbours became greater and greater centres of consumption. Difficult routes across the mountains of Afghanistan could be avoided by taking the sea route to India, where access could be gained to the increasingly powerful cities of the Indus Valley. A gift to the goddess Ningal at Ur included two shekels' weight of lapis lazuli, carnelian, other prized stones and 'fish-eyes' (pearls); these goods had arrived from Dilmun, 'the persons having gone there by themselves from the month Nissannu till the month Addaru'. The names of these months were eventually passed all the way down to the Hebrew calendar as Nisan and Adar, and, bearing in mind the astronomical sophistication of the peoples of ancient Mesopotamia, we can be sure that this means they were absent for eleven months. The gifts had arrived from Dilmun, but they had originated in a scattering of places – the presence of ivory among items listed on some of these tablets suggests links to India, a land of elephants, and its presence was not incidental, for ivory objects were lovingly carved in Ur or were imported ready-carved, like some painted ivory figures of birds, brought from Meluḫḫa, as was much of the carnelian that was so cherished in Sumer. Sometimes, it appears, natives of Dilmun came with these goods; and sometimes men of Ur, such as Lu-Enlilla, set out for Dilmun and carried on their trade there. Some Ur merchants did so as agents of a temple; but, increasingly, others worked on their own.[27] Loans at interest, business partnerships, trading contracts assigning risk, and other indications of a commercial economy with many of the attributes of mercantile capitalism abound, for the first capitalists on record were Sumerian merchants long ago in the third millennium BC:

> Lu-Mešlamtaë and Nigsisanabsa have borrowed from Ur-Nimmar 2 *minas* of silver, 5 *kur* of sesame oil, 30 garments, for an expedition to Dilmun to buy copper there. On the safe return of the expedition, the creditor will not make a claim for any commercial losses. The debtors have mutually agreed to satisfy Ur-Nimmar with 4 *minas* of copper for each shekel of silver as a just price; this they have sworn before the king.[28]

But for the use of weighed silver in place of coin (not such a great difference, all told), and the names, this could almost be a commercial document from Barcelona over thirty centuries later.

The contract just cited forms part of the business correspondence of Ea-nasir, a wealthy merchant of Ur, whose house was identified by Sir Leonard Woolley during his triumphant excavation of Ur of the Chaldees in the 1920s and 1930s; it was not a particularly large house, and consisted of five rooms around a main courtyard, though a couple of rooms had been ceded to a neighbour. He lived around 1800 BC, at the end of the Sumerian ascendancy and at a time, as will become clear, when trade to India had contracted. But he was still a wealthy man. His speciality was copper, which was delivered in ingots, and he apparently supplied the royal palace. He was surely one of the most prominent businessmen of his day, maybe a little unscrupulous, but looking at his wealth it is impossible not to be impressed: one of his shipments weighed eighteen and a half metric tons, of which nearly one third belonged to him.[29] The character of trade had changed somewhat in the century since Lu-Enlilla had lived, and the temples of Ur were no longer (so far as we know) heavily involved in expeditions down the Persian Gulf; this was business conducted by private merchants, and they preferred to pay for their goods in silver, weighed by the shekel, rather than in textiles, as had been the case with Lu-Enlilla. Probably many of the textiles Lu-Enlilla had sent to Dilmun and beyond were woven in temple workshops by female slaves attached to the temple itself. Silver, on the other hand, suited the needs of mobile merchants who constantly and energetically bought and sold, and traded on the open market in Ur.

Far from being a dry enumeration of imports and exports, Ea-nasir's private archive conjures up the passionate disputes that were bound to arise about the quality of goods and the obligations to fulfil a contract:

> Speak to Ea-nasir; thus says Nanni: now when you had come you spoke saying thus: 'I will give good ingots to Gimil-Sin'; this you said to me when you had come, but you have not done it; you have offered bad ingots to my messenger, saying: 'If you will take it, take it, if you will not take it, go away.' Who am I that you are treating me in this manner – treating me with such contempt? And between gentlemen such as we are!' . . . Who is there among the Dilmun traders who has acted against me in this way?[30]

The word translated as 'gentleman' is a technical term for a citizen of a very respectable social position, and 'gentlemen' were bound by a code of honour to which they swore their adherence in the temple of the sun god, Shamash; it was this divinely guaranteed contract that he was being accused of ignoring.[31] This is only part of a longer complaint, and just one of several that Ea-nasir filed away. Even though many of his partners were perfectly satisfied with his conduct, he has been described as a difficult, perhaps sleazy, businessman. This may be unfair; he is far more likely to have preserved documents about transactions out of which claims could arise than others, perhaps the vast majority, that could safely be discarded once everyone was quit of their profit.

<h1 style="text-align:center">IV</h1>

Magan, then, lay close to the exit from the Persian Gulf, reaching up to the tip of the Musandam peninsula, where Oman almost brushes Iran. For many sailors, Magan must have meant the island of Umm an-Nar near Abu Dhabi, a significant settlement where plenty of Sumerian pottery has been found and where copper from the Omani mines reached the Persian Gulf; Umm an-Nar was a sort of storehouse for goods being despatched towards Iraq.[32] The massive reconstructed tomb at Mleiha in the Emirate of Sharjah (UAE), a product of the Umm an-Nar culture, is 13.85 metres across.[33] However, the term 'Magan' was also applied to the Oman peninsula. As Harriet Crawford has observed, 'the ancient scribes seem to have had a rather elastic and foggy concept of location.'[34] But where was Meluḫḫa? Everything suggests that it was a wealthy and desirable trading partner for Sumer. The creation of a sea link between Sumer and another centre of high civilization has special importance in the maritime history of humanity, as one of the first moments, perhaps the first moment, when civilizations that had developed independently to a comparable cultural level entered into dialogue with one another across the sea. Once it has been located it will be possible to return to the question of where Dilmun was to be found, whether it was a specific place or a broader region. Sumerian documents often listed Dilmun, Magan and Meluḫḫa together, because they obviously lay on the same sea route, with Meluḫḫa at the end. Since ivory was one of the most precious exports from Meluḫḫa, the choice is narrowed down to the coast of east Africa or that of India, the two areas from which we could expect elephant ivory to be exported; and it has been seen that Indian goods did reach Sumer.

In much later centuries, when the Assyrians dominated Mesopotamia during the early first millennium BC, the name of Meluḫḫa became attached to parts of east Africa; but that certainly does not mean it was always identified with the area. In the first place, the route out of the Persian Gulf tends eastwards, to lands rich in carnelian as well as ivory; there is a short, clear run from the Strait of Hormuz to the coast of Pakistan. Indeed, the relationship between that coast and Oman has been so close that from the eighteenth century to the middle of the twentieth century the sultans of Oman possessed an outpost on the coast of Pakistan, at Gwadar, 240 miles from Oman proper. Moreover, if ships that left the Persian Gulf then turned south and west, coasting along the shores of Yemen past Aden and maybe as far as east Africa, we should expect evidence of Sumerian contacts in Yemen too, but there is none. Nor is there evidence that the inhabitants of what are now Yemen, Somalia and neighbouring regions were able to launch their own trading fleets, whereas this was certainly true of the Meluḫḫans. Ships from Meluḫḫa and Magan are known to have reached Sumer in the days of King Sargon around 2300 BC and to have docked at his capital, Akkad, where lived 'Su-ilisu the Meluḫḫa interpreter'. There were enough Meluḫḫans around Lagash in the century before 2000 BC to create a 'village of Meluḫḫa', and they had a garden and fields producing barley, so Meluḫḫan migrants were familiar in Mesopotamia at this time.[35] Looking eastwards, the journey along the shores of Iran and Baluchistan to the mouth of the Indus was far less challenging than that to Africa, and perfectly manageable under a captain who understood the monsoon seasons.[36]

It is not beyond credibility that 'Magan' actually meant 'copper' (rather as Cyprus, *Kupros*, did in Greek) and that 'Meluḫḫa' meant 'ivory', in the language of proto-historic India. Or Meluḫḫa may originally have meant 'the place across the sea', rather like the medieval term *Outremer* that Europeans eventually attached to the crusader kingdom of Jerusalem, but could have meant anywhere across the sea before becoming attached to a particular place; this might be deduced from the Arabic term *milaḥa*, possibly derived from 'Meluḫḫa', which was used in the early Middle Ages to mean navigation, seafaring or seamanship.[37] Afghan lapis lazuli could be obtained from Meluḫḫa; this would have been carried down the Indus Valley to ports where Sumerian traders were making their purchases. The area also produced fine woods, including a 'black wood' that must be ebony, and sometimes wooden objects decorated with gold were brought from there, another sign that Meluḫḫa was no backwater. Finally, and conclusively, inscribed Indian seals have occasionally been found on Sumerian sites and in reasonable quantity in the Persian Gulf, so there can be no doubt that contact existed between Sumer and the Indus Valley. Moreover, Indus pottery has been found at Abu Dhabi.[38]

The Indus Valley civilization remains the least known of the great Bronze Age civilizations, for such evidence as there is often remains impenetrable – there are inscriptions in a script that cannot be read and a language that cannot be guessed at, and there is little that can be said about the social and political organization of a culture whose impressive cities stare blankly at the excavator. For the Indus Valley appears to have been dominated in the second half of the third millennium BC by two massive and tightly planned cities, very similar in layout and construction, Harappā and Mohenjo-daro, though these are only their modern names. They lie a full 350 miles apart, and the more southerly city, Mohenjo-daro, stands very roughly 200 miles up the Indus River.[39] These were not, then, cities that had immediate access to the sea, though from Mohenjo-daro it is easy to imagine craft reaching the Indian Ocean, and the Indus civilization possessed many dozens of towns and ports along the ocean shore, in the general area of Karachi, ruling over as much as 800 miles or 1,300 kilometres of coastline, far beyond the Indus estuary. One of the most important harbours lay at Lothal, in the Gulf of Cambay (north-west India), which gave access both to the local river system and to the open sea, and which offered the facilities ships would require at the end of the long journey from the Persian Gulf. Lothal possessed a substantial dockyard and several anchors have been found there. It traded in several directions, for there were contacts with the Neolithic peoples living further south along the west coast of India as well as with the Persian Gulf.[40]

So much attention has concentrated on the mystery of how the two highly organized mega-cities came to be built along the Indus river system that rather little interest has been shown in other places, and even the assumption that these were the twin capitals of a single empire is pleasant speculation. Rigid central control was in place, for, as the archaeologist Stuart Piggott observed, the size of bricks used to build the two great cities, the highly standardized pottery, and the weights and measures show 'absolute uniformity': 'there is a terrible efficiency about the Harappā civilization which recalls all the worst of Rome', while he also observed 'an isolation and stagnation hard to parallel in any known civilization of the Old World'. Over several hundred years during the second half of the third millennium BC not much changed.[41] Although it has proved hard to identify any grand palaces or temples, this was a highly stratified society in which labour gangs were set to work pounding grain into flour. It is assumed that the major rural activity, apart from food production, was the growing of cotton, which is a convenient argument, as this is a product that leaves little residue archaeologically; there is no obvious mention of cotton in Sumerian documents that mention Meluḫḫa, and the Sumerians sent their own textiles to Meluḫḫa, whose main attraction was the luxury items, semi-precious stones, ivory and fine woods, mentioned already. Very occasionally one of the distinctive Sumerian cylinder seals, carved to be rolled across clay, reached Mohenjo-daro, though Sumerian items rarely appear on Indus sites, even though Indus products such as carnelian beads appear quite often in Sumer.[42] A piece from an Omani vase also reached Mohenjo-daro, no doubt by sea and river. The best place to look for signs of contact is the port of Lothal, and, to be sure, gold pendants of Sumerian origin and (possibly) Mesopotamian pottery have been found in a merchant's house there, as has a clay model of a boat. A circular seal found at Lothal, showing goats or gazelles and a dragon, bears close resemblance to circular Sumerian seals.[43]

Seals, however, provide the best evidence for contact the other way, from the Indus Valley towards Sumer. It is not just that seals, being made of stone, survive well; they were also used by government officials, priests, merchants and anyone else who wished to set his seal, literally, on property, and that could include goods sent by ship to foreign ports; they were functional, but they were also declarations of identity, and provided vehicles for some of our earliest written texts. The Indus seals are quite distinctive. Rather than being rolled on clay they were used as stamps, so they are flat and square; they generally portray local animals – tigers, humped oxen (zebu), elephants – and they often carry inscriptions in a distinctive linear script very different to Sumerian cuneiform.[44] So if these seals turn up in the Persian Gulf in reasonable quantity, we have evidence of visits by Indian travellers to the area, evidence, in other words, of merchants passing between Meluḫḫa and Sumer. And they have indeed been found in the ruins of major cities such as Lagash and Ur, sometimes showing the sorts of animals familiar from Indus seals, sometimes also containing a few letters in the Indus script. One seal thought to have been found in Iraq portrays a rhinoceros, which never appears in Sumerian art, for the animal was unknown in Mesopotamia. This seal has some Sumerian characteristics as well, such as its shape, and it may provide evidence for Indians settled in the Sumerian lands, who have already been encountered at Lagash; but maybe a better explanation, more in accord with what we know from the Persian Gulf, is that it originated among the mixed settlements to which it is now time to turn.[45]

V

Having identified Magan and Meluḫḫa with reasonable confidence, we are left with the location of Dilmun. This was another place that wandered around the Babylonian map, or rather acquired several identities: Dilmun the abode of the Blessed; Dilmun as a region; Dilmun as a specific place.

The merchants Lu-Enlilla and Ea-nasir clearly knew what they meant when they talked of Dilmun: for them, it was a place where one could buy copper and other goods, and it had its own community of traders. What began as a general term for (most likely) the Persian Gulf roadsteads that ran all the way down the Arabian shores from Kuwait to the tip of Oman came to mean one place in particular; the term may originally have signified simply 'lands to the south'.[46] Archaeologists have identified where that was, and where its outstations on the route to Magan were as well, notably Umm an-Nar, which has been mentioned already. The discovery of Dilmun was the work of two scholars from a not particularly prominent Danish museum in Aarhus, Geoffrey Bibby and P. V. Glob, later renowned for his book *The Bog People*, dealing with the very different topic of the prehistoric victims of human sacrifice found almost perfectly preserved in Danish bogs. Indeed, as in Denmark, the issue was bodies, or rather the 100,000 burial mounds visible in Bahrain and assumed (though this was exaggeration) all to date to some prehistoric era. Glob and Bibby questioned the easy assumption that Bahrain had been created as a vast isle of the dead, a cemetery island, which might, after a fashion, fit with the idea of Dilmun being located there, as a holy island and the abode of the Blessed.[47] According to one tablet King Sargon of Akkad had conquered Dilmun, which lay in the 'Lower Sea', that is, the Persian Gulf. About 1,600 years later, in the eighth century BC, a warlike king of Assyria, also named Sargon, sent his armies as far as Dilmun, this time said to lie on the 'Bitter Sea' and to include an island; its king was Upēri, 'who lives like a fish' out in the sea.[48] Dilmun could not, then, be very far from Sumer, and the island of Bahrain was an obvious candidate for its location. The connection went back far in time: around 2520 BC King Ur-Nanše, ruler of the Sumerian city of Lagash, asserted that 'ships of Dilmun, from the foreign lands, brought me wood as tribute'. This visit to the king of Lagash fits neatly with archaeological evidence that settlement on Bahrain became denser around the middle of the third millennium BC.[49] The coast of Arabia was an unlikely source of wood for the king of Lagash, and the wood must have been brought to Dilmun from further afield – from Iran or India.[50]

Bibby's team unquestionably made great progress in identifying key sites on Bahrain and then further afield, notably in Qatar and off Abu Dhabi, and even some way into Saudi Arabia; but, precisely because they tried to cover so much ground, they never (to pursue the pun) dug deeply enough into the history of any of these regions. Still, the importance of Bahrain and its identity as the major centre of Dilmun became clear as more and more sites along the Arabian coast were identified. Bibby and Glob uncovered city walls and streets at Qala'at al-Bahrain (Bahrain fort) on the northern tip of Bahrain; but at Barbar a few miles away they made their most outstanding single discovery: a temple of the late third millennium BC, containing a well, for one of the secrets of Bahrain was the availability of sweet water rising, as the Sumerians would have said, from the abyss of *abzu*.[51] The motives for creating a town on Bahrain island are thus not hard to deduce – and as well as water there were abundant supplies of fish, with 700 edible species swimming around the Gulf in modern times, so that fish remains a prominent part of the diet in the Gulf states. It was no different in the Bronze Age: 60 per cent of the bones found at Qala'at al-Bahrain were of fish, though the inhabitants ate a variety of meats as well, even including mongoose, which is not native and must have been brought from India; they also imported dairy goods and cereals from Mesopotamia, so they had quite a varied diet.[52]

One day in Bahrain a workman in Bibby's team found a distinctive round stamp seal made of soapstone and decorated with two human figures; and more seals turned up in the well of the great temple. As he smoked his pipe, Bibby wondered whether round stamp seals, thirteen of which had been found at Ur and three in Mohenjo-daro, made of steatite and even (at Ur) occasionally adorned with Indus script, might be the product of a place halfway between the two great cities, Bahrain/Dilmun, no less.[53] These seals are (like Dilmun itself) intermediate between Sumerian and Indus styles, their patterns matching those of neither grand civilization, but more a mélange of the two to which some individuality had been added, as in the case of a seal showing four stylized heads of gazelles arranged in the shape of a cross – roast wild gazelle was a local delicacy, to judge from the animal bones that have been found in Bahrain. As more seals have come to light, it has been found that around one third carry signs from the Indus Valley writing system, but – before anyone jumps to the conclusion that the Dilmunites conversed in Indus-speak – the letters are combined in ways not found on inscriptions from the Indus Valley itself.[54] Further weighty evidence of the Indus Valley connection came from stone globes and cubes used to weigh goods; Bibby was excited to find that these followed the Indus Valley system of weights and measures and not that of the Sumerians, but the Dilmunites also used Mesopotamian weights, which came to light later.[55] This apparent confusion of weights neatly brings out the role of Dilmun as an intermediary between the cities of Sumer and those of the Indus, a place where goods were exchanged and where merchants both from Sumer, such as Ea-nasir and his agents, and from India congregated and did business together.[56]

Dilmun, then, was both a town that serviced maritime trade between Mesopotamia and the Indus Valley and the capital of a region dotted with

other coastal or island settlements that must have functioned as safe harbours for shipping sailing up and down the Gulf. It was a place where
merchants could hang around doing business all year round – between
the months of Nissannu and Addaru, to cite again one of the Sumerian
tablets. Whether its population was an ethnic mix of Indians and Sumerians or consisted to a large degree of other people is simply unknown, but
it makes sense, bearing in mind the seals, to assume that there was a large
Indian settlement there. Over the many centuries of its existence, this no
doubt became an integral part of local society, as 'native' as anyone else
(indeed, it is a striking feature of several of the Gulf states today that a
massive proportion of the population hails from India and Pakistan).
However, the political life of Dilmun cannot be grasped, beyond the sense
that it was a well-ordered place. Dilmun had tax collectors, a not always
welcome sign of systematic central management. Population was rising in
the region as a whole, which was good for the tax collectors, but this also
suggests that Dilmun acted as a magnet for settlers and stimulated production up and down the coast from Bahrain.[57] Further down the coast, in
Oman, society remained more obviously tribal and mobile, and settlements came and went. We should thus think of Dilmun as a small trading
city with offshoots along the western coast of the Persian Gulf, as far south
as Umm an-Nar, which gave access to the copper of Magan.

Sometimes it is the tiniest and humblest archaeological discoveries that
reveal the most astonishing results. This has been particularly true of
evidence for the types of ships these merchants would have used. A good
point to begin is the description of the boat Ziusudra or Atrahasis built
during the great flood that destroyed the rest of mankind and that was
described on the Sumerian and Babylonian tablets (and later in the book
of Genesis). Here, as a newly discovered tablet reveals, the boat was supposedly a gigantic version of a round hide-covered boat; the hides were
plastered with bitumen and animal fat on to a frame made of miles and
miles of wickerwork, within which a wooden three-storey structure
housed the animals and the hero and his family.[58] Round, keel-less hide
boats were well suited to floating downstream, with the help of a couple
of large paddles, though for the return journey they would have been
dismantled and carried back overland; and a massive round boat with
nowhere to go could happily float in the flood waters that covered the
entire world. But for journeys out into the Gulf long boats were more
suitable; a steering oar could be attached, and a sail provided propulsion.
As along the Tigris and Euphrates, reed boats were widely used within
the Gulf. The fragments of bitumen from Kuwait mentioned earlier leave
no doubt that boats constructed wholly or partially from bundles of reeds

were used out at sea around 5000 BC.[59] It is conceivable that masted reed boats, hugging the shore all the way, made the journey from Dilmun to Iraq and from Dilmun to the mouth of the Indus.

Unfortunately boats made out of reeds tend to leak a good deal, even when coated with tar, but they are still used for fishing in the Gulf; and they are quite buoyant, an ancient equivalent of inflatable craft, since the hollow reeds contain so much air.[60] But in Oman, at Ra's al-Junz, the imprint of long-vanished wooden planks can be detected on pieces of bitumen dated to the second half of the third millennium BC; Ra's al-Junz stands at the eastern tip of Oman, commanding access to the Indian Ocean, and all the evidence suggests that it was a regular port of call for ships that must often have needed repairs in mid-voyage, for its hinterland had little to offer. Moreover, cuneiform tablets mention the caulking of ships bound for Dilmun and Magan.[61] This bitumen was gathered around what are now oilfields, as thick mineral deposits seeped up from below and left pools of tar on the surface of the soil. Bitumen was used for a great many tasks beyond the caulking of ships, including the sealing of earthenware pots, which by nature are very porous.[62] All this serves as a reminder that it is far too easy to concentrate on the traffic in exotic goods such as carnelian and ebony, and to forget that humdrum items – bitumen, dates and fish – were most likely to be found in the cargo space of a boat sailing the Gulf in the Bronze Age, and long after. Such cargoes would have perfectly suited a reed boat able to carry a dozen people at most, with limited storage space. But there is good reason to assume that the ancestors of the dhow had already come into being; the quantities of copper being shifted from Magan towards the Sumerian cities demanded sturdy and well-defended vessels able to carry tons of metal at a time; nor would Ea-nasir and his colleagues have entrusted their shekels of silver to small, open, reed boats that could easily become the prey of pirates. These wooden ships also carried timber from Meluḫḫa and no doubt from the facing shores of Iran. Indeed, some of that wood may well have been used to build ships, as the coasts of Arabia and the marshlands of southern Iraq largely lack suitable timber.[63] Craft constructed out of wood were stitched together; holes were driven through planks and the planks were then bound together using long stretches of coir rope, made out of the husks of coconuts. Bitumen, animal fat and padding were then applied to seal the boat. This type of boat was very resilient, as the hull was quite flexible, and better suited to the open ocean than more rigid construction using a skeletal hull, which was the norm in the ancient Mediterranean.[64] Sewn-plank boats would remain a feature of Indian Ocean sea traffic for millennia.

Dilmun may not possess the grandeur of Ur or the sheer scale of

Mohenjo-daro, but what has come out of the earth is extraordinary evidence for how Ur and Mohenjo-daro interacted in the centuries around 2000 BC. Copper, not gold, was the metal on which Dilmun set its trademark. With the decline of the Indus civilization early in the second millennium BC the history of this connection came to an end. Why this civilization declined has been the subject of lively debate. The traditional view that an invasion of Aryan conquerors, speaking an Indo-European language, shattered the Indus civilization is no longer widely supported. More attention is paid nowadays to the environmental changes that dried out the Indus Valley and resulted in the gradual decline of the great cities, while across the wider region something of Indus culture, even the writing system, lingered for several centuries, in some places until around 1300 BC.[65] The great trade with Mesopotamia became a trickle; an occasional Indus object turns up on sites in Iraq, but routes across the sea had become less important to the inhabitants of north-west India. This did not mean the end of Dilmun, which still appeared (assuming it is the same place) in a document from eighth-century Assyria. And the history of Dilmun is also the history of the first maritime trading route along the coasts of Asia – to all intents the first trade route we know about anywhere in the world that linked two great civilizations. In later centuries, there were severe contractions and long interruptions during which trade and other contact faltered and vanished; but the history of the Indian Ocean as a great seaway began in the Persian Gulf.

4

The Journey to the Land of the God

One great Bronze Age civilization of the Middle East has been left out of this account so far: Egypt. The unification of Upper and Lower Egypt under the early pharaohs, in around 2700 BC, resulted in the creation of a centralized, affluent society able to draw upon the rich resources in wheat and barley of the lands regularly inundated by the Nile. When we speak of the importance of water traffic in the life of Egypt, we refer inevitably, in the first place, to shipping moving up and down the Nile. The term 'Great Green' that appears in Egyptian texts was used vaguely, though it sometimes meant either the Mediterranean or the open sea in general, and could also be used for the Red Sea.[1] In the second millennium BC much of the shipping and many of the merchants who traded with Egypt were foreigners from Syria, Cyprus or Crete. It has already been seen that there is no evidence for contact by sea between Egypt and Mesopotamia at this period, although around the time of the first dynasty in Egypt (c.3000 BC) artistic influences did reach Egypt from Mesopotamia; for instance an ivory knife now in the Louvre portrays a god in what looks very much like Sumerian garb.[2] But such influences are far more likely to have trickled through overland, by way of Syria or along desert routes through what are now Jordan and the Israeli Negev, than by a sea route around the great mass of the Arabian peninsula. Still, Egypt did develop ties to the Indian Ocean in the third millennium BC; the Red Sea highway was used less intensively than the routes the Sumerians and Dilmunites created in the Gulf and beyond – perhaps, indeed, it was only used intermittently. But this highway too can be described with increasing certainty, thanks to extraordinary archaeological discoveries along the Red Sea coast, as well as one of the earliest and most engaging ancient Egyptian texts to survive.

Before one can make sense of the Egyptian expeditions down the Red

Sea, the most important products of the lands they visited need to be examined. There is a danger here of a circular argument: they went in search of incense; the ancient Egyptians' word '*ntyw* found on inscriptions and in papyri must surely mean myrrh, because myrrh and frankincense were the most highly prized ingredients of incense in later times; therefore they visited the lands where these products could be found; which proves these lands were, variously, Eritrea, Somalia and Yemen. However, for all its logical faults, this argument points towards a central feature of the early voyages down and perhaps beyond the Red Sea: these expeditions went in search of perfumes rather than spices. The shift from a trade in perfumes and aromatics to one dominated much more by pepper and the other spices of the east became really noticeable during the Roman imperial period, when ships ranged much deeper into Indian Ocean waters; and in the meantime the trade in aromatics declined precipitously, after the suppression of pagan worship by Christian emperors deprived merchants of a market in the temples of the Middle East – though there was a partial recovery by the sixth century AD as Christian worship made increasing use of the same substances.[3] But the history of the burning of incense before God or before pagan gods goes back very far in time. Pharaoh himself burned the incense called '*ntyw* before the Egyptian gods, to accompany animal sacrifices, and these ceremonies were especially lavish when a new temple was inaugurated, or when the ruler returned in triumph from war. Incense was burned during the elaborate ceremonies that sent off dead pharaohs to the Next World, and it was used extensively for embalming the dead, at which the Egyptians were the unrivalled masters.

It would certainly be helpful to know exactly what '*ntyw* was, so as to be sure where the Egyptian Red Sea expeditions were heading. Since the way '*ntyw* was used coincides closely with the way myrrh can be used, the idea that '*ntyw* was actually some form of myrrh makes sense, though there are other gum-resins such as bdellium that could have been confused with it, and this is also true of frankincense.[4] Gathering these resins takes much the same form, and the collection of frankincense was described with close attention by Pliny the Elder, a man whose obsession with scientific detail was so powerful that he lingered too long in the gas-filled air of the Bay of Naples and fell victim to the famous eruption of Vesuvius.[5] One can wait for the trees to exude a greasy or sticky liquid that may later harden, and collect that; or one can make incisions in the bark of the tree out of which oil will seep; different colours and qualities of incense seep out depending on the process. Frankincense and myrrh are gum-resins that contain volatile oils – up to 17 per cent in the case of fresh myrrh. In the more benign climate of Bronze Age south Arabia and Eritrea

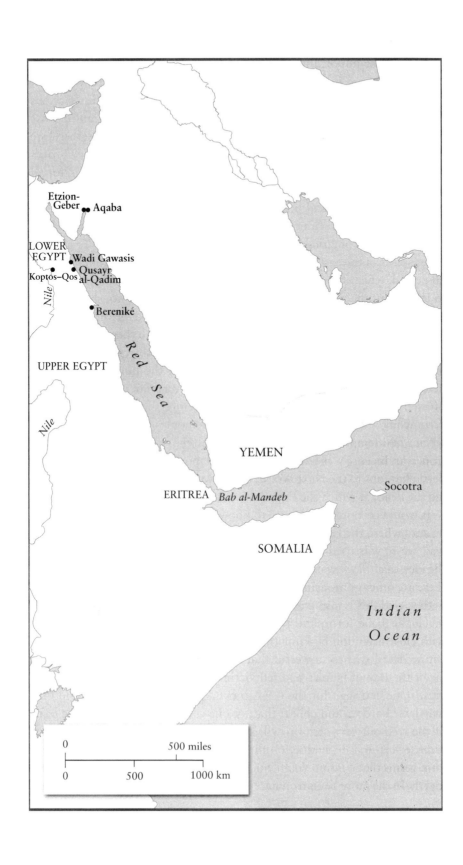

their cultivation spread over a larger area than now, for myrrh has now become a prized rarity in Yemen, which has undergone desiccation over the centuries. Myrrh retains its perfume longer than any other aromatic, and both products have long been prized for their medical uses; myrrh is often an ingredient in high-quality toothpaste. In essence, myrrh was used for anointing, while frankincense was used for burning.[6] These were not the only products that the Egyptians brought back from their expeditions, which also included gold and wild animals, dead and alive. For all of these, they turned southwards to the land of Punt, 'the god's land'.

II

Just as the Babylonians were often vague about where Dilmun, Magan and Meluḫḫa lay, the ancient Egyptians did not have a clear sense of where or what the land of Punt was. This name, which appears in all the modern literature, is a misreading of a name that generally appears in the form *Pwene*, and is sometimes defined as 'the god's land'. Punt appears to be the same place as Ophir, which is said to have been visited by the ships of King Solomon and King Hiram of Tyre in the tenth century BC. But their fleet would have sailed out of the Gulf of Aqaba more than 1,600 years after a ship named *Praise-of-the-Two-Lands* (Upper and Lower Egypt) was mentioned on an inscription containing part of the royal annals that has ended up in Palermo and that dates from the reign of Pharaoh Snefru, around 2600 BC. The ship was built of cedar or pine wood and apparently was involved with sixty or more other boats in a raid on the Nubians that brought back thousands of slaves and an impossible number of cattle (200,000). This ship was impressively large; its length was a hundred Egyptian cubits, or fifty-two metres.[7] In case this is seen as another example of royal boasting, we can point to the funeral boat buried next to the Great Pyramid at Giza. This was built for Snefru's son Khufu, or Cheops, and it lay for nearly 4,500 years in a dismantled state before it was unearthed; it is eighty-five cubits long (nearly forty-four metres), and is made of Lebanese cedar, for one of the eternal problems of Egypt has been the general lack of large quantities of good, hard wood.[8] It is impossible to be sure that the defeated Nubians about whom Snefru brayed were what we would now call Nubians, that is, inhabitants of the upper reaches of the Nile to the south-east of Egypt; maybe they were other Africans, such as the ancient Libyans who lived to the west of Egypt. And maybe this was an expedition down the Nile rather than the Red Sea. Still, the Palermo Stone and the funerary barge between them show that the

Egyptians could build ships with a seagoing capacity, even if many never ventured further than the Nile.

The description in Egyptian texts of Punt as 'the god's land' is reminiscent of the way Dilmun was described in Sumerian texts as 'the abode of the Blessed'. These places had a mysterious aura to those who heard about them in the third millennium BC; and this is a constant feature of maritime history – the news of distant and wonderful lands where (as in Columbus's *Hispaniola* many centuries later) neither food nor fresh water was lacking and paradise lay either here or not far away.[9] And this sense of awe is abundantly present in the finely crafted 'Tale of the Shipwrecked Sailor' written on papyrus somewhere between about 2500 BC and 2200 BC, which tells of a remarkable voyage to the region of Punt, though the story is really a tale of a visit to another world entirely, the world of the spirits.[10] Here, a sailor relates the story of his voyage to a royal courtier, who clearly regards him as an ancient mariner full of yarns, and attempts to brush him aside with the words 'It is tiresome to speak to you.' However, the courtier was being very unfair. The sailor had set out for the royal mines, probably gold mines, in a ship 120 cubits long and forty cubits wide, with 120 sailors 'of the pick of Egypt', for, 'whether they looked at the sky or looked at the land, they were more courageous than lions'. It might have helped them more to look at the sea, because although the sailor praised them for their ability to foretell a storm, a wave of eight cubits smashed into the ship, which broke apart and sank with the loss of all lives apart from this sailor, who was cast upon an island rich in fruit and vegetables, fish and fowl, for 'there was nothing that was not on it'. Indeed, his arms were soon so full of the rich produce of the land that he had to set some of what he had gathered on the ground. Just when he felt so safe and refreshed, a great serpent, with (oddly) a beard two cubits long, came upon him; his body glistened with gold and he had eyebrows of real lapis lazuli. This was a rather different beast to the serpent who led Adam and Eve astray; he wanted to know how the sailor had arrived: 'Who brought you to the island, with water on all sides?' He told his story and the serpent seemed satisfied, saying:

> 'Fear not, fear not, young man! Do not turn pale, for you have reached me. Look, the god has let you live and has brought you to the island of the spirit. There is nothing that is not on it and it is full of all good things. You will spend month upon month until you have completed four months on this island. Then a boat will come from home with sailors whom you know and you will go home with them and die in your city . . . and you will embrace your children, kiss your wife, and see your house. This is better than anything.'

In gratitude the sailor stretched out on the ground in obeisance and promised to bring word of the noble serpent to his ruler, who would certainly send fine presents of laudanum, malabathrum (cinnamon leaves), terebinth, balsam and incense. He said: 'I shall have boats brought for you laden with all the wealth of Egypt'; and he would arrange sacrifices in honour of this divine snake. But the serpent was unimpressed, saying: 'You don't have much myrrh, or any form of incense. But I am the ruler of Punt, myrrh is mine. That malabathrum you said would be brought, a large quantity is from this island.' And he gave the sailor a cargo of myrrh, malabathrum, terebinth, balsam and camphor, as well as black eye-paint (much in demand among noble Egyptian women, as contemporary paintings show), and a big lump of incense. He also gave him hunting dogs, apes and baboons, 'and all kinds of riches'. Elephant ivory and giraffe tails were there too, the latter presumably used as fly-whisks. He was able to load all this on to the boat, which had duly arrived to pick him up as predicted; and he was told it would take two months to reach home, but when he did so he would feel like a young man again.

He and the sailors respectfully thanked the serpent-god and travelled north back home, where the ruler was delighted to see what he had brought and publicly expressed his thanks to this god; besides, he rewarded the sailor by making him a 'follower', meaning a feudal lord attached to his court.[11] So it is a curious tale that addresses the relationship between the creature comforts of home and a world beyond everyday human experience. But the story also sets out clearly some important features of the land of Punt: what could be obtained there, how long one would need to stop over, how long it would take to return, and the simple fact that it lay to the south, which must mean down the Red Sea. Conceivably the island upon which the sailor was cast was Socotra, which was visited in the first few centuries AD by ships in search of resins and other luxury goods, and which stands 240 miles off Yemen.[12]

III

The existence of southward voyages is confirmed by the major expedition sent out by Queen Hatshepsut or Hashepsowe in the early fifteenth century BC, probably a few years before her death in 1458. She was one of a small and remarkable group of female pharaohs (having previously served as regent), and she aimed to restore the economic vitality of Egypt after the overthrow of the dynasty of the Hyksos, Asiatic rulers under whom political power had fragmented. She took great pride in rebuilding the temples in central Egypt, abandoned since the Hyksos had ruled Lower Egypt, 'roving hordes of them overturning what had been made'. She won the deep, indeed passionate, devotion of her officials. Ineni, a much-favoured courtier and master of the royal works, proclaimed: 'people worked for her, and Egypt bowed the head.'[13] This was commemorated in reliefs and accompanying inscriptions within the queen's magnificent funerary temple at Dair al-Bahri, close to Luxor in Upper Egypt. One of these inscriptions makes it plain that the history of trade with Punt was not a continuous one, as one could easily assume. The fantastic land of the serpent-god was only gradually coming into focus. For the god Amun-Ra makes a curious statement:

> No one trod these incense-terraces, which the people did not know; they were heard of from mouth to mouth by hearsay from our ancestors. The marvels brought from there under your fathers, the kings of Lower Egypt, were brought from hand to hand, and, since the time of the ancestors of the kings of Upper Egypt who lived in olden days, they were brought in return for numerous exchanges, and no one reached it except for your royal trading expedition.[14]

It is reasonable to assume that, before Upper and Lower Egypt were united, fine luxury items such as spices and aromatics brought from further south would have passed through Upper Egypt first; and the same would apply to gold mined further south in Africa. The union of Upper and Lower Egypt to which the god referred must be the relatively recent restoration of native rule by her own dynasty, rather than the original unification of the two kingdoms that had occurred 1,500 years before. But the sense behind the inscription, even allowing for typical pharaonic exaggeration, is that Hatshepsut was in some way a pioneer – perhaps reviving the trade to Punt, and integrating its many stages into a single maritime route managed by royal, rather than private, fleets.[15] This may also have meant that she was bypassing the straggly overland routes heading off from the Nile or leading down the west coast of Arabia that were at many times in the past an alternative to the sea route down the Red Sea. Her ambitious building plans and her determination to restore the glittering grandeur of pre-Hyksos days prompted her to look far afield for unguents such as myrrh, luxury materials such as ebony and ivory, exotic animals such as baboons and, of course, gold. That myrrh was a particular prize is clear from the use to which this 'ntyw was put: it would anoint the limbs of the statue of the god Amun-Ra, which is a possible use for oil of myrrh; however, the inscriptions do not mention the burning of incense, which suggests that large quantities of frankincense were not brought from Punt.

The presence of royal fleets in Punt was intended to make a powerful impression on its inhabitants. The reliefs even portray the 'great men of Punt', actually the chieftain Parekhou and his corpulent wife Jtj (vocalizing ancient Egyptian is often pure guesswork, so she is best left in this unpronounceable form). Although one distinguished Egyptologist described Jtj as 'hideously deformed', it is more likely that the distortion of her body was a crude attempt to contrast her primitive, servile condition with that of the true queen, the elegant and in some representations beautiful Pharaoh Hatshepsut. So too the portrayal of the people of Punt is hardly flattering; they lived in round huts and had to climb a ladder to go inside their houses. This was not the sophistication of courtly Luxor. The Puntite chieftains subject to this king and queen prostrated themselves before the royal standard, invoking her favour with the words: 'Hail to you, king of Egypt, female sun who shines like the solar disc.'[16] The inscriptions were intended to show that the dignitaries of Punt were Pharaoh's subjects, even if until now contact had been intermittent or indirect; and therefore what was brought back was not commercial exchange but humble tribute – a common way to conduct trade with supposedly inferior peoples, widely practised throughout Chinese history as well. The tribute was paid over to Pharaoh's messenger; and back in Egypt Pharaoh herself would appear under a special canopy, 'the dais of the bringing of tribute', to receive gifts sent from African peoples to the south of Egypt. Thus one inscription runs: 'Arrival of the Great Chief of Punt laden with his gifts by the shore of Wadj Wer before the royal envoy.'[17] But even Pharaoh bartered for tribute, and before they left Egypt the ships were loaded with gifts of beer, meat, fruit and wine to be sent down to Punt, and these, or supplies for the journey, were illustrated in the reliefs of Hatshepsut's temple, which display a fleet of rather magnificent ships with billowing sails, oarsmen at the ready and long, heavy stern rudders; even the details of the long, taut ropes can be seen.[18]

Such ropes actually survive. Admittedly, those that have been found are earlier than Hatshepsut's expedition, which may have been one of several or many in the period of the so-called New Kingdom. The ups and downs of trade between Egypt and Punt are unknown; the picture is much more blurred than in the case of Dilmun. But, as with Dilmun and Meluḫḫa, there are some basic questions that have to be answered: where Punt was and what route was taken to reach it. And as with Dilmun and Meluḫḫa, a consensus has only slowly come into being, largely as a result of major archaeological discoveries, though they have been made closer to the Egyptian than the Puntite end of the route. For the coast of the Red Sea has yielded more and more fresh evidence for how trade between Egypt and the Indian Ocean operated at key moments in its development: Roman remains at Bereniké; medieval ones at Qusayr al-Qadim; and now Bronze Age ones at Wadi and Mersa Gawasis. All these sites lie relatively close to one another; Qusayr is only fifty kilometres to the south of Wadi Gawasis.[19] Their proximity is easily explained: to reach the Red Sea from the Egyptian desert there were a number of overland routes that linked the coast to Nile ports, where goods were reloaded on to freighters for passage downriver. There is good evidence that a channel was dug that would enable boats to sail from the Lower Nile through the eastern arms of the delta into the lakes above Suez, and then down into the Red Sea; but it is unlikely that it was used for the large ships that Queen Hatshepsut launched, and the best option remained a short trip overland from the Nile to the coast of the Red Sea. One of the most important Nile stations was at Koptos near Luxor, which gave relatively easy access to Wadi Gawasis because it lay in a bend that carried the river a little way eastwards, and reduced the distance between sea and river, as well as granting access through low passes through the desert. In the Middle Ages it still functioned as the departure point for merchants bound for the Red Sea; medieval Qos was one of the largest towns along the Nile. Koptos–Qos was also well supplied with local timber, which was relatively rare in Egypt. The harbour at Wadi Gawasis (technically known as Mersa Gawasis) was in use between 2000 and 1600 BC, to judge from Carbon 14 dating and from some fragments of pottery from Minoan Crete of around that time, though there are earlier and later dates as well, so it was evidently one of the major trans-shipment stations on the route down the Red Sea.[20] But the Egyptians also, at one or two points, left a pile of rubbish in the local caves (or, some think, dedicated some of their equipment to the gods in sealed caverns). The extraordinary dryness of the Red Sea environment has preserved forty-three wooden boxes in which cargo would have been transported, as well as about thirty coils of rope woven from papyrus plants that are still in excellent condition; these date from the Twelfth Dynasty (Middle Kingdom period), c.2000– c.1800 BC. There are also discarded timbers from ships built out of cedar, pine and oak, including the blades of ships' rudders, for barnacles and worms that had been gathered on the open sea often made heavy repairs necessary; and there were limestone anchors too.[21]

Once again it is not always the glossy discoveries that really explain the past. Some of the most eloquent evidence about where Punt actually was comes from fragments of smashed pottery: ceramics from Nubia, Eritrea and Sudan, but also from the area around Yemen on the other side of the Bab al-Mandeb Strait. Enough ebony survives to show that it was a favourite export, and it was even prepared before export, because some of the finds consist of wooden rods already fashioned in their place of origin, which, again, was Eritrea.[22] Gold was mined in an area known as Bia-Punt, which explains the reference to the 'royal mines' in the 'Tale of the Shipwrecked Sailor'. This too seems to have lain in the highlands of what is now Eritrea. But the most important exports leave few traces other than occasional blocks of resin: the perfumes and aromatics carried up the Red Sea which were intended not just for the living, if they were wealthy enough to afford them, but for the dead, if they were of high enough status to be properly embalmed.

Taken as a whole, the discoveries at Wadi Gawasis confirm the suspicion of many Egyptologists that Punt was a broad region encompassing the southern shores of the Red Sea on both sides, the Eritrean and the Yemeni. Where the Punt fleet tied up when it reached Punt is still a mystery; it does not seem that there was a place called Punt in the way that there was a place called Dilmun, but rather there was an extensive 'land of Punt'. There must have been roadsteads similar to Mersa Gawasis that provided the facilities any seagoing fleet would require if, as once again the shipwrecked sailor makes plain, a layover of several months was needed before winds and currents made the return journey safe. Some ships may have penetrated further south still, reaching what is now Somalia, but there is no evidence that Egyptian fleets turned east at Aden and encountered vessels from the Persian Gulf. The Red Sea and the Persian Gulf were still separate worlds, and the role of the Red Sea as the principal funnel through which goods from much further east reached the Mediterranean lay long in the future. Indeed, the Egyptian Red Sea trade went into recession around 1100 BC, and the reasons are not hard to guess: the pharaohs were preoccupied with attacks attributed to 'Sea Peoples' who came overland from Libya and Syria and from the waters of the Mediterranean; in addition, their control over the Nile Delta was undermined by local separatists. As their power weakened, their ability to fund lavish expeditions to Punt, or to maintain quite such luxurious courts, also faltered.[23] This does not mean that the trade in perfumes and resins vanished; over many centuries others, including the Nabataeans of Petra, would maintain the connection by sea and by land.[24] For the creation of this route marked an important moment in the expansion of the trade not just of the Red Sea but of a much vaster world.

IV

What happened to the Red Sea trade following the crisis in Egypt has to be reconstructed out of very short references in the Bible that speak of the trade not to Punt but to Ophir, which seems to have been more or less the same place, since it lay in a similar direction and produced similar goods. Curiously, though, the Bible speaks of gold from Ophir but seems uninterested in incense, even though vast quantities of it were burned in the Temple; rituals requiring the waving of censers containing incense by the High Priest Aaron and his successors are described in some detail in the books of Exodus and Leviticus, which it is now generally agreed took their current shape around 500 BC. Since these texts, at least in the form we have them, are so late, archaeology provides the best clues to the use of incense in the area inhabited by the Canaanites and Israelites at the end of the second millennium BC. Incense stands or vessels have been found at sites in modern Israel such as Hazor (from the fourteenth century BC) and Megiddo (from the eleventh century BC). But the incense may well have been made out of substances other than frankincense. Sumerian and Assyrian incense was not made from frankincense (which is further proof that there was no contact with south-western, as opposed to south-eastern, Arabia); aromatic wood from the cedar, cypress, fir or juniper tree was favoured instead; some myrrh was used, but probably a lesser grade of Indian origin.[25] According to the Talmud, the incense used in the Jewish Temple was very carefully mixed from a great variety of ingredients, beaten fine: eleven spices, including frankincense, balm, myrrh, cassia, saffron, cinnamon and Cyprus wine; 'he who omitted any one of the ingredients was liable to the penalty of death', though there is no evidence anyone ever committed such carelessness.[26] Even if this is an elaboration of what was actually used, it is a reminder that the creation of incense, like that of modern perfume, was a complex art and that no single ingredient was likely to be used on its own.

The Israelites were content with their supply of incense, for when, in the tenth century BC, the king of Israel, Solomon, and his great ally Hiram, king of Tyre, launched their own expeditions down the Red Sea, the aim was to acquire gold rather than resins. Archaeologists argue, almost at fisticuffs, about how real the picture of Solomon in the books of Kings and Chronicles was; they differ profoundly about the reliability of the stories that record the foundation of the Davidic dynasty, though the latest evidence, from Khirbet Qeiyafa and Tell Qasile in Israel, shows that the biblical version is not all fantasy. Kings tells how Solomon put together a fleet of ships at a place called Etzion-Geber on the Gulf of Aqaba–Eilat, where Israel and Jordan share one of the two northern tips of the Red Sea. The fleet was accompanied by sailors familiar with the sea, supplied by King Hiram, who was presumably also closely involved in the building of these ships. They travelled down to Ophir, where they obtained 420 talents' weight of gold, a massive amount (about sixteen tons), which they brought back to King Solomon.[27] Soon after, following the famous visit to Jerusalem of the queen of Sheba (who came overland in a great camel caravan), more ships were sent south, described this time as King Hiram's ships, which makes more sense. They brought gold, sandalwood and jewels from Ophir, and Solomon used the wood in the building both of the Temple in Jerusalem and of his palace next door. Some of the fine wood was even fashioned into harps and other stringed instruments, for 'it was the best sandalwood anyone in Israel had ever seen'. Kings then asserts that at that time silver was of no special value, so everything was made of gold, even cups and dishes; after this expedition, he received 666 talents of gold, according to the Bible, whose authors were almost certainly conjuring a figure out of the air. 'Solomon had many ships of Tarshish. Every three years he sent them out with Hiram's ships to bring back gold, silver and ivory, as well as monkeys and peacocks [or baboons]' – a passage that suggests silver was not quite so worthless after all.[28] So much silver was being brought from Spain by the Phoenicians at this period that it is conceivable silver was not exactly worthless, but was at least easy to obtain and lacked prestige.

This was the time when the Phoenicians were beginning to create their outposts as far afield as Cádiz, even if their settlement there is not as old as the traditional date, 1104 BC (the term 'Phoenician' was invented by the Greeks and refers to Canaanite traders, whether by sea or by land, who thought of themselves more as natives of particular cities such as Tyre or Carthage than as a distinct people).[29] The land rich in silver that they were visiting was called, in classical sources, Tartessos, and it corresponds to parts of southern Spain; it is often assumed that 'Tarshish', mentioned again and again in the Bible, was the same place, but the Bible is emphatic that Solomon's ships were launched on the Red Sea, and the goods they brought back were not the produce of the Mediterranean.[30] The phrase 'ships of Tarshish', rather like the term 'argosy' derived from the city of Ragusa (Dubrovnik) in early modern times, indicated any fleet of capacious sailing vessels able to breast the high seas. Hiram supplied Solomon with fine timber not just from distant Ophir but from the cedar forests of Lebanon in the hinterland of Tyre; and he sent other goods from all over the Phoenician trading world, as can be seen from the biblical account of how the Temple was built. The Red Sea was a subsidiary, but exotic, addition to the Phoenician trade routes that led across the sea to north Africa, Sardinia and Spain and overland to Assyria. In the sixth century the prophet Ezekiel poured verbal fire and brimstone on Hiram's erstwhile capital, Tyre, and listed all the lands where Tyre traded – among the easiest to identify are Persia and Yavan (Ionia, that is, Greece), but also Arabia and Sheba, meaning Yemen or somewhere nearby.[31]

It is possible that the story of Solomon's fleet is a projection backwards from later times, and it is even possible that a memory lingered of Queen Hatshepsut's mission to Punt. Reading between the lines, one can see that Hiram played a bigger role than Solomon in this enterprise. But the gold of Ophir was not an illusion; even if the fleets of Ophir were not sailing in the tenth century, they aroused interest in the ninth. A curious passage in Kings, accompanied, as usual, by a much later recasting in Chronicles, tells how Jehosaphat, king of Judah (c.873–849 BC), 'made ships of Tarshish to go to Ophir for gold, but they did not go, for they were wrecked at Etzion-Geber; then Ahaziah the son of Ahab said to Jehosaphat, let my servants go with your servants in the ships. But Jehosaphat was unwilling.' Chronicles knew, or pretended to know, rather more than Kings, though the author was thoroughly confused between Ophir and Tarshish and offered a different chronology. Jehosaphat received quite a good press in the Bible; for instance, just before the decision was made to build the ships he had expelled the male temple prostitutes against whom the prophets inveighed. Ahaziah, on the other hand, aroused the ire of the authors of the Bible; he was the king of the rival northern kingdom of Israel, which came into existence after the death of Solomon; yet the two kings set aside past enmities, political and religious, and joined together in a pact, constructing a fleet of ships at Etzion-Geber bound for 'Tarshish'. A mercantile consortium of this type, guaranteed by the ruler's protection, was perfectly normal at this time. With the prospect of high profits but the danger of heavy losses, the royal court had the resources to bear the risk, and at the same time welcomed the opportunity to acquire gold and luxury goods.[32]

All went well until Jehosaphat, who tended to have trouble with the very many prophets telling him what to do, became the target of a certain Eliezer, son of Dodavahu, who strongly disapproved of the alliance with the ruler of Israel, a king still tainted with the Canaanite beliefs that his father Ahab had willingly tolerated. 'And the ships were wrecked, so they were unable to go out to Tarshish.' The exact meaning of the term *vayishaberu*, translated here as 'wrecked', is not clear, as it could mean 'destroyed' in all sorts of ways, and in the standard English translations the word 'broken' is used instead. But surely what the Bible points to is ships coming apart, whether because they were poorly constructed, or because they foundered in a storm or on the many reefs of the Red Sea. For even with Phoenician help it cannot have been easy to navigate a little-known sea, either for Hatshepsut's fleet, or Solomon's, or this one.

The obvious task of the archaeologists would be to locate Etzion-Geber. The meaning of the name is not much help; it may indicate something like 'town of the cockerel'; this is not an area, like some in the Middle East, where fairly continuous occupation has preserved old names. However, since the Red Sea ends in a point, now marked by the modern Israeli city of Eilat and its older Jordanian neighbour, Aqaba, one should not have to seek too far. In 1938 the American archaeologist Nelson Glueck, much respected for his work on biblical sites, identified the hillock of Tell el-Kheleifeh, which stands just inside the Jordanian border with Israel, as the location of Etzion-Geber. He thought he had found tenth-century pottery there, of varied origin but dating roughly to King Solomon's time; but more recent investigations have shown the pottery to be somewhat later, later even than King Jehosaphat, and dating to the eighth to early sixth centuries BC, around the time that the book of Kings was probably being pieced together. Still, it contains clues: some pieces are stamped with the inscription 'belonging to Qaws'anal, servant of the king', who may well be the king of Judah.[33] Another discovery at this site was a potsherd with south Arabian writing, dating from the seventh century BC or a little later, so traffic up the Red Sea certainly existed. Others looking for Etzion-Geber have pointed to 'Pharaoh's island' a little offshore, the site of a crusader castle; the island possesses an enclosed inner harbour of a type familiar from the Phoenician colonies. The Phoenicians preferred to found their trading settlements on offshore islands, as can be seen at Tyre itself and at Motya near Sicily or Cádiz beyond the Strait of Gibraltar. It would not have been odd to have done the same when they tried to set up a sea route down the Red Sea, whether in the tenth century BC or, more likely, in later centuries.[34]

All this may appear very tenuous, so the best piece has been saved up till last. The mound of Tell Qasile, now contained within the Land of Israel Museum in Tel Aviv, contains the quite substantial remains of a town that the Philistines established on the coast a little north of Jaffa when, arriving from Crete, Cyprus and the Aegean, these Mycenaean warriors migrated across the Mediterranean during the convulsions that saw the collapse of the great Bronze Age civilizations in the region. The town was still active in the eighth century BC, when someone threw away a fragment of a pot inscribed in early Hebrew: 'the gold of Ophir to Beth-Horon, thirty shekels'.[35] As for Beth-Horon, this was either a temple dedicated to the god Horon or a town a little way to the north-west of Jerusalem, in the West Bank, which – rather than lapsing into obscurity – is now the seat of one of the Israeli settlements that have become an obstacle to peace in the Middle East.

V

'And when they were come into the house, they saw the young child with Mary his mother, and fell down, and worshipped him: and when they had opened their treasures, they presented unto him gifts; gold, and frankincense, and myrrh.'[36] It has been seen that these three luxuries already shared their history 1,450 years before the birth of Jesus. About fifteen years ago, a colleague at Cambridge was returning from a visit to the Middle East around Christmas-time. When his luggage was inspected by British customs officials they asked him what he had bought, and he declared that he had been visiting Yemen and that his luggage contained frankincense and myrrh. 'And gold as well, I suppose!' came the ironic reply, and he was let through without further ado. These items were certainly the prestige products of the earliest trade routes to navigate down all, or most of, the Red Sea. On the other hand, preferences shifted. The Egyptians had a special interest in myrrh, though they were also great burners of incense; the Phoenicians and the Israelites were most interested in gold and had other sources for their incense. And, as in the case of the early navigators down the Persian Gulf, the expeditions to Punt and Ophir were punctuated by long periods of silence, during which, if Queen Hatshepsut is to be believed, contact was lost. Fits and starts characterized this maritime route even more than that of the Persian Gulf. Difficulties in navigating past the reefs and shoals of the Red Sea were one discouragement; the possibility of using land routes was another. One could reach Eritrea by river and land, and one could reach Arabia by following the coast of western Arabia overland. This traffic was rendered much easier by the domestication of the camel, whose date is disputed but may have been achieved, at least in parts of Arabia, by 1000 BC.[37] Competition between land and sea routes to south Arabia and the facing shores of Africa would last many centuries. It was not always clear what comparative advantage a sea route offered those seeking frankincense and myrrh. The Red Sea would only be used intensively when ships regularly sailed south beyond the fabled lands of Punt, Sheba and Ophir into the wide expanses of the ocean, and that would only happen when the attractions of the Indies and of the shores of Africa became clear. In other words, the Red Sea flourished not for itself but as a passageway linking Egypt, and beyond that the Mediterranean, to Africa, India and even Malaya.

5

Cautious Pioneers

I

During the first millennium BC, political convulsions in the eastern Mediterranean and the competition between the rulers of Egypt and Babylonia for control of the lands inhabited by Canaanites and Israelites, Philistines and Phoenicians, turned the attention of the great powers away from the Persian Gulf and the Red Sea; and it was this, perhaps, that enabled the navies of Solomon and Hiram to take over management of the sea route to Ophir. But there is little evidence in the literary sources, in surviving tablets, or in archaeological finds, for regular and intensive movement by merchant ships up and down these seas. This does not mean contact came to an end; but the emergence of a powerful Persian Empire, which by the sixth century had absorbed Iraq as well, brought land routes into the highlands of Iran to the fore, and Indian goods could also be obtained via the cross-country routes, while caravan traffic from south Arabia kept consumers supplied with frankincense and myrrh.

Following the conquest of Babylon by the Persian ruler Cyrus the Great in 539 BC, Cyrus proclaimed himself 'king of Babylon, king of Sumer and Akkad, king of the four corners of the world', setting himself firmly within a 2,000-year-old tradition that had originated in Bronze Age Sumer. Under his successors the Persian Great Kings expanded their power as far as Ionia on the coast of Asia Minor, and were keen to take charge of Greece proper as well. Greeks visited the Persian court and were hungry for information about the vast empire that had come into being, embracing Egypt, Persia, Babylonia and Lydia in Asia Minor; but it was difficult to make sense of the information that trickled through to Ionia and the Aegean. Judging from the geographical writings that survive in whole or in part, the ancient Greeks were curious about the shape of Africa, Arabia and India; they were also excited by stories of bold explorers who had travelled for years around Arabia or even the whole continent of Africa.

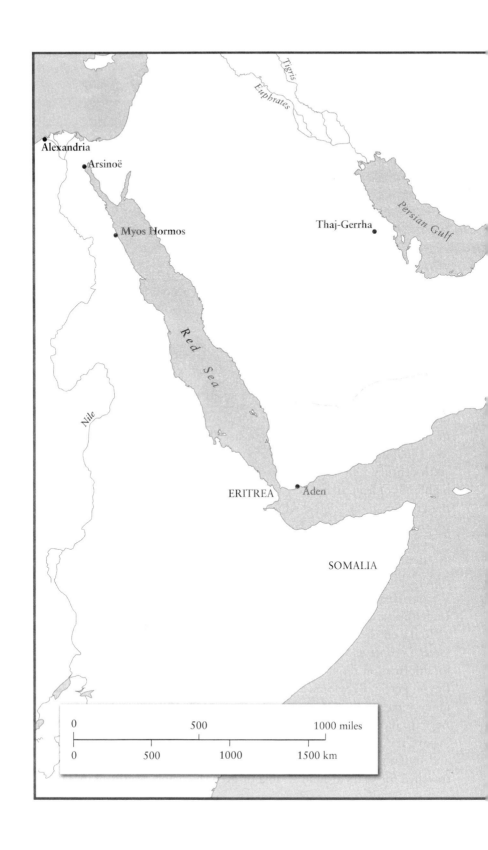

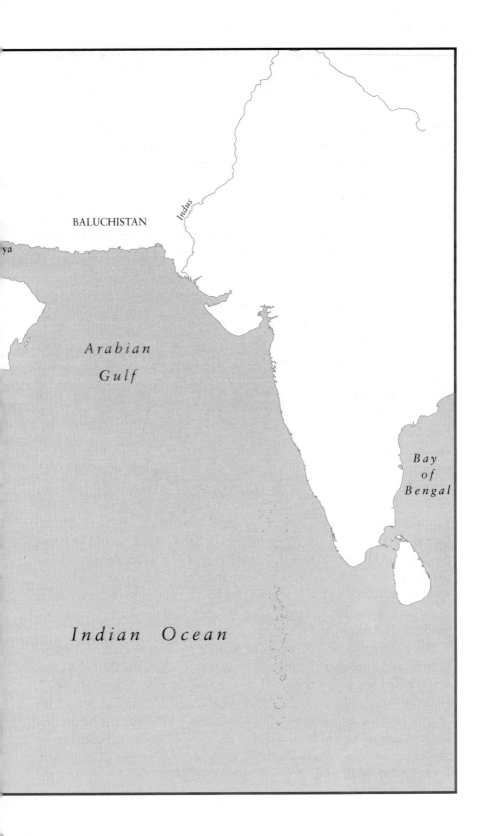

BALUCHISTAN

ya

Indus

Arabian
Gulf

Bay
of
Bengal

Indian   Ocean

Around 500 BC the historian Hekataios, only known from fragments quoted by later writers, mentioned the Gulf and called it the *Persikos kolpos*, 'Persian Gulf', which revealed something about the new political order that had come into being. During the following century the Ionian polymath Herodotos described a remarkable sea voyage around the Arabian peninsula that took place around 510 BC, which suggests attempts were under way to re-establish routes from India to Arabia. Skylax, who came from Caria on what is now the Turkish coast, and was therefore a near neighbour of Herodotos, was commissioned by the Great King Darius Hystaspis to sail with a crew not from the mouth of the Tigris and Euphrates but from the Indus, which he reached overland, and to head out into the ocean and westwards round Arabia and up the Red Sea. The voyage towards the port of Arsinoë near Suez took thirty months.[1]

There is no reason to be sceptical about Herodotos' story. Darius was attempting something that was, potentially at any rate, revolutionary. He aimed to draw together the Indies and Egypt; and this meant that heavy engineering work was needed at the Egyptian end of the route too. Darius re-created the ancient channel through the delta that led up the Nile in one direction, and out to the Mediterranean in the other. This was not exactly a precursor of the Suez Canal, for the route ran westwards from the bitter lakes a little north of Suez; and the ancient Egyptians appear to have laid the groundwork. The new channel, Herodotos avers, was wide enough for two triremes to pass one another, and it took four days to navigate its length.[2] Once this channel was in operation, shipping could, in theory at least, travel from the Egyptian city of Babylon (the present-day Cairo) all the way to the Indus River. An Egyptian inscription from this period found along the route of the canal boasted that ships could 'sail directly from the Nile to Persia by way of Saba', which would be south Arabia, and Herodotos saw this canal as part of a wider Persian scheme to conquer the whole vast area between India and Greece; nor was Darius' ambition confined to the landmass, for he also aimed to become master of the seas: 'after they had made their voyage round the coast, Darius both subdued the Indians and made use of this sea'.[3]

Since there was already a port at Arsinoë towards the top of the Gulf of Suez, and since south Arabian pottery was reaching the Gulf of Aqaba, was the Red Sea such a neglected area during the first millennium BC? It is always very risky to argue from silence, and Herodotos, for all his charm, is often unbelievable, and sometimes confessed that he did not really accept all he had been told. But the story of Skylax is backed up by the bigger, and more easily verifiable, story of Persian imperial ambitions. Less credible, with its description of harvests planted and reaped off the coast of Africa, is another tale Herodotos told about navigation out of the Red Sea into the Indian Ocean during the reign of the Pharaoh Necho, or Nekau (610–594 BC):

> Libya [i.e. Africa] reveals that it is surrounded by sea, except for the part that borders on Asia; and as far as we know this originally was demonstrated by Necho king of Egypt. Once he had finished digging the channel which leads from the Nile to the Arabian Gulf [i.e. Red Sea] he sent out Phoenicians aboard ships, commanding them to sail on and to return past the Pillars of Herakles into the Northern Sea [i.e. the Mediterranean] and from there to head to Egypt. The Phoenicians therefore set forth from the Red Sea and sailed through the Southern Sea [i.e. Indian Ocean]; and whenever autumn came, they would put to shore and sow the land, wherever in Libya they might happen to have arrived; and then they waited for the harvest. So, having reaped the grain, they would sail on, and after two years had passed, they turned through the Pillars of Herakles in the third year and arrived in Egypt. And they reported a thing which I cannot believe, but others might choose to believe, namely that in sailing round Libya they had the sun on their right hand.[4]

Herodotos also reported a voyage sent by a later Persian king, Xerxes (485–465 BC), which was supposed to go round Africa anti-clockwise. The captain, who this time was a Persian named Sataspes, had been sent on this expedition as an alternative to being impaled for raping or dishonouring a noblewoman; but he turned back somewhere in the Atlantic after meeting some small and primitive folk on the shores of Africa and returned to Egypt. There, Sataspes was promptly impaled after all by the unimpressed Great King.[5] The problem in Herodotos' mind was the shape and dimensions of Africa, and whether the Indian Ocean led into the Atlantic, as he and in due course Alexander the Great were convinced it must do. Even so, the geographer Ptolemy would later insist that the Indian Ocean was a closed sea, bordered on its southern fringes by a broad strip of torrid, uninhabitable lands that stretched from southern Africa towards south-east Asia.

This is one of the many great expeditions that have been credited to the Phoenicians, all too often without much evidence; more recent enthusiasts have sent them to the Azores, if not America, and to India, if not Malaysia, and they have even been credited with the building of the city of Great Zimbabwe in southern Africa a mere 1,800 years after the reign of the Pharaoh Necho. The point about the direction in which the sun lay has often been cited to show that they must have sailed along the Atlantic coast of Africa, though other Phoenicians certainly crept down that coast from Gibraltar (maybe including the unfortunate Sataspes), definitely as far as Mogador. Arguments that might disprove the voyage include the rather short length of time, especially when compared with the more reasonable duration of Skylax's voyage around Arabia, all the more so if the Phoenicians stopped for long periods to watch the grain grow. How would they maintain and repair their boats? And what sort of ships did they use anyhow?[6] The most important conclusion from Herodotos' short and puzzling account is that, whatever they observed, these Phoenicians did not open up new routes into the Indian Ocean. East Africa would be integrated into the great trading network of that ocean in due course; but the pioneers in long-distance traffic across this ocean were the Greeks and the Romans.

Once the Greeks had wreaked their revenge for past attacks by Darius and Xerxes, and had conquered the Persian Empire, following the lightning campaigns of Alexander the Great in the fourth century BC, the Indian Ocean attracted increased attention both from rulers and from writers. Alexander's dreams of unlimited empire were only enhanced when he pressed on into north-western India, leaving behind Greek army veterans and a legacy of Greek culture that became intertwined with Buddhism. He was learned in geography, as one might expect of a pupil of the polymath Aristotle, and on one occasion he delivered a speech in which he set out how the various seas, including the Persian Gulf, were related to one another. No doubt Alexander had read about Skylax, who was quite famous, and about other expeditions under the Persian banner. He obviously knew about the circumnavigation reported by Herodotos, for he insisted that 'from the Persian Gulf our fleet shall sail round to Libya, right up to the Pillars of Herakles', and opined that one result would be the extension of his rule over all Libya, or Africa, not to mention Asia – his aim was to reach 'those boundaries which God set for the whole earth'.[7]

In 325 BC he commissioned a Cretan officer named Nearchos to set out from the Indus and head up the Persian Gulf. Nearchos was an old and trusted companion of Alexander, and the choice of someone so close to the king to make this voyage indicates that this was not a trivial enterprise, but that it had strategic objectives as well as scientific ones. Alexander was at first reluctant to appoint Nearchos, because he placed such value on his friendship and was well aware of the risk Nearchos would face leading his fleet into uncharted waters; but Nearchos insisted he wanted to do this, and as they reviewed the names of other possible commanders they realized that all of them would prove unreliable, even chicken-hearted. Nearchos said, if Alexander's biographer Arrian is to be believed:

'O king! I undertake to lead your fleet! May God help this enterprise! I shall bring your ships and men safe and sound to Persia, if the sea is indeed navigable and this enterprise is not beyond human power.'

The sailors for this expedition were from Phoenicia, Cyprus and Egypt, though individual ships were placed under Greek commanders from Alexander's entourage. Some of the ships were partly brought from Cyprus and Phoenicia, extraordinary as this may seem. In accord with common practice, they were dismantled or constructed only in sections on the coast of Lebanon and carried overland to the river system of Mesopotamia. They were taken down to Babylon, where other vessels were built; how they then reached the Indus across the Persian mountains is a mystery.[8] The Phoenicians and their Carthaginian descendants were experts at the assembly-line construction of ships, and would number the planks and fittings so that everything could be put together exactly as intended.[9] Alexander was hoping for a report on the people, ports and products of the sea coast between Mesopotamia and India, and this voyage became widely known when not just Nearchos but several officers in the fleet recorded their own account of the journey. Alas, only fragments of these accounts have survived, though Arrian offered a connected account based on Nearchos' words. His account combined high adventure and quite specific description, for the records left by the captains were not, in the main, stirring sea yarns but detailed navigation guides that recorded in great detail the information the king of Macedon had requested.

There was, though, more than enough material for yarns as well: having travelled down the Indus, the ships were delayed by the monsoon for more than three weeks close to what is now Karachi. Then several ships were lost in gales, even though the men managed to swim to safety; Nearchos cannot have had much understanding of the monsoon season at the start of his voyage, but experience taught him and his captains how important it was to respect the ocean winds. Mastering high seas was only the first serious problem; their reception by the inhabitants of the coastline was often extremely inhospitable. On one occasion, as they sailed along the coast of Baluchistan, Nearchos was challenged by hundreds of half-naked Indians, who are described as extremely hairy, 'not only their heads but the rest of their bodies'. They had no knowledge of iron, but used their claw-like fingernails as tools with which they ripped apart the raw fish they ate, and otherwise they relied on sharp stones for tools; they dressed in animal skins or even whale skins. He sent a phalanx of men, all capable swimmers, over the side of his ships; these men had apparently swum, or at least waded, to shore in their armour, and they struck terror into the Indians.

As they moved beyond what Nearchos regarded as India, down the coast of Iran, they encountered peaceful town-dwelling folk who fed the sailors with bread made not from grain but from pounded fish meal obtained from large sea creatures whose flesh had been dried in the sun; they regarded wheat and barley as delicacies. Fresh fish were generally eaten raw; and, rather than being caught out at sea, the fish were scooped out of hollows along the beaches where they, along with crabs and oysters, were found when the tide receded. At one settlement, the local sheep tasted of fish because, according to the report, there was no pasture for animals and so the sheep were fed on fish meal. Even the beams with which they constructed their houses were large whale or fish bones. Food was sometimes hard to find as the fleet coasted along, and those on board had to resort to palm hearts cut from trees along the coast. Apart from the occasional slaughtered camel, they found little on which to gorge themselves in the land of the fish-eaters, and were glad to press on.[10]

It was perhaps inevitable that the fabulous should become mixed up with the real, and Arrian reports a visit to an island sacred to the sun where no human had set foot, and where one of the demi-goddesses known to the Greeks as the Nereids had once lived. She had lured sailors to the island, but once they arrived she turned them into fish. The sun god was not amused by this sport and expelled her, as well as turning these fish back into human beings, whereupon they settled on the shore and became fish-eaters. Nearchos had no difficulty in reaching the island and proving that there was nothing magical about the place. But there was still a sense of being half-lost, only vaguely knowing where they should be heading. Mapping the contours of India and Iran was confusing, especially as they approached the Persian Gulf and the Musandam peninsula that juts out from Oman and almost closes off the Gulf. Should they sail down the ocean flank of the peninsula past Arabia or carry on into the Gulf along the coast of Iran? On that side Nearchos had already found land rich in cinnamon, but he realized that the Arabian coast was the outer edge of sandy desert, 'quite denuded of water', and rejected the advice of one of his captains that he should follow the shore of Oman south-westwards. He understood that the route up the Gulf would eventually take him to Babylonia. As they sailed up the Gulf they encountered more unconquered tribes living by the shores, and even a wandering Greek, still wearing his Greek cloak, who had become detached from Alexander's army; so, even when coasting along the shores of the Persian heartlands, they were making discoveries and helping the king of Macedon understand how his territories fitted together.[11] The voyage was rated a resounding success.

II

The expedition had explored a small but important segment of the coast between modern Pakistan and the Persian Gulf; the distance was modest compared to the voyages attributed to the Phoenicians, but the framework for a maritime network spanning the Indian Ocean was gradually coming into being. Alexander ordered the creation of a port named (predictably) Alexandria at the mouth of the Tigris–Euphrates system, to facilitate trade down the Gulf; so there was some hope of capitalizing on Nearchos' achievements. But Alexander's ambitions were soon thwarted by his early death at Babylon; for the next few years his generals squabbled over and finally divided his empire. He had sown some seeds: his successors, the Ptolemies in Egypt and the Seleucids in Mesopotamia (actively competing for Syria), became increasingly interested in naval power; and the Persian Gulf gradually re-emerged as an important channel for traders seeking to reach the Indies. Alexander had stretched the Greek world as far as India; partial Hellenization also occurred in the Gulf region, as Greek settlers were encouraged to establish small trading towns that would service the trade in Arabian aromatics and Indian spices. Yet Alexander's successors were generally more interested in Syria and the Mediterranean, where the Seleucids played out their rivalry with the Ptolemies of Egypt, than they were in the Gulf and the Indian Ocean. Elephants rather than warships were the great symbols of Seleucid military power. Still, the Seleucid kings operated a fleet in the Persian Gulf whose task was to make sure that the sea routes to India remained open, particularly when resurgent Persian power threatened free access to these waters; Parthian soldiers in Persian service may have managed to occupy the northern tip of Oman.[12]

This was an age of urban revival in the Gulf. The Seleucid kings dreamed of creating a network of Greek towns along its shores. Such a network could never match the networks created in the Mediterranean, but at least six towns, and maybe nine or more, were established. Exactly where they were has been much debated, for they have vanished from the map. Graves found at the ancient settlement of Bidya, in the small part of the UAE that faces out across the Indian Ocean, have been described as 'Hellenistic', in other words from the Seleucid period; they overlaid graves dating back to the second millennium BC. So maybe the Greeks, or rather people infused with Greek culture (including, to judge from finds in the town, fine glass), reached as far as this.[13] One town which seems to have developed independently from, and rather more successfully than, the Greek settlements lay at what the Arabs later knew as Thaj, in what is now

Saudi Arabia. Most of its inhabitants were probably Arabs, and it was the seat of a state that controlled part of the eastern flank of Arabia.[14] On the one hand, there are the ruins of a large city of whose original name no archaeological record survives; and, on the other hand, there are the enthusiastic reports of classical writers, going right back to the time of Alexander the Great, that describe land and sea trade between a place they called Gerrha and Babylonia, making it plain that this was by far the most important trading centre in the region.[15] According to the Greek writers, the great speciality of these Arabian merchants was, predictably, incense, which they carried northwards to their city; Gerrha was an entrepôt between the lands rich in frankincense and myrrh and the great empires and royal courts that craved these products and had the means to buy them, to be used in temple worship and to render ever more magnificent the ceremonies of the Seleucid and Ptolemaic courts.

King Antiochos III was so keen to benefit from this trade that he made a state visit to Gerrha in 205 BC; although he was showing the Seleucid flag in the Persian Gulf, he did not come to Gerrha as a conqueror, and the Greek historian Polybios emphasized that he gladly recognized the 'perpetual peace and freedom' of the citizens of Gerrha.[16] Antiochos was, however, also happy to go away with massive gifts in frankincense, myrrh and silver; and he hoped he had persuaded the Gerrhaeans to send their merchants to Babylonia rather than to Persia or towards his rivals, the Ptolemaic kings of Egypt, who at this point controlled Syria. To reach the lands of the Ptolemies, as several papyri from Egypt make plain, south Arabian incense travelled overland via Petra or other towns on the edges of Syria in the camel caravans of the Nabataean merchants, and not by ship around Arabia and up the Red Sea. But, in the second century BC, Syria fell under Seleucid rule; and as a result the route from Gerrha to the lands of the Nabataeans was unblocked, as the Seleucid king now stood to gain as much from taxes collected in Syria as from those collected in Babylonia.[17]

That is what is known of Gerrha from the Greek historians and geographers. Then there is the physical evidence from Thaj. Whether or not it stands on the site of Gerrha, Thaj had a long history as a centre of trade. Thaj was still being mentioned by pre-Islamic writers of Arabic, fragments of whose works were preserved by the Muslim Arabs as exemplars of fine writing: 'the flowing wells of Thaj invite the wild she-asses', wrote 'Amr ibn Kultum some time in the late sixth century AD.[18] But much earlier, in the third century BC, this substantial walled town had been taking delivery of Greek black-glazed pottery that had filtered through from the Mediterranean. Rather more pottery arrived from Seleukeia, which was the grand eastern capital of the dynasty, named with typical contemporary immodesty after themselves.[19] Seleukeia lay some way up the Tigris, at a point where the distance between the Tigris and Euphrates narrowed briefly. Thaj therefore had distant connections. The city grew and grew, so that it is the largest known archaeological site in the Gulf region. Its area was over 800,000 square metres (Pliny the Elder said the circumference of Gerrha was five Roman miles, making it much the same size).[20] But although it had plenty of fresh water it lay more than fifty miles inland from the coast, with good access to a port at al-Jubayl, but also, without doubt, to caravan routes that trekked down the eastern side of Arabia, and that were still being used by coffee traders plodding their way up from Yemen on their camels in the nineteenth century.[21] This resolves a difficulty that has left some historians unconvinced that Gerrha and Thaj were the same place. Greek writers thought of Gerrha as a place by the sea; one early Greek description insists that rafts (perhaps he meant reed boats) were sent from Gerrha up the Gulf towards Babylonia; and the geographer Strabo first said it lay by the sea – and then said it lay some way inland.[22] Gerrha, like Dilmun, was both a specific and a general term: it was a twin city, of a sort that has been by no means uncommon in the past, combining a large inland metropolis with a small but handsome harbour on the coast; and Gerrha was also a general word for the political unit, of whose government we know nothing, that encompassed both city and port. The greater success of the inland half of Gerrha may not be evidence that the maritime trade of the Gulf was at last taking off; but it is evidence that the broader region was experiencing a renaissance. Even so, the real transformation would occur when the business affairs of the great kings and of the merchants who served them became still more ambitious, and regularly reached as far as India.

III

The Ptolemies were not idle while their rivals tried to expand their influence in the Persian Gulf.[23] News of Nearchos' expedition reached Egypt, for some of the crewmen were Egyptian. Ptolemy I, who reigned there from 325 to 285 BC, was more interested in building up Alexandria as a major political, commercial and naval centre from which he could exercise command over the eastern Mediterranean than he was in the treacherous waters of the Red Sea. Even so, there were some important initiatives under the early Ptolemies. One was the re-digging of the 'Red–Med' canal that had already been re-dug at the orders of the Persian king Darius; by 400 BC it had silted up and no one had shown much interest in clearing it, even though its closure cut off the trading town of Pithom from its water traffic, and sent it into decline. It was an ancient town, notorious among Jews as one of the 'store-cities' built for the pharaohs with the labour of Hebrew slaves. Then, under Ptolemy II Soter, around 270 BC, the city revived as the canal was reopened.[24] This initiative was thought worth-while because an earlier experiment, under Ptolemy I, had been so successful. That king had sent an admiral named Philo down the coast of Africa, in the hope of obtaining elephants for his army, or, if not live animals, ivory for his court. The Ptolemaic army maintained a special elephant contingent, and the elephants were housed in their own park, where the royal animal-keepers could attend to their every need.[25] Ptolemy II was agitated to learn that the inhabitants of the lands where elephants roamed were in the habit of slicing steaks off the flanks of living beasts; he wanted his elephants whole and healthy. Since African elephants are rather larger than Indian ones, he had the chance to acquire bigger and more aggressive battle-tanks than his Seleucid rivals.[26]

Elephants alone could not sustain the economic life of the small ports that sprang up along the Egyptian coast of the Red Sea, and the trickle of sea trade up the Red Sea from Somalia turned into a regular flow. Egyptian sea captains were venturing with some confidence beyond Aden to the Horn of Africa, but hugging the African coast, while those in Seleucid service were keeping within the Persian Gulf, or close to the shores that led from the Gulf to the edges of India. As for south Arabia, the land of Sabaea, rich in frankincense and myrrh, this was an area that was uncon-quered and unwelcoming; it sent out its goods, and profited greatly from trade, but the only foreign traders it welcomed were the Nabataeans, who dominated the caravan route up to Petra and the Mediterranean coast. Sabaea's own merchants were avid buyers of cinnamon from the Horn of Africa. Not just Sabaean isolationism but problems with navigat-ing the open ocean kept Egyptian merchant fleets and Seleucid ones apart. The monsoons still had to be mastered. The ocean was still a place of unpredictable dangers. In the first century AD, Strabo looked back at the attempts made under the Ptolemies to penetrate the Indian Ocean, and stressed how in his day regular traffic linked Alexandria to the Indian Ocean by way of Myos Hormos on the Red Sea, 'but earlier, under the rule of the Ptolemies, very few people had been bold enough to launch their ships and trade in Indian goods'.[27] Myos Hormos will be visited shortly, for it is an extraordinary archaeological site. The early voyages of exploration along the coast of Iran and north-west India had proved that a sea route existed but had not actually opened that route; and one reason was the challenge presented by the monsoons.

An 'Arabian barrier' therefore existed, and the challenge of finding a way past the Sabaean lands only made the Ptolemies keener to bring the barrier down. These rulers were, after all, patrons of the great library of Alexandria, which was the home of scholars who knew, or thought they knew, how all the lands of the world were joined together. Euergetes II, who ruled Egypt in the middle of the second century BC, enjoyed the company of Alexandrian scholars who were experts in geography; the most important was Agatharchides of Knidos, who wrote a book about the Red Sea, mostly lost. He based his account on a wide variety of travellers' tales and documents in the royal archive.[28] One lengthy passage from his writings, preserved in a Byzantine manuscript, gives some clues to the ambitions of the Ptolemies, for pure knowledge was not the end of the matter. Agatharchides whetted the appetite of the Ptolemies, who were big spenders and big consumers. Offering a survey of Arabia, Agatharchides described lands rich in pure gold nuggets, the smallest the size of a fruit pip and the largest the size of a walnut, mined from the earth by native peoples who regarded gold as utterly commonplace, and who valued iron, bronze and silver much more highly; in their eyes silver was worth ten times the value of gold, weight for weight. Rather than Gerrha, Agatharchides took the view that Sabas, the capital of the Sabaeans, rich in frankincense and myrrh, was the finest town in Arabia. Between them, he says, the Gerrhaeans and the Sabaeans 'have made Ptolemy's Syria rich in gold'.[29]

The adventures of one mariner, Eudoxos of Kyzikos from 118 BC onwards, were long remembered by ancient writers. When an Indian traveller was swept across the seas by the winds and cast all alone upon the shore of the Red Sea, royal guards found him and had the clever idea of carrying him off to the court of the inquisitive King Euergetes. This was someone who would surely know the route to the Indies. He guided the sailor Eudoxos to India, and they brought back a splendid cargo of aromatics and spices. Eudoxos had been looking forward to enjoying the profits from the expedition, but his greedy king took everything for himself. However, after Euergetes died, Queen Cleopatra II of Egypt sent Eudoxos out once again. Once again the royal court took everything. After his ill-treatment by the Ptolemies, Eudoxos was exasperated, for he had hoped for a better outcome under what he assumed to be the benign patronage of the queen. Eudoxos decided he would find a different route to India, this time without royal interference; he would set out from the Mediterranean and circumnavigate Africa to reach India. He invested a great amount of money in this expedition, and even took boy and girl musicians with him, hoping to impress the kings of India with them. But he never reached much further than the Canary Islands, or somewhere in that region, and had to turn back. He attempted the route round Africa a second time, but his little fleet was shipwrecked and everyone, including Eudoxos, was lost, presumed drowned.[30] Eudoxos was, then, a pioneer whose career was filled with frustration and failure, for even when he reached the Indies he was not able to enjoy the fruits of his expeditions. Yet his career also shows that the route to the Indies was now a subject of serious interest at the court of the Ptolemies. The question how best to reach these rich and fabled lands by sea fascinated kings and sea captains long before Columbus and Vasco da Gama.

Once a sea route to India was open, the Ptolemies amassed vast amounts of Indian goods, and the next king of Egypt, Ptolemy Soter II, was said to have been very popular among the merchants of Delos at a time when this island had become the hub of eastern Mediterranean trade routes. The eminent ancient historian Rostovtzeff remarked that he was so popular because the Delians thought of him as Soter, 'the man of business, the great merchant', rather than Soter, the king of Egypt. The presence of all these Indian luxuries brought further riches to an island that was already experiencing a great boom. So much ivory arrived from Egypt that Delian merchants were forced to sell it at lower prices than they had wished.[31] Gradually the Mediterranean and the Indian Ocean were beginning to interact. Those placed in the middle – the kings and merchants of Egypt – were fully aware of the advantages this would bring, in profits and in the luxuries they could enjoy.

6

Mastering the Monsoon

Strabo's remark that there was now constant traffic between Egypt and the Indies is all the more remarkable because this traffic must have built up in a relatively brief period of no more than a century and a half. This was exactly the period when major changes within the Mediterranean were taking place, which saw first Rhodes and then the much smaller holy island of Delos become the focal points of commercial networks that tied together Alexandria, Rome (which was becoming the master of wider and wider tracts of the eastern Mediterranean) and the Syrian coast. Perfumes carried by the Nabataean merchants filled the market stalls on Delos, which was described as 'the greatest emporium on earth', and boasted a population of 30,000 people crammed into not much more than one square mile.[1] Alexandria, with its teeming population of Greeks, Jews and Egyptians, buzzed with business, and that business looked not just towards Syria, Greece and Rome but towards the Red Sea and, at last, the Indian Ocean. A tariff list from Alexandria, probably from the start of the second century AD, offers a pungent list of the spices and aromatics that mainly arrived from the Indian Ocean; to read it is to enter the spice markets of the modern as well as the ancient Middle East, before moving to the jeweller's souk: cinnamon, cardamom, pepper, ginger, myrrh, cassia wood; and then pearls, diamonds, sapphires, emeralds, beryl, turquoise; and beyond that silk, raw and processed, as well as wild animals – lions, leopards, panthers – and, amid all these wonderful cargoes, Indian eunuchs.[2]

The route across the desert linking the Nile to the Red Sea ports was made as safe as possible by setting up watchtowers manned by Roman soldiers, and by providing inns for caravans where both people and camels could be watered and fed, and goods could be stored safely overnight. According to Strabo, the Romans invested funds and energy in digging great cisterns to collect the sparse rainwater of the desert.[3] When trouble

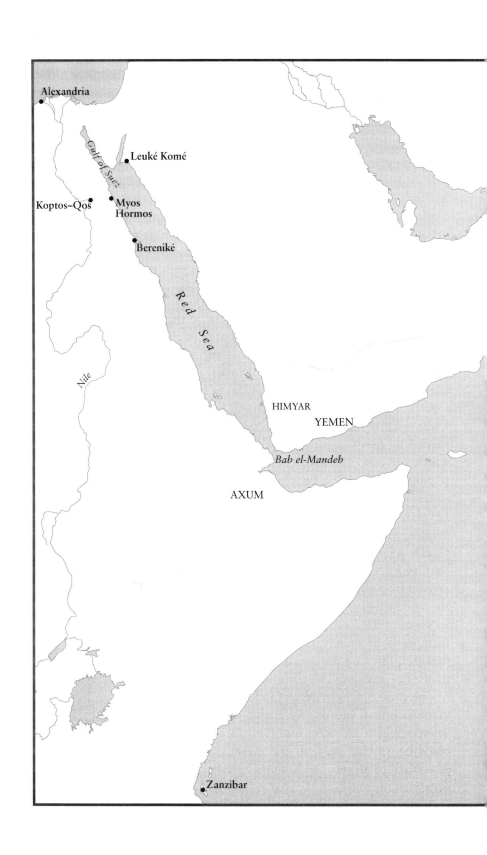

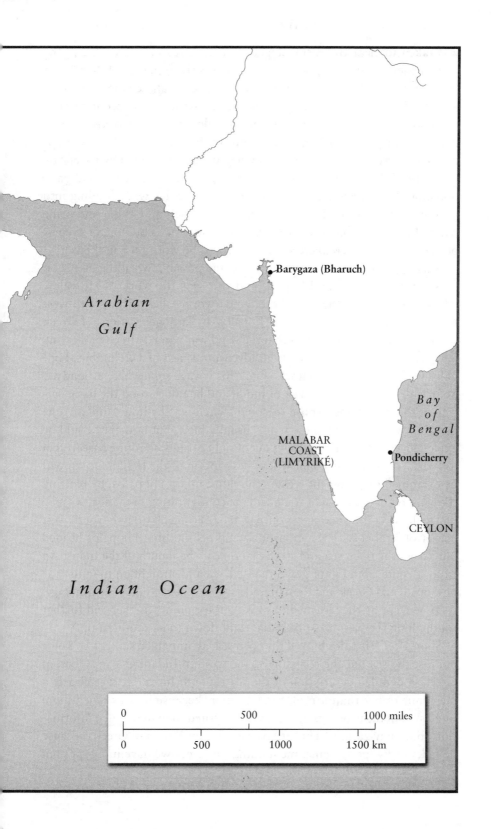

Arabian
Gulf

Barygaza (Bharuch)

Bay
of
Bengal

MALABAR
COAST
(LIMYRIKÉ)

Pondicherry

CEYLON

Indian   Ocean

| 0 | | 500 | | 1000 miles |
| 0 | 500 | 1000 | 1500 km | |

was taken to clear the easily clogged canals that linked the Nile to the Gulf of Suez, it was even possible to travel directly from the Nile to Klysma (modern Suez) and then down the Red Sea, generally changing boat at Klysma. The satirist Lucian of Samosata, who wrote in the second century AD, told the tale of a young man who went down the Nile to Klysma and decided to take ship for India; meanwhile his friends, puzzled at his disappearance, assumed he had been drowned while travelling downriver.[4] By the reign of Augustus, who died in AD 14, the India trade was already booming. By the reign of Tiberius (AD 14–37), coins were flooding into northern and western India, and were even reaching Ceylon and some parts of eastern India. They were used as money or as bullion, or even as ornaments (some were pierced, so they could be worn on a necklace).[5]

Mastering the ocean would only become possible when the monsoon season was properly understood, and this was the work of Hippalos, whose discovery of the way these winds worked led to the south-west monsoon being given the name 'Hippalos' by later generations of Greek sailors. Eventually they forgot that the wind was named after a pioneering navigator who showed some of the adventurousness of a Columbus. Hippalos was a Greek merchant who made his voyage somewhere around AD 20. He already knew the coast of India; and he understood the basic pattern of the monsoons, whose seasonal switch was by now familiar. The question was not when these winds usually blew, but how they could be exploited to make faster journeys out of sight of land, shooting past Arabia to India.[6] A Greek merchant whose description of the Indian Ocean will be examined in a moment wrote: 'the ship captain Hippalos, by plotting the location of the ports of trade and the configuration of the sea, was the first to discover the route across open water'.[7] Setting off from the south-west corner of Arabia with the monsoon wind behind him, Hippalos headed out across the open sea and struck land near the mouth of the Indus. An express route from Egypt down the Red Sea and straight on to India was now open, and Greek and Roman traders were quick to take full advantage. As time went by they learned to strike out for points further and further south along the west coast of India, right down to its southern tip.[8]

Soon after Hippalos braved the open sea, an unnamed sailor who knew not just the sea but the coastline of the western Indian Ocean wrote, in Greek, a detailed description of the sea route to India. He was clearly a merchant rather than a professional sailor, because he was much more interested in the products of the lands he visited than in detailed information about navigation.[9] The author was also an Egyptian Greek, because he talks of Egypt as home, mentioning 'the trees we have in Egypt'; but he was no armchair traveller: he described how his ship set a course and put on speed. His style was matter of fact and lacks grace, but he was capable of literary flight as well, for he offers a dramatic description of the fearsome tides off Barygaza in north-west India. Sir Mortimer Wheeler enthused: 'I should describe it, indeed, as one of the most fascinating books to have come down to us from antiquity.'[10] The original title of this work is *Periplous tēs Eruthras thalassēs*, 'Sea journey around the Red Sea', for the term 'Erythraean Sea' literally meant that, though what he intended is what is now called the Indian Ocean. What is now known as the Red Sea was often termed the 'Arabian Gulf', not least by the author of the *Periplous*.[11] Around AD 900 someone in the Byzantine Empire thought it worthwhile to make a rather messy copy of this work, which is how it has survived; but when it was originally written is not certain, and some of those who reject a date in the first century AD would prefer to assign a date in the early second or even early third century instead.[12] The *Periplous* describes a thriving network of trade that begins at the Red Sea ports of Myos Hormos and Berenikē, which will be discussed later since they have yielded superb archaeological finds. But Berenikē was devastated by an epidemic in AD 166, after which its trade withered, so the *Periplous* was surely written before then. Moreover, the author became very vague when he attempted to describe the waters beyond India, and the little book must have been written before ships under the Roman flag began to pass beyond Ceylon, and before Ceylon was identified as an island rather than the tip of another continent, as he believed.[13] It is clear that the tentative exploration of the early Seleucids had been transformed, perhaps within a century, into regular, intensive traffic. Not merely the scale was unprecedented; the creation of links between India (and also Ceylon) and Alexandria, a connection that would thrive during many later centuries, vastly expanded the range of contact by sea. For, even if Greek and Roman merchants did not venture into the eastern Indian Ocean at the time when the anonymous author sailed the seas, by reaching southern India he and his contemporaries made contact with the spice merchants from barely known lands much further to the east.

One cannot do better than follow the author on his *Periplous*, before backtracking to examine some equally eloquent archaeological sites and what contemporary Romans, such as Pliny the Elder, had to say. This way one can gain an idea of which areas were valued by sea traders and which they tended to avoid, whether because they produced little or because the inhabitants were regarded as hostile barbarians. Interestingly, such people could be found not far south of Berenikē, well within the Red Sea (following modern use of the term). Overall, the image of the Red Sea is of an unwelcoming place, a passageway that for long stretches offers little of its own apart from tortoise shell at a harbour-less port, suitable only for small boats, named Ptolemaïs Thērōn, whose name indicates that it had been founded before the Romans conquered Egypt, and while the Ptolemies ruled there. The south-western shores of the Red Sea were much more promising. The big attraction of Adulis was that elephant ivory and rhinoceros horn were carried there from the lordly city of Axum and from the Ethiopian highlands; sometimes the great beasts themselves wandered down to the shore near Adulis. But the serious drawback to Adulis was that raiders interfered with shipping, and it was vital to moor by an off-shore island for safety's sake.

Further south lay the realm of King Zoskales, 'mean in his way of life and with an eye to the main chance, but otherwise high-minded, and skilled in writing Greek'.[14] Greek cultural influence had, then, penetrated far south, and it is easy to see why: the author lists the goods that the Adulians bought, including Egyptian cloths, linen goods, glassware, brass, copper pans, iron for the spears with which they brought elephants low, and some, but not much, olive oil and Syrian or Italian wine. They clearly craved the products of Egypt and the Roman Mediterranean, but their parsimonious king was not terribly interested in gold or silver objects, unless the price was low.[15] That, however, was only part of the story. You could also sell them goods you had brought from India. They liked Indian steel and iron, as well as Indian cotton fabrics. Carrying on southwards, the *Periplous* mentioned harbours either side of the Bab al-Mandeb Strait that offered cassia, myrrh and sometimes frankincense. It noted too that shipping would arrive regularly from India bearing basic foodstuffs such as grain, rice, clarified butter (ghee) and sesame oil. There is a particularly precious reference to 'the cane honey called *sakchari*' – cane sugar, still an exotic product of India and lands even further to the east, which the Romans used therapeutically rather than as a sweetener.[16] Ships from Egypt might tramp up and down the coast, making up and disposing of their cargoes as they went, or they might head straight for one of the ports the *Periplous* singled out.

The Indian Ocean of the *Periplous* stretched in two directions. The author was keen to explain what can be found along the east coast of Africa as well as to spell out the route to India. The whole arc from somewhere near Zanzibar to western India was becoming a single, vast trading zone. Indeed, the king of part of Yemen, Charibaël, also ruled part of the African shore. Unfortunately it is impossible to be sure where the last port of trade in 'Azania', that is, east Africa, that the author mentioned might have stood; it could be Pemba island, or it could be Zanzibar itself. The name he used was Rhapta, which means 'sewn', and referred to the sewn-plank boats that the locals used for fishing and for hunting turtles.[17] A remarkable feature of this piece of coast is, the *Periplous* says, that it is ruled by the Arabians of Mouza, which corresponds to part of Yemen. This relationship was to last many centuries; in the nineteenth century the sultans of Oman based themselves at Zanzibar. When the *Periplous* was written, the main attraction of this region was ivory, rhinoceros horn and very good tortoise-shell. But beyond that lay an unexplored coastline, of which the *Periplous* could only say that the land tended westwards, until finally the Indian Ocean joined the 'western sea', that is, the Atlantic. This traveller was not, then, convinced by the argument that the Indian Ocean was a sealed sea surrounded by a greatly elongated tongue of land that stretched from southern Africa to the Golden Chersonese (Malaya). However, this view gained great influence in later centuries, as it was confidently supported by the great Alexandrian geographer Ptolemy.[18] Finds of Roman and Indian coins along the African coast, mainly of the fourth century AD, confirm that contact with 'Azania' was maintained over a long period.[19]

Arabian captains sailed back and forth from Mouza, and some of them intermarried with the native population, among whom the men were big-bodied and independent-minded; these Arab sailors learned to speak the local language.[20] The author of the *Periplous* was impressed by the Arabian merchants. Describing Mouza itself, he says that 'the whole place teems with Arabs – shipowners or charterers and sailors – and is astir with commercial activity. For they share in the trade across the water and with Barygaza, using their own vessels.'[21] Barygaza is Bharuch in north-western India, so this acts as a reminder that the arrival of Greek and Roman merchants in the Indian Ocean did not mean that the newcomers gained a monopoly on business. At some stage, impossible to determine, Arabian and Indian seafarers had followed or anticipated Hippalos, and had forged links across the Indian Ocean.[22] Local Indian rulers decorated their coins with pictures of ships, notably in the Satavahana Empire between AD 88 and 194; this empire embraced large tracts of central India as well as part of the east coast.[23] The ocean was awakening; and this was the work of its own inhabitants as much as, very probably more than, it was the work of subjects of the Roman emperor.

II

The author of the *Periplous* was aware that something new had been happening. He talked of a seaside village on the site of present-day Aden, named Eudaimōn Arabia, or 'Happy Arabia', that had previously been a proper city, 'when, since vessels from India did not go on to Egypt and those from Egypt did not dare sail to the places further on but only came this far, it used to receive cargoes of both, just as Alexandria receives cargoes from overseas as well as from Egypt'.[24] He thought it had been sacked by someone named in the manuscript as 'Caesar', which could be a reference to an attempt by Augustus to attack Aden with 130 warships. Strabo believed this expedition had been a success, but all the evidence suggests the opposite.[25] The author of the Periplous was much more interested in offering a vivid explanation of how frankincense formed on the bark of trees, in a mountainous, misty corner of Arabia that was so unhealthy that slaves and convicts were put to work collecting the gum; it was dangerous even to pass this coast on a ship because it was so disease-ridden, and the frankincense workers died of either sickness or malnutrition. This would be the western corner of modern Oman, celebrated today precisely because it is cool and misty, and unusually fertile by comparison with the rest of Arabia. The local ruler had the foresight, though, to construct a sturdy fort and warehouse in which to store the frankincense.[26] The rulers of southern Arabia were beginning to become not just prosperous but powerful. Describing a bay on the south coast of Arabia, the Periplous declared that frankincense can only be loaded with the king's permission; royal agents exchanged frankincense for grain, oil and cotton textiles.[27] Maritime trade was drawing a great variety of people to their land.

The Greco-Roman merchants who sailed in the wake of Hippalos were keen to make the fast connection between Egypt and India, and had no interest in the Persian Gulf. For the Periplous, the Gulf was best avoided; the best one could say of this 'vast expanse' was that there were plenty of pearls to be had near its opening.[28] The author of the Periplous was happy to jump across the strait and to reach a Persian port called Omana, which was not the same as modern Oman. Wherever it was, Omana gave access to a hinterland rich in dates, wine and rice, even though the coastline only produced bdellium, not that this was to be despised – it is another aromatic resin, a close cousin to myrrh. This was one of the ports to which merchants of Barygaza, in India, sent ploia megala, large ships, loaded with fine woods such as teak, as well as copper and ebony. They took away large numbers of pearls of modest quality compared to those of India itself, cloth, including luxurious purple textiles, gold from the Persian interior and slaves.[29]

Then, following the coast, one eventually reached 'the mightiest of the rivers along the Erythraean Sea', the Sinthos, or Indus, which emptied so much freshwater into the ocean that long before you reached terra firma you could see the river water coming out to meet you. One of the seven channels linking the Indus to the ocean was home to Barbarikon, whose exact location, after centuries during which the Indus has dumped silt all around its mouths, is unknown. Barbarikon gave access overland to Minnagar, a major city lying inland, whose royal court was hungry for textiles, plain and coloured, glassware, silverware, frankincense, coral and gems that were probably the attractive light green stones now known as peridots.[30] At such points the author of the *Periplous* most clearly revealed that what he had written was more a manual for merchants than a book of sailing instructions. But the attractions of Barbarikon were as much in buying as in selling. Bdellium, nard, turquoise, lapis lazuli, indigo and Chinese skins, cloth and yarn were all mentioned. These Chinese cloths, however they reached the mouth of the Indus, were made of that rarest and most coveted of fibres, silk.[31]

Yet even the excellent opportunities offered by the marketplace at Barbarikon were not enough. The *Periplous* braved difficult seas, full of whirlpools, sea snakes and turbulent waves to edge down the coast of India as far as the Gulf of Barygaza.[32] Sailing into the port at Barygaza was a challenge; ships had to negotiate a narrow gulf, with sharp reefs on the right-hand side, and a rocky, rough sea bottom that could slice through anchor cables. This took one through to a desolate landscape where it was hard to see the low-lying shore, and shoals made navigation even more difficult. For this reason fishermen in the king's service would come out to pilot ships through these waters; oarsmen attached their boats to incoming vessels and tugged them along, playing along with the tides, which were critical for access, but also extremely dangerous: 'they are much more extreme in the area around Barygaza than elsewhere'. At the flood tide, when there was a great rumbling, hissing rush of water upstream, one would suddenly see the sea floor, and channels used by ships would turn completely dry. During the flood tide ships would be ripped from their anchorage. Not for the only time in history, a major port was built in an unpromising, seemingly inaccessible location (compare Bristol, with quite similar tidal problems).

Barygaza was the real focus of attention in the *Periplous*. Known in Sanskrit as Bhārukaccha, and nowadays called Bharuch or Broach, it ought to be an important archaeological site, for its great mound awaits adequate excavation. It must be one of the most promising but neglected archaeological sites in the world; occasional finds in the general area include late Roman pottery and Roman coins.[33] From lands to the east of Barygaza 'everything that contributes to the region's prosperity' arrived in the port; this included semi-precious stones, such as onyx, and Indian cotton cloth, both fine and ordinary, as well as ivory, nard and bdellium transported from upcountry. Long pepper, *Piper longum*, was readily available; this was a type of pepper that was greatly prized in Rome, where in the first century AD it sold for fifteen *denarii* per pound against four *denarii* for standard pepper.[34] Pliny the Elder could not understand what attracted people to pepper, and even less could he understand why anyone should spend vast amounts of time and money bringing it all the way from India.[35] At the top end of the scale, there were Chinese silks to be had too.

It is worth pausing to think about the implications. Roman citizens in Egypt, and beyond that the Mediterranean, were being supplied with clothing from as far away as India, and it was not necessarily luxury clothing. It was worth the while of ordinary merchants trading in the Indian Ocean to carry these goods by sea past Arabia and up the Red Sea. More than once in its description of India the *Periplous* remarked, in an entirely matter-of-fact way, 'for those sailing to this port from Egypt, the right time to set out is around the month of July'.[36] Here are the first signs of what, with a little exaggeration, can be called a global maritime network, linking the sea entirely controlled by Roman authority, in the west, to the open spaces of the Indian Ocean; and how far into that ocean these routes penetrated would be revealed as the *Periplous* made its way ever further east. The same considerations apply when one looks at the trade coming by sea from the west. Wine arrived not just from Arabia but from Laodicea in Syria and from Italy too. What condition it was in when it reached India is a question better not asked, all the more because it was often treated with salt to preserve it. But the Indians also had an insatiable appetite for copper and tin, the ingredients of bronze, as is shown by many of the beautiful cast figurines that survive from this period; the Barygazans were happy to buy the same coloured or plain textiles as the inhabitants of Barbarikon, as well as coral and peridot. Away from the royal court, they preferred cheap perfumes to anything costly. They were very happy to accept Roman gold and silver, which, as will be seen, was said to haemorrhage out of the Mediterranean into India. The royal court also purchased slaves, both to play music and to sleep in the king's bed.

Barygaza, in the north-western corner of India, seems like the obvious final destination for India traders coming down from Egypt; for many no doubt it was, just as this area had been the normal limit of the ships bound from Babylonia for Meluḫḫa nearly two millennia earlier. But Greco-Roman captains headed further south as well to official ports of trade (the word the *Periplous* uses is the familiar *emporion*, 'emporium'). One kingdom after another along the Indian coast established ports of trade; these were places where foreign merchants could be both welcomed and supervised. Rulers wanted to encourage them, because, quite apart from the goods they brought, luxuries and necessities, they were worth taxing; and yet once one started taxing merchants, a system had to be in place to make sure that smugglers were kept under control, and that the quality of goods was adequately guaranteed.[37]

Having braved more sea snakes, black ones with blood-red eyes and heads like a dragon – whatever these beasts really were – Greek ships could stuff their holds full along these shores: 'ships in these emporia carry full loads because of the quantity of pepper and malabathron'. Malabathron, already encountered in the Egyptian tale of the shipwrecked sailor, is the leaf of the cinnamon tree, rather than its bark, though ancient authors did not make the connection between the spice they also knew well and the dried leaves that were used in medicine, perfumes and food recipes, and to dispel mouth odour. Malabathron was also ideal for making mothballs. The drawback in ancient Rome, though not for merchants such as the author of the *Periplous*, was that the best-quality malabathron was hideously expensive, as much as 300 *denarii* per pound. On the other hand, ordinary Greeks and Romans could buy adulterated malabathron much more cheaply, for as little as one *denarius* per pound. Top-grade malabathron was by a long distance the most expensive spice to come out of India, followed by the best nard at a third of the price.[38] One reason for the high cost was that it was probably gathered some way into the interior, while much of the pepper was local.

The *Periplous* jumps quite quickly from north-western India to the far south of the country; the book enumerates several ports, but the account of what they supply or buy becomes monotonous, despite occasional vignettes that show, for instance, Hindu 'men who wish to lead a holy life for the rest of their days' and are celibate.[39] This may well reflect the ease with which ships setting out from south Arabia could strike the coast some way below Barygaza, if they heeded the advice of Hippalos about when to sail. A route running directly east-south-east from Arabia to the kingdom of Limyriké in south India would arrive near the bottom tip of the subcontinent.[40] The big question is how far Greek and Roman merchants penetrated beyond Ceylon, into the eastern Indian Ocean, in the first century AD. The author of the *Periplous* knew a fair amount about the eastern shores of India. He identified Ceylon, under its ancient name of Taprobané, but he imagined that it somehow stretched ever westwards till it came close to Azania, that is east Africa; his Ceylon was, in a sense, the precursor of the great, semi-mythical Southern Continent of later centuries. Ceylon was rich in pearls, gemstones, cotton textiles and tortoiseshells, about which he was so enthusiastic throughout his book that they must have been one of his specialities.[41] Beyond Ceylon he evidently relied on hearsay. He had heard of barbarian peoples with flat noses, and others called the Horse People, who were reputed to eat human flesh. The change in the character of the *Periplous* from fact to near fiction is entirely typical of travel literature throughout the centuries; it is found in Marco Polo, for example. When the author of the *Periplous* described the Ganges, which he knew was 'the greatest of all the rivers in India', comparable, he said, in its rise and fall to the Nile, he was clearly relying on rumour: 'it is said that there are also gold mines in the area'.

He had heard too that beyond the mouth of the Ganges there lay 'an island in the ocean, the furthest extremity towards the east of the inhabited world, lying under the rising sun itself, called Chrysé', that is, 'the golden place'. And, not surprisingly, it attracted his attention because it produced the best tortoiseshell in the whole Indian Ocean. Whether this land was pure fancy, or a distant acknowledgement of what later generations would call the Golden Chersonese (the Malayan peninsula), or perhaps Sumatra, does not greatly matter, as he was by now well out of his depth, and the short tract ends with the admission that there are remote, cold and stormy lands far out to the east that nature and the gods have made impenetrable. But the conclusion that he or people with whom he had worked knew south-western India is inescapable. This was the real limit of knowledge and, for the moment, it was the limit of navigation by the so-called Roman merchants, though not for south Indian or Malay ones.

III

Recent archaeological research in the Red Sea, at the Roman port of Bereniké, has transformed our understanding of the scale and intensity of Indo-Roman trade that passed up the Red Sea on its way to Alexandria and the Mediterranean. Bereniké Troglodytika was founded by the Ptolemies in the third century BC, and its site was chosen with close attention to the currents in the Red Sea, from which a convenient cape protected it. Its greatest asset was, however, water, for even the Eastern Desert receives rain in the autumn, and as the wadis either side of the town swelled with water a strong, if sandy, flow became accessible.[42] Still, it was hardly the most comfortable place in which to live. Drawing no doubt on plenty of horrible experiences, its excavator has written with feeling of the 'adverse weather, with almost constantly blowing winds carrying stinging and blinding sand, swarms of biting and annoying insects – both terrestrial and airborne – scorpions, termites, snakes, large spiders, mice, and rats'.[43]

The Ptolemies knew what they wanted from Bereniké, and as early as the late third century BC they were taking delivery there of the African elephants they so greatly prized. The animals were carried on short, broad, deep sailing ships called *elephantegoi* that were a challenge to the best captains, because their deep draught placed them at risk in a sea filled with sandbanks and coral reefs, and one classical writer, Diodoros the Sicilian, comments that they were often shipwrecked. A papyrus from 224 BC tells of an *elephantegos* that was wending its way south from Bereniké when it was shipwrecked; fortunately it was travelling in convoy and, since it was on the outward journey, had no elephants on board. An urgent message was sent to land and another boat was promptly despatched from Bereniké, so these ships were not in short supply.[44] On at least one occasion elephants were transferred from the Red Sea to the Nile through the canal that linked the two stretches of water; but the strong prevailing winds in the upper reaches of the Red Sea made journeys to its two northern tips hazardous, and it made much more sense to stop off at Bereniké or one of its rivals, and to send goods overland to Koptos on the Nile.[45] Excavation of Bereniké's harbour has revealed that (at least by the Roman period) the berths had been built for large ships, bigger than those one might expect to find in the contemporary Mediterranean, including those elephantine elephant transports.[46] Bereniké was, then, already prospering under the Ptolemaic rulers of Egypt, who actively promoted new economic initiatives, including shipbuilding; their main ambitions lay in and around the Mediterranean, where they built some vessels so large that there is some doubt whether they could have floated, but the Red Sea and Indian Ocean entered their calculations too.[47]

It would be rash to suggest a population figure for Bereniké. Its size fluctuated over the centuries; its site moved as accumulated silt transformed the shape of the harbour; its merchants came and went. It is wisest to be vague and to talk of a population of several thousand, concentrating instead on who the inhabitants were. For this was a true 'port city', a place where Egyptians, Greeks, Africans from Axum, south Arabians, Nabataeans, Indians, even visitors from Ceylon, found a temporary or permanent home. A tax collector from the early Roman period was named Andouros, a name harking back to Gaul or Germany. People with Latin names also appear, and some at least must have been from Italy. The illustrious and powerful Jewish family of Marcus Julius Alexander had agents here – more of this family shortly. Some *naukleroi*, or shipowners, were women; around AD 200 Aelia Isadora and Aelia Olympias used that Greek word to describe themselves, and operated from Bereniké or nearby. Many languages were spoken, or at least incised as graffiti – Greek appears most often, as one would expect in the eastern Roman Empire; but Latin, the south Arabian language, Tamil from south India, the language of Axum in east Africa all appear. A high-protein diet was available to many of these people: fish, sea mammals (dugong), turtles, beef, chicken and pork, which was a favourite in the Roman army. *Garum* sauce was made locally from the innards of Red Sea sardines. Nile catfish were also consumed in Bereniké, probably dried and then reconstituted; edible snails were a firm favourite in the town's kitchens. The inhabitants tried to make Bereniké an attractive place to live, decorating their houses with textile hangings; and the richer citizens owned gems, even pearl and gold earrings.[48] Temples to deities such as the composite Egyptian god Sarapis were scattered around the town. By the sixth century Bereniké possessed a pillared church with space for about eighty people, as well as side rooms used in part to prepare meals.[49]

The difficult conditions along the shores of the Red Sea were no deterrent, then, and other settlements also came into being on the sea's inhospitable western shore. Myos Hormos was an important base for Roman trade towards India, and revived to become a lively centre of trade once again in the thirteenth century, when it was called Qusayr al-Qadim; it too has been excavated, with truly impressive results that confirm Strabo's impression of the place; he heard that 120 ships sailed every year from Myos Hormos to India.[50] Fortunately, the history of Bereniké can be traced not just in the physical remains of the town but in papyri and ostraka; these were broken fragments of pottery used for recording notes, contracts and several remarkable customs passes issued in Koptos and then carried to the Red Sea ports, where they had to be presented to the authorities. These customs passes mention particular goods: 'Rhobaos to those in charge of the customs gate, greetings. Let Psenosiris son of Leon pass with eight *italika* of wine for loading.'[51] Here the merchant, Psenosiris, has a thoroughly Egyptian name, though his father sounds Greek. And the goods being carried are wine brought all the way from Italy. Myos Hormos too was home to a mixed population: one building constructed out of limestone and mud brick, with stucco decoration, was perhaps a synagogue, though to base this identification on a single fragment of pottery inscribed in Hebrew may be wishful thinking.[52]

Sometimes not just objects found on site, but ostraka and papyri from other parts of Egypt, talk of links to the Red Sea ports. An Egyptian papyrus known as the 'Muziris Papyrus' tells the story of the transfer of cargo all the way from Muziris in southern India, where it was loaded on board a ship called the *Hermapollon*, a good Greek name celebrating two gods; then it was sent across the desert to the Nile and up to Alexandria. This papyrus records a value of 9,000,000 *sesterces* for the goods brought back from India on the *Hermapollon*, of which the state could be expected to claim 2,000,000 in taxes. At Koptos a whole archive of ostraka has been unearthed, known as the Nikanor archive. Nikanor was the head of a small transport company that specialized in the carriage of goods across the desert, and every time he sent goods to the Red Sea ports, or anywhere else, he expected a receipt to be sent back, written on a piece of broken pottery. While it is always interesting to watch the ordinary businessmen like Nikanor in operation, his ostraka also reveal links to the Alexandrian plutocracy, notably Marcus Julius Alexander, the nephew of the Jewish philosopher Philo and the son of the official who administered customs and excise in the desert east of the Nile. Around AD 40 Marcus Julius maintained agents in Koptos and the Red Sea ports. His wife, Berenice (Bereniké), was a member of the Herodian royal family, and would later earn notoriety as the mistress of Titus, the general in charge of the suppression of the Jewish revolt in Palestine.[53] That someone of great wealth and power should become seriously involved in the India trade indicates both its prestige and its profitability.

The impression, both at Roman Bereniké and at Myos Hormos, is that these were intermediary ports, and not in themselves significant centres of consumption; they did not contain splendid buildings, even if their better houses were comfortable enough; and they owed their existence entirely to the need to have somewhere on the dusty shores of the Red Sea where it was possible to do business and to sit out contrary winds. These ports were funnels through which trade from the Red Sea and far beyond reached Egypt and the Mediterranean, and vice versa – as far away, indeed, as Vietnam, Java and Thailand, to which some beads found in Roman levels at Bereniké have been attributed. The express passage first navigated by Hippalos, or other routes that struck India even further south, became the standard routes to and from India, and the lack of finds from the Persian Gulf in Bereniké underlines this fact: ships bypassed the Oman peninsula, and headed across open water to Barygaza and southern India. Some of the Indian pots found at Bereniké were no doubt used by Indian merchants who had taken up residence there, for the port acted as host to a varied population; inscriptions in Indian scripts and the distinctive script of south Arabia are no real surprise, and there are such close similarities between some south Arabian inscriptions found at Bereniké and others from Myos Hormos that it seems the same Arabian merchant was author of both sets, and moved back and forth between these two ports and his homeland in Yemen.[54]

The principal Indian product to reach Bereniké was pepper, particularly black pepper from south India, for there can be no doubt that traders regularly set out from Bereniké for India in search of this commodity. This is confirmed by passages in Tamil poetry dated somewhere between 300 BC and AD 300 that tell of the *Yavanas*, broadly meaning 'westerners' (though derived from the term 'Ionians'), 'whose prosperity never waned'. They were not just merchants but mercenaries, 'the valiant-eyed *Yavanas* whose bodies were strong and of terrible aspect'; they wielded 'murderous swords', with which they guarded the gates of the south Indian cities. The *Yavana* merchants paid in gold for what they called black gold, that is, pepper: 'rich Muziris, the place where the large and well-crafted ships of the *Yavanas* come with gold and leave carrying pepper'. Muziris, we are told, 'resounded with the noise' of this trade.[55] One poem speaks of 'the gifts of gold brought by the ships' to the port of Muziris, and 'those who crowd the port in the turmoil created by the sacks of pepper piled up in the houses'.[56] Late in the first century AD, the *Horrea Piperataria*, or 'Pepper Warehouses', were built in Rome; the ground floor alone had capacity for 5,800 tons of pepper, though it was also used for other spices and for storing incense. The aroma of all these spices, rather arbitrarily mixed together under one roof, turned into a stink, and the *Horrea* were fitted with troughs of water that were intended to increase humidity and somehow offset the pungency.[57]

The evidence from Roman and Indian literature is confirmed by the excavations at Bereniké, which have unearthed two Indian storage jars in the temple of the Egyptian deity Sarapis, dating to the first century AD; one of these contained considerable quantities of peppercorns (7.55 kg). Nowhere else in the Roman world have so many peppercorns been found as in Bereniké, where they appear not just within the temple precincts but on house floors, in the street and in piles of refuse. Many were burnt, notably within another shrine dedicated to a number of gods ranging from the Roman emperor to a god worshipped in Palmyra, in Syria, called Yarhibol; they were almost certainly used in religious rituals.[58] The archaeologists were also able to identify grains of Indian rice, and they surmise that rice-based meals were eaten off the Indian plates aplenty they found on the same site. Sorghum, a staple foodstuff of east Africa, was also found, indicating connections with Africa as well as India, as do finds of the Ethiopian pea. Other Indian products included coconuts, Indian sesame, mung beans and Indian gooseberries. But there was also plenty of evidence that fruits arrived from the Mediterranean, including walnuts, hazelnuts, almonds, peaches, plums, apples, grapes and olives. The presence of these foods does more than add colour to the picture of life in the Red Sea ports. It serves as a reminder that the *Periplous*, with its elaborate lists of luxury items, does not tell a complete story. Spices, gems and exotic luxuries such as ebony and ivory were certainly a great attraction for

India-bound merchants. But even the pepper they brought back was for general consumption. The standard of living in the greatest cities of the Roman Mediterranean – Rome, Carthage, Alexandria, eventually Constantinople – was perhaps higher than at any time before the eighteenth century, and the India trade contributed to the comfort of the wealthy, the urban middle classes and, in some measure, people of more modest means as well. Meanwhile the inhabitants of Bereniké and other Red Sea ports had their own expectations, of south Italian wine and olive oil among other items. These reminded them of their homes in Egypt, Syria, Greece and further afield, and could also be passed on to the towns and courts of India to their great profit.[59]

The identification of these foods shows how archaeology has applied ever more sophisticated methods to analyse the smallest finds, those that would once have been discarded or not even noticed. Traditionally, pottery has been the humble but trustworthy source of information. At Bereniké it is certainly a rich source of data. Among the finest pottery from Bereniké are pieces of 'rouletted ware', which hails from eastern India. The Indian ceramics are not the only evidence of exotic contacts. There is pottery from the kingdom of Axum, which, as has been seen, possessed a port on the Red Sea at Adulis. Not much pottery arrived from south Arabia before the fourth century, when a fair amount reached Myos Hormos and Ayla (Aqaba–Eilat) at the very top of the Red Sea. From the first century BC onwards a Roman port on the Arabian side of the Red Sea, across from Bereniké and Myos Hormos, serviced sea traffic from Yemen towards Petra – ships would dock at Leuké Komé, 'White Village', and unload Arabian incense for carriage overland. Here is proof that sea transport, with the opportunity to load very large amounts of goods in each vessel, had now become entirely standard and was regarded as a safe, efficient way to keep goods on the move.[60] Some marble slabs were brought up to Bereniké from south Arabia. At the same time, the fine red tableware of the Mediterranean, much of it made as far away as Gaul, was also used in Bereniké, while the amphorae used for storing wine and oil came from all around the Mediterranean – southern Spain, Italy, Rhodes, and maybe Gaza, as well as Ayla. Bereniké merchants were active in the jewellery trade as well. Gemstones could be found in the hills around Bereniké itself, notably at Mons Smaragdus, 'Emerald Mountain', a source of rather indifferent emeralds and of beryl stones; and peridots have also been found. The best evidence for a trade in gemstones comes from a couple of sapphires which are thought to have been brought from Ceylon.[61]

It is important to distinguish the different phases in the relationship

between Bereniké and the Mediterranean. In the early phases, the Red
Sea ports could obtain all they liked from the Mediterranean; Roberta
Tomber remarks that 'essentially everything that was available in Alexandria was found along the Red Sea coast in varying amounts'. It has been
seen that among the most exciting finds from Bereniké are inscribed
ostraka dating to the first century AD that were issued as customs passes
in Koptos. Several of these mention amphorae filled with Italian wine.
Some of this wine may have been consumed locally and some of it may
have been drunk by sailors. But a reference in a Tamil poem to 'cool fragrant wine brought by the *Yavanas*' leaves little doubt that wine, whether
Italian, Greek or Syrian, was gratefully received in India. Up to fifty sites
in India have yielded fragments of amphorae from the Mediterranean, and
Roman writers insisted that Indian kings greatly enjoyed a tipple. Hard
physical evidence of the wine trade also comes from the rare wrecks that
have been discovered in the Red Sea: one boat from the early first century
AD that sank near Myos Hormos was carrying south Italian wine amphorae; and another, wrecked off the coast of Sudan, apparently carried
wine of the Greek island of Kos, another source of wine treated with salt.[62]
All this confirms the claim found in the *Periplous*, which at first reading
seems extraordinary, that wine was exported all the way from the Mediterranean to the Indian Ocean. So was olive oil, to judge from the ostraka, and
the stinking fish sauce known as *garum*, to judge from amphorae found at
Arikamedu in southern India.[63] In this sense, the label 'Indo-Roman' trade
makes sense, even if the merchants whom historians obstinately call
'Roman' were predominantly Greeks and Hellenized Egyptians. This was
not just trade between Egypt and the Indies, but between the Roman
Mediterranean and the Indies. Investors lived as far away as Italy, whether
they were spice merchants in Rome or prosperous citizens of towns such
as Puteoli near Naples; there, the Annii, a prominent business family,
extended the sweep of their maritime trade far beyond the Mediterranean
and took a healthy interest in the Indian Ocean as well.[64]

It was a trade route that, according to the Elder Pliny, sucked valuable
specie out of the Roman Empire:

> Each year, India, China and the Arabian peninsula take at the very least one
> hundred million *sesterces* from our empire; that is what our luxuries and
> women cost us. For what fraction of these imports is intended for sacrifices
> to the gods, I want to know, or on behalf of the spirits of the dead?[65]

Pliny wanted to make a traditional patrician point about the way love of
luxury eroded established Roman values, and whether quite so much was
paid for the goods of the East is doubtful. Even so, there were Roman

senators whose wealth can be valued at 600,000,000 *sesterces*, in which case the amount of money lost to India was not as vast as it sounds.[66] Pliny's comment has given the business affairs of Greco-Roman traders such a high profile that it becomes easy to forget the role of the Indians themselves, or other intermediaries; this is particularly true of the routes that stretched beyond Ceylon towards the Malay peninsula. The excavator of Bereniké, Steven Sidebotham, has hazarded a guess that Roman objects found as far afield as Korea and Thailand may have arrived through the Red Sea, though they would have been passed down a lengthy chain of merchants rather than being carried most of the way by a single merchant.

IV

Most of what has been written about navigation in the Indian Ocean at this time has been constructed around the assumption that the term 'Roman trade' carries some meaning. It does, in the sense that links between the Indian Ocean and the Mediterranean heartlands of the Roman Empire were forged by generations of hardy sailors and traders who funnelled pepper and the exotic produce of the East up the Red Sea into the Mediterranean. But, as one historian wrote, 'to the Indians Rome and Roman meant Alexandria and Alexandrians', so that Egyptian merchants, and the Jews who now began to arrive on the Malabar coast, were all 'Romans'.[67] It is always important to remember that the economy of coastal India was not sustained simply by contact with the Roman Empire. Whispers about native merchants are frustrating, because much more needs to be known about them, not least in order to place the 'Romans' in perspective. A twelfth-century writer from southern Italy, Peter the Deacon, quoting a fourth-century pilgrim named Egeria, mentioned Indian merchants who regularly brought their fine ships all the way to Klysma in the Gulf of Suez, though braving the stiff north winds of the northern Red Sea was always a challenge, and that was one reason why Bereniké and Myos Hormos further down the Red Sea coast were preferred.[68]

To write about the opening of the Indian Ocean solely from the perspective of Roman trade is to look at the sea through blinkers. But the evidence from the Indian side is too fragmentary. One must work with the evidence that is there, and at least 90 per cent of it concerns the 'Romans'. Indian historians have debated the impact of these long-distance connections on the development of the urban civilization of their country. Such controversies are part of a much wider debate, often intertwined with increasingly obscure ideological discussions, about the way external economic factors can generate social change; they can be inspired as much by Karl Marx as they are by the hard evidence. The neatest argument is that the Romans reached India because it was worth their while to visit already flourishing towns, whose business life had been stimulated by demand for fine products at the courts of local kings and at the Buddhist monasteries that were spreading in the region, for the monks, with their substantial resources, were not averse to a little luxury. After all, the vast majority of objects found on these ancient sites are not connected with Roman trade but are the day-to-day products of local industry and short-distance commerce.[69]

Two areas should be examined more closely, because they provide clues to the presence or absence of the Roman navigators known to the Tamils as *Yavanas*. One is Ceylon, or Sri Lanka, and the other is the great expanse of sea between India and the Malay peninsula, including the Bay of Bengal. The second-century geographer Ptolemy, who was fascinated by the Indies, said a great amount about Ceylon. Sometimes his imagination triumphed; his assumption that one could capture tigers there was simply wrong. But he knew that the island was a source of ginger, sapphires, beryl, precious metals and a type of 'honey' which must be sugar; and Strabo reported that ivory and tortoiseshell were sent from Ceylon to the Indian towns where Roman merchants picked up these goods. The impression from Ptolemy is that Ceylon had only just become well known to the Roman emperor's subjects, and it is striking that the Roman coins that have been found in Ceylon are mainly later than his own time, dating from the third to the seventh centuries AD. As well as Roman coins, some coins of the Sasanian kings of Persia and even the rulers of Axum in east Africa have turned up.[70] So by the end of this period Ceylon had become the hinge of Indian Ocean trade and navigation, looking both eastwards to Malaya and westwards to Arabia, Byzantine Egypt and the Horn of Africa. In the early twentieth century, those who found these coins, mostly of base metal and well worn, would often pass them into circulation, so one might receive money of Emperor Arcadius in one's small change.[71] As in the *Periplous*, Ptolemy magnified the island; but he only made it fourteen times its true size, and he abandoned the idea set out in the *Periplous* that it was the tip of a great southern continent. His southern landmass consisted, rather, of a belt of uninhabited, uninhabitable, land stretching from the southern tip of Africa eastwards to the Golden Chersonese that transformed the Indian Ocean into a closed sea, a massive Mediterranean.

Beyond Ceylon, the presence of these *Yavanas* was surely more intermittent, as the more enterprising, or perhaps foolhardy, captains tried their luck in less familiar waters. In the second century AD, the geographer Ptolemy named nearly forty Tamil towns and kingdoms that lay inland, and the sheer detail of his knowledge of southern India has led to speculation that Romans (by whom should be understood subjects of the emperor, probably Greek or Egyptian) lived in some of these places, and continued to spread eastwards into the Bay of Bengal. The *Periplous* described how Kamara (Puhar), Poduké and Sōpatma were the home ports of local ships which sailed as far as Limyriké, which is the author's name for the far south-west of India, and this is precious evidence that the mastery of the seas was shared by 'Romans' and Indians. A Tamil poet eulogized Puhar and its trade in these words:

> The sun shines over the open terraces and the warehouses near the harbour. It shines over the turrets that have wide windows like the eyes of a deer. In different places at Puhar the gaze of the observer is attracted by the residences of the *Yavanas*, whose prosperity is without limits. At the harbour there are sailors from distant lands, but in all appearance they live as one community.[72]

The town was ablaze with colourful flags and banners, and contained fine houses with platforms above street level that were reached by ladders. However, this was not for fear of robbers; the Tamil poets were sure that it was a safe and prosperous city, and they delighted in the comings and goings of the great ships that came into port. Some may have come from the Red Sea, but most must have been Indian and Malay vessels, Arab dhows, maybe even the occasional ship that had wended its way from the South China Sea – links to the Pacific will be examined in the next chapter. Archaeology has not offered much help in confirming the vivid images of the Tamil poet. Puhar seems to have disappeared beneath the waves around AD 500; a tsunami may well have destroyed the city in a few hours, and one theory places the blame on an early eruption of Krakatoa in 535, even if it was less violent than the astonishing one of 1883.[73] Both Puhar and Poduké began as Indian towns; they were not created by the *Yavanas*, and it was the *Yavanas* who came to seek them out.

One place thought to have been settled by merchants from the Far West lay at Arikamedu, a village that stood just inside the small enclave of Pondicherry, ruled by France for roughly two centuries until 1954. Seventeen years earlier a French collector had become excited when some children showed him what may have been a cameo carved with a portrait of a Roman emperor, though it was carried away to Hanoi and has now vanished. Then a few years later a trial excavation there uncovered wine amphorae brought from the area around Naples, as well as olive oil jars from the northern Adriatic and jars of fish sauce from Spain. It has been suggested that the oil and *garum* sauce were for foreign settlers, and the wine (which was often resinated) was for everybody, as further fragments of wine amphorae have turned up inland. Setting aside doubts about whether Western goods betoken Western settlers, which have been expressed by the most recent excavator, Arikamedu looks like a classic 'port city', a meeting place for locals and foreigners, including some who had come from very far away.[74] This was a town where different communities intermingled and probably intermarried – in the first century AD a woman called Indiké, 'the Indian woman', who lived in Egypt, wrote a letter on papyrus to a female friend or relative, and there must have been many women like her.[75] In these emporia, there were plenty of opportunities to mix in social life, in religious cults and in doing business. The excavators found pieces of the typical red pottery made in Roman Arezzo, in faraway Etruria, dating from the first quarter of the first century AD – the date of the settlement can probably be pushed still further back in time, as far back as the third century BC.[76] As they probed further into a site that has, unfortunately, been partly washed away by the river on which it stands, the archaeologists also brought to light Greco-Roman glassware. There were upmarket objects too: a gem made of rock crystal and decorated with a figure of Cupid and a bird may have been made in the Mediterranean or, more likely, be of local workmanship, but in the latter case that would still show the cultural influence of the Greco-Roman world as far away as south-eastern India.[77]

The settlement expanded, becoming a pole of attraction for Indian and foreign merchants. No doubt it was at first simply a place beyond the normal range of Greco-Roman shipping that accumulated Mediterranean goods as they were passed on from hand to hand through the ports on the western flank of India, most often in Indian boats. With time Arikamedu drew these westerners to its harbour, and what some like to think of as a Roman settlement in the Bay of Bengal came into existence, during the reigns of Augustus and Tiberius, when the town had already been flourishing for a century or more. It seems to have remained a lively place until the mid- to late second century AD. Among the excellent facilities it offered was a warehouse close to the river, 150 feet long. There were areas given over to industry, easy to identify from the large number of beads, bangles and cheap gemstones that are said to 'litter the area', and there were what excavators identified as vats for dyeing cloth, where the inhabitants manufactured the fine muslins that are mentioned in the *Periplous* as favourite exports of south India. Oddly, Roman coins are absent from Arikamedu.[78]

They were either sucked into royal treasuries or melted down; yet this did not inhibit intensive trade. Arikamedu was convincingly identified by Sir Mortimer Wheeler (who helped excavate the site) as one of the emporia in south-eastern India mentioned in the *Periplous*, specifically Poduké. This name also appears in almost the same form in Ptolemy's *Geography*, and is a corruption of the Tamil word *Puduchchēri*, which simply means 'New Town', so one can imagine that the Greeks may also have called it *Neapolis*, which means exactly the same. Then, over time, the Tamil name was corrupted by the French and British into Pondicherry.[79]

The lure of the Ganges can already be detected in the *Periplous*. Once this area became known by repute, the temptation to sail there in search of silk, pearls and other luxuries became overwhelming, though numbers were probably much smaller than in the western Indian Ocean.[80] Strabo talked of traders who sailed from Egypt to the Ganges; he described them as 'private merchants', suggesting that these were people who went under their own steam; and he did not believe everything they told him, so whether they had actually reached as far as the mouth of the Ganges he could not really say.[81] Ptolemy knew a fair amount about the city of Patna, on the Ganges; and he was aware that a thin tongue of land stretched downwards from south-east Asia, which he called the Golden Chersonese. This area was explored early in the second century AD by a sea captain named Alexander who may well have rounded the southern tip of Malaya, by way of the Strait of Malacca, and have entered the South China Sea, arriving at a place called Kattigara, which will be revisited in the next chapter. Greeks and Romans were not terribly sure where China lay, but they knew it was a source of fine silk, and that was probably the motive for occasional forays towards the South China Sea; an embassy from the court of Emperor Marcus Aurelius may have reached the South China Sea in the late second century, for Chinese records describe the embassy of 'Antun' (Antoninus, the emperor's *cognomen*, or additional name), though they dismissed it as of little consequence because the goods offered as gifts – or, as the Chinese would prefer to think, tribute – were regarded as commonplace. This came as a surprise, because the Han court was aware, though vaguely, that the Roman Empire was a vast polity comparable to their own great empire. Since the embassy had set out with rhinoceros horn, elephant ivory and tortoiseshell the diplomats had probably lost their goods en route.[82] Generally, though, even Burma was a stage too far; a few Roman imperial subjects settled there, as court entertainers in search of a patron, but there was no port city with a mixed population and markets full of goods from each end of the ocean and from the hinterland, in other words another Puhar or Poduké.[83] In reality, Greco-Roman navigators very rarely ventured beyond Malaya, so that Ptolemy's misunderstanding about what lay at the bottom of the Golden Chersonese was perpetuated for over 1,300 years.

V

From the late second century onwards Bereniké went into decline, and one explanation may be the pandemic (whatever disease it was) that struck the Roman Empire in the year 166. By the middle of the third century, Bereniké had not exactly vanished from the map, but there is no evidence that it was still a major emporium linking East and West. Recovery came, however. By the fourth century Bereniké was benefiting from developments further south: the creation of vigorous kingdoms on either side of the Bab al-Mandeb Strait, in Himyar (Yemen) and Axum (Ethiopia/Eritrea), ancient sources of incense, ivory and ebony. Meanwhile, goods from the western Mediterranean ceased to arrive in this part of the Red Sea. One view is that this reflected a growing fracture in the Mediterranean between east and west, though maybe what this reveals is, rather, the economic vitality of eastern Mediterranean ports such as Rhodes, Laodicea (Lattakiah), Gaza and Alexandria, which found themselves more than able to supply the needs of the Roman outstations in the Red Sea. This was accompanied by new opportunities to do business in south Arabia and east Africa, which are suggested by the discovery of a coin from Axum and another from western India dating to AD 362. Trade with Ceylon around 400 has even been described as 'brisk', and the town of Bereniké revived physically too, as new temples dedicated to Isis, Sarapis and other Egyptian gods were built, as well as a church and several warehouses.[84]

The best indication of the manner in which this port looked two ways, towards the Indian Ocean and towards the Mediterranean, can be found in the preserved fragments of wood found on this site, which included a small quantity of Indian bamboo and large amounts of south Asian teakwood, including a beam more than three metres in length from one of Bereniké's shrines.[85] Teak was also widely used in shipbuilding, for instance by early Arab mariners. Yet the material remains also included cedar beams brought from Lebanon or somewhere in that area, and found in the remains of the temple of Sarapis. Meanwhile, at Myos Hormos, wood from ships taken out of commission was re-employed in everyday building. Just as these ships were put together in what amounted to a giant three-dimensional jigsaw puzzle, they could be taken apart quite easily, and the planks, beams and masts reused in quite different ways; wood was precious along the dry edges of the Eastern Desert. Beams and planks discovered during the excavation of the town buildings of Myos Hormos bore traces of pitch, iron nails and barnacles.[86]

We are still left with the question of why Bereniké was abandoned in the sixth century, and its collapse can probably be attributed to a rich combination of factors: bubonic plague in the Mediterranean and Middle East, the so-called plague of Justinian; local wars out of which Axum in east Africa and Himyar in south Arabia emerged as the dominant political forces, under Christian and Jewish kings who were keen rivals; the ascendancy of Axumite and Himyarite merchants, with bases at Adulis on the African side and Kané on the Arabian side. Bereniké did not come to a cataclysmic end. It declined throughout the sixth century, and when it was finally abandoned no one lived close enough to raid the site for wooden beams or building stone. The result was that the dust of the desert blew over the town, and the dry atmosphere preserved its sand-immersed remains.[87] What continued, however, was traffic up and down the Red Sea; what changed was in whose hands control of this traffic lay. Over time, the location of the key ports that linked the Nile, and beyond that the Mediterranean, to the Red Sea changed, as Myos Hormos, once a minor competitor to Bereniké, emerged in the medieval period as an important link in the chain connecting the Red Sea to the Indian Ocean and the Mediterranean, under its Islamic name of Qusayr al-Qadim. The connection was broken only for short periods, and the links between the Indian Ocean and Egypt, and beyond that the Mediterranean, were not severed even when different people to the Greco-Roman merchants took charge of the carriage of cargoes from India and east Africa.

7

Brahmins, Buddhists and Businessmen

I

Looking at the Indian Ocean from the perspective of the *Periplous* and Bereniké presents one overwhelming difficulty. The illusion is created that its ports interacted when the Greco-Roman ships arrived with merchants on board who craved the spices of the East. When Bereniké and Myos Hormos were in decline, it might then be assumed, the whole of this network crumbled away. Without the Romans, it is true, the Indian kings would not be able to accumulate so much treasure; but whether they actually put much of this gold and silver into circulation remains doubtful. Fragments of evidence suggest that Barbarikon and Barygaza, or at any rate ports in their vicinity, remained lively centres of trade and industry in the fifth and sixth centuries, and that many of the stopping places and links that would be described by late medieval travellers such as the Venetian Marco Polo and the Arab al-Mas'udi were already in place.[1] In a word, the question concerns continuity, and relates directly to the idea that the opening of the Indian Ocean routes, whether it was achieved by Romans, Indians or Malays, or all of them in collaboration, should be seen as the first step in the creation of global networks of trade, in which sea routes functioned as the major links. In that case the India trade of the Cairo Jews around 1100, which will be examined before long, or the irruption of the Portuguese in the Indian Ocean in 1497–8, were only further stages in the bonding together of the Indian Ocean with the Mediterranean and with the markets of Europe that lay beyond.

When the evidence for Roman trade is so rich it is tempting to dismiss that for 'native' trade as mere disconnected fragments. But the fragments can be connected, and they tell a remarkable story in which the Romans no longer appear as the main actors. To make sense of this story, places very far apart will have to be examined – as far apart as Madagascar and Malaya, and beyond Malaya to the very edges of China. This will reveal the sheer expanse of the area that was tied together by navigators in the first half of the first millennium AD. It will also show how the links in a chain that stretched all the way from southern China to the Mediterranean were being forged and attached to one another, so that the spice trade that had already obsessed the inhabitants of imperial Rome extended far beyond India and Ceylon. In particular, the mariners of Indonesia and Malaya became the great intermediaries sailing regularly between China and India; it was they who knitted together the networks that had previously functioned apart from one another; and it was they who made traffic by sea, rather than the arduous overland route, first of all worthwhile and then supreme.

The subject of this chapter is a dizzying expanse of sea, then, encompassing the entire Indian Ocean and, beyond that, the South China Sea, which is ringed by southern China, Vietnam, the Philippines, Indonesia and the Malay peninsula. But the place to begin is a relatively small island very far from there, in the north-west of the Indian Ocean, with an area of 3,800 km² (which still makes it the second largest island in the western Indian Ocean, after Madagascar). Socotra lies about 240 miles south of Arabia and the same number of kilometres east of Africa.[2] It was not, therefore, visited by coast-hugging vessels, but by those who had mastered the monsoons and were willing to range out of sight of land, which was worth their while, since it functioned as a trading hub linking east Africa, the Red Sea and the routes to India. Even so, the local currents were difficult to manage; in addition, it could not offer a decent harbour and ships had to anchor off the coast. Between May and September it was unreachable, because the south-west monsoon was blowing. It was often chosen as a pirate base, though the pirates must have been constrained by the same difficult conditions as the traders. Yet the traders came. The *Periplous* gives an impression of exact knowledge garnered by a merchant whose passion for tortoiseshell knew no bounds:

> In the open sea is an island called Dioskourides; though very large, it is barren and also damp, with rivers, crocodiles, a great many vipers, and huge lizards, so huge that people eat the flesh and melt down the fat to use in place of oil. The island bears no farm products, neither vines nor grain. The inhabitants, few in number, live on one side of the island, that to the north, the part facing the mainland; they are settlers, a mixture of Arabs and Indians and even some Greeks, who sail out of there to trade. The island yields tortoise-shell, the genuine, the land, and the light-coloured varieties, in great quantity, and also the oversize mountain variety with an extremely thick shell . . . The so-called Indian cinnabar is found there; it is collected as an exudation from the trees.[3]

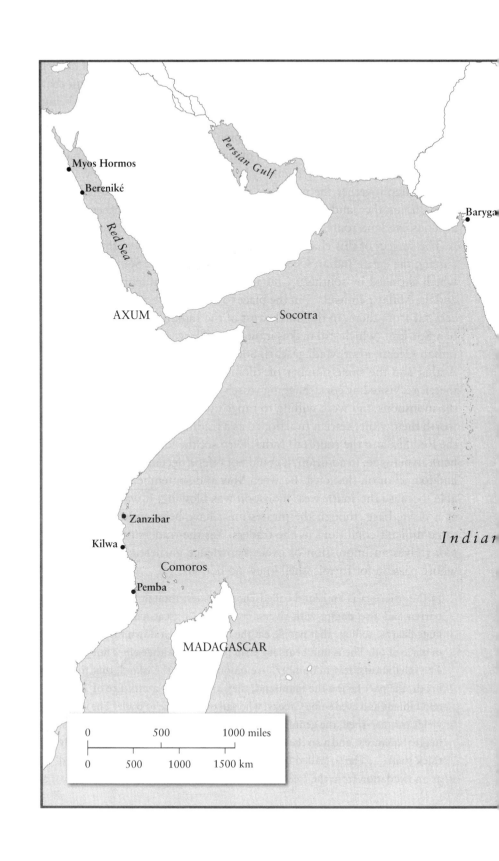

The *Periplous* also explains that the island was ruled by the king of the opposing shore of south Arabia (Hadhramawt); it has often fallen under the control of the rulers of south Arabia, and at present it forms part of the Republic of Yemen. It used to be visited regularly by sailors from southern India and Barygaza; 'these would exchange rice, grain, cotton cloth, and female slaves', against great quantities of poor-quality tortoise-shell. The author then states, mysteriously, that 'the kings have leased out the island, and it is under guard'. There are strong hints here that this island is neither worth visiting for its tortoises, nor worth the trouble of having to negotiate with the current tenant, who seems to discourage trade.[4] Reading between the lines, it sounds as if the island had once again become a pirate base, for which its position suited it very well, in seas that are still notorious for piracy. Over the centuries, though, this island was visited by large numbers of travellers, for they have left about 250 inscriptions and drawings incised on the walls of a cave discovered in 2000, all of which happily confirm the insistence of the *Periplous* that Socotra was visited by people of very diverse origins. These inscriptions are in a great variety of languages, Indian, Iranian, Ethiopic, south Arabian, even Greek, and date from the period between the first century BC and the sixth century AD.

The Hoq cave is very long – two and a half kilometres – and at some points as much as a hundred metres wide and thirty metres high, so it must have appeared an awe-inspiring place, and a cool one on an island baked by the sun. It was apparently a cult centre for one god or more, and the graffiti on its walls are not so very different from those that can be found on tourist sites today: *bhadra prapta*, 'Bhadra arrived', or simply the name of the visitor, most often in Sanskrit characters.[5] One can imagine that sailors and other travellers who had braved the seas to reach Socotra were keen to offer their thanks to the gods for a safe journey there, and their prayers for a safe journey home. Who these gods were is far from clear, but the fact that the vast majority of inscriptions are in Sanskrit suggests that they were Indian gods, linked to Hindu or Buddhist cults; quite possibly the cave contained an image of Buddha himself. For at this period in Indian history the links between religion and trade were close; the Buddhist monasteries, in particular, saw no evil in honest profit. They discarded the caste system that relegated merchants to a less respectable role in society than the priests and warriors who were acclaimed as the leaders of the Hindu communities. The spread of Buddhism is generally thought to have stimulated the Indian economy.[6]

The evidence that this island was visited over several centuries by Indian merchants is overwhelming; the earliest inscription is thought to date from before AD 100, but after 400 the number declined and the visits, or the practice of recording them, gradually died out – more likely the latter, for, as will be seen, the coming of Christianity rendered the cave cult obsolete. Amid the names there are several that speak loudly of contact with India: 'Samghadasa, son of Jayasena, inhabitant of Hastakavapra' had reached Socotra from a town close to Barygaza on the Gulf of Cambay; the town is still there, under the name of Hathab, but it was already known to the author of the *Periplous* and to Ptolemy under the name Astakapra. The *Periplous* mentioned it in its description of the hazardous approach to Barygaza, and excavation there shows that it flourished from the fourth century BC to the sixth century AD.[7] Even more noticeable among the inscriptions are direct references to Barygaza: 'Śesasya Visnusena from Bharukaccha arrived'; or a graffito simply saying *Bharukacchaka*, 'the Barygazan'; and best of all: 'the sea-captain Visnudhara from Bharukaccha'.[8] Evidently, ships bound from north-west India for the Horn of Africa often stopped in Socotra. At a village now known as Kosh, archaeologists discovered Indian artefacts but could produce little or no evidence of links between Socotra and the Mediterranean; Kosh lies on the northern side of Socotra, confirming the statement in the *Periplous* that this was where the inhabitants chose to settle. It is even possible to say something about the boats that reached Socotra, as the Hoq cave also contains several drawings, the clearest of which shows a boat with two rudders and maybe three masts. This compares closely to a sixth-century image of a boat in the famous Ajanta caves in India, where a triple-masted ship with two rudders can be seen.[9]

Some of those who came into the cave to worship were not Indians. The inscriptions include a sizeable wooden tablet in the Aramaic language of Palmyra far away in Syria. The tablet records the prayers of a Nabataean sea captain. The arrival of a Nabataean on the island makes sense: there were Indian embassies to the rulers of south Arabia, whose main motive must have been to discuss the trade in incense; and south Arabian pottery was found by a team of Soviet archaeologists who were let loose on Socotra.[10] Some Nabataeans, then, ventured out across the sea and did not rely on the camel caravans across Arabia. And then there were the westerners. One mysterious scrawl says: 'of the *Yavana* Cadrabhutimukha', which is certainly not a Greek name, even though the term *Yavana* generally means Greek, Roman or someone from the Roman Empire. A perfectly good explanation would be that a *Yavana* living in India had become assimilated into Indian culture, so much so that he bore a Sanskrit name and used the Brahmi script in which Sanskrit was written. Certainly, there were real Greeks on the island as well, not just because the *Periplous* and others insisted they were there. Early in the third century a Greek *naukleros*, or sea captain, left an inscription in Greek in the cave: 'Septimios Paniskos the *naukleros* kneeled before the gods and before that [or those] of the cave.'[11] Greeks had worshipped Indian gods in far-off Bactria since the time of Alexander the Great. To show them respect while sailing around the outer edge of the world was to follow the natural instinct of the Greeks, Romans and many other peoples.

The history of Socotra was also a story of change. An uninhabited island had been transformed into a centre of exchange, but its people could only survive by trading the tortoiseshell and incense they produced for foodstuffs from Arabia, India or Africa. The greatest change occurred when the inhabitants became Christian, some time around the fourth century; and Socotra remained largely or partly Christian until the seventeenth century. This conversion (assuming it was that, and not a mass migration) took place at a time when the southern Red Sea was becoming the scene of bitter confrontation between the Jews, who had converted the kings of south-west Arabia, and the Christians, whose power was based across the water at Axum in Ethiopia. As Axum flourished, it attracted trade from across the Red Sea and sent its own merchants overseas to sell ivory and other prestige products of the Ethiopian highlands, and to buy incense and spices for the Axumite court; over a hundred Indian coins of the late third century have been found at the monastery of Däbrä Damo in Ethiopia (though there is a mysterious complication: the monastery was only founded a few centuries later). Socotra benefited from this renaissance of trade; the Hoq cave offers proof that Ethiopians visited the island around the sixth century, for one or two left their own names there.[12] The early Byzantine traveller Kosmas Indikopleustes (meaning 'Kosmas who sailed to India') wrote his own *Periplous* in the sixth century, in which he described how the Socotrans spoke Greek, 'having originally been colonists sent thither by the Ptolemies', and noted that the local priests were ordained by bishops in Persia. Kosmas did not land there, though he coasted past the island; however, he met Greek-speakers from Socotra on the coast of Africa who had evidently come to believe this version of their history.[13] His story circulated widely, as the Arab geographer resident at the court of King Roger of Sicily, al-Idrisi, said much the same in the middle of the twelfth century, as did the tenth-century traveller al-Mas'udi, whose works were widely read. Al-Mas'udi also mentioned that Socotra was a nest of pirates, and that was one recurrent feature of its history; the pirates he mentioned were Indian ones, who chased after Arab ships bound for India and China, but Greek and Arabian pirates must also have been installed there at different times.

All this proves that a historian ignores the smaller, apparently insignificant places at his or her peril. Socotra was no Barygaza or Bereniké; but this improbably remote island has thrown up evidence for the real nature of contact by sea that is, in its way, as rich as anything in the *Periplous* or in the excavations at Bereniké and Myos Hormos. The names of its visitors, generally unadorned by profession or origin, still provide enough evidence to remind us what sort of people lived on what they must have thought to be a place on the outer edges of the world.

II

All this is rich evidence for the routes that were not dominated by seafarers from the Roman Empire, but by dhows from Arabia, sewn-plank vessels from India, and ships manned by Malay and Indonesian sailors. Malays would certainly play a prominent role at the end of the Middle Ages, but much changed in a thousand years, with the rise and fall of trading empires on Sumatra and on the Malay peninsula. There is, however, extraordinary evidence that people travelled all the way to east Africa from the eastern end of the Indian Ocean, speakers of the Austronesian languages that include Filipino, Malay and the Polynesian languages. They arrived not just in the ports that marked the southernmost limit of Roman trade, around Zanzibar, but much further south, where they first visited and colonized the Comoros archipelago off the coast of Africa (later famous for its ylang-ylang perfume), and then settled in the greatest of all the Indian Ocean islands, Madagascar. Whether they took a direct route across the ocean to discover Madagascar, until then empty of humans, or edged around the coasts of the Indian Ocean has been much debated. The general consensus is that Malay-speakers gradually made their way along more and more ambitious trade routes leading them to southern India and far beyond. Mostly these Malays were absorbed into host populations over the centuries; but in Madagascar they were alone, apart from Bantu slaves they themselves brought from east African ports such as Kilwa and Zanzibar. So what they created was a Malay–Indonesian society in African waters. Later European observers recognized the distinctive features of Malagasy society when they expressed the view that Madagascar was really part of Asia, not Africa.[14]

Language provides rich evidence for the links between Madagascar and the opposite end of the Indian Ocean. Glottochronology is, among other things, the science of dating the moments when languages began to diverge into dialects that gradually became mutually incomprehensible, to the point where they can be described as separate languages. It has been seen that Māoris and Hawai'ians could still make sense of what the other side said in the eighteenth century. It is clear that the first settlers in Madagascar spoke a language close to Malay; Malagasy is a language whose cousins mainly lie on the far edge of the Indian Ocean or deep within the Pacific, and the closest relative to the Malagasy language is a dialect spoken in Borneo. Glottochronology suggests that the time of their arrival was late in the first millennium BC; and the evidence of language is confirmed by that of DNA – mitochondrial DNA reveals that 96 per cent of the population is descended at least in part from Asiatic settlers. However, over the centuries the island has received Bantus, Arabs and many others, so that there are other elements in both the bloodline and the language; the Bantu settlers probably arrived from the start of the second millennium AD onwards. There is also similar evidence to suggest the presence of Austronesians on the coast of east Africa, around Pemba and Zanzibar. Finally, there is the unspoken evidence of the plants that have thrived on Madagascar since humans arrived: rice, saffron, coconuts, yams, plus, very probably, a humble addition to the otherwise exotic animal population – chickens.[15]

Part of the fascination of both Socotra and Madagascar is that these were uninhabited islands far from the mainland that were settled by humans who had to work out what sort of society they would establish there. On Socotra, which was frankly desolate, they could only hope to set up a trade counter to sell what little it offered, and maybe to careen the hulls of passing ships, or send out pirates to capture them. Madagascar offered a very different opportunity. This was a landmass that had floated away from India and had been isolated from the rest of the world for maybe 88,000,000 years, so that, rather like Australia, its animal population developed independently from that of the rest of the world; the lemur, a very early primate, is found nowhere else in the world. The richly forested interior took centuries to tame, but around the coast early visitors may have been attracted by apparently unlimited supplies of spices and resins.[16] That is to assume with Philippe Beaujard that Madagascar was a happy discovery of Indonesian merchants in search of spices, following on from a series of what he calls strategic commercial voyages; they would then have left behind a core population of settlers, who would have supplied spices to the traders as they came year after year in search of the natural wealth of Madagascar. Why people from what became known as the Spice Islands would go in search of spices on the other side of the ocean then becomes a mystery; taking these spices home would have been the equivalent of carrying coals to Newcastle; but there have been attempts to link this demand to the emergence of the great trading empires of the South China Sea, especially the early medieval kingdom of Śri Vijaya, based on Sumatra, which will be examined shortly.

According to this theory, the settlers expanded in numbers and moved ever inwards into the heart of the island, which they gradually denuded of its thickest tree cover, and where they exterminated some of its most remarkable inhabitants – giant lemurs and massive elephant birds, which may be the enormous *rukh* that appears in the late medieval tale of Sindbad the Sailor.[17] Meanwhile other Indonesian settlers arrived who were attracted by the tales they heard from seafarers who described the lush paradise of Madagascar.[18] That is one plausible scenario; another view would present the Indonesians as seafarers similar to the Polynesians, setting out in their catamarans in search of new lands to settle, without a particular interest in the Indian Ocean spice trade. Unfortunately, Malagasy archaeology is in its infancy, and the results of excavations shed little light on this problem. One promising site in the north of Madagascar cannot be dated further back than AD 420, and evidence from earlier times is very patchy. Fragments of locally made pottery from roughly AD 700 have emerged from a rock shelter that may have been used by sailors stopping over on the island before making the long voyage back to Malaya.[19] This could be taken to prove that waves of Austronesians arrived over many centuries, with contact continuing right through to the fourteenth century or later, by which time Arab travellers were reporting the existence of this extraordinary miniature continent.[20] The settlers knew iron, and their technology was therefore much more sophisticated than that of the Polynesians, who around this time were reviving their colonization of the farther reaches of the Pacific. What their boats looked like and where else they sailed is far from certain, though big ships with outriggers feature among the sculptures at Borobodur in Indonesia, and outriggers are still used on boats both in Indonesia and in east Africa, including Madagascar.[21]

Even if the first Austronesians to reach Madagascar were not spice merchants, and even if contact between the island and the inhabitants' mother country was spasmodic, there is enough evidence to show that the Greco-Roman merchants were not the only pioneers in navigating the Indian Ocean at the end of the first millennium BC and the start of the first millennium AD. The great arc from south-east Africa to the East Indies was a space in which human beings moved impressive distances far out of sight of land. They may not have possessed the extraordinary navigational skills of the Polynesians (though conceivably the discoverers of Madagascar possessed some of that knowledge), but the navigators of the

Indian Ocean required and acquired a detailed knowledge of its shores and islands.[22] The different corners of the Indian Ocean were slowly becoming more connected to one another, and beyond that to the seas that lap the shores of Vietnam, Java and China.

III

These Malay navigators are the unsung heroes of trade and migration in the Indian Ocean and in the South China Sea: unlike the Indian travellers, they are not praised in the Brahmin poems and, unlike the Greco-Roman travellers, they have left no *Periplous*; the earliest written history from Malaya, the so-called *Malay Annals*, dates from the early seventeenth century and is rich in stories about fifteenth-century Singapore and Melaka (Malacca), but for earlier centuries it only offers garbled legends about Indian ancestors.[23] The boats of the Malays and Indonesians are impossible to describe in any detail, though finding the right woods was no problem: no one knows whether they resembled dhows, junks or catamarans (and the simple term 'dhow' is a broad description of a variety of roughly similar ships, varying greatly in size and equipment). Yet they played a crucial part in transforming the links between furthest Asia and the Mediterranean, so that south India became a transit point rather than a terminus, and the terminus shifted eastwards as far as the East Indies and even at times southern China. The decades when Bereniké was beginning its slide under the sand were also those in which south-east Asia and its Malay sailors became a powerful force on the oceans.

The first question is what was known of this region and its inhabitants by those who lived outside it. The *Periplous* was vague about a 'golden land', Chrysé, beyond the Ganges; this indicates that contact with its inhabitants was still quite limited, in the first and second centuries, whether that contact was effected through very rare visits to the land of Chrysé (for example, by embassies trying to reach China, such as the Antun embassy mentioned earlier), or through meeting Malay sailors in the ports of southern India, such as Arikamedu/Poduké. Sometimes Chrysé simply appeared in late classical writings as an island beyond India, on the very edge of the habitable world, but not too distant from the land of the Seres, that is, the silk-weaving Chinese.[24] Chrysé and another island called Argyré were said to be so rich in gold and silver that the metals had given their names to these two islands; around AD 40 the Roman writer Pomponius Mela reported a legend that one had soil that consisted of gold, and the other had soil made of silver, but he was not so credulous as to believe the tale.[25] This rumour was repeated by the sixth-century Spanish encyclopaedist Isidore of Seville, who knew his classical sources extremely well, and who became the first port of call for many who wished to understand the shape of the continents in later centuries. The Jewish historian Josephus assumed that this was where one could find Ophir, to which King Solomon had sent his ships a thousand years before his own day.[26] Ptolemy, as preserved by later Byzantine editors, who may have added their own knowledge and opinions, had a different view: he presented Malaya as a lump sticking out of south-east Asia, so that its shape is closer to that of Indo-China than to the Malay peninsula. He arrived at this conclusion more by accident, no doubt, than because of confusion between precise information about the two neighbouring regions.[27] As for information about the people who lived in and around Chrysé, this was the usual mish-mash of startling tales of dark-skinned peoples with barbaric customs, largely conjured out of thin air.

The people outside the region who knew the area and its inhabitants best were the Chinese. They have not appeared often in this book before now. Chinese civilization had developed along the great river systems of east Asia, and the Chinese connection to water involved freshwater more often than the open sea. There were important maritime links to Japan, of which more will be said; and there was plenty of coastal navigation in sizeable junks, 'storeyed ships', or *louchuan*, the sea being a source of fish and salt.[28] Evidence for regular long-distance voyages by Chinese sailors is hard to come by in the early centuries of the first millennium AD. Boat traffic was dominated by ethnic groups other than the Han Chinese, who lived in the north and would eventually rule vast expanses of China; perhaps the most practised sailors were the Yueh in southern China, whose culture fell under increasingly strong influence from Han China, but who were not yet fully sinicized. The Yueh created lively commercial links to the coasts of central China.[29] Around 221 BC, when the Han dynasty was founded further north, there existed four Yueh kingdoms, maybe more; one of them possessed a capital somewhere in the region of Hanoi, at a place known as Lo Yueh. Here, one could obtain luxuries that were much in demand at the Han court: 'rhinoceros horns, elephant tusks, tortoise-shells, pearls, fruits and cloth', as well as kingfisher feathers, silver and copper, which were brought to the Yueh city of Panyu near Guangzhou (Canton) and bought by Chinese merchants who, according to a Chinese writer of the first century AD, enriched themselves greatly.[30] Links to western Asia were maintained across the famous but difficult Silk Road, which took caravans across great swathes of empty desert and through the lands of the Sogdian merchants to the north of

Iran, until the route reached trade centres north and south of the Caspian Sea. Exotic products, of which silk was only the most famous, arrived by this route; but it was a hard and slow journey whose safety could only be assured by plenty of guard posts along the way.[31] The Silk Road functioned effectively in the first century BC and up to about AD 225, while the Han dynasty could provide this degree of protection.

However, the third century BC was also a period of intense conflict among the 'Seven Warring States' of China, and this conflict deflected the Chinese from expansion southwards. Then, between 221 and 214 BC the ruler of the Qin Empire extended his rule over Yueh territory in the face of tough Yueh resistance, and briefly gained control of much of the coastline of the South China Sea, around the Gulf of Tongking. The conquest of the Yueh towns was accompanied by the settlement in the region of 'criminals, banished men, social parasites and merchants', according to a snooty Chinese historian of the time, but the long-term effect was that the Han Chinese population grew, particularly in the cities, and flourished through trade with Chinese lands further north. How much of this trade was carried by sea is unclear, as is the degree of contact between the Yueh or the Chinese merchants living in their lands and the inhabitants of the Malay peninsula. Such goods from the Indian Ocean as arrived dribbled through passageways linking the South China Sea to the Indian Ocean.[32]

This marked the beginning of a much closer relationship between the Han Chinese and the sea. Its characteristics were trade, but also naval warfare. In 138 BC a Chinese navy sailed south from the River Yangtze to fend off Yueh pirates. Over the next few years a series of Chinese naval attacks maintained firm pressure on the Yueh statelets along the coast of the South China Sea. Guangzhou, the capital of the Nan Yueh, fell to the Chinese and was used as the base for a raid into the Gulf of Tongking; the king of Guangzhou was captured as he tried to flee by sea. This was a period when the Han Chinese could confidently extend their power as far south as Vietnam; but holding the Han Empire together was only possible by firmly suppressing the centrifugal tendencies of all the many regions and peoples that lay under Han domination. When Han power disintegrated, Chinese refugees flooded south; they had already begun to do so during a crisis in northern China between AD 9 and 25, and this further stimulated the emergence of Guangzhou as a major centre of trade and culture, a city that was able to draw up from Vietnam exotic birds and animals and tropical plants.[33]

The Han Empire divided, and the Wei in the north found themselves at odds with the Wu dynasty, who came to control the south from AD 220 onwards. As a result, the Wu were cut off from the land routes. On the other hand, the Wu state acquired a long coastline facing out towards the South China Sea, which the Chinese began to exploit more intensely than before. Wu Chinese began to look in new directions for the luxuries they had known while they lived in the cities of the north.[34] These even included the frankincense and myrrh of Arabia, as well as coloured glass from Phoenicia and amber that might well have originated in the Baltic, all of which had once percolated down the Silk Road.[35] The question was how they could obtain these goodies, and the answer lay in their relations with the regions between China and India, in other words Indo-China and Malaya/Indonesia. As will be seen, they also hoped to create a series of links to the land of birth of Buddhism at a time when Buddhist texts and relics were enormously prized in China.

These links could be laid down in two main directions. One route led from the ports of southern China and along the coast of what is now Vietnam, to the territory the Chinese called Funan.[36] From there one could follow the coast right round till one reached the Isthmus of Kra, the narrow neck of land that links the Malay peninsula to Asia. After crossing the isthmus by land, which could take a good ten days as the terrain was covered with forests hilly and, travellers could take ship once again in southern Thailand and then leap across the Bay of Bengal from Burma to north-eastern India. For a while Funan was able to maintain a stranglehold on the movement of people and goods from the South China Sea towards the Indian Ocean, and the isthmian route, despite its awkwardness, was preferred. The alternative route went all the way by sea from Indo-China along the Malay coast, past what is now Singapore and through the Strait of Malacca, jumping across the Bay of Bengal from somewhere on the western side of Malaya.[37] Chinese ships avoided the open sea, to judge from a text known as the *Liang shu*: 'the Zhang hai [South China Sea] is of great extent and ocean-going junks have not yet crossed it directly'.[38] The dividends for those in power were considerable. Around AD 300, Shih Chong was the governor of a region that lay along the trade routes towards Canton and Hanoi, and he accumulated enormous wealth by taxing merchants and ambassadors who passed through his lands laden with goods; he also traded on his own behalf, sending out merchants to collect ivory, pearls, scented woods and perfumes, while he was particularly proud of half a dozen coral trees that stood three or four feet high and were beautifully coloured. He also possessed thousands of beautiful female slaves:

> He asked a few tens of them each to hold various scents in their mouths; and when they talked and laughed, the fragrance was wafted by every

breeze. He then had powdered gharu-woods as fine as dust sprinkled over an ivory bed, and asked those that he specially loved to step on it. Those who left not a trace he presented with a hundred *p'ei* of pearls [50,000 pearls!]. Those who moved the fine powder were ordered to eat and drink less in order that they might be lighter.[39]

Although he was not typical of his contemporaries, the South China Sea trade had brought Shih fabulous wealth – fabulous in the sense that accounts of his wealth no doubt grew in the telling. And yet Guangzhou and Hanoi derived their wealth from the fact that these towns were collection points, rather than centres of production – 'prosperous frontier towns', in the words of Wang Gung-Wu, and the luxurious life of Shih Chong and his successors was rendered possible by the remoteness of these provinces from the central imperial government. As with other frontier regions, the area around Guangzhou, Guangdong, was plagued by pirates and bandits who hoped to set up their own fiefdoms along the coast. This held back the expansion of trade across the South China Sea. One of these pirates, Lu Xun, was resoundingly defeated at the start of the fifth century, a victory that ushered in a period of quiet in Guangdong. Strife further south, along the coast of Annam, left Guangzhou largely free to develop its trade across the South China Sea, so that 'the governor of Guangzhou need only pass through the city gates of Guangzhou just once, and he will be enriched by thirty million strings of cash'.[40] By the sixth century AD Guangzhou was at its peak, and the local officials operated a tax system that, for all its severity, did not slow down the economy, was tolerated and became normal practice: the goods of foreign merchants were bought at half the official price and then sold on at the full price. It seems unlikely that the beneficiaries were anyone other than the greedy officials.[41]

An early Chinese description of the sea route to India survives in the *Qian Hanshu*, a compilation of Han history created in its present form after the fall of the Han, but incorporating older material. It is very difficult to identify the places in India whose ancient names, now imperfectly known, if known at all, were rendered into Chinese sounds. That they included Barygaza and Muziris is very likely. The Han history does contain the earliest surviving description of Malaya, or at any rate the Kra Isthmus, in any language.[42] But the voyage towards India was slow, each stage taking months at a time, as one would expect when the monsoons were blowing; what made the endless wait worthwhile was the produce that could be found:

These countries are extensive, their populations numerous and their many products unfamiliar. Ever since the time of the Emperor Wu [141–87 BC] they have all offered tribute. There are chief interpreters attached to the Yellow Gate [the Department of Eunuchs] who, together with volunteers, put out to sea to buy lustrous pearls, glass, rare stones and strange products in exchange for gold and various silks. All the countries they visit provide them with food and companionship. The trading ships of the barbarians transfer the Chinese to their destination. It is a profitable business for the barbarians, who also loot and kill. Moreover, there are the hazards of wind and wave to be encountered and the possibility of death by drowning. If these are avoided the outward and return voyages take several years. The large pearls are at the most two Chinese inches in circumference.[43]

The impression that had to be created was that of subject peoples, but the pretence could not be maintained; much of this description is concerned with trade for profit. Around the third century AD, the clear aim of the 'chief interpreters' was to reach India; officially, at any rate, they were the emperor's agents sent on a diplomatic mission, but in reality they had gone west to buy the rarest of luxury goods from far-off lands.[44] Malaya was an inconvenient barrier with nothing obvious to offer, whereas Indian products were rare and unusual. The transformation of Malaya into a desirable destination would be slow; but, even before that, Malay seamen had become active. The essential point is that the Han Chinese remained wary of the open seas, and everything suggests that the Malays were emerging as one of the most active seafaring nations of east Asia. There is every reason to suppose that they, not Indians and certainly not Chinese, sailed the boats that took 'chief interpreters' and other Chinese merchants from the west coast of Malaya to eastern India; the historian Wang Gung-Wu, writing in 1958, expressed puzzlement at the fact that his Chinese sources did not specify that ships reaching the Indian Ocean were Chinese or Yueh or Indian, and the answer that he missed is that they were operated by Malays. As will be seen, we even have detailed descriptions of them, with their measurements (over 200 feet long, 20–30 feet high, and with four adjustable sails).[45] In the fifth century the 'southern barbarians' provided everything from rhinoceros horn and kingfisher feathers to pearls and asbestos (then regarded as a mysteriously wonderful mineral).[46] For Malays who ranged further and further across the ocean, as far as Africa, the journey across the Bay of Bengal was nothing special.

For a few centuries Funan in southern Vietnam was the main intermediary between China and India. It is thought to have been the largest kingdom lying between China and India, and to have dominated the coasts of the Gulf of Siam and the eastern shores of Malaya.[47] Only the Chinese name of this territory is known; but many of its inhabitants were probably related to the Mon-Khmer people who later built the great temple cities in Cambodia.[48] Funan's maritime successes date to a period when the shipping that moved through the South China Sea carried Chinese passengers, Indian monks, and merchants and Malay sailors, with, no doubt, a good sprinkling of local Vietnamese hands on board as well. By the middle of the third century Funan was attracting admiring comments from Chinese travellers. At this period a king of Funan named Fan-man or Fan Shiman by the Chinese expanded his power over his neighbours and created a kingdom that combined lively international trade with the successful exploitation of large tracts of land suitable for rice and other foods. Funan's cities were walled, they were rich in libraries and archives, and its taxes, it was said, were paid in gold, silver, pearls and perfume. Funan was also a centre of shipbuilding.[49] In short, the Funanese met Chinese criteria for being classed as reasonably civilized barbarians.

The origins of Funan were said to have lain in the sea, so its vocation was always trading. According to a legend recorded in China, at some time in the first century AD a local queen sent a pirate raid to attack a merchant ship, but those on board defended themselves well, and the ship was able to put in to land. A passenger from 'beyond the seas' with the Brahmin name Kaundinya set foot on dry land, drank some of its water (this symbolized taking possession of the lands of the water queen) and married the queen. Thereupon he became king of Funan, acting as overlord over a group of seven chieftains in different towns around the Mekong delta. The marriage between a sky god and a princess born, rather like Aphrodite, in the foam of the sea was a longstanding motif of Malay and Polynesian mythology, and the story presented here bears the imprint of these earlier legends.[50] Even so, the story has been interpreted as evidence that Indians arrived in Vietnam by sea and inserted themselves into the highest echelons of local society, which they increasingly indianized and indeed commercialized. The kingdom of Funan was a joint enterprise of Indian merchants and colonizers, with an interest in maritime trade, working alongside native Vietnamese with an interest in harvesting the produce of the fields.[51] However important the sea was to the prosperity of Funan, the inland regions were also of great economic importance, and the capital, which still needs to be identified, lay some way inland.[52] Its indianized character was acquired more by osmosis than by colonization; and when colonization took place it occurred in the port cities, and was the work of merchants and Brahmin priests who merged deliberately with the local population, as will be seen. Indian culture fascinated the Funanese, as it did later rulers of lands around the South China Sea; the Khmer kings of Cambodia, the builders of the great temples at Angkor Wat, claimed descent from Kaundinya and the kings of Funan. This does not mean that the townsmen were all Indians. Rather, as in other port cities around the world, the ports of Funan hummed with the bargaining of Indians, Chinese, Malays, Indonesians, Vietnamese, Burmese and many other ethnic groups.

The remains of one of their trading ports, at Oc-èo at the top of the Gulf of Siam, confirm Chinese reports; it had originated in the first century AD as a Malay fishing harbour, but soon afterwards it underwent a spectacular transformation, and it remained a great centre of trade until the early seventh century. Just as no one knows the local name for Funan, no one knows the original name of the town that has been excavated at Oc-èo, which lies not far from Ho Chi Minh City, or Saigon. Oc-èo is not simply one site among many, though other Vietnamese ports of this period await discovery; everything suggests that it was the earliest trading port of any significance in the history of south-east Asia, and it is the first place in the region where writing has been found, in the form of Sanskrit inscriptions, not just on stone but on gold rings. The site itself is large, covering 450 hectares.[53] The inhabitants lived in houses partly built of stone and brick but raised on piles above the ground, to avoid flooding, as is still so often the case in south-east Asia. Larger palaces for the elite had two storeys.[54] Oc-èo did not actually lie on the seashore but twenty-five kilometres inland, and was connected to the open sea by canals. These canals were a typical feature of the south Vietnamese landscape; they ran through the waterlogged countryside and serve as a reminder that the rulers of Funan were able to mobilize a considerable labour force to construct and maintain a whole network of waterways. It has been well said that one word describes the Funanese environment: 'watery'.[55]

Oc-èo tied the sea to the Funanese possessions that lay down the watercourses of the Mekong River, and it had access to vast paddy fields sown with rice that flooded naturally when the Mekong rose; if nothing else, Oc-èo was a place mariners would want to use to resupply their ships on the long haul from southern China to Malaya and back.[56] Objects found there have included coins of the Antonine emperors of Rome, from the second century, Chinese bronzes of the first to sixth centuries, and polished gems thought to have been brought from Sasanid Persia, though many of these items would have been carried to Funan in stages and passed from hand to hand over a long period. Imported materials were used to manufacture ornaments, jewellery and utensils, including silver dinner plates: the people of Oc-èo fashioned gems from diamonds, rubies, sapphires, topaz, garnets, opals, jet and much else, and they imported gold, probably in the form of gold wire, which they then melted down to make rings, bracelets and other high-value objects. More modest metals moved around the South China Sea, such as iron, which arrived from north-east Borneo.[57] Interestingly, more goods have been found that originated in the Roman Empire than from China, even though China was much nearer and more accessible, so Oc-èo, although it lay beyond the Indian Ocean, was certainly linked to those trade routes that brought 'Roman' merchants at least as far as southern India – the question is who then transported these goods to the South China Sea. But Funanese relations with Wu China were constantly being sealed by embassies that carried tribute to the imperial court. In the fifth century embassies to China arrived again and again, bearing gold, sandalwood, ivory and incense.

During much of this century and the early sixth, contact between Funan and China was especially lively. Not just state emissaries but monks were sent back and forth between China and Funan; on one occasion the king of Funan sent a Buddhist monk to southern China with the text of 240 *sutras* that he wanted to share with the imperial court. Funan thus acted as a bridge between the birthplace of Buddhism and the great empire that was at this period enthusiastically embracing Buddhist doctrines. Even so, the Funanese ambassadors were not always welcome, and occasionally, as in 357, they were kept waiting and then sent back without the tribute being accepted, perhaps because the emperor preferred other allies in the region, or perhaps because the tribute itself was regarded as paltry. One reason the Wu emperors cared about Funan was not because of an interest in the trade in fine gemstones but their love for Funanese music, which was still greatly appreciated at the Tang court in seventh-century China. Unfortunately neither the instruments nor the sounds are known; but an 'Office for Funan Music' existed at Nanjing in 244, so the infatuation lasted many centuries.[58]

The ships of Funan were described by Chinese writers, and fell into two categories. There were ships whose average length was said to be twelve *xin*, or eight Chinese feet, which were also six *xin* broad. They would therefore have been quite tubby in shape; a striking feature was the bow and stern, said to look like fish, so the boards were evidently gathered together into something like a point. They were powered by oars and the largest ones could carry about a hundred people. Relatively small vessels of this sort would have been suitable for carrying low-bulk, high-value goods such as jewellery, rare spices and incense. Another account describes much larger vessels, able to carry 600–700 passengers and crew and a very large cargo (more than 10,000 *ho*), and these ships were powered by four sails. They sound more like the junks that traded along the coast of China, and may have been copied from foreign ships by the shipbuilders of Funan. The Chinese texts call the Funanese ships *bo*, which has been linked to a Malay word, *perahu*, that the Chinese language would have struggled to turn into a manageable sound. And this has led to the assumption that the ships and sailors were Malay, which makes a great deal of sense, particularly bearing in mind the description of the smaller ships, which have a strongly Malay feel. For the descriptions that survive of the people of Funan suggest that there were many Malays living in the area where the Chinese would have had contact with this kingdom – the port cities. The Chinese texts speak of dark, curly-haired people, whom they found ugly (though that was a common enough way of expressing superiority over 'barbarians'); they were big people who wore their hair long at the back and went around virtually naked, with nothing on their feet, and like many who display their flesh they adorned their bodies with tattoos.[59] They do not sound like the handsome Khmers who lived further inland in Funan. Oc-èo in particular was a place where people of varied origins came together – Khmers, Indians, Malays, Chinese, only to mention the most obvious among the very many peoples of south-east Asia – a large cosmopolitan port city whose identity was created by generations of settlers and their descendants, and whose daily life was dominated by trade across the seas and by the need to prepare goods, such as gems, that could be sent on its ships to China and elsewhere.

A place of this significance could not be missed by commentators even as far away as the Roman Empire. When Ptolemy mentioned Kattigara in south-east Asia, visited by the Greek sea captain Alexander in the second century, he may have had one or all of the ports of Funan, including Oc-èo, in mind, but he set off a debate about where Kattigara lay that was to fascinate scholars and explorers in sixteenth-century Europe. However, Ptolemy confidently placed Kattigara on the Indian Ocean rather than near the South China Sea.[60] For Kattigara may well have been a name created by Greco-Roman merchants out of a misunderstanding. An eleventh-century Brahmin collection of tales is known as the *Kathāsaritsāgara*, meaning 'ocean of streams of story', and an earlier version of that word, or *Kathāsāgara* ('oceans of story') may well have been heard as 'Kattigara'; the name would then signify something like 'fabled place across the seas'.[61] Oc-èo and Funan remained prosperous until the fifth century, with the peak of their prosperity probably in the second century, under the warrior king Fan-man. During the fourth century, the growing attractions of spices and resins from the Moluccas and other parts of Indonesia gradually rendered the south coast of Vietnam less interesting to sea traders; and this change in direction had major consequences not just for the history of the region but, as will be seen, for the history of the oceans and of the entire world.

Fan-man's wars of conquest resulted in the creation of a land and sea realm that encompassed large areas of Indo-China. His empire spilled over into the Bay of Bengal after he led victorious armies into the Kra Isthmus, conquering a Malay kingdom called Tun-sun (in Chinese); it lay in the innermost north-west corner of the South China Sea, at the top of the Malay peninsula, where it joins Thailand. Chinese commentators were impressed by this victory, because they knew that the Malay peninsula was an inconvenient barrier to access to India. Once Tun-sun was in Funanese hands, the journey to the Bay of Bengal became a little easier; one could arrive in Tun-sun's main port by sea, and then trek across the isthmus through lands that were now all under the sovereignty of the king of Funan. The Chinese were also impressed that the main city of newly conquered Tun-sun was a port where 'East and West meet together so that every day great crowds gather there. Precious goods and merchandise – they are all there.'[62] There were 500 Indian families in the town and 1,000 Brahmins, who were encouraged to marry local girls, 'consequently many of the Brahmins do not go away'. Chinese observers were dismayed by these parasites, as they saw them: 'they do nothing but study the sacred canon, bathe themselves with scents and flowers, and practise piety ceaselessly by day and night.'[63] The Indianization of Vietnam meant, therefore, not just the presence of Indian traders and settlers, but the arrival of Hindu and Buddhist cults, which spread in Indo-China from this time onwards. An early Sanskrit inscription from Funan dates from soon after Fan-man's death, showing how the sacred language of India was beginning to take root in Indo-China.

IV

Trade and religion were closely intertwined. Beyond Funan, the Brahmins had their rivals. From the first century AD Buddhism began to take a strong hold on China, and Chinese Buddhists regularly travelled to India to study Sanskrit texts and acquire mementoes of the life of Buddha. Faxien (or in older spelling Shih Fa-Hsien) was a Buddhist monk who spent about fifteen years away from China at the start of the fifth century; he took an overland route to India, and returned to Guangzhou by sea from some place in India.[64] By now mariners were not interested in hugging the coast of Indo-China, and Faxien was forced to confront the terrors of the open sea. His description of how he reached China by sea from India is full of the dramatic images that so many pilgrims included in their travel diaries. But, even allowing for exaggeration, it offers precious details: there were 200 people on board what he calls a large merchant ship, 'astern of which there was a smaller vessel in tow in case of accidents at sea and destruction of the big vessel'. That, at any rate, was the theory. But after two days of good sailing eastward, propelled by fair winds, they ran into a severe gale in the Bay of Bengal, and the main ship began to take on water.

> The merchants wished to get aboard the smaller vessel; but the men on the latter, fearing that they would be swamped by numbers, quickly cut the tow-rope in two. The merchants were terrified, for death was close at hand; and fearing that the vessel would fill, they promptly took what bulky goods there were and threw them into the sea. Faxien also took his pitcher and ewer, with whatever he could spare, and threw them into the sea; but he was afraid the merchants would throw over his books and his images, and accordingly fixed his whole thoughts on Guanyin, the Hearer of Prayers, and put his life into the hands of the Catholic Church [i.e. his Buddhist sect] in China, saying, 'I have journeyed far on behalf of the Faith. O that by your awful power you would grant me a safe return from my wanderings.'[65]

It took thirteen days for his prayers to be answered, whereupon they reached an island, probably one of the Andamans, and were able to plug the leak in the ship. Even so, he says, pirates abounded in the vast sea, for 'the expanse of ocean is boundless', and navigation by the sun or stars was only possible when the skies were clear; 'in cloudy and rainy weather our vessel drifted at the mercy of the wind, without keeping any definite course'. The sea was too deep to cast anchor; and it was full of threatening sea monsters that showed themselves, somehow, in the middle of the night.

Finally, after ninety days, the ship arrived in a land known as Yepoti, thought to have been northern Borneo, or possibly southern Sumatra, which was not bad navigation; they had evidently passed through the Strait of Malacca and had followed the broken south and east coastline of the South China Sea. Yepoti disappointed Faxien, because it was full of Hindus and 'the Faith of Buddha was in a very unsatisfactory condition'. He did not notice any Chinese merchants in this land, which suggests, yet again, that the trade of the South China Sea was dominated by other peoples.[66] Despite his misgivings about this place, he stayed there for five months, and then boarded a different merchant ship that was large enough to carry 200 passengers. They sailed for Guangzhou, but after a month they encountered another tempest, and Faxien immersed himself yet again in prayer. This nearly became Faxien's involuntary Jonah moment. The Hindu Brahmins on board (whose purpose in travelling to China can only be guessed at) decided that it was precisely because a devout Buddhist was on board that the gods had sent storms against the ship. They did not suggest throwing him overboard, but had a more humane solution: 'We ought to land the religious mendicant on some island; it is not right to endanger all our lives for one man.' But Faxien had a protector on board who promised to report the Brahmins to the ruler of China if they treated him this way; Faxien's friend insisted that the Chinese ruler was also a devout Buddhist who favoured Buddhist monks. 'At this the merchants wavered and did not land him just then.'[67] In any case, they were lost in a typhoon in the middle of the South China Sea, so there cannot have been any islands upon which to abandon the poor monk. For seventy days they wandered, even though they had provisions for only fifty, the normal amount of time required to reach Guangzhou. They had to cook their food in seawater. And when they reached China it was far to the north of Guangzhou, way beyond Taiwan, closer to Shanghai and Hangzhou than to the Wu domains in the south.

The stories of Faxien and other monks who followed the same route are not just picturesque accounts of the terrors of the open sea. They are also valuable testimony to the way the opening of sea routes stimulated the spread of cultures and religions. Later, there will be a chance to examine how Buddhism jumped across the relatively narrow space of the Japan Sea to challenge and then co-exist with the native cults of ancient Japan. The seaways from India eastwards played a particularly important role in the spread of religious ideas, and the art associated with them, as Hindu texts and practices struck roots in Indo-China and Indonesia (so that Bali remains an isolated Hindu island to this day); and after that Buddhism and eventually Islam spread eastwards along the trade routes, refertilizing China, which had also received Buddhist texts along the Silk Road. In the third century over 500 monks lived in twenty or more temples by the Red River delta in Vietnam, and this spot became a favoured halt for pilgrims and merchants bound for and from China. Statues of the Buddha as *Dīpamkara*, 'calmer of waters', have been found on many sites in south-east Asia, often dating from this time.[68] Chinese writers also spoke of the ivory images, painted stupas and even a Buddha's tooth, all of which arrived from the Malay peninsula and the islands, notably from the land of Panpan in what is now southern Thailand.[69] These are excellent testimony to the spread of Buddhism along routes favoured by the merchants.

V

By the sixth century the fortunes of Funan now began to turn dramatically: a neighbouring ruler, the king of Zhenla (in whose temples human sacrifice was said to be practised), invaded Funanese lands and shoved the local economy further into decline; at its greatest extent Funan had exercised suzerainty over Zhenla.[70] Even allowing for the disappearance of Funan, the increasingly important ties between India and China transformed the role of Indo-China, Indonesia and Malaya in the maritime networks of the first half of the first millennium. Their role was not reduced but enhanced by the gradual decline of Roman trade in the Indian Ocean. Others began to enter the ocean, notably the people the Chinese called the *Po-ššu* or *Bosi*, subjects of the Sasanian emperors of Iran, who sailed down the Gulf and were present in Ceylon, or *Si-tiao*, by the sixth century; their main interest was the trade in silk. A Chinese text avers that 'the *Bosi* king asked for the hand of the daughter of the king of *Si-tiao* and sent a gold bracelet as a present'. Yet the Persians did not penetrate further than this, and sense can only be made of their undoubted success in Ceylon by deducing that others brought Chinese silk to the island; and those others were, or included, the mariners of Malaya, Sumatra and Java. This is apparent from the comments of Chinese writers about the constant arrival at Guangzhou, several times a year, of foreign ships, while the Chinese sent their own ships no further than western Indonesia. These Indonesians managed at last to intrude their own produce into the trading network between India and China that they so effectively serviced; the first Indonesian product to be rated highly was camphor, used as a perfume at the Sasanian court (rather an overpowering one, perhaps) and later as a drug. Some unfortunate Arabs who were celebrating the sack of a Persian-held city on the Tigris in 638 sprinkled camphor on their food, thinking it was salt, and were taken aback by the taste.[71]

What might seem to be a curious footnote to the history of food takes on a much greater significance when the gradual adoption of camphor by merchants and their wealthier customers is seen as the first step in the emergence of south-east Asia as the home of most of the world's finest spices. Already expert in the handling of pepper and other spices from the coasts of India, and even perhaps the spices they garnered in Madagascar and east Africa, the Malays and Indonesians were becoming the true masters of the international spice trade. In the centuries that followed, they would substitute their own resins and flavourings for those that had been handled by the Greco-Roman traders. This would be the foundation of the wealth of the great maritime trading kingdom of Śri Vijaya, with its capital at Palembang on Sumatra. The ripples of its influence reached not just China and India but the heartlands of Islam and even medieval Europe.

8

A Maritime Empire?

I

At the eastern end of the Indian Ocean and in the South China Sea, the sixth and seventh centuries saw transformations that turned the spasmodic contact between lands bordering the western Pacific and the Indian Ocean into a two-way traffic lane. This brought prosperity to lands on the southern fringe of the South China Sea that had previously lain on the outer margins of the trade routes. The kingdom of Śri Vijaya, based around Palembang in Sumatra, has been mentioned already. Early in the twentieth century French archaeologists and orientalists were convinced that they had brought to light a great trading empire of the early Middle Ages, whose impact could still be felt in the fifteenth century when the founders of Melaka (Malacca) traced their descent to the ancient rulers of Palembang.[1] The difficulty was that material remains were few; on the other hand, literary references were rich, allowing for the constant problem of the Chinese transcription of foreign place names. Compared to Oc-èo, the physical evidence for a great trading station at Palembang was virtually non-existent.[2] It is therefore no great surprise that more recent research into the history of early south-east Asia has cast doubt on the very existence of this trading empire, which has been described by one of its detractors as a 'vague supposed thalassocracy'.[3]

That a kingdom existed in Sumatra, flanking the South China Sea, is not in doubt; but how long it flourished, and whether it achieved such great wealth as has been assumed, is now less certain. One of its first historians, Gabriel Ferrand, admitted that 'one will search in vain for the name of Śri Vijaya' in books of geography and history, while he also argued that the empire enjoyed no less than seven centuries of prosperity; its reputation was carried across the South China Sea to the Heavenly Kingdom. This place was visited by Chinese travellers such as Da Qin, described as a master of legal study, who followed in the tracks of a

Chinese ambassador in AD 683, to reach the island of *Shili foshi* (a Chinese attempt to transcribe Śri Vijaya), where, interestingly, he immersed himself in Sanskrit books. Only six years later the Buddhist monk Yijing (or I-Ching) set out from Guangzhou on a merchant vessel, and coasted along the shores of Annam, eventually reaching *Foqi*, evidently the same place, as is the *Sanfoqi* mentioned by a historian writing for the Song dynasty between 960 and 1279.[4] According to the Chinese geographer Zhao Rugua, writing in the thirteenth century, this land lay between Cambodia and Java, which fixes its location in Sumatra, the great island to the south of the Strait of Malacca. Moreover, when he wrote of Arab lands, Zhao Rugua noted that 'the products of this country are for the most part brought to *Sanfoqi*, where they are sold to merchants who forward them to China', making this place the intermediary between the trade of the Indian Ocean and that of the South China Sea.[5]

Nor was this a remote place of mystery, to judge from continuing evidence for the exchange of ambassadors, though we can be sure that the Chinese treated the envoys of Śri Vijaya as supplicants. These embassies came laden with gifts from Sumatra and further afield.[6] In 724 the Śri Vijayan ambassador brought two dwarves, a black African slave, a troupe of musicians and a parakeet with feathers of five different colours. He received in exchange a hundred bolts of silk, as well as a title of honour for his master in Sumatra. Yet there were occasions when the Śri Vijayans made demands of the Chinese authorities, and got their way, which was unusual in these unequal relationships. Around 700 the Śri Vijayans 'sent several missions to the court to submit complaints about border officials seizing their goods, and an edict was issued ordering the officials at Guangzhou to appease them by making enquiries'.[7] The Chinese authorities clearly valued their relationship with Śri Vijaya, then. Nor were the contacts solely with the Chinese mainland. An account of a voyage from Sri Lanka in 717 suggests that the traffic heading back and forth across the Indian Ocean was also regular. The monk Vajrabodhi arrived aboard a fleet of thirty-five ships, and then stayed in *Fo-chi* for five months, while awaiting favourable winds.[8] Śri Vijaya benefited directly from the monsoons: the north-east monsoon that blew throughout the winter prevented travel back from there to China for several months, but the south-west monsoon that blew in the summer rendered the journey swift and direct. Coming from China, equally, one had to take advantage of the winter winds to head south and then west. As a result, journeys towards Malaya and India were slow; there was little chance of returning in one year if one wanted to do business in remote markets, and a trip from India to China and back was a three-year affair; however, the monks

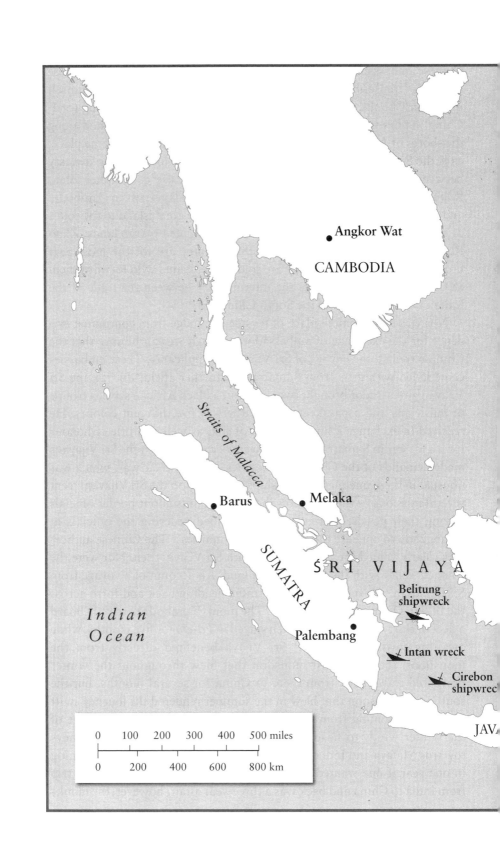

Angkor Wat

CAMBODIA

Straits of Malacca

Barus

Melaka

SUMATRA

ŚRI VIJAYA

Belitung
shipwreck

Indian
Ocean

Palembang

Intan wreck

Cirebon
shipwrec

JAVA

| 0 | 100 | 200 | 300 | 400 | 500 miles |

| 0 | 200 | 400 | 600 | 800 km |

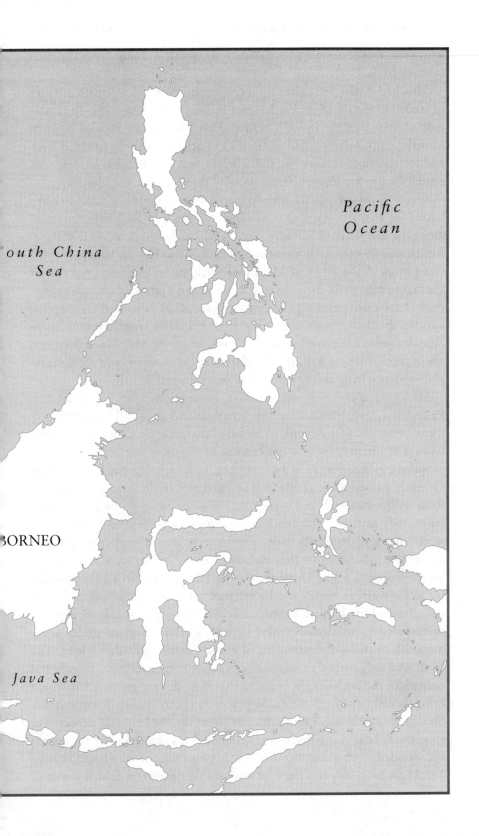

Pacific
Ocean

South China
Sea

BORNEO

Java Sea

who took this route were in no hurry to return – Yijing spent eighteen years in India.[9]

This had important cultural repercussions. Not just a certain amount of trade but the desire of Far Eastern Buddhists to gain access to fundamental texts brought India, China and even Japan into regular contact. Lengthy stopovers by Buddhist monks in Śri Vijaya as they moved back and forth between China and India meant that their religion became well established in Śri Vijaya; Yijing proudly recalled that the kingdom contained a thousand monks who followed Indian Buddhist rituals to the letter. He also remarked that the political reach of Śri Vijaya extended along the east flank of Sumatra, even reaching Kedah in western Malaya. Kedah was by now an important and prosperous link on the trade route tying India to the Strait of Malacca, which, as will be seen, was one of the main props of the Śri Vijayan economy; and Yijing had enough experience of the open sea not to take it for granted; he described a voyage by another monk that took him down from Hanoi or Guangzhou as far as Sumatra, where the overloaded ship sank in a tempest.[10] Much is known about these ships, as a result of underwater excavations, and the remarkable evidence from their cargoes will be examined shortly.

Śri Vijaya is certainly not a mirage. Inscriptions from its capital city, Palembang, state the name of this kingdom and say a little about its political structure. It is difficult to be sure how accurate Chinese or Arabic reports of life in Śri Vijaya were; some of the most colourful detail was supplied by Zhao Rugua in around 1225, by which time the kingdom had certainly passed its peak. But his comments were in large part recycled from earlier material; and even if they are not based on intimate knowledge, they testify to the exotic reputation that Śri Vijaya obtained. He wrote of a kingdom with many provinces or dependencies, though it is impossible to believe that they included *Xilan*, Ceylon; more to the point, his reference to Ceylon is further proof that the reach of Śri Vijaya extended far to the west, as Malay and Indonesian mariners sailed back and forth to India and Sri Lanka. Reports reached him of a sizeable capital city surrounded by solid walls, ruled by a king who processed under a silk umbrella to the accompaniment of guards carrying golden lances. The king, who only bathed in rose-water, was not permitted to eat cereals, but only sago; the Śri Vijayans believed that if he did eat cereals, this would bring drought and high prices. At grand court ceremonies (assuming that his diet of sago brought him sufficient strength), the king was expected to wear a very heavy crown adorned with hundreds of jewels. The succession was decided by choosing from among his sons the one who could bear its weight on his head; and the new king would dedicate a golden statue of the Buddha, to which the king's subjects would bring offerings such as golden vases. The death of a king was treated as a national calamity: the people shaved their heads and many courtiers even immolated themselves in the royal funeral pyre.[11]

The Śri Vijayans used Sanskrit letters, in which one of the rare inscriptions from Palembang was written (though in an early form of the Malay language); but there were experts who could read and write Chinese characters, required when writing to the Chinese court. The inhabitants of the main city lived not within the town walls but around it in suburbs, and even on riverboats – it will be seen that the Chinese writers were actually describing a snake-like town that stretched for miles along the riverbank. The image was conveyed of a state that was ready to go to war against troublesome neighbours, with a competent army and brave soldiers. Rather than adopting the currency favoured by the Chinese, the copper coins known to Europeans as 'cash' that were threaded together through a central hole, the Śri Vijayans made use of hack silver, pieces of silver that were cut into pieces and weighed. (The term 'cash' is apparently derived from the Portuguese word *caixa*, 'cash-box', and the Chinese word was *wén*.)[12] They imported both silver and gold, and also acquired – certainly from China – porcelain and embroidered silk, as well as rice and rhubarb. Camphor, cloves, sandalwood, cardamom, civet perfume, myrrh, aloes, ivory, coral and many other spices and luxuries were for sale on the island. Its markets sold both local products, including some of those spices such as aloe wood, and goods brought from further afield, such as cotton goods carried across the Indian Ocean by *Dashi*, Muslim merchants from Persia and Arabia; and one could also find slaves brought all the way from *Kunlun*, the coast of Africa.[13] There must have been a lively traffic from the smaller Indonesian islands towards south-eastern Sumatra, bringing the resins and spices that the Chinese and Arabs keenly sought. By about AD 500, the Chinese valued benzoin resin from Indonesia as much as or more than Middle Eastern myrrh, while pine resin from Śri Vijaya was used, honestly or dishonestly, as a substitute for Arabian frankincense. One Chinese writer described the trade in frankincense, some no doubt genuine, some adulterated, some substituted by similar resins:

The Arabs bring their goods by ship to San-fo-chi and exchange them for goods. Thus this perfume is usually found in great quantities at San-fo-chi. Each year great ships leave San-fo-chi for Guangzhou or Quanzhou. At these two ports the shipping officials examine the amounts of perfume and establish its value.[14]

Zhao Rugua thought that Śri Vijaya and China began to make contact in the Tang period, at the start of the tenth century; but it has already been seen that contact can be traced back two centuries earlier. And the Song histories mention a whole series of embassies sent to China around 960, which were taken as recognition of Chinese overlordship; it is interesting to find sugar listed among the gifts, for at this period sugar stocks were only slowly becoming known in India and further west, and they are native to Indonesia. These gifts were regarded as tribute, to be sure; but the ambassadors received rewards for their efforts, including such wonders as yaks' tails and white porcelain. As well as official visits, which conformed to the Chinese idea of what trade with the imperial court was all about, there were visits by merchants of *San-fo-chi*: in 980 a Śri Vijayan merchant reached the south coast of China after a sixty-day voyage, carrying rhinoceros horns, perfumes and spices. This was a rather longer voyage than many experienced – a month was normal, or even three weeks.[15]

One might ask why the Śri Vijayans were so keen to acknowledge the distant ruler of China as their lord. Precisely because the emperor was so distant, the chance of direct interference was slim, but imperial approval would enhance the authority of the king of Śri Vijaya over sometimes troublesome vassals; it might even be of some use in fending off claims from independent neighbours with their own ambitions to create a commercial network, such as the Javans, who invaded Sumatra in 992, and who sent a particularly magnificent embassy to China the same year, conveying the message that Java (rather than Śri Vijaya) was the place with which to cultivate friendships and do business.[16] So it hardly comes as a surprise that in 1003 the Śri Vijayan king sent the Song emperor an embassy, declaring that he had erected a Buddhist temple in his home town specifically to pray for the long life of the emperor. Nor is it a surprise that the emperor sent temple bells in return, as well as a title of honour for his faithful subject. A few years later the favours of the emperor extended even further. Instead of the belts adorned with gold embroidery that most ambassadors received on taking leave of the emperor, the Śri Vijayan ambassadors were given belts entirely covered in gold. In 1016 Śri Vijaya was granted the rank of 'first-class trading state', though Java also received the same promotion.[17]

The value that the Chinese emperors placed on ties with Śri Vijaya becomes more and more obvious; and the main motive, without a doubt, was the desire to channel perfumes, spices and exotic goods from Sumatra to the Tang court and its Song successor. In the best tradition of the Chinese bureaucracy, officials such as the *ya fan bo shih*, or Superintendent of Barbarian Shipping, were established in the ports along the Chinese coast; they registered the goods being brought into the Heavenly Kingdom and provided essential services such as translation to and from Chinese to the 'barbarian' merchants who flocked to these ports as early as the eighth century. One term used for port superintendents, *shiboshi*, may be derived from the Persian word *shahbandar*, with a similar meaning, providing further evidence of the links between China and the western Indian Ocean. In one Chinese port, 'rhinoceros horns were so numerous that bribes were offered to the servants and retainers'. The local governor was unimpressed by some of the practices he observed. The goods of foreign merchants who died in China were confiscated if they were not claimed within three months; but the governor pointed out that it could take much longer to reach China, from barbarian lands, so this practice was unfair and should be banned.[18]

All this supervision of trade does little to explain why Śri Vijaya was such an important place in the early Middle Ages; and Zhao Rugua provided a clear answer: 'the country is an important thoroughfare for the traffic of foreign nations, the produce of all other countries is intercepted and kept in store there for the trade of foreign ships.' This statement suggests a rather aggressive policy on the part of the kingdom's rulers, who were as careful as the Chinese to check ships, cargoes and merchants that arrived in their lands.[19] Elsewhere, they blocked one of the straits that gave access to their waters with an iron chain, to keep at bay pirates from neighbouring lands. With the coming of peace, the chain lost its usefulness; it now lay coiled up on the shore, and people travelling on passing ships treated the chain as a god and sacrificed to it, rubbing it with oil until it glistened; 'crocodiles do not dare pass over it to do mischief.' However, the Śri Vijayans too behaved no better than pirates. Zhao Rugua accused them of attacking any ships that tried to pass by without coming into port, for they would rather die than let unaccounted ships through their domains.[20] Yet it might be asked whether their location was quite so perfect. The capital, Palembang, does not even lie on the seashore, while the area of Sumatra in which it lies is some distance from the strait that, in later centuries, would form the vital link between the Pacific and the Indian Ocean: the Strait of Malacca. Somewhere like Singapore, at the entrance to those straits, might seem a much better location from which to control trade.[21] Bearing all this in mind, it makes sense to look elsewhere for clues to the special attraction of the kingdom of Śri Vijaya.

II

The answer to the puzzle can be found in writings produced much further west, in Arab and Persian lands. In the ninth and tenth centuries,

Arabic works of geography expressed wonder at the kingdom of Zabaj, which was visited by the merchant Abu Zayd Hassan in the tenth century; he hailed from Siraf on the coast of Iran, at a time when trade through the Persian Gulf, and particularly Siraf, was very lively. This writer claimed that the normal sailing time from Zabaj to China was one month.[22] Although a Tamil inscription of 1088 uses the term *Zabedj* to describe the inhabitants of the camphor-laden lands of north-western Sumatra, and accuses them of being cannibals, this was a word whose meaning was much wider. *Zabaj* can best be translated as 'East Indies' or Indonesia, and is related to the name 'Java', while the name *Sribuza*, obviously a corruption of Śri Vijaya, was used for the main island, Sumatra. Arab travellers were impressed by a fiery volcano in the lands of Zabaj, but they also noted that its king ruled over a considerable empire, which included the trading emporium of Kalahbar, thought to have lain on the western flank of the Malay peninsula, and therefore some distance from Palembang.[23] Zabaj's other wonders included multilingual white, red and yellow parrots that had no difficulty learning Arabic, Persian, Greek and Hindi, and 'beings in human form who speak an incomprehensible language' and who eat and drink like humans – perhaps a description of the Orang-utan, or perhaps another example of a common fantasy about lands over the horizon.[24] Around the same time, the maharajah of Zabaj, ruler of the isles, was reputed to be the richest king in the Indies, thanks to his massive revenues, derived in part from the extensive trade between Zabaj and Oman, which had begun to flourish in the early tenth century.[25] An earlier king had been so rich in gold that a ceremony was concocted to prove the point: every morning the head of his household stood before the king and threw a gold ingot into a tidal inlet beside his palace. As the water receded a golden glow would arise from the inlet. His successor had a more practical attitude, and trawled every last piece of gold from the water; however, he then distributed it to his family, his staff, the royal slaves and even the poor of his kingdom.

Arab writers also knew that Zabaj faced China, which could be reached by sea in a month, or less when favourable winds blew. It lay midway between China and Arabia. Not just its position but its own resources – large brazilwood plantations, massive camphor trees, rich supplies of benzoin resin, and so on – brought it great commercial wealth. In the *Arabian Nights*, Sindbad the Sailor's graphic description of how camphor was extracted has its origins in tales told of Arab merchants who ventured across the Indian Ocean to Indonesia, as the reference to rhinoceros horns (another very desirable item) makes plain:

And on the morrow we set out and journeyed over the mighty range of mountains, seeing many serpents in the valley, till we came to a fair great island, wherein was a garden of huge camphor trees under each of which a hundred men might take shelter. When the folk have a mind to get camphor, they bore into the upper part of the bole with a long iron; whereupon the liquid camphor, which is the sap of the tree, floweth out, and they catch it in vessels, where it concreteth like gum; but after this the tree dieth and becometh firewood. Moreover, there is in this island a kind of wild beast, called 'Rhinoceros', that pastureth as do steers and buffaloes with us . . . It is a great and remarkable animal with a great and thick horn, ten cubits long, amiddleward its head; wherein, cleft in twain, is the likeness of a man.[26]

Arab writers were struck by the simple fact that the rich, fertile countryside covered the whole of the island of Sumatra on which the maharajah resided. There are no deserts! one of these writers exclaimed. The rare spices that could be obtained from Zabaj included cloves, sandalwood and cardamom – indeed, 'more varieties of perfumes and aromatics than any other king possesses'.[27] Stories of Zabaj grew in the telling, and Mas'udi, a tenth-century traveller, asserted that two years would not be sufficient to visit all the islands under the rule of the maharajah. By the tenth century the fame of the maharajah of Zabaj had reached as far west as Muslim Spain. Al-Idrisi from Ceuta in northern Morocco, writing at the court of Roger II, the Christian king of Sicily, in the middle of the twelfth century, was an enthusiastic geographer whose description of the world was more ambitious than anything that had been attempted before. For sure, he knew about Śri Vijaya, even if he had never been near there; he knew that the natural resources of Sumatra attracted merchants keen to obtain its spices; but he also knew why Śri Vijaya had become such an important market:

It is said that when the affairs of China were affected by rebellions and when tyranny and disorder became too great in India, the Chinese transferred their business to Zabaj and the other islands dependent on it, and became friendly with its inhabitants, for they admired their equity, their good behaviour, the agreeable nature of their customs and their good business acumen. This is why Zabaj is so well populated and why it is visited by foreigners.[28]

Yet this was only part of the story, as al-Idrisi also indicated. The inhabitants of Zabaj were not simply passive recipients, who took advantage of their geographical location to host visits by Chinese, Arab and Indian merchants, and sold them the perfumes and spices of their islands. They were also busy navigators, whose voyages reached as far as Sofala on the south-east coast of Africa, where they bought iron that they carried back to India and to their homeland. They were accompanied to these African markets by people from Komr, Madagascar, which makes sense since, as has been seen, the first settlers on the island were not of African origin but hailed from the islands of Indonesia, whose language they carried with them.[29]

This rich evidence for a wealthy kingdom is derived almost entirely from the writings of those who lived outside Śri Vijaya, though a few Arab travellers did visit the kingdom and recorded their impressions. Its own records are few – some inscriptions from Palembang and elsewhere that extol the king of Śri Vijaya as a maharajah (literally, 'great king') above many other kings, and records of conflicts with island neighbours in Java and with mainland neighbours in the Khmer kingdom, whose greatest city was Angkor Wat in Cambodia. One important inscription in Malay dates from the seventh century, when Palembang already possessed 'overseers of trades and crafts'; it also mentions sea captains.[30] And it has to be said that Arabic writers, prone to repeat one another, can leave the impression that there was a wide consensus about a fact or a place, when they actually go back to a single rumour made real; in other words, they are not independent voices.

The capital, Palembang, has yielded rather few significant finds, though the modern city stands on top of the ancient site, rendering very difficult any attempt to identify its medieval buildings. After a team from Pennsylvania declared that there was nothing on the site that was really ancient, further investigation turned up Tang pottery and demonstrated that there were wharves and warehouses all along the northern bank of the river on which Palembang stood, the River Musi. These installations stretched across a distance of twelve kilometres. The archaeologist John Miksic has pointed out how similar this long, narrow town of wharves is to the extraordinary town described in the nineteenth century by the great naturalist Alfred Russel Wallace. What he found at Palembang was a 'city' about half as long as the medieval evidence suggests, but one that consisted simply of a strip along the river bank; the houses stood on stilts above the River Musi, and Zhao Rugua had already pointed out that everyone in Śri Vijaya lived either 'scattered about outside the city, or on the water on rafts of boards covered over with reeds', which enabled them to claim exemption from government taxes.[31] In the nineteenth century, only the sultan and a couple of his chief advisers lived on land, on low hills close to the river. The building material was wood, which decays easily; however, it can be taken for granted that the maharajah lived in some style, in a large wooden palace with finely decorated timbers, the lineal ancestor to the fifteenth-century royal palace at Melaka described in the *Malay Annals* and now handsomely reconstructed in modern Melaka.[32] As for the extensive town walls described by Zhao Rugua, sections of earth ramparts, probably from the seventh century, have been discovered. The use of brick and stone was rare, though in 1994 the stone foundations of a seventh-century temple were uncovered by French and Indonesian archaeologists. And yet there was enough debris to indicate that Palembang had trading links with both China and India; 10,000 fragments of imported pottery were excavated in the centre of Palembang, though only 40 per cent were actually of Śri Vijayan date. The temple contained sixty Chinese bowls, admittedly from the twelfth century and therefore deposited after Śri Vijaya had passed its peak; other sites have produced an impressive range of green or white Chinese ceramics, though nothing dating earlier than about 800; the Śri Vijayans particularly liked the glazed greenware fired in Guangdong, in southern China. But another source of fine glazed pottery lay far to the west: iridescent lustre-wares from Arab lands and turquoise pottery made in Persia also arrived in Śri Vijaya during the ninth and tenth centuries. Several statues of the Hindu god Vishnu have also been found, though that is not to say they were actually made in India. A statue of a Buddhist divine being, Avalokitesvara, may date from the late seventh century.[33]

This, then, was a city on the water, a city with length but no breadth whose raison d'être was water traffic. Yet the river poses a problem: a significant objection to tales of the great glories of Palembang is that the site lies some way inland, beside a river, in what was a marshy area – the distance from the coast is eighty kilometres, but more if river traffic had to wend its way upriver – and arguments that the coastline lay much further inland in the early Middle Ages have not won universal approval.[34] Still, a major oceanic port can develop some way inland. Seville is a perfect example, and neither Canton nor London stands on the coast. The shores of Sumatra were no doubt dotted with settlements that provided ready services to shipping that did not come all the way up to Palembang itself. Śri Vijaya was not a myth, but that does not mean that its period of efflorescence was as long as has often been assumed. Palembang was at its peak in the seventh to ninth centuries. Later, competitors in Java, Malaya and elsewhere blunted the power of the maharajah.

That is to assume the power of the maharajah was in some sense 'imperial'. Here too care is required. Rather than thinking of a centralized empire stretching over hundreds of islands and as far as the Malayan peninsula, one should think of a commercial hub at Palembang, a wealthy and militarily powerful city ruled by a widely respected king; but whether, as the oriental scholars who first translated Sanskrit, Chinese and Arabic texts concerning Śri Vijaya assumed, these texts speak of empire and provincial governors is a moot point. Maybe the term *vanua Śri Vijaya* on one of the

Sanskrit inscriptions from Palembang was intended to convey the impression not of an 'empire', as once translated, but of a much more modest region under the direct authority of the maharajah. Maybe too the idea that this inscription talks of 'provincial governors' is a misconception, and it really describes autonomous regional lords who, given half the chance, would reject the authority of the maharajah, but were kept under sufficient pressure to maintain their ambiguous and insincere loyalty. The Javanese rulers also received tribute from lesser rulers in Borneo, the Moluccas and eventually Malaya and northern Sumatra, while not neglecting the usefulness every now and again of sending an embassy to the Son of Heaven in China and acknowledging his remote and very loose overlordship.[35]

Sometimes, as in 853 and 871, embassies from Indonesia to China came not from Śri Vijaya but from rival states, suggesting that Śri Vijaya did not enjoy a total monopoly on trade with China. Malayu, later known as Jambi, fell under the control of Śri Vijaya, according to the monk Yijing; and yet it had earlier sent its own embassies to the Tang court. On Java, a number of rulers did the same, and occasionally fought wars against Śri Vijaya.[36] And then there were parts of Sumatra and lands nearby that became rich because of their association with the ruler of Palembang. Barus stood on the opposite side of the island from Palembang, facing the Indian Ocean. Here, as at Palembang, archaeologists have begun to unearth goods brought from as far away as Egypt, Arabia, Persia and India, including not just ceramics but pieces of glass in nearly all the shades of the spectrum, precious stones and other beads, as well as coins, not forgetting 17,000 fragments of Chinese porcelain from the late tenth century up to about 1150. The character of the ceramics found at one of these sites in Barus is remarkably similar to the character of the ceramics accumulated by the inhabitants of Fustat, or Old Cairo, in the same period. So we could think of Barus as one of the links in the chain connecting southern China to the capital of the Fatimid Empire on the River Nile. Barus was also a centre of production, where one could buy bronze caskets and statuettes, made locally from Sumatran copper and tin. As for the inhabitants, they must have been a varied bunch of people, Sumatrans alongside Arabs, Nestorian Christians from Persia and Tamils from India, though many merchants and other travellers were temporary residents, waiting for favourable winds. It would be good to know how Barus was linked, politically and commercially, to Palembang; and the obvious, simple answer is that ties varied in intensity as the power of the maharajah waxed and waned.[37]

All this begins to make the 'empire' of Śri Vijaya look rather like a loose

1. Polynesian boats used several shapes of sail. This boat is equipped with a claw sail, and an outrigger is attached, adding greatly to its stability. Such boats have sailed the Pacific for millennia.

2. By the ninth century AD Polynesian navigators had settled the Hawai'ian archipelago. This early image of a boat with a claw sail, carved on a rock in Maui, may date back to the early settlements.

3–4. Around 1450 BC the female pharaoh Hatshepsut sent a fleet down the Red Sea to collect myrrh, ivory, ebony and exotic animals from the 'Land of Punt'. Her expedition was commemorated in her funerary temple near Luxor, which contains inscriptions describing her fleet as the first to have been sent out since 'the olden days'. The detail, showing men loading two ships with sacks of goods and entire frankincense trees, is clearer in the line drawing below.

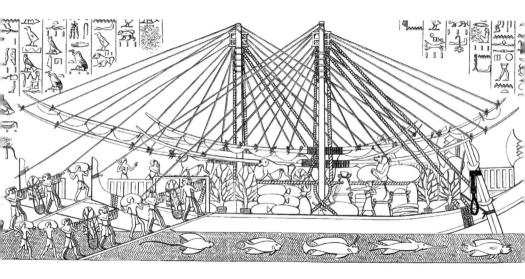

5. Four gazelles on a seal of the late third millennium BC from the trading centre of Dilmun (Bahrain).

6. An Indian seal of the fourth or fifth century AD showing a sewn-plank ship. Similar ships were probably sailing the Indian Ocean two millennia earlier.

7. A coin of the Roman emperor Victorinus minted in Cologne c.AD 270, found in Thailand.

8. Head of a Persian or Arab merchant, seventh or eighth century AD, from Thailand.

9. White porcelain ewer, decorated with the image of a phoenix, that reached Cairo from China c.AD 1000.

11. Multilingual copper plates from Kollam, in south India, of AD 849 testify to the presence of Zoroastrian, Jewish and Muslim merchants.

10. Sixth-century intaglios from Oc-èo in southern Vietnam, the meeting point of traders from China and Persia.

12. Reconstruction of a typical Arab sewn-plank ship based on the ninth-century Belitung wreck from Indonesia. The ship may have been travelling from the Chinese imperial court to an Indonesian ruler carrying gifts in return for tribute.

13. The Belitung wreck contained 70,000 pots, the largest collection of late Tang pottery ever found, including many pieces from Changsha in central China. It probably carried silk as well, but that has disintegrated.

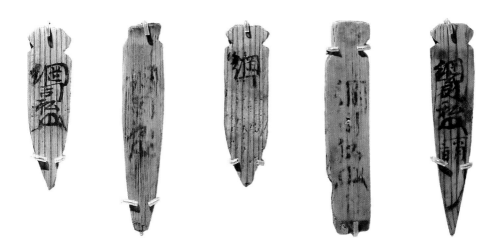

14. In 1323 a Chinese junk was wrecked off the coast of Korea, carrying more than 8,000,000 coins to Japan. Tags such as these were attached to bundles of coins, indicating that the voyage was carried out on behalf of the Tōfuku-ji monastery in Kyoto.

15. The same wreck contained a large cargo of top-quality celadon decorated with animal motifs.

16. Medieval Chinese currency consisted of low-value copper coins strung together. Drainage of bullion out of China led the Song and Yuan emperors to create a paper currency.

17. An early fourteenth-century scroll commemorating the heroism of the warrior Takezaki Suenaga in the wars against the Mongols. Here a Mongol ship is under attack from Japanese warriors in 1281.

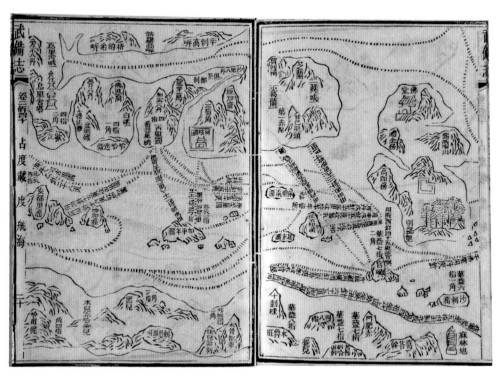

18. A seventeenth-century printed map of the voyages of Admiral Zheng He at the start of the fifteenth century. His ships reached east Africa and the Red Sea.

19. A late medieval image of a sewn-plank ship bound from Basra in Iraq. Black slaves bail out water and work on deck, while Arab, Persian and Indian passengers sit below.

feudal relationship, when it worked at all. It was a political network generally dominated by Śri Vijaya, in which the maharajah had to accept the
autonomy of his neighbours, who for the most part recognized his general
claim to be their sovereign, but carried on as far as possible without allowing him to interfere, and were perfectly prepared to challenge his authority
at the first sign of weakness – hence, indeed, his large armies and navies.
In return, these neighbours were allowed to take part in the trade that
linked Śri Vijaya to India and China, but in a subordinate role. And this
explanation of how Śri Vijaya functioned also makes sense because it
shows how the greatest resource of the maharajah, his prosperous riverside
port at Palembang and the region close by, kept him afloat politically and
financially – it was an enormous source of strength, backed up by his
armies and, as will be seen, his navies too. In this view, Śri Vijaya flourished and survived precisely because it was not an empire, and not even a
centralized state, but the focal point of a trading network with offshoots
around the southern edges of the South China Sea and even as far west
as Kedah on the Indian Ocean shores of Malaya.[38]

III

This uncertainty about whether the Arabic and Chinese accounts of the
empire of Śri Vijaya are grossly exaggerated (for they are certainly exaggerated in some degree) does not compromise the basic argument: that Śri
Vijaya flourished as a mid-point between China and India, looking in both
directions and servicing the trade of both great landmasses; and in doing
so it functioned both as an entrepôt where the goods of India and China
could be exchanged by visiting merchants, and as a place to which to turn
in search of the spices and perfumes that were native to Indonesia and
Malaya. Yet there is still an important element missing. Who were these
merchants? Some were clearly Indian and Arab, and Chinese also arrived
as knowledge of these waters grew. References in Chinese writings to the
Bosi led the pioneers of the history of south-east Asia to conclude that
they were Persian, which is the literal meaning of the Chinese term. Some
certainly were Persian like Yazd-bozed, a late eighth-century merchant
whose name appears on a jar found in a shipwreck off Thailand in 2013.
But identifying merchants is never simple. Cargoes of *Bosi* goods were
carried across the Indian Ocean, and the term in that context evidently
meant not just the exotic produce of Persia and the Persian Gulf, but goods
from the Muslim world as a whole. *Bosi* was a generic term for Arabs as
well, since the Chinese often failed to distinguish between these two sets of

people, even though the Arab lands were also known as *Dashi* and there were large settlements of Muslim merchants within China itself.[39]

Ethnic muddles of this sort are exceptionally common, and the earnestness with which scholars of the Orient have chased these will-o'-the-wisp terms round and round provides more entertainment than enlightenment. However, accepting that the term *Bosi* refers to Western goods, one then needs to ask who actually carried them towards Śri Vijaya; and here, alongside Indian and Arab merchants, a prominent place has to be found for Malays or Indonesians who, as has been seen, ventured as far as Madagascar and east Africa at this period, and were also found in China – in AD 430 an Indonesian embassy took ship for China with gifts of cloth from as far away as India and Gandhara. The king of Java wanted the emperor to promise not to interfere with his ships and merchants.[40] Indonesian and Malay sailors looked in the other direction too, and the crucial link between the Indian Ocean and the South China Sea, the Strait of Malacca, fell for a time at least under the sway of the ruler of Śri Vijaya.[41] Although it is not possible to describe the Malay and Indonesian ships in any detail, it comes as no surprise that the inhabitants of the peninsula and islands around the South China Sea should have taken to the water, first to exchange goods among themselves, and then to range much farther afield.[42]

Several shipwrecks discovered at the end of the twentieth century in Indonesian waters have, in a very short period of time, massively enlarged knowledge of how the connections between China, Indonesia and India worked. The word 'massively' is doubly appropriate, since the quantity of finds is staggering: 55,000 ceramic objects were recovered from the Belitung shipwreck out of an estimated cargo of 70,000 pots weighing twenty-five metric tons; and roughly half a million pots were raised from the Cirebon shipwreck found off the north-west coast of Java. The estimated weight of the cargo carried by this ship is as much as 300 metric tons.[43] The shipwrecks of the South China Sea compensate handsomely for the lack of finds on land, especially at Palembang itself.

The Belitung shipwreck was found off the coast of an Indonesian island midway between Sumatra, Borneo and Java.[44] The wreck took place not far from Palembang, but due east of the town; it is more likely, as will be seen, that the ship was Java-bound. Its date can be established without much difficulty: there is a mirror that carries the Chinese date equivalent to 759, a bowl from Changsha in central China that carries the date 826, and there are coins of a type minted from 758 to about 845.[45] It lay in shallow waters, where it was discovered by divers looking for sea cucumbers, and it had apparently struck a reef about three kilometres offshore; since no human remains were found in the shipwreck, it seems that the crew and passengers managed to escape to dry land.[46] It had not suffered violent damage; its cargo of pottery was nearly all intact – the pots and bowls had been carefully packed in larger storage jars by people who knew how to protect fragile ceramics from the turbulence of the sea.[47] It was constructed out of a variety of woods, but some of this material came from east Africa, and the planks were lashed together in the traditional Indian Ocean way.[48] The ship was not Chinese, but one passenger must have been Chinese, and perhaps a monk, for an inkstone, engraved with the image of an insect, of the sort used in Chinese calligraphy, was found in the wreck. Something too can be said about life on board: bone dice and a board game filled idle hours.[49]

As revealing as the ship itself are the goods carried on board. The first item to bear in mind is one that is too fragile to have survived centuries of immersion in seawater, but one that is known from Chinese and Arabic writers to have been a favourite import from China into the Indian Ocean: silk cloth. An inscription from a Buddhist monastery at Nakhom Si Thammarat, an ancient city in Thailand on the shores of the South China Sea, refers to 'banners of Chinese silk', and dates from a period when the region was under the influence, or possibly dominion, of Śri Vijaya; but Chinese silk travelled much farther afield, and on occasion the covering of the Ka'aba in Mecca was made from Chinese silk.[50] Turning to what has actually survived on the site, the ceramics command immediate attention. The early ninth century saw a vigorous expansion of trade in Chinese glazed ceramics, both from northern China (whence they were ferried by river and canal down to ports in the south, especially Guangzhou), and from Changsha in central China, a city located a long way from the sea, but famous for its quite massive industrial output of pottery. Demand for good-quality ceramics was closely linked to the spread of a new and important fashion: tea-drinking.[51] The Belitung wreck contains the largest collection of late Tang pottery ever found: white pottery from northern China, green wares from southern China, as well as gold and silver vessels and bronze mirrors. A single blue and white bowl is the ancestor of the blue and white porcelain that came to dominate the external trade of China over many centuries, and was imitated centuries later in Portugal and Holland.[52] Another unique bowl shows a ship being attacked by a massive sea monster; this is the earliest depiction of an ocean-going ship in Chinese art.[53] The wreck contained several beautiful examples of the Chinese goldsmith's art, unquestionably objects of high luxury.[54]

The cargo is so impressive that it is easy to conclude that at least part of it consisted of the return gifts sent by the Chinese court upon receipt of tribute from the ruler of Śri Vijaya or from one of the Javanese kings – there were at least six embassies to China from Java between 813 and 839.

A Javanese gold coin was found in the wreck. The ninth century was the golden age of Java, the period during which the great temple complex at Borobodur, decorated with more than 500 statues of Buddha, was constructed under the Sailendra dynasty; it is the largest Buddhist temple anywhere.[55] The exchange of gifts, as has been seen, provided the official and very formal framework for bilateral trade overseen by the imperial court, also intended to demonstrate the submission of lesser rulers to the imperial throne. But the quantity of goods, especially pottery, on board the Belitung wreck was so vast that it is clear other interests were also involved: merchants, whether Malay, Indian, Persian or Arab, who sent their orders for fine pottery to the kilns of distant Changsha by way of agents in Guangzhou, and who took advantage of the sailing of an important cargo vessel to book space on board for their own consignments.

This vast cargo of Chinese ceramics has prompted the question whether the ship was bound for the Indian Ocean, rather than Java or Śri Vijaya, particularly since it is quite likely the crew was from there. Moreover, demand for Chinese ceramics had reached such a fever pitch that Abbasid potters in Iraq in the age of Harun ar-Rashid, the period when this ship sank, began to imitate what they saw arriving from the Far East. Still, there was no substitute for the real thing.[56] Some of the pottery found on board was clearly for everyday use, by passengers and crew, and is similar to the turquoise glazed wares produced at this time in Iraq and Iran, which might suggest that the ultimate destination was Siraf deep within the Persian Gulf. Examples of this pottery have been found not just at Siraf but at Barus in Sumatra and at Guangzhou, so it certainly travelled along the entire sea route.[57]

The Belitung shipwreck is not unique. The Intan wreck, found off south-eastern Sumatra, was probably heading to Java, laden with pottery and metal goods, which included many tin ingots, which are likely to have originated in Malaya. Coins found in the wreck date its voyage to between 917 and 942. The combination of Chinese ceramics and Malayan tin suggests that the goods were loaded in some great emporium that gathered together goods from all around the South China Sea, or that the ship itself tramped around the same sea. The variety of the cargo has been described by one of its excavators as 'astounding': small bronze staffs that Buddhist monks used as symbols of a thunderbolt; bronze masks representing the Demon of Time, sometimes used as door fittings; some gold jewellery. It was common practice for merchants from Śri Vijaya to bring copper to China and to have temple decorations cast in bronze there. The presence of tin, the other ingredient of bronze, in the hold of the Intan ship confirms the importance of this movement of raw metal back and forth until it was transformed into gleaming objects in bronze or other metals. For the ship also carried iron bars and silver ingots, plus as many as 20,000 pots and bowls, some of a high quality, and much of it from southern China. Fragments of resin indicate that the ship had called in at a port in Sumatra, while the presence of tiger teeth and bones suggests an interest in rare medicines. The ship itself was not Chinese; but its construction differed from that of the Belitung ship, and it is thought to have been Indonesian, with a displacement of roughly 300 tons and a length of about thirty metres.[58] Its circuit was most likely limited to the South China Sea, whereas the Belitung ship, smaller in size, was better suited to the long voyage that had brought it all the way from Arabia or Persia. Yet another wreck, discovered in Chinese waters, is the so-called Nanhai I, a very large vessel that contained 60,000–80,000 pieces of pottery, mainly porcelain from the Song dynasty, as well as 6,000 coins, the latest of which date from the early twelfth century, although some may be as old as the first century AD. The impression given by the wreck is that this was a Chinese ship and that it was bound from Guangzhou or another port in southern China for a destination in the South China Sea.[59]

This evidence for goods being collected from different corners of the South China Sea on sizeable ships affects how one might think about this space. It has often been compared to the Mediterranean, but the Mediterranean is not an ideal model, for three large continents meet there, while the southern and eastern rims of the South China, Sea are chains of islands separating the sea from the open spaces of the Pacific; and the mainland to the north has always been dominated by China which, even when fragmented, has possessed an economic and political weight far in excess of anything that rulers over Śri Vijaya could hope to achieve.[60] Yet the South China Sea has also been an area in which the great power to the north has taken a relatively passive role in the conduct of trade, compared to the inhabitants of Indonesia, Malaya, Thailand and Vietnam. China, with its massive continental concerns, often looked away from the South China Sea, and yet its rulers valued enormously the produce of far-off lands that came through that sea. And this provided the perfect opportunity for Malay, Arab and other traders to take charge of the maritime trade routes. These, by the seventh century, were routes that spanned vast distances, from the coasts of Arabia and Africa to southern China, bringing together the Indian Ocean and the western Pacific more intimately than had been the case even in the days when Greco-Roman traders penetrated to India and transmitted some of their goods to the Far East. In the era of Śri Vijaya, a network had come into existence that linked together half the world.

9

'I am about to cross the Great Ocean'

I

Śri Vijaya lay at one end of a route that stretched from Alexandria through the Red Sea and around Arabia and India to the Spice Islands. The Red Sea lost and gained primacy during the early Middle Ages, because a rival passageway, the Persian Gulf, also flourished for a while. Which of the two narrow seas was the more important depended on the political convulsions that were taking place within the Middle East, but the really significant point is that the sea route, whether it passed Aden bound for Egypt or the Strait of Hormuz bound for Iraq and Iran, remained busy, functioning not just as a channel along which fine goods from East and West were passed, but as an open duct along which religious and other cultural influences flowed: Buddhist monks, texts and artefacts; and Muslim preachers and holy books. Islam was a new arrival, but Buddhism too intensified its contact and influence in south-east Asia during the early Middle Ages, as it became increasingly fashionable at courts in India, Sri Lanka, Malaya, Indonesia and, along the shores of the Pacific, in China, Korea and Japan. The crisis of the Roman Empire within the Mediterranean during the fifth to seventh centuries, even if it shrank the market for eastern perfumes and spices in the West, did not fatally damage the networks that had come into being in the days of Pliny and the *Periplous*, and the overall sense is of continuity of contact across the seas.

In the decades before the emergence of Islam in the early seventh century the southern Red Sea was a turbulent area.[1] The opposing shores were the seats of kingdoms with radically different religious identities. On the African side, around Axum, a Christian kingdom, Ethiopia, warily watched developments in Himyar, roughly corresponding to Yemen, where the rulers had chosen to adopt Judaism, or possibly were descended from ancient Jewish tribes. Yūsuf, also known as 'he of the locks' (Dhu Nuwas), was the Jewish king of Himyar; he was accused of massacring hundreds of Christians and of desecrating churches. As reports of these killings spread, enthusiasm for a holy war against the Jewish unbelievers mounted. It is important to stress that the accounts of the massacre are found in Christian writings, and – despite the excitement of several modern historians at the sight of Jews ruthlessly persecuting Christians, rather than the other way round – no one really knows whether these reports were just a trumped-up charge to justify an invasion of South Arabia that has been seen as nothing less than a 'crusade'.[2] For in 525 the Ethiopian ruler, encouraged by the Byzantine emperor, invaded with an army said to number 120,000 men; a great navy was constructed and the troops set out from Somalia as well as Ayla at the top of the Red Sea. Yūsuf ordered a massive chain to be stretched across the water, to prevent the enemy from landing; but this ruse did not prevent the Ethiopians from penetrating into Himyar. The Christians gave as good as they had got, not just destroying synagogues but apparently killing large numbers of Himyarites in revenge. This and other campaigns back and forth across the southern Red Sea must have greatly disrupted traffic; and the war of 525 certainly destabilized the region, which became a battleground between the great powers of the Middle East, the Byzantine Empire and the Sasanian Empire in Persia.[3]

Despite these severe crises, there are enough references in Mediterranean writings to traffic from Ethiopia and Yemen reaching as far north as Ayla to suggest that contacts remained alive, added to which finds of Axumite coins and pottery at Ayla confirm the literary evidence. This trade route would have fed into the land routes that passed through the famous city of Petra. Following his conquests in Syria and Palestine, in the early seventh century, Caliph 'Umar promoted Ayla as a centre of maritime trade, and a grid-shaped new town was constructed next to the old Byzantine port. Ayla had easy access to the minerals of Sinai and the Negev that had already captured the interest of past rulers, maybe even King Solomon. By the mid-eighth century, after some interruptions, trade through Ayla was once again in full flow, as was the exploitation of copper mines in the region (the Negev Desert); there was gold there as well. Fragments of textiles made from cotton, linen, goat's hair and silk have survived in the dry desert setting, and they testify to a lively trade reaching Yemen and well into the Indian Ocean. An overland route joined Ayla to Gaza, at this time a major port which functioned as an intermediary between the Mediterranean and the Indian Ocean.[4] Even if the sixth, seventh and eighth centuries appear to have been a relatively, but not totally, quiet period in the trade of the Red Sea, the foundations were being laid for the network linking the Mediterranean to the Indian Ocean that is clearly visible by the tenth century, and that would expand and expand

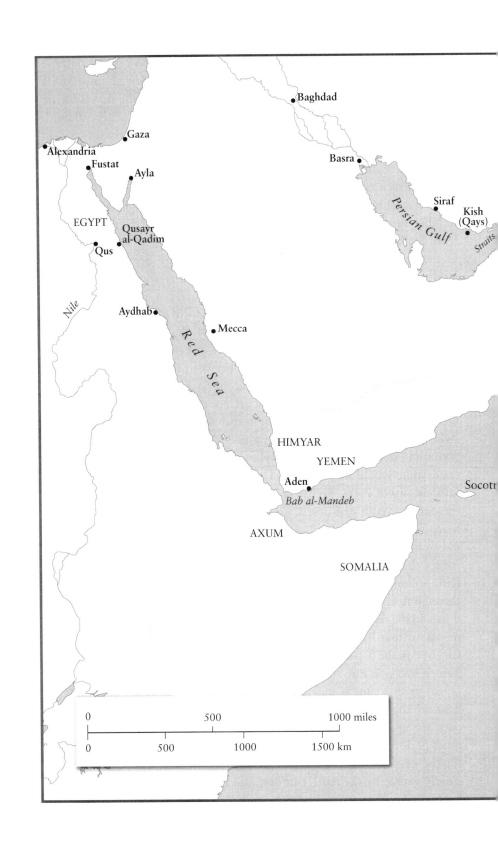

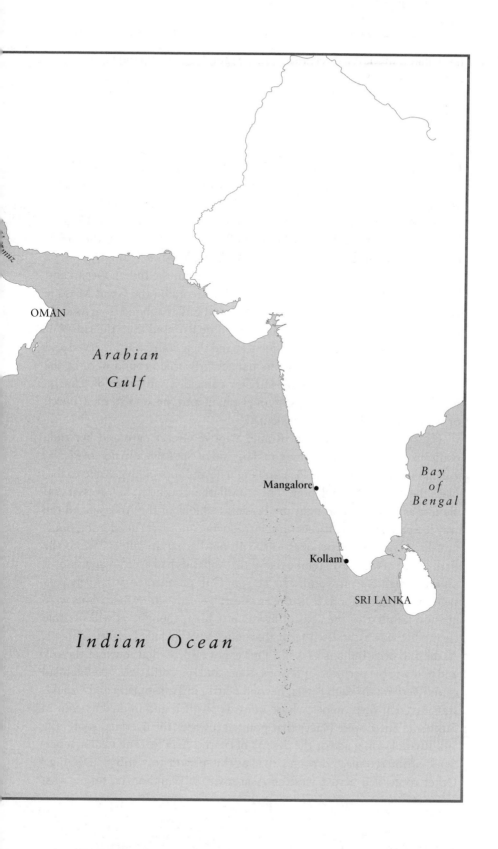

(as demand in the Mediterranean also expanded and expanded) through-out the Middle Ages.[5]

II

But it was not, to use an obvious cliché, all plain sailing. In the middle of the eighth century, the dissensions and rivalries within the Islamic caliph-ate saw a new centre of power emerge in Iraq, at Baghdad, not far from ancient Babylon, where the Abbasid dynasty ruled in place of the Umayy-ads of Damascus, the last of whom had fled to the very ends of the earth, to found the emirate of Córdoba in al-Andalus, Muslim Spain. Damascus had been a glorious city, drawing in luxuries from the Indian Ocean and artists from Byzantium (such as those who decorated the Great Mosque with mosaics). Nothing much survives of mud-built Baghdad from its early days, but the new dynasty became even more exposed than the rulers of Damascus to Persian cultural influence, and their court was observed and envied across the world. This was particularly true around 800, in the days of Harun ar-Rashid, whose reign coincided with that of Charle-magne, to whom he sent gifts of an elephant and the keys to the Church of the Holy Sepulchre in Jerusalem.[6]

The poet Horace wrote of Rome: 'captive Greece captured her rude conqueror'; and much the same could be said of the Arab invasion of Persia, which did not displace the Persian language and took a long while to dis-place the Zoroastrian religion.[7] The scintillating couturier, hairdresser and choir-master Ziryab brought the Persian fashions of the Abbasids all the way to Spain in the eighth century, introducing underarm deodorant, bouf-fant hairstyles and artichokes to the all-but-barbarian lands close to the dark ocean of the West. Yet the rise of the Abbasids had even greater impact on the Indian Ocean world. The Persian Gulf re-emerged as a lively pas-sageway bringing goods from the Far East; 'Persian' (*Bosi*) merchants were already familiar in the coastal towns of China, though, as will become clear, this was a catch-all term that must have included plenty of Jews, Arabs and even Indians as well.[8] This is not to deny that much of the silk and many of the perfumes, precious stones and spices that reached Baghdad came overland through Persia, beyond which, in Transoxiana and Uzbeki-stan, lay rich silver mines whose ore was purified and minted as coin in Bukhara. These were places that pointed towards the overland route, the Silk Road, leading across the deserts of central Asia to Tang China, a net-work of interconnected routes that at this period was still flourishing.[9] Other routes led across western Asia towards Scandinavia, taking vast amounts of silver and swatches of Chinese silk through the empire of the White Bulgars and that of the Jewish Khazars towards the gloomy and frozen lands of the Swedes and their neighbours.[10]

That there were links to China is plain from a statement by the tenth-century Arab geographer ibn Hawqal. Here he is describing the port of Siraf on the Iranian shore of the Persian Gulf:

> Its inhabitants are very rich. I was told that one of them, feeling ill, made his testament; the third part of his fortune, which he had in cash, amounted to a million dinars not counting the capital which he laid out to people who undertook to trade with it on a commission [*commenda*] basis. Then there is Ramisht, whose son Mūsā I have met in Aden, in the year 539 AH [AD 1144–5]; he told me that the silver plate used by him was, when weighed, found to be 1,200 *manns*. Mūsā is the youngest of his sons and has the least merchandise; Ramisht has four servants, each of whom is said to be richer than his son Mūsā. I have met 'Ali al-Nili from the countryside of al-Ḥilla, Ramisht's clerk, and he told me that when he came back from China twenty years before, his merchandise was worth half a million dinars; if that is the wealth of his clerk, what will he himself be worth! It was Ramisht who removed the silver water-spout of the Ka'aba and replaced it with a golden one, and also covered the Ka'aba with Chinese cloth, the value of which cannot be estimated. In short, I have heard of no merchant in our time who has equalled Ramisht in wealth or prestige.[11]

The same Ramisht appeared in letters written by Jewish merchants based in Cairo and in India as the fabulously wealthy owner of massive ships, the sort of businessman whose palatial style of life is celebrated in the *Thousand and One Nights* (as in the case of Sindbad the Sailor, loaded with wealth after his return from his voyages).

Sirafi merchants implanted themselves in many corners of the Indian Ocean: some traded to Zanzibar, while the head of the Muslim community at Saimur, near Bombay (Mumbai), was from Siraf.[12] Other Arab writers describe complex maritime routes carrying dhows laden with goods beyond Ceylon to the Spice Islands and China itself. A ninth-century Arab merchant, whose name was probably Sulayman of Basra, knew China particularly well, and he reported that Siraf was the departure point for the ships carrying goods all the way to China. Whether these were actually Chinese ships is very doubtful, and whether they often went all the way to China is also uncertain, despite a reference to a ship leaving Siraf for China. Very long voyages that involved waiting out the monsoons were best conducted in stages, as the same manuscript indicates later on ('the trading voyages from Oman go, these days, as far as Kalah, then return from there to Oman'). However, Sulayman (or whatever he was called) insisted, against the other evidence, that few Chinese goods reached either his home city of Basra or the Abbasid capital at Baghdad, and that attempts to export cargoes from China had been hampered by fires in the wooden warehouses in China, by shipwrecks and by piracy.[13]

Another author, Abu Zayd Hassan of Siraf, added extra chapters to Sulayman's book, in which he complained that all maritime ties between Siraf and China had been sundered after a rebel named Huang Chao seized power in Guangzhou in 878: 'because of events that occurred there, the trading voyages to China were abandoned and the country itself ruined, leaving all traces of its greatness gone and everything in utter disarray.' His conquest was accompanied by ruthless massacres: 'experts on Chinese affairs reported that the number of Muslims, Jews, Christians and Zoro-astrians massacred by him, quite apart from the native Chinese, was 120,000.' Moreover, the conqueror did the trade and industry of southern China no favours when he cut down the mulberry trees that provided raw silk: 'owing to the destruction of the trees, the silkworms perished, and this, in turn, caused silk, in particular, to disappear from Arab lands.' The rebel leader was defeated, but damage of this order could clearly not be repaired overnight.[14] On the other hand, this writer was perfectly famil-iar with Chinese copper cash which had turned up in Siraf inscribed with Chinese characters. He was surprised that the Chinese had little interest in gold and silver coinage, but relied instead on strings of vast numbers of very low-value coins; the Chinese took the view that it was much more difficult to steal large amounts of money if it consisted of heavy strings of copper coins, each of which was worth only a tiny fraction of a gold dinar. He was also familiar with Chinese painting, drawing and craftsmanship, which, he admitted, was the finest in the world.[15]

Siraf is especially interesting, because, in addition to the testimony of these writers, there is the evidence from excavations conducted by the British Institute of Persian Studies in the 1960s. Siraf turned out to be rather older than had been assumed: inhabited by Zoroastrians, the town acquired the distinctive red pottery of the Roman Empire, and a gold coin of a mid-seventh-century Byzantine emperor, Constans II, was found as well. Its high point was in the ninth to the tenth centuries, but it was already a lively centre of business soon after AD 700. In the eighth century coins from Iraq, Afghanistan, Persia and even Spain were buried in a coin hoard, only to be rediscovered 1,200 years later. During the excavation of what had been the platform of the Great Mosque, plenty of Tang pot-tery from the same period was found. However, in 977 an earthquake damaged the town, and thereafter merchants trading up the Persian Gulf concentrated their attention on the island of Kish (or Qays), which became the seat of a small but successful pirate kingdom, and by the end of the twelfth century Siraf had disappeared off the map. Ramisht lived at a time when Siraf was long past its best. Another factor, to which this chapter will return, was the increasing importance of the rival route taking spices up the Red Sea, following a political revolution in Egypt. At its peak, Siraf was rather less than half the size of the circular inner core of Baghdad, but that actually speaks for its very great size, given the vastness of the Abbasid capital. Shops and bazaars stretched along the seafront for a kilometre or more, which was about half the length of the town. Two-storey buildings with paved courtyards were probably the residences of prosperous merchants and officials, but one building, said to be larger than Hatfield House in southern England (an odd comparison), was, one would imagine, the palace of someone like the merchant-prince Ramisht.[16] The town lay in an unpropitious setting, dry and stony. It was not easy to produce food locally. But, as a citizen of another city set in a rocky land-scape, Dubrovnik, argued several centuries later, the very sterility of the surrounding countryside made trade an imperative.[17]

While it would be a mistake to underestimate the importance of the Persian Gulf in the eleventh and twelfth centuries, changes further west stimulated the revival of Red Sea commerce from the tenth century onwards. The Abbasid Empire began to fragment; the greatest challenge came from the rise to power of the Shi'ite Fatimid dynasty, first in Tunisia (where they founded the city of Qayrawan, 'the caravan', with its Great Mosque), and then in Cairo, where they were able to compete for domination over the Levant. Partly as a result of these political changes, the Mediterranean began to reawaken, and this reawakening was further stimulated by the emergence of Christian trading republics, first Amalfi and Venice, then Pisa and Genoa, that eagerly bought the spices of the East and passed them across the sea to Europe, and then along land and river routes that reached as far as Flanders, Germany and England. And all of these developments had major repercussions in the Indian Ocean as well. The sea routes across the Mediterranean have already been traced in the accompanying volume on 'the Great Sea'.[18] But now it is time to trace a sea route that leads all the way from the Nile to Indonesia and China.

III

By 1000 Persia and Mesopotamia lost their primacy; the Gulf did not exactly become a backwater, for it was home to the pirate kingdom of

Kish, but the old Greco-Roman routes down the other coast of Arabia were reborn. The Red Sea revival is plain from the archaeological record along its shores. From the late ninth century onwards, sherds of Chinese celadons and of white porcelain from distant Jingdezhen appear in excavations as far north as Ayla.[19] Goldmining in Sudan began to produce handsome returns. Egyptian emeralds were exported in the direction of India, and were traded by Chola Tamils from there towards Sumatra and beyond. Further afield, Chinese ceramics arrived in Cairo. An off-white ewer, decorated with an engraved portrait of a phoenix, arrived there by 1000, but now lies in the British Museum. Hundreds of thousands of sherds from shattered Chinese pots have been found on medieval sites in Cairo. As time went by, the strong demand for Chinese porcelain in Egypt prompted Egyptian potters to manufacture their own imitations, but they never compared seriously with the genuine article.[20] Another sign of growing familiarity with celadons and white wares from the Far East was the request to a rabbinical court to investigate whether the impurity attributed in Jewish law to a menstruating woman would be communicated to a porcelain cup were she to touch it. Different categories of goods – earthenware, glass, metalwork – were deemed susceptible to impurity in differing degrees, but what about fine glazed wares from the East?[21]

This curious request comes from the mountain of papers, or rather fragments of paper, that make up the Cairo Genizah documents, most of which were sold to Cambridge University following their discovery in the attic storeroom of the Ben Ezra Synagogue in Fustat, or Old Cairo, at the end of the nineteenth century. The Genizah is not an ordered archive, but a giant rubbish basket, a random assortment of documents thrown away because no one could be bothered to sort out those that might contain the divine name (and thus need to be preserved with reverence, or buried if too dilapidated). Precisely for this reason, the documents, including merchant letters, pages of account books, rabbinic decisions, or *responsa*, magical, medical and religious texts, shed a brilliant light on the daily life of Jews and also Muslims in Egypt between the tenth and the twelfth centuries. In particular, they expose the business affairs of Egyptian Jewish merchants who traded westwards into the Mediterranean, particularly towards Tunisia and Sicily, but who also had very substantial trading interests in the Red Sea and the Indian Ocean up to the late twelfth century.[22] The first scholar to conduct intensive research on this material, S. D. Goitein of Princeton, rather assumed that the character of the trade of these merchants was static, whereas the Red Sea and Indian Ocean trade became increasingly important during the twelfth century, in response to growing demand within the Mediterranean for exotic eastern products used as food flavourings, dyestuffs and medicines. There is a flipside to this argument: the increasing dominance of the Genoese, Pisans and Venetians in the spice trade linking the Levant to Europe, and the success of their navies in dominating the Mediterranean sea routes, prompted the Genizah merchants to turn away from the Mediterranean and to look with greater interest at the opportunities offered by the Red Sea and the route bringing spices from India, where some of them even installed themselves. The letters left by these merchants trading towards Aden and India permit an intimate portrait that goes beyond their account books and reveals their daily life, their contacts with Muslim and Hindu merchants, and the trials and tribulations of those seeking to bring goods across what were for those times vast distances.

In the late tenth century Fustat, long the nucleus of Cairo, was displaced by a new city built a couple of miles away by the new Fatimid caliphs. The new Cairo lay around the imposing citadel of Ptolemaic Babylonia. The creation of a new capital transformed Fustat into a suburb inhabited by non-Muslims: one of its Coptic churches was said to stand on the site where Joseph, Mary and Jesus had taken refuge following their flight into Egypt. Competing legends about the Ben Ezra synagogue went much further back in time, so that it became known as the synagogue Moses had used when he was living in Egypt. Be that as it may, it was certainly the synagogue where another famous Moses, the philosopher Moses Maimonides, based himself after his own flight to Egypt, which had taken him from Córdoba and Fez, both ruled by the hardline Almohad caliphs, all the way to Egypt. Not surprisingly, then, the Genizah documents contain several handwritten letters and discarded notes from the great Maimonides. His brother David was one of the India traders, and when he was drowned in the Indian Ocean in 1169 Maimonides was plunged into despair for several years. David had set out on his journey by sailing down the Nile and then crossing the desert in the company of a caravan to reach Aydhab. Or, rather, that was the intention; David and another Jewish merchant became detached from their companions, and had to make their way to Aydhab without anyone to protect them from bandits. David wrote back to Moses, admitting that everything had gone wrong because he had acted in ignorance:

> When we were in the desert, we regretted what we had done, but the matter had gone out of our hands. Yet God willed that we should be saved. We arrived at Aydhab safely with our entire baggage. We were unloading our things at the city gate, when the caravans arrived. Their passengers had been robbed and wounded and some had died of thirst.[23]

Anyone reading those documents, or indeed this book, might well conclude that robbers, pirates and typhoons made these long-distance journeys risky to the point of foolhardiness.[24] David ben Maimon seems to have thought that when he wrote to his brother from Aydhab. He was also worried about how the boat was built: the sight of an Arab dhow whose planks were tied together by ropes, in the traditional way, could shock a traveller familiar with the vessels that sailed the 'Sea of Tripoli', that is, the Mediterranean: 'we set sail in a ship with not a single nail of iron in it, but held together by ropes; may God protect it with His shield! . . . I am about to cross the great ocean, not a sea like that of Tripoli; and I do not know if we will ever meet again.'[25] They did not, for, once out in the ocean, David's ship went down with all hands.

The Genizah documents have transformed knowledge of the India trade and have shown how torn and discarded letters thought to be of no value can shed more light on the conduct of trade than official records. Yet this material, though quite plentiful, is not unique. And one is bound to ask whether the Jews of Fustat were typical of a society in which, after all, Jews were only a minority. It was obvious, for instance, that Jews were not especially interested in the grain trade, but were very interested in flax and silk. No one can say whether the family ties that bound together Jewish trading families from Sicily, Tunisia, Egypt and Yemen were replicated among Muslim trading families – probably not. That is why it was so exciting when the excavators of the so-called Shaykh's House at Qusayr al-Qadim on the Red Sea found the remains of about 150 documents that had mostly been torn to shreds, but could nonetheless be reconstructed.[26] This material is a little later than the vast bulk of the Genizah documents, but should be looked at now, as the maritime route down the Red Sea into the Indian Ocean is followed stage by stage. The Qusayr documents reveal the business affairs of an early thirteenth-century merchant named Abu Mufarrij, and the information they contain can once again be compared with the archaeological record, including evidence that ceramics arrived in the Red Sea from as far away as China, and gold probably came up the African coast from Kilwa and Zanzibar.

The sheikh was very seriously interested in flour and other foodstuffs, which marks him out from the Jewish merchants of the Genizah: 'to be delivered to Sheikh Abu Mufarrij from the south are: one and a quarter loads of grain and an oil strainer, to be loaded on the vessel *Good Tidings.*'[27] Qusayr was another place in a barren spot, so there was a constant need for basic supplies. It is not surprising that wheat was much more expensive in Qusayr than in the great Egyptian cities; it could cost four times what one would expect to pay in Alexandria and twice what people paid in Cairo.[28] The letters from Qusayr al-Qadim fill out our picture of trade in the region by shifting the emphasis away from the spices and fine goods enumerated in the Genizah documents towards humbler but more vital products such as wheat, chickpeas, beans, dates, oil and rice, the staples of daily existence. The wheat sometimes came in the form of grain, sometimes ground down into flour. The quantities mentioned were considerable: as much as three tons in one document, which was enough to feed four or five households for an entire year.[29] In view of the arid setting in which Qusayr al-Qadim stands, the grain may well have been grown some distance away, whether in the Nile valley, arriving by way of Qus, or in Yemen, in the corner of south Arabia exposed to the monsoon rains. Qusayr was known to Arab writers as *Qusayr furda al-Qus*, meaning 'Qusayr the gateway of Qus' (the word *furda* had overtones of 'government checkpoint', a place where tiresome customs officers would tax everything that came and went).[30] Yemen was certainly seen as an especially important trading partner; the geographer Yaqut ar-Rumi, who was of Greek origin and who died in 1229, wrote of Qusayr: 'there is a harbour for ships coming from Yemen'.[31] Unfortunately it is often hard to work out whether Abu Mufarrij was exporting or importing the products he handled.

Using these documents, we can see what was happening in the upper reaches of the Red Sea, in a port that gave access to the Egyptian trading station at Qus on the Nile, and thence by way of the River Nile to Cairo and Alexandria.[32] Qusayr lay at the closest point to the Nile of any of the Red Sea ports. This did not make Qusayr into a truly major centre of Indian Ocean traffic, and some of its business was directed at other ports within the Red Sea, including those directly opposite that led into the Arabian desert, and pointed towards the holy city of Mecca, which – because of its barren environment – drew in supplies of wheat and other basic necessities from Qusayr and similar small ports. One constraint on Qusayr's growth was the lack of good-quality water; in the nineteenth century, drinking water was brought from a well six miles away, although the water stank of sulphur, while another spring in the area produced saline water laced with phosphorus, which was only good for animals, if that.[33] Still, one should not underestimate Qusayr's importance: fragments of ships have been found there, sometimes used to line graves, and they were taken from both sewn-plank and nailed-plank ships similar to dhows.[34] Ships that arrived in Qusayr would sometimes be taken to pieces and carried on the backs of camels across the desert to Qus, where they would be reassembled and refloated, this time on the Nile.

Sheikh Abu Mufarrij had the support of loyal servants who wrote to him regularly, reporting on what they had despatched:

> By God, by God! Anything you want, let me know. Whatever you, the Master, need, write me a memo and send it through the porters; I will ship off your orders. Upon the delivery of the crops as ordered hereby, you should send us the full payment. Peace be upon you. God's mercy and blessings.[35]

Physical remains from Qusayr confirm the passage through the little town of a great variety of foods brought from all around the Indian Ocean. Some tubers of taro, which is a south-east-Asian vegetable, have been found, along with coconut shells, as well as citron, the large lemon-shaped citrus fruit that was much in demand in Jewish communities, for use during the rituals of the Feast of Tabernacles. Dates, almonds, watermelons, pistachios, cardamom, black pepper and aubergine all appear among the finds from Islamic Qusayr.[36] Archaeology fills out the picture that can be drawn from the sheikh's correspondence. Almonds and eggs comprised a third of one cargo handled by Abu Mufarrij; the letters testify that the town bought fresh and dried fruit, including watermelons and lemons, which were not for export, except perhaps to supply ships in port. The sheikh's overriding desire for grain is nicely matched by the finds of seeds on the site of Qusayr al-Qadim.

The sheikh's agents bought and sold humdrum items such as hawsers and mattocks; but perfumes and pepper were also of interest. Thousands of finds of fragments of cordage confirm that the sheikh's interest in supplying ropes continued over the centuries, and many were evidently used on board ship.[37] So too were clothes, some quite ordinary, such as good-quality *galabiyah*s, and others 'decorated with gold and gems', or woven from pure silk, or 'Ethiopian gowns'. Slaves were not one of his strong interests. Like the Jewish merchants, he was interested in buying large amounts of flax, and he handled fine coral too, probably of Mediterranean origin, because that was where very good coral, bright red in colour, could most easily be obtained.[38] Abu Mufarrij ran something grander than the Qusayr General Stores, but his interests were very eclectic, and he was evidently one of the town's main provisioners, whether in food (especially grain) or in what would have been called fancy goods in the nineteenth century. And now and again he revealed that he was interested in more ambitious trading enterprises. One letter sent to the sheikh explained how some valuable Persian goods would soon arrive by sea on a couple of ships: 'semi-precious stones, pearls and beads'.[39] Abu Mufarrij was well versed in the commercial practices of his day, offering credit and arranging transfers, which avoided the need to handle cash.[40]

The fascination of the Qusayr letters derives from their sheer ordinariness. The sheikh was a wealthy man, at least by the standards of his small, hot, dust-blown town, and the grand trade routes that linked Aydhab and Qusayr to the Far East were not his real concern. Those routes produced great profits for some people, but they had to be serviced, and Qusayr was a convenient service station. It was not a place of high culture – even less so than its ancient predecessors Myos Hormos, on whose remains it stood, or Bereniké, with its profusion of temples to many gods. But eastern influences seeped into Qusayr. These links to a wealthier and more exotic world are well represented by an inscribed ostrich egg, bearing a funerary poem:

> Leave your homeland in search of prosperity; depart! Travelling has five benefits: dispelling grief, earning livelihood, seeking knowledge, good manners and accompanying the praiseworthy. If it were said that in travelling there is humiliation and hardship, desert raid and overcoming difficulties, then certainly the death of the young man is better than his life in degradation between the slanderer and the envious.[41]

A pious pilgrim had perhaps died en route to or from Mecca, and was being commemorated with high honour on a giant African egg – the egg being the symbol of resurrection. Exotic links are also well represented by the fragments of Chinese pottery recovered at Qusayr al-Qadim. The types of pottery found are typical enough: green celadons and white or bluish white wares, the sort of pottery that was becoming familiar on the streets of Fustat in the eleventh, twelfth and thirteenth centuries. If anything, Qusayr produced fewer Chinese objects than one would expect; most of the porcelain passed through the port en route to the great cities – around 700,000 sherds of Chinese pottery have been found at Fustat.[42] However, one influence from China was block-printing. A few Arabic texts have been found in Qusayr which were printed from a carved wooden block, rather as Chinese printed texts were created in this period, and the view has even been hazarded that the blocks used for printing were made in China, and texts were then printed off there and exported to Middle Eastern consumers. These printed texts were used as amulets: 'he who wrote this amulet, and he who carries it, will stay safe and sound.'[43] These amulets may seem banal: praying to stay safe and sound was a natural reaction to the perils of the open sea. Yet they are a reminder that the account books of Abu Mufarrij, or of the Genizah merchants, only tell part of a human story of worries about how to survive in a maritime world full of danger from storms, reefs, pirates and capricious rulers.

IV

Heading down from Aydhab and Qusayr al-Qadim, the strait linking the Red Sea to the Indian Ocean (the Bab al-Mandeb) was of crucial strategic importance. Just beyond the strait, ships entered a small gulf that debouches into the Indian Ocean. There the major centre of exchange was Aden, a thriving town sunk in the crater of an extinct volcano that was well situated to watch comings and goings through the strait.[44] Aden possessed its own resources, which were in part derived from the sea and the coastline: salt, fish and the highly prized whale product ambergris, which was occasionally washed up on the shore and was used in the production of perfume. Water, however, was in short supply, and an ingenious feat of engineering exploited the fact that the town lay within a crater by channelling water that had fallen on higher ground into a series of cisterns. There were even filters that removed some of the impurities from the water as it flowed downwards.[45] Inland and further up the coast towards Oman, there were some fertile and well-watered areas that in good years produced plenty of grain to feed not just Aden but places further away such as Mecca.[46] The overall picture is, then, not vastly dissimilar from that of Siraf: the city flourished as a centre of trade precisely because local resources were rather meagre; and Aden was very well placed to supervise the traffic heading out of the Red Sea towards India, as well as down the coast of east Africa.

This attracted the envy of rivals. The rulers of Kish, or Qays, just inside the Persian Gulf, hoped to gain control of the trade routes not just through the Gulf, which had withered by the mid-twelfth century, but along the southern flank of Arabia, past Oman and Yemen. So in 1135 they attacked Aden, hoping at the very least to seize the port installations and customs house; Aden was already divided between two cousins, one of whom was in charge of the port. The lord of the port offered to surrender and then plied the attackers with so much food and wine that they were unable to resist when the lord's men waded into the staggering mass of invaders, and it was later said that they beheaded so many of them that this district was henceforth known as 'The Skulls'. In reality, Aden was besieged for a couple of months, and relief arrived in the form of two large ships that belonged to Ramisht of Siraf; these were boarded by Adeni troops who were able to attack the aggressors from the rear:

> Finally, Ramisht's two ships arrived. The enemy tried to seize them, but the
> wind was good, so that they were dispersed on the sea to the right and to

the left. The two ships entered the port safely, where they were immediately manned with troops. At this juncture, the enemy could do nothing more, either in the harbour or in the town.[47]

So wrote a Jewish merchant based in Aden to a business partner in Egypt.

Its rulers were well aware that Aden was the jewel in their crown. There were eagle-eyed customs officers who prodded and probed the merchandise that passed through the government checkpoint, or *furda*; detailed records were kept as every piece of cloth was patiently counted in front of the no doubt impatient merchants. This was the sort of treatment Genizah merchants were familiar with from the customs house at Alexandria, and all this acts as a reminder that the high cost of spices was less the result of rarity or even the long voyage that brought them to Aden and Alexandria, than of a sequence of payments to one government after another, not to mention bribes and sweeteners – it would be good to know how much smuggling took place, but Aden looks as if it was the sort of walled and well-guarded city where that was well-nigh impossible.[48] Jews, Christians and other non-Muslims were supposed to pay twice the taxes of the faithful, but the rule was rarely applied. From the *furda*, one door gave on to the harbour front and the other on to the city streets with their multi-storeyed merchant houses built of stone – whether they were quite as tall as the town houses of modern Yemen is uncertain, but the most desirable houses stood near the sea, from which cooling breezes blew that could not reach the lower depths of the crater.[49] The general impression is of communities of diverse origins living peacefully side by side, but the atmosphere changed at the end of the twelfth century, when the sultan insisted that all the Jews of Aden and the rest of Yemen must accept Islam, though foreign merchants passing through seem to have been exempt (presumably because they were the subjects of other rulers, whom the sultan preferred not to annoy). A few Adeni Jews resisted and were beheaded, but even the head of the Jewish community embraced Islam. This event stirred the Jewish world. Maimonides wrote a famous tract in which he counselled the Yemenite Jews to be patient; he saw this forced conversion as a sign that the coming of the Messiah and the redemption of Israel were imminent. However, the persecution waned and the community recovered.[50]

Aden was also a base from which the Cairo merchants sent letters eastwards to India, with information about the state of the pepper market – anticipating where prices would be profitable was fundamental to the business practice of these merchants, who were not mere passive agents.[51] The sailing season out of Aden was, by natural circumstances, well co-ordinated with that of the Mediterranean, with ships setting out for India at the start of autumn, which gave time for goods that were being carried down the Red Sea to reach their eastern Mediterranean destinations from as far away as Sicily, Tunisia and Spain. Aden was therefore a nodal point not just in the Indian Ocean maritime networks, but in what can reasonably be called (before the discovery of the Americas) a global network that stretched from Atlantic Seville to the Spice Islands of the Indian Ocean. Broadly speaking the port was very lively from the end of August to May of the following year. Ships converged on Aden from India, Somalia, Eritrea and Zanj (east Africa), so that Aden became a market where the produce of Africa, Asia and the Mediterranean was exchanged.[52]

V

Moving deeper into the Indian Ocean, the Egyptian merchants who had called in at Aden took advantage of the monsoons to head across the open sea to India. At first sight, the chances of reconstructing the maritime world of India in the tenth to thirteenth centuries might seem slim. Apart from some inscriptions and occasional literary references, the lack of letters and account books appears to be a fundamental obstacle. But this is not the case if the letters of the Jewish merchants from Fustat are taken into account, particularly letters to and from figures such as Abraham ibn Yiju, who actually lived for a while on the coast of India. The Fustat traders had plenty of contact with Indian princes, merchants and shipowners. For instance, Pidyar was an Indian, or possibly Persian, shipowner with whom they dealt; he possessed a small fleet, and employed at least one Muslim captain, of whatever ethnic origin.[53] There were also local Jewish and Muslim shipowners, such as the head of the Jewish community in Yemen, whose brand new ship named the *Kulami* sank five days out of Aden even though it had set out with a sister ship, the *Baribatani*:

> The sailors of the *Baribatani* heard the cries of the sailors of the *Kulami* and their screams and shrieks in the night as the water inundated them. When morning came, the sailors of the *Baribatani* did not encounter any trace or evidence of the *Kulami*, because from the time the two ships had left Aden they had kept abreast of each other.[54]

Distressing as this was, it was a less disastrous fate than that facing a certain ibn al-Muqaddam, whose religion is unknown; after several voyages from Aden to the Malabar Coast he lost his ship at sea, replaced it, and lost the replacement. These were not everyday occurrences; they are known from the legal cases that then arose – it was very important in Jewish law to be able to certify that those who had been shipwrecked had indeed died, so that any widows could remarry without fear of the particularly severe but fortunately quite rare bastardy that any new children would bear if the first husband were still alive.[55]

Remarkable Indian inscriptions survive that shed light on the maritime connections and town life of the Indian coast around this time. The light they shed is obscured by the great difficulty in making sense of a series of copper plates in the difficult Malayalam language. They are legal documents, such as a royal grant of land and privileges to a Christian church, and they were inscribed in the port city of Kollam, or Quilon, in the far south-west of India not far from Ceylon, in AD 849. Important privileges were preserved in this permanent form in order to express the intention that they would hold 'for as long as the Earth, the Moon and the Sun shall endure'. The simple fact that the texts carry signatures in several scripts brings into focus the ethnic and religious diversity of the major trading towns along the coast of India at this period: twenty-five witnesses to these texts wrote their names in their everyday alphabet and language, whether Arabic and Middle Persian (written in Arabic script) or Judaeo-Persian (written in Hebrew script); some were Jews, others Christians, Muslims, Hindus or Zoroastrians, who described themselves uncompromisingly as 'those of the Good Religion'. The copper plates mention the two guilds that brought together merchants trading out of Kollam; one, called 'Manigraman', specialized in Sumatra and the Malay peninsula, and the other, 'Ancuvannam', looked in the other direction entirely, towards Arabia and east Africa. While the Sumatra-bound merchants were themselves south Indian Tamils, those trading towards Asia were Arabs, Persians and Jews, the sort of people who signed the copper plates. The guilds operated under royal supervision; as one of the plates states: 'all royal business whatsoever, in the matter of pricing commodities and suchlike, shall be carried out by them.' What this meant was that the guilds, on behalf of the rajah, would collect taxes on the goods that came and went through the port and out of the land-gates.[56] This also shows that the rajah believed he could trust both native and foreign merchants to act responsibly on his behalf; it was only natural that he should show such a warm welcome to the foreign traders, because without them Kollam would have been nothing, and his own income would have shrivelled.

In 851, at almost the moment when these plates were being prepared, the Muslim merchant probably named Sulayman placed on record his voyages around the Indian Ocean and beyond, as far as China, to which he devoted most of the space in his book. Sulayman knew about the place he called Kûlam of Malaya (which here signified Malabar, not the Malay peninsula), that is, Kollam; he placed it a month's sailing beyond Muscat in south-east Arabia. He knew that ships arrived here from as far away as China. He saw Kollam as the major interchange point between the trade of the eastern and the western Indian Ocean, which matches closely what is known about the activities of the two merchant guilds.[57] As far as he was concerned, the sea route was the obvious way to China. No doubt different places along the Malabar Coast enjoyed greater success at different times. In Sulayman's time, the route from Siraf and the Persian Gulf to India was particularly active; but Sulayman was active before Fatimid Egypt took command of the maritime routes across the western Indian Ocean. Therefore it is no surprise that the copper documents mention Muslims and Jews of Persian origin, while the Genizah letters survive from an era when Jews and Muslims of Egyptian or even Tunisian origin were just as likely to be found in the coastal cities of southern India.[58]

The risks of travel did not prevent ambitious Fustat merchants from reaching India, rather than simply relying on the Indian and Muslim shippers who reached Aden. The greater the risks, the higher the profits. In the mid-twelfth century a group of Jews, including Salim 'the son of the cantor' and several goldsmiths, set out from Aden to Ceylon in partnership with a very wealthy Muslim merchant named Bilal. Ceylon was considered a good source of cinnamon. A north African merchant who had been living in Fustat, Abu'l-Faraj Nissim, went to India to buy camphor. He wrote to his family saying the voyage had been a terrible experience, but he managed to buy plenty of camphor, worth at least 100 dinars, and sent it to Aden, where it arrived safely. Two years passed and nothing was heard of him, so it was time to divide the profits from his shipment.[59] A happier fate awaited the ben Yiju family, very active in Mediterranean trade but also seriously interested in the produce of the Indies. This family provides a marvellous example of how spices were transmitted all the way from India to major Mediterranean cities such as Palermo and Mahdia, a flourishing centre of exchange on the coast of Tunisia. Abraham ben Yiju set out for India in around 1131, and one of his correspondents commiserated with him for his difficult journey, but prayed that God would 'make the outcome good', that is, bring him great profit.[60]

In 1132 Abraham found himself at Mangalore on the Malabar Coast. This area was known as far away as China, where, in the early thirteenth century, the geographer Zhao Rugua described the people as dark brown, with long earlobes; they wore colourful silk turbans and sold pearls fished locally, as well as cotton cloth; they used silver coins and they bought silk, porcelain, camphor, cloves, rhubarb and other spices that arrived from further east, but in his day (he claimed) few ships made the long and difficult journey from China.[61] This was a pessimistic judgement, echoing, consciously or otherwise, the reservations of the ninth-century merchant Sulayman about Chinese trade with Iraq, because the quantities of Chinese goods found in Egypt and other parts of the Middle East prove that contact was intense and continuous, and also very profitable. For Abraham ben Yiju prospered while he was based in Mangalore. He bought a slave girl there; he then freed her, which had the effect in Jewish law of converting her to Judaism (he gave her the Hebrew name Beracha, or 'Blessing'), and after that he married her and raised a family. Meanwhile, he was sending goods up and down the coast of western India; he made a lengthy visit to Aden around 1140, but he stayed most of the time in India until 1149.

Abraham set up a factory where bronze goods were produced – trays, bowls, candlesticks, sometimes quite intricate in design, to judge from a letter from Aden ordering some custom-made metalwork from him. He imported arsenic from the West, for he was told there was strong demand for it in Ceylon, where it was used in medicine. He brought in Egyptian cotton, and sent out iron, mangoes and coconuts, working with Muslim, Jewish and *Banyan*, or Hindu, partners. The Muslim partners of ben Yiju included the wealthy merchant of Siraf, Ramisht, whose large ships were well trusted; but even then things could go badly wrong, for one letter says that two of his ships were 'total losses', including valuable cargo belonging to Abraham ben Yiju.[62] Wealthy merchants needed some resilience; it was important not to place all one's eggs in the same basket. Not for nothing did they interest themselves in a variety of goods, for one never knew what would prove most profitable, however closely one read letters coming in from Palermo, Alexandria, Fustat and Aden, with their information about prices, political conditions and which merchants should be trusted.

Among the goods that Abraham ben Yiju appreciated most were consignments of paper, which was in short supply in India and even in Aden, for, as his correspondent in Aden wrote, 'for two years now, it has been impossible to get any in the market'.[63] Foreign merchants such as ben Yiju preferred using paper to writing on palm leaves or cloth, and ben Yiju had special reason to want more paper, as he was something of a poet in his spare time, and, even if his own poetry was not much good, he admired the great Spanish writers who in his day were producing beautiful religious poetry that was soon to be incorporated into the Jewish liturgy. He dabbled in Jewish law and took part in a religious court of law, or *bet din*, in India – there seems to have been another Jewish court at Barygaza, the ancient centre of the Indian Ocean trade in the north-west corner of India.[64] All this suggests that he was far from alone in Mangalore; there were other Jews up and down the coast, and there must have been even larger communities of Muslim merchants, not to mention the Indian merchants who sailed westwards but also (along with the Malays) ensured that connections to Malaya and Indonesia, and even China, were maintained. The news network of which he was part extended all the way from India to Sicily and perhaps Spain. Now wealthy, he had hoped to settle for the rest of his days in Mahdia or somewhere near there; but just after he left India for Aden he heard that the king of Sicily had conquered the coast of Tunisia (he assumed that there had been massacres, but the conquest was relatively peaceful).[65] It is hard to recover a sense of what it was like to live in Mangalore, so far from home; but the nostalgia for north Africa that ben Yiju showed when he had made his fortune reveals that he saw his trading career in India as just that, a career which would eventually, if luck held, make him rich enough to return to the land of his ancestors, taking with him his Indian wife and his children, for whom this would be a new world.

The Malabar coast looked in two directions, as it had in Roman times. The Chinese geographer Zhao Rugua remarked that one could reach that part of India from Śri Vijaya 'in little more than a month'.[66] Not very often, but sometimes, Jewish traders ranged far beyond India. A tenth-century book called *Wonders of India* was composed by a Persian author called Buzurg, but written in Arabic. Buzurg told the 'curious tale' (his own words) of Isaac the Jew who was sued by a fellow Jew in Oman and took flight to India somewhere around AD 882. He was able to take his goods with him, and for thirty years no one back in the West knew what had happened to him. In fact, he had been making a fortune in China, where he was taken for an Arab (as Jewish traders often were). In 912–13 he turned up in Oman once again, this time aboard his own ship, whose cargo was estimated to be worth 1,000,000 gold dinars, and on which he paid a tax of 1,000,000 silver dirhams. This may have amounted to a tax of about 12 per cent and it kept the local governor happy, but it also aroused the jealousy of other merchants who had no hope of supplying treasures of comparable quality. (Since a lower-middle-class family could subsist quite well on twenty-four dinars per annum, 1,000,000 dinars can be thought of as comparable to nearly 1,000,000 pounds sterling or more than a billion and a half dollars, though such comparisons are not particularly meaningful.)[67] Silks, Chinese ceramics, jewels and high-quality musk were just some of the exotic goods he brought to Arabia. So after three years he decided he had experienced enough hostility, and commissioned a new ship, which he filled with merchandise, and sailed east in the hope of reaching China once again. This meant that he had to pass 'Serboza', which must be the maritime kingdom of Śri Vijaya. Its rajah saw a good opportunity to mint money, and demanded a fee of 20,000 dinars before he would let him leave for China. Isaac objected and was seized and put to death that very night. The rajah expropriated the ship and all the merchandise.[68]

Later generations were more circumspect about making such ambitious voyages. The Genizah merchants were generally content to stay in India or even Aden, and to wait for Chinese goods to reach them; these included the glazed porcelain bowls that aroused such concern about their ritual purity should they be touched by a menstruating woman.[69] India was the interchange point between what at first sight appear to be two trading networks, or even three: from Egypt via Aden to the Malabar Coast, and from the Malabar Coast to Malaya and Indonesia, with a further extension to Quanzhou and other Chinese ports.[70] But when the goods traded come under consideration this looks more like a single line of communication linking Alexandria in the Mediterranean to China, along which silk, spices, porcelain, metalwork and also religious ideas were transmitted, along with all those humdrum materials – wheat, rice, dates, and so on – in which the sheikh of Qusayr, among many others, mainly dealt.

VI

The twelfth century saw important changes in the character of the merchants who passed up and down the Red Sea, even though the goods they carried probably did not alter very significantly, except to increase in volume. The increasing sensitivity of the Muslim rulers to the presence of non-Muslims in the Red Sea was in large part the result of the attempt by a crusader lord, Reynaud de Châtillon, to launch a fleet on the Red Sea during the 1180s, with the aim of attacking Mecca and Medina, and of launching pirate raids on traffic passing through the Red Sea. Although Reynaud's activities were suppressed, his pirates came dangerously close to Medina; this resulted in the closure of the Red Sea to non-Muslims.[71] A corporation of Muslim merchants was created in Egypt who excluded the old generation of Genizah merchants from the India trade. These *karimi* merchants, as they were known, benefited from the goodwill of the government in Cairo, which saw how profitable taxation of the spice traffic could be.[72]

Yet the intimate relationship between Egypt and India continued, and the flow of precious metals that resulted from these exchanges can be likened to a pair of rivers that converged on India. India was, as it always has been, a land in which a rich elite lived a luxurious life far removed from the daily grind of the poor, and the same picture can be painted of medieval China. Payments for Indian luxuries continued to flood into the coffers of the rajahs, in gold and silver, and some of this income was spent on courtly magnificence and warfare. But the *thésaurisation* (to use a handy French word) of bullion flowing in from the West and from China proceeded apace, as the treasuries of Indian princes immobilized the precious metals that came into the country; Egypt, Syria and north Africa found themselves short of silver, which was needed for smaller payments, though expedients to solve the problem included glass tokens and lead coins. They could obtain silver from northern Iran, to some extent; but Iranian silver tended to drain towards Baghdad. They could obtain silver from western Europe; and the growing demand there for eastern spices, from the late eleventh century onwards, meant that merchants from Venice, Genoa and Pisa were keen to establish a presence in Alexandria and other Levantine cities, and to pay in white money for prodigious amounts of pepper, ginger and other Indian or Indonesian goods. It will be seen too that vast amounts of Chinese cash were being taken out of the Middle Kingdom towards surrounding lands, including Japan and Java. It is often said that the beating of a butterfly's wings can affect the climate of the whole world. It can at least be said that the transactions which took place along a series of maritime trade routes that stretched from Spain – and eventually the Atlantic – to Japan had knock-on effects capable of reaching far down the line. Setting aside the Americas, still unknown to the inhabitants of other continents (ignoring for the moment the Norsemen), a global network existed, one that had gained in strength and permanence since the days of the Greco-Roman trade towards India.

10

The Rising and the Setting Sun

I

As well as merchants and travellers from the Far West, merchants and travellers from lands further east – Japan and Korea – converged on China. It has long been assumed that trade had little impact on daily life in Japan. A classic account of Japan in the years around 1000 simply states: 'trade and commerce played a minimal part in the country's economy.'[1] In this view, everything really depended on the cultivation of rice and other basic necessities, and we see the gradual emergence of a society in which power was exercised through control over landed estates, a system with many similarities to the feudalism of medieval Europe. But this is greatly to simplify a much more complex picture. At court, whether in Korea or Japan, the desire for access to Chinese culture was overwhelming; and that contact was effected by sea and was made real through the transfer of people, objects and texts. Moreover, Chinese cultural influence became so powerful that these neighbours started to imitate the Chinese imperial court and began to see themselves as imperial powers in their own right. By virtue of his mastery, real or imagined, over parts of Korea, the Japanese ruler asserted in a cheeky letter sent to the Chinese emperor in 607 that 'the Son of Heaven in the Land of the Rising Sun sends this letter to the Son of Heaven in the Land Where the Sun Sets'.[2] Even so, the Japanese emperors were realistic: they still sent occasional tribute to their supposed Chinese counterpart. The Chinese paid no respect to these claims to equality, and the Japanese learned that it was more diplomatic (in the modern sense of the word) to use a Japanese term, *sumera mikoto*, 'Great King who rules under All Heaven', for their own emperor in the credentials their envoys presented, which the Chinese conveniently pretended was just his personal name.[3]

It is hardly surprising, then, that the history of Sino-Japanese relations begins cordially, turns sour and ends with a break. The mariners who set

out from Japan towards Korea and China, across often difficult seas, were Japanese and Korean; once again the Chinese took a passive role, and embassies from China to Japan were a rarity.[4] As Sir George Sansom pointed out, 'the phenomenon of Japan's isolation is a comparatively late feature in her history.'[5] On the other hand, there is little to say about Japan's links to the Asian mainland before the first millennium AD. Japanese raids across the sea afflicted Korea in the first century BC and are recorded in the official Korean chronicles: 'Year 8 [50 BC], the Wae [Japanese] came with troops intending to invade our coastal region but, hearing of the Founder Ancestor's divine virtue, they withdrew.'[6] There was some contact with the Han Chinese at the start of the millennium, with embassies reaching China and Korea in the first century, but Japan was not of enormous interest to the Chinese: it was seen as a land of warring kinglets (which it would become again in later centuries); its inhabitants 'are much given to strong drink', but many of them live till they are a hundred, and robbery and theft are rare – certain things have changed little in Japan.

One important feature of early Japan was its great ethnic variety, with native peoples in north and south (Hokkaido and Kyushu islands) refusing to submit to central authority. Only in the late seventh century did the rulers of much, though not all, of central and southern Japan begin to use the name *Nihon*, or *Nippon*, 'Land of the Rising Sun', from which the Western term 'Japan' is derived; and even then the ancestors of the Ainu, now few in number, dominated the cold expanses of Hokkaido. Korean culture had an enormous impact on early Japan, and there were close, and not always friendly, ties between the rulers of Japan and those of Silla, one of the Korean kingdoms that lay close to Kyushu island. The small island of Okinoshima, close to Fukoaka in northern Kyushu, was a cult centre visited by fishermen and other sailors, for the produce of the sea has always mattered a great deal in the Japanese diet (the sea was also a good source of fine pearls); since very early times Japanese men (but not women) have gone there to pray for the safety of those at sea. Archaeological finds from the island include artefacts from Korea and even the Middle East, as well as many jade symbols in the shape of an apostrophe, whose exact function is unclear. The great shrine at Munakata was dedicated to the sea gods and now attracts travellers of all sorts, including those who wish their cars to be blessed by the Shintō deities.[7] And then, beyond Okinoshima and halfway to Korea, the island of Tsushima was regarded as the outer boundary of the Japanese Empire.[8] Tsushima provided a base from which Japanese sea raiders repeatedly attacked the coast of Korea during the fourth century.[9]

It goes without saying that the entire population of Japan had arrived from elsewhere at some time, even though the Japanese themselves long believed that their emperors were descended from the sun goddess Amiterasu, and noble families claimed descent from lesser gods.[10] A series of peoples moved into various corners of the archipelago over several millennia. Migration from Korea was easiest, across a relatively narrow stretch of water, and a wave of refugees arrived from Korea in the fourth and fifth centuries AD, a time of turbulence in their homeland; they were welcomed by the Japanese court, for they brought skills that were lacking in Japan itself, until then a largely rural society with a subsistence economy. The immigrants taught the art of silk cultivation; they were experienced weavers; they were metalworkers; they also brought the art of writing, though at this stage this was Chinese writing, which was ill-suited to the polysyllabic language that had taken root in Japan.[11] Korean culture was itself heavily influenced by that of China, so Korea was really a filter through which a more advanced civilization moulded the culture of Japan. By the ninth century AD, though, increasingly regular direct contact with

China itself reduced Japanese dependence on Korea as an intermediary. Japan's maritime horizons took many centuries to expand, as this chapter will show.

Cultural dependence on Korea was not matched by political dependence; indeed, later tradition insisted that the three Korean kingdoms of Silla, Koguryō and Paekche began to pay tribute to Japan in the sixth century, as did some of the islands to the south of Kyushu. These tales grew in the telling, and claims that early Japanese emperors ruled the territory of Mimana, on the strait between Korea and Japan, from the third to the seventh century, were used by early Japanese chroniclers to support the right of their emperor to tax the inhabitants of southern Korea.[12] This points to a fundamental paradox in Japanese history: on the one hand, the island identity of the Japanese reinforced the idea that Japan was an empire set apart by the gods from the rest of humanity; and, on the other hand, the Japanese sought to draw the nearest parts of mainland Asia under their influence. This sense that Japan too was an empire was heavily compromised by an awareness that China was the seat of a more ancient, powerful and sophisticated civilization that the Japanese tried hard to emulate. This love–hate relationship has endured over many centuries of Japanese history.

Korean contact with Japan was quite intense during the seventh century A D. The Japanese even took sides in an armed struggle between the two kingdoms in southern Korea, Silla and Paekche. The Tang dynasty in China was wooed by Silla, and Paekche turned to Japan for help; in 663, a naval battle between the Chinese and Japanese off the coast of Korea, known as the Battle of Hakusuki, proved the decisive superiority of the Chinese fleet over that of Japan, and henceforth Japanese aggression in these waters was limited to pirate raids.[13] The rulers of Silla succeeded in suppressing Paekche and became a significant regional power in their own right. At first, they failed to realize that the Tang emperor intended to absorb Silla once he had helped finish off the other Korean kingdoms. However, between 668 and 700 twenty-three embassies arrived in Japan from Silla, which was now trying to keep its distance from the rulers of China, and saw the Japanese as useful allies. These diplomatic exchanges were an important conduit along which mainland cultural influences reached the island empire. Handsome gifts of Korean, Chinese and east Asian luxury goods could be understood as tribute (though that was not the idea in the king of Silla's mind); on one occasion, in 697, Emperor Monmu even invited the Korean emissaries to his New Year audience, alongside the 'barbarian' peoples of northern Japan, and presumably the envoys from Silla were not quite sure whether to be flattered or embarrassed by what was obviously an attempt to flaunt Japanese imperial authority. And when, in 752, the Sillan prince T'aeryŏm turned up with seven ships and 700 men, the Japanese records insisted that his precise purpose was to bring tribute to the empire of Japan, for he is said to have said:

> 'The king of Silla addresses the court of the empress who rules gloriously over Japan. The country of Silla has from long times past continuously plied the waters with ships coming to serve your state . . . There is nowhere under Heaven that is not part of the royal domain, and no one on even the furthest shores of the realm who is not a royal subject. T'aeryŏm is overcome with happiness to have been blessed with the opportunity to come to serve you during your divine reign. I respectfully present some small items coming from my own land.'[14]

Oddly, or perhaps not oddly at all, there is no mention of this voyage, or other embassies to Japan, in the Korean annals of the Silla kingdom, which are quite detailed. They only mention T'aeryŏm as a leader of a rebellion against the king, in 768, which ended with the execution of the prince and 'their three generations: paternal, maternal, and wife's relatives', clearly a traditional method for dealing with opponents of the regime that is still loyally maintained by the Kim dynasty in North Korea.[15] However, the Korean annals do mention Japan very occasionally: 'the country of Wa changed its name to Japan. They say they took this name because they are near to where the sun rises', which is indeed the meaning of Nihon.[16] And the Koreans noted embassies *from* Japan, even though they actually consisted of protocol officers sent to accompany Sillan embassies to the Japanese emperor back to their homeland. Nonetheless, the Sillans did not feel it was beneath their dignity to admit that they were sending embassies to the Tang court in China.

Most curious is the embassy from Japan that arrived in Korea in 753. This was surely another visit by protocol officers accompanying Prince T'aeryŏm back home, but the Sillans were upset at something – perhaps the long delays in receiving T'aeryŏm at the Japanese court. The Korean annals state: 'Year 12 [753], autumn, eighth month. An envoy arrived from Japan. As he was arrogant with no propriety, the king did not receive him, so he returned home.' Relations were better in the ninth century when, we are told, the Japanese presented the king of Silla with large amounts of gold, having 'concluded an agreement for the exchange of envoys and friendly ties' some years earlier, in 803.[17] Everything really depended on whether the Japanese were friendly to other Korean kingdoms, and whether the Sillans were keen to make friends with Tang China. Relations with Japan were based on the principle 'my enemy's enemy is my friend'.

The 'small items' conveyed by ambassadors were not in reality quite so small. Descriptions of Korean embassies mention rather curious gifts: in 599, Korean envoys presented a camel, a donkey, goats and a white pheasant from the kingdom of Paekche; the Paekche embassy of 602 had a more lasting effect, since this time a monk named Kwallûk brought exciting books that dealt with exorcism, astronomy and the calendar; besides, Kwallûk remained in Japan and trained three Japanese followers in his esoteric knowledge; he was followed by other Buddhist monks from the different Korean kingdoms who displayed an impressive range of knowledge – not just how to manufacture ink, paper and colouring materials, but even how to build a watermill. Embassies from Silla brought gold, silver, copper and iron, as well as bronze statuettes of the Buddha. The northern Korean kingdom of Parhae, which stretched beyond the present borders of North Korea towards present-day Vladivostok, sent tiger-skins and other rare pelts to Japan, so that when Japanese painters portrayed tigers and leopards they were not totally dependent on Chinese artistic models. In 659 an envoy from Koguryō was seen in the market trying to exchange a bearskin for silk floss, which for some reason the Japanese thought was highly amusing. That, perhaps, was on his private account, since gifts to the Koreans in return for tribute lavishly demonstrated the growing wealth of the Japanese emperor: dozens of bolts of silk in any number of forms and colours; hemp cloth, furs, axes and knives.[18]

Some, perhaps most, of the trade with Korea took place outside the narrow confines of official embassies, and one 'register of products purchased from the Koreans', of 752, lists products from all over east Asia, not just from Korea itself: gold, frankincense, camphor, aloe wood, musk, rhubarb, ginseng, liquorice, honey, cinnamon, lapis lazuli, dyestuffs, mirrors, folding screens, candelabra, bowls and basins. A special feature of these imports is that Japanese nobles were allowed to petition the court for permission to buy goods brought by the envoys who accompanied T'aeryŏm. The petitions they submitted were later used to line folding screens that have been preserved in the remarkable eighth-century imperial treasury at the Shōsō-in, still kept at the Tōdaiji temple in Nara. Their letters reveal a less stuffy world than the highly formalized rituals of Japanese diplomacy might suggest, for the official visits masked a more mundane reality: people traded on the side, with the blessing of the imperial court.[19] Their goods also helped shape Japanese civilization – one has only to think of the white lead used in the face-paint of court ladies in the era of *The Tale of Genji*.

This relationship between Japan and Korea, of necessity conducted by sea, did not, then, take the form of a continuous flow of shipping back and forth across the strait between Japan and Korea. Embassies could be made to wait months, even years, before being rudely told to go away. Permanent diplomatic representatives based in foreign capitals simply did not exist.[20] Nor was diplomacy the only way Korea and Japan came into contact. All these accounts of embassies underestimate the scale of piracy and open warfare in the seas between the two lands. Although not much can be said about the ships that fought in these waters, Wa (later known as Japan), Silla and other states in the region could mobilize navies when they wanted to do so. Japanese raids on Korea had a long history, and Kyushu, the southern island of Japan, was seen as a defensive barrier against Korean aggression; in the seventh and eighth centuries, thousands of recruits known as *sakimori* were based in Kyushu and on Tsushima to defend imperial territory against invaders. The Japanese were worried that Kyushu was so easily accessible from the continent: 'various foreign countries come there to pay tribute, their ships and rudders face to face with ours. For this reason we drill horses and sharpen our weapons in order to display our might and prepare for emergencies.' An eighth-century poet described the agony of leaving home and family ('his mother of the drooping breasts' and 'his wife like the young grass'), for:

> A great ship is set with myriad true oars
> In the royal bay of Naniwa
> Where men cut reeds,
> On the morning calm
> They row out in cadence,
> On the evening tide
> Pull the oars till they bend.
> 'May you who set off rowing
> To the boatman's chant,
> Thread your way between the waves
> And safely reach your port.
> May you keep your spirit true
> As ordered by our sovereign lord,
> And when your time of sailing round
> From cape to cape is done,
> May you come safely home,'
> Thus his wife must pray,
> Setting a jar beside the bed,
> Folding back her white hemp sleeves,
> Spreading out her seed-black hair –
> Long days she waits with yearning.[21]

I I

Prince T'aeryŏm's visit to Japan took many months. These long, exhausting and not very comfortable trips across the sea were frequent enough for the Japanese court to set up a reception centre for foreign visitors in Hakata Bay, within the precincts of the large modern city of Fukoaka (earlier known as Hakata). No one knows what route T'aeryŏm followed towards Nara (Heijō-kyō), the imperial capital, but the fact that he stayed at Naniwa, on the site of modern Ōsaka, while returning to Hakata strongly suggests he travelled mainly by sea. En route to Nara, 'the guests must not be allowed to converse with people. Nor should officials of the provinces and districts they pass through be allowed to look at the guests and vice-versa.'[22] His problem was not so much getting to Nara as getting out of Hakata, where he and his entourage were penned in the foreigners' compound under the strictest supervision.

This compound, whose site lies underneath an old baseball stadium, was excavated in 1987–8, exposing structures from the late seventh to ninth centuries, as well as massive quantities of Chinese ceramics, the latest of which date from the eleventh century. It was known as the Kōrokan, and in the eighth century, the 'Nara period' of Japanese history, a channel to the sea probably reached as far as the building, before sedimentation spread Fukoaka well beyond the early medieval shoreline. The Kōrokan contained two quadrangles of the same size (seventy-four metres by fifty-six metres). Presumably the VIPs stayed under cover while the great majority of the party bedded down in the large courtyards, or even outside the gates and on board the ships that had brought them to Hakata Bay. Analysis of latrines discovered within the compound revealed that one latrine was used by people who followed a diet not far distant from the traditional Japanese diet of fish and vegetables, while two upper-class latrines showed high consumption of pork, including wild boar. Even more pungent evidence was provided by small wooden slats that had been attached to food shipments and that indicated what was in each cargo and where it came from (they survived because they were used to wipe one's behind before being thrown away). Here was proof that fish, rice and venison were carried to the Kōrokan from northern and central Kyushu – the centre of the island, containing the vast caldera of Mount Aso, offered rich volcanic soil. The sea provided an important part of the diet of the inhabitants of eighth- and ninth-century Kyushu: shellfish such as oysters and abalone, as well as jellyfish, tuna, whale, salmon and, as now, seaweed such as kelp. Occasionally the more distinguished emissaries would be summoned from the lodge and taken to Dazaifu for feasts at which the governor of Kyushu was their host. Isolation was not total.[23] Yet the Kōrokan was different from the inns that existed in, say, the medieval Mediterranean, which were situated within ports. Hakata Bay was an empty area at this time; the Kōrokan was not simply a large, enclosed quadrangle but an isolated, distant place; in this sense it was also different from the more famous enclosure at Deshima, the island off Nagasaki where Dutch merchants were permitted to trade in the seventeenth and eighteenth centuries.

The physical isolation of the lodge meant that the Japanese authorities had to supervise the Kōrokan from their administrative centre thirteen kilometres inland, at Dazaifu. This was the command centre for the defence of Kyushu as well. All this points to the deep-seated fear that Kyushu would fall under the sway of foreigners, and that it was a border region in constant need of protection. Prince T'aeryŏm and other ambassadors came with more than 700 followers; and there was an uneasy feeling that several hundred foreigners could just as well be warlike marauders as peaceful envoys. It was vexing for the visitors to have to suffer the long wait as Japanese protocol officers travelled back and forth between Hakata and Nara, bringing news of whether the embassy was actually welcome at the imperial court.[24] The fear of contact was also fear of contamination. The Japanese court developed a sense of the distinct purity of the Japanese race, which culminated in the purity of the emperor himself. This was in part an elaboration of the Chinese attitude to other peoples, who were seen as 'barbarians', but another source of these ideas was the Shintō conception of pollution, often also associated with the dead. One must distinguish these theories from everyday practice: in time large numbers of Chinese would settle in Hakata and marry Japanese men and women. But in dealing with official delegations the imperial court had, by the eighth or ninth century, become aware of the distance separating the emperor and his great nobles from foreign peoples, especially those of Korea, who were regarded as a political threat as well as a source of pollution.[25]

By the end of the eighth century the Koreans of Silla had made clear their rejection of any idea that their official trade with Japan consisted of tribute payments to a greater power. The area that remained in regular official contact with Japan was the kingdom of Parhae, in the north of Korea, spilling over into what are now the borderlands of China and Russia, and surviving until it was overthrown by marauders from the interior in 926. The inhabitants of Parhae were of varied origins, some related to the Mongols, some more closely related to the Koreans. They were useful allies when, as happened early in the eighth century, the rulers of Silla decided to link their fortunes to Tang China rather than Japan; but they had less to offer in gifts: furs rather than silk, and none of the spices that Silla had obtained from further south and west. Trade with Parhae was not exactly encouraged, at least at the Japanese court: in the ninth century a mission from Parhae was only allowed to visit every six years, an interval which was soon increased to every twelve years, because the Parhaeans were bringing more than the court really wanted. The king of Parhae was unhappy with this arrangement and continued to send embassies even when they were unwelcome, whereupon the Japanese authorities sent them back with their goods, which, in 877, included two exceptionally beautiful *sake* cups made out of tortoiseshell and carved in the 'South Seas' that some at court would have been delighted to keep in Japan.[26]

The relationship between Korea and Japan soured, but not before the peninsula had implanted some fundamental features of mainland Asian culture in the islands, notably Buddhist beliefs. With the fall of Parhae, however, Japan lost interest in attempting to assert its influence on the mainland. Memories of the links with Korea persisted, and a Korean embassy appears in the very first pages of the great tenth-century Japanese novel, *The Tale of Genji*; there, a wise Korean physiognomist skilled in Chinese poetry recognizes the great talent of the young boy who will one day become the hero Genji.[27] As will be seen, in the long term the cooling of ties with Korea fostered a new type of relationship across the sea, based on everyday trade rather than formal diplomatic exchanges, but in the meantime the weakening of ties between Japan and its closest neighbours left the Sea of Japan and the East China Sea open to pirates capable of operating their own fleets and of preying on such merchant shipping as existed.

Early Japanese rulers appealed to the Chinese for help against local rivals; and often these appeals were directed at Chinese governors of parts of Korea that had fallen under Han control.[28] But increasingly they turned to the Chinese imperial court. This was with certain reservations: the journey there was regarded as very risky – every embassy but one experienced serious danger at sea or on land; and they were uneasy about Chinese claims to superiority, since the Japanese preferred to think of themselves as the civilized subjects of a sovereign empire comparable in status, if not in size, to Tang China.[29] The sea was an important part of a world view that was, nonetheless, firmly centred on the Japanese islands. Most eloquent of all are the dramatic scenes of ships amid the storm-tossed waves that appear in medieval Japanese paintings.[30] In the eighth century the embassies sent to China were already elaborate affairs, with whole teams of participants: a principal ambassador with two or three deputies; scribes and interpreters; craftsmen such as carpenters and metalworkers; a specialist in divination – always useful if one wanted to turn up at court on an auspicious day. A hundred people would constitute a rather small embassy; in this period four ships each capable of carrying 150 people might not be unusual (twelve embassies are known in the years between 630 and 837). To guard against illness a vast pharmacopoeia was carried on board, including pills made of rhinoceros horn, plum kernels and juniper, more often of Chinese than of Japanese origin.[31]

The route started in the bay of Ōsaka, through Japan's Inland Sea, and along the Korean coast, though a direct route to the mouth of the Yangtze (close to the trading city of Yangzhou) became common as navigators gained greater experience; moreover, sailing past Korea was risky when local rulers, such as the king of Silla, were hostile. From Yangzhou, part of each delegation would head much further inland to the imperial capital at Changan, so their journey was by no means over when they reached Yangzhou. However, Yangzhou was a collection point for goods that came overland or along the coast from Canton (Guangzhou), so there they could choose from the luxury goods of the Indian Ocean route and from those that arrived along the Silk Road. They still had to face the horrors of the return journey. On one occasion, in 778, the high seas washed a Chinese envoy coming to Japan with gifts off the deck of his ship, along with twenty-five members of his entourage and one of the Japanese ambassadors who was on his way home. The same ship broke in two but each part stayed afloat, and the exhausted survivors made land on Kyushu.[32]

With such experiences on record, Japanese travellers regarded sea travel with awe, and made sure that they prayed to the gods of the sea before setting out, celebrating with feasts if and when they managed to return. A litany that used to be recited at an event known as the Ceremony of National Purification conjures up a vivid image of Japanese seafaring: 'as a huge ship moored in a great harbour, casting off its stern moorings, casting off its bow moorings, drives forth into the vast ocean . . . so shall all offences be swept utterly away.' In a prayer to the sun goddess the Shintō priest described the lands bestowed on the emperor 'by the blue sea-plain, as far as the prows of ships can go without letting dry their oars and poles'.[33]

The dividends for Japan were enormous. The coming and going of monks ensured that Japanese Buddhism was firmly rooted in Chinese and Indian Mahayana Buddhism; the *Lotus Sutra*, a very lengthy lecture by the Buddha on the theme of eternal bliss, was a particular favourite in

China, and consequently became one in Japan as well.[34] Cultural influences across the sea were not confined to Buddhism. Something was learned from Confucianism about hierarchy and filial respect, though public examinations for government service did not quite follow the Confucian model: opportunities to be trained for office were confined to the sons of the well born rather than being open to all talents. The Chinese model extended to town-planning as well: the handsome new capital at Nara was constructed around a grid, like the major Chinese cities. At the start of the eighth century the imperial court began to issue silver and then copper coins, in imitation of Chinese practice, but silk was used as the medium of exchange in high-level dealings with Japan's neighbours.[35]

The influence of China on the fine arts was incalculable, even if Japanese artists developed their own sensitive eye. The texts that Buddhist monks studied were in Chinese, and the creation of a workable Japanese script took time; when it did come into being, it made use of a great many Chinese characters, while also using syllabic signs better suited to the phonetics of Japanese. Until then, Chinese was the language of administration, and Chinese books on astronomy, divination, medicine, mathematics, music, history, religion and poetry were eagerly devoured by civil servants, monks and scholars in Japan; a 'catalogue of books currently in Japan' of 891 knew of 1,759 Chinese works.[36] At the same time, traditional cults, the 'way of the gods' or Shintō, ensured that native traditions remained alive. Still, the cultural flow was nearly all one way: in later centuries, as will be seen, there were a few Japanese articles that attracted the attention of Chinese buyers, especially high-quality paper, which was made according to a different formula in Japan. But Japanese admiration for Chinese culture was not matched by Chinese admiration for Japanese culture. The Japanese could not escape from being classed as barbarians by those they sought to emulate; one effective way of dealing with this was to treat others (such as the Koreans, rather ungratefully) as barbarians in relation to themselves.

The evidence from the embassies to China is as good a way as any of measuring the steady growth in Chinese influence, and the build-up of trade as well as official exchange across the Japan Sea and the Yellow Sea. Yet here, as with Korea, the tributary relationship did not last; after 838 no more embassies were sent to Tang China. In any case, these embassies had been sent at very long intervals. Twenty-seven years separate the embassy sent by Emperor Kammu to the Tang court in 804 from its immediate predecessor, and thirty-four years passed before the next embassy was sent to China, one that is very well documented and that will be examined shortly. During the rest of the ninth century, the Japanese showed no interest in sending an embassy to the Tang emperor, and by the time they did decide to send one, in 894, the Tang empire was beginning to disintegrate. In the event, that embassy was cancelled when Sugawara no Michizane, the notable who had been chosen as ambassador, advised the Council of State to think again:

> Last year in the third month, the merchant Wang No brought a letter from the monk Chūkan, who is in China. It described in detail how the Great Tang is in a state of decline, and reported that the emperor is not at court [because of the rebellion] and foreign missions have ceased to come ... Investigating records from the past, we have observed that some of the men sent to China have lost their lives at sea and others have been killed by pirates ... This is a matter of national importance and not merely of personal concern.[37]

Maybe that final sentence should not be taken too seriously; the ambassador evidently did not want to risk his life. He was perhaps the greatest Japanese expert on Chinese culture, and a skilled poet who enjoyed exchanging verses with the ambassador of Parhae.[38] Yet his reluctance to lead an official delegation masks the reality of day-to-day contact across the sea. In another letter Michizane reported that 'many merchants have told us of conditions in China', so there were more people crossing to China than the Wang No he mentioned in his appeal to the Council of State. Private traders were coming and going with ever greater frequency and, to judge from Wang No's name, many or most or even all were Chinese. As a result, at the end of the ninth century the character of Chinese trade with Japan was changing decisively. The cancellation of the embassy in 894 was not a sign of isolationism, but rather the opposite: these very formal exchanges of goods by extremely large embassies were not cost-effective. Japan was becoming more and more integrated into the 'Asian Mediterranean' that stretched south beyond Taiwan and joined the South China Sea to the seas around Japan itself.

Silk dominated the list of goods sent from the Japanese court to China, while large quantities of silver also featured, and the distinctive silky paper the Japanese manufactured also impressed the Chinese, though for the moment it was more an object of curiosity than a common article of exchange. The diplomatic team would also bring to China large quantities of silk that each member had been awarded by the emperor of Japan, and would use this to finance the voyage, selling goods in the ports and cities the envoys visited. Chinese gifts, not just to the emperor of Nihon but to the envoys, included suits of armour and books – one Japanese visitor to

China, who stayed there for eighteen years at the start of the eighth century, brought home a handbook of court ceremonial, which must have had quite an impact in his homeland.[39] But the best evidence for the impact of China and east Asia upon eighth-century Japan comes from the extraordinary collection of artefacts still preserved at the Tōdaiji temple in the new capital of Japan, Nara, which are placed on exhibition once a year. This collection was formed in 756, when the widow of Emperor Shōmu presented his treasures to the Great Buddha. Further gifts in the next few decades brought the number of items in the collection to more than 10,000. Influences from the West can be traced both in designs imitated from Persian, Indian and Chinese models (for instance, in painted screens that recall Tang iconography), and in actual objects brought across the seas (such as lapis lazuli belt ornaments from Afghanistan). Musical instruments from the eighth century, including flutes and lutes, Chinese board games, writing cases, brushes and inkstones, furniture and caskets, armour, glass, ceramics and magnificent court robes testify either to the quality of the gifts received and objects bought through trade, or to the manner in which Japanese artists copied faithfully the models they saw – over time modifying them in a distinctively Japanese way.[40] The more the Japanese studied Chinese art and customs, the more they were inclined to stress their own special identity. Physical separation from China meant that these powerful influences operated at a court level; movement back and forth by sea, across difficult waters, constrained contact but also sustained a regular flow of goods from the high culture the emperors in Nara secretly envied, and never dared to despise.

III

The Japanese Buddhist monk Ennin (793–864) became an important religious leader, and was later known to the Japanese as Jikaku Daishi, 'Great Teacher of Compassion and Understanding'. The diary of his pilgrimage, which took place between 836 and 847, offers a unique record of the delicate relationship between China and Japan in the early Middle Ages, and has much to say about the journey across the treacherous waters between the two empires. Only one medieval manuscript survives, finished in wobbly characters in 1291, and copied by a Buddhist monk named Ken'in when he was seventy-two years old and was 'rubbing my old eyes', which was his way of apologizing for the errors of transcription in the text he transmitted. These errors were magnified because he was not copying his native Japanese, but a text written in Chinese, which remained the literary language of the intellectual elite at Nara.[41] Ennin was already forty-one years old when the imperial court appointed members of the diplomatic team it was sending to China, which was to be led by Fujiwara no Tsunetsugu, a member of the great Fujiwara clan. It was to set out in four ships under the direction of 'Ship's Loading Masters'; the title suggests that they were responsible for the cargo of tribute. Two of the loading masters were of Korean descent and one claimed to be descended from a past Chinese emperor, no less. However, there were also skilled navigators who captained the ships while they were at sea, as well as scribes and Korean interpreters, whose task was less to translate from Japanese into Korean than from Japanese into Chinese.[42] It was a motley band of envoys that included a 'Provisional Professor' from the government university, who was also a skilled painter and waited upon the ambassador himself. Several archers who travelled in the convoy were of good birth, one of them serving in the imperial bodyguard, though there were also many artisans, including carpenters, porters and simple sailors who were clearly of more modest origin. Altogether there were 651 people on board the four ships, which, judging from the size of the earlier Korean embassies to Japan, was the expected size of an embassy designed to create a good impression. Alongside the diplomats and their support staff, another important component of this great party consisted of the monks and laymen who were travelling to China to deepen their knowledge of Buddhist beliefs and practices and of Chinese art and letters. The monks represented various sects of Buddhism that existed in Japan, for one feature of Japanese Buddhism was the relative ease with which the different strands of Buddhism, the 'greater' (Mahayana) and 'lesser' (Hinayana), co-existed side by side, one stressing the role of Buddhism in society at large and the other concentrating more on inner perfection.[43]

This team was put together from 833 onwards, but it took a few years to set off on the voyage. For, in addition to those sailing to China, there was another large team at work on land. The ships were not actually ready; Ship Construction Officers were needed who could supervise their building. The imperial court was also well aware that making a good impression on the Tang emperor would depend on the rank of the people sent into the Chinese ruler's presence. Therefore in the New Year Honours List several of the envoys were raised to higher ranks in the complex court hierarchy; the ambassador himself now attained Senior Fourth Rank Lower Grade, which was a little more than halfway up the *cursus honorum*. Previously he had held the rank of Junior Fourth Rank Upper Grade. Solely while he functioned as ambassador he was an acting member of the Senior Second Rank. Progress up the ladder took place at a snail's pace.

There were handsome gifts of silk and other cloths for the leading partici-pants. One reason for this largesse was the simple fact that the journey was thought to be perilous, which, as events would prove, was an accurate judgement.[44] If contrary winds blew, it was quite possible that the ships would be blown on to the shores of Korea, so a further embassy was despatched to the king of Silla, with whom relations had been poor, to guarantee safe passage for the Japanese embassy to China. The Koreans sent back this embassy with a flea in the ambassador's ear. Silla was full of tension at this time, as rivals contended for the throne and as fighting spread into the palace compound itself. Meanwhile a pirate king named Chang Pogo had established himself as master of the waters off southern Korea, and Ennin mentioned the threat that he might pose to the ships carrying the embassy – more of Chang Pogo shortly.[45] It is not surprising, then, that the Koreans had other preoccupations than the renewal of ties with Japan.[46] The Sillan court even suggested that the envoy who had arrived at their court, Ki no Misu, was some sort of mischievous impostor, and he was roundly blamed for his failure when he returned to Nara.[47]

The first part of the voyage, which began in the middle of 836, was easy enough. The four ships set out from Naniwa, not far from Nara, and sailed down the Inland Sea, reaching the coast of Kyushu after four days. Prob-lems began to mount when they set off from Kyushu for the coast of China, on 17 August 836. The weather had been calm, but the typhoon season was imminent. Everything suggests that the Japanese mariners were hope-lessly optimistic about their chances of all arriving unscathed on the mainland, and that their expertise was limited to navigation between the islands of their home archipelago across small distances. The four ships were beaten back by the fierce winds; three of them made land on Kyushu once again, but the fourth was smashed to pieces, and a raft carrying sixteen survivors was washed up on Tsushima island, followed by a few other survivors who floated ashore later – a total of twenty-eight survivors. The story they told was horrifying: its rudder broken, their ship had been at the mercy of the high sea, and the captain had ordered his crew and passengers to break the ship to pieces, so that they could escape on rafts; but nearly all these rafts were lost at sea, with over a hundred men. When the emperor heard of these events, he sent orders for the repair of the three remaining ships; Fujiwara no Tsunetsugu assured him that he was still keen to make the passage, even though he and his men felt half-dead after their experiences (this, in true Japanese fashion, was expressed as a humble apology for failure, even though the circumstances had clearly been well beyond Fujiwara's control). A second attempt to reach China, in 837, fared little better, for the ships were blown back to Kyushu and to islands off

Japan; the imperial court had sent offerings to the shrine at Ise of Amiterasu, the sun goddess and notional ancestress of the imperial family, but
to no avail.[48]

With no obvious help from the Shintō gods, the opportunity was taken
to redouble spiritual efforts before sending the party to sea a third time.
This was achieved by bringing into play the Buddhist monasteries as well
as the Shintō shrines of Kyushu, while right across the Japanese Empire
there were to be daily readings of a Buddhist sutra, *The Scripture of the
Dragon-King of the Sea*, who was a cult figure in Korea, Japan and parts
of China. The envoys felt very doubtful about setting out yet again: they
had witnessed the perils of the sea, and had lost a ship on the first attempt.
Takamura, the deputy ambassador, fell sick with a diplomatic illness and –
while Fujiwara insisted that he was ready to die 10,000 times to serve the
emperor – his deputy and several other high-ranking envoys were sent into
exile for disobeying imperial orders, which was at least a better fate than
being strangled to death, the penalty the emperor could have imposed.[49]

What has been said so far is based on the reconstruction of events
from the Japanese official archives by the editor of Ennin's diary, Edwin
Reischauer. But at this point the words of Ennin himself become audible,
as he describes the third voyage towards the coast of China, cutting
across the open sea so that the Japanese ships did not have to coast along
the mildly hostile shores of Korea. Off the coast of China, however, the
ships encountered a fierce east wind, and Ennin's vessel was blown on
to a shoal, whereupon its rudder snapped in pieces. To add to their confusion, their Korean interpreter was worried that they had already
overshot the entrance to the canal that would lead them down to the
Yangtze River and towards Yangzhou, the first city they hoped to reach
en route to the Tang capital further inland. Ennin, the ambassador and
their fellow passengers were stranded offshore on a ship that was breaking up. The ambassador managed to reached the shore in a lifeboat, but
Ennin was among those left on board: 'The ship eventually fell over and
was about to be submerged. The men were terrified and struggled to
climb on to the side of the vessel. All bound their loincloths around them
and tied themselves with ropes here and there to the ship. Tied thus in
place, we awaited death.'[50]

The broken ship shifted back and forth in the mud, and Ennin and his
companions were forced to switch from one side to another as the waves
pushed it from side to side and as 'the mud boiled up'. When a small Chinese cargo vessel came alongside, the first act of those still on board was to
pass across the 'national tribute articles' destined for the emperor of China;
but in reality they lay very close to the shore and eventually they landed

on *terra firma*, dried out the tribute items that had been soaked in seawater, and made their way upriver, finding out that the ambassador and his secretaries had survived their own harrowing experiences and were heading in the same direction. Two other ships experienced easier crossings, though one of them did begin to break up, and several crew members died of mysterious and sinister 'body swellings' before being rescued by more Chinese ships.[51] Not surprisingly, members of the party of monks were keen to present gifts of gold to a monastery where they were lodged for a while, as thanksgiving for surviving the perils of the sea, and as they travelled they offered simple feasts of vegetarian fare to monks they visited.[52]

The disasters at sea prove that the Japanese had not mastered the art of ship construction. Ennin's terrifying account of his shipwreck is not the only report he offers of a rudder that broke under strain, nor of ignorance of the art of navigation. The Japanese were a maritime people, but the sheer proximity of their islands meant that long journeys across the open sea were rare, although there is good evidence that the Koreans could handle more ambitious voyages. Ennin had come to China to make contact with fellow Buddhists, and his travels along the rivers and roads of the Tang Empire took him far from the sea, but he says that the crew of one Chinese boat, carrying Fujiwara himself back to Japan in 839, was Korean, and the crew was knowledgeable about the coastline of northern China and about the best routes towards Japan.[53] While it is no surprise that they prayed to the Shintō and Buddhist gods on setting out on a voyage, the Japanese were willing to rely on a soothsayer for information about weather prospects. Ennin described how the sailors on board one ship lost all sense of direction once they could not see the sun, and 'wandered aimlessly'; when they saw land the soothsayer first declared it was Silla and then decided it was China – the matter was resolved when two Chinese were found who knew where Korea actually lay.[54] The Japanese attitude to the open sea can be summed up in Ennin's terse comment: 'we saw the ocean stretching far and mysterious to the east and south.'[55] It was not an inviting place.

Following the disasters of the outward journey, from which only one ship had survived, new ships had to be commissioned in Yangzhou, the great commercial city that was China's gateway to the open ocean. It was vital to find people 'familiar with the sea-routes', and more than sixty Korean sailors were hired, along with nine Korean ships.[56] The larger fleet suggests that the ships themselves were smaller, or that a rich cargo of gifts and surreptitious purchases was now ready for loading. However, when members of the delegation attempted to trade privately in the marketplaces of Yangzhou they were arrested and held overnight; they had 'bought some items under imperial prohibition'; and other delegates were in such a hurry to escape the market inspectors after detection that they left behind more than 200 strings of cash, each made up of 1,000 copper coins and threaded together through the hole in the middle. Unfortunately, there is no record of what they were trying to buy, which may have included the rare medicines, spices and incense that wealthy Japanese consumers craved. When they set out, the crews underwent purification according to Shintō rites, praying to the sea gods for a safe journey; and at one point a Japanese sailor was prevented from boarding because he had polluted himself by having sexual relations with another man. Once the ships were at sea, a sailor who was thought to be dying was placed on land so that his dead body would not pollute the ship on which he was sailing. The fearsome sea had to be treated with punctilious respect.[57]

At the last minute, Ennin and a few of his fellow monks decided to stay in China, with the approval of Ambassador Fujiwara but without permission from the Chinese authorities; the ambassador tried to warn Ennin that the Chinese authorities would be furious at his breach of the imperial order that the delegation should now depart, but he understood that Ennin's first priority was to study Buddhist scriptures. So Ennin conspired with Korean merchants to be left on the shore of the Shandong peninsula, which sticks out of China to the west of Korea. A bribe of gold dust and a Japanese girdle helped; the Korean response was a gift of powdered tea and pine nuts, which seems a rather modest exchange.[58] And yet thick *matcha* tea, widely known for its use in the tea ceremony, was valued by Buddhist monks, as it kept them awake through long hours of study and meditation; documents preserved in the Shōsō-in at Nara show that it remained extremely costly in the late eighth century, worthy of being brewed by the abbot himself before it was offered to the emperor as he processed past the great temples of central Japan.[59]

Ennin felt it was important to send some Buddhist scriptures back to Japan, which he asked to be placed on board one of the Japanese ships in a bamboo box.[60] But the embassy had not satisfied his craving for deeper knowledge of Buddhist law and lore. He hoped to reach the holy places of Chinese Buddhism, and he and his companions tried to pose as Koreans. How this worked when they met some Korean sailors is a mystery – what language did they speak? They had not gone very far when they encountered a village elder called Wang Liang, who sent them a written message:

> You monks have come here and call yourselves Koreans, but I see that your language is not Korean, nor is it Chinese. I have been told that the ships of the Japanese tributary embassy stopped east of the mountains to wait for

favourable winds, and I fear that you monks are official visitors to China who have fled to this village from the ships of your own country. I dare not let official visitors stay.[61]

So in China, as in Japan, envoys from afar were expected to be tightly controlled and shepherded from place to place. When the police arrived Ennin claimed to have been suffering from beri-beri, and insisted that he had come ashore with his companions because he felt so ill; but now they wished to join the Japanese ships, which were said to be anchored not far away. They were duly accompanied to one of the Japanese ships that stood close to a temple of the Dragon King of the Sea, and put on board.[62] Ennin was in despair at the failure of his plans: 'we have tried every idea, but we cannot stay. The officials are vigilant and do not permit the slightest irregularity.'[63] No doubt Ennin's wish to stay was also prompted by fear of what lay before him as he crossed the open sea once again. Once he was back on board ship, fog rather than wind proved to be the greatest danger; becalmed, the passengers found that supplies were running low, and Ennin made offerings to the Shintō sea gods, an act which was seen as perfectly compatible with his Buddhist faith. Then they faced storms that left the ships sheltering off the Shantung coast. Still desperate to stay in China, Ennin made his way to a Korean monastery and the ships carried on without him – seven reached Kyushu within three weeks or so, though those aboard the ninth ship took nine months to find Japan: 'find Japan' because, with a broken mast, it wandered all over the western Pacific, and may even have floated as far south as Taiwan, 'the region of the southern brigands'.[64] It is surely significant that this ship was manned entirely by Japanese sailors, whereas the others carried Koreans as well. After an attack by hostile islanders, new boats were fashioned out of the ruined hull of the ship, and some of the exhausted travellers eventually reached Kyushu.

Ennin's difficulties with the Chinese authorities resumed. Fortunately the Korean prior of the monastery on Mount Chi where he had taken refuge was willing to support his request to stay in China; this monastery had been founded by the great Korean warlord Chang Pogo, who had endowed it with estates rich in rice.[65] However, in Tang China, Confucian bureaucracy reigned supreme, and Ennin had to battle with a sequence of officious jobsworths before he could gain the credentials and travel permits he needed; the fact that he wished to study Buddhism was at first largely ignored.[66] Ennin would spend nine years in China, during which he witnessed a fearsome persecution of Buddhist monks and nuns at the behest of Emperor Wuzung, a fanatical supporter of the Daoist faith; the suppression of the Buddhist monasteries by the 'Commissioners of Good Works' and other imperial officials has even been described as 'the most severe religious persecution in the whole of Chinese history'.[67] Ennin submitted requests for an exit visa which were repeatedly ignored, until the persecution reached a point where foreign monks were being expelled. At one point a ship was being built on his behalf to take him back home, or so he claimed, but there were endless bureaucratic obstacles. Ships came and went but he was not aboard them.[68] He finally left China in 847 and sailed back to Japan, where he arrived at the imperial court the next year, to face a hero's welcome. His return voyage past Korea to Hakata Bay was uneventful compared to the trials experienced on the way to China, and, predictably, the ship in which he sailed was under Korean ownership.[69]

Ennin's vivid account of his experiences not merely lights up the social and religious history of Tang China, but helps one understand the distant yet watchful relationship between Japan and China at this period. His simple references to ships sailing back and forth between China, Korea and Japan break through the silence of many official records to show that, despite the infrequency of the Japanese embassies to Tang China, dedicated to the formal presentation of tribute and to the receipt of handsome gifts, the waters between the two empires were populated, if not exactly crowded, with shipping. Much of it was operated by Korean sailors whose prime purpose was undoubtedly private trade. These boats tramped up and down the coast between Yangzhou or other towns in northern China and the coasts of Silla and Kyushu. Nonetheless, these seas were not calm: not just the storm winds and periodic fogs but the depredations of pirates made these waters dangerous, and no doubt many of these Korean shipowners were happy to turn to piracy when trade failed to pay. Among the pirate lords of the waters off Korea the most famous was Chang Pogo, who appears several times in Ennin's diary, and also in the Korean chronicles.

IV

Chang Pogo, or Jang Bogo, has become a national hero in South Korea, and has even been made the hero of an adventure film; well before that, he was worshipped as a god. His Korean name was Kangp'a, and his status at birth, in a land very conscious of rank, is unknown; but he began his career as a soldier in the service of the Tang Empire before returning to his native land in 828. By then he was already a wealthy man, and he set up a garrison said by the Korean chronicler to have numbered 10,000 men (that is, a large number) at Ch'ŏnghae-jin on Wando island, an important command post off south-western Korea that lay alongside the sea routes linking Silla to Tang China.[70] In a thirteenth-century collection of legends about the Korean past, he appears as Kungp'a, 'a man of chivalrous spirit'.[71] When he was living in Tang China, he had witnessed the wholesale import of Korean slaves by Chinese traders, and, with the approval of the king of Silla, he used Wando as a base for attacking the slavers. The king appointed him his Commissioner at Ch'ŏnghae-jin, so officially, at least, he acted as a crown agent. The problem was that as his command of the sea grew so did his independence from the king of Silla. He had taken up residence on Wando to suppress piracy; but his role there had made him into the greatest pirate of all. This was an era during which powerful local lords were intruding themselves into the turbulent politics of the Sillan court, and Chang Pogo too was tempted to try his hand there; what distinguished him was that his power was based more on the sea than on land and that he managed to exercise such power in Silla, for a few years that coincided with Ennin's stay in China.

Ennin thought of him as an independent warlord who might well interfere with his sea voyage. On the other hand, Ennin had plenty of reason to be grateful to him, as the founder of the Korean monastery that gave him asylum when he was trying to stay in China and to escape from the prying Chinese authorities. Chang Pogo was a merchant-prince as well as a warlord; he tried to set up a triangular trade linking China, Korea and Japan, but an attempt to interest the Japanese court in 841 was rebuffed when his merchants were accused of inventing tales about what was going on in Korea and were refused permission to trade.[72] However, he had his own commercial agent at his monastery whose task, Ennin relates, was to sell goods in China. This agent, Ch'oe, became a good friend to Ennin, and offered to provide transport on a Korean ship so Ennin could travel south along the coast of China towards the Buddhist centres he really wanted to visit. Ennin was overwhelmed by this kindness, even if this did not actually come about. He wrote a series of letters to Chang Pogo himself:

> Although I have never in my life had the honour of meeting you, I have for long heard of your great excellence, and I humbly respect you all the more . . . I find it difficult to express in words anything but great happiness . . . I do not know when I shall have the honour of meeting you, but in my humble way I think of you all the more from afar . . . In order to seek the Buddha's teaching, Ennin has come here from afar, moved by your virtue, and has tarried in your region. He has been fortunate enough to enjoy your benevolence. Being a mere nobody, he is overcome with gratitude.[73]

Ennin even suggested that he might call on Chang in Ch'ŏnghae-jin. However, just at this moment, in 839, Chang Pogo was busy at the court in Silla; he helped a royal ally seize the throne, declaring, 'a person who sees an injustice and does nothing is without courage'.[74] According to Korean accounts, he would have married his daughter to the king, had not the Korean nobles vigorously opposed the wedding of the daughter of a mere 'islander' or 'low-ranking commoner' to a princess. He duly paid the price of being an interloper and was assassinated in 841 or 846. A Korean tradition described how he plotted a dastardly coup against the king, and then was deceived by a refugee courtier named Yomjang or Kim Yang whom he had taken in, having failed to realize that this man's flight from the court was just a ruse intended to win his confidence:

> 'I have offended the king,' Yomjang repeated, 'and so I have come to seek asylum under your command in order to escape death.'
>
> 'You are lucky,' Kungp'a [Chang Pogo] said. 'Raise your cup. I drink to your health and your successful flight.'
>
> When Kungp'a was fairly in his cups, Yomjang suddenly drew the long sword from the scabbard which hung at the rebel's waist and cut off his head with a single stroke. When they heard of this, all of Kungp'a's officers and men prostrated themselves before Yomjang in fear and astonishment.[75]

Before long Yomjang had married his own daughter to the king and been promoted to a high rank, for he was worthy whereas Chang Pogo definitely was not, in the hierarchical society of early medieval Korea.[76]

The career of Chang Pogo offers another reminder that the commercial networks across the sea have often been maintained by maritime nations that stood between great empires, rather than by the inhabitants of those empires. Silla in the north and Śri Vijaya in the south were home to skilled mariners who effected links between great civilizations such as Tang China that looked inwards away from the sea, but also saw opportunities across the sea to obtain precious goods and flattering recognition of their political power. The Koreans, Malays and Indonesians prove to have been the real pioneers in crossing the open sea.

11

'Now the world is the world's world'

I

The term 'insularity' conveys a sense of isolation and looking inwards. Sometimes historians seize upon any word ending with -*ity* out of an unbridled love for abstract terms that are supposed to bring sophistication and 'theory' to their writings. But much of what has been said so far in this book demonstrates how lacking in that sort of insularity island societies were. Even when contact with the mainland was restricted by order of a court or government, ways were found to elude these rules, and such official contact as there was could be both intense and productive. Japan provides the perfect example of this apparent but unreal insularity during the early Middle Ages. The nature of its ties across the sea changed significantly in the twelfth century, and is richly documented. A new era of more open trade began, and the continuous presence of foreign merchants, nearly all Chinese, became a fact of life, especially around Hakata. Maritime trade within the Japanese archipelago also flourished; the seat of government at Kamakura (from 1185 onwards) possessed a viable port and consumed so much *sake* that a decision was made to ban its sale. 32,274 jars of the drink were confiscated, while around the Inland Sea port towns mushroomed, serving the megalopolis of Kyoto. The Japanese became much more expert shipbuilders too, although this was a slow development and even in the early thirteenth century the *shogun* only trusted a Chinese shipbuilder to construct a vessel capable of reaching China.[1] The government, or *bakufu*, became worried by the rapid growth of trade from Hakata through the Inland Sea to Kamakura, partly because there were government ships to which the *bakufu* wanted to give priority; Chinese interlopers seemed to be winning the competition to dominate this sea passage.[2] Overall, contrary to the view of Japan as a society that was not greatly involved in or influenced by its maritime links to Asia, what emerges is a picture of a society that revelled in its outside contacts, which were now mainly with China.

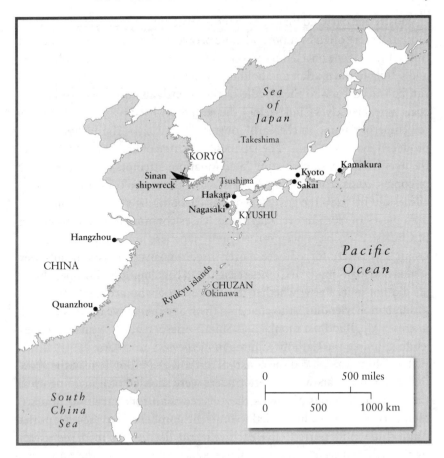

These contacts did not affect the lives of the very poor – the peasants who planted rice for demanding masters, whether warlike nobles or wealthy monasteries, or the fisherfolk or 'People of the Sea' whose livelihood depended upon the sea, but who did not take part in the trade networks that reached towards the great cities of China under the Song, Yuan and Ming dynasties. The People of the Sea owed the imperial court tribute in seafood and salt, for consumption of fish was much more common among richer members of society, while Buddhist disapproval of killing animals for meat made fish even more desirable. The People of the Sea operated boats up and down the coast under the protection of emperors, nobles and abbots to whom they owed allegiance. Under the patronage of nobles and abbots, guilds, or *za*, became a feature of town life.[3] All this was part of a process of commercialization that transformed medieval Japan between about 1200 and 1400. Gradually, markets and fairs took on a more cosmopolitan character; one could buy textiles, paper and metal goods, even luxury items and weapons made in the big cities of Japan and, occasionally, in China.[4]

Mostly one bartered for goods in the market, but copper coinage was used more and more often by more and more people, including peasants; a delightfully painted scene on a temple scroll from this period portrays people buying and selling in the market and holding strings of cash.[5] This reliance on cash can be traced back to the middle of the twelfth century, if not earlier. The coins were themselves Chinese, for – despite a short-lived plan to mint coins in the emperor's name in the early fourteenth century – the Japanese rarely produced their own coins. The Japanese government had its doubts, because the massive influx of cash stimulated inflation; attempts to ban the import of copper coins from China, at the start of the Kamakura period, had no effect, and by 1226 the government was encouraging the use of coin rather than pieces of cloth in everyday trade. Vases containing tens of thousands of Chinese coins have been turned up by Japanese archaeologists.[6] As economic links were forged across ever larger expanses of Japan, bills were settled and loans made in Chinese cash. As in contemporary Europe, observers did not quite know whether to admire those who accumulated wealth through moneylending or to condemn them as exploitative usurers (though, interestingly, Buddhist monks and Shintō priests tended to favour moneylending, unlike the Catholic Church in medieval Europe).[7]

The Chinese deplored the constant outflow of bullion to feed the growing economy of Japan; Japanese traders were accused of hoovering up all the coins in the coastal towns they visited within twenty-four hours of their arrival. When China tried to limit the number of Japanese ships that could trade in its ports to five each year, the decree was rendered useless by the willingness of customs officers to accept bribes, so the number of ships was closer to fifty. It was easy to hide coins in the hold or simply to wait for the customs officers to disappear before taking the cash on board.[8] This passion for Chinese coins was stimulated by a simple, obvious feature of cash: copper coins did not deteriorate, whereas payment in silk, common earlier, involved the use of material that could be soiled, torn or burned; and an alternative to silk was rice, which was far more bulky and no less likely to deteriorate. The use of coin reduced transaction costs for itinerant merchants, as it was no longer necessary to shift bulk goods around in order to make payment.[9] Besides, there was a sense of connecting to Chinese culture when using Chinese coins, and this was felt as much in Korea or Vietnam as it was in Japan; these coins may have been plentiful, but they possessed prestige.

The Japanese court came to prefer private trade to formal exchanges of tribute for gifts, but that did not mean they were keen to see foreign merchants turning up all over their empire. In the tenth century, suspicion of these outsiders led the government to control the number of times a merchant could visit Japan – Chinese visitors were limited to one trip every three years and trips overseas by Japanese traders were strongly discouraged. The obvious way round this for Chinese merchants who were stopped by the Japanese authorities was to claim that the fierce currents of the open sea had carried them willy-nilly to Kyushu. And, once they had arrived, local officials declared they could not go back until the winds turned, a polite way of allowing them to stay without breaking out-of-date rules. Or Chinese merchants might simply claim on tenuous grounds that they were acting on behalf of a high official.[10] Hakata Bay remained the point of contact with China, and the government made up for the disappearance of handsome gifts from the Tang court by insisting on the compulsory purchase of the luxury goods it required, setting its own price.[11]

Chinese books were in special demand at court, including Buddhist religious texts such as the *Lotus Sutra* and collections of Tang poetry; in the early eleventh century the regent Fujiwara no Michinaga was given the Tang anthology three times, and in 1010 he gave a printed copy, with commentary, to the emperor. The first printed book to arrive in Japan was brought by a monk named Chōnen in 986, and consisted of a collection of the main Buddhist texts that had recently been produced in Chengdu after twelve years spent laboriously preparing the woodblocks. Thereafter the Japanese fell in love with printing.

Buddhist rituals also demanded specific perfumes for different occasions, so any chance to obtain these across the sea needed to be seized, while fine perfumes appear again and again in *The Tale of Genji*.[12] Admiration for Chinese culture remained the key to Japanese trade with China. In the later Middle Ages a more self-confident Japan became less embarrassed at presenting itself as culturally the equal of its old teacher, while Japan remained hungry for Chinese goods, so that trade burgeoned, achieving much greater volumes than in the years around 900. Yet the appetite for Chinese books, though strong, weakened somewhat as the Japanese began to produce their own court literature, in their own script and language.

One of the most lasting influences across the sea was the popularization of tea, which was originally a very special drink; the Zen Buddhists spread knowledge of tea-drinking in the twelfth century, as an aid to contemplation. Tea parties enhanced by a tasting of fine dishes made of rice, noodles, tofu and exotic fruit, as well as poetry readings, became fashionable in high society from 1185, during the Kamakura period. Japan began to produce its own excellent tea (the imperial court demanded tribute in tea as early as 815); but it was common to sample both Chinese and Japanese teas at these events, and high-quality Jian bowls were imported all the way from southern China for just this purpose. Rather later, in the eighteenth century, the tea lodge and tea ceremony came into fashion, and the rituals were codified. At first, tea was drunk after steeping the leaves, or part of a brick of powdered tea, in water; tradition attributes the arrival of whisked *matcha*, powdered green tea drunk thick and strong, to the traveller Eisai, who had tasted something similar in China at the end of the twelfth century. Both documents and material finds (Chinese tea bowls) show that this type of tea was known earlier.[13] Still, the crucial point is that the sea route from China continued to bring ideas and practices to Japan. Tea, with its close links to Buddhism, had a special impact, but there were other favourite luxuries that came across the waves. Imported parrots had already fascinated the Heian court in the eleventh century, especially since they seemed to be perfectly capable of learning Japanese. Even while the imperial court in Tang China officially disapproved of private trade across the sea, the desire for gold, in which (as Marco Polo later pointed out) Japan was rich, richer than much of China, made tolerance of this traffic inescapable; and the same applied to pearls, whether from Honshu or from the island of Tsushima, a product that is still the pride of Japan:[14] 'Their trade ships arrive on our shores by a north-easterly wind, and they bring us all sorts of merchandise: products of high value – gold leaf, gold dust, decorative pearls, pearls for medicinal use, mercury, stag horn . . .'[15] To these could be added lacquered boxes and folding fans.[16] All this testifies to the fact that not just Japanese merchants but Japanese mariners were gaining in confidence after the disastrous China voyages of Ennin's time.

It proved impossible to control foreign traders once they began to arrive in large numbers. At Hakata, a town began to develop where, in the early days of the Kōrokan, there had been only very limited facilities. Moreover, Hakata contained a large colony of Chinese settlers, some of whom married Japanese women and produced a generation of mixed parentage, who could then claim to be Japanese and exempt from any restrictions on foreigners. Good connections helped; in 1150 just such a merchant exchanged Chinese books for thirty ounces of gold dust from the Minister of the Left, the senior minister at court, and was asked to bring even more Chinese books to his patron. In the twelfth century 1,600 Chinese families are said to have lived in Hakata Bay; meanwhile the Koreans gradually disappeared from the maritime trade routes.[17] During the excavation of the metro at Fukoaka, the city on Kyushu which incorporates the medieval port of Hakata, 35,000 fragments of native and Chinese pottery were found, the latter coming mainly from centres of production on the Chinese coasts. Some of this pottery was of very high quality. The fragments included sherds of pale green celadon wares, as well as the white pottery of Yuezhou which was known sometimes under the name *hisoku*, or 'forbidden object', because it was originally reserved to the Chinese imperial family alone, but here it was in Hakata on its way, presumably, to the imperial court at Kyoto (also known as Heian, which had replaced Nara as the seat of government several centuries earlier).[18] Everyone tried to cash in on this trade. At the start of the eleventh century, the Fujiwara clan were happy to obtain foreign goods such as furs, medicines and perfumes by way of the estates they held on Kyushu, even though direct contact with foreign merchants had until recently been officially prohibited. Among these luxury imports were pigments such as verdigris, a by-product of oxidized copper used to make green paint.[19]

This trade between Japan and the mainland underwent a series of distinct phases in the Middle Ages. By the eleventh and twelfth centuries, there is fuller evidence for regular commercial exchanges. At least one well-laden vessel a year reached Hakata full of luxury goods for the Japanese elite.[20] This does not sound like very much, and the presence of Chinese settlers at Hakata, not to mention the mountains of pottery, suggests that there was much more movement back and forth to China. Some of the settlers were keen to introduce their own artisan skills to Japan, whether in pottery, metalwork or woodwork, and (as the objects in the Shōsō-in depository at Nara reveal) the court collected both objects from distant parts of Asia and local copies of them. Hakata stood at some remove from the centres of power at Nara and Kyoto. Hakata stood even further from the new power base that was created after 1185 at Kamakura, beyond modern Tokyo, following a brief but violent civil war between the Minamoto and Taira clans.[21] The *bakufu* based at Kamakura was less well able to control the day-to-day affairs of Kyushu island; provincial nobles gained greater power in areas far from the centre, and towns and trade and fairs expanded under their patronage.[22]

The wreck of a Chinese junk found off the Korean coast, the Sinan wreck, provides eloquent testimony to this commercial expansion. Over the centuries, half the hull had been destroyed by the waves; but the area below decks had become buried in mud, and beneath the hatch, within a hull divided into seven partitions, there survived a treasure trove of Chinese goods, some of which were still neatly packed in the wooden containers in which they had been loaded on board. Twenty-eight metres long and about a quarter of that at maximum width, the ship could carry up to 200 tons of cargo. Eighteen thousand pieces of pottery, predominantly Chinese (including about 2,900 celadon wares), were found on board, along with thin-walled, high-quality porcelain bowls made in China and vases with pedestals that had originated in south-east Asia. The light-green celadons, from the period of Mongol rule in China (the Yuan dynasty) include delightful jars with dragon-shaped handles and with floral relief, as well as the classic plain bowls whose trademark is their sheer simplicity. On the other hand, the lack of the famous blue-and-white porcelain among the finds suggests that these wares were still jealously confined to China itself, on the eve of the great expansion in their production that would make them the favourite product of China, exported all over the known world.[23] Another impressive part of the cargo consisted of eighteen tons of Chinese copper coins, generally strung together and carrying a wooden tag with their owner's name, making a total of more than 8,000,000 coins; this gives some idea of the sheer scale of the drainage of bullion out of China.[24] One chest had been packed full of pepper. Very few Korean goods were found in the cargo, so it is unlikely that the ship stopped for any length of time at a Korean port, even though it coasted past Korea itself. The ship was apparently wrecked while it was sailing from Ningbo on the Chinese coast to Japan, on the account of the Tōfuku-ji Zen Buddhist monastery of Kyoto, whose name appears on several of the wooden tags, as does a date corresponding to 1323, which is the probable date of the disaster at sea. This was one of the great monasteries of Kyoto, but it had burned down a few years earlier and was seeking to finance its rebuilding programme by investing in a grand trading expedition.[25] Korean experts think that the ship was actually bound for Okinawa and south-east Asia after it called in at a Japanese port, presumably Hakata.[26]

The private trade was increasingly compromised by the activities of the pirates from Tsushima and western Kyushu known as *wakō*; this became a particularly severe problem from the fourteenth century onwards, and provides further evidence that trade was flourishing, since there was clearly good business to be done by interlopers.[27] Once they had seized other people's cargoes, these pirates would turn into merchants and sell the goods for profit. Surprisingly, since it is such a narrow space that one would have expected it to be easy to supervise, the Inland Sea through which shipping had to pass to reach the outports of Kyoto from Hakata was a particularly pirate-infested area. It had long been a lively zone of exchange where large quantities of goods such as rice were transported from the islands of Shikoku and Kyushu to the province of Kinai, where Nara and Kyoto lay; it has been seen that the Japanese had excellent experience of short-range navigation, but for a long time were hopeless navigators out in the open ocean. However, by the late Middle Ages there is plentiful evidence of lively trade out of one of those outports, Hyogo, in a customs register of 1445, which reveals that nearly 2,000 vessels passed through one tollgate in a year, heading in the direction of Kyoto.[28]

One historian speaks of the twelfth to the fourteenth centuries as a time of active free trade, culminating in the fifteenth century in a balance of trade that was favourable to the Japanese.

The end of the Middle Ages saw major political transformations in Japan, Korea and China, as earlier dynasties were supplanted – the Mongol Yuan were replaced by the longlasting, native Ming dynasty in 1368, and an even longer-lasting royal house, the Li, took charge in Koryŏ (Korea). Fourteenth-century Japan was a battleground between rival clans that sought political power, though not the imperial throne, for the emperors had been pushed to one side by the shoguns and had become ciphers. These conflicts within Japan seem actually to have fostered trade; the shoguns encouraged trade since they were keen to raise ever larger sums from taxation, and the land alone could not meet the expense of maintaining the military establishment they required. During this period, the coastal village of Sakai, on Ōsaka Bay, with its ready access by road to Kyoto, grew into a commercial city trading as far afield as China, and enjoyed the support of the Ashikaga shoguns. Sakai grew and grew and in the early sixteenth century it was home to 30,000 people; it retained a degree of autonomy, while remaining dependent on the favours of the warlords who controlled the area around Kyoto that Sakai was well placed to service.[29]

Contact with China was not always peaceful, and the first Ming emperor, Hung Wu-ti, delivered a severe telling-off to the Japanese when he sent a messenger to Kyushu in 1369, carrying a letter that complained bitterly of Japanese piracy. The sending of a mission was not a signal that Japan was being treated as an equal: the Ming emperor was determined to reclaim Chinese sovereignty over the entire expanse from Java and Cambodia to Korea and Japan; and Hung was also conscious of his peasant origins and therefore anxious to present himself as an emperor in the great Chinese tradition. And yet, paradoxically, the Chinese emperor banned Chinese merchants from trading overseas, preferring to revert to the old system of tributary embassies – those from Korea were welcome to come several times a year, and those from other kingdoms, such as Okinawa, much less often. The Japanese rulers did not react kindly to the reproofs that kept coming from their Ming counterparts, which even included hints that China would invade Japan:

The Chinese Minister of Rites: You should look into the events of the past thousand years for reference. Examine them carefully! . . . If you really wish to find out who would win and lose and which of us is right or wrong, and which side is the stronger or weaker, I am afraid it would not be to your advantage. Examine this carefully!

Prince Kanenaga: Heaven and earth are vast; they are not monopolised by one ruler. The universe is great and wide, and various countries are created each to have a share in its rule. Now the world is the world's world; it does not belong to a single person.[30]

Defiance, which was very rare, only made relations more difficult, and the Japanese learned that the political price was an occasional admission that even the Japanese emperor was a vassal of the Chinese one. However, this admission could bring great dividends: at the time of the early Ming voyages, around 1400, the Chinese sought to take tribute from a vast swathe of east Asia and the Indian Ocean; but the Japanese were compliant and were rewarded with gifts of silk, silver and lacquer, and were able to maintain their exports of horses and armaments to the mainland. Later, in 1432–3, these included over 3,000 sabres, and nearly 10,000 sabres in 1453. And then there was the massive political dividend, for acceptance of Ming overlordship, which involved no interference in the government of Japan itself, helped secure the claims of the Ashikaga shoguns to rule Japan.[31]

This was a period in which control of the shipping routes off the Asian coasts shifted away from the Chinese, who had dominated navigation for several centuries, into the hands of other peoples, including the Japanese, though many of these were *wakō* pirates. The ban on foreign travel that applied to Chinese merchants and mariners left others free to ply the seas, and opportunities were seized by all the peoples of the islands that flank China, from Japan to Java. Japan was visited by ships from Siam and Java around 1400. In 1406 a Javan ship bound for Korea was carrying parrots, peacocks, pepper and camphor, and not surprisingly it was seized by Japanese pirates; however, five years later a Javan mission reached Kyushu safely.[32] A particularly important role was played by the autonomous kingdom in the Ryukyu islands, with its centre at Okinawa, on the southern edge of this Japanese Mediterranean; this region provided southward links, connecting the Japanese seas to some of the longer-distance trade routes as far as the Malacca Strait (home to Melaka, Palembang and Temasek, the modern Singapore), which had become once again a very significant centre of the spice trade in the fifteenth century. Chinese withdrawal thus had the paradoxical effect of opening up the seas.

II

Although there are occasional accounts of sea battles off Korea, and although the *wakō* pirates became an increasing worry, the maritime history of the waters between Japan, China and Java is mainly a history of relatively peaceful relations. There were many tensions, revealed by the attempts to ban private trade by Japanese merchants, or to prevent the export of coin from China, but mass invasions were a rarity. The great exception is the Mongol attacks on Japan, news of which reached as far as western Europe, thanks to Marco Polo; indeed, his account of what happened furnishes valuable details that have been corroborated, as will be seen, by marine archaeologists, and by remarkable illustrated scrolls dating from between 1294 and 1316 that were copied again and again over the centuries for Japanese scholars.[33] The Mongol attacks both were the product of the Mongols' own insistence that the Great Khan was appointed by Heaven to rule the world (and woe betide those who opposed the divine command), and also betray the influence of earlier Chinese ideas about the superiority of the Middle Kingdom over all other territories. The Chinese ideas were adopted and adapted by Khubilai, the member of the Mongol royal house who seized control of China and established the Yuan dynasty, conquering the Southern Song capital at Hangzhou in 1275.[34] Khubilai also coveted Japan's famed wealth in gold and pearls. He proposed to tap into the wealth of Japan by exacting a large tribute, if at all possible, but if that were to prove impossible, the single-word answer any Mongol khan was bound to give was 'war'.

Although doubt has been cast on the claim that Khubilai Khan and Marco Polo even met, Polo's account of Japan must reflect stories that he heard somewhere out in the East:

> I will tell you a wonderful thing about the palace of the Lord of that island. You must know that he has a great palace which is entirely roofed with fine gold, just as our churches are roofed with lead, insomuch that it would scarcely be possible to estimate its value. Moreover, all the pavement of the palace, and the floors of its chambers, are entirely of gold, in plates like slabs of stone, a good two fingers thick; and the windows are also of gold, so that altogether the richness of this palace is past all bounds and belief. They have also pearls in abundance, which are of a rose colour, but fine, big, and round, and quite as valuable as the white ones. They also have quantities of other precious stones. Khubilai, the Great Khan who now reigns, having heard much of the immense wealth that was in this island, formed a plan to get possession of it.[35]

A contemporary Buddhist monk from Japan, Togen Eian, thought that the Mongols were awestruck by the quality of Japanese armour and the excellence of Japanese archers: 'our armour makes even the gods tremble . . . Once Japan's warriors are under their control they will be able to conquer

China and India.' He argued that 'with the strength of Japan and the Mongols combined, no country could resist. That is why the Mongols now desire to subjugate Japan.'[36]

Even so, Khubilai might well have left Japan alone and might have concentrated more on Vietnam (another obsession), but for the breakdown of Mongol relations with Koryŏ, whose king was now master of all Korea. At the start of the thirteenth century, as Mongol power spread over vast tracts to east and west, the Koreans had co-operated with the Mongols, even sending troops to help them subdue troublesome neighbours in northern China in 1219, though they had to agree to send a heavy tribute to the Mongol khan, and the Mongol treatment of the Koreans swung between extremes. The Koreans had their own grievances against the Japanese as a result of the raids by the *wakō* pirates, which carried on until 1265.[37] A Korean supporter of the Mongols named Ch'oe-I fed information to Khubilai, who seems to have been impressed by Ch'oe-I's account of the sophisticated customs of the Japanese. He suggested that Khubilai Khan might like to send an exploratory embassy to Japan, and when a letter from the khan reached Japan, at the start of 1268 (though it had actually been written in August 1266), the message was unusually friendly from a Mongol perspective, even though the letter threatened war if the Japanese did not agree to cordial relations, with the not so diplomatically phrased question: 'it will lead to war, and who is there who likes such a state of things? Think of this, O king!'[38] There was a second letter from the king of Koryŏ begging the Japanese to take heed, and pointing out that Khubilai had no intention of interfering with the running of the Japanese Empire. At this stage Khubilai was not inclined to go further than mild threats. He still had to take control of the lands of the Southern Song in China's deep south, and was building up his power in Korea. He may have felt that he could not ignore Japan, because of its strong trade relations with his Southern Song enemies; the Japanese were probably sending essential supplies to the Song, such as weapons. Song refugees who reached Japan included dozens of very influential Buddhist monks of the Zen school; in a sense, the Japanese kept Song culture alive when China lay under Yuan rule, for the *bakufu*, the Japanese military elite, wished to project an image of themselves as refined followers of Chinese fashion able to compete with the scholars and poets of the closeted imperial court at Kyoto. On the other hand, Khubilai had no particular quarrel with Japan, which posed no direct military threat.[39]

The shogun's government was, however, wise to Mongol wiles; precisely because there was now regular contact across the sea with the Song, the shogun knew perfectly well what the Mongols demanded of their subjects, notably punitive amounts of tribute. The islands themselves seemed safe. The Mongols had never ventured across the sea. Why should one concern oneself with empty threats? So the *bakufu* in Kamakura chose to send back the envoys with no reply. There was the same reaction at Kyoto from the court of the emperor, in whose name any recognition of Mongol superiority would have been made, even though real power rested with the shogun and *bakufu*. In 1269 seventy Mongols and Koreans turned up on Tsushima and demanded an answer to the khan's letters; once again the shogun did not deign to answer and the mission returned home with a couple of captives, who were allowed to visit Khubilai's palace before being sent home, in the hope that their reports of his power and grandeur would shock the *bakufu* into a response; even then there was silence in Japan.[40] But after rejecting the khan's approach and hearing rather more about Khubilai's character and aims the Japanese began to show signs that they were more rattled than they had been willing to admit while the original envoys were in their midst. They even drafted a reply at long last; but it was never sent. They required prayers for peace to be recited, and they issued a ritual curse against the Mongols. In addition, the Japanese laid plans for a raid on the coast of Korea, to knock out whatever facilities were in place for building a fleet to attack Japan. When it became more obvious that the Mongol threat was not an idle one, the Japanese decided that attacking Korea would only make things worse.

In October 1274 the first Mongol assault duly struck Japan. In fact, it was a joint attack by the Mongol khan's army and navy and by the army and navy of his vassal the king of Koryŏ. Nine hundred ships took the predictable route past Tsushima island to Hakata Bay, the shortest direct route from the southern tip of Korea.[41] There were said to be nearly 30,000 men on board, though this figure should be taken with a pinch of salt. To strike terror into their foes, the Mongols are said to have nailed the naked corpses of Japanese women to the thwarts of their ships.[42] Hakata was set on fire, but the Japanese put up a very tough resistance. The samurai Takezaki Suenaga recorded in his illustrated scrolls how he encountered another Japanese warrior who had had a productive day:

I met a warrior on a dapple grey horse at Komatsubara. He wore purple armour with a reverse arrowhead design, and a crimson billowing cape and, having just defeated the invaders at their encampment, was returning with a hundred horsemen. The pirates had fled. Two had been taken. He looked most brave and had two retainers walking before him on his left and right carrying heads – one pierced on a sword, the other on a *naginata* [rather like a halberd].

'Who passes here looking so brave?' I asked, and he replied:

'I am Kikuchi Jirō Takefusa of Higo province. Who are you?'

'I am Takezaki Gorō Hyōe Suenaga of the same province. Watch me attack!'

Saying so, I charged.[43]

After a day of fighting against such highly motivated heroes, the Mongol–Korean forces withdrew discomfited.[44]

Khubilai was even more determined to conquer Japan after the humiliation of the rapid defeat suffered in 1274; but for the moment he concentrated on a much more important target, the conquest of southern China. The year after the Japanese fiasco he could take pride in the occupation of Hangzhou; in 1277 the great port of Quanzhou, which Marco Polo claimed to know well, surrendered, after its leaders realized that any hope of maintaining its prominent position in maritime trade would be left in ruins by a Mongol assault on the city. In 1279 the Mongols proved that they could win a major battle at sea: only nine Song ships escaped destruction or capture, out of a fleet of 900; and the admiral not merely committed suicide by jumping into the waves, but threw the child emperor into the sea as well. The Song dynasty was extinguished.[45]

The second attack on Japan took place six and a half years after the first; the Mongols conscripted large numbers of former Song soldiers into their army for the new attack on Japan. This time the Great Khan intended not just to impose Mongol overlordship but to settle the land, for the ships carried farm tools as well as weapons. Those awaiting death sentences were released so long as they agreed to serve in the vast army Khubilai Khan was putting together. But the Japanese were once again confident, to what might seem a foolhardy degree, in their ability to survive this assault. They decided to admit the Mongol ambassadors to Kamakura, which must have seemed a good sign; but once the ambassadors arrived, they were beheaded and their heads were put on display, rendering attack inevitable.[46] Painfully aware that Hakata had been destroyed during the brief attack in 1274, the government ordered a long stone wall, twelve and a half miles long, to be built around Hakata Bay, bits of which still survive.[47] And Hakata Bay became the scene of intense fighting on sea and on land, as the Japanese ships and ground troops harried the much larger invasion force that had come by way of the islands of Tsushima and Iki, while a second wave of attackers gathered at the western tip of Kyushu, off the little offshore island of Takeshima.[48]

Among acts of bravery those of Kawano Michiari stand out; he had already helped resist the invaders in 1274, and this time he showed how brave he was by standing outside the defensive wall and engaging directly with the invaders. One day he saw a heron pick up an arrow and drop it on one of the Mongol ships. This was surely an augury of Japanese victory; so he and his uncle decided the time had come to strike a blow at the heart of the Mongol fleet. They set out across the bay in a couple of small boats; they had no difficulty penetrating the Mongol fleet, because the Mongols thought they must be bringing an offer to submit; so they came alongside one of the flagships whose astonished crew surrendered after Kawano had killed a fearsome giant of a soldier.[49] Kawano took one of the Mongol generals prisoner, even though he was wounded in the shoulder, and even though his uncle was killed. Kawano then had time to write a poem commemorating his achievement while he was heading back to dry land.[50] These exploits made him a Japanese hero. Under the military rule of the *bakufu*, esteem for the martial prowess of the samurai had risen to new heights; one or two defenders of Japan against the Mongols were even worshipped as gods by later generations.

All these efforts were not enough to hold back the waves of invaders. Korean ships arrived in Tsushima; the islanders tried to escape to the hills, but the cries of their children gave away their hiding places, and the Koreans ruthlessly massacred the islanders. The invaders then bombarded the inhabitants of Iki, the next island between Korea and Japan, with exploding ceramic spheres launched from catapults. On the other hand, the cramped conditions on board the Mongol navy helped disease to spread, with the loss of 3,000 men, as Chinese sources admitted. The Mongol commanders found it impossible to co-ordinate the actions of the different detachments arriving from Korea and from much further south, and they realized that Hakata Bay was well defended and not suitable for a mass landing. The naval detachments that had arrived near Hakata Bay lashed their ships together to create a continuous line of boats, a sort of counterwall, facing off the Japanese but without very clear objectives about what to do next.[51] Small Japanese boats pestered the Mongol fleet like wasps, crowding the waters. Takezaki Suenaga described the chaos in Hakata Bay:

'I am acting on secret orders. Let me on the boat!'

I brought my boat by Takamasa's.

'The *shugo* [provincial governor] did not order you here. Get your boat out of here!'

Having no recourse I replied: 'As you know, I have not been called up by the *shugo*. I am the deputy *shugo* but arrived late. Heed my command.'

'Lord Tsumori is on the boat. There is no more room.'[52]

In the end, Takezaki was allowed to board, and fought with vigour, even though he was wounded.

Nonetheless, all was going quite well for the Mongols, who managed to hold a patch of land for a while, though they were beaten back to the offshore islands. That was not the same as seeing them off; the threat remained real. And then, in answer to the defenders' prayers, 'a green dragon raised its head from the waves', the sky darkened and suddenly a great typhoon struck. Many ships, still fully loaded with soldiers, were tossed around the sea or on to dry land, and others collided with one another. It has been suggested that it was no more than an easterly wind that blew the Mongol ships back to the Asian mainland just when they were inclined to withdraw anyway. Some Japanese writers, notably the warrior Takezaki Suenaga, who was there, do not mention this 'divine wind'.[53] Yet the hard physical evidence that will be confronted in a moment tells a different, and more traditional, story. Japanese, Chinese and Korean descriptions of what happened largely concur, so the fact that this 'divine wind', or *kami-kaze*, became such a powerful Japanese legend should not obscure its historical foundation. It is said 100,000 men drowned and 4,000 ships sank, for which read perhaps 10,000 men and 400 ships.[54]

One of the most fascinating accounts of the Mongol invasion was provided by the Venetian Marco Polo. He was only aware of one attack on Japan, the second one – he knew the name of one of the commanders of the second invasion force, Abacan; Chinese whispers apparently transformed the name of the other, Fan Wenhu, into Vonsainchin.[55] According to Marco Polo, these two 'barons' in charge of the expedition deeply disliked one another. They were 'able and valiant men', and they set out as ordered from the ports of Zaytun (Quanzhou) and Quinsay (Hangzhou), important centres of trade towards south-east Asia. They landed in Japan, and Polo tells a vivid atrocity story in which eight Japanese men were sent for execution, but it proved impossible to cut off their heads or to inflict any wound whatsoever, as they possessed a magic stone inserted under their skin; and as a result the cruel Mongols beat them to death instead. Before long, however, a very great wind came and the Mongols were forced to leave; many ships sank, but 30,000 men under the command of one of the barons took refuge on an uninhabited desert island, hoping that the remaining fleet, which was under the command of the other baron, would come and rescue them. They could see the fleet moving ahead under full sail, but 'the baron who escaped never showed the slightest desire to return to his colleague who was left on the island'. Thereupon the Japanese sent their own fleet to this island; the shipwrecked army fled into the hills and, while the Japanese sought them out, the Mongols crept down to the Japanese ships and commandeered them; they then sailed with Japanese banners flying to what he calls 'the Great Island', where they were greeted as returning Japanese heroes. So they landed and marched on the Japanese capital, which they seized. The Japanese counter-attacked and besieged the capital, and after seven months the Mongols agreed to surrender, 'on condition that their lives should be spared'. Meanwhile, the fate of the two barons was much grimmer: they did manage to reach home, but they were sent off to be executed, because one had fled and the other 'had never behaved as a good soldier ought to do'.[56]

It is obvious that Marco Polo's stories of Japan are a mixture of truth and fiction, as are his stories of other parts of east Asia. At some points in his account of the Mongol attack he seems to inhabit the world of fairy tales, with magic stones and a non-existent occupation of Kyoto or another city. Polo's account of the rivalry between the commanders is certainly credible; and the Japanese chronicle mentions their disappearance, presumed lost at sea. In the Japanese version a commander fell ill and the other did not quite know what to do; the impression is of chaotic lack of leadership rather than a falling-out between rivals. Polo should not be ignored, then, but the best evidence for what happened comes from the physical remains of the Mongol fleet and army. One clue was a bronze Mongol seal dating from 1277, the property of an army commander, that was found on the island of Takashima, visited by the second wave of Mongols en route to Japan. This seemed to confirm that the anchors, cata-pult balls, pottery and other equipment discovered offshore by a team of divers were the residue of the shattered Mongol fleet. When pieces of wood were raised from the deep, it proved possible to date them to the twelfth or thirteenth centuries, and the presence of white porcelain from southern China also seemed to confirm that this was the fleet the Great Khan had sent from there against Japan. These were very large ships, as much as 200 feet long, and they were largely constructed out of camphor wood. As proof that the archaeologists had not simply found the shipwreck of a merchant vessel carrying fine ceramics, there were the swords, arrows, crossbow bolts and bombs made of baked earth and packed with shrapnel – and even part of the skeleton of a warrior surrounded by his helmet and the remains of his leather armour. There were the anchors of ships that had broken their cables, which pointed towards the shore, suggesting that the ships had been hurled by the wind towards the coast, where those that had survived so far had been smashed into pieces. The decision to lash the ships together and to create a floating wall had proved utterly disastrous. As one ship was picked up by the surging seas, it carried along its neighbours.[57] But the most telling evidence of all came from analysis of the wooden fragments of the ships themselves. Rust marks showed that the planks had been nailed together in a rather haphazard way. Either the ships had been poorly repaired after previous outings, or they had been incompetently constructed from the start. Preparing a vast fleet against a deadline had an inevitable consequence: ships were approved for service when they had not been properly checked (even though one piece of wood found underwater was an inspection certificate issued after something, very probably a ship, had been repaired). Many pots taken on board were poorly made, as if they had been rushed through the kilns, and there are doubts about the efficiency of a large stone anchor made in two pieces, again in apparent haste.[58] The conclusion is that the Mongol fleet may well have been overwhelmed by a storm, but that the ships had much less chance of surviving a typhoon because they had been so poorly constructed, and they fell apart under stress. The discovery of part of the remains of the Great Khan's fleet is one of the major achievements of marine archaeology, and fits well with the narrative accounts.

When the second attack failed, Khubilai Khan turned his main attention to Vietnam and Java, with no more success. Marco Polo knew that Khubilai's efforts to conquer Java had failed. Here again Khubilai's interest was surely prompted by the wealth of the island and its close trading links to China, which Polo particularly stressed. In the case of Vietnam, his excuse for conquest was that the kingdom of Đại Việt had offered refuge to leading members of the Song government, while another Indo-Chinese kingdom, Champa, was an important centre of trade and piracy. The defenders of Đại Việt also witnessed the destruction of a Mongol fleet, during the battle of Bạch Đằng, which was fought in a river mouth against tens, maybe hundreds, of thousands of invaders in 1287; but this time the destruction of the fleet was accomplished by human efforts, after the Vietnamese attacked the fleet with blazing arrows and then sent burning bamboo rafts towards the ships.[59]

The Yuan dynasty not surprisingly played down the embarrassment of its defeats at sea, in Japan, Vietnam and Java. Relations between China and Japan recovered remarkably quickly after 1281. Trading ships moved back and forth between the two countries as if nothing much had happened; the Yuan government licensed regular visits to China by Japanese ships. However, their victories against the odds became the subject of great pride for the Japanese, who were convinced that their prayers to the gods had been answered; at the imperial court in Kyoto, it was argued that the prayers of the Shintō priests at the great shrine of Ise had persuaded the gods to send the great black cloud that emerged out of a clear sky; out of it sped the arrow of the gods that roared like a typhoon, while the sea rose up in a great mountain of a tsunami and crushed the invasion fleet into splinters.[60] The victory not merely brought prestige to the imperial court and the Shintō establishment, but confirmed the wisdom of the warrior *bakufu* in Kamakura, with their links to the Zen Buddhists. Both sides in the complex system of rule therefore benefited. More than that, continuing mobilization, made necessary by the threat of a third invasion, justified the extension of Kamakuran authority over larger areas of Japan, including tracts of the islands of Shikoku and Kyushu. It has been argued that 'the *bakufu* became a truly national power only after this war'.[61] And the 'divine wind' would be invoked nearly seven centuries later by the *kami-kaze* pilots of the Japanese imperial air force.

III

The chain of the Ryukyu islands, of which the best-known is Okinawa, is a perfect example of a small and apparently insignificant archipelago that profited from its middle position to acquire wealth and influence. Its rulers insisted that they lived on poor and barren islands, which was precisely the reason that their subjects learned to make money by acting as intermediaries with the rest of the west Pacific rim. In 1433 the king of Chuzan in the Ryukyu islands wrote to the king of Siam: 'this country is deficient in articles of tribute', and proceeded to send a ship to Siam loaded not with local goods but with Chinese porcelain.[62] There were a few local products that were admired overseas: horses, mother-of-pearl and red dye, but the products of Chinese and Japanese craftsmanship took priority when loading a cargo.[63] What was distinctive about the people of the Ryukyu islands was that the inhabitants took the initiative themselves, seizing the opportunity created by the withdrawal from the sea of their mighty neighbour Ming China. The Ryukyu islands were colonized from many directions in the very remote past, but links to Japan have always been especially strong; one can sail in good weather from the island chain towards Kyushu without losing sight of land, and over the centuries settlers arrived in the islands from southern Japan. Early in the seventh century AD the Chinese emperor, perhaps seduced by the idea that these islands were the Land of Happy Immortals, sent an expedition in this direction and carried off many prisoners, and Chinese coins from this period prove that there was indeed contact with the mainland at this stage.[64] Even so, it was only at the end of the seventh century that Japanese officials began to take serious notice of their southern neighbours. No doubt a particular reason for doing so was that the Japanese emperor was keen to show that he, like the emperor of China, received tribute from subordinate peoples.[65]

Bitter strife between the great noble clans of Taira and Minamoto in Japan in the middle of the twelfth century spilled over into the Ryukyu island chain. A keen opponent of the Taira named Tamemoto no Minamoto was a skilled archer; he had been brought up on Kyushu and he joined a Minamoto assault on Kyoto, only to be captured. He was lucky to escape execution, but his punishment was still cruel: the sinews of his bow-arm were severed, and he was sent to the Izu islands off the tip of Kyushu, where he spent fourteen years of dull exile. From there, in one tradition, he is said to have been blown across to Onigashima, 'Devil's Island', which may be Okinawa, after his boat was caught in a storm. He had only intended to travel the small distance between two Izu islands, but now he seized the opportunity to make friends with the king, and ended up marrying his daughter. A child, Shunten, was born who would later rule the Ryukyus; but Tamemoto was always keen to return to the fray, and so, leaving behind his wife and child, he sailed back to Japan, where the Deputy Governor of Izu smashed his little army to pieces. Rather than submitting, Tamemoto committed *seppuku*, better known as *hara-kiri*, a ceremony that was coming into fashion about now. That, at least, is the story, but it probably elaborates a less dramatic history of wandering warriors who offered their services to the chieftains of Okinawa, of whom the partly Japanese Shunten was one.

Japanese influence grew on the islands, marked by the arrival of a writing system based on the syllabic signs of Japanese script. However, the Ryukyuans did not adopt the additional and complex Chinese characters that had become locked into Japanese script, and relied on the plain syllables only – something most people staring at Japanese writing would consider a very wise decision.[66] The Japanese port of Sakai entertained very close trading ties with Ryukyu in the fifteenth century, and contact was stimulated by tea-drinking – this generated a passion for tea bowls and other tea equipment that passed into the islands, while Zen vegetarianism seems to have brought new fashions in food and new types of shredding bowl suitable for ascetic Zen menus. In return, the Japanese could acquire Chinese paintings, pottery and metalware, which also passed through the islands.[67] Once again one has to rely on late traditions, but Buddhism is said to have spread within these islands only after a monk named Zenkan was shipwrecked there around 1270.[68] Uniting the islands, which stretch over hundreds of miles, was beyond the capacity of the chieftains of Okinawa, much the largest island, which stands two thirds of the way down the chain and lies closer to Taiwan than to Kyushu.

Further fragmentation of power in fourteenth-century Japan had serious consequences in the Ryukyus. The Ashikaga shoguns recognized a noble family from Kyushu as 'Lords of the Twelve Southern Islands', though they had already been holding that office for a while. This did nothing to solve internal problems in Okinawa (the 'kingdom of Chuzan'), for Chuzan, like Japan itself, was divided among competing warlords. One of these, Satto, had seized power after the death of the king in 1349, and was dazzled by a Chinese embassy that arrived in 1372 with the intention of asserting the imperial authority of the Ming dynasty, which had launched a coup against the Mongols four years earlier. Satto was evidently impressed with the gifts he received, along with those that arrived following a trip to the Ming court by his brother, who returned with a seal of investiture, as if the Chinese had conferred the crown that Satto had usurped nearly twenty years before the Ming revolution had even succeeded. The Okinawan ambassadors won praise for their punctilious observance of the exacting rituals that tributary embassies had to undergo, including the nine ritual prostrations known as *koutou* (kowtow); they were the first people to accept Ming claims, before the Vietnamese, Siamese and others, and they continued to pay tribute for many centuries without complaint.[69] Not for nothing did the king of Choson in Korea write to the king of Chuzan in Ryukyu: 'we reaffirm that every nation washed by the oceans is under the influence of China.'[70]

The pay-off was the lively trade conducted through official channels, as well as a certain amount of surreptitious trade: in 1381 the interpreter attached to the Ryukyu mission was discovered attempting to smuggle a sizeable cargo of spices out of China. Other prized products were porcelain and silk.[71] Yet the Okinawans did not simply look towards China; they could offer little from their own resources, so the answer was to create a much wider network that tapped into the supplies available in Korea and Japan to the north, and the South China Sea to the south. The creation of this network was deliberate; these words were inscribed on a bell which in 1458 was deposited in a temple on the islands:

> The kingdom of Ryukyu is a place of pure beauty set in the southern seas. Gathered together there, the treasures from three countries, Korea, the Ming Empire and Japan, are to be found. It is a fabled island, which arose from the seas between China and Japan. Its ships are a bridge between 10,000 nations.[72]

To cast this bell, metal had to be imported and the techniques of bronze-casting to be learned. On the other hand, at the start of the sixteenth century, when he was about to send off an expedition to Melaka, the king of Chuzan reflected on the fundamental problem the Ryukyu islands faced:

> This country's products are meagre and inadequate as articles of tribute, causing great inconvenience. For that reason, we are now despatching Chief Envoy Kamadu, Interpreter Kao Hsien, and others aboard a seagoing ship ... with a cargo of porcelain and other goods, to proceed to the productive land of Melaka in order to purchase such products as sapanwood and pepper through mutually satisfactory arrangements, and then to return to this country to make preparations for the presentation of tribute to the Ming Celestial Court in a subsequent year.[73]

The capital of Okinawa, Naha, became a flourishing and cosmopolitan centre of trade, comparable to Hakata and Melaka, with a significant immigrant population from Japan, though many Chinese preferred to live in their own town, Kunemura, a little way off, and included mariners and scribes, who were always chosen to compose diplomatic correspondence with China and south-east Asia. Coins, copied from Ming examples, were produced as Chinese metal flowed into the island, so that the economy was increasingly monetized, rather as was the case in medieval Japan.[74] Excavations on ten sites in the islands have revealed a great variety of ceramics that arrived from all directions: among the finest pieces there are pale green celadons, blue-and-white pottery and whiteware, all from China, as well as Imari blue-and-white from Japan, Korean celadon, and both Thai and Vietnamese pottery.[75] At the northern end of the island chain, a base was created for commerce with the Inland Sea in Japan; Ryukyuans brought the spices and other luxuries of south-east Asia to Nagasaki in western Kyushu, obtaining a range of delicacies for home consumption, some of which sound not very appetizing – sea slugs, shark fins, abalone and seaweed – and also weapons and Japanese gold.[76]

Meanwhile, the king of Chuzan was corresponding with neighbours in Siam, Melaka, Indonesia (including Palembang) and Korea; the oldest known letter in the Ryukyu archives dates from 1425 and reports an embassy to Siam in 1419, though there is other evidence that links went back at least as far as the reign of Satto.[77] The Ryukyu archives once contained an extraordinarily rich collection of correspondence, conducted in Chinese, between the kings of Ryukyu and their neighbours; however, the letters were destroyed in the Second World War during the American assault on Okinawa before they had been closely studied. The patient reconstruction of the documents from decaying photostats and scattered transcriptions has brought to light a lively network of political and commercial contacts in which Ryukyu functioned as a centre of princely demand and a hub for redistribution.[78] Porcelain, raw silk, Indian cloth and perfumed sapanwood all reached Ryukyu, while gifts sent by the king of Ryukyu to the ruler of Korea in 1470 included peacock feathers, glass vases, ivory, ebony, cloves, nutmeg and one mynah bird.[79] Siam was particularly attractive, since it offered spices, perfumes, ivory and tin. The letter of 1425 told how the Ryukyuans were chided by the Siamese for attempting to conduct private trade in sapanwood and porcelain, which the king of Siam regarded as royal monopolies. The affronted king of Chuzan requested that his merchants and mariners should be treated equably: he hoped that 'you will offer sympathy to the men from afar who have to undergo the hardships of the voyage', for 'it is enough of a difficulty to go through the winds and the waves', before discovering on arrival that they have to follow the strict instruction of Siamese government officials.[80] It was a dangerous route, as the Siamese discovered when the Ryukyuans sent an embassy to Siam in 1478, losing their ship, whereupon the next year the king of Siam ordered a new ship to be prepared at his end: 'when the ship approached Ryukyu, it again encountered a storm and sank into the ocean, its men being lost and its property scattered . . . Such is the will of Heaven.'[81]

As junks from the islands became more visible across the sea routes, the Ming court issued letters of protection to ships of Ryukyu. The idea that the royal court should monitor contacts with the outside world had some attraction in Ryukyu as well, and the local rulers began to issue their own voyage certificates, whose seals had to be reconciled with government ledgers as proof that the voyage was officially approved. The court of Chuzan also imitated the Chinese and Japanese by according special ranks to those it sent abroad on government missions. This, it was hoped, would bring them greater respect when they arrived at the court of Siam or wherever.[82] Generally, the crews of Ryukyuan ships are thought to have included Japanese and Chinese sailors as well as locals, reflecting the ethnic mix in the islands themselves. During the fifteenth century, a lively trade network encompassed Sumatra for a time and saw dozens of sailings between the island chain and Siam.[83] From 1432 onwards, the kings of Chuzan were in contact with, and by 1463 they were sending trading expeditions to, lands as far distant as Java and the newly established Malay trading centre at Melaka, the gateway to the Indian Ocean, which could normally be reached in about fifty days; however, out of twenty known journeys in this direction between 1463 and 1511, four culminated in shipwreck. They brought the sultan of Melaka gifts of blue satin, swords, big blue vases, fans and similar objects, begging him to 'accept them with a smile'; they also brought flattery: 'we know well that the people of your country lead a rich life and that your products are abundant. We ascribe these virtues to you, the Wise King.'[84,85]

In 1439 the islanders were granted a permanent trading station at Quanzhou in China, which included areas in which to store goods, to reside and to receive visitors. Thereafter they stuck stubbornly to it, and it was last used in 1875, a trading history of 436 years. This was the base where Okinawan students absorbed Chinese culture, which was no mere veneer, and their home islands developed a culture all of their own that was more influenced by Chinese than by Japanese models. Okinawan textiles imitated Chinese examples, and other influences on the design, colour and material of Okinawan cloth came from Malaya and Indonesia. Important Buddhist texts reached Ryukyu from Korea as well as China – between 1457 and 1501 the *Great Collection of Buddhist Sutras* was presented to Ryukyuan envoys in Korea on five occasions.[86] Overall, the impression is of a society that was open to outside influences, ruled by a royal court that was remarkably cosmopolitan and that appreciated the importance of trade to the point where the kings of Chuzan saw token tribute payments to foreign rulers not as demeaning but as practical, profitable and prestigious.

The final voyage from Ryukyu to Melaka, licensed in September 1511, and yet again carrying porcelain to be traded against pepper and sapan-wood, brought the islanders into contact with western European interlopers, the Portuguese, for the first time. The Portuguese had only captured the town a few weeks earlier, so that news of their victory cannot have reached the court of Chuzan before their ship sailed. Disconcerted by the sudden change of regime, the Ryukyuans sailed away, never to return.[87]

Tomé Pires, a Portuguese chronicler of his nation's conquests in the Indian Ocean, reported that his fellow countrymen met some people called *Guores* at Melaka; they hailed from islands known as the *Lequíos*, which sounds like a corruption of 'Ryukyu', bearing in mind the way the letter 'l' is pronounced in Chinese and Japanese. They sent three or four junks, the limit of their small capacity, to trade along the Chinese coast, near Guangzhou, and they also visited Melaka. 'They are great draftsmen and armourers,' he said, famous for their swords, fans and gilt boxes – he obviously confused what they brought with what they produced. They are truthful and dignified and detest the slave trade. Even so, 'the *Lequíos* are idolators; if they are sailing and find themselves in danger, they say that if they escape they buy a beautiful maiden to be sacrificed and behead her on the prow of the ship.'[88] Probably this says more about the lack of direct contact with the Ryukyuans than about his knowledge of their way of life.

IV

In late medieval Japan, a distinction remained between official and unofficial trade, but by this period it was clearly impossible to prevent the movement of unauthorized vessels. Under shogun Yoshimitsu, legitimate shipping bound for China was provided with government seals, using different colours to indicate whether the cargo was official or private, and under this scheme two ships each year crossed to the mainland between 1401 and 1410. The shoguns and the wealthy monasteries such as the Kōfuko-ji at Nara were great patrons of such large-scale enterprises throughout the fifteenth century. Although the focus of the Japanese trade in luxury items was the court and the great monasteries, the impact of trade on the wider economy of medieval Japan should not be underestimated. The French scholar of Japanese history Pierre-François Souyri has shown how trade helped transform quite a conservative society.[89] To this should be added the overwhelming impact of Asian religion and the exceptionally powerful influence of Chinese culture: books, images, social values. All this had been carried across Japan's Mediterranean, and had been carefully filtered, in the formative period of the early Middle Ages, by government control and by attempts to keep contact with the mainland within carefully prescribed limits. The result was the creation of a distinctive society that combined indigenous with mainland Asian features. By the late Middle Ages, Japanese society was able to produce significant quantities of goods that were in demand on the mainland and to reverse the balance of trade, which was now in favour of Nippon.

12

The Dragon Goes to Sea

I

When the rulers of China and Japan thought about trade they were constantly aware of the distinction between tribute, received in exchange for gifts, and private trade. Buddhism tended to encourage moneymaking, and even Buddhist monasteries traded actively, including those in Kyoto. In ancient and medieval China, attitudes were more complicated. From the perspective of some of the most influential exponents of Confucian thought, as in ancient Rome, trade was something inherently rather disreputable. Tribute, on the other hand, expressed acknowledgement of the superiority of Chinese (or Japanese) civilization over those who brought it, and fitted very well into Confucian ideas of hierarchy and the respect of those lower down the social and political scale for those higher up. Nations had to be ranked just as courtiers were; and calling many of them 'barbarian' was a way of saying that, if they knew their manners, they would pay tribute. Japan and Korea were occasionally treated as civilized nations, but this was not automatic, and the assumption that they were culturally inferior remained firm. The condescending attitude to Roman envoys, which was mentioned earlier, reflected both an awareness that there did exist another great empire far to the west, and an unwillingness to treat it as the equivalent of the Heavenly Kingdom ruled by the Chinese emperor. Tribute had another function beyond the political: the imperial court genuinely craved exotic luxuries, either for its own use or for redistribution to members of the ruling clan, great nobles and the army of scholar-officials who had earned their place at court by passing the most difficult examinations in human history. The imperial court was not greatly interested in the availability of foreign luxuries to the wider population, while the vast majority of the emperor's subjects in any case lived barely above subsistence level. For many of them, ship-borne trade meant the thousands of large rivercraft that carried huge amounts of grain

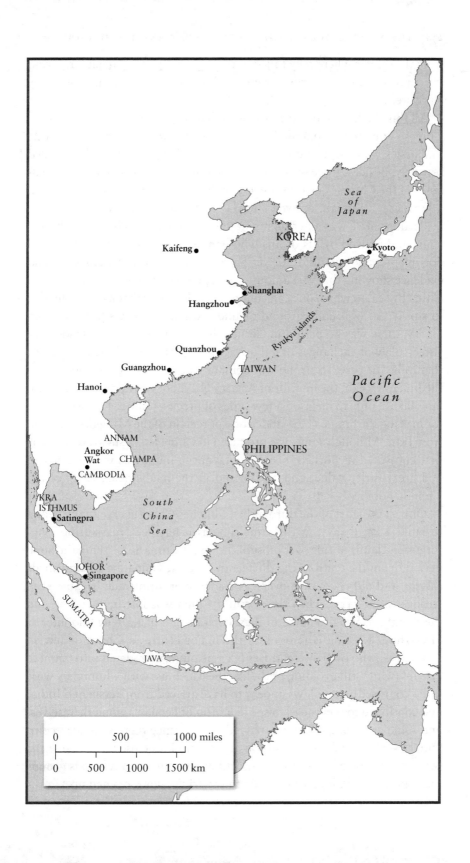

from the estates where they toiled to the big cities that – particularly from the tenth century onwards – were gobbling up the grain and rice they cultivated.

All this should not be taken to mean that trade was outlawed when the Chinese emperors demanded that exchanges should consist of tribute. Embassies were large and their members carried goods that they traded privately. Besides, there were plenty of opportunities to escape the surveillance of the Chinese customs offices, or *shibo*, whether one was a Chinese, a Japanese, a Korean, or even a Malay or Indian merchant. The tribute/trade alternative was a fiction maintained at some periods at the Chinese court and revived by historians who had perhaps read too many official documents, and who did not yet have access to the rich archaeological evidence showing that vast amounts of copper and porcelain left medieval China by sea, to which one can confidently add goods that have not tended to survive so well underground or under water, notably silk textiles. In reality, there was no period in Chinese history when overseas trade consisted solely of exchanges of tribute against gifts; nor did the court want that to be the case, so strong was demand at court for exotic goods from the Indian Ocean, the interior of Asia and beyond: emeralds, rock crystal, lapis lazuli, only to mention a few types of precious stone. The best cobalt for making the famous blue-and-white porcelain of the Ming period came from Iran. Although some was produced in China itself, sugar, which was first cultivated in Borneo, became a favourite import as well, for it still had great rarity value, and was prized in the medicine cabinets of the Chinese nobility.[1]

Only at the start of the third millennium has China energetically begun to build a large navy, at the same time as it has been reasserting long-forgotten claims to rule over most of the South China Sea.[2] Yet in the Song period, from the tenth to the thirteenth century, China did turn towards the sea and did encourage overseas trade; interest in trade became even stronger after 1126, when the north of China was lost by the Song and the 'Southern Song' reigned in their capitals first at Kaifeng and later at Hangzhou. Kaifeng is famous as the major centre in China of Jewish merchants, who over the centuries became quite assimilated into Chinese culture (while still avoiding pork, like the Muslims, with whom they were often confused); these Jews appear to have arrived from Persia and India, and continued for centuries to speak a form of Persian among themselves, and some are thought to have arrived by sea, since there were also communities in Quanzhou, Hangzhou and other cities close to or beside the sea.[3] This is just one example of the different ethnic and religious groups that filtered into China as its trade to the wider world opened up.[4]

Meanwhile, Chinese merchants established themselves in overseas ports as far south as what is now Singapore; there, they were rather modest folk, and rather than trading all the way to China they made it their business to wend their way back and forth across the strait, visiting the Riau islands (now part of Indonesia) and Johor (the southernmost province of mainland Malaysia), working closely with Malay partners and with the big-time Chinese traders who passed their way every now and again. A Chinese colony in Korea can be traced back to 1128. Sometimes these expatriate Chinese married local women, as in Japan. This also occurred in Champa, in Indo-China; there, some of the Chinese women were wealthy enough to invest in trade, though it is unlikely that they would have taken the risk of actually travelling long distances on board ship.[5]

The Song dynasty presided over what has been called a 'commercial revolution', during which a major international centre of trade emerged at Quanzhou, which will be examined shortly; and it was a time during which the central government reaped rewards in sizeable tax revenue.[6] Still, the scale of this revenue should not be exaggerated. It stood at less than 2 per cent of total revenue from all the economic activities in lands under Song rule.[7] That said, the wish to foster overseas commerce reflected new attitudes: the imperial dynasty did not simply require luxury goods for itself; it also had to find the means to pay for its exceptionally heavy spending programmes, which were consumed as much by grandiose projects at Hangzhou and other centres of power as by constant warfare on the Song frontiers, notably with the Chin dynasty that held on to power in northern China. By encouraging trade and industry (including the production of silk and porcelain, both of which were exported in large quantities), and by building shipyards and harbours, the Song emperors moved a little way towards closing the large gap between income and outlay.[8]

The turn to the sea took place gradually. The first Song emperor, Taizu, had experience of naval warfare before he gained the throne in 960; he maintained a war fleet and enjoyed staging mock sea battles, although most of this force was deployed along the rivers and close to shore. Naval wars against Annam and Korea took place during the tenth century, suggesting that the knowhow for ocean voyages did exist; however, the major task of the navy, which was treated as an auxiliary service lower in status than the army, was the suppression of piracy. Piracy betokens trade. Trade was the motive for the majority of sea journeys away from the coast of China in this period – either that or pilgrimage, which accounted for much smaller numbers of travellers.[9] In 982 the imperial court gave way to pressure from Chinese consumers, who were complaining that they could not buy the foreign aromatics they craved. No doubt the need to use these perfumes in temple worship influenced the decision to permit thirty-seven different perfumes to be released from government control. Merchants could now trade in them without having to take them to official markets. This did not bring about a business revolution, but it marked the beginning of gradual relaxation of control over the movement of goods. Within a few years, the government had doubled customs duty from 10 to 20 per cent, while withdrawing further from control of the markets. The imperial court now saw commercial taxes rather than the direct management of goods as the best way to profit from trade.[10]

All this was accompanied by a shift away from reliance on tribute to an acceptance that overseas trade was profitable not just for merchants but for the government: foreign merchants were increasingly welcomed in ports along the coast of the South China Sea, and, from 989 onwards, Chinese merchants were given the freedom to sail abroad. They still had to register their arrival and departure, and they were expected to return within nine months to the port from which they had originally sailed, so that their goods could be weighed and taxed. This meant that they could only be absent for a single monsoon cycle, and that they could not range as far as they would have wished, beyond the Strait of Malacca and into the Indian Ocean. A very intense network of exchanges within the South China Sea came into existence, as Chinese merchants with their substantial amounts of cash boosted existing networks within the area, and as Song traders did business alongside Malays, Thais and other non-Chinese peoples.[11] At the start, only two ports, Hangzhou and Mingzhou, were designated as departure points, with Guangzhou added later; but it became obvious by 1090 that these restrictions did more harm than good, and thereafter ships could set out from any prefecture that was willing to issue permits. In the middle of the eleventh century foreign products officially imported into China were said to be worth over 500,000 strings of cash, and the amount continued to rise, reaching 1,000,000 before 1100. Meanwhile, in 1074 a century-long ban on the export of copper cash was abolished, enabling Chinese merchants to satisfy strong foreign demand for Chinese bullion; payment in cash became the normal way to settle foreign bills, rather than barter and exchange, though every now and again paper money was issued in the hope of stemming the flow of copper outwards, and there were schemes to mint iron coins for the use of foreign merchants.[12] Liberalization of maritime commerce worked; a commercial revolution was indeed under way. The fact that another commercial revolution was under way in the Mediterranean and northern Europe (particularly in Italy and Flanders) at the same time is a curious coincidence. However, both commercial revolutions would have a similar effect in the Indian Ocean and south-east Asia: demand for spices and perfumes grew exponentially, and the produce of the Indies was sucked north to China and west towards the Red Sea and the Mediterranean.

What has been described so far was not simply a change in economic orientation. It was also a change in China's attitude to the outside world. The land routes that traversed the long and fragile Silk Road across Asia were too vulnerable to withstand the pressure of nomadic raiders; their importance, always overestimated by romantic historians, diminished still further, though there was a revival later during the Mongol period (from the late thirteenth to the late fourteenth century). But the sea was the great highway, and in the Song period Chinese travellers as well as Malays and Indians followed its routes. The Song period stands out as a period of three centuries during which China remained more accessible, and took more interest in contact with its neighbours, than at any other time. This openness, though only relative, became more obvious after 1126, when the Song capital at Kaifeng was captured by northern nomads, the Jurchen, who created an empire of their own in large tracts of northern China, with the result that the Song court decamped from Kaifeng and made Hangzhou its centre of operations.[13] The northern lands were the very areas that had been afflicted by floods, droughts and wars, and their wealth seemed to be in sharp decline, while southern China flourished: new irrigation works boosted the production of rice, and stimulated population growth, while gold, silver and copper flowed into the Song court from taxpayers in the southern provinces.[14] This boded well for the maritime traders, as Hangzhou lay near the coast and already functioned as a licensing station for ships setting out across the South China Sea.

The imperial court was not blind to the opportunities that now loomed. Honours (consisting of an official rank) were showered on merchants who brought in foreign goods worth 50,000 strings of cash, and tax officials who had managed to collect more than 1,000,000 strings from the massive trade in frankincense were also accorded higher rank. Lists were compiled of the types of goods that were arriving by sea, and differential rates of tax were imposed, depending on whether they were regarded as high- or low-value commodities. Reversing earlier decisions to cash in on trade by sea by charging high customs rates, the imperial court pushed these rates down to 10 per cent, and to 6⅔ per cent for lower-value items in 1136; and, far from depressing revenues, this acted as a stimulus to private shipowners, so that by the middle of the twelfth century the imperial court could congratulate itself on revenues of 2,000,000 strings of cash each year. Oddly, the rates on some luxury goods required at the imperial court, such as rhinoceros horn, were increased in 1164 and remained at the same level until the Mongols overthrew the Song in 1279; but this only pushed the maritime traders towards a greater emphasis on the lower-value goods, such as drugs and perfumes, which were moving around in much larger quantities and which were in demand beyond the narrow circles of the imperial court.[15]

The effects of urban growth reached much deeper into Chinese society. As people moved towards the cities and as the balance between urban and rural population changed, demand for foodstuffs in the cities soared. This led to the development of commercial networks in the countryside as well, as farmers produced for the urban market.[16] Foreign demand for Chinese goods stimulated the industries for which China was most famous: silk production and the ceramics industry. Other exports to south-east Asia included Chinese metalwork, iron ore (sometimes found in wrecks) and rice wine, contained in ceramic jars.[17] But copper, whether as ingots or as cash, was in constant demand.[18] One way to ensure that the outflow of copper cash did not drain all the bullion out of coastal China was to dump vast amounts of ceramics in foreign markets (though the term 'dump', favoured by economic historians, should not be taken to indicate that what was dumped was rubbish – the ceramics were much appreciated, but the quantities were massive).[19] Commercialization proceeded rapidly. The coastline grew in importance as a source of wealth for rulers and ruled. China was being transformed. All this seems uncannily similar to what has been happening in China since the 1980s, even if the scale of economic growth in modern times is immeasurably faster and vaster.

II

The great transformation that occurred under the Song was the emergence of a large class of native Chinese merchants willing to brave the open seas. It is important, though, to remember that the term 'native Chinese' has to be understood very broadly, for some of the leading businessmen and government agents entrusted with the care of commerce were of non-Han descent. Several were of Muslim descent, of either Arab or Persian origin, like the ruthless Pu Shougeng, who was superintendent of maritime trade at Quanzhou when the city fell to the Mongols in 1276; an eager collaborator with his new masters, he authorized the massacre of 3,000 members of the Song imperial clan.[20] As well as the favours shown to Chinese merchants, a policy existed that encouraged foreign merchants to come to China. Early in the twelfth century a Chinese businessman, Cai Jingfang, recruited foreigners to the port of Quanzhou; he brought Quanzhou's maritime trade office a profit of 980,000 strings of cash over the six-year period from 1128 to 1134. One of his recruits, Pu Luoxin (Abu'l-Hassan), was an Arab merchant specializing in frankincense; he brought incense to the value of 300,000 strings to the port, and around the same time frankincense from Śri Vijaya was imported that was valued at 1,200,000 strings; demand was insatiable. Impressed by Cai's success, the Song government enthusiastically offered an official rank to Chinese merchants who persuaded foreign merchants to ship large amounts of goods to China.[21] Yet what this case shows is that private initiative spurred the government towards the encouragement of yet more private initiative. This was not a setting in which those in power deplored or discouraged trade across the sea.

The sea had, then, come into focus as never before. Chinese and foreigners worked side by side; China was not simply the passive recipient of goods brought across the South China Sea. Much of the shipping that reached Chinese ports was foreign, but there were also large Chinese junks; and this was a period of technological innovation during which the Chinese developed a type of marine compass using a magnetized needle suspended on a string: 'the ship's pilots are acquainted with the configuration of the coasts; at night they steer by the stars, and in the daytime by the sun. In dark weather they look at the south-pointing needle', to cite a text from the start of the twelfth century.[22] Knowledge in China of magnetism and direction-finding went back to around 500 BC, so that this was old knowledge that had taken a very long while to be applied; in earlier centuries the main interest in direction-finding lay in divination and in the doctrines of *feng shui*, so that a magnetized piece of iron made it possible to align a building properly towards north and south. The late development of the marine compass shows that demand for navigational skills had grown as the Chinese became accustomed to sea voyages. Contrary to the passionate beliefs of the famous scholar of Chinese science, Joseph Needham (who managed to combine Maoism, Daoism and High Anglicanism in his long life), the use of lodestones by Vikings, sailors of Amalfi and others was almost certainly the result of independent discoveries far to the west, and not the diffusion of Chinese technical knowhow through the Islamic lands into Europe.[23] Undoubtedly, the use of the compass resolved a longstanding problem in Pacific navigation, for cloudy skies in the rainy seasons meant that it was all too easy to become lost on the open sea. Even then, there is a hint in the passage just cited that the Chinese still preferred to hug shores.

Many of these foreign merchants gathered in a port whose reputation was to travel all the way to medieval Europe, where it was known under its Arabic name of Zaytun, 'Olive City'. However that name came into existence, it was known to Chinese-speakers as Quanzhou (in older spelling, Ch'üan-chou), and lies across the strait that divides Taiwan from the Chinese mainland. The rise of Quanzhou was the result of a power vacuum in that corner of China; its sustained role as a great centre of trade was the result of its eventual incorporation into the Song Empire. For Quanzhou first emerged as an alternative port where merchants could hope to escape the supervision of Chinese customs officials, since during the mid-tenth century the region of Quanzhou lay under the rule of an independent warlord. However, as this area was brought forcibly under Song rule and as imperial power in the region grew, so did the ability of the imperial court to supervise what was happening there. This was all to the immense advantage of the central government, which began to receive greater and greater tax income from Quanzhou's foreign trade: half a million strings of cash around 980, but 1,000,000 at the start of the twelfth century, rising to 2,000,000 by around 1150. Merchants could expect to pay about 40 per cent in taxes and were expected to collect a certificate from the *shibo* official in charge of customs; but even so they flourished as business boomed.[24] Some merchants arrived from as far away as Bahrain, though the majority of ships travelled to Quanzhou from the shores of the South China Sea, including the Philippines, Sumatra, Java and Cambodia, or from Korea, whose traders carried gold, silver, mercury and their own silk cloth.[25]

Tamil merchants reached the city, and the Muslim community possessed several mosques, the oldest of which, the Qingjing or Ashab Mosque, was built soon after 1000 and still survives; it is the oldest mosque in China. Tombstones recording visitors from far to the west survive not just in Arabic but in Persian and Turkish.[26] Satingpra, a Siamese port on the shores of the South China Sea, enjoyed a brisk trade with Quanzhou, importing masses of porcelain; it lay close to the narrow neck of the Malay peninsula, the Kra Isthmus, thereby giving access to the Indian Ocean as well.[27] It is not really surprising that the ambitious rulers of the Khmer Empire in Cambodia should have encouraged maritime trade with Song China; in the first half of the twelfth century, King Sūryavarman II was himself a shipowner, and he was also happy to receive silk and porcelain carried to his realms on Chinese ships; Song pottery has been found at Angkor.[28] Ceramics from the towns around Quanzhou turned up in the Ryukyu island chain.[29] Encouraged by what they saw happening at Quanzhou, the Song emperors built harbours elsewhere along the long coastline of China, for instance at Shanghai and along the rocky shores between Guangzhou and Hanoi, where underwater reefs were torn away to make the passage of shipping safer. These harbours were also vital refuges when typhoons blew.

Quanzhou became the unrivalled centre of trade; it became a distribution centre from which goods were transferred along the rivers and canals of eastern China all the way to the great city of Hangzhou, now the Song capital. Public works enabled this great economic boom to gain further momentum: canals and rivers were dredged, breakwaters were built, warehouses were put at the disposal of foreign and native merchants. As more and more traffic crossed the sea, the temptation to pirates grew exponentially, and convoy escorts were sometimes provided to protect merchant ships; a navy came into being, and commanders such as Weng Chao were given the task of clearing pirates from the waters around the Yangtze estuary, while the corsair Zhu Cong, defeated in 1135, merged his fleet of fifty ships and 10,000 sailors into the Song navy; he was rewarded with the rank of admiral, and others followed the same course. A brief poem circulated: 'if you wish to become an official, kill and burn and accept a pardon.' One early twelfth-century official blamed the government for actually stimulating piracy by offering such generous amnesties: 'the officials are incompetent and seek to placate the pirates by granting them amnesty and, in more flagrant cases, by conferring on them rank and offices.' Merchant ships had to register their departure and were expected to travel in small convoys, and the government was careful to control the traffic to different destinations. Officially, only two ships a year were supposed to go to Korea, returning the next year, and the merchants trading there were supposed to be extremely wealthy, possessing 30,000,000 strings of cash (surely a mistake for 30,000 or 300,000); but there were colonies of merchants from Quanzhou in Korea, and in Vietnam too.[30]

While 30,000,000 strings seems a gigantic amount, there is the story of Wang Yuanmao from Quanzhou, who vastly enriched himself in the late twelfth century. There were several Buddhist monasteries in the city, and the sons of the well-to-do often took monastic vows. Wang, however, was a servant or handyman, and of low social status. But the monks taught him how to read 'the books of the southern barbarian lands', perhaps Indian Buddhist scriptures, as well as Chinese books. He was sent on a mission to the kingdom of Champa, in Indo-China. Champa was an old trading partner of China: as early as 958 the Cham king had sent the Arab merchant Pu Hesan (Abu Hassan or Husain) to the emperor with an explosive gift: flasks of an inflammable weapon similar to Greek fire (in Champa, the expectation was that the elite would be Hindu, the ordinary population Buddhist and the merchants Muslim). Once in Champa, Wang came to the attention of the king, who was so impressed that Wang could read both Chinese and foreign books that he offered him a post at court and even married him to one of his daughters; the trousseau was worth 1,000,000 strings of cash. After ten years in Champa, 'his lust for gain became still fiercer, and he next went trading as the master of an ocean-going junk'. Before long senior Chinese officials noticed him and married their own children into his family. He sent an agent overseas for ten years between 1178 and 1188 on one of his ships, and when his crew returned 'they had obtained profits of several thousand per cent'. But then an argument broke out after a sailor tried to cheat Wang of half the profit; the sailor was murdered, though not by Wang, but Wang was blamed and duly disgraced.[31]

Stories about Quanzhou merchants stress the extraordinary social mobility that agile businessmen could achieve. Chinese tales from this period emphasize again and again how people described as 'serfs' or 'penniless' could break free of their humble origins, accumulate great wealth and marry into grand families. This is further testimony to the transformations that took place in the society of the Quanzhou region during the Song period. And one significant effect of this economic expansion was what has been called 'the generalisation of the consumption of luxury items', as those who rose up the social ladder became somewhat contemptuous of the simple life their grandparents had led:

> I would rather say that after three generations of holding government office, the sons and grandsons are bound to be extravagant, and given to the utmost indulgence. They will be unwilling to wear coarse cotton, coarse silk, coarse padded garments, worn-out hemp quilting or any clothes that have been laundered or patched, insisting on openwork silk, thin silk, damask silk, crêpe silk, figured silk, natural silk and fresh, fine and luxurious linens and silks ... They will be unwilling to eat vegetables and will look on greens and broth as coarse fare, finding beans, wheat and millet meagre and tasteless, and insisting on the best polished rice and the finest roasts to satisfy their greedy appetites, with the products of the water and the land, and the confections of human artifice, set out neatly before them in ornamentally carved dishes and trays. This is what is meant by 'being able to dress up and dine'![32]

Rice, tea and pepper, previously upmarket items, were increasingly seen as three of the 'seven necessities' of life, along with more obvious items such as firewood and salt.[33]

Yet Quanzhou did not lie in a particularly fertile or wealthy part of China. Although some high-quality products such as lychees and oranges were cultivated, the lack of extensive arable land and poor returns from the soil made the region depend on imported supplies of rice and grain.[34] Lack of good local resources has often been a stimulus to commercial expansion, for obvious reasons – in exactly the same period Genoa and Venice were becoming great centres of trade, but relied on imported food as supplies nearby were restricted. The parallels between the 'commercial revolution' in Song China and in the medieval Mediterranean are quite striking.[35] Trade through its harbour created the Quanzhou phenomenon; but as the city grew, so did its role in the most famous Chinese industries. Notwithstanding the arrival of silk from Korea and Japan, Quanzhou became a centre of silk production, but nothing compared in scale with the export of fine porcelain, produced in the smaller towns in the hinterland behind Quanzhou and exported en masse to clients as far away as the Middle East: beautiful celadon wares carrying floral decorations in light relief, many produced in Dehua, a town that lay just across the mountains to the north of Quanzhou.[36]

III

Shipbuilding was another industry that kept Quanzhou prosperous – many of the ships built for Khubilai Khan came from there.[37] A wreck found in the approaches to the harbour of Quanzhou has been identified as a Chinese junk and can be securely dated to 1277. Its cargo consisted in large part of precious woods, but there were also ceramics on board that carried inscriptions identifying the owners as the 'Southern Family', that is, the branch of the Song imperial clan that governed this part of China on behalf of the emperor.[38] There was no evidence that anyone on board had drowned, and its sinking remains a mystery. A reasonably cogent theory about this ship is that it reached Quanzhou just as the Mongol armies overwhelmed the city, and that its crew scuttled the junk rather than allowing it to fall into the hands of the new masters of China or the bloodthirsty superintendent of trade, Pu Shougeng. It was more than twenty-four metres long and more than nine metres wide, and the hull contained thirteen cabins.[39] Chinese junks did not possess a pointed bow, and the stern too consisted of a flat end.[40]

The interest of this wreck lies not just in its physical remains but in its similarity to what Marco Polo described in his book of travels in a chapter that follows directly after his account of Zaytun/Quanzhou. There he spoke of ships with as many as sixty cabins and two or three hundred sailors, capable of loading up to 6,000 baskets of pepper; by contrast, the

Quanzhou boat was only of middle size, and could be an example of one of the 'large barks or tenders' that he said travelled alongside the bigger ships. But in some versions of his book he mentioned ships constructed around thirteen compartments stacked with cargo, with the aim of affording greater strength to the hull and of reducing the danger of sinking if the hull were pierced 'by the blow of a hungry whale' or by a rock (a similar technique used on the *Titanic* did not work). Other medieval travellers such as the Arab explorer ibn Battuta, of the fourteenth century, offered very similar descriptions of these large Chinese ships.[41] But Marco Polo is helpful in other ways too. His description of Zaytun does not match in enthusiasm his account of Hangzhou, known in medieval Europe as Quinsay, but it does match quite neatly the evidence from Chinese writers and from archaeology. Zaytun is 'frequented by all the ships of India, which bring thither spicery and all other kinds of costly wares'; but the inhabitants of Manzi (that is, southern China) also flock to the city, in search of precious stones and pearls, 'and I assure you that for one ship-load of pepper that goes to Alexandria or elsewhere, destined for Christendom, there come a hundred such, yes, and more too, to this haven of Zaytun; for it is one of the two greatest havens in the world for commerce' – maybe he thought the other one was his native Venice. He knew that the porcelain produced in a town nearby was not merely of superlative quality, but very inexpensive. And he described a lucrative system of taxation obviously inherited by the Mongols from that of the Song emperors.[42]

Even so, Quanzhou had reached its peak by the time the Mongols overwhelmed the city in 1277. Khubilai Khan was not responsible for its relative decline, though it remained a place of note under his Yuan dynasty as well. Nor was this decline the result of pirate raids on the all-too-successful merchant fleets of Quanzhou and other ports. War with the Chin or Jin dynasty in northern China was certainly a factor, but not so much because of the military outcome; it was more a question of the strain this constant conflict, renewed in 1160, placed on state finances. The commercial policies of the Mongol rulers of China may also carry some blame. In 1284 the Yuan court tried to ban private foreign trade, reverting to the classic position whereby contact with the outside world was carried out under state auspices. But the ban, despite strict penalties, only lasted ten years; and then twenty years later it was reimposed, only to be followed by its relaxation, reinstatement and final relaxation (1323) – all of this generated great uncertainty. Following the ban, Quanzhou did become the headquarters of the Mercantile Shipping and Transportation Bureau, which oversaw government-sponsored expeditions across the seas, but the freedom of Quanzhou merchants to come and go as they pleased had been curtailed. Another development was the creation of the Bureau of Ortaq Affairs, the Ortaqs being a guild of traders from central Asia who were actively patronized by the Mongol rulers, but who then, in the early fourteenth century, found themselves challenged by factions at court that resented their tight hold on Chinese trade. The Ortaqs hoped to create a shipping monopoly, but they had no experience of the sea, and therefore relied to a significant degree on the Arab and Persian merchants they encountered in Chinese ports. These developments do suggest that the trading community of Quanzhou lay under increasing pressure by 1300.[43] However, most explanations of the decline of Quanzhou stress the fiscal legacy of the Song dynasty, which had never managed to ensure that revenues matched expenditure. In part this was because the trading system they had helped to create contained some fundamental flaws.

The very success of Quanzhou resulted in a massive outflow of copper coinage; those figures of millions of strings of cash speak for themselves, since constant demand for Indonesian spices and Indian Ocean jewels percolated down to the urban middle class. By the middle of the twelfth century the Song rulers tried to meet this deficit by taking advantage of their mastery of the printing press, issuing a form of paper money. Marco Polo described the paper money of the Mongol rulers of China, which was used as currency throughout China and completely substituted for cash. But the Song paper money took the form of IOUs, credit notes that could be exchanged at some time in the future for hard cash. Merchants very much wanted to be paid in cash, as copper had a stable value based on the fact that it was a commodity in its own right, and in high demand in Japan and elsewhere; merchants knew perfectly well how to smuggle it to small ports from which it could be collected after their ships had been inspected in Quanzhou to see if they were carrying bullion.[44] Meanwhile, the temptation to print more and more notes grew. The result was inflation, which comes as no surprise nowadays, but which crept up on an unsuspecting Song Empire. The imperial court had developed an intelligent economic policy when it improved harbours and cleared rivers; but when it came to the effects of issuing paper money it had no experience of what to expect. The long-term effect was to dampen the enthusiasm of foreign traders. What were they supposed to do with these printed chits that had no value outside China itself? But there were other factors that made life more difficult in Quanzhou. A Mongol attack on Korea at the end of the twelfth century damaged a profitable maritime link. Champa was embroiled in power struggles with its famous neighbour, the Khmer kingdom of Angkor, and disorder there made that part of Indo-China a less attractive destination. Śri Vijaya had passed its peak by the mid-thirteenth century, though there were good business opportunities for spice merchants in Java.[45] All this meant a contraction but certainly not a collapse in the maritime network that had been dominated for nearly three centuries by Quanzhou.

One unanswered question is how typical or exceptional Quanzhou was. The Song capital at Hangzhou was a larger and grander city; but everything suggests that Quanzhou was the prime gateway into China for people coming across the sea with the luxury articles that the Song rulers were so eager to obtain. Looked at in a much wider setting, taking one far beyond the shores of China, Quanzhou can be seen as the command centre of a network of trade and navigation that extended right across the South China Sea, the East China Sea and into the Indian Ocean. At the start of the fifteenth century interest at the imperial court in these waters was to revive with results as remarkable as the rise of Quanzhou, though much more temporary.

13

Light over the Western Ocean

I

It has been seen that the Chinese emperors tended to treat Japan as a subordinate nation, while according it more honour than most other kingdoms. The shogun Yoshimitsu was roundly condemned by his son and successor for admitting that he was China's inferior. When writing to the Ming court at the start of the fifteenth century, Yoshimitsu had described himself as 'king of Japan', and the term 'king' was understood to mean that he accepted the sovereign authority of the Son of Heaven in China. After all, the Chinese emperor, Jian-wen, wrote to Yoshimitsu:

> You have sent envoys to come to the court, crossing over waves and billows ... You make tribute of precious swords, fine horses, helmets and armour, paper and inkstones, together with pure gold, with which We are well pleased ... Keep your mind on obedience and loyalty and therefore adhere to the basic rules.

And the shogun wrote a letter that, following the overthrow of Jian-wen, was received with gratitude by the new emperor, Yong-le:

> Your subject, the king of Japan, submits: your subject has heard that when the sun rises in the sky, there is no dark place not lighted by it; when the timely rain soaks the earth, there is nothing that is not moistened ... Thus the ten thousand directions come under his influence, and the four seas adhere to his benevolence.[1]

This emperor, the third in the Ming dynasty, which ruled China from 1368 to 1644, is a figure of exceptional interest. Earlier known as Zhu Di, he took the regnal name Yong-le (Yung-lo), meaning 'Perpetual Happiness'; the name of the dynasty, 'Ming', meant 'light', and had been chosen by his father. Yong-le was a ruthless and extravagant ruler with grandiose plans – not just naval expeditions and land campaigns, but the

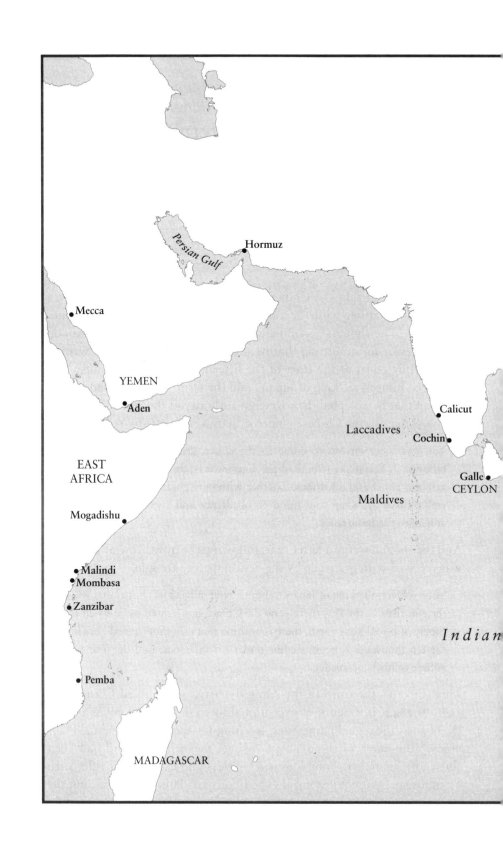

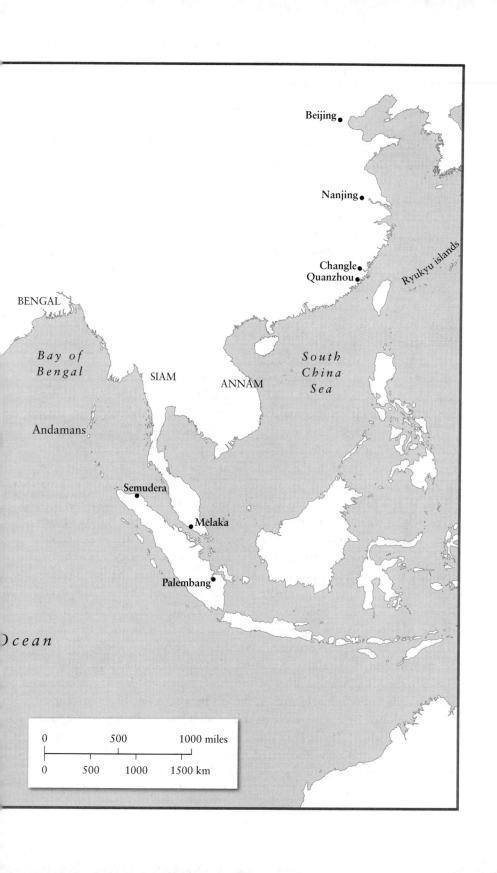

beautification of Beijing and the active patronage of culture. He rebuilt the Grand Canal linking Beijing to the Chinese rivers and assuring the capital of regular grain supplies.[2] His overseas expeditions, led by Admiral Zheng He (Cheng Ho) have attracted attention not just in modern times but under later Ming rulers – a certain Luo Mao-deng wrote a novel about the Ming voyages that was published in 1597 under the title *The Grand Director of the Three Treasures Goes Down to the Western Ocean*, and, despite its obvious fantasy, including a visit to the Underworld, attempts have been made to use it as a reliable source for all those aspects of these voyages that are not recorded in the official histories and inscriptions that survive.[3] Precisely because of the sheer scale of the Ming voyages, Zheng He has attracted most of the attention from historians of Yong-le's reign: there were 255 ships on the first voyage and 249 on the second, and a total of seven voyages, according to his biographer, Edward Dreyer, who counts 27,550 men on the final voyage, roughly the same as the first. Some of these figures will be questioned later; but, when they read about the voyages, later generations were astonished at the number and size of the ships, the number of those on board and the distances traversed: Chinese ships reached east Africa, Yemen, Hormuz, Ceylon and the lands around the South China Sea, and Zheng He created a spacious Chinese base at Melaka.[4]

The Ming voyages have attracted comparisons with Christopher Columbus, very much to the detriment of the latter, where the point is made that Columbus's flagship, the *Santa María*, was a small fraction of the size of Zheng He's treasure ships, and his initial fleet consisted of only three ships. That is to assume that Columbus and Zheng He had similar objectives, which was far from being the case. Nonetheless, the failure of the Ming emperors to repeat these very expensive expeditions after 1434 raises that hoary question in Chinese history: if Chinese technology was in many respects so far in advance of that of western Europe in the late Middle Ages, why did China fail to create a world empire, or have an Industrial Revolution, or indeed open up to the world? This question lay at the heart of the Marxist-inspired account of *Science and Civilization in China* composed by Joseph Needham.[5] Needham speculated about visits to South America, Australia and around the Cape of Good Hope towards Brazil in the Ming or some other period; his enthusiasm for things Chinese was literally unbounded. However, the voyages have also been unscrupulously exploited by a sensationalist writer who has woven together a vast narrative in which Zheng He's ships went much further than Africa and Arabia, and supposedly discovered Antarctica, Alaska, the Atlantic and just about every corner of the world long before the arrival of the Spaniards, Portuguese, Dutch or British; in addition Zheng He's arrival in Italy supposedly kick-started an Italian Renaissance that was already well under way. Needless to say, this 'research' is utter nonsense and pure fantasy, and the truth is far more interesting.[6] Equally, the claim that Marco Polo knew about, and perhaps even visited, Alaska, making him the first European since the Vikings to set foot in North America (though the other side), is unfounded, this time based on what may be sixteenth-century manuscripts rather than modern-day fancy.[7]

The first question is why seven massive expeditions were sent out from China between 1405 and 1434, when nothing on that scale had been tried before. Yet there had been some seafaring activity before Zheng He. A Chinese envoy, the eunuch Yin Qing, had visited Melaka in 1404, a year before Zheng He set out; the town's founder and rajah, Parameśvara, was granted the title of king, legitimizing his position as master of the Malacca Strait and of the trade route linking the Indian Ocean to the South China Sea.[8] Yong-le was as active in securing the submission of his neighbours in central Asia by means of land embassies as he was in winning that of maritime nations on the routes Zheng He followed. Landlocked kingdoms as far away as Samarkand were expected to assimilate into Chinese culture. However, its monarch proved less than happy at being treated as a vassal and sternly insisted that Yong-le would be best advised to stop talking nonsense about being ruler of the world and should instead become a Muslim.

The Middle Kingdom over which Yong-le directly ruled was supposed to be surrounded by a ring of subordinate barbarian states. He was also determined to recover lands that had once been ruled from China and to draw them into the Chinese cultural world. Like the Mongol rulers of China in the thirteenth century, he aimed to gain control of Annam, roughly northern Vietnam, even though his father, the first Ming emperor, had warned against ever trying to achieve this (and he gave the same advice about Japan and the Ryukyu islands).[9] Yong-le put together a large fleet, supposedly of at least 8,600 ships, captured from Annam, but he had to face tough resistance that was accentuated by the policies he adopted after victory, such as the requirement to wear Chinese dress.[10] Another area best reached by sea that Yong-le eyed was Bengal, where his ambassador intervened to head off a war with the ruler's neighbour; the king became a fan of the Chinese emperor, sending rare animals such as one which was identified as the *qilin* known from Chinese mythology, and which was a giraffe, obtained from distant Africa by the ruler of Bengal.[11] Yong-le did in fact describe his aims very clearly during the very first year of his reign:

> Giving and nourishing lives is the utmost virtue of the Heavens. A humane
> ruler needs to learn from Heaven; hence, loving the people should become

the principle of his rulership. The four seas are too broad to be governed by one person. To rule requires delegation of powers to the wise and the able who can participate in government ... My late father Hong-wu received the mandate of heaven and became the master of the world. During the thirty years of his rule, there was peace and tranquillity within the four seas. There was neither catastrophe nor tumult.[12]

On the one hand, the Chinese emperor was master of the world; on the other, he could not actually rule over the entire world – a difficulty all claimants to universal imperial power have had to face. But that did not mean he should pass by the opportunity to demand from countries right across the world recognition of his superiority. Once again, what comes through powerfully is the insistence of the Chinese on their superiority as a moral force – Confucian ideas blended with those of Yong-le's Mongol predecessors, with their ruthless demands for recognition of their own 'Mandate from Heaven'. Ming court culture owed much to the Mongols, including many of the costumes worn at court and the passion the Ming emperors showed for hunting and archery.[13]

Sending fleets overseas under the command of Admiral Zheng He was, then, a highly conspicuous and extremely expensive way of doing what earlier Chinese emperors had long been trying to do. Some historians have looked for quite different explanations. The most peculiar is that Yong-le was trying to run to ground his predecessor and rival, Jian-wen, who, according to one rumour, had escaped to a remote island across the sea.[14] Other arguments that have been advanced include the simple idea that Zheng He's voyages were motivated by curiosity. In other words, Zheng He was an explorer, even more so than Columbus, who, after all, was certain of his destination (China or Japan) and had read a book (by Marco Polo) that told him what to expect.[15] The arrival at court of the giraffe would have prompted questions about the land from which it came, somewhere in the outer reaches of the 'western sea'.[16] The emperor required exotic goods from all over the known world, for tribute was supposed to contain things that could be treasured – rare animals, precious jewels – as well as disposable items such as spices and perfumes. That is not quite the same as curiosity about the human and physical geography of the Indian Ocean. Chinese advances in technology, such as the use of the maritime compass and of woodblock printing, did not form part of a wider scientific endeavour built around the pursuit of knowledge for its own sake.

Those who went on the voyages did have exciting experiences to remember; and the short books left by two travellers on several expeditions, Ma Huan, an Arabic and Persian interpreter, and the soldier Fei Xin, are rich in details about the customs, religion, products and topography of the lands of the Indian Ocean.[17] Although Ma Huan claimed to come from a modest background, describing himself as a 'mountain woodcutter', he knew his Chinese classics and had read Buddhist literature. Yet his account of the 'Western Ocean' took several years to be printed and published (probably in 1451), and was little read. Fei Xin aroused more interest among sixteenth-century Chinese scholars, which may reflect the continuing interest in Zheng He, about whom Ma Huan said rather less, his main concern being the countries he visited in the Indian Ocean. Fei Xin also paid attention to the lands around the South China Sea, which, as near neighbours and past targets of military campaigns, aroused special interest.[18]

The argument that the aim of the voyages was to create a trading network is easy to challenge. Yong-le forbade private trade. Earlier attempts to ban private trade had been widely ignored, all the more so when the imperial throne was in contention.[19] Yong-le was only interested in the exchange of tribute for gifts, which was a political act in the first place. It is true that a well-established custom existed that when the government had claimed its share, members of a diplomatic mission could trade the remaining goods placed on board ship for local produce, and this made participation in overseas embassies very desirable – there were big profits to be made and some prestige to be gained from bringing, say, Chinese ivory to the court in Japan or Java. But the prestige Yong-le sought was his own prestige, as emperor of the Middle Kingdom; he 'wanted to display his soldiers in strange lands in order to make manifest the wealth and power of the Middle Kingdom', and sent his ships 'to the various foreign countries, proclaiming the edicts of the Son of Heaven and giving gifts to their rulers and chieftains. Those who did not submit were pacified by force.'[20] Setting aside Vietnam, which was seen as a borderland within range of Chinese areas of settlement, this 'pacification' did not involve the sending of governors or sinicization. Ports would only be visited if they acknowledged Chinese sovereignty, so that those that failed to do so lost out on the chance to obtain Chinese goods and to offload their own products.[21] These are by no means the only interpretations of the Ming voyages. Another view of the voyages, which took place around the time of the conversion of the ruler of Melaka to Islam, is that they stimulated the spread of Islam in what are now Malaysia and Indonesia; but this is doubtful, and at best it would have been an accidental effect of the voyages, and obviously not their intention. Buddhist hopes of acquiring a sacred relic in Ceylon have also been brought into play, without any real evidence.[22]

The role of Islam in Zheng He's life is an interesting problem. The admiral (though he did not actually hold such a title) was born a Muslim in 1371. He hailed from south-western China, from the province of Yunnan, which had a large Muslim population descended from traders who had been arriving throughout the Middle Ages. His own family had rather distinguished antecedents: they originated in Bukhara, making him more a son of the Silk Road than of the Silk Route of the Sea, and had been in the service of the early Mongol khans. His father and grandfather must have been quite devout Muslims, as they were known as *Hajji*, 'the pilgrim', implying they had both visited Mecca. As a boy, Zheng He was taken prisoner after his father was killed resisting the Ming invasion of Yunnan. He was castrated and sent to the Chinese imperial court; and there he rose among the ranks of the court eunuchs, whose closeness to the emperor was often a great source of irritation to the bureaucrats who expected to gain their ruler's ear.[23] He became head of the Directorate of Palace Servants, a government office heavily involved in building projects, and these, like shipbuilding, required the use of enormous quantities of wood. It was his experience in organizing construction rather than his experience as a naval commander, which was non-existent, that made him a very suitable choice to take charge of the emperor's fleet.[24]

All this time, his links to Islam must have been weakening, and, like the Chinese around him, he became eclectic in his religious practice, joining his crew in praying to the sea goddess Tianfei at the start of his expeditions. To cite an inscription he laid down in 1431, 'the divine majestic spirit of the Heavenly Princess, who is entitled by imperial edict "she who defends the country and shelters the people, whose miraculous spirit responds visibly to prayers, and whose vast benevolence saves all", spreads across the oceans'. The goddess, also known in local dialect as Mazu, was said to have been the daughter of a humble fisherman; she was born in AD 960 and possessed the power of prophecy; she could therefore warn her brother that he was at risk of being drowned at sea, and so saved his life.[25] Zheng He became very large, supposedly seven feet tall and ten feet around the waist, though the Chinese 'foot' was shorter than the twelve-inch foot of today. He had a small nose but high cheekbones and a broad forehead. There are a good many pictures and statues of him, the product of imagination, as he was deified after his death and has been worshipped by expatriate Chinese as their patron ever since – his cult continues in the oldest surviving Chinese temple in Malaysia, the Cheng Hoon Teng temple in Melaka, built in 1645.[26]

II

The story of Zheng He has grown in the telling, then, and the question that needs to be asked is whether the size of the fleet and the number of those on board have also been exaggerated. The novel by Luo Maodeng fantasized about the size of the ships, but many of those who subsequently wrote about the voyages assumed that Luo had access to precise information. Fei Xin, who was there, wrote of '27,000 government troops' aboard the fleet that set out in 1409, and the numbers given for each expedition are broadly comparable. Very large figures in the thousands were just a Chinese way of saying 'innumerable'; it is quite reasonable to insist on scaling down these numbers, which represent a large medieval city on the move, and which raise insoluble problems about how it was possible to feed all these people, even if the fleet put into port every week or two. Interestingly, Fei Xin also mentioned '48 sea-going ships', and that looks a very tight fit for 27,000 troops and an entire storehouse of fine porcelain, silks and other gifts (even bulkier on the return, when the tribute included a menagerie of lions, giraffes and zebras).[27] And yet other estimates for these fleets suggest that at least 250 ships set sail, so one could try to argue that Fei only counted the Treasure Ships. One has to distinguish big junks from small sampans, lighters and supply ships, including those filled with fresh water and towed behind larger vessels. Marco Polo's description of the largest Chinese ships insists that they were manned by 200 sailors, even, in one text of his book of travels, by 300. He describes tugs that were used to help these great junks along, with fifty or sixty sailors at the oars. Ships were constructed out of fir wood, to the best of his knowledge, though evidence from underwater archaeology and the written sources we have indicates that cedar and camphor wood were often used as well, and they would have lasted better; the Yuan shipbuilding industry had denuded parts of China of tree cover, and Yong-le's schemes, if they were really on the scale that was reported, must have had the same disastrous effect. Polo described capacious vessels, bigger than those that sailed the Mediterranean, and others who saw or heard about them knew that they contained many cabins for the wealthier or more important passengers. They do seem to have been much more comfortable than European ships, where everyone was crowded together under the open skies and living, sleeping and cooking space was very confined.[28]

A reconstruction in print of the ships by Edward Dreyer sets the size of the largest vessels in these fleets, the so-called Treasure Ships, at around 400 feet long and about 170 feet broad, with nine masts.[29] It is generally assumed that those who built these ships adapted the design from the traffic that regularly sailed up and down the Yangtze and the other broad Chinese rivers and canals, where big ships were constructed with flatter bottoms than one would expect to find at sea and with large numbers of masts. Detailed records of shipbuilding survive from this period, and the sheer scale of the industry is very impressive; even so, most vessels never ventured into saltwater.[30] What was suitable for the relatively calm and shallow waters of a river would certainly not suit the open ocean, where a proper keel would be needed to guarantee stability, and where too many sails could make ships more difficult to manoeuvre in storms. A displacement of over 18,000, or even 24,000, tons would make these ships into the very largest ones constructed out of wood, setting aside one or two of the vanity vessels built for the Ptolemaic rulers of Hellenistic Egypt that probably never ventured out of the harbour at Alexandria.[31]

All this sounds incredible, especially since there are no references to the loss of ships at sea during the expeditions, though that must have happened occasionally. The arguments in favour of smaller fleets with fewer people on board are compelling. At 200–250 feet in length, manned by about 200 crew, these ships enter the realms of plausibility.[32] This scaling-down of the size of the ships and of the fleets and their crews should not suggest that the arrival of a grand imperial navy in Melaka or Calicut or Aden was anything less than an extraordinarily impressive event, as ship after ship came into sight offshore, unfamiliar in its rigging, with dragon pennants flying. Even if we reduce the size of the company to, say, 10,000 on each expedition, we still have that sizeable medieval town on the move, with all the logistical problems of supplying water and food and of maintaining discipline and health on board during voyages that reached as far as Africa and Arabia.

III

The first expedition took place in 1405–7, soon after Yong-le had gained power. The sixty-two Treasure Ships built in the Lonjiang shipyard in Nanjing and floated down the Yangtze River to reach the sea stood at the heart of the fleet; these were the ships on which the gifts to China's vassals were to be loaded. From Champa, which was happy to recognize Yong-le's authority as a defence against its neighbour and rival Annam, the first voyage headed towards Java, where the local kings had been a source of trouble to Hong-wu, but where a large community of Chinese merchants lived, servicing the island's booming economy based on spices and other rare goods. The current king was 'arrogant and disrespectful and wanted to harm Zheng He. He heard about this and went away.'[33] For the moment Zheng He was content to parade his ships and awe the Javans, as his destination lay through the Strait of Malacca, past Melaka itself and around the Andaman islands (described by Marco Polo as a wild and dangerous

place) and right across the Bay of Bengal to Ceylon, where he expected
no favours from the local ruler, so he pressed on up the western coast of
India to Calicut and Cochin. Calicut made a good impression on Zheng's
officers, to judge from positive comments by Ma Huan: 'the people are
very honest and trustworthy. Their appearance is smart, fine and distinguished.' He called Calicut 'the great country of the Western Ocean', while
Fei Xin noted that 'it is also a principal port for all the foreigners of the
Western Ocean'. Ma Huan also reported a garbled story about 'Mou-xie
who established a religious cult' and the Golden Calf that he heard in
Calicut, not realizing that this was the same person as the Musa, or Moses,
revered by his fellow Muslims. And yet he also recognized that there were
very many Muslims in Calicut; a past king of Calicut had said: 'You do
not eat the pig; I do not eat the ox.'[34]

After spending winter 1406–7 in Calicut, Zheng He made his way back
past Melaka, with an eye on the troubled situation in Sumatra, where a
Chinese pirate named Chen Zu-yi had taken control of Palembang. The
old capital of Śri Vijaya was no longer the great trading centre it had once
been, a role that was passing even now to Melaka, but the town had
recovered something of its lost importance at the end of the fourteenth
century, as closer ties with China were created.[35] The Ming ban on private
trade seems to have caused no problems, for it was easy to ignore commands from Beijing in far-off Sumatra. However, the presence of a
powerful Chinese pirate threatened this special relationship, and Zheng
He was determined to assert Ming authority over the South China Sea;
as a result, the Chinese merchants in Palembang greeted the Ming fleet
with delight. However, Zheng was unimpressed when Chen Zu-yi came
to offer his submission. Suspecting that this was simply a ruse to gain time
before Chen and his pirate fleet could slip away, Zheng He attacked the
pirates, who had at least seventeen ships – no match for Zheng's fleet. An
official history of Yong-le's reign claims that more than 5,000 pirates
were killed, while Chen Zu-yi was carried back to Beijing and beheaded
by imperial order; 'after this the seas were restored to peace and order'.[36]
This was the one violent confrontation in what had otherwise been a
peaceful mission, or rather a display of Chinese power so impressive that
no one in his right mind would oppose the power of the Ming emperor.
The Ming navy had taken advantage of the monsoons to time its journeys
out and in, but even so on the final leg a great storm arose and the sailors
were struck with fear. They prayed fervently to Tianfei and were rewarded
with a miraculous light that settled on the top of the mainmast of one
of the ships and that they knew was a sign of the goddess's protection
(St Elmo's Fire, a common electric effect during storms at sea). To cite a

later inscription on which Zheng He recorded his memories of earlier expeditions:

> We have traversed over a hundred thousand *li* of vast ocean and have beheld great ocean waves, rising as high as the sky and swelling and swelling endlessly. Whether in dense fog and drizzling rain or in wind-driven waves rising like mountains, no matter what the sudden changes in sea conditions, we spread our cloudlike sails aloft and sailed by the stars day and night. Had we not trusted her divine merit, how could we have done this in peace and safety? When we met with danger, once we invoked the divine name, her answer to our prayer was like an echo; suddenly there was a divine lamp which illuminated the mast and sails, and once this miraculous light appeared, then apprehension turned to calm.[37]

Zheng He's fleet arrived back in Nanjing in October 1407, accompanied by emissaries from around the South China Sea and from as far away as Calicut and Melaka, who presented their tribute to the imperial court and were rewarded with copper cash and paper money, though it is not clear what use paper money would have had in far-off kingdoms.[38]

Aware that the gifts of money were not entirely what was expected, the emperor began to plan Zheng He's second voyage, of 1407–9, whose declared function was to present letters of appointment to the king of Calicut, including a silver seal of office, and to present gifts of silk robes, caps and belts to the king and his chief advisers, who would be ranked in best Chinese fashion. Similarly, the rulers of territories en route to Calicut, such as Siam, Java and Melaka, were to be honoured with imperial letters.[39] The expedition probably split up into squadrons that visited different ports and then regrouped. However, a particular show of force was needed in Java, whose king had resisted Chinese authority in the past and was wise enough to agree to a tribute payment and compensation for past offences.[40]

The wish to discipline those who were reluctant to accept Ming overlordship was also apparent on the third voyage (1409–11), which this time did not avoid Ceylon. The king of Ceylon, Alagakkonara, was accused of insulting Zheng He and even of trying to assassinate him, luring Zheng inland and plotting to send his own 'bandits' to raid the Chinese fleet. Zheng's way back to his ships was blocked by felled trees, though messages were sent to his fleet via unblocked roads. Zheng led his soldiers into battle across back roads and launched a surprise attack on the capital; he captured the king, who was carried back to China, although the emperor decided he was just an ignorant barbarian, and did not execute him. Instead, in a show of Ming authority, he nominated a replacement for him from the royal family of Ceylon, 'in order to continue the sacrifices of the kingdom of Ceylon'.[41] The Sinhalese version of these events is rather different, and reveals that the court in Ceylon was trying to save face: here, Chinese envoys arrived at the royal palace loaded with gifts; but this was just a ruse, and once inside the compound they seized the king and carried him off.[42]

It has also been suggested that the real aim of the attack on Ceylon was to steal a tooth relic of the Buddha, one of the most important of all Buddhist relics on the island. In 1284 Khubilai had already despatched ships to Ceylon requiring this relic to be handed over; the king of Ceylon demurred. A later account of the voyages does claim the relic was carried back to China, and attributes the calm seas through which the fleet passed to its magical power.[43] The story is surely a fable; but this would fit well with the idea that Yong-le's political programme was moulded as much by Khubilai's ambitions as by those of his father. The nearest one can reach to the argument that this expedition was a Buddhist project is the text of an inscription that Zheng He left at Galle on the coast of Ceylon. The inscription uttered praise to Buddha for watching over the fleet:

> Wherefore according to the Rites we bestow offerings in recompense, and do now reverently present before the Lord Buddha, the World-Honoured One, obligations of gold and silver, gold-embroidered jewelled banners of variegated silk, incense-burners and flower-vases, silks of many colours in lining and exterior, lamps and candles with other gifts in order to manifest the high honour of the Lord Buddha.[44]

But that was only the section in Chinese; the text was repeated in Persian and in Tamil, and there it was Allah and a Hindu god who were invoked. Allah, Buddha and the Hindu god are all offered 1,000 pieces of gold, 5,000 pieces of silver, as well as silk, perfumes and temple ornaments. Taken as a whole, we witness here 'a co-ordinated imperial offensive to persuade the heavens and their diverse deities to smile on Chinese maritime activities'.[45] This eclecticism was typical of Chinese attitudes to religion.

IV

The three first expeditions had happened in rapid sequence. After Zheng He's return in mid-1411 the emperor, distracted by plans for a land campaign against the Mongols, waited until December 1412 before he ordered

Zheng He to set out once again, bearing gifts for sundry kings in the South China Sea and beyond. Among the places visited were Palembang and its replacement as the main trading centre near the Malacca Strait, Melaka, ruled by Parameśvara. A lengthy inscription left there by Zheng He included an eloquent poem:

> The vast south-western sea reaches unto the Middle Kingdom,
> Its waves cresting high as the heavens,
> Watering the earth, the same way for countless aeons . . .
> Its righteous king, paying his respects to imperial
> Suzerainty, wishes his country to be treated as one of
> Our imperial domains and to follow the Chinese way . . .[46]

Melaka was developing into an important base for Zheng He's activities, thanks to its strategic position and to the creation of the Chinese settlement there. Zheng He needed to find a place where the fleet could be serviced, and Melaka was as much a naval base as a centre of Chinese trade.[47] The rise of Melaka thus owed a great deal to Chinese influence, and to the patronage of Zheng He just at the moment when Rajah Parameśvara was bringing the city into existence. Fei Xin saw Melaka when it was still 'a single hill with few people on it', located in an unproductive area, with simple houses; but once Zheng He had brought it under Chinese sovereignty and had raised it to the status of an imperial county things clearly improved.[48] Still, it had its rivals, notably Semudera on the northern tip of Sumatra, 'the most important port of assembly for the Western Ocean'. On his return from the Indian Ocean, Zheng He would display another rare show of force and send in his troops to suppress a rebellion against the king of Semudera, thereby showing what advantages could be gained from submission to the Chinese emperor.[49] Yet India was not the intended destination. The Chinese fleet majestically sailed past the Maldive and Laccadive islands, but its target was a place the Chinese must have heard about at length when they visited Calicut, Hormuz at the gateway of the Persian Gulf.[50] The voyage from Calicut to Hormuz took thirty-four days, which was rather slower than the norm (about twenty-five days), but this was surely due to the need to keep a fleet together and to the less flexible manoeuvrability of the very largest ships, by comparison with Arab and Persian dhows.[51] The mystery is what Zheng He can have wanted from a trading city so far from China. Perhaps, then, it would be wrong to rule out curiosity entirely, or even the traditional Ming contempt for trade, since the Chinese court was fascinated by exotic goods from the 'Western Ocean' and beyond. The interpreter Ma Huan was impressed with the place and took special interest in the jugglers, acrobats and street magicians, above all by acrobatic goats that could balance on a couple of tall poles and dance a jig up in the air.[52]

One voyage generated another, as tribute was received, as ambassadors from foreign kingdoms were received at court, and as Zheng He was ordered to return to distant waters with letters of appointment and seals of office. He departed on his fifth voyage by way of Quanzhou in summer, 1417, leaving behind a tablet on which he recorded his offering of incense to the sea goddess; he took on board a massive cargo of porcelain, of which more shortly. He was now sent beyond Hormuz ('Ho-ru-mo-ssu') to a town on the southern shores of Arabia called Lasa, thought to have been a port in Yemen. In Luo Maodeng's romanticized account of the voyages, Zheng He encountered greater resistance as he ventured into uncharted waters, and had to blast the walls of Lasa with his cannons, though there is no other evidence for that happening.[53] But a much more important destination was the Rasulid kingdom of Yemen, whose capital, Aden, had for centuries been a control centre for traffic heading up to Egypt, down the coast of east Africa and across to western India, including Calicut. Its prosperity boomed in the fourteenth and fifteenth centuries, partly thanks to the lively India trade of the Egyptian merchants of Cairo and Alexandria, but also thanks to its command of a surprisingly fertile interior. It has been seen already that this was an area where frankincense and myrrh were easy to obtain, and tribute paid in this form would please the Ming court enormously, in view of the difficulties and expense of obtaining these luxuries overland or by way of endless intermediaries along the 'Silk Route of the Sea'. It is hardly surprising that its rulers were determined to protect their independence in the face of attempts by the Mamluk rulers of Egypt and Syria to extend their power right down the coasts of the Red Sea, and accepting Chinese claims to overlordship, and subsequently sending a series of missions to Beijing, did not seem a ridiculous idea, when Zheng He could come all that way with his grand fleet.[54] Ma Huan thought that 'the people are of an overbearing disposition' and noted that the sultan had a large, well-drilled army. He was impressed by the wealth of Aden, visible for instance in large precious stones he called 'cat's eyes', and in the fine filigree jewellery worn by women.[55]

Zheng He's purpose was not, however, to intervene directly in the politics of Yemen. His fleet was bound for Africa; the arrival at the Chinese court of the giraffe sent by the king of Bengal had already alerted the Ming dynasty to the extraordinary treasures of Africa, and on past expeditions there had been plenty of chances to examine African ivory and ebony. Mogadishu in what is now Somalia was named on the sailing instructions given to Zheng He, and it was the first African town his fleet reached. The

Chinese were unimpressed by the arid setting of a city that lacked supplies of wood, and in stark contrast to Chinese towns was entirely built of stone, even if the buildings were several storeys high. The Chinese considered the Somalians rather stupid, and were only interested in what they could bear away: frankincense, ambergris and wild animals, including lions, leopards and zebras. Further south, at Brava, they saw more of the same type of housing but were able to add myrrh, camels and 'camel-birds', that is ostriches, to their booty, and as they reached the Kenyan coast at Malindi they acquired African elephants and rhinoceroses, as well as the much-vaunted *qilin*, or giraffes, so that the returning Treasure Ships must have resembled Noah's Ark.[56]

The Chinese were not totally ignorant of Africa. The earliest Chinese reference to Africa so far identified dates from the ninth century; there, as in the accounts of the Zheng He voyages, the Horn of Africa is presented as an arid land, and the inhabitants are described as nomads who drain blood from the veins of their cattle and drink it mixed with milk, rather as the Masai have continued to do. By the thirteenth century, the Chinese had heard of Zanzibar; in 1226, it was mentioned under the name 'Cengba' by the geographer Zhao Rugua, who even understood that the name 'Zanzibar' was derived from the term *Zanj*, which indicated black-skinned people. Zhao was aware of the River Nile and of Alexandria (Egentuo) with its great lighthouse, so anyone reading his work would have understood how Aden was linked to a wealthy land to the north.[57] By the fourteenth century, Egypt had become a great consumer of Chinese pottery and metalwork, to the extent of making reasonable imitations of Chinese bronzes in order to satisfy ever-rising domestic demand.[58] Large amounts of Chinese ceramics also reached Zanzibar, as the archaeological evidence clearly shows. Zhao also looked at the coastline south of Zanzibar and knew that black 'savages', as he condescendingly called the inhabitants, were carried off by *Dashi*, that is, Arab, slavers. He imagined that these black Africans lived on Madagascar, which was an error (Madagascar was even now being colonized by people of Malay and Indonesian origin); but he had time for stories about a great bird similar to Sindbad's *rukh* whose massive wings blotted out the sun, and whose diet included camels swallowed whole. He knew too that this was a land that produced rhinoceros horn and elephant tusks.[59] One might conclude from the Chinese coins that have turned up all along the coast from Mombasa northwards that Africa was already the target of Chinese merchants well before the arrival of Zheng He; a hoard discovered by a farmer in Zanzibar in 1945 consisted of 250 Tang and Song coins, dated between 618 and 1295. At Mogadishu six coins of Yong-le have been found, so it is quite possible that they arrived on board Zheng He's fleet. As for porcelain, the island of Pemba, like Zanzibar an important centre of trade, has yielded pieces from the Song and Ming dynasty, and African demand for Chinese pottery grew during the fourteenth century.[60] But to say that they were interested in African produce and that Chinese cash has been found along the coast is not the same as saying that Chinese traders travelled as far as this. Chinese cash remained in circulation long after it was manufactured (normally by casting rather than striking); a Song coin might have arrived in Ming times.

Once again Zheng He brought back to the Ming court ambassadors, including representatives of Hormuz, but they were kept waiting a couple of years for their return trip. Meanwhile, forty-one Treasure Ships were fitted out from October 1419 onwards, setting out at some point in mid-1421. However, the emperor was losing interest in the voyages, and concentrated his energies on the construction of his new capital at Beijing and on war in Mongolia instead. Around the same time he ordered the suspension of further voyages, although he let this one depart. After they entered the 'Western Ocean', the ships did not stay together; a eunuch named Zhou Man led part of the fleet to Aden, but much of the fleet apparently stayed behind in India, based at Calicut. By September 1422 the fleet had returned to China, bringing envoys from Siam, Semudera and Aden. But, after spending so much on Beijing, the emperor had run out of money to pay for these great worldwide displays of Chinese magnificence. Then, in 1424, Emperor Yong-le sent Zheng He on a further voyage, but this was a much more modest expedition than those Zheng He had commanded earlier, and it went no further than Palembang, a territory which happily acknowledged Chinese supremacy; Zheng delivered the letter and seal appointing the head of the 'Pacification Commission' at Palembang, the figure who was responsible for managing the large Chinese community there. But by the time Zheng He returned home, his patron was dead.[61]

This was not quite the end of Zheng He's naval career. The new emperor, Hong-xi, only lasted a few months, and he was hostile to these projects; on the very day of his accession he abolished the expeditions to the 'Western Ocean', and a day later he released an opponent of Zheng He from prison, Xia Yuan-ji, who had been warning of the excessive cost of the maritime expeditions.[62] Hong-xi's successor, Yong-le's grandson Xuan-de, also had other plans for Zheng He, including a military command at Nanjing and the building of the great Bao-en Temple at Nanjing, also known as the Number One Pagoda, which became a seat of Buddhist scholarship and the main temple in the city. So a perhaps disconsolate

Zheng He was sent back to his duties as overseer of construction projects, and languished in prestigious but not politically important tasks, while his foe Xia Yuan-ji held the emperor's attention and counselled against further expeditions; as Minister of Finance, Xia could see no justification for the waste of money they involved. However, Xia's death in February 1430 prompted a rethink; Xuan-de became worried that the prestige of his empire was suffering because 'the foreign countries, distantly located beyond the sea, still had not heard' of the stable and successful rule he had inaugurated. The ships built for the expedition he launched bore names that set out the fundamental principles Xuan-de was trying to broadcast: *Pure Harmony* was one, *Lasting Tranquillity* another.[63]

Once again Zheng He set out to proclaim Chinese overlordship across the Western Ocean, and once again he left inscriptions that helpfully set out the aims of the expedition. One of these inscriptions was carved on a tablet in the Temple of the Heavenly Princess Tianfei at Liujiagang on the Yangtze River, newly constructed by Zheng He in honour of his divine patron, while the other was erected on the admiral's behalf by the chief Daoist priest of Changle, 400 miles from Liujiagang, just as the fleet was about to set off from the coast of China. Both date from 1431, and both reveal how happy the Muslim eunuch was to worship other gods (whether traditional Chinese ones or Buddhist deities) rather than Allah: 'if men serve their prince with the utmost loyalty, there is nothing they cannot do, and if they worship the gods with utmost sincerity there is no prayer that will not be answered.'[64] Zheng He commemorated his past voyages 'to the various barbarians' aboard 'over a hundred seagoing ships', and carrying 'several tens of thousands' of soldiers. Just to give an idea of how easily numbers were inflated, when he mentioned the number of countries he had visited the figure for 3,000 crept in where modern scholars believe the intention was to write 'thirty'. Zheng He had no objection to the lively trade between 'barbarian' peoples, and even thought of himself as its protector: 'the sea routes became pure and peaceful and the foreign peoples could rely on them and pursue their occupations in safety. All this was due to the aid of the goddess.'[65] Yet the second inscription makes abundantly plain the unique achievement (so it is claimed) of the Ming dynasty, which has surpassed the Han and Tang dynasties in encompassing the peoples of the world: 'from the edge of the sky to the ends of the earth there are none who have not become subjects and slaves'.[66] Their reward has been not just material gifts but, more importantly, imperial favour. For these voyages had a more important moral than material purpose.

The main fleet headed first for Champa and then across the South China Sea to Surabaya on Java, which meant the Chinese had arrived in the heartlands of the Majapahit kingdom. They arrived on 7 March and only left Java after more than four months, suggesting the need for ship repairs as well as politicking; they visited Sumatra next, calling in at Palembang, but they only stopped there for three days, for they had had plenty of time to resupply their ships in Java. At the start of August they were in Melaka, where they halted for another month, and then on to Semudera, where they remained for about seven weeks. No doubt they were also factoring into their calculations knowledge of the monsoons and of the typhoon season, but that was not enough to save them from severe storms as they headed through high seas into the Indian Ocean. Zheng He's boasts in the two inscriptions that described how the goddess Tianfei had saved them on earlier expeditions must have seemed like wishful thinking. But they found safe anchorage in the Nicobar Islands and bought plenty of coconuts from the friendly natives. Once calmer weather arrived, they headed straight for Cochin and Calicut, and then on to Hormuz. Possibly detachments were sent further, as far as Aden or even east Africa, but without Zheng He on board; ambassadors from Arabia and Somalia travelled back with Zheng He after joining his fleet at Hormuz, but someone must have been sent to fetch them.

Even earlier, several ships had been sent off to Bengal, which lay well to the north of the route the Ming fleets always took towards India but which, as has been seen, was ruled by kings who cultivated friendship with the imperial court, and had even sent a giraffe as a present. Fortunately, the chronicler of this voyage, Ma Huan, joined the Bengal-bound squadron; he admired the country's fertility and its fine textiles, but was less pleased by the heat. Fei Xin enjoyed a feast of roast beef and lamb but was a little surprised that no wine was drunk, 'for fear that it might disturb someone's character and prevent him from conforming to the ceremonial'. So they drank sweetened rose-dew or sherbet instead.[67]

Yet the most remarkable connection was yet to be made. In Calicut the Chinese found a ship bound for Mo-qie, that is, the kingdom of Mecca (by way of the Red Sea port at Jiddah). Some Chinese, including Ma Huan, were allowed on board, and returned in due course with plenty of wild animals, some of which were oddly un-Arabian (giraffes and ostriches, though lions still existed in the Middle East); these were marvellous things they had bought rather than been given, but along with the animals came tribute-bearing ambassadors, or so the Chinese sources claimed. Ma Huan, who was himself a Muslim, also called Mecca Tianfang, or 'Heavenly Cube', referring to the shrine of the Ka'aba (which indeed means 'cube'), and he described the Great Mosque and some of the *hajj* ceremonies.[68] However, he does not give the impression of knowing a great deal about his religion, without being quite as detached from Islam as Zheng He; he rather distanced himself from the Muslims of Arabia by noting that they were punctilious in their religion, 'not daring to commit the slightest transgression'.

In early July 1433 the fleet was back at Liujiagang. On board were ambassadors from ten countries around the Indian Ocean. The official history of the reign of Xuan-de quotes the words of the emperor himself, which, were he not an emperor, one might describe as churlish: 'we do not have any desire for goods from distant regions, but we realise that they are offered in full sincerity. Since they come from afar they should be accepted, but their presentation is not cause for congratulations.'[69] Indeed, having revived the Ming voyages, Xuan-de sent no more expeditions to solicit submission from the peoples of the Indian Ocean. A year or two after his return, Zheng He died and around the same time Emperor Xuan-de also died, leaving a vacuum, since his heir was only eight years old. The eunuchs, who are usually supposed to have favoured lavish spending, lost influence at court, and interest in maintaining a navy plummeted. Foreign ambassadors arrived bearing gifts, but the Ming emperors received tribute from Siam, Java and elsewhere without any longer sending their fleets to collect it.[70] Once again China looked away from the sea. Foreign adventures went out of fashion as domestic difficulties accumulated. The sea voyages had always been controversial, and even those who strongly believed in the special place of the Middle Kingdom under Heaven were not necessarily convinced that they brought much gain. Indeed, it is quite likely that the emperor's words quoted a moment ago were put in his mouth by a later chronicler, who wanted to cast doubt on the wisdom of the Ming voyages without showing disrespect to the emperor.

Modern Chinese historians like to insist that there was a great difference between Zheng He's voyages and those of the Portuguese and Spaniards (which were just beginning in the 1420s and 1430s, in the case of Portugal): the Iberian voyages aimed to conquer territory, if need be by force, and to impose trade networks under their exclusive control, whereas the Ming voyages were by and large peaceful – allowing for the eradication of pirates – and aimed to show the flag rather than to create colonies. Zheng He is seen as the potential star of a counterfactual history in which 'Vasco da Gama and his successors would have found a powerful navy in control of the Indian Ocean'; and even 'Christopher Columbus might have encountered Chinese junks exploring the Caribbean'.[71] This contrast between Europe and China involves an oversimplification of Iberian aims, which evolved slowly; but this view also underplays the imperial dimension to the Ming voyages. Although the settlement of foreign lands by

Chinese soldiers and sailors was not on the Ming agenda, a Chinese compound was created in the new trading town of Melaka, and support was offered to the sizeable community of Chinese merchants in Java and Sumatra – indeed, the Chinese in Palembang were governed by a Commissioner whose power clearly extended beyond his own ethnic group. The emperor expected, demanded and received recognition of his superiority. But this came at a price, for the tribute brought back did not compensate for the cost of fitting out the expeditions, nor for the value of the gifts generously bestowed on the emperor's vassals in the South China Sea, India, Arabia and Africa. Even if fewer and smaller ships than is often assumed set sail, these voyages were an impressive technical achievement for a navy that had little or no knowledge of the Indian Ocean.

14

Lions, Deer and Hunting Dogs

I

At the centre of vast webs of trade and tribute, feeding their products into the routes leading towards both China and the Indian Ocean – and beyond that to the Red Sea and the Mediterranean – there lay what Marco Polo called 'the greatest island in the world', 3,000 miles in circumference and ruled by a great king who, he confidently asserted, paid tribute 'to no one else in the world'. Inhabited by 'idolaters', Great Java was of 'surpassing wealth, producing black pepper, nutmegs, spikenard, galingale, cubebs, cloves, and all other kinds of spices'. It was visited by huge numbers of ships, and the merchants who traded there, including many from Quanzhou and other southern Chinese cities, made an enormous profit. But in reality, as the exaggeration about its size implies, Polo was confused between the real Java (Java Minor) and an imaginary landmass of great wealth lying to the south (Great Java).[1] In modern works Java tends to be subsumed into a large mass of East Indian islands that were famous for the production of high-quality spices, some of which ended up on tables in Venice and Bruges. The truth is a little more complicated and rather more interesting, especially as it helps explain the eclipse of the maritime state of Śrī Vijaya and the emergence of Singapore and Melaka as important links between the Indian Ocean and the South China Sea. The success of Java was built upon its rivalry with Śrī Vijaya. The rulers and merchants of both kingdoms aimed to supply high-grade spices to the Chinese to the north and the Indians, and little-known peoples beyond them, to the west. At first, Śrī Vijaya proved stronger than Java. In 1016 the Śrī Vijayans sent their fleet against Java, and scored a notable victory. This was not a battle for territory but for command of the trade routes across the South China Sea and of the many subordinate towns that acknowledged the higher authority of the rajah of either Śrī Vijaya or Java.

However great the success of Palembang may have been in the heyday of Śri Vijaya's trade, by the time of its victory over the Javans its glory days were coming to an end. One reason was that its very success had brought upon Śri Vijaya the envious attention not just of the Javans but of a ruler much further to the west, in southern India, whose subjects knew Sumatra through their lively trade there, and the lively trade of the Indonesians in the Tamil-speaking kingdom of Cōḷa, or Chola. Chola had a long reach; objects in the Chola style dating to the tenth and eleventh centuries have been found in the Kra Isthmus, the narrow strip of land attaching the Malay peninsula to the great landmass of Asia; and in 1025 the king of Chola launched a violent attack on Śri Vijaya that has been credited with permanently disrupting the kingdom's trade. Śri Vijayan bases beyond the Strait of Malacca were also in the firing line. After the Chola invasion, even though it did not result in permanent occupation, Śri Vijaya was no longer able to count on its tribute-bearing dependencies in northern Sumatra and the western Malay peninsula.[2] In addition, for whatever reason, the Śri Vijayans shifted their capital away from Palembang towards another city, Jambi, that took advantage of its position closer to the Strait of Malacca to become a new centre of trade, though it too lay some way upriver (which in a time of raids and counter-raids made good sense). The Chinese continued to write about *San fo-chi*, their transliteration of Śri Vijaya, and both Jambi and Palembang were still visited by Chinese merchants; but the kingdom had lost its leadership to its rivals. That said, the rajah of Śri Vijaya made every effort to foster good relations with China, sending tribute to the Song emperors in 1137, 1156 and 1178, while the Śri Vijayans also asked the customs administration at Guangzhou to reduce the duty payable on frankincense from 40 to 10 per cent, suggesting that the flow of aromatics from south-east Asia continued to be managed in part from Jambi. In 1156 a native of Śri Vijaya was invited to act as the official head of the community of foreign merchants in Guangzhou, with five Chinese assistants appointed to serve under him.[3]

Song liberalization of trade had allowed a hundred flowers to bloom: there were now Chinese as well as south-east Asian competitors to Śri Vijaya's dominance of the sea routes. Among those who benefited from this were sundry petty kings who had previously operated in the shadow of Śri Vijaya, notably the rulers of Semudera – Pasai on the Indian Ocean tip of Sumatra, with which, as has been seen, Zheng He had a sometimes difficult relationship. According to legend, its first ruler chose the site of his new town at Semudera when he saw one of his hunting dogs being attacked by a mouse deer – apparently a good augury. However, similar tales explain the choice of other city sites in virgin territory, notably

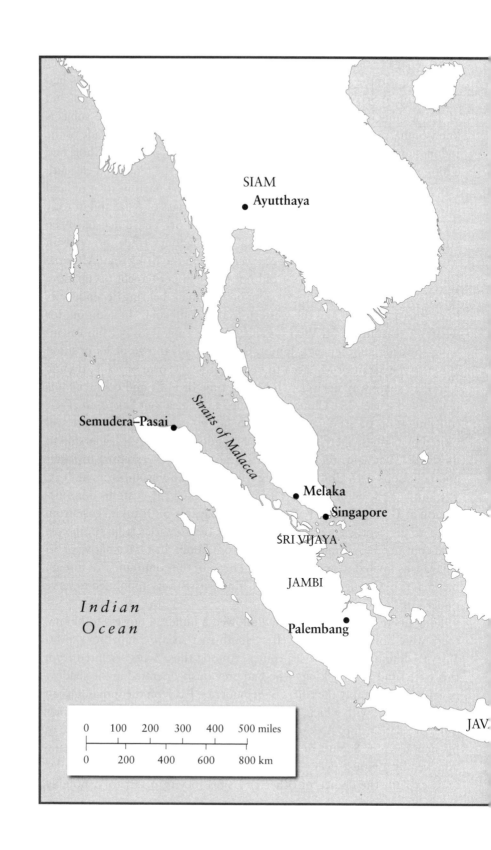

SIAM
● Ayutthaya

Semudera–Pasai ●

Straits of Malacca

● Melaka
● Singapore

ŚRI VIJAYA

JAMBI

*Indian
Ocean*

● Palembang

JAV

0	100	200	300	400	500 miles
0		200	400	600	800 km

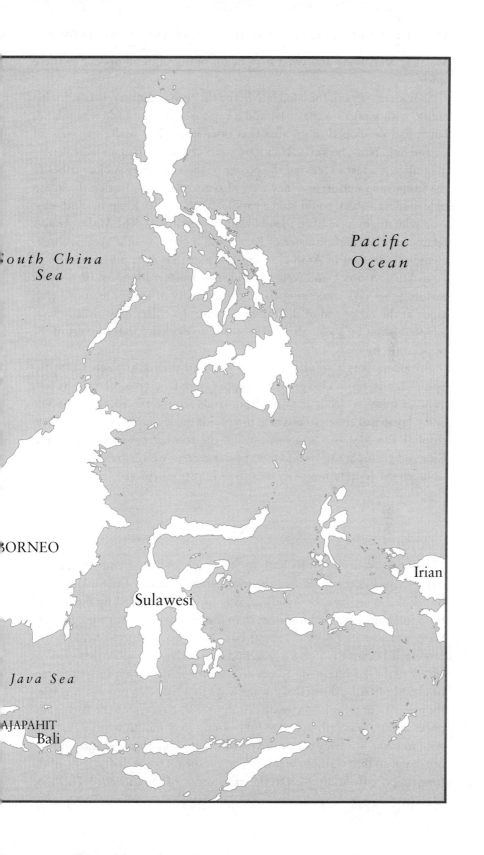

Melaka; deer, lions and what may be an orang-utan all appear in these stories.

Semudera – Pasai, founded late in the thirteenth century, was a double entity, with a port on the coast and a capital at Pasai a little way inland, but it had developed in an area that once had fallen under the sway of Palembang. Now, however, elaborate court ceremonials at an increasingly magnificent court expressed the power of the ruler over subject tribes in the Sumatran interior; and they were also intended to show that the sultan of Semudera – Pasai could hold a candle to other petty kings in south-east Asia who might have liked to gobble up his territories. The *Malay Annals* relate that the chief minister of Pasai built a ship, bought 'Arabian merchandise', dressed in Arab clothing 'since at that time all the people of Pasai knew Arabic', and went on a visit to another kingdom on a secret mission; this says something about the intensity of Pasai's relations with lands at the other end of the Indian Ocean.[4] Its rulers may already have adopted Islam by 1300, although there is no evidence that the rest of the population followed suit.

Semudera was a staging post for ships on their way deeper into the Spice Islands, but it also provided pepper from its own hinterland as well as other spices which it acquired from lands around the South China Sea; and it lay in just the right position to provide basic supplies to ships bound through the Malacca Strait or around the southern shores of Sumatra. Rice and grain for sailors and their passengers, as well as fresh water, were as much the foundation of its wealth as luxurious spices.[5]

II

There were plenty of rivals both to Śri Vijaya and to Semudera. A major city emerged in the middle of the fourteenth century a little inland from Bangkok. Ayutthaya, or Ayudhya, was formally founded by the king of Siam in about 1350 and for more than four centuries it was the capital of Siam, not just its political capital but also a great centre of trade, well protected because it stood in the midst of a river complex that ensured access to the sea but made access difficult for raiders from the sea. Sometimes, admittedly, the maze of waterways that led to Ayutthaya was itself the hazard – in the mid-sixteenth century the ship on which the Portuguese poet Camões was sailing entered the wrong river mouth when its captain tried to make headway towards Ayutthaya; the ship then ran aground and broke up, so that Camões was lucky to escape on some driftwood, all the time supposedly holding on to the manuscript of the *Lusiads*.[6] The flood plain on which it was constructed had only risen out of the sea during recent centuries, so when the rivers were in full flood the area around the city became completely waterlogged; but this was exactly what the rice fields needed, since the heads of grain kept above the level of the flood and the grain itself could be conveniently reaped from boats. Villagers round about lived in houses built on stilts so that they would be safe whenever the waters rose.

The town was not brand new – a massive golden Buddha was installed in the area a quarter of a century before the city was founded, as a thank-offering for the prosperity brought to the area by Siamese trade with China. As with its neighbours, how it was founded soon became the stuff of legend. In one version, the site had been visited by Buddha himself before it was founded by Prince U Thong, who displayed his talents by eating iron and by revealing that he was the reincarnation of a famous ant that had lived at the time of the Buddha and had been praised by Buddha for carrying a single grain of rice; that was all he could possibly do, whereas if a horse carried one grain of rice this was a worthless act involving no effort. In another version, recorded by a Dutch visitor, Ayutthaya was created by Prince U Thong, who was really Chinese, and who had been disgraced at home after he seduced the wives of the emperor's courtiers. He turned up in Siam, where he also supposedly founded Bangkok, a rather smaller settlement downriver from Ayutthaya. But when he discovered the magnificent but empty site that was to become Ayutthaya he was nonplussed. Why was it empty? He learned of a great dragon that breathed noxious fumes and lived in the marshes; all the inhabitants of an earlier settlement had been suffocated. Of course, U Thong killed the dragon and drained the marshes, on which he built his city.[7]

This was a different sort of city to the great Chinese ports of Hangzhou, Quanzhou and Guangzhou that hummed with officials and merchants. Ayutthaya was vast, but it was also surprisingly empty: the perimeter of the city was over eleven kilometres long. Much of the capital was given over to temples and pavilions, with a few streets of merchants, and there were plenty of open spaces, some still swampy.[8] Ayutthaya was a seat of government and the base from which the fourteenth-century rulers of Siam extended their control over lands to east and west – as far to the east as Angkor, for the great Khmer civilization had fallen on hard times. The Siamese kings were keen to show the surrounding world that they were the masters, and they expected those who came to trade with them, such as the inhabitants of the Ryukyu islands south of Japan, to bring gifts which they saw as tribute. Like many rulers in the region, they exercised close control over trade, imposing monopolies on the most desirable items such as pepper and sapanwood. By the seventeenth century, when the Dutch were active at Ayutthaya, Siam was exporting formidable quantities of elephant ivory: in sixty years, the Dutch sold 53,000 pounds of ivory to the Japanese, and the volume sent to Taiwan was much the same. An exotic perfume was made from Thai 'eaglewood', a type of aloe-wood that was scraped from rotting trees. Not surprisingly, given its use in Chinese medicine, rhinoceros horn was another favourite export, while millions of deer hides were also carried away by the Dutch. Tiger skins and shagreen, that is, shark-skin, also had a place in this trade.[9]

It may sound anachronistic to make use of much later evidence from a time when Dutch capital was being injected into the region, but the evidence for close links to China is not simply the product of foundation legends. Lacking a maritime tradition of their own, the Siamese kings were happy to employ Chinese merchants and sailors, so that 'Siamese' ships were not actually crewed by Siamese sailors. The readiness of the Chinese to serve is easy to explain. So long as the Ming government in China itself forbade its Chinese subjects to trade overseas, those who wished to do so ended up living in settlements away from home, and away from the everyday interference of the Ming government. So there were plenty of Chinese merchants in Siam, not to mention neighbouring lands.[10] In the 1370s the king of Siam sent several embassies to China, loaded with remarkable gifts, such as six-legged turtles and elephants. The Siamese king was not simply motivated by awe at the might of the Ming, nor by the lustre that would accrue to him when the Chinese emperor recognized him as a legitimate king; he also had commercial instincts of his own since he would expect to receive silk cloth and fine ceramics, and his agents would be able to pick up plenty of desirable goods in the marketplace of Guangzhou as they made their way home. Some of these were sold on to private traders for a handsome profit. Embassies were sent year in, year out with only a few exceptions, during the last years of the fourteenth century and the first half of the fifteenth, and ties were strengthened further when the large fleets of Chinese junks commanded by the eunuch Zheng He made their appearance in the South China Sea at the start of the fifteenth century.[11]

Ayutthaya would remain a centre of power and a focal point for the trade of the South China Sea until it was sacked by the Burmese in 1767. Although the documents tend to record the movement of exotic goods back and forth to China and other western Pacific lands, its strength also lay in local resources, notably its rice, which Thai boats (not this time manned by Chinese sailors) carried up and down the coasts of Malaya and Indo-China. This too helped to integrate Ayutthaya into a network of maritime routes that stretched towards the Strait of Malacca in one direction, towards the East Indies in another direction, and upwards towards southern China and even beyond – to Okinawa and Japan.

III

Java was always a rival to Śri Vijaya, whether the kingdom's capital lay at Palembang or Jambi. In 1275 the ruler of Singhasari, a kingdom in eastern Java, sent his forces against Jambi, which was sacked.[12] Meanwhile, with the Mongol conquest of the Song Empire, an outside power began to take an unhealthy interest in the little states of south-east Asia. Even before the Mongols launched their naval expedition against Java in 1292, they had been issuing commands to the rulers of states such as Semudera, which were told to send tribute to the Yuan emperor; the Mongols did not wait for their rajahs to volunteer. Jambi, rebuilt after its sacking, sent three missions to the Mongol emperor between 1281 and 1301, this time antici-pating the demand for tribute, rather than awaiting the command to deliver it; but if the Śri Vijayans hoped to gain favour at the Yuan court there is no evidence that they succeeded, for the Mongols, unlike the Śri Vijayans, were not as interested in trade as they were in proclaiming the universal authority of the Mongol khan. Mongol rule brought no obvious advantages to Jambi, Semudera or any other towns around the inner edges of the South China Sea.[13] Another potent threat emerged in Siam, whose Thai rulers extended their influence by land and sea as far south as an island that will feature prominently later in this chapter: Temasek, soon to be known as Singapore. A Sumatran tradition tells how a Thai army led by a renegade Śri Vijayan prince sacked Jambi, while Sumatra's own chroniclers praised the ports of Semudera–Pasai for their efforts in repel-ling Thai attacks. The impression that all this disorder conveys is of rampant piracy and of the fragmentation of the Śri Vijayan political net-work. The Strait of Malacca was particularly dangerous, according to an early fourteenth-century Chinese writer named Wang Dayuan.[14] Getting spices out into the Indian Ocean was therefore not at all straightforward, and this was where the authority of the sultans of Semudera was of some help. In the longer term, the answer would have to be the foundation of a control centre within the strait itself.

The beneficiary from all this chaos was the rajah of Java. The Javanese kingdom of Majapahit came into existence in the thirteenth century, around the same time as Semudera. While Semudera's success, though impressive, was rooted in control of its own local area, Majapahit sought to replicate the trading empire of Śri Vijaya. At its peak, its network of vassals extended as far as Singapore.[15] Its rulers favoured Hinduism and Buddhism, and they liked to portray themselves to their awed subjects as semi-divine beings. But they were also very pragmatic: untouched by the Confucian dislike for trade, they enthusiastically fostered trade, as a means to support themselves and to pay for their ambitious building programmes. For, although the great temple complex at Borobodur had been built around AD 800 and had been abandoned to the jungle a couple of centuries later, the royal passion for large-scale building did not fade, particularly in eastern Java.[16] Ports, markets and roads carried the life-blood of their kingdom, so much so that a Javan epic poem of the fifteenth century celebrated the sacred character of a set of crossroads that lay close to the royal palace.[17] Among the documents that survive from this kingdom is the 'Canggu Ferry Charter', dated 1358, which was a royal privilege inscribed on metal plates; it offered protection to those carrying goods up the River Brantas to the town of Canggu, which would later be mentioned as a place of note in Ma Huan's account of Zheng He's visit to Java. With this decree, the royal court detached the ferrymen of Canggu from the noble lords on whom they had earlier depended, and placed them under the direct protection of the royal court, which – of course – wanted to gain special access to the goods they carried from the coast to the king's palace.[18] These road and river networks within Java are the key to the success of the Majapahit kingdom. From the interior, rice was humped down to the ports along the coast, loaded on boats and transported to other ports, often beyond Java itself, in the easternmost Spice Islands such as Sulawesi, Bali and Irian. There, it was exchanged for pepper, cloves and other exotic products, which were carried back to what Marco Polo had called 'Great Java' and put on sale in the ports along its north coast. In other words, the commercial system of the Majapahit kingdom was very well integrated; and the ruler was well aware of the advantages – some of the other royal charters preserved on metal plates dealt with taxes payable to the crown, and royal interest in business initiatives even included part-ownership of a fish farm.[19]

The kingdom of Majapahit was, then, wealthy; during much of the fourteenth century it also remained quite stable. As with the Chinese rulers, its success depended on the devolution of power in the provinces to local nobles, often members of the royal family. But the internal tensions were obvious when Zheng He visited the island during his first and second voyages. At the start of the fifteenth century civil war broke out between a nephew and a son of King Hayam Wuruk of Majapahit (d. 1389), who had divided Majapahit between them, and several hundred Chinese merchants were killed. During his first voyage, Zheng He had not even tried to intervene in the conflict, though he had noted the rudeness of one of the kings towards the Ming emperor.[20] After one of the two Javanese kings had been captured and beheaded by the other, Yong-le demanded 60,000 ounces of gold in satisfaction from the victor.[21] In fact, the king was hardly in a position to make this massive payment.

Along the coast, merchant communities took advantage of the contest for power to take charge of their own affairs. The faster these towns detached themselves from the central government, the more royal revenues, which had been so heavily based on trade, began to shrink, and royal troubles were magnified still further when local nobles also exploited the chaos to insist on their own independence; sometimes they worked with the towns, assuring them of vital food supplies in return for help fighting their rivals, but just as often the port cities waged war against the nobles in order to conquer the land they needed for rice cultivation.[22] What all this meant was that Java's brief ascendancy came to an end in the early fifteenth century. The authority of the semi-divine kings was further eroded by the spread of Islam in Indonesia. As disorder increased, the Chinese court began to wonder how it could secure peace in the South China Sea. This attempt to bring stability helps explain Zheng He's voyages, and in particular the close connection that the Ming court developed with the new town of Melaka. But before looking at the rapid rise of Melaka it is necessary to examine its antecedents in Singapore, which have been exposed to view by archaeological discoveries that have transformed knowledge of the 'Silk Route of the Sea'.

IV

Fort Canning Park consists of a hill in the middle of the colonial heart of Singapore, rising above what one might imagine to be the buildings of old Singapore – the Armenian Church, the synagogue, Raffles Hotel, and what remains of the creeks and river that once connected this part of Singapore island to the sea. From its paths one can look across at the cluster of giant office buildings and hotels that delineate the skyline of new Singapore, located next to land reclaimed from the sea. The history of this city is commonly assumed to have begun in the early nineteenth century, when Sir Stamford Raffles chose it from a shortlist as the site for a British trading station commanding the entrance to the Strait of Malacca. Yet his motive for settling on this site was not simply its convenient location; he was deeply interested in the history of south-east Asia, and the fact that a trading city had once stood here fascinated him, even though little or nothing remained of medieval Singapore.[23] Raffles acquired a copy of the most important chronicle of the early history of Malaya, the *Sějarah Mělayu*; generally known as the *Malay Annals*, the title should really be translated as *The Malay Genealogical Tree*. Amid legends about the foundation of Singapore and then Melaka, this chronicle wove together fact and fancy so as to extol the dynasty that had brought both cities into existence. It has also served as a key text for those in Malaysia who have, since the country's independence, insisted upon its predominantly Malay (rather than Indian or Chinese) identity, and on the special place of Islam in Malaysian history. A constant theme is how the resourceful and crafty Malays were able to outwit their rivals in Java and Siam, and even in China. Although the text we have was written at the start of the seventeenth century, the *Sějarah Mělayu* incorporated a great amount of much older material, going back centuries – or indeed well over a millennium, if one believes the claims the book makes.[24]

The legitimacy of the later rulers of Melaka could (according to the *Sějarah Mělayu*) be traced right back to Alexander the Great, who appears as 'Rajah Iskandar, the Two-Horned, son of Rajah Darab, a Roman of the country of Macedonia'.[25] This supposed fact betrays the strong cultural influence of India and Islam on Malaya at the end of the Middle Ages; the early stories in the book are about India, not south-east Asia. But gradually the history of that area comes into focus. The author told how an Indian prince called Rajah Chulan decided to attack China, for 'the whole of India and Sind was subject to him and every prince of East and West was his vassal' – every prince except the ruler of China, here cast not as an emperor but as a weakling who pretended to be 'Lord of the Earth', but who knew that if the army and navy of Chulan arrived, 'assuredly this country of ours will be destroyed'. The Chinese could not rely on greater military force, so they had to rely on a ruse. When the rajah was already at Temasek (later known as Singapore) a Chinese ship came to meet him; to the surprise of the Indians it carried a crew of very old men, and on board they found a number of fruit trees. The men claimed that they had boarded the ship when they were twelve years old, when the trees were mere seeds. That was how long it took to sail from China to the Strait of Malacca. The rajah reflected on this and decided that 'China must be a very long way away. When should we ever get there?' Instead of advancing against China, he decided to explore the sea. He had a sort of glass submarine made in which he visited underwater cities and was received with honour at the court of one of the sea princes. The two rajahs became good friends, and the sea prince offered Chulan the hand of his daughter; they married, lived under the sea for three years and had three sons, before Chulan decided he had to abandon his distraught family so that his kingdom on earth would continue to be ruled by his dynasty. A winged steed carried him out of the sea, and once back home he took another wife, who came from Hindustan.[26]

Surprisingly, this fable does have some historical value. There is the simple fact that the sea fascinated the Malays, in this and other stories in the same book. More specifically, Rajah Chulan is thought to be a distant memory of the same Chola king who launched an attack on Śri Vijaya in 1126; and this legend not merely mentions the site of Singapore but it immediately precedes a story about the old capital of Śri Vijaya, Palembang: 'formerly it was a very great city, the like of which was not to be found in the whole country of Andelas [Sumatra]'. The three princes born under the sea were adopted by the ruler of Palembang and became rajahs in their own right; the youngest, blessed by a miraculous being who emerged out of sea foam, took the name Sri Tri Buana, which has strong Buddhist overtones and means 'Lord of the Three Worlds' in Sanskrit; he took up residence in Palembang, whose ruler abdicated in his favour.[27] But one day he announced: 'I am thinking of going to the coast to find a suitable site for a city. What say you?' He set out with a great navy:

> So vast was the fleet that there seemed to be no counting it; the masts of the ships were like a forest of trees, their pennons and streamers were like driving clouds and the state umbrellas of the rajahs like cirrus. So many were the craft that accompanied Sri Tri Buana that the sea seemed to be nothing but ships.[28]

During his travels, Sri Tri Buana went hunting; and one day, while chasing a deer, he climbed a high rock and found himself looking across a stretch of water towards a pure white beach in the distance.[29] He asked what that land was and was told that it was called Temasek; archaeology confirms that a white beach would have fringed the southern shores of what was then Temasek island during the Middle Ages. The channel separating Temasek from where he was (which would be one of the Riau islands, now under Indonesian control) proved much more difficult to cross than he could have imagined; a storm blew, and the rajah's ship began to fill up with water. The best the sailors could do was to throw overboard all the goods on board, to lighten the vessel; but one item, the rajah's crown, was kept on board. The boatswain insisted that this too should be cast in the sea, and Sri Tri Buana replied, 'Overboard with it then!' So over it went and the storm abated.

None the worse for this experience, Sri Tri Buana went on land and saw a strange animal bigger than a he-goat that had a red body, a white breast and a black head. Mystified by this, the rajah was told that it was some sort of lion, though the description hardly matched that of a lion, and it has been suggested that the author might have been thinking of an orang-utan instead. Whatever the animal was, it was considered a good augury, and Sri Tri Buana decided to build a city on that site, which he named 'Town of the Lion', *Singapura*. Like Sri Tri Buana's new name, this was a Sanskrit rather than Malay word, and was intended to show that the ruler and his court were in contact with the high civilization of the Buddhist and Hindu lands to the west.[30] 'Singapura' was a common name for towns in this region, but that a new town came into existence on this site somewhere around 1300 cannot now be doubted.[31] The *Sĕjarah Mĕlayu* reported that 'Singapura became a great city, to which foreigners resorted in great numbers so that the fame of the city and its greatness spread throughout the world.'[32]

In south-east Asia that was not entirely good news. The ruler of Majapahit enters the story told by the Malay chronicler at this point. He had 'heard that Singapura was a great city but that its ruler did not acknowledge the Batara [rajah of Majapahit] as its overlord'. This made him exceedingly angry. He sent a strange gift to the rajah of Singapore, an extremely thin wood shaving seven fathoms long, rolled up to look like a girl's earring. At first confused and irritated, Sri Tri Buana realized that he would have to show that his own carpenters were just as skilled as those of Majapahit, and he ordered a carpenter to shave a boy's head with an adze rather than a razor, which proved he was as adept with his adze as the Javan carpenter had been. On hearing of this, the rajah of Majapahit jumped to the conclusion that the ruler of Singapore was threatening to invade and to shave the heads of all the Javans. He ordered a fleet of a hundred warships to be prepared, and launched a vicious attack on Singapore. Nonetheless, he was beaten off.[33] So too were equally vicious garfish (a type of small swordfish) that leaped out of the sea and stabbed anyone who was on the seashore; in modern times, fishermen in the waters around Singapore have been attacked and killed by these fish, which jump out of the water when they see the bright lights of lanterns aboard the fishing boats, and woe betide anyone in their way. The ruler was unable to work out how to stop these attacks, and thousands died until a young boy suggested the Singaporeans should make a barricade out of the stems of banana trees along the beach; after that, each time a garfish jumped out of the water it buried its snout in the foliage, and could be cut down and killed. However, the ruler was jealous of the boy who had come up with a solution that had eluded him, and put him to death, after which 'the guilt of his blood was laid on Singapura'.[34] The story therefore foreshadows the fate of Singapore, which the rajah was soon to lose to his old enemies.

This event was an unpleasant interlude before the next Javan attack, which was prompted by dissension at the court of the current ruler of Singapore, Iskandar Shah. One of the king's mistresses, who was the beautiful daughter of the royal treasurer, was accused of carrying on with other men; the angry rajah ordered her to be displayed naked in the town marketplace. Her father would have preferred her to be put to death rather than let her face this humiliation; and he wreaked revenge by sending a letter to the rajah of Majapahit, promising his help if the Javans attacked again. So the Javans made ready 300 large ships and countless smaller craft, bearing (supposedly) 200,000 soldiers. Soon after their arrival the treasurer opened the gate of the fort that was supposed to protect Singapore, and the Javans streamed into the city; the fort was flooded with the blood of those killed on either side.[35] Yet Iskandar survived, and fled from the city, which remained in the hands of the ruler of Majapahit. The lesson of these events was that Iskandar had lacked wisdom: he had been unable to deal with the garfish, and he provoked his treasurer into treachery when he disgraced the daughter of a loyal officer of the crown.

These extraordinary tales established not just a dynastic genealogy going back, it was claimed, to ancient Macedonia, but a genealogy of cities: Palembang was the mother city of Singapore, which itself, as will be seen, was the mother city of Melaka. By the time the author reached the end of the fourteenth century, his knowledge of the past became much more precise; the magical atmosphere of his early chapters gave way to a more factual, though not entirely credible, account of what happened, without underwater princes and prophets born out of sea foam. The general picture of Singapore as a thriving emporium in the fourteenth century can now be confirmed, thanks to broken sherds, a shattered inscription, and bits and pieces of brick foundations. Moreover, there is other written evidence, this time from far beyond Singapore, that speaks of Temasek before it took its new name, and that shows how it had already become a centre of trade and piracy by the early fourteenth century.

V

Wang Dayuan was a merchant who was born in 1311 and who lived for a time in Quanzhou. In the 1330s he set out twice across the South China Sea, and recorded his impressions in a book entitled *Description of the*

Barbarians of the Isles. Although his style is considered poor, he enjoyed composing poetry and was a keen geographer – writing from the perspective of someone who had sailed the seas, he divided the world into two oceans, an eastern one and a western one, corresponding to the Pacific and the Indian Oceans. Dan-ma-xi (his transcription of Temasek) in his view marked the point where the two oceans met. He described the people who lived there and whom he had visited: they tied their hair in a bun and they manufactured rice wine; they wore short tunics made of cheap cloth coloured dark blue; but this was a place where one could trade gold, silk, metal vessels and fairly ordinary ceramics. However, the goods they traded 'were obtained by piracy'. Ships sailing out into the Indian Ocean would be permitted to pass without interference, because what the pirates wanted was for them to return laden with goods. As these ships came back past Temasek 'the sailors have to install arrow guards and special cloth screens and sharpen weapons to prepare for defence'. With a fair wind, one could sail straight through and escape being attacked, but if the pirates did manage to seize a ship, they ruthlessly killed those on board and took their possessions. The most dangerous place was Longya-men, 'Dragon's Tooth Strait', a narrow passage off the southern tip of Singapore, separating a small skerry from the main island. And yet Wang also described how the governor of Temasek insisted that everyone should 'live in harmony with the Chinese people', or, in an alternative translation, 'men and women reside beside Chinese people'.[36] In other words, a Chinese settlement existed on Temasek in the early fourteenth century, at a time when the town lay under Javanese dominion. Precisely because it was so exposed, the town was very vulnerable and at the same time in a good position to reap great benefits from the sea trade that passed its doors – which, in the early days, it chose to do by piracy, although the presence of pirates would also draw the armies and navies of Siam and Majapahit towards the Malacca Strait. The people of Temasek, for their part, tried to make friends in the region: there is evidence that they sent gifts to the king of Vietnam.[37] In the end, as will be seen, it was the Ming Chinese who cracked this nut, and not at Singapore but at its replacement, Melaka.

Before that, however, the Ming dynasty set off a crisis in the region. The accession of the first Ming emperor in 1368 was followed by tighter and tighter restrictions on foreign trade, aimed at Chinese traders or Chinese settlers overseas, who were ordered to return to their native land, but evidently did not do so. Under the new regulations, Chinese worshippers were expected to burn Chinese rather than foreign incense. This might have greatly eased the outflow of bullion, which had been a serious problem under the Song, but it also undermined the relationship that had been

built up with the rulers of Java and other lands around the South China
Sea, as well as Japan and Korea. By 1380 the relationship between Java
and China had worsened still further. The Javans intercepted and put to
death Chinese ambassadors who were on their way to Jambi to invest
the maharajah of Śri Vijaya as a vassal king. The ruler of Majapahit
insisted that the rajah of Śri Vijaya was his own vassal, and it seems that
this rajah was hoping to free himself from Javan tutelage by turning to
China instead. The attempt backfired; Java asserted its control over
Sumatra. Following this outrage, the Ming emperor wanted nothing
to do with the peoples of Indonesia.[38] This left the Javans free to pursue
their own aggressive policies.

Meanwhile Sumatra was in turmoil. At Palembang, a prince named
Parameśvara had taken charge; this is the figure the *Malay Annals* named
as Iskandar, although, to add confusion, the real Iskandar may have been
his son. There are as many versions of who was who and what happened
as there are accounts of Parameśvara's stormy life. Palembang, as has
been seen, was no longer the great emporium that it had been in the glory
days of Śri Vijaya, but Parameśvara aimed to throw off Javan overlordship. The Majapahit navy attacked Palembang; after only three years in
charge there, Parameśvara fled westward, landing in Singapore. His ten-
ure of power there was brief: enemies would unseat him in 1397, and he
would acquire his third princedom with the foundation of Melaka.[39]
Before looking at early Melaka, a close examination of early Singapore
is required.

The *Malay Annals* described how Sri Tri Buana was buried on the 'hill
of Singapura', and the author of the *Malay Annals* and other writers
mentioned additional royal burials in what is now Fort Canning Park.[40]
Memories of these tombs remained alive, and the area came to be known
to those living there when Raffles arrived as the 'Forbidden Hill'; it was a
taboo area, perhaps because of the graves, and it was also credited with
being the site of the royal palace. One story told how earlier rulers had
forbidden anyone to ascend the hill unless the king summoned them; and
there was a stream where the queen would bathe, and that too was forbidden ground. Here, in the time of Raffles, the first antiquarians to take
an interest in the remote past of Singapore found tumbledown sections of
ancient walls and brick foundations; since most buildings, including the
royal palace, would have been of wood, and since many would have stood
on stilts, the lack of extensive remains is no surprise. But with the coming
of British rule no one bothered to investigate further; the sacred hill
became the British headquarters, and the ground was levelled.[41] Over the
years other discoveries have taken place, but by accident: some elaborate

gold jewellery in an Indian style, including a bracelet and earrings, was turned up in 1928 and evidently belonged to someone of very high rank.

One potentially important written record inscribed on stone (the so-called Singapore Stone) was blown to smithereens by the British army, which needed the site near the mouth of the Singapore River where it lay for a new fort. No one has deciphered the writing on the small surviving fragment that is proudly displayed in the Singapore History Museum.[42] Here myth and history once again become entangled. The *Malay Annals* mention a giant named Badang who came to Singapore and challenged a rival strongman from nearby Kalinga to a contest:

> Now in front of the hall of audience there was a huge rock, and the Kalinga champion said to Badang, 'Let us try our strength in lifting that rock. Whichever of us fails to lift it is the loser.' 'Very well', answered Badang, 'you try first.' Thereupon the Kalinga champion tried to lift the rock but failed. He then put forth every effort and raised it as far as his knees, then he let it down again with a crash, saying, 'Now it's your turn, sir.' 'Very well', said Badang, and he lifted the rock, swung it into the air and hurled it as far as the bank of Kula Singapura [Singapore River]. That is the rock which is there to this day.[43]

The Kalinga champion had to hand over the seven ships laden with goods with which he had arrived in Singapore, and, humiliated, he headed back home. More importantly, perhaps, Badang was credited with stretching a chain across the river mouth, to block free access to the port of Singapore – evidence, for what it is worth, that efforts were being made to create a working harbour, and one that could be closed off when pirates or enemy navies threatened.[44]

Only in the 1980s and after did serious investigation of what remained under the surface of the hill begin, confirming that this was an important fourteenth-century centre of trade.[45] The evidence mostly consists of fragments of pottery, in their thousands, though plenty of glass beads and coins complement the pottery, and all point in the same direction: fourteenth-century Singapore was an important trading emporium with links to China, Java and the lands around the South China Sea, and westwards to the Indian Ocean. The most striking feature of the discoveries on the hill is the predominance of Chinese ceramics even over local ones; those from China nearly all date from the Yuan dynasty, that is, before the Ming dynasty threw out the Mongols in 1368.[46] Chinese silence after then reflects the new Ming hostility to foreign trade; there is simply not much early Ming porcelain to show from the excavations. But before the trade with China dried up the Singaporeans made much use of

good-quality Chinese porcelain: light-green celadon, some of it from Fuk-
ien province in the neighbourhood of Quanzhou; white porcelain, very
typical of the Chinese export trade and produced in large quantities at
Dehua not far from Quanzhou; the famous blue-and-white porcelain, one
piece of which is especially remarkable, as it carries the Chinese characters
for compass directions.[47] This bowl is more likely to have been used in
divination, for *feng shui*, than at sea, but at least it is clear that it arrived
along the sea lanes. These good-quality bowls, vases and cups were
found in the area where the royal palace must have stood, so they give a
clue to the standard of living of the princely court during the fourteenth
century.

Bearing in mind that other small-scale discoveries of pottery, glass and
metalwork have been made on the flat ground below Fort Canning Hill,
now occupied by buildings of the colonial era and by the new parliament
house, it becomes clear that Singapore was a place of note, with a palace
on a hill and trading quarters down below by the river exit. Its rulers ably
took advantage of its excellent position astride the trade routes and –
remembering Wang's slightly obscure words – Singapore seems to have
started life as a pirate base and then to have transformed itself into an
honest trading settlement. As it grew it attracted the envy of powerful
neighbours in Java and Siam, while the Ming ban on foreign trade had a
dampening effect on its fortunes.

VI

The sixteenth-century Portuguese writer and traveller Tomé Pires
described in his *Suma Oriental* the foundation of Melaka by 'Paramjçura
king of Palembang', or Parameśvara. The word means 'Supreme Lord' in
Sanskrit, and was an epithet frequently attached to the Hindu god Siva,
though there was also a god called Parameśvara, and the name was often
used by royalty.[48] Really it was not so much a name as a title, one that
expressed the link between a royal prince on earth and the Hindu gods
in heaven. Stories linking Palembang, Singapore and the new foundation
at Melaka, which Parameśvara ruled in succession to one another,
bestowed a special legitimacy on the later rulers of Melaka, creating a
genealogy that in theory stretched back to ancient Śri Vijaya and even to
Alexander the Great, for the *Malay Annals* call him not Parameśvara but
Iskandar, an arabized form of Alexander.[49] However, Tomé's Parameśvara
does not emerge as a particularly savoury character, any more than
Iskandar does in the *Malay Annals*. In the Portuguese version, apparently

derived from tales current in Java, Parameśvara was ruling Palembang when he rebelled against his overlord, the Javanese ruler, at the end of the fourteenth centry. He was soundly defeated and fled from Sumatra to Singapore, where he murdered the rajah and seized power, which he held for only six years at most. During his reign, Parameśvara relied on the support of the piratical 'Sea People', in Malay *Orang Laut*. They did not actually live with him in Singapore, but on an island that stands astride the strait between Sumatra and Singapore, and therefore astride the main trade routes from the South China Sea up the Strait of Malacca, a good location from which to prey on merchant shipping.[50]

Speculation about what happened at the end of Parameśvara's brief reign in Singapore, somewhere around 1396, ranges from a Javanese attack, which fits with the Malay account, to a revenge attack by Malay allies of the Thais who had been benefiting from a marriage alliance with the previous ruler.[51] All this adds up to a picture of vigorous piracy and local conflicts, into which every now and again more substantial powers – the rajahs of Majapahit and the Thai rulers based at their lively capital, Ayutthaya – threw themselves, because interference with their shipping was proving intolerable. No doubt the Sea People entered into agreements with various neighbours to allow them passage, in return for some material benefits, but the coming of Parameśvara signalled a return to the piratical ways of the founders of Singapore: 'he had no trade at all except that his people plundered their enemies.'[52] Hunger for Chinese and other goods only increased as the Ming emperors made it more difficult to obtain them legitimately.

The existence of two names, Parameśvara and Iskandar, in accounts of the foundation of Melaka has caused endless confusion, and there are grounds for believing that the real Iskandar was in fact the founder's son and successor. Further confusion results from the similarity between the account of the foundation of Melaka and the accounts of the foundation of both Semudera–Pasai and Singapore, all contained within the *Malay Annals*. But even if the annals are fanciful they record the legends in which the inhabitants of Malaya believed, which have influenced the way the early history of Melaka is written even today. The *Malay Annals*, where he is called Iskandar, describe his search for a new home after he was thrown out of Singapore. He edged up the coast of the Malay peninsula until he came to a river mouth that looked promising.

> And as the king, who was hunting, stood under a tree, one of his hounds was kicked by a white mouse-deer. And Sultan Iskandar Shah said, 'This is a good place, when even its mouse-deer are full of fight! We shall do well

to make a city here.' And the chiefs replied, 'It is indeed as your Highness says.' Thereupon Sultan Iskandar Shah ordered that a city be made, and he asked, 'What is the name of the tree under which I am standing?' And they all answered, 'It is called *Melaka*, your Highness'; to which he rejoined, 'Then Melaka shall be the name of this city.'[53]

What is not said here is that there were striking physical similarities between the site of Singapore and that of Melaka, which has been described as a 'mirror image' of Singapore. Just as Fort Canning rises above the city of Singapore, St Paul's Hill – though smaller and lower – is the high point of Melaka; these hills were defensible vantage points, and they were also good locations for a royal palace. They were seen as sacred places to which access had to be specially granted. Moreover, both towns were situated close to a river mouth, which provided a convenient berth for shipping.[54]

The Malay annalist was well aware that ships transformed the fortunes of Melaka. The book describes the success of the city's rulers in fostering trade, which also meant that it attracted many foreign merchants and settlers, who were made welcome there.[55] There were endless naval engagements with neighbours in the strait, such as the rulers of Siak across the water in Sumatra. After all, everyone wanted to gain control of the lucrative trade that passed through the strait. Not just goods arrived from the other end of the Indian Ocean. Rajah Tengah, who according to these annals would be the grandson of the founder of Melaka, 'showed in the treatment of his subjects such justice that no other rajah of his time in the world could equal him'. So it is little surprise that he was chosen to fulfil an important part of Melaka's destiny. He had a dream in which he was visited by none other than the Prophet Muhammad, who taught him the Muslim declaration of faith, or *shahadah*, and gave him a new name – appropriately, Muhammad. The Prophet told him: 'tomorrow, when it is time for the afternoon prayer, there will come hither a ship from Jiddah; and from that ship a man will land on this shore of Melaka. See that you do whatsoever he tells you.' When he awoke, he found that he had been circumcised. He spent the day repeating the *shahadah*, and his ministers thought he had gone mad. They informed the Bendahara, or vizier, who was reluctant to accept the miraculous circumcision as proof, but who agreed that if a ship came from Jiddah at the promised time he would know that the dream was true. Sure enough, the ship did arrive, and one of the people who disembarked, the Makhdum (or teacher of Islam) Sa'id 'Abdu'l-aziz, began to invoke Allah on the quayside.

And all who saw him were astonished at his behaviour and said, 'What means this bobbing up and down?' And there was a general scramble to see him, the people crowding together so thickly that there was not a space between one man and another and there was such a disturbance that the noise of it came to the ears of the rajah inside the royal apartments of the palace. And straightaway the rajah set forth on his elephant escorted by his chiefs and he perceived that the Makhdum's behaviour in saying his prayers was exactly as in his dream. And he said to the Bendahara and the chiefs, 'That is exactly how it happened in my dream!'[56]

The Makhdum was invited to mount the elephant and was borne back to the royal palace with the rajah. The Bendahara and the chiefs all became Muslims, 'and every citizen of Melaka, whether of high or low degree, was commanded by the rajah to do likewise'.

Whatever actually happened, Melaka was always, and remains, a city inhabited by people of several faiths. But there is no reason to doubt that the rajahs became Muslim early in the fifteenth century. Rather than a sudden event, this conversion was the product of years of contact and of pondering the advantages of such a conversion. Even before Tengah's time, the rajahs had flirted with Islam. Pasai, not far away, had a reputation as a beacon of Islam in south-east Asia. Tengah/Muhammad had actually married a princess from Pasai. In fact, earlier in his career he had quarrelled with the sultan of Pasai over whether he should convert. He tried to draw towards Melaka Javanese Muslim merchants who traded regularly with Pasai, but he found that the sultan was unwilling to let them trade with Melaka unless Tengah converted to Islam; after all, if they made heavy use of Melaka, these merchants would contribute less to the tax revenue of Semudera–Pasai. For the moment Tengah was reluctant to convert; but the quarrel did not last long, and eventually Muslim merchants from Pasai went to live in Melaka as he had hoped; they built the town's first mosques. But Tengah's ambitions extended further: he encouraged Muslim merchants from Java itself to come to his city. Islam and trade were two sides of the same coin. The Portuguese writer Tomé Pires wrote: 'trade began to grow greatly and the king derived great profit and satisfaction from it . . . The Moors were great favourites with the king, and obtained whatever they wanted.'[57] The conversion of Melaka marked a major step in the emergence of the city as the centre of commerce in the region.[58] The sultan of Pasai, allied to the newly renamed Sultan Muhammad, acquiesced in the erosion of Semudera–Pasai's commanding position in the Strait of Malacca, where the upstart town of Melaka now seized the initiative. After all, its location, actually within the strait, was better, not just because it lay right along the direct trade route but because it was better placed to challenge pirates.[59]

This is not to say that Tengah was uninterested in his new religion; his conversion may appear opportunistic, but it may just as well have been the result of a slowly dawning conviction that he wanted to become a Muslim. Quite apart from the influence of his wife, Tengah had visited China, where he met the ambassadors sent to the Ming court by Muslim rulers, including the envoys of Pasai. The Melakans would have been perfectly familiar with people 'bobbing up and down' five times a day. Yet the conversion of this and other rajahs in south-east Asia changed the religious balance significantly. Buddhism and Hinduism, as well as local cults, had become interwoven, and religious syncretism was the general rule. Islam, as the rajah's supposed insistence on the conversion of all his subjects makes plain, was exclusive; while there was still space for Hindus and Buddhists in these lands, the Muslim population could not, officially at least, share their festivals, customs and in certain cases their food. But to be seen as the patron of Muslim merchants right across the region would greatly enhance the prestige of the sultan of Melaka, and he could present himself as the champion of all Muslims whenever the conflict between Melaka and Siam flared up again.

The guarantor of Melaka's security was Ming China. Contact was established between Melaka and China within a few years of the creation of the new town. Even before Zheng He set off on his great voyages, the imperial eunuch Yin Qing arrived in Melaka in 1404 on a friendly visit, offering Parameśvara a crown; and Parameśvara responded by sending tribute to the Ming court.[60] Here was an opportunity to throw off the overlordship of Siam by accepting as new overlord a far greater power. But this was not without risks: Siam was a local power, and China was very far away. The fact that Zheng He's voyages were on such a large scale – even if the scale has been exaggerated – meant that for a time the Melakans could develop their trade and send campaigns against local pirates without too much fear of Siamese intervention. The Chinese came past Melaka again and again during Zheng He's voyages; but they also made it more secure by their actions in cleaning up Palembang, suppressing Chinese piracy off Sumatra and holding the Javans in check. The Chinese presence thus acted as a brake on the rivalries that had, until the start of the fifteenth century, made the Strait of Malacca one of the most dangerous sea passages in the region. Paradoxically, then, the Ming emperor's great distaste for overseas commerce resulted in greater freedom of the seas, as the tribute-seeking expeditions of Zheng He proclaimed a Chinese peace, a *Pax Sinica*, across the South China Sea and beyond. The moment it was shattered can be identified easily enough. When Xuan-de suspended further voyages, the sultan of Melaka was himself in China, on the third visit by a Melakan ruler, and hoping to present tribute to the emperor. He and other ambassadors, from as far away as Ceylon, were embarrassingly stranded far from home; and in any case Xuan-de died soon after. His successors were not interested in spending vast sums on fleets bound for the ends of the earth.

Looking back from the start of the seventeenth century, the author of the *Malay Annals* was unwilling to admit that this was the real shape of things. From a Melakan perspective, it seemed to be Melaka rather than China that exercised thalassocracy:

> When news reached China of the greatness of the rajah of Melaka, the rajah of China sent envoys to Melaka: and as a complimentary gift to accompany the letter he sent needles, a whole shipload of them. And when the envoys reached Melaka, the king ordered the letter to be fetched from the ship with due ceremony and borne in procession. And when it had been brought into the palace it was received by a herald and given by him to the reader of the mosque, who read it out. It ran as follows: 'This letter from His Majesty the Rajah of Heaven is sent to the Rajah of Melaka. Of a truth there are no rajahs in this world greater than ourselves, and there is no one who knows the number of our subjects. We have asked for one needle from each house in our realm and those are the needles with which the ship we send to Melaka is laden.'[61]

Needless to say the rajah then sent back his own cargo, this time of grains of sago, to make an identical point, so that the emperor had to admit: 'Great indeed must be this rajah of Melaka! The multitude of his subjects must be as the multitude of our own. It would be well that I should marry him with my daughter!'[62] The annalist was well aware that a Chinese trading settlement across the river from the hill on which the royal palace stood, known as Bukit China, dated back to these times, and occasional finds of objects in that area, around the Cheng Ho Museum that commemorates Zheng He's voyages, prove the point further: not just fragments of pottery but what seems to have been a well used by the Chinese community.

Siam was a constant thorn in the flesh of the rajahs of Melaka, as it had been to the rulers of Singapore. It is, as ever, difficult to disentangle the involved stories in the *Malay Annals*, and it might make more sense to look at what can be described as the received version of the history of Melaka, as it is portrayed in the impressive displays of the Melaka Historical Museum on St Paul's Hill. The Siamese attacks of 1445 and 1456 are presented as a response to the prosperity and commercial rivalry of Melaka. On the second occasion, the Bendahara is said to have lit up the river mouth, deluding the enemy into thinking that a massive force lay in wait. The enemy exclaimed: 'What a vast fleet these Malays must have, no man can count their ships! If they attack us, how shall we fare? Even one of their ships just now was more than a match for us!' After that the Siamese kept well clear of Melaka.[63] Melaka's own historians like to present the image of a heroic city whose defence of its independence laid the foundations for an Islamic nation consisting of Malay people, strict in their adherence to Sunni Islam but also willing to permit Hindus and Daoists, among others, to settle and erect the ancient temples in Melaka that still stand. In fact, the situation was not so clear. Sometimes the Melakans found it convenient to pay tribute to Siam (forty Chinese ounces of gold each year, at one point); sometimes they could get away without doing so. A small but wealthy city surrounded by enemies was not in a position to declare itself independent of all higher authority. It was much safer to accept an overlord so long as he did not interfere greatly with day-to-day business, which was what really mattered: 'the ships, large and small, were past counting in number; for at that time the rajah's subjects in the city alone numbered 90,000', though the Malay annalist, who wrote those words, then went on to claim that there were 190,000 people in the city alone, not to mention the coastal areas it controlled, and foreigners also flocked to the city.[64]

The sultan began to boost his standing in the world by introducing elaborate protocol at court and by building a spacious and stately palace on the present-day St Paul's Hill. The wooden palace, with its beautifully carved panels, no longer survives, but it has been reconstructed, partly from the description in the *Malay Annals*. The ceremonies that were held there drew on both Indian and Chinese models. There were strict rules about who might wear yellow robes or be shaded by umbrellas, for yellow was the Chinese imperial colour, reserved for members of the ruler's family. Gold ornaments, including anklets, were the prerogative of the sultan and his close advisers. The sultan sat enthroned with ministers on either side, rather as the Chinese emperors did; everyone who was permitted to attend upon the sultan knew exactly where to stand or sit in the throne room.[65] The pirate kingdom of Parameśvara, for that is what Melaka had originally been, had been transformed within a couple of generations into an emporium that linked the Indian Ocean to the Spice Islands and to Ming China.[66]

If an outside force intruded itself into the Strait of Malacca, everything would be set spinning once again. And this is what happened when the Portuguese arrived at the start of the sixteenth century: 'there came a ship of the Franks from Goa trading to Melaka: and the Franks perceived how prosperous and well-populated the port was.' Those are, once again, the words of the anonymous Malay annalist, but the Portuguese too were impressed, as Tomé Pires bore witness and as the greatest Portuguese poet, Luis de Camões, would write in his epic of his country's overseas expansion, the *Lusiads*: 'farther on lies Malacca, that your countrymen will make known as a great emporium for the wealth and merchandise of all the territories bordering on this vast ocean.'[67] Before long the Portuguese came back to Melaka with an armada and captured the city, after a tough fight, in 1511. To understand how they arrived there it is necessary to return to the far-off waters of the eastern Atlantic.

PART THREE

The Young Ocean: The Atlantic, *22,000 BC–AD 1500*

15

Living on the Edge

I

A history of the oceans might be expected to say little about the Atlantic before Columbus, or at least before the Portuguese discovered and settled islands out of sight of land in the fifteenth century, apart from a glancing reference to Vikings who reached America after they were lost off the coast of Greenland. 'Atlantic history' has become an entire industry, and it is mainly concerned with connections after 1492 between the four continents that border the Atlantic Ocean: North America, South America, Africa and Europe.[1] At first sight there is nothing in prehistoric and ancient times to compare with the astonishing feats of the Polynesian navigators, nor with the mastering of the monsoons by those who crossed the open Indian Ocean. There are plenty of crackpot theories about ancient Egyptians or Phoenicians who reached Central America, and the name of Thor Heyerdahl comes up once again here. And yet, going back as far as the fifth millennium BC along the European flank of the Atlantic, and, quite separately, as far back as 2000 BC in the Caribbean, people moved across parts of the ocean, and the sea exercised massive influence on their social and economic life (the Caribbean will be described within a later chapter). Reconstructing these worlds depends on archaeology, but not just in one place – it is only possible to make sense of what was happening by looking at the links between societies separated by considerable distances, whether in the form of trade connections or similarities in culture, including art and architecture. For several archaeologists have identified a common north-eastern Atlantic culture that was formed by the communities living along the edges of the Neolithic Atlantic, from Orkney in the far north past Ireland and Great Britain to Brittany, northern Spain, Portugal and even the Atlantic coast of Morocco, a distance of about 4,000 kilometres. A spur leads down the English Channel to Holland, Denmark and Sweden, bringing parts of the Baltic into this Atlantic world, the world of what have been called 'the Western Seaways'.[2]

Norwegian Sea

NORWAY

SWEDEN

Cape Wrath

Orkney

Atlantic Ocean

SCOTLAND

Oronsay

North Sea

DENMARK

IRELAND

GREAT BRITAIN

Doggerland

WALES

CORNWALL

HOLLAND

BRITTANY

Cape Finisterre

GALICIA

PORTUGAL

SPAIN

Cape St Vincent

MOROCCO

0		500		1000 miles

0	500	1000	1500 km

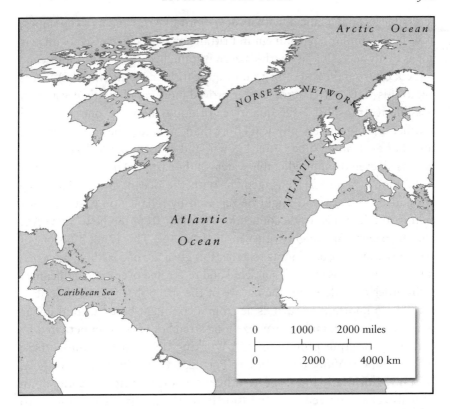

Still, there are several ways of interpreting the clear evidence that people built similar monuments in Portugal to those that were built in Scotland and Ireland. Traditional 'diffusionist' interpretations have gone out of fashion among archaeologists, and there is much more emphasis among 'processual' archaeologists on the internal dynamics of society, so it might be argued that similar physical conditions created similar solutions: pressed between the rough seas of the Atlantic and rugged shores, the inhabitants of Galicia, Brittany and northern Scotland found the same solution to the problem of how to subsist. And when connections can be demonstrated between communities hundreds or even thousands of kilometres apart, was this the result of direct contact, or did artefacts and ideas seep slowly from one area to another and another and another, in slow stages? Then there is the problem of how contact might have been maintained, either locally between shore-side settlements or over longer distances. Evidently sturdy boats were needed in order to reach Britain and Ireland from Brittany, and there are good reasons to assume that contact between Brittany and Galicia tended to be by sea. Land routes cannot be ruled out; but the coastal communities that are going to be examined here were not easily accessible by land: Galicia, with its deep fjord-like *rías* and its steep slopes, as well as a similar environment in Brittany or Wales. Even Cornwall was not as easily accessible as south-eastern Britain, because its hilly landscape was cut off from the rest of Britain by quite forbidding moorland. According to this view, travel across water proved more rapid, while it was also possible to transport large quantities of goods between one place and another with much less physical effort than on land. The sea had its terrors; but as it came to be better known, and as astronomical knowledge increased, even the unpredictable waters of the eastern Atlantic were found to be manageable.[3] Yet engagement with the ocean varied over time. Dependence on seafood might be replaced by reliance on pasture, agriculture and hunting. Trade connections familiar from the New Stone Age and the Bronze Age might wither in the Iron Age. This is not a history of ever-closer integration binding together this great arc of coastline, but a history of connections created, sundered and re-created over many millennia.

In order to understand the nature of the space that will be described here, it is important to turn aside from a continent-based mental image of ancient Europe, and to visualize long stretches of coast punctuated by massive projecting promontories.[4] Working up from the south, these include Cape St Vincent in southern Portugal, Cape Finisterre in Galicia, Brittany, Cornwall, and Cape Wrath at the northern tip of Scotland, an area also characterized by a profusion of rocky islands and easy access to the granite that has ever after been the chosen building material of many Scots. Strong winds from the ocean brought heavy rainfall, which favoured those trying to produce crops in low-lying corridors along the shoreline. When metalworking became widespread in the Bronze and Iron Ages, the ready availability of good-quality ores, including Welsh copper and gold, Cornish tin, and Iberian silver, tin and copper stimulated the creation of trade networks linking these lands and bringing in other lands, such as western Scotland, that were rather poor in metals but sought to acquire them.[5]

Describing the resources only goes so far; finding out who the people were who exploited them, and whether they were of common ancestry or culture, is also important. Here even the most sober accounts of what has been found in the soil become entangled with the idea that the inhabitants of this Atlantic arc were 'Celts', whose ancestors had originated somewhere in central Europe and had migrated stage by stage until they could reach no further. The fact that classical writers used this term to describe peoples living in large areas of western Europe does not mean that 'Celt' is a precise ethnic label. As for the debatable question of what language they spoke, that will be addressed in a later chapter.[6] Nor, indeed, is there much agreement about the role of the sea in drawing together prehistoric communities that were largely self-sufficient. Some communities, even close to the sea, depended on food they foraged from the land for their survival; but often their self-sufficiency extended to the sea itself, which was a magnificent source of food, some harvested along its shores, including the molluscs whose shells were dumped in vast, mountainous middens that altered the seaside landscape, while fishermen also used nets and hooks to catch large fish that swarmed in coastal waters. This is, then, a rather different story to the great maritime adventures of those who struck out across the open sea in the Pacific and, eventually, the Indian Ocean. It begins as a series of histories of local connections.

I I

The effects of falling and rising sea levels have been felt much more dramatically in the Atlantic than in the Pacific or the Indian Ocean, and have had a powerful influence on how the edges of Europe were settled in Palaeolithic and Mesolithic times (the Old and Middle Stone Ages). About 11,500 years ago significant changes occurred, which geologists mark as the start of the Holocene period that has continued ever since; 'Holocene' means 'wholly new', and yet the Holocene is understood as a temporary warm phase in the middle of a continuing Ice Age that (in theory) should some day return; temperatures were not consistent, and fell by about 2°C early in the first millennium BC, at the end of what is regarded as the Atlantic Bronze Age. These higher temperatures did not exactly make the climate in places such as Orkney balmy, but they did facilitate crop production and hence the growth of population.[7] The changes that were taking place were geological as well as climatic. Long before the Holocene, the massive accumulation of ice far beyond the poles had sucked away water from the oceans and had lowered sea levels by thirty-five metres or more, exposing the floor of what are now shallow seas such as the North Sea. The Baltic began as a freshwater lake and was only joined to the salt sea as water inundated the land bridge between what is now Denmark and Sweden; the North Sea was partly blocked by the large expanse of Doggerland that linked the east of Britain to the continent before it sank beneath the waves to become what is now known as the Dogger Bank. The end of the Ice Age saw seawater levels rise as melted ice returned to the sea, and also made the climate more congenial for the limited number of humans who inhabited Europe around 8000 BC; Doggerland was one of the areas where they flourished.[8] The process was more complicated than that, however, since the sheer weight of the ice had pushed the land hundreds of metres lower in some areas, such as Scotland, and as the weight was removed the land itself began to rise; Great Britain is still slowly tilting, with the result that the coast of East Anglia is gradually falling into the sea.[9] Several islands around the British coast that were now clear of ice found themselves joined to the mainland for several centuries; it is possible that one could walk from Scotland to Orkney for a while, or at least wade across the tidal waters.[10] In other parts of Atlantic Europe, the glaciers had scored deep gashes in the landscape, which remain in southern Norway and along the deeply indented western coast of Galicia in north-western Spain, creating the dramatic scenery of the Rías Baixas; their appearance was accentuated by the Atlantic winds and waves that stripped away softer stones and left behind the hard rocks of the Galician coastline. This area will be revisited shortly, since Galicia has provided rich evidence for prehistoric communities that exploited the sea and enjoyed ties to other parts of the Atlantic shoreline.

For the human population of Europe, the Ice Age had also been an era of extinction and repopulation. By 8000 BC, the Neanderthals of the Upper Palaeolithic, who had found a way to survive in the cold of Ice Age Europe, were long extinct.[11] In the early Holocene period the modern human population remained very thinly spread around Europe, but some families were beginning to reach the Atlantic seashore, beyond the current coastline of France, Britain, Holland, Germany and Denmark. The cultures that were emerging in these lands are broadly described as 'Mesolithic', or Middle Stone Age, yet this is a troublesome term. It indicates that these people retained many characteristics of the Palaeolithic lifestyle, notably their reliance on hunting and gathering food, including, along the coast, seafood. The term 'Mesolithic' recognizes some innovations in toolmaking, for much of what is known about these societies depends on the close examination of stone tools that were becoming smaller, even very small (microliths); blades, harpoons, arrowheads and scrapers became everyday objects in the toolkit of Mesolithic hunters. These changes took many centuries, yet they occurred more or less in sequence across one area after another of western Europe, which shows that technical knowhow was spread by contact between groups of hunters. This improvement in the quality of tools in turn indicates that the tasks being performed in Mesolithic societies were becoming more complex, such as sewing together animal skins to make more effective clothing, and, using the microliths, the creation of delicate secondary tools made of wood, reed and bone. In some areas, simple pottery was created. It is a moot point whether Atlantic Europe learned from or developed independently techniques that can be observed in the Middle East in the twelfth millennium BC. In the Middle East the Mesolithic inhabitants gradually developed an interest in farming, by taming the wild grasses they had been gathering since time immemorial; large villages and even fortified towns became home to more and more of those who lived off the soil. But along the Atlantic coast of Iberia around 5000 BC the relationship with the soil was different; grass seeds formed part of quite a rich diet, but were still casually gathered as they grew wild in fields and meadows, alongside berries, bulbs (notably onions) and legumes.[12]

Each environment was different in detail, and each small pocket of population exploited what was to be had without having the need to develop close interaction with neighbours, or at any rate trade in foodstuffs – no doubt other forms of interaction, such as the exchange of brides or warfare to gain control of valleys rich in game, were quite frequent. During the Mesolithic period, populations became more settled, and villages began to emerge; the inhabitants would mark out the territory they exploited, though it is unlikely they thought of this as rule over a chunk of land. They sought control of the material assets of the land, not the land itself. A harsh winter or a boiling summer could suddenly deplete resources to dangerous levels as the seasons changed. From this point of view, living by seas and river mouths was a sensible strategy; what mattered was variety, rather than reliance on a staple foodstuff. The more diverse the habitat, the easier it was to survive, and that made the coastal fringes of Europe the most attractive places to settle. In addition, it was as far as one could go by land. By the fifth millennium BC these areas hard by the shore were therefore quite densely settled, and as the population rose pressure was placed on the food supply, which, again, fostered movement – the voluntary or forced departure of superfluous people for new lands. With time, migrants needed to search further afield for empty spaces, whether by trekking along the coast or by braving the sea in boats made from animal skins, wicker or felled trees – since the evidence for boats comes from the Bronze Age, the design of their boats will be looked at later.[13]

Unfortunately, much of the best information about these shore-dwellers is now buried beneath the sea, for the shoreline that they knew has been inundated, and the remains of what appear to be coastal communities often come from settlements a little way inland. But this is not always the case, since the melting of the ice also allowed landmasses in some areas to rise. For that reason a good many archaeological sites from this period survive in northern Scotland, including middens, mounds of food debris. Oronsay, to the south of Mull, is a tiny island off western Scotland that already stood offshore in the Mesolithic period; archaeologists have been able to deduce the exact time of the year at which the type of pollock known as the saithe was caught, because its ear-bone grows longer according to a strict schedule. This shows that people moved around from midden to midden; these people were either inhabitants of the island itself, who over the centuries gobbled down gargantuan amounts of fish and shellfish, or, bearing in mind the minute size of the territory, they came across from bigger islands nearby (Islay, Jura, and so on) on seasonal visits, because they knew that its intertidal outcrops were a perfect breeding ground for shellfish.[14]

Brittany too is a rich source of information, with plenty of middens containing the remains of seafood that indicate how, by 5000 BC, the inhabitants had become heavily pescatarian in taste. The fact that they neatly deposited the shells in reserved piles indicates that they did not simply comb the beach for throw-away snacks, but brought their catch to places where their family could enjoy what they had found. They took up residence on little islands off the coast such as Hoëdic, where there was not much hunting, apart from netting birds or shooting at them, but plenty of food from the sea, and the right sort of rocks from which they could knap their tools. These early Bretons ate a great variety of shellfish: periwinkles, limpets, cockles, mussels, as well as many types of crab. They exploited the Atlantic tides to cross the sands and collect the rich harvest of the sea. Consumption of seaweeds such as samphire and of plants that grow close by the seashore such as sea kale made the seaside a very attractive place to live.[15]

In several parts of Atlantic Europe milder temperatures caused a spurt in the growth of forests, and the opportunities for hunting declined as wild animals such as deer were crowded out of their habitat by the trees. This prompted people to move in ever greater numbers towards the coast, away from impenetrable lands in the interior. In Denmark, at a place now known as Ertebølle, the late Mesolithic inhabitants hunted any animals they could find, even including lynx, wolves and pine marten. But they loved fish – herring, cod and flounder were favourites – and they also exploited freshwater supplies, taking eels and pike from rivers and lakes. They took seals from the sea and ate them too. They paddled around in log-boats, which were sometimes at least ten metres long, and they built fish traps out of wickerwork; organic objects of this sort have survived in the marshy conditions of Denmark, to be unearthed by Professor Glob (of Dilmun fame) and his colleagues. And then there were the piles and piles of oysters, cockles, mussels and periwinkles. It was, after all, much less work to go beachcombing than to rely on catching deer, elk and aurochs, which might escape the hunter for days at a time, a change 'away from the high-risk, high-yield, high-energy expenditure strategy of game hunting to a low-risk, moderate-yield, low-energy expenditure strategy', in the concise words of Barry Cunliffe.[16] One could go further: the dependence of these folk on the produce of the sea must have affected their system of values, which would place less emphasis on the martial skills associated with hunting (casting spears, shooting arrows, and so on) and more on the nautical skills needed to master even inshore waters.

III

By the fifth millennium, as new technology began to spread in Europe and many other parts of the world, with the gradual domestication of animals and the adoption of farming, not merely the diet changed. Although the term has come into and gone out of fashion, this is often described as the age of the 'Neolithic Revolution'; it turns out to have been a very slow revolution, and it is increasingly obvious that many of its apparent innovations reached back into the late Mesolithic period, particularly in the Middle East. Farming the soil, if not the herding of animals, encouraged settlement in permanent villages; this was often the case even when the early farmers followed the widespread practice of slash-and-burn cultivation, which involved the clearance of forest, the planting of the soil, and the cultivation of another patch of cleared forest after the original piece of land had been exhausted of nutrients. The new grain-based diet was not necessarily healthier: body sizes appear to have shrunk from an average of 1.7 metres for men and 1.57 metres for women in the Upper Palaeolithic period to 1.67 and 1.54 in the Neolithic age. This may not seem a significant amount, but skeletal remains also reveal a decline in dental health and an increase in diseases associated with malnutrition, especially among children – infant mortality was high, life expectancy was low.[17] As tasks within society became more specialized, political elites emerged who organized production and defended the community's territory. A distinguished archaeologist has spoken of 'population stress' along the Atlantic seaboard within the period from about 4800 BC to about 2300 BC.[18]

This leaves the important but controversial question of where the Neolithic peoples of the Atlantic coast, and of western Europe in general, came from, assuming they came from anywhere and were not just the descendants of the old Mesolithic inhabitants who had learned new skills as these skills filtered from one community to another and, higgledy-piggledy, were copied by the existing population. The easiest way out of this dilemma, but also without doubt the most accurate answer, is that both answers are correct in different measure and in different places at different times.[19] One could hardly expect all the communities that had developed along the coastline from Iberia to Scotland by the late Mesolithic age, say 8000 BC, to have responded in an identical way to the arrival of farming, for each of these communities exploited different resources in the sea, in the rivers and along the edges of the forests. One case, at first sight surprising but in fact only to be expected, is the shift in diet that took place in Brittany as the Mesolithic faded into the Neolithic around 4000 BC. The people of Hoëdic, which has been mentioned earlier, lost much of their interest in seafood and seabirds, which would have left a strong signature in their skeletons, and became fashionably Neolithic in their preference for grain, dairy products, meat and other non-marine products. It is possible that these areas had been taken over by migrants from the interior, which would explain their lack of interest in the sea.[20]

Even if these early Bretons were less interested in the harvests of the sea, they may still have been keen to cross the sea, either to settle other lands or to acquire objects they could not obtain or produce locally. The great triangle of Brittany, standing in the way of direct passage by sea from south-western France to the English Channel, looked in several directions. In the sixth to fourth millennia BC sea contact along this coast becomes visible to archaeologists, who would not exclude the strong probability that this is the second or third chapter in a story of maritime connections that began in the Middle Stone Age, or even in the late Palaeolithic. A marvellous example of Breton links across the sea is provided by a small passage tomb in Scotland from around 4000 BC; these passage tombs, entered by a corridor and lined with stone, are characteristic of the 'megalithic' culture that will be discussed shortly. It is located at Achnacreebeag, on the west coast not far from Oban. Its most remarkable feature is that it contained pottery at a time when the art of pottery was unknown in Scotland. The pots found in the tomb are from Brittany and Lower Normandy, and they were carried at some point across the open sea, most probably up the Irish Sea directly to western Scotland, since a few fragments of similar pottery have turned up in north-eastern Ireland. Among the scenarios that archaeologists then envisage is the movement of a small group of Bretons around 4000 BC, just when tombs of this type were becoming fashionable in Brittany.[21] Some of these Bretons reached as far as Scotland, others, whether at the same time or earlier and later, made their landfall in Ireland, passing also through Cornwall, Wales and the Isle of Man, all of which were inhabited by people using similar 'Tardenoisian' flint tools as early as the Mesolithic period.[22]

Meanwhile, objects from Iberia turned up in Brittany and were buried alongside its inhabitants.[23] While they may have filtered up the coast of France overland, it is clear that early Neolithic travellers possessed the knowhow to cross tracts of the Atlantic Ocean: if Bretons could reach Scotland by sea, they could reach Spain. And Spain stands at the centre of a bigger argument about Neolithic culture, the debate about the megaliths.[24] The origins of the large stone structures found along the coast of Spain and Portugal, as well as inland, and in great numbers in Brittany, not to mention northern France and parts of Britain, have long been debated. They are best described as large stone structures rather than structures made of large stones, as not all the stones used were *mega*, or 'large'.[25] The most famous of these structures, Stonehenge, is far from the sea; however, even setting aside the more bizarre arguments about its use as a Neolithic computer, this and other Neolithic structures reveal a knowledge of the heavens that was surely exploited by sailors as well as the priests and rulers of Late Stone Age southern England.

Most of the structures are classed as graves, though whether they really were that, or just that, is a complex issue. The traditional assumption has been that two distinctive types of tomb appeared over large areas of Atlantic Europe during the Neolithic period: the passage grave, which consisted of a corridor leading into an often circular inner chamber, all carefully constructed out of large blocks of stone; and the gallery grave, which lacked the inner chamber but was once again built of stone and often covered over with earth. Elaborate theories were built on the argument that they represented different cultural streams. Modern dating using Carbon 14 and other methods established that the earliest passage graves so far identified are to be found in Brittany, and go back to the fifth millennium BC. On the other hand, a series of passage graves from southern Spain were built about a millennium later.[26] This style of funerary architecture was not a passing fancy; passage graves were constructed in northern Scotland, in northern, central and south-eastern Ireland, in Brittany and along the coast south from there; and all around the Iberian coast from Galicia to southern Spain; but they also appeared in Denmark and northern Germany, with 7,000 identified in Denmark alone, maybe one third of the number in existence 4,500 years ago.[27] They range in date from 4800 BC to 2300 BC, and none can be found more than 300 kilometres from the Atlantic or North Sea coasts.[28] But they did not all develop at the same time, and they originated in different places in different ways – in Great Britain the custom around 4000 BC was to build unchambered long barrows, still a feature of the British landscape; and these developed into passage graves later. Meanwhile the Bretons constructed grander graves ahead of everyone else. To say that knowledge of these Breton monuments influenced the architecture of passage graves in England or Iberia is not the same thing as claiming that the same people, of the same ancestry and language, built all these monuments. There is general agreement that different places developed this style of monument independently, with Brittany coming first, and once the megaliths were a common feature of the landscape along the shores of western Europe, different communities copied details of the design and structure from one another, to make their own monuments more perfect.[29]

When speaking of perfection, the megalithic settlement at Skara Brae in Orkney has a special claim to attention. This is not just because it, and above all the passage grave at Maes Howe, is very well preserved; it also sits in the midst of other important Neolithic sites from the period 3600–2100 BC. The first Neolithic settlers on Orkney (assuming they were not descended from Mesolithic predecessors) arrived from the facing shore of Scotland around 3600 BC with their animals – cattle, sheep and deer – and took advantage of the excellent fishing to be had around the islands.[30] There were very many deer on the Orkney island of Westray, and it is possible they were herded rather than allowed to run completely wild. Catching birds and collecting birds' eggs was another way of ensuring a high-protein diet. The consumption of shellfish, as elsewhere along the Atlantic coast of Europe, was prodigious. The predominance of limpet shells can be interpreted in several ways. Since this is a low-nutrition shellfish, reliance on limpets could indicate that during periods of shortage or famine the islanders relied on this second-class food. Or they may have been used as fish bait, a practice that has not disappeared from the area. The fish the islanders caught was probably used not just for human consumption but to produce fish meal, of the sort already encountered in the Indian Ocean; and this would be fed to animals.[31]

This style of life was very stable and lasted for maybe half a millennium. The islanders' use of stone slabs, easily obtained, to construct their houses means that there are some truly remarkable archaeological sites on Orkney, which offer a very clear idea of how their occupants lived; for once, it is possible to move beyond evidence about how people disposed of the dead and to gain an intimate idea of how they lived from day to day. Half a dozen or more stone houses, sunk a little into the earth, were constructed at Skara Brae on the main island, and fitted out with stone cupboards and shelving, most likely box beds, benches and hearths, and even what has been described as a dresser, which may have served as a display cabinet, one of whose functions was to impress visitors. Storage boxes were let into the floor – one contained beads, pendants, pins and a dish containing red pigment made out of one of the vertebrae of a whale. These houses formed

a compact group, linked by semi-subterranean passages.[32] Another structure at Skara Brae was evidently a workshop, where flints were knapped
using sophisticated techniques that involved the heating of the chert out
of which stone tools were manufactured.[33]

The inhabitants of the Orkney archipelago lived in small communities
scattered across the islands, and apparently obtained enough food and
raw materials to meet their needs. Many mysteries about their social and
religious life remain. One puzzle is why their chambered tombs so often
contain vast amounts of human bone from disarticulated skeletons, but
many bones are missing: at Isbister there were many foot bones but few
hand bones, and plenty of skulls. Bodies were allowed to decompose and
then the bones were collected and redistributed. This suggests the existence of elaborate rituals in which bones were rearranged – perhaps a
moderately efficient sorting process so that individual chamber tombs
specialized in particular parts of the body. This surely demonstrates that
the tombs were not places for the long-term burial of individuals but were
seen rather as part of a single greater funerary monument that stretched
across an entire island and in some sense embodied the spirit of the island.

The houses at Skara Brae are remarkable enough, but the chamber tomb
at Maes Howe has been described as 'one of the supreme achievements of
Neolithic Europe'. It even left a bizarre impression on the Vikings, who
covered the walls with runic inscriptions thousands of years later, and
mentioned it in the *Orkneyinga Saga*: 'during a snowstorm Earl Harald
and his men took shelter in Maes Howe and there two of them went
insane'.[34] The quality of the craftsmanship was exceptional: stones were
neatly fitted together and were carefully dressed to create flat surfaces in
the low corridor leading to the core of the monument, as also in the central
'hall', even though some of the stones used to line the walls weighed as
much as three tons.[35] The islanders were learned in astronomy, and carefully aligned the monument at Maes Howe with the solstices, indicating
that sun and moon rituals were conducted here. This was not unusual –
one of the greatest megalithic monuments, New Grange in Ireland, was
similarly aligned, and the decoration on its stones matches that at Maes
Howe, so connections between Orkney and Ireland must have been close,
with regular visits to Ireland by Orcadians.[36] The Orkney archipelago
provides inherent evidence for the use of the sea passages by Neolithic
navigators: they crossed the sea to arrive there in the first place, and all
the evidence suggests that they prospered, despite living on what is not
the most welcoming climate in Britain. More than that, Orkney, when
compared with Ireland and elsewhere, provides evidence for cultural contact between communities separated by the sea – not just art but ritual

was shared between communities. The communities on these islands were reasonably self-sufficient, but they did not become cut off from the outside world.

Away from Orkney we depend on the evidence from tombs, or structures that at first sight appear to be tombs. That gallery and passage graves became a widespread fashion is not in doubt, but what caused this change in burial practices is far from clear. Archaeologists were tempted to compare evidence from the eastern Mediterranean (some of it actually much later, but dating methods have taken time to improve); they then concluded that the practice spread from the east by way of Malta, Sardinia and the Balearic Islands, each of which has its own impressive stone monuments. It was also tempting to link this to the cult of the Mother Goddess or Earth Mother who may well have been worshipped in the great stone temples of Malta around 4000 BC.[37] Admittedly, the great stone towers, or *nuraghi*, of Sardinia are much later, and a subtle distinction has resulted in the classification of the *talayot*, or prehistoric stone monuments, of Minorca and its neighbours as 'cyclopean' rather than 'megalithic'; but it was easy to draw lines on a map showing how the megalithic culture of the Atlantic was diffused out of the Mediterranean towards Iberia, and then out of Iberia towards Brittany and the British Isles. British experts expressed polite differences of opinion with Spanish archaeologists, who, with a nationalist flourish, were determined to show that Galicia and northern Portugal were the obvious places to find the origins of the megalithic culture of Neolithic western Europe. However, the dates of the Spanish tombs were relatively late – the end of the fourth millennium BC for the very earliest. To be sure, the grave goods found in southern Spanish megalithic monuments show both Atlantic and Mediterranean influences; this was a place where the Atlantic and the Mediterranean worlds converged.[38]

In the end, though, the old 'diffusionist' approach to Megalithic culture, arguing that it was spread by migrants from the Mediterranean, was abandoned even by its former champions such as Glyn Daniel, the Cambridge archaeologist who also did much to promote archaeology in the early days of television.[39] Carbon 14 dating produced surprises and pushed the date of these monuments much further back in time, so it made no sense to see them as massively reduced imitations of the pyramids, not that it had ever made much sense to do so. Yet these differences of opinion converged at one point: the megalithic tombs were characteristic of the lands along the Atlantic seaboard. Moreover, they do share some features. Plaques inscribed with designs that seem to show boats, axes, snakes and undulating lines are found in several areas, so that similar snake designs were used in Galicia, Brittany and the Irish Channel, and there are similarities between snake patterns found carved on slabs in passage graves from Anglesey and patterns used by megalithic builders in Galicia, who were versatile builders, using carvings and paintings in their structures.[40] Rather than showing that the megalithic tradition spread slowly out of the Mediterranean and into first southern and then northern Spain, all this suggests that there was a good amount of to-ing and fro-ing between Iberia, Brittany and Britain, so that the north-west corner of Spain, the north-west corner of France and the Irish Sea were linked by regular sea voyages. Brittany stood at the centre of this Atlantic world, and was more precocious in its use of this architecture than its maritime neighbours to north and south.

Were these monuments actually tombs? In some, no human remains have been found. But even when there is evidence of burial this does not mean the prime purpose of the megalithic mounds was to dispose of the dead with honour. They may also, or primarily, have been used to mark out territory at a time when a more settled Neolithic population was beginning to think of ownership of the land itself and not just (as in the Mesolithic era) the exploitation of its resources. This makes good sense because the coming of farming tied humans to the land in a way that did not apply to a hunter-gatherer society. These were small, localized societies, for there is no evidence of great power centres nor of large settlements similar to the towns that had emerged in the Middle East during the early Neolithic period. In such a fragmented society, subject to constant pressure as agriculture and pastoralism brought population increase, it was important to know who belonged where. Monuments to, and often containing the remains of, the ancestors of the leaders of the community acquired special importance. For this reason it made sense to raise large mounds over the chambers these people carefully constructed. Whether they stood at the edge of a territory, to mark out borders, or at the centre, to function as cult centres and hallowed places where the leaders of the community would announce important decisions, they were places for the living as well as for the dead. When no evidence can be found that they were used for burial, the likelihood still remains that they were built to commemorate ancestors, sometimes so distant in time that there were no bones to show for them; or sometimes the mounds may commemorate people lost at sea whose remains were simply not available for burial. Quite often, indeed, the corridor was left open so people could come and go into the inner chamber.[41] For us, they also open a door – one into the political world of these early Atlantic societies.

16
Swords and Ploughshares

I

The societies of the Neolithic Atlantic have left behind few signs of major changes during the second millennium BC. This was the period when great Bronze Age civilizations came into being in the eastern Mediterranean and the Middle East: Minoans, Mycenaeans and Hittites in Greece and Anatolia, not to mention the high civilizations of Egypt, Babylonia and the Indus Valley. The Atlantic fringes of Europe remained dependent on high-quality stone for tools, and consisted of village communities that did not compare in size and sophistication with the cities, palaces and temples of the East. Atlantic societies were not literate, although claims have been made that signs incised on pottery found in France consist of a rudimentary type of writing.[1] Even the use of bronze did not greatly alter life in the Atlantic arc. Between about 1200 BC and about 900 BC bronze objects filtered into the coastal lands from the European hinterland, but the low level of finds of foreign goods from this period indicates that they came through gift exchange and were owned by members of the local elite, rather than being everyday commodities.[2] The trade routes of Bronze Age Greece had reached no further west than Italy, though Mycenaean objects have occasionally surfaced in southern Spain, and very occasionally as far afield as the British Isles: a copper axe from Topsham in Devon has been identified as Mycenaean.[3] Indeed, it would be surprising if some goods had not been handed on from place to place until they reached the Atlantic, by which time they would be seen as exotic curiosities from an unknown world. And then, as the Bronze Age civilizations of the eastern Mediterranean experienced severe crisis in the twelfth century BC, the opportunity to create links to their once prosperous lands was lost.

The Atlantic Bronze Age was out of phase with that in the eastern Mediterranean. According to the rough definition applied by archaeologists, it lasted until around 600 BC, when iron technology spread more

widely in the Atlantic lands; its high point, the Late Bronze Age, can be dated to its last 300 years, beginning in 900 BC. It may or may not be important that the Late Bronze Age was a period of cooler climate throughout Europe, after several warmer and drier centuries, though the effects of a changing climate in Atlantic Europe and in the Mediterranean were not necessarily the same.[4] This is just when the discussion of ancient Italy or Greece adopts the label Iron Age. Of course, this well-established way of defining societies by the materials out of which their members made their tools is crude and one-sided. One very good reason for preferring bronze was quite simply the ready availability of copper in the Atlantic lands, along with tin; tin could be found in the north-west of Iberia and copper in the south-west, while the area round Nantes, where the Loire debouches into the sea, was a source of both metals, and eventually of a distinctive type of sword.[5] Although bronze implements were not as strong as the best iron ones, early ironmaking was unsophisticated, and in a duel between the two an iron sword was as likely to shatter as a bronze one was to bend. Many other criteria, such as political and social organization, cannot be used as labels because the evidence is so hard to unearth. On the other hand, there is almost certainly a political dimension to the appearance and diffusion of bronze weapons. Precisely because bronze remained precious and because it provided material for sharper weapons, the people who owned bronze goods were members of the warrior class, or merchants who aimed to sell metalwork to the warrior class. This means that the finds of bronze objects from Atlantic Europe, plentiful though they are, speak much more loudly about princes and nobles, and occasionally about traders, than they do about the vast majority of the population, who still relied on their traditional stone tools.[6]

Although a number of archaeologists have been keen to present the Atlantic arc as a single interacting zone of culture and contact, there was great variation between, say, southern Portugal, which was exposed to influences coming out of the Mediterranean, and lands to the north such as Brittany or Ireland. Broadly, Ireland, Wales and southern Britain display differences but had much in common; Brittany had close relations with the British Isles but a strong identity of its own; within Iberia one can distinguish Galicia and northern Portugal from southern Portugal, but the Iberian coastlands also had much in common; and, taken together, an Atlantic world can be drawn on the map, stretching from the Scottish isles to Cape St Vincent, though Scotland was less well integrated into this world than it had been in the days of Maes Howe; western France, south of Brittany, was oddly disconnected from this network.[7] The linked areas shared styles of metalwork, which was quite distinct in appearance from that produced in inland France and western Germany, home to the Urnfield Culture, of which more in a moment. Even so, weapons and implements brought into Britain from the Continent were probably melted down and refashioned in the specific shapes that had become traditional on the island.[8] The important question here is whether these societies remained in maritime contact with one another or whether the deep dip in trade and contact within the Mediterranean was matched by similar inward withdrawal among the communities living beside the Atlantic.

Certain features of Atlantic Bronze Age society reveal new ritual practices. The custom of casting precious bronze objects such as shields and swords into rivers and lakes presumably had a powerful religious significance. These were not objects that one would simply discard as rubbish. The abandonment of the custom of building megalithic chamber tombs covered by great barrows is equally mysterious, because it is not obvious how people now disposed of the dead – cremation seems the obvious answer, but, in contrast to the large number of urn burials in central Europe (which have given a whole culture the name 'Urnfield'), urns were not adopted and cremated remains must have been scattered – most likely into rivers, along with some of the bronze objects just mentioned. When rituals change significantly – notably the shift from inhumation burial to cremation – it is tempting to assume that this indicates that migrants have arrived, marrying into, outnumbering or entirely replacing the existing population, but a moment's thought about religious change in more recent centuries (for instance, the rise of Protestantism) should be enough to show that radical changes can occur without a sudden shift in population. DNA tests suggest that a significant proportion of the inhabitants of south-western England, specifically the area around Cheddar, are descended from Neolithic forebears. And some experts would like to claim that what united the Atlantic peoples was their use of Celtic languages; but the lack of written texts makes this just a hypothesis.[9]

The period before 950 was a rather quiet phase of contact. The evidence for contact before then has to be teased out of bronze objects as diverse as Irish cauldrons and Portuguese or British flesh-hooks, while the exact design of a sword handle often reveals significant long-distance contacts. The cauldrons, whose weight and craftsmanship made them into highly prized objects, turn up in south Wales, the lower Thames region and, interestingly, Galicia and northern Portugal, though there they are often of a slightly different design.[10] Since rather few have been found in the French interior, it is plain that they reached Iberia by sea, either by way of Great Britain or directly, while swords of a type found frequently in the lower Thames area quite often reached south Wales and Ireland. They are evidence for an Atlantic society that took delight in noble feasting, as great hunks of meat were stewed in cauldrons and the meat extracted with hooks that were sometimes elaborately decorated with figures of birds that resemble swans and ravens, their necks and beaks cleverly moulded to make them function as the teeth of these hooks.[11]

Many of these cauldrons must have been offered by chieftains to one another as magnificent gifts. Feasts at which gifts were exchanged speak of contact between centres of power, and of warriors travelling short and long distances to seek one another's company. For this elite was not simply a local aristocracy; the cauldrons are evidence of a shared culture along the Atlantic arc. The voices of these warriors are silent, but what one sees in the literature of Anglo-Saxon England, such as *Beowulf*, or in the Icelandic sagas, may portray a similar sort of culture, given to braggardly display and, no doubt, the consumption of large amounts of beer and mead. It was also a culture in which fighting with a sword as well as a spear was the mark of a noble warrior. Close combat also required good protection for the body, so armour, more often of thick leather than of bronze, was an important part of a warrior's equipment. The expense of producing or acquiring these goods increased the distance between those who could afford to do so and the wider population. For swords became prestigious articles of trade. There were distinct cultural preferences in the design of high-quality weapons, rather as in much later centuries scimitars were favoured by Turks and straight swords by Spaniards – in other words, there is a hint here of a common sense of identity, at least among the warrior elites who used these fine weapons. In order to be socially respectable, it was important to follow the traditional British fashions. Unfamiliar continental ways were regarded as socially unacceptable.

The best evidence for wide contacts comes from what are known as 'Carp's Tongue swords', on the basis of a rather remote resemblance between the ribbing along the length of these swords and the appearance of a carp's tongue. 'The Carp's Tongue sword', it has been said, 'is truly an Atlantic armament.'[12] This ribbing greatly strengthened the blade, so it had a practical as much as an aesthetic purpose. Since these swords did not vary very much in appearance, and were also regarded as a high-quality product, there is a whole history to be reconstructed out of their first appearance in north-western France, and out of their diffusion to other places, at first by trade and subsequently through the spread of technology. Soon, such swords were being produced in south-eastern Britain, though the design followed in Iberia was not exactly the same as that used in northern Europe. Still, there is enough similarity between Iberian and northern swords to suggest cultural influences and maritime trade along the Atlantic arc, and the adaptation of a model known through sea contact to local needs and conditions. In the late eighth century BC, these contacts reached as far as the bay of Huelva, on the Atlantic coast of south-western Spain, where a substantial bronze hoard was found underwater in 1923. The hoard contains plenty of these swords and may be the remains of a shipwrecked vessel carrying metalwork that was cast in Spain and was being taken out to sea, rather than being delivered from afar, although mixed in with this were cloak pins (*fibulae*) from distant Cyprus; another view is that this was a sacred deposit, such as an offering to the sea gods.[13] The list of places where these swords have been found is impressive: northern Germany, southern Portugal, but also within the Mediterranean.[14]

Overall, there was an increase in, or rather renewal of, contact between Brittany and Britain, on the one hand, and Spain and Portugal, on the other, by 600 BC.[15] The English Channel was regularly crossed by Bronze Age boats, so that Brittany and Normandy (or Armorica) and southern England (or Wessex) were in close and constant contact, without losing their cultural individuality, made evident, for instance, in different burial rites. North-western France had more in common with southern England than with eastern France, well away from the ocean; Breton biconical urns turn up in Wessex.[16]

II

Maritime trade across the English Channel was also fed by more remote contacts. An extraordinary discovery from Langdon Bay near Dover, together with a similar but smaller find at Moor Sand in Devon, sheds light on the character of trade within and beyond Atlantic waters. The overwhelming advantage of looking at evidence from wrecks is that one can see goods in transit, gathered together, and clearly in these cases intended for trade. At Langdon Bay, underwater archaeologists found forty-two 'median-winged' axes, thirty-eight palstaves (another type of axe-head), eighty-one dagger blades and sundry other bronze goods; Moor Sand yielded seven French bronzes, including four daggers.[17] The axes would not have found their way to the bottom of the bay had not a Bronze Age ship, most probably bound for what is now Dover Harbour, foundered, perhaps in a gale that blew the boat beyond its destination. By looking closely at the origins of these objects archaeologists have concluded that the cargo was gathered together in the mouth of the Seine, for it did not all originate in the same place – the winged axes are typically eastern French, and yet the palstave axes are recognizably Breton. The winged axes belong to a type not actually found in the British Isles, so these axes were not imported to be used, even though they seem to have been in good condition when the ships sank. Rather, the bronze objects were valued for their metal content, and were melted down on receipt, so that they could be turned into bronze objects of the sort Bronze Age Britons preferred. The traders of Langdon Bay and Moor Sand were scrap metal merchants – though in addition they doubtless carried all sorts of perishable goods such as food and textiles that have decomposed.[18] Among foodstuffs, salt was being traded around the Atlantic shores, as it would be for many centuries to come; and nothing of that can survive a ship-wreck in saltwater.[19]

Some of the bronze goods moving around the Atlantic region may have been used in payment as ingots of standard weight, rather than as tools and weapons, for, as has been seen in the Indian Ocean, the history of money does not begin with the invention of coinage. The modern history of these ingots began in 1867, when a clog-maker called Louis Ménard discovered the first great pile of them, which his friends thought were a hoard of gold, but which he insisted on taking to the local museum.[20] By now 32,000 socketed axes of several standard designs have been dis-covered at sites not far distant from the Atlantic, originating in Brittany and Normandy, and generally called 'Armorican axes' after the classical name for Brittany. They turn up in southern Britain, in Ireland and along the shores of the Netherlands and northern Germany, but not in Galicia and Portugal. By the late seventh century BC they were being produced with a bronze alloy that used lead rather than tin, and this would have rendered them extremely inefficient as tools or weapons, strengthening instead the argument that they were a way of storing wealth. Many have been found packed in cylindrical holes in the ground, or in jars, and neatly arranged in circles, with the cutting edge pointing inwards. Two hoards from Finistère contained 800 at a time, and at another site archaeologists uncovered more than 4,000 axe heads in several deposits. They have been described as 'currency axes', objects that were versatile enough to be used as a form of money but also as ingots, and in some cases as tools too.[21]

Evidence from settlements is scarce, but it enables archaeologists to reach closer to the domestic life of these Atlantic people. Away from the coast, banks and ditches divided up the land, indicating that ownership of territory was now sharply defined. These field systems were created in areas close to the Atlantic before this type of land division became wide-spread in continental Europe. The availability along the Atlantic arc of copper ores and of the tin needed to make the alloy bronze stimulated community life by creating specialist activities: mining, smelting, manufacturing, exchanging and selling. Just as political elites became more visible and more powerful through their acquisition of deadlier weapons and stronger armour, smiths and traders acquired a distinct place in these societies, which grew in complexity.[22] One expression of this complexity was the creation of soundly built circular villages with dry-stone house foundations, themselves circular, and strong perimeter walls. Circular stone houses were not themselves a novelty – they have been encountered already at Skara Brae on Orkney. The novelty lay in the spread of this type of structure from Britain and Ireland down to the coasts of Iberia, though unfortunately the surviving remains from Brittany are few. On the one hand, this type of village speaks for a sense of insecurity, whether from warlike neighbours after one's land or from brigands after one's goods; after all, this was, as the evidence from the swords and spears reveals, a society dominated by warriors. On the other hand, this type of settlement speaks for permanence, the intention to stay put. Interestingly, these villages are characteristic of the Atlantic arc, while in central Europe the preference was for oblong houses; so it is tempting to think that they are the product of a common culture embracing the British Isles and the Atlantic flanks of France, Spain and Portugal, a culture with deep roots in Neolithic Europe that gave the settlements along the Atlantic edge of Europe a different appearance and that expressed a distinct identity. Whether that identity was expressed in a common language is less clear.[23]

Judging from the finds at Langdon Bay and Moor Sand, stretches of water were crossed by several routes, including a route from Brittany to south-west England and one from the mouth of the Seine north-eastwards to the Strait of Dover; the English Channel is exposed to gales and strong tides, so the best route across is not necessarily the shortest, and even these longer routes would not generally follow a straight line.[24] A few rock carvings from Spain give some idea of the appearance of ships around this time, though they are difficult to date and the outlines are crude: several images are of sailing ships, and in at least a couple of cases sail power was combined with oar power.[25] Sturdy watertight boats constructed out of a wooden shell covered in hides, some quite sizeable, are attested from Iron Age Britain and are hardly likely to be an Iron Age invention; the description of these ships by Julius Caesar will be examined later.[26] A number of log-boats found near Peterborough in eastern England give a good idea of what sort of boat could be used along rivers and in open water such as the Wash, and similar boats have been found in France in a tributary of the Seine, dating right back to the Middle Neolithic (roughly 4000 BC).[27] How far out to sea such boats were wont to go is unknown. Landing places lay within existing natural harbours, for at this period there is no evidence that ports had been set up. Occasional rock carvings from Denmark, Sweden or Galicia offer crude outlines of oared and sailing vessels.

Once built, a ship was put to maximum use, for trade, fishing and transporting people. And people were constantly on the move. Colin Renfrew has listed eleven reasons why one might have travelled in prehistoric Europe: to obtain goods; to sell goods; for social meetings; out of sheer curiosity or to acquire exotic information; to a holy place as a pilgrim; to learn or train; to find work; as a mercenary; to visit friends and relatives; as an emissary; and, in his view one of the most important and most easily forgotten reasons, to find a spouse.[28] The fact that the British Isles were a distinct but not a totally separate cultural world provides simple proof of the readiness with which Bronze Age sailors traversed the English Channel over many centuries.

III

One element missing from this picture of the Atlantic world, already fragmentary and tentative, is the connection between the ocean and the Mediterranean. For although the eastern Mediterranean, during its own Bronze Age, had experienced little or no direct contact with Iberia, in the age of the Minoans of Crete and the Mycenaeans of Greece (who were hardy navigators), the Mediterranean network of trade and settlement that the Phoenicians created from about 900 BC onwards stretched right across, and beyond, the Mediterranean; legend attributed the foundation of a Phoenician trading settlement on the island of Cádiz to 1104 BC, which is certainly too early, but there can be no doubt that Cádiz, or Gadir as the Phoenicians called it, was up and running in the ninth century BC, well before the Iberian ship – if it was Iberian – foundered in the bay of Huelva with its bronze cargo. It is no surprise that the Phoenicians were attracted to this area. It gave access to the silver-rich realm of Tartessos in the southern Iberian hinterland; and around the bay of Huelva lay several settlements that had flourished since at least the end of the Neolithic era, attracted by rich supplies of salt and fish, while the Phoenicians were attracted by sources of tin in Iberia and in further reaches of the Atlantic; whether they reached Cornwall, as is often maintained, is far from clear. They still had to meet the considerable challenge of battling their way against contrary currents and often strong winds as they made the passage past Gibraltar (coming in was always much easier). Some Phoenicians stopped at Gorham's Cave, a fissure in the Rock of Gibraltar, to invoke the gods before daring to enter the open ocean, leaving behind pottery and votive objects.[29]

Phoenician traders made their way down the coast of Morocco as well as northwards. Their objectives included the collection of murex shellfish, which provided them with the purple dye after which the Greeks had named them *Phoinikes*. As was their custom, they established themselves on a small offshore island, taking charge of Mogador, or Essaouira, which provided a base from which to trade with the native Berber population. It lies 1,000 kilometres south of Cádiz and it apparently marked the furthest limit of their regular trade. Mogador was probably visited seasonally by traders coming down from Cádiz or out of the Mediterranean, and was as much a camp as a settlement; the traders feasted on shellfish and even whale meat, and left plenty of debris behind. It was very possibly the place named Kerné by Greek writers; if so, we have a credible description of how these merchants operated: they arrived in their big merchant ships, set up booths in which to live, and unloaded the pottery, perfumes and other fine goods they had brought south. These they loaded on to smaller boats, which took the traders and their wares to meet the 'Ethiopians' on the African mainland. They bought ivory and the skins of lions, leopards and gazelles in exchange for the products they carried down from Gadir. It was assumed that one simply could not travel beyond Kerné.[30]

Mogador flourished in the late seventh and early sixth century, but it never proved as successful a settlement as the towns the Phoenicians founded on either side of the entrance to the Strait of Gibraltar, at Gadir/Cádiz and at Lixus near modern Larache. Yet goods filtered through from as far away as Cyprus and Phoenicia itself; Greek and Phoenician jars arrived in quantity, trans-shipped through Gadir; several carry the name 'Magon', who was no doubt a wealthy merchant.[31] Gadir, then, was the capital of a network of trade dominated by Phoenician merchants who flourished in the years up to about 550 BC. After that, pressure in the East, from Persians and Assyrians, damaged the trade of the Phoenicians within and beyond the Mediterranean, though this enabled the Carthaginians, themselves of Phoenician origin, to pick up the pieces and create their own flourishing network. However, the Moroccan settlements did not recover.

Mediterranean artefacts did occasionally reach sites in Atlantic Spain other than Gadir, and since what has been found can only be a fraction of what remains to be discovered, which itself must be a fraction of what was originally there, this contact, even in the Mediterranean Bronze Age, should not be ignored. Several sites in Spain and Portugal where Mediterranean goods have been found – Villena, Baiões, Peña Negra – lie inland and could have been reached by following rivers upstream, whether in a boat or along a land trail. And a burial at Roça do Casal do Meiro just south of Lisbon brings us up to the water's edge. This vaulted tomb contained two people, who were surrounded by grave goods from the Mediterranean, such as an ivory comb and a cloak pin. The date is uncertain and could be as early as the eleventh or as late as the eighth century BC. The tomb may have been a memorial to Mediterranean traders who had reached this far when they died as it is hardly representative of the burials in Bronze Age Portugal. Baiões lies further inland in an area quite rich in tin, which would have attracted Phoenician or other visitors; a hoard found there, and unfortunately hard to date precisely, once again reveals links with the Mediterranean, including bronze wheeled vessels similar to those found in Cyprus and an iron bit attached to a bronze chisel. The chisel is of Atlantic origin, but the bit is Mediterranean, so someone created this composite tool, even before iron-working had begun to spread in Iberia. Nor was this traffic one way. An Atlantic roasting-spit has turned up in Cyprus.

The main candidate for the role of intermediary is the island of Sardinia, because ships entering the Mediterranean from the Atlantic could take advantage of prevailing winds carrying them in that direction. Sardinia, the home of the rich but enigmatic 'nuraghic' culture in the Bronze and Iron Ages, looked both west to Spain and east as far as the Levant in the years around 1000 BC (the term 'nuraghic' derives from the thousands of prehistoric castles, known as *nuraghi*, that still dot the island). The typical heavy sword of nuraghic Sardinia followed Atlantic models, even if it was made locally using the plentiful copper of the island; thus the 'Carp's Tongue' extended as far as Sardinia, and Atlantic sickles appear in Sardinia.[32] But though much of the copper used in Sardinia was local, the tin was not: they had to obtain it in places such as Spain and southern France, and this would explain the intensity of contact, commercial and cultural, between this part of the Mediterranean and Iberia.

Other Sardinian similarities to the Iberian cultures of the Neolithic and Bronze Ages include stone tombs not vastly different in structure from the Atlantic megaliths – as also in the Balearic islands – and walled villages composed of circular houses arranged in a similar way to the *castros* and *citânias* of Atlantic Spain and Portugal, of which more shortly.[33] To suggest that the Strait of Gibraltar was not an impenetrable barrier and that the Atlantic world spilled over into the Mediterranean makes sense. Whether this Atlantic world also encompassed the Atlantic coast of Morocco is, however, uncertain, in the present state of knowledge. But it is hard to imagine that Atlantic Morocco, which the Phoenicians penetrated without great difficulty, escaped close contact with the Atlantic culture of Iberia and the great arc stretching up to the British Isles. The idea of Bronze Age Atlantic Europe as an area joined together by a common culture makes good sense; but it is also an unnecessarily Eurocentric approach. Those living in southern Iberia had no concept of Europe, and it was easier to sail back and forth to Morocco than to Sardinia.

One might, and should, dispute the usefulness of the terms 'Neolithic', 'Bronze Age' and 'Iron Age', at least in the Atlantic, for the life of those living along the ocean's edges changed gradually; the coming of copper and then bronze did not bring traditional stone-cutting to an end by any means. There were changes in burial practices, there was the abandonment of megalithic architecture; there was a new warrior elite, though whether native or immigrant is still far from certain. All the time, though, the awareness that the picture we have is built on little bits of evidence – first funerary, then about bronze weapons – troubles anyone who hopes to understand these societies in the round. Maritime communication was certainly an important feature of life along the Atlantic arc. However, it is only in the Iron Age, roughly from 600 BC onwards, that there is a little more clarity – though not a great deal of clarity – about who the people living along the edges of the Atlantic were. Here at last there is evidence from travellers that bears comparison with the *Periplous* of the Indian Ocean; and there is the much disputed evidence of inscriptions found in Iberia, as well.

17

Tin Traders

I

By the second half of the first millennium BC the Atlantic arc had ceased to function as a lively network binding together distant parts of the west European coastline; it became the outer margin of a new world whose main centres of activity lay in the heartlands of continental Europe. This was the age of the two successive cultures known as Hallstatt and La Tène that interacted strongly with the peoples of the Mediterranean, such as the Etruscans, and became masters of iron production. Iron remained largely out of favour along the Atlantic edges, probably because it was not as readily available as it was in central Europe; but this itself indicates how the coastline had become disconnected from developments in the hinterland.[1] When Etruscan bronze figurines turn up in Devon, Greek coins appear in Brittany or Iberian pin-brooches (*fibulae*) are found in Cornwall, this is an exciting event in archaeology, for after 500 BC such exotic items had become increasingly rare; and it has been seen that the apogee of the Phoenician penetration into the Atlantic, judging from the case of Mogador, can be dated to the sixth century BC.[2]

Sea traffic certainly did not cease; but some of the most impressive connections, such as that linking Orkney to the Irish Sea and beyond, either were sundered or became much less regular, to judge from the very limited finds of 'foreign', that is, non-Orcadian, goods on Iron Age sites within the Orkney archipelago. As along the shores of the Scottish mainland, the coasts of these islands were now dotted with small castles, or brochs, whose function is as much a mystery as the Sardinian *nuraghi*, to which they bear an outward resemblance.[3] Like the *nuraghi*, they were often surrounded by small outhouses, and became the nucleus of village settlements. Indeed, stone roundhouses, not quite as imposing as the broch towers must have been, characterized settlements all along the Atlantic arc, from Portugal to Shetland.[4] More generally, there is a sense that

society was turning inwards, and that local communities lived off both the land and sea. In the British Isles these communities based themselves in small settlements that it would be hard to dignify with the title of town, though that would be a suitable description of several of the large settlements that have been discovered along the maritime edges of Galicia and northern Portugal. Brittany may also have possessed a few imposing settlements close to the sea. Writing about his invasion of north-western Gaul, Julius Caesar described the settlements of the Veneti in Brittany as 'towns', but he wanted to impress his readers with the scale of his conquests. It would not have sounded quite right if Roman armies had had to struggle to master scattered seaside villages.

Evidence for exchange of goods across the sea is so sparse that the argument for contact up and down the coasts of Atlantic Europe has to depend on cultural similarities all the way from Portugal to northern Scotland. There were broad similarities in the decoration of pottery; there was the common practice of building villages made up of roundhouses constructed on stone foundations. The similarities between the culture of Brittany and Cornwall, and their difference from the rest of France and England, suggest that the links across the sea should not be underestimated.[5] Between about 600 and 200 BC, a striking common feature across great swathes of the Atlantic coastline was the construction of promontory forts overlooking the sea; these were lines of walls, generally double or triple lines, that cut off the tip of a small promontory. There is no certainty about their function. It is unlikely that they marked out trading centres, because they are by and large in elevated positions and not close to an obvious harbour. Excavation of the promontories has produced little evidence that they were continuously inhabited. More likely, they were places of refuge and strongpoints to which warriors and their dependants could retreat in times of war. Julius Caesar described the defensive use of promontories in Brittany in his *Gallic Wars*:

> The positions of the strongholds were generally of one kind. They were at the end of tongues and promontories, so as to allow no approach on foot, when the tide rushed in from the sea – which happens every twelve hours – nor in ships, because when the tide ebbed again the ships would be damaged in shoal water.[6]

On the other hand, they could not all benefit from the tide this way. They generally looked out to the west, from western Ireland, Galloway in south-west Scotland, or the Pembroke peninsula in Wales; they were abundant in Cornwall and Brittany, and they appear on the islands of the north Atlantic: Shetland, Orkney, the Hebrides and the Isle of Man.[7] This suggests that they may sometimes have had a religious rather than a defensive use, as points of land on which to propitiate a god of the sea or of the winds, bearing in mind that the prevailing winds came from the west. Another common feature of the northern Atlantic coastal communities was what are known as *souterrains*, underground corridors built out of stone with some care; and, once again, their function is unclear – maybe they were for storage, maybe for shelter, though they would have been clearly visible above ground, so it is hard to see what advantage that would have brought. Once again, it is the presence of the same subterranean architecture on both sides of the English Channel that suggests mutual influences, rather than any objects found in the ground.

Settlements of varying size made up of roundhouses could be found as far south as Iberia. The *castros* or *citânias* of Galicia and Portugal were often substantial settlements occupying good strategic locations. One example is the very substantial *citânia* at Santa Luzia, high above the modern Portuguese town of Viana do Castelo; unfortunately, a large part of the site was destroyed early in the twentieth century in order to build a luxury hotel, but more than enough remains to indicate that the term 'town' rather than 'village' would be appropriate here. It overlooked the River Limia where it debouches into the Atlantic; this was a superb defensive position. Whether the inhabitants made much use of their access to the Atlantic is unclear. The site at Santa Luzia eventually acquired three lines of walls; the area within the walls contains dozens of circular houses closely packed together, as well as solid towers built into the retaining walls. The houses, several of which contained vestibules, were entered from the south-west or the south-east, since a southerly entrance was better sheltered from the winds and rain that tended to strike from the opposite direction. While the walls were of stone, the conical roofs of these houses would have been built of wood covered with straw. Loom weights have been found, indicating that weaving was a local industry, as one might expect; otherwise, the main sources of livelihood were agriculture and stock-raising.[8]

Bearing in mind the cultural similarities between the roundhouse settlements all the way from Portugal to the Scottish isles, the question then arises whether the inhabitants of these places possessed a common origin. Some archaeologists and philologists have seized on the idea that what united these people was a 'Celtic' identity. Language and race are quite different things, and people of similar ancestry switch languages, so that it becomes impossible to identify the 'original' language of those groups. Indeed, the term 'Celts' has several plausible meanings: the peoples called *Keltoi* by the ancient Greeks, and *Galli* by the ancient Romans; the assumption that the Hallstatt and La Tène cultures in central Europe were essentially 'Celtic' in character; the peoples who spoke Celtic languages, several of which survive to this day.[9] A case has been made for the use of Celtic dialects not just in Scotland, Ireland, Wales and Brittany but in Galicia. Its modern inhabitants have seized on their 'Celtic' identity in the struggle to gain greater autonomy from the government in Madrid, though whether a modern-day fondness for bagpipes proves Celtic identity is a moot point. Beyond that, in south-western Iberia, in the lands rich in silver visited by the Phoenicians, lay the area known to the Greeks as Tartessos.

A significant number of Tartessian inscriptions survive, written in a distinctive script whose remote origins probably go back to the same Phoenicians. If, as John Koch has controversially maintained, they are written in a Celtic language, that only mildly reinforces the argument that the lands of the Atlantic arc shared a number of cultural traits, as well as being somewhat isolated from the cultures of the rest of western and central Europe. It would be good to know that *talainon* really does mean 'the country of the blessed headland', an ambitious extrapolation from a proto-Celtic term assumed to mean 'having a fair brow', but with such limited material these efforts at decipherment appear far-fetched.[10] On the other hand, a general case can be made for the archaic character of the form of Celtic, known as Q-Celtic, spoken in Ireland and then, partly as a result of later Irish settlement in Scotland, in the far north of Britain as well; and this would imply that in the first millennium BC an 'Atlantic proto-Celtic lingua franca' was a feature of a common culture that flourished around the Irish Sea and at least as far south as Brittany, only to be over-taken in Wales and Cornwall, and later on in Brittany, by more recently formed languages that are known as P-Celtic and that were closer to the languages spoken by the ancient inhabitants of Gaul.

Knowing who these people were is certainly desirable. To what extent they saw themselves as people wedded to the sea is uncertain, but it is interesting that the term 'Armorica', a latinization of the ancient name for Brittany, means 'dwellers by the sea'. Some of the peoples encountered by Julius Caesar during the Roman war of conquest in Gaul (58–50 BC) were excellent navigators. A famous passage in Caesar's boastful memoir of his victories, mentioned already, describes the ships of the Veneti of Armorica, which he encountered in 56 BC. They are said to be built quite differently from Roman ships: they have much flatter keels, because they have to deal with tidal waters where the water level changes significantly; they have high prows and sterns, to carry them through rough seas and storms; they have strong cross-beams bolted together with thick iron fastenings; they are made of stout oak that can tolerate the violence of the open sea; they have anchors suspended from iron chains; their sails are made of hides; altogether they are much better suited to the mighty winds and waves of the open ocean than Roman vessels.[11]

There were also smaller vessels that were strong enough to withstand the waves. At the end of the nineteenth century an Irish farmer ploughing his field at Broighter in County Derry turned up a hoard of gold artefacts dating from around the time of Caesar's wars in Gaul, or maybe a little later. The most remarkable piece the farmer found was a miniature boat, twenty centimetres long, and modelled in gold with loving detail. The model contains nine benches for oarsmen, and eighteen delicate oars, as well as a steering oar at the stern, a mast and an anchor (or grappling hook). It has been estimated that a boat built to this specification would have been 12–15 metres long.[12] Boats of this type were constructed out of wickerwork that was fitted around a wooden frame; all this was then covered with skins and coated with animal fat to create a solid waterproof vessel. They have been constructed around the world from prehistoric times to the present day, and include circular Mesopotamian rivercraft, Welsh coracles (also circular) and Irish currachs, of which the gold model is a very ancient example.[13] Caesar's description of the sturdy Venetic ships offers powerful evidence that the Atlantic coastline was indeed connected by sea. And to the evidence of Caesar can be added that of Greek travellers, notably the intrepid Pytheas of Marseilles.

II

It is no surprise that the Greek travellers who became interested in the Atlantic should have had close links to Massalia, the port now known as Marseilles that had been founded by migrants and merchants from Phokaia in Asia Minor. They had, according to rather dubious accounts, fled from the conquering army of the Persian Great King, and then from a colony they had established in Corsica, out of which the Etruscans and Carthaginians flushed them in a great naval battle in 541 BC. Southern France was already the target of Etruscan traders, who made contact with the Gauls in the interior, selling them prodigious amounts of wine from the mid-seventh century onwards. Massalia experienced a golden age in the sixth century, because it was able to service demand in central France for wine and other Mediterranean goods, in the lands characterized by the so-called Hallstatt culture, which was dominated by powerful princes wealthy enough to acquire Mediterranean goods, long seen as a

great marker of status. But then the focus of economic activity, and presumably political power, shifted eastwards within central Europe towards
the scattered villages of the La Tène culture, around 500 BC, and Massalia
lost its special advantage, though it has never ceased being a significant
centre of trade.[14] While the Massalians certainly exploited the land routes
across Gaul and the river route up the Rhône, their skill at navigation
made them curious about the lands that lay beyond the Strait of Gibraltar
and the Phoenician base at Gadir; and what attracted them above all was
the possibility of gaining privileged access to tin, which was required for
the production of bronze goods – bearing in mind that the coming of iron
had in no way depleted demand for bronze, as can be seen from the large
number of bronze figurines and utensils being produced at this time within
the Mediterranean (such as the massive Greek crater which arrived at Vix
on the Seine in central France, perhaps as early as 530 BC).

Around this time an unnamed Greek sailor compiled a sailing manual,
or *Periplous*, that described the coasts of Spain from Galicia through the
Strait of Gibraltar along the coast all the way to Massalia. Today, it is a
major source of information about Greek knowledge of the Atlantic, just
as in its own day it was evidently treasured for its account of both Atlantic
and western Mediterranean waters. Indeed, it was still being read in the
late fourth century AD, when Avienus, a very indifferent pagan poet living
in north Africa, based much of his work entitled *The Maritime Shores*
(*Ora Maritima*) on this *Periplous*; and without Avienus, whose work was
published by a Venetian printer in 1488, the text would now be lost.[15] It
is a sort of palimpsest, as one has to scrape beneath the clumsy Latin to
ascertain the views of the ancient Greek traveller. This is not too difficult,
as he omitted several places that later became important, which inspires
confidence in the very early dating; at the same time, his insistence that
several ports were already in decay provides evidence, confirmed by
archaeology, that the Phoenician network in the Atlantic had already
passed its apogee.[16]

The original Greek author's account of the lands where tin could be
obtained was especially precious to the inhabitants of Massalia in the
sixth century BC.[17] Avienus spoke at length about Tartessos, which had
also passed its peak by the fifth century BC, and confidently and incor-
rectly identified it with Cádiz ('here is the city Gadir, formerly called
Tartessos'), while insisting that 'now it is small, now it is abandoned, now
a heap of ruins';[18] he described how the Tartessians traded with their
neighbours, and how the Carthaginians reached these waters; he pointed
out a glittering mountain rich in tin which would have greatly interested
early traders.[19]

Tin and lead, Avienus related, were also the great asset of a group of widely scattered islands known as the Oestrymenides that lay beyond a great promontory and that some commentators have identified with Great Britain and Ireland. However, a good case can be made for identifying this place with Galicia, which is surrounded by a number of offshore islands and was, it has been pointed out, 'the most prolific tin-producing region in Europe'.[20] Most probably, Avienus was drawing together disparate material and, having heard about tin supplies coming from Cornwall, Brittany and Galicia, was conflating all these into the Oestrymenic islands and mainland. Avienus' traveller was impressed by the inhabitants:

> There is much hardiness in the people here, a proud spirit, an efficient industriousness. They are all constantly concerned with commerce. They ply the widely troubled sea and swell of monster-filled Ocean with skiffs made of skin. For these men do not know how to fashion keels with pine or maple wood. They do not hollow out sailing vessels, as the custom is, from fir trees. Rather they always marvellously fit out boats with joined skins and often run through the vast salt water on leather.[21]

The poem also described how the 'holy island' inhabited by the Hierni lay a two-day journey from the tin islands, while 'the island of the Albioni' stood close by as well – these were evidently references to Ireland and Great Britain, and Avienus believed that the Carthaginians and the Tartessians used to trade as far as the Oestrymenides.[22] Particularly mysterious is what then follows, an account of the wider spaces of the Atlantic Ocean that had supposedly been explored by a Carthaginian navigator, Himilco; Avienus described sluggish seas and windless days, as well as waters blocked with masses of seaweed. In general, though, Avienus' account of the Atlantic, as one might expect from a Mediterranean author, emphasized the high waves, the strong winds and the marine monsters that would be encountered by anyone daring to venture into the ocean. There were inhospitable islands and there were miraculous places such as the isle of Saturn, which was thickly covered in grass but possessed a strange natural force: if any ship approached, the island and the sea around it would quake violently.[23]

Avienus did know of a route down the coast of Portugal, past Cape St Vincent: 'rising high where the starlight sets, this extremity of rich Europe extends out into beast-filled Ocean's salt water.'[24] 'That', Avienus said, 'is the Ocean which pounds the far-flung world. That is the great deep, this is the swell that encircles the shores. This is the supplier of the inner salt water, this the parent of our sea.'[25] This was a Mediterranean perspective on the stormy, tidal Atlantic. The sailor from whom Avienus derived his material had evidently experienced a frightening but highly educative voyage towards the lands of tin. He deserves the title pioneer at least as much as the better-known, but not much better-recorded, fourth-century Massalian who followed in his footsteps and then ventured even further, Pytheas of Marseilles.

III

Pytheas was both an explorer and a writer. Since they had to rely on his own words, composed around 320 BC, later Greek authors whose description of the world ventured into the Atlantic felt themselves free to scorn what he said; they included Polybios, a serious historian who wrote in the second century BC, and Strabo, an equally serious geographer, who wrote in the early first century AD. Much that needs to be said about Pytheas has to be filtered through their hostile comments, and through remarks by Pliny the Elder, active a little later than Strabo.[26] In the face of his classical critics, two modern historians of ancient exploration have boldly claimed that Pytheas 'has the best claim among ancient travellers to rank with the great discoverers of modern times'.[27] He has even been described as 'the man who discovered Britain', though Avienus' traveller knew about Britain centuries earlier.[28] The problem is that Pytheas' own writings have vanished; too many people simply refused to take him seriously. He was accused of 'errant deception'.[29] Strabo and Polybios agreed that Pytheas' voyage was simply implausible: 'how could it happen that a private individual, and a poor man at that, could cover such distances by ship and by foot?' Pytheas claimed to have reached the 'limits of the cosmos, which a person would not believe if Hermes himself were speaking'.[30]

Pytheas' motives for travelling as far as Britain, and maybe still further, might seem obvious. He shared a curiosity about the shape of the habitable world with his later rivals Eratosthenes and Strabo. This was the age of the great Alexandrian cosmographers. Even in faraway Massalia some of the major Greek works of *historia* (meaning 'enquiry') must have been known and read, not least Herodotos' account of the Persian Wars, which also contained rich descriptions of barbarian lands, such as the territories of the Skythians to the north of the Black Sea. Then there is the possibility that Pytheas was keen to promote trade, or at any rate to identify places where useful trading connections could be made. It has been seen that, with the rise of the La Tène culture north of the Alps, trade routes carrying Greek and Etruscan goods through southern France had shifted eastwards, to the advantage of Etruscan and Greek towns in northern

Italy and the upper reaches of the Adriatic. There was still strong demand for their goods in continental Europe, but the problem was that it was the wrong part of continental Europe from the perspective of Massalia. It has therefore been suggested that Pytheas set out with a grand fleet to break the Carthaginian monopoly on the Atlantic tin trade; but it seems much more likely that he was a lone traveller, and it was precisely because he was alone that he could range so far and wide and collect information about places, distances and products that would be precious to his compatriots.[31] Moreover, there was always a question about where to turn for supplies of tin. The rocky promontories of northern Europe, in Brittany and Cornwall, beckoned.[32]

Despite the chorus of disapproval led by Polybios and Strabo, there is no reason to doubt Pytheas' claim to have travelled at least as far as the British Isles during the fourth century BC, setting out from Marseilles. Nor is there reason to doubt that he made use of local ships rather than fitting ships out at his own expense. Ships powered by sail and oar were well suited to coastal navigation in the Mediterranean; but it is impossible to imagine a trireme battling against the high seas of the Bay of Biscay and the English Channel without it being rapidly swamped and sunk.[33] A further complication was that during the fourth century BC the Carthaginians controlled key points along the coastline of Mediterranean Spain, and it is unlikely they would have waved a Greek ship past the great rock of Kalpe, later known as Gibraltar.[34] Although Pytheas apparently knew about Kalpe and Cádiz/Gadir, whose existence was common knowledge in Massalia, it is much more likely that he followed a mainly overland route from Massalia to the Atlantic coast of Gaul, and went on board a Gaulish vessel there. After all, these land routes out of southern France were as much a part of Massalia's rationale as the sea routes linking the city to Italy, Spain and the Mediterranean islands. Barry Cunliffe has suggested that he did indeed set out by sea from his home town, but only travelled a short distance: in his view, he passed the Greek settlement at Agde in what is now southern Languedoc and then arrived at Narbo (Narbonne), a 'native port'; from there he would have headed to the river system that debouches into the ocean near the Gaulish settlement of Burdigala, or Bordeaux. The journey this far might only have taken a week.[35]

After three days at sea he reached Ouexisame, or Ushant, off the western tip of Brittany, but what he did there, or even whether he stayed for any length of time there, is pure speculation. Cunliffe places him on the north shore of Brittany, in the handsomely defended Iron Age port of Le Yaudet, at the point where the River Léguer joins the sea; this was a centre for trade across the Channel to southern Britain.[36] There is no evidence Pytheas ever went there, but, if he had done, he would have experienced a strong contrast between his bustling home city of Massalia, with its imposing stone temple façades and its grand covered marketplaces, and any port along the coast of northern Gaul or southern Britain. This puzzlement at the more primitive life of the northern peoples is reflected in a romantic account of the simple lives of the early Britons, written by the Greek author Diodoros the Sicilian in the first century AD and possibly derived from Pytheas' own book, *On the Ocean*. 'Far removed from the cunning and knavishness of modern man', they lived in wattle-and-daub huts and ate a thick gruel made from the ears of the grain they grew. Diodoros' image of simple innocence formed part of a great literary tradition celebrating poverty rather than the corruptions of wealth that survived into the Middle Ages and Renaissance.[37] The peoples encountered on these Atlantic travels were not derided for their simplicity, which was, rather, seen as very praiseworthy.

The Channel ports were a vital link in the tin trade that reached all the way from Britain to the Mediterranean. An account of the tin trade in south-western Britain also survives, once again from the hand of Diodoros, and possibly echoing the lost words of Pytheas.[38] Diodoros described a promontory called Belerion where seams of tin could easily be quarried. The tin was worked into the shape of knucklebones, and then it was carried to an offshore island named Ictis that was linked to the mainland by a natural causeway which flooded at high tide. Whole wagonloads of tin were taken across to Ictis at low tide and the tin was sold to merchants, who brought it first across the Channel to Gaul, and then overland all the way to the mouth of the River Rhône, whence it would presumably have been ferried to Massalia. Pliny provided slightly different information, calling the island Mictis, and stating that the Britons took their goods there in wicker boats covered in skins rather than across a causeway. One possible location for Ictis is St Michael's Mount, off the coast of Cornwall, though no remains from that period have been found that might confirm the story.[39]

Even more speculative is Pytheas' route northwards along the coasts of Britain as he island-hopped his way towards the edges of the known world on British boats. In trying to work out where he went, everything depends on measurements of the height of the sun at midday, cited (often scathingly) by his later readers such as Strabo. Strabo himself misjudged the orientation of the north European lands, even placing Ireland to the north of Great Britain, whose east coast in his view lay parallel to northern France and the Netherlands; but Strabo had an eccentric view of Ireland, which he saw as the very edge of the world, 'just barely habitable'.[40] The difference between Pytheas and Strabo, of which Strabo was keenly aware, was that Pytheas had visited most of the lands he described, while Strabo was an armchair traveller. One good candidate for a stop on Pytheas' route is the Isle of Lewis, off the north-west shore of Scotland; and Pliny offered a very brief description of the Orcades, or Orkney archipelago, which he perhaps derived from Pytheas.[41] But the big question is how far he travelled beyond that. Pliny repeated Pytheas' claim that an island called Tyle lay six days' voyage north of Britain, in a part of the world where the sun was hidden from view for half the year and continuously in view for the other six months (rather an overstatement of the phenomenon of the Midnight Sun).[42] No part of Pytheas' journey has attracted as much attention as his visit to what the dramatist and thinker Seneca would later call 'Ultima Thule', conjuring up the image of a remote and uninhabited land at the very edge of the world. Strabo refuted the claim that Pytheas had reached this place, declaring that this was a tissue of lies.[43] On the other hand, early medieval writers such as the Irish monk Dicuil would associate 'Thule' with Iceland; Dicuil was a keen cosmographer and he wrote his *On the Measurement of the Globe of the Earth* in the early ninth century at the court of the Frankish emperor, Louis the Pious, Charlemagne's son. By this time, his fellow monks from Ireland were visiting Iceland, where some of them were found by the first Norse settlers in the ninth century.[44] However, there are other good candidates for Thule, such as Shetland or the Faroe islands, for there is no indication that Pytheas' Thule is an island on the scale of Iceland.

More significant, really, is the question whether Pytheas circumnavigated Britain and entered the North Sea. All this depends on glancing references – one that may concern Kent, which would suggest he passed through the Channel from the east. There is Pliny's striking description, derived from Pytheas, of an island called Abalus where amber dumped by waters flowing out of a great estuary accumulated. The inhabitants had no interest in amber and used it in place of firewood; still, the Teutoni who lived a day's journey away on the mainland valued it, and were happy to buy it from them.[45] Pliny understood that amber was a resin and that it was found washed up on the shores of parts of northern Europe.[46] At this point, speculation is once again let loose, and debates rage as to whether this was Baltic amber or Jutish amber, which certainly seems more likely, and whether the great river was the Rhine or, more probably, a number of rivers that all flow into the North Sea along the coast between the Low Countries and Denmark. It appears that by Pytheas' time supplies of Jutish amber were diminishing; and, just as he searched for sources of tin, he may have intended to gather information about sources of amber.

Baltic amber, which is still strongly dominant, was already filtering south-wards in payment for bronze goods from as far away as the Etruscan cities of the Mediterranean. Some of it reached modern Slovenia, suggesting that the routes carrying amber were overland ones and that they lay well to the east of the routes to which Massalia had access. It was the old problem of the displacement of the centres of demand for Mediterranean products eastwards, leaving Massalia high and dry.[47]

Maybe, then, Pytheas was really a commercial spy. But, by way of Diodoros and Pliny, he offers brief glimpses of the Atlantic world, and above all of its unfamiliarity compared to not just the Mediterranean but the Black Sea, the Red Sea and the Indian Ocean. For the Atlantic coastline of Europe was still the outer edge of the known world, whereas the Indian Ocean was already functioning as the link between the Mediterranean and the South China Sea, between the high cultures of the Roman Empire and those of the Far East.

18

North Sea Raiders

I

Descriptions of northern waters by Mediterranean travellers ignore the perspective of its own inhabitants. Although writing spread northwards across the Alps, in the form of the runes, which may be derived from Etruscan or another north Italian script, no texts survive from the shores of the Atlantic in the first centuries AD. Archaeological evidence is patchy: it is richest in those areas where waterlogged and boggy soil has preserved the remains of wooden boats and even sacrificial victims, such as the 'Bog People' studied by Professor Glob in Denmark. Denmark provides some of the richest evidence, with its many islands and its profusion of inlets that could be used as harbours; the land had lifted out of the sea in the seventh and sixth millennia BC as Arctic ice had melted and sea levels had risen. Setting aside the interior of Jutland, this was a land that was best traversed by sea, with easy connections across to the Scandinavian peninsula as well. The first boats were made out of limewood, alder or oak tree trunks, hollowed out and turned into small fishing boats, maybe only suitable for a handful of passengers; but by the middle of the fourth millennium BC boats were heading out into open waters, to judge from a jar fished out of the Baltic twenty kilometres off the outlying Danish island of Bornholm.[1]

As well as fish, these boats carried amber, 'the gold of the north', which was used as jewellery but also for offerings to the gods – a pot from the fourth millennium BC contained 12,849 amber beads, though none was large (the total weight of all these beads was only four kilograms). It has been seen that Jutish amber supplies were diminishing by the first century AD, but this stimulated a greater interest in Baltic amber instead; the Baltic was stirring into life, after long centuries as a backwater. Amber was the gift of the sun, and by the second millennium it had become a favourite article of trade along overland routes that, stage

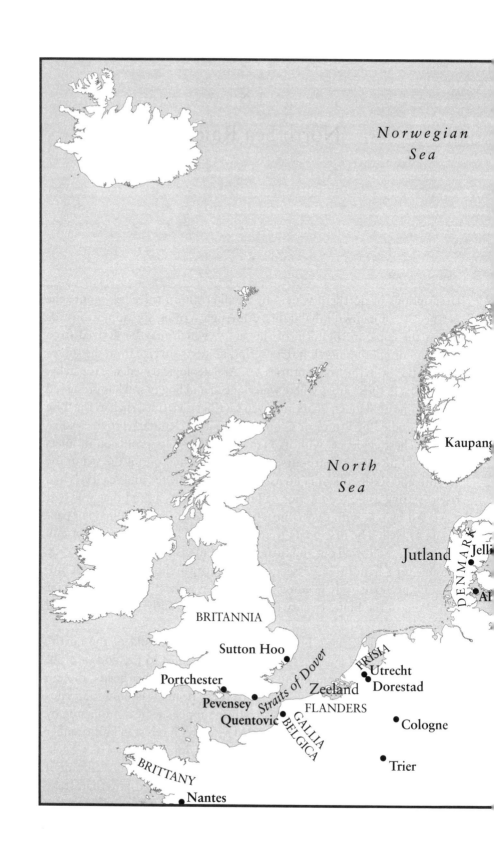

Norwegian
Sea

North
Sea

Kaupang

Jutland Jelli

DENMARK

Al

BRITANNIA

Sutton Hoo

Portchester

Straits of Dover

FRISIA

Utrecht

Pevensey

Zeeland

Dorestad

Quentovic

FLANDERS

GALLIA
BELGICA

Cologne

Trier

BRITTANY

Nantes

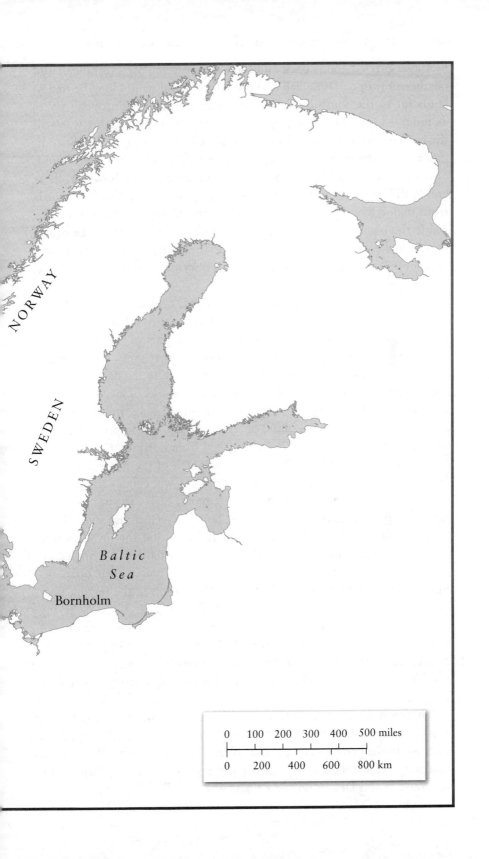

NORWAY

SWEDEN

*Baltic
Sea*

Bornholm

| 0 | 100 | 200 | 300 | 400 | 500 miles |
| 0 | 200 | 400 | 600 | 800 km |

by stage, carried goods back and forth between the Mediterranean and northern Europe.[2] Denmark and the Baltic world would long be tied to lands far to the south by way of the central and east European rivers as much as, or more than, by long-distance sea routes; this was still the case in Viking times.[3] Roman goods did seep into ancient Scandinavia, with Denmark receiving well over half of what has been found, Norway just over a fifth and Sweden a little over a sixth; however, these goods did not travel very far by sea: they were brought northwards from major Roman cities such as Trier and Cologne.[4] But within the Baltic the island of Bornholm, conveniently situated astride sea routes that linked eastern Denmark to lands further east, was a notable centre of shipping, to judge from the practice of burying local notables in boat-shaped graves.

Around the time of Pytheas' voyage evidence comes to light for the use of small ships in warfare. That is not the same as naval warfare, which even in the age of the Vikings was rare: in this part of the world, ships were used for transport, whether of warriors or merchants, or they might be used in the pursuit of enemies (a task entrusted to the disconcertingly named Ulf the Unwashed in one of the greatest works of medieval Icelandic literature, *Njál's Saga*), but they did not often engage in battle at sea.[5] A battle took place on the island of Als in the late fourth century BC following a raid that may have been launched from northern Germany (Als lies on the eastern side of Denmark, just north of the modern German border); at least three, and maybe as many as six, war canoes about twenty metres in length pounced on the Danish coast, each carrying twenty or more warriors, all armed with spears, lances, javelins and swords, and some dressed in chain mail armour. It is likely that the invaders were soundly defeated, because what survives from the battle is a mangled pile of their weapons, sacrificed in a bog into which one of their boats was also dragged.[6] Owing to the physical configuration of the region, boats were an important feature of everyday life in early Scandinavia; carvings showing long and narrow boats survive from the second millennium BC, and sometimes, as an example from Östergötland in Sweden shows, the figures on board seem to be engaged in sexual intercourse – what this signifies is a mystery, and these scenes may be drawn from myths about the gods.

The impression remains that even in the earliest centuries AD sail power was little used and not very effective, and power was generated by oars or paddles. In the first century AD Tacitus refers in his *Germania* to the boats of a people called the Suiones, apparently living somewhere around southern Sweden and Denmark; these boats were paddled:

Next come the communities of the Suiones, situated in the Ocean itself, who, besides their strength in men and arms, also possess a naval force. The form of their vessels differs from ours in having a prow at each end, so that they are always ready to move forward. They make no use of sails, nor do they have regular benches of oars at the sides: they row, as is practised in some rivers, without order, sometimes on one side, sometimes on the other, as occasion requires. These people honour wealth.[7]

Only with the development of higher freeboards, stronger keels, and the larger masts and sails that the new keels could support did wind power fully come into its own, possibly as late as the Viking age. But ship design was certainly changing in the early centuries AD. A warship found at Nydam in Denmark (very close to Als) was sunk as a sacrifice, along with plenty of weapons, by about AD 350, after several decades of service; it was made out of oak and possessed an anchor. Its prow and stern were less steep than those of the famous Viking ships built five centuries later, but this was no longer a hollowed out tree-trunk: as was so often the case in northern waters, the boat was clinker-built, constructed out of overlapping strakes of wood; it is the oldest clinker-built boat to have survived. It was twenty-three metres long, and four metres wide at its widest point, and was constructed using five large strakes of wood on each side, each about fifteen metres long. Iron nails were used to fix the strakes to one another, though the strakes, rib and keel were bound together by fibre, which created greater flexibility in the hull. The vessel had space for fifteen pairs of oars and a side rudder.[8] There is no way of knowing whether the sinking of the ship indicates that the vessel was captured in war, or whether this was seen as the best way to dispose of a worthy sea companion after years of loyal service; but it had been built not far away around AD 320, for it was made of local wood, from Jutland or Schleswig.

A second ship, made from pinewood, was found only in fragments, and this too appears to date from the fourth century AD; it was not quite as long or broad, and it may have arrived from Norway, Sweden or even Britain, since fir trees were few in the area surrounding Als.[9] On the other hand, it would be a mistake to assume that, just because the inhabitants of the Danish marshes did not make much use of sails, no one did so. A flat-bottomed boat found at Bruges, dating to the second or third century AD, was most probably a merchant vessel, well suited to North Sea conditions, with plenty of room for cargo and a large central sail; its lack of a keel made it suitable for sailing over sandbanks, where it would rest when the tide was out. The remains of Rhine barges from this period often include stepped beams into which a mast was inserted, and the Romans certainly used sailing vessels in their Rhine fleet based at Cologne.[10] The problem with wind power was that it was more difficult to control when one could set out and where one could go. The use of paddles or oars made more sense if the aim was to launch an unexpected raid.

The finds at Als and Nydam conjure up a world in which raiding across the sea was a frequent scourge. The question that then arises is whether these were, by and large, local raids or much more ambitious expeditions that could range right across the North Sea. And this takes one into the vexed question of the identity of the Angles, Saxons and Jutes who crossed from the region where these ships have been found to settle the land that became known as England. They themselves were the successors to Germanic raiders who were active from the first century AD. Indeed, the first references to Germanic pirates come from Tacitus' account of the pacification of Britain by the Roman general Agricola; some rebel Germans, from the tribe Tacitus called the Usipi, mutinied, seized some galleys, and fled northwards, circumnavigating Britain, clashing with other Germans and ending up somewhere near their native territory, which lay a little way down the Rhine in Frisian territory. The Frisians enslaved those whom they spared. But the Usipi were not skilled navigators, and it had been a miserable journey; they ran out of food and ended up eating one another.[11] The mouth of the Rhine had a very different configuration to later centuries, with many inlets poking deep into what are now Belgium and the Netherlands; and to the east of that, all the way to the borders of Denmark, stretched sandy shores and lines of small islands. These wetlands could only be made habitable by building up mounds, or *terpen*, above the likely floodline, and some of the villages along this coast prospered not just as fishing ports but as trading centres that received Roman glassware and metalwork – after all, one of the major Roman cities in northern Germany, Cologne, lay on the Rhine, and Roman Britain also lay a short distance away across the North Sea. This was an area where the Frisians, who became very active in North Sea trade during the early Middle Ages, lived side by side with other Germanic groups, notably those whom Tacitus called the Chauci.[12]

What tribal labels such as 'Chauci' really signified is a puzzle that ancient and medieval historians have enjoyed chewing over, but it is likely that the Chauci were one of the groups that eventually became part of the still larger wave of migrants we know as the Angles and the Saxons. In the first century AD their piracy was an irritant and Roman fleets were sent against them – the Romans even mobilized their shipping based at Cologne. For a time the Chauci were led by an ambitious Germanic warlord named Gannascus, whose bold sea raids against the province of

Gallia Belgica culminated in his capture and execution by the Romans in AD 47.[13] However, his defeat stirred the emotions of the Chauci still further, and trouble in the lands bordering Gallia Belgica flared up again and again in the second half of the first century; nothing is heard of them after raids in 175, no doubt because they were now subsumed in the general category of 'Saxons'. In one engagement the Germans arrived aboard a medley of different ships, some captured from the Romans, some powered by oars in the traditional German fashion; but they also strung up their colourful cloaks to convert their vast array of boats into simple sailing craft.[14] Tacitus, who tells us about these events, took a not very secret delight in the energy and freedom of the Germanic peoples, and in the failure of the Roman emperors and their generals to tame them. Nonetheless, there is no reason to disbelieve his insistence that the Romans were time and again defeated by Batavians and other peoples living on the edge of the Roman Empire, often following the defection of Germanic auxiliaries to the naval forces opposing Rome.[15] The simple reality was that by about AD 200 it was not safe to live by the sea. Villas in Brittany that were burned to the ground, coin hoards buried at spots along the Breton coast, and severe damage to Chelmsford and to nearby villages in the part of Britain that the Saxons would call Essex all strongly testify that raids from the sea, rather than internal strife, rendered the coastlines unsafe.[16]

By the third century, raiding had become severe enough for forts to be constructed along the coast of eastern Britannia and along the shore of Gallia Belgica. The 'Saxon Shore', under its commanders, or counts, was the first line of defence against Germanic raiders who came by sea, although there were plenty too who raided across the *limes*, the frontier dividing Roman Germany from neighbouring peoples. These raiders might sometimes be persuaded to become confederate allies of the Romans, but might instead become confederate allies of one another, notably the large groups known in later history as the Franks, or 'free people', and the Saxons. The Saxons were then living close to the North Sea, and their confederation (including the Chauci) came into existence after Tacitus wrote his *Germania* in the first century AD, since he mentions a great many tribes but omits the Saxons, who were, however, known to Ptolemy in the mid-second century. Whether or not these tribes had become greedy for the wealth of the Roman lands across the border in Gaul and across the sea in Britain, they were under constant pressure from the third century AD onwards: rising sea levels were eroding their habitable lands along the shores between Flanders and Frisia, a phenomenon of uncertain cause grandly known as the Dunkirk II Marine Transgression. The loss of land prompted migration out of the territories that had been settled by the

Chauci and their Saxon descendants; meanwhile the emergence of swamps and marshes encouraged the Romans to pull back from their forts in Gallia Belgica, allowing what land there was to be occupied by Frankish tribes.

Piracy became a means to a livelihood for those who were increasingly forced to depend upon the sea for their existence. Sometimes land raids and sea raids were combined, as during the first major Frankish raid on the Roman Empire in the mid-third century, when Franks reached as far as Tarragona in Spain and then appropriated the ships they found in the harbour, after which they raided north Africa. Later, another Frankish party even reached the Black Sea. These people were certainly highly adaptable. Such high-profile adventures captured the imagination of Roman writers, but what really affected the North Sea and the English Channel was the sequence of raids on Brittany and Gallia Belgica that saw the continuing destruction or destitution of dozens of villages, or *vici*, traceable in the archaeological evidence.[17] How effective the forts built along the shoreline at places such as Portchester in southern Britannia and Nantes in western France actually were is a moot point. What is striking is the sheer range of the raids, if they could penetrate as far as Nantes. Admittedly, the purpose of these forts was not simply to act as watchtowers: they were bases from which Roman fleets could be launched against attackers, and from which the neighbouring seas could be policed. All the same, large stretches of the eastern flank of Britannia lay exposed to lightning raids, and it has been suggested that only in the Strait of Dover could anyone realistically expect to control movement across the sea, and even then not very successfully: the construction of the great fort at Pevensey near Hastings in the early to mid-fourth century indicates that stronger defences were needed to protect southern Britain.

Defence of the sea was, however, a matter of deep concern: when an experienced naval commander named Carausius set up active patrols in the North Sea and seemed to have stemmed the threat from piracy, the emperor turned against him in a fit of jealousy, even accusing him of collaborating with the Franks (and no doubt diplomacy as well as warfare was used to achieve such good results). Carausius responded by declaring himself emperor in Britannia and northern Gaul in 286, and the Roman army and navy struggled hard to reconquer Britain during the next ten years. This did, however, prompt the Romans to build a substantial fleet, and they seem to have kept it in operation after the recovery of Britannia, since piracy ebbed, though it did not disappear – around this time the inhabitants of Godmanchester, near Cambridge, were massacred by raiders who must have penetrated the river network of East Anglia from the sea.[18] By the late fourth century there was no let-up in raids on Britain launched by the Saxons and their neighbours, while overland raids by the Picts and the Scots increased still further the misery of the inhabitants of Britannia; Ammianus Marcellinus, the late Roman historian, wrote of the 'continuous vexation' of the borderlands of the entire Roman Empire, including Britannia; and once the raiders began to work together in 367, in what Ammianus saw as a great 'barbarian conspiracy', Roman authority in Britain was stretched to breaking point.[19]

There are grounds for believing that Saxons arrived as settlers as well as raiders, and, with the help of fragments of pottery in a Saxon style, it has even been suggested that the title 'Counts of the Saxon Shore' conferred on the commander of the defence network against the sea raiders reflects the fact that this was a shore inhabited by, rather than attacked by, Saxons.[20] In reality, though, Roman power was crumbling and the Saxons were raiding with greater and greater impunity, even reaching the Orkney islands some way beyond the borders of Roman Britannia. So with the withdrawal of Roman legions in 410, and the recognition that Rome could no longer control the destiny of Britannia, the door was left open: Angles from the south of Denmark and the north of Germany, as well as Jutes from Jutland, joined the Saxons in colonizing Britain, a process that was accelerated by the continuing depletion of their own lands as the sea claimed more territory along the coasts of northern Europe.[21] There are still many unanswered questions about the Anglo-Saxon settlement of what became England, and evidence from DNA suggests that the invaders often took British wives or perhaps had children by enslaved British women, while an underclass of British slave workers known as *wealhas* persisted for some centuries – the term *wealhas* meant 'foreigners' and was applied by speakers of Germanic languages to any number of outsiders, notably the inhabitants of what became known as Wales. But, outside the areas in the west and far north that became Celtic refuges, the invaders were numerous enough to impose their Germanic language and pagan religious beliefs on what had been a Celtic-speaking and increasingly Christianized population.

Anyone who knows anything about the Viking raids is likely to see striking similarities between the attacks by the Saxons and their neighbours on late Roman Britain, followed by their conquest of parts of Britain, and the activities of the Danes and Norsemen in the ninth and tenth centuries. Although, as will be seen, Viking ship construction had developed rather further, the combination of piracy, violent attacks on the shoreline and subsequent settlement were a continuing feature of the North Sea world over many centuries. The Viking age marks an accentuation of something long present. Moreover, Scandinavia was often the source of the fleets that ravaged the shores of northern France, and sometimes penetrated a good way down the complex river system of the Rhine delta as well. The best-documented attack was that of a Danish king called Hygelac, which occurred between 516 and 534, targeting the territories of the Franks; the raiders carried away goods and people, but the Frankish king, Theodoric of the Merovingian dynasty, despatched his son with an army that attacked the Danes, apparently at sea; the Franks were victorious and Hygelac was killed, and all the booty and captives were supposedly recovered.[22] This conflict was long remembered, for it featured in the great Anglo-Saxon poem *Beowulf*, written at least a hundred and maybe 400 years after Hygelac's raid: after killing the monster Grendel the hero Beowulf was presented with the neck-ring worn on his last raid by Hygelac, who had been his kinsman: 'I am Hygelac's kinsman, one of his hall-troop. When I was younger, I had great triumphs.' The poet recalled the tragedy of Hygelac's death in 'Frisia', in a battle where Beowulf fought as well, escaping from danger by swimming away loaded with a great pile of armour that he had seized as booty (all his achievements verged on the superhuman).[23]

Something is missing from this account of contacts across the North Sea. What has been presented so far is a history of violent contact followed by settlement on a scale sufficient to wipe out most traces of the culture of Roman Britannia. Even the boats that have been unearthed are generally warships. Yet, as the ship from Bruges indicates, despite its early date, cargoes moved back and forth as well as raiders. The raiders themselves often passed the goods they had seized through markets. Indeed, it was because they craved products which they could not easily obtain at home that they set out on pirate raids. Some of their grave goods indicate how much they valued the manufactures of the Roman cities.[24] A commercial network linking the lands facing the North Sea did, as will be seen, emerge by the seventh century, but it would be hard to argue that such a network already existed in the age of the Saxon raids, a period that saw the decline of towns as centres of trade and industry or, to put this more dramatically, the fall of the Roman Empire in the West.[25]

II

The arrival of the Angles, Saxons and Jutes in Britain not surprisingly saw the introduction of their practice of ceremonial boat burial. The most impressive example, even though all that remained of the boat's fabric were its nails, is the lavish Sutton Hoo ship burial, excavated in Suffolk in 1939. The burial took place in the early seventh century, and shows traces of Christian influence, so it seems to document a period when Christianity was gradually impregnating a society that still abided by pagan values – indeed, the lavish ceremony of ship burial is a clear indication that pagan practices still prevailed. The site was probably the tomb of the powerful East Anglian king Rædwald; by the time of his death he appears to have established himself as the leading Anglo-Saxon king among the many competing for power in southern England. Some years before he died, he did receive baptism, but he also maintained a pagan shrine, so that his attachment to his new faith seems to have been opportunistic, an attempt to curry favour with the Christian king of Kent, not far away. Among the grave goods was Byzantine silver plate. Twenty-seven metres long and four metres wide, this was a large ship that had undergone repair in the past, to judge from the impressions left in the soil by its timbers. The strakes used in its clinker construction were not single planks of wood but were composite strips made out of several lengths of wood bonded to one another, a technique that appears here for the first time in northern Europe, though there is no way of knowing at what stage between the Nydam boats and Sutton Hoo the method was introduced. The bow and stern posts were raised an impressive four metres above the level of the keel. If there was a mast step it was apparently taken away, to allow for the insertion amidships of a burial chamber for the king. Unfortunately other finds from the same period, in Jutland as well as East Anglia, still leave the question of propulsion up in the air. But it is hard to avoid the conclusion that sails were used at least as an auxiliary source of power when wind conditions were suitable. Since the use of wind would have made journeys much shorter, the presence or absence of sails raises significant questions about the ease of contact between the new lands settled by the Anglo-Saxons and their original homeland. It is even possible that sailing skills known to earlier generations were lost, because the need for cargo ships powered by the wind was much reduced as Roman power and Roman cities contracted, and as demand for luxury goods plummeted; one result of the collapse of Roman authority was the abandonment of carefully constructed harbours with quaysides, and the use instead of beaches for loading goods and passengers. And ships drawn up on sand would need to be constructed differently from those that remained afloat – their keel, for instance, should not be too prominent or else they were likely to overbalance.[26]

The history of Anglo-Saxon shipping can be reconstructed from evidence other than ship burials. One notable feature of Anglo-Saxon literature is the survival of written accounts of journeys at sea. Allusive, alliterative poems celebrated voyages and voyagers. In 'The Wanderer' an exile recounts the hard life of one who could not return home:

> *Ond ic hean þonan wod wintercearig ofer waþema gebind . . .*
> Wretched I went thence,
> winter-wearied, over the waves' bound;
> dreary I sought hall of a gold-giver,
> where far or near I might find
> him who in meadhall might take heed of me,
> furnish comfort to a man friendless,
> win me cheer.[27]

Another powerful poem, 'The Seafarer', one that moved Ezra Pound to produce his own eccentric version, tells of the fear every traveller must experience before setting out:

> *Forþan cnyssaðnu heortan geþohtas þæt ic hean streamas . . .*
> Now come thoughts
> knocking my heart, of the high waves,
> clashing salt-crests, I am to cross again.
> Mind-lust maddens, moves as I breathe
> soul to set out, seek out the way
> to a far folk-land flood-beyond.
> For no man is so mood-proud,
> so thoroughly equipped, so quick to do,
> so strong in his youth, or with so staunch a lord
> that before seafaring he does not fear a little
> whither the Lord shall lead him in the end.[28]

Whether this poem records a real sea voyage, as has been claimed, or whether it conveys an underlying Christian message, awareness of the sea and its dangers became a common theme in the lively literature of the Anglo-Saxons. They remained conscious of their maritime heritage.

The *Beowulf* poet was also well acquainted with the sea, and with the Danish lands from which Hygelac hailed; Beowulf was a 'Geat', the term the author used for the Danes, for the oldest English epic poem is not a poem about England. The story begins with a boat burial, though, unlike those that have been excavated, this one took place at sea; and for all one knows this was the favourite way of honouring someone whose grand status earned him, or her, a boat burial:

> A ring-whorled prow rode in the harbour,
> ice-clad, outbound, a craft for a prince.

They stretched their beloved lord in his boat,
laid out by the mast, amidships,
the great ring-giver. Far-fetched treasures
were piled upon him, and precious gear.
I never heard before of a ship so well furbished
with battle-tackle, bladed weapons
and coats of mail . . .
And they set a gold standard up
high above his head, and let him drift
to wind and tide, bewailing him
And mourning their loss.[29]

There are also eloquent descriptions of warships ready to leave harbour, 'their wood-wreathed ship' and 'steep-hulled boat', in Seamus Heaney's sensitive translation, which 'flew like a bird until her curved prow had covered the distance'.[30] And these vessels carried sails:

Right away the mast was rigged with its sea-shawl;
sail-ropes were tightened, timbers drummed
and stiff winds kept the wave-crosser
skimming ahead; as she heaved forward,
her foamy neck was fleet and buoyant,
a lapped prow loping over currents,
until finally the Geats caught sight of coastline
and familiar cliffs. The keel reared up,
wind lifted it home, it hit on the land.[31]

Then a harbour master came to greet the ship and ensured that it was fastened to the beach with its anchor cables, 'in case a backwash might catch the hull and carry it away'. This was a world in which fear of the sea was countered by a sense that the sea could be mastered, with the help of the great wooden seabirds that the English and the Danes knew so well how to build – and how to describe. It was also a society in which the exchange of gifts between people of high status sealed personal relationships – Beowulf's neck-ring was a gift from a queen. And it was a society in which raiding was an accepted reality, and showing prowess in a raid was a way to win wealth but also a way to win honour.

III

Movement across the North Sea was not conducted solely by warships. As early as the sixth century, ship-borne merchants were setting out from an area broadly defined as 'Frisia', stretching from southern Jutland down the marshy, boggy coasts of northern Germany and the Netherlands. It was not an area that an army could easily hope to conquer, with its creeks and inlets, its rivers and streams, and its patches of land that lay perilously close to sea level; land was lost and gained, for the delta was in constant flux as riverbeds moved across space and as new waterways carved themselves into the shifting alluvial soil. The best hope for anyone trying to live there was to settle in the *terpen*, the mounds that rose above the waters, and some of these evolved into ports, or *vici*, from which archaeologists have recovered gold and silver coins that reveal how the *terpen* were by no means isolated communities. 'The sea', it has been observed, 'was omni-present': water, water everywhere. Yet the water offered valuable resources, such as salt and fish, while the use of what dry land there was for pasture enabled the Frisians to trade in the wool and leather that became standard cargo aboard their ships. Cattle were as important to them as boats, for they followed a diet rich in meat and milk. The Frisians were both merchants and peasants, exploiting such local resources as there were, while building links that extended further and further afield.[32] To build their ships they required plenty of wood, and that had to be brought down from the Rhine, along with grain and other staple goods they found it hard to produce. Thus the early Frisians provide an excellent example of the way that an unbalanced local economy and the necessity of specializing stimulate trade. They began to trade not in order to accumulate wealth and to live in luxury, but in order to ensure their day-to-day survival. Their success in guaranteeing survival provided the basis for more ambitious trading voyages that, as will be seen, offered wine, textiles and other finished products to consumers around the North Sea.[33]

This was the obstinate land, unwelcoming to conquerors, in which King Hygelac had met his death. This region had earlier been the home of Angles and other peoples who had invaded what became England, and the Frisian language remains the closest Germanic language to Anglo-Saxon and indeed modern English. The inhabitants, up to and beyond their conversion from paganism, were regarded as 'ferocious' and lived largely free of outside interference until the Frankish 'Mayor of the Palace' (and to all intents the ruler of the Merovingian kingdom), Charles Martel, launched an ambitious campaign against that 'most fearsome race', the Frisians.[34] But Christianity was already gaining a purchase in Frisia, for the inhabitants were evangelized by an early archbishop of York, Wilfred, late in the seventh century, while another missionary, Willibrord, set out from Ireland to complete the conversion of the Frisians at the very end of the century. The fact that the missionary campaigns were initiated in the

20. Irish legend told of the intrepid navigator St Brendan, who sailed into the Atlantic with his monks looking for remote islands where they could live far from ordinary human company.

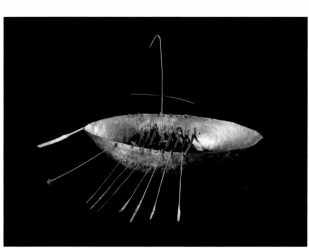

21. A golden model of a boat, twenty centimetres long, from Broighter in Northern Ireland dating from the first century BC or AD. Early Irish ships were made of wicker frames covered in skins.

22. Overlooking the Atlantic, this Iron Age settlement at Viana do Castelo in northern Portugal contained dozens of roundhouses and was ringed by walls with watchtowers.

23. A bronze hoard from the Bay of Huelva in south-western Spain contained several 'Carp's Tongue' swords fashionable along the Atlantic coasts around 800 BC.

24. The Oseberg ship from Norway, of c.AD 820, was superbly carved out of oak. It was used for the burial of a queen or high priestess and carried an array of grave goods.

25. Viking sails were made of plaited strips of cloth, producing a lozenge effect. Viking picture stones often portray the journey to the next world aboard a ship.

26. A coin from Haithabu in southern Denmark found in Birka in central Sweden provides evidence for trade between these early Viking towns.

27. Inuit carvings from Greenland, thought to show the Norse inhabitants with whom they made contact.

28. The crozier of Bishop Olafur of Gardar (d. 1280), brought to Greenland from Scandinavia.

29. Fifteenth-century clothing from Greenland, reflecting current European fashions.

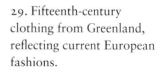

30. In the thirteenth century or later two Norse Greenlanders sailed as far north as 72°55'N. and left this record of their visit in runes.

31. Wealthy Lübeck merchants built fine houses along the waterfront, containing offices, storerooms and accommodation.

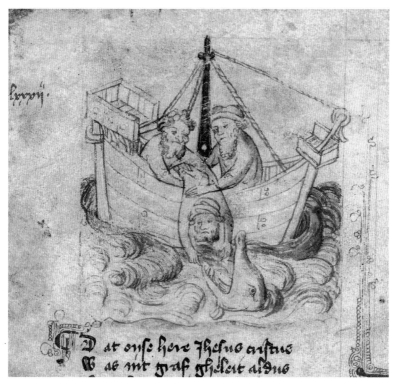

32. Jonah and the Whale from an early fifteenth-century Dutch manuscript. The ship closely resembles the Hanseatic cogs of this period.

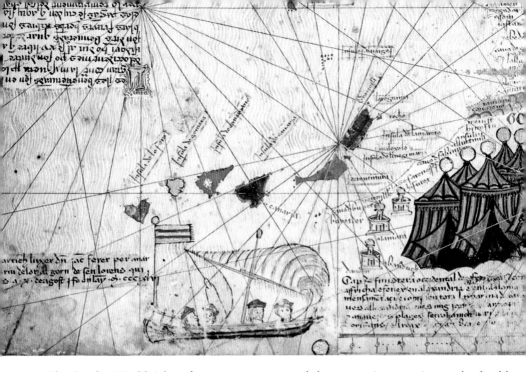

33. The Catalan World Atlas of 1375 commemorated the voyage in 1346, in search of gold, of Jaume Ferrer of Majorca, past the Canaries, which are shown, and down the coast of Africa, from which he never returned.

34. A late sixteenth-century image of a noblewoman from La Gomera in the Canaries. The pagan islanders, mostly naked and ignorant of metal, were a surprise to explorers.

35. A magnificent glazed bowl from fifteenth-century Málaga, in the Muslim kingdom of Granada, showing a Portuguese caravel under sail.

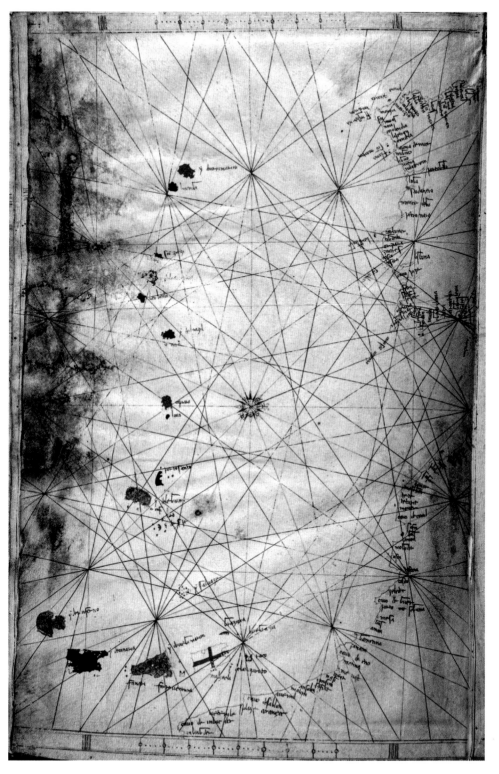

36. A Venetian atlas of the early fifteenth century shows a scattering of Atlantic islands, including Madeira (south-west of the central compass), the Canaries and several imaginary ones.

37. The Portuguese fort at Elmina in Ghana was a centre of trade in gold and slaves, founded in 1482 and built out of stones brought from Portugal.

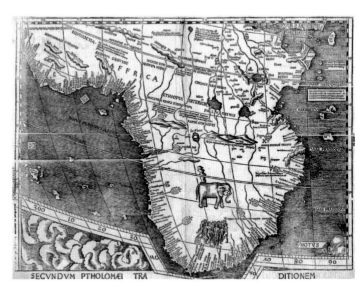

39. Portuguese *padrões* also appear on Martin Waldseemüller's massive world map of 1507, along the coasts of southern Africa.

38. In 1894, following the German colonization of Namibia, this *padrão* marking the arrival of the Portuguese at Cape Cross in 1486 was carried off to Berlin. In May 2019 Germany agreed to return it to Namibia.

British Isles already provides proof that there was traffic between Frisia and lands across the North Sea.[35]

The traffic went both ways: the Venerable Bede, writing in the north of England, knew that in 678 a noble war captive from Northumbria named Imma had suffered the ignominy of being taken down to London to be sold to a Frisian trader. The merchant was kind-hearted enough to allow him to go and seek ransom money in Kent, which Imma managed to do. This way the Frisian was not left out of pocket when Imma was released.[36] By the late eighth century, on the eve of the first Viking attacks, there were plenty of Frisian merchants living in England, notably at York, Ipswich and Hamwih, now known as Southampton, as well as across northern France and along the lower Rhine. Silver coins minted in Frisia have turned up repeatedly in eastern England and gold coins minted in Frisia have been found at Kaupang near Oslo and Jelling in Jutland; these date from the 670s. Brooches from Scandinavia have been found in Frisia, and brooches from Frisia in Scandinavia.[37] A particularly important centre of Frisian trade lay at Dorestad near Utrecht, within the Rhine delta, and another major trading hub existed by about 600 a few miles upriver beyond Boulogne, at a place known as Quentovic. Some of the Frisian bases in and around Flanders had been Roman trading centres, while others were new, or at least revived, ports of trade. Here one could buy wool and woollen cloth, hides and slaves; down the rivers feeding into the North Sea came high-grade Rhenish pottery, glassware and good-quality millstones.[38]

No country can match the Netherlands for the intermingling of sea and land, and the major Frisian port at Dorestad linked the maritime to the terrestrial world. Although it already existed in some form in the late Roman period, Dorestad experienced particularly fast growth during the early Middle Ages, so that it encompassed 250 hectares by the end of the eighth century. Its merchant houses, long, hall-like structures surrounded by a palisade containing a well and a refuse pit, were joined to the rivers that flowed past the town by lengthy wooden jetties, and here barrels or jars filled with Rhineland wine were loaded for transit to small ports along the coast that stretched northwards towards Jutland and into the Baltic as far as Gotland and eastern Sweden, where fragments of Rhenish pottery and glass abound. Eighty per cent of the pottery recovered at Dorestad is not local but foreign, predominantly Rhenish. Nonetheless, the Frisian towns, including Dorestad, were modest-looking places, for all their wealth: 'monumentally they were far from impressive; Dorestad would have looked very utilitarian to a visitor from Cologne, or maybe even one from Tours, though it was more active as an urban centre than the latter by far.'[39] Ships travelling from Cologne to Denmark in the early ninth century passed through Dorestad, which functioned as the key link between the Rhineland and the open North Sea. Dorestad was also the home of an exceptionally important mint during the eighth and early ninth centuries, which makes sense, as its prominence in trade brought plenty of bullion to the town; indeed, it became the most important mint in the realms of Charlemagne, who reformed the currency of his empire, abandoning the minting of gold in favour of silver, which was much easier to obtain.[40] Dorestad, Quentovic and other towns benefited from the presence of Frankish royal officials once Carolingian power had been imposed on the region; and the high point of their fortunes coincided with the high point of the fortunes of the Carolingian dynasty. As, towards the middle of the ninth century, the Carolingian empire fragmented, the importance of these towns waned.[41] This suggests that one of the best sources of profit was the court of the Carolingian rulers themselves, who are known to have welcomed other merchants, such as Jews from the Mediterranean, and whose attempts to project themselves as a new generation of Roman emperors were expressed through luxury and magnificence.

The Frisians were not just masters of the trade networks of northern Europe; they were also expert navigators. Judging from their coins, they built round-bottomed ships that lay low in the water but were suitable for medium-range voyages across the open sea, all the way to England. These were possibly the ancestors of the late medieval cargo ship known as the hulk. Ships sailing closer to the shore or up and down the rivers were flat-bottomed and had higher sides, resembling another type of late medieval cargo ship, the cog. Beyond the schematic images on coins, there is the evidence of a Frisian ship that was unearthed at Utrecht in 1939; it has now been dated to the high point of Frisian commercial activity, around 790, using Carbon 14 analysis. This ship, which resembled the banana-shaped boats shown on Frisian coins, was built out of oak, and it was nearly eighteen metres long; its maximum width was four metres, with a displacement of about ten tons. What sort of mast and sail it possessed has been much debated, and without an answer to this question it is impossible to be sure that this ship could cope with the open sea.[42] This, then, was a proto-hulk. But Frisian coins found in Birka, in Sweden, also portray flat-bottomed cogs with big central masts, rigging and large square sails. Whichever types of ships Frisian sailors used, they preferred to hug the shore as much as possible, taking shelter in the Wadden Sea amid the North Frisian islands when bound for Denmark and beyond. This way they could make the voyage all the way to Ribe in south-western Denmark without heading further out to sea than Heligoland. Heading west too there was the shelter of islands that have now become part of the European landmass, in what is now the Dutch province of Zeeland; following this course, they could travel from Dorestad almost all the way to Quentovic. They seem to have travelled in convoy when they were out on the open sea, and they would not set out in winter: sea journeys were strictly seasonal. Their dominant position in the trade of the North Sea led contemporaries to call the waters between Frisia and England the 'Frisian Sea'.[43]

Although the Frisian merchants obviously worked together (as the use of convoys suggests), there is no hard evidence for the existence of trading companies; individual merchants apparently traded on their own account. It has been suggested that their palisaded houses expressed their strong individualism: at Dorestad, 'the houses by the Rhine were packed closely but each made itself into an island', so that they possessed 'all the connection and the isolation of the *terpen*'.[44] At any rate, the fact that they stored their goods in their own houses rather than using communal stores indicates that they had a strong sense of private property. On the other hand, they may have been pioneers in the creation of guilds of merchants, which formed the basis for the famous urban guilds that flourished in Bruges, Ghent and other Flemish cities.[45] Whether or not that degree of continuity existed, the most important point about the Frisian merchants is that they did lay the foundations for the great trading network of medieval Flanders; they operated from towns that lay well within the borders of what later became the county of Flanders, and they were open to new opportunities. Their towns absorbed immigrants from Frankish lands, from England and in due course from Scandinavia; and they set up their own trading stations far from Frisia, in places such as Kaupang, in the Oslo fjord, and Birka, beyond Stockholm, about which more will be said later. They were open to the excellent new opportunities that arose on the other side of Jutland, in the Baltic, at the start of the ninth century, around the same time that Viking marauders began to exploit the wealth of the Frisian and Anglo-Saxon trading world. By the tenth century the term 'Frisian' had become a generic word for merchants, just as in Merovingian Gaul the terms 'Syrian' and even 'Jew' had conveyed the same idea. So, although the Frisians originated among their *terpen*, the world they explored and the experiences they underwent far from home generated a cosmopolitan identity that enabled them to act as intermediaries between the peoples living by the shores of the North Sea.

This chapter has set alongside one another the peaceful traders of eighth-century Frisia and the aggressive invaders who set out from Jutland and northern Germany, transforming large parts of Roman Britannia into

Anglo-Saxon England. But the line between pirates and honest merchants has always been fuzzy; with the irruption of a new wave of Scandinavian raiders into the North Sea and the Atlantic Ocean the distinction between raiders and traders becomes even more difficult to sustain. In some respects, as will be seen in the next chapter, the Vikings represented more of the same; but in other respects – the scale of their assaults and the development of new shipping technology – the Viking world differed dramatically from what had come before.

19

'This iron-studded Dragon'[1]

I

Changes in ship design elevated the level of threat posed by the Scandinavian raiders to a new level. This can be seen thanks to the remarkable excavations in Norway and Denmark that have brought to light both sunken and buried ships, while memorial stones from the Swedish island of Gotland carry images of ships that are rich in information about the parts that do not survive – sails and rigging. Then there is archaeological evidence for the towns and trading networks of the Scandinavians, extending far from their homeland, which helps answer the question whether these attacks had economic motives.[2]

The other evidence that has attracted continuous attention comes from the written texts that describe the first arrival of the 'Danes' on the shores of England, and the horror of monks and others at the first appearance of 'heathens' and 'Danes', a generic term that also included raiders from 'the Northern Road', the meaning of the name 'Norway', and occasionally from Sweden as well. These accounts of murder and theft are interspersed among accounts of equally bloody conflicts among the competing kings of Anglo-Saxon England, so that the main source of information, the *Anglo-Saxon Chronicle*, which in any case survives in several versions, leaves the reader puzzled as to how England could have become the prosperous and well-ordered state that it eventually did become under Anglo-Saxon rule: in 878, we are told, a 'great part of the inhabitants' of Wessex fled across the sea, while the English king, Alfred, took refuge in the woods and marshes.[3] England's prosperity was one of its attractions, as far as the Vikings were concerned. They perhaps realized that they should not kill the goose that laid the golden egg, though some accounts of Viking devastation give the impression that great swathes of territory were 'harried' to the point of ruin.

The Viking raids on England began, according to the *Anglo-Saxon*

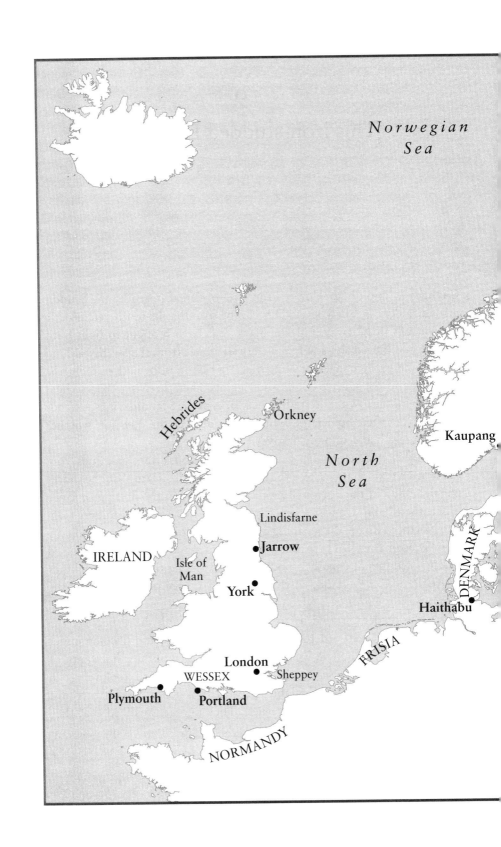

Norwegian
Sea

Kaupang

Hebrides

Orkney

North
Sea

Lindisfarne

IRELAND

Isle of
Man

Jarrow

York

DENMARK

Haithabu

London

FRISIA

WESSEX

Sheppey

Plymouth

Portland

NORMANDY

NORWAY

Staraya
Ladoga

Åland
Islands

Birka

Gotland

*Baltic
Sea*

oskilde

Wolin

0   100   200   300   400   500 miles

0   200   400   600   800 km

Chronicle, in 789, with a small Norwegian, or possibly Danish, raid on Portland in Dorset: 'these were the first ships of the Danes to come to England.'[4] But terror struck in 793, when, amid great portents ('fiery dragons were seen flying in the air') and severe famine, heathens came and laid waste the monastery at Lindisfarne on the coast of Northumbria, the pride of the Northumbrian Church. The next year the monks of Jarrow were attacked, though the chronicler recorded with satisfaction that some of the Danish ships were wrecked in stormy weather and that a good many Danes were drowned or killed.[5] The Viking raids became intense by the 830s, and a striking feature was their range: the Isle of Sheppey, off Kent, was a target in 835, and a group of Vikings wintered there in 855; but they also appeared close to Plymouth, where the Danes entered into an alliance with the Cornish Britons, and where King Egbert of Wessex scored a victory in 838; and this victory was all the sweeter as the year before Egbert had been defeated by a Danish warband that had arrived off Somerset aboard thirty-five, or possibly twenty-five, ships.[6] How big these warbands were has been a topic of controversy. The authors of the *Anglo-Saxon Chronicle* referred several times to the *mycel hæþen here*, 'the great heathen host', that arrived in 865, although massive Danish fleets were recorded earlier too, as in 851, when 350 Viking ships penetrated the Thames, ravaging London and then marching inland, where they were soundly defeated. This is exactly ten times as many ships as were recorded in 843, so either the scale of the attacks had changed dramatically, or the monks who wrote about the attacks became more and more prone to exaggeration.[7] The Vikings had learned what rich pickings were to be found in England, as also along the northern coasts of the Frankish Empire, and their ambitions began to expand in new directions: in Kent the Vikings were promised money in the hope that they would remain peaceful, but this was to underestimate the lure of war booty, and they devastated eastern Kent nonetheless.[8]

Danish ambitions became ever greater, as groups of Scandinavian settlers arrived, and as plans evolved for the conquest of parts of England. The individual raids of the early ninth century, where a group of like-minded warriors set out in search of booty and adventure under a war-leader, often in just a few ships, gave way to much larger expeditions led by kings and other great lords, although as early as 810 the Danish king, Godfred, invaded Frisia, nearby, with 200 ships and carried off 200 pounds of silver as tribute from one of the most prosperous provinces of Charlemagne's great empire. No doubt the idea of earning a pound of silver for each ship had a certain attraction, quite apart from helping to cover the cost of putting together such a large fleet. This, however, has to be understood from the perspective of regional politics, as a conflict between neighbours. Still, it provides evidence that Danish kings could mobilize large fleets if they chose to do so; further away, in Norway, royal control was yet to be imposed, and individual enterprises were the norm.[9] A Scandinavian kingdom was established at Jorvik, or York, while King Alfred, later in the ninth century, agreed to divide much of England between himself and the Viking ruler Guðrum, who, however, did accept baptism. On the English side, there was some awareness that preventive action at sea would be more effective than attempts to overwhelm the *mycel here* on land, and Alfred's newly formed fleet managed to defeat a small Danish squadron in 882; one result was that the 'great host' was deflected away from Alfred's realms and travelled instead up the River Scheldt, to make a nuisance of itself in northern France and Flanders.[10] So, by 896, King Alfred built up his naval defences, and in some accounts of British naval history this was the moment when the English navy was founded: the king

> ordered warships to be built to meet the Danish ships: they were almost twice as long as the others, some had sixty oars, some had more; they were both swifter, steadier, and with more freeboard than the others; they were built neither after the Frisian design nor after the Danish, but as it seemed to himself that they could be most serviceable.[11]

Exactly what these ships looked like remains a mystery, as we are only told what they did not look like, although their size sounds impressive. Thereafter, well into the reign of King Athelstan, an English navy was able to defend the shores of the Anglo-Saxon realm. However, one difficulty was that raids did not simply start in Scandinavia.[12] Even after 911, when the Frankish ruler conceded control of what would henceforth become Normandy to the Northmen from whom it took its name, sea raiders arrived in southern England from northern France, sailing up the River Severn; they also raided the Welsh coast, for the Celtic lands, notably Ireland, were constant targets of Viking attacks and, in the case of the area around Dublin, long-term settlement.[13]

A detailed chronicle of Viking raids on England would show how, even as the Christianization of Scandinavia was under way, the raids did not cease; the arrival of Svein Forkbeard and his son Cnut in England early in the eleventh century, followed by the submission of England to these rulers and by the creation under Cnut of an empire that embraced England, Denmark and Norway, did not mean the end of Scandinavian raids.[14] In 1066 the Norwegian king, Harald Hardraða ('hard ruler'), brought the claimant to the English throne, Tostig, across the sea to northern England, where both were defeated and killed by Tostig's half-brother king, Harold Godwinsson, just as Duke William of Normandy (himself of Scandinavian descent) launched his own combined assault on southern England.[15] Viking raids only gradually petered out, for when conquest was not the motive there was always the lure of being paid off with handsome bribes. Like all forms of blackmail, a gift of what came to be known as Danegeld simply acted as an invitation to return later and to demand more.

So far, then, a bare chronicle of some of the most vicious Viking raids tells a story of murder, theft and eventual partial conquest. But this does nothing to explain who the raiders were and why the attacks were launched in the first place. Even the word 'Viking' has been the subject of debate. The most reasonable explanation is that it means 'men of the *vik*', that is, the inlets from which raids were launched, whether the majestic steep-sided fjords of Norway or the low-lying creeks of Denmark and southern Sweden. The term *víkingr* was used in Scandinavia to mean a pirate; these people went *í víking*, that is, raiding across the sea, and were celebrated for doing so on the runestones that commemorated their life.[16] This term has been applied rather too widely, so that even the Scandinavian settlements in late medieval Greenland (of which more later) are often presented as 'Viking', a term best applied instead to the raiders who have been described in this chapter. Within the Baltic, the Swedish Vikings who raided the southern coasts and sent their ships down the river systems of eastern Europe, to reach Mikelgarð, 'the Great City' (Constantinople), are often described as Varangians, another term of uncertain origin, derived from the Greek word *Varangoi*, which was applied particularly to the Scandinavian and also Anglo-Saxon mercenaries who were greatly valued by the Byzantine army. Raiding within the Baltic did not cease in the late eleventh century, and later Swedish wars of conquest along the shores of what are now the Baltic states had much in common with the Varangian raids of earlier centuries, even if a strong element of Christian mission sometimes intruded.[17]

It is already obvious that the raids did not have a single cause, and that attempts to ascribe them to overpopulation or political strife within Scandinavia (leading to an exodus of dissenters) may fit some of the evidence, but fail to account for the great variety of Viking attacks: lightning strikes from the sea, aiming at wealthy monasteries where the raiders could seize great treasures in gold and silver; attempts at political conquest; migrations in which women as well as men crossed the sea (as in the case of Iceland and the lands beyond); to which should be added peaceful trading expeditions in the sort of ship that will be described shortly.[18] The colonization of Iceland was apparently launched after King Harald Fairhair gained control of large swathes of Norway in the late ninth century and demanded the payment of new taxes, so that discontented Norsemen who had lived free from royal interference set off to create their own new commonwealth in a virtually empty land across the ocean.[19] But it is impossible to ignore one very distinctive feature of Viking society (using the term to mean the select group of those who went raiding). Far from possessing a sense that stealing treasure and murdering one's victims was disgraceful, the Vikings gloried in their achievements. They expounded a cult of the violent hero:

> Cattle die, and kinsmen die,
> And so one dies one's self;
> But a noble name will never die,
> If good renown one gets.[20]

A good name was to be won through heroic deeds, and death in battle brought the glory of fame, which was more valued than life itself.

The greatest glory was to be found through winning a reputation not just as a great war leader but as a generous host. Indeed, it was impossible to become a generous host without raiding. Arriving back at home laden with booty and distributing prizes to one's followers marked the high point in the Viking year. The Orkney Saga describes an eleventh-century Viking named Svein Asleifarson who used to take Hakon, whose father was earl of Orkney, on raids 'as soon as he was strong enough to travel with grown men . . . doing all in his power to build up Hakon's reputation'. Svein would spend each winter in Orkney, 'where he entertained some eighty men at his own expense'. After a winter of hard drinking and carousing, and a spring spent sowing the soil, he would go off raiding, once in late spring and again in the autumn, reaching the Hebrides, the Isle of Man and Ireland. As well as raiding on land, Svein and his men would attack merchant ships, such as two English vessels they found crossing the Irish Sea; these ships carried a rich cargo of fine cloths, which the Vikings seized, hoisting some brightly coloured pieces of sailcloth as a visible boast of their success.[21] Piracy and plunder sustained an aristocratic lifestyle, and one's greatness was measured by one's generosity as well as by deeds in war, but that generosity could only be funded through war.

The Vikings shared their culture of warfare and feasting with neighbours around the North Sea, including the Anglo-Saxons and the Celtic peoples of Scotland and Ireland, with whom they often intermarried. Scandinavians based in such places as the Orkney Islands were as content to plunder Norway as they were willing to raid the Scottish isles or Ireland.

Scandinavian Vikings shared a language (already fragmented into mutually comprehensible dialects), though they could probably make sense of Anglo-Saxon speech as well. The major distinction between Vikings and their neighbours was not so much ethnic origin or the culture of feasting and warfare; it was their paganism – for their victims, the most important feature of the raiders who attacked Lindisfarne in 793, and Irish monasteries in later decades, was not that they came from Scandinavia, but that they were heathens, lacking all respect for Christian holy places and for the accumulated treasures of the Anglo-Saxon and the Irish Church.[22] Yet the Viking raids continued even in the eleventh century, when the Scandinavian kings had adopted Christianity (which is not to say that all their subjects had abandoned paganism). The Orkney Saga saw no contradiction between belief in Christ and a life of raiding; indeed, the twelfth-century earl of Orkney, Rognvald, went on pilgrimage to Jerusalem, travelling out by sea, and returning home by way of Rome. The culture of raiding was very deeply ingrained.

II

One question is whether larger changes in economic relationships across Europe and western Asia stimulated the Vikings into action. So long as the routes across the Baltic and down the river systems were open, the Varangians managed to make contact with prosperous, urbanized societies in the Steppes, and conveyed large quantities of silver northwards, either in the form of coin or as silver bullion (including hack silver, silver objects cut into pieces and valued by weight); Varangian merchants reached as far as the shores of the Caspian Sea, while several widely read Arab writers noted their peculiar ways, including boat burials and the custom of sacrificing a slave girl at the funeral of her master, after her master's companions had one by one taken advantage of her.[23] More than 100,000 Islamic coins have been unearthed in Scandinavia, and the number of finds is still growing.[24] The Caspian gave access to northern Iran, with its silver mines, and beyond that to the Abbasid empire in Iraq.

All this coincided with the emergence of the first towns in Scandinavia. Sweden's oldest town was Birka, which lay on a small island in Lake Mälaren, the large island-studded lake that extends westwards from present-day Stockholm; in this period, many of its islands had not risen out of the sea or were much smaller (Birka's own island was half its present size), while the lake consisted of saltwater and was in effect an extension of the Baltic Sea. Across the many thousands of islands of the Stockholm archipelago small settlements came into being that were linked to one another by boat traffic, and every community had its little fleet of boats, from small fishing vessels to larger ships suitable for Viking raids or longer-distance trade. All this meant that Birka was quite easily accessible from the open sea by boat. The town benefited from the protection of the king of central Sweden, who maintained a manor house just across the water on the larger island of Hovgården. Without royal protection, who would ensure the safe passage of Birka's boats through a dense network of islands, stretching far beyond the coast of Sweden, each of which might provide a base for Viking pirates? On the other hand, if one could make the journey across the Baltic in safety, the riches that were now to hand were the stuff of fable: furs from Russia and the silver of the Orient, accessible in such places at Staraya Ladoga only a little distance down the rivers that led towards the principality of Kiev, also known as Rus. By the tenth century, Birka was home to about a thousand people, boat-builders, artisans, sailors and merchants, who lived in sturdy wooden houses on little plots of land. A similar story can be told of the nameless trading centre not far from modern Oslo that looked out towards the North Sea; known to archaeologists by the convenience name of Kaupang ('trade centre'), it was the first town to emerge in Norway.[25]

The history of another town, the port of Hedeby, or Haithabu, situated on the Baltic side of Schleswig where Denmark and Germany meet one another, helps us connect the Baltic to the North Sea world. It has been said that 'the remains of Haithabu lie in one of the richest archaeological zones in all of Europe'.[26] Although an earlier and much smaller trading settlement may have existed nearby, the foundation of Haithabu can be securely dated to the war between King Godfred of Denmark and his neighbour Charlemagne around 810, since timbers found on the site date from 810 or soon after. While campaigning on the eastern side of Denmark against Charlemagne's allies, Godfred raided a port established by the Slav people known as the Obodrites close to present-day Lübeck, and deported its merchants to his own new town of Haithabu. The Obodrites had obligingly provided the Frisian merchants from the North Sea, and their customers in northern France, with goods that came through the Baltic, most importantly furs and amber.[27] Godfred's idea was, then, to create a Danish entrepôt that would dominate traffic between the Baltic and the North Sea. Charlemagne regarded this as intolerable interference and set off with an army (accompanied by the elephant that Harun ar-Rashid, caliph of Baghdad, had presented to him). Godfred built up his defences, but there was rivalry at court and he was murdered by Danish foes.

All the same, Haithabu survived and flourished, particularly between about 850 and 980. It was a centre of amber crafting, and its mixed population included Scandinavians, Slavs and Frisians, who found the town's location much better than anything that had existed before: it lay on an inlet as close as one can get to the western flank of Jutland, so that goods unloaded in the North Sea could be funnelled through to Haithabu very easily – the analogy in the ancient Mediterranean would be with two-facing Corinth. Haithabu was surrounded on its land side by a strong defensive wall, while its harbour offered plenty of jetties to incoming boats. Among goods that reached this port were tin and mercury that may have originated in Spain or England.[28] A canal ran through the middle of the town and, rather as at Dorestad, the houses were built of timber and wattle, on their own little plots of land connected to one another by narrow pathways. The expansion of Haithabu marked the first stage in the creation of commercial networks that linked two regions which were experiencing exponential economic growth: the North Sea and the Baltic.[29]

The Baltic was coming alive. Its many chains of small islands fostered sea traffic by their very nature. The Åland Islands between Sweden and Finland became a meeting point between Scandinavians from the west and Finno-Ugrians from the east; many of the stories in the Finnish national epic, the *Kalevala*, only recorded in the nineteenth century, probably originated in the watery world around these islands.[30] Nowhere was the liveliness of Baltic networks more obvious than on the island of Gotland off the southern coast of Sweden. The decline of Birka brought Gotland to the fore, for the island was beautifully situated with easy access across the sea to all the shores of the Baltic. Silver dirhams from the Abbasid caliphate have been found at Paviken on Gotland, which was only one centre among many for the trade of the Gotlanders.[31] The Gotlanders hoarded even greater quantities of German and other continental coins, and this *thésaurisation* of bullion that flooded into the region, whether it was acquired through trading or raiding, must have placed quite a severe strain on the economies of both western Europe and western Asia. Exotic luxuries sometimes reached Scandinavia along with the silver – the most famous example is a small Buddha cast in Kashmir that turned up in central Sweden.[32]

Generally, the fate of Islamic dirhams was to be melted down, for the only Viking coins before the end of the tenth century were some imitations of Carolingian money made in Haithabu soon after it was founded.[33] Sometimes, as the Anglo-Saxon *Beowulf* poet shows, precious metals were deployed in gift exchange, as kings and famous warriors conferred armbands and other signs of status on one another. Often too European coins were sent back to Germany as payment for Rhineland wines, for one constant feature of the Viking world was its love for strong drink, confirmed by the mass of fragments of Rhenish wine jugs found in Scandinavia. What the merchants of Haithabu, Birka and Gotland knew was that there was persistent demand for the goods they sent out of the Baltic and brought into the Baltic, demand that extended to England, France and beyond, and that servicing this demand provided them with a good livelihood.

That this trade was conducted by sea goes without saying, but the connections with the Muslim world were only rendered possible by the penetration of the river systems that flowed south towards the Steppes, and by the creation of a Varangian-ruled polity based at Kiev, the principality of Rus; Scandinavian merchants trading towards Staraya Ladoga and Novgorod pioneered routes into the interior that gave access to seemingly limitless supplies of furs and that were once again to become important in the heyday of the German Hansa.[34] One important town that linked the Baltic to the Eurasian landmass was Wolin, whose site lies just across the present-day German–Polish border; it flourished from the tenth to the twelfth century, and, like Haithabu, it was no mere village: its houses were strung along four kilometres of wooden pathways, and they were impressive structures, sizeable and handsomely decorated. Wolin supplied the Baltic and areas beyond with goods from the interior, and vice versa, but it also had its own lively potteries, amber workshops and glass-makers. Adam of Bremen, who wrote in the late eleventh century, claimed that 'it is truly the largest of all cities that Europe has to offer', and insisted that the inhabitants even included Greeks. But the local population 'all still remain captive to their pagan heresies', which he regretted, as they were in all other respects as trustworthy and friendly as it was possible to imagine. Christians were best advised to keep their beliefs secret.[35] Adam of Bremen wrote a history of the archbishops of Hamburg, and he played up the success of the Christian Church in defeating the heinous pagan beliefs of its opponents – he wrote with lurid fascination of Viking human sacrifice at Uppsala. The fact that he lived not very far away should not mask his delight in exaggeration; but there was an underlying truth about the importance of Wolin.

III

Ships were a matter of exceptional pride to the Vikings. Memorial stones for dead warriors often depict Viking longboats, carrying a complement of warriors, with their big square sail fully set. The island of Gotland has yielded large numbers of these stones, portraying the entry of the warrior into Valhalla and scenes from Norse mythology, as well as one stone showing a majestic ship, battle scenes and the sacrifice of a human victim on an altar – a brief Swedish history of Gotland known as the *Gotlanders' Saga* also tells of human sacrifices conducted by a supreme council of the entire island.[36] The evidence from the Gotlandish picture stones goes back before the Viking period, beginning around AD 400; the Gotlanders at first used these stones as grave markers, but, as with the inscribed rune stones found across Sweden, they were increasingly set up at the roadside to draw attention to the person they commemorated. In the Viking world it was entirely appropriate that the journey to the next world should be aboard a ship, even if not everyone merited the elaborate ship burials that were already conducted by the Angles in England. If one could not be buried in a ship, then to be buried under or near a stone that displayed a ship in bright colours was the next best option. In the Bronze Age (before about 500 BC), the Gotlanders already buried their dead in boat-shaped graves lined with stone, and there and on the mainland carvings on rock showing oared ships were common currency. The picture stones from the Viking period include sails and rigging, and are detailed enough to show that sails were being made out of strips of cloth plaited together, because local looms could not produce single pieces of cloth wide enough to serve as sails. Plaiting was a more efficient way of bonding the strips than sewing, because it meant that there were no seams and the wind would not tear the sail apart; in the 1980s a replica Gotlandish boat was built and sailed all the way to Istanbul, and its plaited sails, though heavy, were well up to the task and did not disintegrate. The strips out of which sails were made were of different colours, arranged in a lozenge or chessboard pattern; the striped sails beloved of modern film-makers did exist, but appear less often.[37] More importantly, the masts that carried these sails were now sturdy enough to function as the main source of propulsion when the wind was favourable.

Such advances in shipping technology rendered possible the great Viking voyages in the North Sea and the Atlantic. The Vikings continued the tradition of clinker-built ships, constructing the hull out of overlapping strakes before they inserted a relatively light frame which was bonded to the hull by rivets or nails.[38] As has been seen, this method of shipbuilding produced flexible boats that were well suited to the high seas of the Atlantic. Fortunately, several magnificent examples survive, of which the oldest is the Oseberg ship from Norway, built out of oak around 820 and used for a ship burial roughly fourteen years after that; one of the two skeletons found in the boat was that of a woman who died around the age of eighty, and must have been either a queen or a high priestess.[39] The Oseberg ship was excavated at the start of the twentieth century, and nearly all the original boat survives; in addition to superb carvings decorating the prow and stern, it contained a burial chamber with a wonderful assortment of grave goods. On the other hand, its mast cannot have been particularly strong, and its low sides made it unsuitable for journeys across the high seas. It has been suggested that it was a 'royal yacht', used for display, but rarely sent out to sea. It is 21.5 metres long and a maximum of 4.2 metres wide, and there were fifteen oar-holes on each side, as well as a steering oar, so the size of its crew can easily be calculated.[40] Another very fine ship, the Gokstad ship, unearthed around the same time, is a little longer and wider, with one more oar-hole on each side; this was constructed towards the end of the ninth century and buried around 910; its sides were built up rather higher, and the fact that little round shutters were attached to each oar-hole, so they could be closed off in high seas, suggests that this vessel did venture across the ocean. The mast and keel were strong enough to take the strain of a large and heavy sail.[41] But whether its greater seaworthiness compared to the Oseberg ship reflects increasing sophistication in shipbuilding, or whether it reflects different use, cannot be said for certain.

In the early ninth century, it is quite likely that Viking ships were used indiscriminately for raiding and trading. The Oseberg, Gokstad and other ships offered plenty of space in their hull for the storage of goods, whether obtained by trade or seized as booty. The 'longship' was well suited to quick and devastating ventures across the open sea, and it could penetrate deep into rivers such as the Thames and the Seine, allowing its crew to wreak havoc far inland. The sturdiest Viking warships reached Spain and entered the Mediterranean. The geographer az-Zuhrī, who wrote in Muslim Spain (al-Andalus) in the mid-twelfth century, knew of Viking raids by Viking ships in earlier times:

> There used to come from this sea [the Atlantic] large ships which the people of al-Andalus called *qarāqīr*. They were big ships with square sails, and could sail either forwards or backwards. They were manned by people called *majūs*, who were fierce, brave and strong, and excellent seamen. They

only appeared every six or seven years, never in less than forty ships and sometimes up to one hundred. They overcame anyone they met at sea, robbed them and took them captive.[42]

The term *qarāqīr* passed into European languages as 'carrack', though carracks were late medieval cargo ships that looked quite different to Viking longships. The fearsome nature of these people was further emphasized by the use of the term *majūs* to describe them; originally applied to Zoroastrian magicians (or Magi), it was now being applied to ruthless heathens from the edges of the known world. The terror they brought with them extended as far as southern Spain.[43] In 844 they sailed by way of Lisbon and Cádiz to the mouth of the Guadalquivir River, and then made their way, still aboard their ships, to Seville, where they are said to have looted the city for a whole week, enslaving or killing men, women and children – modern research shows, however, that the often lurid descriptions of the havoc they created are embroidered accounts of embroidered accounts of embroidered accounts of an attack that did, for sure, take place.[44]

This ability to reach southern Spain, and on later occasions the Mediterranean as well, speaks for advanced skills in navigation, although the *leiðarstein*, or lodestone, a very basic form of compass, is only mentioned in texts from the fourteenth century or later. It is a little more likely that Norsemen navigated with the *sólarstein*, also, however, first mentioned in texts from the late Middle Ages: these were light-sensitive crystals of cordierite that enabled sailors to locate the sun even through thick cloud; an Icelandic saga relates how a king challenged a certain Sigurð to tell him where, above snow-laden clouds, the sun actually stood. Sigurð was sure he knew, and so the king asked for the 'sun stone' to be brought, which enabled him to verify Sigurð's claim: 'then the king made them fetch the solar stone and held it up and saw where light radiated from the stone and thus directly verified Sigurð's prediction.' Viking navigators were helped on their way at night by close observation of the Polar Star, while in the Faroes the inhabitants developed a system for measuring the declination of the sun over the year, though, once again, it may not have been known to their Viking ancestors.[45]

The discovery of a group of ships at Skuldelev near Roskilde in Denmark has enlarged our understanding of the types and functions of the vessels used in this period. Roskilde lies at the end of a short and shallow fjord, and at some point in the Viking age several ships were scuttled to block sea access to Roskilde itself.[46] These ships, which survive in a much more fragmentary state than those preserved in Oslo, were built rather later than the Oseberg and Gokstad ships, and several date roughly from the time of the Norman Conquest of England – the Bayeux Tapestry includes images of ships not very different from the Roskilde ones, though one especially large longship from Roskilde may have been constructed somewhat earlier in the eleventh century for King Cnut, ruler of Denmark, Norway and England, or for one of his successors.[47] Cargo ships, less obviously associated with the image of Viking marauders, have received less attention, but one of the ships found at Skuldelev was a cargo boat, eleven metres long, and built in western Norway in the early eleventh century. It is thought to have been manned by only a dozen oarsmen, though it also had a mast, and its shallow draft was well suited for navigation around the sandbanks and creeks of the Danish and Frisian coasts. Another, rather larger, Skuldelev ship built out of Norwegian pine in the early eleventh century had a carrying capacity of about twenty-five tons, and sat lower in the water, so that it would have needed to make use of the jetties at Haithabu or other ports it might have visited; and Haithabu has yielded fragments of a trading vessel that might have been able to load as much as sixty tons of cargo. This is the type of ship that would have been described as a *knǫrr*; they were ocean-going cargo ships that were well suited to voyages to Iceland and beyond, carrying not just colonists but cattle and even household furniture. The deeper draught of the *knǫrr* made it much safer in unpredictable seas.[48] Scandinavian ships, whether they were built for war or trade, possessed flexible shells of a sort that seems not to have been perpetuated in later centuries. As ships grew in size, so did it become necessary to make them sturdier. Lightness gave way to solidity.

In the early days of the Viking raids, then, light longships best suited the tactics of hit-and-run raiders who swooped down on the monasteries of Northumbria or the little ports of northern France. With the growth of Haithabu and the emergence of a lively trading network which in some respects replicated that of the Frisian merchants, it became more likely that the colourful Scandinavian sail poking over the horizon belonged to a rather tubby cargo boat whose passengers proposed to pay for what they wanted, rather than seizing it, and who were Christian rather than pagan. Moreover, these ships, whether longships or cargo vessels, were making more and more ambitious voyages, carrying them over the top of Scotland and out of the North Sea, towards Orkney, Shetland, the Faroes, Iceland, and far beyond. This was the ocean that, in Norse mythology, was encompassed by the vast body of the Miðgarðr serpent; when the monster released its tail from its mouth, the world would come to an end. These were risky waters.[49]

20

New Island Worlds

I

It has been seen that the attack on Lindisfarne Abbey in 793 attracted special attention because it was the work of heathen raiders who dese-crated a Christian shrine. That does not mean that the history of Viking raids began on the north coast of England. Quite probably raids across the North Sea reached Orkney and Shetland before they penetrated Eng-land, and it is even possible that the raiders of 793 arrived from the Scottish isles, rather than from Norway. Heading westwards, Vikings began to harass the Hebrides and to work their way into Irish waters, as far south as the Isle of Man and western Ireland. Under the year 794, the *Annals of Ulster* state that there was 'a laying waste by the heathen of all the islands of Britain'. Viking graves on Orkney and Shetland, and a hoard of silver found in the Shetlands, can be dated back to about 800, while the Scandinavian settlement at Jarlshof in Shetland included a substantial farmhouse that dates back to the early ninth century.[1] This does not prove that the northern isles were settled before raids on England began, but settlement is very likely to have followed a period of raiding and explor-ation, so we can safely say that it was at the northern tip of the British Isles that the Vikings first arrived; and their descendants would remain loyal to the Norwegian Crown right up to the fifteenth century. They created a maritime empire, if that is not too grandiose a term, that stretched down into the Irish Sea, and that was ruled at various times by earls, or *jarls*, of Orkney and by kings of Man.

Neolithic Orkney, with its rich archaeological sites, lay towards the end of the 'Atlantic arc' that stretched all the way down to the coast of Portu-gal. In the early Middle Ages, the importance of Orkney lay not in its position at the end of a line, but its position in the middle of a line; this line linked Norway, Scotland, Ireland, the Faroe Islands, Iceland and lands even beyond that. The islands offered plenty of pasture, and sheep-rearing rather than fishing or agriculture was probably the main activity. Still, as one can see from the career of Svein Asleifarson (mentioned earlier), Vikings living in the Orkneys took care to sow grain and to reap the harvest, in his case between his spring and autumn Viking raids: 'he stayed till the cornfields had been reaped and the grain was safely in. After that he would go raiding again.'[2] With the extension of rule from the Orkneys and Shetland to parts of the Scottish mainland, the supply of food must have been adequate, while heavy cloth could be produced from the wool of local sheep. In Orkney and Shetland, the production of oats increased significantly when the Norse colonists arrived, reflecting its use both as food for humans and as fodder for animals; it is a hardy grain, well suited to a northerly environment. Shellfish were sought out as food, and cod became ever more popular, to judge from finds of fish bones. Linen too was hardy enough to flourish this far north, as archaeological evidence from Quoygrew in the Orkney Islands has revealed.[3] The great virtue of the islands was their strategic position, both from the perspective of naval power and from that of commercial networks – under Norse rule trade links developed towards Ireland and Iceland, Norway and York.[4]

The early history of the Orkney Islands was recorded, with a good amount of elaboration, in the *Orkneyinga Saga*, one of the liveliest of all the Icelandic sagas. There, of course, is the problem, for it was written a long way from Orkney around 1200, which means that its coverage of events in the twelfth century, such as the pilgrimage of Earl Rognvald, is based on exact knowledge; but its account of the ancestors of the first earls of Orkney conjures up fantasies of a half-remembered pagan world in the far north inhabited by Finns and Lapps as well as by Norsemen. Yet the story of how the kings of Norway gained overlordship in the Scottish isles is plausible. In the ninth century King Harald Fairhair became irritated by Viking raiders who set out from Orkney and Shetland, their winter base, and reached as far as Norway itself. Determined to teach these raiders a lesson, the king seized control of lands much further to the west than any of his predecessors, right down to the Isle of Man. He agreed to install a certain Sigurð, whose nephew Rolf later became the first Norse ruler of Normandy, as earl of Orkney and Shetland, and Sigurð then pressed ahead with his own local empire-building; the result was that the shores of Scotland to the south of Orkney, Caithness, fell under Norse rule.[5] Over time, the earls of Orkney would acknowledge the king of the Scots as their overlord in Caithness, while continuing to accept the king of Norway as their overlord in the islands; and this was easier to do as the Scots and the Norwegians sealed their own relationship in marriage alliances – the real problem was not so much rivalry between those two kings, though that

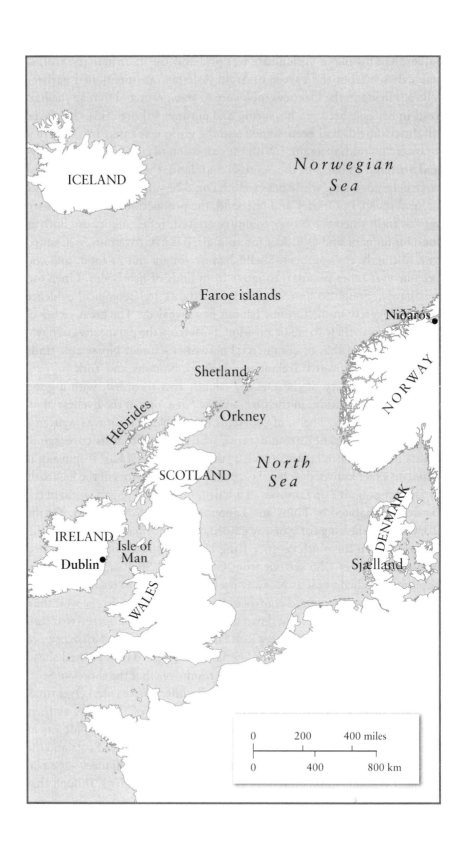

ICELAND

*Norwegian
Sea*

Faroe islands

Niðaros●

NORWAY

Shetland

Hebrides

Orkney

*North
Sea*

SCOTLAND

DENMARK

IRELAND

Isle of
Man

Dublin●

Sjælland

WALES

0	200	400 miles
0	400	800 km

did break out, as the internal strife within Scotland whose ripples sometimes reached as far as the Orcadian realm. The word 'realm' is appropriate, since the authority of the Norwegian king was exercised through what has been called 'indirect lordship', leaving Sigurð's descendants largely free to conduct their own affairs so long as they acknowledged Norwegian supremacy. This continued until 1195, when the king took the islands under direct control. The title *jarl*, or earl, can be translated as 'chieftain' or even 'prince', and a *jarl* was not very different in status from a king. The earls of Orkney, like the kings of Norway, waged gruesome struggles against rivals to gain and hold on to power, and being burned to death in one's house was an occupational hazard, as in other parts of the Norse world.[6]

Sigurð's mainland conquests generated tension with Mælbrigte, earl of the Scots (as the Orkney Saga calls him), and the dispute could only be resolved by battle. Sigurð, victorious, decapitated Mælbrigte and attached his head to the saddle of his own horse. While he was riding around with this ghastly trophy, his leg was grazed by Mælbrigte's tooth, and sepsis set in. Sigurð was soon dead, and although the succession was sorted out, Orkney fell prey to groups of marauding Danes and Norwegians with nicknames such as Tree-Beard and Scurvy who would take up residence on the islands and launch their Viking raids from there.[7] Once order was restored, the Norsemen in Orkney established their own reputation as raiders: 'Earl Havard had a nephew called Einar Buttered-Bread, a respected chieftain with a good following. He used to go plundering in the summer.'[8] At the end of the tenth century the earl of Orkney became involved in bigger issues than control of northern Scotland, as the warlord Olaf Tryggvason went on the rampage in the British Isles, partly on his own account and partly in support of Svein Forkbeard, king of Denmark, who eventually overwhelmed the Anglo-Saxon kingdom and handed it on to his more famous son Cnut.

Olaf was baptized (in the Scilly Isles, if the Orkney Saga is to be believed) and suddenly decided to insist on the baptism of his putative subjects as well. During Olaf's own bid for the crown of Norway, which he held until 1000, his five longships reached Orkney, where they encountered three ships that the current earl of Orkney (another Sigurð) was leading on a Viking raid. Sigurð was summoned to Olaf's ship. 'I want you and all your subjects to be baptized,' Olaf demanded. 'If you refuse, I'll have you killed on the spot, and I swear that I'll ravage every island with fire and steel.' 'After that,' the Orkney Saga tersely relates, 'all Orkney embraced the faith.' This must have made it possible for Sigurð to marry the daughter of Malcolm, king of the Scots; Sigurð's mother was an Irish Christian, and such mixed marriages between Scandinavians and Celts were common in Ireland as well – further evidence that the Viking raiders were often a mixture of Scandinavians, Celts and Celto-Scandinavians. Sigurð's mother, described in the Orkney Saga as a 'sorceress', did not close her mind to magic, and bestowed a magical raven banner on her son; it would bring victory to the person in whose honour it was carried, but death to whoever carried it. Sigurð, on campaign in Ireland following his baptism, found that none of his followers would carry it; so he decided he would have to do so himself, whereupon his mother's prophecy came true, and he was cut down.[9]

Naval power enabled the lords of the isles to hold their own, and to extend the long arms of their reach as far as Man. An eleventh-century earl, Þorfinn, defended his territory in Caithness with 'five well-manned longships', described in the saga as 'a considerable force'. Unfortunately the king of the Scots, Karl Hundason (possibly the king who is also known as Macbeth), came upon his fleet with eleven longships, and their navies engaged:

> Confronting the foe, Þorfinn's
> fleet of five ships
> steered, steadfast in anger
> against Karl's sea-goers.
> Ships grappled
> together; gore, as foes fell,
> bathed stiff iron, black
> with Scots' blood;
> singing the bows spilt
> blood, steel bit; bright
> though the quick points quaked,
> no quenching Þorfinn.[10]

This was a real sea battle, with the ships coming up close to one another and catching hold of the enemy's ships with grappling hooks; after a tough fight, Þorfinn's men tried to gain hold of the king's ship and Þorfinn followed his banner on to the deck of King Karl's longship – Karl escaped, but most of his crew were killed.

Even allowing for some artistic flourishes in the saga's account of this battle, the description of a fight at sea is important, because it proves that warships were not simply used for the rapid transport of warriors and their booty, but were used as platforms on which to fight bitter contests in open waters. If we take the size of the Oseberg ship as a very rough guide, we can expect that about thirty oarsmen powered each vessel, though there must have been other troops on board as well, ready to change shift. This might leave us with a figure of about 300 warriors in Þorfinn's company, with more than twice as many in King Karl's fleet, so it is possible that around 1,000 troops were involved in this sea battle, and at the very least half that number. Þorfinn became one of the most successful and most powerful earls of Orkney, exercising control in the Hebrides and even in parts of northern Ireland. His career demonstrates how the Orkney islands were very well situated as bases for control of much wider spaces of ocean.

The strategic significance of Orkney was not lost on the kings of Norway. In 1066 Harald Hardraða decided to support the claims of Tostig, who was challenging the right of his half-brother Harold Godwinsson to the throne of England. The Norwegian king took ship for Shetland and Orkney, collecting new recruits to his army there, before edging his way southwards to defeat and death at Stamford Bridge in October 1066. At that time power in Orkney was shared between two brothers; they too had accompanied Harald to Yorkshire, but they survived the invasion, only to find themselves outmanoeuvred by a later king of Norway, Magnus Barelegs (d. 1103), who decided to impose Norwegian rule over a wide swathe of territory stretching as far as Anglesey; he set out with a fleet in 1098. He deported the two earls from Orkney and installed his young son in their place, though he placed the government of the islands in the hands of regents. His reversal of earlier policy, which had left the earls responsible for the day-to-day running of Orkney and Shetland, formed part of these wider ambitions, for he needed a naval base from which he could control lands further away. Meanwhile he took with him to Wales the heirs to the earldom, one of whom, Magnus Erlendsson, proved irritatingly unco-operative:

> When the troops were getting their weapons ready for battle, Magnus Erlendsson settled down in the main cabin and refused to arm himself. The king asked him why he was sitting around and his answer was that he had no quarrel with anyone there. 'That's why I have no intention of fighting,' he said. 'If you haven't the guts to fight,' said the king, 'and in my opinion this has nothing to do with your faith, get below. Don't lie there under everybody's feet.' Magnus Erlendsson took out his psalter and chanted psalms throughout the battle, but refused to take cover.[11]

This was an early sign that Magnus was destined for sainthood; in Orkney some years later, as disputes with his co-earl flared, his rival's chief cook stove his head in, and he became a martyr for the faith, capable of working miracles. Whether or not his life was as holy as his supporters insisted, the cathedral that was built in Orkney was named in his honour, and his wrecked skull has been unearthed in the church.[12] Magnus Barelegs 'took an intense dislike to him', even though young Magnus was his cupbearer. As the fleet moved northwards past Scotland, Magnus Erlendsson was able to sneak away at night and swam to shore. He was in his night clothes, and he scratched his bare feet badly as he stumbled through the undergrowth. That morning at breakfast the king noticed his absence and sent a man to his bunk to find him. When they discovered that he was no longer on board they sent a search party out on land, supported by bloodhounds; but young Magnus was up a tree and he scared off the one dog that had found him. He made his way to the Scottish court and to England and Wales, where he was made welcome, and awaited the news of King Magnus' death.[13]

The king was more interested, however, in gaining Anglesey, 'which lies as far south as any region ever ruled by the former kings of Norway and comprises a third part of Wales' – that, at least, is what the anonymous saga-writer believed.[14] Magnus' intervention in the Isle of Man formed part of a wider contest for control of this small but strategically valuable territory, with its command over access to central and southern Ireland; there was a local king, Guðroð Crovan, who reigned from 1079 to 1095, and who was of mixed Norse and Irish descent, while enough Gaelic names have been found on inscriptions from the island to indicate that either the old population or Irish settlers played a large part in the life of Man. After his death, Magnus saw an opportunity to gain control, but his plans were challenged by Irish rivals, and by 1103 Guðroð's son was in charge, founding a line of succession that lasted until 1265.[15] However, Man was only the key to a vaster space, and King Magnus of Norway had limitless ambitions. It was even alleged that the king was being urged to avenge the death of his grandfather Harald Hardraða by invading England. Later, in 1103, he was to die in battle in Ulster.[16] Magnus Barelegs was one of a series of Norwegian kings who, during the eleventh century, transformed the predatory and diffuse raiding of the Vikings into a co-ordinated project: there were still plenty of opportunities for booty and glory, but control of the Norse expeditions was becoming centralized, and raids were now a means by which royal power was extended across the north Atlantic, though with questionable success: after Barelegs was killed the Orkney islands reverted to rule by local earls.

How Norse rule affected these islands, and other British islands that came under Norwegian sovereignty such as the Hebrides, is not entirely clear. The pre-existing native population may well have been enslaved or absorbed through intermarriage. Ancient Celtic systems of land division were perpetuated. On the other hand, there is no evidence for the survival of Celtic Christianity in these islands after the Norse conquest; as with the Anglo-Saxon conquest of England, paganism triumphed for a while, and the conversion of Sigurð is not likely to have brought the old cult to an end – more important in that respect was the spread of the cult of St Magnus, which gave Orkney, and the Orcadians, a distinct religious identity. That the Norse character of the Orkneys and Shetlands is not a modern affectation should be clear from the long survival of a Norse dialect, Norn, in the islands; it only died out in the mid-nineteenth century, and appears to have been spoken across the water in Caithness during the Middle Ages, in the mainland territories under Orcadian rule.[17]

The distinctive mixture of Norse and Celtic culture can be seen most clearly in Ireland, whose very name was forged by the Vikings.[18] Rather than chronicling the successive waves of Viking attacks on Ireland, it makes sense to look at the pattern of Norse penetration into that country. It is striking that the early raids, at the very end of the eighth century, came down from the north, as Viking ships swept down the great arc linking the fjords of Norway to Orkney, the Hebrides and then down to Ulster and as far south as the Isle of St Patrick (Inispatrick), close to the site of what would become the major seat of Norse power in Ireland, Dublin. Not surprisingly, early targets included monasteries, even though the Vikings also carried away women and children, whom they enslaved; many of these women gave birth to a new generation of Vikings who were of mixed ancestry. A major settlement lay at *Duibhlinn*, 'Blackpool', but other towns as well as Dublin, right across the island, owe their origins to the Vikings. They were thus creators as well as destroyers. Endemic warfare between the different Irish kings was complicated by the involvement of Scandinavian settlers, who were sometimes the target of Irish attacks, but who were increasingly active alongside Celtic armies. In 871 a boastful Scandinavian warlord named Ivar styled himself 'king of the Norsemen of all Ireland and Britain'. Yet by the middle of the tenth century the Norse in Ireland were at each other's throats, even though Dublin flourished as a great centre of trade within the Irish Sea – some of this trade being fed, to be sure, by plunder from continuing raids deep into the island and across the sea towards Wales, for Welsh captives were in good supply in its slave market.[19]

The Viking raids caused great damage to the flourishing Celtic Church on the island, even though the Scandinavians learned something from the intricate styles of decoration in the fine manuscripts they pillaged; 'Viking art' was not immune to Celtic influences. When the Irish king and 'high priest' Brian Boru led his armies to victory over the Norsemen at Clontarf in 1014 (though he himself died in the battle), the Norse were not expunged from Ireland. They continued to meld into Irish society, and one of the most significant markers of their assimilation was the adoption of the religion they had so mercilessly pillaged: Christianity was restored throughout the island, but it also needs to be said that Irish kings had seen the rich monasteries of Ireland as fair game, and the devastation reported in the Irish annals was as often the work of Celtic as of Norse armies.[20]

II

It is a moot point whether one can seriously use the word 'Viking' to describe the complex maritime world that was brought into being across the northern Atlantic by Norse settlers in long-inhabited lands such as Orkney and in barely inhabited lands such as Iceland and Greenland, where the Norse created brand new societies on virgin soil. The age of the marauders was still far from over when Greenland and North America were discovered; but Greenland was inhabited by the Norse for over 400 years, long past the time when violent Viking raids occurred. Moreover, the term does harm by emphasizing images of violence that appeal to those who like their history well spattered with blood. In Iceland, certainly, bloody conflicts between neighbours, conjured into the vivid tales of the sagas, show that Norse men, and indeed Norse women, were perfectly capable of creating havoc at home, without needing to take their weapons across the open seas. But settled societies did emerge out in the Atlantic, prospering through trade: in the Faroes, in Iceland and in Greenland.

The colonization of the Faroe Islands is said to have begun under Harald Fairhair at the end of the ninth century, a good hundred years after the first raids on England, so it probably resulted from King Harald's attempt to impose rule across great swathes of Norway, and from the decision of unruly Norsemen to escape from the taxes he was trying to impose.[21] On the other hand, the first colonist mentioned in the admittedly jumbled saga record was a certain Grim Kamban, whose second name is Gaelic, which suggests once again that there had been a continuous injection of Celtic blood into the Norse community ever since the Scandinavians entered British waters. The other implication is that many of the early settlers came not from Norway but from the Scottish isles, Ireland and the growing 'Viking diaspora'. The obvious attraction of this chain of rocky islands was pasture, and the meaning of the name Faroe is 'sheep island', *Færeyjar*.[22] Cultivable land is very limited, amounting to only 5 per cent today, but there was plenty of driftwood available, which was carried across from America, while better-quality timber had to be brought from Norway or Britain. There was nothing to take away as Viking booty. The climate was milder than one might expect so far north, as the Faroes are bathed by warm currents coming across the Atlantic.[23]

Whether or not these islands had been seen by Pytheas centuries earlier, the only regular visitors when the Norse settlers began to take an interest in them were Irish hermits, who may already have been living in the Faroes by 700. It is now known, from the carbon-dating of some peat ash and burnt barley grain, that there were settlers there in the fourth to sixth centuries, and again in the couple of centuries thereafter, but their presence was almost certainly spasmodic – conceivably they were seasonal migrants moving north from Shetland.[24] They were not sitting on the spectacular wealth that had been accumulated in abbeys such as Lindisfarne. According to the Irish monk and geographer Dicuil, the monks still felt threatened by the occasional Viking visits to their remote hermitages:

> On these islands hermits sailing from our country Scotia [Ireland] have lived for nearly a hundred years. But just as they were always deserted from the beginning of the world, so now because of the Norse pirates they are emptied of anchorites and filled with countless sheep and a great variety of sea fowls.[25]

The anchorites would have brought sheep to the islands, and these, along with seabirds, eggs and fish, provided them with a rich diet; moreover, just about every part of a sheep can be used for some purpose, whether making cloth, fashioning tools out of bone, manufacturing cheese, butter and tallow, or (less likely among the monks) a feast of roasted lamb. Whales were driven ashore, a thirteenth-century Faroese law code says, but once they were above the high-water mark the owner of the land could claim a large share of the animal, and the hunters would only receive one quarter.[26]

These references to ancient anchorites raise issues concerning the voyages of the Irish monks, which have generated an interest out of proportion to their real significance. One of them, St Brendan, has been presented as the first navigator to cross the Atlantic, so that the Irish voyages have become entangled with the hoary, and in many ways unenlightening, question of who reached America first. Irish saints' lives tell of adventurous monks who, in their wish to escape normal human company, set out in small leather-hulled currachs for islands in the open sea, from at least the sixth century onwards: 'thrice twenty men who went with Brendan to seek the land of promise', to cite an ancient document known as the *Litany of Oengus*. St Brendan became associated with a good many points along the western flank of Ireland and Scotland which he is said to have visited in the early sixth century. The list is so long that it sounds as if it was formed out of 'the collective sea experience of successive generations of Irish mariners', which suggests that one or another Irish saint did indeed set foot at these places.[27] In other words, St Brendan the Navigator was not one person but several, based on the image of a real Brendan of Clonfert (the home of a monastic school), who inspired his followers to take ship with him and sail into the open ocean. Brendan was of noble birth – indeed, his birth in the Irish kingdom of Munster was accompanied by miracles and prophecies.[28]

Brendan's search for paradise is recorded in the short text known as the *Navigatio Brendani*, which tells how Brendan was inspired by the stories of the adventures at sea of a fellow monk to find some of the communities that were said to be scattered across the open ocean. He decided to take fourteen monks on his own expedition to find the 'Land of the Promise of the Saints', but all the detail in the text is generic: rocky islands with steep cliffs; islands crowded with flocks of pure white sheep; a barren island that proved to be the back of a whale; an island where the birds sang psalms in praise of Jerusalem for an hour; but also an island inhabited by devout monks who never suffered from illness and never grew old, and another one inhabited by three classes, boys, young men and old men – the absence of women does make one wonder where all the boys came from. The *Navigatio Brendani* eloquently portrays the dangers of the seas, such as fogs and waterspouts, not to mention battling sea monsters and angry savages on remote shores, as well as 'Judas the most miserable of men', who was given a day's rest from the torments of Hell every Easter Sunday.[29] It is hard to see how anyone can read the description of Brendan's voyage as an account of a real journey across the Atlantic, rather than a series of exhortations about the life a devout monk should lead.

Monks did set off across the open sea without much idea of where they were heading, other than a desire to find 'a desert in the ocean' (sought out by a certain Baitán), or Cormac ui Liatháin, who repeatedly set out in his currach on a voyage that took him from Ireland up to Orkney; Cormac also penetrated far into the ocean, without finding land, but turned back when he was confronted by a great shoal of red jellyfish.[30] Another intrepid monk, St Columba, sailed 'through all the islands of the ocean', according to his Irish biographer, and once again communities of monks came into being on the spurs of rock and offshore islands that he visited, including the windswept Aran Islands off the coast of Galway and Skye off western Scotland. These achievements are certainly more credible than those attributed to St Brendan; and the voyages were the work not just of the famous monks celebrated in the saints' tales but of their crews (presumably monks) as well, for, paradoxically, the foundation of solitary hermitages on remote islands had to be teamwork. On the other hand, through its popularity the tale of St Brendan stimulated speculation about what lay out in the Atlantic Ocean, and ideas about Islands of the Blessed, which were fed by classical as well as by Christian writings, continued to fascinate medieval navigators throughout the Middle Ages; the isles supposedly visited by St Brendan were freely confused with the Canary Islands, for instance.[31] Rather than those sunny islands, which were already inhabited by Berbers, the Irish monks found distinctly cooler places in the north Atlantic: first the Faroes, and then Iceland.

Settlement by monks was obviously incapable of generating permanent colonies, unless there was a constant stream of new arrivals (rather as the monastic houses on Mount Athos are sustained to this day). Unfortunately for the monks, the new arrivals, who did bring women with them, were pagan Scandinavians. The paganism of the first Norse settlers in the Faroes is reflected in the name of the capital, Torshavn, 'Thor's harbour'. However, the islands had accepted Christianity by the early eleventh century, possibly at the insistence of the same Olaf Tryggvason who had engineered the Christianization of the Orkney Islands. They eventually fell under the ecclesiastical control of the archbishop of Niðaros (modern Trondheim), which was the northernmost archdiocese in the world. This encroachment reflected the growing power of the Norwegian monarchy in the north Atlantic during the late twelfth century, but until then the Faroe islanders managed their own affairs at the annual parliament, or Þing, which was dominated by the wealthiest local families. These islands did not possess the strategic advantages that had made possession of the Orkneys a matter of close interest to the Norwegian court. Even when shipping from Norway to Iceland became very regular, the direct route bypassed the Faroes, although once a route from Norway to Greenland had become established ships did stop there. All this may lead to the con-clusion that the Faroes were not of major significance; but their interest lies in the creation of a brand new society on what was to all intents empty land (the sheep apart), a social experiment that was to be repeated on a much larger scale in Iceland.[32]

III

Iceland has been described as the 'highest point' of Norse civilization, not just because there were virtually no previous inhabitants to disturb, but because of its cultural achievements, represented by the remarkable saga literature, recited in dark winters when Icelanders took the opportunity to recall and to embroider their past history, and that of their ancestors in Scandinavia. The sagas are one of the great literary achievements of the Middle Ages, and all the more extraordinary for having been produced almost at the limits of the world then known to Latin Christendom.[33] Iceland was probably discovered from the Faroes. The stories that survive about the discovery of Iceland tell one more, no doubt, about the twelfth, thirteenth and fourteenth centuries, when they were recorded, than they do about the ninth century – more about an island under increasing threat of a takeover by the Norwegian crown than about an earlier community of independent farmers and sailors. Thus there is an emphasis in many of the texts on the tyranny of Harald Fairhair, king of Norway, but perhaps the Icelandic authors had contemporary Norwegian kings in mind instead.[34]

In one reasonably plausible version, preserved in an Icelandic history of the 'land-taking', or *Landnám*, a settler in the Faroes named Naddoð was swept off course early in the ninth century and came upon a land in the far north; noticing snow on the mountains, he named it *Snæland*, 'Snowland'. Another story tells of a sea-roving Swede named Garðar Svávarsson who lived on the Danish island of Sjælland (Zealand), although his wife came from the Hebrides; he had heard about 'Snowland', and his mother, a sorceress, urged him to go and look for it. He sailed all round Iceland, proving that it was an island, and then he spent what must have been a tough winter there in a roughly built house. Later, his son travelled to Iceland, hoping that the Norwegian king would make him its earl, rather as earls had been appointed in Orkney, but this idea did not meet with the approval of the other settlers, who had arrived with him and who were careful to keep Norwegian power at arm's length.

Both Naddoð and Garðar thought very highly of the land they had discovered. This was not true of a 'great Viking', Flóki Vilgerðarson, whose visit to Iceland ended in disaster when his men failed to make hay and all his sheep died from lack of fodder; meanwhile he and his companions had been happily living off fish and had failed to think about their animals. 'When asked about the place, he gave it a bad name.' That name, Iceland, is the one that stuck. Finally, according to Icelandic writers, a certain Ingolf Arnarson was inspired by news of Flóki's discovery to look for Iceland, and when he had scouted out the south coast he returned to Norway, and then went back with his foster-brother, a Viking raider named Hjǫrleif, some time around 870; Ingolf took care to sacrifice to the gods before setting out, and once he was close to shore he threw into the sea the high-seat pillars that had been set up in his house back home.

These were pillars that were placed either side of the ceremonial seat of the head of a Norse household, and they would probably have been carved with images of Thor and other gods. He watched to see where they would land, for this would reveal where the gods were sending him (they ended up at the spot that is now the capital of Iceland, Reykjavík, 'Smoke Inlet', named no doubt after the steam rising from its hot springs). His brother had not bothered to sacrifice and was set upon by his slaves. They were furious because he had yoked them to his plough, for lack of enough oxen – he had only brought one along with him. They seized the women and goods in Hjǫrleif's ship; but when his own slaves found Hjǫrleif's battered body, Ingolf was horrified at what had happened, chased after the slaves, and killed all of them.[35] It is impossible to prove that events unfolded in quite this way, but the image of a ship arriving loaded with some farm animals, supplies, slaves and women (whether free or enslaved) is credible.

The land they had discovered lies athwart the tectonic North American and European plates, though this does not mean that half of Iceland is geologically part of America, since the island was spewed out of the sea (as were the Faroes) by volcanic eruptions that continue to this day. Unlike other volcanic areas, it is not particularly fertile, owing to its location just below the Arctic Circle; but much more pasture land existed when the Norse settlers arrived than can be found nowadays, and the effects of overgrazing were soon felt – sheep grazed lands that had little time to recover from the harsh island winters. Farmers harvested grass and made it into hay; some barley was produced, but the islanders had to import grain, or else had to feed themselves from their sheep and from the rich local wildlife: seabirds and their eggs; seals; whales too – 'Þorgils worked hard at acquiring provisions, and every year he went out to the Strands, an area on the northern tip of Iceland. There he collected wild foods and found whales as well as other driftage.' One summer he found a beached whale, but a pair of dishonest traders, landless men, arrived in their cargo ship and tried to take control of the parts of the whale that Þorgils and his companions had not already cut up. A fight broke out and Þorgils was killed.[36] Whales were valued for their blubber as well as their meat, while walrus had the additional advantage of ivory.[37]

The first settlers left Norway not in Viking longboats but in tubby *knǫrr*s, sailing vessels that were capable of carrying thirty tons of goods, sheep and whatever else the colonists required to build a life from scratch. For they were leaving their old home for good. Some of the settlers came on ships they already owned, so these people were not impoverished refugees; rather, it seems, they were escaping the tough regime of Harald

Fairhair.[38] Maybe 20,000 people, and certainly more than 10,000 people, migrated to the island between about 870 and about 930, principally from Norway, although the colonists also included Swedes, Danes and people of mixed Norse and Celtic origin. DNA testing has revolutionized our understanding of the ancestry of the Icelanders, particularly now that it is possible to trace both matrilineal and patrilineal ancestry (through analysis of mitochondrial DNA and Y-chromosomes respectively). About two thirds of modern male Icelanders appear to be of Norse descent, and one third of Celtic descent; but when one looks at the matrilineal line the proportions are reversed. This confirms how very substantial the Celtic element was, represented by female slaves whose children by free parents were accepted into Icelandic society, as well as by the Celtic wives of Vikings from the Scottish isles and Ireland. A similar picture can be drawn in both the Faroes and the Western Isles of Scotland (but not in Orkney and Shetland, where matrilineal and patrilineal lines are to an equal extent of Norse origin, suggesting that entire families migrated from Norway, not just warrior males).[39] The name of the hero of one of the finest of the Icelandic sagas, Njáll, is of Irish origin (Niall, Neil). The Icelandic records of settlement from the twelfth and thirteenth centuries also mention Irish settlers, *Iskr*, such as a certain Ketill; and most of the slaves who arrived against their will were probably Celtic too.[40] It is generally accepted that by the end of the eleventh century there were about 40,000 people living in Iceland, and maybe even twice that number. They could benefit from the fact that the climate was relatively benign in this phase of the Middle Ages, but even so there were occasional famines caused by volcanic ash, a bad summer and the failure of supplies to arrive from Norway. The life of the Icelanders was not exactly precarious, but (as in much of western Europe) it was all too easy to run out of basic food supplies.[41]

As in the Faroes, the first settlers found some inhabitants, people they called the *papar*, and these too were Celts, more Irish hermits who left their imprint on the island not in the bloodline but in place names such as Papey, a small island off southern Iceland. Some of them migrated back and forth each year in their simple leather boats, avoiding the Icelandic winter, and probably guided by their faith more than by sophisticated navigation. Dicuil, the Irish monk whose description of the Faroes has already been cited, marvelled at the midnight sun: 'a man could do whatever he wished as though the sun were still there, even remove lice from his shirt, and, if one stood on a mountain-top, the sun perhaps would still be visible to him.'[42] Irish monks returning from Iceland may have carried with them tales of a land of fire and ice that fed the appetite of Irish listeners, and it has been suggested that the Irish monks first learned of the existence of Iceland when Arctic mirages projected an image of the coast of Iceland as far south as the Faroes, which can happen soon after dawn at that latitude.[43]

The *landnám*, the Norse settlement of the land, was recorded with great care in later Icelandic tradition. For the land was divided up according to strict rules; and a curious tradition attributes the division of the land to the king they were trying to escape, Harald Fairhair. He is said to have persuaded the settlers that 'no man should take possession of an area larger than he and his crew could carry fire over in a single day', although female settlers, who were also welcome, could only claim the area they could walk around during a spring day, with a two-year cow in tow.[44] The fundamental principle was that each landowner should be free to run his or her own affairs, subject to the laws that were agreed in the *Alþing*, the parliament that met every June from the year 930 onwards, when there was plenty of light in the sky, and that was attended by the wealthy and powerful landowners known as the *goðar* (literally, 'gods'); they were not just political leaders but priests, charged with maintaining sacrifices and other rituals on behalf of the community over which they presided. It was not the democratic people's assembly that many would like to imagine, but it enabled this distant island to govern itself according to laws its own inhabitants made, without any but the loosest recognition of the authority of the Norwegian king. To describe Iceland as a 'republic' or 'Commonwealth' is therefore quite acceptable.[45]

Most Icelanders were pagan during the first century of the island's history; but there were also Christians who lived there, including many of the settlers and slaves who had come from Ireland. One Norse Christian was Ketill the Fool, so named because his pagan neighbours ridiculed his beliefs. He lived on Church Farm (Kirkjubœr), which had earlier been an Irish hermitage. The story went about that pagans could not live there, and after Ketill died a pagan arrived to occupy his farm. No sooner had he crossed the boundary than he fell dead.[46] With the conversion of Iceland to Christianity in 1000, the *goðar* were not displaced; the landowners built their own churches, seeing them as private property in just the way their pagan shrines had also been their personal possessions. King Olaf of Norway knew that Iceland depended on trade with Scandinavia to keep itself fed, and he banned trade with the island so long as it remained staunchly pagan. This, as much as the longstanding presence of Christians on the island, prompted urgent discussion in the *Alþing*, where the winning argument was that the refusal of pagans and Christians to live together would destroy the entire community. The *Alþing* declared law; but there could only be one law. So it was agreed that baptism would be universal and compulsory, although individuals could still continue to worship the pagan gods privately; they could also carry on eating horse-meat, which was one of the few forbidden foods of the Catholic West. A bishop only arrived in the middle of the eleventh century, and until then the goðar retained religious functions, serving the new religion. As in other parts of the world, religious ideas moved across the sea and helped transform the societies they penetrated. That did not make the Icelanders more peaceful, as one can see from the tales of feuding and violence in the sagas, which hailed from a world that was, by now, Christian, but still well aware of its pagan past and still fascinated by the stories of the Norse gods.[47]

The Faroes and Iceland are precocious examples of a phenomenon that would become widespread in the Atlantic by the end of the Middle Ages: the creation of a brand new society on uninhabited (or virtually uninhabited) islands. In the fifteenth century, the Portuguese became pioneers in exploiting virgin islands. Both the Scandinavians and the Portuguese brought into being societies that were in some respects similar to the mother country, but that all possessed very distinctive features – they were not clones of the Old World. The political structure of Iceland, built around the principle of local autonomy under powerful goðar, expressed a conscious rejection of royal interference; the islanders were trying to create an idealized society, based on the Norway they would have liked to inhabit, and perhaps imagined that their forebears had inhabited before royal power began to intrude into the fjords. Even so, they learned that an annual assembly and a common system of law was necessary to ensure a degree of order among communities riven by feuding and competition for territory. Although they were proud of their autonomy, the Icelanders were also obsessed by the history of the Norse ancestors, to the point where they celebrated Viking raiders and their pagan cult, long after Iceland had accepted Christianity. They told tales about the Norwegian kings and their mental horizons extended as far as Constantinople, Spain and the Baltic. As the next chapter will show, these mental horizons also extended westwards, right across the Atlantic Ocean.

IV

The sea provides a constant backdrop to many of the Icelandic sagas, whether they are concerned with events in Norway and Europe, or with the affairs of Iceland and the lands to the west. Since they were written down in the thirteenth century and after, the sagas tell us more about how Icelanders of the central and later Middle Ages viewed their relationship with the sea than they do about conditions at the time of the first settlement. One of the best-known sagas, *Egil's Saga*, was written down in the early thirteenth century, and is full of tales of bloodthirsty treachery set alongside honourable displays of loyalty. Woven into its fabric are matter-of-fact accounts of conditions at sea as its main characters journeyed from Norway to Iceland, supposedly at the time when Harald Fairhair was imposing his will on the Norwegians, leading his opponents to seek their fortune in distant lands. Thus Kveldulf, a sea captain, dies on board his ship and his body is cast overboard in a coffin. The ship approaches Iceland with an accompanying vessel and enters a fjord, but before the crews can steer to land heavy rain and fog separate the two ships and they lose sight of one another. Then when the weather turns better they wait for the tide and float their ships upriver, beach their boats and unload their cargo. As they explore the shoreline they find Kveldulf's coffin where it has washed ashore and place it under a mound of stones.[48] This series of events, told to add local colour to a much bigger story of rivalries among the settlers, surely reflects the everyday experiences of travellers from Norway to Iceland.

Notable too is a casual account of how a ship bound from Shetland to Iceland, with a crew of men who had not sailed the route before, was blown quickly across the ocean towards its destination, but was then caught by a contrary wind and sent westwards beyond the island.[49] These contrary winds or dense fogs would, as will be seen, lead to some extraordinary discoveries in the waters to the west of Iceland. An image that must be from the thirteenth century shows how trading ships would arrive and be berthed in rivers, channels and streams.[50] Another image, perhaps from earlier centuries, presents Egil as a Viking who goes plundering and killing as far away as the Baltic, along the coast of Courland, in present-day Latvia, though by the thirteenth century Scandinavians (mainly Danes and Swedes) were still raiding the Baltic coasts, now under the banner of crusades. Egil is said to have burned down the house of a prosperous Courland farmer who was drinking with his companions, and thought nothing, apparently, of killing all these people; he had, however, seized a treasure chest which turned out to be full of silver. After that he decamped to Denmark: 'they all sailed to Denmark later that summer and sat in ambush for merchant ships, robbing wherever they could.'[51] On another occasion, Egil visited the English king, Athelstan, who presented him with 'a good merchant vessel, and a cargo to go with it. The bulk of the cargo was wheat and honey.'[52] This and other Icelandic sagas are impregnated with the smell of the sea.

Yet Iceland did not, at this period, possess any towns; nor did there exist a distinct group of merchants whose livelihood was derived solely from trade, even though those who raided also traded, sometimes to sell their plunder, and sometimes to make some profit on the side.[53] Norway, it is true, possessed very few towns in the Viking period – the foundation of Niðaros on the site of present-day Trondheim was a deliberate royal act, providing an opportunity to detach the Church in Norway from the oversight of the see of Lund, which (though now part of Sweden) then lay in Danish territory. There were one or two trading stations, such as that at Kaupang, near Oslo, which was well situated for access to the silver and other fine items coming up through the rivers of eastern Europe in the early Viking age. By the thirteenth century, though, Bergen had become an important centre both of royal power and of North Sea trade, with 5,000–10,000 inhabitants, and it established itself as the major port for the Iceland trade.[54] This trade had several peculiarities. The Icelanders did not mint coins, though they were happy to use hack silver. If you wanted to buy goods on the island, you normally resorted to barter. But as trade with Norway took off in the eleventh and twelfth centuries it became obvious that some sort of standard of value was needed. Since the major Icelandic product that was in demand in Scandinavia was the heavy woollen cloth known as *vaðmal* that is still the most prized export of the island, this was chosen. *Vaðmal* made up in warmth for what it lacked in softness. The ell, or *ǫln*, was adopted as the standard measurement of cloth; it is said to have been based on the length of the arm of King Henry I of England, from his elbow to his fingertips. Two ells made a yard. The *Alþing* decreed that all *vaðmal* woven in Iceland would be two ells broad; a piece of cloth measuring two ells by six counted as a 'legal ounce' of silver, though over time there were changes in ratios and different types of ells as well – the fundamental point is that the 'money' of early Iceland consisted of pieces of woven cloth. Documents sometimes speak of *vaðmal* cloth as a monetary unit, and sometimes as a physical article of trade.[55] Overall, the system seems to have worked well – better, anyway, than having to depend on imported (or plundered) silver. Sheep were Iceland's silver mines.

Cargo ships of the *knǫrr* type found near Roskilde (Skuldelev I) could carry about three tons of *vaðmal*, thirty tons of fine meal grain or five tons of coarse unmilled barley, and grain was one of the European products that the Icelanders craved, for lack of suitable soil at home. The Icelanders were familiar with a variety of ships, operated increasingly by Norwegians rather than by islanders; after all, wood was in poor supply on the island, as was metal for nails and rivets and much else that was needed in shipbuilding. As well as the *knǫrr* they were visited by the *búza*, or buss, a ship with high gunwales that was better suited to rough seas, and that came into fashion in the early eleventh century; its high sides meant that there was a deeper hold, with more space for cargo, but its deeper draft, accentuated by its heavier cargo, made this type of ship slower and less well suited to the shallow waters in which the *knǫrrs* tied up. Still, the use of bigger ships shows that this trade was growing in value.[56] Above all, this was entirely licit trade, in an age when piracy was rampant, and it took place under the protection of the king of Norway, who had his uses even for republican-minded Icelanders. Around 1022 the king of Norway entered into a commercial treaty with Iceland, to guarantee the arrival of woollen cloth in return for grain. Icelanders visiting Norway were to be granted the same privileges as free Norwegians; they could even take wood and water from the king's forests; the interests of Norwegians visiting Iceland were also protected, for instance their property was to be kept safe if they died there. Admittedly, the Icelanders did have to pay quite heavy landing fees in Norway (in *vaðmal* should they so wish); but the king would not interfere even when they traded with third countries. This agreement remained in force for a couple of centuries, and its origins no doubt lay in an attempt by the king to demonstrate his authority over Iceland, though in the most benign way.[57]

Providing grain to Iceland became less attractive as Norway's population grew, and as its new towns placed pressure on food supplies. The English, who exported grain to Norway, came to the rescue; Egil's going-away present from the king of England was, as has been seen, a boat loaded mainly with wheat.[58] In 1189 a priest turned up in Bergen aboard a ship that had set out from England loaded with grain, wine and honey, and the intention was to sail on all the way to his native Iceland; but it turned out that the cargo had been stolen.[59] Norway could obtain heavy cloth from many sources; the relationship with Iceland was vital to the islanders but hardly essential for Norway. However, there were other items that made it worthwhile to brave the seas on the route to Iceland (a route that could only be taken in the late spring and throughout the summer). Iceland was the only source of sulphur for northern Europe, and its falcons, along with those of Greenland, were in demand at the great courts of Europe.[60] It has been suggested that polar bears sometimes arrived off Iceland on ice floes, were captured and were taken to Europe – the charming tale of the white bear that Auðun wanted to present to the king of Denmark will be examined shortly. Walrus tusks were probably brought from Greenland by this stage, since the Icelanders appear to have exterminated what walruses there were around the shores of the island within a few decades of their arrival. Since Iceland lacked reliable sources of iron, this was imported from, or by way of, Norway, along with all sorts of implements and articles of clothing.[61]

The maritime route from Norway to Iceland formed part of a remarkable trading network that survived long after the Vikings had become a memory, though, as it was expressed in the Icelandic sagas, a very powerful one. For this network extended still further afield, however, right across the north Atlantic, all the way to the shores of North America.

21

White Bears, Whales and Walruses

I

Greenland is often described as the world's biggest island.[1] Geologically, though, it forms part of North America, and to include Baffin Island as one of the American discoveries of the Norse navigators, while excluding Greenland, is another example of what might portentously be called 'the social construction of continents'. Even in the sixteenth century it was sometimes assumed that Greenland was somehow linked to Asia, which had already been the view of Adam of Bremen in the late eleventh century, while around 1300 an Icelandic geographer remarked that 'some people think' the American continent must in reality be part of Africa; Adam, on the other hand, took the view that it was part of Asia, a view that survived up to and beyond the days of Columbus and Cabot.[2] This was hardly the issue that worried navigators, however. The seas that lap Greenland are as unsafe as the environment, dominated by a truly vast ice cap, is hostile and impenetrable. Only a small part of the island was suitable for settlement, and it is a tribute to the persistence of its first Norse explorers that they searched out the fjords that gave access to grasslands, even though they lay on the western flank of the island.

To reach these distant lands in the types of ship that the Norse operated was a challenge of endurance: when Eirík the Red led the first settlers across the sea to Greenland in around 986, he set out from Iceland with a fleet of twenty-five ships, but only fourteen reached Greenland, some sinking and others having to turn back.[3] Although an awning would be spread over the crew and passengers at night, space was tight in the hold, especially when it was as crowded with animals as it was with humans. The journey from Norway to the east coast of Iceland was estimated at seven days' sailing, and from western Iceland to the Norse settlements in Greenland took four days, while from Iceland to Ireland was a five-day voyage. By the thirteenth century, Norse ships had discovered lands even

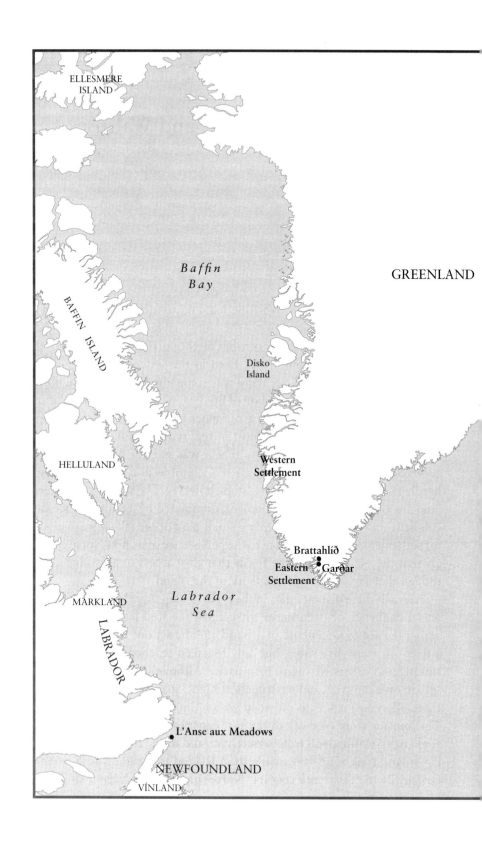

ELLESMERE
ISLAND

*Baffin
Bay*

GREENLAND

BAFFIN ISLAND

Disko
Island

HELLULAND

**Western
Settlement**

Brattahlíð

Eastern •**Garðar**
Settlement

*Labrador
Sea*

MARKLAND

LABRADOR

• **L'Anse aux Meadows**

NEWFOUNDLAND

VÍNLAND

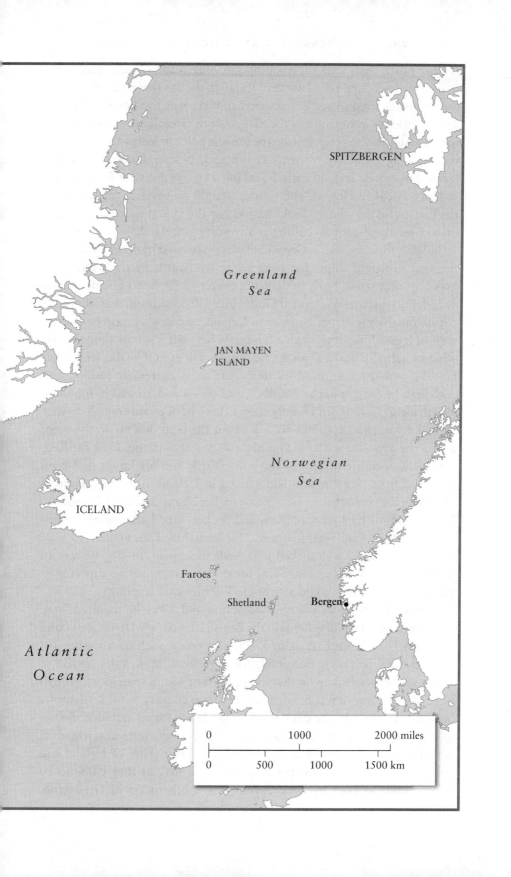

SPITZBERGEN

*Greenland
Sea*

JAN MAYEN
ISLAND

*Norwegian
Sea*

ICELAND

Faroes

Shetland   Bergen

*Atlantic

Ocean*

0		1000		2000 miles
0	500	1000	1500 km	

further north than Iceland, reaching Jan Mayen Island and Spitsbergen (which lay four days' travel north of Iceland), though these were not places the explorers tried to settle – the environment was too hostile. Another very hostile environment was the east coast of Greenland, even though it took a single day to reach it from the nearest point in Iceland. Once traffic was moving regularly towards Greenland, Norwegian captains also learned to bypass Iceland entirely, taking a course due west from a place in Norway called Hernar, and sailing straight on between Shetland and the Faroes, 'so that the sea looks halfway up the mountainsides', and then on to Greenland without calling at any ports in Iceland.[4]

Judging from the sagas, Greenland was discovered by accident; bearing in mind stories of ships that were swept westwards by the winds, this makes perfect sense. Early in the tenth century a nephew of Naddoð, one of Iceland's discoverers, named Gunnbjorn Ulf-Krakuson, was blown off course on a voyage from Norway to Iceland, and saw a group of skerries west of Iceland, together with a landmass beyond; it is now thought that what he actually saw was an Arctic mirage, but even if he did see Greenland he would have found its steep east coast extremely forbidding.[5] Although he did not explore further, and was not interested in founding a settlement, Gunnbjorn's family seem to have been proud enough of what he had achieved to continue to talk about the land that lay to the west; and in the 970s one settler in Gunnbjorn's neighbourhood, Eirík the Red, clearly listened attentively to the story. Eirík and his father had been outlawed from Norway and had arrived in Iceland in the vain hope of obtaining the sort of broad estates that earlier Norse settlers had acquired. But by the time they reached the island the best land had long been occupied by the goðar and their followers.[6] Eirík had killed one man in Norway, and before long he was sucked into feuds in Iceland. By 983 he was an outlaw there too; the sentence was for three years, but if he appeared in public any of his foes could attempt to kill him with impunity.

Leaving Iceland was the obvious option and, since he required land, Eirík chose not the Norse lands in the British Isles but the far-off ice-bound land that Gunnbjorn had sighted. The east coast, with its towering ice-covered cliffs, was quite unsuitable for settlement. Many tales survive of Norse sailors washed up on this shore, some of whom were lucky enough to be found, some of whom tried to trek across country to the settlements but were defeated by the cold, their bodies being found and identified as much as fourteen years later. In one case wax tablets were also found on which a traveller from Bergen recorded how his journey to Iceland had gone awry.[7] Eirík avoided these 'unsettled wilds', as they came to be known, and worked his way beyond the southern tip of Greenland, identifying two areas suitable for settlement: to the south, following water-courses away from the rocky coast, and navigating past islands teeming with bird life, he found the grassland of the so-called Eastern Settlement (though it might better have been called the Southern Settlement). Four hundred miles to the north he identified another area, much cooler, which he thought would make a good base for hunting expeditions, and this became known as the Western Settlement, and was always smaller than the main base further south. It is likely that he returned from this area laden with sealskins, walrus tusks and other polar prizes, all of which advertised the wealth that skilled hunters could draw from the region. The promise of the Eastern Settlement, with its green fields, led him to name the territory Greenland, 'for he argued that men would be drawn to go there if the land had an attractive name'.[8] It was not really dishonest to use the name Greenland, for the part he proposed to colonize was indeed green, and a global rise in temperatures made the land even greener. After three years he returned to Iceland, no longer an outlaw; a severe famine in 976 had demoralized the Icelanders, and, with his brightly painted oral prospectus for Greenland, he had little difficulty in recruiting somewhere around 400 settlers from Iceland.[9]

Following convention, as he approached the lands marked out for the Eastern Settlement, Eirík threw his high-seat pillars overboard, watching to see where they would be washed ashore; he thus relied on the gods to show him where to settle. The place he chose, Brattahlíð, has been identified and excavated, for it was occupied for hundreds of years; it lay some way back from the water, in a broad plain that led down to a fjord giving access to the sea. The settlements were not real towns, any more than the Icelandic settlements were; they consisted of a scattering of nearly 200 farms in the Eastern Settlement, while the Western Settlement possessed ninety. Some of these farms were occupied by later waves of settlers who had heard good reports of the opportunities this new land offered.[10] The Eastern Settlement also contained a cathedral at Gardar, following the Christianization of the Norse settlers, and there were several churches in the other settlement too. The hardy inhabitants of the two settlements would sometimes head north in small six-oared boats, which many of the farmers owned. They might go as far as Disko Island (70°N), in search of walrus, polar bears and narwhal, whose spikes were often believed in Europe to be unicorn's horns. The famous Lewis chessmen were made out of walrus ivory, though they are thought actually to have been made in Niðaros on the coast of Norway.

In the mid-fourteenth century this commerce in walrus tusks began to fall away, and one can only wonder whether the exploitation of these resources had reached such a fever pitch that the walrus population had begun to vanish. Another explanation that has been mooted is the increasing ease of access within Europe to elephant ivory, by way of west Africa and the Red Sea, but, at least as far as west Africa is concerned, this was a development of the fifteenth and not the fourteenth century. Walrus hide was valued in northern Europe because it could be twisted into tough rope. Two tiny amulets preserved in the National Museum of Denmark are in the form of a polar bear and a walrus.[11] A Greenland falcon made a perfect gift for the falcon-crazy Emperor Frederick II in thirteenth-century southern Italy; twelve Greenland falcons are said to have constituted the ransom paid for the crusading son of the duke of Burgundy when he was captured by the Turks in 1396.[12] Greenland did, therefore, play a role in the international trade of the Middle Ages, and was by no means a disconnected territory inhabited by Norse exiles. A thirteenth-century Norwegian writer explained that there were three good reasons to sail to Greenland: curiosity; the search for fame; and the search for wealth – precisely because Greenland was so remote, and was visited less often than other lands, it offered 'a good profit'. This was not just because it was a source of rare Arctic products; traders could also exploit the shortage of iron and timber, for 'everything that is needed to improve the land must be purchased abroad'.[13]

The great difference between Greenland and Iceland was the fact that part of the western coast of this vast land was already inhabited, not, as in Iceland, by a handful of chaste priests but by Eskimo peoples. The term 'Eskimo' has gone out of fashion, because it was a native American word meaning, rather contemptuously, 'raw-meat eaters'; but it is used here as a blanket description of different people with different cultures: the so-called Dorset people, named after a small island off Baffin Island, and then the more familiar Inuit, who still inhabit Greenland and who have sometimes been called 'Neo-Eskimos' instead. The term 'Inuit' simply means 'human beings', for (not unreasonably) many peoples have no name for themselves other than 'ourselves'.[14] The Dorset Eskimos may have been clinging on to Greenland at the time of the Norse discovery, for the 'Iceland Book', the *Íslendingabók*, relates that Eirík and his companions 'found many settlements, towards the east and towards the west, and remains of skin boats and stone implements'; and the author assumed that the people who had lived in these places were of the same origin as the troublesome inhabitants Eirík would later encounter in Vínland, some way down the eastern flank of America.[15] Archaeological evidence is less secure, and the 'Iceland Book' may well have been embroidering the account of Eirík's discoveries with information gathered much later; still,

Dorset Eskimos may have been present in Greenland up to about 1000, though further north than the two areas settled by the Norse migrants. Legends circulating among the next wave of Eskimo settlers, the Inuit, recorded seal-hunting landsmen who had been pushed southwards as the Inuit entered Baffin Island, between Greenland and the Canadian mainland; these predecessors of the Inuit would have crossed over to Greenland in kayaks, but they were not really a maritime people, and they were defeated by conditions in Greenland: they lived in lightly constructed houses warmed by open hearths, and fuel was hard to find in a land so poor in timber as Greenland.[16]

The Inuit, on the other hand, learned to work the waterways of the Arctic in increasingly well-constructed kayaks, and made their way from Siberia and Alaska along the far northern coasts and islands of Canada into north-western Greenland, which they entered by about 1000, that is, at the same time as the Norse settlements took hold. By about 1200 these Inugsuk Inuits (to give them their exact name) had made themselves known to the Norse Greenlanders. Contrary to the popular image of Eskimos living in igloos built out of ice-blocks, the Inuit lived in slightly sunken houses entered through narrow passageways, and made out of piled-up stones, stone flakes, turf and whalebone; like the Norse, they hunted walruses and seals, and they were very active whalers who were armed with heavy but handsomely crafted harpoons and who could even capture massive baleen whales. Objects of Norse origin found on Inuit sites in Greenland – a piece of tusk with symmetrical decoration, a fragment of a bronze spoon and of a bronze pot, and so on – indicate that trade (or possibly plunder) connected the Norse and Inuit communities. Contact became much more frequent as the Inuit moved slowly southwards, and as Norse explorers searched ever further north; on the other hand, very few Inuit articles have turned up on Norse sites in Greenland.[17]

In the larger Eastern Settlement, there was more of an attempt to create a self-sufficient community. As in Iceland, this was not really possible, as there was no hope of sowing large areas with grain, and the mainstay of the Greenland settlers was their flocks. A thirteenth-century Norwegian text, the *King's Mirror*, described how the settlers were rich in cheese and butter, and raised cattle for meat, as well as hunting reindeer, whales and seals, which they turned into meat or fat, as well as local fish (notably cod) and Arctic hares. The milky drink known as *skýr* was a favourite food. Timber was sparse and of poor quality; even the driftwood that came down from Siberia along the ocean currents was not suitable for building ships, though it burned well as fuel. They would have to go in search of wood – which, as will be seen, took them still further west. But they, like the Icelanders, produced heavy woollen cloth that found its way along the trade routes; a warp weight found in Greenland was decorated with a hammer, the symbol of the god Thor, suggesting that the pagan gods still had their attraction among the Norse settlers. So little grain was grown that (if the *King's Mirror* is to be believed) most Greenlanders had no idea what bread was.[18] The settlers were tough: when Eirík the Red called on his cousin Þorkell the Far-Travelled, Þorkell needed to offer him dinner but realized he had no boat available to travel to the island a mile away across the water where his sheep were pastured. So he swam to the island and killed a ram, which he then heaved on to his back, before swimming the whole way back and serving a meal of roast mutton.[19]

The first settlers were pagan, and the circumstances of Greenland's conversion to Christianity are not clear. According to the *Saga of Eirík the Red*, the founder remained a convinced heathen, and was disconcerted to find that his family was keen to adopt the new faith. His son Leif the Lucky had spent some time at the court of Olaf Tryggvason in Norway, and the king urged him to go back to Greenland and to spread Christianity there; Leif was no doubt thinking of his father when he objected that this would be a difficult task, but the king was persistent, and on his arrival (having first been blown to North America) he immediately converted his mother, whereupon she refused to live with Eirík, and 'this annoyed him greatly'. The annoyance was magnified when his family built a small church, only six metres long by three metres broad, that has been excavated at Brattahlíð.[20] It is probably an exaggeration to suppose that King Olaf added Greenland to the list of countries he converted, and the story of his involvement was intended to boost still further the reputation he developed by the thirteenth century of being the father of Norse Christianity. No more than he succeeded in imposing the new religion on the more remote corners of Norway did he succeed in stamping out paganism in Iceland and Greenland; but gradually the population was won over, and the effects can still be seen in the remains of the cathedral at Gardar and in the intermittent line of succession of bishops of Greenland, sent out to the Eastern Settlement from the early twelfth century onwards. The church at Brattahlíð was built, for lack of good timber, out of chunks of turf set around a sparse wooden frame in the same way as the farmhouses of both Greenland and Iceland.[21] For a long time, Greenland was not a dependency of Iceland; its system of government was closely modelled on that of Iceland, with a *Þing* that brought together the leading inhabitants and that passed laws under the direction of its Law-Speaker. This territory had the same ambiguous relationship with Norway as did Iceland, and by

1261 it, like Iceland, had accepted the authority of the king of Norway, not that he was able to do much to control its affairs.

A charming tale from medieval Iceland recounts the career of an Icelander named Auðun, who travelled all the way from Norway to Greenland, where he bought a bear, 'an absolute treasure', with all the money he possessed. He decided to return to Norway and then to travel south, with the aim of presenting his bear to Svein, king of Denmark. But when he reached Norway the Norwegian king, Harald, a rival of the Danish one, heard that Auðun had arrived and summoned him to his court. The king courteously asked Auðun, 'You have a bear, an absolute treasure?' Auðun gave as non-committal an answer as he could, because he could guess what was coming next: 'Are you willing to sell him to us for the same price you gave for him?' Auðun politely but firmly refused. So the king asked what he did propose to do with the bear, and when he heard that Auðun wished to present it to the king of Denmark he expostulated: 'Is it possible that you are such a silly man that you have not heard how a state of war exists between our two countries?' Still, King Harald was polite enough to let him go on his way, so long as he promised to tell Harald on his return about the reward King Svein would give him. As he travelled south, Auðun realized that he had no money left and no way to feed either himself or his bear. He persuaded the steward of the Danish king to sell him some food, but the price was half-ownership of the patient bear. After all, the steward pointed out, if the deal was not struck the bear would die of starvation, and what profit would that bring to Auðun? 'When he looked at it that way, it seemed to him that what the steward said went pretty close to the mark, so that was what they settled on.'

Auðun entered the royal presence with the steward, and explained why he had come, and that there was now a new problem: he could not present the bear to the king, because he only owned half of it. The king scolded the steward for his lack of generosity to a traveller who had come to court with such a fine gift, when even Svein's enemy King Harald had let him go on his way in peace. The steward was exiled forthwith, while Auðun was invited to stay at court as long as he wished. After a while, Auðun's love of travelling reasserted itself, and he decided to go to Rome with a group of pilgrims; the king offered him every support. But by the time he returned to Denmark he was once again destitute, and he skulked around outside the feasting hall, not daring to show himself in his rags. Eventually the king realized that there was someone who was hanging back, and worked out who he was. Yet again Auðun was invited to stay for the rest of his days. Once again Auðun's wish to be on the move triumphed: 'God reward you, sire, for all the honour you would do me, but what I really have in mind is to return to Iceland.' He was worried that his mother was living in poverty on the island while he might be carousing at court.

> One day, towards the end of spring, King Svein walked down to the jetties, where ships were being overhauled in readiness for voyages to many lands, to the Baltic and Germany, Sweden and Norway. He and Auðun came to a very fine ship which men were making ready, and, 'What do you think of this for a ship, Auðun?' asked the king. 'Very fine, sire,' was his answer. 'I am going to give you this ship,' said the king, 'in return for the bear.'

But the Danish king was worried that the ship might be wrecked on the dangerous shores of Iceland, so he gave him a purse full of silver and a gold arm-ring that he himself was wearing, charging him only to give it to someone to whom he found himself under a very special obligation.

First Auðun sailed to the court of King Harald, and received a hearty welcome. He told the king how his rival had willingly accepted the bear and had given such handsome gifts in return. Auðun said: 'You had the opportunity to deprive me of both of these things, my bear and my life too; yet you let me go in peace where others might not', and saying this he presented the Danish king's arm-ring to King Harald, and then set off for Iceland, where 'he was thought to be a man of the happiest good fortune'.[22] Alas, the tale does not relate what happened to the bear. However, the story of Auðun does not simply present evidence for the capture of Greenland polar bears, which were carried all the way to Scandinavia; it also conjures up a trading world that linked Greenland to Norway, sometimes by way of Iceland and sometimes directly. The story of the gift of a polar bear to a great prince is corroborated by evidence that both the eleventh-century German emperor Henry III and King Sigurð of Norway, known as 'the Jerusalem Traveller', who went on crusade to the Holy Land early in the twelfth century, received just such a gift. The idea behind the gift to this Norwegian king was that he would support the creation of a Greenland bishopric.[23]

II

Contact between Greenland and Europe began to diminish in the fourteenth century. Even so, contact was maintained to a greater degree than used to be supposed, proving that over a period of more than 400 years Greenland was linked to Europe by regular trade; by the late Middle Ages only one *knǫrr* a year was reaching Greenland, and maybe not even that, for no ships are known to have reached Greenland between 1346 and 1355, which was just as well, since Greenland was out of touch with Norway just at the time when Europe was being ravaged by the Black Death. By the fourteenth century, only ships granted a royal licence were permitted to trade towards Greenland. If anything, though, this proves that the king of Norway saw real value in the Greenland trade, and was keen to hog a large share of the proceeds. The arrival of ships from Greenland tended to be noted down in Norwegian annals, as was the case in 1383 when a ship loaded with Arctic goodies reached Bergen directly from Greenland (the ship itself was owned by an Icelander); it brought news that the bishop of Greenland had died a few years earlier, which suggests contact was intermittent. It turned out that the captain had never obtained a royal licence to trade in Greenland; but the crew insisted that the ship had been blown accidentally towards Greenland, and that no one had really intended to go there. The tax authorities preferred to believe what was probably a tall story – the cargo was too interesting for the Norwegians to complain. This sort of thing happened several times, and was conveniently over-looked; another Icelander turned up in Greenland in 1389 with four ships full of Norwegian cargo, and the Icelandic merchant breezily claimed that the Greenlanders, led by the king's agent in Greenland, had absolutely insisted that he unload his cargo and take on board Arctic goods.[24]

Still, the very insistence of the Greenlanders on their need for European goods shows that contact was less intense than it had been. The last bishop of Greenland officiated there from 1365 to 1378. There are several possible reasons for the decrease in contact: the end of the Middle Ages may have seen a cooling of temperatures, with the result that pack ice appeared ever further south, so that the voyage to Greenland became increasingly per-ilous; the Greenlanders themselves were more and more reluctant to pay the papal tax known as Peter's Pence (paid in *vaðmal* cloth or walrus products); the king of Norway faced a cash crisis and became heavily dependent on the merchants of the German Hansa, who had not been involved in the past with the ambitious route across the north Atlantic; the Black Death reached Iceland in 1402 – much later than in Scandinavia – and sailings to Greenland were at least for a time suspended.[25] The warm period stretching from about 800 to about 1200 was at an end. Drift ice certainly was an increasing problem: around 1342 the Norwegian priest Ívar Bárdarson, who had been sent to Greenland to look after the lands of the bishop of Garðar, described the sea route from Iceland to Green-land. He took as his point of reference the skerries Gunnbjorn had discovered when he accidentally came across Greenland centuries earlier. The priest knew of an old set of sailing instructions, for he went on to say: 'This was the old course, but now ice has come down from the north-west out of the gulf of the sea so near to the aforesaid skerries, that no one without extreme peril can sail the old course, and be heard of again.'[26]

The Western Settlement succumbed to a combination of worsening weather and to competition between the Inuit and the Norse for access to hunting grounds; the Inuit had been moving south as the seals they hunted tried to escape the bitterly cold weather of the very far north. When the Norwegian priest Ívar Bárdarson visited the Western Settlement in 1342, he found that it contained only 'horses, goats, cattle and sheep, all wild, and no people, either Christian or heathen', though he had heard rumours that the Skrælings, that is, the Inuit, had been harassing the inhabitants of the settlement.[27] Its rationale had always been the supply of walrus ivory and other Arctic products to Europe. It has long been assumed that the smaller settlement had therefore ceased to exist by 1342. Rather different, though, is the evidence from archaeology. The 'Farm beneath the Sand', excavated after its discovery by Inuit in 1990, survived all the way from the eleventh to the fifteenth century. No evidence was found of furniture, suggesting that the last human inhabitants had taken most of their possessions away when they left. However, animals continued to roam the farmhouse, for an unburied goat was found beside an inside wall, having starved or frozen to death when its owners left it behind.[28]

Although a papal letter from 1492 proclaims that ships had ceased to travel to Greenland since the early fifteenth century, archaeological evidence suggests otherwise: fragments of fifteenth-century Rhenish pottery have been found in the walls of a Greenland church. The Eastern Settlement, or at least some of the homesteads, kept up contact with the outside world well into the fifteenth century, as the remarkable costumes excavated in graves from a farm at Herjólfsnes prove: late fifteenth-century Burgundian fashion is reflected in a headdress, and more generally the cut of the clothes accords with fifteenth-century European styles. The harbour at Herjólfsnes was the first port of call that ships were likely to encounter as they approached the Eastern Settlement, for it lay, unusually, directly on the sea coast, and further south than the other homesteads.[29] A small silver shield from the early fourteenth century carries the coat of arms of Clan Campbell, suggesting some sort of connection between Greenland and the British Isles. The obvious conclusion is that, even when Norwegian shipping failed to set out for Greenland, and even when contact with Iceland was lost for years at a time, there were other visitors to Greenland, most probably English and Basque sailors who by the end of the Middle Ages were exploring the superbly stocked fishing grounds of the northern Atlantic. By 1420 English ships dominated the approaches to Iceland.[30]

Still, this was not enough to save the Norse settlements from extinction.

A mass grave at Herjólfsnes may be evidence that when, as was almost bound to happen, the Black Death spread from Norway and Iceland to Greenland it wiped out a large number of people. Amid all the explanations that have been offered – the Black Death or other disease, famine and malnutrition, climate change, Inuit attacks, a European preference for elephant ivory, sheer lack of interest in sending supplies from Europe – nothing quite explains the evidence, which has all the character of an Agatha Christie mystery.[31] In 1769 a Lutheran minister from the north of Norway named Niels Egede recorded a legend he had heard in Greenland. This told of Inuit who came to trade with the Norse settlers, and of how one day three small boats arrived carrying men who attacked the Norsemen, though they managed to fend them off; meanwhile the Inuit fled in terror. Then a year later a fleet came over the sea; the raiders massacred the Norse inhabitants and carried off their cattle. After another raid the following year the Inuit returned to the coast and saw that the settlement had been ravaged; the Inuit found some Norse women and children and took them away; the women married into the Inuit community, and harmony prevailed. After a long while an 'English privateer' arrived in the same region, but the Inuit were happy to find that all he wanted to do was to trade with them. Since the settlement that is described here lay right on the coast, it is once again assumed that it must have been Herjólfsnes. This is very late testimony from an oral source that could have been embroidered over the centuries, and further embellished by Niels Egede, who must have been influenced by conditions in his own day, when English pirates were known to be roaming the Atlantic.[32] Even so, the idea that a third party, neither Inuit nor Norse, had a role in the downfall of the Greenland settlement is an interesting solution to the mystery.

The mystery is compounded by archaeological finds at a farmhouse at the end of one of the fjords that led down to the main part of the Eastern Settlement. This was a sizeable building, with fifteen rooms; in a passageway a skull and human bones were found, leading to the unprovable claim that maybe this was the last Norse Greenlander, who had no one to bury him – the skull has been identified as that of a Norseman. The evidence is made still more mysterious when one takes on board the report of Jon Grønlænder, from Iceland; he had taken passage on a German ship bound for his home in about 1540, but the ship was blown off course towards Greenland. There, deep within a fjord, he saw houses ranged along the beach, as well as huts for drying fish; then he found the body of a man dressed in woollen cloth, a fine hood and sealskin, who seemed to have collapsed and died right there.[33] So here is another candidate for the title of last Norse Greenlander, though he could have been a lost visitor from somewhere in Europe, or even an Inuit who had managed to acquire Western clothes. For the Inuit certainly raided Norse farmhouses, which was easily done since the settlers continued to live in scattered homesteads rather than in a town. In 1379, for instance, the Skrælings killed eighteen Norse Greenlanders and enslaved two boys.[34]

A simple but important question is why the Inuit survived and flourished, while the Norse population disappeared. The Inuit proved much more adaptable than the Norse; they had the whole coastline of western Greenland, and the Arctic islands beyond, as their domain, whereas the traditional economy of the Eastern Settlement was based more on pastoralism within the small area of what was truly green Greenland than on hunting and fishing.[35] It was long assumed that the Norse colonies in Greenland died out because the unbalanced diet left the population physically weak, a sign of which was the poor state of several skeletons recovered at Herjólfsnes. This degeneration was supposedly visible in the small size of the skulls of the Greenlanders (457 skeletons having been analysed). Much of this research was based on questionable assumptions, not just about the date of the bodies but about how representative they were of the wider population, and about the imagined difference between six-foot-tall Viking warriors and the shorter folk actually dug up from the ground. After all, one would expect to find similar evidence of physical ill-health in any medieval European cemetery, without assuming there was a process of constant degeneration. On the other hand, the high proportion of young women found in the graves suggests that death in childbirth was higher than in western Europe, or maybe that women stayed put while men went further afield – more of this in a moment. Evidence for malnutrition in the bones is very slender. The most convincing demographic explanation for the extinction of the Greenland colonies is a slow but steady trickle of emigration, as the inhabitants, particularly young males, went to search for a more profitable livelihood in Iceland or Norway.[36] In that case, the ships carrying Arctic products back to Europe were also, very probably, carrying Greenlanders who had no intention of returning to the land where their ancestors had lived since the year 1000. Moreover, these Arctic products were more difficult to obtain as access to the hunting grounds was cut off by the Inuit, who were happy to trade bearskins and walrus tusks but expected more in exchange than curdled milk and woollen cloth. Meanwhile, manpower became a major problem: the fields around Brattahlíð, Eirík the Red's original settlement, were allowed to revert to meadow, suggesting that there were fewer people around to work the soil, and perhaps fewer mouths to feed. Some Greenlanders may have merged into the Inuit population, for it has been seen that the Inuit themselves preserved tales of intermarriage. Some, it has been suggested, went in search of pastures new in America, an opinion that can be traced right back to a seventeenth-century Icelandic bishop, who insisted they all turned pagan as well.[37]

The routes from Iceland to Greenland and then from Norway to Greenland had been in regular use during the summer months throughout the eleventh to fourteenth centuries; there was an occasional hiatus, but the fact that Pope Alexander VI wrote about his spiritual concern for the Greenlanders in the year that Columbus reached the Caribbean indicates that memory of this vast island did not evaporate: 'the church at Gardar is situated at the world's end', he stated.[38] By 1492 the Greenland settlements were deserted. But, if they ended around then, they had been in existence for half a millennium, about as long as the period between the Portuguese rediscovery of Greenland at the start of the sixteenth century and the writing of this book.

III

The volume of European trade with Greenland and the size of the Norse colonies that were established there may have been small, but knowledge of the north Atlantic was widely diffused, in works of geography produced in northern Europe, and the discovery of Greenland and of lands beyond was narrated in two sagas, the *Greenlanders' Saga* and the *Saga of Eirík the Red*, both of which were copied and edited over the centuries, with the unfortunate effect that it is difficult to recover the original story amid later embellishments.[39] These sagas are richer in information about the Norse discovery of what came to be known as America than they are in information about Greenland. Even so, they only reveal the first phase of contact; Norse mariners certainly continued to visit Labrador long after Leif Eiríksson sailed down the coast of North America around the year 1000, in search of timber and other raw materials. But, whereas the settlement in Iceland proved permanent, and that in Greenland lasted for centuries, it proved impossible to create anything more than temporary settlements in North America. The Norse voyages to America testify to the skill of these navigators, but they proved to be a dead end.

Before looking at the much more famous voyages to the east coast of America, to the lands the Norse called Helluland, Markland and Vínland, a word needs to be said about voyages northwards from Greenland that brought the Norse to the edges of the Canadian Arctic. Here, a mass of islands vast and small, from Baffin Island and Ellesmere Island to tiny

Dorset Island, offered opportunities to Greenlanders of the Western Settlement in search of narwhal and walrus ivory, polar bears and seal or whale blubber (used in lighting as well as in food). On at least one occasion in the thirteenth century or later Norse Greenlanders penetrated as far as 72°55′N, leaving a runic inscription: 'Erling Sigvaðsson and Bjarni Þordarson and Enriði Ásson on the Saturday before the minor Rogation Day [25 April], built these cairns.' In 1266 an expedition to the north saw Inuit houses but was frightened off by the large number of polar bears, which prevented the Norsemen from landing; and a couple of small Inuit carvings from sites in western Greenland are thought to portray a European with whom the Inuit came into contact.[40] An arrowhead found on a farm in the Western Settlement was manufactured out of meteoric iron obtained in north-western Greenland, which suggests that the Norse traders sometimes obtained iron from the Inuit, not just from Norwegian merchants.[41] A case has been made for Norse visits to an improbably welcoming environment, Ellesmere Island, at 83°N, one of the northernmost large islands in the world, which turns out to be largely free from snow (though not from ice), and in past times hosted a large population of musk oxen, as well as plenty of plants and lichens on which they can graze; in some areas, summer temperatures hover between 10 and 15°C. Fragments of Norse chain mail and an iron rivet have been found there, underneath the remains of an Inuit house; but, despite the enthusiastic assertions of some writers, these and other bits and pieces do not prove the Norse went there – rather, they suggest that Norsemen traded with Inuit who travelled up to Ellesmere Island.[42] There were no doubt extreme cases where adventurousness carried Greenlanders beyond their normal hunting grounds, but trips to Disko Island were much more regular: here a great amount of driftwood would arrive, carried down from Siberia.[43]

A tiny fragment of larch assumed to be from a ship tells a story that is in its own way as rich as the two sagas. Found in Greenland, it comes from a tree that did not grow in Greenland, Iceland or Norway, but existed in profusion in north-eastern Canada.[44] It is not driftwood: that was not of sufficient quality for building anything large and strong, and it degrades in the water. Then there are the tiny traces found at the 'Farm beneath the Sands' on the Western Settlement in Greenland: fragments of bear fur, not from local polar bears but black or brown bears, of the sort that inhabit northern Canada, as well as bits of bison hair. An arrowhead found near graves in the same area originated somewhere around Hudson Bay. Moreover, two sets of Icelandic annals tell of a ship that arrived unexpectedly from a place beyond Greenland called Markland; this was in 1347, and it had been blown off course: 'There came also a ship from

Greenland, smaller in size than the small Icelandic boats; she came into the outer Straumfjord, and had no anchor. There were seventeen men on board. They had made a voyage to Markland, but were afterwards storm-driven here.'[45] The assumption is that the ship had sailed to Markland in search of timber. The place name would have been familiar to an Icelandic, and indeed a Scandinavian, audience.

The geographical treatise from Iceland which suggests that Africa somehow embraced lands to the west of Greenland seems to go back to the twelfth century, even though the surviving text dates from around 1300. This states:

> To the north of Norway lies Finnmark [Lapland]; from there the land sweeps north-east and east to Bjarmaland [Permia], which renders tribute to the king of Prussia. From Permia there is uninhabited land stretching all the way to the north until Greenland begins. To the south of Greenland lies Helluland and then Markland; and from there it is not far to Vínland, which some people think extends from Africa.[46]

This describes a closed Atlantic (rather in the way that Ptolemy had assumed there existed a closed Indian Ocean), with Greenland linked to Europe by way of an Arctic landmass. The statement may be even older than the *Greenlanders' Saga*, of about 1200, and the *Saga of Eirík the Red*, written down in the mid-thirteenth century. Of these, the *Greenlanders' Saga* claims to record the memories of one of the key participants in the discovery of the three territories of Helluland, Markland and Vínland, Þorfinn Karlsefni, while the *Saga of Eirík the Red* is richer in obvious fantasy, such as an attack launched on Norse visitors to these new lands by a Uniped, a single-footed humanoid who was supposed to inhabit Africa – hence, in part, the assumption that Vínland was linked to Africa. And this betrays the influence not just of medieval bestiaries and other imaginative literature, but of classical writers since, as has been seen, the Icelanders were devouring Latin texts from Europe with an enthusiasm barely matched anywhere else (a possible source is Isidore of Seville, writing around AD 600).[47]

Medieval fantasies about lands to the west are well matched by modern fantasies about who 'discovered' America. That the Norse reached North America is not in doubt. But, in one version, Norsemen reached as far as Minnesota, where a bogus rune-stone clearly manufactured in the nineteenth century proves their presence in 1362. In another version, a forged fifteenth-century map bought in an uncritical moment by Yale University supposedly demonstrates that exact knowledge of parts of North America was circulating in Europe in the fifteenth century, information that might have reached the ears of Columbus, who probably visited Iceland as a young man. A little more attention might attach to a late eleventh-century Norse penny found on a native American site in Maine in 1957; it has excited great interest, but it had been perforated for use as jewellery and had almost certainly worked its way south along the existing trade routes, passing from hand to hand.[48] It is better to turn to the sagas and to try to make sense of what they say and of how it fits with archaeological evidence from North America.

IV

In the *Greenlanders' Saga* we learn that new land to the west of Greenland was first spied out by Bjarni Herjólfson, who was trying to reach Greenland from Iceland in around 985 but was blown off course. He realized that the hills and woodland that came into view could not be craggy, icy Greenland and refused even to land to take on water and wood. He also saw what he called a 'worthless' land, with mountains and a glacier, before putting in at Herjólfsnes, which was named after the farm of his father, Herjólf. 'People thought he had showed great lack of curiosity, since he could tell them nothing about these countries'; on the other hand, 'there was now great talk of discovering new countries'.[49] The most enthusiastic Greenlander was Leif Eiríksson, the son of the colony's founder, Eirík the Red, who was by now too old and tired to take part in new adventures. Leif has been described as 'a tremendous sailor, and the first skipper reported to have made direct voyages between Greenland, Scotland, Norway, and back again'.[50] The sagas disagree whether there were six or three expeditions to the new lands, and the *Saga of Eirík the Red* does not even mention the incurious Bjarni.

Leif and his men came first to the land Bjarni had considered worthless, and they agreed with that view; it was given the name Helluland, meaning 'the land of slabs of rock'. Further south, though, they discovered white sandy beaches that fringed a flat, forested interior; this land they called Markland, 'the land of forests'. After another two days at sea they reached an island and a headland; 'in this country, night and day were of more even length than in either Greenland or Iceland', and the river they saw teemed with salmon. There was an abundance of rich grass, and when one day a German slave named Tyrkir staggered back to their camp drunk from eating too many wild grapes they decided to call this land Vínland, 'the land of wine'. They built some large houses, and wintered in Vínland.[51]

At this point one can see how the saga-writer or his source added colour to the story. Eating grapes does not make one drunk, though those living so far north of wine-producing lands might be forgiven for imagining that this could happen. The naming of the land and the story of Tyrkir have set off a debate about where the Norse explorers landed and whether *vín* in Vínland really means 'wine'; the term *vin* for 'fertile land' is sometimes presented as the true etymology, but in Old Norse the vowels *i* and *í* were quite distinct, and it really does seem that the travellers reached a land where fruit that at least looked like grapes grew in profusion. One suggestion is that they actually found gooseberries, which do resemble a rather hairy grape, or that Old Norse confused currants and grapes. If, on the other hand, they did find wild grapes, they must have arrived in southern Nova Scotia or the borderlands of Canada and the United States, while it is possible they reached as far south as modern Boston.[52]

A second expedition, led by Leif's brother Þorvald, returned to Leif's houses in Vínland, and the prospects for settlement seemed good, until they found three skin-covered boats that lay upturned on a beach, with three men underneath each boat. There is no evidence these men meant any harm, but they killed eight, though one escaped; and then they realized that there was some sort of settlement not far off, and before long they came under attack from a swarm of skin-boats, manned by people they called 'Skrælings', a term that they also came to apply to the Inuit. Its meaning was something like 'wretches'.[53] Leif was known as 'Leif the Lucky' after he rescued a shipwrecked crew off Greenland; but Þorvald might have been called 'the Unlucky', because, while he was away from Leif's camp, he was hit by an arrow that passed through a narrow opening between the gunwale of his ship and his shield. Þorvald died in Vínland; and this was a portent of future trouble between the Greenlanders and the native Americans.[54]

Soon after, back in Greenland, Þorfinn Karlsefni, a successful Norwegian trader, went to stay with Leif Eiríksson and fell in love with the beautiful widow Guðrið, whom he married. They became a formidable pair; stories of Vínland continued to be told, and Guðrið urged her husband to fit out an expedition – in the end he recruited sixty men and five women. 'They took livestock of all kinds, for they intended to make a permanent settlement there if at all possible.' They based themselves at Leif's camp, cutting a cargo of timber and living comfortably off the land. Only after one winter did they encounter the Skrælings. At first things went badly. The Norse settlers had brought a bull that became excited by the great number of Skrælings who suddenly appeared out of the woods. Bellowing at them and charging, the bull frightened many of them away.

Curiosity and the wish to trade (rather than fight) gained the upper hand, and the Skrælings returned, offering furs and pelts in return for weapons. Karlsefni, sensibly anticipating the trouble that trade in weapons would bring to much later generations of settlers in North America, insisted that the Norse could only offer milk, which the women in the colony carried out to the Skrælings, who were delighted by this – 'the Skrælings carried away their purchases in their bellies.'[55] Just in case relations turned sour, Karlsefni had a palisade built around the settlement, and Guðríð gave birth to the first European known to have been born on American soil. However, the Skrælings were turning troublesome; they were caught trying to steal weapons, and before long a battle broke out between the Norse and the Skrælings. Karlsefni decided that the time had come to load his rich cargo of furs and pelts on his ship and return to Greenland; his instincts as a trader came to the fore. Eventually he took his cargo all the way to Norway, where he sold his wares, 'and he and his wife were made much of by the noblest in the country'.[56]

As he was about to sail back towards Iceland a German from Bremen called on him. He wanted to buy a decorative wooden carving that was displayed on Karlsefni's ship. 'I do not want to sell it,' Karlsefni replied. 'I shall give you half a mark of gold for it,' said the southerner. Karlsefni realized what a good offer this was and agreed. But he did not know what type of wood it was; however, 'it had come from Vínland'.[57] Maybe it was the work of a native American, and that was why the Bremen merchant thought it so remarkable.

Another attempt at settlement in Leif's camp followed later, and now Freydis, the illegitimate daughter of Eirík the Red, went out with the colonists. However, this time the trouble that flared was between the settlers themselves, with one group being reproved for storing their wares in the houses Leif had built. They went off and set up their own settlement not far from Leif's original one, but Freydis, whose brutality places her at the other end of the spectrum from the firm but good-natured Guðríð, had them killed, and when she found that none of her male companions would kill her victims' womenfolk, she took an axe and murdered five women as well, a 'monstrous deed' for which she was never punished in Greenland, but which brought her disgrace. Maybe one reason she escaped punishment was her heroic behaviour diring a Skræling attack, recounted, perhaps fancifully, by the *Saga of Eirík the Red*: 'when the Skrælings came rushing towards her she pulled one of her breasts out of her bodice and slapped it with the sword. The Skrælings were terrified at the sight of this and fled back to their boats and hastened away.' She was a latter-day Brünnhilde. However, the saga says, 'although the land was excellent they could never live there in safety or freedom from fear, because of the native inhabitants. So they made ready to leave the place and return home.' On the way they captured a couple of Skræling boys in Markland and took them home, learning something about the ways of the people they had encountered. These boys may well have been Inuit, but further south they had probably met the Mic-Mac Indians, who would see Europeans once again when John Cabot landed in Newfoundland in 1497.[58] Guðrið had a much more honourable life than Freydis, and eventually went on pilgrimage to Rome, and the longhouse where she lived after her return from Vínland and Greenland has been plausibly identified. She ended her life as an anchorite living in Iceland, celebrated for her Christian piety. Through her American son, Snorri, and another child, she was also the ancestress of generations of distinguished Icelanders.[59]

So much for the information contained in the *Greenlanders' Saga*, and to some extent the *Saga of Eirík the Red*. Even so, the fantastic elements throw the reader off balance. Did Þorstein Eiríksson and his wife, Grimhild, really sit up in bed after they had died of a plague that ravaged Þorstein's crew – maybe some disease they had picked up in America?[60] And that is a story from the less fanciful of the two sagas about Vínland. This is where archaeology has once again come to the rescue, even if the physical remains are rather less impressive than those still standing in Greenland. In 1960 Helge and Anne Stine Ingstad, who had spent many years scouring the areas of North America within reasonable range of Greenland, identified a site on the northern tip of Newfoundland as a Norse settlement, even though it became obvious that it was only occupied for a score of years at the start of the eleventh century. It would be tempting to identify L'Anse aux Meadows as the place where Leif Eiríksson struck camp, although the location does not match the description in the sagas: this is some way north of the area where wild grapes can be found, and questions have been raised about its suitability as a harbour and about the mildness of winter weather, which was a point made in the saga description of Leif's camp. A harbour it must have been, though, as the finds included boat sheds in which rather small boats could be stored, the sort of vessel that, as has been seen, was often used by Norse hunters travelling north from the Western Settlement in Greenland.

There can be no doubt that this was a Norse site. As well as a bath-house, there was a charcoal kiln and a forge; the site contained a deposit of bog iron, which may be why the Norse stopped here – this was certainly something the native population never used, and yet access to iron and to smelting facilities would make a settlement much more viable: ships could be repaired, tools could be made, altogether the settlers would become less dependent on Greenland, which in any case could not offer them iron.

A spindle whorl indicates that women inhabited the site, as spinning was women's work. It is certainly possible that the buildings were constructed by another group of Greenlanders than those we hear about in the sagas; but the best bet is that the sagas were optimistic about the resources of Vínland, or at least the area around Leif's settlement, and that this was indeed where the explorers created a base. From this base they did travel further south, as remains of butternut squash, which does not grow at such a high latitude, were found on the site. Thus, even if it originated as Leif's camp, it became a service station on the route south; but whether the Norse built other settlements in the south, or simply travelled down for trade (as they travelled up Greenland for hunting) is an open question, as is the question whether they would have counted this area as Markland or Vínland.[61] The obvious conclusion is that, for a brief period, there did exist trade in American furs and pelts, against which the Norse increasingly preferred to offer strips of cloth (according to the sagas); but dealing with the Skrælings was not straightforward, and the risks were rapidly seen to outweigh the advantages. On the other hand, the Norse stay was so short that there was no need to create a cemetery: no skeletons have been found on the site.

Whether or not Norsemen reached as far north as Ellesmere Island, it is certain that Markland supplied the Greenlanders with wood. It was easily reached by following currents that headed north from the two Greenland settlements and then curved round, taking ships themselves built out of Markland wood past Baffin Island to the coast of Labrador and, eventually, the forested areas close to the sea. Unlike the voyages linking Greenland to Iceland and Norway, then, the Norse voyages to Vínland and Markland did not become regular, and settlement among hostile native inhabitants was not an option. The Norse traders' presence in America did not transform the maritime world in the way that the expeditions of Columbus, Cabot and Vespucci would do 500 years later, yet links to North America did not cease. This is not to claim that the Norse traders knew that Markland and Vínland were anything but large islands comparable to Iceland and Greenland – or maybe part of Asia, but this was not something about which they greatly cared.

22

From Russia with Profit

I

During the centuries of the Iceland trade and the Greenland trade, much more intensive maritime networks were developing further to the east, in the connected space of the Baltic and the North Sea, the 'Mediterranean of the North', into which, by way of Bergen, the Arctic luxuries discussed in the previous chapter were fed.[1] This became an organized space; that is to say, the activities of merchants were controlled with increasing attention by a loose confederation of towns that had itself emerged out of corporations of merchants. During this period, from about 1100 to about 1400, the Mediterranean became a theatre for contest between the Genoese, the Pisans, the Venetians and eventually the Catalans, who were often as keen to challenge one another as they were to join campaigns against the real or supposed enemies of Latin Christendom in the Islamic lands and in Byzantium.[2] In the 'Mediterranean of the North', by contrast, the unity of purpose of the merchants is striking – there were, of course, rivalries, and efforts were made to exclude outsiders from England or Holland, but co-operation was the norm.

This confederation of merchants from towns along the shores of the Baltic and the North Sea, and across great swathes of the north German hinterland, is known as the German Hansa. *Hansa* or *Hanse* was a general term for a group of men, such as an armed troop or a group of merchants; in the thirteenth century the term *Hansa* was applied to different bodies of merchants, German or Flemish, from a variety of regions, for instance the Westphalian towns that gravitated around Cologne, or the Baltic towns that were presided over by the great city of Lübeck; but in 1343 the king of Sweden and Norway addressed 'all the merchants of the Hansa of the Germans' (*universos mercatores de Hansa Teutonicorum*), and the idea that this was the Hansa par excellence, a sort of super-Hansa embracing all the little Hansas, spread thereafter.[3] The phrase *dudesche hanze*

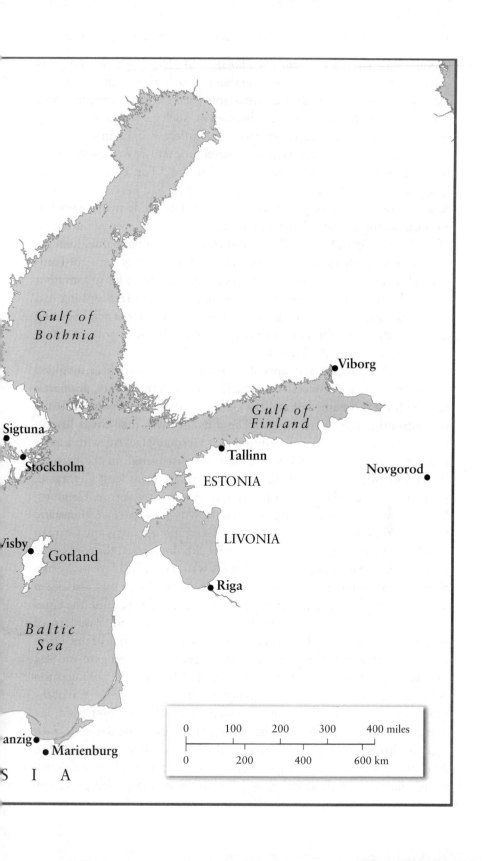

Gulf of
Bothnia

Viborg

Gulf of
Finland

Sigtuna

Tallinn

Stockholm

ESTONIA

Novgorod

LIVONIA

Visby

Gotland

Riga

Baltic
Sea

anzig

Marienburg

S   I   A

0	100	200	300	400 miles
0	200	400		600 km

(Middle Low German – *Deutsche Hanse* in Modern High German) was used informally; but the official term that the early Hanseatic (or, as they are sometimes called, Hansard) merchants used for themselves in places where they successfully installed themselves, such as Bergen in Norway or the Swedish island of Gotland, was rather different: in Latin *mercatores Romani imperii*, or in Low German *coepmanne van de Roemschen rike*, both meaning 'merchants of the Roman Empire'.[4] For, even in German lands far beyond the Rhine and the Danube that had never fallen under Roman rule nobles, knights and merchants took pride in the imperial authority of the medieval German kings, most of whom received the crown of the Holy Roman Empire. The major Hansa city in the Baltic, Lübeck, was elevated to the special status of a free imperial city by Emperor Frederick II in 1226, having already received privileges from his grandfather Frederick Barbarossa in the twelfth century. Since the Danish king had been making his own bid to gain control of Lübeck and the neighbouring lands of Schleswig, the German ruler understood how important it was to win the loyalty of the Lübeckers.[5]

To a striking degree, accounts of Hanseatic history have been moulded by modern political concerns. In the late nineteenth century, Bismarck and the Kaisers dreamed of making Germany into a naval power capable of confronting the British at sea. The difficulty was that Great Britain appeared to possess a naval tradition that Germany lacked; with a little probing, however, just such a tradition was discovered, in the fleets of the Hansa cities. That the Hansa was a German, or at least Germanic, phenomenon was easy to demonstrate: there were, it was true, Flemings, Swedes and other non-Germans whose towns took part in Hanseatic trade, but these people shared a common Germanic ancestry, and German merchants in such centres as Visby and Stockholm formed the core of the original merchant community. Such ideas were taken still further by historians writing under the Third Reich. By now the Hansa was associated not just with racial purity but with German conquest, because the cities founded along the shores of the Baltic by merchants and crusaders, of which more shortly, could be presented as glittering beacons of the 'Drive to the East' that had subjugated, and would once again subjugate, the Slav and Baltic peoples. Even after the fall of the Third Reich, the politicization of Hansa history continued, though in new directions. Since several of the most important Hanseatic towns, such as Rostock and Greifswald, lay along the shores of the now vanished German Democratic Republic, East German historians took an interest in the Hansa. They were wedded to Marxist ideas about class structure, and they made much of the 'bourgeois' character of these cities, which were by and large self-governing communities, able until the fifteenth century to fend off the attempts by local princes to draw them into their political web. East German historians also laid a strong emphasis on evidence for political protest among the artisan class in the Hansa towns, and they asked themselves whether these were places where a precocious proto-capitalism came into existence (whatever that term might mean).[6]

Following the collapse of the discredited East German regime, inter-pretations of the history of the Hansa have swung in a different direction, with German historians once again taking the lead. The Hansa is now held up as a model of regional integration, an economic system that crossed political boundaries by linking together Germany, England, Flanders, Norway, Sweden, the future Baltic states and even Russia. Andrus Ansip, Prime Minister of Estonia, celebrated the entry of his country into the Eurozone by declaring: 'the EU is a new Hansa'. Modern German accounts of the Hansa barely conceal their authors' satisfaction that German economic dominance within Europe has what appear to be inspiring precedents going right back to the Middle Ages: the German Hansa encouraged free trade among its members and constituted a 'superpower of money'.[7] There was even a degree of political integration, since commercial law followed a limited number of models; at first many maritime cities followed the sea law of Visby in Gotland, but over time the commercial law followed in Lübeck became standard. However, a leading French historian of the Hansa, Philippe Dollinger, took exception to the common term 'Hanseatic League', because the German Hansa was not one league with a central organization and bureaucracy, like the European Union, but a medley of leagues, some created only in the short term to deal with particular problems. He very sensibly suggested that the term 'Hanseatic Community' fits best of all.[8]

All these ways of reading the history of the Hansa distort its past in a broadly similar way. The German Hansa was not simply a maritime trading network. By the fourteenth century it had become a major naval power, able to defeat rivals for control of the waters where its members traded. Less often noticed is the significance of the inland cities that played a very important role in Hanseatic trade with England, operating under the leadership of Cologne.[9] Of its three major trading counters outside the network of Hanseatic cities, places where the Hanseatics were permitted to create their own towns within a town, one, Novgorod, lay inland, though the other two, Bergen and London, were only accessible by sea. The Hansa was a land power (or maybe one should say river power) as well as a sea power, and its ability to draw together the interests of cities in the German hinterland and cities that gave access to the sea lent it enormous economic strength. It was a source of supply for luxury goods such as furs from Russia, spices from the Levant (by way of Bruges) and amber from the Baltic; but its members were even more active carrying uncountable barrels of herring, vast supplies of wind-dried cod, or the rye produced along the shores of the Baltic on the lands of the Teutonic Knights. Indeed, the link to this crusading order of knights, lords of large parts of Prussia and Estonia, was so close that the Grand Master of the German Order, to give the Knights their correct name, was a member of the Hanseatic parliament, or Diet. As well as supplying a good part of the food the Hansa cities required if they were to survive and grow, the Grand Master was overlord of several towns that the German merchants had set up along the southern shores of the Baltic.[10]

The presence of a crusading Military Order in the deliberations of the German Hansa acts as a reminder that the medieval conquest of the Baltic was not simply the result of merchant endeavours. Just as the Genoese, Pisans and Venetians took full advantage of the crusades in the Mediterranean to install themselves in the trading centres of the eastern Mediterranean, the arrival of German merchants in Prussia, Livonia (roughly Latvia) and Estonia was rendered possible by the victories of the 'northern crusades', wars against pagans and sometimes against the Orthodox Russians in which two German Military Orders, the Sword Brethren and the Teutonic Knights, played a leading role, as did the Danish and Swedish kings. The Sword Brethren came into existence at the start of the thirteenth century, when Albert von Buxhövden, an enterprising cleric with close family links to the archbishop of Hamburg–Bremen, arrived in Latvia with twenty-three ships, carrying 500 crusaders. His aim was always to create a permanent German presence in the area, and so he established a trading centre at Riga in 1201. This also became the base for the crusading brethren, whose mission was to convert the local Livs (a people related to the Finns and the Estonians), if need be by force. The 'northern crusades' borrowed concepts and vocabulary from the more celebrated crusades to the Holy Land, portraying their wars as the defence of lands dedicated to the Mother of God, just as the expeditions to Jerusalem were conducted in defence of the patrimony of the Son of God; in due course the Teutonic Knights would name their command centre in Prussia Marienburg, 'the fortress of St Mary'. Without constant supplies of state-of-the-art weaponry brought across the Baltic on Hansa ships, these campaigns against wily, well-trained, obstinate native peoples had little chance of success; as it was, the ferocity of the German onslaught did more to unite the opposition than to break it down.[11]

Very soon the conquest of Livonian territory became an end in itself, and interest in the spiritual life of the Livs waned, if indeed it had ever been strong. A contemporary writer named Henry, who wrote a chronicle of the conquest of Livonia, insisted that all the violence against the Livs was in a good cause; as pagans, they had robbed, killed and committed sexual depravity, including incest, but after baptism they were subject to holy correction, which often seemed to work. On one occasion Sword Brethren fighting Estonian pagans maintained a siege of a heathen strong-hold for several days, calmly killing their prisoners in sight of the besieged, until the Estonians had had enough: 'we acknowledge your God to be greater than our gods. By overcoming us, he has inclined our hearts to worship him.' As at the time of the conversion of the Scandinavians, the message was that Christ was a warrior to be respected above all other leaders.[12] The Brethren formed part of the bishop of Riga's entourage until they began to interfere in the Danish lands that had been carved out of Estonia, including the trading city the Danes had created there – Reval, or Tallinn (which may mean 'castle of the Danes').[13] By 1237, this and other scandals had reached the ears of the papacy, with the result that the Sword Brethren were incorporated willy-nilly into the larger and better-organized Teutonic Knights; but by then the Sword Brethren had already extended the German military presence, and by extension the German trading presence, far along the southern shores of the Baltic.[14]

As the foundation of Tallinn suggests, the thirteenth-century conquest of the Baltic was not solely achieved by Germans. The political ambitions of the Danish and Swedish kings, often in competition with one another, also transformed this area, and offered yet more opportunities to German merchants. From the foundation of Stockholm, around 1252, German merchants were made welcome in the island city, because the Swedish rulers understood that the resources they needed for their wars of conquest had in large part to come from the profits of trade. Scandinavian raids brought the Finnish coast under the rule of the Swedish kings, and Estonia fell under Danish rule for a time, until it was handed on to the Teutonic Knights. Without violence to the evidence, these attacks can be seen as a continuation of the wars fought by earlier Danish and Swedish rulers, and by Viking raiders, in the days when Haithabu and Wolin were major trad-ing bases perched on the edge of pagan principalities.

The history of this period, known largely from German and Scandina-vian writings produced by Christians who were fiercely critical of their pagan neighbours, is too easily presented as a one-way movement of ruth-less crusading armies and navies eastwards into the Baltic lands. The reality on the ground was more complex. By the twelfth and thirteenth centuries the Slavs, Balts and Finno-Ugrians who inhabited the Baltic shores, mostly pagan, were launching their own Viking-style raids against German and Danish ships and settlements. Just as the Anglo-Saxons had once prayed for deliverance from the wrath of the Northmen, so in medieval Denmark prayers were uttered beseeching deliverance from Curonian raiders, the pagan inhabitants of what is now the west coast of Latvia; in 1187 Estonian raiders reached as far as the important trading base of Sigtuna, on Lake Mälaren, which they sacked, having outwitted the Swedish defences. It was a feat worthy of those Vikings who in earlier centuries had navigated down the Seine or the Guadalquivir with the aim of sacking the rich towns of France and Spain.[15] Looking further ahead, the Swedish king, Birger, informed the Hansa in 1295 that he had conquered the Karelians, in southern Finland, and had converted them to Christianity; this was perfectly just, he argued, since they had been launching pirate attacks on Christian shipping, and had routinely disembowelled their victims. He had also constructed a castle at Viborg 'to the honour of God and the glorious Virgin, both for the protection of our kingdom and for the safety and peace of seafarers'. From Viborg, King Birger proposed to keep a watchful eye on trade towards Russia, even limiting the number of Russian merchants who could board Baltic shipping. What he really wanted was a stake in the fur trade out of Russia, and to extend his political control over the southern shores of Finland.[16] As trade across the sea grew in volume, German and Scandinavian ships became more obvious targets for raiders of all descriptions. Imposing order on these dangerous seas would, however, produce handsome returns. Trade and crusade were intimately entangled, whether in the Baltic or in the Mediterranean; but political ambitions also counted for much in the calculations of the crusading kings of Sweden.

II

Why the Germans became dominant in the Baltic and the North Sea is a good question. After all, around 1100, German ships were not seen as often in the North Sea or the Baltic as Scandinavian ones, while the Flemings were a notable presence on the river routes of northern Europe, and further south in Germany there were busy communities of Jewish merchants, especially active in the wine trade; whether deliberately excluded or simply not interested in the far-flung north, the German Jews took no part in the transformation of the Baltic and the North Sea led by the Hansa.[17] Until Lübeck began to flourish in the twelfth century there were no German towns on the Baltic, and the area that became the German

Democratic Republic did indeed have a different identity to the rest of Germany: its inhabitants were pagan Slavs, notably the Wends, or Sorbians, who still survive in the Spreewald near Berlin. The predecessor of Lübeck, Liubice, or Alt-Lübeck, consisted of a fortress established by a *knes*, or prince, of the Polabian Slavs, while not far off another very small Slav settlement lay at Rostock, in Abotrite territory; beyond lay Rugians, Wagrians, Pomeranians – Szczecin (Stettin), close to the modern German–Polish border, was famous for its three pagan temples and its strong walls.[18] There was an enormous variety of different peoples speaking different languages or dialects, and the fragmentation into small groups rendered all of them much more vulnerable to the organized onslaughts of the Germans and the Danes. But there was plenty of peaceful contact too; several of these Slavonic peoples were happy to trade across the sea, which was also visited by Russian merchants, who were arriving in Gotland off Sweden, and reaching Schleswig in 1157. There can be no doubt that they were arriving much earlier, because links to Russia went back to the period when Scandinavian princes had become rulers of Kiev; Varangian merchants from Sweden had long been familiar with the river routes that extended far to the south, through Ukraine and, with a short hop overland, to the Black Sea. However, the twelfth-century Russian merchants came from Novgorod rather than Kiev, selling furs and pelts from the edges of the Arctic that had filtered down to Novgorod itself.[19]

The transformation of this region was, however, the work of Germans, by which one means speakers of a group of languages which (in their late medieval written form) goes under the name of Middle Low German, and which, at first glance, looks more like Dutch than the High German of further south, meaning that relations with Flemings and Hollanders were easy to maintain. Two places dominated the Baltic in the early days of the Hansa: Gotland, particularly its largest town, Visby; and Lübeck. It might seem odd that one of these places was not in German territory at all, but on a Swedish island; but, as has been seen, Lübeck too was barely in Germany, if by Germany is understood the area inhabited by German-speakers. Lübeck was not on exactly the same site as the old town of Liubice, which was more exposed.[20] The foundation of the new city happened in stages, first with the destruction of Liubice in wars between Slavs and Germans, and then with the creation of a new town by the ruler of Holstein, Adolf von Schauenburg, in 1143. This was a bad moment, since soon afterwards the papacy declared a crusade on three fronts – not just the Second Crusade, which took the French and German kings off to Syria in the vain hope of conquering Damascus, but encouragement to the Christian armies fighting the Muslims in Spain, and a war against the pagan Wends which the pope would have preferred the German king to join.

The pope was rightly worried that two kings on crusade to the East would only obstruct one another, which is exactly what happened. In 1147, during the war against the Wends, the Abotrite ruler, Niklot, attacked Lübeck; but it was already well enough defended to resist him. On the other hand, it proved more difficult to resist the growing power of Henry the Lion – the duke of Saxony and one of the greatest princes in Germany – who refounded Lübeck in 1159, and granted it the *iura honestissima*, 'the most honourable charter of town rights', rights that were confirmed by the German emperor, Barbarossa, even after he had destroyed the power of his rival Henry in the 1180s. This gave the leading citizens power over law-making, and established them as the city elite.[21] A German chronicler, Helmold von Bosau, was strongly of the view that Henry was only interested in making money, and did not really care whether the Slavs in the surrounding countryside turned Christian; but Henry certainly had a good sense of what was needed to make his new city flourish:

> The duke sent envoys into the northern towns and states, Denmark, Sweden, Norway and Russia, offering them peace and free right of access through his town of Lübeck. He also established there a mint and a market and granted the town the highest privileges. From that time onwards there was ever-increasing activity in the town and the number of its inhabitants rose considerably.[22]

He was particularly keen to attract merchants from Visby, for he understood that a network linking Gotland, situated right in the middle of the Baltic, and Lübeck, with its access to the interior, would be extremely profitable. From 1163, Gotlanders were allowed to come to Lübeck free of tolls, though Henry expected reciprocal rights for Lübeckers visiting Gotland. Lübeck grew and grew; although the size of its population before 1300 is pure guesswork, the city is thought to have had 15,000 inhabitants at the start of the fourteenth century, and in the late fourteenth century – a time when plague had depopulated much of Europe – the population may have reached 20,000.[23]

Lübeck looked in two directions. Westwards, a short overland route connected the new city to Hamburg, giving access to the North Sea, and this was guaranteed by a formal agreement between the towns in 1241; by the fourteenth century, the narrow sea passage through the Øresund, or Sound, between Denmark and what is now southern Sweden, took priority. Naturally, use of that route depended on the approval of the king of Denmark, and relations between Lübeck and the Danes were not always easy. In the very early days, Henry the Lion boosted Lübeck by working closely with King Valdemar of Denmark to conquer the coastline that stretched east from Lübeck towards the large island of Rügen, where the statue of the Slav god Svantovit was 'hacked to pieces and cast into the fire'. That done, the Danish king seized the temple treasures he found there. There was always the danger that the king of Denmark would come to regard these shores as his own little empire. One important result of these conquests was the foundation of satellite towns within the commercial orbit of Lübeck, towns that followed the Lübeck legal code; Rostock has been mentioned, established at the start of the thirteenth century, and a similar story of foundation, with the blessing of local territorial lords, applied at Danzig and elsewhere. These princes, whether German or Slav, were keen to draw in the profits of expanding trade; but the new towns acted as agents for the growing population of the German heartlands, who took the opportunity to settle the countryside alongside or in lieu of the existing Slav population – Netherlanders arrived as far afield as the Upper Elbe, where they introduced drainage schemes they had learned in their own boggy homeland, and left behind Dutch dialects that were still to be heard at the start of the twentieth century. This 'Drive to the East', *Drang nach Osten*, was both maritime and terrestrial.[24]

Only defeat in 1226 checked the apparently irresistible rise of the Danish coastal empire, which for a time even included Lübeck. The German emperor, Frederick II, looked on, but those who led the assault were the count of Schwerin, one of his often troublesome subjects, and the Lübeckers themselves.[25] However, the Danes refused to stop interfering, and the ambitions of Valdemar IV Atterdag, the Danish king, who reigned from 1340 to 1375, drew together the Hansa cities. His relentless attempt to overwhelm Visby and Gotland, and to create a base there for Baltic expansion, was checked amid massive slaughter in 1361; the hideously wounded skeletons of the besiegers are a ghoulish motif of Swedish museums.[26] When they at last made peace with the Danes at Stralsund in 1370, the Hansa cities were even able to insist that Valdemar's successor would need to meet with their approval before he could be crowned king. That was a prestigious prize; but there were other prizes that were more valuable still: the Danes were forced to cede to the Hansa the towns that controlled traffic through the narrow passage of the Øresund – Helsingborg, Malmö and other places.[27]

This, then, was a glorious future, whose triumphs were expressed in the handsome Gothic buildings that the Lübeckers constructed at huge expense out of brick; there were grand churches, such as the Marienkirche and Sankt Petri in Lübeck, but also streets of gabled merchant houses, and these became the model copied by the masons of Rostock, Greifswald, Bremen, and of city after city along the great arc that stretched from Bruges to Tallinn. The design of these houses was determined by the simple need to incorporate a warehouse as well as an office and living quarters, because the Hanseatic merchants looked after their own goods rather than depositing them in central warehouses, as often happened in the Mediterranean. Yet the most successful merchants also sought to show off their wealth with Gothic frills and other touches of grandeur, such as a façade coated in imported stone to distinguish their home from the frontages on either side.[28] Artists from Lübeck such as Bernt Notke and Hermen Rode, the creator of massive carved altarpieces, were in great demand as far away as central Sweden, so that cogs sometimes carried not just rye and herrings but carefully wrapped masterpieces destined for the churches of Stockholm and elsewhere.[29] A common legal standard, the maritime law of Lübeck, ensured that commercial disputes would be solved by similar means in places very far apart. A common language, Low German, took over from Latin as the medium in which to record business transactions. The middle classes in the Hansa towns did not learn letters in order to dispute the ideas of St Augustine or Thomas Aquinas, even though Lübeck and other cities had their share of wealthy convents, and both Rostock and Greifswald acquired universities that still survive, founded in 1419 and 1456; an ability to read and write oiled the wheels of commerce.[30]

III

Late medieval Lübeck gloried in the title *Caput Hanse*, 'head of the Hansa', but in the early days of what was to become the German Hansa, Visby exercised more influence than Lübeck, benefiting from its excellent position in the middle of the southern Baltic.[31] A self-governing community of German traders began to coalesce; on its seal it proudly proclaimed itself to be the *universitas mercatorum Romani imperii Gotlandiam frequentantium*, 'the corporation of merchants of the Roman Empire visiting Gotland'. This word *universitas* had not yet become a term of art for places of advanced learning, and retained its generalized meaning of 'community', 'corporation', not so different from the vernacular term *Hansa*. In the thirteenth century, enough Germans had settled permanently on the island to form a second, parallel, self-governing group, using a similar seal, but with the word *manentium*, 'remaining in', replacing *frequentantium*, 'visiting'. The Germans had their own very magnificent church, St Mary of the Germans, which now serves as Visby cathedral; the Germans also, as was typical at the time, used it as a safe place to store goods and money. In addition to a quite formidable line of walls, more than two miles (about 3.5 km) in length, Visby contains over a dozen sizeable medieval churches, but following the city's decline at the end of the Middle Ages all but St Mary's fell into disrepair. Birka may have been the first town in Sweden, but Visby was its first city.

One of Visby's grandest churches, Sankt Lars, betrays the influence of Russian architectural styles, and a small church in the south of the island contains frescoes in a Byzantine–Russian style; there was also a Russian Orthodox church in Visby, though this is now buried underneath a café. For Gotland was the great emporium where Russian goods such as furs and wax were received, having travelled part of the way by river, through Lake Ladoga and up the Neva into the Baltic, and then across what could be dangerous waters to Gotland itself. At the other end of the route, in Novgorod, the Gotlanders possessed their own trading colony, or 'Gothic Court', which included a church dedicated to the Norwegian king, St Olaf, in existence by about 1080.[32] Novgorod was not an ancient city, as its name, 'New City', suggests: tests carried out on the wooden streets of medieval Novgorod, excavated in the 1950s, take the city's history no further back than 950.[33] The Baltic connection was thus of great importance to Novgorod, just as the Russian connection was of great importance to Gotland; and Henry the Lion and the Lübeckers were keen to tap into that. At first, the Germans rode on the backs of the Gotlanders. In 1191 or 1192 Prince Yaroslav III of Novgorod entered into a treaty with the Gotlanders and the Germans, but it mentions an earlier treaty, now lost – whether this included the Germans is unknown.[34]

Within twenty years another prince of Novgorod, Konstantin, granted the Germans the right to operate from their own courtyard, dedicated to St Peter – the Peterhof. Actually they had already set themselves up there, and had built a stone church. The use of stone was a necessary luxury, since the merchants stored their wealth here. Then they would go back to Visby at the end of each winter, carrying the chest containing the funds of the community until their return in the summer. Between the winter, when trade in ermine and other Arctic goods was brisk, and the summer, which was a good time to collect wax or buy the luxury goods arriving circuitously from the Black Sea and beyond, German merchants would be absent from Novgorod. Attempts were also made to build ties to other Russian cities, but they were never as successful as the links to Novgorod, which had the advantage of lying not too far inland. Once again, the sea is only part of a bigger story, since Cologne absorbed many of these Russian goods before they were sold on to Flemish and English businessmen.[35]

There was enormous demand throughout Europe for high-quality Russian wax, most of which evaporated into the atmosphere when it was used in church ceremonies; and the range of furs that could be obtained from Russia and Finland was unmatched: not just plenty of cheap rabbit and squirrel furs, but pine marten, fox, and at the top of the scale white ermine (*de rigueur* at princely courts).

IV

Benefiting from their links to German cities as far away as Cologne, the early Hansa merchants could raise the capital they needed for ambitious ventures into Russia, carefully managed through legally binding contracts. This gave them an advantage over traditional Scandinavian traders, who operated with less sophisticated methods. The purchase of shares in ships rather than ownership of an entire ship meant that one could spread the risks associated with sea voyages across a number of investments. Contact with Russia provided essential priming for the rise of the German Hansa; but the Baltic and the North Sea became increasingly important to the Hanseatic traders, as England and Norway became the focus of their longer-distance sailings, while within the Baltic rye, herrings and other basic foodstuffs became ever more important as the German cities grew, and as their persistent demand for food outstripped local resources. These towns had been founded as centres of trade and industry, but their very success turned them into major consumers of agricultural goods. This was greatly to the advantage of those who produced such food, above all the Grand Master of the Teutonic Order, who was also master of extensive estates where subject Prussians and Estonians laboured on behalf of the Christian conquerors in slave-like conditions. Trade in grain, principally rye, became the lifeline of cities as far afield as Flanders and Holland, and this dependence would only increase over the centuries, long after the Grand Master of the Teutonic Order had become a distant memory in Prussia and beyond.[36]

The ships that the Hansa merchants used were, in the early days, mainly cogs, with their shallow draught but generous cargo capacity; they had developed in the North Sea and the Baltic over several centuries. A late fourteenth-century example was found in the mud of the River Weser in 1962 and has been carefully restored for the German Maritime Museum in Bremerhaven. Her timbers can be securely dated from their tree rings to 1378. She was twenty-four metres long, three times her maximum breadth, and her capacity was somewhere in the region of 100 tons. She originally possessed a square sail and a rudder at mid-stern. But she never went to sea, to judge from the fact that not much was found on board apart from the tools of a shipwright, so it is likely she was dragged underwater during a tidal surge. Her construction was slightly odd (carvel planking around the keel, with planks laid flush, rather than the clinker planking one generally expects in northern Europe); but this was a fairly old-fashioned type of ship by 1380: the Hansa fraternity were making increasing use of larger vessels, mounted with 'castles' at each end, the 'hulks' that appear on many a medieval town seal from this part of the world.[37] All this has set off technical arguments about when a cog is really a cog, though quirks of construction are only to be expected; the term *kogge* was a generic description, and these ships were not produced on an assembly line, unlike the big Venetian galleys of this period. They were no more uniform than modern city trams, but were perfectly recognizable as the same object; and what mattered was their seaworthiness first and their capacity second.[38]

Typical or not, the Bremen cog represents the humble realities of Hansa seafaring; silk and spices certainly reached the ports of northern Germany, whether they had been carried all the way from the Mediterranean down elongated sea routes favoured by the Venetian, Catalan and Florentine galleys of the late Middle Ages, or humped overland from the warehouse of the Germans (*Fondaco dei Tedeschi*) in Venice, past Bolzano and over the Alpine passes until they reached the rich cities of southern Germany – Nuremberg, Augsburg, Regensburg – and then embarked on further travels to reach Lübeck and its neighbours. A modern visitor to Lübeck who did not visit the famous marzipan emporium of the Niederegger family, founded in 1806, would be missing a great treat; but before Niederegger the city attracted ginger, sugar and cloves as well as almonds, and – most probably during the golden age of the Hansa – the north Germans discovered how they could manufacture sweetmeats and spicy sausages from the exotic trade goods that reached their cities. Fine *Wurst* is a Hanseatic legacy.

The fortunes of the Hansa were not, however, built out of marzipan and gingerbread. Fish, grain and salt, apparently humble animal, vegetable and mineral staples, were not quite such modest sources of profit as might be supposed when they were traded in the astonishing quantities handled by the German Hansa. Herrings had a special place in the diet of European Christians, as far away as Catalonia: when Lent arrived, they provided the perfect substitute for forbidden meat, all the more because methods of preserving them became more sophisticated. The difficulty with herring is that it is a very oily fish, and oily fish rot much faster than those with a very low fat content, notably cod. For this reason it was possible to produce wind-dried cod, which remained edible for a good many years (after soaking), whereas herring had to be salted and pickled as quickly as possible after it was caught.[39] Tradition records that a Dutch sailor, Willem Beukelszoon from Zeeland, transformed the future of the herring fisheries in the fourteenth century, when he devised a method of pickling partly eviscerated herrings and placing them between layers of salt in great barrels, which had to be done immediately after they were brought on deck (the secret was to leave the liver and pancreas in place, which improved the flavour, while removing the rest of the guts). This seems already to have been standard Hanseatic practice, and it was adopted in Flanders only around 1390, when fighting in the North Sea interrupted the flow of herrings to Flanders.[40] Pioneer or plagiarist, Beukelszoon has been rated as the 157th most important Dutchman in history, not surprisingly in a nation that loves its *Nieuwe Haring* so much, but also in tribute to the fortune that the Dutch made out of exporting this humble fish in later centuries.

Nothing, though, compared to the quantities of herring to be found in the Baltic when the fish spawned off the coast of Skania, now the southernmost province of Sweden but during the Middle Ages generally under Danish rule. It was said that you could wade into the sea and scoop them out of the water with your hands; rather than sea, there was a mass of wriggling fish: 'the entire sea is so full of fish that often the vessels are stopped and can hardly be rowed clear through great exertion', to cite an early medieval Danish writer.[41] All this gave great impetus to the fair held on the shores of Skania, which dealt in many goods, but was most famous for its herring market; temporary shacks were set up as housing for the thousands of people who came to the fairs, also providing factory space for the labour force that cured, dried and, in a myriad of other ways, treated the fish. The fairs became an ever more attractive centre of trade as demand for these fish expanded and as the reputation of Skania as the unsurpassed centre of this business became known: visitors arrived from northern France, England and even Iceland.[42]

In the course of the fifteenth century, the herrings began to gather further north, for an unexplained reason (maybe connected with climatic conditions), and the glory days of the Skania fairs came to an end. But at its peak it was not unusual for 250 ships all loaded with herring to come into port at Lübeck alone, as happened in 1368. Annual totals just for Lübeck may have reached 70,000 barrels.[43] Yet none of this could have happened without the availability of salt to preserve the silver harvest of herrings – indeed, some Dutch observers went further, and less poetically called it a 'gold mine'. Here lay Lübeck's great advantage. Not far away, near Lüneburg Heath, lay very extensive supplies, consisting of strong brine that was boiled down to produce salt; this was not the cheapest process, and when in the early fifteenth century rivals in western France began to flood the market with their own cheaper salt (sometimes half the price, even after long-distance transport), Lüneburg fell into decline, and Hansa merchants proved happy to range much further afield, all the way to the Bay of Bourgneuf or even Iberia.[44]

This Hanseatic world, at once contentious and co-operative, thus extended its sights far beyond the Baltic and the North Sea. It has been seen that the search for cheap salt took German ships all the way to western France. There they might encounter ships from another land that were learning their way around the Atlantic: the Portuguese, whose own base in Flanders lay at Middelburg, close to the modern Belgian–Dutch frontier. But by the fifteenth century the Hansards were travelling even further, reaching Portugal itself, which they recognized as another source of salt (including the flat lands around Lisbon); and they also recognized that Portugal was short of grain, which they could easily supply from the rich reserves of the Baltic. They brought all sorts of other foods to Portugal, including beer and beetroots, and even salted fish, which was something the Portuguese could supply to themselves in vast quantities. After the Portuguese captured the Moroccan port of Ceuta in 1415, in the campaign where Prince Henry the Navigator won his spurs, German ships began to bring grain as far south as Ceuta itself, which was desperate for supplies as it was cut off from the rich grain fields that still lay under Muslim rule. Nor was this a casual relationship: Hansards interested in Portugal included prominent burghers of Danzig experienced in trade with Scotland, England, Flanders and France.[45] As Portugal emerged as a significant maritime power in the fifteenth century, its Hanseatic connections gave it access to a much larger world than the waters off Iberia.

23

Stockfish and Spices

The calamity of the Black Death struck first the Mediterranean and then northern Europe from 1347 to about 1351, followed by further periodic visitations of bubonic and pneumonic plague. The heavy toll on human life – as much as half the population in some areas – reduced pressure on supplies of the most basic foodstuffs, notably grain, but had distorting effects on the production and distribution of food. Land went out of cultivation as villages lost their manpower and became unviable; migration to the towns, where artisans were in short supply, shifted the balance between urban and rural population, so that it was no longer broadly true that up to 95 per cent of the population of western and northern Europe lived and worked in the countryside; and even those peasants who remained in the countryside often managed to cast off what remained of the shackles of serfdom. This was the beginning of a great economic transformation, but the reconfiguration of the economy depended on the easy movement of large quantities of food. Here, transport by sea was of crucial importance, since it rendered possible the movement of really substantial quantities of grain, dried fish, dairy goods, wine, beer and other necessities or desirables, and the ability of the Hansa merchants to exploit these opportunities meant that the years around 1400, often characterized as a period of deep post-plague recession, were for them, as for merchants in many other parts of the Atlantic and Mediterranean, a time when it was possible to reap handsome profits and to answer back to rulers who up to now had seen them as rather troublesome creatures, valuable only as suppliers of prestige items, and greedy and unreliable.

It comes as no surprise, then, that within a few years of the Black Death the Hansa merchants began to organize themselves much more tightly, holding regular Diets, or *Hansetage* (which were also an opportunity for Lübeck and some other leading cities to throw their weight around). This has generally been interpreted as a shift from the 'Hansa of the Merchants' to the 'Hansa of the Towns', even the creation of what one might call a

'Hanseatic League', which (in this view) would be one of a great many city-leagues that were emerging in the fragmented territories of the German Empire at this time, of which the most famous, because it still exists, is the league of cities and peasant communities in southern Germany that we know as Switzerland. Still, these leagues had no pretensions to what might be called statehood, not that the concept of statehood would have meant much to the Hansa merchants. Moreover, the Hansa was different from other leagues since it included a large number of places that lay outside the Holy Roman Empire, such as Riga and Tallinn.[1] The first Diet was held at Lübeck in 1356, following pirate attacks, unsatisfied demands for indemnity, and the breakdown of relations with the counts of Flanders and with the city of Bruges; solidarity between cities was the best way to force the Flemings to restore the rights of the Hansards.[2] As will be seen, the relationship between the Hansa and Bruges was always a delicate one, because each side needed the other, while complaints about the abuse of existing rights abounded, and the Hansards again and again threatened to move their business to one of Bruges's lesser rivals. Issues of this order bound the Hansa cities together, and by 1480 seventy-two Diets had been held. It is no surprise that fifty-four of these gathered in Lübeck; and, apart from a single meeting in Cologne, they were always held in towns next to or quite near the sea, such as Bremen.[3]

This development did not mean that the Hansa had become a state-like body; it remained a loose super-league, bringing together groups of allied cities from regions as diverse as the Rhineland, where Cologne dominated, the southern or 'Wendish' Baltic, which was Lübeck's informal *imperium*, and the newer cities of the eastern Baltic, of which Riga was the most important. Minutes of the Diets were kept; but there was no administrative superstructure, and there were no formal treaties that members signed to gain entry to the Hansa. Maybe, indeed, this was one of its sources of strength. On the other hand, the lack of a constitution allowed the citizens of Lübeck to turn their *de facto* leadership of the Hansa to their advantage, and, despite grumbles from Danzig and Cologne, the special status of Lübeck was never really in doubt; its size, wealth and location gave it formidable advantages. Including every city that at some stage was regarded as a Hansa town, the total comes to about 200, too many to fit into the assembly hall provided by the good burghers of Lübeck; most members were far too small to exercise any political influence, and what they sought was tax advantages and trading opportunities. This was particularly true of the horde of inland towns, such as Hamelin of Pied Piper fame, or Berlin, not as yet a place of great significance. The sections consisting of Baltic members were much smaller in number, but their importance was

Gulf of
Bothnia

Gulf of
Finland

Tallinn

Novgorod

Tartu

Stockholm

LIVONIA

Visby

Gotland

Riga

Baltic
Sea

Danzig

0	100	200	300	400 miles
0	200	400	600 km	

out of all proportion to their slight numbers, given the presence of Lübeck, Danzig, Riga and Visby.[4] In addition, the member cities lay under very different political regimes. Further east, the Teutonic Knights exercised overlordship, and the host of inland cities that occasionally sent representatives to the Hansa Diet were by and large subject to a local duke or count, which was not a great problem around 1400, when princely power in Germany was very weak, but did become more problematic once the princes began to claw back their power in the middle of the fifteenth century, sometimes forbidding towns from sending representatives to the Hansa Diet.[5]

After 1356 the Hansa showed much more muscle, resisting not just the Danes but predatory pirates known as the *Vitalienbrüder*, who made a nuisance of themselves at the end of the fourteenth century; they probably earned their strange name, the 'Victual Brothers', from their role as privateers who kept Stockholm supplied with food during a Danish siege in 1392. This siege was a dramatic moment in a war of succession that would, by the start of the fifteenth century, see a personal union of the three Scandinavian kingdoms; but the war spilled over into the Baltic, since the major actors included the duke of Mecklenburg as well as an exceptionally capable and determined royal consort, Queen Margaret of Denmark; one of the issues in the Swedish succession was the fear that the arrival of a north German duke as king would extend still further the powerful German influence in the country, which was already strongly expressed through the sizeable German community living in the boom city of Stockholm. Queen Margaret was, however, canny enough to realize that she should cultivate the Hanseatic cities, which were reluctant to be drawn directly into a conflict that was likely to redraw the political map of northern Europe. She had already extended Danish authority over southern Sweden (Skania), the area that had been ruled from Denmark for most of the past centuries.[6] Once the siege of Stockholm was over, the *Vitalienbrüder* held on to their ships and preyed on Hanseatic and other vessels in the Baltic. The herring fisheries fell under threat, and for a few years supplies to the rest of the world faltered. Queen Margaret even appealed to King Richard II of England for naval aid, to help clear the Baltic and reopen the supply lanes. This appeal failed, and if anything the result was to stimulate the search for good-quality herring in the North Sea – admittedly, the quality was never quite as good as that in the Baltic, but thanks to the methods attributed to Beukelszoon the fish could be competently preserved.

Queen Margaret gained what she sought, mastery over the three Scandinavian kingdoms, and saw her son Erik, duke of Pomerania, crowned as ruler over this Nordic union in 1397. Even then, everyone wanted to fish in Baltic waters: the Teutonic Knights, not Queen Margaret, expelled the *Vitalienbrüder* from Gotland in 1394, although fifteen years later they sold the island to the Nordic queen and Erik. These were years when the Teutonic Knights were at a loose end: the ruler of the great Lithuanian duchy, extending all the way across Belarus and much of Ukraine, at last accepted Christianity in 1385, as part of a marriage treaty with his Polish neighbours, and the Knights found themselves with fewer excuses for the conquest of pagan territory in the east, though Orthodox Russia now came within their line of sight as a land of heretics. The Nazis made heroes of the medieval Teutonic Knights, but over the centuries the *Vitalienbrüder* have acquired a more romantic image; plenty of novels and films present one of their pirate leaders, Klaus Störtebeker, in a better light than he deserves. When conditions in the Baltic became too risky, they decamped to the East Frisian islands in the North Sea and carried on marauding there. Störtebeker was captured, and in about 1400 he and dozens of his companions underwent a grim execution at the hands of the resentful citizens of Hamburg. Even so, piracy remained a major worry in the North Sea, and the next generation of pirates were making a nuisance of themselves as far north as Bergen in 1440.[7]

All this meant that the Hansa Diets did have matters of real political and military (or rather naval) importance to discuss.[8] The Hansa Diet expected to make its decisions unanimously, but delegations would often insist that they had no authority to support a particular position; the Diet was not a parliament where common problems were aired, discussed and resolved, but a place where decisions (often those of Lübeck and its allies) were recorded and announced – that was how late medieval parliaments functioned. Cities might not bother to send delegates to the *Hansetag*, though not surprisingly the larger and more powerful ones were more careful to do so. Still, it must have seemed that this was Lübeck's opportunity to show off its commanding position. The effectiveness of the Hansa lay in the expertise of the merchants who inhabited its cities rather than in its institutional structure, which remained fragile.

II

The different communities that made up the Hansa were bonded together by the presence of travelling merchants, some passing through briefly and others settling alongside their fellow Hansards. Hansards felt at home in the ports of a great swathe of northern Europe. In the early fifteenth century, two brothers, Hildebrand and Sivert von Veckinchusen, worked with family members and agents in London, Bruges, Danzig, Riga, Tallinn and Tartu (also known as Dorpat), as well as Cologne and distant Venice, sharing the same work ethic, business methods and cultural preferences. In 1921, a pile of over 500 letters between members of the family was found buried in a mass of peppercorns within a chest that is now in the State Archives of Estonia at Tallinn. In addition, their account books survive. No other Hanseatic family is as well documented. The Veckinchusens are of interest precisely because they were not always successful, and their careers show clearly the risks that needed to be taken if the trade routes were to be kept alive at a time when piracy remained a constant threat, when the Danes were still flexing their muscles in the Baltic, when English sailors were trying to carve out their own niche in the market, and when internal tensions within the Hansa towns threatened to upset the apple cart.[9]

The Veckinchusen brothers originated in Tartu in what is now Estonia, although they eventually became citizens of Lübeck.[10] They are known to have been based in Bruges in the 1380s. They therefore operated between the two most important trading centres of northern Europe, which were linked by the Hanseatic sea route through the Øresund.[11] The Hansa community in Bruges operated rather differently from Novgorod, London and Bergen, where the German merchants possessed a reserved space and were closely concentrated together. As befitted a cosmopolitan centre that attracted businessmen from all over western Europe, notably Genoa and Florence, as well as from the Baltic, the Hansards were dispersed across the city, living in rented accommodation, though they did hire a meeting space in the convent of the Carmelite friars, whose church they attended. In 1478 the Hansards began building the handsome 'House of the Easterlings', or *Oosterlingenhuis*, that can still be seen (though much rebuilt) in the heart of the old trading area of Bruges. It possessed its own courtyard and stood on a plot of land that the city fathers had assigned to the Hansa several years earlier. Now they had a base for meetings, and some office space, situated close to the house of the great Florentine trading firm of the Portinari (patrons of Jan van Eyck), and to the Genoese consulate, a fine Gothic building that has been raised to new glories as the Belgian national fried-potato museum. Everyone wanted a base in Bruges, and around 1500 the English, the Scots, the Portuguese, the Castilians, the Biscayans, the Lucchesi, the Venetians, the Genoese, the Florentines and no doubt others as well also possessed business houses in the centre of the city.[12] Many of these communities, including most of the Hansards, were to decamp to Antwerp only a few years later; Bruges became less attractive for business as the water channels leading to the open sea silted up and as international politics (the ascendancy of the Habsburgs) favoured the growth of the more accessible port of Antwerp.[13]

Until then, the concentration of merchants of different backgrounds provided Bruges with its raison d'être. Bruges was a very large city by medieval standards, with up to 36,000 inhabitants on the eve of the Black Death; but it was not the prime target of all those traders who came there, even though the arrival of large amounts of Baltic rye and herring did help to keep the citizens well fed. In the fifteenth century, one of the main functions of the merchant communities in Bruges was quite simply to settle bills. The city became the major financial centre in northern Europe, which meant that even as its port silted up and fewer goods passed through the city, there was still plenty of work for those well practised in the art of accounting. The Veckinchusens were primarily dealers in commodities, but currency exchange and the provision of letters of credit was a source of profit for them and their peers, even though the Hansards left the creation of international banks mainly to the Italians – the Medici had an important branch in Bruges.[14] Generally, the Hansards showed a suspicion of reliance on credit that meant their financial methods never reached the sophistication of those achieved by the Florentines and Genoese. Even so, late medieval Bruges was to the economy of large swathes of Europe what modern London has become within the global economy.[15]

From the Hansa perspective this had both advantages and disadvantages. The usual pile of grievances – confiscations of goods, quarrels over tax exemptions, the rights of the resident community, interference by the counts of Flanders and their mighty successors the Valois dukes of Burgundy – soured relations between the Hansa and Bruges, and during the late fourteenth century the Hanseatic merchants were thinking seriously about moving their business away from Bruges, northwards towards Dordrecht. In the 1380s the Hansards lost not just property but lives in Bruges, during a period of revolutionary disorder that ended with the assumption of power by Philip the Bold, duke of Burgundy. Yet Philip was not willing to meet their demands for compensation, so in 1388 the Hansards did decamp to Dordrecht. This was not the back of beyond: in 1390 Hildebrand Veckinchusen was there, sending Flemish cloth and a fair amount of wine all the way to Tallinn. After a couple more years, relations with Bruges had been restored, and Hildebrand had become an Alderman of the Hansa community there; he had earned enough trust to be appointed an inspector of weights and measures, a task that was performed jointly with local officials.[16] For, in reality, the Hansards and the citizens of Bruges were happiest working closely together.

The Veckinchusens were not wedded to Bruges. Indeed, when Hildebrand found a bride, she was a young woman from a prosperous Riga family.[17] Going to Riga for his wedding, which had been arranged by one of his brothers, gave him the chance to experience the route to Novgorod, where the Hansa *Kontor*, or 'Counter', continued to flourish, and where he brought for sale thirteen bolts of cloth of Ypres, in other words a sizeable quantity of some of the best woollen cloth Flanders looms were then producing; each bolt would have been twenty-four yards long and one yard wide (approximately 22 by 0.9 metres). These he sold for 6,500 furs, which gives some idea not just of the high value of Flemish cloth but of the easy availability of squirrel, rabbit and finer skins in fifteenth-century Russia. On another occasion his brother Sivert forwarded 15,000 furs from Estonia to Bruges, where Hildeband had re-established himself – by 1402 he was renting a building in the city that included storage space as well as an apartment for his wife and his seven children.[18] In good years, the Veckinchusens could hope for profits in the range of 15–20 per cent.[19] Meanwhile his brother Sivert, now living in Lübeck, warned him that he was taking too many financial risks – 'I've warned you again and again that your stakes are too high' – which led him to send his wife and children to live in Lübeck; but he was convinced he could make money by staying put in Bruges.[20] This obstinacy in his business dealings was to cost him dear over the next few years.

Despite his warnings to his brother, Sivert also faced an uncertain future. His reputation in the city stood high, for he was invited to join the Society of the Circle, an influential club to which only members of the merchant elite were admitted. However, Lübeck was facing the same sort of political strife that was creating turmoil in Bruges, Barcelona, Florence and many other European cities in the years either side of 1400.[21] Lübeck's butchers, for instance, had already led two revolts, the 'Bone-Cutter Rebellions', in the 1380s, neither of which was successful. Much depended on the solidarity of the rebels, and in 1408 a New Council, on which the city's guilds were heavily represented, challenged the authority of the existing city council, which was seen as a high-spending and closed elite that spoke more for the Society of the Circle than for the city, and had failed to respond to the economic changes of the late fourteenth century. The increasing prosperity of the urban middle class in the decades after the Black Death, when reduced pressure of population gave access to better food and a higher standard of living, needed to be reflected in the government of the cities. The New Council attempted to keep its membership broad, so Sivert Veckinchusen, whose natural sympathies lay more with the old order, found himself elected to it; but he then followed many of the members of the Old Council into exile in Cologne. The Holy Roman Emperor, Sigismund of Luxembourg, had the unenviable task of sorting out who should govern the Imperial Free City of Lübeck, which was a matter of great importance to the rest of the Hansa, in view of its role as honorary head of the league. Sigismund ignored principles and was inclined to favour whichever side in Lübeck could offer him more money; when the New Council failed to satisfy his insatiable demands (24,000 florins), he sided with the Old Council, although its members had the sense to include some of their rivals in a government of reconciliation that came into being over the next few years; this helped restore much-needed stability to Lübeck.[22]

Meanwhile, Sivert turned his attention to landward connections between Germany and Italy, setting up a *venedyesche selskop*, or 'Venice Company', in Cologne that supplied the Italians with furs, cloth and rosaries made from Baltic amber (a monopoly of the Teutonic Knights). His brother Hildebrand joined the company; for a time everything looked very promising, but then things began to go awry: they were cheated of money that was owed to the firm, as well as making unwise choices about what to bring to Lübeck and the north (both by sea and overland), and what to send down to Venice, where they proved to have misjudged the appetite for furs and amber. Sivert had to report to his brother that the family should really have stayed with what it knew best, the sea trade from Bruges to the eastern Baltic; 'I wish I had never become involved in Venice,' Sivert complained.[23] But even the Baltic trade of the Veckinchusens fared less well than expected: woollen cloth despatched to Livonia was found to be riddled with moth-holes; and rice carried from Bruges to Danzig became waterlogged. For whatever reason, market conditions were poor in the years around 1418, whether in Danzig, Novgorod or the inner German cities, so the Veckinchusens were not the only ones to suffer; it seems the markets were saturated with goods, and that the whole decade from 1408 to 1418 saw poor profits.[24] In 1420 Hildebrand heard that the salt normally collected in the Bay of Bourgneuf was not available, so he thought he could restore his fortunes by snapping up the salt supplies of Livonia and sending them westwards towards Lübeck; but poor information about where in Livonia he should buy the salt and the simple fact that other merchants had the same idea meant that the attempt to corner the market failed.[25]

Hildebrand returned to Bruges and tried to keep himself afloat with Italian loans, but he could not repay them, and fled to Antwerp in the vain hope of escaping his creditors. Lured back to Bruges by promises that his friends would help him sort out his affairs, he was thrown into the debtors' prison, where he lingered in misery for three or four years, during which even Sivert was unwilling to offer any help; meanwhile Sivert was doing rather well, and was elected to the Lübeck Society of the Circle, the club of the wealthy and powerful that had honoured his brother some years earlier.[26] Conditions in the prison were not too bad, if means could be found to pay for food and the rent of a private room; but by the time he was released, in 1426, Hildebrand was evidently a broken man. One of his old partners wrote in pity: 'God have mercy on you, that it has happened to you this way.'[27] He set out for Lübeck but he died within a couple of years, worn out by his trials.[28] His ambitions had never been matched by his success.

Hildebrand was let down by his family, and family solidarity was the key to the success of these Hanseatic trading families. There is no reason to suppose the Veckinchusens' rise and fall was unusual; trade was about risks, and in an age of piracy and naval wars the chances of always making a profit were slim. The places that attracted the strongest interest of the Veckinchusen clan were cities on or close to the sea, with the exception of the Hanseatic outlier Cologne and their mistaken ventures overland through the south German cities to Venice. This suggests that the routes across the sea carried the lifeblood of the Hansa, and that the many towns of northern Germany which became members were mainly interested in the goods that traversed the Baltic and the North Sea. When the Kaiser's historians laid all the emphasis on the Hansa fleets and ignored the inland towns, they were not completely distorting the character and history of the German Hansa.

III

The cod fisheries of northern Norway, and the opportunities for catching the same fish out in the open Atlantic off Iceland or even Greenland, brought prosperity to the Hansa and to the Norwegian rulers. There were several types of dried and salted cod, but the development of wind-drying in little harbours along the coast of Norway, where Atlantic winds turned the supple flesh of these large fish into leathery triangular slabs, created an article of trade that lasted for years without rotting, and that satisfied the increased demand for high protein foodstuffs that the smaller post-Black Death population found itself able to afford. Norway also became a good source of dairy goods, for grain production was poor, while mountain pastures were abundant, and dairy products were exchanged for imported rye and wheat. As diet improved, so did the revenues of the

Hansa merchants and the king of Norway. The German merchants had
long identified Bergen as the obvious centre in which to concentrate much
of their North Sea business. It was the seat of a royal palace, and not much
could be achieved without the king's protection. The town had emerged
by the twelfth century – tradition recorded its foundation by King Olaf
the Tranquil in 1070, but evidence from excavations shows that the
wooden structures that lined the shore began to be constructed around
1120, though again and again (even in very modern times) fire has laid
waste this cluster of buildings, the Bryggen, or 'wharves', that became the
home to the Hansa merchants in the city. Yet the prosperity of Bergen was
not created by the German merchants; they chose this site as their base
because it was already a flourishing centre of exchange for furs, fish, seal
products, and all the other products of the forests, fjords and open sea
further to the north; it was already the harbour to which ships moving
back and forth to Iceland would come, a 'natural gateway' and 'nodal
point of trans-shipment', to cite a Norwegian historian of the city's
origins.[29]

Unexpected evidence for the vitality of Bergen as a centre of Norwegian, rather than just German, trade has been revealed following the
discovery of many dozens of strips of wood dating from the fourteenth
century and inscribed, surprisingly, with runes, which runologists had
thought long extinct by this time. Some were just tags, not so very different from modern luggage labels, and in two cases the tags state that they
were attached to bales of yarn. One inscription even appears on a walrus
skull, pithily stating 'John owns'; even if the skull was just a curiosity, this
can be taken as evidence that a couple of tusks, which would have had
real value, had arrived from the Far North, most likely from Greenland.
There are also carefully checked receipts marked (in runes) *uihi*, which is
thought to be a corruption of the Latin *vidi*, 'I have seen', the origin of
the modern sign ✓. And there are a few longer letters, in one of which
Þorer Fair despondently writes from southern Norway to his partner,
Havgrim: 'things are bad with me, partner. I did not get the beer, nor the
fish.' He is worried that a certain Þorstein Lang, presumably his backer,
will hear about his failure; he seems to be suffering from the cold – 'send
me some gloves!' he adds. But the Bergen runes also contain short love
letters: 'the belt from Fana makes you still prettier'. A few fragments of
Latin poems also survive, written in runic script. All this suggests that the
art of writing was not confined to a small network of merchants; plenty
of people read and wrote runes, taking advantage of the ease with which
the mainly straight strokes could be carved into slivers of wood. The vitality of the Norwegian community in Bergen should not be underestimated,

even if we know much more about the Germans in their *Kontor*, and even if the Germans were becoming more and more dominant in the Bergen economy.[30]

In the years before the Black Death food supplies were under increasing pressure as Europe's population grew, peaking by about 1315. In the twelfth and thirteenth centuries English wheat and barley were regularly exported to Bergen. King Sverre of Norway gave a speech in Bergen in 1186 in which he said: 'We thank all Englishmen because they came here, those who brought wheat and honey, flour and cloth. And we further thank those who have brought linen and flax, wax and kettles.' At the same time he thanked everyone who had come from all the north Atlantic islands, such as the Faroes and Orkney, 'who have brought here to this country such things as we cannot do without and which are of great use to this country'. He was much less positive about the Germans: 'the German men who have come here in great numbers and in great boats wish to take away butter and codfish and their export is of great ruin to the country.' The reason the king resented this German intrusion was not just that they grabbed hold of the best that Norway could offer, but that they brought dangerous produce in the holds of their ships: wine. The people of Bergen have taken to drink; 'many have lost their lives, some their limbs, some are damaged for their entire life, others have suffered disgrace, have been wounded or beaten, and all this comes from too much drink.'[31] It is difficult to know how seriously to take a colourful speech that was recorded in an Icelandic saga (even though the author knew the king personally), but there is an interesting hint here that the German network extended down to the vineyards of central Germany; Cologne and its neighbours would have ferried the wine downriver, where it would have been pumped into the North Sea networks of the early Hansa.

However, England too began to feel the pressure of rising population, and there was greater reluctance to export grain across the North Sea when supplies at home were frequently stretched to the limit. The Norwegian kings became more generous to their German visitors as they began to see how essential their presence had become. Baltic rye was turning into black gold. In 1278 King Magnus assured the Germans – represented by two merchants of where else but Lübeck – that they were welcome to come to Bergen, and encouraged them to buy hides and butter. The German merchants were brought under the protection of the crown; the king insisted that 'the Lübeck citizens are shown all possible favour and goodwill'.[32] Even so, the Hansa merchants were not given an entirely free hand. By 1295, alongside further guarantees of immunity, they were forbidden from travelling north of Bergen into the land where Norwegian traders obtained their wares, and they were forbidden from exporting fish during part of the year unless they had carried grain of similar value to Bergen: 'such foreigners as sit here during the winter and do not bring flour, malt or rye, shall purchase neither butter, furs nor dried fish between the Cross Masses' (14 September to 30 May).[33]

By 1300 the German community in Bergen consisted not just of those who arrived by sea each spring, but the 'winter-sitters', and alongside them there were shoemakers and other German craftsmen who had been settling in the town since at least 1250. By 1300 the Hansa merchants in Bergen had learned how important it was to work together in the face of the combination of suspicion and welcome that they faced in their dealings with the kings of Norway. Within Bergen, a corporate identity emerged, and this was recognized by the crown: in 1343, for the first time, the Hanseatic traders were described as 'the merchants of the Hansa of the Germans' (*mercatores de Hansa theotonicorum*). What came into being over the next few years (certainly before 1365) is known as the *Kontor*, or 'Counter', a tightly controlled organization that negotiated for and managed the lives of the German merchants trading through Bergen. It was, in effect, a body of Lübeckers, operating under the commercial law of Lübeck, though there were also members from Hamburg, Bremen and elsewhere: 'the counter was a branch office of Lübeck', in effect an extra-territorial enclave.[34] The fact that the Germans lived under their own law is just one sign of their separation from the other inhabitants of Bergen, but after the middle of the fourteenth century the great majority of Hansa merchants lived in Bryggen, in the closely packed wooden houses right by the harbour that formed a German enclave.[35]

Such enclaves were a common feature of the medieval trading world (and probably provided a model for Jewish ghettos); the example of the Peterhof in Novgorod has already been encountered, and that of the Steelyard in London will be examined shortly. They enabled rulers to keep an eye on merchant communities; but they also provided an opportunity for the mother city of the merchants, in this case Lübeck, to set up an administration, ensuring that the running costs of the community were covered by internal taxes, and offering justice according to the legal system with which the members were familiar. Above all, the members of these communities could form a united front whenever they believed their interests were being threatened by the local ruler, as often happened in Bergen.[36] In the Mediterranean, these enclaves were usually created by order of kings and sultans, but the creation of the Hansa enclave in Bergen was a gradual process, as the German merchants acquired more and more houses within the wharfside area; and for at least a hundred years there were houses that remained in Norwegian ownership within the area. Besides, the plots of land on which the German warehouses stood were rented from local nobles or from the Church.[37]

The Bryggen area was a tight fit; around 1400 there were about 3,000 Germans in a city of 14,000 inhabitants. Many were quite young apprentices and journeymen who faced a tough life during the seven to ten years that carried them up a strict hierarchy from the modest status of *Stuben-junge* to the honourable status of *Meister*. Living conditions were strictly controlled, and for part of the year apprentices were largely confined to the house where they resided. They were male-only settlements, and the apprentices lived in narrow dormitories, working a twelve-hour day, excluding mealtimes. Many crept out at night, finding their way to the red-light district that lay just behind the Hansa quarter; but to do so meant avoiding massive guard dogs that were placed around the outer edges of the Bryggen houses, to deter not just intruders but escapees. Fear of liaisons with Norwegian women stemmed from the notion that people living in the *Kontor* would give away to local wives or to whores all the trade secrets they had learned: they might 'tell the native woman under the influence of her charm, as well as that of liquor, things she had best not know'. On the other hand, the fine for being found with a 'loose woman' was a keg of beer – the woman suffered much worse, by being thrown into the harbour. Journeymen were subjected to brutal initiation rituals, which might include such wholesome entertainment as being roasted by a fire while suspended in a chimney, being half drowned in the harbour and being ceremonially flogged, though a little mercy was shown by making sure that they were already drunk.[38] These, admittedly, are negative images of life in the community, and back home in Lübeck there was, by the mid-sixteenth century, some concern that the initiation rituals were now out of control. Allowing for feast days and periods when trade was slack, and allowing for the strong sense of community that was created within the Hansa community, life in the *Kontor* can best be described as harsh and hard, but not insufferable. The *Kontor* was a place where German merchants learned the art of honest trade, and where they were made fully conscious of the fact that they were Hanseatics (mainly Lübeckers) first, and inhabitants of Bergen second.

24

The English Challenge

In the fifteenth century, two challenges to the ascendancy of the Hansa emerged, one from within the area where some Hansa towns already existed, the Netherlands, and one from a kingdom that had already become one of their favourite trading destinations in the North Sea, England. The Hansa monopoly, such as it was, was being slowly broken, even though it had already suffered from strains when Cologne or Danzig challenged Lübeck, or when the *Vitalienbrüder* harassed shipping in the Baltic and the North Sea. In order to understand the new challenges, it is best to stay for the moment with the Hansa, and to look at the bases that they created in England, not just in London but in Lynn, Boston, Hull and Ravenser, a port near Hull that long ago was washed away by the waves.

London, by far the largest city in England, was, not surprisingly, their headquarters. There, they operated from their *Kontor* next to the Thames at what was known as the *Stahlhof*, or 'Steelyard'. The name seems to be a corruption of the term *Stapelhof*, 'courtyard for trading staple goods', and has nothing to do with steel. The site of the German *Kontor* in London has been covered over by Cannon Street Railway Station, constructed in the middle of the nineteenth century; the builders swept away the entire Steelyard, down to its foundations. Very little was found during excavations in 1987 (even the pottery turned out mainly to be English). However, some plans and descriptions survive from the sixteenth century. There were three gateways, and there was a great hall; there were warehouses and sleeping quarters, as well as administrative offices. Nonetheless, the Steelyard was not a particularly imposing place, compared to the courtyards and quadrangles that existed elsewhere in London, such as the Inns of Court, by now an enclave for lawyers. Rather, the Steelyard was a packed space, a business quarter where hardly an inch of space was wasted. The Hansards wanted privileges, not fine buildings.

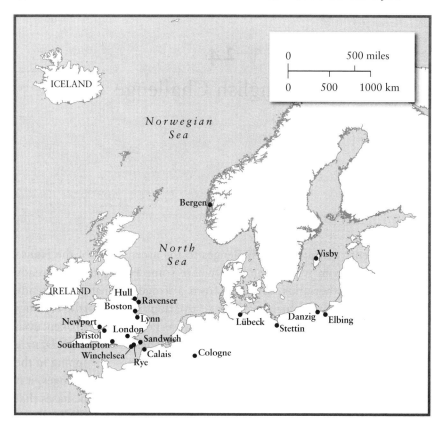

As in Bergen, the London *Kontor* formed a privileged enclave, enjoying both royal protection and self-government, and, like the settlement in Bergen, it took time to coalesce. In London, recognition of the special status of the German merchants did not take place as a result of the efforts of the Lübeckers, but through the activities of merchants first of Cologne and then of Gotland; in the thirteenth century the English royal administration talked of several *hanses*, applying the term to groups of Flemings, as well as to those who would eventually become the Hansards. England was a highly desirable market for both Flemish and German traders. The country supplied excellent wool, which was hungrily consumed by the looms of the Flemish cities, while the English had long ago developed a taste for Rhineland wines. Yet wine was by no means the most important item to cross the North Sea from Germany. So strong was demand for English produce that silver flooded into the kingdom, which was able to maintain a high-quality silver currency in the thirteenth century while other parts of Europe constantly devalued their silver coinage by adding base metals. No other European kingdom was as rich in silver and of no other kingdom can it be said that the silver content of its coinage remained stable all the way from the ninth century to 1250. By 1200 the influx of silver, mainly from the rich mines that had been opened up in Germany, led to quite serious price inflation that affected basic commodities such as foodstuffs.[1] 'Sterling silver', today set at a standard of 925‰, has a long history. It comes as little surprise that the one place in northern Europe to match the quality of English coinage was the mint of Cologne, for this was the distribution centre from which English goods fanned out across the Continent; even the availability of local silver supplies could not prevent a serious decline in the quality of the coinage elsewhere in Germany.

The English kings rather took the silver imports for granted, and when they extended their favours to the merchants of Cologne it was in recognition of their accomplishments as dealers in good wines. By the middle of the twelfth century, the men of Cologne lay under the protection of the English Crown, and they were assured of the right to sell their wine on the same terms as French wine merchants; they already possessed a *domus*, or operations centre, later described as their *gildhalla*, 'guildhall', implying that this was not a random group of visitors but an organized body of men; exactly where this guildhall lay is not clear. Circumstances outside their control brought new advantages to the German merchants in London. King Richard I had been imprisoned by the German emperor, Henry VI of Hohenstaufen, while he was trying to make his way home after the Third Crusade failed to recover Jerusalem. One of the German princes who was willing to give him help was the archbishop of Cologne. The grateful king of England therefore extended the privileges of the Cologne merchants in 1194, so that they would henceforth be free of taxes and tribute. They could operate their own internal customs system among themselves, which would be important if the costs of running their guildhall were to be met. Admittedly, the attitude of later kings to this generous grant wavered, but the political motives never went away: King John also relied on an alliance with the archbishop of Cologne, who supported the same claimant to the German throne after the death of Emperor Henry as did John (with disastrous consequences for the English king). So even the money-grubbing King John was minded to let the Cologne merchants retain their special privileges. These Cologne merchants possessed their own seagoing ships, and they also hired Flemish vessels, acting as intermediaries in the wool trade linking England to the Flemish cloth towns.[2]

Gradually, the German community broadened its character, as visitors arrived from Visby, Lübeck, Bremen and Hamburg; they came not just to London but to accessible places on the east coast, such as Lynn and

Boston, where Lübeckers could be found buying wool in 1271.[3] When Emperor Frederick II gave Lübeck its special privileges in 1226, he insisted that its merchants trading in England should be exempt from taxes imposed on them by the merchants of Cologne, and over the next few years King Henry III, who was related by marriage to the German emperor, also took the Lübeckers under his protection.[4] The Cologne merchants took umbrage at the presence of these rivals, which serves as a reminder that family disputes often disrupted Hansa brotherhood. These groups were granted their own corporations, or Hansas, so that during the thirteenth century there was not one consolidated group of Hanseatic merchants, but several sub-Hansas vying for royal favour. The citizens of London complained that the Germans had greater freedoms in their own city than they did.

Then, when King Edward I attempted to rationalize all the past grants to merchants visiting his kingdom, the Hansa gave him vocal support; in 1303 he issued the *Carta Mercatoria*, legislation that levied higher taxes on foreign than on native merchants, but the Germans saw it as a relatively good deal; they wanted guarantees, they wanted stability, and they understood by now that it was more important to work together than to feed the pride of Cologne, Lübeck and other rivals. Unfortunately that was by no means the end of the story, as the next king, the unfortunate Edward II, suspended his father's law in 1311. The Hansards insisted on their exemptions, and Edward II wanted as much money as he could squeeze out of his subjects for wars in Scotland. Nonetheless, in bits and pieces, and subject to all sorts of temporary reversals, by the middle of the fourteenth century they had clawed back many of the rights they had obtained in 1303.[5]

It was not all plain sailing thereafter. Once Edward III had taken charge of his kingdom, he launched vastly ambitious wars in France that frequently disrupted movement across the sea. Flanders might be cut off; ships might be pounced upon by rival navies. The English Channel and the North Sea became important, and dangerous, theatres of war.[6] Fortunately for the merchants, he needed to borrow funds and, having drained the great Florentine banks of capital in the 1340s, he turned to German bankers, pawning his Crown Jewels; and this meant that he had to be polite to merchants from that part of the world (interestingly, his creditors included Jewish bankers, excluded from England for the past half-century). There were ugly moments when Germans were accused of piracy against ships bearing English wool across the North Sea, leading to exemplary confiscations of German property in the kingdom. The relationship between the Hansa and the English Crown was not, then, a smooth one, but on balance the two sides needed one another. Not just silver but furs, wax and stockfish were in high demand. By 1400 the English had begun to realize how desirable Baltic herrings were; ships were reaching Hull that carried nothing but herrings, loaded at the expense of English import-ers. In the past, many of these goods had been supplied by Norwegians, but the Germans increasingly muscled in on this business: by 1300 they had already acquired a commanding position at Bergen. And much the same was true of Flanders, as Hansa cogs plied back and forth between the Flemish coast and England – the Flemings tending to concentrate more on producing cloth.

In the fifteenth century the entire space between England and the east-ern Baltic was abuzz with trade. Ties were built to Danzig and the towns along the coast of Prussia (which then included Danzig), and direct contact between eastern England and the further reaches of the Baltic became common. Nor did this simply consist of visits by enterprising citizens of Danzig or Elbing to England, for a constant complaint of the Prussians was that their towns were being invaded by English cloth merchants.[7] This reflected an important change in the character of English trade at the end of the Middle Ages. Although England had always exported some finished cloth of very high quality, its real speciality in the twelfth and thirteenth centuries had been the export of raw wool, leaving others, in Flanders and elsewhere, to turn it into the fine woollens for which northern Europe was famous, goods that might find their way to Morocco and Egypt. Trade wars with Flanders during the early fourteenth century occasionally blocked the import of Flemish cloth, and even after the trade wars were at an end high tariffs made the import of this cloth unattractive. This created a strong incentive to manufacture cloth at home and not to rely on imports. Flemings were encouraged to come and settle, importing the secrets of Flemish cloth-making; the wealthy towns of East Anglia became home to many Flemish weavers. By the late fourteenth century enterpris-ing Englishmen had, then, stimulated their own cloth industry into new life, and English woollen cloth rather than unprocessed wool became the export of choice. England was transforming itself from a country that concentrated on the export of raw materials into one that concen-trated on the export of finished goods – a process of what might loosely be termed proto-industrialization.[8]

Just as Flemish cloth had been sent deep into the Baltic and all the way to the Mediterranean, English cloth could increasingly be found in places very far from the wool towns of East Anglia and the Cotswolds. The pres-ence of growing numbers of Englishmen in Prussia is not as surprising as it may seem; when things were working well, Englishmen from Lynn and

Boston rented Hanseatic ships and carried the cloth of England all the way to Danzig and beyond. Richard Schottun from Lynn was the sort of character who gave English merchants a bad name in Danzig. He boasted about ignoring the tax regulations, and he brought back poor-quality timber known as *wrak et wrak-wrak*, probably taken from rotting hulks and driftwood, while pretending that he only obtained his timber from Danzig itself. He and three other Englishmen bought a ship, the hulk *Krystoffer*, in Danzig, but he overextended himself, for he then found himself being pursued for debts there. Even so, his links with Danzig lasted a good ten years, so his reputation was not bad enough to force him out of the city. By 1422 fifty-five English merchants were frequenting the port of Danzig, to judge from existing records. Ordinary folk in England built marriage ties as far away as Prussia; the son of the celebrated English mystic Margery Kempe married a woman from Danzig, and Margery herself visited the city.[9]

Prussia was also a favourite destination for English crusaders, and joining the Teutonic Knights on one of their sprees into pagan territory was regarded as good military entertainment, whether or not it was also good for the soul. Among the participants was Henry, earl of Derby, who after his return would seize the English throne from the increasingly tyrannical Richard II; he arrived in Stettin (Szczecin) with up to 150 servants and recruits, so keeping him supplied was big business for those who carried him over the waves. Indeed, during the 1420s the Grand Master of the Teutonic Order remained friendly to the English, even when the Prussian members of the Hansa sternly demanded their arrest in return for alleged insults against German merchants in England.[10] Relations between the Hansards and the Teutonic Order had plummeted following the massive defeat of the Knights at the Battle of Tannenberg in 1410, when the Knights paid for their folly in turning against what was now, officially at any rate, a Catholic kingdom embracing Christian Poland and newly converted Lithuania. A three-cornered contest for power was taking place between the king of Poland–Lithuania, the Teutonic Knights and the Prussian members of the Hanseatic League. It is hardly surprising that outsiders sometimes found themselves caught up in rivalries that they had no part in creating.[11]

Between 1469 and 1474 relations deteriorated to the point where England and the Hansa found themselves at war with one another, although predictably Cologne was opposed to action, and the warmongers were Lübeck and Danzig, both of which had suffered from English piracy. The problem was English intrusion into the Baltic, which was of little interest to Hansa cities more connected to the North Sea.[12] Underlying all this is a simple fact: there was a greater will for peace and the restoration of good relations than for conflict, and if that involved compromise over the rights of access of the English to the Baltic, it would simply have to be accepted. Once peace was signed between the Hansa and the English Crown in Utrecht in 1474, a decade of peace followed. In reality, though, the English had found a place for themselves on the sea, and were now impossible to shift; the men of Bristol, in particular, had become familiar figures who sailed with impunity across broad swathes of the North Sea and the Atlantic.[13] By the 1490s it was obvious that the great age of German trade with England had come to an end. Not just the economic climate was difficult: the complications of early Tudor politics made merchants from the Holy Roman Empire, the subjects of Henry VIII's rival Charles V, wonder whether they were still welcome on English shores.[14]

Something remained, all the same. The Steelyard, briefly confiscated, was restored to the Hansards in 1474, and was only closed down by Queen Elizabeth I in 1598. Indeed, the Utrecht treaty for the first time assigned full ownership of the site in London to the Hansa, along with property at Lynn and Boston. The management of the new Steelyard at Lynn was entrusted to the merchants of Danzig, because, the Hansa Diet insisted, 'your merchants frequent Lynn more than any other Hanseatic merchants, and therefore this matter is of more concern to you than anyone else'.[15] The building the merchants received still stands, though it was converted into dreary local government offices. Still, enough of its wooden framework survives outside, and enough of its beams inside, to justify its claim to be the only Hanseatic structure still in existence in England. The building originally contained a kitchen, hall and courtyard, and the property was formed out of seven houses joined together. The great advantage of using Lynn was that it gave access to the riches of East Anglia, which, as has been seen, was drawing great wealth from the production of woollen cloth. The great wool churches of Lavenham and Long Melford stand testimony to the prosperity of the region, and this prosperity depended in significant degree on the sea trade out of the east of England.

II

Wool attracted many besides the Hansards to medieval England. The opening of a sea route from the Mediterranean to the North Sea at the end of the thirteenth century was closely linked to the surge in demand for fine wool in Italy. Florence emerged from relative obscurity during the thirteenth century, making itself famous through the quality of its cloth, and then through its ambitious decision to launch a gold coinage in 1252. As the cloth industry developed, moving from the finishing of other people's cloth (the cleaning and dyeing of cloth from Flanders and France), to the manufacture of cloth from raw wool, the Florentines understood that they could only rival the high-quality output of Flanders by obtaining the very best wool, even if that meant looking all the way towards England. They lacked a fleet of their own; but by 1277 Genoese ships had learned how to pass out through the dangerous waters of the Strait of Gibraltar and sail on towards Flanders. From 1281 onwards Majorcan as well as Genoese ships began to reach London from the Mediterranean, breaking open a route that, on and off, would be maintained by the Genoese, and later by the Venetians, the Catalans and the Florentines themselves, during the fourteenth and fifteenth centuries. The ships that stood in the Port of London in 1281 are known to have been loaded with wool before they departed. This new route enabled much greater quantities of English wool, or, for ships sailing from the outports of Bruges, many more bolts of fine cloth, to be carried into the Mediterranean; large galleys sent from Venice and Pisa, the port of Florence, in the fifteenth century brought sugar, spices, fine ceramics and exotic silks to northern Europe, including goods that were collected in the ports of the Muslim kingdom of Granada, or in the outports of Seville, which had become the lynchpin linking the trade of the Mediterranean to that of the Atlantic. Italian bankers, from Lucca, Florence and elsewhere, established themselves in England late in the thirteenth century, and until a great crash occurred in the 1340s – partly the result of the bad debts of the English king incurred during his wars against the French – the Italians acquired considerable leverage at the English court.[16]

London was one target of the Italians; but it made more sense for those who also wished to visit Flanders to stop somewhere on the south coast instead, and this stimulated the development of a town that already had a history of close contact with France (commemorated in its 'French Street'): Southampton.[17] By comparison with the cities of the Mediterranean, or with the greater Hansa cities, Southampton was tiny: its population stood at around 2,500 in 1300, and in the wake of the Black Death it had dropped to a mere 1,600 in 1377.[18] Just at this point a distinguished Genoese emissary, Janus Imperiale, came to the court of Edward III with the proposal that Southampton should be declared a staple port, the only point of access for foreign merchants seeking wool. The Genoese clearly hoped to corner the market, but Janus's body was found outside the front door of his lodgings in London on the night of 26 August 1379. He had been assassinated by his English rivals. For the king had already established Calais, which he had brought under English rule, as the staple port for wool exports, and his assassins could see that the Genoese project would undermine their own ascendancy.[19] However, Italians continued to flock to Southampton in the late fourteenth and early fifteenth century. Fifty to a hundred Italians took up residence in the town, though they lacked a quarter reserved for their use. Sometimes, as in the case of the Florentine agent Christopher Ambrose (Cristoforo Ambruogi), the Italians decided that their future lay in the colder climes of England, and they applied for English citizenship, though there was also a middle status, giving them the right of abode as 'denizens', that suited a great many. Ambrose even became mayor of Southampton.[20]

London hosted Spaniards as well as Italians. Catalans arrived on galleys from Barcelona and Majorca, but pirate attacks often discouraged them.[21] Most of the Iberian visitors came from the northern coast of Spain, bringing iron, woad and leather, rather than the sugar, ceramics and silk collected by the Italian galleys as they passed the kingdom of Granada.[22] Cantabrians, Galicians and Basques from Atlantic Spain plied the waters around Iberia, also penetrating into the Mediterranean; and they worked their way up the western flank of France towards Bourgneuf, Normandy and Bruges.[23] Spaniards such as Andrés Pérez de Castrogeríz arrived in London from Burgos as early as 1270, and he also traded in Gascony, which lay under English rule and was the major source of wine for English markets; he had many successors. The reward for their hard work came in the form of royal privileges that offered tax exemptions in London and Southampton – the English kings wanted them to keep coming.[24] In the early fifteenth century a doggerel poet, the author of the *Libelle of Englyshe Polycye*, a tract in verse that extolls the foreign trade of England, wrote that:

> Bene fygues, raysyns, wyne, bastarde and dates,
> And lycorys, Syvyle oyle and also grayne,
> Whyte Castell sope and wax is not in vayne,

and went on to praise the iron, saffron and mercury that Spain also offered (*grayne* does not mean wheat but *grana*, a red dye made from crushed insects, and a Spanish speciality).[25]

The most prominent communities of foreign businessmen in London were the Genoese and the Germans, but the fifteenth-century city was quite cosmopolitan. From faraway Dubrovnik, Ragusan merchants arrived on their own ships or those of the Venetians, bringing sweet Malmsey wines from Greece. One particularly enterprising Ragusan was Ivan Manević, who became a naturalized subject of the Crown and a landowner, and also farmed the taxes due to the Crown from the textile workshops of a large area of southern England. By the early sixteenth century, the Ragusans became the masters of the English cloth trade towards the eastern Mediterranean, benefiting from their cosy relationship with the Ottoman court in Constantinople.[26] The impression all this might give is that the English played a rather passive role, welcoming the Hansards, the Genoese and the Spaniards (up to a point), while not themselves being very active on the water. If that was ever true, it was certainly not the case in the late Middle Ages, as the examples of Winchelsea and Bristol clearly show.

III

Winchelsea was one of the 'Cinque Ports' that had been entrusted with the defence of the eastern end of the English Channel since the eleventh century. Now some way inland, Winchelsea stood alongside an irregularly shaped, shifting, marshy coastline. In the 1280s the town was moved at royal command to a higher site away from the encroaching waves, which meant that it could still function as a port. The new town, with its square street pattern, was modelled on the *bastide* towns, defensive positions built by the English and the French in the contested lands of south-western France, with which King Edward I was very familiar.[27] Its inhabitants and those of Rye, nearby, made use of relatively peaceful times to launch raids on shipping in the English Channel, so that piracy as well as trade created the wealthy community that emerged on the new site. William Longe was a Member of Parliament early in the fifteenth century; he was also one of the Rye officials appointed to keep an eye out for pirates by patrolling the Channel, and yet he himself turned pirate, attacking Florentine and Flemish ships. The courts could not ignore this, and Longe was sent to prison for a while, but his popularity only grew, and he was re-elected to the House of Commons time and again.[28] As ever, the borderline between piracy and officially sanctioned warfare was easily crossed.

Outrages were committed on both sides. In 1349 a surprise attack by a Castilian admiral, who had seized English ships loaded with wine off Gascony, created consternation in England; the time for revenge came a year later when a Castilian convoy laden with Spanish wool passed through the Channel on its way to Flanders. This was understood in England to mean that the Castilians were cocking a snook at the English and their commanding position in the wool trade towards Flanders. Led into the fray by a very large cog from Winchelsea, the *Thomas*, the English pounced on the Castilian fleet as it returned from Flanders. The battle of

Winchelsea, as it is known, though ships from Sandwich, Rye and elsewhere also took part, was a resounding victory for the English, even though
the Castilian ships were larger than the English ones. This was possibly
the first naval battle in the west in which cannon were used. The battle
was won, but, to use the old cliché, the war was not: the English Channel
remained an unsafe area, and to avoid capture by the French or their
Castilian allies the English had to sail in convoy. This was not enough to
protect the town, though. In 1380 Winchelsea was sacked by Castilian
raiders.[29]

No doubt the stone-lined cellars that still exist in Winchelsea were often
used to store the proceeds of piracy; but this was not a nest of pirates –
there was plenty of licit trade. The citizens of Winchelsea were wine
merchants; in 1303–4 twelve ships from Winchelsea went to Bordeaux,
where they collected 1,575 tuns of wine, very roughly 4,000 gallons.
Winchelsea had the most successful wine trade of any of the towns along
this coast, and its shrunken state today makes it hard to imagine the thriving, well-connected port that it once was.[30] But the town that was best
placed to handle the traffic in wine had a much brighter future: it was
Bristol, soon to become the third greatest city in the English realm.

IV

Bristol, originally *Brig-stowe*, 'the place of the bridge', is one of the most
unusual harbours in the world. It lies beyond the gorges of the River Avon,
which narrow where the Avon meets the majestic River Severn. When the
tide is in, the water level rises alarmingly, sometimes by as much as twelve
metres, or forty feet; ships bound for Bristol would await the high tide and
be swept up towards the city. At low tide, the muddy bottom of the harbour was exposed, and ships would balance their keels on the soft
ground.[31] Bristol lay in a fertile part of England, and in the early days its
trade with Wales and Ireland brought the town some wealth; but even in
the fourteenth century ships trading with Ireland remained small, reflecting the relatively low volume of business (their capacity was generally
around twenty to thirty tons). As the Irish linen industry took off at the
end of the Middle Ages, opportunities along this route did improve; but
the ships themselves were mainly Irish-owned, and the real prosperity of
Bristol was the result of contacts much further afield.[32] One reason for
the port's increase in trade was the rise of the English cloth industry,
for when it came to the manufacture of fine cloth, the Cotswold villages
east of Bristol were keen rivals to the wool towns of East Anglia, while

objects carved in alabaster, the waxy stone out of which the English sculpted highly decorated altarpieces, were brought down from Coventry and sent abroad from Bristol. Bristol dealers also kept up their links with Southampton, so that even when they were not sending their cloth through the home port, they despatched it across Salisbury plain towards Italian galleys waiting there, while Bristol cloth was also carried on the roads to London, to be sold to Hansa merchants, who were said to offer better terms than their English counterparts.[33]

The real reason for Bristol's success, however, lay with the wine trade.[34] This success was built on political as well as commercial links: the acquisition of English rights in Gascony following the marriage of King Henry II to Eleanor of Aquitaine in the twelfth century. Even then, the reputation of Gascony for wine took time to be established. By the end of the thirteenth century, encouraged by the businessmen of Bordeaux, the flat lands of the Bordelais were given over almost entirely to vineyards. This was made possible not just because the soil was suitable for wine production, but because of the ease with which wine could be transported down the little tributaries of the Gironde towards Bordeaux. The merchants of Bordeaux carved out a monopoly for themselves, ensuring that they could tax the wine to their heart's content as it passed through the city. Since the administration of Gascony was autonomous, despite English rule, the English merchants had to put up with these taxes despite their objections, which reached the House of Commons in 1444; these objections were a little exaggerated, since English merchants did not pay any dues on the goods they imported into Gascony, and the great majority of the ships that plied back and forth between England and Bordeaux were English. At the start of the fifteenth century, something like 200 ships each year could be expected to set out from Bordeaux loaded with wine, arriving in autumn or early spring and leaving in December or March; the voyage normally took about ten days.[35]

The fortunes of the Bordelais depended on reasonable harvests and, crucially, on the possibility of exchanging these vast quantities of wine for staple foodstuffs. At a time when grain was the staple foodstuff and rising population was placing increased pressure on supplies, the Bristol connection offered a lifeline. There was grain to be had from southern England, and English merchants made every effort to send it to Gascony, even when there were shortages at home, which was common in the early fourteenth century. The size of the wine cargoes grew and grew, right up to the final war that culminated in the French occupation of all of Gascony in 1453. In autumn 1443 six Bristol ships carried almost as much wine out of Bordeaux as would, near the start of the century, have been loaded in a whole year. As English cloth cornered the market in northern Europe, this too became a prized export bound for Gascony, and the Gascons reciprocated by supplying Bristol with large amounts of woad, the blue dye that was a speciality of south-western France.[36] English defeat did not bring this wine trade to an end, for the French king, Louis XI, was not the sort of person who would turn away the opportunity to rake in taxes. By the end of the fifteenth century, as many as 6,000 English merchants are said to have flocked to Bordeaux to buy wine, even though the wine trade had now passed its peak, as had Bordeaux itself.

Other opportunities beckoned for the mariners of Bristol, or for foreign mariners hoping to sell their produce in Bristol. Basque ships, and ships from further along the coast of northern Spain, came to Bristol in growing numbers during the fifteenth century, and Bristol merchants recognized the quality of Basque seamanship by sometimes loading their own goods on Basque vessels; Basques and Bristolians shared curiosity about the open Atlantic and its fish stocks, while the Basques, whose native lands were poor in resources, looked outwards to the open sea and developed an expertise in whaling that made them the unrivalled masters of the sixteenth-century whale industry – a sixteenth-century Basque whaling vessel has been meticulously excavated off Labrador.[37]

The hull of another Basque ship, from around 1450, has been found underneath the Welsh city of Newport across the estuary from Bristol; it is said to be the largest fifteenth-century hull yet discovered, with a capacity for 160 tons of cargo (quite likely wine). Coins and pottery found on site indicate that it travelled as far as Portugal, which in the mid-fifteenth century was one of England's closest trading partners. For a time it may have been operated by a mainly Spanish or Portuguese crew; but it was probably owned by English merchants (possibly even by an English nobleman) by the time that it toppled over and sank in the shipyard at Newport, where it was undergoing repairs, around 1469.[38] For a while, English merchants had the good sense to try out the wines of northern Spain, which this ship almost certainly carried. But traffic to northern Spain was not all concerned with trade, and the Bristol ships that set out for its north-west corner, Galicia, carried passengers – pilgrims bound for Santiago de Compostela who preferred not to trek overland on the famous *Camino*. Beyond the lands that lay under Castilian rule, there were good opportunities in Portugal, whose dynasty was related by marriage to the royal house of Lancaster. As Portugal itself emerged as a maritime power the English were able to take advantage of its successes, importing wine from mainland Portugal, and eventually buying *grete salt*, that is, sugar, from Madeira, though by way of intermediaries.[39]

All this generated great wealth, displayed to this day in the great church of St Mary Redcliffe, in which the wealthy shipowner William Canynges built chantry chapels and a tomb for himself and his wife. His endowments resulted from a sad fact: his sons predeceased him and left no heirs. The city of Bristol became his heir instead. He was a member of a trading dynasty whose members had been making their money out of cloth since the late fourteenth century (a much later member of the same family was George Canning, the nineteenth-century British politician). The Canynges traded at first with Bayonne and Spain, but by the middle of the fifteenth century, when William Canynges was in his prime, they were looking much further afield: he despatched ships to the Baltic and to Iceland, as well as Portugal, Flanders and France.[40]

Another Bristol merchant is remembered for his failures rather than his successes. Robert Sturmy enriched himself by supplying the English army in Gascony with grain. In 1446, his ambitions turned in an entirely new direction, the Mediterranean.[41] By the mid-fifteenth century Bristol had become a place where shipowners and seamen planned voyages to the limits of the known world – to Prussia, Portugal, Iceland and eventually right across the Atlantic. The Mediterranean was a better-known area; Sturmy had received news of the expulsion of the prosperous Venetian colony from Alexandria, and he hoped to capitalize on that by creating a direct spice trade from the Levant to England. He had a ship, the *Cog Anne*, and was prepared to risk it on this venture. He obtained a licence to export wool all the way to Pisa, for the looms of Florence, with the intention of then moving east to the Holy Land. His crew consisted of thirty-seven sailors, but there were 160 pilgrims on board as well, on one-way tickets, since his idea was that on the return journey the hull would be filled with the spices of the East rather than with human beings. The pilgrims disembarked at Jaffa, and made their way to Jerusalem. But his crew showed their inexperience by attempting to cross the eastern Mediterranean as Christmas approached. No doubt they imagined that Mediterranean squalls could never match the high seas of the open Atlantic. As they approached the Venetian naval base at Modon, on one of the southern tips of the Peloponnese, a storm began to blow; they lost control of the *Anne* and it was torn to pieces on the rocks. Not a soul survived.[42]

Sturmy had stayed at home, and his wealth had not been lethally dented. Over the next few years, he held high office in Bristol, and was elected mayor. When Parliament asked for help in the war against piracy, Sturmy funded the building of a new ship. All the while, he was listening to news from the Levant, which included the fall of Constantinople to the Turks in 1453. He hoped that, with this new political configuration in the eastern

Mediterranean, he could at last break his way into the highly profitable Levant trade. So in 1457 he put together another cargo bound for Italy and the Levant, including wheat, tin, lead, wool and cloth; the cloth alone was worth an enormous amount, £20,000. All these goods were to be sent 'beyond the mountains by the straits of Marrok' on the ship *Katharine Sturmy*, which had already proved itself the year before by sailing all the way to Galicia with pilgrims for the shrine of St James. The *Katharine* reached the Levant, where not just spices were loaded aboard but the seeds of green pepper which, it was hoped, would be made to sprout on English soil. On the way back, however, in 1458, his ship was seized by Genoese sailors off Malta and his goods were stolen. Back in England, the news of the outrage stirred up ever-present hostility to the Italians; the Genoese community in London was arrested en masse. Sturmy was never fully compensated for his losses and died towards the end of the year.[43] English merchants realized that attempts to penetrate beyond Portugal were simply too risky, and it was another half-century before regular traffic from England to the Levant was established. That still left vast swathes of the Atlantic, up to and beyond Iceland, open for exploration and exploitation.

V

During the fifteenth century the English, particularly the merchants and shipowners of Bristol, became determined to break into the Norwegian monopoly of trade with Iceland, taking advantage of its increasing isolation. Sheer distance meant that the Norwegian king was hardly in a position to maintain tight control of what happened in Iceland, even though it had submitted to his authority in 1262 on condition that the Norwegians send six ships a year to the island; again and again the Icelanders complained that this was not happening.[44] The Hansa merchants based in Bergen, who conveyed Icelandic goods further into Europe, were not themselves supposed to enter Icelandic waters. Occasionally, though, they did venture to Iceland, since no one seemed very interested in stopping them.

In these circumstances, the Icelanders had no compunction about welcoming ships loaded with the foodstuffs and other supplies they needed that had arrived from elsewhere than Bergen. King Erik wrote to the Icelanders, grumbling that they were trading with 'outlandish men'; he might have added that the English found it easier to fish in Icelandic waters because the *hirðstjóri*, or governor, of the island had started issuing his own licences for fishing and for trade on the island itself. The governor carried this letter to the court of King Erik:

Our laws provide that six ships should come hither from Norway every year, which has not happened for a long time, a cause from which your Grace and our poor country have suffered most grievous harm. Therefore, trusting in God's grace and your help, we have traded with foreigners who have come hither peacefully on legitimate business, but we have punished those fishermen and owners of fishing smacks who have robbed and caused disturbance on the sea.[45]

His justification cut no ice; he was not sent back to Iceland. Forbidding this trade would hardly help the islanders to survive, particularly if, as is often argued, harsh weather conditions were making access to Iceland (and Greenland) more difficult in the fifteenth century. English ships were ready to face these risks, even when twenty-five vessels sank in storms in one day. At Lynn there was an association of English Iceland merchants.[46] What attracted them was the swarms of codfish that had migrated towards the waters off Iceland.

By 1420 the situation had become critical. A German merchant went to Iceland to spy for the Hansa and for King Erik, and insisted that Iceland itself would be lost to the English if the king did not take decisive action. This may sound like exaggeration, but English freebooters did invade the island, 'in full battle array with trumpets and flying ensigns'. One of their targets was the Danish governor King Erik had appointed; his attempts to maintain tight control of the island's economy aroused deep resentment, and he catalogued the sins of the English traders, who had been seizing the islanders' sheep and cattle and even wrecking the island's churches. The grumbling governor was captured and carried off to England, where he registered a lengthy complaint about the conduct of the English visitors to Iceland, leading to embarrassment at court and, in 1426, official attempts to ban the Iceland trade, a move that went down badly with the merchants of Lynn. The sailings to Iceland simply continued. English smugglers, because in a sense that was what they had become, enjoyed outwitting port officials, and the occasional confiscation of Icelandic goods in English ports did not dent the Iceland trade, which often used out-of-the-way ports like Fowey in Cornwall, though Icelandic stockfish also turned up at Bristol, Hull and elsewhere. Moreover, it was still possible to obtain official approval. An application to the Crown for a licence would cost money, but could be seen as insurance against forfeiture. The Scandinavian king could also be approached in the same spirit. So in 1442, for instance, fourteen English ships were licensed to travel to Iceland; they carried just about everything, from kettles to combs, from beer to butter, from gloves to girdles.[47] Over the next few decades, the arguments between the English court, the English merchants, the Danish court and, increasingly, the Hansards continued. It was no help that English raiders killed the governor of Iceland in 1467. King Richard III complained to the city of Hamburg that three English ships had been seized in Iceland by Hanseatic rivals; but the Hansards could tell their own stories of attacks by sailors from Bristol in the very same waters.[48]

One way of dealing with this constant turmoil was to turn one's back on Iceland, however desirable its fish might be, and to look for other stretches of the north Atlantic that teemed with cod. In the 1480s, the shipowners of Bristol sought out these waters, and the big question is whether, in the process, they crossed as far as the fishing grounds off Labrador. The claim that English sailors reached America in the 1480s is not simply speculation. An Englishman named John Day addressed a letter to an Admiral of Spain, probably Christopher Columbus, soon after John Cabot's voyage to Newfoundland in 1497; he wrote:

> it is considered certain that the cape of the said land [Newfoundland] was found and discovered in other times by the men of Bristol who found 'Brasil' as your Lordship knows. It was called the Ysle of Brasil and it is assumed and believed to be the mainland that the Bristol men found.[49]

('Mainland' does not mean an entire continent, and could just mean a large island.) This name 'Brasil' should not be confused with that of modern Brazil, discovered by the Portuguese in 1500, which became attached to the area because it was rich in brazilwood, much prized as a dyestuff. Rather, 'Brasil' was one of the legendary islands of the Atlantic that featured in late medieval maps, and can be traced back to stories of an island out in the ocean woven by Irish mariners in the early Middle Ages.

More important than the name is the evidence that sailors from Bristol were setting out on journeys deep into the Atlantic in the 1480s.[50] On 15 July 1480, John Jay sent a ship out from Bristol; its master was a highly reputable mariner named Thloyde, or Lloyd, and its destination was 'the island of Brasylle in the western part of Ireland'. But after nine weeks at sea it was forced back to Ireland by bad weather and found nothing.[51] John Jay or his namesake (this was a prominent trading family) had been importing *stokffish* from Norway in 1461.[52] In 1481, just under a year later, the *Trinity* and the *George*, also from Bristol, set out 'to serch & fynde a certain Isle called the Isle of Brasile'.[53] Although their owners also insisted this was not a trading voyage, the ships were loaded with salt, which makes one think that the aim was to catch fish, which would have had to be preserved without delay. There is no evidence that these ships found whatever they were seeking. The master of the *Trinity* and other ships bound for 'Brasil' would not be the first or last to mask their real destination behind a fanciful one. In 1498 the king and queen of Castile, Ferdinand and Isabella, received a report from their agent in England which stated that for seven years the men of Bristol had been sending from two to four ships in search of Brasil and the 'Seven Cities', another mythical territory out in the Great Blue.[54] If fishing was the aim, then they had very different ambitions to John Cabot, who set out in 1497 to gain access to the fabulous wealth of China and the East, sharing with Christopher Columbus the assumption that Asia could be reached by sailing westwards. Myths of lands such as the Isle of the Seven Cities, inhabited by Christian refugees fleeing from the Muslim invasion of Spain, remained potent, and there were romantic dreams of making contact with long-lost Christian brethren. In the same decade, Ferdinand van Olmen, a Fleming in the service of the Portuguese king, set out from the Azores in the hope of finding the Seven Cities; he was never heard of again.[55]

There are other possibilities. The Bristol ships may have made their way to Greenland, of which knowledge certainly survived, even though the Norse population had probably vanished by now; they might then have realized that following the currents down the Labrador coast would net them much bigger catches. The explanation might also be more humdrum. Only in 1490 did the king of Denmark relax his ban on direct English trade to Iceland. Some ships did set out from Bristol bound for Iceland in 1481, as the city's customs records reveal; but there were still people who preferred not to pay for formal licences.[56] Even if they did reach Labrador, a secret discovery by men of Bristol was no discovery at all. Another Atlantic destination that was within the sights of Bristol merchants was Portuguese Madeira, with its abundance of fine sugar, to which they were sending goods on Breton ships in 1480, and beyond that the Azores; there were plans to create a route to Morocco, but the Portuguese objected, as they did when English merchants contemplated a trip to west Africa in 1481.[57] It is time to see what the Portuguese were doing in Atlantic waters, and how their little kingdom became the seat of a great empire.

25
Portugal Rising

I

The north-east Atlantic was becoming a well-integrated maritime region by the end of the Middle Ages. The history of the early Atlantic cannot, however, be written without paying attention to the shorelines further south. Even so, the vast expanse from the Canary Islands to the southern tip of Africa remains blank. The Canary islanders, whose ancestors had unquestionably arrived by sea, had lost the art of navigation by the time that European explorers chanced on their islands, in the fourteenth century. The peoples of sub-Saharan Africa did not venture out to sea, and long-distance sea routes down the coast of west Africa were first developed by Europeans – by the Portuguese in the second half of the fifteenth century. The ambitious voyages of the Portuguese southwards along the coast of Africa and westwards towards the Atlantic islands have overshadowed the earlier maritime history of Portugal and Atlantic Spain, for when Prince Henry the Navigator launched the first expeditions southwards the major interest of Portuguese sailors lay in northern waters, in Bruges, Middelburg and England.[1] The first aim of this chapter is to see whether the maritime history of Portugal really began well before the fifteenth century.

Even before the Portuguese and the Castilians launched fleets in the Atlantic (having secured the service of highly competent Genoese admirals), the ocean waters off Iberia were far livelier than is generally supposed. The Viking raids on Spain prompted the rulers of al-Andalus to create an Atlantic fleet, and to take more seriously the dangers that might threaten from the open Atlantic. In 859 Muslim fleets set out to challenge the Viking raiders, carrying on board flasks of Greek fire and teams of archers; they scoured the seas as far away as the northern coast of Spain, so that the presence of these 'Moors' (*Mauri*) alarmed the Christians who ruled there as much as did the arrival of the Vikings. But Muslim fleets

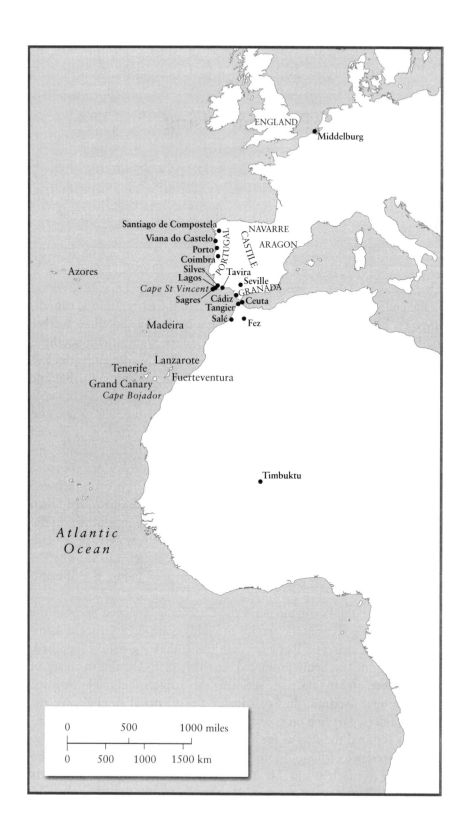

ENGLAND

Middelburg

Santiago de Compostela
Viana do Castelo
Porto
Coimbra
Silves
Lagos
Cape St Vincent
Sagres

NAVARRE
ARAGON

PORTUGAL
CASTILE

Tavira
Seville
GRANADA

Cádiz
Tangier
Salé

Ceuta

Fez

Azores

Madeira

Lanzarote
Tenerife
Grand Canary
Cape Bojador

Fuerteventura

Timbuktu

*Atlantic
Ocean*

0	500	1000 miles

0	500	1000	1500 km

kept up the chase and scored a series of successes, culminating in the destruction of fourteen Viking ships near Gibraltar; in 966 a Muslim fleet from Seville scared off Vikings who had penetrated right up to Silves, an important town that lay a little way upriver in what is now the Portuguese Algarve.[2] All this shows that the Muslims were perfectly capable of launching fleets in the Atlantic, often based upriver at Seville; moreover, since the Viking raids were lightning attacks, these fleets were not specially built for the occasion, but were clearly part of the standing forces of the emirs and caliphs of al-Andalus.

The problem with tracing the activities of the Muslim fleets, and still more of Muslim traders, in Atlantic waters is that the evidence is very sparse, mainly consisting of stories about battles that have been reported at second or third hand, or references to rare goods brought to the heartlands of Islam from *al-Andalus al-Aqsa*, the furthest reaches of Spain.[3] Seville, it is true, looked eastwards, and sent the olive oil of southern Spain through the Strait of Gibraltar to the eastern Mediterranean; but this did not mean that the resources of the Atlantic were neglected. In the Muslim period, up to the early thirteenth century, the shores of Portugal and Atlantic Andalusia were scoured for the whale vomit known as ambergris, which, despite its inauspicious source, has long been an expensive ingredient in perfumes, and which could be found washed up on the shore in fatty lumps; this, along with Atlantic coral, was forwarded all the way to Egypt, while the ocean was also exploited for its fish, sold in local markets; the tunny caught off Cádiz and Ceuta was specially prized. The fishermen were both Muslims and Mozarabs, that is, arabized Christians largely descended from the pre-Islamic population of Spain and Portugal. Wood suitable for shipbuilding could be found in the Algarve. The inhabitants of Silves sold their elegant ceramics far afield, and the town possessed its own arsenal in the eleventh century, when it was ruled by the Muslim kings of Seville.[4] Nor did the inhabitants of al-Andalus ignore the coast of Morocco, for they sailed down to Salé opposite Rabat in the twelfth century; and other ports along the Moroccan coast, including Arzila and possibly Mogador, were being visited in the ninth century.[5] While the waters off Atlantic Iberia did not match the Mediterranean for intensity of contact, the Atlantic was not a sea of darkness for the Muslims.

The relative quietness of the coastal waters off Morocco and Mauritania contrasts with the increasing liveliness of contact between Christian and Muslim in the waters off Iberia itself. In the twelfth century, as the Christian county (later, kingdom) of Portugal carved out territory in western Iberia around Porto and Coimbra, the Muslims found they had to face a challenge on the sea as well as on land. This was just when Muslim power in Iberia seemed to have recovered under the fundamentalist Almohads, whose radical revivalist movement originated among the Berbers of the Atlas Mountains. The first shock that the Almohad caliph faced was a surprise attack on Lisbon by a substantial navy, said to have numbered 164 ships or more, which had set out from Dartmouth in England en route to the Holy Land in 1148, following the call to arms of the Second Crusade. When they arrived in Porto the city's bishop eloquently reminded the English, Flemish and German sailors on board the crusading fleet that they would be coasting past Muslim-held territory even before they entered the Mediterranean. Convinced that an attack on Lisbon would serve the purposes of a grand crusade which was being fought not just in Syria but in the Wendish lands bordering Germany and in the Muslim lands bordering Catalonia, the crusaders eagerly joined a Portuguese expedition against Lisbon and, after great violence, forced the city's surrender; predictably, this was followed by its sack, and even the bishop of the Mozarabic Christians whom they found within its walls was slaughtered.[6] The capture of Lisbon gave the Portuguese a superb base in southern Iberia; in the thirteenth century the weakness and then collapse of the Almohad Empire in Spain and north Africa left them free to chip away at the Algarve, and they were masters of Silves by 1242.

Portuguese sea captains were already harrying Muslim ships and shores well before that date. A Portuguese fleet was built in response to constant raids on central Portugal by the Almohad navy, so it seems that Almohad policy had backfired: the Portuguese began to organize themselves as never before. By the late 1170s an intrepid admiral named Dom Fuas Roupinho was launching his ships into the Atlantic and led attacks on Almohad al-Andalus, all the way down to the coastline near Seville, as well as attacking Ceuta on the northern tip of Morocco. Between 1177 or 1178 and 1184 the two sides fought what a French historian has called 'a veritable battle of the Atlantic', marked by dramatic episodes such as the capture of the Almohad flagship and eight other vessels in 1180. In the long term, though, things did not always go well for the Portuguese: in 1181 the Almohads captured twenty, or maybe forty, of Dom Fuas's ships, and he was killed, while three years later the Almohads attacked Lisbon from the sea, though they were unable to repeat the success of the crusaders thirty-six years earlier.[7] Almohad power in Spain was only broken in 1212, in the land battle of Las Navas de Tolosa, in which – uniquely – the kings of Castile, Aragon, Navarre and Portugal set aside their differences and launched a joint attack on a Berber empire that was already suffering from the strains of overextension and abandonment of its founders' rigid principles.

II

Lisbon benefited from growing interest in routes linking the Mediterranean to England and Flanders at the end of the thirteenth century, as did the ports of northern Spain: Basque sailors become more and more noticeable in the records from this time onwards, while the pilgrim traffic to Santiago, which lay under Castilian rule, brought increasing numbers of pilgrims across the sea. Inland, Portugal remained poor in resources, though demand for its wines grew during the Middle Ages. The ports, notably Lisbon and Porto, but also smaller places such as Viana do Castelo in the north of the country, were the real hives of economic activity. And the Portuguese kings recognized the importance of these places in one privilege after another: royal letters of 1204 and 1210 mention a 'commander of the ships' (*alcaide dos navios*), and around the same time Portuguese merchants were being made welcome in England by a ruler who was always on the lookout for sources of revenue, King John; his son Henry III was prodigal in safe conducts for Portuguese merchants, dispensing more than a hundred of these privileges in the single year 1226.[8] Following the grant of the *Carta Mercatoria* to all foreign merchants by King Edward I in 1303, the Portuguese, like everyone else, had to pay higher customs dues, but England became even more attractive than before, because the merchants now lay under the protection of the Crown. That was something worth paying for. A commercial treaty in 1353 was followed by the Treaty of Windsor in 1386, a political alliance that reflected the common interests of the two kingdoms during the Hundred Years War, and English support for the dynasty of Aviz that had seized the throne in 1383 (largely to prevent it from falling into the hands of their hated neighbours, the Castilians). Marriage ties also bound the kingdoms together, after Philippa of Lancaster married the king of Portugal; her sons included the pioneers of Atlantic exploration Henry the Navigator and Prince Pedro.[9] So began an alliance that both sides in later centuries liked to think had never been sundered.

The Portuguese kings were, not surprisingly, even keener to promote Portuguese trade than foreign partners; King Dinis established an innovative mutual insurance scheme in 1293, whereby risks at sea were shared among the trading community. He understood that an effective fleet was needed in troubled times, and in 1317 he hired Manuel Pessagno, a Genoese admiral, to organize the construction of a fleet – the Castilians and even the French also relied on Genoese talent in their fleets.[10] Well before then, by 1200, Portuguese products were flowing into Bruges: a burgher of the city wrote that 'from the kingdom of Portugal come honey, skins, wax, hides, grain, ointment, oil, figs, raisins and esparto grass'.[11] By 1237 there was a royal arsenal in Lisbon, though it had surely existed for some time already. No one could have claimed that Portugal was already a major maritime power, and one should be wary of assuming that these achievements led in a straight line to the successes Portugal was to enjoy in the fifteenth-century Atlantic, but without the groundwork of King Dinis and others it is hard to see how Portugal would have emerged as a naval power on a scale out of all proportion to the size and natural resources of the country.

If Portugal was to flourish as a centre of business, it was vital to attract capital to Lisbon; and the obvious source of capital lay in the north Italian cities. The Crown was therefore keen to make the Italian merchants feel comfortable in the capital. In 1365 the Portuguese king generously exempted merchants from Genoa, Milan and Piacenza (a major centre of banking) from the authority of the royal officials who supervised the loading of goods on ships. It would not do to discourage the wealthiest businessmen in Portugal from trading through Lisbon. A few years later another king of Portugal found himself apologizing to the Genoese for Portuguese pirate raids on their ships, which had been seized along with a precious cargo of Flemish and French cloth. These kings offered special privileges for the Genoese and others in Lisbon, without extending them to other ports in the country. The city became home to branches of several of the most powerful Genoese families, such as the Lomellini and the Spinolas.[12] Lisbon was being slowly transformed into a major port city.

Notwithstanding these initiatives by the Portuguese Crown, interest in the sea depended on the initiative of the shipowners, sailors and merchants who set out from Lisbon and other ports, bound for Flanders and England in one direction, but also for warmer waters further south. By the fifteenth century Portuguese shipping was making regular appearances in the Mediterranean, bringing dried fruits and other relatively modest goods through the Strait of Gibraltar, over which the wealthy Muslim city of Ceuta, on the northern tip of Morocco, majestically presided.[13] The presence in the Mediterranean of ships from Atlantic Iberia – not just Portugal but Galicia and Cantabria, including many Basque vessels – demonstrates how the Strait had ceased to function as a barrier, and had become a link in the chain connecting the vigorous trade of the Mediterranean world with Atlantic networks.[14] From the eastern end of the Indian Ocean to the Red Sea, from Egypt and Syria to Venice, Genoa and Barcelona, from there out through the Strait to Atlantic waters all the way to Bruges, and from Bruges to Lübeck, Danzig and Riga, goods were conveyed stage by stage;

and the ports of Portugal were especially well placed to benefit from these world-encompassing connections (world-encompassing at least in an age when the existence of the Americas was not suspected). One stimulus to their interest came from the increasing concern of mapmakers to sketch accurately the shores of Europe and the lands beyond. By the middle of the fourteenth century, maps were being drawn in Majorca, Genoa and elsewhere that showed interesting-looking islands out in the Atlantic, as yet unsettled: certainly Madeira and possibly also the Azores, which lie so much farther out that this would speak for quite bold attempts to sweep the eastern Atlantic in the search for lands to exploit, whether by conquest or trade.

Exploration of the coast of Africa had begun by 1291, when the Vivaldi brothers from Genoa set out by way of Majorca and the Strait of Gibraltar to find a sea route all the way to India. They disappeared somewhere off the coast of Africa, no doubt overwhelmed by waves or wrecked on sandbanks along shores that were still unmapped and therefore extremely treacherous. The idea that they were precocious predecessors of Columbus, bound westwards for the opposite shores of the Atlantic (and for what they supposed would be China) holds no water. Still, their unfinished exploits remained the subject of wonder and speculation in Genoa even 200 years later, in the days of Columbus. The sense that there was something out there was reinforced when ships began to edge their way past Ceuta to ports along the coast of Morocco. As early as 1260 the king of Castile launched a fleet against Salé, the port opposite modern Rabat that for centuries was seen as a hive of pirates. King Alfonso failed to capture the port or to make inroads into Morocco, but peaceful visits by Catalan ships showed that there were good opportunities to make money along this coast. Around Fez, vast amounts of grain were cultivated, and this explains the arrival of ships from Barcelona and Majorca in Moroccan ports. Then the question beckoned: what lay beyond? Visitors to Morocco could not fail to see that this country had close ties with lands much further south, to which it was linked by caravan routes carrying gold and slaves from sub-Saharan Africa. Catalan mapmakers speculated that a 'River of Gold' stretched across the Sahara and might be reachable by ships that carried on along the African coast. A Genoese explorer named Lançalotto Malocello apparently reached the Canary Islands in 1336, and his name is commemorated in that of one of the easternmost islands – Lanzarote.[15]

The Canaries had been vaguely known for centuries as the 'Happy Islands', *Insulae Fortunatae*, but they were rarely visited. The twelfth-century geographer al-Idrisi, who came from Ceuta but had taken refuge at the court of Roger II, the Norman king of Sicily, mentioned failed attempts by the Muslims to conquer the Canary Islands, which were, however, still largely the stuff of myth: he reported that there existed a strange and magnificent temple in the islands, and that the inhabitants sold amber to the Lamtuna Berbers of north-west Africa, who came to trade.[16] The islanders, also of Berber origin, had arrived long before Islam swept into north Africa, and had lost the art of navigation, leaving them isolated in their (to all intents) Stone Age existence on all seven major islands, which probably did not even have contact among themselves. The most famous group were the warlike Guanches of Tenerife, whose massive volcano, Mount Teide, was visible from afar and was even mentioned by Dante in the *Divine Comedy*.[17] Lançalotto Malocello must have encountered the Majos and Majoreros of Lanzarote and Fuerteventura, who were just as capable warriors as the Guanches, despite the reliance of all the Canary islanders on weapons made of hardened wood and stone.[18]

After Malocello's visit, the race for the Canaries began. In July 1341 an expedition set out from Lisbon, apparently funded by Italians and consisting of three vessels manned by a motley crew of Portuguese, Castilians, Catalans and Italians. An extraordinary survival, a letter by the great writer Giovanni Boccaccio based on a report he had received from Florentine contacts in Lisbon, describes what happened.[19] The explorers took horses and heavy armaments on the ignorant assumption that they would be waging war against well-defended towns and fortresses. When they first saw the islanders they were astonished: they found rocks and forests inhabited by naked men and women, whom they described as 'rough in manners'. They obtained some modest goods: goatskins, sealskins, fats; but they were not tempted to create a base there, so they sailed on. What they really wanted was access to the gold of sub-Saharan Africa, which featured prominently on the world maps that were being produced around this time in Majorca and elsewhere. Any delusions they may have had about gold-rich Canary Islands soon vanished.

Moving on, the little fleet reached a second, rather larger island, Canaria, the island now known as Grand Canary. Standing close offshore, their ships attracted the wonder of the natives. The explorers saw a great gathering of men and women, who had come to watch them; most were naked, including unmarried girls, though some wore dyed leather kilts and were obviously of higher status. The islanders seemed welcoming enough, so twenty-five armed sailors went to shore; showing the sort of tactlessness that would be repeated again and again in the history of European overseas conquests, they broke into some stone houses, one of which proved to be a temple made of dressed stone blocks, from which they stole a statue of a naked man. Boccaccio evidently assumed this idol was similar to the classical statues he knew from his native Tuscany, which is hardly likely. The explorers also persuaded or coerced four young Canarians into travelling back to Portugal with them; they were handsome and gracious, and, judging from their kilts, must have been members of the Canarian elite. On board ship, it became obvious that they had never encountered bread or wine, and – to the disappointment of the explorers – they had never seen gold and silver; this suggested that the 'River of Gold' was beyond their reach. 'These do not appear to be rich islands,' Boccaccio reports, and those who had planned the expedition found that they had to recoup their investment from the sale of goatskins, tallow and dyestuffs picked up on the islands.[20] The disappointing outcome of the Portuguese voyage failed to deter the Catalan king of Majorca, James III, a mentally unbalanced ruler who dreamed of creating an island empire embracing both the Balearics and the Canaries. James sent his own heavily armed expeditions to the islands; and then, after 1343, when he was thrown off his throne by his cousin the king of Aragon, further visits by Catalan–Aragonese ships resulted in the creation of a missionary bishop on Grand Canary.[21]

The voyage of 1341 marks the first time medieval western Europeans had come into contact with isolated Stone Age societies, and Boccaccio's account wove together an idealized view of a society that lived in a prelapsarian state of innocence, of which their unashamed nakedness was a clear and beautiful sign. On the other hand, there was also a darker image: of peoples living in the Canaries as wild men (and women) of the forest, in a state of primitive and naked brutishness. This was the view of Boccaccio's friend and fellow littérateur Petrarch, and it could be used to justify European conquest both in the islands and, in due course, on the American mainland.[22] Another dark aspect of the Portuguese voyage of 1341 was that it planted in the mind of European merchants the notion that these primitive folk could be carried away without compunction and enslaved. Nothing is known of the fate of the four Canarians who were brought back to Lisbon; but documents from the late fourteenth century often speak of Canary islanders who were working as slaves on estates in Majorca, beginning in 1345, only three years after the first Majorcan expedition. In the decades after the Black Death, which hit Europe in 1347 and killed perhaps half the population, manpower shortages stimulated an active slave trade out of the Canaries, operated by Catalans and Castilians who kidnapped islanders without compunction. Intensive raids on the archipelago depopulated Lanzarote, a situation made far worse when Norman adventurers seized Lanzarote and Fuerteventura around 1400, with the intention of setting up an independent lordship there. By the early fifteenth century the papacy was seriously concerned about attempts to carry off islanders who had accepted baptism from the missionary friars in the islands.[23]

European explorers were much more interested in finding a sea route to the 'River of Gold' and in bypassing the camel routes across the Sahara and towards Timbuktu that were off-limits for Christian merchants. Understandably, they cared rather less about low-profit voyages to remote islands that were a source of truculent slaves and a not very interesting violet dyestuff – orchil, which was made from lichens found across the Canaries. An expedition by the Majorcan explorer Jaume Ferrer, in 1346, may well have reached some way down the African coast, anticipating Portuguese efforts to pass the supposed obstacle of Cape Bojador in the fifteenth century. However, nothing is known for certain, apart from the fact that Ferrer was commemorated on one Catalan map after another, beginning with the beautifully illuminated atlas presented to the king of France in 1375, preserved in the Bibliothèque nationale de France. This shows his solidly built ship, of the type known as an *uxer*, making headway southwards, carrying on board not just merchants and soldiers but priests ready to spread the word of Christ.[24]

All this demonstrates that the fascination of later generations of Portuguese with African gold formed part of a longer and wider tradition of thinking about ways of reaching the sources of gold by sea. Even so, it would be wrong to conclude that Portugal was turning away from colder Atlantic waters towards the coast of Africa. Links to England and Flanders, sealed by treaties and strengthened by marriage alliances, were intended to confirm Portugal's growing importance within the politics and trade of the northern Atlantic. But political convulsions in Portugal during the 1380s brought to power a new dynasty, that of Aviz, and during this turmoil there was little opportunity to challenge the Castilians, Catalans and Normans who were interfering in the waters off Africa. Only after about 1400, as the new dynasty in Portugal gained wide acceptance, not least among townspeople, did new schemes emerge that revealed how a royal family poised on the edges of Europe had begun to dream of grander achievements in the name of God and profit.

III

Ceuta occupies a narrow neck of land that joins the lesser of the Pillars of Hercules, a hill now known as Mount Hacho, to the mainland of Africa. Ceuta still preserves an impressive set of walls, parts of which date back to the long period of Arab domination, from the late seventh century to 1415; and Mount Hacho was also well defended, serving as a beacon (or *hacho*) overlooking the Strait of Gibraltar. On either side of the tiny isthmus lively harbours could be found, offering shelter to ships depending on whether the winds were easterly or westerly. Many of these ships plied down the coast of Morocco, making headway through the difficult waters of the Strait and then putting in at ports such as Salé, where they loaded with grain from the plains around Fez – Ceuta brimmed with granaries (there were forty-three mills in and around Ceuta), and some of the keenest clients who came to buy this grain were the merchants of Genoa and Barcelona, who would face severe shortages at home if they did not supply their cities with wheat from Sicily, Sardinia and Morocco.[25] As early as the twelfth century, whenever political crises, which were frequent, shut off access to the rich wheat fields of the Norman kingdom of Sicily, the Genoese headed for Ceuta to make up the shortfall.[26] Fine wool and hides from the Merino sheep, who derived their name from the ruling dynasty of Morocco, were other powerful attractions, though these sheep were eventually bred in vast numbers in Castile.[27] In the past – though it is less certain that this was still true around 1400 – Ceuta had been an important terminal for the camel caravans that carried gold dust across the Sahara in exchange for European textiles and Mediterranean salt.[28]

During the late thirteenth century and early fourteenth, Ceuta enjoyed a period of virtual independence as a city-state controlled by a local family, the 'Azafids; these 'Azafids helped keep the Castilians at bay when they tried to conquer Algeciras next door to Gibraltar, but they also, for several decades, managed to steer an independent course between the Marinid dynasty that took control of Morocco during the thirteenth century and the Nasrid dynasty that ruled over Granada, which included the other Pillar of Hercules, the Rock of Gibraltar.[29] Fragments of wooden decoration from its public buildings suggest that Ceuta's palaces and mosques were quite luxurious; besides, the city is said to have contained dozens of madrasas and was home to scholars of high repute, such as the great twelfth-century geographer al-Idrisi (before he went off into exile on Sicily), and ibn Sab'in, a philosopher who corresponded (in a rather condescending way) with the thirteenth-century Holy Roman emperor and king of Sicily, Frederick II.[30]

The strategic value of Ceuta was obvious, and it had been targeted by European navies as well as by the Marinids and the Nasrids. By 1400, when traffic heading from Italy and the Catalan lands through the Strait towards Flanders and England had become quite regular, the city was booming, and was seen as a wealthy prize. Even so, the decision by the Portuguese court to make Ceuta the target of a massive naval crusade took Europe and the Islamic world by surprise. Portugal did not seem to possess the resources for a campaign across the water against a well-fortified city that others had failed to conquer. But the surprise was all the greater because the Portuguese court kept its destination a closely guarded secret. From 1413 onwards it was obvious that something was being planned in Lisbon. A sign of what was in the air that no one seems to have understood was a ban that the Portuguese king, João I, imposed on trade with north Africa, targeting not just the export of weapons to Islamic lands, something that the papacy had long, and often fruitlessly, been forbidding, but the export of the dried fruit and other humbler products that Portugal regularly placed on the market.[31] This was hardly likely to shake Ceuta, Tangier or any other trading partner of the Portuguese to their foundations, though it would at least discourage Portuguese merchants from being stranded in Moroccan cities when an attack was launched.

Some speculated that the Portuguese intended to launch a raid in the northern Atlantic, as far away as Flanders or northern France, conceivably in conjunction with King Henry V of England, who was about to launch the Agincourt campaign. More probable was an attack on the last Muslim kingdom in Spain, Granada, though there existed a longstanding agreement among the Iberian rulers that Granada was reserved as a future prize for the kings of Castile. Indeed, the Portuguese had signed a treaty with the Castilians in 1411, despite a history of hostility between the two kingdoms that had culminated in a Castilian siege of Lisbon in 1384.[32] Letters passed back and forth between the Portuguese and the Castilian court, in which the Portuguese proposed to help in campaigns in Granada, while the Castilians, at that point preoccupied with other matters, gave them no encouragement.[33] On the other hand, there were those at court, notably Prince Henry, who remained deeply suspicious of Castilian intentions, and the treaty of 1411 lessened but failed to dissipate tension; to cite a fifteenth-century Portuguese king: 'after twenty years of bitter war between the two kingdoms treaties of peace cannot remove from the hearts of men so great a foundation of hatred and ill-will.'[34] Henry and his brothers, imbued with passion for the crusade and chivalric achievements, were determined to prove themselves on the field of battle, and constantly pressed for action.

The expedition of 1415 cost 33,600,000 *reais brancos* ('white royal coins'), and though this was a heavily devalued currency, equivalent to about 280,000 golden *dobras*. That is still a mountain of gold. This was just the immediate outlay, but there were also loans and purchases on credit that inflated the cost much further. In part the money was raised by demanding that anyone with reserves of silver or copper, the ingredients of the white, or rather off-white, coins, should surrender their bullion to the Crown; the Crown also bought in vast quantities of salt at an artificially low price and sold it on at much higher prices, which was a classic way for medieval kings to make money quickly. Even so, it is hard to believe that such orders can have had much effect; the king was scraping the barrel.[35]

Then there was the problem of finding a fleet. This involved the expropriation of ships in harbour in Portugal. Half the fleet that set out in August 1415 consisted of non-Portuguese ships. There were many vessels from north-western Spain and from the Bay of Biscay, because Galician and Basque sailors used Lisbon and Porto as stopping points on their way towards the Mediterranean. But there were also twenty-two Flemish and German ships, for it has been seen that the German Hansa had quite close ties to Portugal, and these included a 'great ship' from Flanders that displaced 500 tons; there were ten English vessels. As well as the ships themselves, there were the mariners, several hundred of whom were not Portuguese. Among the fighting force there were, again, some north European knights, though the English, despite their alliance with Portugal, were distracted by Henry V's war in France – Henry landed in France during the very days when the Portuguese fleet was beating its way towards its own destination.[36]

The participation of knights from outside Portugal exposes one motive for the campaign. Capturing a wealthy city was certainly an objective, but this war was a crusade, a continuation of the conflict between Christians and Muslims in Iberia (the so-called Spanish Reconquista) that was nearing completion now that the small kingdom of Granada was the only Muslim state left on Spanish soil; the *conquistadores* had long intended to continue their campaigns in Africa once, or even before, all Iberia lay under Christian rule. The problem was that Castile had reserved Morocco for itself, and Aragon had reserved Algeria. This left no space for the newcomer, Portugal. And yet, lacking a frontier with Muslim territory, the kings of Portugal were forced to seek glorious victories in Christ's name away from their own frontiers. So the army and navy were entertained with crusading sermons from the king's confessor while they stood off the Algarve, presenting the campaign as King João's act of repentance for shedding so much blood in his wars – wars with Castile, which shed Christian blood, whereas war against the Infidel was quite another moral issue.

In early August the Portuguese fleet moved south-east from the Bay of Lagos in the Algarve and headed into the troublesome waters of the Strait of Gibraltar. Scattered by the winds and currents, only part of the fleet was able to draw near to Ceuta, and before long a storm blew the fleet back towards the bay of Algeciras, the western part of which lay under the rule of the Castilian king, who had become suspicious enough of Portuguese plans to forbid his officials to offer any help. Discouraged by the hostile weather, some of the Portuguese commanders argued that Gibraltar was just across the bay and, since it was in Granadan hands, was a much more accessible target. But others, notably Prince Henry, were fixated on Ceuta; besides, the failed attempt a few days earlier had given the fleet a chance to inspect its fortifications on Mount Hacho and to see what sort of land-walls the city possessed. And by now it was so obvious that Ceuta was the intended target that the Portuguese would have looked silly in the eyes of their Christian neighbours if they had chosen any other target. One advantage of which they were not aware was that the *qadi*, the governor of Ceuta, had decided that the threat from Portugal had receded once the fleet was blown back towards Spain. He dismissed troops he had brought in from Morocco, and no effort was made to ring the city with Marinid warships. The Portuguese certainly made mistakes in the early stages of their campaign; but the Ceutans made even more serious ones. On 21 August 1415 the Portuguese returned, and the *qadi* brought his troops down from the battlements to prevent them from landing. He failed to stop them, and left part of his defences exposed.

The battle for the city lasted a whole day, but by evening Ceuta was in Christian hands. So it has remained ever since, allowing for a change from Portuguese to Spanish rule in the seventeenth century. But if the Portuguese expected to take charge of a prosperous and well-connected city they were at once disappointed. The attack had already prompted the great majority of Ceutans to flee into the Moroccan hinterland; maybe they expected to return, but Portuguese victory scared them away – after all, the Great Mosque was converted into a cathedral. Not just the Muslims but the Genoese, who had played such an important part in the business life of the city, disappeared. They were hardly encouraged by what they saw: a Portuguese noble seized all the grain owned by a Sicilian merchant who was residing in Ceuta, and then tortured him until he signed a deed handing over gold coins he had stored away in distant Valencia.[37] The Portuguese made Ceuta into a garrison city inhabited by 2,500 soldiers, and sent there all sorts of undesirables, so that it became Portugal's Siberia; what had once been one of the great cities of the Maghrib had to all intents ceased to exist as a city, and it never recovered its past glories. Lack of access to the interior meant that Ceuta had to be supplied from Tavira in the Portuguese Algarve, which was a constant drain on public finances.[38]

This victory infuriated the Castilians, alarmed the Moroccans, and boosted the prestige of the royal house of Portugal, and especially that of Prince Henry, the king's third son, who had displayed bravery to the point of foolhardiness on the streets of Ceuta – even at one point becoming trapped among Muslim soldiers, from whom he was rescued by a loyal knight who lost his own life in the process. Henry was knighted when the fleet returned to Tavira and was made absentee governor of Ceuta as a reward for his bravery. His obsession with chivalry and crusade lasted throughout his life, as his biographer, Sir Peter Russell, showed, to the consternation of the old generation of Portuguese historians, who saw him as the first builder of what became the worldwide Portuguese empire.

The big question, though, is whether the events of 1415 really mark 'the origins of European expansion', to cite the title of the conference held in Ceuta to mark the 600th anniversary of its conquest – a rather low-key affair, given the sensitivities in Morocco about the two, now Spanish, cities on the coast of north Africa. It has not been easy to shake off the assumptions about Portugal's imperial destiny that are enshrined in the greatest work of sixteenth-century Portuguese literature, Luis Camões's *Lusiads*:

> A thousand swimming birds, spreading
> Their concave pinions to the winds,
> Parted the white, turbulent waves
> To where Hercules set his pillars.[39]

Yet a strong case can be made that the Portuguese hoped to expand not across the world, but from this foothold on the northern tip of Morocco down the coast to Tangier and other cities close to the Strait. An attack on Tangier in 1437 proved a total disaster, and Portugal was almost cornered into a position where it would trade Ceuta for one of Henry's brothers, who had been taken captive; but Henry preferred to let him die in a Moroccan jail – he loved Ceuta more than his brother. Yet the Portuguese kept coming back to Morocco, well into the late sixteenth century, leading to the extinction of their dynasty when King Sebastian, leading a crusade against Islam with Messianic fervour, died in the Battle of the Three Kings in 1578.[40] The Moroccan crusade lay right at the top of Portuguese foreign-policy objectives.

The traditional view of Prince Henry was that he fostered the science of navigation, making him in matters maritime the equivalent of the great cultural figures of the Italian Renaissance. He supposedly established a revolutionary school of navigation in his palace at Sagres, near Cape St Vincent on the southern tip of Portugal, enlisting the help of a certain

Jaume de Mallorca, a Majorcan Jew or convert from Judaism, who brought to Portugal the cartographic and astronomical knowledge that Majorcan Jews had been cultivating since at least 1300. It is just possible that he did bring a member of the famous mapmaking family of Cresques to Portugal, but the myth of a fully fledged academy at Sagres does not hold water.[41] Thoroughly modern Henry is a myth. The statue of Henry that looms over the quayside at Belém, near Lisbon, pointing the way of his navigators out into the far ocean, was built for an exhibition in 1940 and reconstructed for the 500th anniversary of Henry's death in 1960. It says more about the imperial myths of Portugal under Dr Salazar than it does about Portugal in the days of Prince Henry.

26

Virgin Islands

To deny the capture of Ceuta its accustomed place as the starting point for the 'Expansion of Europe' is not to deny Prince Henry a central role in the opening of Atlantic waters. His ambitions stretched in many directions; in 1424 he launched an assault on the Canaries that was rebuffed by the islanders, and he was probably well aware of the Portuguese expedition to the Canaries in 1341, and the claim to the islands that followed. It is certain that he was looking for lands over which he could rule in his own right under loose Portuguese dominion. Throughout his long career (he died in 1460), he juggled the crusade in Morocco, ambitions in the Canaries, the management of newly colonized Atlantic islands and the exploration of the west African coast in search of gold, though he himself never sailed further than Ceuta. These objectives were not separate from one another: gold would pay for crusades; so would the profits from the sugar industry that began to flourish in the Atlantic islands. As governor of the Order of Christ he administered a crusading Military Order that had come into being when the disgraced Order of the Temple was disbanded early in the fourteenth century; its Portuguese properties were handed over to the new order, in whose name the Atlantic voyages were conducted.

The uninhabited Atlantic islands that fell under Portuguese rule have a special claim to attention. As with the Pacific islands, they were places where the human presence decisively transformed the environment, exploiting or in some cases destroying their fertility. They were places where settlers, living far from home in simple conditions, had to create a society that could function effectively despite the inability of the royal government back home to keep an eye on day-to-day affairs. They were also places where different social mixes came into being, whether through the arrival of Genoese in Madeira and Flemings in the Azores, or the presence of Jewish converts, black slaves and Portuguese convicts in the remotest

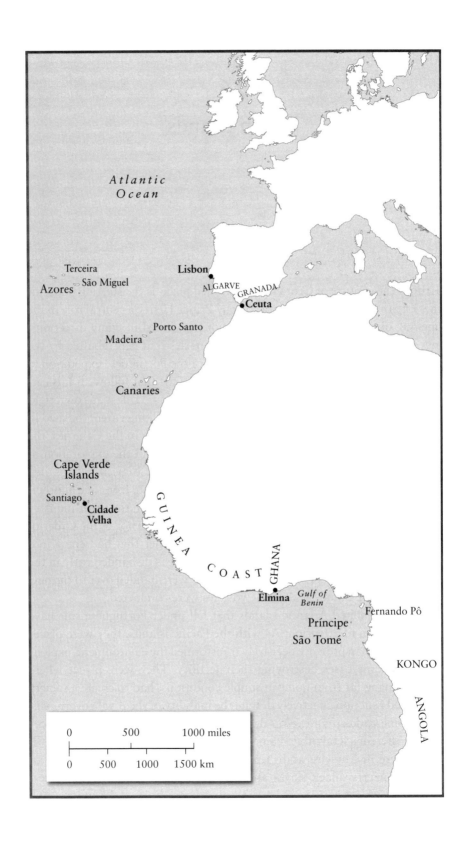

Atlantic
Ocean

Terceira
São Miguel
Azores

Lisbon
ALGARVE
GRANADA
Ceuta

Porto Santo
Madeira

Canaries

Cape Verde
Islands

Santiago
**Cidade
Velha**

G U I N E A

C O A S T

GHANA

Elmina
*Gulf of
Benin*
Fernando Pô

Príncipe
São Tomé

KONGO

ANGOLA

| 0 | 500 | 1000 miles |
| 0 | 500 | 1000 | 1500 km |

island, São Tomé. They also offer insights into the very earliest phases of the European slave trade out of Africa, insights that can now be developed further following excavations in the Cape Verde Islands. For this was a clean New World, the first New World, newer than the New World that was soon to be discovered, because all the island groups in the eastern Atlantic apart from the Canaries were uninhabited. The rape of this virginal world by greedy Europeans is one of the themes of this chapter.

Geographers have given these scattered islands the common name of 'Macaronesia', derived from the Greek term 'Fortunate Isles' (Μακάρων Νῆσοι, *Makarōn Nēsoi*), which was used in antiquity to describe the Canaries; this has too much of the flavour of macaroni and has often been shortened to 'Macronesia', by analogy with Micronesia in the Pacific. Some historians have preferred to use the term *Méditerranée Atlantique*, seeing the eastern Atlantic archipelagoes as an interconnected world that came into existence as merchants and migrants expanded beyond the familiar waters of the Mediterranean and the eastern Atlantic shoreline into open seas that had rarely been navigated before the fourteenth century.[1] The first of the Atlantic islands to be colonized were those in the Madeira archipelago. Although later legend told of a pair of storm-tossed and star-crossed English lovers who had been swept towards Madeira, the islands were uninhabited when the one-eyed João Gonçalves Zarco and his colleague Tristão Vaz, squires of Prince Henry, explored them in 1420. The low-lying island of Porto Santo close to Madeira was placed under the authority of another sea captain, named Perestrello, whose family had originated in Piacenza in northern Italy but settled in Portugal; later, Christopher Columbus would marry into this family and quite possibly gained knowledge of Atlantic waters by studying information the family had kept to itself.[2]

The islands were already known to Italian and Catalan navigators of the fourteenth century: Madeira appears on the portolan charts as the 'Isle of Wood', *Legname*, which is exactly the meaning of the Portuguese word 'Madeira'; and anyone sailing back from the Canaries after a slave-raid would have known how to catch the prevailing winds by swinging out north-westwards, which would have brought them in sight of Madeira, while an even greater swing might bring navigators to the Azores. It is an extraordinary fact that the colonization of the Pacific had already been completed with the settlement of New Zealand about a century earlier, while colonization of the Atlantic islands lagged far behind. In part this was because the Atlantic islands were fewer and more scattered; in part it was the result of relatively slow advances in shipbuilding. Eventually the Portuguese caravel became the trademark ship of the early Portuguese explorers.

This versatile lateen-rigged ship, of around fifty tons, had a shallow keel that made it suitable for travelling upriver, an important advantage for those seeking the 'River of Gold' in west Africa. There were other advantages in its small size, compared to the great *naus* and cogs that visited Lisbon on their way to and from northern waters, or the ocean-going galleys of the Venetians and the Florentines that linked Flanders to Italy. For Portuguese timber resources were limited, and (as it turned out) the best timber was not to be found in Portugal itself, but out in the Atlantic.

The colonization of Madeira really took off after 1433, when the old king, João I, died, and Henry found himself in full charge of the island; even then, he arrogated to himself greater powers than the Crown was willing to concede, and tussles between Henry and the kings of Portugal over jurisdiction in Madeira were still going on in 1451.[3] Yet it was thanks to Henry, if his biographer is to be believed, that this small island became an economic powerhouse. According to Zurara, Henry supported the first settlers by sending them seeds and tools. His interest in the island grew as his attempts to gain a further foothold in Morocco met with complete failure; following defeat at Tangier in 1437, he turned his attention to the Atlantic islands. Although he saw these islands mainly as a source of revenue, he also boasted to the pope that he had freed the inhabitants of Madeira from Muslim rule and had brought them back to the Christian faith – a nonsensical statement that reveals more about his love for self-promotion than about the crusade against the Muslims.[4]

Madeira lies 350 miles from Morocco and about the same distance from the Canaries. The island's abundant hardwood became one of its best exports; it was said to be so strong that the inhabitants of Lisbon could use it to build new storeys on their houses.[5] It was of great value to the growing Portuguese fleet; Madeira as well as Lisbon became a centre of shipbuilding. The discoverers divided up the territory, and one-eyed Zarco made his base at the 'place of fennel', O *Funchal*, now the island capital, where he and his followers flourished. The fertile, well-watered soil, left untended since the island rose out of the sea, yielded vast quantities of wheat; since the settler population was small (150 households in 1450, according to Zurara), Madeira offered a lifeline to Lisbon, which was suffering from lack of access to Moroccan grain now that the Portuguese were launching campaigns against the Marinid sultanate. Prince Henry's Venetian captain, Alvise da Cà da Mosto (or Cadamosto), stated that around 1455 Madeira produced 68,000 bushels of wheat each year. All this meant that the ecology of Madeira underwent massive transformations following the arrival of the first human settlers, and the same applies to the other Atlantic islands that the Portuguese colonized.[6]

Nonetheless, flat land suitable for wheat production was not easy to find on such a mountainous island, and Henry had grander plans. Da Mosto was travelling past Cape St Vincent on a Venetian galley bound for Flanders; the ship had to put in, and Prince Henry lured da Mosto into his service by showing him samples of sugar grown in Madeira, something that would tempt any Italian merchant.[7] Demand for sugar was booming, just as supplies of sugar from the eastern Mediterranean were threatened by the Turkish advance to Constantinople; princely courts and prosperous merchants were enthusiastic consumers of luxury foodstuffs, including crystallized fruits and little caskets containing blocks of white sugar.[8] Sicily, Valencia and Muslim Granada were among the great sugar centres of the Mediterranean, and Madeiran sugar was cultivated from either Sicilian sugar stocks or southern Portuguese ones recently set up by Genoese entrepreneurs in the Algarve. But to produce sugar in the subtropical climate of Madeira was an inspired idea; Madeira was superbly equipped for this, with its vast amounts of wood (needed for the boiling of the cane) and of water, running down the steep hills. Its sugar could then be supplied to Flanders via Lisbon, or, before long, directly – many of the splendid Flemish paintings in the Museum of Sacred Art in Funchal were acquired as payment for sugar by Madeiran merchants of the late fifteenth and early sixteenth century.

Da Mosto thought that the island was already producing 1,600 *arrobas*, or about 24,000 kg, of sugar by 1456. But these were small beginnings: by 1498 something like 600,000 kg of sugar were being sent to Flanders alone, with 225,000 bound for Venice and only 105,000 for consumption in Portugal – the total for just these places approaches 1,000,000 kilograms, but that year a decision was made to limit the quantity exported to 1,800,000 kg (120,000 *arrobas*), which was just as well, as the sugar cane was beginning to exhaust the land.[9] Europe had developed a sweet tooth. And the quantity being produced grew and grew. The Portuguese *Cortes*, or parliament, of 1481–2 noted that twenty large ships and forty to fifty smaller ones were loading sugar and some other goods, 'for the nobility and richness of the merchandise of great value which they have and harvest in the said islands'. Pope Paul II praised Zarco and his colleagues for all they had done to supply the Iberian kingdoms with sugar, wheat and other 'comforts'.[10]

Administering places a long way from Lisbon was a challenge. The 'sub-donatories', Zarco and Vaz on Madeira and Perestrello on Porto Santo, who had discovered the islands and were Henry's agents there, were authorized to operate local courts; they received one tenth of the revenues from their lands, passing the remaining nine tenths to Henry, or rather the Order of Christ. Their share might seem paltry, but it was not paltry so long as the Madeira archipelago continued to export its sugar and wheat on such an enormous scale. Madeirans at large benefited handsomely from exemption from trade taxes on goods sent to Portugal, which the Crown renounced in 1444 to encourage trade. It is no wonder, then, that, by the end of the fifteenth century, Madeira was attracting settlers from Portugal, Genoa and Tuscany; others arrived from Flanders and Germany, given the close links between Madeira and the sugar trade to Flanders. In 1457, some German settlers were allowed to plant vines and sugar and to build a chapel and houses. The Portuguese imposed few restrictions on settlers, though the Madeirans were keen to expel the enslaved Canary islanders who had been imported to work the sugar mills, and were proving extremely truculent.[11] The Genoese brought capital and enterprise, and helped kick-start the sugar industry. Among them was Christopher Columbus, who visited the archipelago in 1478, aiming to buy sugar in exchange for cloth; and his business partner in Madeira was Jean de Esmerault, a Fleming. This mixed population had reached about 15,000 by 1500, which included the full panoply of priests, merchants and artisans as well as the descendants of the original cultivators of the soil. Of this total, some 2,000 were slaves, either from the Canaries or from west Africa. This is a surprisingly low figure, since the sugar industry demanded plenty of cheap labour for back-breaking work; the main labour force was Portuguese and Italian.

Another source of stability was the simple fact that the first European proprietors lived a long time, Zarco remaining in charge of southern Madeira for about forty years. It is not hard to see why they lasted so long. They lived far from the centres of plague and other disease in western Europe; their diet was a plainer but healthier one than that of minor nobles in Iberia or Italy; the water was clean; they fought few or no wars. Nature could be remoulded: whether by the planting of sugar stocks or by the cattle and sheep that first populated the Azores. Sometimes, admittedly, this did not work well: when rabbits were introduced to Porto Santo they gobbled up the vegetation and turned the island into a semi-desert; it has never recovered. Madeira lost part of its tree cover as its timber was sent for export or burned in the furnaces of the sugar mills.[12]

II

The Azores too were evidently known to mapmakers before their colonization; they are recognizable in fourteenth-century Majorcan portolan charts.[13] Lying between 800 and 1,000 miles due west of Lisbon, these nine volcanic peaks gradually became valued for themselves, rather than any notional value in the fight against Islam in north-west Africa. Although they lie much further out from Portugal than Madeira, ships returning from Madeira or the Canaries would have taken advantage of the prevailing winds to follow a great curve that took them towards the Azores before they turned eastwards in the direction of Lisbon; the story grew that the Portuguese had reached the legendary 'Isle of Brazil' that was said to lie out in the Atlantic, or possibly the 'Isle of the Seven Cities', inhabited by refugees from the Muslim conquest of Spain more than 700 years earlier.[14] Impressed by the hawks that hovered over the islands, the Portuguese gave them the name 'Hawk Islands', *Açores*. These islands were completely uninhabited by humans, and attempts to argue that the Phoenicians knew the islands or that stone structures on the island date back to Neolithic times are based on very flimsy evidence. In 1439 Henry the Navigator received permission from the Crown to settle 'the seven islands of the Azores', so they already had their name and a number; and, though it was the wrong number, it was the number of units in the Isle of the Seven Cities.

In the 1450s, Henry claimed, with typical bravado, that the Azores 'had never known any lordship but his'. This was a blatant lie, as the king had earlier insisted he must share the lordship with his brother Dom Pedro, but by the time Henry made his claim Dom Pedro had rebelled against the Crown, had been defeated and had died, so his rights could be ignored. As at Ceuta, convicts were regularly dumped here, though in 1453 one convict was able to argue that he should not be transported to the Azores for the rest of his life, because conditions on the islands were still so primitive. No doubt he had friends in high places, for his argument, which succeeded, hardly stands up – solid buildings existed and dairy products and wheat abounded. The main concern back in Lisbon was not how to punish criminals but how to populate far-off islands and make sure the settlers stayed put.[15]

Wetter and windier than Madeira, though still blessed with a benign climate, the Azores seemed ideal terrain for cattle rather than for people, and as the islands were opened up to settlement ships would arrive carrying cows, sheep and horses rather than human beings, leaving them awhile until they had bred, spread and cleared some of the meadows. The Azores are still a major source of dairy goods in Portugal, and are famous for their butter and cheese; there was some attempt to produce sugar, but the climate was not quite warm enough and manpower was in short supply – the inhabitants of one island, Santa Maria, had to send their canes to São Miguel across the water for processing, since they did not have the machinery themselves. In 1510 the Azores exported only about 6 per cent of the sugar exported by Madeira, and sometimes it was even less than that.[16]

The Flemish connection was as important as the Portuguese one. Enterprising Flemings came and colonized, but not, as in Madeira, because of a sweet tooth. On the third island to be settled, appropriately known as Terceira, or 'Third Island', James of Bruges established a dominion around the little beach of Praia da Vitória in the north-east, building an elegant church with a Gothic gateway and stone-vaulted side chapels, out of materials that were brought all the way from Europe. Henry sent him a charter urging him to settle the island, 'which had never before been settled by anyone in the world', with good Catholics, and in the wake of this so many Flemings arrived that the whole group of islands was often called the 'Flemish Isles' rather than the Azores.[17] The products they cultivated included the dark-blue substitute for indigo, woad, much in demand in the Flemish cloth workshops; by 1500, up to 60,000 bales of cured woad leaves were exported annually. Gradually, an intertwined network of islands emerged, as the Azores, Madeira and the Canaries exchanged goods and manpower: native Guanches from Tenerife were settled against their will in Madeira; Portuguese labourers emigrated to the Canaries; Genoese and Flemings arrived in all the islands. This network was itself tied to the emerging emporium of Lisbon, no longer a city of moderate size and importance, but the centre of a maritime trading world that stretched across great swathes of the eastern and northern Atlantic.[18] By the late sixteenth century, the Azores became the strategic centre of a network of trade routes; ships arriving from South America and round the Cape from India gathered at Angra on Terceira, before proceeding in convoy to Portugal, in order to escape predators such as the English pirates who lurked in those waters. They were also important resupply centres for long-distance shipping.[19]

III

The exploration of the coast of Africa, the subject of the next chapter, resulted in the discovery of yet more uninhabited islands, west of Senegal. The debate about who first sighted the Cape Verde Islands, around the time of Henry the Navigator's death in 1460, is not very instructive – maybe it was the Venetian captain of Prince Henry, Alvise da Mosto, maybe a Genoese named Antonio da Noli, maybe a Portuguese named Diogo Gomes, but the fact that two of the three were Italian says something about the reliance of the Portuguese on Italian navigational know-how. After their discovery, the islands were placed under the command of Antonio da Noli as captain-general. He proved to be yet another long-lived colonial master, and he held on to power even though for a brief period in 1486–7, when Castile and Portugal were at war, he was carried off to Spain, where he apparently abandoned his loyalty to the king of Portugal and recognized Ferdinand and Isabella as his overlords.[20] He probably never returned to the islands; but neither Spain nor Portugal could really maintain control of such distant possessions, and once Castile and Portugal were at peace again, and once the pope had adjudicated these islands to Portugal, as he did in 1493/4, Portuguese claims to rule the islands could no longer be challenged from Spain.

Like the Azores, these islands were stocked with animals, not so much to feed the exiguous population as the sailors who passed by, heading from Europe to the west. However, when livestock was introduced to the Cape Verde Islands goats and sheep uprooted the plants, the soil no longer retained such water as there was, for rainfall is low; and the landscape became even more parched and bare than it was already. The animals somehow survived; but hopes of making the islands into a second Madeira were foiled. The royal privilege establishing Portuguese settlement in the Cape Verde Islands, dated 1462, grandly talked of the rivers, woods, fisheries, coral, dyes and mines, but the reality was that these islands could offer very little apart from the ubiquitous lichen orchil, used to make purple dye, and salt from the island appropriately known as Sal, which could be used to salt the meat sold to passing ships. One island was being used as a leper colony by the time of Christopher Columbus, and others, including Sal, were left unoccupied.[21]

Limited resources on the islands themselves were not an overwhelming problem; if anything, these sparse resources stimulated close interest in trade with west Africa as a much more viable source of profit, and the king permitted islanders to trade freely on the Guinea coast opposite, with the result that slave-trading and slave-raiding became their speciality (the arrival of the Portuguese in west Africa will be explained in the next chapter).[22] It cannot, therefore, have been easy for the islanders when, during the 1460s, the Crown insisted that only Caboverdean goods, including foodstuffs, could be used in payment if the settlers visited the Guinea coast for trade, but one effect of this regulation was that it stimulated the cultivation of cotton and the weaving of cotton cloth in the islands.[23] Horse-breeding became another speciality – mounted troops were a familiar sight in African armies, but obtaining good horses was a headache everywhere.

The main article of trade through these islands was quite simply, and quite horribly, human beings young and old, male and female.[24] As the coast of west Africa became a major source of black slaves, the Cape Verde Islands began to be used as a way station for slaves exported from Africa to Europe (and, in the sixteenth century, to Brazil and the Caribbean).[25] Although Portuguese merchants penetrated into west Africa, and even set up home there, there were great advantages in using the islands as a base. In Africa, there was always the delicate problem of dealing with the local rulers, and convincing them that the presence of these outlandish Europeans, with their bizarre clothes, was worthy of attention. Living on Portuguese territory and visiting the Guinea coast solely for business was a much more practical option; one might have to pay taxes to Portuguese officials, about whom the merchants naturally grumbled a good deal, but the protection of the Portuguese king, even so far from Lisbon, was preferable to that of African rulers who were often at war with one another – indeed, these wars were the major source of slaves for European buyers. In the three years 1491, 1492 and 1493 around 700 slaves were brought to the island of Santiago, or, at least, that number was recorded; in reality there must have been many more who were sneaked past the royal tax officials, and it is likely that as many as 25,000 African slaves passed through the island between 1500 and 1530, as demand for labour grew not just in Europe but in the newly discovered lands across the Atlantic.

Most of the population lived on the main island, Santiago, and a town called Ribeira Grande, later sacked by Francis Drake, was founded in about 1462; after it was abandoned for the present capital, Praia, it became known by its present-day name of Cidade Velha, 'the old city'. Taking advantage of the 'Great River' that gave the town its original Portuguese name, and that ensured an unusually lush setting in an otherwise arid island, the Portuguese were quick to develop their trading base. They built stone houses, which have now vanished, and churches, beginning with Nossa Senhora de Conceição, whose construction probably began only a few years after the islands were discovered. The foundations of this church have been unearthed by a team of archaeologists from Cambridge University, marking the site of the earliest European building in the Tropics.[26] Only one of the churches in the old capital survives intact, Nossa Senhora do Rosário, built in the 1490s close to the earlier church. It was reputedly visited by both Vasco da Gama and Christopher Columbus, who passed through the Cape Verde Islands in 1498 on his third voyage. Today much of the church has been remodelled, but there are still clear traces of the original building: a side chapel has retained its ribbed Gothic ceiling, manufactured in Portugal for reassembly in Ribeira Grande; for it was common Portuguese practice to send dressed stones to overseas settlements, and the vaulting of James of Bruges's church in the Azores, also brought from Portugal, is quite similar.

Half a century later Ribeira Grande was still tiny: in 1513 it contained 58 Portuguese citizens, or *vezinhos*, 56 visitors or foreign settlers, 16 free African males, 10 free African women and 15 churchmen, who were all outnumbered by the uncounted slaves; and the foreigners included Genoese, Catalans, Flemings and even a Russian. (By 1600 it may have risen as high as 2,000, though never higher.)[27] The Town Council of Ribeira Grande saw slaves as the foundation of the islands' prosperity, and stated in 1512 that 'merchants from Castile, Portugal and the Canary islands would not come to the Cape Verde islands if they were not able to purchase enslaved Africans'; by this time the slavers were already sending captives across the Atlantic to the Caribbean, to replace the native population of Hispaniola and other islands, which was heading towards rapid extinction.[28] In 1518 the Spanish king arranged the purchase of 4,000 slaves from Portuguese merchants, to be sent to the Caribbean.[29]

Ships put in at Ribeira Grande and at a rival town called Alcatrázes, whose location remained unknown until the archaeologists from Cambridge identified the site at the start of the twenty-first century. Archaeology has also come to the rescue of historians of the Atlantic by showing that large numbers of slaves lived in Ribeira Grande just after 1500, many of them apparently converted to Christianity. To judge from the graves found by the same team from Cambridge, there may be as many as 1,000 burials under and close to the church of the Conceição, and the simplicity of many of the burials, along with preliminary DNA analysis, suggests that half or more were slaves. There were also some free black inhabitants, and they eventually merged with the European settlers to create the Creole, or *Krioulu*, society that persists. For long, though, a white elite dominated the islands, including New Christians of Jewish descent who hoped to keep the Inquisition at arm's length; their blood also runs through the veins of many modern Caboverdeans.[30]

Millet and rice were imported from Guinea, mainly, it seems, to feed the African slaves.[31] The islands depended on the income from the sale of slaves and other goods, which provided the cash to buy in the most basic supplies. The manifest of a single ship that carried 139 slaves and a quantity of hides back to Europe in 1513 is very revealing. The *Madanela Cansina* was a Castilian caravel under the command of Diego Alonso Cansino. It carried a vast variety of products to Santiago in 1512: linen cloth, dark-green Castilian cloth, Flemish cloth, figs, flour, wine, biscuit, raisins, almonds, cheeses, saffron, wheat, olive oil, beans, soap, shoes, tablecloths, bowls, brooms, just to cite selected items.[32] In addition, the new excavations at Cidade Velha on Santiago have brought to light pottery from Portugal and Africa (and, rather later, from China), building materials, especially marble, tiles, coins, nails and buckles, once again indicating how dependent Santiago was on finished goods, particularly those from Europe. African ceramics arrived from Senegal and from Berber areas of north-west Africa; European ceramics included small drinking cups and other everyday wares from Portugal, 'giving', according to the archaeologist Marie Louise Sørensen, 'a sense of the attempt to maintain a similarity in daily life routines' among the settlers.[33]

IV

There is no reason to doubt the misery of the African slaves who either languished labouring in the Cape Verde Islands or were sent on to Portugal, and from there across Iberia to Valencia and other slave-trading centres in the western Mediterranean.[34] As Portuguese expeditions reached further south and east, they made contact with local rulers who were happy to sell them slaves from the Gulf of Benin and from the areas they knew as Kongo and Angola, a little to the north of the present-day country of Angola. Once again the Portuguese made use of uninhabited islands off the coast of Africa as collection points for slaves, while at the same time they tried to work out how they could capitalize on the resources of these fresh territories. In 1472 Portuguese ships reached the island of São Tomé, tucked into the corner of Africa and lying right on the Equator. Within ten years it had become the collection point for the thousands of slaves who were brought (and bought) from Ghana, while the nearby island of Príncipe was the major Portuguese base for trade with the Benin coast.[35] When they discovered that the third island in the Gulf of Guinea, Fernando Pô (modern Bioko), was already inhabited, the Portuguese held back from settling the island. For what they wanted was territories they could mould exactly to their own uses.

It took some years for the Portuguese Crown and Portuguese merchants to express much interest in São Tomé, whose thick tropical forests left them wondering what they could hope to extract from the island. Its usefulness only became obvious as the slave trade out of Ghana took off in the 1480s.[36] Unlike the Cape Verde Islands, this island played an insignificant part in the trade towards the Indies that developed after 1500, lying as it did well away from the great parabolas that carried ships around the southern tip of Africa or up to Portugal from Brazil. Gradually, though, the Portuguese attempted to cash in on the island's own resources. At the end of the fifteenth century they tried to make São Tomé into a centre of sugar production.[37] Labour was cheap, consisting of Kongo slaves and, as will be seen, Jewish children from Portugal, although São Tomé offered its first inhabitants little apart from palm oil and yams, leaving them hungry, so that, at the start, staple goods such as flour, olive oil and cheese had to be imported from Portugal and the nearby, better-endowed, island of Príncipe. That said, the Portuguese made a great effort here, as in other Atlantic islands, to transform their colony into a place suitable for settlement. They brought in all sorts of domestic animals, figs, citrus trees, plantains, and, in due course, American varieties of coconut and sweet potato. By 1510 there was a surplus and they were now feeding, rather than being fed by, the colonists at Elmina, the main Portuguese base in Ghana.[38]

Sugar came to dominate the economy of the island, along with the handling of slaves brought from the mainland. One item, essential for sugar manufacture, was plentiful: water. São Tomé has high rainfall as well as plenty of wood for burning; and there are steep slopes off which the water runs. Water was also a problem. It was needed while sugar was being manufactured; but the finished product had to be allowed to dry out, and the humid climate made this much more difficult. What the São Toméans put on sale was far inferior to the highly prized sugar of Madeira. Sugar from São Tomé was described as 'the worst in the world'; it often contained live insects that survived transport to Portugal. Moreover, mortality from malaria, overwork and generally unhealthy conditions was extremely high, particularly among Portuguese settlers unused to the tropics; it is hardly surprising that Portuguese churchmen appointed to serve on this island made every effort to avoid setting out. At a rough estimate half of those who came to São Tomé died from disease and other factors within a few months of their arrival.

The population remained small at the start of the sixteenth century, when about 1,000 heads were counted by a German geographer and printer based in Portugal named Valentim Fernandes. But these were just the settlers; 2,000 slaves resident on the island and 6,000 slaves destined for export have to be included as well. The free settlers included liberated slaves, among whom there were women who bore children to Portuguese men, so that a free mulatto population emerged quite early.[39] Like other Atlantic islands, São Tomé was considered a suitable place of exile for the so-called *degredados*, people convicted of crimes in Portugal.[40] São Tomé, as a place of exile, had one very special feature to its early population. In

1493 King João II decided to settle the island with Jewish children, forcibly taken from their parents in order to ensure that they were baptized
and brought up as Catholics. These were Jews who had fled from Spain
to Portugal in 1492, at the time of the expulsion of the Jews from Spain,
and who had overstayed the eight-month period the king had reluctantly
allowed them to remain. This was one stage in a process that culminated
in the mass conversion of all Portuguese Jews in 1497.[41]

The Jewish settlement of São Tomé is described in several Jewish and
Christian sources. The court chronicler Rui Pina wrote soon afterwards
of João II:

> The king gave to Alvaro de Caminha the Captaincy of the island of São
> Tomé by right and inheritance; and as for the Castilian Jews who had not
> left his kingdom within the assigned date, he ordered that, according to the
> condition upon their entry, all the boys, and young men and girls of the
> Jews be taken into captivity. After having them all turned into Christians,
> he sent them to the said island with Alvaro de Caminha, so that by being
> secluded, they would have reasons for being better Christians, and the king
> would have a way for the island to be better populated, which, as a result,
> grew rapidly.[42]

The Christian writer Valentim Fernandes thought there were 2,000 children, while the estimates of numbers among Jewish authors varied between
800 and 5,000. It appears that they were mostly very young, from two to
ten years old, so that they were placed with foster parents, mostly convicted *degradados*.[43] According to the Portuguese Jew Samuel Usque
'almost all were swallowed up by the huge lizards on the island and the
remainder, who escaped these reptiles, wasted away from hunger and
abandonment'. Fernandes said only 600 were still alive in 1510.[44] The
harsh conditions – the searing heat, the uncleared jungle, the heavy
manual work involved in sugar production, along with diseases such as
malaria – killed many of the settlers, whatever their origin; and it was for
that reason that black slaves began to be imported to work the sugar
estates. In the sixteenth century, Portuguese New Christians, descended
from Jews, did settle in the island, but the Jewish children were by then
long dead, or had merged with the other Portuguese settlers and with the
African slaves. Memories of the Jewish connection survived: one bishop
reported, as late as the seventeenth century, that he had been awoken by
a 'Jewish' procession, in which a Golden Calf was being carried along the
street underneath the windows of what passed for his palace. His knowledge of Judaism, or indeed of the biblical story of the Golden Calf, was
evidently very limited.[45]

Valentim Fernandes noted that there were about 250 wooden houses in the main town, and that there were stone churches, constructed out of materials sent in 1493 with those early Jewish and Christian settlers. Despite the miserable conditions, the island proved a lucrative source of income, from which the Crown could hope to draw as much as 10,000 *cruzados* a year at the start of the sixteenth century.[46] A privilege to Fernão de Mello and the inhabitants of São Tomé, dated 20 March 1500, explains the Crown's thinking:

> Since the said island is so remote from these our kingdoms, people are unwilling to go there unless they have great privileges and franchises; and we, observing the expenditure we have ordered for the peopling of the said island and likewise the great profits which would come from it to our kingdoms, if the island were peopled in perfection, as we hope with the help of the Lord it will be, have resolved to grant him certain privileges and franchises, whereby the people who go there, may do this more willingly.[47]

The basis of this success was initially trade towards the African mainland, using home-made ships, which were quite small (thirty tons) and simple, and which were supplied with cowrie shells rather than metal currency for payments in Angola and Kongo.[48] The regular traffic in slaves between São Tomé and Elmina reached its peak in the thirty years after 1510, when up to half a dozen vessels moved back and forth almost continuously between the two points, laden with African slaves when bound for Elmina. The journey normally took up to a month and departures from São Tomé occurred about every fifty days; some ships were large enough to carry one hundred slaves, others only about thirty.[49]

V

The Portuguese began to see the Atlantic as an island-studded ocean. In 1469 and 1474 the king of Portugal had already made generous grants of islands in the far west to two of his knights. One was granted two islands, which suggests some vague reports had arrived of specific places; the other was simply granted the isles 'in the parts of the Ocean Sea', which implies little more than a general assumption that there were more places like the Azores to be found. If there were islands, these might well be the islands that were known to lie off the coast of Asia, notably Cipangu, Marco Polo's Japan, or bits and pieces of the Spice Islands whose costly products were on sale in Alexandria and Beirut.[50] The best authorities, such as Admiral Morison, have rejected modern Portuguese claims that there was real knowledge of land to the west, kept secret in Lisbon for fear of Spanish or other competition.[51] A good reason for this doubt is the fact that the Crown was not willing to pay the costs of an expedition to find new land. If individual entrepreneurs wanted to apply for a licence to look for land, that was another matter, so long as they reached into their own pockets.

King João II therefore had no objection when the Flemish sea captain Ferdinand van Olmen approached him in summer 1486 requesting permission 'to find for him a large island, or islands, on the coast of a continent, situated where it was thought the Island of the Seven Cities was to be found, and that he would undertake this at his own expense', winning in return hereditary rights of jurisdiction. He would travel in the company of a Madeiran named Estreito, who would provide two caravels; if the land was found and the natives resisted, the king airily promised that he would despatch an armada to keep them in check. Van Olmen thought that the journey could be accomplished in less than forty days. He set out from the Azores full of hope, probably in spring 1487, heading north-west, only to disappear from history. For, even if he had heard rumours of distant lands, vague reports of Greenland or of Bristol fishermen off Labrador, he knew little of the winds and currents out in the open ocean, and he almost certainly sailed into storms he could not manage.[52] If anything, van Olmen's disappearance proved that this route led nowhere. It might indeed be possible to reach the Indies, but the obvious routes were down the 'River of Gold' that in some accounts crossed the waist of Africa, or even around the southern tip of Africa – assuming, that is, that it had a southern tip and that the Indian Ocean was not a closed-off Mediterranean completely surrounded by land, as Ptolemy had maintained, and who could quarrel with such a great authority?

27

Guinea Gold and Guinea Slaves

I

The different groups of Atlantic islands participated in the slave trade in different ways: the Canaries as exporters of native slaves, and eventually as importers of black slaves to replace the depleted population; Madeira and the Azores as consumers, especially in the growing sugar industry; Cape Verde as a base for the despatch of slaves first to Portugal and later to the Caribbean and Brazil; São Tomé as another consumer of slaves, another point of despatch, and as the last home of captive Jewish children of Spanish descent. It is difficult to read the bare documents listing slave exports out of Cape Verde without a feeling of deep sadness and disgust. Children as young as two or three years old were transported through Santiago to Portugal (assuming they survived the journey); families were split up, as the slaves were divided into equally numbered groups and as one fifth of these animate trade goods were assigned to the Crown, with another share for the crusading Order of Christ. Prince Henry's biographer, Zurara, described the misery of slaves arriving at Lagos in the Algarve in 1444:

> It is not their religion but their humanity that makes me weep in pity for their sufferings. If the brute animals, with their bestial feelings, understand the sufferings of their own kind through natural instinct, what would You have my human nature do when I see before my eyes that miserable company and remember that they too are of the generation of the sons of Adam? . . . To increase their sufferings still more, there now arrived those who had charge of the division of the captives, and they began to separate one from another in order to make the shares equal. It now became necessary to separate fathers from sons, wives from husbands, and brothers from brothers . . . You others, who are so busy in making that division of the

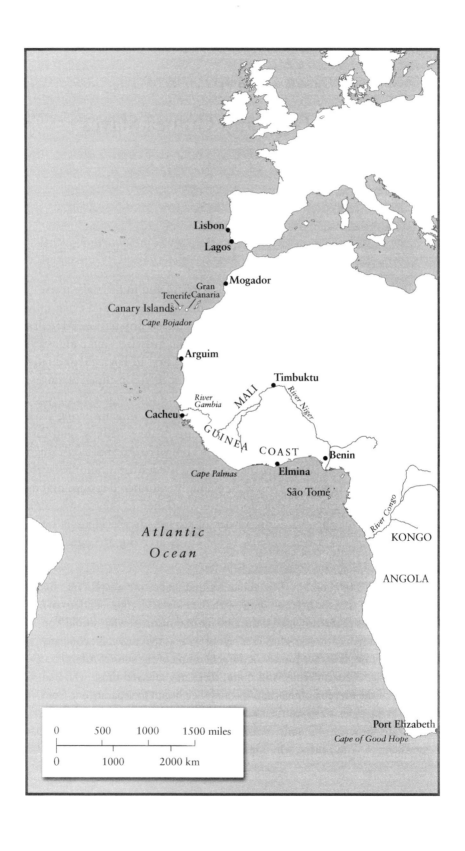

Lisbon

Lagos

Mogador

Gran
Tenerife Canaria
Canary Islands

Cape Bojador

Arguim

Timbuktu

River
Gambia

MALI

River Niger

Cacheu

G U I N E A

COAST

Benin

Cape Palmas

Elmina

São Tomé

River Congo

KONGO

Atlantic
Ocean

ANGOLA

Port Elizabeth
Cape of Good Hope

| 0 | 500 | 1000 | 1500 miles |
| 0 | 1000 | 2000 km |

captives, look with pity upon so much misery and note how they cling to one another so that you can hardly separate them![1]

In the thirteenth century Thomas Aquinas had insisted that slave-traders must not break up families, which would be contrary to natural law; but Prince Henry and his successors let this happen without a second thought. Zurara was not, however, alone in reasoning that enslavement also brought an inestimable advantage to these miserable people; they were given the opportunity to become good Christians, so captivity was in fact their road to salvation – a notion that was still in the air in the southern United States in the nineteenth century. Zurara had his prejudices too. He believed that black races were condemned to slavery because of sin – specifically the sin of their supposed ancestor, Ham, who mocked his naked and drunken father, Noah.[2] Zurara complained that the black slaves he saw were very ugly, like monsters from Hell. Physical difference had not been an issue while the slaves traded in Iberia and the Mediterranean were white or light brown, and similar in colour and facial characteristics to southern Europeans – descriptions of Canary islanders stressed that their physique was similar to that of Europeans, that they were intelligent, and that, if anything, they were taller, though sometimes a little darker.[3] No one was very interested in the intelligence of the black slaves, even though, as will be seen, many of them came from sophisticated, partly urbanized societies whose technology far surpassed that of the Neolithic Canary islanders.

The slaves delivered to Portugal were callously seen as commodities, for all the talk of Christian salvation. Portuguese trading documents from around 1500 never name the slaves, any more than they would have attached names to the pieces of ivory that they also sent towards Portugal. No questions were asked about how these people were obtained. In one bare list from 1513 four 'lots' of African slaves are mentioned, consisting of two men in their early thirties, a teenage boy, two mature women and five children, one of whom, a girl of between ten and twelve years of age, was retained as a tax payment to the king's officials; and this composition of a slave cargo was fairly typical of the time.[4] The bare facts do not explain how the slave trade came into existence, what needs it was thought to satisfy, or where the slaves originated. But it is important to understand the origins of the transatlantic traffic in human beings that lasted for another 400 years and that, amid massive misery, reshaped the ethnic map of large areas of North America, South America and the Caribbean. This takes one back to the early history of Portuguese exploration in the Atlantic – exploration this time of coastlines rather than islands.

II

The challenge of Africa was of a very different order to the challenge posed by the occupation of uninhabited islands. Broadly, there was a difference between the lightly islamized peoples of the savannah, who controlled the great rivers, notably the Niger, and the peoples of the forests, who were animists, and who often became the target of the Muslim *jihad* against pagans. The pagan Serers, for instance, lived in present-day Sierra Leone and were flanked entirely by Muslim principalities or by the sea; not surprisingly, they would find common cause with the Portuguese. West Africa was known to be inhabited by people of high culture, many of them Muslim, many also living in large towns. These towns were the home of leather, cloth and other industries; payments were often made in cowrie shells, individually worth very little, so that a piece of cloth might cost tens of thousands of units. Many west African kings relied on cavalry; even when they were pagan, their courts welcomed Muslim merchants from the north, who lived in reserved areas not far from the court itself. Although war captives were enslaved, slavery in much of west Africa had many similarities to the serfdom of medieval Europe: slaves were occasionally sold, for instance to buy war horses; but the main task of slaves was to cultivate the land on behalf of their masters. Many features of these societies were therefore familiar to western Europeans.[5]

Reports reached Europe of wealthy courts, such as that of Mansa Musa, king of Mali, whose fabulous wealth in gold was no fable; he continued to be shown on Catalan world maps well into the fifteenth century, and memories of his visit to Egypt, where he had scattered gold in the streets of Cairo and had set off rampant inflation, increased the certainty that the gold of Africa was within reach if only it were possible to bypass the caravan routes of the Sahara, dominated by Muslim Tuareg Berbers. Europeans were unaware that the power of the Mali empire had peaked by 1400; in 1431 the Tuaregs even managed to take control of Timbuktu, holding it for thirty-eight years.[6] It has been seen that adventurers such as the Majorcan Jaume Ferrer, who vanished off the coast of Africa, were already heading out in search of the 'River of Gold' in the mid-fourteenth century. Around 1400 demand for gold was very high in Europe, and western Europe was experiencing a bullion famine, as gold and silver leaked out in payment for spices and eastern luxuries, targeted by an increasingly prosperous urban middle class as well as by princely courts that often spent beyond their means.[7] Availability of sugar in southern Spain and the Atlantic islands helped ease the outflow of bullion to the

Islamic world; the jury is still out on the question of whether this bullion famine was as severe and universal as some have argued. Economic warfare against Islam was an integral part of the grand strategy of late medieval crusaders; if the gold that north Africa and the Middle East received from sub-Saharan Africa, by way of Timbuktu and its neighbours, could be diverted to Christian Europe, a double blow would be struck: Christendom would be enriched and Islam would be impoverished.[8]

In 1444 a Genoese spy, Antonio Malfante, penetrated deep into the Sahara in search of the sources of gold; but, if his trek proved anything, it was that an overland route managed by European traders was out of the question. Then the occupation of the Canary Islands opened up the prospect of European bases being created along the flank of Africa, but as it turned out the islands lay a long distance north of the sources of gold; moreover, the islands, being already inhabited, proved difficult to tame (Tenerife was only conquered in 1496, and Gran Canaria in 1483). It made more sense to see what could be found on the coast of Africa itself. The traditional date for the breakthrough into west Africa is 1434, when, under the patronage of the Order of Christ (and therefore of Prince Henry), Gil Eanes worked his way past the reefs of Cape Bojador into what were thought to be unknown waters, though it is quite possible pioneers such as the Genoese Vivaldi brothers in 1291 and Jaume Ferrer in 1346 had already gone beyond. However, Eanes not merely went beyond – he returned home. And he returned home a year later from a second expedition with reports of footprints left in the sand by human beings and their camels, as well as of rich fishing grounds, for, as ever, the Portuguese were on the lookout for good fish.[9] Gradually the Portuguese gathered information about who lived along the outer shores of north-west Africa; these were lands inhabited by Sanhaja Berbers, or Aznaghi, some of whose ancestors had formed the mainstay of the terrifying Almoravid armies that invaded Iberia in the late eleventh century.

The Portuguese did not involve themselves in any depth with the complicated politics of western Africa. Their aim was to find allies with whom they could trade, preferably in gold or ivory. Henry's resources were far from limitless, although he made a handsome profit out of Madeiran sugar; and the Ceuta garrison was a constant drain on the resources of a kingdom that was only now lifting itself out of relative poverty. Alternative sources of revenue had to be found by Henry's explorers. This led to the foundation of an offshore trading base at Arguim, on an island off the coast of modern Mauretania. The choice of a small island made excellent practical sense. No one lived there apart from a few Sanhaja fisherfolk. No ruler's sovereignty was being challenged. The island was easily defensible. Offshore islands and defensible promontories had again and again been chosen by merchants in the Mediterranean, at least since the time of the Phoenicians, as safe places from which to penetrate the hinterland opposite.[10] The Portuguese also briefly occupied the islands off Mogador, which had themselves been Phoenician bases in the days of the trade in purple dye.[11]

It was all very well to create a base; but there were no big profits to be made out of sealskins, orchil dye or even fish. Ten years after the rounding of Cape Bojador one of Henry's Genoese captains brought back to Lagos caravels crammed with 235 Berber (or 'Moorish') slaves he had captured along the coast of west Africa. They were put on show in Lagos, where Prince Henry and Zurara saw them, one taking pity and the other not.[12] The first slaves to arrive en masse from Africa were therefore white or brown, not black; the trickle of Canary islanders towards Spain and Portugal had continued for a century already. But what Henry wanted to prove was that he could obtain more and better slaves with greater ease. In the years that followed, raids penetrated further south, and the expeditions returned with black slaves as well as brown ones; and eventually they came only with black slaves. Arguim and later the Cape Verde Islands served as way stations from which the captives were sent on to Portugal.[13] Raiding was not the most satisfactory way to achieve this; trading was more effective. This required the Portuguese to make treaties with local rulers who might see some advantage in an alliance – whether the provision of trade goods, armaments or even mercenaries willing to fight on their behalf and to train local warriors in skilled horsemanship. This happened when the Portuguese made contact with the Serer people, animists who made no use of horses, but who realized how useful they would be in fending off the cavalry of the Muslim Mandinga and Wolofs on their borders. As a result the Cape Verde Islands became an important centre of horse-breeding within easy sailing distance, able to supply Serer needs. Even so, the islanders had to import a great amount of basic equipment such as bridles, bits and spurs from Portugal, before passing them on to their African allies.[14]

The Portuguese were not dealing with maritime peoples. The boats they encountered as they crept down the coast of Africa were either rivercraft or vessels that kept close to shore, like the boats used by the fishermen of Arguim. There were no ports along the coast, although it was not too difficult to find safe harbours in river mouths. All this meant that it was much easier to make contact with local rulers inland than along the coast. However, by making full use of the virtues of the caravel, the Portuguese could navigate a long way upriver, whether in search of African towns and villages, or in the hunt for the 'River of Gold'. In 1455 the Venetian nobleman in Prince Henry's service, Alvise da Cà da Mosto, took his caravel up the Senegal River and reached the court of Budomel, an African king who extended a hearty welcome to the insatiably curious traveller, although one of his motives for doing so was his wish to increase his sexual potency still further – he already, as da Mosto discreetly wrote, 'has a different dinner each night'.[15] These river journeys continued: the Portuguese would travel as much as sixty miles up the river from their base at Cacheu-São Domingos, which was their largest base on the African coast by the end of the fifteenth century, trading in honey and fine-quality beeswax with the Mandinga in the interior.[16] By 1500 too the Portuguese were not simply living in the Cape Verde Islands, Arguim and Cacheu. Some, the so-called *lançados*, or 'thrown ones', by and large people who had good reasons for not wishing to return to Portugal, were living among the Africans and had taken African women to their bed, with the result that a mulatto generation came into being.[17] These good reasons included being under suspicion as New Christians who had not abandoned their Jewish religion. The *lançados* played an important role as cultural intermediaries, inspiring African ivory craftsmen to produce the extraordinary carvings of Portuguese soldiers and merchants that started to appear towards the end of the fifteenth century.

This still leaves in the air the controversial question of how the Portuguese obtained the thousands of slaves they were exporting. Modern politics dominate discussion, and admitting that black rulers sold slaves to white merchants has not come easily to historians of the slave trade. The idea that these rulers sold their own people is certainly an oversimplification. The Serers did not enslave fellow Serers. War captives were another matter, and the intense struggles for power on the frontier between the savannah and the forest made sure that there were plenty of such captives. Further south, in Kongo and Angola, the situation was more complicated, and at the start of the sixteenth century the Portuguese leaned on local rulers to ensure that they delivered large numbers of slaves, even from their own population. The truth is that the slave trade could only come into being because plenty of different people collaborated: back in Portugal, Prince Henry and then the Crown; merchants of various origins, including Spaniards and Genoese as well as Portuguese; settlers living in the Cape Verde Islands; *lançados* living in west Africa; local African rulers; and even parents who imagined that selling their sons and daughters to the Portuguese would offer them new opportunities in rich lands far away. Payment often came in the form of *manilhas*, brass bracelets that could be worn or melted down to satisfy the craving of the African elite for copper and brass goods, for which they generally depended on imported raw materials. One slave might be worth forty to fifty bracelets.

A ship called the *Santiago* that set out for Sierra Leone in 1526 carried 2,345 *manilhas*, which might be enough to purchase fifty or sixty slaves; and slaving in Sierra Leone and Guinea Bissau before returning to Portugal by way of the Cape Verde Islands and Terceira in the Azores was the main aim of the voyage.[18] Not every ship was carrying slaves; one Flemish ship captained by a well-born Portuguese sailor was only interested in ivory and raw cotton. The peoples who lived upriver were keen to receive raw cotton, which grew quite well in the Cape Verde Islands; and these peoples then sold cloth made out of this cotton.[19]

III

So long as the sources of gold lay out of range, the Portuguese continued to trade in slaves and ivory along what became known as the Guinea Coast, and the king of Portugal adopted the grandiose and not totally empty title 'lord of the navigation of Guinea'. The discovery of a hot spice, named Malagueta pepper after the stretch of coast where it was first found, increased the attraction of the Guinea trade, even though this pepper did not compare in quality with the true pepper that continued to arrive in the eastern Mediterranean along the Indian Ocean sea routes; Malagueta pepper is not actually a botanical pepper, but a member of the ginger family. However, the Crown waited a while before it took direct control of traffic along the Guinea coast; a wealthy merchant and shipowner, Fernão Gomes, was granted licences that permitted him to trade beyond Sierra Leone. Gomes not merely had to pay a handsome sum each year for his special privilege; he had to sell all his ivory to the king at a knock-down price (before resale at a grand profit by the king) and promise to explore 100 miles of coast each year. Even without the gold, the profits were attractive enough for King Afonso to keep increasing his share of the Guinea trade, claiming a monopoly, for instance, on the import of civet cats, whose anal gland produced a foul-smelling excretion that perfumiers knew how to turn into one of the most prized scents in the world.[20]

The more attractive Guinea became, the greater became the danger of interlopers, especially since the Canary Islands were occupied (as yet only partly) by Castilian forces, and provided a good base for pirates looking for business on the Guinea Coast. This problem became more serious still when the Portuguese king set out his claim to the crown of Castile following the death of King Henry 'the Impotent' in 1474 – he was not really impotent, but his half-sister, Isabella, who had married the heir to the throne of Aragon five years earlier, took the view that anyone accused of homosexuality must *ipso facto* be unable to father a child. So she pushed aside the claims of Henry's daughter Juana and seized the throne; thereupon Afonso, already Juana's uncle, married her and invaded Castile. The contest was settled on Iberian soil, with the victory of Ferdinand and Isabella; but events in the Atlantic, even if they were a small sideshow, had lasting effects too.[21] These were the circumstances in which the Castilians gained control of the Cape Verde Islands for a while, in the hope that they could establish a Spanish stake in the Guinea trade.[22] Ferdinand and Isabella hoped to intercept Portuguese fleets bringing Malagueta pepper, ivory and maybe even gold, while claims to Castilian dominion over the Guinea Coast were also put about, though it is hard to see what they might have been based upon, since by now the Portuguese could wave several papal bulls that confirmed their possession of the Guinea Coast. Meanwhile, Spanish traders arrived aboard three caravels at the mouth of the River Gambia, and started trading with the local ruler, buying slaves in return for brass bracelets and other goods. The king had no reason to suppose these Europeans were anything other than Portuguese. Tricked into visiting one of the ships, he and 140 of his best men were seized and carried off to Spain; King Ferdinand thought the capture of a king was a disgrace, and in solidarity with his fellow prince he sent him back to Africa, but several of his companions were less fortunate, and were sold as slaves in Andalusia.[23]

This conflict was resolved fairly amicably in the Treaty of Alcáçovas of 1479: the Portuguese retained their rights in the Atlantic islands, including those yet to be discovered, and along nearly all the Guinea Coast, while Castile was allowed to keep hold of the Canary Islands and a notch of the mainland opposite. This was a less generous concession than it might seem, since Grand Canary and Tenerife, the two largest islands, were still unconquered.[24] The Treaty of Alcáçovas was the first step to the more ambitious division of the world between Spain and Portugal by drawing a line down the Atlantic that followed Columbus's discoveries in the Caribbean.

By now Portuguese (and rival) ships had rounded Cape Palmas, which lies on the present-day border between Liberia and the Ivory Coast, and which marks the beginning of the roughly horizontal coastline of the southern shore of west Africa, several degrees north of the Equator. At the western end, along the 'Ivory Coast', there were swamps and lagoons, so obtaining ivory there was not as easy as the name given to this area suggested; still, it was elephant country, and when one did reach land, tusks were there for the asking. Moving ever eastwards, a further stretch of coast was discovered in 1471; here the Portuguese found villages whose inhabitants hardly gave a second thought to adorning themselves with gold ornaments. The story grew: it was assumed that there must be a massive gold mine somewhere near these villages, so this stretch of the shore was baptized 'Mina', or 'mine'.[25] In reality this was the steamy environment in which the Portuguese eventually made contact with rulers who would supply them with gold that had been brought down from the River Niger through the thick belt of forest that separates the savannah from the sea. These were also lands into which Islam had not yet penetrated; they included the seat of wealthy kingdoms such as Benin, famous nowadays for its ivories and bronzes; ruled over by its Oba, or king, Benin contained a massive city but, like the other towns of west Africa, it lay nowhere near the Atlantic Ocean.[26] For the moment Benin City was beyond reach; but Portuguese ships reached the sharp bend of Africa by 1472, discovering the uninhabited islands that were to become major bases later on – São Tomé and Príncipe, on the Equator.

Finding the route to gold was more difficult than the optimistic first generation of Portuguese explorers had ever imagined; but with the discovery of the Mina coast Fernão Gomes became wealthier than ever – and the king began to think about what would happen when Gomes's licence expired in 1474, which would provide an ideal opportunity for the Crown to take charge of such a lucrative sea route. Observing the ever-increasing flow of gold from Mina, and aware that the Castilians and others would like to muscle in on the success of the Portuguese, King Afonso decided that Gomes's contract should not be renewed; but Gomes would be rewarded for his service with a grant of noble status and of a coat of arms bearing the heads of three black slaves.[27] Thirty-seven years had elapsed between the rounding of Cape Bojador and the discovery of the gold-rich villages. The Portuguese advance along the coast of Africa looks rapid in retrospect, and was certainly purposeful; but the speed of advance only increased rapidly from 1469 onwards, and then slowed down again in the decade before Vasco da Gama left for India (in 1497).

Under Gomes, and still more under the Crown, the Portuguese assumed the right to a trading monopoly in Guinea. Still, both the Portuguese and the Spanish interlopers did begin to obtain gold along the Mina coast; in 1478 Joan Boscà of Barcelona visited Mina, exchanging gold for cowrie shells, brass and other sundry goods; he thought things were going well until the Portuguese sent out ships to intercept him – in 1479 his treasure of gold was seized; but even after the Treaty of Alcáçovas Spanish ships kept trying to intrude.[28] Even more interesting is the presence of Flemings so very far from home; the North Sea and the southern Atlantic were beginning to connect well before the end of the fifteenth century.[29] Eustache de la Fosse from Tournai in Flanders was one of several north European merchants and travellers who penetrated this region in 1479, setting out from Bruges and conducting business in northern Spain before moving down to Seville, where he collected the merchandise he would be taking for sale at *la Minne d'Or*.[30] It is obvious from the account he left of his voyage that precise knowledge of the geography of west Africa had spread all the way to northern Europe, with which, after all, Portugal had close commercial and political ties. En route to the Mina coast his ship not surprisingly had to dodge Portuguese caravels.[31]

As he travelled down the coast of Africa, Eustache marvelled at the sight of Malagueta pepper, or 'grains of Paradise' as he called them; he also marvelled at the naked inhabitants of the Guinea Coast, but not enough to dissuade him from buying several women and children in return for brass bracelets and other metal goods; however, he and other merchants had it in mind to sell the slaves along the Mina coast in return for gold. This shows that there was a market for black slaves among the black population further east; it has been seen that there was reluctance to enslave one's brethren, but less reluctance to own or sell slaves from neighbouring ethnic groups. In due course, Eustache was delighted to find a place where he and his partners could buy gold – as much as twelve or fourteen pounds of it. All seemed to be going well in what was, after all, a fairly deserted area of ocean until his ship was pounced upon by a Portuguese squadron of four ships commanded by Fernando Pô and Diogo Cão, an intrepid explorer who would before long be travelling very much further along the coast of Africa; 'we were pillaged of everything' – *fumes tout pillez*.[32] Taken back to Portugal, Eustache and his colleagues were clapped in prison; the penalty for unlicensed trade on the Mina coast was death, for it was seen as a pure act of piracy. Eustache bribed his jailer with 200 ducats and was able to sneak out of prison at night-time, escaping to Castile.[33]

Everyone wanted to cash in on the Guinea trade. In 1481 there were plans afoot in England to send ships to west Africa. The Portuguese king prevailed upon his English ally, Edward IV, to forbid the English ships to sail, though it has been suggested that the ringleaders, John Tintam and William Fabian, may have visited Africa a year or so earlier, and that an English expedition far into the Atlantic just now should come as no surprise: as has been seen, this was the period when English ships were ranging deep into the Atlantic in other directions too.[34]

IV

Trading with villagers by anchoring offshore was one way of doing business; but what appealed much more to the Portuguese Crown was the creation of a permanent base on the Mina coast, comparable to Arguim and Cacheu.[35] For the Portuguese kings were claiming to be masters of 'the navigation of Guinea', rather than planning to build an empire on the African mainland, even if an occasional African king loosely acknow-ledged their overlordship. The so-called Portuguese empire began as a network of trading stations, and for much of its early history it would continue that way, as it spread into the Indian Ocean and Pacific, as far as Goa, Melaka, Macau and Nagasaki. But trading stations needed a patch of territory and a guarantee of safety, which made negotiation with local rulers essential. The decision to build a fort at what became known as São Jorge da Mina, or Elmina, followed logically from the success of the Por-tuguese in buying impressive amounts of gold along the Mina coast; they had been trading through an African village called Shama, but its water supplies were limited and the Portuguese caravels, standing offshore, were sitting ducks so long as there were no defensive walls behind which the merchants could hide and so long as interlopers continued to evade Portuguese patrols.

In 1481 King João II of Portugal put together an expedition under the leadership of a faithful and experienced commander, Diogo de Azam-buja.[36] The king even obtained a crusading privilege from the pope, promising a plenary indulgence to anyone who might die in the castle of 'Mina': its name preceded the choice of its exact site, let alone its construc-tion. The pope was terribly confused about who lived in this part of Africa, speaking of 'Saracens' ripe for conversion, but also permitting trade in weapons with them – the term 'Saracen' often being applied to pagans as well as Muslims. Oddly, given papal approval, the expedition made no attempt to spread the Gospel in Mina; the priest or priests who accom-panied the voyage ministered to the Portuguese alone. Although the Portuguese did not lose sight of missionary opportunities, they were already placing the lure of gold higher than the lure of souls; they would have argued that all this gold would eventually pay for victorious wars against the Muslim Infidel, even though the people of the Mina coast were not Muslims. In the sixteenth century an influential Portuguese chronicler, João de Barros, insisted that the real plan was to tempt the Africans with trade goods, and then to tempt them still further with the inestimable goods of Heaven, but this was a much later rereading of the evidence.[37]

Ten caravels were assigned to the expedition, carrying 500 soldiers as well as 100 stonemasons and carpenters, but two further ships, sturdy *urcas*, were sent ahead, loaded with dressed stone prepared in Portugal, so that prefabricated windows and gateways could be fitted quickly on site; and there were plenty of tiles, bricks, timber joists and other essential supplies that would not be available along the Mina coast. The big *urcas* were to be broken up when the fortress was built, which would put to good use the mass of timber they contained.[38] Early in 1482 the ideal spot was identified about twenty-five miles beyond Shama, at a place called the Village of the Two Parts, perhaps because the village lay on the boundary between two tribes; this offered a rocky promontory, some high ground and access to the river that led inland, and it was already known to be a good base for trading in gold. This was not the gold that had for centuries been traded through Timbuktu and other towns and then carried north-wards across the Sahara; sources were local, in the thickly forested interior that was cut off from the goldfields the Portuguese had so long hoped to reach – still, it was gold, and there was plenty of it.[39]

On 20 January, after only a couple of days at the site, Azambuja was ready to hold an interview with the local ruler, who is known to history as Caramansa, though this was probably his title rather than his name. This interview was a comedy of errors: Azambuja, like many an explorer of his day, chose to meet the king dressed up to the nines, with a bejew-elled golden collar around his neck; his captains wore festive costumes. Caramansa was not to be outdone. He arrived with his soldiers, accom-panied by drummers and trumpeters who (Barros related) produced music that 'deafened rather than delighted the ear'. Whereas Europeans imag-ined that fine clothes (hardly suitable for the tropics) were the way to display power and prestige, Caramansa and his followers arrived naked, their skins shining from the oils they had rubbed into them; all that was covered was their genitals, though the king wore gold bracelets, a collar from which little bells dangled, and gold bars in his beard, which had the effect of straightening the tightly curled hairs.[40]

Barros piously but implausibly insisted that Azambuja did raise the question of conversion at the start; but the conversation mainly turned on the question of building a Portuguese fort on the site of the meeting. Cara-mansa was promised that this would bring him power and wealth, and that, rather than religion, was the argument which convinced the king. However, Caramansa was also aware that the Portuguese had considerable firepower, and he was anxious to avoid a clash with the hundred well-armed soldiers aboard the caravels. He did complain that previous European visitors to his village had been 'dishonest and vile', but graciously conceded that Azambuja was not of that ilk – indeed, his lavish clothes proclaimed that he too was the son or brother of a king, a statement that the over-dressed commander had to refute with embarrassment.[41] So building was allowed to begin; there were hitches, when the Portuguese began to cut into a sacred rock, because they still needed some local stone in addition to what they had brought. Fighting broke out, but Caramansa's subjects were appeased with extra gifts. A fort was thrown up in three weeks, and, once a secure area had been created for a Portuguese garrison, it was extended to include a courtyard and cisterns. All that was built outside the walls was a small chapel. Sixty men and three women stayed behind after the fort was built, and the rest of the Portuguese went back home.[42]

Just as important as the creation of the settlement, which lasted for many centuries first under Portuguese and then under Dutch rule, was the creation of a set of rules controlling trade from the Castelo de São Jorge (generally known simply as Elmina, 'The Mine'). Trade was conducted in the courtyard of the fortress, not within the African village that developed beneath the castle walls.[43] These rules were refined over the next few decades, but they testify to the difficulty in keeping control of movements over the unprecedented distances (by European standards) that the Portuguese ships were now sailing. The most important rule was that ships had to sail directly from Lisbon to Elmina, a journey that would normally take a month. Everything was carefully regulated: the provisions on which the sailors would depend during their long voyage included prescribed amounts of biscuit, salted meat, vinegar and olive oil, not just to make sure the crew was fed but to make sure they did not load surplus goods and sell them in Elmina at a profit. On leaving Lisbon, special pilots stayed on board until the ship left the Tagus; their job was to check that no skiffs came alongside, loading contraband out in the estuary. On arrival in Elmina there were further strict rules about signalling arrival by raising a flag and waiting for the Elmina garrison to answer back with their own flag. These rules applied not just to the ships coming in from Lisbon, but to the small craft that plied between São Tomé and Elmina, bringing fruit, fish and above all slaves who had been taken off the shores of Kongo and Angola or were bought in the kingdom of Benin.

Ships were supposed to be sent out from Portugal once a month; in most years fewer ships came from Lisbon – in 1501 only six ships arrived from there, although the slave ships from São Tomé kept coming even in years when nothing at all arrived from Portugal. Whereas single ships set out from Lisbon in the early days, from 1502 onwards the Portuguese sometimes put together a small convoy, which was a much safer way to travel. On the return journey the chests containing gold were sealed and the sailors' own sea chests were often closely inspected for contraband gold, which was easy enough to carry, as the gold took the form of small nuggets and gold dust. The value of these cargoes was out of all proportion to their weight, so on the return journey ships had to be weighted down with rock ballast.[44] Coming out to Africa, the Elmina caravels brought textiles, not just European ones but striped Moroccan ones which were in strong demand in west Africa; they brought brass goods, as elsewhere; they brought cowrie shells. Paying for the gold was not a problem. Relations with the local inhabitants were increasingly cordial, and African soldiers helped to man the battlements of the fort from 1514 onwards; the Portuguese and their African neighbours came to depend on one another.[45] There were also Portuguese private traders who travelled into the interior and made sure that Elmina was well supplied with food, as the settlement could not simply rely on Lisbon for sustenance.[46]

Meanwhile slaves brought through São Tomé were assigned menial tasks in the fort, including the unloading of goods from the supply ships. Many slaves were sold to black African masters in Caramansa's kingdom, and Caramansa's subjects preferred to be paid for their gold not in cowrie shells or cloth but in slaves.[47] Ships plied back and forth between São Tomé and Elmina, carrying up to 120 slaves on each four-week voyage to Elmina; a rough calculation would suggest that somewhere around 3,000 slaves were coming through Elmina each year.[48] Even so, Elmina was not seen as a centre of the Portuguese slave trade. The Portuguese king was determined to extract literally every ounce of profit from the gold trade. By 1506 Elmina was bringing in a revenue of nearly 44,000,000 *reis*, more than ten times the revenue from Guinea slaves and Malagueta pepper.[49] This was what funded the imperial expansion of Portugal as the little kingdom's fleets broke their way into the Indian Ocean.

V

Reaching the Indian Ocean had always been on Portugal's agenda. The search for the 'River of Gold' had been based on the assumption that the river flowed right across Africa, linking the oceans, as if any known river did such a thing. But the aim was to gain mastery over gold; slaves were a convenient substitute when gold was not to be had; Malagueta pepper whetted the appetite for the real pepper of the Indies. The pioneer who was entrusted with the exploration of further stretches of the African coast was Diogo Cão, who first appears in the record as captain of a caravel that became involved in the arrest of the Flemish interloper Eustache de la Fosse. For de la Fosse, Cão was *ung bien rebelle fars*, 'a very bad sort', who bought de la Fosse's ship from his captors, forced de la Fosse to sell his own expropriated goods up and down the African coast, and then made him render an account of his sales each evening.[50] The Portuguese explorers possessed the ruthlessness of pirates even when they were serving their king.

Cão's commission from King João II was described by a sixteenth-century writer, Fernão Lopes de Castanheda, as the discovery of 'the dominions of Prester John of the Indies of whom he [the king] had report; so that by that way it would be possible to enter India and he would be able to send his captains to fetch those riches which the Venetians brought for sale'.[51] Since the term 'India' was used to describe any lands along the shores of the Indian Ocean, including east Africa, it seems more likely that the king of Portugal aimed to send his men to Ethiopia rather than to India, hoping that he would find a Christian ally willing both to satisfy his craving for gold and spices and to join when appropriate in the war against Islam. This 'Priest John' had surfaced in the twelfth century and appeared to live for ever, while his kingdom moved around in the medieval imagination from India to further Asia to Africa. However, the assumption that a Christian kingdom existed in east Africa was perfectly well founded, and João was not alone in seeking out the ruler of Ethiopia. During his long reign (1416–58) King Alfonso V of Aragon sent friars to Ethiopia and even dreamed up a plan for a marriage alliance between an Aragonese princess and an Ethiopian prince.[52]

Cão was not offered very large resources. Most probably he set out with just two caravels. But the fact that these ships carried stone columns known as *padrões* provided a clear sign that the expedition intended to mark out new land. These *padrões* were inscribed and decorated with the royal coat of arms and installed on headlands, where many of them still stood until the late nineteenth century, when they were carried back to museum collections in Europe. Part road signs, part statements of Portuguese sovereignty, the *padrões* did not signify control of the African interior: the king remained 'lord of the navigation of Guinea', and he charged Cão with making the Guinea coast still vaster than it already was. Cão moved smoothly beyond São Tomé down the southward-pointing coast of central and southern Africa, erecting his first *padrão* at the mouth of the Congo; uniquely, this *padrão* was inscribed in Arabic as well as Latin and Portuguese, even though Cão had passed some way beyond the lands of Islam. The use of Arabic suggests that the Portuguese navigators thought it would not be long before they reconnected with the Muslim world.[53]

Cão was not convinced that the River Congo was the 'River of Gold'; he sent a detachment of men upriver to greet the local king, promising to wait for them; when they failed to reappear he kidnapped four of the most prominent villagers, thinking of them both as hostages and as potential sources of information. Reaching a large bay off Angola that extends a long way eastwards, Cão wondered whether he had reached the southern tip of Africa, erecting his second stone *padrão* with the inscription:

In the year 6681 of the creation of the world, and 1482 of the birth of Our Lord Jesus, the very high, very excellent and mighty prince King Dom João II of Portugal ordered this land to be discovered and these *padrões* to be erected by Diogo Cão, squire of his household.[54]

Having displayed the royal coat of arms far beyond the Equator, Diogo Cão was granted his own coat of arms on his return in spring 1484, as well as an annual pension, for what the king evidently saw as a very worthwhile expedition.[55] Later that year, the Portuguese ambassador at the papal court extolled his countrymen's achievements in a speech before Pope Innocent VIII, and boasted that Portuguese ships had reached the very edges of the Gulf of Arabia, by which he meant the Indian Ocean.[56] By insisting that it was possible to break into the Indian Ocean from the Atlantic, the speaker, the learned Dr Vasco Fernandes de Lucena, was openly challenging the Ptolemaic orthodoxy that continued, in maps being copied at this very time, to show the Indian Ocean as a vast closed sea, with the southern tip of Africa merging into a long southern continent that reached as far as the Spice Islands.

The claim that Cão had already reached the southern tip of Africa was hopelessly optimistic; but it tempted King João to offer him a second commission in 1485, once again with two caravels; and aboard the caravels were his four captives, now conversant with Portuguese customs and willing to act as King João's emissaries to the king of Kongo. When Cão reached the village from which they had been kidnapped, everyone there rejoiced; but Cão cannily sent only one of the hostages to the African king, for he was determined to secure the release of the Portuguese men he had sent inland during his first voyage. The presents carried by the released hostage helped convince the African king that he should send the Portuguese men back to their captain, and after they arrived Cão himself headed inland to meet the king. This time Cão and his colleagues clearly hoped to find a river route deep into Africa; they sailed right up to the limits of navigation of the River Congo, and, seeing they could go no further, carved a surviving record of their extraordinary journey on the rocks that now prevented them from penetrating any further: 'Here reached the vessels of the distinguished King Dom João II of Portugal: Diogo Cão, Pero Añes, Pero da Costa'.[57] After that, Cão pressed on to meet the king of Kongo, returned to his ships, and managed to explore further stretches of the coast of southern Africa.

Cão's expeditions have been rather overlooked, even if Portuguese historians living under Dr Salazar around 1960 extolled him as one of the founders of an empire that eventually controlled large swathes of southern

Africa.[58] Cão had shown that it was possible to press on beyond the new Portuguese bases in Elmina and São Tomé, and to find a welcome in lands untouched by Islam that should be the gateway to the Indian Ocean. However, that gateway lay much farther to the south than Henry the Navigator, João II, or their cartographers and navigators had supposed. It made obvious sense to fit out a third expedition, this time under the leadership of Bartomeu or Bartholomew Dias. A third ship, loaded with supplies, was now added to the flotilla, with the notion that it could be parked somewhere off the coast of Africa and could be used to resupply the other caravels on their return from a journey that might well stretch their own supplies to the limit. Setting out in 1487, Dias's ships were eventually caught in storms off southern Africa; they headed out to sea, moving south-westwards, and in the process made as important a discovery as the discovery of land: the strong winds blowing from west to east could be harnessed to propel their vessels back towards Africa and a more southerly latitude. This led Dias to the coast that stretches beyond the Cape of Good Hope (not in fact the southernmost point of south Africa), reaching hundreds of miles further, as far as the bay in which the modern town of Port Elizabeth stands. By this point it was obvious that the winds and currents continued to trend eastwards and that the ships had rounded the bottom of Africa, entering the Indian Ocean by a brand new sea route.[59] Dias set up a *padrão*, which vanished from sight over the centuries, until a young South African historian, Eric Axelson, scrabbled in the sand on a headland at Kwaaihoek, where he thought it was most likely to be, and found many fragments of it – confirmation of the not always reliable stories in the sixteenth-century narratives.[60] Dias's voyage was a tremendous achievement, and Dias would have liked to carry on further; but his crew was worried at the lack of supplies on board – the next voyage in these waters, by Vasco da Gama, had no great difficulty in obtaining supplies from the local population – and were determined to work their way back to the supply ship. In the process they mapped the parts of the coast they had missed when they had swung out to sea. Dias was back in Lisbon towards the end of 1488, and Christopher Columbus recorded that he saw and was impressed by Dias's map of Africa, though he remained attached to his own theories. But the king of Portugal failed to reward Dias with either the honours or the money that Cão had received. He had returned to Portugal without exploring the Indian Ocean.[61]

Suddenly, though, the search for routes to the East acquired much greater urgency. A Genoese mariner, as boastful as he was learned, was washed up on the shores of Portugal in 1493, claiming to have discovered a new route across the oceans all the way to China and Japan.

PART FOUR

Oceans in Conversation, AD 1492–1900

28

The Great Acceleration

I

So far this book has been concerned with separate oceans. Admittedly, the western Pacific rim and the Indian Ocean enjoyed close ties through maritime trade during the Middle Ages, whether by means of Tamil and Malay or Chinese navigators; but these sailors never targeted the wide-open spaces of the island Pacific. Links between the Indian Ocean and the Atlantic were mediated through the Red Sea and the Mediterranean, after the opening of a regular sea route from Italy to Flanders and England at the end of the thirteenth century. The 1490s, however, saw a great acceleration in contact between western Europe and what were fondly imagined to be the Indies, for in the case of two discoveries they were not the Indies at all, even if Columbus's voyages resulted in the term 'Indies' being applied to the great landmass of the two American continents, whose inhabitants were classed as 'Indians'. The three European attempts to reach the Indies were those of Christopher Columbus, whose four voyages to the New World spanned the years from 1492 to 1504;[1] John Cabot, who sailed west in search of China and the Indies in 1497;[2] and Vasco da Gama, whose first expedition to the real India departed the same year. Amerigo Vespucci, sailing in the wake of Columbus, wrote about the lands to the west, often tendentiously, but his name, not that of Columbus, became attached to the Americas.[3] The second Portuguese expedition to India should also be added to this list, as it resulted in the accidental discovery of Brazil in 1500 – a voyage that linked four continents. This linking of the oceans was completed remarkably quickly during the sixteenth century, once the routes from the Atlantic to the Pacific had been mapped out by pioneers such as Ferdinand Magellan, the Portuguese captain in the service of Spain, Juan Rodríguez Cabrillo, the Spanish discoverer of California, and Francis Drake, sailing in the service of England. The world, as a book describing Drake's voyages proudly proclaimed,

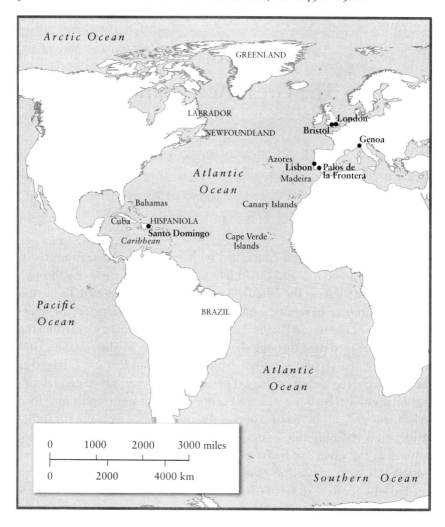

had now been 'encompassed'.[4] The linking of the oceans culminated in 1565 with the despatch of the first Manila galleon tying the western Pacific (and, beyond that, China) to Mexico and, ultimately, the Atlantic trade networks. Bearing these developments in mind, the chapters that follow will concentrate mainly on the navigators, routes and goods that passed between different oceans, rather than continuing to portray the history of three separate oceans. It may then seem odd to begin with Columbus and Cabot, whose expeditions were confined to a single ocean; but they assumed that the waters off Europe and Africa and the waters off China and Japan were part of one great ocean, in modern terms the Pacific combined with the Atlantic.

It is often pointed out that the Canary islanders, the Taíno Indians of

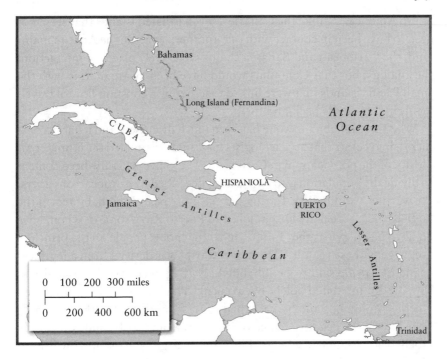

the Caribbean, the Tupinambá Indians of Brazil and all the other peoples previously unknown to the Europeans were perfectly well known to themselves; their 'discovery' was a two-way process. The Arab traders who already knew the Swahili coast far down the flank of east Africa were surprised to encounter Vasco da Gama as he worked his way into the Indian Ocean in 1498; but they were aware that Christian lands existed beyond the frontiers of Islam, and da Gama even met traders who knew the Mediterranean. 'Discovery' was not a purely European phenomenon, but those who were carving out new routes across the oceans were Europeans.

II

So far, the history of the Atlantic has been presented as the history of the north-eastern Atlantic, and (by the end of the Middle Ages) the history of navigation all the way down the Atlantic coast of Africa. Another maritime network existed in the Atlantic, within and a little beyond the Caribbean, a 'New World' that would be exposed to European view by Columbus's voyages. It was in reality a very old world, first settled in the fifth millennium BC, with new waves of settlers arriving periodically from

South America.[5] Unlike the Canaries, seven isolated islands that seem not even to have been in contact with one another, let alone the African mainland, the Caribbean and Bahama chains were lively places of interaction; the analogy, not that Columbus would have been aware of it, is with the small Pacific islands that were linked together by a constant flow of travellers bringing goods back and forth.

Who these inhabitants were has been much discussed, and it has become increasingly clear that archaeologists have underestimated the ethnic complexity of the pre-Columbian Caribbean. They have generally been content to divide the population into two groups described by European observers, the warlike, cannibalistic Caribs and the more peaceful inhabitants of the large islands, especially Hispaniola and Puerto Rico, some of whom have come to be known as the 'Taínos', meaning 'noble people' in the principal language of these islands.[6] The name 'Carib' was derived from a mythical island of *Caribe* said to be inhabited solely by men (another island was supposedly inhabited solely by women). The Taínos at first wondered whether Columbus and his crew had come from there. But the Spaniards seized upon the negative image of islanders from Caribe and collectively labelled all islanders who paddled their large canoes northwards to Hispaniola in the fifteenth century man-eating 'Caribs'; that they did occasionally eat human flesh is very likely. These 'Caribs' represented a further wave of migrants of Arawak descent, warriors seeking to establish themselves in the lush islands of the Greater Antilles; it is likely that the Lesser Antilles, the line of islands stretching from the South American coast towards Puerto Rico, were becoming overpopulated, and they were looking for new lands to settle. The problem was that some of these lands, notably Hispaniola, were already very densely settled. This set off violent confrontations.

While it suited the Spaniards to distinguish between those who were regarded as legally free subjects of the king and queen of Castile, and hostile cannibal invaders from the south, who could legitimately be enslaved, the reality on the ground was rather different. On the largest island, Hispaniola, a variety of languages could be heard, reflecting different waves of immigration from South America.[7] Jamaica was only settled in around AD 600, as also the Bahamas, at the end of a period known to archaeologists as the 'First Repeopling'. Although there are uncertainties about the route that the very earliest settlers might have taken, evidence from pottery suggests that the main route taken during this phase was a south-to-north one, along the line of the Lesser Antilles. As in the Pacific, movement was slow, and just as 'Melanesians', 'Polynesians' and 'Micronesians' overlapped and intermingled, here the very earliest settlers were eventually outnumbered by a wave of migrants related to the Arawak population of northern South America, who created a particularly elaborate group of societies on Hispaniola by the time of the arrival of the first European explorers. The Taíno idols, or *cemís*, often carved out of stone, survive as evidence of a lively culture, dependent on a reasonably nutritious food starch, cassava, and organized into small political units that jostled for power on the main islands.[8]

This was a well-connected world. The sea lay at the centre of their elaborate myth-making, which included strange stories about all the fish and all the water in the seas raining down from a great gourd, recorded by a puzzled friar named Ramon Pané whom Columbus had sent into the interior of Hispaniola to find out about the islanders' religious beliefs.[9] Hispaniola is a fairly large and mountainous island, and there were certainly Taínos and other groups who lived in the interior and did not have much to do with the sea. Their aim was to achieve self-sufficiency, and this they did by and large manage to do, which led occasional admiring Europeans to speak in glowing terms of their societies: 'theirs is a Golden Age', an Italian scholar at the court of Ferdinand and Isabella opined, describing a society where envy and property were absent, and there was no need for laws and judges – the writer Peter Martyr never actually went to see for himself, but his words set off some fantastic ideas in the mind of Thomas More, recorded in his *Utopia*.[10] But that is not to say that there was no trade. The inhabitants of the Bahamas, which they called the *Lucayos*, were familiar with the bigger islands to the south, trading goods such as coloured stones, foodstuffs, cotton thread and carved *cemís*: Columbus was amazed to find that glass beads and coins traded by his men on 13 October 1492, the day after he arrived in the New World, were already being taken south in a native boat he encountered off Long Island (Fernandina) on 15 October, along with some dried leaves and food. Not just European goods but reports of the coming of the strangely attired visitors in their flying boats were diffused at top speed throughout the island chain.

A maritime highway ran all the way from Cuba to Trinidad and the South American mainland. Inter-island trade was conducted using the dugout canoes, propelled by paddle power, which attracted Columbus's attention from the moment he made contact with the Lucayan Taínos. The largest of these canoes, made from a massive felled tree trunk, could seat as many as a hundred Taínos, and the chieftain's boat might be specially painted and carry on board a canopied area. The process of making these boats was long and complex, involving a massive collaborative effort by the village. The tree trunk had to be split open and hollowed out, by burning away the wood and chopping away at the residue. The outside of the boat was trimmed and 'marvellously carved in the native style', to cite Columbus's first reaction.[11] The smallest, carrying a single person, were also very seaworthy, skimming back and forth between the islands. Not for nothing was the native word *canoa* adopted in western European languages. In 1492 the Caribbean was not home to static cultures rooted in centuries of unchanging traditional practices; it was a little world on the move.[12]

III

Yet this Caribbean world could only be the outer edges of the luxurious empires crowded with great cities described by Marco Polo. From the European perspective, da Gama's voyage to India was the true success story. Columbus and Cabot were convinced that they had reached the edges of Asia, and yet Columbus's first voyage did not reveal the silks and spices of China and Japan, as he so confidently promised Ferdinand of Aragon and Isabella of Castile. Instead, he brought back some strips of gold foil (though not a shipload of gold), some attractive feathers and some interesting but puzzling inhabitants of the Caribbean, who, he had to admit, were little more advanced in technology than the Stone Age Canary Islanders being conquered at the same time. It seemed that the islands he had reached were richer in cotton than in gold; and the mystery remained: where were the teeming cities whose harbours were crowded with massive junks, ruled over by the Great Khan, of whom Marco Polo had informed western Christendom two centuries earlier?[13] Cabot's voyage in 1497 was even less satisfactory: he was almost certainly aware that Bristol ships had strayed towards distant coasts somewhere near Newfoundland, but once he returned home he had to admit that the best chance for profit came not from rich ports and courts but from codfish – it was so plentiful that English fishing boats would no longer need to sail to Iceland.[14]

It is important to keep remembering that the first American voyages were conceived as voyages to Asia and as ways of opening up access to the spices of the East. They were planned according to exact expectations of finding gold and spices. The waters they reached were deemed to be part of what would now be regarded as the western Pacific. Some gold and spices were indeed found, though not by Cabot. Oddly, therefore, it makes sense to play along with the geographical assumptions of Columbus, and to assume that the routes they had found did lead to Asia, and that the goods the Spaniards acquired in the Caribbean were from the

'Indies'. Only then can one understand how more and more Spanish efforts were pumped into the transatlantic voyages, which became quite regular within ten years of Columbus's arrival in the Caribbean. Even the discoveries claimed by Amerigo Vespucci at the start of the sixteenth century did not definitively disprove the idea that South America was somehow connected to Asia; the idea that there might be a land bridge between the continents was only decisively rejected in the late nineteenth century. The Americas and Asia and indeed eastern Africa were all *las Indias*, 'the Indies'. After he had heard of da Gama's success in reaching Calicut, Columbus even speculated about carrying on westwards to meet the Portuguese in India. What discouraged him from an attempt to circumnavigate the globe, according to his son (and biographer) Ferdinand, was the lack of supplies on board his ships, rather than any notion that this was an impossible achievement.[15]

Just like the Portuguese, Columbus and Cabot were guided by the grand strategy of bypassing the Red Sea and eliminating dependence on the dhow traffic carrying spices across the Indian Ocean. The aim was not simply to make a grand profit: Columbus shared with the Portuguese the ambition of undermining the economy of the Muslim world by diverting the spices of the Indies directly to Christendom; and he shared with King Manuel (and with Ferdinand and Isabella) the messianic expectation that the discovery of a new route to the Indies would fund a massive attack on Islam that would culminate in the reconquest of Jerusalem by the greatest crusade of all time, in which, it was fervently hoped, various Christian kings of the East would also take part – Prester John was never far from the thinking of these new-style crusade strategists. Ideally, Christian navies would force open the Red Sea and clear the way to the Mediterranean – the spice route, but also the route to the Holy Sepulchre in Jerusalem. Columbus's apocalyptic thinking dipped and soared depending on circumstances, and he was generally most obsessed by his sense of a divine mission when he found himself in a tight corner, but his combination of materialistic greed and the conviction of having been chosen by God never left him. Whatever riches he acquired in the 'Indies' were also to be understood as God's gift; the material and the spiritual were intertwined like the strands in a rope.[16]

At no stage did Columbus express serious doubts that he had reached Asia, even if the geography of the Indies had proved far more mysterious than his reading of existing maps had led him to believe it would be. This is not to deny that Columbus had private doubts: when he made his sailors swear that Cuba was part of the Asian mainland, subject to a penalty of 10,000 *maravedís* and excision of the culprit's tongue, he was unconsciously expressing his own uncertainty about where on earth he had arrived.[17] But such evidence as existed for lands across the Atlantic seemed to confirm the assumption that Asia was within reach. The bodies of strange people had been cast up on the shores of Ireland, and their features were rather like those of Tartars, in other words, the 'Orientals' with whom westerners were reasonably familiar through political contact and through the trade in slaves from the Black Sea into the Mediterranean. Almost certainly these were the bodies of native North Americans which had been washed out to sea. If, as is possible, the young Columbus travelled to Iceland he might well have heard tales of lands to the west visited by Norse sailors in the past. In Bristol he could also have picked up rumours of lands to the west, because several Icelanders had taken up residence there, and because English expeditions had penetrated deep into the Atlantic in the 1480s. Besides, he seems to have read some mysterious papers in the possession of the Perestrello family of Porto Santo near Madeira (into which he married), which provided further evidence of land to the west.[18]

Building into their work the mass of rumours that circulated throughout the Middle Ages, several fifteenth-century cartographers liberally sprinkled the Atlantic with imaginary islands. One such mapmaker was Andrea Bianco, a citizen of Columbus's own home town of Genoa, who made charts in 1436 and 1448. Still, the distances looked formidable, unless one followed the argument presented by the Florentine geographer Paolo Toscanelli, who shrank the distance between western Europe and the Far East by arguing for a narrow Atlantic that separated the continents, a judgement that also stretched the distance overland from Portugal to China, making it greater than Ptolemy had assumed.[19] Columbus conveniently slotted Toscanelli's version of the Atlantic into Marco Polo's description of Japan to show that *Cipangu*, or Japan, was within relatively easy reach of Europe. Moreover, it was virtually paved with gold:

> The people are white, civilized, and well-favoured. They are Idolaters, and are dependent on nobody. And I can tell you the quantity of gold they have is endless; for they find it in their own Islands, *and the King does not allow it to be exported. Moreover* few merchants visit the country because it is so far from the mainland, and thus it comes to pass that their gold is abundant beyond all measure [*passages in italics* appear only in some manuscripts].[20]

The emperor of Japan was said to have a palace roofed with gold, 'just as our churches are roofed with lead', with golden floors made of great golden slabs, 'so that altogether the richness of this Palace is past all bounds and all belief'.[21] Conceivably this description was based on Chinese whispers about the Golden Pavilion and other beautifully decorated temples in Kyoto.

The assumption that Japan lay across his line of travel was not unique to Columbus and Toscanelli. Martin Behaim, a German cartographer who had made the lucky decision not to join van Olmen's ill-fated voyage west of the Azores in 1487, produced the first proper globe that has survived; now in the Germanisches Nationalmuseum in Nuremberg, it dates from around the time of Columbus's first voyage, and does not include any of his discoveries. However, the globe shows Cipangu athwart the western Atlantic, about two thirds of the way across; superimposed on a modern map that would place Japan just above the Guianas, while to its south-east a scattering of smaller islands leads down to 'Java Minor' and 'Seilan', or Ceylon, the Bay of Bengal having evaporated. Even though there is no evidence Columbus and Behaim knew one another, the similarity between their view of what lay out there in the western Atlantic is very striking. In that sense, Columbus was not quite the eccentric fantasist he might at first appear.[22]

He was, after all, a citizen of Genoa, a port whose inhabitants had saltwater in their veins – despite many counterclaims there is no doubt about that, for the Genoese archives prove that he was the son of the weaver Domenico Colombo; he was an imposing figure, six feet tall and red-haired, capable of great charm as well as great fury.[23] It is certainly striking that three of the pioneers who opened up the Atlantic on behalf of kings in Spain, Portugal and England were Italian. John Cabot appears to have been Genoese by birth, but he lived long enough in Venice to acquire Venetian citizenship, always a long process.[24] Amerigo Vespucci was a well-connected Tuscan who lived in Florence and Piombino, a little maritime state on the coast. It has been seen that the Genoese were very active in the colonization of the Atlantic islands, which explains why Columbus was made so welcome when he called on the Perestrello family in Porto Santo.[25] At that stage in his career, the young Columbus was interested, like many of the Genoese who sailed the Atlantic, in the sugar trade.

Wealthy Italian businessmen based in Lisbon and Seville were of crucial importance in funding both the transatlantic voyages and the Portuguese expeditions. Columbus came to depend on Florentine backers, since the king and queen insisted they had run out of money after spending all they had on the war to conquer Muslim Granada. The solution was to combine their financial support, over a million *maravedís* (less than it sounds, as this was a low-value coin), with backing from Italians in Seville, notably a certain Giannetto Berardi; this way Columbus was able to inject half a million more *maravedís* into the preparation of his tiny fleet.[26] John Cabot received monetary support from the London manager of a bank operated on behalf of an ancient and illustrious Florentine family, the Bardi, with the intention of seeking out 'the new land' (the fact this land is preceded by the word 'the' rather suggests prior knowledge of its existence, but may simply refer back to knowledge of Columbus's discoveries much further south).[27] As for Amerigo Vespucci, he was for a time an agent of Berardi's bank, which brought him into contact with Columbus, and they held one another in respect.[28]

Why then did these Italians not set out across the ocean on their own initiative? Political power was an important issue here. By the 1470s the Portuguese and the Spaniards were already sparring for control of Atlantic waters, so lone interlopers travelled at their own risk. And in delivering grandiloquent letters to the Great Khan, of the sort Columbus carried on his first voyage, it would surely make a difference if they were written in the name of Europe's greatest monarchs, the king and queen of Castile and Aragon, rather than the tiny, if highly influential, republics of Genoa or Florence – even though they were addressed to the 'dear friend' of the king and queen, the letters Columbus carried contained blank spaces so that he could fill in the unknown name of whatever ruler he managed to visit.[29] Besides, the Italians living beyond Italy were probably better placed to raise funds and take risks; the 1490s were troubled years in Italy, marked by a massive French invasion of the peninsula and by Savonarola's revolution within Florence. Finally, there was the fact that the Italians had for hundreds of years been selling their nautical skills to the kings of Portugal and Castile.

Neither Cabot nor Vespucci shared Columbus's apocalyptic vision. Cabot, at the court of the money-hungry King Henry VII, well understood that the king expected good financial returns from whatever lands Cabot might find. Vespucci was a cultured product of Renaissance Florence, and, though he enjoyed exaggerating his achievements, he did not boast about how his discoveries would end the Turkish threat or usher in the Last Days before the Second Coming of Christ. While Columbus fantasized about how he had discovered the source of all the world's great rivers and was closing in on the Garden of Eden, Vespucci, even in his most extravagant moments (describing cannibal feasts, for instance), was keener to shock than to moralize. Columbus saw himself as a crusader; Vespucci did not.

IV

Columbus's first voyage, conducted by two caravels and a slightly larger *nao*, the *Santa María*, set out in August 1492 from Palos de la Frontera in Andalusia, passed through the Canary Islands, and reached its first stop in the Bahamas on 12 October.[30] His crew included at least one convert from Judaism, Luís de Torres, whose great virtue was that he knew both Hebrew and Arabic and would surely, therefore, be able to communicate with the peoples of the East. Oddly, there was not a single priest or friar on board, although Columbus claimed in his own logbook (which survives in a heavily re-edited edition) that one of his aims was to 'determine what method should be undertaken for their conversion to our holy faith'; but if anything the lack of a priest made Columbus even more conscious that he himself was God's agent on board the voyage. Also lacking were impressive trade goods that could be offered to the Great Khan; however, the native population of the Bahamas and the Caribbean was only too happy to be given beads, little red caps and other items of truck, which, as has been seen, immediately passed into the trading networks of the Taínos.

Over the next few months Columbus explored the Bahamas and the coast of Cuba, but decided that the large island he called Hispaniola (modern Haiti and the Dominican Republic) would be most suitable as a base. Although his initial relations with the Taíno population of these lands were by and large friendly, and he wrote very positively about how sweet, docile, good-looking and innocent they were, he had great difficulty fitting them into his world view; they were, for one thing, naked, which was not what one expected of the subjects of the Chinese or Japanese emperor, who would surely be clad in silk. The closest parallel he could find was with the Canary islanders: they too were naked island people, ignorant of metal tools (although the Taínos were, he was glad to report, familiar with a gold and copper alloy called *guanín*); and they too were pagans who lived without any 'law', by which he meant that they were not Christians, Muslims or Jews. Some early accounts and maps show the newly discovered islands as *Novas Canarias*, 'New Canaries', reflecting the view that he had found more of the same on the same latitude, but much further away.[31] He attempted to found a small settlement in the north of the island. He returned to Europe in March 1493, after a difficult voyage through the Azores that washed him up in Lisbon, where King João II was deeply disconcerted to learn of his discoveries, having previously ignored him as a fantasist.[32]

Had he really reached India? Evidently there was something out there, and after Columbus had presented himself, and the Taínos he brought back with him, to Ferdinand and Isabella at court in Barcelona he received a second commission, setting out in September with a much more impressive armada of seventeen ships; and this time there were priests on board. Much of his energy was spent trying to subdue the interior of Hispaniola, as he became sucked into rivalries between the different chieftaincies on the island. He established a new centre of operations at La Isabela in northern Hispaniola, of which more later; and the Taíno Indians were subjected to harsh demands for tribute in gold. Accusations of incompetence reached the court in Spain

When the first inspector, named Juan Aguado, was sent out to Hispaniola in 1495, Columbus was deeply resentful. Normally such inspections took place when a governor demitted office, but the king and queen had appointed him 'Admiral of the Ocean Sea' and governor of all newly found lands for life. Columbus, an agile social climber, expected to make a fortune out of the share of the wealth of the Indies that the king and queen were willing to assign to him. His pretensions did not endear him to people back at the court of Castile. The Genoese were not popular, even though their contribution to the Castilian economy, notably in Seville, and to the creation of a Castilian navy had been crucial; some of the hostility that had been building up against the Jews, expelled as Columbus set out on his first voyage, was redirected towards the Italians. Columbus was also accused, with good reason, of attending too much to the interests of his family, promoting his brothers and his son to high office in Hispaniola and exploiting the resources of Hispaniola to enrich himself – there was a real issue as to whether he was legally entitled to one tenth of the value of goods sent back to Spain, or merely one tenth of the tax of one fifth that the Crown would receive on goods sent back to Spain, in other words one tenth or a mere fiftieth.[33]

The result of all this was that Columbus hurried back to Spain in 1496.[34] He had a difficult time making his case to the Catholic Monarchs, but – taking into account his undoubted skill as a navigator – he was allowed to go out a third time in 1497, and now he headed further south, through the Cape Verde Islands, in the hope that he would find a route to the Far East somewhere to the south of Hispaniola. He discovered 'a very great continent, which until today has been unknown', the north coast of South America, but not too much should be made of this: the term 'continent' simply meant a large area of mainland, which could still be connected to, or lie just offshore from, Asia. Still, the mystery of what was out there deepened further. Columbus was convinced that he had reached the outskirts of the Garden of Eden, which, as the Book of Genesis explained, was guarded by angels bearing flaming swords and could not be entered. He decided that the garden stood at the top of a great protuberance 'something like a woman's nipple' – the earth was not round, but pear-shaped.[35] Sometimes he insisted that these were not just the Indies; he had discovered Paradise – even its Taíno inhabitants, tame and beautiful, unashamedly naked, seemed to live in prelapsarian innocence.

Back in Hispaniola, reality intruded: trouble with the Taínos was compounded by trouble with his fellow Europeans, and he faced a series of rebellions by his Spanish lieutenants. These culminated in the despatch of yet another official investigation under a somewhat dubious figure, Bobadilla, and in the arrest of Columbus. In 1500 he was sent back to Spain in chains that he refused to have removed until he stood in the presence of the king and queen, whom he was still, remarkably, able to charm.[36] Even so, it is surprising that he received a fourth commission, hedged about with conditions about where he could put in, since his presence in Hispaniola was rightly seen as a source of trouble. He was only able to raise funds for four ships, while the governor of Hispaniola, Nicolás de Ovando, sailed out to the Indies ahead of him with thirty.[37] In June 1502 Columbus's ships stood off Santo Domingo, the third attempt at European settlement in Hispaniola and now the island's capital; but they had to sit out a hurricane, as he was not supposed to set foot on the island that he had discovered and ruled.

The conviction that he was called by God to make ever greater discoveries became still more powerful during his final voyage. His knowledge that he was God's agent was confirmed even more strongly at a low point in 1503, during his fourth voyage, when his men were beaten back by the Indians of Panama, where he was hoping to found a colony. Suffering from a high fever and deeply depressed by his failures, his troubled sleep was disturbed by a voice from heaven that said:

> 'O fool and slow to believe and to serve your God, the God of all! What more did He do for Moses or for his servant David? Since you were born, He has always had you in His most watchful care. When He saw you at an age with which he was content, He caused your name to sound marvellously in the land. The Indies, which are so rich a part of the world, He gave you for your own; you have divided them as it pleased you, and He enabled you to do this. Of the mighty barriers of the Ocean Sea, which were closed with such mighty chains, he gave you the keys.'[38]

On the coast of Panama and Costa Rica, he gathered information about a rich civilization in the interior, probably a mixture of memories of Maya glories from centuries earlier (his men found what were almost certainly some Maya buildings), and vague knowledge of the Aztec empire in Mexico. The evidence was there in solid gold ornaments worn by the local Indians, some of which must have been traded from the interior. This gold awakened yet again the greed of Columbus and his followers. He once again tried to found a settlement in lands he suspected were genuinely rich in gold; but when he was beaten off by the locals and when his ships were tossed to and fro in another hurricane, he found himself washed up on the shores of Jamaica, an island he knew vaguely but had never tried to conquer. For a whole year from June 1503 onwards he was allowed to languish there, since the Spanish governor of Hispaniola rather enjoyed leaving him to rot, but one of his companions who had already escaped from Jamaica sent him a ship, and in early November 1504 he was back in Spain, only to discover that his eager patron, Queen Isabella, was on her deathbed; her husband had other priorities, mainly in Italy (following his conquest of Naples a year earlier), so now Columbus was stranded once again, but at least it was in his adopted country; and he himself died there a year and a half later.[39]

As has been seen, Columbus saw the Taínos as innocent and beautiful creatures quite different from the dog-headed monsters some had predicted would be found in southern climes; in his logbook Columbus wrote: 'on these islands until now I have not found any monstrous men, as many expected; rather, they are all people of very beautiful appearance.' Occasionally he looked over his shoulder at what the Portuguese were doing in Africa (he had visited Elmina), and speculated that they were so docile that they would make excellent slaves or servants, but Queen Isabella was adamant that they were her free subjects and must not be enslaved.[40] Attempts to convert the Taínos were half-hearted; a friar was sent into the interior of Hispaniola to learn about their ways, but evidence revealed as recently as 2006 shows that Columbus was unhelpful over conversion, to the point of being obstructive.[41] These ambiguities and inconsistencies in his attitude occur again and again. He still had room in his thinking for monstrous peoples, especially when he heard tales of man-eating Caribs (whence the term 'cannibal', whose first letters echo the Latin *canis*, 'dog'); these Caribs were said to be invading Taíno lands from the south, coming up in their war canoes and seizing boys, whom they castrated and raised for the pot, or women, who bore them children that faced the same terrible fate.[42]

Whether they, or indeed the Taínos, occasionally feasted off human meat has become a controversial question. Historians and literary scholars who claim the label 'post-colonial' argue that cannibalism was a European invention, employed to justify the subjection of the American Indians. On the other hand, it is surely the height of colonial condescension to assume that the Caribs or indeed the Taínos must have had the same moral values as western Europeans either now or in the sixteenth century; there is no serious reason to doubt that some American Indians, whether in the Caribbean or in Brazil, did occasionally eat their captives.[43] Such stories of monstrous conduct led Columbus to divide the inhabitants of the New

World into good Taínos, whom he had made into notionally free subjects of the king and queen, and evil Caribs, who were fair game for slaving expeditions: 'when your Highnesses order me to send you slaves, I expect to bring or send the majority of them from these people.'

However, the Taínos could not produce nearly as much gold as he had hoped, and as he continued to promise to the Catholic Monarchs in Spain. He therefore put them to work sifting and mining for gold in increasingly oppressive conditions, laying the foundations for the *encomienda* system that effectively enslaved the Indians not just of the Caribbean but, in later generations, of Mexico and Peru as well. Rather than being actually slaves, the Taínos were understood to be legally free; but like other subjects they had to render some service to their rulers, which for Columbus meant tribute in gold dust, an amount per head sufficient to fill a hawk's bell. The Crown did occasionally try to improve the conditions under which they lived, but European slavers made no effort to distinguish between 'good' Taínos and 'evil' Caribs. The first major legislation in favour of the Taínos, the 'Laws of Burgos', dates from twenty years after Columbus first reached the Caribbean; by then it was far too late to save them. Unaccustomed to heavy labour and corralled into settlements, with families often broken apart for months at a time, the Taínos began to disappear: falling birth rates, ill-treatment by Spanish masters, even massacres, resulted in their rapid extinction. Demand for labour in the gold fields of Hispaniola led to the depopulation of outlying islands, so that the Bahamas were largely deserted by 1510. As will become clear, the disappearance of the Taínos led to the importation of cheap labour from Africa, black slaves who were not even notional subjects of the Spanish rulers and had even fewer benefits of protection. The economic viability of the West Indies was only sustained by a radical transformation in population, both African and European.

Columbus, torn between his duties as governor of the new Spanish lands and his sense of mission as bearer of God's word, neglected the people of Hispaniola because he was still convinced that he stood on the edge of the Fabulous Orient and that he would unlock the door that would lead Christian armies and navies to Jerusalem. He had radically different views about how to reach Asia from most of his contemporaries; but that does not make him into an example of 'Renaissance Man'. When he used the classical writer Seneca to demonstrate that Europe would overwhelm the Indies which lay not too far to the west, he read Seneca as a prophet, indeed as a Christian prophet, for it was often argued that he had been a secret Christian at the court of the Christian-hating Emperor Nero.[44] His thinking was rooted in medieval ideas of crusade and

Christian redemption as much as it was rooted in the commercial outlook of medieval Genoa.

V

Columbus set out on his first voyage with three ships; John Cabot only had one, the 'shippe of Bristowe' named the *Matthew*, a medium-sized boat of around fifty tons. This was not even a new ship, but a commercial vessel that had probably traded towards Ireland and France before Cabot took charge.[45] One has to say 'probably' because the evidence about Cabot is very fragmentary. His early career was punctuated by failure and scandal: he seems to have fled from Venice to avoid his creditors, and in both Valencia and Seville he offered his services as a harbour engineer, but his projects were never brought to a finish, raising doubts about his competence.[46] A respected British historian announced that she was writing a radically revisionist life of Cabot that would, it seems, have brought to light not just his connections with Italian bankers but his attempts to explore large tracts of the North American coastline and even to settle friars and others along that coast. However, she died before her work was complete and left adamant instructions that all her notes and drafts were to be destroyed.[47] So there is still plenty of speculation about his origins, his career and his impact, speculation that is further muddied by the insistence that he was the real discoverer of America, because Columbus only reached the mainland of America (South rather than North) in 1498, and felt too ill to set foot there, though he did send his men ashore. In reality, the discovery of America was a gradual process of working out that two large continents blocked the way to a further ocean which would present an even greater challenge to navigators than the Atlantic.

Cabot knew perfectly well that Columbus had found land in the west, but his voyage was designed to show that the Spaniards had been sailing too far to the south in their search for Asia, a route partly determined by the lust for the gold that the sun was believed to have generated in hot latitudes.[48] The Milanese ambassador in London reported that Cabot was searching for the real Cipangu, for he was unconvinced that Cuba or any other land Columbus had found was Japan; Cabot, he said, 'believes that all the spices in the world have their origin' in Japan, and Cabot supposedly knew about this because he had intrepidly journeyed to Mecca as a young man and had asked where spices originated.[49] If Cabot's hunches were correct, London stood to become an even more important spice market than Alexandria. In March 1496 King Henry blithely granted John

Cabot extensive rights of conquest, trade monopoly and dominion in the lands he would discover: 'whatsoever islands, countries, regions or provinces of heathens and infidels, in whatsoever part of the world placed, which before this time were unknown to all Christians', though King Henry left it to others to finance the expedition, and evidence collected in the last few decades shows that the Bardi of Florence provided essential backing.[50] The fact that the king specified these were to be previously unknown lands avoided a direct clash with the interests of Columbus and the Crowns of Castile and Portugal.[51] It was simply assumed that Christian discoverers could raise the flag of England in whatever non-Christian land they visited, without reference to the native inhabitants or to the papacy, which, as will be seen, had already divided the globe into Spanish and Portuguese hemispheres.

After a first try in 1496, when he was defeated by the weather and the pessimism of his crew, his first full voyage, in 1497, apparently took him to the 'New-found-land', and possibly to Labrador.[52] As has been seen, spices were not to be had; but there was an astonishing amount of cod. It was widely assumed that Cabot had found more islands, rather than a continent – the duke of Milan was told by his agents that Cabot had found the Island of the Seven Cities.[53] The Englishman John Day wrote to 'the Lord Grand Admiral', almost certainly Columbus (then back in Spain, between his second and third voyages), with a description of Cabot's voyage; he patriotically claimed that 'the cape of the said land was found and discovered in the past by the men from Bristol who found "Brasil", as your Lordship well knows'; what Columbus made of any of this is unknown, and he was never tempted to try a northerly route across the Atlantic. Day reported that Cabot reached land in late June, but there were only a few clues that any humans lived there.[54] So the claim that this was Japan or China did not fit at all well.

Another, larger expedition set off under John Cabot, in 1498. This time he was more willing to take into account Columbus's discoveries, for as far as is known he headed towards Newfoundland, with the idea that the ships would strike southwards towards the tropics, in search, perhaps, of a route to India, or at least Japan and China. John Cabot himself disappeared, though it is possible that some sailors made their way back to Europe with three Indians.[55] For the *Great Chronicle of London* reported that in 1501 or 1502 there 'were browgth unto the kyng iij men takyn In the Newe ffound Ile land'; 'These were clothid In bestys skynnys and ete Rawe fflesh and spak such spech that noo man cowde undyrstand theym, and In theyr demeanure lyke to bruyt bestis.'[56] John Cabot's son Sebastian, himself an explorer of North America, warned of a 'very sterile land', inhabited by polar bears, moose ('large stags like horses'), sturgeon, salmon, soles a yard long and an infinity of codfish.[57] It was not, then, the semi-paradise about which Columbus enthused so poetically, in which seasons were of little importance and crops almost shot out of the soil. The ocean and the rivers, not the land, were the greatest assets of this new-found-land.

There are hints that Cabot or later visitors from Bristol travelled very far to the south. In June 1501 one of Columbus's rivals, Alonso de Hojeda, received a commission from Ferdinand and Isabella, instructing him to 'follow that coast which you have discovered, which runs east and west, as it appears, because it goes towards the region where it has been learned that the English were making discoveries'. He was to set up the Spanish equivalent of *padrões*, to make public the Castilian claim to this shoreline, 'so that you may stop the exploration of the English in that direction'.[58] This was despite the marriage alliances that bound the house of Tudor to Spain through Catherine of Aragon. These explorations were probably conducted by Bristol merchants; in 1527 Hugh Elyot and Robert Thorne were both credited with the discovery of Newfoundland some years earlier, which may have been not so much a snub towards the Cabot family as a recognition that further new-found-lands were reached around 1500, and the American Indians brought back to the court of Henry VII may have arrived on one of these later sailings, which seem to have continued until 1505 or thereabouts.[59] Although a patriotic English historian has claimed that Cabot made entirely clear the fact that North America was not Asia, in reality the discombobulation continued – this was both a New World, of previously unsuspected existence, and at the same time somehow attached to the Old World. Its inhabitants lived so far from the Old World that they might even have been created separately by God; yet they were also 'Indians', sharing ancestry with the peoples of the Old World. None of it made much sense.

How hard it was to connect the mass of new information to existing knowledge became apparent when Greenland once again entered the consciousness of western Europeans. King Henry VII was interested to hear of the rediscovery of Greenland by Gaspar Corte Real, from the Azores, in 1500, news brought to his court by a Portuguese sailor named João Fernandes Lavrador ('the Farmer') from Terceira in the Azores. Lavrador received a privilege from the English king and set up an Anglo-Portuguese syndicate that explored the western Atlantic out of Bristol.[60] The Corte Reals subsequently, at the cost of their lives, explored the coast of Labrador right down to Newfoundland – confusingly, they applied the name Labrador not to the Atlantic coast of Canada, meant here, but to

Greenland.[61] A map of 1502, the Cantino Map, drawn in Lisbon, attached a caption to Greenland describing it as the land 'discovered by licence of the most excellent prince Dom Manuel king of Portugal, the which is believed to be the peninsula of Asia'.[62]

Enough reports filtered back to Portugal to confirm that this stretch of sea was good for fishing, but the land had little to offer beyond ice.[63] It has been suggested that the real motive of these explorers was to find a North-West Passage to Asia over the top of Canada, which would become a longstanding obsession of navigators; however, it is more likely that they were curious to look further at whatever Cabot had found, and that they concurred with the general view that Greenland was a spur sticking out of Asia.

29

Other Routes to the Indies

I

It took nine long years to capitalize on Dias's rather amazing discovery that Ptolemy was wrong, and that the Indian Ocean has an open bottom. One factor that delayed action was that the Portuguese once again became interested in campaigns in Morocco, though their meddling continued to irritate the Castilians, who sent an expedition to Morocco's Mediterranean coast, capturing Melilla in 1497, and holding it ever since. The Portuguese king was surrounded by doubters who pointed out that the monarchy did not have unlimited resources, even with the profits that accrued from gold, sugar and slaves; surely it made more sense to concentrate on maximizing these profits? It was easy too to insist that little was really known about political conditions in and around the Indian Ocean. Quite apart from the difficulty in keeping such elongated trade routes open, little was known about the Christian prince who was supposed to come to the aid of the Portuguese, Prester John, who had been cited again and again for four centuries.

In preparation for new voyages, spies were sent into Muslim lands, in the hope that they could penetrate still further, all the way to both India and Ethiopia. Between 1487 and 1491 an agent of King João, Pero da Covilhã, explored the land route to India and ended up in Ethiopia, where he saw out his days. His account of conditions in India was sent back to Lisbon via Portuguese Jews trading in Cairo.[1] The Portuguese court also applied the knowledge of the skilled Jewish astronomer Abraham Zacuto, who had taught at Salamanca University before being exiled from Spain in 1492.[2] Zacuto was a great specialist in astronomical tables, vital for long-distance sailing; for the aim in sending Covilhã to India was not to create a land route, which was obviously impossible while Turks and Mamluks stood in the way, but to spy out the cities of India, find out what could be bought there, and obtain some sense of the geography of the lands bordering the Indian Ocean.

Portuguese interest in a westward route across the Atlantic was limited. Columbus had not been taken seriously when he delivered his sales pitch about a short transatlantic route to Asia, still less after Dias rounded the Cape of Good Hope and gave the Portuguese good hope of a route to the Indies; Columbus's calculation of the size of the earth was simply not credible, and his idea that Cipangu (Japan) was within easy reach of the Canary Islands made no sense.[3] The Crown had given its blessing to Ferdinand van Olmen's expedition westwards in 1486, but had invested nothing in it, and, after all, van Olmen never reappeared.[4] King João was therefore shocked when Columbus returned from his first voyage to the Caribbean in 1493, carrying Taíno Indians on board. One issue was which newly discovered lands should fall under the dominion of which kingdom; the solution agreed in the Treaty of Tordesillas, in 1494, was to divide the Atlantic, and by extension the globe, vertically down the middle of the ocean; the treaty was mediated by the pope, Alexander VI Borgia, who took the opportunity to express his own overarching authority across the entire world. Spain was granted rights to the west of the line of division, Portugal to the east. The Portuguese therefore remained confined to the eastern flank of the Atlantic during the 1490s.

Seen from a maritime perspective, this was the lull before the storm. A new king succeeded to the throne late in 1495; Manuel I was the cousin of João II, and he was driven as much by messianic ideas of Portugal's role in the struggle against Islam as he was by his support for the now wealthy trading community of Lisbon; he had been educated by Franciscan friars who imbued him with his sense of a messianic mission, which was accentuated when, against the odds, he found himself heir to his cousin's throne.[5] Manuel's decision to expel both Jews and Muslims from his kingdom in 1497 reflects his apocalyptic view of human history: Christ would return when the Jews became Christians and when the Infidel Moors were defeated at home, as far east as Jerusalem, and in Asia. (In the event, most Jews were forced to convert to Christianity when Manuel closed the ports to prevent them leaving, with the result that a large and prosperous community of New Christians, often secretly loyal to their old religion, came into existence.) Voyages to the heart of Asia would divert the gold and spices of the East away from the Islamic heartlands, and help to undermine the power of the Mamluks in the Middle East and of the Ottomans in Turkey and the Balkans.

So, amid great celebration, in July 1497 Vasco da Gama set out with four ships, at first following the classic Portuguese route along the west coast of Africa and past the Cape Verde Islands.[6] Two of these ships were not caravels; much energy had gone into designing a sturdier type of ship,

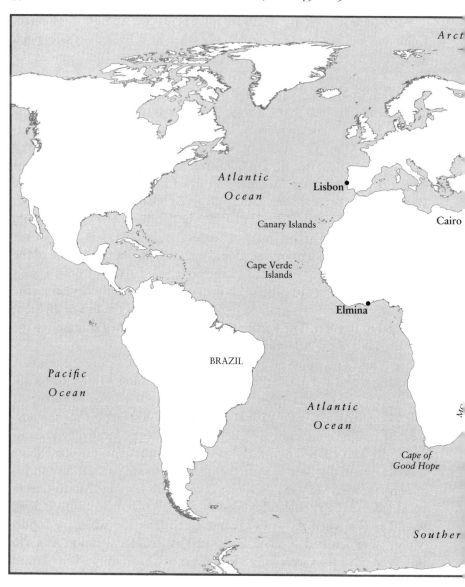

with square sails, that would be better suited for the bold route Dias had identified. This route would take the ships through powerful winds across open ocean well out of sight of land, rather than the coastal route Cão had taken, which took advantage of the ability of caravels to sail a good way upriver. Dias advised on the design of the new ships, but the king mysteriously chose da Gama, a minor nobleman with no experience of command at sea, to lead the expedition; Manuel was more interested in placing someone who might be able to negotiate with foreign rulers at the

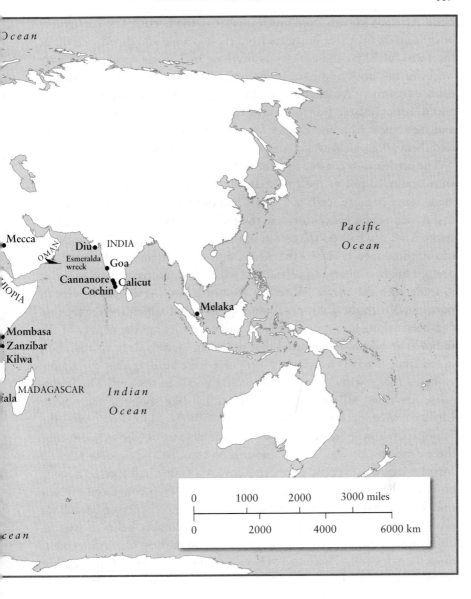

head of the expedition, rather than an old sea dog like Dias.[7] Bearing in mind Dias's advice, da Gama swung far out into the ocean once past the Cape Verde Islands, describing a route that traversed three times the distance covered by Christopher Columbus in 1492. His ships were swept along, arriving somewhere along the coasts of modern Namibia and South Africa. There they met naked, tawny-coloured Bushmen who were disappointingly ignorant of spices, gold or pearls;[8] further south, Vasco da Gama's chronicler described people who looked and acted more like the

black Africans known from much further to the north.[9] The Portuguese
bought an ox for three bracelets from these people and dined well off it,
for it was full of fat and as tasty as anything back home – a great joy after
weeks of salt pork and hard biscuit.[10] The good news was that, as they
rounded southern Africa, the Portuguese began to realize that the inhabitants were not isolated from the world; they were 'handsome and well-made'
and they knew iron and copper, and the Portuguese met one man who
told them about his travels far up the coast, where he had seen big ships.

The further they coasted into the Indian Ocean the more the Portuguese
were reminded not of the Christian but of the Muslim world, and this
made sense because Arab merchants had been trading up and down the
east African coast for centuries in their dhows.[11] Many of the inhabitants
spoke Arabic, whatever the colour of their skin (for there had been plenty
of intermarriage between the Arabs and the Africans). These people
dressed finely in linen and cotton and wore silk turbans; they were active
in trade with the 'white Moors' to the north, and Arab vessels were in
port, piled with the gold, pearls and spices about which the Portuguese
had been asking everyone they encountered, including the pepper of the
Indies. The merchants boasted that pearls and jewels were so abundant
in the lands towards which the Portuguese were heading that one simply
gathered them, without any need to offer goods in return.[12] The Portuguese absorbed all the rumours they heard like sponges: there were
Christian kingdoms to the north, at war with the Moors; there was the
Ethiopian realm of Prester John, still busy in defence of Christendom after
three centuries. It was all too good to be true. By the time he reached
Mombasa in what is now southern Kenya, da Gama had entered a much
more familiar world of princes and traders. He even convinced himself
that he had met some Christians when two merchants of Mombasa
proudly showed the Portuguese what the newcomers believed was an
image of the Holy Spirit drawn on paper.[13] With the help of a willing pilot,
often though wrongly assumed to have been ibn Majid, the Muslim author
of several tracts on navigation, da Gama was at last able to make his way
to Calicut in India, where he arrived on 20 May.[14]

Here he was entering a world which had close links to home. He found a
couple of Moors from Tunis, who spoke Spanish and Italian, and who un-
enthusiastically greeted the Portuguese with the words: 'May the devil take
you! What brought you here?' The Portuguese were, nonetheless, convinced
that they had reached a Christian land. It was certainly not a land under
Muslim rule. The Portuguese were mightily impressed by a building they
identified as a church; it was made of stone, and was the size of a monastery,
with a great bronze pillar at the entrance. Within the church there was an

imposing chapel, and 'within this sanctuary stood a small image which they said represented Our Lady'. The figure carried a child, so the identification was as certain as could be. Therefore Vasco da Gama entered the compound with some of his companions, and they said their prayers. The local priests threw holy water over the Portuguese visitors and presented them with 'white earth' made of cow dung, ashes and sandalwood, with which the local Christians were accustomed to anoint themselves. The local Christians were also devotees of any number of saints, whose images were painted on the walls of the church, some with several arms or with giant teeth.[15]

It was all, of course, a great mistake. Their first encounter with the Hindu gods was transmogrified in the fertile imagination of the Portuguese into an encounter with the Virgin and Child. The panoply of gods painted on the walls was read as a cycle of Christian saints.[16] The Virgin and Child was probably an image of Krishna being suckled by his mother Divaki. The Portuguese knew these people were not 'Moors', whose places of cult had no images and whose language and practices were easily recognizable – as has been seen, Islam was banned in Portugal only in the year when da Gama left home.[17] But India was a land of kings, of scheming Moors, of undoubted wealth, in which the Portuguese were not really welcome. Da Gama's attempts to negotiate with local rulers were frustrated at every turn, and his constant recourse to violence, which became the trademark of Portuguese conquerors, made it more difficult still to win the respect of local rulers and establish trading stations. Still, da Gama was able to leave loaded with samples of pepper and other goods, and to reach Lisbon again in September 1499.

The king of Portugal optimistically began to call himself 'king of Portugal, lord of Guinea, lord of the conquest and navigation and commerce of Ethiopia, Arabia, Persia and India'. This title was not quite as empty as it may sound: within five years an astonishing eighty-one ships were despatched from Lisbon to India. A second fleet was put together under the command of Pedro Álvares Cabral, setting out in 1500; this fleet consisted of thirteen ships and swung so far out into the Atlantic that it made landfall in South America, in what the Portuguese called the 'Land of the Holy [or True] Cross', soon to be rechristened Brazil. This land happened to fall on the Portuguese side of the line of demarcation that had been established by the Treaty of Tordesillas six years earlier. Although it has often been suggested that the Portuguese already possessed secret knowledge of Brazil, and that Cabral knew where he was heading, contemporary reports indicate that this was an accidental discovery. The Portuguese took a long time to capitalize upon it.[18]

Cabral took care to carry along Arabic interpreters, including a certain Gaspar da Gama, named after his godfather Vasco, who was an enthusiastic and well-informed Jew of Polish descent da Gama had found wandering in India and had brought back to Portugal. Cabral's method for convincing the *Samudri*, or king, of Calicut to do business was crude in the extreme: ships with hundreds of passengers aboard were sunk; the town was bombarded by cannon; no quarter was given; elephants as well as people were massacred (and the elephants were eaten); but in the end permission was given for spices to be loaded, though not enough to fill all the holds. These goods were only acquired because Cabral was able to take advantage of the intense rivalry between the ruler of Calicut, whose town he had ravaged, and the rajah of Cochin, better disposed to the interlopers because he saw them as well-armed allies.[19] Seven of the ships finally returned to Lisbon, but only five carried merchandise; one ship wandered off and reached Madagascar, the first European landing there. In June 1500, along the coast of Africa Cabral's ships encountered a fleet carrying the Italian explorer Amerigo Vespucci, a sign that this vast world was in some respects still a small one – in these enormous spaces Europeans somehow managed to find one another. Vespucci was bound for the north coast of South America; but he was fully alive to the implications of these Portuguese voyages. He sent a long letter back to Florence, recounting the achievements of Cabral's fleet and describing the geography of maritime Asia to his patron, a member of the Medici family; he thought that the lands Cabral had visited in South America were an extension of those Columbus and others had been revealing under the Spanish flag, whereas the Portuguese view was that Brazil was a large island.[20]

King Manuel was so carried away by enthusiasm that even before Cabral had returned he sent out yet another fleet, in March 1501, under the Galician commander João de Nova. Nonetheless, de Nova managed to learn what Cabral had been doing: Cabral left a message in a shoe suspended from a tree near the southern tip of Africa; astonishingly, the message was found, and de Nova was warned that he should stay wary of the hostile *Samudri* of Calicut. De Nova was able to use his cannon to fight off attacks by ships from Calicut, and he captured several cargo vessels, one of which belonged to the embattled *Samudri*. Cochin and Cannanore proved good sources of spices, although the downside was that the Indians had only limited interest in the goods the Portuguese had brought. Still, de Nova managed to establish a 'factory', that is, a warehouse and office, for the Portuguese at Cannanore; this is what da Gama had aimed to achieve at Calicut, but his bloodthirsty behaviour there made the creation of a permanent base impossible. So de Nova was able to return to Portugal in September 1502 with hundreds of thousands of pounds of pepper, cinnamon and ginger. Some of the cargo was without doubt loot from captured Cochin ships. The Portuguese would long appear to many of the inhabitants of the shores of the Indian Ocean as pirates and interlopers, and it is impossible to disagree.[21]

In 1502 da Gama went out to India for a second time, departing just as de Nova left Indian waters. Twenty ships set out, divided into three squadrons: one squadron of ten ships to collect cargoes of spices, one to clean the sea of Arab traders hostile to the Portuguese, and one to stay in India, protecting the Portuguese who were taking up residence there. The self-confidence of the Portuguese is impressive: they assumed that the ships that went out would – with some losses – eventually return, despite the danger of war with the ruler of Calicut and the sheer difficulty of a journey through stormy seas and past many potentially hostile towns in east Africa. The tone of the expedition was set by a visit to Kilwa, long an important port on the east coast of Africa, where the threat of unleashing his firepower on the town convinced the local ruler to declare himself a vassal of the king of Portugal and to offer a substantial tribute in gold.[22] The message that Portugal would achieve its aims by force was never allowed to fade from sight. Once off India, the level of violence increased to horrific levels: the burning of a merchant ship full of men, women and children returning from Mecca was only one ghastly episode, as da Gama bombarded towns and rejoiced in Portuguese firepower, ever intent on humiliating the *Samudri* of Calicut and of forcing his way into the spice markets of India. Potential friends were harassed too, like the rajah of Cannanore, who was found to be in cahoots with Muslim merchants and had to be warned that in no circumstances must he interfere with the Portuguese agents based in his port.[23]

These actions even stirred da Gama's enemy, the ruler of Calicut, to begin negotiations, though in the hope of trapping da Gama and destroying his fleet; early in February 1503 the Portuguese and the navy of Calicut clashed, and da Gama won a handsome victory. One reason for the defeat of Calicut was that the *Samudri* was unable to persuade the Arab merchants to lend him their ships, so his navy consisted of a few dozen ships provided by his Indian subjects. The Portuguese took home an extraordinarily rich cargo of over 3,000,000 pounds' weight of spices, mainly pepper but also plenty of sweet-smelling cinnamon. Brightly coloured parrots were brought back, described as 'marvellous things'. If this could be repeated year in, year out in more peaceful conditions, the trade routes of the world would be radically transformed.[24]

Even when these pioneers were able to fill their ships with pepper, the high risks of these voyages, with the loss of up to half the ships, began to raise doubts back home about their viability; the wreck of what may well be one of da Gama's ships, the *Esmeralda*, which foundered off the coast

of Oman, was first identified in 1998, although its location was kept secret
until 2016. It is the earliest known wreck of a European ship from the age
of discovery. This is one of those cases where archaeological evidence and
the documents converge neatly, for the story of this shipwreck is well known,
thanks to reports in contemporary chronicles and in a letter sent to King
Manuel.[25] The sinking of the *Esmeralda* and its sister-ship, the *São Pedro*,
was even illustrated in a manuscript of 1568, such was the fame of these
events. These vessels had been sent to hunt down Arab ships off Arabia, but
unfamiliarity with the winds and waves did the Portuguese vessels far more
harm than clashes with Arab dhows – the *Esmeralda* was torn from its
anchorage close to an offshore island by a storm and hurled against the
rocks. The name of its captain, Vicente Sodré, was commemorated in the
inscription 'VS' carved on to the stone shot kept on board for use in battle;
Sodré was da Gama's uncle and was to be his substitute if da Gama died
on the expedition. A bell carrying the number '498', that is, 1498, and some
gold *cruzado* coins minted in Portugal help to confirm the ship's identity;
one coin, a silver *indio* of King Manuel I, is only known from one other
surviving example, but it was a famous coin in its day, minted for trade with
the Indies.[26] Among the most recent finds is a mariner's astrolabe, of which
very few other examples survive, and none this early.

Growing experience of these waters reduced these dangers, and growing
profits increased their attractiveness to those trying to make their fortune.
Venetian writers began to panic, fearing (wrongly) that all the pepper they
had been buying through Alexandria would disappear; they were also disconcerted to learn that 'it is impossible to procure the map of that voyage.
The king has placed a death penalty on anyone who gives it out.'[27] In his
diary the Venetian Girolamo Priuli kept repeating his fears about the future:

> Some very wise people are inclined to believe that this thing may be the
> beginning of the ruin of the Venetian state, because there is no doubt that
> the traffic of the voyage and the merchandise and the navigation which the
> city of Venice made each year thence, are the nutriment and milk through
> which the said republic sustained itself . . . With this new voyage by the
> king of Portugal, all the spices which should come from Calicut, Cochin
> and other places in India to Alexandria or Beirut, and later come to
> Venice . . . will be controlled by Portugal.[28]

Venice was quick to act, and sent its own galleys out of the Mediterranean
to Flanders, dumping the spices it had obtained in the Levant and trying
to head off Portuguese competition.[29]

Portuguese pepper was plentiful, but by the time it reached Europe it
was often waterlogged, and Portugal did not gain supremacy in the spice

trade overnight. The Venetians were relieved when the Portuguese king failed to make much money from the pepper brought back in 1501. It took a few years for the effects of da Gama's breakthrough to be visible. After 1503 the price of spices in European markets fell, reflecting the presence of spices brought by the Cape route. Venice did suffer, but a sudden and catastrophic collapse did not occur, and there was even a Venetian recovery in the late sixteenth century.[30] Portugal's success depended on the strength of demand in north European markets; Antwerp was to be Portugal's salvation, a market close to the cities and courts of northern Europe where Portugal could unload its goods and undercut the Venetian galley trade out of the Mediterranean. That said, it is important to remember that the major overseas market for Indian spices lay eastwards, not westwards, in China, which was a voracious consumer even in the face of Ming attempts to concentrate production at home; and India itself consumed far more spices than the whole of Europe – even before the Mughals brought their cuisine to the subcontinent, there was plenty of spicy food to be had in India. European demand for spices did not have much effect on the price of spices in the Indies. The opening of the route to India and beyond by Portugal was of massive importance, laying the foundation of the first of the great European maritime empires; yet it is important not to exaggerate the effect of the European spice trade on the economy of Asia.

Some Italian businessmen did, however, benefit from the new opportunities. Bartolomeo Marchionni was a very wealthy Florentine businessman who had been based in Lisbon for nearly thirty years when da Gama first set out; he traded in sugar, slaves and wheat and built up interests in both Madeira and the Guinea Coast before he became an enthusiastic backer of the India project. He was a naturalized Portuguese subject, and he believed that his family's future lay in the booming city of Lisbon, where, by about 1490, he was the richest merchant in the city. He had a long history of supporting India ventures even before da Gama; he had provided the letters of credit that Pero da Covilhã cashed as he travelled eastwards on his spying mission. Marchionni was the proud owner of the *Annunciada*, one of Cabral's ships, which returned carrying gems obtained in India, and he also funded de Nova's expedition.[31]

II

The Swahili coast also entered the consciousness of the Portuguese. Although the Swahili population was not much interested in taking to the sea, the Portuguese could hardly prevent Arab dhows from carrying on their trade down the east African coast; Arab, Indian and quite probably Malay ships used to visit the ports along this shore, stopping at Kilwa, Mombasa and other towns, whose faraway links extended, according to Tomé Pires, the early sixteenth-century Portuguese writer, all the way to Melaka.[32] The main aim of the Portuguese was to intimidate local Muslim rulers, so that they had free passage through their waters; they needed stopping points where ships could be careened and leaks could be plugged; and above all they hoped to blockade the Red Sea, cutting off the supply routes that brought the spices of the Indies to Alexandria. There was one place along this coast that really did attract them: Sofala, in modern Mozambique, which was a terminal point for the gold that was brought from the African interior towards the coast. By controlling the coast of Mozambique, the Portuguese would be able to block Arab access to Sofala, while the region was within surprisingly easy sailing distance of India, once the monsoon winds were blowing in the right direction. Otherwise, they were not enormously interested in what they could buy and sell along this coast: the aroma of Indian spices was addictive.[33]

Most histories of da Gama and his successors pay rather little attention to Portuguese projects in east Africa, but success there was vital if the Portuguese were to master the route to India and gain some degree of control over an ocean so far from home. There was no point in creating bases in India, at Cannanore and Cochin, and later at Goa and Diu, if the route past Africa was not protected by strong alliances and by impregnable forts that would remind local rulers how important it was not to irritate the Portuguese; much the same policy had guided them down the coast of Morocco and all the way to Elmina, so fortress-building far from home was in their bones. This understanding of how east Africa fitted into their wider plans was apparent as early as 1503, when Manuel sent António de Saldanha into the Indian Ocean with three ships. Such a tiny squadron might seem laughably small, but the firepower of the Portuguese was terrifying; the cannons on board were the weapons of mass destruction of the early sixteenth century, as one of Saldanha's captains showed when he seized some ships based at Mombasa and then blockaded Zanzibar. However, the attack on Zanzibar is a perfect example of the repeated failure of the Portuguese to think their actions through. The sultan of Zanzibar had never opposed the Portuguese. When the Portuguese bombarded the beach they killed the sultan's son; they also captured three ships standing in Zanzibar harbour, whereupon the sultan felt obliged to make a humiliating peace agreement, consisting of a large tribute in gold and thirty sheep each year, as well as a hefty ransom payment for one of the ships that had been seized.[34]

Local rulers hoped that the Portuguese would go away within a few years, once they discovered how unwilling the Muslim and Hindu rulers were to host them, after which they would leave the Indian Ocean in relative peace. Yet they kept returning for more, and began to dig themselves into east Africa by constructing Portuguese forts at Sofala and Kilwa. The commander who was sent out to build these forts, Francisco de Almeida, exploited the fact that the local sheikhs had accepted the overlordship of the king of Portugal, but it was clear that they would only be permitted to stay in power so long as they continued to pay tribute and to help the Portuguese.[35] This type of relationship was inspired by the surrender treaties that the Christian rulers in medieval Spain and Portugal had forged with Muslim princes: a combination of an alliance, into which the Muslims had been coerced, with loosely defined submission.

Almeida, who became the first Portuguese viceroy in the Indian Ocean, was sent to the Indian Ocean with the largest Portuguese fleet so far: there were 1,500 men aboard twenty-two or twenty-three ships, and those on board included many high-ranking Portuguese and captains with experience of these waters (such as João de Nova), because the aim, set out in a 30,000-word set of instructions, was to gain mastery over the western half of the Indian Ocean.[36] When he found that the sheikh of Kilwa was less than welcoming – the sheikh argued that he could not meet Almeida as a black cat had crossed the road in front of him – Almeida's willingness to compromise turned into fury at obvious delaying tactics, and Portuguese troops were unleashed on the town. Almeida's men overran the town, the sheikh fled through a postern gate, and the next day the victorious Almeida began to build the promised fort. Still, he had to sort out the government of what could become a restive city. A compliant Muslim leader whom the Portuguese knew as Anconi was installed as king of Kilwa; conveniently, Almeida had brought along a crown that Manuel was sending to the rajah of Cochin, and this was used in Anconi's lavish coronation ceremony, which was attended by the Portuguese commanders all dressed up to the nines.[37]

A similarly revolting story can be told of the attack that was now launched against Mombasa: intimidation followed by ruthless bombardment, the landing of troops, the looting and burning of the city, and the massacre of many of its inhabitants. The sultan wrote to another Arab ruler: 'in this city the stench of death is such that I dare not enter it.' The victors divided up loot, some of it from as far away as Persia, that included gold, silver, ivory, silk, camphor and slaves, as well as a carpet so magnificent that it was set aside as a gift to King Manuel. So much was seized that loading the ships took a fortnight.[38] The Portuguese preferred to be feared rather than loved. They were particularly interested in Sofala, with its reputation as a centre of the gold trade, even though its harbour was difficult to enter, making it less suitable as a supply station. Their reputation had preceded them, and the sheikh, aged about eighty and blind, was hardly in a position to resist them, especially when they offered to defend Sofala against attacks by African raiders from the interior. They were allowed to build a fortress and commercial base, which they created from scratch in a couple of months during the autumn of 1505. This gave them charge of the gold trade out of Sofala, from which the Arab traders were now excluded.

The Portuguese also began to eye the great inland empire of Monomotapa, the source of much of the gold they craved; in 1506 a report by a Portuguese agent demonstrated that the gold lay in a kingdom ruled from a place called *Zimbaue*, which it took about three weeks to reach – the first European reference to a successor kingdom to the empire of Great Zimbabwe, whose rulers had once dominated large stretches of south-east Africa. Clearly, the more gold they could extract from this area (later the Portuguese colony of Mozambique), the more easily they could pay for the spices of the Indies, and a lively exchange network developed, linking Portuguese Sofala with India and importing into Africa Indian cloths and carpets, ranging from the finest silks to linen shirts.[39]

One of the most striking features of this Portuguese takeover in the Indian Ocean is that they were confidently seizing control while they still knew little about the geography and resources of the lands where they were building their forts. One of the ships in da Cunha's fleet landed by chance in Madagascar, which had already been discovered by the Portuguese, but was still unknown territory. When they saw that young men on the island wore silver bracelets, and realized that cloves and ginger could be found there as well, the Portuguese became very excited. Maybe there was no reason to go all the way to India and fight wars against the Muslims and Hindus, when the spices and precious metals of the Indies were accessible on this massive island inhabited by generally friendly inhabitants. João de Nova informed King Manuel that 'great ships' arrived every other year in Madagascar from further east, and that it would therefore be possible both to exploit the island's own riches and to tap into the trade between Madagascar and Melaka in the Far East; as one historian has said, 'it would be a case of large profits, quick returns'. Manuel became very excited. In 1508 an expedition was sent out to see if these expectations were realistic. But no silver and no cloves were found; interestingly, the Portuguese came to the conclusion that the cloves they had been shown had been collected from the wreck of a Javanese junk. In the years around

1500, traffic continued to ply between the East Indies and south-east Africa, especially Madagascar, which had not lost its connection to the islands far to the east from which its own population had originated.[40]

The Portuguese had scored remarkable successes in east Africa and India. Yet the waters of the Indian Ocean could never be entirely theirs: not just Javanese junks but Arab dhows and Ottoman war galleys had to be taken into account, for, as will become clear, the Turks had their own ambitions in this vast arena.

30

To the Antipodes

I

It seemed that Asia could be reached in two directions. But gradually doubts began to accumulate. Amerigo Vespucci's writings were distributed and translated even more widely in Europe than those of Columbus, thanks to ever more energetic printing presses; they suggested that there really was a New World that might not even be connected to Asia. Vespucci's claim to have taken part in four transatlantic voyages does not have to be taken at face value. His letters describing the New World, some of which survive in manuscript and some in print, combine the tendentious with the factual, for he had a very good eye for his market, which consisted of readers as interested in feasts of human flesh as in the geography of the world. The printed versions, which play up this theme in especially lurid detail, may well have been rewritten by his editors, and the real question is not whether Vespucci saw what he claimed, so much as how his works influenced Europeans at a time when awareness was growing that access to Asia through the Atlantic was blocked by massive continents. One of his admirers was Sir Thomas More; the fictitious narrator of his description of an ideal society somewhere out in the Atlantic was Raphael Hythloday, who 'accompanied Amerigo Vespucci on the last three of his four voyages, accounts of which are now common reading everywhere'.[1]

Vespucci claimed that he joined a Spanish expedition across the Atlantic in 1497, led by Alonso de Hojeda, who had been entrusted with the command of the first small fleet to break Columbus's monopoly on exploration.[2] These ships were heading into areas which lay beyond the area opened up by Columbus's first two voyages, and were therefore not automatically part of the massive grant of dominion and rights of exploration that had been made to him by the Catholic Monarchs. The rival voyages gave rise to lawsuits between the Columbus family and the Crown that lasted a generation; the Columbuses saw the newcomers as interlopers in their own

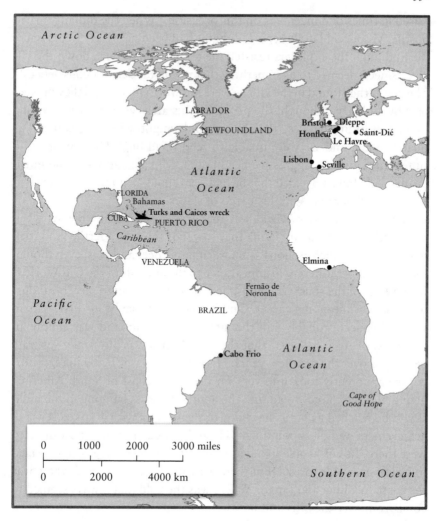

Caribbean. It is quite possible that Vespucci did not actually accompany Hojeda, and that he first crossed the Atlantic two years later; however, whether his first voyage took place in 1497 or 1499, he was drawn across the Atlantic by news that there were pearl fisheries in the southern Caribbean, and he may have fancied himself as a jewel merchant.[3] But it became clear that the real source of profit was to be found not in pearls but in human bodies: the crew carried off more than 200 slaves.[4]

As Hojeda's ships coasted along the southern shores of the Caribbean, they entered a land where the natives lived in villages built above the water, just like Venice; this was the origin of the name 'Venezuela', which means 'little Venice'.[5] Admittedly, the houses were not Venetian *palazzi* but huts raised on stilts and linked to one another by drawbridges which could be raised in times of danger – as on this occasion.[6] When the Indians turned hostile, Vespucci blandly reported that it had been necessary to massacre them, though the explorers resisted the temptation to burn down the village, 'since it seemed to us something that would burden our consciences'.[7] The goods they found in the village were not worth much, and they pressed on.[8] By and large, though, the people in this area were friendly, offering food, performing dances; 'there we spent the night, where they offered us their women, and we were unable to fend them off'.[9] These people did suffer from raids by aggressive neighbours, who also attacked the Europeans, and Hojeda decided that he had seen enough and that the time had come to return home with his cargo of slaves.

How new this New World was to Europeans became obvious when they studied the flora and fauna they saw. For this was a fertile land, rich in wild animals such as 'lions' (that is, jaguars), deer and pigs, even though they were rather different in appearance to the animals of the Old World.[10] Knowledge of the southern hemisphere was only acquired piecemeal during Vespucci's seagoing career. On his second, or maybe his first, trip, in 1499, Vespucci probably still thought that the mainland was simply an extension of Asia; his sense that the New World was physically separate developed over the next few years. His third (or was it really his second?) voyage apparently took him very far down the coast of South America, giving him the chance to admire the Southern Cross hanging in the night sky. If he reached as far as he claimed, then it was with a mixed sense of achievement and disappointment. He had visited lands no one suspected were there, full of people living a simple life on the edge of what seemed to be impenetrable forests. But there were no great cities. And where was the route to China and Japan? Where was the gold that always seemed to come from over the hills and far away?

Eventually Vespucci concluded that this was the southern continent. 'We learned that the land was not an island but a continent, both because it extends over very long, straight shorelines, and because it is filled with countless inhabitants.'[11] As has been seen, the term 'continent' did not have quite the meaning it has now, and in a general sense indicated a large area of mainland that could be part of Asia, Africa or Europe, the three known continents in the modern sense of the term. However, Vespucci concluded that this was indeed a separate landmass; he was convinced these were the 'Antipodes', the southern continent that had occasionally been mentioned by geographers but that were assumed to be not just uninhabited but uninhabitable, in view of the torrid heat of southern climes: 'I have discovered a continent in those southern regions that is inhabited by more numerous peoples and animals than in our Europe, or Asia or

Africa.'[12] So how had the people arrived there? As the puzzle grew, later commentators would sometimes suggest that God must have created them separately, and that even if they were somehow descended from Noah, the common father of all mankind, they were not fully rational beings but were destined to serve their European masters as 'natural slaves'. These views were still being promoted in the seventeenth century.[13] Vespucci's descriptions of cannibal peoples reinforced the idea that the inhabitants of the southern continent were human in shape, but monster-like in behaviour.

Others came to the conclusion that these lands were not Cathay or Cipangu with the help of their mercenary instincts. The silks and spices of the East were not to be had; but slaving expeditions became more and more frequent. Vicente Yáñez Pinzón had captained the *Niña* on Columbus's first voyage; in 1499 he set out under royal licence for the New World. He was ordered not to bring back Caribbean natives as slaves, though Africans were acceptable if he entered eastern Atlantic waters; in fact he took thirty-six slaves from the New World.[14] But the most persistent slavers were the Guerra brothers. Luis Guerra and a colleague went to Brazil in 1500–1501, taking slaves from 'Topia', the land inhabited by the Tupí Indians; they sold one girl named Sunbay in Spain for 6,000 *maravedís*, though this was an exceptionally high price, and it was not a good deal – Sunbay fell ill. The Guerras raided into Topia with impunity, because this land lay in the Portuguese sphere, and therefore the natives had no right to the protection of the Spanish monarchs.[15] These captives were called *indios bozales* – the term *bozales* indicated that they were primitive, even savage, and was also used of untrained black slaves from west Africa. In 1504 the Guerra brothers were allowed to go slaving anywhere except the lands of Columbus and the king of Portugal, which concentrated their efforts on Carib territory in the southern Caribbean; the Spanish historian Oviedo wondered about this: 'I do not know if these merchants were authorised to enslave the people of that land because they are idolaters, savages, sodomites, or because they eat human flesh.'[16] Thus, a sad routine of slave-raiding developed.

Linked to the slave-raiding was the incessant search for sources of gold; one Spanish explorer, Juan de la Cosa, met people along the coast of South America who went around naked, though the men wore penis sheaths, sometimes made of gold.[17] The explorers begged some gold off them, but when the natives asked for it back they wisely agreed; rumours reached the Europeans of a great temple with gold-plated idols, suggesting that the real riches lay a little further inland. These rumours coalesced into the story of El Dorado, the kingdom awash with gold. De la Cosa had accompanied Columbus, Hojeda and Vespucci on voyages to the New World, and is best known for his remarkably well-informed world map of 1500, showing great stretches of the South American coast and daring also to include what looks like the coast of Texas and areas still further north. Without engaging in the argument that Hojeda or others penetrated that coastline to keep the English at bay, as defenders of Cabot's reputation like to think, one can still see that de la Cosa had clever intuitions: he realized that Cuba was not Japan nor part of the Asian mainland, showing it as a humpbacked island looking not vastly different from its real shape.

These uncertainties stimulated further expeditions that gradually mapped out parts of the North American as well as the South American coast. Inevitably, the presence of European ships on the coast of what much later became the United States of America has created a whole industry built around the nonsensical question: 'Who discovered the USA first?' The credit, if that is the right term, for landing on future United States soil is usually granted to Juan Ponce de León, one of the more attractive figures in an age of brutal Spanish *conquistadores*, although there is not much doubt that slave-raiders had arrived first.[18] The great defender of Indian rights, the Dominican friar Bartolomé de las Casas, told of the disappointment of Spanish slavers that they could not find any victims in the now-deserted Bahamas, already emptied of their population by earlier raids; so they travelled further north to the land las Casas knew as Florida, and brought back from there the first slaves captured on the North American mainland, who would have belonged to the relatively sophisticated Calusa or Timucua peoples.[19]

The oldest wreck found in the western hemisphere was found off the Turks and Caicos Islands, close to the Bahamas; it was very probably manned by slave-raiders. Although its exact date is unknown, let alone the name of the ship, of which only a small part of the hull survives, the pottery and firearms found on board indicate that the ship hit a reef within the period 1510–30. The lack of personal equipment belonging to the sailors suggests that they survived and salvaged their own possessions. Life on board was evidently very simple, to judge from the coarse tableware. Tiny glass beads found in the wreck would have been used in trade with the Taíno Indians. A more sinister aspect of Spanish trade is represented by a number of leg irons, used to restrain captives. The ship's ballast, in the form of big stones placed at the bottom of the hull during construction, is especially revealing. Analysis shows that the stones originated in various places: near Bristol; from the mid-Atlantic islands; and above all from Lisbon. This does not prove that the ship visited those places, but it does show how bits and pieces of ships were recycled, and what sort of maritime connections dominated the trade of the eastern Atlantic around 1500.[20] The Casa de Contratación in Seville that took charge of trade with the New World was founded in 1503. The fact that the Crown took an intense interest in these routes does not mean that its supervision was very effective. There were plenty of interlopers, and not just Spanish ones.[21]

Ponce de León represents the official side of trade with America. His career was moulded by the changing fortunes of his principal backer, King Ferdinand of Aragon, who was spending his money on Italian wars that brought him control of Naples but also deeper and deeper immersion in the quagmire of Italian politics. At the same time, he was trying to maintain his influence in the politics of Castile, which had been checked by the death of his wife, Isabella, in 1504, whereupon he had to cede control of Castile to his short-lived son-in-law, Philip of Burgundy, and his unbalanced daughter, Juana, later known as 'the Mad'. As if these developments were not enough, he also knew that the situation in Hispaniola was deteriorating, as the governor, Ovando, struggled to keep the claims of the Columbus family at bay; every move the Spanish government made in the Caribbean seemed to be challenged by Christopher's son Diego Colón, on the basis of the exceptionally generous grant of rights conferred on the admiral by the Catholic Monarchs way back in 1492.[22]

If Hispaniola was such a nightmare, the answer was to capitalize on the opportunities for finding gold in the other large Caribbean islands, beginning with Puerto Rico; Cuba was only invaded in 1511. Ponce was in Puerto Rico by 1508, if not sooner; he built a Spanish town and his stone house still survives. He tried to encourage the Taíno Indians to work with their new masters, and began to collect gold, providing the king with 10,000 *pesos* of tribute in 1511. But the chance that he would avoid the interference of Diego Colón was slim. In a great show of its independence from Ferdinand, the Royal Council in Castile decided that Ponce was treading on the legal rights of Diego Colón, and Ponce realized that he now had little chance of carving out a dominion in Puerto Rico. He must have known of previous attempts to explore a mainland to the north of Puerto Rico, and he was aware of legends about an island called 'Bimini' somewhere to the north. When in 1511 Ferdinand's commissioner based in Hispaniola invited him to sail north, this seemed the golden opportunity to break free from the tortuous political struggles dividing supporters of the Crown, supporters of the Columbus family and the Indian chieftains that were ruining Hispaniola and had spilled over into Puerto Rico.

More controversial is the idea that Ponce de León was sent by the ageing king of Aragon to search for the 'Fountain of Youth'.[23] This fountain would restore his virility and offer him the chance to father a child by his second wife, Germaine de Foix, giving him an heir in Aragon (though not Castile, which would pass to Juana the Mad's son, the future Habsburg emperor Charles V) – better Aragon without Castile than a Habsburg Spain. That was the practical dimension to a fantasy about the 'Fountain of Youth' that drew on both Indian and European myths, and acts as a reminder that the miraculous and strange were still an important part of European ideas about the New World.

II

Meanwhile, demand for maps of the lands Vespucci described grew and grew. A small coterie of scholars interested in geography gathered in the little town of Saint-Dié among the hills of Lorraine, under the patronage of their duke, René II, titular king of Naples. They reprinted one of Vespucci's most popular pamphlets and added to it a massive world map by Martin Waldseemüller, published in 1507, which portrayed the New World as a separate pair of continents to the linked-up continents of Europe, Asia and Africa. A small part of the southern continent was labelled AMERICA in honour of Amerigo Vespucci.[24] Although the west coast of South America was drawn as a straight line, for want of any information about it, only a fragment of North America was shown, and on the main map (though not in a miniature version in the margins) North and South America are separated by a short stretch of water close to the land Columbus had explored on his fourth voyage, without, obviously enough, finding such a channel. Vespucci's explorations southwards had revealed plenty of large rivers but no seaway that would take one towards Asia. It was becoming more and more obvious that the transatlantic routes tried so far did not and could not reach the true Indies. Waldseemüller optimistically assumed that Japan lay close to South America; he had no conception of the vastness of the Pacific. At least his judgement was more accurate than that of the maker of the small globe now preserved in the Jagiellonian University in Kraków and thought to date from around 1510. There, a transatlantic continent resembling South America is labelled as 'New World', 'Land of the Holy Cross' and 'Brazil', while an irregular chunk of land in the eastern Indian Ocean becomes 'Newly Discovered America'; here is the work of a cartographer who was thoroughly puzzled by the news that Vespucci had been exploring unknown lands in the Indies.[25]

Amid all this confusion about how to reach the Indies, John Cabot's son Sebastian set off with two ships and a royal licence, in 1509, right at the start of the reign of Henry VIII, on a voyage to Labrador and, he hoped, the route to the wealth of Asia. He reasoned that Newfoundland was blocking the way to Asia, but the strait that he found north of the island, which was probably the entrance to the large sea that became known a century later as Hudson Bay, was full of ice and his crew refused to take the ships any further.[26] In any case, Henry VII was not really interested in the sea, and his son Henry VIII was much more interested in building a fleet which would outrank that of France – one can imagine his annoyance when the French king built a ship with a tennis court and windmill on board, and his delight when it proved too heavy to float. In England, the American lands only came into focus in the second half of the sixteenth century, when Spain was a bitter enemy, and serious colonization only began when Jamestown was founded in 1607. By then Protestant England had no reason to accept the pope's division of the world between Spain and Portugal.

The French also attempted to join the race to reach the spices of the Indies by choosing a westward route. The first reported journey across the Atlantic by a French ship happened, rather like Cabral's voyage, by accident; and like Cabral its captain, Binot Paulmier de Gonneville, was not trying to reach land across the Atlantic but the ports of India. The phrase 'reported voyage' is important, because sceptics have argued that the surviving narrative of this voyage was cooked up in the seventeenth century to bolster French claims to authority in Madagascar, or South America, or some other land such as the massive, temperate 'southern continent' that was believed to encompass the bottom of the world, counterbalancing the continents of the northern hemisphere. After he published the account of Gonneville's voyage, one of the captain's descendants received the reward he craved and in 1666 was nominated as Papal Vicar in the southern continent.[27] What follows can therefore be treated as fact or fantasy.

The *Espoir*, of 150 tons, is said to have set sail in 1503; its captain came from Normandy and was named Binot Paulmier de Gonneville, and before then the furthest the *Espoir* had ever travelled was to Hamburg. This was a private expedition, not a royal one, but Gonneville was well connected and had persuaded a group of businessmen from Honfleur to invest in his risky venture.[28] Gonneville knew a certain amount about what the Portuguese had achieved in India, and he even secured the services of two Portuguese pilots, who had been out to India and who might well have been executed had they fallen into Portuguese hands.[29] Nevertheless, the ship was loaded with a good supply of armaments, to fend off enemies in the Atlantic or the Indian Ocean, including cannon, harquebuses and muskets; there were enough salted fish, dried peas, local cider and water for over a year, and enough ships' biscuit for two; and then there was the merchandise – scarlet cloths, fustians, a velvet cloth, a cloth embroidered with gold, but also simpler goods such as fifty dozen little mirrors, knives, needles and other hardware, as well as silver coins.

Claims have often been made that Norman sailors (particularly from Dieppe) knew as much about the Atlantic – or more than them – as the men of Bristol, even that they reached America a few years before Columbus in a ship commanded by a certain Jean Cousin; but like all these claims it is based on an optimistic reading of very vague evidence – in the case of Cousin the so-called evidence dates from 1785.[30] More to the point – bearing in mind that Gonneville in any case was trying to round Africa – is the simple fact that the ports of Normandy were undergoing a lively revival in the late fifteenth century now that war with England was at an end, and now that the western European economy was returning to stability after a century and a half of plague and disruption.[31] A school of mapmakers existed in Dieppe by 1540, though one can assume there were earlier mapmakers in the town, simply because it was home to ambitious merchants and mariners. Many of the maps seem to have been plagiarized from Portuguese models, despite the extreme reluctance of the Portuguese to permit others to peruse their charts.[32]

According to the surviving narrative, the *Espoir* set out from Honfleur on 24 June 1503; avoiding a landfall in the Spanish Canaries, the ship hugged the African coast and was fortunate to pass the Portuguese Cape Verde Islands without challenge. The crew spent ten days at Cape Verde itself, on the African coast; there, they traded some of their iron goods with the native Africans, buying chickens and *couchou*, 'a sort of rice', in other words the thick couscous still eaten there. The ship then swung out to sea, hoping to catch the Trade Winds and to be swept eastwards in the wake of da Gama. Instead, it was caught by fierce gales, and was swept westwards, as Cabral had been, though the crew were convinced that they were in the right latitude to pass the Cape of Good Hope – they saw *Manche-de-velours*, 'velvet sleeves', or penguins, which someone, no doubt the Portuguese pilots, identified as birds that lived on the southern tip of Africa. For weeks they were tossed about, and then drifted. However, on 5 January 1504 'they discovered a great land', which reminded them of Normandy itself.[33] The sailors felt they had gone far enough and that the ship would bear no more; they persuaded Gonneville that it was pointless to try to recover their route to India.

The inhabitants of this land were fascinated by everything they saw in the ship: 'had the Christians been angels who had come down from heaven, they could not have been more loved by these poor Indians'. Simple items of truck like knives and mirrors meant as much to them as gold, silver or even the philosopher's stone meant to Christians. They were particularly fascinated by the sight of written words on paper, for they could not understand how paper could be made to 'speak'. But the spiritual dimension was not neglected by Gonneville. The Normans built a great wooden cross in time for Easter 1504, and this was carried in barefoot procession by Gonneville and his senior crew, joyously accompanied by the Indian king, Arosca, and his sons, one of whom would later join Gonneville's ship, be taken back to Europe and marry Gonneville's daughter. Gonneville inscribed his cross with the names of King Louis XII of France and of the pope, thereby staking some sort of French claim to these lands.[34]

The *Espoir* had no better fortune on its return journey than on its outward journey. Foul weather forced the ship to put in twice on the coast of Brazil before it was able to cross the Atlantic. They found Indians whom they regarded as more primitive than Arosca's followers. They were cruel eaters of human flesh: *au reste, cruels mangeurs d'hommes*. This accusation was not levelled against Arosca's people. No less extraordinary was evidence that these man-eaters had had some contact with Christians in recent times; they possessed some trinkets that must have come from Europe, and they were not very surprised to see the ship, though they were well aware of the threat posed by European artillery. Gonneville had probably arrived in the areas visited by the slave-raiders in the last few years. The Normans were desperate to leave, and sailed off as soon as they could; the voyage home past the Azores was slow, but it was easy enough until they came within sight of home. For as they entered the waters off Jersey and Guernsey the ship fell prey to two pirates, Edward Blunth of Plymouth and Mouris Fortin, a Breton corsair. After such a long voyage the *Espoir* was in no condition to escape. The pirates caught up with, pillaged and sank the ship; many of the sailors were massacred. Only twenty-eight men reached Honfleur alive; but among them were Gonneville and his future son-in-law, Essomericq, who aroused considerable wonder, 'since there had never been anyone in France from such a distant land'.[35] However, the logbook went down with the ship, and only in the nineteenth century was a detailed narrative of the voyage discovered in the archives. Gonneville had promised King Arosca that he would return after 'twenty moons', but he never did so, and Arosca was left wondering what had happened to his long-vanished son.

Without the backing of the French king, who was more interested in laying claim to Milan and Naples, Gonneville was unable to set in train a French bid for whatever parts of Brazil he had reached. For the time being, Portugal's priorities remained in Africa and India and colonization was slow. Nevertheless, a small series of commercial ventures was aimed at Brazil. An expedition in 1501 reported that, frankly, there was little to be loaded apart from brazilwood. But this was a prized dyestuff that produced a rich reddish colour, so the next year a royal licence was granted to Fernão de Noronha or Loronha, a wealthy New Christian merchant, who agreed to send six ships each year to Brazil to collect brazilwood; in 1504 he brought back some parrots as well, and we also hear of monkeys being sent back to Lisbon. Noronha already knew the eastern Atlantic, trading in gold and slaves through São Tomé and Elmina, and he was thus a pioneer in joining together the three continents of Africa, Europe and South America. On his first journey to Brazil, Noronha discovered a beautiful offshore island that still carries his name.

King Manuel also wanted to know more about what had been discovered. It had become obvious that the assumption made by Cabral that the 'Land of the Holy Cross' was just a fairly large island did not match the news that was filtering back by way of Vespucci and others. The shoreline went on and on. So Vespucci was commanded to explore 300 leagues of the coast each year, and the Portuguese decided to set up a small fort, subject to a sliding scale of royal taxation, from zero in the first year to one quarter in the third year. In 1503–4 just such a fort and factory were built at Cabo Frio close to modern Rio de Janeiro, which already lay to the south of the areas Cabral is thought to have visited. It was staffed by twenty-four men.[36] These ships were soon bringing back about 30,000 logs (about 750 tons) each year. The ships often carried black slaves and other labourers, whose task was to trim and cut the brazilwood. Brazil's African connection therefore can be traced back to the very origins of Brazil itself. Here Noronha, with his interest in the African slave trade, played a crucial role. It turned out that the Tupí Indians were willing helpers too. In exchange for small items of truck, such as little mirrors, combs and scissors, they were happy to load logs on the Portuguese ships.[37] A small-scale trade in Brazilian slaves also developed, war captives of the Tupís for whom the expected fate was that they would be ceremoniously killed and eaten at a cannibal feast. What they thought about escaping the cooking pot, or rather griddle, for a life of captivity is not recorded.[38]

In February 1511 a ship named the *Bertoa* set out for the factory at Cabo Frio in Brazil, where it spent two months before heading back home, reaching Lisbon in October of the same year. By good fortune a manifest listing what was on board still survives. Everything in the account of the voyage suggests that trips to South America were becoming routine: the *Bertoa* set out via the Canaries and returned via the Guinea coast and the Azores, making the best use of the prevailing winds. By now it will be no surprise that the principal investors included, among the Portuguese, Fernão de Noronha, and, among the Italians based in Lisbon, Bartolomeo Marchionni, although they did not travel out with the ship. One of Marchionni's servants was aboard, however, as was one of his black slaves. The Crown also took a strong interest in the voyage, which was being conducted under royal licence, and this meant – as with the contemporary voyages to Elmina – that every stage of the journey was tightly managed and recorded. The instructions were very clear: every inch of available space was to be filled with logs of brazilwood, which seems to have left little room for the slaves, wild cats and parrots that were also to be brought back. In the end 5,008 logs were loaded, as well as thirty-six slaves, one of whom was acquired by Marchionni's servant, who also brought back cats, monkeys, parrots and parakeets. The *Bertoa* was ordered not to dally in the islands or along the coasts that lay on its route back home, but to head straight for Lisbon. No harm was to be done to the natives of Brazil. Indians who insisted they wanted to come to Portugal were under no circumstances to be allowed on board; were they to die in Europe the Tupís would assume they had been eaten by the Portuguese, 'just as they have the custom of doing among themselves'. Sailors who blasphemed were to be carried off to prison in chains when they returned to Lisbon, until they paid a hefty fine.[39]

Brazil was, then, a sideline, valued up to a point but not able to compare with Elmina or the India trade as a source of profit. Still, the arrival of loggers in Brazil was the first stage in the binding together of this corner of the Portuguese Empire with lands in Europe, Africa and Asia; after 1500 Portugal had a stake in four continents and two oceans.

III

It has been seen that French interlopers planned to reach the Indian Ocean but arrived in Brazil instead. By 1500 the reach of Dieppe extended as far as Seville in one direction and the Danish Sound in the other; among the products that reached Dieppe in this period was Madeiran sugar, brought from Portugal, while Norman ships even edged their way into the trade out of Morocco and Guinea, which the Portuguese were unable to seal off hermetically. Gonneville's expedition, if it really took place, was an exceptionally ambitious example of this constant attempt to break the Portuguese monopoly on movement across the ocean. The Normans were as adept at piracy as they were at trade, exploiting the rivalry between the French king and the duke of Burgundy in the 1470s to prey on ships trading with Burgundian Flanders. The Portuguese often thought of the Normans as 'thieves', accusing them of greed and jealousy towards the ever-growing wealth of Portugal.[40] Meanwhile the Bretons established a reputation as hardy fishermen, leaving open the possibility that they, like the Bristolians, occasionally crossed to the Newfoundland Grand Banks in search of cod even before Cabot's first voyage; and they were certainly there by 1514, when the monks of Beauport were levying a tax on cod brought back to Brittany from Newfoundland. In 1508 a Norman, Jean Aubert, sailing out of Dieppe, reached as far as Newfoundland and brought back seven Mic-Mac Indians, the first north Americans to be seen in France.[41]

One family, the Angos of Dieppe, played a particularly prominent role in the creation of the French merchant marine. Jean Ango the Elder was a fairly typical merchant, dealing in herrings, barley and other humdrum products (though also some sugar) during the 1470s and 1480s. However, his son, also Jean, greatly enlarged the family business; his interest in the sea was intellectual as well as commercial, for he seems to have received a rich education in geography, hydrography, mathematics and literature. His trade in England and Flanders brought him great wealth – he was still alive in 1541, when a report on his activities was sent to no less a person than the Holy Roman Emperor, describing Ango as 'a most rich person', and noting that 'because of his trading affairs, people call him the Viscount of Dieppe'. This also made his ships obvious targets for attack by the Portuguese: he lost boats to them off Guinea, but it is hard to see how he could complain, as his way of tapping into Portuguese trade with the Indies, or the sugar trade out of Madeira, was to launch pirate attacks on ships returning from those parts loaded with precious cargoes. The booty included Chinese silk and jewels that originated in Bengal and China. At least a million ducats' worth of loot was seized by Ango's pirates between 1520 and 1540.[42] Ango was presented to the king and became a favourite of the king's sister, Marguerite of Navarre, the famous author of the *Heptaméron*.

The king took an increasing interest in the possibilities for trade in Asiatic spices by way of the western Atlantic. By the 1520s Francis I was determined to receive a cut of transatlantic trade and gave his backing to the plans of Giovanni da Verrazano, a Florentine navigator who also had the support of Jean Ango and – not surprisingly – of Italian merchants, though from Lyons rather than Dieppe; and he made use of the new and successful Norman port of Le Havre as departure point.[43] Verrazano's name is now commemorated in a bridge linking Brooklyn to Staten Island, although the aim of his expedition was not to explore the coast of North America but to find a way to Asia: 'my intention on this voyage was to reach Cathay and the extreme eastern coast of Asia, but I did not expect to find such an obstacle of new land as I have found.'[44] He concluded that the continent he reached in 1524 was bigger than Europe or Africa, and maybe even Asia. He had hoped that he could find a route round the top of the newly discovered continent, the North-West Passage; he may well have known that Magellan had recently explored the southern tip of the Americas, which did not seem to offer a promising route to the Indies; a big ocean west of America had already been spied out by the Spanish commander Balboa standing on his 'peak in Darien' in 1513.[45] But if one could go round the bottom, maybe one could go round the top, an idea which shows that the assumption that the Americas were a gigantic isthmus sticking out of Asia was beginning to lose its power. Verrazano was *chapitano dell'Armata per l'India*, 'captain of the India Fleet', engaged on a voyage to the *espiceryes des Indes*, 'the spice-lands of the Indies', and as far as can be seen the idea of taking this route was his own.[46]

Verrazano has divided historians. In 1875 Henry Murphy looked closely at the documents and concluded that Verrazano's description of his voyage was a fiction built out of earlier descriptions of the coasts and peoples of the New World.[47] For a time that seemed to be the end of the matter, and Verrazano dropped out of history. That his systematic demolition of the story Verrazano told was rather too enthusiastic was proved when a new manuscript came to light in 1909; it is now impossible to doubt that the voyage of 1524 took place. But that is not to say that his letter contains accurate information; he may well have inflated his account, rather as Vespucci did, in order to impress his audience, especially if the audience included the vain King Francis. Murphy may not have been completely wrong. What is clear is that Verrazano sailed out on a second voyage in 1526. His fleet of four ships was scattered, and he reached Brazil, where he loaded brazilwood; but one of his ships entered the Indian Ocean, apparently trying to reach Madagascar. Instead it was blown towards Sumatra and then made its way back past the Maldives to Mozambique, where the Portuguese governor took charge of the crew and reported back to Lisbon in alarm.[48] Verrazano had apparently abandoned his idea of looking for a North-West Passage, and the obvious alternative was to break the Portuguese monopoly on the spice trade linking the Indian Ocean to the Atlantic. But the voyage can hardly be called a success. On his third voyage, in 1528, Verrazano is said to have been eaten by cannibals, though this did not deter his brother from making another remarkable

voyage the next year, from Le Havre to Brazil, then through the Mediterranean to Alexandria and back to Le Havre.[49] Long and ambitious voyages
in search of spices had become the trademark of the Verrazanos.

The story of the Verrazanos takes one well into the sixteenth century.
However, they built cleverly on the information acquired by an earlier
generation, that of Jean Ango the Elder, which was also the generation of
Columbus and Cabot. They shared with Columbus and Cabot the backing
of Florentine businessmen who were willing to chance several thousand
ducats on the possibility – and, increasingly, the likelihood – that these
voyages would produce valuable returns. In the three decades after Columbus first arrived in the Bahamas, roving explorers were increasingly
outnumbered by fleets of merchant ships that knew exactly where they
were going and had a good enough understanding of the seasons (vital in
the hurricane-ridden Caribbean) to reach their destination safely. Although
it has been suggested that in these decades roughly one fifth of the ships
on the India route eventually foundered, this figure does not mean that
one in five voyages ended in disaster, as ships were reused, repaired and
given new life. Many ended their days being broken up so their timbers
could be recirculated. The transatlantic crossing had become a trade route.

31

The Binding of the Oceans

I

And then there was the third great ocean. The first person to set eyes on it and to realize that another expanse of water separated the newly discovered continents from Cipangu and Cathay was Juan Núñez de Balboa, a Spanish *conquistador* who in 1513 was trying to create a Spanish settlement on the coast of Panama. His discovery was commemorated, under the wrong name, by John Keats:

> Or like stout Cortez when with eagle eyes
> He star'd at the Pacific – and all his men
> Look'd at each other with a wild surmise –
> Silent, upon a peak in Darien.[1]

Advised that Balboa, not Cortés, had stood upon that peak, Keats retained the name of Cortés, so that the scansion would not be ruined. Yet Cortés, conqueror of Mexico, also enters the story: at this point he was secretary to the governor of Cuba, which the Spaniards had invaded in 1511, and, as voyages to the coast of Central America became more frequent, news of a civilization rich in gold somewhere in the interior began to spread.[2] Moreover, Ponce de León's discovery of Florida suggested that the big continent to the north was probably connected by land to the big continent to the south.

If there was no route across Central America, there were three options. An icy North-West Passage over the top of America might be accessible if Asia and North America were not joined together, as they were often thought to be. This was an idea that motivated Sebastian Cabot as he tried to follow up his father's discoveries, and it was still alive in 1845, when Sir John Franklin led his ill-fated expedition into the ice floes of northern Canada.[3] Another Arctic route entered the calculations of mid-sixteenth-century English explorers, who wondered whether a North-East Passage

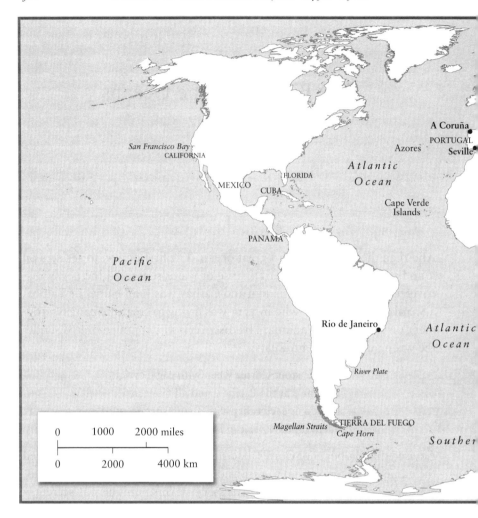

over the top of Russia all the way to China was feasible.[4] Both of these ideas, or rather fantasies, will be examined in another chapter. But there was a third possibility, based on Vespucci's observations, accurate and otherwise, about the extended coastline of South America. Just as Catalan and Portuguese explorers of the fourteenth and fifteenth centuries had imagined that a channel or river might cut right across Africa, Spanish explorers now held out hope for a more direct route to the Spice Islands rather than the long haul around south Africa through hostile waters in which, as will be seen, Ottoman navies contested control with the sparse and scattered fleets of Portugal. A route round South America might offer Spain its chance to dominate the spice trade, by taking the spices eastwards out of the Indies towards America and then Europe.

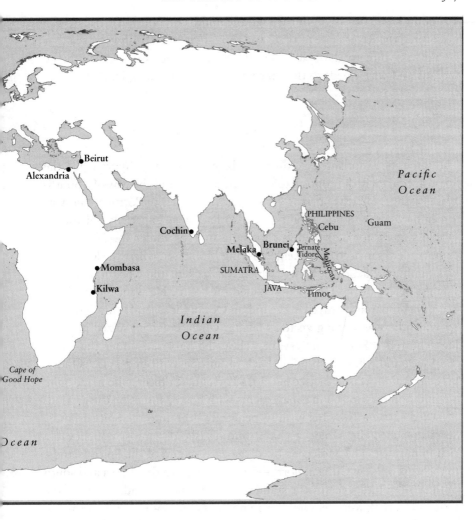

At the end of his life King Ferdinand of Aragon was playing with several ideas about how he might challenge Portugal's dominance of the oceanic trade in spices. It makes sense to use the adjective 'oceanic' because there were still spices to be had in the eastern Mediterranean, though the conquest of Egypt and Syria by the Ottoman Turks had only increased the risks of going to Alexandria and Beirut to buy them. In 1512 Ferdinand gave his support to a plan to send ships round the Cape of Good Hope, in the wake of Portuguese ships; the target was to be *Maluco*, the Moluccas, 'which lie within our demarcation', and ultimately China, but the challenge to the Portuguese in the Indian Ocean was too obvious, and the scheme never materialized. Three years later he commissioned the same commander, Juan de Solís, to lead a voyage westwards that would find a way round the bottom of, or through the middle of, South America. Solís discovered the River Plate in 1516, and thought it was a freshwater sea that would take him to the Spice Islands. However, Solís fell out with the Indians and was killed, so the survivors turned back to Spain.[5]

II

The same idea motivated Ferdinand Magellan when he approached the Spanish court with a proposal to reach the Spice Islands by way of a South-West Passage. He was born as Fernão de Magalhães in Portugal and was a member of the minor nobility; he also had close experience of Indian Ocean waters, for he sailed out to India in 1505 under the Portuguese commander Francisco de Almeida, visiting Mombasa, where the local ruler was summarily deposed; Kilwa, which was sacked; and Cochin, where he saw the spices of the East being loaded on board. He went out again in 1507, and apparently stayed in the Indian Ocean for several years. The fleet on which he was serving visited Melaka, which Portugal seized in 1511. He acquired a Sumatran servant, whom he baptized under the name 'Enrique', and whom he brought back to Europe in around 1512.[6] One of his companions was Francisco Serrão, a Portuguese officer, who made quite a reputation for himself in engagements with hostile forces on the ground.

Lured eastwards by his wish to penetrate deep into the Spice Islands, Serrão reached the Molucca chain, finding islands almost unbelievably rich in nutmeg. The Moluccas lie at the eastern end of the Spice Islands, to the west of New Guinea, north-east of the eastern tip of Java and south of the Philippines; even by the standards of the ancient trade routes of the East Indies they were remote. But remoteness did not erode their fame – rather the opposite; these were seen as the most desirable of all the Spice Islands. After a number of adventures, during which he lost his ship and took over a pirate vessel that had been chasing him, Serrão sorted out a bitter dispute between the rival Moluccan sultans of Ternate and Tidore, both of whom were Muslim. The sultan of Ternate was so impressed that he appointed this Portuguese Christian as his vizier. Serrão sent letters to Magellan in Melaka in which he told of his luxurious life at the court of the sultan of Ternate, and described the lush lands full of precious spices in which he now lived: 'I have found here a New World richer and greater than that of Vasco da Gama.'[7] India was already an extraordinary distance by sea from Portugal, Melaka another great leap, but reaching the Moluccas meant making a half-circle around the world. Serrão was very possibly the first European to find his way to the Moluccas, and it is one of those constant ironies of the age of exploration that his extraordinary career has received so little attention. (A rival case can be made for the Italian traveller Ludovico di Varthema, who travelled extensively in Asia between 1503 and 1508 and claimed to have seen cloves growing in a place he called Monoch, which may be one of the Moluccas.)[8] Serrão showed that it was all very well to control Melaka, but Melaka was itself the main point of trans-shipment for the spices that came from still further to the east; and, while the pepper of south India was a great prize, the cloves, cinnamon and camphor of the Spice Islands might be accessible at their point of origin. This would be the culmination of all those schemes to reach the source of spices, for the Portuguese still relied on middlemen to obtain the spices they bought in Melaka.

Magellan therefore knew a great deal about the lands he was trying to reach from personal experience and from his friend's enthusiastic letter; and Varthema's book of travels had been published in 1510. However, despite his rich experience, Magellan was not made welcome at the Portuguese court, where he was accused of trading illicitly with the Moors in north Africa; and King Manuel was determined to press on with what had already been achieved by breaking into the Indian Ocean.[9] The Portuguese capture of Melaka in 1511 seemed to guarantee access to the Spice Islands through the traditional routes followed by Indian Ocean navigators over many centuries. There was no obvious reason to look for a westward route, especially because this would dissipate precious resources that needed to be spent on keeping open the supply lines through Guinea, south Africa and the Indian ports where Portuguese factories had been established.[10]

Selling the scheme to the new king of Castile, Charles of Ghent, was therefore somewhat easier than selling it to King Manuel. It is important to realize that Magellan never had it in mind to circumnavigate the globe, for all his extraordinary achievements.[11] The purpose of his expedition was to reach the East Indies, to load his ships with spices, and to return the way he had come; the fundamental error, which he shared with Columbus, was to assume that the distance between Europe and Asia, sailing westwards, was much smaller than it actually is. Moreover, Magellan was killed in the Philippines at a point 124°E, and did not enter the Indian Ocean. (He had, however, sailed as far east as 128°E earlier in his career, so that he went round the world in separate journeys.)[12] The captain who did leave from and return to Seville was the Basque Juan Sebastian Elcano, who took command of the expedition after Magellan was killed and managed to steer one leaky, rotten hull back to Spain through the Indian Ocean and the Atlantic, travelling through four oceans, since he sailed through the Atlantic twice. Nor did Magellan open a regular route linking

Spain to its Pacific Ocean possessions in the Philippines; as will be seen, the solution to the question of how to reach those islands was quite different. None of these reservations undermines the claim of the Magellan–Elcano voyage of 1519–22 to be the most ambitious and impressive act of seamanship in the age of discovery. But, as with Columbus, what was planned and what was achieved were very different.

The basis for Magellan's expedition had to be the past agreements between the kings of Castile and Portugal, mediated by the pope. But one can also see the influence of past agreements at a lower level: as in the case of Columbus, Magellan and a cartographer named Faleiro were to enjoy a monopoly on trade to the lands they found, but the Crown had learned a little from its mistakes, and this monopoly was limited to ten years, to avoid the endless lawsuits that were still being pressed by Columbus's heirs. They also received handsome tax privileges, 20 per cent of the profits from the first voyage, and the hereditary office of governor of the lands they brought under Spanish rule, always bearing in mind the need to avoid interfering in lands that lay under Portuguese rule. This, however, was the real complication: Magellan and Faleiro had managed to persuade King Charles that the Moluccas lay within the Spanish half of the world, assuming one could extend the Tordesillas line through the North and South Poles and wrap it round the world, but there was no chance the Portuguese court would accept that. Faleiro has been described as 'something of a madman', 'a brilliant but deranged man', who encouraged Magellan to underestimate the breadth of the Pacific, rather as Columbus had underestimated the distance to Cipangu and Cathay.[13]

III

Charles agreed to send five ships under Magellan's command in search of the passage to Asia. When they set out from Seville in 1519 they carried a motley crew of 260 men that included forty Basque sailors, among them the future commander, Elcano, although there were also Portuguese, black Africans, Germans, Frenchmen, Flemings, Irishmen, Italians and Greeks, as well as a single Englishman, Andrew of Bristol, who was chief gunner, plus Magellan's Sumatran servant, Enrique.[14] The identity of the crew serves as a reminder that the voyages of discovery were not simply the work of Portuguese, Castilians and the occasional Italian. But aboard Magellan's ships was one of those occasional Italians: a patrician from Vicenza, Antonio Pigafetta, signed up as a passenger, adding his name to the list of curious Italians who were prepared to risk their lives to see unknown parts of the world, a successor to Vespucci and Varthema. He wrote an account of the entire voyage, which remains the principal source of knowledge about what happened.[15] He was a great admirer of Magellan, which skews his account in one direction; but he survived the entire voyage, carrying on westwards under the command of Elcano, whom he disliked so much that he never even mentioned him by name in his narrative.

The challenge Magellan faced was not simply that of keeping a hostile crew (Pigafetta apart) under control; nor was it simply that of finding an unknown passage to India. He also needed to sail clear of his own compatriots, for Portuguese patrols were looking out for Spanish and other interlopers, and news of his plans had infuriated the Portuguese court, even if King Manuel had never believed in Magellan's scheme. The journey across the Atlantic followed a peculiar route, staying close to the Guinea shore in worryingly calm waters before the ships were tossed about in November storms as they attempted to reach South America. Magellan's unorthodox route down the African coast irritated his Spanish officers, who had expected to strike out for the New World from Spanish-controlled Tenerife. The lack of trust between them and Magellan was a constant problem, fed by the traditional dislike of Castilians for their Portuguese neighbours. There was some comfort in the safe arrival of the little fleet off Rio de Janeiro in December 1519, which was high summer in the southern hemisphere, but lack of faith in Magellan's abilities revived when the estuary of the River Plate was decisively shown not to offer a route through South America to Asia. Travelling south from there in February 1520 the ships met late summer storms, and the slower they progressed the greater became the danger that food supplies would be exhausted. The crew were put on short rations. The officers demanded that Magellan should keep them properly informed about what route he planned to take. The frustration of blindly following orders without knowing the why and the wherefore of Magellan's decisions undermined still further their belief in his abilities.

All this led to mutiny, with Elcano among those condemned to death, though in due course he was pardoned and even promoted.[16] Magellan was perfectly well aware that he could not execute forty of his own crew as mutineers. The main punishment was symbolic; the mutinous captain of the ship *Victoria* had already been killed in fighting between Magellan's supporters and the mutineers. His body was hung upside down from the yardarm as a warning to all who dreamed of opposing the admiral. The rebellion gave Magellan the excuse to appoint Portuguese officers to the command of his ships – one of them, João Serrão, was the brother or cousin of his old friend Francisco Serrão, who had ended up as vizier of the sultan of Ternate, and whom Magellan was determined to meet when he reached the Spice Islands. Pigafetta, meanwhile, was fascinated by the Patagonian 'giants' whom the sailors met as they penetrated further and further south. Their ability to live almost naked in such a cold climate was only one of their remarkable features; tall and thin, the Patagonians had adapted well to the cold, since their body surface was actually smaller than that of the more compact but relatively tubby population further north. Their willingness to eat rats found on board ship, unskinned, surprised and rather disgusted the explorers.[17]

The greatest challenge of all, however, came when Magellan's fleet reached the strait that he correctly identified as a passage through the southern tip of South America, later known as the Strait of Magellan. Pigafetta claimed that Magellan knew all about the strait already because he had seen a chart in the treasury of the king of Portugal made by 'Martin of Bohemia', who must be Martin Behaim, the creator of the globe made in around 1492 that still survives in Nuremberg and does not show any part of America. Behaim died in Lisbon in 1507, so Magellan may well have met him. However, a German globe of 1515 did speculatively include a channel between South America and a great southern continent. This globe was created by Johannes Schöner, who, like Behaim, hailed from Nuremberg; it also included a channel between North and South America and placed Japan only a few degrees west of America.[18] It was not obvious to Magellan that the land on his southern quarter, which became known as Tierra del Fuego (owing to the fires he saw there, possibly lit by Patagonian inhabitants), was simply a medium-sized island that ended at a great cape, Cape Horn. To him it seemed to be another vast landmass. This idea persisted, so that the first world map of the famous cartographer Mercator, of 1538, marked the Magellan Strait as the channel between two continents, one of which, the *Terra Australis*, covered the entire southern tip of the world, like a great enlarged Antarctica.[19]

Navigating these stormy waters, through channels that led in different directions, and that were constantly buffeted by the so-called williwaw winds, cold blasts that seemed to explode from nowhere, depended on a combination of intuition and luck, and one of his captains decided to turn back to Spain. The desertion of the *San Antonio* reduced his fleet to three ships, as one had already been wrecked while exploring the South American coast. By the end of November 1520 he had entered a new ocean. Pigafetta remarked: 'during these three months and twenty days, we sailed in a gulf where we made a good four thousand leagues across the Pacific sea, which was rightly so named. For during this time we had no storm.'[20] The experiences of later navigators would give the lie to the name 'Pacific', but at last the greatest of all oceans had a European name and – more importantly – it became obvious how gigantic this sea is: leaving Tierra del Fuego on 28 November 1520, Magellan only reached Guam on 6 March 1521. This was the first proper landfall, for, oddly, the three ships did not encounter the islands and peoples of Polynesia and Micronesia as they headed for what they hoped were the Moluccas. Nor, apparently, did they meet any Pacific islanders in their splendid outrigger boats until they arrived at Guam. This is testimony to the sheer vastness of the Pacific Ocean, but it also shows that the land-sighting skills of European navigators accustomed to the very different waters of the Atlantic Ocean were quite different to those of the Polynesians, who could find needles in the Pacific haystack without great difficulty.

The real difficulty that Magellan's crew faced as they crossed the Pacific was not the weather but the lack of supplies of fresh food that left the sailors trading in rat meat and chewing rehydrated oxhides for their dinner, so long as they could chew anything. The scourge of scurvy made these long voyages a deathtrap, not just because of the dramatic effects of this disease on skin, bones and blood vessels, which to all intents fall apart, but also because of its side effects: it was impossible to eat what food there was with massively swollen gums. Thirty-one men died of scurvy or other illnesses during the Pacific crossing, including a Patagonian giant and a Brazilian Indian. When the ships at last reached land, islanders swarmed aboard, robbed the ships and were fought off; the sick sailors asked for the entrails of the islanders who had been killed in this engagement, in the belief that by eating them 'immediately they would be healed'. The true solution was there to be seen: when the crew started to eat fresh fruit and vegetables, the swelling shrank away. Moreover, the officers on board, with a more luxurious diet, by and large escaped from the disease, so that Pigafetta, for one, 'being always in good health', observed scurvy without suffering from it: 'yet by the grace of our Lord I had no illness', which was still the case when he returned to Spain.[21] The discovery that lemons or limes kept scurvy at bay was the result of trial and error between 1746 and 1795, when the Royal Navy began to include lemons or limes in the diet of British sailors, and only the identification of ascorbic acid (vitamin C) in the early twentieth century explained how and why limes worked so well.[22]

IV

When Magellan reached the islands of the western Pacific, he encountered lands very different in culture and social structure to those he had left behind in Patagonia. Admittedly, the first islands he reached, around

Guam, revealed societies that made no use of metal and where people walked around almost naked; because the islanders had run amok on board the Spanish ships, seizing everything they could carry away, Magellan's men called this place the 'Island of Thieves'. Pigafetta thought that the islanders believed that they were the only people in the world, but he was relying, as he admitted, on sign language, and what they were no doubt expressing was their disbelief that the shaggy-looking sailors on their vast wooden ships were of the same genus as themselves. They were people of the sea, whose boats decorated with palm leaf sails and outriggers 'are like dolphins jumping from wave to wave'.[23]

Gradually, though, the ships navigated their way through islands blessed with an abundance of chickens, palm wine, coconuts and sweet oranges (a novelty, as the oranges known in the west were the bitter Seville oranges introduced to Spain by the Arabs). There was even some gold, which was used to decorate the islanders' daggers. As the ships penetrated deeper into the Philippine chain in March and April 1521, they found new friends among the local rajahs; it was a great help that Magellan's Sumatran servant, Enrique, was able to speak with one of these rajahs in Malay and make himself understood. The rajah presented Magellan with porcelain jars filled with rice, and offered presents of gold and ginger; Magellan gave the king a red-and-yellow robe, 'made in the Turkish fashion'. The rajah organized a reception for the officers, and Pigafetta found himself eating meat on Good Friday, 'being unable to do otherwise'; on the other hand, it was a relief to discover that the rulers of these islands were 'heathens' and not 'Moors'. An even greater luxury than dinner with the rajah was the chance to sleep in a soft bed made out of a mat of reeds, with cushions and pillows.

In the spirit of previous explorers under the Spanish flag, Pigafetta noted that this rajah had a brother who ruled over a neighbouring island that contained 'mines of gold, which is found by digging from the earth large pieces as large as walnuts and eggs', with the result that the king dined off gold plates as a matter of course.[24] The sight of Chinese porcelain here, and on islands they visited later, was a sure sign that they were not far from the luxurious empire that a generation of explorers had been trying to reach: 'porcelain is a kind of very white earthenware, and is fifty years underground before being worked, for otherwise it would not be fine. And the father buries it for the son. And if poison or venom is put into a fine porcelain jar, it will immediately break.'[25] This was evidence for trade between the Chinese ports and the Spice Islands, but Magellan preferred to find a route to the clove-scented Moluccas; after all, his fleet was the *Armada de Molucca*.

All this promised good results; yet the deeper Magellan's ships penetrated into this island world, the more the captain-general became aware of the difficulties he still faced in winning the confidence of the rajahs. The rajah of Cebu expected to receive tribute or taxes, which he levied on all boats that called at his shores. A *iunco*, or junk, had come in from 'Ciama', either Vietnam or Java, four days before Magellan arrived; the rajah introduced one of Magellan's officers to a Muslim merchant who had reached Cebu aboard the junk, and the merchant not very helpfully warned the rajah:

> 'Have good care, O king, what you do, for these men are of those who have conquered Calicut, Malacca, and all India the Greater. If you give them good reception and treat them well, it will be well for you, but if you treat them ill, so much the worse it will be for you, as they have done at Calicut and at Malacca.'[26]

Fortunately Enrique, the Sumatran interpreter, understood what was being said, and 'told them that his master's king was even more powerful in ships and by land than the king of Portugal, and he declared that he was the king of Spain and emperor of all Christendom', a fair point since Charles had already been elected to the throne of the Holy Roman Empire. This riposte was combined with threats of a Spanish invasion which cannot have made Charles of Spain sound a better friend than Manuel of Portugal.

These threats did not destroy increasingly warm relations between Magellan and the rajah. If Pigafetta is to be believed, he swore fealty to the king of Spain and joined in the mass baptism of hundreds of islanders, as well as the querulous Moorish merchant. It hardly needs to be said that this did not result in the Christianization of Cebu, and that the inhabitants slipped back to their 'heathen' ways when the ships departed, just as loyalty to King Charles was easily forgotten. However, the insistence on conversion is something that can easily be lost to sight when looking at the voyages of discovery. There was a genuine desire to spread the faith; at the same time, the conversion of the rajahs of these islands would help bond them closer to the Spanish masters to whom they were nominally subject.[27]

Cebu brought disaster upon the little fleet. A number of outlying islands refused to accept Magellan's demand that they should place themselves under the control of the rajah of Cebu, who was henceforth to be the Spanish king's representative. In other words, the real issue was not the authority of the king of Spain, about which the islanders cannot have cared, but the authority of an overweening rajah whom Magellan was enthusiastically supporting. In April 1521 Magellan, against the advice of João Serrão, insisted on joining an armed attack on one of these islands, Mactan. There, the invaders faced stiff resistance, and Magellan was killed.[28] Soon after, the rajah of Cebu turned against the Spaniards and massacred twenty-seven men whom he had invited to a feast; they included João Serrão. This was a world of which the Spaniards knew very little indeed, apart from the existence of spices, and it had been a foolish mistake to become embroiled in local rivalries; after all, Magellan did not think of Cebu as his destination; he was still searching for the fabled Moluccas. Clearly it was time to move on, and in July 1521 the ships visited Brunei in Borneo, with their captains still determined to find a route to the Moluccas. Then as now Brunei had a wealthy court, and Elcano, soon to be the leader of the remnant who returned to Europe, found himself riding an elephant and being instructed in the elaborate protocol required when one entered the presence of the rajah. One was not allowed to address the ruler directly; instead one told a courtier, who told a brother of the ruler, who whispered the message to the rajah through a speaking tube, which cannot always have resulted in very accurate messages reaching his ear. The Spaniards were not at all awestruck by the solemnity of their interview and found these rules quite comic.[29]

They set sail for the marvellous Moluccas, and reached the islands in November 1521. The sultan of Tidore, Rajah Sultan Mansur, told his visitors that he had had a strange dream a long time ago which foretold the arrival of ships sailing to the Moluccas from far-off lands. He was friendly, to the point where he proposed renaming Tidore 'Castile' out of love for the Spanish king. Pigafetta took great delight in the clove trees and learned how the spices were harvested, and was interested to see how the inhabitants made bread out of sago, a starchy food extracted from palm stems that was the staple crop in the Moluccas and remains a firm favourite in south-east Asia. But there was bad news about Francisco Serrão. He had become the commander of the troops of the rival ruler of Ternate, and during a struggle between the two sultanates he had carried off many of the chief men of Tidore as hostages. After peace was made, he visited Tidore to buy cloves. But he was deeply resented; he was given poisoned betel leaves to chew and died within a few days. This had happened only eight months earlier; Serrão had still been alive when Magellan set out from Spain.[30]

The *Armada de Molucca* had now reached waters that were also being probed by Portuguese based in Melaka, even if their appearances were spasmodic and their expeditions unofficial. The Spaniards met a Portuguese merchant named Pedro Afonso de Lorosa in Tidore; he arrived in a local boat, or *prao*, and he, like the late Serrão, lived in Ternate. He claimed to have spent sixteen years in India and ten years in the Moluccas. He knew of a 'great ship of Malacca' that had reached the Moluccas just under a year ago, commanded by a Portuguese captain, Tristão de Meneses, who had already heard that the Spanish king had sent a fleet out of Seville towards the Molucca Islands. Pedro Afonso was delightfully garrulous and quite incapable of keeping a secret. He told the Spaniards that the king of Portugal had reacted furiously to reports of Magellan's voyage. He sent ships to the River Plate and to the Cape of Good Hope to block Magellan's armada, since he did not know which route it would actually take. He also encouraged one of his captains in the Indian Ocean to sail to the Moluccas in search of Magellan with six heavily armed ships; however, when this commander heard that the Ottoman Turks were planning an expedition against Melaka he headed westwards instead, towards the coast of Arabia, sending a smaller convoy, which was forced back by contrary winds. Pedro Afonso claimed that the Moluccas were already loyal to Portugal, and that the ever-secretive court in Lisbon had simply not wanted anyone to know of its success out there.[31]

Maybe he imagined that all this would deter Elcano; far from it. He loaded one ship, the *Victoria*, with cloves and set out for Spain by way of the Indian Ocean, carrying a crew of forty-seven sailors who had endured the voyage so far, but sixty in all as they had taken on board some native inhabitants during their travels. A handful of sailors were left in Tidore so that they could set up a Spanish base there. The other seaworthy ship, the *Trinidad*, would take the trans-Pacific route home with a crew of fifty-three men and nearly fifty tons of cloves, but not by way of the Strait of Magellan; the idea was to send it to Panama and then trans-ship its cargo across Central America and into the Caribbean, always assuming it could find its way and that there was anyone in Panama waiting to greet its arrival. The *Trinidad* struggled to find a route, ending up in the latitude of Japan and then turning back to Tidore. Alas for her, Tidore had already been visited by a Portuguese squadron which was searching for the Spanish flotilla; the Portuguese closed down the Spanish station, set up their own on Ternate, and found the *Trinidad*, from which they seized the cargo. Just as importantly, they seized the charts they found on board; the Portuguese were quite determined to keep knowledge of these waters a secret. If anything, the Spanish expedition had drawn the Portuguese deeper into the Spice Islands. Eventually one survivor escaped and three were sent back to Lisbon, where prison awaited them – one found that his wife had remarried, assuming he had died at sea.[32] Yet the idea that the only way for Spain to maintain contact with the East Indies across the

Pacific was by way of Central America, rather than through the Magellan Strait, was a sound one, as later events would show.

Elcano also faced a Portuguese threat. His route home would take him right through the waters that the heirs of da Gama were now trying to dominate. He could expect to pass Portuguese patrols, and calling in at coastal stations to take on water and food was beyond consideration. His voyage did start well, though, with a useful visit to Timor, where excellent sandalwood was to be had. Between early February and early May he was at sea between Timor and the southern tip of Africa, sailing far to the south, avoiding Java and Sumatra, where the Portuguese were known to trade; meat taken on board turned rotten, and a landfall in south Africa took them to sterile land where no food was found: as Elcano wrote to the king of Spain after his return, 'when we had left the last island behind, we subsisted for five months on nothing but corn, rice and water'. Fifteen Europeans and ten inhabitants of the Spice Islands died on this stretch. Worse was to come, as the *Victoria* still had to wend its way past the Portuguese bases in west Africa. The only solution to the lack of supplies was to put in at Ribeira Grande, the capital of the Cape Verde Islands. The crew told the Portuguese customs officials that they had got lost on their return from the Caribbean, but when an attempt was made to pay with cloves for food and slaves (needed as extra hands), it became obvious that the ship had been poaching on what the Portuguese regarded as their part of the world. Elcano was alert enough to realize that he must set sail at once, but he still had to cope with the prevailing winds, which demanded he should take a convoluted route past the Azores to reach Iberia. On 4 September his lookout spied Cape St Vincent and by 8 September the worm-eaten hulk of the *Victoria* was tied up on the quayside at Seville. Eighteen Europeans had survived the trip.[33]

Elcano had brought specimens of the crops he had found in the Moluccas and Philippines as well as descriptions of crops he had seen and their location; the emperor was impressed enough to write to his aunt, Margaret of Austria, that 'one of our ships has returned laden with cloves and with specimens of all the other spices, such as pepper, cinnamon, ginger, nutmeg, and also sandalwood. Further, I have received tokens of submission from the rulers of four of the islands.'[34] Elcano also brought home something much more valuable than a large cargo – intelligence about what could be found in the eastern extremities of the Spice Islands. The actual weight of the cargo he brought has been estimated at about 20,800 kg, of which more than a twentieth belonged to Elcano. This meant that the costs of the expedition were met, with a small profit – very roughly the same amount as Elcano's share. A return of 5–6 per cent was rather feeble, but it was also obvious that the profit would be very much higher if this could made into a regular sea route.[35]

V

How to create such a sea route was the problem. The Portuguese would continue to stand in the way, denying that the large western Pacific islands fell within the Spanish half of the world. Discussions with Portugal about where the lines between the Spanish and the Portuguese hemisphere should be drawn achieved nothing, because it was impossible even to agree on where the line sliced through the Atlantic; for a start there were conflicting views about which of the scattered Cape Verde Islands should be used as marker.[36] In addition, not everyone was happy about Elcano's conduct as captain, and still less about Magellan's, so that commissions of enquiry delayed plans for a second expedition along the same route round South America. Elcano's fears for his life, which led Charles V to assign a bodyguard to him, were mainly prompted by the knowledge that the Portuguese would happily kill to reserve their monopoly.[37] A new expedition set out in July 1525 under the leadership of Garcia Jofre de Loaísa, who was no sailor and who would therefore depend on his pilot-major – Elcano. The fleet consisted of seven ships, carrying 450 men, including four gluttons for punishment who had served with Magellan. But these men had seen what the Far East had to offer and were eager bounty hunters. Moreover, the great Augsburg banking house of the Fuggers, the wealthiest bank in Europe, was willing to invest in the expedition. No doubt this was an opportunistic throw of the dice; the Fuggers can have had few illusions about the dangers involved, whether from natural hazards or enemy attacks, but they were rich enough to be able to take a chance and threw 10,000 gold ducats into the pot. The Spanish dream was to make A Coruña in Galicia the new Lisbon, the base from which the spices of the East Indies would be shipped on to Antwerp and from there into the wider European market.[38]

Though much was gained from past experience, only four ships out of seven actually reached the Strait of Magellan, and Loaísa himself died, with the result that Elcano once again found himself in charge – for a week. For he too did not survive the journey across the Pacific, and three of his brothers also died on the voyage. He had been hoping to achieve the great ambition of Christopher Columbus: to find the route to Japan. The plan was to head for Japan and then to turn southwards towards the Moluccas. The crew of the ship on which Loaísa and Elcano had been sailing did reach Tidore, only to find that the Portuguese were now installed nearby in rival Ternate, and had recently sacked Tidore. Disaster struck another ship, which struggled to reach Mexico and made contact with the *conquistador* Hernán Cortés. Finding Cortés was the salvation not just of these Spanish castaways but of Loaísa's ship, which had ended up in Tidore, where the survivors spent their time fending off the Portuguese; little did they realize that they would end up spending more than a decade in these islands before being sent home.

Cortés had already been corresponding with the Spanish court about routes to the Indies, and the court was keen for him to find out what had happened to Loaísa's ships. With an eye on the profits he could make as an intermediary in the spice trade, he saw that a route from Mexico to the Spice Islands made much more sense than the elongated route around the bottom of South America, which risked capture in Portuguese waters off Brazil. What the Spaniards really wanted was to carry off some clove bushes and replant them in Mexico, which would render the Portuguese spice route around Africa redundant. Somehow Cortés launched three ships on the Pacific, under the command of his cousin Saavedra, who then set off for Tidore with the aim of carrying off the survivors from Loaísa's ships (about 120 people in all). Two ships went down near Hawai'i. But in an all too typical act of the time, the crew of the third ship, the *Florida*, reached Tidore, looked at what was going on, decided there were too many people to take off the island, and filled its empty spaces with a cargo of cloves instead. Trying to beat its way back to Mexico, the *Florida* made no progress and was forced to return to Tidore. Several attempts to sail away were frustrated by the winds, and all these Spaniards languished in the East Indies for years as unwilling guests of the Portuguese, who were not clear what to do with them; eventually, in 1534, most of them were sent back to Lisbon. Andrés de Urdaneta, who was on board keeping the ship's accounts, did not reach Spain until 1536, and will be met again in a later chapter.[39]

The Spaniards were keen to find out much more about the ocean Magellan had entered, with an emphasis on the Pacific shores of their growing American empire that now embraced not just Mexico but Peru. Cortés and the viceroy of New Spain, Mendoza, were eager patrons of voyages up and down the American coastlines as well, leading to the mapping of the coast of Lower and parts of Upper California between 1539 and 1542. The name most closely associated with the opening up of Upper California to Spanish shipping is that of Juan Rodríguez Cabrillo (although the Chumash Indians around Santa Barbara are still there to object that they knew about the coast all along). Cabrillo set out with three ships, the largest of which was a small galleon named the *San Salvador*, of about 200 tons' displacement. In many ways his most impressive achievement was the construction of these ships, as well as ships for other explorers, in an inhospitable river mouth on the Pacific coast of America. He brought in Spanish artisans and used native labour, and African slaves for the most unpleasant work: hauling objects as heavy as anchors from the Atlantic coast across to the shipyard in Guatemala. The great advantage of this site was that there was plenty of good, hard wood to be had.

Cabrillo tested the *San Salvador*, and the quality of his crew, by taking the galleon on a trading voyage to Peru, where he sold horses at the highly inflated prices they then fetched in a land where they had been unknown until the arrival of Pizarro's conquering armies a little more than a decade earlier.[40] Traffic continued to grow along the stretch of coast linking Central America to Peru, so that even before the Spaniards had mastered the art of sailing right across the Pacific, they were adept at navigation along the eastern shores of the ocean. Cabrillo's Californian voyage reached as far north as San Francisco Bay, without discovering what they had hoped to find: a channel that would enable ships to pass through the North American continent, which had a name, the Strait of Anían, but no existence. Even if they did not find the strait, there was the lure of a mythical kingdom, that of Queen Calafia, who ruled over a population of black Amazons. It was rich in gold, and man-eating griffins were used to carry heavy goods around.[41]

Elcano and the *Victoria* had crossed three oceans. A few Portuguese had already passed all the way through the Atlantic, had crossed the Indian Ocean and had penetrated the Pacific as far as the eastern Spice Islands. But the sheer stamina, determination and fortitude involved in bringing one ship the whole way around the world continues to astonish. It might seem odd, then, to finish this chapter on a negative note, not just because Magellan, Elcano and Loaísa were not thinking of circumnavigating the world when they planned their expeditions, but because the route taken by the *Victoria* was proved not really to work. More thought was needed about how to extend Spanish dominion across the Pacific, and about how to use a route from Mexico to the Spice Islands in order to ferry silks, spices and porcelain from the Far East to America and Europe.

32

A New Atlantic

I

Even though Columbus took a long while to set foot on the American mainland and even though he soon became *persona non grata* in Hispaniola, his voyages completely transformed Atlantic navigation. Spanish sailors seized the opportunity to look for profit in the New World with enthusiasm. The constant warnings from Queen Isabella that they must take care not to enslave the native population, at least on those islands that were claimed by the Spanish Crown, provides clear evidence that this did happen on an increasing scale by 1500, as does the complete depopulation of the Bahamas by about 1520, after their inhabitants were carried off to work in the gold mines and sugar plantations that were the main attraction of Hispaniola, or were captured by slavers. The history of European relations with the Taínos of Hispaniola and neighbouring islands offers a devastating indictment of Spanish policy in the New World, even if no one could have predicted that the arrival of European diseases such as smallpox would wipe out tens, and maybe hundreds, of thousands of Taínos before these diseases wreaked even worse havoc on the American mainland. The increasing demands laid upon the Taínos by Columbus and his successors also destroyed their communities: backbreaking work in the gold fields demanded more energy than their simple diet of cassava bread could supply; the separation of males from their families meant that the birth rate fell – these and other changes wiped out the Taínos within thirty years of Columbus's arrival in the New World. The persistent pleas of the Dominican friars Montesinos and Las Casas, enriched by terrifying stories of the mistreatment of the Indians (treated like 'excrement' according to Las Casas), fell on deaf ears in the Caribbean. Eventually, it is true, Las Casas gained an audience among conscience-stricken courtiers back in Spain. By then it was too late. Isabella's great-grandson Philip II sat on the Spanish throne. The Taínos had long ago disappeared.[1]

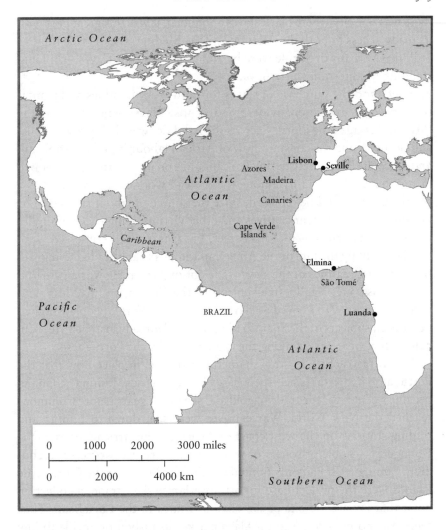

Today, the genetic profile of the inhabitants of the Dominican Republic, constituting the greater part of Hispaniola, reveals how massive this collapse in population actually was: taken as a whole, modern Dominicans are 29 per cent southern European in ancestry (including 0.5 per cent Neanderthal), and only 3.6 per cent Taíno. The largest single element in Dominican DNA is west African, accounting for nearly 45 per cent, with a further scattering of DNA from central and southern Africa.[2] Denuded of native workers, the Spanish lords of the Caribbean began to import thousands of west Africans, easily available by way of the Portuguese trading stations on the other side of the Atlantic. The Spaniards were already perfectly familiar with slaves from sub-Saharan Africa, many of whom could be found on the streets of Seville around 1500; indeed, if there was one city where black slaves abounded, it was this great port with its ready access to both the Atlantic and the Mediterranean trade routes.[3] Still, the Africans of Seville were by and large domestic slaves, in a long-standing Mediterranean tradition.

After 1500 the purchase of slaves for hard work in mines and plantations became ever more widespread. Those slaves who survived the 'Middle Passage', the journey across the Atlantic, were likely to be robust and resilient, and the constant flow of African labour into the Caribbean, and, once the Portuguese decided to capitalize on its resources, into Brazil, meant that high mortality among the African workers was not seen as a problem: they could be replaced, since the source of labour seemed to be bottomless: African war captives and other victims of internecine conflict in west Africa. For much of his career, Las Casas was so obsessed (with good reason) by the fate of the American Indians that he failed to register the appalling realities of the slave trade out of Africa. He was aware that the Indians were, legally, free subjects of the Crown, and had less sympathy for those who arrived as slaves in the New World, people who had never been subjects of the Spanish kings but had already lost their freedom before they were passed along the trade routes by the Portuguese.

The infrastructure for this shameful trade was in place now that the Portuguese had established their bases in west Africa. Elmina in Ghana became a centre for the trade in gold and slaves ten years before Columbus reached the New World. War captives were sent down to Elmina and trading stations on the west coast of Africa by the African allies of the Portuguese – noble prisoners of war, peasant farmers, women and children. Elmina itself had only limited holding facilities; but the Cape Verde Islands were the perfect base for a transatlantic slave trade, a collection point that lay astride one of the obvious routes to the Caribbean. Thus there was no need to go to the slave market in Lisbon or Seville to buy slaves. The economy of the Cape Verde Islands was transformed by the growing demand for African slaves. Originally, many of them had been kept on the islands in the hope that they could conjure life out of the poor soil of the islands. This was not a success. The transit trade to the Americas began in earnest in 1510. After that, the islands' slaves fell into three categories: 'trade slaves', destined for the slave market in Portugal or, increasingly, America; 'work slaves', for sugar and other plantations on the Cape Verde Islands; and domestic slaves, bought to serve in settler households, who were certainly the most fortunate. In recognition of its growing importance, Ribeira Grande – which was not at all *grande* – was granted city status in 1533, when it became the seat of the Portuguese bishop responsible for west Africa. Even so, most of those who slept in the little city were merchants and slaves who were passing through the islands. Even towards the end of the century there were probably only about 1,700 settlers in the whole archipelago, and about six times as many slaves.[4]

The towns of Hispaniola had a different character. For the moment, until Cortés and his successors conquered vast tracts of the American mainland, this was the end of the line. Columbus had not had much luck with his town foundations. The inhabitants of La Navidad, constructed out of the timbers of the *Santa María* on Christmas Day, 1492, had met with disaster – all the Spanish settlers were dead, turned on by the Taíno chief and his men, by the time Columbus returned to Hispaniola. The next settlement on the north of the island, named after Queen Isabella, was founded a year later, but the site was unhealthy and the settlers quarrelled among themselves. La Isabela had slightly better fortune than La Navidad: it lasted four years. Columbus did not see the town as the capital of a new Spanish province, so much as think of it as a trading station, or *feitoria*, modelled on Elmina in west Africa. Just as Elmina functioned as a funnel through which great quantities of gold from the interior were channelled to Portugal, so La Isabela would be the collection point for the gold and spices of the Indies.[5]

The settlers needed to eat as well as to trade, and their numbers were much larger than the small team who kept Elmina in business. Excavations at La Isabela show that it was built with defence in mind, as one might expect after the experiences at La Navidad; it was constructed mainly of packed earth, but the builders used a limited amount of stone as well, and what was probably Columbus's own house had a stone doorway. Many colonists had to make do with thatched huts not totally dissimilar to the houses of the Taínos. But the Spaniards tried to be as self-reliant as possible: there was a sizeable community of artisans, not just masons but workers in wood and metal, makers of tiles and bricks and boat-builders. Some people lived on a second, satellite, site at Las Coles, on the opposite side of the river, which, it was hoped, would help feed the new town, for the main business there was agriculture, along with pottery-making. The Spaniards were none too happy with the Taíno diet of cassava bread, along with the occasional iguana, manatee, conch and large rodents. Las Casas thought the Spaniards ate in a day what the Taínos would eat in a month, adding, 'just think what 400 of them would consume!' The Indians marvelled at the voraciousness of the settlers, and wondered whether they were so hungry because they had run out of food at home.[6]

The Spaniards within La Isabela and the Indians outside its stockade kept apart; yet children of mixed origins must have been common, because there were so few Spanish women in early Hispaniola. For the moment, though, sharp lines were maintained between the communities. The Spaniards had little interest in Taíno products, and made only limited use of Taíno pottery. The proportion of Spanish pottery found on the site of La Isabela is actually higher than one would expect to find on a contemporary archaeological site in Spain, where plenty of Italian and other foreign goods normally appear. The style of Spanish goods found on the site is typical of the arabized culture of southern Spain, and includes plenty of glazed maiolica that was brought from Seville and its sister ports during the brief life of the town.[7] Columbus attempted to place all trade with the Indians under his own control, acting in the name of the Crown. No gold objects have been found; any golden artefacts or nuggets of gold passed quickly through the colony to the Old World. On the other hand, over a hundred Spanish coins have been found, mainly low-value coins made of the heavily debased silver alloy known as billon; real silver coins were a rarity. The coins themselves were not just from Spain but from Genoa, Sicily, Portugal and elsewhere, palely reflecting the trading world of late medieval Seville.[8] So it is clear that the residents did business among themselves, operating a modest money-based economy, but mixing little with the Taínos.

II

In 1498, as it became more and more obvious that La Isabela was never going to flourish, Bartholomew Columbus, Christopher's brother, made the fateful decision to move the centre of Spanish operations right across the island to the shores of the Caribbean. In deference to his brother he at first called his new capital Nueva Isabela, but Santo Domingo was the name that stuck until 1936, when the ruthless Dominican dictator Trujillo modestly renamed it Ciudad Trujillo – it has been Santo Domingo again since his fall. Even then the Columbuses did not get it quite right. The city lies on the River Ozama, in those days a broad passageway offering a reasonable harbour for ships arriving from Seville; but Bartholomew's town was blown to smithereens by a hurricane, and within a few years the town was moved across the river to what was thought a better-protected site.[9] There, Nicolás de Ovando, who had replaced Christopher Columbus as governor of the Indies in 1502, decided to build a true Spanish city, so Spanish that he and his successors brought stonemasons and carpenters from northern Spain to construct monumental palaces and

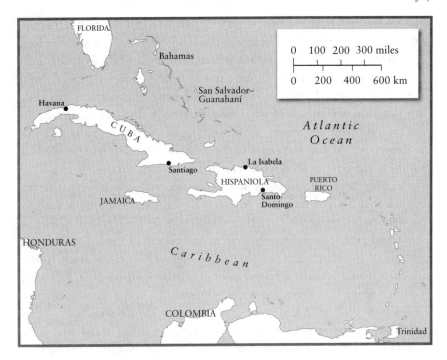

churches in the latest Iberian styles. A longstanding rival of Columbus, Ovando had arrived in the New World accompanied by the largest number of sailors, soldiers and settlers yet seen there, well over 2,000.[10]

Ovando's aim became the creation not just of a Portuguese-style *feitoria*, but a city with broad streets, stone houses and, above all, a permanent population. The *Zona Colonial* of Santo Domingo is the oldest, largest and best-preserved colonial quarter anywhere in the Americas. Ovando's palace, now a luxury hotel, still survives as testimony to his sense of grandeur, and he built at least fourteen more substantial stone houses. His immediate successor, Diego Colón, son of Christopher Columbus, who took up office in 1509, constructed a particularly imposing residence with an excellent view over the harbour and out to sea. These governors of the Indies, later graced with the title of viceroy, were keen to place their capital at the centre of the New World. At first they could only see as far as Spain; but as new explorations and conquests opened up first Cuba, in 1511, and then Mexico, whose capital fell to Cortés (an old Santo Domingo hand) in 1520, Ovando's city seemed poised to become the nerve centre of an entire western Atlantic trading network.

Making Santo Domingo work would present many challenges. In the early days food supplies were scarce; the Spanish settlers came to rely on imported grain brought all the way from Spain, though this was good news for Spanish businessmen, since they needed to fill the outbound ships with something saleable. Wheat was the food of the rich, maize the food of the relatively poor, and cassava was left for those at the bottom of the social pile, who, by definition, were not Spaniards.[11] Royal officials were set in place in Santo Domingo, where an imposing headquarters was built; their function was to record what passed through the port, especially the gold brought from the mines, while keeping an eye out to make sure that the Crown received its fair share of the profits. Columbus had pointed out that the areas poor in gold were very rich in cotton; but no one in Europe was terribly interested in New World cotton, since there were plentiful supplies that arrived from the Mediterranean. Even Columbus realized this and began to argue that the inhabitants of Cathay and Cipangu, China and Japan, would surely snap up the cotton of the Indies – a good example of the fantasies that often wandered across his brain.[12] Rather later, salt would become a prized asset of northern Hispaniola, picked up by Dutch ships that were not really supposed to visit Spanish territory; but for now gold, gold and more gold was what people sought.

By 1508 forty-five ships were coming each year to the island, and Santo Domingo was firmly established as the prime port of call in the Spanish Indies. Some of its settlers came from well-connected families, such as the Dávila of Segovia, and it is no coincidence that many of the stone buildings recall those of Segovia itself.[13] Santo Domingo attracted the attention of the two busiest men of affairs in Seville, who were of Genoese origin, Juan Francisco de Grimaldo and Gaspar Centurión. In 1513 and 1517 their loans to merchants and ship's masters sailing to the new port mounted higher and higher, one loan being worth 214,000 *maravedís*. Admittedly, the sort of product the settlers required was at first relatively modest, as had been the case when the Canaries or the Cape Verde Islands had first been settled: chickpeas, vinegar, paper, coarse cloth. But there was every hope of bringing back gold by return. By the middle of the sixteenth century, demand for luxury goods in the new colonies had begun to rise, including fine cloths from all over Europe, and increasing numbers of African slaves, all of which (or whom) helped to make the fortune of yet more Genoese families. One not very popular imposition by King Ferdinand was a tax of 7½ per cent on imported European goods, which included silk shirts, velvet hats and other luxuries for the Spanish elite. If one compares the excavated remains of La Isabela with the grandeur of Ovando's city of Santo Domingo, one can see how the standard of living of the colonial elite was beginning to soar.

In the early days, the Taíno Indians had simply panned for gold in river beds, but the point came when the large lumps had, by and large, been collected, while other lands across the Caribbean began to look much more promising as sources of gold – on his final expedition Columbus had uncovered evidence of gold-rich peoples some way inside Central America. The Spaniards now resolved to transform the island economy in new ways, always with an eye on demand from Europe: just as Madeira, the Canaries and São Tomé had become major sources of sugar, there seemed to be no reason why the same should not happen in Hispaniola.[14] The tropical climate guaranteed heavy rainfall, and water was essential in sugar production. The newly arrived African slaves were thought to be better suited than the vanishing Taínos to the exceptionally harsh conditions within a sugar mill: punishingly high temperatures as the sugar was boiled, not to mention very demanding work in the fields cutting the thick and fibrous stalks of the sugar cane with knives or machetes. Even so, the history of sugar production in Hispaniola is a story of mixed success. In 1493 Columbus apparently took sugar cane from La Gomera in the Canaries to Hispaniola, though several attempts were necessary before the Caribbean sugar industry took off.

The first serious attempts to start sugar production in Hispaniola began in 1503, and the first proper mill was only built in 1514, on the initiative of a Spanish landowner named Velloso; growth was slow, depending as it did on securing experts who could advise on the machinery needed in the mills, some of whom Velloso brought over from the Canaries.[15] An even more important problem was lack of capital, in short supply before the Genoese and the Welsers became involved. A state-of-the-art mill could cost as much as 15,000 gold ducats, way beyond Velloso's modest means; however, he did enter into a partnership with wealthy local officials, and his project was soon under way. More money was pumped into this industry by the Jeronymite friars, who had become a major influence in the government of Hispaniola by 1518 and who petitioned the Crown for investment in what they advertised as a golden opportunity. Royal loans enabled dozens of settlers to build sugar mills in the years around 1520, and they made little effort to pay the money back; the whole sugar industry was littered with debt to the Crown, to Genoese investors and to merchants in Seville.[16] Thereafter sugar mills spread across the island and the income from sugar was, for a while, handsome: over half a million *pesos* each year in the 1580s, from about 1,000 tons of exported sugar. Labour supply remained a problem because the African slaves rarely lived much longer than seven years before overwork and disease took their toll. The answer was to increase the number of imported slaves; some of the largest estates had a workforce of 500 slaves, and many had 200.[17]

Among the pioneers of the Caribbean sugar industry were pioneers of the sugar industry in the Canaries, such as the Genoese businessman

Riberol (a victim of local xenophobia), and the Welsers, a German banking family from Augsburg that was keen to profit from the new discoveries across the Atlantic, and that would eventually send expeditions deep into Venezuela in search of the gold-rich kingdom the Spaniards called 'El Dorado'. For the moment, in 1526, the Welsers were content to set up a branch of their bank in Santo Domingo managed by two Germans, one of whom would go on to become governor of Venezuela. They valued Santo Domingo not just as a source of goods such as sugar, but as the capital of the Spanish Indies, the place where they would be able to work side by side with the viceroy and the king's other agents.[18]

European participation went much further, thanks to the presence on the Spanish throne of a king who was also ruler of the Holy Roman Empire, Charles V; he was in hock first to German bankers and later to the Genoese. The Welsers of Augsburg responded with enthusiasm, even though this stretched their existing resources to and beyond wise limits. In the seventeen-year period beginning in 1518, 1,044 ships sailed from Seville to Santo Domingo, an average of sixty-one each year, and of these ninety-three were owned by the Welsers – a number were then put to use in intra-Caribbean trade towards Venezuela.[19] They overextended themselves both in Venezuela and in Hispaniola, and when it became obvious that they would never find El Dorado and be able to use its fabulous wealth to pay off their mounting debts they closed up shop in both places in 1536.[20]

Then the conquest of Mexico and Peru pulled the centre of gravity of the Spanish Indies much further westwards, so that by mid-century Santo Domingo had become a seat of government but had lost its pre-eminence in trade – not just to Mexico but, as will be seen, to newly subdued Cuba. Santo Domingo was no longer the focal point of the Spanish Empire in the Indies; its governors were looking for new ways to maintain the status and wealth of Hispaniola, and another option was to import cattle and to try to make a profit from ranching.[21] The sale of hides from Hispaniola on the other side of the Atlantic became big business, but turning the land over to cattle also spelled the end of the old intensive cultivation practised by the Indians (of whom, in any case, there were now very few), and generated increasing dependence on food supplies, other than meat, from outside the island. Had the Spaniards been willing to change their diet things might have turned out differently; but, rather like British colonial officials in India who expected to be served English food, the Spaniards were slow to adapt to Caribbean tastes. Once the ranches were in place, meat and more meat became the daily diet of the entire white population – it has been suggested that in Hispaniola a plate of beef cost one hundredth of what one would have paid in Spain. Before long there were forty cattle for every person on the island. Since Spain required leather, not fresh meat, which would hardly survive an Atlantic crossing (although some was taken on board to feed the sailors), there was a glut of beef in Hispaniola. Nearly 50,000 hides were exported in 1584, though that was about a quarter of the number of hides exported from the Caribbean islands, for the passion for ranching went far beyond Hispaniola.[22]

The city of Santo Domingo stood frozen in time. Its magnificent Gothic cathedral was completed just as the downturn was beginning. The remarkable survival of its buildings is testimony to decline, not to success. Other ports were seizing the lead: Veracruz in Mexico and Nombre de Díos in Panama.[23] So long as Santo Domingo was the redistribution point for the goods being sent to Europe, it had some role to play, but a powerful rival emerged that was better placed to handle the wealth of Mexico: the new capital of Cuba, Havana.

III

The pre-eminence of Havana within the Spanish Indies was clear by 1571, when an English observer wrote:

> Havana is the principal and most important port of all the king of Spain has in the Indies: because all the ships coming from Peru, Honduras, Puerto Rico, Santo Domingo, Jamaica, and other parts of the Indies, touch there upon their return to Spain, this being the port in which they take food and water, as well as the largest part of their cargo.[24]

This was not the result of any great resources that Cuba could offer; indeed, it was slow to develop the sugar industry for which it eventually became so famous, and was generally a tardy developer within the Spanish world, for it had only been conquered twenty years after its discovery by Columbus – if Las Casas is to be believed, the conquest was accompanied by hideous acts of violence. Even so, the *conquistador* Diego Velázquez seems to have been an urbane man who made some attempts to treat the native population with consideration; after all, it was by now obvious that the treatment of their cousins in Hispaniola had led to utter disaster and population collapse. Realizing that the island had little gold to offer, Velázquez tried to introduce cattle and pigs, in the hope of re-creating Mother Spain on its soil. The production and export of hides exceeded even that of Hispaniola, but the price that had been paid was the same: nothing could protect the Taíno Indians from disease, and they too disappeared within a few decades.[25]

Havana was founded in 1519. Its real strength lay in its position astride the Gulf Stream, which made it the ideal transit point between the two American continents and Europe.[26] Settlers were attracted by the excellent natural harbour and by the quality of fresh water in the nearby river. Havana was able to supplant the original capital of Cuba, at Santiago, which lay well within range of Santo Domingo but shrank rapidly in the face of competition.[27] This was the point where fleets coming from all over the Caribbean, including those bringing the silver of Mexico and Peru, converged, which also made it a very attractive target for pirates. As early as 1538 a French pirate had a go at Havana, and in 1555 another one managed to sack the town; old Havana had been built by Taíno labour, but new Havana was built by African slaves, for lack of native manpower.[28] And then it flourished: it was the great centre of inter-colonial shipping, that is, trade within the Spanish Indies, with ships arriving from the Yucatán peninsula, Florida, Honduras, Colombia, Trinidad and Hispaniola; but it also received goods (some in human form) from Africa, the Canaries, Spain and Portugal, and the inter-colonial trade fed and was fed by the transatlantic connections – literally in the case of the Canaries, which in those days were celebrated for their wines, and which were also the home base of some of the liveliest merchants trading through Havana. In the last fifteen years of the sixteenth century, the volume of trade conducted by Francisco Díaz Pimienta of La Palma in the Canaries reached 1,800,000 *reales*. He was mainly a wine merchant but he did not scorn the slave trade out of Angola.

Mexico was Havana's second most important trading partner, after Seville; in a later chapter it will be seen how Chinese goods reached Mexico all the way from Macau and Manila, and some of these found their way to Havana, from where they could be passed on to Spain. Sometimes they were just plain ceramics used as much as ballast as they were used as sale goods, but sometimes they were fine silks or delicate porcelains. Havana was a centre of shipbuilding too.[29]

Havana, then, was a city that lived from servicing international trade; it was more closely integrated into the commercial world of the Spanish Atlantic than it was into the narrower and poorer world of early colonial Cuba. A local elite of Spanish landowners, office-holders and merchants emerged, tightly bound together through marriage and common financial interests. All stoutly denied any Jewish or Moorish ancestry; if you wanted to heap the worst possible insult on someone you called him a *puto judío toledano*, 'a fucking Toledan Jew'. But there were Portuguese businessmen who were strongly suspected of being secret Jews, settlers who chose Havana in order to escape as far away as practicable from the Inquisition.

Still, the total population was much smaller than one might expect in a town of considerable strategic and economic importance: sixty citizens in 1570, 1,200 in 1620. And then there were high-status slaves, for not all slaves toiled in the sugar plantations or in construction projects: as in ancient Rome, some were sent abroad on business by masters who trusted them and recognized their talent.[30] In 1583 royal slaves, many of whom were set to work on the city's fortifications, numbered 125. They were mostly brought, via holding stations in the Cape Verde Islands, from Upper Guinea, which supplied the great majority of slaves before 1600. Other royal slaves reached Santo Domingo and Havana from Luanda in Angola, so that the slave trade out of south-western Africa towards the Caribbean had the dual effect of strengthening Portugal's grip on Angola and reinforcing Spain's control of the Caribbean, particularly after 1580, when the king of Spain held the throne of Portugal as well. Not all the Africans were kept in permanent slavery: a free black population gradually came into existence in the islands, among whom there were black ranchers who possessed their own slaves.[31]

All told, the Caribbean was quite unlike the world Columbus had so confidently expected to find. A new series of relationships emerged within the Atlantic. The sugar islands of the eastern Atlantic, notably Madeira and the Canaries, taught the sugar islands of the western Atlantic the necessary skills. There was constant to-ing and fro-ing between these groups of islands. The Caribbean towns, notably Santo Domingo and then Havana, functioned as supply stations for shipping bound from one great continent to another, just as the Cape Verde Islands and the Azores kept ships stocked with meat and dairy goods. In that sense, the claim that Columbus had discovered 'New Canaries' in the Caribbean was not totally mistaken. The slave trade and slave labour kept these islands afloat, not just under Spanish rule but in later centuries when the English, the Dutch, the French and the Danes staked out their own claims in the Caribbean. This New Atlantic was constructed out of the resources of the Old Atlantic.

33

The Struggle for the Indian Ocean

I

The richness of the evidence in the archives of Lisbon and Seville has made the maritime history of the sixteenth century appear to be a story of ever-expanding overseas empires that would inevitably create well-functioning and profitable trade networks stretching right around the globe. The challenges the Portuguese faced are usually, therefore, listed as the Spaniards in the first place, and later on the French, the English and, in particular, the Dutch. However, the major challenge that the European merchants and navies faced in the Indian Ocean during the early sixteenth century was that of another partly European political power that was already heavily involved in the Mediterranean and that was beginning to turn its attention to the Red Sea and the Indian Ocean as well: the Ottoman Empire.[1] The capture of Constantinople in 1453 had transformed the Ottomans from doughty warriors of Islam on the western fringes of the Muslim world into Sunni emperors who saw their mission as not just the extension of Turkish power into Italy and western Europe but as the imposition of Ottoman rule over neighbouring Muslim states as well. In 1516 the Ottomans overwhelmed Syria, ruled since the late thirteenth century by the Mamluk sultans of Egypt, and the next year they brought Egypt too under their authority. They were careful not to dismantle completely the Mamluk state, with its elaborate tax system geared to the exploitation of the spice trade through the Red Sea; but their presence in Egypt and Syria caused as much concern to the Venetian merchants buying spices in Alexandria and Beirut as did the penetration of the Portuguese into the Indian Ocean. The reaction of the Indian and Arabian inhabitants of the ports along the coasts of the Indian Ocean is much more difficult to judge, since much of what is known is derived from Portuguese or occasionally Ottoman reports.

During the twenty years after da Gama first set out from Lisbon the

Mamluks were still trying to control the Red Sea, facing political challenges from not just the Ottomans but rebels in Yemen, as well as the danger that Portuguese fleets would break through beyond the Bab al-Mandeb strait and threaten Jiddah and even Mecca. These difficulties were compounded by the fact that revenues from Venetian trade, which was protected by a whole series of Venetian–Mamluk treaties, were an important source of revenue for the Egyptian sultans, whose political grip on the lands they had ruled for two and a half centuries was slipping even before the Ottomans invaded their lands: in 1505/6 Bedouin raids were so persistent that the pilgrimage route through Syria to Mecca had to be suspended. And this had a knock-on effect on trade, since the raids undermined confidence in the ability of the Mamluks to keep the commercial routes open. The Venetians were canny enough to look in other directions, making eyes at the Ottomans, with whom in any case they had enjoyed quite good commercial relations since the fall of Constantinople; but for the moment only the Mamluks could ensure large-scale access to the spices Venice sought. Rather than tightening control, the Mamluks tried to raise funds for their campaigns against the Bedouins and other enemies by increasing taxes in Alexandria, and by constantly bending the rules – Mamluk officials, whether for themselves or for the government, would add arbitrary levies, impound goods, and generally make life difficult for Italian merchants. In 1510 the Venetian consul was thrown into prison and accused of plotting against the Mamluk state. As early as 1502 an Egyptian historian, ibn Iyas, took the view that these policies were ruining Alexandria, that is, even before the effect of the Portuguese breakthrough into the Indian Ocean was measurable.[2] However, his pessimism may have been the result of naval warfare in the Aegean which led to a suspension of the Venetian spice convoys between 1499 and 1503. If anything, the suspension of the convoys confirmed that the prosperity of Alexandria depended on the spice trade towards Europe.

Still, the Venetians knew that they had to work with the Mamluks, at least for the moment, so when in 1504 they heard that the Portuguese had started to bring back Indian pepper they sent a messenger named Teldi to the sultan in Cairo, where he arrived posing as a jewel merchant. He wormed his way into the palace and warned the Mamluk government about the danger Egypt, along with Venice, faced following the Portuguese entry into the Indian Ocean. Teldi had a whole armoury of arguments: if the Mamluks did not help to suppress the Portuguese, Venice would turn its spice trade westwards, sending its ships to Lisbon instead of Alexandria (a vain boast as what Venice sought was a near monopoly over distribution within Europe, which it could never obtain in Lisbon). At the very least,

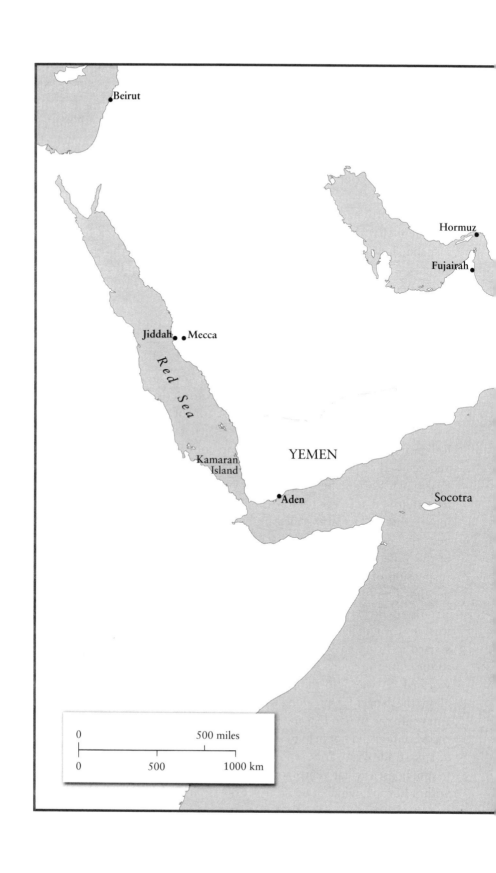

Beirut

Hormuz

Fujairah

Jiddah Mecca

Red Sea

Kamaran Island

YEMEN

Socotra

Aden

| 0 | | 500 miles | |
| 0 | 500 | | 1000 km |

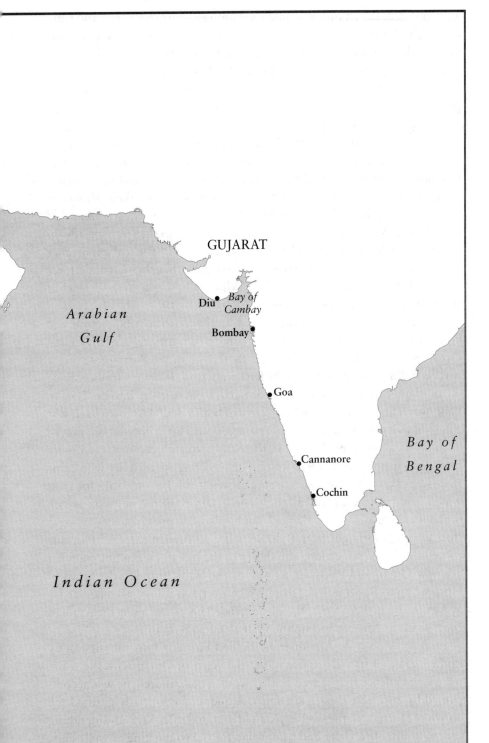

Teldi insisted, the Mamluks could send ambassadors to Cochin and Cannanore, ordering their rulers, who were also Muslims, to have nothing more to do with the Portuguese, who before long would surely be threatening the holy cities of Islam by way of the Red Sea.[3] The Mamluk sultan slowly took action: in 1505 he built up the defences of Jiddah, so as to protect Mecca, and in 1507-9 a Mamluk fleet at last ventured out against the Portuguese. It was well advised to do so, as the Portuguese had thought up a plan to seize Socotra, the island to the south of Yemen that, since the days of Greco-Roman trade, had functioned as a sort of commercial watchtower for traffic leading to Arabia, the Red Sea and east Africa, making it seem a perfect acquisition if only it could be taken. However, the Portuguese soon discovered that it was a barren wasteland and that it lay too far from the Red Sea entrance to give them the strategic advantage they sought, so they abandoned it after four years.[4] The real importance of Socotra is not its brief Portuguese occupation but the magnetic force the island exercised upon the Mamluks, who saw how crucial the defence of the waters off Yemen had become.

The son of the ruthless Portuguese admiral Afonso de Albuquerque had noted that there were three places that command the markets of the Indian Ocean: Melaka, Hormuz and Aden.[5] By this point the Portuguese threat was becoming more intense and the flashpoint was Hormuz. Hormuz, lying on an island on the Iranian side of the narrow passageway into the Persian Gulf, was a first-class strategic objective of both sides.[6] The town itself was a dust-blown port with no natural resources but a large population, maybe as many as 40,000 inhabitants in the early sixteenth century, even more than densely populated Aden. Ralph Fitch, an English traveller who came there in 1583, wrote: 'there is nothing growing in it but only salt; for their water, wood or victuals and all things necessary come out of Persia, which is about twelve miles from thence.' But he also saw piles of spices, a 'great store of pearls' brought from Bahrain, silk and Persian carpets.[7] Hormuz commanded the traffic along the shores of the Indian Ocean linking what are now Oman and Pakistan, as well as the traffic through the Strait of Hormuz up to Basra in Iraq, from which overland routes stretched as far as Aleppo in northern Syria. Its ruler extended his power along the Arabian coast as far as Muscat and up the Gulf as far as Bahrain.

In 1507 Afonso de Albuquerque bullied Hormuz into submission by raiding some of its outstations along the coast of Oman with the usual terrifying violence that spared neither women nor children; he was accompanied by 460 men aboard six ships. Albuquerque formally granted the crown of Hormuz to the twelve-year-old nominal ruler Sayf ad-din, taking care to nominate a vizier and a guardian for the young king as well. This, along with a tribute payment, did not amount to much more than a formal acknowledgement of Portuguese supremacy in a kingdom that was already being torn apart by power struggles within its royal family, quite apart from the fact that the shah of Persia was meddling in its affairs. The shah sought an outlet to the sea, and he even sent the king of Hormuz a ceremonial bonnet indicating Persian suzerainty over Hormuz.[8] At the time there was some prospect of an alliance between the Portuguese and the Persians, whose Shi'ite shah was said to have his own ambitions to capture Mecca. He was known in the West as the 'Great Sophy', meaning *Sufi*, and the idea of a Persian–Catholic alliance had been bruited about since the late fifteenth century, in the awareness that the Sunni Turks could not abide this Shi'ite rival. The Portuguese mooted a project whereby spices would be sent through the Persian Gulf rather than up the Red Sea, with the help of the shah, and encouraged the shah to march all the way to Cairo, at which point, presumably, the Red Sea route would come back into operation.[9] This was an agreeable fantasy, no doubt, but the Portuguese began to have their doubts about the Great Sophy when the Ottomans scored a great victory over the Persians at the battle of Çaldıran in 1514.

Determined to strengthen the Portuguese position in the Indian Ocean, Albuquerque was back in 1515, having now become 'governor of India'; this time he had 1,500 Portuguese troops with him, impressive testimony to the scale of Portuguese penetration into the Indian Ocean. No rewards were on offer for the earlier submission of Hormuz; the vizier was killed, the fortress of Hormuz was garrisoned, and even the shah of Persia, who was shocked that the Portuguese had seized what he regarded as one of his vassal states, had to accept the new reality, especially when Albuquerque made soothing noises and talked of an alliance between Persia and Portugal against their common enemies, the Mamluk sultan in Egypt and the Ottoman sultan in Turkey.[10] Soon after that the dreaded Albuquerque died, but the Portuguese held on to Hormuz for over a century. They did Hormuz some favours, though: in 1518 the Portuguese sent a fleet up the Persian Gulf to defend the claim of the sultan of Hormuz to suzerainty over Bahrain. The Portuguese were faithful to their vassal in Hormuz.[11] Its acquisition enabled Portugal to create a line of ports and forts defending its route towards India; the coastline of Fujairah, the part of the UAE that faces out towards the Indian Ocean, is dotted with pinkish-brown Portuguese forts of impressive solidity. Creating this line of forts was especially important once the decision had been made to make Goa, captured in 1510, the seat of Portuguese government in India.[12]

The Portuguese relied, quite simply, on brute force. They were well aware that their spice trade would never flourish if they had to compete with rivals. Although they were successfully bringing large cargoes of pepper and other spices to Europe, for sale in Lisbon and Antwerp, the quality did not compare well with spices carried through the Red Sea – the long journey in ships filling up with bilge water did not improve the quality of their goods. Therefore they sought as total a monopoly as possible, an enormously ambitious aim in view of the logistical difficulties they faced in maintaining contact across the Atlantic and the Indian Ocean. As far as the spice trade was concerned, the struggle against first the Mamluks and then the Ottomans in the Indian Ocean was a life-and-death struggle. They were well prepared for naval engagements, but the results were mixed. One Mamluk victory, over the fleets of Almeida, the first Portuguese governor of India, in 1508, was followed by humiliation of the Mamluk navy at Diu in northern India, even though several Indian princes had sent aid to the Mamluks.[13] In 1511 the Venetians even urged the Mamluks to make common cause with the Ottomans against the Portuguese, for they could see that the lack of wood for shipbuilding was, as ever in Egyptian history, causing problems; so they invited the Mamluks to obtain wood from the Turks, while offering supplies from Venice as well.[14]

There were two issues here: the exclusion of the Portuguese from the spice trade, but also the defence of the Red Sea, for it was becoming increasingly obvious that the Portuguese hoped to force their way into the Red Sea and gain mastery over the spice trade through Alexandria via the back door. The route around Africa was only an expedient. Once they had conquered the Indian Ocean – as if that were at all possible – the Portuguese dreamed of restoring the Red Sea route, abandoning the costly and dangerous Cape route, and becoming lords of not just Alexandria but Jerusalem. In going after pepper, the Portuguese did not forget their crusading past.[15] Whenever the Portuguese sent fleets into the Red Sea they tried to make contact with the emperor of Ethiopia, whom they recognized as the real Prester John, the Christian king who would join their great crusade. An attempt to send two caravels to what were assumed to be the coasts of his empire met with disaster when one of the captains was killed even before his skiff reached the shore. But in 1518 there was some direct contact, generating the recurrent dream of uniting with him in the conquest of not just Egypt but Jerusalem.[16]

The redoubtable and violent Portuguese commander Albuquerque already had it in mind to force his way into the Red Sea in 1510. His plan was to sail all the way to Suez and destroy the Mamluk fleet anchored there; but in the end he turned against Goa. The Red Sea remained a priority all the same, and was Albuquerque's target in 1513, when he once again attacked Aden, this time with twenty-four ships, 1,700 Portuguese troops and 1,000 Indian troops. He aimed to set up a blockade preventing shipping from reaching the spice markets of Alexandria. The Portuguese occupied Kamaran Island, much closer to the Red Sea entrance than Socotra, though they were unable to hold it for very long.[17] That was the central problem: the Portuguese had to find a way of maintaining the blockade year in, year out if they were to establish the monopoly they sought. Even when they failed to achieve their objectives in the Red Sea, the Portuguese wreaked havoc: in 1517 an armada of thirty-three warships carrying 3,000 troops attacked Jiddah; the threat to Mecca was now real. The Portuguese were thrown back with the loss of 800 lives and several ships.[18] Still, the spice markets of Cairo, Alexandria and Beirut were said to be empty in 1518 and 1519. During his campaigns Albuquerque took detailed notes on the layout of the Red Sea, and convinced himself that, following its defeat at Diu, there was no Mamluk fleet left to challenge his supremacy – just fifteen pinnaces at Suez. He told the king of Portugal: 'if you make yourself powerful in the Red Sea you will have all the riches of the world in your hands.'[19]

II

In the event, neither the Persians nor the Portuguese gained control of the Red Sea, which fell under Ottoman sovereignty following the Turkish invasion of Egypt in 1517. Historians have made rather a meal of the question why the Ottomans seized Egypt at a time when they were actively competing with the Persian shah in the Middle East. But the Ottoman claim to world dominion had already been made plain by Mehmet II when he conquered the Byzantine Empire and attacked Italy. To occupy a wealthy and populous country that stood at the very heart of the Islamic world was an obvious step.[20] The Ottoman conquest of Egypt encouraged the Venetians to continue to work alongside the Turks, who by and large had been willing to protect their shipping; the Venetians traded through Constantinople as well as Alexandria, and the Ottomans enthusiastically fostered the economic revival of their capital, which had shrunk to a collection of villages under late Byzantine rule. The main impulse for the invasion of Syria and Egypt came from an increasingly powerful sense of the role of the Ottoman sultan as a world ruler, ideas derived from Byzantine conceptions of the ruler as Roman emperor, from Turkish ideas of the ruler as Great Khan and from Muslim ideas of the ruler as caliph, a title the sultans began to use with increasing frequency, even if their descent from the Companions of the Prophet was, to say the least, hard to prove.

The sultan began to add to his already long list of titles claims to Yemen, Arabia, Ethiopia and Zanzibar, at a time when his direct control of waters connected to the Indian Ocean was limited to the Red Sea port of Jiddah. This was surely a rebuke to King Manuel of Portugal, who had also appropriated a grand array of titles to lands and coasts he did not control. Strategically, though, the move into Egypt made sense: it gave the Turks access to Mecca and Medina, of which they could now claim to be the protectors, and it gave them control of the Red Sea in the face of Portuguese incursions. As masters of the Red Sea they were sucked into the struggle for mastery over the spice trade as well, whose profits accrued to them as rulers of Egypt – so long as the spices actually reached Egypt.[21]

This reorientation was encouraged by allies in the Indian Ocean; the Muslim kingdom of Gujarat played a central role in the politics and trade not just of north-west India but of the entire Indian Ocean, because its main port, Diu, had become one of the great commercial centres of the entire region and a key ally of first the Mamluks and then the Turks.[22] Malik Ayaz, the governor of Diu, a man of uncertain origins (it is even possible he was born in Dubrovnik), had witnessed the failure of the Mamluks to follow through their victory over the Portuguese in 1508, and had witnessed the victory of Almeida's fleet over the Mamluk navy at Diu the next year. He was a businessman as well as as political leader, so he took a strong interest in the spice trade. He was fortunate that the Portuguese commander, Almeida, was not interested in capturing Diu; one of Almeida's main demands was the surrender of Muslim mercenaries, who were subjected to the most ghastly punishments: having their hands and feet lopped off before being thrown on a massive funeral pyre; being forced to kill one another; being bound to the mouth of a cannon and then blown to smithereens.[23] This was yet another example of the ruthless terror that da Gama, Cabral, Almeida and after him Albuquerque spread in the belief that it was the best way to subdue the cities of the Indian Ocean.

These methods only encouraged Malik Ayaz to look in a different direction: the Mamluks were a failure and their state was in disarray, while the Ottomans must surely be the great power of the future not just in the Mediterranean but in the Indian Ocean. Moreover, following the Ottoman victories, the new governor of Jiddah on the Red Sea coast wrote to Malik Ayaz and to the ruler of Gujarat (who was Malik Ayaz's superior) informing them that twenty ships from the former Mamluk fleet were now in Jiddah and that the Ottoman sultan, Selim, had ordered the construction of fifty more: 'if God so wills, with numberless troops he will soon undertake to push these perfidious troublemakers towards a destiny of blackness.'[24] Albuquerque even warned the king of Portugal that the

Ottomans might be about to invade India; he said that the whole Indian Ocean was in turmoil now that the Ottomans had marched into Egypt, even though just a few years before, when he had captured Melaka (in 1511), everything had been peaceful. More Portuguese fears were realized when Sultan Selim made peace overtures to Venice and Dubrovnik. He also sent an expedition to Yemen, hoping to bring the mouth of the Red Sea under his control, but his death in 1520 put an end to this project. He clearly had every intention of restoring the Red Sea pepper route.[25]

Under Selim's successor, Süleyman, known to history as 'the Magnificent', these steps into the Indian Ocean were taken further. Süleyman relied on his closest friend, Pargalı Ibrahim Pasha, who had been born to a Greek Orthodox family in the Greek–Albanian borderlands, and had been carried off to Constantinople as a slave while still a young boy. There Süleyman had befriended him (they even slept in the same bedroom, which raised the eyebrows of many a courtier); Ibrahim attained great power at court, becoming Grand Vizier, and masterminded Süleyman's policy in the Indian Ocean and beyond (he was involved in negotiations with the king of France that led to the notorious Franco-Ottoman alliance in the 1530s).[26] Ibrahim simplified the commercial taxes levied in Egypt so that merchants were no longer compelled to buy a set amount of pepper at inflated prices from government agents. A basic 10 per cent tax was to be levied instead. The aim was to make Egypt an attractive place to trade in spices, now that Europe was receiving eastern spices via the Cape route as well as through the Red Sea. As a result income from the spice trade held up well, and even in 1527 the Ottoman administration in Egypt seems to have been making more money out of this trade than the Portuguese Crown. The idea that from da Gama's time onwards the spice trade through the Red Sea dried up, and that Portugal seized a commanding lead at the very start of the sixteenth century, is a myth.[27]

Lower taxes were a wise means of attracting business; but first of all one had to make sure the goods reached Alexandria. So Ibrahim revived the plans for the conquest of Yemen. In 1525 a corsair in Ibrahim's service, Selman Reis, reported that

> at the moment Yemen has no lord – an empty province. It deserved to be a fine *sancak* [province]. It would be easy and possible to conquer. Should it be conquered it would be possible to master the lands of India and send every year a great amount of gold and jewels to the Sublime Porte [Constantinople].[28]

Securing Yemen proved far more difficult than Selman had supposed; its lawlessness and lordlessness returned as the Ottoman commanders, including Selman, became immersed in quarrels among themselves about who was really in charge; this was a regular problem in Ottoman armies and navies. The result was that by the time Selman's rivals assassinated him in his tent, in 1528, Yemen had been lost and the Portuguese were able to raid into the Red Sea once again. The Portuguese had the added advantage that Süleyman the Magnificent had been focusing on a massive land campaign in Europe that took him to the gates of Vienna. It hardly seemed possible to flush the Portuguese out of the Indian Ocean, and the Ottomans had to concentrate on the defence of the Red Sea, not just as a trade route but as the route to Mecca and Medina.[29] In 1531 spices were so hard to find in Alexandria and Beirut that the Venetians ended up filling the holds with grain and beans.[30] But there was constant flux. In 1538 the Ottomans at last captured Aden, securing control of access to the Red Sea, and in 1546 they took Basra, leading to control of the Persian Gulf. Six years later, though, they failed to capture Hormuz, the gateway to the Gulf, which the Portuguese had been ruling continuously since 1515; after their defeat at Hormuz, the Ottomans temporarily lost interest in naval campaigns in the Indian Ocean. Süleyman was now looking in other directions: he was increasingly anxious to lay his hands on Cyprus and to challenge Habsburg naval power in the Mediterranean, and relations with Persia continued to fester.[31]

Just as it makes no sense to consider the Portuguese successes in the Indian Ocean without bearing in mind the Mamluk and Ottoman counter-attack, it makes no sense to concentrate on the Turks and the Egyptians to the exclusion of native Indian merchants who also challenged the Portuguese, but more by means of trade than by launching armadas. Gujaratis had been enjoying great success along the trade routes of the Indian Ocean until the Portuguese came along, mainly through their flourishing port at Diu. When Melaka was seized by Albuquerque in 1511, it became more difficult to maintain their links with the spice trade to the east; but there was still plenty of profit to be made by looking westwards towards the Red Sea and Alexandria, so long as Portuguese blockades remained inter-mittent. Every now and then the Portuguese raided the shores of Gujarat, but Diu on its island in the Bay of Cambay was too well fortified to be taken, and an ambiguous relationship between the rulers of Gujarat and the Portuguese 'State of India' became the norm.

Only in the 1530s did Portugal acquire first a small port on the coast, including the fishing harbour of Bombay, and then Diu itself. In 1535 the ruler of Gujarat granted the Portuguese control of the Diu customs house and they were allowed to build a fortress in Diu. His motive was self-preservation: he had already been defeated by Mughal armies invading

India from the north, and had taken refuge in Diu. But he really wanted neither the Mughals nor the Portuguese, 'Mongols by land and infidels by sea', to be his masters. Once the Mughal threat had diminished, he appealed to Süleyman to send his navy and recapture the fort at Diu. Süleyman took the request seriously, not simply because the Gujarati envoy offered him a magnificent bejewelled girdle and 250 chests containing 1,270,600 'measures of gold'.[32] He was turning his attention back to the Indian Ocean after ten years during which the Ottomans had looked away while the Portuguese took charge of the coasts. The Ottomans fitted out their largest-ever Indian Ocean fleet, made up of ninety ships and 20,000 soldiers. Attempts, not always successful, were made to create a pan-Arabian alliance that would knock out Portuguese power for ever (the ruler of Aden was so terrified by the choice between the devil and the deep blue sea that he fled from the city). The aims were clear and simple:

> Since Diu is the centre of all the maritime trade routes of India, from there war can be made against all the principal strongholds of the Portuguese at whatever time desired, none of which will be able to resist. The Portuguese will thus be expelled from India, trade will once again be free as it has been in times past, and the route to Muhammad's sacred residence will once again be safe from their depredations.[33]

It was hard to see how they could fail to win Diu, which was defended by a small garrison. The problem with sending out such a large expedition was that it had to be kept watered and fed, and there was no longer any support from the current ruler of Gujarat, his troublesome predecessor Bahadur having been disposed of by the Portuguese. Rumours began to spread that a Portuguese fleet was arriving from Goa any day to relieve Diu. Within twenty days the Turkish commander, Hadım Süleyman Pasha, decided that his siege of Diu was futile and turned back to port in Suez.[34] Amazingly, Hadım Süleyman was not beheaded when he returned home after this humiliation, but lived to fight another day. Even after this upset and another failed siege of Diu in 1546, Portuguese relations with Gujarat did not completely disintegrate: in 1572 there were about sixty Portuguese living in the Cambay region, many of whom had become involved in local trade and had intermarried with local women, in the same way that Portuguese settlers in west Africa took local wives.[35]

The Portuguese began to see that they could not actually create the complete monopoly over the spice trade of which they dreamed. The Ottomans would not let go of the Red Sea; they had trumped the Portuguese by taking Aden in 1538, which ensured that some traffic continued to pass up the Red Sea to Egypt; after about 1540 the Red Sea spice trade underwent a revival. When the Turks took Basra in 1546 they acquired a base in the Persian Gulf, though at the wrong end – what they really needed was control of the passage past Hormuz. Still, with ever-expanding demand for spices in Europe and increased production of spices to meet this demand there was room for more than one route linking the Indian Ocean to Lisbon, Antwerp and other Atlantic ports.[36] The Portuguese compromised with the Indian merchants: they allowed local shipping to carry goods back and forth so long as those on board had bought a licence, or *cartaz*, and they insisted that customs dues were paid at the three major Portuguese stations in the Indian Ocean, Hormuz, Goa and Melaka. They well knew that they were unable to control movements east of Melaka, despite a signal victory over a navy of Javanese junks in the Malacca Strait in 1513. This victory helped guarantee free passage for Portuguese ships as far as Ternate and Tidore, the places Francisco Serrão had identified as centres of the trade in cloves and other costly spices; but, to cite Charles Boxer, 'Portuguese shipping in this region was merely one more thread in the existing warp and woof of the Malay–Indonesian interport trade.'[37]

The conquest of Melaka by Albuquerque in 1511 did not bring Portugal mastery over the Malacca Strait, since the expelled sultan still held lands right opposite Melaka in Sumatra; Portuguese territory was limited to a densely populated town and its harbour. As time went by, Indonesians learned to avoid the strait completely, sending spices round the bottom of Sumatra by way of the Sunda Strait, the opening between Sumatra and the next big island, Java. A modus vivendi was reached in the Spice Islands: there was no Portuguese monopoly, but there were enough advantages in letting the Portuguese come and pay for spices to allow them access to the islands. Local rulers learned how to play the Portuguese off against the Spaniards once Spain had gained access to the Moluccas and the Philippines. Generally the Hindu rajahs were more open to contact with the Portuguese, while the Muslim sultans were deeply suspicious of them, with good reason. In many ways the biggest worry back at home in Lisbon was not competition from native merchants so much as the constant attempts by Portuguese merchants to break the Crown monopoly on trade in the most precious spices. Many a Portuguese ship in the South China Sea and the Moluccas was privately owned; and, once again, the Crown had to put up with the situation. The Portuguese also had to face the simple reality that most of the spices garnered in the East Indies were sent not into the Indian Ocean but across the South China Sea to China, as had been the case for centuries. Admittedly, few Chinese ventured out across the waters a century after the Ming voyages had come to an end, but junks from Java kept up the connection instead.[38] All this, as will be seen, acted as an allure to the Portuguese as they attempted to build ties to China itself and even to Japan.

The effects of the Ottoman–Portuguese encounter could, then, be felt as far away as the south-western corner of the Pacific Ocean, in the Spice Islands. In the second half of the sixteenth century Ottoman-led fleets even challenged the Portuguese in the East Indies; Melaka came under attack in 1581.[39] Although the conflict with the Spanish Habsburgs in the Mediterranean took priority (culminating in the massive defeat of the Ottomans at Lepanto in 1571), a parallel conflict between the Ottomans and the Portuguese continued in the Indian Ocean, and both sides saw themselves as warriors of the faith, even when they were battling for control of lucrative trade routes.

III

At the start of the sixteenth century the Turks were not as well informed about the Indian Ocean as one might expect. Selma Reis, writing in 1525, asserted that 'the accursed Portuguese' had captured Melaka 'from Hindu infidels', whereas it had been under Muslim rule for many decades.[40] One man, however, had the curiosity and the connections that enabled him to situate the Ottoman Empire in the wider world: Piri Reis, corsair, admiral, cartographer and geographer extraordinary.[41] Born not later than 1470, in Gallipoli, the seat of a major Ottoman naval arsenal, he began his career while still a boy in the fleet of his uncle, Kemal. Kemal was one of the most successful Barbary corsairs of his day, raiding the Balearic Islands, Sardinia, Sicily, Spain and France with the blessing of the Ottoman sultan.[42] Piri took command of his own vessel in a squadron led by his uncle during a bitter war with Venice between 1499 and 1502 that saw key fortresses in the eastern Mediterranean fall to the Turks. After serving briefly under the most feared of all corsairs, Hayrettin Barbarossa, Piri returned to Gallipoli and in 1513 he prepared a world map, of which more shortly.

Next, seeing the direction world affairs were taking, he gravitated towards the Ottoman court, sailing with Ibrahim Pasha, who has been met already, to newly subdued Egypt, where he presented his world map to Sultan Selim. But he had grander ambitions as a geographer; in 1521 he completed the first version of his *Book on Navigation*, whose importance was rapidly appreciated by Ibrahim Pasha.[43] During a storm Ibrahim saw that Piri was consulting his piles of notes and was duly impressed. 'Finish the book and bring it to me, and we will present it to the Great Ruler of the World, Sultan Süleyman the Lawgiver' (Selim having died by now). Piri presented Süleyman the Magnificent with a revised edition in

1526, followed by a second world map two years later. He was still active in his seventies, taking command of the Red Sea fleet anchored at Suez, and in 1552 he launched a long-expected attack on Hormuz. At first everything went well: Turkish forces landed on Hormuz Island and surrounded the citadel, which proved to be so impregnable that Ottoman cannons had little effect. When he heard that a Portuguese fleet was heading his way he prudently took refuge deep within the Persian Gulf at Basra, but this was seen as an act of cowardice. The charge of treason was strengthened when he sailed off to Suez on his own with a pile of booty, even though the Ottoman governor of Basra forbade him to do so. Now, without Ibrahim to protect him, his enemies at court turned against him. Earlier in the century Hadım Süleyman had been spared after making a mess of Ottoman naval plans, but Piri Reis was not so lucky; everything depended on the sultan's whim, and in 1554 he was beheaded in Istanbul.[44]

At least twenty-six copies of the first version of Piri's book are known, most of which were copied in the seventeenth century, but one manuscript, now in Dresden, dates from 1554, and another, in Oxford, from 1587. Of sixteen copies of the revised version, several once again are late in date; they are thought mainly to be presentation copies, whereas it has been suggested that the copies of the first version, which are less grand in appearance, were aimed at mariners and used at sea.[45] This would make one think that the text was read and had influence over many decades. But, surprisingly, his maps and his book had a limited afterlife; it is not clear that they moulded Ottoman thinking about the world, and this may have been the result of a curious feature of Ottoman civilization: the refusal to permit printing in Turkish and Arabic for several centuries, although Jews and Christians were allowed to set up printing presses in places such as Safed in Galilee.[46] At a time when printed versions of Ptolemy's admittedly incorrect *Geography* were being widely disseminated, not to mention the enormous world map of Waldseemüller depicting 'America', information about the rest of the world was failing to reach a wider Turkish audience. Oddly, by writing in Turkish, Piri Reis cut himself off from the more exalted readers who might have been able to put his information to some use; the languages of high culture in the Ottoman world at this time were Arabic and Persian, and it is not even clear that Piri could write Arabic – it is likely that his second language was the *lingua franca*, the mix of languages with a base in Spanish and Italian that was used on the seaways of the Mediterranean to communicate with merchants and slaves.[47]

Since the time of Mehmet the Conqueror, in the mid- to late fifteenth century, the Ottoman court had taken an interest in Western art and letters; but Piri Reis's connections went deeper, since he had access to secret information. He drew on a very wide range of sources, not by any means all Islamic; the Ottomans were well acquainted with the portolan charts produced by the Catalans, Genoese and Venetians, and a good number of Turkish versions of these maps survive from the period of Piri Reis.[48] Piri would have been perfectly familiar with this type of map from his time as a corsair in the western Mediterranean. He said that he used twenty individual maps as well as several world maps to complete his map of 1513; these included an Arab map of India and a Portuguese map of both India and China.[49] How he obtained these is a puzzle, especially since the Portuguese were so careful to embargo any information about their discoveries, particularly maps. Further evidence that the Ottomans gained access to western European maps comes from an extraordinary world map of 1519 made in Portugal but preserved in the Topkapı Palace Library in Istanbul. The map shows a circular projection with the South Pole at the centre; it is thus a global map of the southern hemisphere, conceivably created in Lisbon by the court cartographer, Pedro Reinel, and anticipating the route taken by Magellan and Elcano – Magellan would have displayed similar maps while attempting to gain attention first at the court of King Manuel and then at that of Emperor Charles.[50] Quite how such a map reached the Ottoman court is a great mystery. The finger has been pointed at Venetian spies, or one could think of Portuguese New Christians of Jewish origin who fled their homeland for the safer setting of the sultan's capital city. Its apparent theft and its arrival in Istanbul would certainly make an ideal topic for a novel by Orhan Pamuk.

The surviving maps of 1513 and 1528 are just fragments of larger charts showing the entire world, maybe one quarter and one sixth of the total, preserved by accident – most likely they were the parts of the bigger chart that were thought to be not very interesting, while the other parts, showing the Indian Ocean, were worn to bits.[51] For these fragments both show the New World, but in a way that would have removed any Turkish fears that Spanish or Portuguese navigators had found a back door into the Spice Islands by taking a westward route across the Atlantic. South America slants south-eastwards and joins a massive southern continent, and there is no break anywhere along the Atlantic coast letting ships pass through somewhere around Panama.[52] The 1513 map shows a number of beautifully drawn ships, such as the ship of 'Mesir Anton the Genoese', Antonio da Noli, discoverer of the Cape Verde Islands.[53] One ship, standing off the coast of South America, carries this label: 'this is the barque from Portugal that encountered a storm and came to this land', and another label on the map describes how a Portuguese ship bound for India was blown on to the shores of a new land. Piri knew, correctly, that a ship had been sent back to Portugal with news of the discovery of Brazil, although he did not know that there was a larger fleet that carried on to India. Another label, placed over the point where South America merges into the great southern continent, begins: 'it is related by the Portuguese infidel that in this place night and day are, at their shortest period, of two hours' duration', which shows that Piri Reis was using Portuguese sources of information, and very early ones at that – Magellan had yet to sail, but Vespucci claimed to have reached a long way down the South American coast.[54]

Piri Reis was aware of the importance of Columbus, to whom he devoted another label, much the longest on the map. There were quite a few crossed wires: he told how 'Qulunbu' had presented his idea about crossing the ocean to 'the eminent men of Genoa', who replied: 'O foolish man, the end and boundary of the world is to be found in the West. It is full of the mist of darkness.' But Piri's uncle, Kemal Reis, had a Spanish prisoner who claimed to have travelled to the newly discovered land with Qulunbu on three occasions. After a long description of the lands Qulunbu visited, Piri Reis remarked: 'now these regions have been opened to all and have become well known . . . The coasts and islands on this map are copied from the map of Qulunbu.'[55] Piri tried to reproduce the names of places all along the shores he was mapping, and in the Atlantic islands in between. He understood the importance of this information not just in the grand strategy of the Ottoman Empire face to face with Spain and Portugal, but also as valuable knowledge about the world. In that sense he was the intellectual kinsman of the geographers of Renaissance Spain and Italy, even if he wrote in the Turkish vernacular. This does not mean that he was any the less agitated about the intrusion of Christian infidels into the Indian Ocean or that he had any positive feelings towards the Portuguese whose maps he had been exploiting:

> Know that Hormuz is an island. Many merchants visit it . . . but now, O friend, the Portuguese have come there and built a stronghold on its cape. They control the place and collect the customs – you see into what condition that province has sunk! The Portuguese have vanquished the natives, and their own merchants crowd the warehouses there. Whatever the season, trading cannot happen now without the Portuguese.[56]

Piri Reis understood, then, that the European irruption into the Indian Ocean had dramatically changed the political and commercial relationship between the Ottoman lands and the rest of the world. Yet, paradoxically, his warnings about the Portuguese were based on knowledge he had derived in part from Spanish and Portuguese maps. Both the Ottomans and the Iberians had acquired a much larger view of a world joined together by maritime connections.

34

The Great Galleons of Manila

I

The Ottomans were not alone in wishing the Portuguese ill-fortune in the Indian Ocean. When Andrés de Urdaneta reached the court of Charles V at Valladolid in 1536, after more than eleven years spent stuck in the East Indies under Portuguese detention, he was not discouraged by his experiences. He was still young, twenty-eight years old. He could only deliver a verbal report, after the Portuguese had confiscated all his maps and papers, but 'he was very well informed, and able to relate, stage by stage, all that he had seen', according to the polymath natural historian Oviedo, who witnessed his performance.[1] Forty-four years had passed since Columbus had set out for the Spice Islands by the western route, and Urdaneta was keen to show that a western route was still feasible, even with America in the way and the Pacific to be mastered. He told the emperor: 'If Your Majesty were pleased to order commerce to be maintained with the Moluccas, there might be brought from there every year over 6,000 *quintales* of cloves [roughly 600,000 lb], and there are years when there is a harvest of more than 11,000 *quintales*.' In addition, gold, nutmeg and mace could be found there; 'there are many rich and valuable conquests to be made round the Moluccas, and many lands with much trade, including China, with which communication might be made from the Moluccas.'[2] It was still unclear whether the Moluccas lay in the Spanish or Portuguese half of the world, as defined by the treaty of 1494, but seven years earlier Charles had renounced Spanish claims in return for a cash payment from Portugal of 350,000 ducats, which was much-needed money at a time when Charles was busy with his Italian wars.[3] As the Spaniards consolidated their hold on Mexico, under Cortés, and Peru, under Pizarro, it became clear that vast amounts of silver could be extracted from the New World, and the Genoese were willing to advance money in anticipation of the arrival of the silver fleets from America.[4]

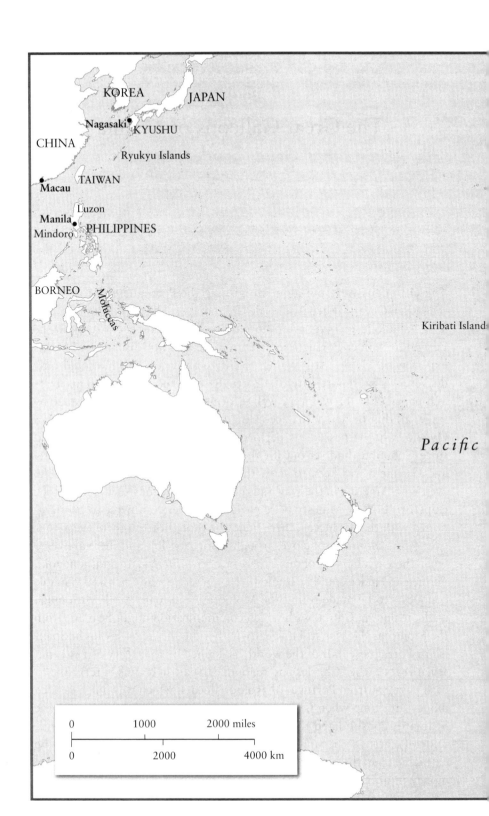

KOREA
JAPAN
Nagasaki
KYUSHU
CHINA
Ryukyu Islands
TAIWAN
Macau
Luzon
Manila
PHILIPPINES
Mindoro
BORNEO
Moluccas
Kiribati Island
Pacific

0   1000   2000 miles

0   2000   4000 km

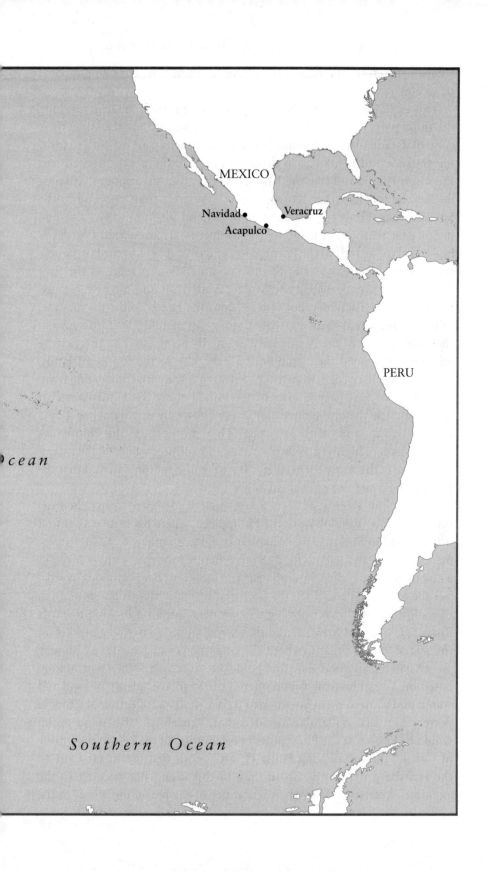

Charles therefore had reason to believe his money worries would come to an end.

This explains the rather slow progress the Spaniards made in marking out those parts of the western Pacific that they wanted to take under their control. Gradually they learned that the Pacific was studded with islands, but they took little interest in them – an expedition in 1536 headed into the south Pacific and saw the Kiribati Islands, but the captain, Grijalva, decided he would rather return to South America than press on to the Spice Islands. However, his crew mutinied and killed him. Grijalva had had cogent reasons for avoiding the Moluccas: he knew that Charles V had ceded the islands to the Portuguese, and engaging with the Portuguese was always the great fear of Spanish commanders en route to the East Indies. The sailors reached the Moluccas after all and most were massacred by irate islanders, but two fell into the hands of the Portuguese, with the result that their unsavoury story can be told.[5] Still, the gaps in the Spanish map of the Pacific were gradually being filled in. In 1542 the Spaniards extended their ambitions all the way to the Ryukyu Islands, which, as has been seen, were lively centres of trade with China and Japan. The idea that was germinating in the minds of the Spaniards was that they could use the Philippines (not as yet known by that name) as a base from which to trade with east Asia. They did not rate the Philippines themselves very highly; greedy for cloves and nutmeg, which fetched startling prices in the Antwerp market, they were disappointed to find that the Philippines could not offer them either spice.

In 1542 the viceroy of New Spain (that is, Mexico) despatched his brother-in-law, Villalobos, to the Philippines, where his crew was at first discouraged to find that the inhabitants did not bother, or need, to produce a surplus and had no food to offer. Before long they were reduced to a diet of grubs, psychedelic crabmeat and luminous but poisonous lizards. Yet the Spaniards could see the potential of these islands not as sources of wealth in their own right but as a strategic location looking towards Borneo, China and Melaka, and they were impressed to find a market on the island of Sarangani, where the Spanish crew spent seven hungry months; here, silk, porcelain and gold were to be had. When a local king based on a neighbouring island offered the Spaniards plenty of food and water, and showed them his wooden palace with its collection of Chinese pottery and silk, Villalobos decided that, henceforth, the island group would be known as the Philippines in celebration of the heir to the throne of Castile, the future King Philip II, an honour that meant far more to the Habsburg dynasty in Spain than to this king.[6] But once again the explorers were stymied by their ignorance of the prevailing winds in the

Pacific; when they tried to reach Mexico, they could not make any headway, and Villalobos died on Amboyna, an island west of New Guinea, in
1544. The Spaniards began, however, to see that the Philippines were not
a complete desert, even if they were less sophisticated than some parts of
the East Indies. The native peoples wore gold ornaments made out of local
metal; there was cinnamon bark; and ginger, long the second most popular
eastern spice, grew in the islands. The inhabitants were drawn from
several peoples; the area had been settled in the remote past by Malay
navigators, and the different languages spoken in the Philippines were
related to Malay and the Polynesian languages. The coastal peoples had
often retained the skill in seamanship for which the Pacific peoples are
famous.[7]

The problem was that the Philippines seemed so inaccessible. Only in
the 1550s did the Spanish king, now Philip II, decide that the time was
ripe for a new expedition, and his decision may have been influenced by
short-term inflation in the spice market: between 1558 and 1563 spice
prices nearly trebled in Old Castile, and cloves and cinnamon were
particularly badly affected. Quite why this occurred is not clear – one
explanation is runaway speculation in the spice market of Antwerp.[8] The
plan to reach the Philippines was all very well, but the question remained
whether there was anyone who knew enough about the Pacific to guide a
new venture across the ocean. There was one person: Andrés de Urdaneta,
who, moreover, was conveniently convinced that the Philippines lay within
the Spanish hemisphere of the world. However, Urdaneta was well into
his fifties and had entered a convent of Augustinian friars; no one in his
right mind wanted to join such a risky voyage, which ensured that many
of the crew were not Spanish at all but Portuguese, Italian, Flemish and
even Greek. But a personal appeal from the king of Spain to Urdaneta
persuaded him to leave his convent and take up the position of senior pilot,
advising the captain-general, Miguel López de Legázpi.[9]

The fleet was to consist of two galleons and three smaller vessels, and
the first problem was that no shipyard capable of building large galleons
existed on the Pacific shore of Mexico. Everything had to be created from
scratch, including a workforce; and the right sorts of wood had to be
obtained and hauled down to the coast. The cost of building this tiny fleet
was 7,000,000 *pesos*.[10] It set out from Navidad, a port on the Pacific coast
of Mexico, late in 1564.[11] One of the small ships, of a type known as the
patache, or pinnace, became detached from the rest of the flotilla but
reached Mindanao in the Philippines on its own; after patiently waiting
for the other ships, which had headed off elsewhere, its captain, Arellano,
decided that he did not have enough food to stay any longer and returned

to Mexico, having spent eight and a half months away from Navidad. This was the first really successful return journey, because Arellano had the good sense to seek out the east winds that would blow his ship back to the Americas. In the process he discovered a route back from the Philippines, ignorance of which had frustrated previous attempts to reach Mexico. There was a Kafkaesque finale, though: he was accused of abandoning his commander and avoiding any attempt to find him in the Philippines. After his own return to Mexico, Legázpi submitted a request to the *Audiencia*, the highest court in New Spain, demanding that Arellano be put on trial. Arellano was forced to defend his conduct before the *Audiencia* but he was never actually punished for his supposed crime.[12]

As for Legázpi, he made good progress in extending Spanish dominion over the Philippines. Local rulers, including Muslim ones, were willing to enter into pacts with him when they saw the glitter of American silver, invaluable in trade with China. When the Filipinos objected, Spanish firepower proved irresistible. Less blood was spilled than during the Portuguese entry into the Indian Ocean, but Legázpi could be ruthless when he thought occasion demanded a show of strength. His expedition was not all about conquest, however; he informed King Philip that Chinese and Japanese merchants came to trade in the big Philippine islands of Luzon and Mindoro year in, year out; but he was also aware that he had come into an area where Portuguese merchants occasionally wended their way. To keep them at bay he really needed a base in the islands, and he needed to convince the local sultans, even if they were Muslim, that Spanish overlordship was a good thing.[13]

Like Arellano, Legázpi's men found their way back to Mexico. Urdaneta once again proved to be an able pilot, and the maps he made were not, this time, lost to the Portuguese but were copied for generations. He found a much better route than Arellano, but even so the voyage from the Philippines to Mexico proved to be much longer than the journey outwards; the south-west monsoon took the galleon *San Pedro* (sometimes referred to as the *San Pablo*) up to the latitude of Japan, and then into the wind system of the northern Pacific, which drove the ship eastwards in a great arc until it reached the Santa Barbara Channel off California.[14] It took a little over four months for the galleon to reach Acapulco, in October 1565. The bare recitation of the route taken does not do justice to the misery the sailors experienced on the long homeward run. As with da Gama's fleets, scurvy took the lives of several men (sixteen died en route, but the crew numbered more than 200, so the ratio of deaths was much better than on many earlier voyages). The Legázpi expedition is generally taken to mark the beginning of the Manila galleon trade, which lasted for

250 years from 1565 to 1815, punctuated by occasional interruptions during periods of conflict or following the shipwreck of a galleon.[15] These
galleons frequently displaced 1,000 tons and were perhaps the largest
trading ships afloat at the time.

Once they lay under Spanish rule the Philippines were treated as part
of the viceroyalty of New Spain, in other words as an extension of Mexico;
and the inhabitants, like the native Americans, were indiscriminately
called 'Indians', *Indios*, or, in the case of the large number of Muslims in
some parts of the archipelago, they were called 'Moors', *Moros*. These
were the traditional broad-brush ethnic categories into which the Spaniards divided much of humanity.

II

While the circumnavigators, notably Magellan and Elcano and then
Drake, have attracted a great deal of attention, the really important circumnavigation, conducted in stages, was that which was created following
the opening of the Manila galleon route, and this has been oddly ignored
by historians.[16] The Philippines were linked to China and Japan, but also
to Mexico and Peru; goods transported across Central America reached
Veracruz on the Gulf of Mexico, were ferried to Havana and were then
carried across the Atlantic to Seville and Cádiz. And in the opposite direction, despite the longstanding hostility between the Spanish colonizers
and the Portuguese, goods filtered from Manila to Macau, Melaka,
Goa and then into the Portuguese spice trading network all the way to
Lisbon and Antwerp. The oceans had been joined together, and the nails
that held the network together were all these cities. Chinese silk and
ceramics might reach a table in Spain by way of Mexico or the Cape of
Good Hope. Spanish *hidalgos* in Mexico, and the native elite, could dine
off Chinese porcelain and dress in fine silks brought by galleon once a
year from Manila.[17] For, as the Spaniards and their Portuguese rivals
penetrated deeper into the trade networks of the South China Sea, the
search for ever greater quantities of spices was matched by a passion for
the exotic products of both China and Japan. These ambitions were independently boosted by the decision of the Ming emperor in 1567 to permit
Chinese merchants to trade abroad, after a century and a half during which
the Ming court had strongly discouraged foreign trade.[18]

To achieve their aims the Spaniards would have to identify the best-
placed harbour from which they could conduct their trade. An expedition
sent out in 1570 had the pleasing result that the sultan of Manila, a

settlement on the island of Luzon, entered into a pact of blood brother-hood, in the traditional way (which involved drinking a liquid containing drops of the blood of the parties to the agreement). However, there is a difference between sworn amity and submission, and Sultan Soliman was upset when he realized that the Spaniards now thought he was their sub-ject and owed the king of Spain tribute. This meant that the Spaniards resorted to force, but in 1571 they formally established Manila as the capital of their Philippine colony, a title confirmed by King Philip in 1595, when the city, now booming, was recognized as *Cabeza*, head, *de Filipi-nas*.[19] The Chinese had their own story about the foundation of Manila:

> When they perceived that the country was weak and could be occupied, they bestowed rich presents upon the king and demanded a plot of land as big as an oxhide for building houses and living there. The king did not suspect any trickery and assented. These men thereupon cut the hide of an ox into narrow strips, pieced these together until they extended the length of a thousand fathoms, and in this way encompassed the whole land of Luzon, which they then claimed, in accordance with their agreement.[20]

This was the story of how Dido founded Carthage, which had found its way, perhaps in the storytelling of Portuguese travellers, all the way to China.[21] Yet the gloomy view of Legázpi was that 'this land cannot be sustained by trade', by which he meant not that the creation of a trading base there would fail, but that the resources of the Philippines were not sufficient to keep Manila alive. Its future depended on becoming the hub for Pacific trade – which is what did happen.[22]

Remarkably, the Manila galleon – often just one very large ship – was the main source of income for the Spanish population of Manila. The life-line linking Manila to Mexico was fragile and was easily snapped. Even so, sailors and settlers were prepared to risk taking this route in the search for profit or sometimes out of curiosity. A vivid account of a journey to Manila survives from the hand of Francesco Carletti, a Florentine merchant who set out across the world in 1594, when he was about twenty-one years of age. He had been living in Seville with his father, learning 'the profession of merchant', and after three years there his father suggested that they should hire a small ship of about 400 tons, sail to the Cape Verde Islands, load the ship with black slaves, and transport them to the West Indies. This was (it is sad to say) a normal enough operation, apart from the fact that the Carlettis were Italian, and only subjects of Spain were permitted to ply these routes. It was therefore essential to find a Spanish backer; this was a woman from Seville who had married a Pisan businessman, and who agreed to front the expedition.[23] The Carlettis arrived in the Caribbean safely, mourning the loss of slaves thrown into the sea after they died (so they said) from eating fresh fish, and on a whim they penetrated deeper and deeper into the New World, reaching Panama and Peru, and then up to Mexico, visiting Acapulco and next trekking up to Mexico City with a load of silver, buying and selling, and recording the wonderful sights they saw, for Francesco had decided that his account of the voyage was to be sent to Ferdinando de' Medici, the Grand Duke of Tuscany and an enthusiast for the promotion of trade – he showered the free port of Livorno with privileges that enabled Armenians, Jews and others to settle in the city.

The Carlettis had it in mind to buy goods and take them back to Lima. The maritime route along the coast from Peru to Mexico was now fully functioning; it was a Spanish creation, for the Aztecs and the Incas had barely been aware of one another's empire. But the longer they spent in Mexico, the more Carletti's father was convinced that this was only halfway to where he needed to be: the Philippines. Once again they had to find a way of being taken on board when only Spaniards were allowed to buy passage to the islands. However, those who served on board were exempt from this rule – after all, the crews included large numbers of Filipinos, Chinese and even black Africans. The Carlettis were appointed as officers on board, though the captain agreed to find two sailors who would perform their duties so long as they renounced their officers' pay. There was also an official limit of half a million golden *escudos* (converted into silver) on the amount of silver, mined in Peru and Mexico, that could be taken to the Philippines to pay for the goods available there. The Crown wanted to treat the Manila trade as a royal monopoly, but in reality there was plenty of opportunity to smuggle money into the islands, and goods out of them; the captain was fully complicit, for 'he was used to carrying such things for various people who shipped money', with the result that the amount of bullion on board was worth 1,000,000 *escudos*. Out of this, the captain was entitled to take 2 per cent as a fee, so one can see why he was perfectly willing to defy the Spanish authorities despite threats of confiscation and worse.[24]

The outward journey was generally less of a trial, and after setting out in March 1596 the Carlettis enjoyed a 'prosperous and very happy navigation'; there was always a following wind, so that the journey lasted sixty-six days, compared to the six months that a return trip might take. The ships took on fresh water in the Marianas, the islands Magellan had called the 'Islands of Thieves'; it was loaded in the form of very stout lengths of bamboo cane, filled with water. All the inhabitants wanted was bits and pieces of iron, which were prized more than gold: 'they were asking in the friendliest way, rubbing the palm of their hands along the side of their hearts, saying "*Chamarri, her, her*," which means "Friends, iron, iron."' Francesco Carletti was especially impressed by the boats the islanders built, 'so well made of the thinnest boards painted and worked with various colours, these mixed with much artistry, and sewed together without nails in a capricious and beautiful way and style, so light that they appeared to be birds flying over that sea'. He admired the outriggers that made sure the boats could never capsize or sink, because they buoyed up the boats, and the long, narrow sails 'made in the manner of rush mats'.[25] He was less impressed by the 'barbarians' themselves, whose men went around shamelessly naked.

In many respects, the approach to Manila was the most dangerous part of these voyages. Manila lies on the western side of the large northern Philippine island of Luzon, and to reach it ships had to pass through the Luzon Strait between Taiwan and Luzon, and then manoeuvre through narrow channels and past shoals into Manila Bay. Even before the galleon carrying Carletti had passed Taiwan, a typhoon started to blow, and at that point the sails were at last lowered, and the galleons were immobilized for eighteen days, running short of fresh water. Carletti described how water was rationed and orders were given not to cook any food, on the grounds that this made people drink more (the meat taken on board was heavily salted); all one was allowed was ship's biscuit moistened in water and oil, and sprinkled with sugar. These privations seemed distant memories once the storm abated and the ships anchored off Luzon, taking on fresh fish and marvellous fruits: 'truly those bananas in that region seemed to me one of the most delicious fruits to be found anywhere in the world, and in particular certain ones that had a very subtle odour, so that one could desire nothing more welcome or more flavoursome.'[26]

Carletti was not as overwhelmed by Manila as he was by Philippine bananas. He recognized that its layout and the style of its houses were similar to what he had seen in Mexico City, which was much larger, though he thought Manila was better defended by its thick walls and a garrison of 800 Spanish soldiers, which made sense as they faced many enemies in a sea that contained, he said, 12,000 islands. But he was impressed by the profits that the Spanish settlers were able to make: 'from the merchandise brought there by the Chinese and then transported to Mexico, they still earn 150 and 200 per cent.'

> Whatever those islands lack is brought there from outside. From Japan comes the wheat flour from which they make bread to serve to the Spaniards; from there also come divers other things that they bring on their ships and sell. And the Chinese – that is, those from the province of China – also

come there each year with some fifty ships laden with raw silk that has been
spun and woven into pieces of velvet, satin, damask or taffeta, as well as
much cotton cloth and musk, sugar, porcelain, and very many other sorts
of merchandise, from all of which they make very noble trade with the
Spaniards, who buy it from them to take it to Mexico in New Spain.[27]

The year Carletti arrived there were only about a dozen of these junks in
port, and everything was snapped up quickly. Carletti attributed the lack
of Chinese goods to a big fire in the Chinese quarter of the city; but, as
will be seen, there were other interruptions: pirate raids, riots by Chinese
settlers, and so on.

Carletti did not simply report on business opportunities; he was also
fascinated by the Filipinos themselves: the *Moros*, who enjoyed gambling
on cockfights, and the heavily tattooed *Bisaios*, the pagan population,
whose men pierced their penises with studs, which somehow increased
their 'lustful pleasure', though at first, at any rate, the studs made their
female partners extremely uncomfortable. But he was full of praise for
the islands – 'everything is good in those islands.'[28] Aware that the Spanish
government made it very difficult for foreign merchants to trade out of
Manila, the Carlettis next conceived a plan to sail by way of Japan to
China, the East Indies, Goa and Lisbon. This was no more straightforward
than attempting to load merchandise on ships bound for Acapulco. Castilians were forbidden to enter the Portuguese area of trade, under pain of
confiscation of goods and imprisonment. This rule still held even though
Philip II of Spain had succeeded to the throne of Portugal in 1581, following the death of King Sebastian in battle against the Moroccans and of his
childless heir shortly afterwards. It was a way of keeping the peace between
enemies who had a common monarch but not a common purpose.

The answer to the problem the Carlettis faced was to steal out of Manila
at night carrying their bars of silver on board a Japanese ship, for Japan
was 'a free region in which neither the Portuguese nor the Castilians rule'.
This ship was similar to a junk, and Carletti was fascinated but not entirely
convinced by the sail, which, he said, folded up like a fan but was really
quite weak, and he was intrigued also by the fragile rudder.[29] Portuguese
ships arrived each year at Nagasaki, sailing in from Macau on the coast
of China, so that there would be no great difficulty in heading for the
South China Sea after looking around parts of Japan, which was not yet
closed to foreign traders, and where Carletti encountered a leaf called *cha*,
or tea, and warm rice wine – his experiences in Japan will be examined
later.[30] Carletti's account of Manila clearly demonstrates the city's place
at the hub of networks linking the Spanish Philippines not just to Mexico,

and through Mexico to Spain, but also to China (when the junks arrived) and northwards towards Japan; nor in reality were the Portuguese always unwelcome in the city. As a centre of exchange, Manila was connected to the maritime trading centres of the entire known world.

III

Manila, with its fine harbour and its fertile hinterland, was a cosmopolitan city, though that is not to say that relations between its many different peoples were always cordial. The Spanish presence was complicated by the fact that the conquerors were Catholic and that they were in constant contact with Muslims, Buddhists, Daoists and pagans. While the Spanish settlers in Manila, numbering 7,350 in 1650, confined themselves to a fortified city, which came to be known as *Intramuros*, 'within the walls' (still the name of old Manila), the suburbs of Manila teemed with Chinese, Japanese and Filipinos.[31] There had been a settlement at the site the Filipinos called *Maynila* for some time, and the Spaniards thought of calling the city 'Sweet Name of Jesus', but somehow a hispanized version of the old name seemed simpler.[32] The Chinese presence in the Philippines already had a long history when the Spanish conquerors arrived. In the Song period, from the mid-tenth to the late thirteenth century, Chinese junks regularly visited the islands, for this was a period when the imperial court encouraged private trade. But private trade continued unofficially even under the sterner policies of the early Ming emperors; the Philippines were among the places visited by Zheng He's fleet, since the Yung-lo emperor was keen to draw the islands under his overlordship and had already sent an official to the island of Luzon in 1405 in the expectation that he would take charge of the place.[33] Two years later Zheng He's fleet arrived, and then and on other occasions tribute reached China from the islands, including gold, precious stones and pearls, but Filipino boats continued to come to China, and spices from Java and the Moluccas were collected in the Philippines by Chinese merchants who evaded the official ban on private trade. The clearest evidence for intensive contact between China and the Philippines before the arrival of the Europeans comes from the description of local chieftains dining off porcelain in Pigafetta's account of Magellan's voyage, while archaeological finds even in the Philippine uplands, away from the coastal areas visited by shipping, show that gifts of Chinese ceramics were used to bond the highland chiefs to the powerful *datus*, or petty rulers, of low-lying regions. Admittedly, the *datus* kept the finest porcelain for themselves.[34]

It rapidly became clear that Manila could not live without China, just as it could not live without Acapulco. After a great massacre of the Chinese in 1603, a Spanish commentator complained that the city ran out of food, even out of shoes, for the Chinese were not just traders but artisans: 'it is true that the city can neither go on nor maintain itself without these Chinese'.[35] The Spaniards knew the Chinese as *Sangleys*, a corruption of the term *seng-li*, which in the Amoy dialect of Chinese meant 'trade'.[36] The Sangleys arrived on big junks that carried up to 400 passengers, some of whom could be expected to stay put in Manila, settling in the *Parían*, or Chinese quarter. The junks were quite unlike European or Filipino vessels; each end was square, and the deck was covered with little huts roofed with palm leaves, while the hold was divided up by partitions, so that if the ship sprang a leak only one partition at a time would be flooded. Merchants rented space in these partitions, storing their cargo for a fee of 20 per cent of the price the goods fetched; another 20 per cent or more went to the Chinese brokers in Manila who helped manage the sales, if need be by handing out bribes to Spanish officials, although officially goods were sold through a system of wholesale bargaining which met the needs of Spanish merchants – with little or no knowledge of Chinese, they remained suspicious of the bargaining ability of the Chinese.[37] Already familiar with old Maynila, the Chinese junks came in ever greater numbers once the Spanish city had come into being, recorded arrivals rising from only six in 1574 to forty or more each year by 1580, and generally at least thirty could be expected to arrive, so long as the Chinese knew that the Manila galleons had come into port with the silver needed for settling bills. The visit was brief, to allow for the monsoons and the danger of typhoons: out from China in March, and leaving Manila by early June.[38]

This trade was dominated by silk and porcelain. At first some of the Spaniards were rather dismissive when talking about the quality of the silk coming from China, but once the Chinese had a good sense of the distant markets they were trying to reach all this changed. They imitated the silks of Andalusia, and opinions differed about which was better, Chinese or Andalusian silk cloth. The business community of Seville looked with disapproval on the expansion of the silk trade from China to Manila and from Manila to Mexico, having assumed that Mexico would be their own special market. Chinese kilns showed similar adaptability to Chinese looms. In the seventeenth century Chinese potters knew what the Europeans and the Japanese wanted, and modified their designs accordingly. What resulted was a European and Spanish colonial taste for Chinese goods, subtly altered to meet the cultural preferences of the purchasers; this was an important moment in the encounter of Chinese civilization with the West. Antonio de Morga, president of the high court, or *Audiencia*, at Manila late in the sixteenth century, itemized the goods that arrived on these junks:

> Raw silk in bundles, of the fineness of two strands, and other silk of coarser quality; fine untwisted silk, white and of all colours, wound in small skeins; quantities of velvets, some plain and some embroidered in all sorts of figures, colours and fashions, others with body of gold and embroidered with gold; woven stuffs and brocades, of gold and silver upon silk of various colours and patterns, quantities of gold and silver thread in skeins; damasks, satins, taffetas and other cloths of all colours . . . [39]

That was only the silk; they also brought linen and cotton cloth, hangings, coverlets, tapestries, metal goods including copper kettles, gunpowder, wheat flour, fresh and preserved fruits, decorated writing cases, gilded benches, live birds and pack animals – each junk must have been the sixteenth-century equivalent of a floating department store. So responsive were the Chinese to the demands of the market in Manila and Mexico that they sometimes jumped to the wrong conclusion. A Spaniard had lost his nose, probably from venereal disease, and he commissioned a wooden nose from a visiting Chinese craftsman, whom he paid very generously. On his next trip to Manila the craftsman thought he had worked out how to make himself a small fortune, and brought a whole cargo of wooden noses, only to discover what he should have noticed earlier: that the Spaniards in Manila already had noses of their own.[40]

All this was paid for with enormous quantities of Peruvian, and to a lesser extent Mexican, silver shipped out from Acapulco on the annual galleon voyage. One estimate for the quantity of American silver mined between 1500 and 1800 is 150,000 tons; only some of this was carried west on the Manila galleons (apparently 12,000,000 *pesos* of silver were sent to Manila in 1597, 5,000,000 in most years), but even so the export of American silver had a dramatic effect on the silver-starved Chinese economy.[41] The Ming emperors had tried to deal with the shortage of silver within their empire by continuing the Mongol practice of issuing paper money. Foreign rulers who received gracious gifts of paper money in exchange for their tribute may well have wondered whether this was fair exchange, especially when (as in 1410) an embassy from the Philippines brought the emperor a present of gold.[42] Another possibility was to collect taxes in grain, but Chinese officials responded to the influx of bullion by accepting payments in silver instead, as it was easier to transport; and then a decision to rationalize a whole series of taxes into what was evocatively called the 'Single Whip', in about 1570, made silver payments the norm.

In the very long term the gold:silver ratio in China became less extreme; it stood at 1:5.5 in Canton around 1600, but could be as high as 1:14 in contemporary Spain. In China as in Europe, the arrival of large amounts of bullion pushed up prices, leading to a 'great inflation'; on the other hand, the arrival of so much silver drove economic expansion within Ming China by vastly boosting the money supply.[43] Meanwhile visiting merchants could buy gold cheaply with silver so long as the Chinese exchange rate was much more favourable than elsewhere. There were opportunities to make a considerable fortune by shifting bullion around the world from places rich in silver to places poor in silver, something the Genoese and Venetians had known in earlier centuries.[44] A Portuguese merchant commented in 1621: 'silver wanders throughout the world in its peregrinations before flocking to China, where it remains, as if at its natural centre.'[45]

Chinese trade brought people as well as goods to Manila. The Chinese quarter, the *Parían*, had been set aside by a late sixteenth-century governor of the Philippines as a sort of Chinese ghetto; the name was a corruption of the Chinese word for 'organization'.[46] This lay outside the walled area of Intramuros inhabited by the Spanish settlers, and it grew very rapidly, so that by 1600 there were more than 400 shops in the reserved area and the Chinese population of Manila is thought to have reached 12,000, mainly men, as they tended to arrive from China without women, though many took Filipino wives. The Spaniards were deeply suspicious of the inhabitants of the *Parían*. Some became Catholics, but on one occasion the ringleader of Chinese opposition to the Spaniards was a disillusioned Christian. King Philip III believed that they were a 'great peril'.[47] Tensions increased when Manila was under threat from Chinese ships, as occurred in 1574; that year Chinese pirates aboard seventy large junks commanded by Lin Feng, or Limahon, overran large parts of Manila, and were only beaten back with great difficulty after Spanish reinforcements arrived by sea under the able command of Juan de Salcedo, who was the grandson of the pioneer of the Philippines, Legázpi. Once Limahon and his men had been chased away from Manila, the Spanish ships caught up with the pirates and annihilated their fleet. But there was also trouble inside the colony. In 1593 the Spanish governor and Spanish members of his crew were assassinated by Chinese oarsmen aboard his galley. The governor's son and successor sent out an appeal as far as Macau and Melaka in the hope of tracing the culprits and arresting them, and a few Chinese sailors were sent from Melaka to Manila for execution, though they may just have been scapegoats. Meanwhile (a Chinese account says) the Chinese, from love of trade, continued to live in Manila.[48]

Tension boiled over every fourteen years, on average, during the late sixteenth and seventeenth century. The most bizarre example of Chinese–Spanish tension took place in 1603, and even at the time the Spaniards wondered whether they were witnessing a farce or serious political negotiations. Three mandarins arrived in Manila, and were ceremonially carried to the governor's palace, where they said that they were looking for the gold-bearing island of *Cabit*, which was not far off and belonged to no ruler. There was indeed a place called Cavite near Manila, a port that served as a gateway to the capital, and the mandarins were taken there and were shown that it was not full of gold.[49] It did possess a naval shipyard, and that was surely what the mandarins hoped to inspect. The arrival of the mandarins set off rumours about their real intentions. The Spanish settlers became convinced that they were spies and that a large Chinese fleet was being prepared, bearing 100,000 soldiers who would flush the Spaniards out of the Philippines. On top of this, rumours spread that the Chinese in the *Parián* district were about to rise in revolt. The mistrust between Spaniards and Chinese was nothing new, but Chinese grievances mounted as Japanese mercenaries who formed part of the Manila garrison threatened to head off rebellion by massacring the Chinese. October 1603 saw a series of terrible events, as the Chinese rose in revolt, burned the outskirts of the city and killed the elite soldiers of Spain, including the governor; on another occasion they were able to scatter the formidable Japanese mercenaries. The rebels even massacred fellow Chinese who were not interested in joining the rebellion. The rebellion could only be put down when Spanish reinforcements arrived from elsewhere in the islands; they pursued and killed Chinese rebels everywhere they could find them, and a Chinese chronicle states that the death toll was as high as 25,000.[50]

Even the massacre of thousands of Chinese did not lead to a rupture with China: trade continued and 6,000 settlers came back to the *Parián* within the next two years. The new governor told King Philip III: 'this country has been greatly consoled at seeing that the Chinese have chosen to continue their commerce, of which we were much in doubt.' The Chinese view, not surprisingly, had a slightly different emphasis: 'after that time the Chinese gradually flocked to Manila; and the savages [the Spaniards], seeing profit in the commerce with China, did not oppose them.'[51]

IV

King Philip had even grander plans, going far beyond a trading relationship with the Chinese. As early as 1573 the idea of a Spanish invasion of China had been mooted. The examples of Mexico and Peru seemed to prove that compact Spanish armies, well supplied with arms, could overwhelm mighty empires. The Japanese were known to hate the Ming and could be persuaded to join the invasion. The Ming Empire was dismissed as fragile and ill-defended. As with the other Iberian conquests, the mercenary and the spiritual were intertwined. One only needed to think of the great benefit to Christendom of conquering this heathen land and converting its inhabitants to the Catholic faith. An expedition set out from Manila in June 1575, and many of those on board imagined that they were *conquistadores* who would win control of the legendary wealth of China. However, the first priority was to persuade the Ming emperor that Spanish friars should be allowed to preach the faith in China. Another topic for discussion was the creation of a Spanish trading base on the Chinese coast opposite Taiwan, which the Chinese were quite happy to permit, especially if the Spanish fleet would help clear the waters between the Philippines and China of pirates – one troublemaker, Limahon, was as much of a nuisance to the Chinese as he was to the Spaniards.[52] Over the next few years schemes to invade China were presented again and again at Philip's court, and – though they looked attractive – the defeat of the Spanish Armada by the English navy in 1588 brought Philip down to earth. Hugh Thomas wondered whether these schemes might have been brought to fruition had Philip not lost his fleet that year, while the increasingly bitter rebellion in Philip's north European possessions, the Netherlands, was another drain on resources.[53]

Philip understood that his priority would have to be the promotion of Spain's commercial interests in the western Pacific, rather than dreams of conquering another exotic empire. His Spanish subjects, not just in Manila but in Mexico, Peru and even Europe, were fascinated by Chinese goods.[54] Behind their commercial ambitions lay the old question of rivalry not with Chinese merchants but with Portuguese ones. The Spaniards were aware that their Portuguese rivals had managed to camp on the very edge of China, where, at the mouth of the Pearl River, which leads to Guangzhou (Canton), they had created the outpost of Macau, whose foundation will be examined in the next chapter.[55] After 1580, and Philip's accession to the throne of Portugal as well as Castile, opportunities seemed to beckon for Spanish trade through Macau. The king was not keen, however, banning Spanish visits to Macau in 1593. A few years later he did permit the Spaniards to visit the coast of China, and they tried to copy the Portuguese by setting up their own base at a place they called El Piñal, which also lay close to the Pearl River; it probably stood somewhere in the territory of modern Hong Kong. Not surprisingly, the Portuguese complained vociferously, while a Spanish official who had to endure a freezing winter in El Piñal in 1598 grumbled that not just the Portuguese but the Chinese were an endless source of trouble – rather than robbing the Spaniards by violence they found more subtle means of robbing them 'by other and worse methods', in other words clever trading practices.[56] El Piñal did not survive much longer. Over time, contact between Macau and Manila grew; Manila learned to look westwards as well as eastwards, and the value of goods sent from Macau to Manila reached 1,500,000 *pesos* by 1630.[57] From the perspective of the Manila settlers, what counted was that the Chinese junks kept coming, accompanied by Filipino outrigger craft, Portuguese ships and, importantly, Japanese junks.

V

The Japanese connections of Manila were not as important to the city's prosperity as its Chinese connections, but they were nonetheless significant. It would be wrong to think that Japan always cut itself off from contact with Europeans, once the Portuguese, Spaniards and finally the Dutch had penetrated into their waters. The closure of trade to European merchants for more than two centuries, except through Nagasaki (where the Dutch established a small trading station in 1641), followed a period of close but wary engagement with these visitors from the other side of the world, who were as puzzled by the Japanese as the Japanese were by them. Until 1639 the Portuguese enjoyed an active trade in Japanese silk; problems arose, however, when Jesuit missionaries, also Portuguese, began to proselytize actively in southern Japan, and the shoguns decided that not just they but converted Japanese were a political threat. A Spanish pilot who reached Japan had brought with him a world map on which the many lands of the Spanish Empire were marked. The Japanese were curious to know how these conquests had come about.

> 'Nothing is easier,' the pilot answered. 'Our kings begin by sending into countries which they desire to conquer some friars, who engage in the work of converting the people to our religion. When they have made considerable progress, troops are sent in who are joined by the new Christians. They then have little difficulty in settling the rest.'[58]

News of this tactless conversation is said to have prompted the regent, Hideyoshi, to begin the first of a series of persecutions of Christians in Japan.

In the late sixteenth century, as the example of Manila has already shown, Japanese mercenaries were a familiar and frightening sight, and the high quality of their training and armaments, as well as their reputation for ferocity, made them the prime choice of anyone looking for paid military help. Japanese mercenaries were readily available, following the unification of much of Japan by the regent and chancellor, Hideyoshi, ten years earlier, capped by the success of Tokugawa Ieyasu in defeating his enemies in 1600. There was not much for them to do in Japan itself, so foreign opportunities beckoned. Occasionally, this admiration for the Japanese could take an awkward turn. Maybe they were such skilled soldiers that they would be tempted to launch an invasion of the Philippines? After all, there were plenty of Japanese merchants in Manila by the 1590s.

For this reason the Spanish governor decided that the Japanese, like the Chinese, needed their own quarter, known as the *Dilao*: 'to relieve our anxiety regarding so many Xaponese traders in the city, it would be advisable to assign them a settlement located outside the city, after first taking away all their weapons'. By 1606 there were more than 3,000 Japanese living in the *Dilao*; later, it attracted large numbers of Japanese Christians, for whom life in Japan was becoming increasingly difficult; it was the largest Japanese settlement outside the homeland. Only in the 1630s, with the decline of direct trade between the Philippines and Japan, did this community pack its bags and leave. The governor was also worried by the large number of Japanese servants living in Manila, who had free entry into houses within the city and might set fire to Manila. Antonio de Morga, who has been met already in his capacity as president of the high court, wrote in 1609 that the Japanese are 'of good disposition and courageous . . . of noble bearing and carriage, and much given to ceremony and courtesies', and he insisted that 'the maintenance of friendly relations between the islands and Japan is advisable'.[59]

Admiration was, then, combined with fear. This meant that Japanese ships were by and large untouchable. In 1610 a Japanese trading ship that carried the 'vermilion seal', guaranteeing the shogun's protection, reached Manila just as the Spanish and Dutch fleets engaged in battle with one another offshore. The Europeans suspended action while this ship serenely passed through their ranks, and no attempt was made by either side to come on board. This was not because anyone was afraid of Japanese firepower; trading vessels of this sort would not have carried guns. Both the Spaniards and the Dutch knew that the Japanese were under orders to report any interference to the shogun's court, where reprisals would be launched against the nation that had insulted the empire's subjects. The seizure by a Spanish captain of a Japanese ship off Siam in 1629 showed how things could go wrong if the government, or *bakufu*, was offended.

The Japanese seized a Portuguese ship at Nagasaki in retaliation, drawing the Portuguese (then still subjects of King Philip) into the quarrel. An embassy from Japan to Manila, two years after the incident, failed to soothe either side, and contact with Japan withered, while the Christians in Japan underwent further persecution. The Spanish and Portuguese attempts to spread Christianity in Japan did nothing to help the situation. The governor of the Philippines complained in 1636 that 'the trade with Japan has been spoiled by the indiscretion of certain religious'.[60]

Japan was attractive for other reasons than its formidable mercenaries. The sixteenth century saw the extension of silkworm cultivation, and new centres of silk-weaving also emerged, with the encouragement of the feudal lords who dominated during the age of the shoguns, and who saw good opportunities for profit in the silk industry, as well as wanting to clothe themselves in magnificent fabrics. They encouraged the creation of markets. The regent Hideyoshi cleared the land of bandits and cleared the sea of pirates, as well as encouraging the free movement of goods by abolishing internal customs stations. He also tried to take control of the production of silver and gold wherever he could. Hideyoshi also supported foreign trade, encouraging a trading expedition to Korea and taking charge of the key port of Nagasaki. He snapped up (for honest payment) all the raw silk on board when what was described as a foreign 'black ship' reached his coast, and acted much the same way when a Spanish ship came in from the Philippines loaded with ceramics, or when Portuguese ships arrived bearing gold. His successor, Ieyasu, was so keen to promote good relations with the Spaniards that in 1604 the governor of the Philippines felt able to tell King Philip III that 'peace and friendship with the king of Japan goes on continuing' (though the shogun was not in fact king).

VI

Ieyasu was thoughtful and observant, and he realized how important to Manila was the link to Acapulco. He too wanted a stake in trade with Mexico. He wanted Japanese merchants to have rights of access in New Spain, and he wanted the Manila galleons to make a short detour and put in at a Japanese port en route to Acapulco. The Spaniards prevaricated, but Ieyasu was able to seize his opportunity in 1609 when the *San Francisco*, bearing the ex-governor of the Philippines, foundered on his shores. This official made a treaty with Ieyasu, although his authority to do so was very doubtful; and Ieyasu even promised to permit missionaries to preach in his islands.[61] In 1610 the ex-governor was ferried back to Mexico on a ship provided (partly thanks to a loan from the shogun) that had been built in Japan but according to European standards. Ieyasu was well aware that Japanese navigational skills lagged behind those of the Europeans, and would dearly have liked to create a shipyard on the European model. However, this ship was built under the direction of an English shipwright and merchant, or perhaps one should say pirate, who had managed to reach Japan, William Adams, known in Japan as Miura Anjin. Adams's story was another tale of shipwreck, this time aboard a Dutch vessel out of Rotterdam, *De Liefde* ('The Beloved'), that had ambitiously set out in 1598, taking an elaborate route by way of the Cape Verde Islands, west Africa and the Strait of Magellan before the ship was washed up on the shore of Japan. The expedition was better at marauding than at trading. In the Cape Verde Islands, where the crew hoped to take on food and water, they occupied Praia, on the main island, Santiago; the unsurprising result was that the Portuguese governor sent them packing without new supplies, after telling them that he would have sent supplies but for their awful behaviour (memories of Francis Drake's sacking of the then capital, Ribeira Grande, in 1585 were still powerful). They reached Patagonia, and there were altercations with Patagonian Indians, supposedly eleven feet tall. Passing through the Strait of Magellan, they decided that it was too difficult to return the way they had come, and settled on Japan as a destination, since they were carrying heavy Dutch broadcloth which they realized, belatedly, was not the sort of cloth anyone in the tropical East Indies would want to buy.[62]

Ieyasu met Adams and took a liking to him; but he was suspicious about the intentions of the Dutch and English visitors, and for a time clapped him in prison. These suspicions were justified, since the Dutch crew had probably been more interested in finding Spanish treasure ships, as Sir Francis Drake had managed to do several years earlier, than in creating a new route to the Spice Islands or indeed Japan. Fortunately, Ieyasu concluded that Adams possessed the skill needed to build a ship in the Western style. Adams protested that he did not know a great deal about shipbuilding, but even so he and his colleagues put together a seaworthy vessel.[63] The ship set sail along with an official ambassador and Japanese merchants, and it returned in 1611 bearing a Spanish ambassador, who, however, was as discouraging as he dared to be. Ieyasu was, in any case, having doubts about Spanish ambitions. All the same, a few attempts were then made to set up a Japan–Acapulco route, manned by Japanese ships, but mutual hostility made sure that direct contact soon came to an end; a final voyage to Acapulco took place in 1616.

Nothing, however, compared with the experiences of an official

Japanese party that travelled all the way to Europe, by way of Mexico, setting out from Japan in 1613 and only returning home in 1620. Their journey continues to fascinate readers of Japanese literature, thanks to Shusaku Endo's book *The Samurai*.[64] The travellers reached Seville, where they brought a letter proposing a Japan–Seville trade route, and even promising that Japan would accept the new faith. Their arrival caused great excitement. They moved on to Madrid, where (given the Japanese obsession with rank) they probably understood the consternation of the royal court at the fact that the letter had not been written by either the emperor or the shogun, but by a lower official; so they were offered the same honours as would be provided for the ambassadors of an Italian duke. Their leader, Hasekura, was baptized by the royal chaplain in Spain before the embassy moved on to Rome, where Hasekura was given the title of patrician and senator and was granted an audience by the pope. Ironically, all this was happening just as Ieyasu embarked on another persecution of Christians in Japan; the promise that he would turn Japan Christian was an empty one.[65] By the end of their extraordinary journey, they had not achieved much beyond knowledge of the New World and Europe, and if anything their immersion in the society of Philip III's Christian empire made them more suspicious of the Catholic world, and less inclined to encourage the building of close relations between Japan and either the New World or Spain.[66]

   The issue of 'vermilion seals' by the government to Japanese ships trading southwards was another aspect of the vigorous economic policy the shoguns were pursuing. Roughly fourteen ships set out year after year, visiting eighteen countries, with a preference for Vietnam. At the start of the seventeenth century the most frequent visitors to Japan were the Portuguese, but the first Dutch vessel arrived in 1609, and four years later an English ship came to Japan; both nations aimed to set up trading stations on the island of Kyushu.[67] But as tension grew, particularly over the Catholic missions, the Japanese government turned against the foreigners, banning the Dutch and English in 1616, so their stay was very short indeed. And then the shoguns turned against Japanese traders who ventured beyond their homeland. In 1624 the Japanese were ordered to stop trading in Manila, and such foreign trade as there was became concentrated in Nagasaki and Hirado. The vermilion seal was granted to fewer and fewer merchants, members of a small elite with access to the *bakufu*; remarkably, they included William Adams, indicating the value Ieyasu placed on his ability and knowhow – in 1613 Adams was a useful intermediary between Ieyasu and an English captain, Saris, who hoped to create a trading base in Japan.[68] Gradually, though, prohibitions against foreign trade became stricter: the Spaniards were banned from Japanese soil in 1638, under pain of death, and a ban on the Portuguese followed a year later.[69]

While it lasted, this trade was profitable. Ships carried grain, salted meat, fish and fruit to Manila, all vital supplies; they also carried military supplies, both horses and armaments; beautiful products of Japanese craftsmanship included lacquered boxes and painted screens and high-quality silks. The value of trade in silk alone was estimated at 111,300 *pesos* in 1606. In the other direction, Chinese silk, tea jars, glass, even Spanish wines, as well as spices brought from the East Indies, passed north to Japan. The fact that the Japanese came to Manila to obtain Chinese products underlines the importance of Manila as a trading hub attracting goods from all directions. The eclipse of trade with Japan and the disappearance of the Japanese community in Manila were easy to bear so long as Manila could continue to function as a channel through which Chinese goods passed to Mexico, as it continued to do until early in the nineteenth century; the last return trip to Manila by galleon took place in 1815. By then, the Spanish government had relaxed restrictions on the movement of goods between Asian ports and Mexico, so that Manila lost its central importance and smaller ships than the galleons, sometimes flying the flag of other nations (including the United States of America), were now plying between the western Pacific, including Manila, and various ports along the Mexican coast. The Manila galleons had survived for as long as the Spanish monopoly held, but once it was broken the galleons ceased to sail.[70]

35

The Black Ships of Macau

I

One of the constant and in many ways justified complaints about histories of the seaborne empires of the sixteenth and seventeenth centuries is that they are Eurocentric, even when the subject matter is Goa, Melaka, Macau or Manila. This partly reflects the richness of the archives in Lisbon, Seville, Amsterdam and other European cities compared to what can be found in Asia; and it partly reflects an assumption that the Portuguese and their successors were able to dominate the long-distance movement of goods to the exclusion of any serious rivals. But that was not the case. At best the Portuguese could only blockade the Red Sea, for, as has been seen, they were unable to force their way into it, and much the same applied to the Persian Gulf, where they could control movement through the narrow Strait of Hormuz. But the trouble with a blockade was that it cost a good deal of money to maintain and produced no revenue. It made more sense to treat the Portuguese forts as customs stations through which the Asian merchants would have to pass. The Red Sea did remain open. So long as Gujaratis, Malays and others paid for their trading licences, they were able to carry on their business without further interference from the Europeans, who were more likely to confront one another (once the Dutch arrived in the Indian Ocean around 1600) than to interfere with local shipping. Indeed, paying for one's licence brought a certain amount of protection. It has been well said that 'the Portuguese forced their way into an established trading world; they did not revolutionise Euro-Asian trade.'[1]

Portuguese methods were rooted in traditional medieval practices: they created trading bases, the nodal points of their Asian trading world being Hormuz, Goa, Melaka and Macau, which were backed up by coastal forts and by the Portuguese fleets that moved across the Indian Ocean and into the South China Sea. The Spaniards, on the other hand, did conquer entire territories, as happened in the Philippines, and as had already been

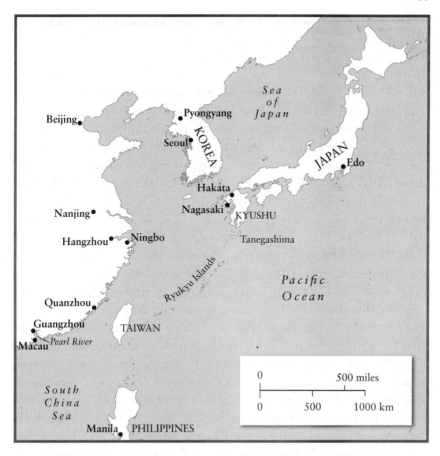

happening in the Caribbean, Mexico and Peru. Their interest in commercial connections across the oceans grew as the silver mines of Peru and Mexico delivered vast amounts of bullion to Manila and Seville, and their conquistadors had been attracted by stories of the gold of the Aztecs and Incas. So the two Iberian empires had very different profiles, one more sea-based, the other more land-based. In reality, the Portuguese made more money out of the taxes they imposed on Asian shipping and out of their own intra-Asian shipping routes than they did out of the spice trade linking the Indies to Lisbon and Antwerp. Rather than pepper, nutmeg and cloves, the source of profit was cotton and calico cloth from western India, carried eastwards to what is now Indonesia (enabling the Portuguese to buy spices with the proceeds), while in the other direction they took these goods to east Africa, exchanging them for ivory and gold.[2] This ability to carve out a role for themselves as intermediaries between Asian (and even African) ports was most clearly demonstrated in the trade route they created between Macau and Japan.

The Portuguese became aware of Japan in stages. The traditional description of 'Cipangu' by Marco Polo placed the Japanese Empire much too far from the coast of Asia, and the major interest of the Portuguese following the capture of Melaka in 1511 lay in trade with China; even when they arrived in Japan, the Portuguese may not have realized that they had reached the land described by Polo. Until the 1540s the Portuguese remained vague about the layout of the western Pacific. The ambassador the Portuguese sent to China, Tomé Pires (who wrote a magnificent account of the Far East, the *Suma Oriental*), arrived in Nanjing soon after Albuquerque seized Melaka, aware that the links between Melaka and the outside world pointed in three directions: towards India, towards the Spice Islands, and beyond those islands towards China, for Chinese junks were a familiar sight in Melaka. It has been seen how Zheng He's voyages, among other visits, brought fifteenth-century Melaka under the notional sovereignty of the Chinese emperor. After Albuquerque seized the town, its deposed sultan urged the Chinese to help him recover control of Melaka. All this created panic among the Portuguese: would the Chinese emperor sit back and permit the Portuguese to hold on to such a valuable possession? Tomé Pires had a frustrating time in China – he played board games with Emperor Zhengde in Nanjing, and he moved on to Beijing ahead of the emperor, hoping to negotiate a trade deal, but the emperor died almost immediately after returning to his capital. The new emperor was much less interested in these barbarians and sent them back to Guangzhou. Once again the Portuguese began to worry about Chinese intentions.[3] No Chinese fleet materialized, and the Portuguese tentatively made their way deeper and deeper into the Pacific, by way of the South China Sea. They began to realize that there was profit to be made not just out of the spices of the East Indies but out of the lands that lay off the coast of China. First, they took an interest in the Ryukyu island chain, which, as an earlier chapter showed, possessed its own lively culture and functioned as the crossroads of the trade routes of the western Pacific. The Portuguese heard that these islands were rich in both precious and base metals, and Tomé Pires offered a description of the islands in his book, though he knew very little about Japan.[4]

The Portuguese discovery of Japan (insofar as it makes sense to use the term 'discovery') was unplanned, though not, surely, unexpected. To understand what was happening it is necessary to begin with a series of Portuguese attempts to penetrate the markets of China. Following the capture of Melaka, Portuguese merchants began to fit out junks, or occasionally (from 1517 onwards) European ships, and reached the south coast of China. The squadron of eight ships that set out in 1517 with Pires aboard was allowed to sail up the Pearl River and to dock at Guangzhou (Canton), where they were able

to observe how the city acted as a magnet for ships coming from all over
the region, including Japanese junks; unfortunately these peaceful Portuguese were followed by others who disregarded royal instructions not to
interfere with other ships, and 'captured islands, robbed ships and terrorised
the population'; they were, this Chinese writer continued, 'a crowd of riff-
raff' who set up 'boundary stones', which must be more of the *padrões* the
Portuguese had been erecting all the way from west Africa to Asia. Skirmishes between the Portuguese and the Chinese in the waters off Hong Kong
kept recurring; the Chinese made clever use of fireships, tactics they owed
to a certain Wang Hong, who is still worshipped as a minor god in Castle
Peak, Hong Kong.[5] Other troublemakers along this coast included the *wakō*,
who have been met already; this term was used mainly for Japanese pirates.
The Portuguese had some contact with them and would therefore have
known something, though not very much, about who the Japanese were.[6]

In 1543 three private traders from Portugal were on their way from
Ayutthaya in Siam to Quanzhou aboard a junk loaded with hides; they
took a long way round because they knew that the Portuguese were
'detested and abhorred' in Guangzhou after events earlier in the century –
a Portuguese ambassador had had the temerity to flog a mandarin.[7] A
Portuguese writer described their unexpected arrival in Japan:

> As this junk was making for the port of Chincheo [Quanzhou], it ran into
> a fearful storm of the kind the natives call typhoon [*tuffão*], which is fierce
> and appalling, and makes such bravado and quaking, that it seems as if all
> the spirits of Hell are whirling the waves and the sea, whose fury seems to
> cause flashes of fire in the sky, whilst in the space of an hour-glass, the wind
> boxes all the points of the compass.[8]

They were blown on to the shores of Tanegashima, a small island off
Kyushu, the southernmost landmass of Japan, where the inhabitants
looked after them well. They had arrived in 'Nipongi which we usually
term Japão'. The Japanese were fascinated by the weapons the Portuguese
carried, and now or subsequently they acquired some firearms and began
to copy them; the term for a wide range of guns made in Japan became
tanegashima, because that was where the lessons had been learned and
where the guns were often made.[9] In other respects the Japanese were
mystified by the Europeans; a Japanese chronicler recorded the opinion
of the Chinese interpreter who had acted as go-between between the
islanders and the surprise visitors:

> They eat with their fingers instead of with chopsticks such as we use. They
> show their feelings without any self-control. They cannot understand the

meaning of written characters. They are people who spend their lives roving hither and yon. They have no fixed abode and barter things which they have for those they do not, but withal they are a harmless people.[10]

Apart from anything else, this passage reveals a very particular Chinese and Japanese attitude to literacy. And harmless they were not.

II

Macau (as Macao tends to be spelt nowadays) became the conduit for trade between Japan and the wider world in the second half of the sixteenth century. Its foundation in 1557 was the culmination of failed attempts to secure a base in the Pearl River, not helped by the all too typically aggressive stance of the Portuguese in the first half of the sixteenth century. Now avoiding the Pearl River, the Portuguese crept into other ports than Guangzhou, such as Quanzhou and Ningbo, near Hangzhou, and even unloaded their goods on to Chinese junks out at sea.[11] Their difficulties in gaining free access to China encouraged them to seize a new opportunity, trade with Japan. Japanese soil contained rich veins of silver, and the Japanese were voracious consumers of Chinese silk, insisting that it was superior to their own excellent products.[12] But the Portuguese knew that they needed a way station between Melaka and Japan, somewhere where they could break their journey, take on Chinese goods bought with Japanese silver, and refit their ships. Tentatively, therefore, they installed themselves about fifty miles from the mouth of the Pearl River, bribed the local officials, and set up their encampment on what they called the 'Island of St John'. At first the imperial court tried to exclude European ships, because the *Ferengi*, or 'Franks', were 'people with filthy hearts', and pirates. But a spice shortage and the loss of revenue from trade were beginning to worry the emperor's courtiers. So by 1555 the Portuguese were at last able to visit Guangzhou so long as they paid their taxes.[13]

St John Island did not satisfy the Portuguese. It was too distant from the Pearl River, so they left after three years. The traditional account of the foundation of what became their base, the future city of Macau, tells how the Portuguese won the approval of the Chinese authorities by defeating a dangerous Chinese pirate. *Wakō* pirates had been making a thorough nuisance of themselves in the 1550s.[14] But the permission granted to the Portuguese also generated a difficult question. The Chinese Empire could not really allow the Portuguese to treat this patch of territory as its own. Equally, the Chinese were perfectly aware that the king of Portugal had no intention of submitting to the Heavenly Emperor. The solution was to keep Chinese tax officials in place whose special (but not unique) concern lay with the taxation of Chinese visitors to Macau. The fact that no formal grant of the territory was made, as did indeed happen with parts of Hong Kong, left Macau vulnerable to China's claim that the territory should be returned to China, as happened in 1999; in the case of Hong Kong, by contrast, the argument for cession of the territory to the People's Republic turned on whether the treaty granting it to Great Britain had been unjustly imposed. The Portuguese appear to have received a scroll commemorating their help in defeating pirates and a document permitting them to set up their trading station; a version inscribed on wood and stone was kept in the Senate House of Macau, but the Senate House burned down and no one kept a record of what the inscription said. Macau was allowed to exist 'completely outside the rules and precedents of the tribute system'; in other words the solution to the problem of its status was for the Chinese largely to ignore the problem.[15]

The name *Macau* was derived from a Chinese term, *A-ma-ngao* in Cantonese dialect, meaning 'Bay of Ama', a goddess whose temple, pre-dating the arrival of the Portuguese, still stands by the site of the original inner harbour. This became *Amacao* and *Amacon* in Portuguese documents, although the Portuguese had, typically, intended to give their settlement a Christian rather than a Chinese name: *La Povoação do Nome de Deos na China*, 'The Town of the Name of God in China', later elevated to the status of *Cidade* or 'City'.[16] Initially the settlement consisted of quite simple buildings made of wood and straw – what are called matsheds in the Far East.[17] The Florentine traveller Carletti, who visited Macau in 1598 aboard a Japanese ship, described it as 'a small unwalled city without fortresses, but having a few houses of Portuguese'; the imposing fortress that now dominates old Macau was built around the Jesuit College after his time, more as a defence against the Dutch than as a defence against local powers.[18] The population stood at 800 in 1562.[19] As the settlement grew, the ever-watchful Chinese authorities tried to ensure that fellow Chinese did not stay overnight, though there were ways of hiding away and there were Chinese servants living in Macau. The Chinese authorities worried that trade relations between Macau and Japan were making the Portuguese too friendly to the Japanese, nearly a hundred of whom were expelled from Macau in 1613 at Chinese insistence.[20]

The Portuguese were not permitted to cross the wall into China proper, which meant that the growing town possessed no hinterland from which to draw its food. This suited the Chinese merchants who profited from supplying Macau with essentials, and it suited the Chinese officials who knew they could blockade Macau if trouble with the Portuguese loomed.[21] The great age of building that threw up the magnificent Church of St Paul (partly built by Japanese craftsmen) and the substantial Dominican church was yet to come, but even before 1600 there existed a cathedral and convents for the three great orders of friars, the Dominicans, the Franciscans and the Augustinians, as well as the Jesuit College from which missionaries passed into China and Japan.[22] A charitable foundation, the Santa Casa de Misericórdia, came into existence in 1569, following a model established elsewhere in Portuguese Asia – the first of these houses had been created in Cochin as early as 1505. This was a sign that the Portuguese saw Macau as a stable base for their operations, as well as a recognition of the need to cater for widows, orphans and others who fell on hard times so far from their original home.[23]

Macau had first of all to make its money, and it did so very successfully. Guangzhou was the source of the silk the Macanese (the term for Macau's inhabitants) sent on to Japan and elsewhere; Carletti believed that up to 80,000 pounds of silk were carried down from Guangzhou twice a year, as well as mercury, lead and musk. Only a select group of Portuguese from Macau were permitted to land in Guangzhou, and they had to travel up the Pearl River in Chinese boats. Carletti was excited by what they brought to Macau, and eagerly bought silk, musk and gold, which, he observed, 'is really another sort of merchandise and is used more for gilding one or another kind of furniture and other objects than as a kind of money', so that its price fluctuated according to seasonal demand. Carletti resolved to send all his goods on to distant Middelburg in the Netherlands and to sell them there. Among these goods were two enormous porcelain vases filled with branches of ginger; the vases were 'perhaps the largest that ever have been brought to Europe from those lands', and the Middelburg merchant who bought them forwarded them to the duke of Tuscany. The very best porcelain was reserved for the emperor, 'but the most beautiful is what one sees ordinarily, white and decorated in blue'. Carletti bought something like 700 pieces of Chinese blue-and-white, all at low cost, a mixture of plates, bowls and other pieces. It is no coincidence that Portuguese tiles (*azulejos*), and later on Dutch ones, also came to be decorated in blue and white, even though the Iberian peninsula had its own long tradition of more colourful tile-making based on Islamic designs.

The English traveller Ralph Fitch was in Macau in around 1590, and he explained the simple strategy of the Macanese:

> When the Portugales goe from Macao in China to Japan, they carrie much white silke, Gold, Muske and Porcelanes: and they bring from thence

nothing but Silver. They have a great Carake which goeth thither every yeere, and shee bringeth from thence every yeere above 600,000 crusadoes [ducats]; and all this Silver of Japan, and 200,000 crusadoes more in Silver which they bring yeerly out of India, they imploy to their great advantage in China: and they bring from thence Gold, Muske, Silke, Copper, Porcelanes, and many other things very costly and gilded.[24]

One writer after another confirmed that the profit to be drawn from the 'great carrack' or (as the Portuguese called it) the 'ship of trade', *Não do Trato*, was truly vast, 'a million in gold', as Diogo do Couto hyperbolically asserted in around 1600. In 1635 an English visitor to Macau believed that one could make a 100 per cent profit on the return voyage between Macau and either Japan or Manila.[25] And yet the Portuguese showed little interest in the beautiful objects produced by Japanese artisans, buying a few writing boxes and an occasional decorated weapon; they craved instead the silver extracted from deep mines. Estimates of the amount of silver exported from Japan on board native, Chinese and European ships during the early seventeenth century reach as much as 187,500 kg per annum.[26]

These carracks were rather different to the galleons that crossed the Pacific from Manila. They tended to be larger, broader and slower, starting, in the middle of the sixteenth century, at 400–600 tons' capacity, and rising by 1600 to as much as 1,600 tons, with occasional 'monsters', as Charles Boxer called them, of 2,000 tons; 'a shipping ton,' he explained, 'was a unit of capacity and not of weight', roughly sixty cubic feet, so that a 2,000-ton carrack had space for 120,000 cubic feet of cargo. They had fewer guns than the galleons, and the disadvantages began to tell once Dutch competitors entered the waters off China and Japan, leading to substitution by smaller and faster vessels known as *galiota*s, 'galliots', and occasionally small frigates and pinnaces as well.[27] All these ships descended from the same basic model, the late medieval galleass, with its lateen foremast and its array of square sails, as well as officers' living quarters at the stern, though the carrack retained the large forecastle of medieval ships. The Japanese made fewer distinctions between the carracks and the galleons than the Portuguese; they looked very different to their own junks, and were simply described as 'black ships', *kurofune*, while the word *galiota* was transmogrified into the Japanese term *kareuta-sen*; the Japanese language has always been very open to foreign terms, and the Japanese word for 'thank you', *arigato*, is said (mistakenly, it seems) to be a corruption of the Portuguese *obrigado*. Japanese fascination with the 'black ships' went much further than their name. A popular way of decorating the silk screens that were required in prosperous Japanese homes was to portray the arrival of a massive black ship, with the crew (occasionally displayed as monkeys) swarming over the rigging, Portuguese merchants strolling along the quay-side in their western garb, and sometimes a Jesuit missionary to add further verisimilitude.[28] Nonetheless, the Portuguese were keen to exploit every opportunity to fill their hold with Japanese silver, and often they hired large junks, manned mainly by Chinese sailors.[29] The Portuguese did not insist on using European ships – which in any case were not made in Europe but in Portuguese bases along the shores of the Indian Ocean, where good, hard teak was ready to hand.

As in the case of Manila, the raison d'être of the town was its intermediary role, rather than anything it could offer from its own limited resources. The secret of Macau's success was that it was not a royal foundation, but had been created by private initiative. It never cost the king of Portugal anything. Macau was governed by its own 'Loyal Senate', or *Leal Senado*, whose members, mainly interested in profit from trade, took advantage of the distance separating Macau from Lisbon to manage the town's own affairs.[30] The accession of Philip II of Spain to the throne of Portugal did not, as has been seen, lead to a merger of the Spanish and Portuguese trading networks in the Pacific or anywhere else. From 1581 onwards the governors of both Goa and Manila deplored what still counted as illicit trade across the imaginary line dividing the Spanish from the Portuguese hemisphere, but in the vast spaces of the Pacific it continued. Wealthy Mexican merchants obtained Chinese silks from Guangzhou by way of Macau and Manila, where the Portuguese sold their silk at a very respectable profit, before the goods were ferried along the galleon route all the way to Acapulco.[31] The route to Japan was the foundation of Macau's fortune, and had the great advantage of being relatively short, compared to the routes from Melaka westwards, or from Manila eastwards.

As the Portuguese became more familiar with the coasts of Japan, they realized that they needed a base there, just as they now had a base in southern China, and the obvious place to look was the south-west of Kyushu island, not too far from important ports such as Hakata. One very promising location was a fishing village within the lands of a great land-owner sympathetic to the Christians, Omura Sumitada. A Jesuit priest had turned up there in around 1569 and, having kindly been offered accommodation in a Buddhist temple, he proceeded to demolish it and to build a parish church out of its planks; he managed to convert the entire population, including Omura. There was a large bay that would provide excellent anchorage for a great black ship. Local wars brought refugees to the village, and it grew and grew – all the more so when the Portuguese chose it as their port of preference in 1571. The name of this place is

Nagasaki, meaning 'Long Cape'.[32] Within a couple of years the risks in sailing seas that were still little known became obvious when a massive carrack bound for Nagasaki and weighed down by a very heavy cargo foundered in a matter of minutes after being violently struck by a summer typhoon. There were a good many Jesuit missionaries on board and a large part of the cargo consisted of Chinese silks the Jesuits were bringing to Japan, where they planned to sell the goods and use the profit to fund their missionary campaigns.[33] Two survivors were pulled from the sea by a passing Melaka junk, under Portuguese command; they were Arabs or Indians, and one soon died.

The constant problem with any attempt to explain the lively maritime connections linking such places as Malaya, Siam, Cambodia, China, the Philippines and Japan is that it easily develops into an account of the links between Melaka, Macau, Manila and Nagasaki, in other words the places where the Portuguese or the Spaniards created their bases. Yet it is obvious from (say) Carletti's account of his voyage round the world that he saw and sailed in non-European ships, and that the Siamese, the Javanese and others were in constant movement back and forth, while far more spices were absorbed by China than ever reached Europe.[34] For under the Ming China was the big economy on the planet. Its own sailors were still discouraged from venturing on to the open sea, but that did not stop them from doing so, nor did it prevent the large Chinese settlements all around the South China Sea from coming into existence. China's hunger for silver shaped the economy not just of the Ming Empire but of much vaster spaces, including Japan and Spanish America. Trade with China from nearly all directions continued to flourish until the 1640s, a decade marked by the collapse of the Ming dynasty and a period of cool weather that damaged production across the globe.[35]

What made the Spanish, Portuguese and later Dutch ships that entered these waters different – even ships constructed in India or in Mexico – was that they formed part of a worldwide network that linked Antwerp and Amsterdam to Melaka, the Moluccas and Mexico. They were the agents of empires that stretched across distances never matched in human history, whether one is thinking of the Portuguese seaborne empire, largely consisting of trade stations and subject ports, or the territorial empire of the Spaniards that encompassed the Americas and saw the Philippines as a dependency of Spanish America. A particularly important aspect of the creation of transoceanic links was the arrival of alien plants in new continents. Obvious cases include the arrival of maize and tobacco in Europe, from Spanish America, but the Portuguese presence in Macau introduced 'the vegetables of the western seas' into Ming China: lettuce, watercress, bell peppers, new types of bean. Several of these new fruits and vegetables, such as the papaya and the guava, were not European at all, but they were still brought by Europeans; both the papaya and the guava were Mexican fruits, and the papaya was native to the area around Veracruz, from where the Manila galleons headed westwards.[36] More sinister arrivals in the Far East were European weapons, not that the Chinese or Japanese lacked firearms of their own; however, they admired European ones, and the existence of their own advanced technology meant that it proved easy to copy what the Portuguese and their rivals showed them. The same applied to navigation, where the superior charts and handbooks carried by the Portuguese gave a distinct advantage; Portuguese sailing manuals, or *roteiros*, were translated into Japanese.[37]

III

Nothing could be achieved in Japan without the consent of the rulers of the empire. However, identifying who actually exercised power was not straightforward. In the mid-sixteenth century the emperor was a cipher, and the power of the *daimyo*, local warlords, remained formidable; occasionally they would send messages to Macau asking for help against their enemies: Omura Sumitada wrote asking for a supply of saltpetre, which was a vital ingredient of gunpowder, while showing due deference to the Catholic Church.[38] The great weakness of the daimyo was that they spent all their resources on the maintenance of their samurai, whom they paid in kind with supplies of rice from their estates, and without whom they could not hope to stay in power. By and large, both daimyo and samurai had little money to spare, and lived simply off rice, vegetables and fruit. The opportunity to make money from the Great Ship of Amacon was too good to miss.[39] However, by 1600 a succession of capable and ruthless shoguns managed to impose control from the imperial capital at Kyoto and their own headquarters at Edo (now Tokyo) over large areas of the country, and they were the people with whom the Portuguese would most need to curry favour, even though the daimyo remained a force in the outlying regions. The relationship between the Portuguese and the shoguns was complicated by the attempts of the Jesuits to introduce Christianity into Japan, and the increasing alarm the shoguns felt at their success; this was exactly the area where the policy followed by sundry daimyo often diverged from that of the central government. An example of this divergence was the daimyo Omura Sumitada, who vigorously encouraged conversion to Christianity.[40]

Much has been written about the Jesuit attempts to bring Christianity to China, and the way the Jesuits tried to make Christianity palatable to the Chinese by themselves adopting Chinese ways of life, and by adapting their teachings to the assumptions of a society dominated by Confucian ideas about rank and honour. Macau, where Jesuits had been residing from the start of its history, and where they built the imposing Church of St Paul, whose façade is now the symbol of the city, was the base from which Matteo Ricci and others launched their missions into China. Before he reached Macau, Ricci had already spent some time in Goa, the major Jesuit centre in Asia, with a Jesuit college containing over a hundred members, so that his Chinese mission can be seen as a spin-off from the creation of the Portuguese trading network.[41] However, from the perspective of maritime history the Jesuit campaigns in Japan, rather than China, have particular interest, because the silk trade from Macau and the missions became closely intertwined in what sometimes proved a very dangerous operation.[42]

The missionaries were well aware that conversion took place by command. An Italian Jesuit, Alessandro di Valignano, who for thirty-two years led the Jesuit mission in Japan, saw a direct link between the Christianization of Japan and the arrival of the Great Ship of Amacon in Kyushu. He suggested that the Pope should ban, under pain of excommunication, visits by the Great Ship of Amacon to 'the ports of lords who persecute Christianity or who are reluctant to allow their vassals to be converted'.[43] Valignano was keen to promote the trade in silk towards Japan because the Jesuits invested heavily in it; from the profits of this trade they funded their operations, and unless someone else could come up with 12,000 ducats per annum they would have to continue to pursue profit, whatever the Franciscans, with their vows of poverty, or the Protestants, with their accusations of hypocrisy, might say.[44] In a text he wrote in 1580 Valignano showed how important the Great Ship had become in the great project of turning Japan Christian:

> The greatest help that we have had hitherto in securing Christians is that of the Great Ship ... For as the lords of Japan are very poor, as has been said, and the benefits they derive when the ships come to their ports are very great, they try hard to entice them to their fiefs. And since they have convinced themselves that they will come to where there are Christians and churches, and whither the padres wish them to come, it therefore follows that many of them, even though they are heathen, seek to get the padres to come thither and to secure churches and convents, thinking that by this means the ships will [in their turn] secure other favours they wish to obtain

from the padres. And since the Japanese are so much at the disposal of their lords, they readily become converted when told to do so by their lords and they think it is their wish.[45]

Valignano opined that, being 'white', the Japanese were 'of good understanding and behaviour', the whiteness of the Japanese being a common motif in European writings at the time. Whiteness might be thought of as a metaphor for the rational behaviour that some contemporaries denied to American Indians, black Africans and other peoples. Valignano expounded a racial hierarchy in which white-skinned Christian Europeans naturally stood at the apex, but his respect for Japanese culture and manners led him to place his hosts very high up his scale.[46]

The dominant figures in Japan during the 1580s, the shogun Nobunaga and his successor, the regent Hideyoshi, were worried that the Jesuits were the secret vanguard of a Portuguese takeover of their islands. Their hostility to the missionaries was demonstrated in 1587 and again ten years later. On the first occasion they ordered the priests out of Japan, but within a few years the Jesuits had argued their way back in; on the second occasion Hideyoshi unleashed a brutal persecution of Japanese Christians, resulting in mass crucifixions of men, women and children in and around Nagasaki. Yet the suspicion remains that Hideyoshi's prime aim was to bring the daimyo of Kyushu, often sympathetic to Christianity, under his control, rather than a deep-seated hostility to the religion itself, for he could also show the Christians favour when it suited his interests. This interpretation is bolstered by the fact that Hideyoshi vigorously persecuted Buddhist monks of various sects, since he regarded the Buddhist monasteries as political rivals, institutions that stood outside the centralized state he was trying to create. Valignano observed that Buddhist monasteries of around a hundred monks were reduced to only four or five after these persecutions. On one occasion Hideyoshi even rejected a plea from Buddhist monks who suspected that the local daimyo, a Christian, planned to destroy the images in their temple; far from supporting them, even though his wife pleaded with him to do so, Hideyoshi had the images brought to Kyoto and chopped up for firewood. On another occasion Hideyoshi visited a church and declared that all that was stopping him from becoming a Christian was the ban on having many concubines: 'if you will stretch a point in this, I will likewise become a convert.' A further reason for his friendly attitude in the years around 1586 was that he was planning the conquest not merely of Korea but of China; he wanted to hire two Portuguese carracks and he promised the Jesuits that he would build churches right across China were his campaigns to succeed. When a Jesuit emissary agreed to obtain the ships Hideyoshi's enthusiasm knew no bounds, and he offered the Jesuits the right to preach throughout his lands and a bundle of privileges greater than those enjoyed by the Buddhists.

No doubt all this was made easier by the gifts of Portuguese wine that Hideyoshi greatly enjoyed. One night in 1587, while Hideyoshi was in his cups, his physician persuaded him that the Christians were up to no good, since they destroyed Buddhist temples and Shintō shrines, ate cows and horses (which could be put to better uses), and carried overseas Japanese servants whom they had enslaved. Literally overnight, if accounts of these events are to be believed, Hideyoshi transformed himself from a friend of the Christians into their bitter enemy. All of a sudden he banished the missionaries, but emphatically not the Great Ship: 'as the Great Ship comes to trade, and this is something quite different, the Portuguese can carry on their commerce quite unmolested.' Yet the Jesuits continued their work in the lands of Christian daimyo beyond the regent's control, and few left the country; before long, the Japanese authorities tolerated the Jesuits as much-needed intermediaries between themselves and the Portuguese merchants, who could not speak Japanese and knew little about the way of life in Japan.[47] Alessandro di Valignano wrote that Hideyoshi was persecuting the Jesuits 'not for love of the false gods of Japan, for he believes nothing, and has done more to destroy their temples and *bonzes* [religious teachers] than we have'.[48] The fact was that both Jesuits and *bonzes* appeared to undermine central authority. The testimony of the Florentine traveller Carletti confirms Valignano's view: 'this king did not believe in any sect, and he often used to say that laws and religions had been founded only to regulate men and to force them to live with modesty and civility'; Carletti sternly reminded his readers that Hideyoshi's lack of a belief in an afterlife was at this very moment being disproved to him, while he burned in the fires of Hell.[49]

At the same time, Nobunaga and his successors brought a greater degree of peace to Japan, and they valued the trade between Japan and the outside world. They saw the Portuguese, and later the Dutch, as useful sources of luxury products that were especially valued at their own courts, but also across the country (which meant that they generated useful tax revenues). Silver was easy to come by under the soil of Japan, so that the outflow of bullion towards China, whether on Portuguese or Asian ships, does not seem to have placed a strain on the Japanese economy, even though, understood in modern terms, the balance of payments was extremely unfavourable to Japan. Japan had not sealed itself off from the outside world, and the European merchants formed only a small part of a much wider trading network dominated by Japanese, Korean and Chinese merchants that tied the islands to neighbouring lands.

For the Florentine traveller Francesco Carletti the sea held few fears. He described the routes across the Pacific, linking Acapulco to Manila, Macau and Nagasaki, and beyond the Pacific to Goa and Lisbon, as if the movement of ships was entirely regular and safe.[50] Just as Hideyoshi was turning his ferocity upon the Christians, Carletti set foot in Japan. His curiosity took a morbid turn at the very start of his visit: as soon as his ship reached Nagasaki 'we went immediately to see the spectacle of those poor (as regards this world) six monks of St Francis ... who had been crucified with twenty other Japanese Christians – among them three who had donned the habits of the Jesuits – on the fifth of the month of February of that same year, 1597'. He described in intricate detail the design of the cross used in Japanese crucifixions, and he noted how a whole family might be executed for the mistakes of a relative or even a neighbour.[51]

Carletti brought back to the duke of Tuscany an elaborate report on the food, manners and products of Japan. It is striking how much has remained the same to this day: he wrote about the Japanese writing system, *tatami* mats, Japanese screens and many other features of Japanese houses. He was particularly fascinated by the food the Japanese ate, including warm rice wine and a sauce that he called *misol*, made out of fermented soya beans, 'taking on a very sharp, piquant flavour'. 'They eat everything by using two small sticks', and when they eat they bring their bowl close to their mouth 'and then, with those two sticks, are able to fill their mouth with marvellous agility and swiftness'. Rice, not bread, was their staple food, and most of the wheat they produced was turned into flour and sent to the Philippines, where the Spaniards baked it into bread; Japanese traders made a profit of up to 100 per cent on these transactions. He noted that the Japanese did have copper coins, used in trade with China, but that many payments were made with weighed chunks of hack silver. Some of this silver was used to pay for the woven and raw silk that was brought each year from Macau aboard a Portuguese ship.[52]

> Most Serene Prince, I say that Japan is one of the most beautiful and best and most suitable regions in the world for making profit by voyaging from one place to another. But one should go there in our vessels and with sailors from our regions. And in that way one would very quickly make incredible wealth, and that because of their need of every sort of manufacture and their abundance of silver as of the provisions for living.[53]

Carletti does not portray a closed-off Japan but an island empire whose elite took great delight in perfumed woods and shagreen, or shark-skin, from Siam and Cambodia. His ambition, which the duke of Tuscany was not in a position to satisfy, was to see his fellow Florentines flocking to make profit out of the trade of Japan.

Some of the most eloquent evidence for day-to-day contact between Japan and its neighbours comes from ceramics rather than chronicles. The Japanese taste for tea dates back to the eighth century, and by the end of the Middle Ages not just Buddhist monks but members of the lay elite consumed delicate teas in carefully chosen cups. Korean tea bowls were in fashion from the fourteenth century onwards, and among the remains of a ship that foundered in 1322 off the coast of Korea during a violent storm were about 15,000 pieces of Chinese pottery, destined for the Japanese market. As demand for tea continued to develop, so did the fashion in tea bowls, but the interest in exotic pieces was constant, so that 'found objects', rustic ceramics made for other purposes in Korea and elsewhere, became specially desirable. This shift in taste took place at the end of the sixteenth century under the influence of Takeno Jôô, a merchant from the port of Sakai, and his protégé Rikyû, tea instructor to both Nobunaga and Hideyoshi and an enthusiast for the strong 'whipped tea' that still features in tea ceremonies. Both rulers made use of tea gatherings to draw around themselves a group of political allies. In the sixteenth century samurai warriors, though often short of resources, dined off Chinese porcelain, and Buddhist temples also possessed porcelain dinner services. By the 1620s Japanese merchants were ordering consignments directly from the porcelain factories at Jingdezhen deep inside China, and within ten or twenty years new styles were being developed specially for the Japanese market, the cobalt-blue porcelain known as *Shonzui*.[54]

In the early seventeenth century the Japanese learned to make their own porcelain, but the high-volume trade in ceramics from China and other lands continued, and the development of Japanese pottery bears witness to the importance of the sea route across the Yellow Sea in the transmission of ideas and technology as well as hard goods. Stories circulated about a Korean potter whom the Japanese knew as Ri Sanpei; he was brought to Japan in the 1590s during the Japanese war in Korea, of which more in a short moment. It is difficult to disentangle legend and fact, but excavations at the site where Ri Sanpei is said to have introduced the manufacture of porcelain in 1616 reveal that its porcelain is slightly later in date than that, and it seems that others were busy making Chinese- and Korean-style porcelain before Ri set to work. A document concerning a master potter whose grandfather had made ceramics for Hideyoshi shows that a porcelain kiln was up and running some years before 1616. Maybe, then, Ri was a merchant rather than an industrialist. But he has become

a national hero in Japan and Korea, and the symbol of the creation of the
Japanese porcelain industry, which depended on the discovery of kaolin
in Japan, since it was impossible to import vast amounts of China clay.
Out of these innovations developed the beautiful Imari wares which in
due course would be carried out of Japan by Dutch merchants.[55] In all of
this, it is hard not to notice how often the name of Hideyoshi crops up.
Cruel and temperamental he may have been, but his vigorous promotion
of a wide range of economic activities both at home and overseas marks
his period of rule as a golden age in the economic history of Japan.

IV

Hideyoshi was interested in more than trade. Having mastered many of
the daimyo, he imagined that he could achieve similar results across the
water. He still dreamed of conquering Korea and ultimately China, and
launched a massive naval expedition to that end in 1592/3. Carletti said
that the army was 300,000 strong.[56] During the land campaign that followed, Seoul and Pyongyang fell to the Japanese, though a Ming-led army
flushed them out of Pyongyang and they proved unable to hold Seoul after
the Chinese threatened to unleash an army of 400,000 men against them:
'Stay here in Seoul and you will be slaughtered.'[57] A second invasion was
unleashed in 1597, following the defeat of the Korean navy at sea. Hideyoshi ordered his army to 'mow down everyone universally, without
discriminating between young and old, men and women, the clergy and
the laity – high-ranking soldiers on the battlefield, that goes without saying, but also the hill folk, down to the poorest and meanest – and send
their heads to Japan'.[58] Rather than collecting heads, the Japanese preferred to send back mountains of noses sliced off the faces of their dead
victims. Just as the ancient Egyptians used to cut off the penises of dead
invaders, this was a useful way of counting the enemy dead: 'To: Kuroda
Nagamasa. Total number of noses taken verified as 3,000. 1597, ninth
month, fifth day.'[59] On land, Japanese troops penetrated deep inside Korea,
though not this time as far as Seoul, and they engaged with both Korean
and Chinese armies; they also set up bases along the Korean coast, but they
failed to achieve the breakthrough they sought. The Ming emperor's support for his Korean vassals made the Korean nut impossible to crack. At
sea, the Japanese needed to keep the supply lines open, as the Korean fleet
was well aware.

Hideyoshi gravely underestimated the abilities of the Korean navy. He
assumed that size was all that mattered. In September 1597 thirteen ships

under the Korean admiral Yi Sun-sin proved capable of holding back the entire Japanese fleet of over 200 ships at the battle of Myongnyang. In the fifteenth century the Koreans had developed a type of fortified ship known as 'turtle ships', with strengthened sides and spiked roofs, making them all but impregnable; they had gone out of fashion, but Yi had new ones built, adorned at the bow with an impressive dragon's head, through which the muzzles of heavy guns poked. Generously provided with additional firepower at port, starboard and stern, they were rather like floating armoured tanks.[60] These ships were also used as rams, because the lighter ships of the Japanese were no match for their heavy prows. Guns blazing, the tiny Korean squadron abandoned all thought of coming out alive and charged the Japanese fleet. The Koreans targeted the Japanese flagship, which was set ablaze and sank; Admiral Yi had the satisfaction of seeing the corpse of the Japanese commander dragged from the water: it was cut in pieces and hung from the mast, so the Japanese could see what had happened to their leader. This was Korea's battle of Salamis, fought in a narrow channel, from which the Korean ships emerged unscathed, but the Japanese lost thirty-one ships.[61]

By 1598 the struggle had become a matter of honour for Hideyoshi. By then, his real intention was not so much to subdue Korea, which now seemed impossible, but to humiliate the Ming emperor, by showing that Korea, a tributary state of China, was open to the armies of the other great empire, that of Japan.[62] After a glittering career of naval victories, punctuated by a period when his jealous rivals had him imprisoned, Yi Sun-sin died in his final battle at the end of 1598, struck down by a bullet in much the same way as Lord Nelson, with whom he is often compared. Estimates of the number of Japanese ships destroyed in this battle hover around 200, with another hundred captured and 500 Japanese killed, quite apart from a great many who drowned. He even became a hero in the modern Japanese navy. A Japanese admiral who scored a great triumph over the Russians in 1905 objected when he was compared at his victory celebrations to Nelson and Yi. 'It may be proper to compare me with Nelson,' he said, 'but not with Korea's Yi Sun-sin. He is too great to be compared to anyone.'[63]

V

These events in Korea might seem to have had nothing much to do with the links between Japan and Macau. However, having spent so much time and money on his futile invasion of Korea, Hideyoshi was all the more inclined to favour trade, in the hope of generating more income. Trade within the Inland Sea was already lively, carrying not just goods but pilgrims between the islands of Japan. With the rise of the new administrative centre at Edo in Tokyo Bay, a new centre of consumption for rice and its much-appreciated by-product, sake, became prominent, and in the early seventeenth century the so-called 'barrel ships', named after their barrels of sake rather than their shape, moved back and forth to Edo following a regular timetable.[64] Hideyoshi was also interested in much more distant connections. He enthusiastically issued 'vermilion seal' passports which allowed Japanese ships to travel back and forth to his lands. As early as 1587 he sent an expedition into Kyushu island consisting of 300,000 troops and 20,000 horses, and both Hakata, the ancient port, and Nagasaki, the new one, were brought under his direct control, which meant that he possessed windows on the world a good distance from Edo and Kyoto. Hideyoshi listened carefully to news of foreign ships, buying Portuguese gold and on one occasion offering to buy all the pottery brought from the Philippines on a Spanish ship – Luzon ceramics, though rather rough, were much appreciated by Japanese tea-drinkers.[65] Japan was not isolated from the outside world, but its rulers were selective about the contacts they were willing to encourage. The importance of the Portuguese lay in the access they gave to fine Chinese silks and the links that extended beyond Macau all the way to Melaka and Goa.

The rulers of Japan also became aware that Spaniards were taking an interest in their dominions. These were not just merchants, whose attempts to integrate Japan into the Manila galleon route have been discussed already. A remarkable Dominican friar, Juan Cobo, had travelled from Mexico to Manila in 1588; he quickly learned 3,000 Chinese characters before moving on to Satsuma in Japan in June 1592. He came as much to spy out the land as to build friendly relations with the regent's court on behalf of King Philip of Spain; Spanish dreams of conquering China could only be realized if Japanese troops came to King Philip's aid. In Satsuma, Cobo encountered a merchant from Peru who claimed he had been cheated by the Portuguese, so together they made their way to the military camp of Hideyoshi, who was on campaign near Nagoya. Hideyoshi was intrigued by a globe that Cobo produced, on which the friar traced the extent of the Spanish empire; but he was not convinced that Cobo's boasts were to be taken seriously, for he was disappointed by the modest presents Cobo had brought from the Philippines, which, in any case, he chose to treat as tribute. Hideyoshi sent a letter to the governor of the Philippines, full of exaggerated boasts about his conquests in Korea and his victories over Chinese armies. He insisted that the Philippines were 'within my reach'.

He concluded with a message that mixed appeasement with threats: 'Let us be friends forever, and write to that effect to the king of Castile. Do not, because he is far away, let him slight my words. I have never seen those far lands, but from the accounts I have been given I know what is there.' Cobo was shipwrecked off Taiwan and was killed by local head-hunters.[66] Spanish Franciscan friars began to compete with the Jesuits in Japan, and one of them, Fray Jerónimo de Jesús de Castro, was thrown out of Nagasaki in autumn 1597, only to bounce back into Japan the next summer; this time the shogun, Ieyasu, who had just come to power, decided that the presence of a Spanish friar in his lands might encourage the Spaniards to strike a trade deal, and Fray Jerónimo was allowed to build a church in Edo in May 1599, even though Ieyasu did not grant him permission to convert his subjects to Christianity. The Jesuits became as busy fending off their Franciscan rivals as they were currying favour at the court of the unpredictable shogun.[67]

The complications in dealing with Ieyasu were clearly demonstrated in 1599. A Portuguese sea captain based in Nagasaki named Francisco de Gouvea got it into his head that he could enrich himself by coming to the aid of the king of Cambodia, who was fighting his neighbours; he recruited a mixed force of Japanese and Portuguese and sailed by way of Macau to Cambodia, where his ship was joined by two Spanish vessels from Manila. Gouvea never made himself rich and was killed in Cambodia, but many of his followers escaped from Cambodia aboard his ship. Still hoping to make some money out of the expedition, they seized a boat heading across the South China Sea from Malaya, and took it with them to Nagasaki. Their exploits were deemed to be acts of piracy; all the Japanese soldiers as well as many of their wives and children were arrested and crucified, with Fray Jerónimo brought in as a witness. Only the intervention of the Jesuits prevented an even worse massacre – the wife and children of Gou-vea had also been arrested but in the end were spared.[68] The arbitrary nature of Ieyasu's rule became very obvious, particularly after he defeated his Japanese foes in 1600.[69] Soon after that Fray Jerónimo died of dysen-tery and his rival Valignano spat out the comment: 'the Lord taught him a lesson!' At the root of the disagreement between the Franciscans and the Jesuits was a sense among the Franciscans that the Jesuits were too willing to respect the strict limits placed on their activities by the regime in Edo: 'they therefore go about in Japanese dress, and they say Mass and administer the sacraments behind closed doors.' Meanwhile the Jesuits, who certainly knew Japan much better, were convinced that the open evangelization favoured by the Franciscans was placing Japanese Christianity in jeopardy.[70]

In 1614 Ieyasu banned Christianity in Japan. By then hundreds of thousands of Japanese had already accepted the faith, mainly in Kyushu. The daimyo were expected to conform and to abandon Christianity for Buddhism. Over the next quarter of a century, horrific persecutions took place.[71] What has been called Japan's 'Christian Century' came to an end in the middle of the seventeenth century. The Portuguese found it more and more difficult to trade, and were thrown out in 1639; an embassy set out the next year from Macau, hoping to restore ties, but the uncompromising attitude of the authorities was made absolutely clear when most of the diplomats were beheaded.[72] This was not simply the result of the ban on Jesuit proselytization and the withdrawal of the Jesuits from the lucrative trade in Chinese silk. Other forces were at work: the Portuguese had new European rivals in these waters who, like them, had once been under the rule of the dour King Philip II of Spain, but had been more successful in throwing off his rule: the Dutch. The English too had resisted King Philip, who had also, briefly, been their own king while he was married to Queen Mary. In England, and then in the Netherlands and Denmark, new ideas were being propagated that suggested there were previously unexplored ways around the seas patrolled by Spain and Portugal, routes that were investigated with extraordinary persistence in the late sixteenth and early century seventeenth.

36

The Fourth Ocean

I

So far this book has looked at three great oceans. Yet most atlases would show that there exist five oceans. One of them, the Southern or Antarctic Ocean, is really a southward extension of the Atlantic, Pacific and Indian Oceans, and might or might not embrace the bottom of Australia and New Zealand, its northern limits being as arbitrary as those laid down by the Spanish and Portuguese treaty that divided the world in 1494. The other, the Arctic Ocean, has barely featured so far, because even the Norse voyages to Greenland were confined to Atlantic waters. An occasional trip northwards up the Davis Strait, or (at the other end of the Norse maritime world) voyages as far as Spitsbergen, brought Norse ships above the Arctic Circle, although the Davis Strait, separating Greenland from Baffin Island, is clearly an extension of the Atlantic. Even before the discovery of North America, the question of what lay far to the north gave rise to fanciful speculation, based on snippets of knowledge about the Sami (or Lapps). Martin Behaim's globe, created around the time of Columbus's first voyage, imagined that the North Pole consisted of a circular island surrounded by ocean, and betrayed the usual confusion about what Greenland was, making it an extension of Eurasia beyond Norway.[1] Before 1555 the Swedish cleric and geographer Olaus Magnus reached the north of Norway and wrote about the midnight sun as well as the fur trade and Sami customs.[2]

The lure of the Arctic to sixteenth-century sailors consisted not of lands within the Arctic Circle but of seas that would take them across the Arctic into warmer waters studded with spice islands. Only at the start of the twenty-first century has the melting of polar ice made the passageways around the top of North America and around the top of Russia look viable. Magellan had shown that a route round the bottom of the Americas did exist; but it was almost beyond human endurance, and the opportunity to find a passageway to the north of either the Americas or Russia that

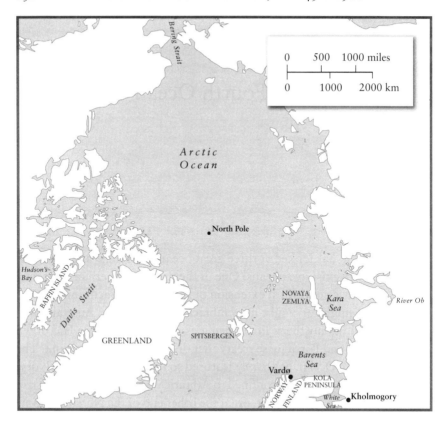

would bring European merchants to Cathay and the Indies could not be passed by – not, at any rate, by the English and later on the Dutch, who hoped to avoid territories over which Spain and Portugal exercised or claimed to exercise dominion. Now and again, it is true, the English could take advantage of close relations with Spain and claim access to Spanish markets as far afield as Hispaniola. But the relationship between England and Spain was bumpy. Henry VIII's alliance collapsed in acrimony over his divorce from Catherine of Aragon, and Philip II's brief period as king of England, through his marriage to Catherine's daughter, Mary, was followed by a Protestant succession.

This was not simply a matter of commercial and political alliances. English merchants trading in Andalusia had established a base at Sanlúcar de Barrameda, an outport of Seville, under the patronage of the dukes of Medina Sidonia, who were something of a law unto themselves and had all sorts of creative ideas about promoting prosperity (including the settlement of Gibraltar with converted Jews in 1474). Now the English claimed that they had become the target of the Spanish Inquisition, which had extended its persecutions beyond crypto-Jews and crypto-Muslims to embrace those who rejected papal supremacy: 'many of our nacion be secretly accused and know not therof so that all the hole company daylly dotth live in great feare and daunger.'[3] Yet the English craved access to the products of the Indies, all the more so as the economy began to expand. One possibility was to create warm ties with the rulers of Morocco, which, it was hoped, would satisfy English hunger for sugar, while an alliance with its rulers would box in the king of Spain close to home and would maintain pressure on the Portuguese, who still controlled several Moroccan ports. So, from the 1550s onwards, a 'Barbary trade' developed, and from the 1580s it was managed by a Barbary Company licensed by Queen Elizabeth and based in London.[4]

Sugar was one thing; but there was a whole pharmacopoeia of drugs and a larder of spices that the English wanted to acquire. Here the twin notions of a North-West and a North-East Passage around either the top of North America or the top of Russia came into play. It is no surprise that the initiative lay with Bristol merchants who had already been heavily involved with first John and then Sebastian Cabot, particularly the Thorne family, wealthy merchants and benefactors (the school founded by Robert Thorne the Elder still survives, as Bristol Grammar School). In 1530 his son, also Robert, wrote at length to King Henry VIII, arguing that the king should seize the opportunity to increase his power and influence by sending expeditions to 'divers New lands and kingdoms, in the which without doubt your Grace shall winne perpetuall glory, and your subjectes infinite profite'. The younger Thorne was now based in London, but had lived for a while in Seville with, it is said, his Spanish mistress; and the advantage he placed second – 'infinite profite' – was the one that mattered more to him. Thorne underplayed the dangers from ice and cold, and emphasized instead the fact that one could keep sailing during the perpetual daylight of an Arctic summer, 'which thing is a great commoditie for the navigants, to see at all times round about them'. He seems to have assumed that the best route would take ships close to the North Pole itself, right over the top of the world. All this led Robert Thorne to an extravagant account of how English ships could then choose to return by way of the Magellan Strait or the Cape of Good Hope, having in the meantime visited 'the richest lands and Islands of the world of golde, precious stones, balmes, spices, and other thinges that we here esteem most'.[5]

These plans were not followed through, and by 1569, when Gerard Mercator published a new version of his very influential world map, the view began to spread that a direct polar route was probably impossible, because the North Pole was supposedly surrounded by four closely packed islands; however, that still left the passages to the north-west and the north-east open, assuming they were not blocked by ice. 'No other map in the *Atlas* proved to be so erroneous,' it has been remarked, all the more so as Mercator credulously included information from a bogus account of the travels of a late medieval Venetian named Zeno, who was supposed to have been washed up on the shores of the mythical Frisland and Estotiland, said to be well-populated mid-Atlantic islands. However, this map did assume the existence of what is now known as the Bering Strait, opening up the route to China around the top of Eurasia.[6]

Thorne's friend Sebastian Cabot was an even more enthusiastic supporter of the idea of an Arctic route, patiently awaiting the day when it would become obvious that this was an opportunity not to be missed. He was still arguing the case half a century after his father had discovered Newfoundland but had failed to open up the promised route to Cathay. Sebastian had explored waters off Canada (and had possibly entered Hudson Bay) while in English service in 1509, and he had returned to the English court by 1548, after spending thirty-four years working for the king of Spain.[7] This time, though, the target of his expeditions was left vague: he took charge of a newly formed 'Companie of the Marchants Adventurers for the Discoverie of Regions, Dominions, Islands and Places Unknowen'. In Richard Hakluyt's remarkable collection of sixteenth-century travel narratives the planned voyage is aptly described as 'a newe and strange Navigation'. Funds were raised by inviting subscriptions of £25, which brought in £6,000, enough to buy and fit out three ships. Given the choice between a north-eastern and a north-western route, the consortium decided in 1553 that the best prospects lay in the direction of Russia; after all, several expeditions already sent towards the American north-west had found no passageway. Sir Hugh Willoughby and Richard Chancellor were to lead the expedition, armed with letters from the young King Edward VI addressed, in time-honoured fashion, to sundry 'Kings, Princes and other Potentates'; the ships attracted enormous attention when they sailed downriver and passed the royal palace at Greenwich: 'the Courtiers came running out, and the common people flockt together, standing very thicke upon the shoare: the Privie Counsel, they lookt out at the windows of the Court, and the rest ranne up to the toppes of the towers.'[8]

The optimism that had led to the creation of the consortium was certainly misplaced. Off the coast of northern Finland, storms dispersed the ships and Willoughby's ship along with one other pressed on into the Barents Sea, which lies between Spitsbergen and the long and desolate pair of islands simply known as *Novaya Zemlya*, 'New Land', before icy conditions forced the ships back to the Kola Peninsula at the very top of

Scandinavia. Forced to spend the winter there, all sixty-three sailors and merchants were in no condition to survive the freezing conditions. A couple of years later the Venetian ambassador in London told how the crews had been found by Russian fishermen, literally frozen to death and still sitting at dinner, or writing a letter, or opening a locker.[9] No doubt these details were embellishments; but the challenge of the north-east route became much clearer, and the Venetian ambassador must have combined satisfaction with horror, aware that his native city already faced quite enough competition in the spice trade from the Portuguese. Better news came from the third vessel. Chancellor's ship ended up on the coasts of the White Sea, from where Chancellor set out on an ambitious but successful overland journey to Moscow, laying the foundations for a successful fur trade between England and Russia which came to be handled by a licensed Muscovy Company. Quite apart from the fascination English reports show at the customs and beliefs of the Russians, and quite apart from the friendly relations that developed between Ivan the Terrible in Moscow and Elizabeth I in London (even extending to a marriage proposal from the psychopathic tsar), the Muscovy trade opened up other possibilities: the road was now open to Persia, but overland, and a trickle of exotic eastern goods reached England by this long and roundabout route. Unexpected success in Muscovy deflected attention from the North-East Passage, and the sense that the north-eastern route was not viable was strengthened when a second expedition, in 1555, was guided some of the way by Russian sailors and reached Novaya Zemlya. However, the ship, a small pinnace, had to turn back because of the frightful conditions at 70°N – not just the ice floes but the unwelcome attention of a massive Right Whale that 'made a terrific noyse in the water' and swam within a few feet of the ship.[10]

The Muscovy Company continued to raise money for expeditions; these reverses did nothing to dampen enthusiasm for voyages across the Arctic, and the Muscovy Company was fortunate in its choice of commander: Anthony Jenkinson, who set out in 1557, proved to be an indomitable explorer of central Asia, reaching Persia and Bukhara, and acting as Queen Elizabeth's representative at the court of the highly temperamental tsar. What Ivan really sought was a military rather than a trading alliance, in the hope of extending his power in the Baltic and keeping the Swedes at bay. Although the privileges to the English also included trading rights along those parts of the Baltic that lay under Russian control, it is hard to see what real benefit a military alliance would have brought England, apart from the opportunity to sell armaments. In 1572 Jenkinson managed to negotiate the restoration of English trading rights when Ivan the

Terrible, in one of his all-too-frequent spasms of rage, had abolished them, and he worked his charm on the tsar so successfully that he was sent back to England bearing 'our hearty commendations to our loving sister, Queene Elizabeth'.[11] The English merchants established a base at Kholmogory, about fifty miles upriver from the White Sea: 'in this town the English men have lands of their own, given them by the Emperour, and fair houses, with offices for their commodity, very many.'[12]

Not deterred, the Muscovy Company tried yet again in 1580, even though the ships the company sent were apparently tiny – a crew of ten on one barque of forty tons and a mere six on the other, perhaps in recognition that passage through the ice would be even more difficult with large vessels of the sort that had been used by Willoughby and Chancellor. The real interest of this voyage lies in its manifest: confident of reaching China, the cargo included a 'large Mappe of London to make shew of your Citie'; plenty of English clothes, including hats, gloves and *pantophles*, or slippers, not to mention glassware from both England and Venice and a great assortment of ironmongery, which makes one think that among the investors were manufacturers of locks, hinges and bolts. In return the explorers were expected to obtain not just plenty of seeds, in the hope that Chinese herbs could be cultivated in Europe, but a map of China. They were also supposed to spy on the Chinese, carefully noting fortifications and naval activity in the places they visited. Needless to say, they did not reach China, although they did penetrate a little way beyond Novaya Zemlya before the ice of the Kara Sea forced them back. Yet Russian sailors already knew how to navigate further along the northern coast of Eurasia right up to the great River Ob.[13]

The English were frozen out of the Arctic; but others were not discouraged. At the end of the sixteenth century Dutch navigators also saw a route across the top of the world as a way to keep their trade in exotic goods alive while immersed in conflict with Spain. They had the support of Prince Maurits, the *Stadhouder*, who occupied a sort of presidential role in the United Provinces of the Netherlands and who in 1593 ensured that money was invested in this route. Here was an opportunity to strike sharp blows against Catholic Spain that appealed to Calvinist ministers of religion such as Petrus Plancius, a forceful hardliner who took an especial interest in geography and navigation, lecturing and publishing on the subject, including maps that outlined a route through the Arctic Ocean.[14] Mapmakers, though, could only go so far, which was not very far at all. What was needed was an expedition. Doing it the hard way, the great Dutch navigator Willem Barentsz sailed into Arctic waters and mapped out parts of the sea that now bears his name, as well as the islands of

Novaya Zemlya on its eastern edge; but even he confused Spitsbergen with Greenland, and in 1596–7 he and his crew had to endure a harsh winter immured in a wooden house built from driftwood and parts of their ship. The ship itself was completely trapped in ice, so they were forced to travel in open boats all the way from Novaya Zemlya to the Kola Peninsula. Barentsz died en route; how anyone survived is the real surprise, although Russian sailors occasionally came to their aid. A bestselling account of this dramatic voyage was in the bookshops as early as 1598. Normally one expects these narratives to be embellished, but, when in 1871 a Norwegian skipper chanced upon the remains of a wooden hut in this remote corner of the Arctic, it became obvious that the basic facts at least were true: the hut was still stocked with all the paraphernalia of the voyage, from spoons and knives to an iron chest with an elaborate lock, to pewter candlesticks, to a 'pitcher of Etruscan shape, beautifully engraved', to small weapons, to Dutch books and engravings (so many of these that they were clearly taken to be put on sale in China), and much else.[15] Nor did Dutch expeditions end at this point; the lesson of the attempts to find a North-East Passage was that failure only increased the appetite. The realization that Arctic waters teemed with whales, including the enormous Arctic Right Whale, attracted the Dutch 'North Company' into the seas to the north of Russia. A Right Whale could be as much as sixty or seventy feet long, and at least 2,000 pounds of baleen plates could be extracted from the carcass, as well as a mountain of blubber.[16]

II

If, as Mercator's atlas and other maps showed, North America was physically separate from Asia, then the North-West Passage was also worth considering. Maybe the world was constructed in such a way that the route did not actually pass through the Arctic: after all, when the French king sent Giovanni da Verrazano on the journey that took him past what became New England, in 1524, Francis I hoped he would find a way through to the Pacific somewhere in those latitudes, and the same idea motivated his support for Jacques Cartier's exploration of the St Lawrence River in Canada.[17] A woodcut of around 1530, made in Nuremberg, seems to reflect Sebastian Cabot's assumption that a long, reasonably wide and accessible *Fretum Arcticum*, or Arctic Passage, passed between Greenland and northern China – on the woodcut Greenland was shown as a peninsula sticking out of Asia, so that Asia was made to reach right across the top of a stunted and much-reduced North America. Some maps and globes of this period followed this model and attributed the discovery of a North-West Passage to the Corte Real brothers from the Azores, who had rediscovered Greenland and Labrador around 1500. The assumption that the route existed became more and more widespread, especially since the idea had the imprimatur of Sebastian Cabot: 'one Sebastian Cabota hath bin the chiefest setter forth of this journey or voyage.'

The Muscovy Company kept its options open, concentrating at first on the north-eastern route but holding a monopoly on the exploration of the north-western one as well. Humphrey Gilbert, Walter Raleigh's half-brother, argued the case for a new route to Cathay, or China, with determination in a tract of 1566 entitled *A Discourse of Discoverie for a New Passage to Cataia*: 'you might justly have charged mee with an un-settled head if I had at any time taken in hand, to discover Utopia, or any country fained by imagination: But Cataia is none such, it is a country, well knowen.'[18] Gilbert presented his arguments to Queen Elizabeth, whose court he attended, and accompanied his tract with a map showing how the two American continents, joined to one another, were still sep-arated by water channels from a large southern continent and from an Asian landmass that did not, this time, include Greenland. He had a vision of large spaces of open water giving access to a channel into the Pacific. No less significantly, he urged the court to think of the advantages explor-ation of this route would bring England, as its relations with Catholic Spain steadily deteriorated following the death of Queen Mary and Philip's loss of recognition as king of England.[19]

Queen Elizabeth did not act on Gilbert's optimistic advice for several years. Then, in 1576, Martin Frobisher set out to explore the North-West Passage, and Gilbert's advice was printed and distributed as a sort of prospectus for Frobisher's voyage. Frobisher had some experience of the west African trade, but he was, in essence, one of those adventurous and unscrupulous privateers who often received tacit support from the queen.[20] This made him all the more suitable as a challenger to Spanish and Por-tuguese mastery over the spice trade. A 'Company of Cathay' came into being, but it only raised £875, enough to equip two thirty-ton barques and a small pinnace, total crew thirty-four men, 'alarmingly small vessels' engaged on a 'madcap venture', in the words of the leading historian of this route.[21] The tiny fleet set out in summer 1576; the pinnace sank with all hands in a storm west of Greenland, and one of the barques, the *Michael*, headed back home.[22]

Frobisher steered his own ship, the *Gabriel*, towards the southern shores of Baffin Island, where the crew encountered their first Inuit out at sea paddling their kayaks. Having assumed that the northern shores of this stretch of water were part of Asia, and the southern shores part of North America, Frobisher knew this to be absolutely correct when he saw the Inuit at close quarters; his colleague the Master of the *Gabriel* reported: 'they bee like to Tartars, with long blacke haire, broad faces, and flatte noses, and tawnie in colour.'[23] This was a similar mistake to that made by observers of Columbus's generation, who had also identified the native peoples of the Caribbean and Central America with Asia.[24] At first, relations with the Inuit were quite good; the Inuit offered the crew salmon and other fresh fish. Five sailors who were taking an Inuit back to the shore to collect his kayak, after he offered to lead the *Gabriel* back to the open sea, disappeared from sight, though memory of them remained remarkably strong among the Inuit, for whom, after all, this was their first encounter with English explorers:

> Oral history told me that five white men were captured by Innuit people at the time of the appearance of the ships a great many years ago; that these men wintered on shore (whether one, two, three, or more winters, could not say); that they lived among the Innuit, that they afterward built an *oomien* [large boat], and put a mast into her, and had sails; that early in the season, before much water appeared, they endeavoured to depart; that, in the effort, some froze their hands; but that finally they succeeded in getting into open water, and away they went, which was the last seen or heard of them.[25]

The Inuit even remembered that there were three separate visits by Frobisher's ships. However, an English narrative of the voyage paints a less positive picture: some English clothes were found in an Inuit camp overrun by Frobisher's sailors on his second expedition, of 1577, and they can only have been left behind, or taken from, the five sailors who disappeared. Frobisher was inclined to think that the omnivorous Inuit had eaten the men rather than looking after them, for by this time relations with the Inuit had deteriorated badly and there were frequent clashes between the Europeans and the native population; besides, the image of the cannibalistic native American was widely diffused during the sixteenth century.[26]

Missing the entrance to Hudson Bay, Frobisher sailed some way down a fjord on Baffin Island, which became known as Frobisher Bay, and decided that this must be the passageway he sought. But in the event he turned back before winter could set in, reaching London with not much to show for his voyage apart from a fairly small piece of black rock, which, on close examination, seemed to contain fragments of a bright metal that the London assayers optimistically thought was gold, estimated to be worth £240 per ton of rock. This raised hopes to such a pitch that Queen

Elizabeth was willing to invest £1,000 in a second expedition by the same two ships, while the Flemish geographer Abraham Ortelius is said to have made a jealous trip to London to see if he could steal some of the secrets of the north-western route, which would certainly have interested the Spanish masters of Flanders. Aware that the ships were venturing into lands that would never keep them supplied with the food they needed, the second expedition carried five tons of salt beef, sixteen tons of ship's biscuit, two tons of butter (enough for half a pound per man per day) and over eighty tons of beer, which would provide eight pints (four and a half litres) per man per day – even so, the ships managed to sail in a straight line when so required.[27] However, there was a subtle change in emphasis, as the Cathay Company now charged Frobisher with collecting many more samples of rock; collecting it in Arctic conditions out of what even in August was frozen ground was no light task, and the ships had to set sail before the end of the month because the Arctic summer ended early and the ice began to close in.[28] Still, the queen was gratified, and, showing off her skill in Latin, she even gave the territories Frobisher had visited a new name, *Meta Incognita*, 'The Unknown Limits' – meaning that this was an unclaimed land to which neither Spain nor any other power had a prior claim.[29]

In a third, massive expedition, of 1578, consisting of eleven ships and 400 men, Frobisher collected still more of the rock, and happened upon the entrance to Hudson Bay. The aim was to create a permanent settlement, dedicated to the extraction of gold-bearing rock.[30] He realized that this was very possibly 'the passage which we seeke to find the rich country of Cathaya', but everyone's attention had turned to the pieces of black rock. Investment in Frobisher's project boomed, as a mineral-processing plant with furnaces and mills was built at Dartford at great expense to render down the rock and extract the gold. The plant was supplied with 1,250 tons of rock when those of Frobisher's ships that had survived the Arctic ice returned – only Frobisher's flagship, the *Michael*, had been provided with a strengthened hull, and other vessels risked being crushed to pieces by the weight of the ice floes.[31] Once processed, the rock mainly delivered iron pyrites, 'fool's gold'. Although iron pyrites tend to occur in places where real gold can be found, it remains astonishing that, in an age when alchemy was the rage, and learned figures such as John Dee gravitated around the royal court, such an elementary mistake was made. So, all too quickly, the bubble burst and the investments evaporated into thin air. Frobisher emerges with more credit than the assayers: he had not set out to find gold in North America, and he seems to have been a demanding but inspiring leader of his men; when digging up rocks became the business of the day, he somehow managed to convince them to put all their limited energy into hard physical labour; and by his third expedition he had recruited hundreds of volunteers.

Like the search for a North-East Passage, the search for the North-West Passage continued despite setbacks. After all, the saga of the false gold could be dismissed as a distraction from the real purpose all along, which had been to reach China. In the 1580s John Davis followed in the wake of Frobisher but then headed off into the strait now named after him between Greenland and Baffin Island.[32] The early seventeenth century saw the heroic endeavours of Henry Hudson (who had already explored the North-East Passage) to work out the nature of the great sea that carries his own name and the all-too-modest qualifier 'bay'. His efforts ended in disaster in 1611 when the crew mutinied, placed him, his son and a handful of crew members in a small boat, and cut them adrift in James Bay, the southernmost part of Hudson Bay. It is unlikely that the captain and his friends survived; they were given neither food nor warm clothing.[33]

A footnote to these expeditions is provided by the circumnavigation of the world led by Sir Francis Drake in 1577 to 1580 aboard the *Pelican* (later renamed the *Golden Hind*).[34] He decided to follow the Pacific coast of not just South but North America a long way northwards, beyond the trajectory of the Manila galleons operated by Spain upon which he planned to prey. He also captured and rifled a number of Spanish ships whose route took them up and down the coasts of South America and Mexico, for the Spaniards were building towns along the shoreline, and the 'wine of Chili' was a fond target of Drake's men.[35] One explanation that has been offered for his insistence on sailing northwards into cooler climes is that he too was looking for a channel linking the Pacific to the Atlantic.[36] Apart from anything else, the discovery of this legendary passage would offer a quick way back to England – his aim was not actually to circumnavigate the globe, but to harass the Spaniards in their own waters, first in the Caribbean and then in the Pacific; once in the Pacific, there was a good chance of capturing Spanish treasure ships where they least expected to face any challenges. Finally, when Drake realized that he could not return by way of the stormy Magellan Strait, he aimed for the Cape of Good Hope instead.[37]

More than ten years later, having been defeated by the Arctic, John Davis led an expedition into the Pacific by way of the Magellan Strait in 1591-2, hoping to resolve the problem of the North-West Passage 'on the backe syde' by following Drake's route up the American coast until he found the way through. Disagreements with the joint leader of the expedition, combined with foul weather, forced Davis back to England before he had reached far beyond the southern tip of the Americas.[38] Had he reached Alaska from Tierra del Fuego his expedition would surely be ranked as one of the greatest sixteenth-century voyages. As it was, Davis may have been the first to land in the Falkland Islands, where his crew were forced to live off penguin meat, on their way home. Inevitably, those mapping the shores of unknown seas kept an eye out for the express routes across continents that had first been postulated as a way to cross Africa and now were being postulated as a way to cross North America.

III

England and the Netherlands were not alone in eyeing these Arctic routes with interest. The Danes were well aware of the long history of Norse involvement in far northern waters, and at the start of the sixteenth century they were already operating a customs station on the northern tip of Scandinavia, at the place they called Vardø and the English called Wardhouse, 'a haven or castel of some name in the kingdome of Norway'; it had been chosen as the meeting point for the ships of Hugh Willoughby and Richard Chancellor on their ill-fated expedition into the Arctic Ocean.[39] Shipping bound for the White Sea stopped there and dues were paid to the Danish king, who was ruler of Norway as well; meanwhile the Danish kings laid down plans to gain control over Greenland: King Frederick II hoped to persuade Martin Frobisher to lead an expedition there, and King Christian IV hired Scottish and English captains to assert Danish rule over the vast icy island. Once he thought he had achieved his aims in the north-west Atlantic, he turned his attention to the North-East Passage. He sent an enterprising and experienced seaman, Jens Munk, as far as the ice would permit. Once this route proved to be impassable, Munk was reassigned to the North-West Passage instead, dreaming, as had the English, of opening a route to China. In 1619 Munk set off with a frigate and a sloop in the direction of Baffin Island and Hudson Bay. Described as 'one of the most vivid and poignant works in the literature of the Arctic', Munk's diary of his voyage still exists, only because he, with two other members of the crew of sixty-four, survived the terrible conditions of a long winter on an inadequate diet which created an epidemic of scurvy: 'the stomach was ready enough,' Munk wrote, 'and had appetite for food, but the teeth would not allow it.'[40] Much of the time, the ground was too hard even to bury their dead companions – in 1717 an English expedition arrived at the same spot and found it littered with the skeletons of unburied Danish sailors. The ships had arrived in Hudson Bay in late August, not realizing that this was actually the time to leave before the ice set in. In the end, Munk and two of his companions steered their sloop back to Denmark, where the king showed his immense gratitude by ordering him to set out again, find the frigate that had been left behind, and map the rest of Hudson Bay. No doubt Munk was very relieved that no one could be persuaded to join the crew for this journey into a frozen hell.[41]

Danish ambitions in Arctic waters were arrested, although these were also the years in which a Danish East India Company came into being, eventually followed by a Danish West India Company, a reminder that the battle for control of maritime trade was not confined to Spain, Portugal, Holland, England and France, not to mention the Ottoman Turks in the Indian Ocean. Among all these powers and nations, however, the Dutch proved to be the most determined and ruthless challengers of the Spanish and Portuguese supremacy over the ocean routes.

37

The Rise of the Dutch

I

Before looking at the history of the Dutch presence across the oceans, something needs to be said about the emergence of the Dutch merchant fleets. Their success in supplanting the Portuguese was one of several extraordinary triumphs over the old order – over the Hansards in the Baltic and over Antwerp in their own neighbourhood. All these victories were intertwined. Antwerp played a vital role in the Asiatic trading system created by the Portuguese, funnelling silver into the Portuguese network in return for prodigious quantities of eastern spices. But Dutch maritime history begins with herrings rather than spices. It has been seen that the Hansa began to lose its grip on the trade of the Baltic and the North Sea as competition from both the Dutch and the English became more lively. Meanwhile German princes were attempting to re-establish their much-weakened territorial power and to rebuild their finances, and were often reluctant to permit subject-towns to participate in the German Hansa, all the more so when the Hansa developed its own foreign policy and sent its fleets into battle against the Danes or the English.

These conflicts, and political struggles taking place within Flanders, had serious effects on Bruges, which lost its position as the great clearing house of maritime and terrestrial trade in the late fifteenth century. The citizens of Bruges stood up to the centralizing policies of the Habsburg regent, Maximilian of Austria, and Maximilian riposted with the instruction that all foreign merchants evacuate the city, issued in 1484 and 1488. Although he made peace with Bruges before long, the expulsion of the foreign merchants prompted many of them, including wealthy Italians, to move their business to Antwerp, which was better situated for access to the sea – the channels linking Bruges to the open sea had been silting up. Moreover, Maximilian encouraged the merchants to choose Antwerp because the city had stood by him during his conflict with the Flemish towns.[1] When Maximilian permitted the foreign business houses to return to Bruges, they demurred.

The Portuguese established an agency in Antwerp as early as 1498, even before they knew the outcome of Vasco da Gama's first voyage to India. They aimed to sell the goods they had acquired along the Guinea Coast, including Malagueta pepper; in the event they were laying the foundations for the 'golden age' of Antwerp. Another Portuguese product was sugar, brought over from Madeira and later from São Tomé in vast quantities; some of this came to be processed in refineries close to Antwerp. In 1560 Portuguese sugar imports into the Low Countries were worth 250,000 guilders, though this accounted for only 1.4 per cent of all imports (other Portuguese spices were worth 2,000,000 guilders, nearly 11 per cent).[2] Unlike the other foreign communities in Bruges and Antwerp, which were mostly branches of banks or private trading companies, the Portuguese *feitoria*, or 'factory', in Antwerp was set up by the Crown, which continued to appoint agents there. By 1510 the city had officially recognized the Portuguese community – indeed, by that date other nations, including the Genoese, the Catalans and the Florentines, watched the peppercorns flowing through Antwerp and established their own agencies. Immigration boosted the population, which reached about 100,000 at its peak in the mid-sixteenth century.[3]

The English Merchant Adventurers were very visible on the streets of Antwerp, as a result of generous privileges enshrined in the treaty grandly entitled the *Magnus Intercursus*, an agreement between the English Crown and the Habsburg rulers of Flanders. They had been active in Antwerp since 1421, when they established a staple there; in other words, all their textiles were to pass through this port alone.[4] The canny Henry VII obtained excellent terms for his subjects, who channelled English cloth into Europe just as England was expanding its cloth production and Flemish cloth production was faltering.[5] The Merchant Adventurers included a large number of Mercers, members of the elite cloth-trading guild, and one of the most prominent English dealers in Antwerp was Sir Thomas Gresham, himself the son of a Mercer, who combined a first-class education at St Paul's School and Gonville Hall, Cambridge, with outstanding business talent. It has been said that he also combined 'political influence and diplomacy with a grasp of finance and a lack of scruple almost equally breath-taking'.[6] His experience of the Antwerp Bourse led him to found the Royal Exchange in London, and he also founded Gresham College, where lectures on the practical skills a merchant or navigator might need were encouraged.

The Venetians had, until now, been sending their Flanders galleys to Antwerp, loaded with spices brought through Alexandria and Beirut, as

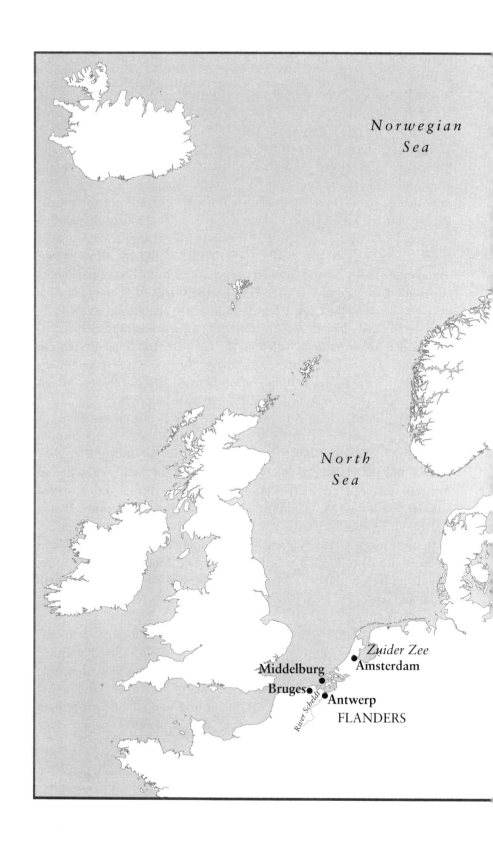

Norwegian Sea

North Sea

Zuider Zee
Amsterdam

Middelburg

Bruges

Antwerp

FLANDERS

River Scheldt

Baltic
Sea

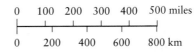

0	100	200	300	400	500 miles
0	200	400	600	800 km	

well as Mediterranean luxuries. In 1501 the first shipment of Asian, rather than west African, spices reached the port from Lisbon, and after this the quantities brought to Antwerp by the Portuguese traders grew and grew. Venetian galley sailings stopped for a few years, though they did resume in 1518, when the spice trade had recovered some equilibrium.[7] Antwerp now became a magnet for south German businessmen keen to buy these goods for consumers in Nuremberg, Augsburg and elsewhere – the great banking houses of the Fuggers, the Welsers and the Imhofs, among others, who enriched themselves greatly from the spice trade, although a modern historian has written of their 'appalling reputation as leeches'.[8] They paid in silver and copper, which was mined in central Europe and now flowed, via Antwerp, towards Portugal. These metals had traditionally been funnelled southwards over the Alps to Venice, so the switch from Venice to Antwerp as the major trading port for spices had wide ramifications, threatening the money supply of the Most Serene Republic. As early as 1508 the precious metals trade was worth 60,000 marks. Having built one Bourse in which businessmen could make their deals in 1485, Antwerp had to construct a larger one in 1515 and a New Bourse in 1531, to cope with expanding trade.[9]

The Antwerpers could not rest on their laurels. Habsburg rivalry with France disrupted maritime trade; in 1522 and the next year the city was deprived of spices as ships failed to reach Flanders from Portugal, Italy and Spain. The Venetians bounced back in the 1530s, for, as has been seen, the Portuguese proved unable to cut off the Red Sea routes, along which spices continued to filter. For Portugal, silver had always been Antwerp's selling point, and once large quantities of Peruvian silver began to arrive closer to home, in Spain, in the 1540s, Antwerp lost its attraction to the Portuguese, who closed down their offices in the city in 1548. On the other hand, the native Flemings took up some of the slack, dealing not just in the produce of the soil but in tapestries, paintings, jewellery and other upmarket goods that belonged in the house of any respectable citizen of means. Antwerp also became an important centre of printing, thanks to the initiative of Christoffel Plantijn. He explained why he had come to Antwerp from France:

> No other town in the world could offer me more facilities for carrying on the trade I intended to begin. Antwerp can easily be reached; various nations meet in this marketplace; there too can be found the raw materials indispensable for the practice of one's trade; craftsmen for all trades can be easily found and instructed in a short time.[10]

And there were still plenty of foreign merchants in the city, including Protestants from Germany and England, and New Christians of Jewish descent from Portugal. In 1550 the city offered the English Merchant

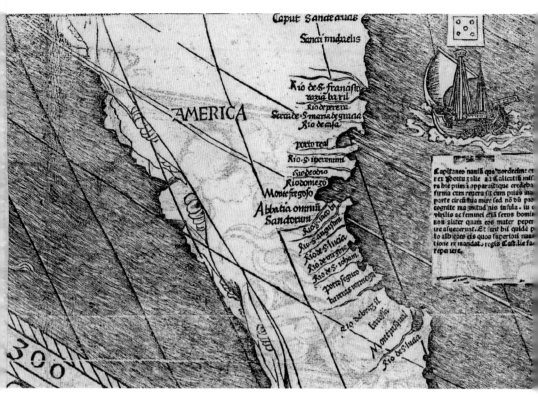

Caput Sande auas

Sancti michaelis

Rio de S. francisco uziā baril
Rio de perera
Sierra de S maria de guinai
Rio de casa

porto real

Rio. S. ipéronimi

Sancto obito
Rio do mezo
Monte fregoso

Abbatia omniū Sanctorum

AMERICA

300

Capitaneo nauis qua nordechint ot r ex Portu zalte a s Calicutiũ miss re bre prim s apparuit que credeba firma cum reuera sit cum prius inu parte circuitua mire sed nō bū pro cognite ma suitud nis insula. in c virilis ac feminei etis feruo bomi nou aliter quam cos mater pepe re asueuerunt. Et sunt bū quidē p lo albicces eis quos superiori naui tione re mandat. regis Cast.lie fa repererc.

40. Martin Waldseemüller celebrated Amerigo Vespucci's voyages by labelling part of the New World 'AMERICA'.

41. A globe of c.1510 in the Jagiellonian University, Kraków, mistakenly labels an imaginary continent south of Ceylon 'Newly Discovered America'.

42. Martin Behaim's globe of 1492 assumes that Japan, China and the Spice Islands can be reached by sailing westwards from Europe, a view shared by Columbus.

43. In 1503, on da Gama's second Indian voyage, the *Esmeralda* was torn from its moorings during a violent storm and foundered off the coast of Oman. The wreck was discovered in 1998.

44. The Spanish seat of government in early sixteenth-century Santo Domingo forms part of the oldest, largest and best-preserved colonial quarter in the Americas.

45. Seville c.1600. Atlantic shipping worked its way up the Guadalquivir River to the wharves of Seville. The Moorish Giralda Tower looms over the city.

46. An early seventeenth-century Indian portrait of the ruthless Portuguese commander Afonso de Albuquerque (d. 1515).

47. Portuguese watchtower at Badiya on the Gulf of Oman, overlooking a fifteenth-century mosque.

48. The first map by the Turkish corsair Piri Reis, of 1513, reveals detailed knowledge of Iberian voyages to the New World, partly acquired from a Spanish captive.

49. In 1642 Abel Tasman's fleet reached the South Island of New Zealand and was met by hostile Māoris who killed four Dutch sailors.

50. Founded in 1350, Ayutthaya in Thailand was an important trading centre linking the Indian Ocean to the South China Sea, from which the Dutch acquired enormous quantities of elephant ivory and rhinoceros horn.

51. Map of Macau showing the imposing façade of St Paul's Church a little to the left, with the fort and Jesuit College behind it. The main port, at the bottom, lay on the western side.

52. In 1597–8 the great Korean admiral Yi Sun-sin successfully deployed 'turtle ships' against a much larger Japanese navy.

53. The regent Toyotomi Hideyoshi blew hot and cold towards Jesuit missionaries and Japanese Christians.

54. Mercator's world map imagined that the North Pole was surrounded by four large islands, and that a route to China through the Arctic Ocean was impossible. This version dates from 1595.

55. In 1596–7 Willem Barentsz and his crew endured a freezing winter in the Arctic, leaving behind pewter candlesticks and merchandise rediscovered by a Norwegian skipper in 1871.

56. A Japanese bowl of c.1800 portrays Dutch ships and merchants, at that time the only foreign traders permitted to visit Japan. They are still shown as they would have dressed 150 years earlier.

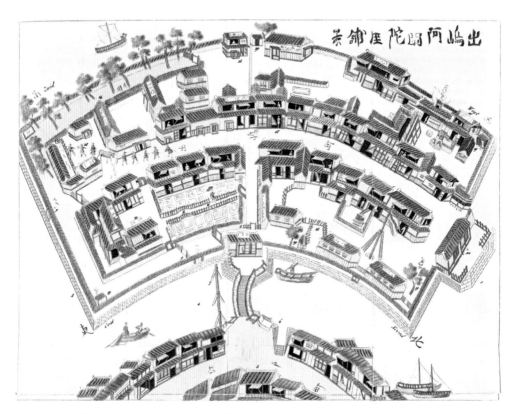

57. The Dutch settlement at Deshima, off Nagasaki, resembled a miniature Dutch town, with a flower garden but no church, as that was banned by the Japanese.

Adventurers an extensive range of buildings with an orchard, garden and four inner courtyards. The Hansards did just as well: the magnificent Oosterlingenhuis of 1568 lay close to the River Scheldt and contained 130 chambers for visiting merchants, though they rattled around in the building, as only a few Germans made much use of it.[11]

In reality, Antwerp was struggling to keep its head above water. Emperor Charles V had been relying heavily on loans raised through banks based in Antwerp. His debts rose from 1,400,000 guilders in 1538 to 3,800,000 guilders in 1554. In the 1550s the rulers of France, Spain and Portugal made it plain that they were unable to repay the capital of loans raised from business houses based in Antwerp, though they were graciously willing to pay 5 per cent interest for ever. This bankrupted the Fuggers of Augsburg, the greatest bankers of their day and pillars on whom the prosperity of Antwerp rested (even if the Genoese were able to fill the gap to some extent).[12] Tussles between English and Spanish sailors disrupted trade with England. The English had seized Spanish treasure ships en route to the Low Countries, carrying the pay of the Spanish soldiers. The Merchant Adventurers decided that Hamburg was a more amenable base, and upped sticks for a while in 1569 and again in 1582. Trade was declining even before the next shock hit Antwerp. This was the persecution of Protestants by the governor of the Netherlands, the infamous duke of Alva, and was one cause of the great Revolt of the Netherlands that erupted in 1572. From 1572 onwards the Dutch 'Sea-Beggars', privateers licensed by the house of Orange, blockaded the River Scheldt and forced Antwerp to find other export routes, as well as scoring victories against Spanish shipping. In 1576 Spanish troops unleashed their fury on Antwerp, in resentment at not being paid for their services. Then, in 1585, after besieging the city for more than a year, Spanish troops captured it. This was the final signal to the foreign merchants to leave, notably the Portuguese New Christians, who would be at constant risk from the Inquisition if they stayed behind (there were 97 Portuguese merchants in the city in 1570, not counting their dependants). It was also the signal to regather in a new port, and attention gradually focused on a city that seemed to have good natural defences and adequate access to the sea: Amsterdam.[13]

II

The rise of once impoverished Portugal and the creation of a Portuguese commercial network stretching round half the world, from Brazil to the Moluccas, is already a surprise. Even more of a surprise is the rise of

Dutch naval and commercial power. It has been claimed that 'the impact of this on a small country was overwhelming, even unparalleled in history', since one outcome was the emergence of a vigorous urban civilization expressed in the art and culture of seventeenth-century Holland.[14] The surprise comes not so much from the muddy, unpromising environment in which the Dutch operated as from the rapidity with which they supplanted the Portuguese in Asia and even for a time in South America. After all, other great trading powers had grown up in equally marginal settings, most obviously Venice. Going far back in time the Frisians had set out from their trading towns that rose above the waters of the same broad region as the Dutch and had mastered the trade of the early medieval North Sea, but had explored no further. And yet, at the end of the sixteenth century and throughout the seventeenth, Amsterdam and its neighbours became the base for operations on a truly worldwide scale. Amsterdam became the greatest trading city in Europe, and it derived its success from the fact that its ships had penetrated into the furthest reaches of the oceans. As Jonathan Israel has written, 'a fully fledged world entrepôt, not just linking, but dominating, the markets of all continents, was something totally outside human experience.'[15] For the Dutch did not simply link Europe to Africa, Asia and the Americas. They were also active in intra-Asian trade, more successfully than the Portuguese.

Any attempt to explain how the Dutch established mastery has to begin a century and a half before they founded their most famous trading institution, the East India Company. In the fifteenth century several Dutch towns were challenging the Hanseatic hegemony in the North Sea, but they were not yet ready to compete with the Lübeckers and Danzigers in what would later be called the 'rich trades', commerce in silks, spices and the other products bought in Bruges or further afield and shipped by the Germans through the Danish Sound into the Baltic. They had to be tolerated, even if they came from ports that had not joined the Hansa (as some did for a while), because they carried humdrum goods that were needed within the Baltic, especially the salt of northern Europe. Without salt there were no edible herrings, for, as has been seen, herring deteriorates rapidly once out of the water. The North Sea herring fisheries were completely dominated by the Dutch by the middle of the fifteenth century, and a century later the Dutch ports were home to about 500 herring 'busses', a type of ship adapted to herring fishery. Baltic herrings were generally considered better in quality but, even so, those from the North Sea found a vast market. Without herrings, a whole area of Hansa business would be placed in peril, not to mention the food supply of large tracts of Europe, especially in Lent. Once within the Baltic, Dutch ships were also welcome because they loaded their holds with grain, much of it rye. Often the ships sailed empty into the Baltic, carrying only ballast, though by the 1590s the Dutch had learned how much Moselle wines were appreciated along the north German shore, not to mention French wines, which passed through Middelburg. The Spanish government in the Netherlands appointed this town, already a favourite of the Portuguese, as the official staple port for French wine in 1523, although this was merely to confirm its status as a great wine emporium since the middle of the fourteenth century.[16]

All this led the Dutch to build hefty, strong ships suitable for bulky goods that needed sizeable crews, a good source of employment in the Dutch towns as population recovered from the ravages of plague. The nature of the goods these ships carried meant that insurance rates were low. By the end of the sixteenth century these ships had evolved into the lightly built *fluyts*, efficient sailers with a simple rig but a large hold.[17] Taking advantage of the middle position of Holland, it was possible to zip down to Iberia to collect salt and then go straight to the Baltic without returning home. All this was combined with a shift in the economic centre of gravity within Germany from the Hanseatic coastline in the north to the banking centres of the south, such as Nuremberg and Augsburg, which had ready access to the spices that were humped over the Alps from Venice. The result was that by 1500 the Dutch found their niche in the North Sea and the Baltic, while the Germans by and large ceded these areas of activity to them. Some simple statistics prove the point. In 1497, 567 Dutch ships passed through the Danish Sound, and 202 German ones. Thereafter German numbers recovered but the Dutch remained well ahead – 890 as against 413 in 1540, so that the Germans only rarely overtook the Dutch, and then it was because of the looming political crisis in the Netherlands created by Spanish attempts to impose authority there.[18]

These advances laid the basis for growth at home and conquest overseas. At home, the Dutch towns enjoyed easy access to large quantities of imported fish and grain, which enabled them to absorb a booming population and to develop their own textile industries. The population balance had already been shifting away from the countryside and towards the towns after the Black Death, but more and more of the population was released for non-agricultural activities as land was turned over to cattle; the dairy industry, already strong in the late Middle Ages, went from strength to strength, offering the cheese and other dairy goods that have almost become a symbol of the modern Netherlands. The drainage of waterlogged land to create the polders enabled Dutch farmers to grow vegetables and fruits, such as plums and strawberries (previously a rarity),

or to keep their animals on land that was not suitable for grain production, since it had only recently emerged out of the salty sea.[19] A well-fed
population was a strong and healthy one, capable of providing perhaps
30,000 mariners by the 1560s.

For centuries the Baltic remained an important focus of Dutch business.
Far from abandoning their ancient concerns, the Dutch integrated them
into the world system that they created around 1600. They extended their
range by taking rye into the Mediterranean and establishing themselves
at Livorno, Smyrna and other nodal points of Mediterranean trade.[20] Even
so, the Dutch were in a difficult position during the 1570s, as opposition
to their Spanish overlords intensified. The city that would become the
commercial capital of the free Netherlands, Amsterdam, stood aloof from
the Dutch Revolt, and its own Baltic trade contracted as a result of its
isolation. Antwerp even seemed to be bouncing back, having extended a
welcome to those of all faiths who were willing to return to the city and
rebuild its fortunes. But once Antwerp had been captured by the Spaniards
in 1585 its fortunes rapidly reversed. Dutch pirates still guarded the mouth
of the River Scheldt so that its ships could not escape into the open sea.
The business community dispersed, not just into the northern Netherlands
but as far west as Rouen, down the Rhine to Cologne, up to Hamburg,
Bremen and the other Hansa towns of northern Germany, down to Venice
and Genoa, and even into the lion's den, taking up residence in Seville and
Lisbon, where a certain Louis Godijn, formerly of Antwerp, built up a
profitable business sending South American brazilwood and sugar to
northern Europe.

Antwerp was not the only place to suffer. In 1585 King Philip II imposed
an embargo on Dutch shipping bound for Spain and his newly acquired
kingdom of Portugal. In the past, as has been seen, Dutch ships would
load salt in Iberia and head straight for the Baltic. This was now virtually
impossible – as the embargo began to bite, the number of Dutch ships
taking this route fell dramatically, from seventy-one the year before the
embargo was imposed to three in 1589, the main beneficiaries being the
Hansards, who took up the slack.[21] On the other hand, the English defeat
of the Spanish Armada brought hope that Philip II would abandon his
overweening ambitions in northern waters, and by 1590 he was becoming
dangerously entranced by civil conflict raging nearer home, in France.
Were the Huguenot Henry of Navarre to become king of France, Philip
might have a powerful Protestant-ruled kingdom on his very doorstep, his
worst nightmare. The Dutch were no longer King Philip's top priority, and
the Spanish king had to abandon his embargo on Dutch ships in Spanish
waters, because there was no other way he could acquire the grain and

ship's stores he needed for his own fleet. Oddly, then, the Dutch found themselves supplying their own enemies, a feature of trade in wartime that has never really disappeared. Many of these goods came from the Baltic, and the Netherlands merchants seized the opportunity to load goods in Seville, Lisbon and elsewhere that had filtered through to Europe all the way from the East Indies and Central and South America.[22]

It is hardly surprising, then, that the upsurge in Dutch commerce was accompanied by a flood of immigrants into Amsterdam and other Dutch cities that had freed themselves from the Spanish yoke. The increasing concentration of the migrants in Amsterdam is surprising, for its location is unpromising; this may explain why many other Dutch towns also became important maritime centres and were closely involved in the foundation of the Dutch East India Company. Amsterdam faced the Zuider Zee rather than the open North Sea, and the marshy setting led to a Venetian solution: the town was built on piles and (like several of its neighbours) riddled with canals, which were good for distributing goods to the warehouses that lined their banks, but only in part compensated for its poor access to the sea. On the other hand, the complex waterways of the Rhine–Maas estuary offered routes into the interior, so that Amsterdam benefited from the fact that it was a middleman between a rich hinterland and the seaways that now stretched right across the world. By the middle of the sixteenth century ships were sailing regularly to Norway, which accounted for 7 per cent of its trade in 1544–5; but Lisbon accounted for more than twice as much, so its long-distance connections were already flourishing. Rye and textiles went to Portugal, and spices came back the other way. The Baltic was always within the line of sight of the Amsterdammers, who took advantage of the so-called Twelve Years Truce with Spain, from 1609 onwards, to achieve more than 2,000 movements through the Danish Sound each year.[23]

The striking feature of the years after 1590 is the speed with which the Dutch in Amsterdam and elsewhere began to commission voyages to much more distant destinations as well. This reflected the increasing concentration of capital in the city as the wealthier migrants decided to settle there. The first new destination was Russia, but not by way of the Baltic route that the Hanseatic merchants had been exploiting for centuries. Having conquered the Baltic port of Narva, the Swedes stood in the way of reviving the old route to Novgorod; besides, under Ivan III and his successor, Ivan the Terrible, Moscow had emerged as the capital of a vigorously expanding Russian state. Ivan IV decided to develop the site of what became Archangel on the White Sea as a terminus for shipping arriving from western Europe. As has been seen, at first much of this shipping was

English, and the motives of those who came were mixed. A more immediate attraction of the Arctic route than the hope of finding a shortcut to China was the availability of Russian forest products, including wax, tallow and furs.[24] Once Archangel had been founded, the Dutch began to edge out the English, who by 1590 were sending up to fifteen ships to Muscovy each year. By 1600 the Dutch had overtaken the English. Thirteen Dutch ships arrived that year, and twelve English ones, and over the next decade the Dutch pushed forward ever more decisively, marketing the pepper they had begun to bring from the East, or at least from Lisbon, as well as their own cloth. They were so hungry for Russian products that they had to make up the balance by paying in the silver of Peru. Thus metals mined on the Pacific side of South America were being used in payment in the most remote port in northern Europe.[25]

At the same time, the Dutch dreamed of using a route through the Barents Sea, past the barren archipelago of Novaya Zemlya, and round the top of Siberia to reach the Indies, just as the English had hoped to do. As has been seen, Barentsz and his colleagues left their names and sometimes their bodies in these frozen realms of the polar bear. Ever-present, then, was the hope of binding together the places that the Dutch were marking out on the world map, and encompassing the entire globe with interlinked and profitable trade routes. And yet if they were to achieve a breakthrough in Asia, or indeed in west Africa and South America, much would depend on their ability to displace the current masters of European traffic to those lands, the Portuguese.

38

Whose Seas?

I

Who has mastery over the sea itself? The question was posed in 1603 after a Dutch ship despoiled a heavily laden Portuguese carrack, the *Santa Catarina*, in the strait near Singapore, and carried its magnificent cargo of bullion and Chinese goods off to Amsterdam, where it sold for more than 3,000,000 guilders. The Portuguese appear to have been betrayed by the king of Johor (the southern tip of the Malay peninsula), who told the Dutch that the carrack was on its way and unprotected. Claims and counterclaims went back and forth. But the Dutch challenge to the Portuguese was theoretical as well as practical.[1] The question that the Dutch raised has still not gone away: in the twenty-first century the South China Sea has become the focus of intense legal debates in which theoretical claims and practical realities are closely intertwined.[2] In 1609 the Dutch scholar and lawyer Hugo Grotius argued learnedly and forcefully that the seas were free spaces where all had the right to come and go.[3] Admittedly, he began with the argument that 'it is lawful for the Hollanders . . . to sail to the Indians as they do and entertain traffic with them';[4] and his views ran up against opposition in Great Britain, where the argument that English or Scottish seas were an English or Scottish preserve was forcefully advanced, notably by another writer on the law of the seas, William Welwod, professor of civil law at St Andrews University.[5] Even so, Grotius's tract, written when he was a young man and first published anonymously, established itself as the starting point for discussion about claims to maritime dominion and continues to exercise influence. No one, Grotius argued on the basis of classical and biblical sources, had the right to forbid free passage, and refusal to do so had justified wars between the ancient Israelites and the Amorites as they attempted to pass through their lands on the way to the Promised Land.[6] The Portuguese had arrived in the Indies not as masters but as suppliants, their presence dependent on the willingness of local

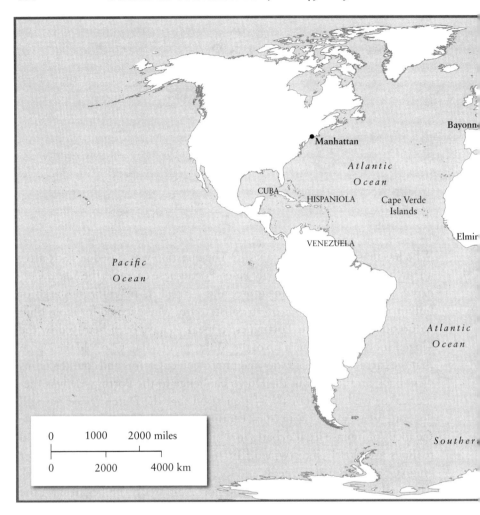

rulers to let them live there 'by entreaty' (this underestimated the bludgeon-ing that the Portuguese applied to anyone who resisted their attempts to create trading stations).[7] They maintained forts and garrisons, and did not control entire territories. Besides, the Portuguese could not even claim to have discovered India – it was known to the Romans.

Citing Thomas Aquinas, from the thirteenth century, and the eloquent Spanish writer of the early sixteenth century Vitoria, Grotius insisted that Christians have no right to deprive infidels, such as the Indians, of domin-ion unless they can show that they have suffered some injury from them. As a Dutch Protestant, Grotius gave no credit to the pope for dividing the world between Spain and Portugal, insisting that papal authority did not extend over those who were not members of his Church. As for the sea,

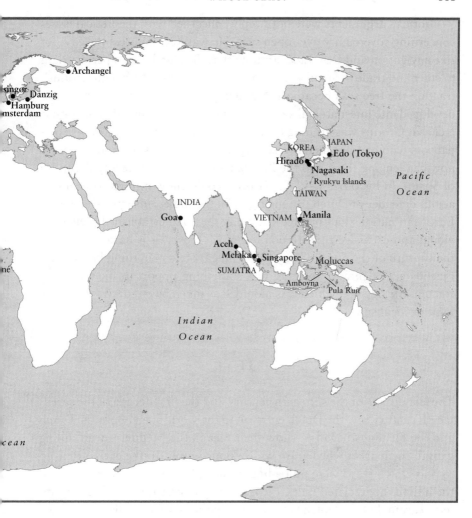

this is a common or public domain: 'it can no more be taken away by one from all than you may take away that from me which is mine.'[8] It is not as if you can build upon the sea. No part of it belongs to any people's territory; when you take fish from the sea, you draw from the common resources that the seas provide; he ticked off William Welwod, whose prime concern was the rights of Scottish fishermen to have unchallenged use of their own waters, with the words: 'the use of that which belongs to no one must necessarily be open to all, and among the uses of the sea is fishing.'[9] Grotius emphasized that he was speaking about the wide oceans rather than inland seas or indeed rivers, for the ocean encompasses the whole earth and is subject to the great tides that man cannot control – this ocean 'more truly possesseth than is possessed'.[10]

Grotius's arguments were not simply concerned with theoretical issues concerning sovereignty over open seas. He was keen to press the case for free navigation and free trade, arguing that the Dutch had a perfect right to enter and trade in Spanish and Portuguese waters.[11] Although Grotius's tract on the free seas became a standard point of reference in what later developed into international law, one should not blind oneself to the simple fact that Grotius was arguing his own partisan case in favour of his compatriots who had not merely challenged the Spaniards on land, but were now challenging them and the Portuguese (who were ruled by Philip III of Spain). In his other writings, Grotius could show himself to be a tenacious defender of Dutch trading rights in the Indies, insisting that where European nations had planted their flag they had established their individual and exclusive right to dominion. Moreover, it is hard to describe the capture of the *Santa Catarina* off Singapore as anything but an outrageous act of piracy. So there was something opportunistic about his tract on the free sea, which was moulded as much by circumstances as by logic or idealism.

II

The last decade of the sixteenth century and the first decade of the seventeenth century saw the Dutch entry on to the world stage. Both the Dutch and the Flemings began to show their face in the Mediterranean, filling gaps in the market when grain was in poor supply. In the early 1590s up to 300 Dutch ships were unloading grain in Italy each year. How much the Italians appreciated Baltic rye is a moot point; this was not their preferred grain. But the Dutch brought other goods into Italy all the way from Archangel, including beeswax and caviar. They made deals with the merchants of Genoa, Venice and Tuscany (where the newly enhanced port of Livorno welcomed people of all nations), enabling them to bring currants from the Ionian Islands and exotic goods such as Turkish mohair back to Amsterdam. It would be a mistake to exaggerate the impact of the Dutch, who were only at the start of their remarkable ascent, and were not always welcome. Conflating Dutch and Flemings, English merchants in the Ottoman Empire complained that 'Flemings merchants doe beginne to trade into these countryes which will clean subvert ours'; the English already saw the Dutch as rivals on the international trade routes, and their sympathy for the Dutch revolt was muted by the awareness that the Dutch were, unexpectedly, making themselves into a world force. Another sign of success was the way they increasingly cornered the market for spices in Lisbon, turning themselves into major suppliers across northern Europe. Hopes for the future were soon dashed. At the end of the century King Philip III renewed the ban on trade between his Iberian kingdoms and Holland, with the result that the number of visits to Lisbon plummeted. In 1598, 149 Dutch ships visited Portugal. The next year there were only twelve. Just as telling is the sharp decline in Dutch traffic heading straight into the Baltic: over 100 in 1598, and twelve the next year. The Hanseatic merchants enjoyed something of an Indian summer as they eagerly filled the gap, sending 153 ships along that route in 1600.[12]

The lesson of the conflict with Spain was that the Dutch would have to extend their ambitions a long way beyond either the Baltic or the Mediterranean. One of the peculiarities of the Spanish and Portuguese embargo on Dutch ships was that it did not seem to apply to Portuguese possessions overseas, and the Dutch were sending about twenty ships each year to the Portuguese trading stations in west Africa at the start of the seventeenth century. The Portuguese had done them the favour of creating the infrastructure they needed, so that when Dutch ships put in at São Tomé there were sugar plantations in place, and plenty of Portuguese settlers keen to shift their sugar.[13] Meanwhile, the near impossibility of loading Portuguese or Spanish salt so long as the embargo obtained prompted the Dutch to look ever further afield. Without salt, there would be no edible herrings. It had to be the right type of salt – French supplies often contained manganese, which turned the herrings black and damaged their flavour. There was plenty of salt on the island of Sal in the Cape Verde archipelago, Portuguese colonies, it is true, but the inhabitants, such as they were, were quite willing to shift it. Better still, the Dutch thought, might be the seizure of some of these islands. They attempted to capture the Cape Verde Islands towards the end of the sixteenth century, and São Tomé in 1600.[14]

The search for salt took the Dutch all the way to the coast of Venezuela, and over six and a half years, starting in the summer of 1599, 768 Dutch ships sailed to the salt lagoons of Punta de Araya; many of these ships sailed out on ballast, simply aiming to load up with salt and take it back to Holland. The outer edges of the Spanish and Portuguese empires were safe enough and the Dutch even carried on business in Cuba and Hispaniola, anchoring well away from Havana or Santo Domingo and carrying away large numbers of animal hides, but discretion was the rule; woe betide interlopers who were captured near the major Spanish settlements. They were likely to be slaughtered without mercy.[15]

These initiatives, and attempts to create small settlements in the Caribbean, would eventually lead to the foundation of the Dutch West India Company (WIC), but the most lucrative breakthrough that the Dutch achieved lay in the East, beginning at the end of the sixteenth century with the establishment of a 'Long-Distance Company' in Amsterdam in 1595. Nearly all of those who set up this company were actually Dutch, even though the immigration of large numbers of businessmen from Flanders, Portugal and elsewhere was gradually transforming the face of what was fast becoming the economic capital of the United Provinces. Just as the search for Venezuelan salt was prompted by exclusion from Iberia, the search for markets in the East was the result of exclusion from the spice market of Lisbon. In the beginning, this seemed to be a very profitable business, and the Portuguese were being pushed into a corner by their aggressive new rivals. Having been excluded from Lisbon, the Dutch went one better and blockaded Lisbon in 1606, preventing Philip III from sending out his spice fleet that year. This was more than the Dutch could hope to do every year, but when the Portuguese, along with the Spaniards, tried to force the Dutch out of the East Indies they soon found that the Dutch were no weaklings and could not be budged.[16]

If there was ever an example of an economic policy that backfired, it was surely the decision to place a trade embargo on the Dutch. By 1601 sixty-five ships had reached the East Indies from Holland, divided up among fourteen separate expeditions launched not just by the Long-Distance Company but by several rivals. Everyone wanted pepper, with the result that suppliers in the East Indies were able to double their prices. However, so much pepper was reaching Holland that the opposite effect was felt: prices began to fall within Europe, and it became obvious that the East Indies trade was already in crisis, producing negligible profits. Investors were bound to pull out of the pepper trade, and what had begun so gloriously would simply peter out. The answer was to consolidate the efforts of all the different companies, and, with plenty of prompting from the States General of the United Provinces, one company, in which representatives from Amsterdam had a near majority, was at last formed: the United East India Company, generally known by the Dutch acronym 'VOC', standing for *Vereenigde Oost-Indische Compagnie*. From 1602 onwards the VOC became the official arm of the government of the United Provinces in the East Indies, and (taking into account the rivalry with Spain and Portugal) it was encouraged not just to conduct trade but to patrol the seas and to set up forts in the Far East. Within three years the Dutch had occupied Tidore and Ternate in the Moluccas, the source of cloves, nutmeg and mace, and much-prized possessions of the Portuguese.[17] The assault on and occupation of Portuguese bases across the world followed throughout the first half of the seventeenth century. Portugal only had itself to blame for closing its own spice markets to the

Dutch. And, although they were not founders of the VOC, the growing community of Portuguese merchants in Amsterdam and other Dutch cities, often refugees from the Inquisition, gave active support to the creation of a Dutch overseas empire. This group will deserve separate examination later.

Early successes were not easily maintained. The Dutch conflict with Spain was renewed in 1621, with turbulent effects on the Dutch merchant navy. Once again the Dutch had to look far afield for salt and for the dried fruits that had become a staple of the middle-class diet across northern Europe; and the Spaniards were alert to this, building a fort to block access to the salt pans the Dutch had been using in Venezuela and swamping salt pans in Haiti that the Dutch hoped to use. Once again the Catholic Flemings became a serious nuisance, as the struggle with Spanish power was brought home to the very coasts of the Low Countries. In 1628 privateers from Dunkirk sent 245 Dutch and English ships to the bottom of the sea, or seized them. It is no surprise that the cost of insuring ships and cargoes rose steeply. As before, the main beneficiaries were the Hansa merchants. In 1621 they sent twenty-two ships from Iberia to the Baltic, and the Dutch sent thirty-six. The next year they sent forty-one and the Dutch managed to sneak out two ships (in several later years, none at all). For a time the Danes also did well out of this situation, bringing goods from Iberia through the Sound, which, after all, they controlled. As the conflict with Spain deepened, the Dutch found themselves short of herrings – no salt, no herrings. This was not just a problem for the Dutch, as consumers further afield who had relied on them were also badly hit, for instance the burghers of Danzig. Difficulties were compounded by the decision of the king of Denmark, in 1638–9, to increase the Sound toll levied on ships passing through the narrows at Helsingør. The Danes entered into an understanding with Spain, Protestant and Catholic working together to suffocate the Dutch. Only a Swedish invasion of Jutland in 1643 distracted the Danes from their hostility to the United Provinces. The Dutch decided that the time had come to face the Danes, and sent an imposing fleet of forty-eight naval vessels plus 300 merchant vessels into the Baltic past Helsingør Castle, where the king had taken up residence. King Christian was hardly in a position to stop them, and before long the Dutch had made an agreement with him that offered lower tolls on shipping passing through the Sound.[18]

One group of people who were willing to act on behalf of the Dutch were the Portuguese settlers in Bayonne, in south-western France, New Christians of Jewish origin who found their new home a good place in which to escape the ministrations of the Inquisition, although they also kept up contact with fellow Jews who remained welcome at court in Madrid, so long as they led Catholic lives in public. Large quantities of goods were smuggled through the Pyrenean passes to Bayonne. No embargo in this period was watertight. The inhabitants of Viana do Castelo in northern Portugal had prospered from Dutch trade and were not going to enforce the rules now. The Spanish government tried to improve its supervision of visiting ships, arresting vessels found in Spanish ports on the grounds that their voyage had been financed by the Dutch, and entering into agreements with Denmark, England and Scotland to make sure that their ships did not carry Dutch goods. They seem to have found it difficult to distinguish between the Danes and the Dutch, confiscating goods that had already been approved by their own officials based in Danish territory close to Hamburg.[19] Still, it cannot have been easy to determine who was in the pay of the Dutch merchants, with so many Portuguese milling around, a mobile population moving constantly between Iberia, south-western France, Holland, and, in due course, England and Hamburg.

For a time it seemed that the rise of the Dutch had been a mere flash in the pan. According to Jonathan Israel, 'the Dutch lost an eighth of the Baltic traffic' in the 1620s and 1630s.[20] However, the economic crisis was by no means limited to Holland. This was a period of internecine warfare in Germany; later, England and France would experience severe tumult. In reality, the Dutch were able to make advances, but they took place far from home. They consolidated their position as masters of bits and pieces of the Portuguese trading empire, even installing themselves for a time in Brazil; they were pushed out in 1625, but this was a harbinger of better things to come. When Piet Heyn captured the Spanish treasure fleet carrying bullion from Mexico to Spain, the West India Company found itself 11,000,000 guilders richer, and other great prizes included 40,000 chests of Brazilian sugar, which were said to be worth 8,000,000 guilders. The Dutch were a significant presence on the Gold Coast of Africa, and even (though not for long) held Elmina. Considering that Elmina had been the jewel in Portugal's African crown, or rather the source of gold for that crown, this was an impressive achievement. With this temporary conquest the Dutch served notice that they were serious competitors on both sides of the Atlantic. The West Indies Company, it is true, was overspending, which is hardly surprising: they had to maintain a fleet, forts, foot soldiers and a whole trading network, and the value of shares in the WIC dipped and dived during the 1630s and 1640s; they were a bad short-term investment. And yet from the Moluccas to Brazil the captains and merchants of the United Provinces were steadily taking charge of the most precious territories in the Portuguese seaborne empire. The awareness that their empire was being whittled away was one factor in the uprising that brought Portugal renewed independence from Spain in 1640.[21] Thus the Dutch advances were not simply important for the global economy; they were also very important in global politics.

III

Many histories of early modern maritime trade and exploration neatly separate the Portuguese, the Spaniards, the Dutch, the English, the French and other rivals into parallel histories. In reality, though, one cannot understand the rise of the Dutch without weaving into that story the rise of English trade in the same period, aiming at the same objectives: trading bases in lands as remote as the Moluccas, Japan and the coast of India. At first, the English attempted to reach the Spice Islands by way of a western route. Francis Drake's circumnavigation, on which he set out in 1577, was planned in part as a sustained assault on Spanish shipping in the Caribbean and along the Pacific coastline of the Americas. A second voyage, led by Thomas Cavendish, or Candish, circumnavigated the globe between 1586 and 1588, but these two voyages only confirmed that the Strait of Magellan was difficult water, a maze of icy and stormy channels. That was the bad news; but the good news was that Cavendish returned home with the spoils of an entire Manila galleon, including 122,000 gold *pesos*, a rich store of silk and spices and two Japanese boys who could read their own language – this implies that he was thinking of trying to reach Japan and of opening up trade there, though in the event he headed for the Moluccas instead. It is said that on their arrival in Plymouth the English sailors were arrayed in silk doublets seized from the enemy. Cavendish was clearly an honourable man, since he set the crew and passengers of the galleon onshore in a place called Porto Seguro, and gave them supplies, including enough wood to make a small ship of their own. Some of his contemporaries would, instead, have been after their blood.

The next English attempt to reach the East Indies, by James Lancaster in 1591, took what contemporaries called the Portuguese route, round the Cape of Good Hope and then across the Indian Ocean.[22] Lancaster decided to follow up rumours that the Portuguese were close to discovering a North-East or North-West Passage above China, which remained an obsession. But his crew was worn down by scurvy and his pilot (picked up in the Indian Ocean) had obviously lost his way, with the result that Lancaster failed to penetrate beyond Penang in western Malaya.

Lancaster's one great prize was 'the ship of the captain of Malacca', a Portuguese vessel travelling from Goa to Melaka, loaded with Canary wine, palm wine, velvets, taffeta, an 'abundance of playing cardes' and Venetian glass, as well as a 'false and counterfeit stone which an Italian brought from Venice to deceive the rude Indians withal', but there was no trace of the treasure the English sailors confidently expected to find on board. After that the English lay in wait for the Portuguese fleet due to arrive from Bengal, which was said to carry diamonds, rubies, Calicut cloth 'and other fine workes', but before long, with their captain now sick, the crew insisted on waiting no longer and on returning to England.[23]

Only the news that the Dutch were sending ships to the East Indies revived English plans to carve out a place for their kingdom in the spice trade. It was particularly galling that the Dutch lured the English explorer John Davis into their service as expert navigator; they also began to bid for the purchase of English ships to increase their capacity. Here was a man who could be relied upon to make an accurate record of the route to the East and of the characteristics of the islands the Dutch visited. Mapping out which islands were rich in cloves and nutmeg became an obsession, since these products could only be obtained from a small area, and the Dutch – as also the English – planned to penetrate right into those areas and gain control of them, rather than relying on local merchants to bring them to bases on Sumatra, Java or other, more accessible places. Within a few years of Lancaster's first expedition, the Dutch had established a 'factory' at Bantam in Java, and then they penetrated as far as Neira, which has been called 'the nutmeg capital of the Moluccas'.[24] In response, a 'Company of Merchants of London trading into the East Indies' came into being, and its first expedition to the East Indies was, perhaps surprisingly, entrusted to Lancaster. His attempt to reach the East Indies had whetted the appetite of the London investors, rather than being seen as a costly disaster. That was the immediate outcome of the formation of what would eventually develop into the English East India Company, but the long-term outcome was a long tussle between the Dutch East India Company and the English one.

Scurvy had wreaked havoc on Lancaster's first voyage. On a second expedition to the East Indies, in 1601, Lancaster foresightedly insisted that each sailor was to be fed three spoonfuls of lemon juice every day, but only aboard his flagship; on the accompanying ships scurvy was rampant. By the time his four ships reached southern Africa, Lancaster had lost over a hundred men to disease, which equalled the complement of one ship.[25] The curative role of fresh fruit was understood, but its preventative role was not noticed. Yet an important observation did result from

Lancaster's second expedition, though it was something the Portuguese had known for a century. On arriving at Aceh, on the northern tip of Sumatra, facing the Indian Ocean, Lancaster found 'sixteen or eighteen sail of shippes of diverse nations'; these were Gujaratis, Bengalis, Malabaris (from southern India), Pegus from Burma and Patanis from Siam.[26] Lancaster had several productive interviews with the sultan, Ala-uddin, to whom a letter from Queen Elizabeth was carried by an elephant twice as high as a tall man, 'which had a small castle like a coach upon his back, covered with crimson velvet. In the middle thereof was a great basin of gold, and a peece of silke exceedingly richly wrought to cover it, under which Her Majestie's letter was put.'[27] Ala-uddin's feasts were sumptuous, and he paid no attention to the Islamic prohibition of alcohol; but one of his requests was not easy to satisfy, his wish to be sent 'a fair Portugall maiden'. Moreover, the price of spices in Aceh was higher than Lancaster had bargained for. If one wanted to obtain spices cheaply the answer was to penetrate to the lands where they grew. Even in Bantam, on the western tip of Java, spices could be bought much more cheaply than in Aceh.[28] In both places the English secured the right to a factory and other trading concessions, so that the investment made by members of the East India Company seemed likely to earn good returns over the years, so long as rivals could be kept at bay. Lancaster returned home very satisfied with pirate raids on Portuguese shipping, but he left behind a small pinnace and instructed its crew to search deeper into the East Indies, all the way to the sources of the best spices.

This brought the English, even if only a small number of them, into conflict with the Dutch. It was an odd situation: the Dutch sometimes declared how grateful they were for the support England had (though not consistently) given the United Provinces in their struggle against Spanish rule, but the fact that they were at peace in the North Sea did not mean that the English were automatically welcome in the South Seas. They saw them as interlopers; as an English factor in the East Indies named John Jourdain wrote:

> The Hollanders say we go aboute to reape the fruits of their labours. It is rather the contrarye for that they seem to barre us of our libertie to trade in a free countrye, having manie times traded in those places, and nowe they seeke to defraud us of that we have so long fought for.[29]

So much for Grotius. Jourdain would die in a skirmish with the Dutch out in the East Indies in 1619, in what has been called 'flagrant disregard' of yet another Anglo-Dutch truce.[30] The Dutch scored major successes against the Portuguese, gaining control of the island of Amboyna in 1605.

The Dutch intended to keep the proceeds for themselves, and on island after island they resolutely sought a monopoly. English adventurers attempted to secure the tiny island of Pula Run for the English Crown, so that King James I was described as 'by the grace of God, king of England, Scotland, Ireland, France, Puloway and Puloroon', these being the spice islands of Ai and Run.[31] This, however, set off a dirty battle for control of Run in which the Dutch shamelessly cut down all the nutmeg trees on what was the nutmeg island par excellence; it was better no one should have the nutmeg of Run than that the English should. The main English defender, Nathaniel Courthope, was shot and killed in 1620, and the Dutch took charge of the island, expelling the native population for good measure; but negotiations about its future dragged on for forty-seven years, until the Dutch and English governments finally agreed that the Dutch could keep Run if the English were allowed to hold on to Manhattan island far away in North America, which they had seized from the Dutch three years earlier.[32] To the inhabitants of the East Indies one lot of Western barbarians was much the same as another, and they easily confused the Dutch with the English.[33]

Even after they captured Run, outrageous acts of violence were still being committed by the Dutch, to intimidate all English interlopers present and future: in 1623 a group of innocent traders based at the English factory in Amboyna were arrested, tortured within an inch of their lives and then executed, on the specious grounds that they had been conspiring with Japanese mercenaries, who met the same fate, to take over this island.[34] The 'Massacre of Amboyna' soured Anglo-Dutch relations, as did the high-handed manner of the Dutch governor-general of the Indies, Jan Pieterszoon Coen, a singularly unattractive figure who had no compunction about wiping out native peoples, European rivals or anyone who stood in his way, and sometimes ignored the instructions of his own government in the Netherlands. Coen rejoiced in the killing of his old foe Jourdain. Such methods did, however, greatly strengthen the Dutch position in the East Indies, particularly after the transfer of their headquarters to the well-placed town of Jakarta, renamed Batavia, the Latin name for the Netherlands.

English attention turned away from the East Indies towards the Indian subcontinent. In part, it is true, English interest in India was generated by the need to find products that would appeal to the inhabitants of the East Indies, because heavy English woollen cloths were not exactly what the near-naked inhabitants of these islands craved. Indian calicoes, though, were lighter and could find a market. Thus the English, like the Portuguese before them, became intermediaries between the far-flung coasts of what they broadly called 'India'. There was already a lively inter-regional trade by sea, and it was not just clever but necessary to insert themselves into it if they were to make themselves welcome in the Indian Ocean and beyond.[35]

The human cost of conflict with the Dutch was high enough; but the financial cost was also difficult to bear. The East India Company already functioned in a rather different way to the other English trading companies, such as the Muscovy Company and the Levant Company, which was active in Smyrna and other parts of the Mediterranean. Whereas the other companies were, in essence, umbrella bodies facilitating and licensing trade by syndicates of members, the East India Company traded as a single operation, 'one body corporate and politick', to cite Queen Elizabeth's charter of 1600. The board made the decision when and where to trade, and investors were not permitted to fit out their own expeditions in parallel with official ones.[36] Over time, and following a number of crises, it evolved into a joint-stock company, much strengthened after 1657 by a generous new charter granted by Oliver Cromwell that attracted record investments, exceeding £700,000.[37]

IV

The most remarkable success achieved by the Dutch was not their series of victories over the Portuguese, for the Portuguese trading empire was already under severe strain by 1600, or their victories against the English, but their installation in Japan. Between 1641 and 1853 the Dutch merchants based in Nagasaki were the only European merchants present on the soil of Japan, and even then they were based on the offshore island of Deshima.[38] Their presence there around 1800 has been beautifully portrayed in a work of fiction by David Mitchell.[39] The idea that this was the channel through which the Japanese acquired scientific knowledge, dealing with navigation, medicine and much else, has been much discussed; the Japanese knew this western knowledge as *Rangaku*, 'Dutch learning', which implies that it was seen as a coherent system, though the tendency nowadays is to stress the higgledy-piggledy nature of the acquisition of Western science and technology over more than 200 years.[40] This seems much more characteristic of the way knowledge was transmitted along maritime trade routes: a slow osmosis, as one can also see with the spread of religious ideas, whether Christian, Muslim or Buddhist.

The Dutch presence in Japan can be traced back to 1600, to the voyage of *De Liefde*, whose pilot was William Adams, the Englishman who later won the trust of the Japanese shogun.[41] Other English merchants managed to win privileges from the shogun, and there was an English factory in Hirado from 1613 to 1623; however, it was regarded as unprofitable, a source of copper to be sure – but taking copper to England was like carrying coals to Newcastle. Later, the Dutch would realize that good profits were to be made by hawking Japanese copper round Asian seas.[42] Since the Portuguese and Spaniards still had some influence in Japan, they did all they could to poison the relations between the first Dutch visitors and the Tokugawa administration. But the Dutch had a particular selling point: they explained how they had thrown off the shackles of Catholic Spain, which, in the eyes of the Japanese, made them into non-Christians. This was enormously helpful just when the Japanese government was becoming increasingly hostile to Jesuit and other missionaries. Prince Maurits, the Stadhouder, sent a polite letter to Ieyasu, which arrived in 1609; and a remarkable correspondence between the Stadhouder and the shogun continued for a while – the Stadhouder took the opportunity to berate the Portuguese and the Spaniards for their 'cunning and deceit', and portrayed King Philip as a power-crazed megalomaniac who planned to use the Christian converts to spearhead revolution in Japan. Oddly, Ieyasu did not respond to the damning indictment of King Philip and his subjects, but diplomacy worked and the Dutch secured trading rights at Hirado.[43] Even so, the Dutch presence remained precarious during the next thirty years: a hasty request for the renewal of their rights following the death of Ieyasu was viewed with deep displeasure at court, since it implied that his son and successor was so disloyal to Ieyasu's memory that he would quash his father's decisions. The Dutch clearly needed to be taught a lesson, and the shogun began to restrict their freedom to trade in raw silk. The governor-general of the VOC, based at Batavia, had a good understanding of how the Dutch should behave:

> You should not get into trouble with the Japanese, and you have to wait for a good time and with the greatest patience in order to get something. Since they cannot stand being retorted, we should pretend to behave humbly among the Japanese, and to play the role of poor and miserable merchants. The more we play this role, the more favour and respect we receive in this country. This has been known to us through years of experience.[44]

He wrote these words in 1638, by which time he could see clear proof that it paid to be patient. By 1636 the Portuguese had been cleared out of Japan, apart from the trading station at Nagasaki on Deshima Island. This was not a permanent factory: the Portuguese were to bring their goods, do their business, and leave, until they came back the following year. At the same time the Japanese were banned from sending ships overseas. The penalty for doing so was execution. Care was also taken to prevent Portuguese travelling on Dutch passports, which by this time was happening all the time – the New Christians of Amsterdam were well installed in Macau and even Manila.[45]

In reality, the Japanese did want to keep a door open, but only by a small crack. They were deeply insulted when the commander of the Dutch fort on Formosa, or Taiwan, Pieter Nuyts, impounded some Japanese ships; rather than breaking off all relations, the Japanese demanded that Nuyts should be sent to Japan, where he was held hostage until 1636. But the shogun was careful not to cut himself off completely by expelling the Dutch. Equally, the Dutch were perfectly aware that they needed to prove that they were nothing like the Portuguese. In 1638 they were happy to support the shogun against rebels, including many Japanese Christians, backed by the Portuguese, and, since the defeat of the rebels culminated in the massacre of maybe 37,000 victims, the Dutch were for ever after blamed for their cynical betrayal of their fellow believers. Yet this confirmed the belief at court that the Dutch were not really Christian, or at any rate were a very different sort of Christian who would not try to spread their faith. In *Gulliver's Travels*, the hero visits Japan, pretending to be a 'Hollander', and in Edo (Tokyo) he witnesses the Dutch trampling on a crucifix, a standard ritual for the Japanese, but obviously rather more questionable for a Dutch Christian.[46] The shogun was shocked to learn that the newly built and elegantly gabled Dutch warehouse at Hirado carried a date on its façade according to the Christian calendar. Forewarned of a plot to massacre the Dutch merchants in Hirado, the Dutch quickly demolished the offending building, while the government, anxious to keep all traces of Christianity at bay, forbade the Dutch merchants from observing the Sunday rest that had become part of the Calvinist religious routine.[47]

In the end, the stand-off was resolved when the Dutch were ordered to go and occupy the former Portuguese base at Deshima. Once again the Japanese government spoke dismissively of the Dutch presence in Japan, in language that, if anything, betrays that the Japanese did value having some access, but mainly for the court, to the exotic goods of the world beyond – whether European guns or Chinese silk:

His Majesty [the shogun] charges us to inform you that it is of slight importance to the empire of Japan whether foreigners come or do not come to trade; but in consideration of the charter granted to them by Ieyasu, he is pleased to allow the Hollanders to continue their operations and to leave them their commercial and other privileges, on the condition that they evacuate Hirado and establish themselves and their vessels in the port of Nagasaki.[48]

Deshima means 'Fore island', since it lies in front of Nagasaki proper, although the modern extension of the city has completely enveloped it in metropolitan Nagasaki. The island was an artificial one, a curved trapezoid shaped like a fan, supposedly because the shogun replied to the question of what shape it should be by snapping open his fan. No larger than Dam Square in modern Amsterdam, Deshima measured 557 feet at the top and 706 feet at the bottom, while the sides were 210 feet long.[49] Such a confined space was rendered even more claustrophobic by its railings of iron spikes and the sentries posted on the stone bridge that linked Deshima to the mainland, checking every entry and exit. The Dutch tried to build houses as similar as possible to what they knew from home, and, being Dutch, they naturally found space for a flower garden on their tiny island. There were few permanent residents: some Japanese officials, and the Dutch captain, the chief merchant, a secretary, a bookkeeper, a doctor and other essential support staff, and a few black slaves and white artisans. They were vastly outnumbered by the Japanese officials, not just guards but a vast horde of interpreters – around 150 at the end of the seventeenth century. The numbers were so swollen because the Dutch had to pay for the upkeep of the Japanese officials. Not surprisingly, then, there were many sinecures. On the other hand, there were other officials who took their job extremely seriously, carefully inspecting all goods that arrived, with special attention to Christian literature – the Dutch were not even permitted to hold church services on Deshima. Meanwhile Nagasaki flourished on the back of Dutch trade and maritime trade within Japan itself – around 1700 the city possessed about 64,000 inhabitants.[50]

Why, it might be asked, did any Dutch merchants agree to live there? The answer lies in the profitability of trade with Japan. During the late seventeenth century Nagasaki proved more profitable than any other VOC base in the Dutch trading world: during the decade 1670–79 Dutch merchants were making a 75 per cent profit on their trade through Japan, though this was a high point. For no one else was on hand to offer everything from sugar and shark-skins to buffalo horns and brazilwood to microscopes and mangoes, not to mention pickled vegetables, lead pencils, amber and rock crystal; but the greatest demand was for Chinese silk. All these paid for gold, silver, copper, ceramics and lacquer-ware, though the Dutch did not neglect sake or soy sauce too. And one can see from the nature of the goods they sold in Japan that the Dutch were by no means specialists in European goods. They brought together goods from India, the Spice Islands, east Africa and the Atlantic – that was the source of narwhal tusks, which had a similar fascination to rhinoceros horns, another product that they eagerly sold through Deshima.[51] So Deshima gave them a Japanese monopoly, and they were prepared to put up with the humiliation of living in a virtual prison in order to maintain access to the court of the shogun.

One of the many curiosities of life in Deshima was that the Dutch captain was treated as an honorary daimyo, or high vassal of the shogun, and was expected to make an annual visit to the court at Edo, bearing presents and conducting himself with meticulous attention to the exacting etiquette of the Japanese court. Once he had reached the ceremonial hall and been sonorously announced as the *Oranda Kapitan*, 'captain of Holland', the Dutch captain was required to crawl past the piles of gifts his embassy had brought towards the platform on which the shogun was seated (though behind a lattice, so he could not actually be seen); that done, he crawled back 'like a lobster' as a European observer wrote – although later in the day a relatively informal session often took place in which the shogun and his courtiers, still out of sight, cross-examined their exotic visitors about the world they had come from.[52] Historians have debated whether the treatment of the Dutch embassies at Edo was a humiliation or a sort of honour, since the VOC had received favours from Ieyasu, and his successors were keen to see those privileges continue. Moreover, the chance to learn about Western science was too good to miss. Intellectual contact was also maintained through the work of interpreters and translators, and this contact became more intense over time, so that by the late eighteenth century Japanese authors were expounding Western medicine in their own books.[53]

A Japanese historian has made the valid point that Japan was not alone in closing off access to European merchants, and in trying to suppress the spread of Christianity. Similar moves can be seen in China, the Ryukyu Islands, Vietnam and Korea.[54] The violence of the Portuguese, the Spaniards and the Dutch had earned them poor reputations. The arrival of the Dutch while the Portuguese were at a weak point in their fortunes and under the rule of the Spanish king gave the Japanese the chance to maintain limited links with European trade. Contrary to common assumptions, they did not cut themselves off completely from the outside world; rather, they chose exactly what sort of contact they wanted, and confined it within narrow parameters.

39
Nations Afloat

I

The complex rivalries among those who aspired to control the ocean routes (whatever Grotius might say about free trade and navigation) can too easily be reduced to an image of national empires in conflict with one another. In public, noble Spaniards scorned trade, as if they were ancient Roman patricians, and left the dirty business, officially at least, to the Genoese and German financiers without whom not just the Crown but the city of Seville would have found themselves short of resources. In reality, financiers and aristocrats were keen to form powerful teams, whose links were strengthened by marriage alliances. This was visible in the close links tying the New Christian families of Spain and Portugal to the Iberian noble houses. When money began to run dry, an injection of funds from wealthy families of Jewish origin made sense, until the doctrine of *limpieza de sangre*, 'purity of blood', began to spread in the sixteenth century, making such marriages undesirable; every attempt was then made to cover up evidence of Jewish or Muslim ancestry.

Frontier regions tend to attract chancers, hustlers, ne'er-do-wells, but also those looking for new and potentially lucrative business opportunities. In the late sixteenth century the Spanish and Portuguese empires acted as hosts to a myriad of different ethnic groups: there were Bretons and Basques, Scots and French Huguenots, Galicians and Corsicans; Basques are found as far away as Potosí in Peru, the source of the apparently endless quantities of silver that were sent to Spain and China. Some, such as the Huguenots, were refugees, leaving their native country to avoid religious conflict. Others were looking for new economic opportunities. Some left their homeland *en famille*, while Portuguese migrants tended to be male and were drawn from a wide range of backgrounds and social classes. It was the classic combination of those fleeing persecution and economic migrants, with a fuzzy boundary between those two groups.[1] However many they were, the European migrants did not come alone – shiploads of slaves diffused black Africans right across the two Iberian empires, in places as far from home as Lima and Manila.[2] By the late seventeenth century, so many slaves were delivered to the Americas as contraband that no one was bothering to buy the *asientos*, or licences, that had long been required in this revolting trade.[3] The European colonization of the lands claimed by Spain and its rivals was not, then, an orderly imposition of authority, though Spanish and Portuguese bureaucrats and soldiers abounded, but a haphazard movement of merchants, religious dissidents, criminals fleeing justice, impoverished peasants and artisans, and slaves. Yet it was hard to find a safe haven: an apparently settled life in the smaller Canary Islands could not guarantee immunity from attention, as those accused of secret adherence to Judaism in the seventeenth-century Canaries were to find.[4]

Solidarity within migrant groups was often maintained by the existence of a community church, typically, in the Portuguese case, dedicated to St Anthony of Padua, a companion of St Francis, who was and is much venerated in Portugal, having been born in Lisbon. These were not just places of worship – after all, some of the Portuguese were more sympathetic to Judaism than to Christianity – but sources of charitable support, and places where one could exchange news and make useful contacts. In Cartagena de las Indias, in what is now Colombia, the Portuguese were prosperous enough to build a substantial hospital.[5] The Genoese and the English tended to name their churches overseas after their common patron saint, St George, and the Huguenots built Protestant chapels wherever it was safe to do so.

In the final analysis, trade generally trumped distaste towards other religions: the Portuguese monarchy tolerated the existence of Jewish communities in the Moroccan towns over which it ruled, even though the open practice of Judaism had been banned in Portugal in 1497.

II

Portuguese settlers had helped set up sugar industries across the Atlantic from the fifteenth century onwards. But the Portuguese diaspora of the late sixteenth and early century seventeenth had a distinctive character. The Portuguese merchants in the Atlantic, Indian Ocean and Pacific attracted suspicion because a high proportion – exactly how many it is

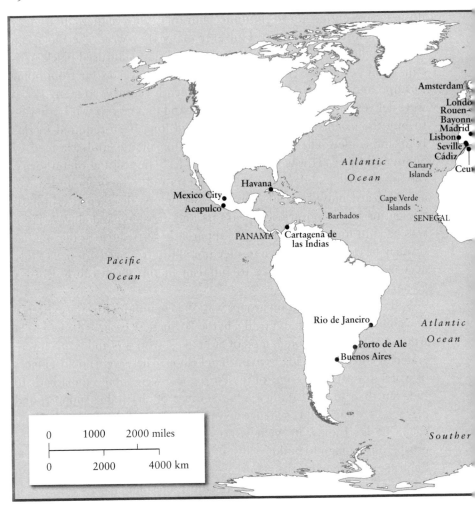

impossible to say – had Jewish forebears. That does not mean they were
Jewish in both the patrilineal and the matrilineal line; and, whereas the
leading Sephardic families, like the Arab elites of al-Andalus and the
hidalgos of Castile, carefully preserved their genealogies going back very
many generations, this was only worth doing if one could live as a Jew
and take pride in one's Jewish ancestry – the image of past times in Spain
and Portugal as a golden age in which Sephardic Jews had risen to eminent positions at court was too attractive to be easily forgotten. For the
New Christians, most of whom had adopted Portuguese or Spanish
names, often as inconspicuous as López or da Costa, Jewish ancestry
was better not advertised. By the middle of the sixteenth century, the
practice of Judaism in secret within Spain had largely disappeared, under

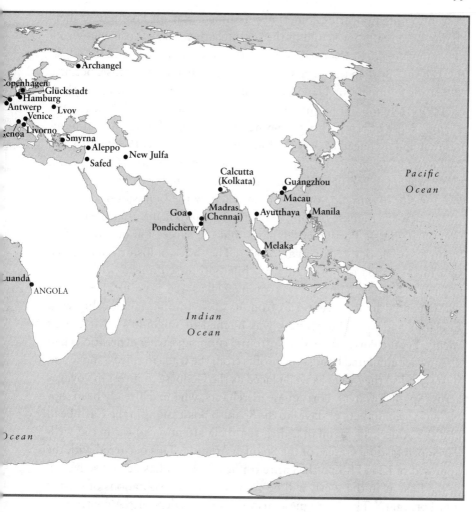

pressure from the Inquisition. But in Portugal the king had promised the
Jews that he would wait for a whole generation until the Inquisition was
unleashed, when he forced the great majority to convert in 1497 – these
were not just native Portuguese Jews but Spanish Jews who had arrived
as refugees only five years earlier after the Jews were expelled from
Castile and Aragon. Portugal therefore became fertile ground for the
practice and dissemination of crypto-Judaism. Then, as the Portuguese
New Christians became more and more involved in trade and finance,
they turned up at the court in Madrid and elsewhere in Spain, seeding
a revival of interest in the religion of their ancestors among Spaniards
of Jewish descent.

Even though the Portuguese merchants were by no means all of Jewish

descent, contemporaries sometimes assumed that all Portuguese merchants were really Jews, and in the seventeenth century those who wrote
about the Nação, or 'Nation', of the Portuguese might even add the adjective hebrea.[6] By then the term made some, though not total, sense, because
increasing numbers of New Christians were openly returning to their
ancestors' religion in Livorno, Amsterdam and London, and there existed
a strong sense of brotherhood binding together these scattered communities that had managed to defy the Inquisition. To this day the Spanish and
Portuguese Synagogue in London, founded by members of the Nação,
offers prayers in Portuguese each Day of Atonement for os nossos irmãos
prezos pella Inquisição, 'our brethren taken by the Inquisition'.

The new Portuguese trading network came into being after the extinction of the native Portuguese dynasty and the succession of Philip II of
Spain to the throne of Portugal in 1581. The shock of losing King Sebastian in the sands of north Africa while he pressed ahead with a vain
attempt to conquer Morocco was commercial as well as political. Portugal
had benefited for two centuries from its close trading relationship with
England, and now the country was hitched to England's most potent
enemy. Yet the Portuguese hit the ground running: earlier generations had
already accumulated handsome profits from the trade in spices, sugar and
slaves, and so they were as well placed as the Genoese to invest in voyages
across Spanish waters. Portuguese merchants, who had already been supplying large numbers of slaves to the Spanish possessions in the Caribbean
and the American mainland, diverted their attention towards the well-
developed trading empire of the Spanish Atlantic. This occurred with the
approval of King Philip: 'the entire traffic of all that has been discovered,
in the East as in the West, will be common to the two nations of Castile
and Portugal.'[7] The Portuguese also became masters of the contraband
traffic that brought Peruvian silver down from the mines at Potosí in the
Andes and across the plains of South America to a small but bustling
Atlantic harbour at Buenos Aires. After all, it was cheaper to trade without having to pay for asientos, or licences, if one could get away with that.
On the other hand, this did not make the Spanish officials love the Portuguese, particularly in the early seventeenth century, when competition
from European rivals such as the Dutch led to a noticeable reduction in
Spanish trade across the Atlantic.[8] There was still the sense that they were
foreign interlopers, chancers skilled in exploiting loopholes, never really
loyal to the Habsburg monarchy both as Portuguese and as secret members
of another faith – exactly what one might expect, in the anti-Semitic
language of early modern Spain, of the Jews.

In this way, Jewish or not, they were often seen as Jews; in any case, there was plenty of intermarriage between New Christians and members of Old Christian trading families, which meant that defining who was a Jew was not straightforward.[9] The Sephardic rabbis in Amsterdam and London were not too worried if the new members of their community could not prove Jewish ancestry in the female line, as orthodox Jewish law requires, or if they knew next to nothing about Jewish practices. The sense of common experience as members of La Nação was good enough. Their observance might be limited to the avoidance of pork and shellfish and the occasional fast, practices that it would be possible to keep alive without attracting too much attention.[10] And what is one to make of families such as the Nunes da Costa, where one brother died in Safed, the great centre of Jewish mysticism in Galilee, and another brother, Fray Francisco de Vitoria, became archbishop in Mexico City?[11] The New Christians crossed a fuzzy boundary between Judaism, crypto-Judaism and Catholicism, and the beliefs of the crypto-Jews were often an apparently unholy mix of prayers, observances and theologies drawn from both Judaism and Christianity, generated in part by their movement back and forth between lands where they had to pose as Christians and lands, such as Holland and Italy, where it was possible to live as Jews if they so chose.[12]

Jewish or not, these Portuguese merchants created worldwide networks that linked all three great oceans. Manuel Bautista Pérez made his fortune after he transported hundreds of slaves from southern Africa to Peru in 1618, thanking God and his uncle (a co-investor) for the fact that he made a profit of over 50,000 pesos. Although his centre of operations lay in Lima, he did business with correspondents in Panama, Mexico City, Cartagena de las Indias, in the Americas; in Luanda in Angola; in Lisbon, Madrid, Rouen and Antwerp. In Peru he handled Chinese silk, European textiles, Caribbean pearls and even Baltic amber.[13] These contacts were by no means unusual. Around 1630 Portuguese merchants were also doing business in Acapulco (linking them to the Manila galleons), Havana, Bayonne (an important centre of New Christian settlement) and Hamburg, whose citizens had begun to welcome Portuguese Jewish merchants into their midst.[14] There they built relations with the rulers of Denmark and Sweden, to whom the Teixeira family provided credit; and eventually a Sephardic settlement sprang up in Glückstadt, a royal foundation in the contested territory of Schleswig–Holstein, and after that in Copenhagen too. That is just to speak of their local business, which extended into the Baltic; but in the seventeenth century the Hamburg Sephardim had links with the Portuguese possessions in India, with Mediterranean ports such as Venice and Smyrna, with Ceuta and the other Portuguese possessions in Morocco, not to mention Barbados, Rio de Janeiro and Angola.[15]

The wealthier Portuguese merchants settled comfortably into the urbane business worlds of Amsterdam and Hamburg, dressing like the local elites and living in equally gracious homes. But the Portuguese network brought their partners to very different societies across the globe. The Portuguese Jews who settled in Porto de Ale, near Dakar in west Africa, from 1606 onwards also took note of local habits and customs, and, just as they managed to win favour at European courts, they gained the protection of Muslim kings in and around Senegal. They were mainly a male community, so they took local women as their wives, and managed to convince the rabbis of Amsterdam that their families should be accepted as Jewish; they observed Jewish rituals and received advice from a Portuguese rabbi sent out from Amsterdam to minister to their needs. Their open profession of Judaism alarmed the other Portuguese in west Africa, who supposedly threatened to kill them; but the king told their enemies 'that his land was a market where all kinds of people had a right to live', and those who caused trouble would have their heads cut off. Just like the Portuguese merchants elsewhere, they rapidly built ties across the trading world of their 'Nation', as far afield as Brazil.[16] By the seventeenth century the New Christians were in the ascendant both on the Guinea Coast and in the Cape Verde Islands. Some became involved in one of the major activities on these dusty islands: the collection of slaves sold by African rulers to Portuguese merchants, and their transmission via the islands to Brazil or the Caribbean. But it would be a grave mistake to treat this as in some way a Jewish speciality.[17]

III

Historians who have written about the Portuguese merchants, particularly those of Jewish origin, have generally concentrated on one ocean or another. Even though this reflects the way historians have divided themselves into Atlanticists, Pacificists, Indian Oceanists and Mediterraneanists, this is a pity, because the really impressive feature of their network is the way it embraced the entire globe. Portugal itself recedes from view as ships move between Africa and South America, or goods are sent up the coast of South America for trans-shipment to Macau. Maybe half the Portuguese traffic in the Indian Ocean was operated on behalf of New Christians. The royal monopoly on trade in this region proved to be only theoretical. The wealth and influence of the New Christians increased exponentially as private trade in the hands of merchant houses became the mainstay of Portuguese prosperity – with effects, as will be seen, on the prosperity of the Habsburg monarchy as well.[18]

All this happened despite attempts to stamp on the New Christians in precisely this area. The mass conversion of 1497 left former Jews free to engage in overseas trade, their involvement having been tightly circumscribed while they were still practising their old religion. Yet in 1501 King Manuel was already trying to exclude New Christians from positions of responsibility in the new trading stations that were being established in Asia, and the decrees became ever harsher – eventually they were banned from travelling there in any capacity, but they continued to arrive nonetheless, giving the Inquisition in Goa a fierce headache. Risks were worth taking when the proceeds were so impressive: the annual trade around the Cape was worth about 5,000,000 *cruzados* by 1600, and the king realized which way things were going, so he levied especially high customs dues on the most precious spices carried along this route, nutmeg, cloves and mace. But the private trade also brought diamonds from India, fine eastern cloths, lacquered boxes and porcelain. Needless to say, all this was managed by very effective, well-connected networks, by and large constructed around families and marriage alliances. There were New Christians in Mexico City such as the brothers Vaaz, who dominated trade to Manila around 1640. Then, in Manila, there were other New Christians who maintained close contact with fellow New Christians in Macau and Melaka.[19] These operations were conducted on behalf of investors far away in Lisbon and Seville.

The Portuguese diaspora included, importantly, Madrid, even though Spain was hardly a safe place for anyone who did attempt to practise Judaism. The Spanish monarchy, having relied heavily on German and Genoese bankers in the past, began to see the Portuguese as ideal financial agents. As with the Genoese bankers, the Crown required advance payments against the income it could expect to receive further down the line, largely from the silver mines of the Americas. In the 1570s the funds advanced by the Genoese had been used to pay the salaries of soldiers serving in Flanders, and an attempt to write them out of existing contracts by Philip II, in 1576, left the troops bereft of funds and sparked a mutiny among the Spanish troops in Flanders.[20] Genoese capital could not appear out of thin air, and as the transatlantic trade between Seville and the Americas declined at the start of the seventeenth century, the ability of the Genoese to service the needs of the Crown also declined. The Genoese were overstretched; they already dominated the banking of the kingdom of Naples, another Spanish possession of great strategic importance where the Habsburgs could not let their control slip.[21] As the Portuguese also found, the role of bankers to the king engendered xenophobia, which in the case of the Genoese was already visible in the age of Columbus. Genoa did develop an interest in the Indian Ocean, but only from the 1640s onwards, and attempts to fund a Genoese East India Company came far too late to enable them to challenge the Dutch or the English.[22] By contrast, Portugal had become master of trade routes in all the oceans, and the political link to Spain meant that the Portuguese had been able to intrude themselves in the Spanish trading world as well. For anyone looking for a source of large amounts of capital, this was where to turn.

However, there were suspicions about the political loyalty of the Portuguese towards the Habsburgs and about their religious loyalty towards the Catholic Church. When it came to politics, the Portuguese merchants doubted whether spending vast sums on a war with the Dutch rebels, renewed in 1621, made sense; from a commercial perspective war with the Dutch rendered contact with their fellow Portuguese, the Sephardim of Amsterdam, much more difficult. Worse still, the existence of sugar-rich Portuguese colonies on the coast of Brazil acted as a magnet drawing Dutch naval forces towards South America. The *feitorias* and little towns in Brazil, as well as Portuguese shipping out of Africa, were much more exposed than the Spanish treasure fleets, for the Spaniards had learned some lessons from Francis Drake and his friends, and made sure their fleets were well armed. Even so, the Portuguese were so keen to gain the contracts offered by the Spanish Crown that they managed to reach an agreement in 1626, and the king's favourite, the Count-Duke Olivares, was not seriously worried about employing New Christians. Indeed, he took the view that Spain should openly encourage wealthy New Christians to settle in what for many was the land of their Spanish Jewish ancestors.

The Portuguese who worked with Olivares in the financial offices of state in Madrid were not all New Christians, but many were: Manuel Lopes Pereira was born in Lisbon to a New Christian family and went to live in Seville in 1621, before Olivares's rise to power; and then he worked under Olivares as *contador*, or auditor, during the 1630s, which left him little time for commercial business of his own.[23] In many respects the New Christian elite replicated the role that the Jewish elite had played in medieval Castile and Aragon, as royal financial advisers and as tax farmers. Public display by New Christians aroused envy, and the fact that some of them lived in the most fashionable parts of Madrid was not appreciated by their often virulent critics, who included the poet Francisco de Quevedo and the playwright Lope de Vega. Despite its heavy dependence on them, the Crown was reluctant to offer leading bankers noble titles or membership of the great Military Orders, for these positions were supposedly reserved for Old Christians of pure blood; but even here exceptions were made. Inevitably there were constant complaints about their political and financial influence, heavily coloured by traditional antipathy to those of 'impure' blood, even where there was no evidence that these people had an interest in the Jewish religion; and the New Christians themselves did not like to be called by that name – still less by the common nickname *Marranos*, which meant 'pigs'.[24]

As with the Genoese and the Germans, these intimate ties to the royal court could not be maintained in the face of constant crisis. Olivares fell from grace in 1643, meaning that the Inquisition was once again able to stake out powerful victims who lacked a protector. Moreover, Portuguese rebellion against the Habsburgs and the re-establishment of a national monarchy in Portugal in 1640 undermined the strong economic base on which the relationship between the New Christians and the Crown had rested. Portugal found itself under increasing pressure from the Dutch, especially in Brazil, and lacked the resources to defend its empire effectively.[25] The Portuguese merchants had moved beyond maritime trade into public finance, but their capacity to keep the Spanish Crown in funds depended on the operation of the Portuguese trading network that encompassed the globe. The collapse of their influence was hastened by the decline in influence of Portugal itself, in the face of Dutch and other competition. Many of the most talented Portuguese businessmen now lived in the Dutch United Provinces. As members of this diaspora in many cases found their way back to Judaism, the Portuguese diaspora began to revolve around Amsterdam rather than Lisbon, Seville or Madrid.

IV

Trading diasporas are found across the world, and they often consist of people distinctive by religion as well as ethnic origin. Another example of a religious and ethnic minority is the Armenians, though it too is a complex one, as the Armenians were split between those who had, since around 1200, accepted loose papal authority and those who rejected it. As exotic Christians within Muslim and Christian states they were able to avoid being sucked into the internecine strife between Sunni and Shi'a or Catholic and Orthodox.[26] Their trading networks were less exclusively maritime than those of the Sephardim, reflecting their very long history of both deportation and trading enterprise. Their major base was at New Julfa, a suburb of Isfahan in the Iranian hinterland. Shah Abbas, the great Safavid ruler of Persia, invited them there in 1605, after he deported about 300,000 Armenians from territories he had conquered during one of his wars with the Ottomans. Many of those who settled in Isfahan came from a town in the Caucasus already called Julfa, and the Julfans had traded in silk as far as Aleppo and even Venice, where the Armenians were so well installed that they were able to set up their own monastery that can still be visited on the island of San Lazzaro.[27]

From New Julfa, Armenian merchants had access to the Persian court, while the relative proximity of the Indian Ocean drew them towards the trade of India – there Madras (Chennai) was their most important centre of operations. The shah conferred commercial privileges on the New Julfans, knowing that they were heavily dependent on his goodwill; particularly valuable was the right to export Persian silk. However, the New Julfans diversified into Indian textiles and jewels. Although they did not ignore other opportunities, such as the cinnamon of Ceylon or the coffee of Arabia, silk, textiles and jewels dominated their activities, with the result that their trading network, despite its impressive physical extent, was always narrower in its focus than that of the Sephardim, who handled spices, sugar and hides among many other goods. All the same, Shah Abbas achieved his aims, which made New Julfa into 'one of the most important mercantile centres in Eurasia'.[28]

The geographical spread of their interests is impressive: by sea, as far west as Cádiz, and as far east as Mexico; by land, as far north as Archangel, London and Amsterdam – overland connections to Russia were generally manageable, as the Englishman Anthony Jenkinson had discovered while travelling on behalf of Queen Elizabeth; they even appeared in Tibet in the 1690s.[29] At the start of the sixteenth century, Tomé Pires had already found Armenians who traded in Melaka by way of Gujarat.[30] Burma and Siam were also familiar ground; they could hardly ignore the commercial attractions of the great Siamese trading city of Ayutthaya. New Julfans turned up in Guangzhou in the 1680s, at a time when India was thirsty for China tea, which they exported to Madras. Mateos ordi Ohanessi, who died at Guangzhou in 1794 (half a century after the New Julfa network had largely fallen apart), took a Portuguese passport and based himself in Macau; he was said to be so wealthy that the annual budget of Macau represented a fraction of his resources. From Macau, New Julfan merchants looked eastwards towards its great trading partner, Manila, and made use of the Manila galleons plying towards Acapulco. In 1668 an Armenian merchant named Surat sent his ship the *Hopewell* to Manila on its maiden voyage.

These Manila voyages were something of a scam. The Armenians sent their own ships across the waves, flying the red, yellow and red flag of the Armenians, decorated with an image of the Lamb of God. This was in effect a neutral flag, respected by the Spaniards and the Portuguese.

Indeed, Armenian-owned ships as a rule travelled without cannon, which may sound like folly, when one takes into account the violence between the colonial powers and the widespread piracy in the Indian Ocean, but this practice was understood as a guarantee of their inviolability. Sometimes the English took advantage of this neutral status and used the Armenians to negotiate on their behalf with tricky parties such as the Safavid shahs or the Mughal rulers of India. Yet these Armenian ships were often trading on behalf of the English or the French – the English East India Company entered into an agreement with the New Julfans in 1688, in the hope that the Armenians would send their silks to London around the Cape of Good Hope, rather than using a route through Turkey and the Mediterranean, in return for which Armenians were encouraged to settle in English forts and trading stations in India, 'as if they were Englishmen born', to cite the agreement. In 1698 an Armenian *khwaja*, or merchant, named Israel di Sarhat, arranged for the English East India Company to receive a rent farm in south-western Bengal; this eventually became the site of Calcutta (Kolkata); and they performed similar services for the French, as well as using the longstanding French base at Pondicherry in their south Indian trading operations – these were particularly lucrative, because they opened up the route to the diamond mines of Hyderabad.

The Spaniards had already got the measure of the Armenians and attempted to crack down on what they saw as contraband trade conducted on behalf of the English and other rivals. They confined the Armenians living in Manila to the area outside the city walls given over to the Chinese, the 'Moors' and others they wished to keep at arm's length. Probably there were never many Armenians in Manila, but they did make use of the port to reach Mexico, where the distinctive nature of Armenian Christianity attracted unwelcome attention from the Inquisition. Silver drew them to Mexico: by selling their goods there and acquiring American silver, they could fund their purchases of Chinese silk in Macau or Manila. Occasionally too international rivalries made things awkward; rather than being treated as neutral, the Armenians were classified as Persian, or in some cases Turkish, subjects; if the latter, they were banned from bringing silk to Marseilles in 1687, but the answer was to pose as Persians, since the French had no quarrel with the shah.[31] Ultimately, what counted was the hunger of consumers in western Europe and other markets served by the New Julfans for the goods they brought from India and beyond.

In their vast diaspora, nowhere compared with Madras in importance; the New Julfan merchants were there by 1666, and they had their own church in Madras from 1712 onwards, even providing aldermen who helped run the city council. They could not set up a church everywhere, for fear of arousing the suspicion of the Christian authorities or because of scanty numbers; on the other hand, they seized what opportunities they could; in the eighteenth century they possessed several churches in Burma, and they also acquired the right to use a chapel in one of the churches of Cádiz, testimony to their ability (at the best of times) to convince Spanish Catholics that they were not heretics, just very different in their practices. And, although the Calvinist Dutch placed tight limits on Catholic worship, the Armenians of Amsterdam were able to exploit their distinctive identity, acquiring a church of their own in 1663–4 – in this period the Amsterdam authorities were keener to allow Jewish worship than Catholic. Most of the Amsterdam Armenians were New Julfans, and they are thought to have numbered only about a hundred people, with a similar figure for other major Armenian bases around the world. Their strength did not, therefore, reside in numbers; but the fact that this rather small number of merchants and their dependants could build a church, and rebuild it early in the next century, suggests no lack of resources. In the same years they set up an Armenian printing press in Amsterdam; setting up these presses was a trademark of the Armenians, as it was of the Sephardic diaspora, and Armenian printing houses were found across the Julfan world, in Venice, Calcutta, even Lvov.[32] However, the Armenian communities were predominantly male, so one reason it was often an advantage to accept normative Catholicism, in Catholic cities such as Venice, was that they could then take local wives.[33]

Looking at the Sephardim and the Armenians, one can see that these diasporas did not conform to a strict model. The Portuguese could bury themselves within a host society when it was safer to do so, notably when the Inquisition was stalking outside; the Armenians were conspicuous in their identity, because they faced less severe threats. Even so, when given the chance to come out into the open, a good number of Portuguese New Christians, even many of mixed ancestry, did declare themselves to be Jewish, in the safety of Amsterdam, London and other places of welcome – even in far-off Senegal. Yet by far the largest diaspora was that of African slaves, a very diverse mix of peoples, mainly from west Africa and Angola, who were to be found not just within the Atlantic world but on the shores of the Pacific. At the same time, there were plenty of other diasporas that added to the variety and enterprise of trading cities around the shores of the oceans that were not particularly exotic: Bretons and Basques and Scots, all (apart from the slaves) seeking the opportunities that the emergence of the great trading empires of the early modern world had brought into being. Willingly and unwillingly, the peoples of Europe and Africa were on the move across vast tracts of sea.

40

The Nordic Indies

I

The history of western European contact with the Americas and with the Indies has been written largely from the perspective of the Portuguese, the Spaniards, the Dutch, the English and the French, and with good reason: their imprint can still be felt in ports as diverse as Melaka, Macau, Santo Domingo and Curaçao. By the late seventeenth century, other European powers also wanted their share of the products and profits that could be drawn from long-distance maritime trade. The Danes and the Swedes created global networks of their own, although their importance does not lie in the scale of their trade, for the Danish slave trade at the end of the eighteenth century accounted for not more than 3 per cent of the European total, while their trade with China accounted for just over 5 per cent of the European and American total – the figures for the fledgling USA are closely comparable, while Great Britain stood highest, with well over one third of Canton trade, followed by France.[1] Nonetheless, looking at the maritime achievements of the Danes and Swedes offers a valuable, oblique slant on the activities of the Portuguese, the Spaniards, the Dutch and the English, with whom, neutral or not, the Danes found that their affairs were closely intertwined.

The Danes and the Swedes bore witness to significant changes in maritime commerce, notably the explosion in the consumption of tobacco, tea and coffee in the seventeenth and eighteenth centuries. They did not stand on the sidelines but participated in the transformation of the maritime world in those centuries. Their involvement in the tea trade was particularly important: Great Britain consumed about three quarters of the tea imported into Europe from China in the late eighteenth century, and around one third of that tea was handled by Swedish merchants based in Gothenburg or by their Danish rivals. The tea trade is not just interesting because it was massive and a good source of profit. It also says much, if

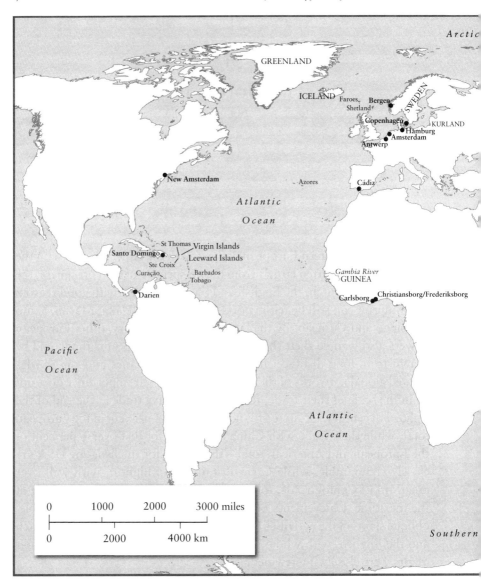

the pun can be excused, about taste and the revolution in consumption that was taking place in eighteenth-century Europe, amply revealing the imprint of maritime trade: the passion for *chinoiserie*; the attempts to develop porcelain or its substitutes in Europe; attempts to replicate Chinese silks and their much-admired colours in Europe, whether by natural or by artificial means. Just as medieval spice-handlers in France or Italy had adulterated and fabricated eastern condiments, fake tea became all too common in Britain, Holland and other centres of consumption. The

inclusion of such tasty ingredients as sheep's dung did nothing, of course, to satisfy the craving for caffeine that the tea, and also the coffee, trade had brought into being.[2]

Scandinavia was the centre of interconnected global operations.[3] By looking at the maritime ambitions of the Nordic peoples in these centuries, one can see how what happened in the West Indies was entangled with what happened as far away as Guangzhou and southern India – how, for instance, many of the cloths carried on Danish ships to the West Indies had arrived in Danish ports from India and even China before being passed on down the Danish maritime trade routes. In the case of the Danes, their insistence that they were a neutral power enabled them to act as intermediaries for other Europeans who were officially in competition with, even at war with, one another, so that Danes could be found supplying goods on behalf of English merchants to the French inhabitants of Mauritius during the Napoleonic Wars.[4] From the very earliest days of Danish operations, intimate ties to other nations came into being: among the founders of the Danish East India Company were Dutch businessmen with past links to the VOC; and later on Copenhagen attracted Portuguese New Christians, who were allowed to set up a small Jewish community there, as they had done in Hamburg and the Danish town of Glückstadt.[5]

Denmark became home to a great many trading companies, eighteen of which were founded between 1656 and 1782, which is something of a European record: an Africa Company based in Glückstadt, close to Hamburg, in 1651; a Morocco Company in 1755; companies trading to and beyond Iceland; the United East India Company of 1616, which evolved into the Danish Asiatic Company, under direct royal control, in 1732.[6] The West Indies and the Guinea coast were also the focus of attention, and Denmark won control of three Caribbean islands, to which its companies exported African slaves.[7] Denmark lost its slice of what is now Sweden, the region of Scania, in 1658, although attempts to recover it continued for many decades; but Denmark was not the small north European state that it became following the loss of Norway and Schleswig–Holstein in the nineteenth century. One should really write not of Danish merchants but of Danish–Norwegian ones, since the Norwegians took part in the enterprises of the Danish trading companies. As overlord of those territories, which in the case of Norway gave access to fishing grounds, furs and other Arctic products, as well as the Faroes, Iceland and (at least in theory) Greenland, Denmark was a significant maritime power even before it acquired colonies and trading stations in the Caribbean, in Guinea and in India.

The Danes made full use of the north Atlantic when sending their ships out to India and China, generally sailing round the top of Scotland, between Shetland and the Faroes, to reach the open ocean – indeed the Atlantic leg was the most dangerous part of a journey out east that could take seven months, for ships set out around December, not the best time to face Atlantic storms. Even so, the Danes lost few ships once they had mastered the routes through the Atlantic and the Indian Ocean – sixty-three ships were sent to China after 1772, and all survived the voyage.[8] Maritime trade was the foundation of the Danish kingdom's prosperity.

The royal castle at Helsingør was world-famous as the gateway to the Baltic even before Shakespeare put 'Elsinore' on the stage, for it was a magnificent source of revenue from ships passing through the narrow opening of the Sound.[9] Within the Baltic, the Danes enjoyed close links to the inhabitants of Brandenburg–Prussia, who muscled in on their West Indies trade. Finally, one of the distinguishing features of Danish trade in India was its strong emphasis on local networks, so-called country trade, reducing dependence on European supplies of silver to pay for goods purchased in India and also in China, which became an increasingly important focus of interest. The main Danish possession in India, Tranquebar in the south-east, was able to carry on its business independently of Europe, inserting itself into the maritime networks of the Indian Ocean peoples and therefore enabling one to glimpse what is often invisible, the magnitude and profitability of maritime trade outside the monopolistic spheres of the Dutch and the Portuguese. There was a twenty-nine-year period when no ships reached Tranquebar from Copenhagen; even so, business carried on, because the colony simply did not depend on metropolitan Denmark for its survival.[10]

II

In 1616 King Christian IV issued the first licence for Danish voyages to the East, which were to be led by the Dutch entrepreneurs Jan de Wilem, from Amsterdam, and Herman Rosenkrantz, from Rotterdam. The king wanted to make full use of Dutch experience. They set out at the very end of December 1618 en route to Ceylon, cheered by the offer of exemption from customs dues on the voyage. These two provided around 12 per cent of the initial capital of the Danish East India Company, whose organization was quite closely modelled on that of the VOC; this was more than the king put up.[11] Jan Pieterszoon Coen, the bloodthirsty governor-general of the Dutch Indies, issued a ban on French and Danish traders even before the ships had left Copenhagen, and this hostility continued for several years, as the Dutch watched the success of the Danes with growing alarm. They were irritated that local rulers seemed to have taken to the Danes. The less aggressive stance of the Danes towards the native peoples of the Indian Ocean, compared to the Dutch, made them not just easier to deal with but genuinely more popular. A VOC agent in Trincomalee, an important port on the east coast of Ceylon, reported with alarm on the willingness of one ruler to assign the Danes a fort at Tranquebar, only twelve miles from the well-known trading station of Negapatnam.[12]

Well might he feel alarm: the Dutch had still not seen off the English, and here was a new threat; besides, the Danish voyages to Ceylon were proving profitable: news spread, and a Latin chronicle from the German–Danish borderland concisely stated that 'in the same year [1622] the king of Denmark received two ships from the island of Ceylon in the Indies, loaded with ebony and spices'. After buying a great deal of pepper, the Danes set their sights on cloves, and an expedition of 1624 managed to obtain 9,600 kg of cloves, trumping the English, who just at this point were suffering humiliation at Amboyna and on Run.[13] If the Danes could make their own capital city into a redistribution centre sending the luxuries of the East across northern Germany and beyond, the Dutch might have cause to worry. The Danes were well aware that their core possessions of Denmark, Schleswig and Norway could not absorb all that they brought. By the end of the eighteenth century 80 per cent of what they brought from India and 90 per cent of what they brought from China was re-exported from Copenhagen, often deep into the Baltic.[14]

The English began to worry about their own access to southern India. An English captain named John Bickley was already complaining in 1624 that the Danes 'had formed [farmed] all the seaports of the Kinges between Napagapatan and Pullacatt for use and benefit of the Kinge of Denmarke; therefore willed us agayne to bee gone, or else they would send us awaye in haste'. For when it came to relations with the other Europeans, the Danes proved rather less charming than they were towards Indian kings: 'moste of all Danes were our deadly and most cruell enimyes.' The value of their trade along the Coromandel coast in the late 1620s was the same as that of the English East India Company, roughly 30,000 *rikstalers* in the best years.[15]

In the event, there were interruptions, as Denmark became sucked, like its neighbours, into the Thirty Years War that devastated Germany. Investors were not, in any case, impressed by the returns, since only seven ships came back from the East between 1622 and 1637, so about one every two years.[16] Trying to help with making ends meet, the king pumped more and more money into the Danish company; by 1624 he was already owed over 300,000 *rikstalers*. This was unsustainable, and the first East India Company was wound up in 1650, but a new one was up and running from 1670. This did not mean the end of the Tranquebar colony, for, as has been seen, there were excellent opportunities to pick up Indian calico cloths and carry them from Tranquebar as far as the Moluccas – this was already happening in 1625. There was a very lively spice trade within as well as beyond the Indian Ocean, notably in cloves, nutmeg and other products that could only be produced in a restricted area – only Indian cuisine cleverly combines spices from all over the Indian Ocean and South China Sea. The Danes were as good at shifting different spices around as they were at moving cloth.[17] However, they worked a standard set of routes and, after gaining Tranquebar, they did not manage to break into new markets. An attempt by the Danish 'President' in Asia, Pessart (who was in fact Dutch), to follow his former compatriots into Japan in the 1640s ended in disaster when the Dutch dissuaded him; he travelled instead to the Philippines, and was killed there.[18]

Paying for eastern goods, as everyone knew, used up silver. Those who followed the mercantilist doctrines popular in contemporary Europe argued that the conservation of silver was vital to national prosperity but that national prosperity would be fostered by vigorous foreign trade. New opportunities offered themselves, now that vast amounts of silver were pouring out of the Peruvian mines, some of it destined for Macau and Canton in payment for the Chinese silks that came via Manila. The pause in trade between Copenhagen and Tranquebar actually did the Danes a favour, because it stimulated the country trade in India, and at the same time the Danes became less interested in obtaining their pepper and spices from their own factory out in India, and began to see that Indian cotton cloths were a better source of profit, whether they were sold in China or taken back to Europe. By the start of the eighteenth century, Danish trade with the East diversified further: increasing demand for Chinese porcelain was accompanied by a passion for tea and coffee. The Danish tea trade became very big business by 1800. A landing document of 1745 from Canton lists seven different types of tea, including *Pecco*, Pekoe tea, as well as sugar, sago, rhubarb and 274,791 teacups with saucers (who counted them so precisely?, one might ask), tens of thousands of coffee cups, and thousands of butter dishes and chocolate cups, plus more than 1,000 teapots.[19] The Danes were not the only Europeans to find this happening. *Chinoiserie* was now in vogue throughout northern Europe, and the presence of the European trading companies was barely able to satisfy demand for porcelain and other exotic goods – so much so that attempts were being made to imitate Chinese and Japanese pottery in English and continental kilns.

III

The trade to India and China was only part of wider Danish ambitions. By working closely with colleagues in Brandenburg–Prussia and in Kurland, roughly corresponding to modern Latvia, the Danes hoped to become masters of the Baltic trade in exotic goods. For the Danish presence was far from insignificant. The Danes occupied parts of the Guinea coast for longer than the Portuguese, and for a time it appeared that their control would extend some way beyond their main trading stations into the hinterland of what is now Ghana. In the seventeenth century the Danes operated fourteen trading stations in Guinea, the English seven, the Brandenburgers three and the Swedes three, though the Swedish ones were all taken by the Danes; by 1837, thirteen years before the Guinea forts were sold to Great Britain, the Danes ruled over an African population of about 40,000 people.[20] Danish entrepreneurs were involved in the sordid slave trade, though to a lesser degree than the Dutch or the English, as their main aim was to provide labour for their three West Indian islands rather than to supply the plantations of Virginia, the wider Caribbean or Brazil; and Denmark was the first nation in Europe to abolish the slave trade. Even so, in 1696 the governor of St Thomas, one of their Caribbean islands, boasted that 'all other trade is nothing compared with this slave trade'.[21]

Their ability to obtain slaves depended on the willingness of local African kings to supply them; many were the subjects of rival kings and had been captured in war, while others were enslaved for debt. The cruelty began well before the slaves had even reached the Danish or other forts where they were sold to Europeans and packed away in the hold of a ship for transport to the New World, for many died during the arduous trek across country to the coast – by definition the slaves were not inhabitants of the areas closest to the European forts, whose rulers would not normally sell their own subjects to the slave-traders. Most captains, with an eye on profit rather than humane treatment, wanted to deliver as large and healthy a human cargo as possible. Therefore they did not make the conditions so absolutely dreadful that their captives died en masse; some time was allowed on deck and the slaves were generally fed well enough to keep them alive; if the conditions below deck were intolerable, disease would spread, infecting the crew as well. Yet some practices such as throwing live slaves overboard when the ship had been so long becalmed that food and water was running out only deepen the sense of horror the modern reader feels.[22]

The foundations of the Danish network in west Africa were in fact laid by the Swedes, their rivals, during the Thirty Years War. At this time the hyper-ambitious Swedish king, Gustavus Adolphus, imagined that, in addition to conquering vast tracts of Germany, he could draw income from a 'General Commercial Company for Asia, Africa, America and *Magellanica*', the last term signifying a supposed southern continent below Cape Horn. This company was the brainchild of a Flemish entrepreneur from

Antwerp named Willem Usselinx who had traded out to Iberia and the Azores, and had been involved with the VOC since its early days but had been dismissed. He looked first to King Christian IV of Denmark, but did not find approval, so he approached the Swedish king instead. The company was chartered in 1626. It operated out of Gothenburg, which had only been founded in 1621, as a Swedish base on the North Sea; Gustavus Adolphus welcomed Dutch and German merchants to the city, and relied on Dutch architects to lay out its network of canals and streets.[23] Usselinx's company set up a colony in the Delaware River which kept going for seventeen years from 1638 onwards, until the Dutch overran it; it was acquired by England, along with New Amsterdam, in 1667.[24] Aware no doubt of what Gustavus Adolphus was up to, Christian of Denmark did issue a charter to Danish merchants in 1625, but then and again a few years later the projects did not get off the ground.

This left the Swedes in pole position. Louis De Geer, a merchant of Liège, trading under the Swedish flag, brought an assortment of goods back to Sweden from a voyage to Guinea in 1648: tobacco, sugar, indigo, ivory, calico cloths and some gold – all very promising, except that some of the goods had been bought not in Africa but in Lisbon.[25] De Geer relied very heavily on the Dutch for both ships and sailors, and he had family in Amsterdam who helped him run his business. The advantage for the Dutch shipowners in this case was that they were able to carry on business overseas under a foreign flag, free from the monopolistic policies of the VOC and its West Indian equivalent. Under the terms of the Swedish king's charter, De Geer was able to run his own business with very little interference, though he did set up a fort named Carlsborg for the Swedish government, on the Guinea coast – oddly, the cornerstone was laid by a Swiss merchant, something of a rarity along these maritime trade routes. The site had been used in the past by the Portuguese, the Dutch and the English, but they had left it empty: there was no proper harbour and ships had to stand out at sea while goods were laboriously brought to and fro from the shore on lighters or in African canoes.

The Danes riposted in several ways. They too had a port which had been founded as an outlet into the North Sea. This was Glückstadt, which lay in Holstein, so it is now part of Germany, and it was founded in 1615. Among its most important settlers were Dutch and Portuguese Jewish merchants. One of the Portuguese Jews even helped to negotiate a trade treaty between Denmark and Spain, and the Crown welcomed Sephardic Jews from both Iberia and the Mediterranean, 'but no German Jews', for the fundamental principle was not toleration but profit, and the Sephardim were seen as better businessmen. In the 1640s and 1650s a group of sea captains from Glückstadt set up their own company to trade in Africa, while two Portuguese Jews opened up a route across the ocean to Barbados, so business out of Glückstadt began to take off. Plans were laid for a company that would embrace all the lands, including *Magellanica* that the Swedes had already shown they hoped to penetrate, added to which was the *Terra Australis*, or 'Southern Land' – both being blanket terms for that vast southern continent that was assumed to reach almost as far as South America, and perhaps included Tierra del Fuego. Some of these activities did produce a return, and when a large cargo of sugar arrived in Copenhagen in 1658 a sugar refinery was built in the expectation that this was the beginning of something big. However, the most satisfying success was the capture of the Swedish forts on the Guinea coast, beginning with Carlsborg, even though it was ceded to the Dutch; they had offered their help to the Danes, more in the hope of expelling the Swedes than in the hope of creating a Danish network of forts.[26]

The Danes did, however, want to create their own bases, and the Glückstadt Company that now ran Danish operations across the sea established a fort at Frederiksborg in what is now Ghana at the end of 1659, with the assent of the local king of the Fetu people. It is no surprise that the Dutch were soon at the throats of the Danes, claiming that they had once controlled that patch of territory – so much for past friendship.[27] But the Danes by and large managed to placate both the Dutch and the English, and their ability to do so reflected the fact that they were seen as only minor rivals. The history of Frederiksborg is a story of constant skirmishes for control, mainly with the Dutch, the effect of which was to soak up funds that would more profitably have been spent on commerce. It is also a history of disease, early death, and mismanagement by governors who were thought by observers to be far too fond of drink and of parties. When the money ran out the fort was pawned to the English, who had no great interest in it and let it decay. Reaching Guinea also meant running the gauntlet of the Salé Rovers and other Barbary corsairs off the coast of Morocco, as well as English pirates who considered that the Danes were fair game, even though they increasingly tried to present themselves as politically neutral.

A similar history can be written of what became the major Danish fort, Christiansborg, founded in 1661 in the region of Accra. One of its commandants held office for eleven days, which were given over to a spectacular feast during which he married a part-African woman; but the Fetu king was disgusted and had him removed from office (this is less surprising than it sounds, as the forts were not sovereign territory, but were at least in theory rented from local kings against a small tribute payment). The Portuguese were deeply irritated by these northern interlopers in what they still liked to think was their Gold Coast, even though fellow Portuguese were active among the Danish merchants – Moses Josua Henriques traded between Guinea and the West Indies around 1675 and became royal factor for trade between Glückstadt and Guinea. Meanwhile the Danish West India Company, like the African kings, expected its share of the proceeds from the Guinea trade. A 'recognition' had to be paid, taking the form of a percentage of profits. For instance, Portuguese Jews based in Holland were permitted to pay a 2 per cent 'recognition' if they sailed under the flag of Denmark to the Danish bases in Africa.[28]

IV

The great scramble for Africa took place in the nineteenth century; but the seventeenth century also saw a scramble, this time for Guinea and the West Indies. Part of the impetus to develop colonies in the West Indies came from an unexpected quarter, soon after the Thirty Years War came to an end with the Peace of Westphalia in 1648. This was Kurland, where Jakob Kettler was duke, and he was determined to promote the economy of his small but strategically important territory. He had spent some time in Amsterdam and had been inspired by the maritime glories of what was, after all, still a small nation. The Swedish king once described Jakob as 'too poor for a king, too rich for a duke'. Kurland was rich in wood and other naval supplies, and Jakob could not be ignored; but his schemes proved overambitious. He could afford to build a fleet of forty-four men-of-war and sixty merchant ships, and from 1650 onwards he began to plant settlements across the Atlantic: in 1651 he established a fort in the Gambia River, and three years later he completed the purchase of Tobago, off the coast of South America, from its impoverished owner, the Englishman Lord Warwick. In one of the most curious episodes in the colonial history of the Caribbean, he sent Latvian peasants, as well as German and other settlers, to this island. This almost inevitably set the Dutch against him, while the English, then under the rule of Oliver Cromwell, proved to be better disposed and entered into a treaty that recognized Gambia as a Kurlander possession. In the end, the Kurlanders were unable to hold back their Dutch and French enemies, who were determined to flush them out of Tobago, setting up their own colonies on the island. First the Dutch seized the Kurlander fort, and then the Kurlanders managed to recover it; but their hold was precarious, and Tobago became a battleground between the Dutch and the English, putting to an end the dreams of this Baltic duke, who died not long afterwards.[29]

Meanwhile the Danes were having only limited success as they attempted to create colonies further north, just to the east of Puerto Rico, in what became the American Virgin Islands after the Danish possessions were sold to the United States in 1917.[30] The Danish West India Company had been revived in 1670 and received its royal charter in 1672, and an unoccupied island in the Caribbean suitable for settlement had already been identified, St Thomas, which the English had briefly held but had abandoned only a few weeks before a Danish–Norwegian ship arrived from Bergen in May 1672. The English were quite co-operative, letting the Danes (or rather their slaves) cut sugar cane on one of their own small islands nearby, a free gift that proved to be the foundation of St Thomas's prosperity, such as it was.[31] The truth was that there were plenty of small islands, at most inhabited by a few Caribs, and (so long as they ignored the native peoples) the Europeans could pick and choose – Jakob Kettler had perhaps been overambitious in setting his heart on Tobago rather than a smaller territory. St Thomas, true to the style of Danish colonization, became home not just to Danes but to Dutch, German, English and Portuguese settlers, the last being mainly of New Christian origin. There were so many Dutch that the islanders mainly used their language.

Inevitably, the arrival of the Danes set off tensions with other colonists in the Caribbean. The English had been hospitable at the start, but gradually became troublesome, though King Charles II, anxious to maintain good relations with the Danish court, sacked the English governor of the Leeward Islands after he laid claim to Danish St Thomas. The French were more dangerous, for when Denmark went to war against Louis XIV in 1675 (in support of the Dutch) St Thomas was seen as a fair prize, and the island was raided; the fortifications were still unfinished, but the French did no more than capture some free and enslaved Africans, and if anything their raid acted as a spur to the completion of the fort.[32] Yet there were also deep internal rivalries, accentuated by the failure of the West India Company to make much money out of its miniature West Indian empire. In 1684 the king deposed the quarrelsome governor of St Thomas and sent out Gabriel Milan as his replacement; he was of Portuguese Jewish descent, an experienced soldier who had served under the French minister Cardinal Mazarin, and had then traded through Amsterdam, becoming Danish factor there. By the 1680s he insisted that he was a loyal Lutheran, but his sixteen-month career in the Caribbean showed little evidence of piety. He arrived with a large entourage, including six or seven dogs, and carrying 6,000 *rikstalers* given to him by the king of Denmark to cover his expenses. However, he regarded St Thomas as a private kingdom, treating the African slaves especially harshly: one runaway was impaled, another had his foot cut off. The Danish settlers complained to the government in Copenhagen, and he was arrested and sent back to Denmark for trial. Condemned to death for abuse of power, he received the good news that the king had agreed to mitigate his sentence: instead of having his hand cut off before being beheaded, whereupon his head would be impaled on a stick, he would simply be beheaded, and this duly happened in March 1689.

Just as Denmark's Asiatic trade had been restructured time and again because of its relatively limited success, none of these activities in Africa or the Americas proved to be as lucrative as the companies or indeed the Danish kings hoped, and in the 1750s the affairs of the West India Company reached the point where the Crown felt obliged to take over the company's assets, as well as the forts of Christiansborg and Frederiksborg (which had been back in Danish hands for quite a while). Admittedly, there were some notable successes: in the late seventeenth century several successful trading expeditions were despatched from Bergen by a wealthy merchant; the acquisition of the island of Sainte-Croix from France in 1733 gave the Danes a stronger base in the West Indies close to the two islands they already held. On the other hand, Danish and Norwegian cargoes sent directly across the Atlantic (thereby excluding the slave traffic out of Guinea) were made up of basic necessities rather than costly goods: tallow from Iceland, Baltic pitch and tar, whale oil from the Faroes and Greenland, base metals and, importantly, all the equipment needed for the manufacture of sugar, such as copper boilers. This does show how Copenhagen, Bergen and Glückstadt were functioning as centres for the redistribution of goods from right across the Danish colonial empire. Guinea, on the other hand, mainly received textiles, foodstuffs and weapons such as muskets; half of the textiles were not European at all, but had been brought all the way from India or even China. The Danes had put together a maritime trading network that tied together their Indian Ocean operations with their Atlantic ones.[33] What came back from the West Indies was, in the first place, sugar, the colonial product par excellence, though a few other products gradually made inroads, notably tobacco, coffee and cocoa.[34]

There were several attempts to reinvigorate West Indian and African trade by forming new companies, such as the 'Royal Danish Baltic and Guinea Trading Company' at the end of the eighteenth century, which was supposed to tie together the Baltic trade of Copenhagen and its trade in the Atlantic, including even the Greenland Trade Office. It was an ambitious project: this company operated thirty-seven ships and did very well in the years around 1780 as a result of the American Revolution, which left a neutral trading power in a strong position while the British battled against the Thirteen Colonies. However, when the Danish government banned the slave trade in 1792 (admittedly with a ten-year delay before implementation) the Baltic–Guinea Company declared that it could see no point in maintaining the overseas settlements. As a result, trade was opened up as never before to all Danes and to foreigners.[35] But the Baltic–Guinea Company pointed to a special characteristic of Scandinavian worldwide trade. Well managed, the Scandinavian ports could serve as distribution centres for large swathes of northern Europe. The Danes never quite succeeded in that ambition; however, the Swedes, making intensive use of Gothenburg, had a very slow start but in the long run proved more successful.

V

Others came up with schemes that would, they hoped, transform the fortune of small, marginal states; from 1715 onwards, the newly created Ostend Company took advantage of the transfer of the southern Netherlands from Spanish to Austrian Habsburg rule, and had grand ambitions in both west and east Africa; but it crashed in 1727 partly thanks to the hostility of the Dutch – they hated the idea of an economic renaissance in Flanders when their own world trade had passed its peak. The Austrians agreed to wind up the Ostend Company as a condition for British and Dutch recognition of the claims of Maria Theresa as heir to the Habsburg throne.[36] The Scottish Company of the Indies was chartered in 1695; in its reincarnation as the 'Darien Company' it was responsible for the disastrous Darien Scheme that pumped its funds into a failed colony on the Panama isthmus. Panama was not an absurd place to choose, since Pacific goods coming up from Chile and Peru, and potentially from the East Indies, were trans-shipped into the Caribbean at that point; but the architect of the scheme, Paterson, had not taken the trouble to find out what sort of place it was; in the words of Lord Macaulay:

> Let but that precious neck of land be occupied by an intelligent, an enterprising, a thrifty race; and, in a few years, the whole trade between India and Europe must be drawn to that point … It was true that the region which Paterson described as a paradise had been found by the first Castilian settlers to be a land of misery and death.[37]

It is the most famous, and in many ways the most important, of these minor companies, because the catastrophic financial collapse that then followed led Scotland into full union with England, and the Darien Scheme still features in debates about whether an independent Scotland is viable.[38] These and other schemes were based on the assumption, which was by no means stupid, that there was always room for companies that were willing to carry the goods of nationals of other countries while those countries forced merchants to trade through monopolistic enterprises such as the VOC and the English East India Company. The Flemish and Scottish companies just mentioned are, however, important in other ways: the Ostend capitalists helped create the Swedish East India Company; and the Swedish company depended heavily on the expertise of Scottish entrepreneurs whose imprint on eighteenth-century Gothenburg was at least as heavy as that of the Dutch on seventeenth-century Gothenburg. Many of the Scottish settlers in Gothenburg were Jacobites, sympathetic to the rebellions of the Old Pretender, son of James II of England, and his own son, Bonnie Prince Charlie. This did not mean that they were Catholics: Colin Campbell, a Scot, founded a Reformed Church in Gothenburg. And there were also English investors; the British presence was strong enough to earn Gothenburg the title 'Little London'.[39]

The Ostend Company left its imprint on what became the Swedish East India Company in several ways. Between them, the English and the Ostenders commanded 80 per cent of tea imports into Europe. In 1731 the king of Sweden granted the newly formed Swedish East India Company a monopoly on trade beyond the Cape of Good Hope; this charter was valid for fifteen years, and it was renewed four times, the last time in 1806. Gothenburg was to be the centre of operations. The Swedes had one advantage over the English that both reflected and compensated for the fact that they were newcomers: they had no Indian Ocean factories whose support ate up a significant part of their income and that would have propelled them into rivalry with the Dutch, the French, the English and the Danes, all well installed on the coast of India by the early eighteenth century.[40] It was touch and go around 1730 whether the Ostend traders would switch their attention to Copenhagen or to Gothenburg, but one or two of them, notably Colin Campbell and his fellow Scot Charles Irvine, built up their interests in Gothenburg, and helped to set the Swedish Company on its remarkably successful course. They focused on the trade route to Guangzhou, knowing that the Swedes would be only one of several nations trading there, but knowing too that the Chinese operated strict controls on access, and that they could count on the protection of the Chinese authorities once they reached the Pearl River.

Campbell took passage on the first Swedish voyage out East, as 'first supercargo', an important position, second only to the captain (whom he detested), with rights of supervision over the cargo on board. He also carried a letter announcing that he was the Swedish king's ambassador to the emperor of China; however, on the return voyage his ship encountered seven Dutch vessels in Indonesia, and the Dutch were unimpressed by the claim to diplomatic immunity. Only his persistence convinced them that it would be wiser to let him, his ship and his crew continue their journey, and in due course the Dutch governor-general in Batavia handsomely apologized.[41] One factor that may have made the Dutch very suspicious was that the other supercargoes were British, and there was every reason to suppose that, as had often happened in the Danish merchant fleet, the Swedes were acting as cover for more serious rivals. The second company ship to leave Gothenburg, which left even before the first one had returned, was built in England and carried four British supercargoes. This ship brought back a profitable cargo, including pepper, silk and cotton cloth, but made the mistake of attempting to trade in India and Ceylon, and, if anything, this voyage made clear the advantages of heading straight to Macau and avoiding waters that teemed with more powerful European merchants. For when the Swedish ship reached Ceylon the Dutch denied the Swedes fresh water for the long haul back to the Cape of Good Hope. Fortunately they had a more humane welcome from the French in Mauritius, when they arrived there panting with thirst in June 1734.[42]

It became more and more obvious that tea, not pepper, was the commodity Europeans wanted to buy, in all sorts of different types and qualities, and by concentrating on that the Swedish companies kept afloat financially. Gothenburg was much less important than Copenhagen, a much larger city serving a whole Danish empire that stretched from Greenland into the Baltic, plus the West Indies and west Africa. And yet the more modest status of Gothenburg, and the less advanced economy of Sweden as a whole, brought advantages: the domestic market was small, but there was an incentive to serve the lands around the North Sea, and, as has been seen, Great Britain was a marvellous target, with its thirst for China tea.

One apparent problem was the lack of interesting products that Sweden could offer the world, particularly the Chinese. But this too could be resolved. Swedish raw materials – Finnish timber, Swedish iron, and the like – were in heavy demand in the shipyards of southern Spain. Cádiz became the preferred port of call on the way out to China, for its streets were paved with the silver of Peru. By selling Swedish goods in Spain, the Swedes acquired the American silver that the Chinese craved.[43] The silver of the Swedes had been carried up the Pacific coast of South America, had passed through Panama or Mexico, across the Atlantic, and would then be taken down the eastern Atlantic, through the Indian Ocean (generally bypassing India entirely), to reach Macau and Guangzhou in the western Pacific. At the end of the eighteenth century, the proportion of silver in the cargo of Swedish ships bound for China reached as high as 96 per cent (figures for Danish trade in China are not very different). If one arrived with cash in hand, no time was wasted trying to sell European goods in the hold of one's ships. Scandinavian businessmen could go straight to the tea and silk markets and snap up the best teas, such as the variety known as *Bohea*, before their rivals had a chance to do so. The Dutch often ended up mixing this tea with inferior teas to fill their tea chests.[44] Importing this tea into Britain was not straightforward: taxes on tea often exceeded 100 per cent, as the British government tried to take full advantage of demand. Inevitably, this created an unofficial tea trade – the word 'smuggling' conjures up a dramatic, even romantic, image, but the Swedes certainly knew how to dump their tea on the English.

A similar story can be told for silks and ceramics. In the eighteenth century 30,000,000–50,000,000 pieces of Chinese porcelain passed through Gothenburg. Admittedly, one reason for carrying so much of it in the cargo of European ships was that it provided ballast, but it was not all needed in Sweden. A Swedish expert who has also thought about rival sources of Chinese ceramics in Europe has pointed out that 'the company brought home the largest quantity of Chinese porcelain not only in relative but even in absolute terms'.[45] Even the very first voyage to China, which set out in 1732, brought back 430,000 pieces of porcelain, including over 21,000 plates and six chamber pots, which were put up for auction in Gothenburg; the ship also carried 165 tons of green and black tea and over 23,000 silk cloths.[46] On each voyage, much of the return cargo took the form of teacups and other paraphernalia for the tea and coffee consumers of Europe, who now encompassed not just crowned princes but city-dwellers of quite modest means – a consumer revolution was taking place in eighteenth-century Britain and elsewhere, and Chinese blue-and-white pottery was a universal obsession.[47] Attempts to imitate Chinese ceramics were matched by attempts to imitate Chinese silks, and a village called Kanton was built outside Stockholm in the hope that the Swedes could develop their own silk industry. This was influenced by a set of attitudes known as 'cameralism', which argued for the creation of self-sufficient national economies. Maybe, indeed, tea could be planted in Sweden; the great Swedish naturalist Carl Linnaeus, who died in 1778, tried various experiments over a period of twenty years, but there was no substitute for the teas of the Far East, as the tea bush could not be persuaded to grow in a cold climate.[48]

During this period 132 ships were sent east, all but a few to China; most returned, for the Swedes had a very good safety record compared to other European nations. Accidents were much more likely to occur in the North Sea on the way out from Gothenburg, in winter, or on the way back, than in warmer ocean waters. One ship foundered on rocks in the Gothenburg archipelago in 1745 when it was almost within sight of home; it is quite possible that this was a deliberate insurance scam.[49] What brought the Swedish expeditions to an end was a combination of factors: a reduction in the heavy tax on tea imposed by the British government, which created a free-for-all in the tea trade; competition from new rivals, the Americans; bad financial management around 1800; the accumulation of vast amounts of unsold tea. But the Swedish East India Company had been, until the start of the nineteenth century, a remarkable success story; more than that, it had helped shape not just Swedish but European culture and society, with its massive imports of tea and tea services.

41
Austrialia or Australia?

The idea that a great southern continent existed can be traced very far back in time. It has been seen that the Romans understood Ceylon to form the northern tip of this mysterious continent, in accordance with Ptolemy's view that the Indian Ocean was an enclosed sea whose southern shores connected Africa and south-east Asia. Even when it became obvious that Ptolemy was mistaken, the assumption that a southern continent existed led mariners sailing in the wake of Magellan to think that Tierra del Fuego was the tip of this southern continent. The sixteenth-century English circumnavigators, Drake and Cavendish, travelled through the Magellan Strait, but their explorations suggested that Tierra del Fuego was a large island; even when the route round Cape Horn was discovered, its high winds and violent seas long discouraged navigators. It was believed that the world needed to be in balance to occupy its position in the middle of the firmament. Therefore a southern land as weighty as the continents in the northern hemisphere must exist. Moreover, once one had crossed the torrid regions, where human survival had long been assumed to be impossible, one would find lands that were 'as fertile and habitable as the northern hemisphere', rich in precious stones, pearls and fine metals, as well as abundant flora and fauna. These lands were sometimes known as *Magellanica*, though this term was quite flexible, and could mean Pacific islands or even South America.[1]

There was plenty of evidence towards which sixteenth-century geographers could confidently point: biblical texts, of which more in a moment; classical texts, culminating in Ptolemy's world map; and also Peruvian legends of an Inca ruler named Tupac Inca Yupanqui who set out across the sea and discovered lands of great wealth; he supposedly brought back gold and slaves, as well as providing encouragement, centuries later, to the bizarre theories of Thor Heyerdahl about trans-Pacific navigation.

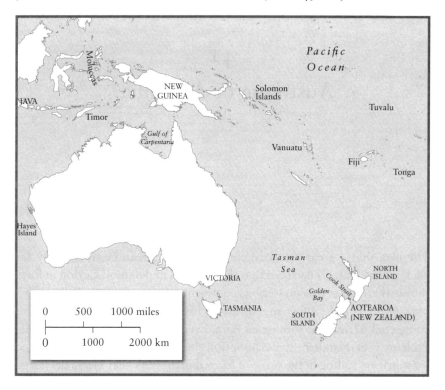

Although the first map to name America, by Waldseemüller, showed no southern continent, certainty that it existed grew in the next thirty years. Mercator's first world map, from 1538, included a massive southern continent, of which he could only say: 'that land lies here is certain but its size and extent are unknown'; however, its northern tip reached as far as the Magellan Strait, and when he issued a more famous world map in 1569 he had not changed his mind. When Abraham Ortelius published his own world map in 1570 he could not improve on this. For him this was the 'Southern Land not yet known', *Terra Australis Nondum Cognita*.[2]

The series of Spanish voyages across the Pacific that followed the Spanish capture of Mexico and Peru brought European ships deep into the Polynesian islands. In 1542, for instance, the commander Villalobos set out from Navidad, which lay along the Pacific coast of Mexico, a little to the north of Acapulco, searching for the islands visited by King Solomon – the distant land of Ophir mentioned in the book of Kings. The idea grew that the gold vessels of Solomon's Temple had been made out of beaten gold from Ophir.[3] Villalobos's journey took his ships towards what therefore became known as the Solomon Islands, amid many hazards: a whale swam underneath the flagship, almost heaving the galleon out of the water before it swam on and the galleon rocked back to normal. In the event, the voyage ended up in the Philippines, and only the fringes of Polynesia had been penetrated. Back in Seville the notion that Ophir lay not somewhere in the Red Sea or western Indian Ocean but across the world in the southern Pacific had gained a certain amount of purchase; Columbus, in his *Book of Prophecies*, which was really a scrapbook of biblical, classical and patristic quotations, had been dreaming of finding Solomon's islands by sailing west. The learned introduction to a Spanish translation of Marco Polo's book of travels, widely circulating by 1530, placed Ophir somewhere in that vast space between Japan and the Moluccas that was still a matter of pure conjecture. A series of Spanish voyages set out from 1567 onwards, looking for a great southern land, or rather for a series of islands that were believed, rather like the West Indies, to lie close to the unknown continent and to offer great riches. The spirit of scientific enquiry was clearly subordinate to the greedy search for gold and spices, though there may have been some hope of bringing the Catholic faith to heathen peoples. The whole enterprise was strikingly reminiscent of that of Columbus over seventy years earlier. As in the Americas, the assumption was that Spain would lay claim to this land, whether it was populated or not, and establish a colony there.

The commander of the first expedition, Álvaro de Mendaña, took his two ships on a conservative route out from Callao, in Peru, and then across a wide space of water until he reached what are now Tuvalu and the Solomon Islands. Mendaña had to face the hostility of the islanders, and just as bad as that was the hostility of his colleague Sarmiento, a military man who had been pressing for the expedition to be launched, and resented being passed over as commander; Mendaña was the viceroy of Peru's nephew, though the viceroy hoped to use this expedition to send away many of the young adventurers who were clogging the streets of Callao. In the event, the ships carried a motley crew of Spanish, mixed-blood and African men, for slaves who had already crossed the Atlantic were arriving as far away as Peru.[4] Sarmiento went along on the voyage, although his exact position on board is, and probably was at the time, unclear. Not much was achieved, apart from planting in Mendaña's mind an obsession with the southern continent and with the supposed riches of the islands he had visited. Mendaña's detailed report on his voyage was not entirely encouraging: the explorers had not always found it easy to obtain food, although they had managed to trade small amounts of truck with the islanders. They had been taken aback by the evidence that the islanders consumed human flesh, not least when a friendly chieftain offered Mendaña a piece of meat that he identified as the shoulder and arm of a boy (the hand was still attached). The islanders were taken aback when Mendaña declined to eat the arm:

> I accepted the present, and, being greatly grieved that there should be this pernicious custom in that country, and that they should suppose that we ate it . . . I caused a grave to be dug at the water's edge and had the quarter buried in his [the native leader's] presence . . . Seeing that we set no value on the present, they all bent down over their canoes like men vexed or offended, and put off and withdrew with their heads bent down.[5]

Although the practice of both cannibalism and human sacrifice could be used as an excuse to justify European hegemony, the revulsion of the Spaniards was genuine. As Montaigne was aware, they forgot that their own form of human sacrifice, practised in the fires of the Spanish Inquisition, was in some respects comparable.[6] Other types of food were hard to come by, and by the time they had returned to America they had even had to consume the white cockatoo which was, perhaps, the only prize they had obtained during their arduous journey.[7]

Unfortunately the new viceroy, Toledo, was much better disposed to Sarmiento and much worse disposed to Mendaña than his predecessor, so Mendaña trailed across the world to the court of King Philip II, to whom he had already written a Columbus-style letter exaggerating the attractions of the Solomon Islands. He did not secure what he wanted until 1574, and even then he had to learn patience on an unusual scale. He arrived in Panama a couple of years later, ready to launch his voyage into the unknown corners of the Pacific, armed with an exceptionally generous royal privilege. The king graciously permitted him to take office as governor and marquis of a new colony in the Pacific, with the right to pass these lands on to his heir, and to recruit a native labour force (for distribution among his followers). He could even mint his own gold and silver coins, presumably out of metals mined by his new subjects – as if the tragic lessons of what had happened in Hispaniola had never been learned. He would be provided with sheep, goats, pigs, cattle and horses, as well as Spanish settlers, male and female. He would have to found three cities, though, and he had to post a bond of 10,000 ducats to make sure that he did not renege on his promises.[8]

Drake's entry into the Pacific in 1578 put a spoke in the wheels of Mendaña's ambitions. The Spaniards had assumed that the wide spaces of the Pacific east of the Spice Islands were Spanish waters, granted by the pope in his division of the world as long ago as 1494. Protestant English privateers had no place in this vast space. The priority became not the launch of a new expedition westwards across the ocean, but the despatch of an armed fleet southwards to prevent foreign ships from slipping into what was still an unguarded space. Sarmiento was sent to the Magellan Strait to bar the way to English shipping. Far from keeping the English out, he was taken prisoner and carried off to London, where he, Queen Elizabeth and Walter Raleigh discoursed together in Latin on the geography of the Pacific Ocean.[9]

The infinitely patient Mendaña was not able to leave Peru until 1595, by which time fortune's wheel had turned again in his favour – there was a new viceroy, who was excited by the plans, and the royal letter of approval made it hard to refuse Mendaña's requests for help. Mendaña's first expedition was a failure; this expedition was a disaster. One fundamental problem was that it was easy enough to determine latitude, with the help of the sun, but impossible to fix longitude until precise chronometers were invented in the eighteenth century.[10] As a result, he was none too clear where he had arrived, and, after passing through the Marquesas Islands, he installed himself on the outer edges of the Solomon Islands, setting up the colony of Santa Cruz, where his followers managed to hang on for a while until they were defeated by disease and by the hostility of the islanders. Disease carried off Mendaña. In the end the remnant of his settler population sailed off to the safety of the Philippines. The new commander, a capable Portuguese named Quirós, was, however, still impressed by the argument for the existence of a great southern continent. Where, he argued, could the inhabitants of the Pacific islands have come from, if not from some great landmass nearby? South America was too far away. The southern continent must be just over the horizon. This was a gross underestimate of the seagoing capacity of the Polynesian canoes that they kept seeing in the Solomon Islands and elsewhere. They arrogantly assumed that European methods of shipbuilding and navigation were infinitely superior to local ones, seeing local craft as impossibly small and light and failing to understand the extraordinary sophistication of Polynesian knowledge of the seas.[11]

Undeterred by failure, Quirós set out again in 1605, accompanied by another explorer, the Spaniard Torres. With Franciscan friars on board, Quirós made plain his desire for evangelization. Once they had left Callao, he and his companions experienced first the emptiness of the broad tracts of open ocean, and then skimmed past uninhabited islands where they deemed it pointless to try to find food and water, let alone people who might direct them towards the great southern continent. Heavy clouds betokened the mainland they sought, or so they imagined at the end of January 1606. Finally they were forced to anchor close to islands thick with foliage, but still uninhabited, where at least they could find fruits and herbs that Chinese sailors on board knew were edible. Water remained the critical problem, though. While up to fifteen jars of water were used each day in normal conditions, Quirós had to cut the quota to three or four.[12] Fortunately early February saw them reach inhabited islands where, at the start, they were welcomed by Polynesians consumed by curiosity at their white skins. As always happened, relations with the native people deteriorated, and the voyage through the islands of eastern Polynesia and Melanesia was not easy, a sequence of good and bad encounters with the inhabitants.

By May 1606 they had reached what is now called Vanuatu, where they found what seemed to be a suitable port, a place that could surely function as the headquarters of a Spanish settlement in these remote islands. The name chosen for the harbour was Vera Cruz, but the name given to the island combined the sacred with the secular: *Austrialia del Espiritú Santo*. Maybe there was a play on words here, but this was not a direct reference to the *Terra Australis*, the southern continent. *Austrialia* commemorated not the Land of the South but the Land of the East, Austria or Österreich, the dynastic home of the Habsburg dynasty, still called *las Austrias*, 'the Austrians', in Spanish history books. Quirós went on to proclaim formally that this land was now in the possession of King Philip II of Spain, after which he appointed a government and founded his own bizarre 'Order of the Knights of the Holy Ghost'. In the ceremonies that followed, two African cooks were publicly freed from slavery, an act of conspicuous generosity that did not please their owners, so they were made to return to their masters once the festivities had come to an end.[13]

It is not surprising that Quirós was keen to celebrate what he was convinced was a great discovery. Otherwise, though, it was the usual story of lots of killing, an occasional baptism, the carrying off of a few young men destined to be baptized, and departure to find other islands, before returning home with the news that the outer edges of a new continent had supposedly been discovered. It was also the usual story of the officers and crew grumbling at Quirós's behaviour, complaining about his decisions, and trying to get him into trouble on his return, though in the event he was able to travel to Madrid and urge the king to follow up his voyage with new ones, begging him in the name of Christ to do so, since his priority was no longer the discovery of great wealth but the salvation of the souls of the miserable and naked people he had encountered in *Austrialia*. Polite noises were made about plans for a new expedition, and he headed west to Panama, but died there in 1614 or 1615, with his dreams unfulfilled.[14]

Quirós's colleague Torres did not follow his commander back to Peru; rather, he decided that the search for a southern land had only just begun.

He set out westwards and passed to the south of New Guinea through the strait that still bears his name. Australia lay close by, and he saw 'very large islands, and more to the south', but he pressed on; he wended his way through the strait and headed through the Moluccas towards Manila. He was satisfied that he had now brought New Guinea under King Philip's sovereignty, although if he thought the headhunting inhabitants would accept that he was deluding himself.[15] From the far-flung islands of Polynesia he and his men had now entered the battleground, for that is what it was, where the Portuguese and the Dutch, not to mention the Spaniards and the English, fought for access to the finest spices of the East, islands far richer in the goods the Europeans sought than those Quirós and Torres had so far discovered.

The southern continent remained elusive. Mendaña and Quirós had cast themselves in the mould of Christopher Columbus. This was not the best model to follow. What was different was the insistence that there were more continents out there, that the wealth of the East Indies was only a pale reflection of the wealth to be obtained from a temperate Antarctic continent. A southern continent was finally reached at the start of the seventeenth century. However, it took nearly 170 years for its edges to be properly mapped out; and the earliest contact was the result not of deliberate searching, in the wake of Villalobos, Mendaña, Quirós and Torres, but of a series of accidents.

II

'Captain Cook,' Graham Seal has pointed out, 'did not discover Australia, despite what generations of school children were once taught and many still believe.' He adds that 'modern Australia was not discovered at all. It was revealed.'[16] Obviously the term 'modern Australia' needs to be emphasized, since the claim that it was a *Terra Nullius*, a land with no inhabitants, or at least no inhabitants who could claim rights over its possession, was used in the nineteenth century to justify its acquisition by Europeans, and the denial of rights to the native population – Aborigines were only allowed to vote in all the Australian states and territories from 1965 onwards.[17]

The Dutch were the first to reveal that they knew about the existence of what they came to call 'New Holland'; but the Portuguese had almost certainly seen its shores before them. The debate about which Europeans first reached Australia has not aroused quite as much passion as the debate about which Europeans first reached the Americas, but it is mired in often credulous interpretations of roughly drawn maps. The sixteenth-century

Dieppe maps did show an extensive southern continent below South America. One historian of cartography has observed that the southern continent was 'a special favourite of the Dieppe school', and that 'fantasy outweighs reality' in many of the charts.[18] These maps were often beautifully decorated with images of local flora and fauna, or even of native villages in South America and Africa. The warning that the coastlines traced on these maps become less reliable the further they are from anywhere Europeans had adequately explored has not always been heeded. A lively attempt to prove that the Portuguese were the first Europeans to reach Australia was published in 1977 and became standard teaching in Australian schools. The argument was straightforward: early maps, ultimately of Portuguese pedigree, show the coast of Australia. What may be one of the earliest Dieppe maps, the Dauphin Map, most probably dating from the 1540s, was clearly based on Portuguese sea charts. The claim that it shows part of Australia in some detail is based on the appearance of a large chunk of land described as *Iave la Grande*, 'Greater Java', which is shown immediately to the south of plain *Iave*, Java, separated from Java by a narrow channel, and lying close to spice islands such as Timor. Along its coastline appear such vaguely named places as *Coste Dangereuse* and *Baye Basse*. There are some agreeable images of scattered huts and of naked inhabitants.[19] Other maps too showed a landmass south of Java or New Guinea. It was simply assumed that the great southern continent reached up towards tropical climates. And as for 'Greater Java', this had already featured in Marco Polo's account of the East Indies, as part of the confused description of lands he had certainly not visited, whether or not he really lived for a time in China – he muddled up Java and Sumatra, and then he talked of Greater Java as the largest island in the world.

III

One way of resolving this issue is to state baldly that the Europeans knew Australia existed even before they had actually touched its shores. Arising out of their theories about a southern continent, and anchored in Marco Polo's certainties, they were as convinced that a large landmass must exist somewhere south of the Spice Islands as Columbus had been that no landmass could exist between Europe and the Far East; and maybe it was a massive island rather than the world-encircling continent that mapmakers generally preferred to show. A sort of mental discovery actually preceded physical discovery, odd as it may sound. After all, much the same might be said about modern cosmology – dark matter and dark energy, it is claimed, must be there, partly to solve the mathematical equations, despite the fact that nothing has, if the pun can be excused, come to light. The universe has to be in perfect balance, just as the assumption in 1600 was that the earth could only be in balance if the southern continent weighed down the Antarctic pole. Discovery, as has been seen in other cases, such as the Norse arrival in America, was a gradual process that could result both in knowing things and in largely forgetting them; and the European discovery of the world beyond depended crucially on gaining some understanding of what has been found, and on making use of it. The problem with Australia, it will become clear, is that no one was terribly interested in what had been found, for no one had much use for what was there.

The finger is usually pointed at a certain Cristóvão de Mendonça, who (it is argued) explored the waters south of Indonesia as early as the 1520s. He is known to have taken fourteen ships to south-east Asia, setting out from Lisbon in 1519; the theory that he was sent to block Magellan's Spanish fleet from passing through Portuguese-dominated waters does not stand up, since, as has been seen, Magellan had not intended to return to Spain by way of the Indian Ocean. No one really knows why Mendonça was sent on his voyage or where his ships went.[20] But it has long been argued that a shipwreck found in 1836 on a remote Australian beach on the coast of Victoria by two men who had gone out to catch seals was none other than one of Mendonça's ships; supposedly made of mahogany, its timbers had disappeared by 1880. Mendonça has been found everywhere, but nowhere does the identification convince: a stone hut well to the south of Sydney, a set of iron keys found near a bay in Victoria, and so on. South-eastern Australia is surely the wrong place to look; later, Dutch ships would sometimes be shipwrecked off western Australia, as they tried to cut across the Indian Ocean to the East Indies, although a swivel gun found in the sands near Darwin, in the north of Australia, might well be from a Portuguese ship, date unknown.[21] These reports, like the discussions of the Dieppe maps, offer plenty of opportunity for semi-informed fantasy. Perhaps the most bizarre of the claims is that a sixteenth-century Portuguese manuscript carried an illustration of a kangaroo. That said, it is highly likely that Portuguese ships were occasionally blown on to these shores, though if they were wrecked it is quite possible that their crews went down with their ships, or died on land, and news of these chance encounters failed to reach the Portuguese bases in Java and elsewhere.

Speculation about a great southern land turned into reality when the Dutch began to take a shorter route across the Indian Ocean, allowing the

Roaring Forties, which had carried their ships out of the Atlantic and past the Cape of Good Hope, to blow the ships still further eastwards, so that somewhere below the underbelly of Java they could wiggle through the Sunda Strait and arrive in Batavia (Jakarta), the Dutch centre of operations. This became regular practice after 1611, after Hendrik Brouwer sailed 4,000 miles across the ocean to reach Java directly from southern Africa.[22] In many ways this was a safer route than one further to the north, since the Malacca Strait was a notorious haunt of pirates, besides which the Portuguese still controlled Melaka until 1641, when it fell to the Dutch (the red-coloured *Stadthuys*, or town hall, is the oldest Dutch building in the Far East).

Speculation about who reached Australia first from Europe comes to an end with the Dutch. The *Duyfken*, or 'Little Dove', is the first of the Dutch ships known to have arrived in Australian waters. Twenty metres long, this was what the Dutch called a *jacht*, or yacht, and she would have carried no more than twenty sailors. After a successful trip to the East Indies under the patronage of the VOC, during which she had engaged in battle with a Portuguese flotilla off the island of Bantam in December 1601, she already had a record of trading successfully in eastern spices. Her captain was Willem Jansz, or Janszoon, and he took her back to the Indies in 1603, from where she was sent south to see what might lie underneath Indonesia. Along the coast of New Guinea there were some ugly encounters with the inhabitants, and the same happened when the ship turned south and landed off the shore of Australia – a sailor was killed after being stuck through with an Aborigine spear. Legends that circulate among one of the native peoples, the Wik, tell of a large wooden ship and of their encounter with those on board, who needed help in digging a well, and who showed the Aborigines how to use metal tools. It seems the Dutch interfered with local women, and then the Wik decided they were unwelcome, so they watched until the Dutchmen had climbed down into the wells they were making, and then set upon them and killed them. Clearly this is a confabulation drawn from many tales and visits, but the story is widespread in several versions.[23]

It became increasingly obvious that the, or a, southern continent had been discovered, as more and more ships, travelling in the wake of Brouwer, ended up willy-nilly on the shores of western Australia or its offshore islands and kerries. The VOC ship the *Eendracht*, captained by an old Baltic and Mediterranean hand named Dirk Hartog, was one of the lucky ships whose landfall in October 1616 took place in relatively calm conditions. Hartog even inscribed a flattened pewter dinner plate with the date and the names of the senior crew and supercargo and left it on an island near the westernmost point of Australia. The plate was seen by another Dutch visitor in 1697; he replaced it with his own, which is now in a museum in Fremantle, Western Australia.[24] Yet a claim to Dutch lordship was not thought worth pursuing. As reports came back of the desolate land (most of the ships visited the bleak, dry edges of Western Australia), it became obvious that this southern continent could supply neither gold nor spices. It was searingly hot and inhabited by unfriendly people whose technology was the simplest one could imagine, in modern terms Palaeolithic peoples, 'a dry cursed earth without foliage or grass'.[25]

The Dutch were not alone in being cast upon these shores. The English traders who were trying to insert themselves into the spice trade took the same risk, crossing the Indian Ocean and occasionally striking land too far south, in Australia rather than in the Indonesian islands. They knew of the new route across the Indian Ocean, tried it successfully and thought that they could repeat the crossing in a straightforward way; but in May 1622 the *Tryall*, or *Trial*, a newly built English East India ship, still out in what seemed to be open water off Australia, ran aground on sharp rocks concealed beneath the waves, and began to break up. About two thirds of those on board, who may have numbered 150 souls, had to be left to their dismal fate after the captain and other crew members used the ship's two small boats to reach Java. *Trial* proved to be an appropriate name: its captain, John Brookes, was accused of negligence – of failing to post a watch, of concealing the evidence that the ship was off course, and of abandoning most of the crew to a certain death. It seems that he lied about the location of these rocks, which meant that they remained a hazard to shipping for a couple of centuries. Disputes about what had happened and about how far Brookes was liable generated vast reams of paper, and reached the highest court in the land, the House of Lords. However, the evidence is even richer than that: a wreck found off Western Australia in 1969 by not terribly scrupulous treasure-hunters is probably that of the *Tryall*, and exploration of the site, sometimes conducted with explosives rather than with a trowel, yielded anchors and cannon. If this is another ship, then it only proves that Brookes's refusal to indicate exactly where the dangerous rocks lay had further tragic consequences long after his own death in poverty and obscurity. The leader of the team who found the wreckage, Alan Robinson, became known as the 'gelignite buccaneer'. He was arrested for interfering with the site of the *Tryall*, found not guilty, and later arrested again for murder; by then he had had enough of life, and hanged himself in gaol.[26]

Knowledge of the continent gradually grew, as stretches of its northern coasts, around the Gulf of Carpentaria, were sketched; but none of the European visitors saw any profit in a desolate land inhabited by often hostile people who entirely lacked the luxurious sophistication of the native rulers encountered in Java. The most famous shipwreck, because of the high drama that followed, remains that of the *Batavia*, a VOC vessel that set out from Holland in October 1628, in a fleet of eight ships bound for Java. On board was the supercargo François Pelsaert, who was the brother-in-law of Brouwers, the man who had discovered the fast route to Java and was now a much-respected director of the VOC; and the ship carried 600 tons of cargo, including twelve chests full of silver with which to pay for the spices of the East Indies. Pelsaert was on his way to join the cabinet of the governor of Batavia, the irascible Jan Pieterszoon Coen, and there were whole families on board – about 300 people.[27]

The *Batavia* had become separated from the rest of the convoy, but the ship was confidently ploughing through the seas en route to Java in June 1629 when, during a night watch, the ship's lookout saw what he thought was surf spray. Since he knew they were nowhere near land, the captain decided that this was just an effect of the moonlight and that they should carry straight on – which bore the *Batavia* on to a coral reef. Pelsaert felt the keel and rudder grind against the reef; 'I fell out of my bunk,' he reported.[28] There was no hope for the ship; it could never be refloated or repaired, but it was not heading for the bottom of the sea quite yet, so there was time to prepare a proper evacuation of those who had not been washed overboard already, using the ship's boats. And the good news was that, with the dawn, scattered coral islands came into view, so that the whole day was spent ferrying the crew and passengers towards a couple of these islands. It was a slow process, and by the evening seventy people were still stuck on board the disintegrating ship. A few saved themselves by swimming to the coral islands, but many drowned; and the islands did not, in any case, have much to offer: there was wildlife, including both wallabies and pythons, but no water.

Desperate for a supply of water, Pelsaert and Jacobsz, the captain of the *Batavia*, spied out what seemed to be mainland, and took a longboat across to what was the western shore of Australia. They saw a few Aborigines, but found virtually nothing to drink:

> We there began to dig in various places, but the water was salt; a party went to the high land, there by luck they found some holes in a rock, where sweet water from the rain had been left . . . Here we quenched a little our great thirst, since we were almost at the end of our endurance, and since leaving the ship had had only one or two small measures a day.[29]

The problem was that the captain, the supercargo and their small group of men were moving further and further from the survivors camped near the wreck of the *Batavia*. They decided that they would head for Batavia, rather than the *Batavia*, in their longboat, report to Governor Coen and request help for the survivors. Coen, unimpressed by what had happened, flung the captain in gaol and sent Pelsaert back; the issue was not simply human lives, for the cargo of silver had been huge, and could not be left lying around for anyone in the world to pilfer. But Pelsaert and Jacobsz had deliberately put the recovery of people above the recovery of cargo; invoking God's name, they had drawn up an agreement in which they stated their 'utmost duty to help our poor companions in their distress', by appealing to the governor.[30]

Pelsaert's ship took a couple of months to find the survivors, arriving at the coral islands in September 1629. Pelsaert was not clear in his mind where the wreck lay, and the weather did not help. Remarkably, some of the crew and passengers were still alive. However, the conditions under which they lived were alarming, not just because of the inadequate supply of food and water. Pelsaert's deputy, Jeronimus Cornelisz, had taken charge and had gathered together on the largest atoll those he thought most reliable. Others were sent to outlying coral reefs, where the chances of surviving were thought to be slim (though some of them found quite generous supplies of food and water before long). That left him with 140 men, women and children under his command. Cornelisz saw every mouth that had to be fed as a liability. He unleashed a psychopathic reign of terror. It has been suggested that his fury stemmed from the fact that he belonged to an extreme wing of a dissident Protestant sect, the Anabaptists, and that he believed that the murder of ungodly folk was licit.[31] But this seems a weak explanation of his crazed behaviour. He would dress up in fancy robes, stolen from Pelsaert's sea chest, as if he were king of his little realm, while his followers adopted a uniform of red cloth trimmed with gold lace, all of which had been recovered from the hold of the wrecked ship.

Cornelisz's followers happily executed anyone who resisted his orders. A *Dominee*, or minister, of the Dutch Reformed Church was travelling out on the *Batavia* with his wife and seven children; most were massacred by Cornelisz's men, though the *Dominee* and one daughter were allowed to live, so long as they did not show any grief at what they had witnessed. The daughter was forced to enter into a mock marriage with one of Cornelisz's toughs, which at least guaranteed her survival; other women were made the common property of the gang, but the number of murders is thought to have reached 115. When Cornelisz discovered that about fifty of those he had sent to another island (now known as Hayes' Island) were surviving quite well, he launched an invasion, though he was captured and his men were nearly all killed. This did not stop his followers from waging war on the defenders of the other island. So when Pelsaert arrived he found chaos, death and stories of horrifying barbarity.[32]

It was not difficult to establish the truth. Cornelisz himself was recovered from captivity on Hayes' Island, where he was still wearing the grand robes that Pelsaert had brought along on the voyage. However, they were filthy by now: he had been kept in a hole in the ground, and was forced to pluck the feathers off birds captured for their food. As a result the beautiful robes were now covered in guano and bits of feather. He was sentenced to be executed, after his hands had been chopped off, and most of his troop of followers were hanged. Seventy-seven people deemed loyal to the VOC remained, to be taken to Batavia. There was another task to perform: Pelsaert set to work recovering the cargo of silver, and, remarkably, ten of the twelve chests were brought up from the sea. A couple of offenders, Pelgrom and Loos, who were guilty of appalling crimes, had somehow gained Pelsaert's mercy, perhaps because he wanted to show that he was quite unlike the vengeful and violent Cornelisz, and they were put ashore on the mainland, along with items of truck – bells, beads, wooden toys, mirrors – to be used in trade with the native population. They were ordered to search for information about sources of gold and silver, and to watch for any VOC ships that were passing, so they could send smoke signals and be picked up. This confirms that there was already regular traffic along the shores of Australia; it was just that the Dutch did not believe there was any profit to be found in the new continent.[33] His handling of the situation should have earned Pelsaert some credit, but instead he lost his place on the governor's council, and went off to fight the Portuguese in Sumatra, dying soon afterwards. As for Pelgrom and Loos, they never managed to hitch a ride on a VOC ship, and must have died somewhere along the coast of Western Australia, the first Europeans to inhabit this strange land.

The *Batavia* had an afterlife: its wreck was found in 1963, and the islands were explored, leading to the recovery of guns, coins and other bits and pieces from Hayes' Island, where a simple stone ruin is now celebrated as 'Australia's earliest European structure'. A number of skeletons have also been found, mostly in mass graves, and many of the bodies bear witness to the extreme violence of Cornelisz and his cronies: one victim was hit over the head with a sword by a right-handed attacker who stood directly in front of him. The sword left a two-inch mark on the victim's skull. The victim was unable to defend himself by raising his arms, which showed no cut marks, suggesting that he was tied up and awaiting execution. The preferred method of execution was to smash open the skull of the victim.[34] These remains of a ship and of murdered people stand as testimony not to an act of colonization, but to the passionate hope of those who resisted Cornelisz that before long they would be taken as far away from Australia as possible.

IV

The wrecking of the *Batavia* and other early experiences of Australia did nothing to encourage interest in a continent that would, nonetheless, soon become known as 'New Holland'. There was, on the other hand, quite a strong interest in mapping the shores of Australia, and in identifying reefs and shoals that could threaten ships plying along Brouwer's route; and that would mean more expeditions along its shores. Dutch ships even penetrated along the southern shores of Australia; in 1626 the ship beautifully named *'t Gulden Zeepaert*, 'The Golden Seahorse', reached what is now the state of South Australia, and its course was duly noted on VOC charts. This meant that half of the southern shoreline of Australia had been mapped.[35] Moreover, the assumption remained that a great southern continent would surely lie to its south, and would be a far more attractive place, with a temperate climate and plenty of riches worth exploiting. Australia, however, was seen as the very negation of the type of place that the Europeans hoped to exploit and colonize, a nightmare world inhabited by black folk who were caricatured as less than human, cannibalistic and (this at least was true) lacking any knowledge of the advanced technology that could be found in the East Indies, or even in the relatively undeveloped societies of the Polynesian islands.

Not surprisingly, then, the aim of two famous expeditions to Australia in the mid-seventeenth century was not the further exploration of the barren continent, but the continuing search for places where the Dutch could trade profitably, particularly a land supposedly rich in gold that had come to be known as 'Beach', a name whose origins went back to Marco Polo's fantasies about the Indies.[36] Abel Janszoon Tasman was a forty-year-old Calvinist who set out from Batavia on a wide sweep of southern latitudes in 1642. He enjoyed his drink; later in his career he was deprived of his command after he hanged a troublesome sailor while he was drunk, not bothering to go through the due process of a trial.[37] He came in sight of Tasmania, not realizing that it is a large island lying off the coast of Australia, and sailed around the bottom, demonstrating that this was not, alas, part of the great southern continent. He was keen to honour the governor-general of the Dutch Indies, so he named this land 'Anthonio van Diemens Landt' after him. He also claimed it for the Netherlands. There was no sight of the inhabitants, the Tasmanian Aborigines who were eventually wiped out by white Australians, but there was good evidence that the land was inhabited: sailors set on shore reported thick smoke rising out of the forest, and for some reason Tasman concluded that 'there must be men, of unusual height' – the usual tropes about giants, monsters and savages were being wheeled into place.[38] Southern Australia, like western Australia, was, frankly, a disappointment.

Slightly more promising was an accidental discovery further east, the other side of what has come to be known as the Tasman Sea. At the end of December 1642 his little fleet reached the northern tip of the South Island of Aotearoa (New Zealand). As soon as the Dutch ships arrived, two Māori canoes drew near; the Māori warriors on board kept challenging the Dutch, calling out to them and blowing on shell trumpets; the Dutch responded in kind, shouting, blowing their own trumpets and attempting to scare the Māoris by firing a cannon. Overnight things remained quiet, but the next morning a Māori catamaran set out to investigate the Dutch ships. Before long eight Māori boats were circling the ships. The first catamaran carried thirteen naked men; they must have been a formidable sight, covered in tattoos and clearly very hostile. The Dutch did try to send a small boat to shore, but one of the Māori canoes headed straight for the Dutch boat, ramming it; the Māori crew tussled with the Dutch sailors, clubbing and killing four Dutchmen, and carrying off their bodies. The Dutch would have assumed that the bodies were taken to be eaten, which is not impossible. The bay where these events happened was given the name 'Murderers' Bay' by an irate Tasman, though it is now known more politely as Golden Bay.[39] This bloody reception had the effect the Māoris had hoped for: the strange visitors in their massive boats left and headed north, not bothering to explore Aotearoa in any depth.

Tasman had been made aware that the people he was dealing with now were very different in appearance and style of life from the native Australians; but he failed to work out the shape of the two great islands of Aotearoa, and imagined that Cook Strait, which divides North from South Island, was simply a large inlet; but he did realize, on sailing north all the way to Fiji and Tonga, that wide watery spaces separate Australia from New Zealand, and therefore Australia must have an east coast that would link up with the areas already discovered by the Dutch. In other words, Australia is a continent, not a protrusion out of the southern continent. Tasman had no idea of the shape of New Zealand, since he only saw a little of South Island and the west coast of North Island, and his bitter experiences there did not encourage him to stay longer.[40] Even so, the islands began to be marked on Dutch maps by the middle of the seventeenth century, patriotically named after the Dutch province of Zeeland. Tasman took the view that he had arrived on the shores of the southern continent, and that the coastline further south trended all the way to South America, but somehow his reports did not convince the VOC that the Company needed to probe deeper. The VOC was apparently more struck by the similarities between Australia and New Zealand than by the differences between the two lands and the two sets of inhabitants.

These mediocre results were not disappointing enough to stop the VOC from commissioning a second voyage, in the hope of understanding how all the different pieces of coast that had been identified linked up, if at all. At the end of another uninspiring trip the verdict was confirmed:

> Thus they secured nothing advantageous, but only poor naked beach-runners, without riches, or any noteworthy fruits, very poor, and at many places bad natured men . . . Meanwhile this great Southland has been gone round by the aforesaid Tasman in two voyages and is reckoned to contain in it 8,000 miles of land as the charts drawn thereof, which we send to your Worships, make known. That such great land lying in various climes . . . shall have nothing of profit to find is scarcely acceptable.[41]

The attitude of the VOC was, then, entirely materialistic. Indeed, one of the tasks assigned to Tasman was the recovery of a treasure chest that had gone down with the *Batavia* – not that he managed to find the wreck or the castaways who had disappeared on land. The verdict of the VOC was typically ungenerous: thanks to Tasman and his predecessors the Dutch now had a fair idea of the dimensions and shape of Australia, the problem being that it was the wrong continent. There was still confusion, long after Torres's voyage, about whether Australia and New Guinea were joined together. A map of around 1690 drawn on fine Japanese paper and preserved in Sydney, known (through its provenance) as the Bonaparte map, reveals that the Dutch voyages to Australia did result in the mapping of its western, northern and southern coasts, and there was clearly an assumption that the eastern coast was not too dissimilar.

Tasman's voyages were important in the mapping of the south Pacific and the northern edges of the Southern Ocean, but they were based on false premises about the southern continent, and the discovery of both Tasmania and Aotearoa was in many respects accidental: Tasman simply came upon these places. There is a striking contrast with the voyages of Captain Cook well over a hundred years later. Cook's voyages were seen as scientific endeavours: Joseph Banks and other scientists were on board; observation of the transit of Venus across the Sun was one aim, but accurate mapping of the Pacific was another. Cook carefully identified areas along the coast of Australia that had been neglected ever since the Dutch had arrived in that continent. He established that Aotearoa was not a spur sticking out of a vast Antarctic continent, but two large islands inhabited by a substantial Māori population. Although one motive was to search out land for British colonization, Cook was also commanded to look for the southern continent, even if many of the dreams of finding the golden realm of Beach had long ago evaporated.[42]

The story of the first European encounters with Australia and New Zealand differs markedly from the history of European encounters elsewhere in the world. Greed remained a powerful motive for exploration, and yet this was greed that neither country could satisfy – Aotearoa because of the hostility of its Māori inhabitants, and Australia because the land was too poor, dry and unproductive to attract interest. But in sailing as far as Aotearoa, Tasman had reached the last significant inhabited coastline as yet unvisited by Europeans. There were still icy lands empty of people to discover further to the south, and coastlines to map, but Europeans had now truly encompassed the entire world, even if the Māoris had no reason to feel grateful for their presence.

42

Knots in the Network

I

Sixteenth- and seventeenth-century maps exaggerated the size of the mid-Atlantic islands. It was hard to believe that places such as the Cape Verde Islands, the Azores and St Helena were mere dots on the ocean, when they possessed such importance as resupply stations for fleets crossing the Atlantic, or passing between the Indian Ocean and the Atlantic. As a result, Madeira might appear to be the same size as the area that now makes up New York State. Yet from a maritime perspective these were not such small territories: the Azores stretch across 360 miles, or 580 kilometres, so that ships in search of shelter were not exactly looking for a needle in a haystack. The islands were also places where it was not too difficult to collect goods from right across the world. Sailors expected to make a little money on the side by buying and selling the spices of the East as they travelled back home from the Moluccas or India by way of the Cape of Good Hope and the Portuguese islands of the Atlantic. In this way the Azores became an unlikely but useful source of tropical spices that the temperate islands themselves were incapable of producing; Brazilian sugar too was easy to obtain in the archipelagoes, as Brazil became the dominant source of high-quality sugar after 1600. Complex trade networks were created by Dutch and Portuguese merchants that exploited all the loopholes in the relatively light Portuguese system of control; Portuguese ships out of Brazil would arrive in the two major Azorean islands, Terceira and São Miguel, pleading that they had been forced into port by storms, or that they were fleeing from pirates. Then they would unload their sugar and despatch it directly to the Low Countries on other ships, without being subject to the customs duties they would have had to pay in Lisbon.[1]

The islands were home to very diverse communities: as well as Portuguese and Spanish settlers, the Atlantic islands were host to English,

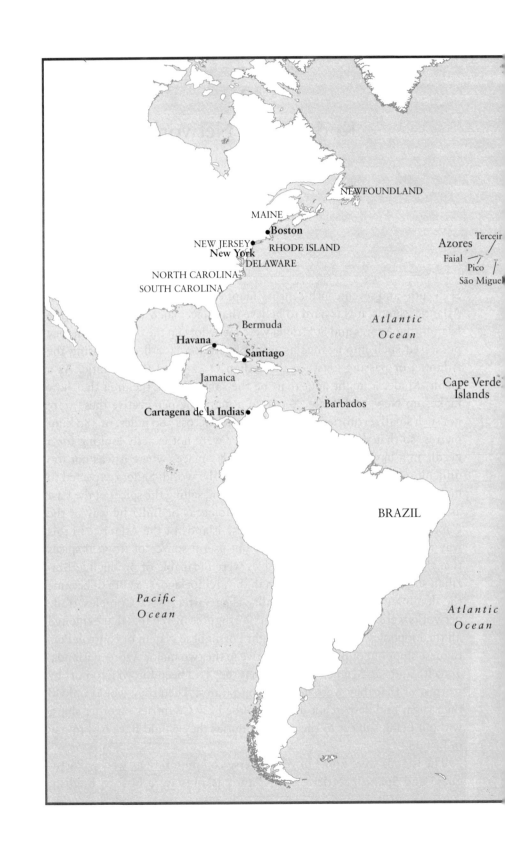

NEWFOUNDLAND

MAINE

●Boston

NEW JERSEY●
New York   RHODE ISLAND
DELAWARE

NORTH CAROLINA
SOUTH CAROLINA

Azores   Terceir

Faial
Pico
São Miguel

*Atlantic
Ocean*

Bermuda

Havana
●
Santiago

Jamaica

Cape Verde
Islands

Cartagena de la Indias●   Barbados

BRAZIL

*Pacific
Ocean*

*Atlantic
Ocean*

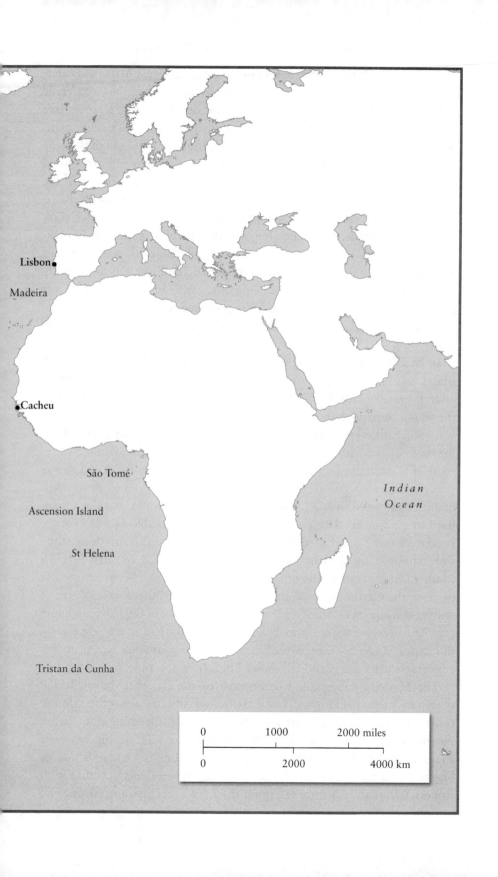

Lisbon

Madeira

Cacheu

São Tomé

Ascension Island

St Helena

Indian Ocean

Tristan da Cunha

| 0 | 1000 | 2000 miles |
| 0 | 2000 | 4000 km |

Scottish, Irish, Dutch, Flemish, Italian, German and west African inhabitants, the last group consisting mainly of slaves, although in the Cape Verde
Islands they mixed with the Portuguese and others to form a partly free
mulatto population.[2] However, the development of large-scale sugar plantations in Brazil, and then in the Caribbean, took the wind out of the sails
of Madeira and other Atlantic islands. The slave economy of Brazil suited
the back-breaking work that took place in the fields and furnaces of the
sugar estates. Transport costs were kept low by relying on mass-produced
Portuguese caravels for the shipping of Brazilian sugar. The Dutch took
a share of this trade, operating alongside the Portuguese, and again making use of cheaply built ships to reduce overheads. Brazil therefore became
a perfectly viable alternative to Madeira or São Tomé, with its notoriously
bad sugar. One measure of the decline of sugar in Madeira is that slaves
disappeared from the island, for their presence was a sure sign, within
the Atlantic world, that sugar or other highly intensive production was
under way.[3]

In Madeira, the hunt began for alternatives, but the rich soil of the
island was becoming exhausted after two centuries of intensive exploitation by sugar-planters. What saved Madeira was the product for which
the island remains famous: its wine. Seventeenth-century Madeira wine
was rather different to the rich dessert wine that is produced nowadays.
It was neither fortified nor nurtured for years into a fine vintage wine;
most of it was red plonk, drunk within a year of the harvest, but it was
very popular with sailors. There were some superior wines made in small
quantities from Malvasia (or Malmsey) and other grapes; but these were
hard to obtain. Yet Madeira wine had some remarkable characteristics.
It seemed to be unaffected by heat or transportation; if anything, they
were thought to improve the wine, and nineteenth-century English
Madeira enthusiasts would often demand wine that had been carried first
of all to the Caribbean or South America.[4] Besides, there were plenty of
willing consumers in Brazil and the West Indies, whom English merchants
supplied not just with slaves but with wine. Barbados was especially
thirsty for Madeira wines, while English settlers in Jamaica became major
consumers after the island fell under English rule in 1655.[5]

The Madeira wine trade was boosted by the fact that the island lay
within easy reach of England, but was also well situated along the Atlantic
trade routes, making it a useful loading point for ships bound for either
North or South America. So began the intimate relationship between
Madeira and England that remains unbroken. English business houses
began to flourish on Madeira, beginning in the late sixteenth century with
Robert Willoughby, whose safety on the island was guaranteed since he

was a Catholic – indeed, he became a Knight of the Portuguese Order of Christ. The seventeenth-century English colony included a good number of Protestants. There were frequent brushes with the Inquisition; however, it was obvious to the Portuguese authorities that the English colony was a valuable asset, so the Protestants mainly suffered insults.[6] In many ways their position was similar to that of the Portuguese New Christians, whose Jewish identity could conveniently be ignored when doing business. These English merchants often lived in some style, possessing agreeable *quintas*, or estates, away from the capital at Funchal. The bonds became closer as the English brought in cloth, which helped balance the cost of the wine they were taking out of the island. The looms of Devon and Essex hummed as English cloth displaced French and Flemish. A firm mutual relationship came into being.[7]

The English presence in Madeira is illuminated by the chance survival of letters written by a merchant from Warwick who traded actively between Madeira and the West Indies, as well as towards England, around 1700. William Bolton was the agent in Madeira of Robert Heysham, a London banker and merchant who had interests in Africa and who also owned lands in Barbados, where his partner and brother, William, functioned as official agent for the British planters.[8] 'African trade' in this period meant, above all, the trade in slaves, imported into the West Indies to work on sugar plantations. That, however, was not Bolton's speciality, even if the goods he sent to Barbados and Jamaica were no doubt paid for with profits from the sugar mills and the slave trade. Bolton's career shows how Madeira was locked into a much larger world than that of the eastern Atlantic. Quite apart from his connections with the Heyshams and Barbados, he found customers in Boston, New York, Rhode Island and Bermuda, and he loaded Madeira wines on to ships that passed the island bound for Brazil, India and the East Indies.[9] His activities also reveal how dependent Madeira had become on Europe for basic supplies, for the shift first to sugar and then to wine had turned the island into a place of monoculture, drawing its wheat from Holland, England, North America and the Azores, its meat and dairy goods from Scotland and Ireland, its fish from Scotland and Newfoundland, its woollen, silk and cotton goods from England. Particularly astonishing is the dependence of Madeira on the West Indies for supplies of the very product that had catapulted Madeira to fame in the fifteenth century, sugar; and timber, another prized export from the island in the days of Henry the Navigator, was now brought from the English colonies in North America.[10]

In mid-December 1695 William Bolton reported on the ships that stood off Madeira. A Portuguese vessel was loading plenty of wine for delivery in Brazil, and a Bristol ship was heading for the West Indies also carrying wine; a ship from New York was 'bound home with about 100 Pipes', approximately 5,700 litres.[11] In July 1696 Bolton described how 'a strang [*sic*] revolution in my affairs' took place: 'I was seized upon and putt into a wett dungeon'; and the complaints against him tell something about the priorities of the Portuguese government of Madeira – he was told by the governor himself that the English ships had stayed for too short a time during a recent visit, with the result that not enough wine could be shipped: 2,000 pipes remained unsold. But, he objected, some of these ships were West Indian and simply did not have the capacity to carry large amounts of wine.[12] In July 1700 he was already thinking ahead and keeping his partners in London well informed: 'We are like to have a plentiful Vintage: the weather is good and above half the vines are out of danger, soe that it wil be your advantage to send a ship to be here the latter end of December, or the beginning of January.' He insisted that 'our Vintage wil be large. The weather cannot be better. Now our hopes is only upon a good season to gather it.'[13] One visitor Bolton observed was the great astronomer Edmund Halley: a ship arrived in January 1699, and 'on borde her was M[r] *Halley*, the Mathematician, bound to the coast of *Brazil* and to the southward of ye *Cape*; his designe is to observe the variation of ye Compass'.[14] Bolton's letters thus expose to view a whole network of contacts mediated through Madeira, which became the meeting point for ships travelling to and from Portugal, the Netherlands, England, North America, the West Indies and Brazil.

II

Like Madeira, the Azores were particularly favoured by the English. Between 1620 and 1694, 279 ships are known to have put in at São Miguel, now the capital of the Azores. Well over half were English, while fewer than 10 per cent were Portuguese. Not just the ships were English: the major routes pointed to and from England, for the Azores, even more than Madeira, depended on the cloths of south-west England, such as the Taunton cottons that, despite their name, were made of wool.[15] The Azorean ports, such as Angra on the island of Terceira, could handle large merchantmen and men-of-war much better than Funchal in Madeira, where there was barely a harbour to speak of. Nor was this simply the story of a close relationship with Great Britain. England's American colonies benefited greatly from access to these Atlantic islands. Horta, on the island of Faial, developed intimate ties with the English possessions in North

KNOTS IN THE NETWORK

America during the seventeenth century. The wine of the neighbouring island of Pico, grown on the steep slopes of its volcano, and comparable to Madeira wines, was a great attraction. As Horta grew, so did its contacts with New England, and it was on its American business, rather than its European, that its flourishing economy was based, since the Bostonians often bought more Azorean than Madeiran wine, and then made a handsome profit redistributing it across the English colonies just at the moment when these colonies were being established along the east coast of North America – in Maine, New York, New Jersey, Delaware, North Carolina and South Carolina. The early newspapers of New York and Boston carried advertisements for wines brought from the Azores. Horta was also a vital stopping point for shipping bound from England to the West Indies.[16] One cannot understand the success of the English in creating a transatlantic network of maritime routes without taking into full account the role of the Azores.

There was, however, a fly in the ointment. East Indiamen would arrive ready to be resupplied with food before making the final leg of their long journey to Lisbon. As has been seen, Portuguese law forbade those on board from unloading their eastern spices and luxury goods, which were supposed to be sent all the way to Lisbon and then re-exported, if the Azoreans still wanted them. Naturally there were ways around this – smuggling, bribery, open defiance of the law. In 1649 a big, heavy ship called the *Santo André* was escorted into the port of Angra, on the island of Terceira, by English and Dutch allies of the Portuguese, since it was under threat from pirates and was carrying a very valuable cargo of cinnamon. Special permission was given to unload the spices but this cargo still needed to get to Lisbon, and the *Santo André* was twenty-six years old and not very seaworthy after its long voyage from the East Indies; besides, there were strong winds against which she would make little headway. The Portuguese therefore hired two English ships, and the precious cargo was divided equally among all three boats. They reached the mouth of the Tagus safely enough, but once again the wind was the obstacle. The English ships were small enough to work their way into Lisbon harbour, but the *Santo André* was a cumbersome galleon, and its master fled before the winds to the inlets off the coast of Galicia, the famous *rías*. But this was Spanish territory, and the Spanish king was still fighting what he regarded as an impudent rebellion by the Portuguese, who had broken free from the Habsburg dynasty nine years earlier. As a result, the galleon and its cargo were impounded, meaning that a good third of the cinnamon was lost to the enemy.[17]

Portugal was able to face up to its Spanish enemy thanks in part to the

support of the English and the Dutch. Angra became the base for merchants from all over Europe; the Dutch consul acted on behalf of other
nations as well, including Denmark, Sweden and Hamburg. Seventeenth-
century Angra has been described as 'one of the nodal points of Atlantic
maritime commerce'.[18] With its spacious harbour, overlooked by a massive
promontory that had already been heavily fortified by the Spanish Habsburgs, it was a safe retreat in times of tension and a much valued port in
times of peace.

III

There is a stark contrast between the lush Azores and the barren Cape
Verde Islands. Yet the existence of both archipelagoes made long-distance
oceanic navigation possible in an age when supplies of food were liable to
be exhausted in mid-voyage – no one could predict the time it would take
to battle against the winds and the waves until the coming of the steamship. The Cape Verde Islands provided goat meat, the flesh of the very
animals that had done most to strip the islands' vegetation bare; there
were cheese and butter made out of goat's milk; they offered salt in great
quantities, at virtually no cost; there were citrus fruits, even though European sailors were slow to make the connection between limes or lemons
and a cure for scurvy. These islands also played a significant role in the
transmission of African and European plants to the New World, including
yams and rice; the links between the Cape Verde Islands and Brazil had
been forged as early as the first half of the sixteenth century. The movement of plants went both ways: arriving by way of the Cape Verde Islands,
American maize became a favoured crop in west Africa, along with man-
ioc. It has been pointed out that this transmission took place within the
space of just a few years; but 'once a certain amount of diffusion had taken
place, it was self-perpetuating'.[19] It was also irreversible, part of a wider
process that transformed the domestic economy of each continent bordering the Atlantic – the example of the potato and its importance in the
nineteenth-century Irish economy hardly needs to be stressed.[20]

   By the 1680s enterprising English merchants were selling Azorean
wheat and Caboverdean salt to settlers in Newfoundland, who then used
this salt to process the cod in which that part of the Atlantic was so rich,
before the salted cod was passed back across the Atlantic to Spain and
Portugal, where *bacalao* remains a national dish to this day. The Cape
Verde Islands were also visited by East Indiamen, whose crews would
stock up with supplies before making the long haul around the Cape of

Good Hope to the Indies. From the sixteenth century onwards, this gave the islands a certain strategic interest; Francis Drake arrived in Santiago, the main island, in 1585, and ravaged its tiny capital, Ribeira Grande.[21] The Habsburg rulers of Portugal reacted by building the Fort of São Felipe, an imposing structure that still hangs high above the remains of the old town, looking far out to sea.[22] This did not protect the bays further east along the coast of Santiago, and other predators arrived, notably the Dutch, who briefly occupied Praia. However, there was not much to occupy. The islanders relied on imported knick-knacks from Europe, cheap ceramics and textiles, simple metal goods, as well as African pottery, some produced locally and some carried across from the Portuguese trading posts on the west coast of Africa.

The real source of prosperity for the Europeans living in or trading through Santiago remained African slaves.[23] As the sugar industry of Brazil took off in the late sixteenth century, the importance of the route past Santiago was magnified. In 1609–10 thirteen ships took something like 5,900 African slaves out of Ribeira Grande to a variety of destinations, Cartagena, in modern Colombia, being the favourite. However, this was just the official trade, and we can be sure that many more Africans were loaded on ships and sent across the Atlantic; the islands remained a useful entrepôt where slaves could be held for a while until slave-merchants came to collect them. Proof of this comes both from the fact that recorded numbers of slaves arriving in Santiago are lower than the numbers of those leaving, and from the fact that the slave cemetery excavated by archaeologists from Cambridge in Ribeira Grande contains the skeletons of so very many slaves who died on the island before being re-exported.[24] By the end of the seventeenth century some attempts had been made to protect slaves from abuse. They were to be baptized within six months of arrival, or else they would be forfeited, and they were to have time off on Sundays. Slaves bound for the Americas were to have a certain minimum space on board, and time for exercise on deck, as well as for instruction in their new faith. The Portuguese view was that their souls had a chance of salvation, so that being a Christian slave had clear advantages over being a free pagan.[25]

There were distinct advantages in picking up slaves in the islands rather than on the African coast. The Portuguese trading bases in west Africa such as Cacheu, inhabited by the so-called lançados, Portuguese often suspected of crime or heresy, built close ties to the courts of African rulers. Many were well assimilated into African society, with African mothers or wives and a good knowledge of both European and African culture. Some were of New Christian descent; local Muslim rulers and their economic usefulness to Portugal protected them from the long arm of the Inquisition. Since many of the Portuguese settlers in the Cape Verde Islands were also New Christians, there existed a natural kinship between the colonists on the islands and on the coast, a network of trust that helped to foster trade.[26] The *lançados* obtained trading privileges and knew what sort of gifts the African kings expected to receive in return for favours, for the kings could be very specific in their demands for weapons or brass goods. This was an art that the slave-merchants and sea captains, who were only transient visitors to these waters, could not be expected to develop.

Dealing with the *lançados* brought another benefit: they supplied the islands with the basic goods that the islands found it hard to produce, such as palm wine and millet. These were required at least to feed the slave population. And the *lançados* were happy to send these goods in payment for the worldwide manufactures that were popular among the west African elites: Europe sent red cloth of Portugal, metal bracelets, buttons, Venetian glass beads; the New World sent silver coins; the Indies sent coral, cloves and cotton, though these were often re-exported through Lisbon.[27] All these goods passed through the Cape Verde Islands, reinforcing their role as a key entrepôt between Africa and the rest of the world. Islanders of African descent began to weave cotton cloths in the African fashion, often coloured blue and white and copying traditional African designs. These cloths, or *barafulas*, were similar to but often better in quality than west African ones; they were produced for the African market, making it possible to exchange Caboverdean products for the captive humans of west Africa. The whole process was helped further by the planting of indigo in the islands, where it flourished. The *barafulas* were used as standard currency (the American silver coins were melted down and turned into jewellery in west Africa). The use of cloths as currency defeated the bureaucrats of Lisbon, who expected customs dues to be paid in coin, with the result that many merchants simply failed to pay their taxes.[28]

The Portuguese rebellion against Habsburg rule in 1640 posed the usual problem that political freedom was one thing, but the risks to prosperity were quite another. The solution was simple: that year, the Portuguese government decreed that Spanish ships could continue to visit both the Cape Verde Islands and Guinea, so long as they arrived from the New World, so long as they deposited a financial guarantee in Lisbon and so long as they paid for the slaves with American silver. This led to a lucrative trade with places such as Havana. Either side of 1640 the slave trade continued to bring profit (and to inflict massive misery): taking the seventeenth century as a whole, 28,000 slaves are known to have passed through the Cape Verde Islands, which is definitely not the full total.[29]

These archipelagoes were not simply part of a Portuguese network but part of a global one. Without the Azores and the Cape Verde Islands it is hard to see how not just the Portuguese but the Spanish and English commercial networks would have functioned reasonably efficiently during the seventeenth century. At the same time, one cannot close one's eyes to the horrors that this trade inflicted on the innocent human cargoes that passed through the Cape Verde Islands towards the Americas.

IV

Far beyond the Cape Verde Islands lay other isolated peaks sticking up out of the southern Atlantic Ocean, uninhabited by humans or by mammals until the arrival of the Europeans: St Helena, Ascension Island and Tristan da Cunha. Historians of St Helena in particular have noticed that this island, mainly known to history as the last abode of Napoleon, had an importance out of all proportion to its size, for what really mattered was its location on the sea routes to and from India; the takeover of the island by the English East India Company reflected a carefully constructed policy of creating stepping stones across the oceans, in the awareness that without resupply the routes across the high seas were quite simply unmanageable. Oddly, the island had been known to European navigators since the Feast of St Helen in May 1502, and it was visited again the next year by Vasco da Gama on his return from his second Indian voyage. St Helena may be tiny; but it was impossible to miss: heading out across the Atlantic from the Cape of Good Hope 'the wind is very constant and carries you in sixteen days into St Helen's road'.[30]

The Portuguese realized that this island could serve its India fleets well, without the need to create a colony there on the model of Madeira or the Azores; they actually discouraged long-term settlement, for they knew that such a remote place would be impossible to control from Lisbon. They wanted to keep St Helena out of the public eye, all the more so as the English and the Dutch began to navigate to and from the Indies. They had not learned from their experiences in the Cape Verde Islands, for they populated the island with goats. At least one Portuguese resident settled there voluntarily in 1516. Fernando Lopez was well born, but was arrested in Goa for desertion and was brutally punished by having his ears, nose, left thumb and entire right hand cut off. Understandably he avoided human company, preferring his pet chicken, but he did some business with visiting ships, selling the skins of the goats he had captured for his dinner with his four remaining fingers.[31]

Aware of the value of this island as a source of fresh food, the Dutch began to prey on Portuguese shipping off St Helena at the end of the sixteenth century. The *Witte Leeuw*, or *White Lion*, a Dutch East Indiaman, attacked Portuguese ships off St Helena in 1613. This proved to be an act of hubris: a cannon exploded on board, and the powder room then blew up, leading to the loss of a hundred tons of pepper and a large cargo of fine Chinese porcelain, some of which has been recovered from the sea and is preserved in the island's museum.[32] This was the prelude to Dutch attempts to push the Portuguese out of the island, without, however, taking direct control. The idea that it could continue to function as a resupply centre, to all intents a neutral territory, still found favour. This was not the view of the English. In 1656 Oliver Cromwell was persuaded by the English East India Company that the Company's trade with the Indies would take off once England took charge of St Helena – 'a halfway house in the midst of a great ocean', as a French traveller described it in 1610. St Helena had already been visited by Cavendish as he headed back into the Atlantic on his round-the-world cruise. He was greatly impressed, for by now he was glad to see melons, lemons, oranges, pomegranates and figs, streams of fresh water, big fat pheasants and partridges, and goats and pigs brought there by the Portuguese.[33] Oliver Cromwell's son and momentary successor, Richard Cromwell, granted the EIC a charter giving it authority to 'settle, fortifie and plant' the island. The EIC thought of St Helena as a base from which to launch expeditions towards the fardistant Moluccan island of Run, which they still dreamed of recovering from the Dutch right up to the exchange agreement of 1667 that sacrificed Run for Manhattan.[34]

Defeated in the Moluccas, the EIC was nonetheless disinclined to let go of St Helena, for the island was thought to have real potential. The quality of its fresh water attracted wonder, making the island 'an earthly paradise'.[35] It was assumed that 'plants, rootes and grains and all other things necessarie for plantation' would transform its lush but wild environment, while fish swarmed in the waters round about, and even the wild grasses provided wondrous cures for 'sailors just dead with scurvy', who would 'recover to a miracle' and bounce back into life. Using plants brought from the Cape Verde Islands, St Helena became a garden island where fruits and roots from across the world were cultivated: from the Americas cassava and potatoes, from Europe oranges and lemons, from Africa plantains, from India rice, all intended to make the island selfsufficient, since a settled population would require rather more than the limited list of items needed for the resupply of passing ships. The animal population was boosted by sending cattle and sheep as well as chickens. Even so, at the start of English colonization, it was difficult to obtain agricultural knowhow. Four free planters could be found on the island in the 1660s; inevitably, the hard work planting and harvesting the new crops was carried out by black African slaves, who were permitted to cultivate their own plots of land, and produced promising yields. This was an island that suffered from underpopulation, not overpopulation: in 1666 there were fifty male inhabitants, twenty women, and six slaves. Male and female slaves were regularly brought from the Cape Verde Islands; Madagascar slaves were specially prized by the English and were taken as far as Barbados, where they trained as highly skilled artisans. It was hoped they could be equally useful on St Helena.[36] In 1673, 119 colonists set out from England, following an abortive Dutch invasion of the island. Some of them were reasonably well-off, with servants of their own, or black slaves. By 1722 the population had reached 924, more than half of whom were free; and of those the majority were women and girls.[37]

The settlers were not a passive body of people, willing to take orders from the EIC. St Helena was a turbulent place in the late seventeenth and eighteenth centuries, as its governors, its garrison, its free planters and its slaves clashed with each other. The colonists held a majority on the island council for a few years, but from the moment the English took control of the island its governors were not inclined to pay the council much attention, and back in London the directors of the EIC were well aware that this high-handed treatment of the settlers was counterproductive. In 1684 the governor responded to an uprising by the settlers by ordering his soldiers to shoot at the rebels, killing some of them; and then others were taken prisoner and executed. Another governor was assassinated. The slaves rose up in rebellion. The leading historian of this island has pointed out that it was only ever a Utopia on paper; theory and reality stood far apart.[38]

The East India Company wanted to keep St Helena for its own exclusive use, and that did not simply mean defending the island against the Dutch or other foreign rivals. Even other English companies were discouraged from making use of the island. This was the EIC's link to India, not England's link, even if it had been established by a charter of the Lord Protector himself. Not for nothing was St Helena known as 'The Company's Island'. In 1681 the EIC resolved that slave ships coming from Madagascar or the adjacent coasts of Africa would be made welcome, if they touched at the island for supplies or were in distress. However, the governors discouraged non-Company ships from attempting to trade. The

Roebuck, an English slaver, reached St Helena in spring 1681, having lost forty of its 346 slaves to disease; sickness had also taken hold of the crew. Medical help was offered, but the governor forbade the sailors to carry on any trade, to the intense annoyance of the planters.[39] Yet this policy was consistent with the monopolistic outlook of the Company.

The EIC hoped to extend its monopoly even further by taking control of another remote south Atlantic island, Tristan da Cunha, although the weather there was worse even than on St Helena and the island was even more barren.[40] The motive was control of the sea routes into the Indian Ocean, and also looking westwards towards Brazil, though Tristan da Cunha stands a little south of the latitude of the Cape of Good Hope, a long way down from St Helena, which lies roughly on the latitude of the border between modern Angola and Namibia. Tristan was not occupied by the British until 1816, although the first attempt to colonize the island took place in 1684, when the English ship *Society* was despatched there with orders to conduct a survey; the East India Company was keen to learn how good its harbours might be. There, or on other promising but empty islands, the ship's captain was to leave a boar and two sows and a letter in a bottle, which was deemed sufficient evidence to establish an English claim to the territory. By the early nineteenth century British enthusiasm for this utterly remote volcanic island had reached the point where it was compared favourably to Funchal, the main town of Madeira, 'from the circumstance of its being a straight shore'; there was sufficient land for cultivation and there were good supplies of fresh water.[41]

St Helena and Tristan da Cunha, and even the archipelagoes much further north, were not simply Atlantic bases. They were tied as closely to the Indian Ocean as to the Atlantic. Just as the oceans flowed into one another, their trade routes were inextricably intertwined.

V

It may seem strange to include the fourth largest island in the world, Madagascar, among these dots on the map, but there are good reasons for doing so: a few points along its coasts were initially seen as potential points for the resupply of ships; and, although it does not lie in the Atlantic, it was seen as a valuable link between the Indian Ocean and the Atlantic, reinforcing the sense that merchants, pirates and indeed governments did not employ the rigid divisions between oceans that tend to be applied nowadays, above all among historians.[42] Later, as the idea of settling larger tracts of the island took hold, the assumption grew that this was a more attractive version of Asia, rather than Africa; the full title of a widely circulated pamphlet by 'Richard Boothby, merchant', published in London in 1646 and reprinted the next year, was *A Breife Discovery or Description of the Most Famous Island of Madagascar or St Laurence in Asia neare unto East-India; with relation of the healthfulnesse, pleasure, fertility and wealth of that country, also the condition of the natives: also the excellent meanes and accommodation to fit the planters there.* Another tract by an Englishman who knew the island well was enthusiastically entitled *Madagascar, the Richest and most Fruitfull Island in the world*; and the author was especially charmed by the 'loving and affable condition' of the people – indeed, in another pamphlet he called them 'the happiest people in the world'.[43] These were some of the many manifestos that praised an island that, in truth, the Europeans did not know well, but one that was much more easily accessible by way of the Cape of Good Hope than Sumatra, let alone the Moluccas. The hope was raised that Madagascar could be a substitute for the East Indies, a new Asia away from Asia proper. As usual, optimism turned to disappointment when the Europeans encountered areas of dry, red earth that seemed to extend for ever. On the other hand, there was truth in the idea that this was a world apart from Africa – a miniature continent, with its own extraordinary wildlife and its historical links right across the Indian Ocean.

The Portuguese had reached Madagascar in 1500, and they found that the island lay under the authority of several different kings. They also found that it was already well connected with the outside world through major east African ports such as Mombasa. In 1506 they conducted a raid on a Malagasy port; it did not produce gold or ivory, but there was so much rice that it would fill twenty ships. These contacts brought Islam as well as goods to Madagascar, but Islam failed to make a strong impact on the island, even though some Muslim practices, such as circumcision and avoidance of pork, became quite widespread. The same applied to Hinduism, whose influence trickled along the trade routes that had brought the first Malay sailors to the island during the Middle Ages; but again it remained weak, and the main cult consisted of ancestor worship (which could, according to some accounts, involve the ceremonial display of ancestors' corpses and even their consumption).[44] Although it became obvious that conquering the island was out of the question, the Europeans exploited the wars between local kings, just as they always had in west Africa, to secure a supply of slaves, which they exchanged for European textiles and cattle. Some of the kings had more upmarket tastes: Dian Ramach had been educated in Portuguese Goa, so it is not surprising that he showed off a lacquered throne made in China, a Japanese vase and both Persian and European robes.[45]

Slaves were the main 'product' of the island in which the Europeans took an interest. As in west Africa, there was a world of difference between the harsh regime to which the great majority of exported slaves would find themselves subjected, whether in Indian Ocean colonies or across the Atlantic, and the much looser style of slavery on the island, a light version of serfdom that only turned vicious when rulers and nobles decided to sell their unfree subjects to the Europeans.[46] Malagasy slaves accounted for a small percentage of the number of slaves who were carried across the high seas by European merchants, less than 5 per cent of slaves traded by Europeans in the Indian Ocean, and a small fraction of those traded in the Atlantic. By comparison, over 2,800,000 slaves are believed to have been transported out of west and central Africa just on English ships during the seventeenth and eighteenth centuries.[47] However, the Malagasies were valued for their intelligence and skills (while their distant relatives, the Malays, were deemed to be too lazy and unreliable); in Barbados, English planters took the view that Malagasy slaves were the 'most ingenious of any Blacks', well suited to be trained as carpenters, blacksmiths or coopers. The East India Company sought 'lusty well-grown boys' on Madagascar – the term 'lusty' being used here without sexual connotations.[48]

However, there was another advantage to Madagascar beyond resupply and the slave trade: piracy. At the end of the seventeenth century, local kings actively tolerated the presence in coastal ports of European pirates, as well as pirates from the English colonies in North America. Well-armed pirates could be recruited to take part in wars between rival kings. And the reason they were well armed was that far away in the Atlantic – as far away as New York – friendly merchants could be found who were keen to supply them with arms as well as strong drink. Casks of beer and spirits were sent all the way from America, despite the objections of the East India Company and the Royal African Company in London. Meanwhile the pirates, who were variously of English, Dutch, French and – interestingly – African descent, supplied Malagasy slaves to willing buyers.[49]

The American backers of these pirates were men of significance back in New York. Frederick Philipse, of Dutch descent, was one of its wealthiest citizens; and, hearing that a pirate named Adam Baldridge had abandoned his old business, piracy in the Caribbean, and had taken up residence on St Mary's Island, off the north-east coast of Madagascar, he saw a golden opportunity to send him supplies in return for Malagasy slaves. Philipse and Baldridge had bought a winning ticket: once the base on St Mary's was up and running, with hundreds of people living in the settlement, all the pirate vessels active in the western Indian Ocean began to call in there for supplies. Baldridge did particularly good business by selling on rum and beer at an appreciable mark-up. Yet he also imported bibles from North America, a reminder that many pirates saw no contradiction between robbery on the high seas or the enslavement of fellow humans and the Christian life. As the settlement expanded, so did the Malagasy population; and while Baldridge was away from St Mary's late in 1697, on a local slaving expedition, the islanders living in the town rebelled, tearing down the fort he had built and killing about thirty of the pirates. Baldridge abandoned St Mary's, and later he would complain that the revolt had taken place because the Europeans had no idea how to treat the islanders gently. But William Kidd, a famous Scottish pirate who was later to hang for his crimes, thought that Baldridge was making excuses for his own mistreatment of the Malagasy inhabitants of his little town, since he would inveigle men, women and children on to his ship, before taking them captive and selling them as slaves to the Dutch in Mauritius and the French in Réunion (then known as Île Bourbon), the two Mascarene islands to the east of Madagascar which were being colonized just at this period.[50] Maybe, then, there were other pirates like Kidd who did read their bibles and did have a conscience.

Some pirates valued their Malagasy slaves highly and appointed them as cooks on board ship, where they occupied positions of some responsibility; making sure that food did not run out and that as much fresh food as possible was served was an important task. One such cook was Marramitta, who was appointed by his master, none other than Philipse, as cook aboard the *Margaret*. His real name is unknown, for 'Marramitta' appears to be a corruption of the Malagasy word for 'cooking-pot', *marmite* in modern French. Malagasy slaves were dispersed across the world. The English East India Company made use of Malagasy labour when it built a fort at its pepper factory in Sumatra, at Bencoolen, towards the end of the seventeenth century. Once there, quite a few headed off into the jungle, no doubt able to take advantage of the fact that they spoke a language not too dissimilar to Malay–Indonesian. But the Atlantic also received increasing numbers, often via a holding station on St Helena.[51] As early as 1628 a slave from Madagascar arrived in the new French colony of Quebec; and at the end of the century ships loaded with slaves were regularly reaching New York. However, the growing cities of North America were less frequent destinations than the islands of the Caribbean, particularly Barbados and Jamaica, or the English settlements in Virginia and the Carolinas. In 1678 three ships out of Madagascar delivered 700 slaves to Barbados, where the intensification of sugar production (with the high mortality this industry produced) led to greater and greater demand for slaves not just from west Africa. By 1700 something like 16,000 slaves on Barbados were Malagasy, about half the total; and just one port in Madagascar is thought to have exported between 40,000 and 150,000 slaves during the seventeenth century.[52] The good news, if it can be called that, is that mortality on English ships carrying Malagasy slaves was low.[53] This may reflect the quality of supplies they were fed, loaded in Madagascar, at the Cape or in St Helena; and it may also reflect the fact that they were often transported in relatively small ships, which reduced the danger of epidemics: average cargoes in the eighteenth century were sixty-nine slaves. In 1717 the Board of Directors instructed the East India agents on St Helena to treat slaves 'humanely', pointing out that 'they are Men'.[54] And, after all, slavers wanted to deliver their human cargo alive; a dead slave meant financial loss.

43
The Wickedest Place on Earth

I

When looking at the centuries after Columbus and da Gama, this book has laid an emphasis on the links between the oceans. The flow of people and goods from one ocean to another created a series of connections, wrapped right around the world, that can justifiably be described as a global network. Whether one would want to call this a global economy is a less straightforward question, since the term 'global economy' might indicate an economy in which global connections moulded the activities of a high percentage of merchants, craftsmen and consumers in all the major centres of economic power, from China to England to the Spanish cities in the New World. The careers of the English and other pirates who plagued the Caribbean in the middle of the seventeenth century may seem a rather unimportant issue, despite the enormous fascination that pirates of the Caribbean have generated among film-makers and film-goers. However, the passage of treasure ships through the Caribbean is not simply a story of Caribbean, or at best Atlantic, history. Bearing in mind the origin of much of this bullion, the Potosí silver mines in Peru (now in Bolivia), and the route the silver had already taken along hundreds of miles of Pacific water to reach the isthmus of Panama, the history of the silver routes shows clearly how the different oceans were bound together by the sixteenth and seventeenth centuries. Nor should it be forgotten that much of this silver was being sent westwards, reaching Macau by way of Manila. In the seventeenth century, though, production was declining and Spain was financially overstretched thanks to its heavy involvement in European and Mediterranean conflicts. The failure of a treasure fleet to arrive, following raids by English pirates, was a bruising blow to a failing empire.

These pirates certainly existed, although many of them are better described as privateers, armed with official letters of marque entitling them to attack the ships of enemy powers, than as freebooters.[1] The term that

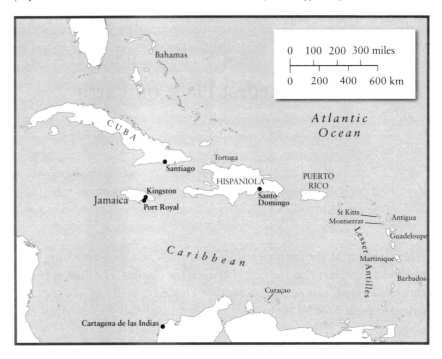

came into use to describe the Caribbean pirates was 'buccaneers', derived from the French word *boucan*, which meant the grill on which they would smoke large slabs of meat, often cut from the sides of animals they had rustled in Hispaniola and other Spanish islands, which were now depopulated of Taíno Indians and heavily populated instead with roaming cattle, easy to find and wholesome to eat. The term 'corsairs', derived from *corso*, 'journey', is usually reserved for a quite different class of pirate, the Barbary corsairs who infested the western Mediterranean and eastern Atlantic waters.[2] It is true that the pirates of the Caribbean tied red cloths around their heads, wielded cutlasses and drank plenty of rum, and that they preferred a rather democratic system of command according to which the ship's captain lived and slept among his men, and decisions were made by consultation.[3]

Nonetheless, the pirates and privateers served the interests of higher powers even when, like Henry Morgan, famous for his raid on Panama, they went about their business without taking direct instruction from above. They were valuable instruments in the creation of a permanent English presence in the Caribbean from the middle of the seventeenth century onwards; they shared with the Lord Protector, Oliver Cromwell, and then the king, Charles II, the ambition of interrupting the Spanish treasure fleets bringing silver from Veracruz in Mexico and Porto Bello in

Panama to Cádiz and the coffers of the Habsburg kings of Spain. Successful piracy depended, however, on maintaining a watchful balance between the capture of treasure ships and their free passage through the Caribbean. The principles underlying this approach were once explained by an economist who developed 'The Pure Theory of the Muggery'. Just as a fishing fleet has to take care not to overfish so that no resources are left behind, a mugger, or equally a pirate, has to ensure that streets or seaways are sufficiently clear to permit most people to pass. Winning too many prizes results in abandonment of the route by those the pirate hopes to despoil. If the route is too dangerous, like Central Park, New York, at 3 a.m., it will be abandoned entirely by potential victims. Equally, the pirate, or the mugger, or indeed the fisherman, has to ensure that competitors are kept at bay.[4]

The idea that piracy remained a constant scourge in the Caribbean needs to be qualified. Licensed piracy aimed at Spanish ships was a serious problem between 1655 and 1671, but after that the problem receded, partly because the English and the Spaniards had hammered out a peace agreement, and partly because the passage of the treasure ships had become intermittent, with several years at a time going by during which no silver ships left Mexico or Panama. The Spanish navy was by now so poorly supported at home that Spain could not always provide ships to carry the bullion to Spain, and there were even occasions when Dutch ships had to be hired to do the job. Returns from raids on treasure ships were, therefore, sinking. Moreover, the major English base in the Caribbean, at Port Royal on the coast of Jamaica, was largely destroyed by an earthquake and tsunami in June 1692. This is not to deny that outbreaks of piracy recurred. Piracy was rather like the plague: it came in waves, but was generally a low-level threat. To give one example: in the first few years of the eighteenth century, the Bahamas became a nest of pirates, what has been described as a 'buccaneer republic'. But once a British governor was in place (himself a former privateer) he offered an amnesty to those who were willing to change their ways, and set them against those who were not. Within a few years the pirate plague was at an end.[5]

II

The acquisition of Jamaica by the English is a good example of Sir John Seeley's dictum that the British Empire was acquired 'in a fit of absence of mind'. Yet it was not the first English colony in western Atlantic waters, even if it became one of the most important ones. Sir Walter Raleigh's attempt to create a colony at Roanoke on the coast of North Carolina during the 1580s had ended with the mysterious disappearance of its settler population.[6] More enduring was the Jacobean colony at Jamestown, founded in 1607 in Virginia, which gave the English their first permanent foothold in North America, over a century after Cabot's first voyage, but only a year after a legal ban on the right to emigrate was abolished.[7] One accidental spin-off from the establishment of Jamestown was the settlement of Bermuda, briefly visited a century earlier by a Portuguese seaman named Bermudez. In 1609 an English ship caught in a hurricane while bound for Virginia collided with rocks off Bermuda; no one drowned but some of the sailors and passengers kept insisting that they would rather stay there than return home once their ship had been repaired – there was even a meat supply, since wild pigs infested the island, having survived an earlier shipwreck. When the Virginia Company back in England heard about this, they seized at once on the attractions of an island that had no previous inhabitants (unlike Virginia) and whose contours had been carefully mapped by the castaways, whereas much of the Virginian hinterland was still *terra incognita*.

It took three years, starting in 1612, to despatch 600 settlers to Bermuda, aboard nine vessels. Bermuda proved to be very suitable for tobacco cultivation, and lumps of ambergris, the enormously valuable secretion from the bile duct of whales, were sometimes washed up on its shores. Soon after settlement began, a large lump worth £12,000 secured the financial future of the new colony. It became the first English colony to make use of African slave labour. However, planters on other English islands learned how to produce far superior tobaccos, and the islanders on Bermuda shifted their attention to food production, first cattle and then sugar. Out of that, by the early eighteenth century, a lively exchange market sprang up, with North American grain and timber passing through Bermuda to the Caribbean, and Caribbean sugar and rum passing the other way. The ships the Bermudians used were put together on the island, built and sailed by slaves as well as free men. These mainly small but fast sloops became a familiar sight in North American ports, which, rather than Great Britain, were before long the focus of the island's trade; the Bermudians also ran their ships down to Dutch Curaçao and all around the Dutch Caribbean. Bermuda's success as a centre of exchange was extraordinary: its ship movements compared well with those of New York and Jamaica, though they fell some way behind Barbados, of which more shortly.[8]

James Evans has pointed out that during the seventeenth century almost 380,000 Englishmen and women migrated to the Americas; a majority,

200,000, headed for the Caribbean. This far exceeded migration by rivals: Spanish migration to the Americas reached about half that of the English, while the number of French migrants was minute, one fortieth of those from England. The figures are all the more remarkable because there was a similar flow out of England towards Ireland.[9] These figures are also greater than those from the eighteenth century. There were many factors driving people across the Atlantic: poverty at home, the wish to practise one's faith without interference, the search for wealth, as rumours of gold continued to spread, notwithstanding Frobisher's fiasco with fool's gold. The sailing of the *Mayflower* with 100-odd passengers has become part of the American national myth, so it is important to remember that most colonists were not Puritan idealists; those in Britain and Europe who remain mystified by the American cult of 'Thanksgiving' are right to wonder how important this voyage really was.[10]

In Virginia, moneymaking opportunities opened up for reasons quite other than gold-digging: the fashion for tobacco had created a seemingly inexhaustible demand for a product that was supposed to have impressive health-giving properties.[11] At first the labour force consisted of indentured servants, English migrants who sought a route out of poverty by signing away their freedom in return for food, clothing and a roof over their head, so that one third of the settler population in Virginia consisted of these people in the middle of the century. The notoriously cold seventeenth century saw several severe famines, particularly in the 1630s, encouraging emigration. This 'Little Ice Age' was a global phenomenon, however: on arrival in North America, conditions were also still unusually cold at this period. Even so, the risk of crossing the sea and of living in a land where unfamiliar and untamed diseases wiped out perhaps half the settlers within a few years of their arrival could seem a risk worth taking.[12]

The Caribbean was a different sort of success story to Virginia. England acquired Barbados, on the outermost edges of the Caribbean, in 1625 after Captain John Powell arrived there and planted the English flag in what had once been a flourishing native settlement, but was now empty of people: the Spaniards had not bothered to occupy the island, and had used it as a source of slaves, since the warlike and probably cannibalistic people they knew as Caribs were treated as legitimate foes of the Spanish Crown; the exasperated inhabitants decamped to other, less exposed points in the Lesser Antilles where they could defend themselves better.[13] That did not solve their problems, as the English had already installed themselves on St Kitts in 1624, at the price of having to fight a war with the Caribs for mastery over the island, which was given over to tobacco plantations. There was much to learn: a hurricane wrecked the first crop. Then England took charge of Antigua and Montserrat eight years later. Meanwhile the French occupied Guadeloupe and Martinique, as each European nation that followed in Spain's wake took advantage of the Spanish failure to establish control of the smaller islands; inevitably this led to bitter battles with the warlike Caribs, and the ruthless extinction of Carib communities.[14]

In Barbados, on the other hand, attempts to grow tobacco were not particularly successful. The economy took off when Sir James Drax observed the success of the sugar plantations that were spreading across the Dutch and Portuguese colonies in South America. Drax brought Sephardic Jews from Dutch Brazil to help him set up the industry. The result of the sugar boom was that the island attracted plenty of English settlers, 2,000 by 1657 just in the new capital, Bridgetown, which attracted admiring comments from a French Catholic missionary: the houses 'have an appearance of dignity, refinement and order, that one does not see in the other islands and which indeed it would be hard to find anywhere'.[15] In this period, Barbados was already able to export 8,000 tons of sugar to England each year; in the early eighteenth century the sugar output of the small Caribbean islands under English rule exceeded that of Brazil. Barbados became England's sugar island, just as Madeira had once been Portugal's. In the early days, the human cost was lighter than it became. About half of those who arrived from England were indentured servants; there were 13,000 servants, mostly young men but also some women, in Barbados in 1652, with an annual flow of roughly 1,500 to 3,000 into the island. It cost up to £8 to bring a servant across the Atlantic, which in mid-century was a cheaper option than buying slaves, the price for which hovered somewhere around £35 – although indentured servants were not slaves and were treated much better than black slaves. As slave prices fell and the numbers volunteering for indentured labour also fell, the slave plantation became the norm, and a new elite of planters emerged, seventy-four of whom appeared in an official list submitted to London in 1673.[16]

Throughout the eighteenth century Barbados continued to satisfy Britain's craving for sugar – and continued to import the enormous numbers of slaves who made that possible, in unspeakable conditions. The English taste for sweet tea helped fuel the expansion of production. Thus the Barbadian sugar producers were in part responding to demand created by the tea trade out of China, another example of the way what happened in one ocean could have a powerful impact on what happened in another. Barbados became the model for other sugar-producing islands: for English Jamaica, but also for the French settlement that was established in 1665 at the western end of Hispaniola, known as Saint-Domingue, the lineal ancestor of modern Haiti. Curiously, these cases apart, the 'sugar revolution' in the Caribbean took off not in the islands settled by Columbus but in the new colonies of the English, the French and the Dutch – Columbus's attempts to cultivate sugar on Hispaniola had faltered once the Portuguese brought sugar to Brazil. Spanish Cuba and Puerto Rico only became major producers much later, during the nineteenth century (though still thanks to slavery, which continued to exist on the islands).[17] In each of the islands, slave labour became the source of the colonists' prosperity. Yet the slaves were not politically passive. In 1675 and again in 1692 slaves plotted to seize Bridgetown and take control over the island and over the ships in its harbour. Both conspiracies were discovered in time, and ninety-three conspirators were executed in 1692.[18]

III

The short but turbulent history of Port Royal began as a result of a series of mistakes. In 1655 Oliver Cromwell, Lord Protector of the Commonwealth of England, Scotland and Ireland, agreed to support an English expedition against the capital of Hispaniola, Santo Domingo.[19] As ruler of Great Britain, Cromwell had an extraordinary ability to swallow his profound religious convictions and to make friends, if necessary, with Catholic powers such as Spain, and enemies with Calvinist ones such as Holland. It was therefore in a spirit of mild threat that he summoned the Spanish ambassador a year earlier, requesting free passage for English trading ships bound for the New World in return for continuing friendship. The ambassador flatly rejected the proposal; but Cromwell was prepared for this already, as he had been thinking for a while that he could exploit Spain's weakness by sending a fleet into the Caribbean. Among those urging the Lord Protector to take this course was supposedly a Portuguese merchant named Carvajal who had taken refuge in London after the Inquisition had run him to earth in the Canary Islands. He is said to have been another of those crypto-Jews who had managed to move around the Iberian lands from which Jews were banned, and he continued to trade in American silver, importing silver bars into England from Seville. In this reading of the very fragmentary evidence, Carvajal is portrayed as a key figure in Cromwell's willingness to permit the Portuguese New Christians living in London to live openly as Jews – though Cromwell's support for the readmission of Jews to England had to face bitter opposition from such prominent but disruptive figures as William Prynne, already punished for his constant abuse of his foes by the loss of both ears. In one highly exaggerated account, based on the testimony of an English boy captured by the Spaniards in the Caribbean, Cromwell had promised to turn a London church into a synagogue, in return for the funding provided by Portuguese Jews keen to support this expedition.[20]

Cromwell cited the cruelty of the Spaniards towards the native inhabitants of the Caribbean and towards people of other nations when he issued his instructions to the admiral in charge of the English fleet, William Penn (the father of the founder of Pennsylvania), in October 1654. By 'other nations' he also meant those like the English who were trying to trade in the Spanish Main. (He had evidently forgotten his own harshness towards the inhabitants of another English colony, Ireland.) Cromwell was strongly encouraged in his view by pamphleteers who insisted on the weakness of the Spanish Empire, among them John Milton. One theme that was taken up by the English invaders was the promotion of evangelical Protestantism in the face of the papist Spaniards – and the Spaniards regarded their fight with the English in the opposite way. The English position was that 'just as the Spaniards had taken Jamaica from the Indians, so we English have come to take it from them. As for the pope, he could neither grant lands to others nor delegate the right to conquer them.'[21]

No doubt some of the New Christians were keen to punish Spain for the continuing persecution of Portuguese merchants by the Inquisition. But Cromwell's plans went askew. He sent sixty ships and 8,000 men against Santo Domingo, 'a genuine riff-raff of criminals and vagabonds', according to a modern Spanish historian, only to find that the campaign was seriously mishandled. For whatever reason, the English camped some way from the city and were soon flushed out of Hispaniola. There was no easy repetition of Sir Francis Drake's triumphant occupation of Santo Domingo several decades earlier, when he had only 1,000 men at his disposal.[22] But the English commanders, who had not helped the campaign by their quarrels, were determined not to return home with nothing. It was the old story, repeated in many armies and navies, of discord between the man in command of the fleet, Penn, and the general in charge of land forces, Robert Venables. They redirected their energies to Spanish-held Jamaica, a poorly defended and neglected island, whose strategic position south of Cuba and west of Hispaniola was, as the Spaniards would learn, much more valuable than they had ever suspected. Cromwell, meanwhile, had no idea what was going on and can at best have had only a hazy notion of Jamaica's existence.[23] When news of the disaster in Hispaniola reached England, it caused deep consternation among the Godly elements of society close to Cromwell: maybe the Almighty had not deemed England virtuous enough to defeat Spanish Catholic power in the Caribbean? But, if so, surely this was a divine test, an opportunity to increase the effort to achieve God's Design, the defeat of popery. The Spaniards were cast in the role of the Philistines, while the English were likened to the ancient Israelites, whose bad ways had led them to well-deserved defeat at Ai, as the biblical book of Samuel recorded.[24]

Yet Divine Providence seemed, on later reflection, not to have abandoned the English. Jamaica was not a negligible prize. No one had previously given much thought to the strategic position of this neglected island – no one, that is to say, of consequence, but a Spanish priest had shown great prescience when he wrote a few years before the conquest:

> The defence of the island is very poor ... If the enemy takes possession there can be no doubt from it he will quickly infest all parts, making himself master of their trade and commerce. As it lies in the way of the fleets voyaging from these kingdoms to New Spain and the plate galleons to Havana ... it can be gathered how harmful it would be for ships in that trade if the enemy should take possession of this island.[25]

So weak had Spanish interest in Jamaica been that the island was granted as a perpetual domain to the descendants of Columbus, who notionally ruled it as a Marquisate, although the benefits were financial – there was no need to go there very often. Columbus's grandson, Don Luís de Colón, was accused of involvement in contraband trade; he managed to stop further investigation in 1568, which seems to provide perfect proof that he was guilty.[26] The lack of rich gold or silver mines was recognized early on, and its sugar industry remained small under Spanish rule, with only seven mills in operation at the time of the English invasion.[27] 'Fulfilling no specific need,' it has been said, 'Jamaica nonetheless had to be kept out of the hands of others.'[28]

From the moment that English troops landed in Kingston Bay, the Spaniards found themselves on the defensive, for their Jamaica garrison was small, and resistance to the English from forts inland was not effective: the English had what they wanted, a base on the coast in what is now Kingston Bay, where they occupied the Spanish forts and were able to interfere with shipping heading across the Caribbean. In any case, the Spaniards assumed that the English had come to raid the island and resupply their ships, after which they would surely up-anchor and sail away.[29] Hearing of the humiliating defeat near Santo Domingo, Cromwell was not particularly impressed with the news from Jamaica; Robert Venables was disgraced and briefly locked up in the Tower of London on his return to England, while Penn fled from the wrath of the Lord Protector to Ireland.[30] Not surprisingly, it took a while for the English to work out the implications and advantages of this conquest. Cromwell was being advised by a committee of West Indies commissioners, and they immediately saw that the island would need to be properly defended and populated; they suggested that as many Scottish Highlanders as possible should be sent over there – but as servants, for many or most would be prisoners taken in Cromwell's Scots campaigns.[31]

In the long term, this failure to establish Spanish mastery over the entire Caribbean left interlopers such as the English, the French and the Dutch free to occupy the small islands of the Lesser Antilles. In 1623 Dutch raids on the Caribbean islands disrupted the trade of Cuba. With an eye, no doubt, on the English occupation of Barbados, the Dutch gained control of Curaçao in 1634, and there too they faced no opposition from the Spaniards; many of those involved in its settlement were Portuguese Jews, active also in the colonization of the parts of Brazil seized by the Dutch between 1630 and 1654. And it has been seen that the Danes too intruded into the area by the 1670s.[32] Spain had become too feeble to stand in the way of any of these maritime powers.

IV

Most of these islands were exploited for sugar and tobacco; but from being a backwater Jamaica was transformed into one of the major commercial centres of the seventeenth-century Caribbean. With an eye on the success of other trading centres such as Livorno and Amsterdam, where people of all religions had been welcomed, Jamaica was thrown open to settlers of all religions and nations, Protestants, Quakers, Catholics alike; and, just as Amsterdam and Livorno, the new colony attracted settlement by Portuguese Jews, whose presence brought Jamaica into a network that embraced London, the Dutch cities and Brazil.[33] These Jewish settlers, who had shrugged off their supposed Catholic identity and operated their own synagogue, have been labelled the 'Jewish pirates of the Caribbean'; but here, once again, sensationalism has corrupted the reading of the evidence. They funded the privateers; they invested in trade, and that trade included contraband goods smuggled past the Spaniards; they built a warm relationship with the English Crown, which protected them from hostile rivals among the other settlers in Jamaica; but the idea that a kosher version of Captain Morgan plied the high seas is fantasy.

What Charles II hoped for was the discovery of mines bearing gold, silver or copper on Jamaica, and some of the Jewish entrepreneurs optimistically built up his hopes. Benjamin Bueno de Mesquita, also known as Muskett, arrived on board the *Great Gift* in March 1663 with a number of Portuguese Jewish colleagues keen to find the mines; he may have been sincere about the mines, but filled his time with contraband trade in ammunition across the straits to Cuba. What was probably a stolen Spanish treasure chest, bearing on its keyhole the royal coat of arms, has been excavated close to a house he owned in Port Royal. King Charles II had high hopes for developing the island's economy, and he was angry when no mines were found, and thought of expelling the Jews from Jamaica (though he was too dependent on Portuguese Jewish loans to think of expelling them from England).[34] Although Jamaica became an important centre of sugar production, the hopes of mineral wealth raised by its conquest had not been realized. It was therefore a relief to find that it was still very prosperous; and the reason for that was not its own resources but its proximity to the main shipping lanes of the Spaniards. Jamaica successfully challenged the Spanish monopoly on trade through the Caribbean. The English sought more than an occasional boost to their fortunes from the capture of a treasure fleet; they wanted rights of navigation on the high seas that (as Grotius had already assured the world of lawyers) should be free to all.[35]

Within four years of its occupation by the English, Jamaica had become the base for successful raids on Spanish shipping. At first the major role was played not by pirates but by the English navy. Gradually the involvement of privateers became greater and that of the navy smaller. The assumption that this was an unlicensed pirate war is based on the constant and contemptuous use of the term *pirata* by the Spaniards, who eagerly dismissed all their foes in the Caribbean as enemies of mankind. This assumption has provided the basis for popular ideas of reckless and bloodthirsty 'Pirates of the Caribbean', whose existence at various times is not in doubt, but whose presence at this period has been greatly exaggerated, especially since the seas around Jamaica were policed by the English navy, which committed its resources to Jamaica even while it was very strapped for cash.[36] So the picture is much more complicated: Cromwell was content to encourage buccaneers to come to Jamaica, so long as they remained under some sort of English command. He could see that they would be the ideal force to deploy against Spanish ships: their relatively small vessels rendered them much more mobile than the heavy treasure ships; they were accustomed to finding hiding places among the creeks and coves of the Caribbean islands; they were strongly motivated and self-sufficient, even if that made them, from the point of view of the English governor, unruly. They were not all English; the first buccaneers in Jamaican service were drawn from the island of Tortuga, off Hispaniola, which had become a nest of pirates of the most varied origins, English, Irish, Scots, French, Dutch, with a smattering of Africans and native Indians as well.[37]

The first privateer to make his mark was Christopher Myngs, who had very modest origins – his father was a cobbler – but he was (literally) a commanding presence, and captained a fleet that sacked four Spanish towns in the Caribbean in 1659, returning to Port Royal with 1,500,000 pieces of eight. He proved to be more of a pirate than a privateer, refusing to hand over part of the proceeds to the governor of Jamaica, which led to his arrest, his despatch back to England and his release by the newly installed king, Charles II, who thought he could tame such a talented sea captain. The king's confidence in him was justified: in 1662 he led what seemed an impossibly foolhardy attack on the second city of Cuba, Santiago, which lay just across the water from Jamaica, an obvious, tempting but well-defended target. He managed to scatter the Spaniards, march his men into the heart of the city and leave them there for five days of wanton pillaging. His crew included a young Welsh privateer, Henry Morgan, who would terrorize the Spaniards even more effectively in the coming decades, and who would also manage to switch back and forth between licensed and unlicensed raiding.[38]

Morgan, who was born in 1635, came from a more prosperous background than Myngs. This casts doubt on the romantic version of his career, which was told during his own lifetime by his Dutch biographer, Exquemeling: that he had run away to sea at Bristol, apparently hoping to make his fortune in Barbados. There he supposedly ended up not as a rich planter but as an indentured servant, at a time when English servants still carried out much of the backbreaking work on the sugar plantations. This led him to run away to sea again, when Cromwell's fleet arrived in Barbados bound for Santo Domingo.[39] It is more likely that he made his way across the sea after paying for a gentleman's passage on a boat bound for Barbados. He did take part in the Hispaniola campaign, and before long he was sailing aboard Myngs's ships.[40] In 1666 he sailed in a substantial fleet of fifteen ships under the command of an English privateer named Mansfield, en route to Porto Bello and the treasure-laden ships bringing the silver of Peru across the Atlantic. Mansfield realized that the Spanish governor had wind of his arrival, and the privateers selected another, lesser target in what is now Nicaragua. However, Morgan's appetite for an attack on Panama had been whetted. In 1668, following successes in other theatres, notably Cuba, Morgan led an attack on the surprisingly ill-defended silver station of Porto Bello. The loot amounted to around 250,000 pieces of eight, though there was also profit to be made from merchandise and slaves seized during the raid. Ordinary crew members might expect to receive around one thousandth of the haul of silver, which was enough to lead a comfortable life, or to spend their loot over many months in the bars and whorehouses of Port Royal.[41] His most famous expedition was once again sent against the Spaniards in Panama, three years later. This time he marched his men across the isthmus and burned Panama City, though the booty was smaller than Porto Bello had delivered. The problem was that this happened just as Spain and England made peace, so he was sent back to England, notionally in disgrace, but the king could not resist the opportunity to grant him a knighthood.[42] And before long he was back in Jamaica, concentrating on the suppression rather than the promotion of buccaneering.

Morgan is a good example of the pirate who, on close examination, does not look much like a pirate. It has been pointed out that he stayed married to his wife for two decades; that he never led an expedition without obtaining a letter of marque from the Jamaican governor; that he won the strong approval of the English Crown despite the destruction of Panama; and he even became lieutenant-governor of Jamaica; he is known to have joined only one expedition, in 1661, whose members were accused of piracy.[43] In addition, he spent the years after 1671 ensuring that piracy was held in check within the Caribbean, to honour peace with Spain and to assert the authority of the English Crown in its Jamaican colony; he saved rather than squandered his money and became a prominent planter on Jamaica.[44] Attempts to argue that he did not torture his captives, as Exquemeling's colourful contemporary account of his career claimed, are less convincing, though if he did so he surely had in mind the methods of the Spanish Inquisition, which were sometimes applied to Protestant sailors. When he read Exquemeling's biography, which had appeared in two competing English translations in 1684, Morgan tried to suppress it; he even won a libel case and £400 in damages from two publishers. He was as angry at being described as an indentured servant as he was at accusations of torture.[45] On the other hand, the wide diffusion of Exquemeling's book, including Dutch, Spanish and German editions, proves that Sir Henry Morgan had acquired a powerful reputation; and it was inevitable that his days as a privateer would be given all the emphasis, rather than his more respectable career spent clearing the Caribbean of buccaneers.

The connection between licensed raids and Jamaica is made crystal clear by the fact that the word 'privateer' only came into use in the English language following the seizure of Jamaica. The specific circumstances of the English presence in the Caribbean and the raids on the Spanish treasure fleets generated this term, which described an old practice but now gave it legal form – in 1671 the English Parliament passed *An Act to*

Prevent the Delivery up of Merchants Shipps, and for the Increase of Good and Serviceable Shipping, which included clauses dealing with the distribution of 'Prize Money as in cases of Privateers'.[46] However, privateering had already passed its peak. The successful raids of the 1660s had left fewer prospects for profit within the Caribbean. The rule that muggers must not over-mug if they are still to find people to mug came into play. Even before Spain and England made their peace in 1671 privateers started to abandon raids on the Spanish towns, choosing instead voyages to empty coastlines where they could load logwood without interference. They were turning themselves into boring but honest merchants.[47]

V

Prize money spent indiscriminately and smuggling allegedly made Port Royal into the 'wickedest city on earth'. Its businessmen were involved in several enterprises that were barely legal or were outright illegal. Contraband trade with the Spanish islands has been mentioned already. In the 1670s and 1680s, as privateering went into decline and overt piracy was suppressed, the best opportunities were provided by this contraband trade. Probate documents from Port Royal not long before the great earthquake of 1692 describe about half of the deceased as merchants, even though at this stage Jamaica was producing much less sugar for export than Barbados.[48] It was easy to smuggle as there were so many inlets and channels that were left unsupervised by the Spaniards after they had turned Hispaniola into a vast ranch from which cattle and meat products could be obtained for little trouble. Then there was the resale of ships seized at sea, assuming they were not simply kept by the privateers. Prize vessels, even those captured by licensed privateers, were sold at Port Royal under the watchful eye of the governor, and not sent back to England. They could be obtained quite cheaply: when Myngs returned from his campaign in 1663, he had nine ships for sale, at a total price of £797, an average price of £89 – in London one might have to pay £2,000 per ship.[49] Salvaging operations also occupied a good deal of energy. The islanders were adept at identifying shipwrecks, and managed to raise large amounts of Spanish gold and silver from the sea, to the frustration of their Spanish neighbours. One ship was the focus of so much attention that it was simply known as 'the Wreck'; it had foundered off Hispaniola several years before the English arrived in Jamaica, but had lain undisturbed on the seabed until one privateer after another found something worth taking away from the site.[50]

One unusual feature of Port Royal was the amount of silver coin that circulated (coins from Peru have been found on the site of Port Royal).[51] Other English colonies still relied heavily on barter, but even when the English no longer raided Spanish galleons there was plenty of coin in people's pockets, because it was easy to sneak into the smaller harbours near Porto Bello or either side of Cartagena, on the coast of Colombia, and do semi-secret business there. Jamaica became an important source of silver for both England and the growing English colonies in North America, for ships plied back and forth between Jamaica and the American colonies – 363 arrived in five years (1686 onwards). These were relatively tiny ships averaging about twenty-five tons, but the number of these little ships was rather higher than the number of larger vessels that arrived within the same period from the other side of the Atlantic, from England and west Africa.[52] The ships brought everything and everyone: convicts who had been spared execution by Judge Jeffreys and his colleagues after the rebellion of the duke of Monmouth against King James II; African slaves who stayed on the island, though most were re-exported; and goods aplenty: every alcoholic drink on the market, from Madeira and Canary wines to naval stores, firearms, tiles, bricks, pots and pans, as well as preserved meat, cheese and cereals, though the islanders preferred fresh turtle meat they could obtain locally to salt pork.[53]

Jamaica became an important source of slaves for the Spanish colonies in central and South America. Spain did not have a direct source of supply for slaves, because the trading stations along the coast of west Africa were held by the Portuguese, later joined by the Dutch and the Danes. The Spanish lands in the Americas therefore depended on intermediaries, who held contracts (*asientos*) to supply slaves. The Genoese normally stood at the top of this chain, but they did not have the ships and slave stations that would be required, something that the English Royal African Company could supply. Spanish slave-merchants were happy to come to Jamaica to buy slaves brought across the Atlantic by the African Company, at a mark-up of 35 per cent; it made the whole business easier for the Spaniards. So far, demand for slaves on Jamaica itself was still quite limited, as the sugar industry had not taken off.[54]

Some of the profits were ploughed back into the island, for, remarkably, there was very little investment from England. The slow but sure development of its sugar plantations was financed from the proceeds of contraband trade and other local activities, licit or illicit. The autarky of the Jamaican economy is striking. And yet all this was sufficient to make Port Royal into the most important harbour in the English colonies, indeed the most important harbour in the Caribbean, to the horror of its Spanish neighbours, who could see that its wealth was not all honestly derived. Contemporary accounts describe how splendidly the richer merchants lived, so that even their slaves were dressed in fine livery, and there was never any lack of meat and fruit. The standard of living was said to be higher than in England, even for artisans. Plenty of luxuries were on sale – archaeological finds at Port Royal include Chinese porcelain that must have arrived by way of Macau, Manila and Mexico, as well as English Delftware with blue-and-white decoration in imitation of Chinese ceramics.[55] The better-off Jamaicans were also well supplied with silver plate off which to dine – a silver wine taster was excavated on the site of one of the town's many taverns, and imported English tableware made of brass and pewter turned up in abundance.[56] Against this must be set the dangers of living in a tropical climate where malaria and other diseases were widespread; the first English invaders had died like flies during the campaign that failed to capture Santo Domingo. Contrary to Columbus's claims, Jamaica was not a branch of Paradise.

To some observers, indeed, it was a branch of Hell. The more colourful accounts of Caribbean pirates enjoy describing it as 'a rollicking town, where rum-drinking was so common that it seemed to flow through the town' – not to mention whores such as Mary Carleton, with her frank statement that 'they have almost delug'd this place in liquor'. She was hanged in 1673 in London, and her notoriety became attached, perhaps unfairly, to Port Royal, which may not have been much worse than other port cities where strong drink and 'hot Amazons' abounded. In reality the large number of places of worship, from a Quaker meeting hall to a synagogue, suggests that a fair number of inhabitants tried, at least outwardly, to lead respectable lives in the sight of God.[57]

Port Royal stood on a low-lying island at the tip of the narrow peninsula that closed off Kingston Harbour. The harbour itself was excellent, though strong winds and earth tremors were always a source of concern. Houses were crowded together in this confined space: 200 in 1660, 400 in 1664 as the town boomed, maybe 1,500 by 1688, containing a population that peaked at about 6,500 people in 1692, including 2,500 slaves.[58] Despite the accounts of luxurious living, there were no truly grand buildings and the streets were unpaved, simply covered with sand; but there were strict building regulations, which required stone foundations and brick walls. As a result the town resembled nothing so much as the English West Country towns from which many of its inhabitants hailed.[59] On its exposed site, Port Royal lay at the full mercy of the elements; and just before noon on Wednesday, 7 June 1692, these elements proved fiercer than anyone could have imagined: a violent earthquake brought down the tower of the Anglican church, as buildings crashed to the earth and people were swallowed up in the great cracks that opened as the entire earth heaved apart. That was only the beginning: a vast tidal wave crashed into Port Royal, sweeping away people, buildings and objects. Even the town cemetery was torn apart, so that decayed corpses were seen floating on the water alongside those who had just drowned. Stone and brick had not been enough to protect the inhabitants of this fragile spit of land, much of which remains submerged to this day. At least 90 per cent of the buildings of Port Royal were wiped out. About 2,000 lives were lost on 7 June, and an equal number in the days that followed, as disease spread among the survivors.[60]

This was not the end of Port Royal. Reconstruction of part of the town, notably its forts (in view of the danger of Spanish or French attack), took place; and trade resumed. But it seemed to make more sense to govern the island from a place a little further inland, Kingston, for no one could guess when another earthquake and tsunami would strike. In any case, Port Royal had already passed its true peak. The days of privateering had come to an official end in 1671, following peace with Spain; even its entrepôt trade began to tail off, as English residents gradually switched their interest from shipping to the exploitation of the island itself. In the eighteenth century Jamaica would be reborn as a full-scale sugar island. Those who really paid the price for this were the many thousands of African slaves carried across the ocean in abominable conditions to work in the equally abominable conditions of the sugar factories and plantations.

44

A Long Way to China

Just as the inhabitants of Amsterdam, London or Copenhagen developed a taste for the spices of the East and took pleasure in exotic objects brought from China and the Indies, a passion for Chinese and Indian imports developed in the colonies that the Europeans were establishing across the Atlantic. It has been seen that English settlers along the east coast of North America were trying to tap into Indian Ocean trade by way of Madagascar in the late seventeenth century, whether by fair means or foul, although the main outcome was the development of a slave trade carrying Malagasy captives to the West Indies.[1] During this period, as Boston, New York and Philadelphia grew into compact but busy trading cities, with populations barely in the tens of thousands, their citizens acquired large quantities of Chinese porcelain, used day to day not just by the rich elite families such as the Philipses of New York but by middle-class townspeople. Around one third of estate inventories from New York at the end of the seventeenth century mentioned Chinese porcelain, and the figure rises to three quarters in the decade before the American Revolution. Chinese silks, already familiar to the inhabitants of Spanish Mexico by way of Manila, reached the north American colonies by way of the Indian Ocean and the Atlantic instead. For, by and large, the American settlers had to rely on imports of these goods either from London, Amsterdam or the West Indies (in which case they had in any case been transported from Europe). The requirement of the Navigation Act of 1651 that the colonies should acquire their eastern goods through London, to which the goods were brought by the East India Company, kept the Company in business, but on the other side of the Atlantic it increased the cost of goods, since the Americans were dealing through middlemen who expected their share of the proceeds.[2]

Early in the eighteenth century goods advertised for sale on Rotten Row in New York included: 'Fine Heyson, Green, Congoe and Bohea Tea;

Coffee and Chocolate; single and double Refined Sugar; Powder and Muscovado ditto; Sugar Candy ... Cloves, Mace, Cinnamon, and Nutmeg; Ginger, Black Pepper and Allspice ...' As its position at the start of this list suggests, there was one product of east Asia that held sway in every household: tea, in a variety of types and grades. It was already being drunk right across New England in the 1720s. Among the customers were not just the citizens of New York or Boston but the Mohawks and their native-American neighbours, who were sold tea by the enterprising Philadelphia trader Samuel Wharton.[3]

The monopolistic East India Company was determined to control the movement of these exotic products, in the face of constant challenges. These challenges were not just from European rivals; the Chinese themselves, despite imperial ukases forbidding precisely such activities, sent their junks to Melaka and beyond. As they became familiar with Western taste, Chinese potters adapted their own designs to suit the preferences of far-away peoples they regarded as barbarians.[4] In America, however, there still existed confusion about what came from where. The term 'East Indies' was a catch-all that described the entire Indian Ocean and the western Pacific; Americans called China tea 'India tea', while the porcelain was known as 'India china', and the colonists had little understanding of the message that Chinese potters were trying to convey in the images of dragons, flowers or rural scenes; this was a language that clients in and near China could follow, particularly if they knew Chinese legends or had read the most popular Chinese classics. Eventually the richer sort of American would opt for custom-made pottery with family monograms or other decorations that had nothing to do with Chinese culture – within a few years of the break from Britain these pieces might be decorated with the coat of arms of the United States and the inscription E PLURIBUS UNUM.[5] Well-heeled Americans would buy porcelain in standard sets of 270 pieces for a dinner service and 101 for a 'long' tea set, forty-nine for a 'short' one.[6] As time went by coarser porcelain, poorly decorated, chunky and cheap, arrived in massive quantities; its function was as much to provide ballast when the ship's cargo consisted of light chests full of tea as to satisfy domestic demand, and these bulk wares were often sold at a loss.[7]

In the growing literature on the opening of America's trade with China there is a tendency to begin the story with the expeditions sent out after British recognition of the independence of the United States in 1783. That is when direct contact was established between North America and Chinese ports. However, American 'Red Sea men' were bringing exotic goods to North America a century earlier – by 'Red Sea' was meant the Indian Ocean. Five or six ships reached Pennsylvania from the 'Red Sea' in April

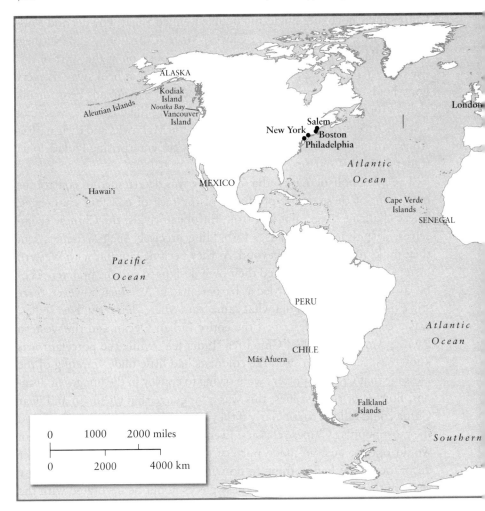

1698, and others arrived at the same time off Connecticut. Among those sending out ships was the wealthy Jacob Leisler, a smart operator with a murky record of contraband trade and privateering, who had manoeuvred himself into the role of lieutenant-governor of New York. He sent the modestly named *Jacob* to Madagascar and India in 1689. Leisler was born in Germany, and he had more experience of the Atlantic than he could have wished: in 1678 he and his ship were seized by Barbary corsairs in one of the Atlantic archipelagoes, where he had been loading wine, and he found himself paying a vast ransom of over £2,000.[8] The *Jacob* was still at sea when his tumultuous career ended with his execution for treason against William and Mary in 1691, but the sailors, who came back to America in 1693, handed out dozens of bribes in gold and silver to

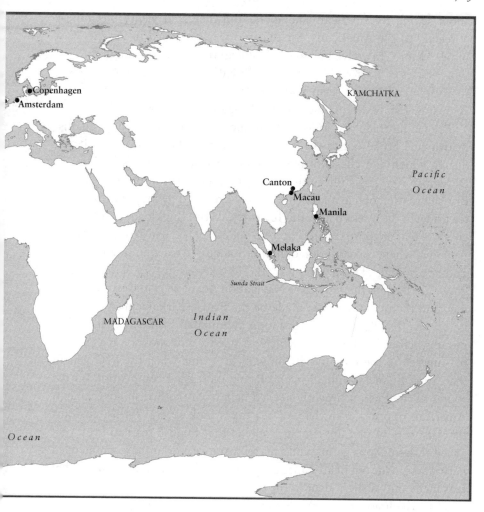

Copenhagen
Amsterdam
KAMCHATKA
Canton
Macau
Manila
Pacific Ocean
Melaka
Sunda Strait
MADAGASCAR
Indian Ocean
Ocean

'prevent them from being put to trouble' by the new governor of New York. The crew told the tale that they had thrown their eastern goods overboard when they heard what had happened to Leisler, but no one can have believed that then and no one does so now.

It was standard practice to unload goods on a deserted American beach, letting most of the sailors disappear with their share, and then to sail into harbour where officials could be, and expected to be, bribed to ignore this contraband trade. The bribe would be made up of silver coins already collected in a whip-round of the sailors before they went their separate ways. Many cargoes contained large consignments of tea, which was easily available in the Dutch West Indies for those willing to circumvent the customs regulations imposed by Great Britain – the Dutch had no qualms about selling to American smugglers, and they sold plenty of Chinese porcelain to the Americans, for that too was smuggled in via the West Indies.[9] More tea arrived by these unofficial routes than through the customs houses of Boston, New York or Philadelphia. When smuggling was so widespread it may seem odd that tea became the catalyst for revolt against British taxation, and ultimately against British rule.

The China trade was an issue from the moment that rebellion against British rule broke out in the Thirteen Colonies. The Boston Tea Party, during which 342 chests of tea were dumped in the town's harbour in December 1773, was the culmination of a long series of protests against British taxation of tea, and the monopoly exercised by British firms in the tea trade. In the weeks before the Tea Party, British ships loaded with 2,000 chests of tea, or approximately 90,000 pounds of tea, had arrived in North America, where consumption of honestly acquired tea amounted to about 200,000 pounds of tea a year by 1770. The complex history of these events goes right back to the restrictive Navigation Act of 1651 and to the adjustments to the taxation of tea made by the British Parliament in the years before the Tea Party. This legislation culminated in the Tea Act a few months before the Tea Party, which assigned a monopoly on tea exports to America to the East India Company at a time when the EIC was in increasing financial difficulty, and facing increasing competition on the routes to the East; it urgently needed help from the British government. American opposition to the new tea taxes took several forms: customs officials were beaten up; rumours spread that English tea had been poisoned with smallpox germs; and a tea temperance movement recommended herbal teas made out of all-American raspberry leaves. In the event, herbal teas made only a slight dent in the tea market. Caffeine was queen.[10]

The British government's new tax regime reduced the price of tea in the American colonies. But if prices fell below a certain point contraband tea traders would suffer, since legally imported tea would be available more cheaply than the tea they picked up in Holland or the Dutch West Indies. Unhelpfully, the EIC produced a list of partners in the North American ports that left out some tea brokers, for whom exclusion spelled ruin. Boston and the other coastal ports had become caught up in manoeuvres whose main aim was not to squeeze the American colonies, but to save the East India Company. In that way, what was happening in the Indian Ocean and along the routes to Macau and Canton was having an effect on what was happening right over the other side of the Atlantic Ocean.[11]

Tea was still on the menu once peace with Britain was signed: the Americans immediately seized the opportunity to explore the sea routes to China. The ambitions of the new nation were clearly expressed by Ezra Stiles, President of Yale College, in 1783 in an early example of the celebration of the Stars and Stripes (though at that time the stars were arranged like the flag of the European Union): 'Navigation will carry the American flag around the globe itself; and display the thirteen stripes and new constellation at Bengal and Canton, on the Indus and Ganges, on the Whang-ho and the Yang-tse-kiang.'[12] So determined were the Americans to reach China directly that the first of their ships to be sent to China, the *Empress of China*, left New York in February 1784 at the same time as another vessel slipped out of the city bound for London and carrying 'the definitive articles of peace' between the United States and Great Britain. Yet the prospects were not quite as bright as the optimistic President of Yale averred. Great Britain continued to block trade between the United States and its own valuable possessions in the Caribbean, which were a prime source of contraband goods from the Far East. It was far from clear that wider European markets would be open to the Americans, and that might well include European colonies in Africa, Asia and South America as well. The answer was to go global, taking advantage of the simple fact that the Americans were now free from the authority of the East India Company.[13]

Sending a ship to China was a dangerous and expensive business. The *Empress of China* was built in Boston, and was about a hundred feet in length, displacing 360 tons. The bottom of its hull was coated with copper, to keep at bay the barnacles and sea slugs that would eat into the wood during a long voyage. But this was only one of the ships that the investors, led by Robert Morris (English-born) and Daniel Parker, intended to send to China; the value of the goods and money on board was said to be £150,000. They were to sail on the riskiest route of all, around Cape Horn and into the Pacific Ocean, whereupon two ships would travel along the coast of South and North America until they reached the islands and ice floes on which seals and sea otters were known to congregate. The aim was to kill and skin as many animals as possible, and take their fur to Canton, where the third ship should already have arrived.

Everything indicated that Chinese traders would leap at the opportunity to buy all this fur: Morris and Parker were relying on information from an American named Ledyard who had taken part in one of Captain Cook's voyages, and had seen what happened when the English ships arrived in Canton carrying the pelts that the Chinese craved. It might be possible to take advantage of the doubts the English had about developing a fur trade in the far north of the Pacific. Captain Cook recorded his thoughts in the journal of his third and final Pacific voyage, in 1778, as he made his way along the coast of Alaska: 'There is no doubt but a very beneficial fur trade might be carried on with the Inhabitants of this vast coast, but unless a northern passage is found it seems rather too remote for Great Britain to receive any emolument from it.'[14] The English sailors discovered that there was intense demand for the sea otter furs, which contain an enormous number of hairs per square inch, making them the warmest furs anyone in China had ever found; besides, the type of fur one wore was an indication of status, sea otter fur being a sign of wealth and distinction. Traditionally, the Chinese relied on Russian fur-traders to supply pelts from the northern Pacific – the Russians could even be found on Vancouver Island, and they ventured right up to the Kamchatka Peninsula and to the Aleutian Islands strung out to the west of Alaska.[15] If the Americans could break into this traffic, they would have something valuable to sell to the Chinese, since it was not obvious what else the Chinese might be willing to buy from the United States.

Morris and Parker dreamed of sending another three ships to China by way of the Cape of Good Hope, but they could not arouse much interest in the idea, and the plan to send ships to seal country in the northern Pacific began to pall. The early optimism of the first investors was soon dissipated. The funds available were only sufficient for one ship after all, the *Empress of China*, and the idea of sending it through the Pacific had to be abandoned; the safe route around the bottom of Africa, created by the Portuguese, was chosen instead. The ship was loaded with thirty tons of ginseng, a product of the Appalachian mountains known to be in high demand in Chinese medicine; $20,000 in Spanish coin; also furs and other goods.[16] Even though the original plans had to be scaled back, the departure of the *Empress of China* was celebrated as the great event that it was, with a thirteen-gun salute representing the thirteen states of the Union.[17]

One New York newspaper printed a poem by a prolific poet, Philip Freneau, that made plain the political as well as the commercial significance of the voyage, invoking the Roman goddess of war at the very start:

> With clearance from Bellona won
> She spreads her wings to meet the Sun,
> Those golden regions to explore
> Where George forbade to sail before . . .
> To that old track no more confin'd,
> By Britain's jealous court assign'd,
> She round the stormy Cape shall sail
> And eastward, catch the odorous gale.
> To countries plac'd in burning climes

And islands of remotest times
She now her eager course explores,
And soon shall greet Chinesian shores.
From thence their fragrant TEAS to bring
Without the leave of Britain's king;
And PORCELAIN WARE, enchas'd in gold,
The product of that finer mould . . .[18]

Freneau had served at sea during the Revolutionary War. He and other Americans keenly awaited the outcome of a voyage during which the ability of the United States to break into new markets was being tested – an outcome, in other words, of significance for the whole of the new country, and not just for Morris, Parker and the other investors.

II

The voyage passed through mainly calm seas of the sort that irritated diarists and letter-writers looking for drama on the high seas. The ship's purser complained that 'it has been one dreary waste of sky & water, without a pleasing sight to cheer us'. One went to sea for excitement, and all that happened was that the captain fell against a railing and bruised his head and arm.[19] When the *Empress of China* reached the Sunda Strait leading into the South China Sea, the Americans found a French ship at anchor whose crew were delighted to hear stories about the American Revolution, which France had supported; so this ship, the *Triton*, agreed to accompany the *Empress* to Macau and Canton, showing the way and helping to fend off any attacks. In Macau the Portuguese welcomed the new arrivals, even though they had never seen their flag before. The Americans had little to fear: as they made their way up the tangled waterways of the Pearl River towards Canton in August 1784 they were greeted not just by the French, the Dutch and the Danes but by the British. The American supercargo, Samuel Shaw, was impressed by the polite conduct of the British, which is all the more impressive as he had served with distinction in the Revolutionary army:

The behaviour of the gentlemen on board was perfectly polite and agreeable. On board the English it was impossible to avoid speaking of the late war. They allowed it to have been a great mistake on the part of their nation, – were happy it was over, – glad to see us in this part of the world, – hoped all prejudices would be laid aside, – and added, that, let England and America be united, they might bid defiance to all the world.[20]

Meanwhile the French let the Americans use their storehouse, or 'factory', until an American warehouse was made ready. Relations between the representatives of the European nations were very harmonious; they knew that their safety depended on mutual support, and that negotiations with a sometimes unpredictable Chinese government could be delicate. So, when a Chinese subject was accidentally killed by a ceremonial cannon shot from the *Lady Hughes*, a British ship that plied between India and Canton, its supercargo, named Smith, was arrested, and all the foreign supercargoes lodged a protest – but the Americans alone stood by the British even though the Chinese briefly suspended trade with them at the height of the row.[21] The Chinese were perplexed that these new arrivals came from a state of which they had not heard, and needed to be shown a map before they were convinced it existed; everything seemed to suggest that they were just more Englishmen, though eventually the Chinese called them 'New People' and later still 'Flowery-Flag Devils', since they thought the stars on the American flag were flowers. The Americans had thought ahead, and the captain of the *Empress* was supplied with a letter that was indeed flowery, addressed to whatever 'Emperors, Kings, Republicks, Princes, Dukes, Earls', and so on *ad infinitum*, he might meet; it was made plain that he was a citizen of the United States of America and Congress, no less, requested that he should be treated 'in a becoming manner' and be allowed to trade freely.[22]

In accordance with closely prescribed Chinese policy, the *Empress of China* had anchored at Whampoa Island, a dozen miles from Canton, rather than in the teeming city itself. The supercargo Smith described the conditions the foreign merchants had to endure:

> The factories at Canton, occupying less than a quarter of a mile in front, are situated on the bank of the river. The quay is enclosed by a rail-fence, which has stairs and a gate opening from the water to each factory, where all merchandise is received and sent away. The limits of the Europeans are extremely confined; there being, besides the quay, only a few streets in the suburbs, occupied by the trading people, which they are allowed to frequent.[23]

As in the merchant fonduks of the medieval world, the ground floor was given over to the goods themselves; the first floor contained parlours and offices where deals were struck; and above that was the hostel where the merchants lived.[24] They were not supposed to bring in women, but occasionally smuggled wives or mistresses in nonetheless. Sometimes Chinese merchants did invite their European counterparts to dinner, but it was impossible to squeeze any useful information out of them; and the tedium of life along the hot and humid riverbank, with a working day of up to fifteen hours, was eased by trips up and down the river to nearby pleasure gardens, and even, in the early nineteenth century, by yacht races along the river, despite official attempts to forbid this.

By the end of the eighteenth century the Europeans decided to advertise their existence more visibly. Individual merchants claimed that they were consuls who represented their home power, and the consuls made sure to run up their flag, so that the factory area became a blaze of colour, beginning with the Austrian consul (who was in fact a Scot) in 1779. The Prussians, Danes, Genoese and Swedes followed suit, and paintings of the European factories were livened up by many of these countries' colours. The trading community also contained people of non-European origin: Armenians, Parsees, Bombay Muslims, although in the early nineteenth century the largest groups were the British and the Americans – after 1812 and the end of a brief spat with the British Navy, the Americans had taken advantage of their neutrality during the Napoleonic Wars to transport tea back to Europe without the interference that every European nation faced as alliances were forged and broken with dazzling speed.[25]

Despite these pretensions, what really mattered was a good relationship with the Hong merchants, members of the Co-hong guild which had been set up in the mid-eighteenth century (on much earlier foundations) to manage trade with the foreigners. By 1831 a complex set of rules, often honoured in the breach, had been imposed in the name of the emperor. Foreign merchants were not supposed to reside permanently in Canton; they were not allowed to bring women into the factories; they were not to take trips in sedan chairs; they could only communicate with the government through the Hong merchants.[26] A 'Canton System' came into being, supervised by a powerful agent of the emperor, known as the Hoppo, whose office went back to 1645. One of the most memorable moments in a voyage up the Pearl River was the elaborate measuring ceremony, when the Hoppo would come on board and check the size of the incoming vessel with long silk tapes. But this was not just a matter of recording length and breadth. The Hoppos were flattered with gifts, and gave gifts in return, consisting of a couple of cows, a store of wheat and some strong drink; these practical gifts were a sign that the emperor cared about the welfare of the foreign barbarians who came to his lands, although the Europeans were known to complain among themselves that the animals were too old or scrawny to be edible. The Europeans would lay on music, make lengthy speeches and dispense plenty of wine; gun salutes would be fired time and again. Doing this again and again became tedious, so the Hoppos would save up ships and try to measure six or seven in one day.[27]

Relations with the Hong merchants were often cordial. Both sides knew that their relationship could be very lucrative. One, Howqua (1769–1843), is said to have become the richest man on earth, worth $26,000,000 by 1824 – he had no trouble in generously abandoning a claim for $72,000 against a Philadelphia opium-trader to whom he had taken a liking. One wonders how credible the account of their conversation is: 'You and I are Number One, *olo flen* [old friend], you belong honest man, only got no chance.' But pidgin English was a standard way for the foreigners and the Chinese to communicate. Howqua fascinated the Americans and was commemorated in countless paintings sent back to America which show an ascetic-looking, painfully thin man wearing silken robes. His investment policy was wise: protecting himself against the ups and downs of the international tea trade, he became a property magnate as well as a tea-trader, owning some of the land on which the foreign factories stood; and he went straight to the tea-growers or even grew the tea himself, cutting out costly middlemen. He entered into close partnerships with his friends from Boston and invested in the new American railway network; he relied on American businessmen to write whatever letters he needed to send abroad. It is not an exaggeration to speak of his American friends: he sent off one American trader, Warren Delano (an ancestor of Franklin Delano Roosevelt), who had spent ten years trading through Canton, with a spectacular fifteen-course dinner that included bird's nest soup, shark's fin, sturgeon's lip and other Chinese delicacies. Some Americans made a fortune in China: John Cushing went back to the United States in 1831 $700,000 richer, though no one could quite compete with that.[28]

The Americans adapted quickly to all this, selling and buying in the Chinese markets through the Hong merchants. When the *Empress of China* set out on her return voyage she was loaded with tea, silk, porcelain and the yellow cotton cloth known as nankeen, named after Nanjing in northern China, which was very popular in North America. She arrived back in New York in May 1785, bringing her investors a profit of at least 25 per cent, which was less than they had hoped but still a good augury for future trade in China. The next year five ships, including the doughty *Empress*, set out for China, and this time Philadelphia and Salem sent ships; by 1790 Canton had been visited by twenty-eight American ships, although they were often only a third of the size of the ships the East India Companies sent out from Europe. In the early nineteenth century the Americans were sending more (but smaller) ships to Canton than the British. Their fast, light vessels could cope more easily with the risks in sailing through poorly charted seas. The turn-around for American ships was quicker, though they had further to go – which raised the question once again of whether they were following the best route to China, especially if the Chinese wanted them to bring furs from the Pacific or, as will be seen, the far south of the Atlantic.[29]

III

The search for furs in the north-eastern Pacific opened up new worlds to the citizens of the United States who explored the shores of what would become Oregon, British Columbia and Alaska; they also provided the Americans with a launching pad for expeditions to Hawai'i, Fiji and other Polynesian islands, where they collected sandalwood, a dyestuff that was in demand in China. The challenge was to find goods that the Chinese were interested in buying, so that one did not have to pay in silver, for silver was in short supply in the early United States, with the effect that the volume of transactions fell and a severe economic depression took hold of the new country, with a heavy impact on merchant shipping.[30] Other sources of credit were therefore essential, and the enormous attraction of fur trapping was that the seals did not need to be bought, although the less said about the revolting methods used to kill them the better. They could be found elsewhere than the Pacific, but the Chinese market was what attracted the Americans there, both to the far north and to the island of Más Afuera off Chile, which was a major sealing station, 'the mecca of the fur seal'. This did not prevent them from looking for seals elsewhere: Captain Cook already knew that the Falkland Islands, not long discovered, were a good source of skins. Captain Cook's journals were printed in London in 1785 and in a shortened version in Philadelphia eight years later. A year before the American publisher went into print, American ships had already begun to exploit Falkland furs.[31]

There were two major obstacles to operation in the eastern Pacific (generally called, from the American perspective, the 'Pacific north-west'). One was the presence of ships flying the flag of other powers: Russians along the coast all the way down to what would become known as Vancouver Island; Spaniards all the way up the coast of California, also very interested in Vancouver Island; and the British, who had come to know these waters after the third voyage of Captain Cook, and once again saw attractive possibilities on the very same island, while reports reaching the United States also made the island sound the ideal base for fur-trapping. The other obstacle was the route around Cape Horn. The *Empress of China* had avoided this route in the end. Its terrors and perils were nowhere better described than in Richard Henry Dana Jr's best-selling

account of *Two Years before the Mast*, recounting a journey out of New
York in 1840:

> Wednesday, November 5th . . . Just before eight o'clock.
>
> Then about sundown (in that latitude) the cry of 'All hands ahoy!' was
> sounded down the fore scuttle and the after hatchway, and, hurrying upon
> deck, we found a large black cloud rolling on toward us from the southwest,
> and darkening the whole heavens. 'Here comes Cape Horn!' said the chief
> mate; and we had hardly time to haul down and clew up before it was upon
> us. In a few minutes a heavier sea was raised than I had ever seen, and as
> it was directly ahead, the little brig, which was no better than a bathing-
> machine, plunged into it, and all the forward part of her was underwater;
> the sea pouring in through the bow-ports and hawse-holes and over the
> knight-heads, threatening to wash everything overboard. In the lee scuppers
> it was up to a man's waist . . . The brig was laboring and straining against
> the head sea, and the gale was growing worse and worse. At the same time
> sleet and hail were driving with all fury against us . . . At daybreak (about
> three, A.M.) the deck was covered with snow.[32]

And this was summertime in the southern hemisphere.

The ship on which Dana sailed had many American precursors. In 1787
the *Lady Washington* and the *Columbia* had set out from Boston, in the
hope of loading furs along the Pacific coasts of North America. News of
the impending voyage set off enormous enthusiasm. Around 300 pewter
medals were struck in the newly founded Massachusetts mint to commemorate the two ships, along with silver and copper versions intended for
grandees such as George Washington and Thomas Jefferson. The pewter
medals were mainly intended to be gifts to the native inhabitants of the
regions the ships were expected to visit, though what they would make of
them is a mystery. Captain Cook had also received the accolade of having
medals struck in his honour by the Royal Society of London. But that
happened after, not before, the voyage.[33]

This voyage contained plenty of high drama, from the moment the ships
reached Praia in the Cape Verde Islands and the surgeon of the *Columbia*,
Dr Roberts, decided he had had enough of the tough rule of Captain
Kendrick. He left the ship and could not even be persuaded to go back on
board when Kendrick found him in the street and threatened him with
his sword. Roberts insisted that without a promise from Kendrick not to
have him flogged for deserting the ship he would stay in Praia. Kendrick
refused to make this promise, oddly acting as if he did not really need the
surgeon on his ship, and let him go. This and other quarrels kept the ships
in the Cape Verde Islands too long: if they did not leave soon they would

face the seasonal hurricanes that plague the waters off Cape Horn – that, at any rate, was the prediction of Captain Gray, who commanded the smaller ship, the *Lady Washington*. Once they were under way, an officer named Haswell struck a sailor who had disobeyed an order to come on deck. Kendrick took the side of the sailor and threatened Haswell with being shot if he ever again set foot on the quarter-deck (reserved for officers); he would have to sleep in the common quarters.[34] These events, recorded by Haswell himself, confirm that Kendrick was a tough captain, though perhaps no tougher than many of his contemporaries, who took the view that keeping order on board demanded ruthless decisions, all the more so when a ship was following an unfamiliar route that exposed it to natural dangers as well as danger from rivals.

The ships rounded Cape Horn by heading hundreds of miles to the south of the cape, experiencing the full diet of gales and sleet before entering what Haswell called 'a perfect hericain'. The two ships were driven apart, and Gray's opinion that time had been wasted in Praia seemed to have been confirmed.[35] The ships would travel separately for many hundreds of miles before they arrived at Nootka Bay on Vancouver Island; and in the meantime they faced constant harassment from Spanish ships along the coasts of Chile, Peru and Mexico. In August 1788 the *Lady Washington* reached the shores of North America and started trading with the native Americans, only to find, as so often happened, that a friendly reception turned sour: at first the Indians brought cooked crabs, dried fish and berries, and were happy with the small items of truck, buttons and bells, that the Americans offered in payment. Captain Gray was also happy, as fresh food was the best cure for the scurvy that raged on board. But when an Indian stole a cutlass that Captain Gray's servant, an African who had boarded at Praia, had left stuck in the sand, the mood changed. The servant, Marcus Lopius, tried to recover the cutlass and was seized; the Indians unleashed their arrows against the American intruders and skewered Lopius with their knives and spears. Even when the Americans scrambled back on their ship, their troubles were not at an end, because the *Lady Washington* was stranded on a sandbank and had to await the tide before it could float out to sea.[36] But the ship and its crew survived, and managed to meet up at long last with the *Columbia* off Vancouver Island.

All this was happening just as the Spaniards pressed further and further north along the same coast, reaching Kodiak Island in late June 1788, while another Spanish ship coasted along the Aleutian Islands in the far north of the Pacific, and met the sole Russian inhabitant of Unalaska Island, Potap Zaikov, who relied on local Aleut hunters to obtain the skins he traded. Isolated he may have been, but somehow he knew, or thought he knew, a great deal about his country's plans: four Russian warships were expected to arrive by way of the Cape of Good Hope. The Russians too were determined to stake their claim to rule this coastline – literally, for the ship *Trekh Sviatitelei* was carrying stakes and copper plates that could be hammered into place as a formal sign that Imperial Russia laid claim to these lands. Moreover, the Russians knew that British ships lay not far off, and they were determined to stop them from establishing a settlement of their own.[37]

The flashpoint was Nootka Sound, which everyone identified as good seal-hunting country; and when the Americans arrived they found a British settlement under construction, with a partly imported labour force – there were Chinese carpenters at work. The Americans also witnessed the arrival of irate Spaniards, who claimed Nootka Sound for themselves, and managed to impound four British ships, as well as arresting all the Chinese workers. These events could easily have set off a war between Great Britain and Spain, but everyone's attention was turning elsewhere at the moment, as the political crisis in France turned into revolution. The Spanish commander was less worried about the Americans than about the British. It seemed extremely unlikely that the Americans would try to create their own settlement on the west coast of this continent; the United States was patently an east-coast entity. When the Boston newspapers reported the friendly encounter between the Spanish and the American commanders at Nootka, they rejoiced in the 'protection and respect of the European Lords of the Soil' for their flag and took wicked delight in the fact that the flag 'of another nation hath been forbidden to be unfurled on the coast'.[38] In the event, the British preferred to make their peace with Spain, signing the Nootka Convention in October 1790, which was a victory for diplomacy (and for Spain) over war – even so, in the long run, this area would fall under British rule, when the boundary between Canada and the USA was fixed in 1846.[39]

The Americans seized the opportunity to find the sea otter skins they knew the Chinese craved. Captain Gray sold his furs in Canton and decided to continue round the world, returning to the United States via the Cape of Good Hope, which made him the first American captain to circumnavigate the globe, after a journey of three years. Kendrick, on the other hand, was killed in a tragic accident while still in the Pacific: a gun salute went wrong and the shot pierced his cabin and blew him to bits.[40] Meanwhile interest in the Nootka Sound continued to grow, but in more peaceful ways. A question that had been raised many times in the past was whether a channel could be found around the top of North America.

Looking for the North-West Passage from the Pacific side made sense after so many failures on the Atlantic side, and was not a new idea – it has been seen that Francis Drake may have been looking for such a route when he sailed up to California on his round-the-world voyage. This was also a reason why British and other ships poked around the waters off Alaska and western Canada. Alejandro Malaspina, an Italian in Spanish pay, led two large ships into these waters in 1791. His expedition set out just as a Spanish publisher issued a specious account of a journey from the Pacific to the Atlantic in 1588 by a certain Maldonado. So Malaspina was sent on a wild-goose chase; even so, he mapped unknown stretches of coast, studied the life of the local Indians, and drew up elaborate and intelligent proposals for the creation of an integrated trade network in the Pacific, involving Russia and China as well as Mexico and the Philippines; but no one at court expressed much interest. After all, he had not found the gateway to the Pacific, and was seen in Madrid as a failure.[41]

The merchants of this new nation were bringing furs from the south Atlantic as well as from the Pacific north-west. In 1792 Captain Daniel Greene led the *Nancy* to China by way of the Falklands. When he came back to the Falklands five years later, he loaded around 50,000 skins, and then added some more at Más Afuera in the south-eastern Pacific. The Falklands were at that time a largely unclaimed space. A French settlement on East Falkland, founded in 1764, had been matched a year or two later by a British settlement on West Falkland; and then the French agreed to hand over the islands to Spain, which sent two priests 'who, beholding their settlement, were overwhelmed with grief'. As a result of these claims, the two islands were known to sailors as the 'English Maloon' and the 'Spanish Maloon', a corruption of their Spanish name, *Las Malvinas*.[42] But the people who did most to exploit the islands at this stage were the Americans, with their raids on the seal population. Meanwhile, first the British and then the Spaniards withdrew from the Falklands early in the nineteenth century, and, although they were eventually reoccupied by Great Britain, the question of their ownership has festered ever since. Beyond the south Atlantic, American ships regularly went in search of seals in the southern Indian Ocean, on islands such as St Paul. Places uninhabited by humans were ideal, as the seals had as yet no reason to fear humans and lay passively on the rocks while the hunters did their bloody work. Later, seals did sometimes grow wise to what was happening, but escaping on land was almost impossible – these are animals made for the sea.[43]

Furs from as far away as Alaska thus fuelled the maritime links between the early United States and China. The fur trade of the United States was truly global, stretching in both directions towards China, around both southern capes. The profits from this trade, and from the China trade more generally, fuelled the recovery of the American economy and the prosperity of great business houses such as that of the German immigrant John Jacob Astor. The first generation of American millionaires came into being, an aristocracy of wealth rather than blood whose prosperity had been created by the China trade and all the other business that was intertwined with it: trade in furs, trade in sandalwood and – as will be seen – trade in opium.[44]

45
Fur and Fire

I

One of the difficulties in dividing up the maritime history of the world between the three great oceans, and several smaller seas, is that the oceans are themselves composite seas. The Atlantic embraces the North Sea and the Caribbean, icy waters off Greenland and warm waters off Brazil; the Pacific is even more complex, which is hardly surprising since it covers about one third of the globe: the South China Sea, and at times the Yellow Sea and the Japan Sea, acted as corridors linking east Asia to the Indian Ocean, rather than looking eastwards into the open ocean; the island worlds of Polynesia, Melanesia and Micronesia were connected across great distances, and yet they had few or no links with the great continents surrounding the ocean; and in the far north another partly island world existed, inhabited by Ainus (the original inhabitants of northern Japan), Aleuts and other peoples, many of whom had adopted a style of life broadly similar to that of the Inuit of northern Canada and Greenland – a life heavily dependent on the resources of the sea, which provided them with food (fish), oil for lighting their homes (seal blubber), clothing (cormorant skins) and even warm overcoats (stretched seal intestines).[1] In the Kuril Islands and the Aleutians, a certain amount of trade was carried on by boat. Along the coast of Alaska, the art of canoeing was taken to a very high level, and the inhabitants could handle choppy seas, strong winds and ice floes with assurance. Yet this maritime world was isolated from the rest of the Pacific. The Japanese and the Koreans did not, as far as is known, explore these waters. Only with the arrival of the Europeans in the seventeenth century did this area begin to arouse interest.

There were several reasons why this remote corner began to attract attention. The most important was the availability of furs, in order to pay for the tea of China. But the first group of Europeans to make their presence felt in the far north of the Pacific had not arrived by sea, even though

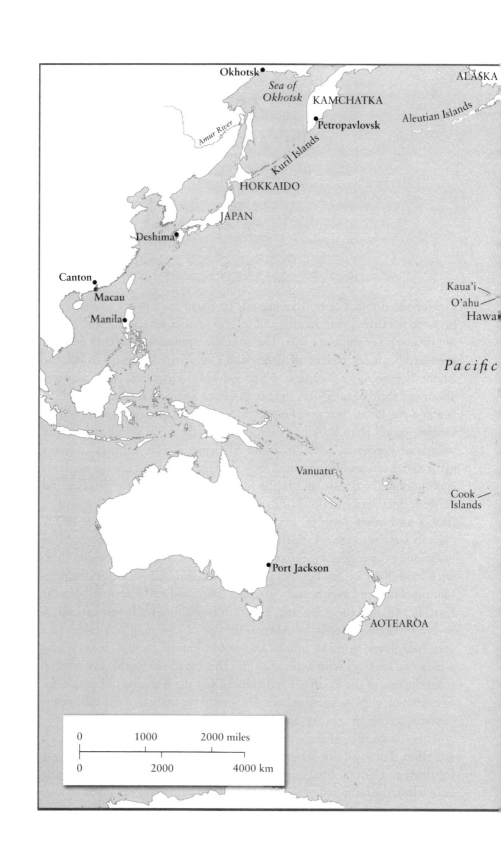

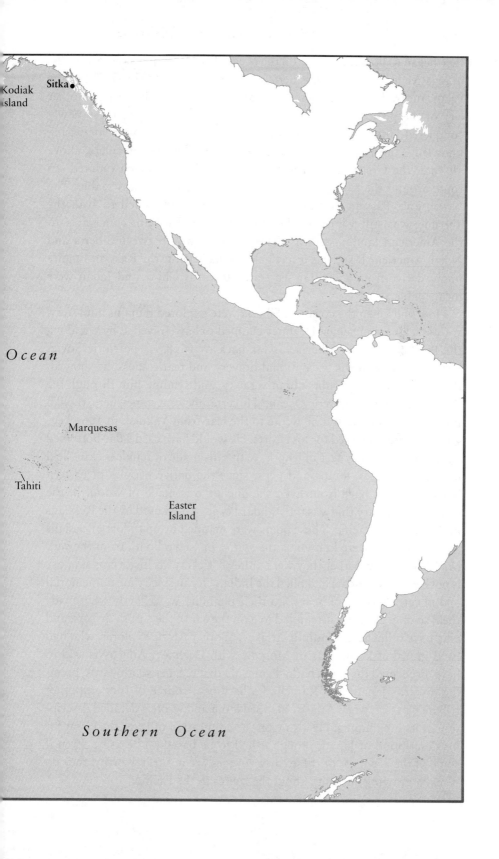

they began to float their ships on the ocean. Russian expansion eastwards, in massive leaps and bounds across Siberia, brought to the shores of the Pacific fur traders who originated as far west as Suzdal, the ancient mother city of the principality of Muscovy. Curiosity about how these newly conquered lands were linked to the oceans grew along with increasing knowledge of the shoreline of eastern Siberia. The Russian rulers, above all Peter the Great, were keen to know whether the much-vaunted sea route around the top of Siberia into the Pacific Ocean was viable. The North-East Passage, which the English had tried to sell to Ivan the Terrible, was still a lure, all the more so as the Russians came close to the American landmass. Was there a passageway between Siberia and North America? If so, was it navigable? The benefits the Russian Empire might derive from a regular sea traffic towards China and Japan were incalculable.

How and when the coasts of Siberia were explored remains a mystery. A Cossack named Semen Dezhnev claimed to have travelled by sea along the Pacific shores of Siberia, as far back as 1648.[2] A patriotic Soviet historian wrote of the 'exceptional bravery and fearlessness' he showed, throwing aside any doubts about veracity, and sending him through the Bering Strait into the Arctic Ocean.[3] He certainly went somewhere, though probably not so far; and he wrote to the tsar from Yakutsk in 1662 begging to be recompensed for his efforts. He would have used a flat-bottomed boat at most seventy feet in length, with sails made of reindeer skin, held together by ropes, straps and pegs, since the native peoples of eastern Siberia did not have iron. Even the anchor was made of wood. In the eighteenth century this was the standard type of boat used by the Russians in the northern Pacific. These boats were manned by up to forty Russians and locals, and were known as the *shitik*, or 'sewn boat', from the verb *shit'*, 'to sew'.[4] Whether they were quite as 'rickety' as historians suppose is not clear: sewn boats had plied the Indian Ocean since time immemorial and in certain types of heavy sea their pliability was exactly what made them strong. Dezhnev attempted to gain the ear of the tsar's advisers, and may have influenced Vladimir Atlasov, another Arctic explorer, who had lived in Yakutsk and was in Moscow with Dezhnev; Atlasov is said to have discovered the Kamchatka Peninsula that reaches southwards, pointing towards Japan; and Kamchatka became a source of furs and other tribute by 1697, when Atlasov mapped it out and wrote a detailed description of its inhabitants. He also won the admiration of Peter the Great for his description of Japan, though it had to be based on hearsay.[5] Even if some of the accounts of these early voyages are not trustworthy, they do reveal a growing curiosity about the routes to the Pacific.

The galloping expansion of Russia's empire also brought Russian officials and colonists to the northern borders of the Qing Empire, which had taken control of China following the collapse of the Ming dynasty in 1644. At first the advantages for Russia seemed to lie in tribute payments imposed on the native peoples of Siberia, although there were rumours of silver mines somewhere along the river routes beyond Yakutsk.[6] But the advantages of trade with China were also clear: if the Cossacks (the main colonists) could break into the Chinese market, they would make great profits for themselves as well as for the tsar. As far back as the 1650s clashes were occurring along the Amur River, which ever since then has been a source of tension between Russia and China; native peoples appealed to the Chinese for help, and Chinese armies advanced into the field. The Russians found it difficult to hold their own.[7]

I I

In 1714 an influential adviser of Peter the Great, Fedor Stepanovich Saltykov, who was an expert on maritime affairs and was then living in London, wrote a series of *Propozitsii* ('Propositions'), which he sent to the tsar in St Petersburg. Saltykov had travelled in Siberia with his father, and he was clear in his mind that an opportunity now existed to create a Russian empire in the Far East. He imagined that it would be possible to build a fleet of ships near the mouth of the Ob and Yenisei Rivers, which debouch into the Arctic Sea in central Siberia, and then to send the ships around Siberia looking for islands that could be brought under Russian sovereignty. Russia too was succumbing to the lure of eastern spices and gold:

> If an open passage can be found to the coasts of China and Japan, your empire will receive great wealth and profit for the following reason. Ships are sent to eastern India from all realms such as England and Holland and others, and must cross the Equator twice, when they go out and when they return. Because of the great heat in those places many of their people die and there are severe food shortages if they are on their voyage for a prolonged period of time. Thus upon the discovery of a [northern] sea route such as this, they will all wish to use it . . . For trading purposes your empire is closer than any other realm.

Foreign shipping using this route should be monitored, and of course taxed, as it passed Novaya Zemlya in the Arctic Ocean; Saltykov observed how much income this type of tax produced at both the Danish Sound and Gibraltar. Silver was to be had both in Japan and in Siberia, where

Saltykov had actually seen abandoned silver mines. Trade 'by water' would be possible with China and the East Indies, bringing gold, porcelain, silk and many other luxury products to Russia, which would become as wealthy as Holland or England. The tsar certainly gave thought to these proposals, saying in 1711 that:

> as soon as he has peace and leisure to apply his mind to it, he will search out whether it is possible for ships to pass by way of Novaya Zemlya into the Tartarian Sea; or to find out some port eastward of the River Ob, where he may build ships and send them, if practicable, to the coast of China & Japan.[8]

The illusion persisted that Arctic waters were safer and easier to suffer than the tropical waters through which European ships passed en route to the Indies.[9]

Peter the Great did find the peace and leisure to apply his mind to all this, but only at the very end of his life. One of his very last acts before he died in 1725 was to order Vitus Bering, a Danish captain in his service, to build boats in Kamchatka and 'to sail on these boats along the shore which runs to the north and which (since its limits are unknown) seems to be a part of the American coast'. The aim was 'to determine where it joins with America', and if possible to visit a European settlement along the American coast, in the hope of learning more about the geography of the region and drawing an accurate chart. Typically, Tsar Peter also ordered the Senate 'to find among the apprentices or assistant master-builders one who could build there a deck ship along the lines of the big ships here'; and, should there be no navigators in Russia with experience of the Pacific, two men should be brought from Holland 'who know the sea in the north and as far as Japan'. As it happened, Bering had experience of the East Indies, having served in the VOC, and was strongly recommended by the Senate and by two admirals.[10] This, after all, was the remarkable tsar who had reputedly laboured in (and had certainly observed) the Dutch shipyards in the hope that he could make Russia too into a great naval power.

That said, the focus of Peter's maritime ambitions remained far from the Pacific. The Black Sea was one area where he hoped to extend Russian naval power, but his major interest lay in the Baltic, which became his home when he established his new capital at St Petersburg. More than anything, he was determined to push back Swedish control of large tracts of the Baltic, and the Great Northern War at the start of the eighteenth century eventually – after some checks – brought Russia dominion over the Baltic.[11] Bering had served in the Great Northern War, but being sent to Siberia, even as captain of a minuscule fleet, was not the reward he sought. Still, he obeyed orders even after the tsar died and even though the first, and in some respects most arduous, part of his journey was the interminable trek across Siberia to the newly established Russian fort and trading station at Okhotsk. The trading station had access to the Sea of Okhotsk that lies west of the Kamchatka Peninsula, and is bounded by the Kuril Islands, strung out north-eastwards from the northern tip of the Japanese island of Hokkaido.[12] It also had enough facilities to build a *shitik*, of the type mentioned earlier, and a second boat was built in Kamchatka. Considering that the number of Russians in the trading stations was still very small, just a few hundred, the ability to put ships together, even if they would hardly have won praise from a Dutch or English captain, was impressive. Bering did manage to sail some way into the strait that bears his name, but he was still unsure whether he had identified a passageway into the Arctic Ocean, or simply a large inlet set into a continuing coastline that linked Asia to America. Fog made progress difficult and he turned back, against the advice of his Russian deputy, Chirikov, who has therefore won the plaudits of Soviet historians for being the man with true vision. A second expedition in 1729 was no more successful, although the work of his crew, including the mapping of previously unvisited shores, should not be underestimated.[13]

There was still an enormous amount to learn about the configuration of the northern Pacific, which remained well into the eighteenth century one of the least known areas of the oceans. One of Bering's deputies, Captain Spanberg, was invited to explore the chain of islands leading towards Japan, which was still unwilling to open its doors to any foreign traders apart from the Dutch.[14] Spanberg was in Okhotsk in 1735, building a pair of ships and making ready a third, older one. Setting out in June 1738, Spanberg's flotilla stood off Japan a year later. Despite official hostility to foreigners, both the locals and the officials who came on board were quite friendly, and the Russians were able to obtain gold coins, rice, fish and tobacco. The officials took Japanese politeness to an extreme, bowing and kneeling – indeed, they stayed on their knees so long that the captain finally felt he had to tell them to rise. Once in Spanberg's cabin, the officials were impressed by the Russian food they were offered and quaffed Russian brandy with pleasure. But Spanberg knew how these brief encounters could turn from friendship to violence, and soon set sail for Kamchatka.[15] Although a further attempt to reach Japan failed, Spanberg had added a great amount to Russian knowledge of the northern Pacific, making it possible to lay more precise plans for the creation of a Russian dominion over the Kuril Islands and beyond.

Since the Pacific was not a high priority back in St Petersburg, Russian penetration of the northern Pacific in the second half of the eighteenth century depended in high degree on the initiative of individual merchants, some of them Russians of modest origins, born as peasants or into Cossack military families, who had managed to heave themselves up the social ladder, some of them Greeks who had taken up residence in Muscovy.[16] Small companies acquired ships and sent them out from the Pacific coasts of Siberia in search of furs; the Russian Senate became increasingly interested in the taxes that could be obtained from the fur trade, and by 1748 merchants were petitioning the Senate for monopolistic rights over patches of territory rich in furs. The Senate was only too happy to fall in with these plans, some of which proved very lucrative: one expedition produced nearly 22,000 roubles for the imperial treasury, one third of the value of the fur cargo.[17] Most expeditions produced more than 1,000 roubles for the treasury, and they penetrated deeper and deeper into areas not previously visited by Europeans, all the way to Alaska. Plenty of ships were wrecked in the difficult conditions of the Far North, but by 1770 the profits were getting larger and larger. This was partly the result of the policies of Empress Catherine II, who encouraged free trade from the 1760s onwards. The Soviet historian of these merchants saw in this 'the power of bourgeois economic development', though she admitted that private trade was already well established before 1760. After all, eastern Siberia, mainly inhabited by native peoples who were not reduced to serfdom, was a very long way from the centres of government power or the estates of the great aristocratic families. The remote frontier offered freedom and the chance to carve out wealth, whether from land or trade.[18]

Not just demand but confidence was growing. One ship that spent several years at sea was the *Sveti Pavel* or *St Paul*, operated by three merchants; it travelled to the Kuril Islands in 1770 and to the Aleutians in 1771, where the Russians befriended the native Sannakh islanders, with whom, as so often, relations were good at first, but then turned sour. The Russians' interpreter was found dead in his yurt. The islanders attacked. The ship's captain, Solviev, hurried off deeper into the Aleutian Islands, where the crew gathered information about the many furry animals to be found – beavers, bears, deer, wolves, squirrels and otters. The crew were back in Okhotsk in July 1775, carrying 150,000 roubles' worth of furs, though thirty out of seventy-one fur-hunters who had set out had not survived the voyage.[19] These experiences were replicated again and again, puncuated by special moments such as an encounter between Captain Cook and the Russians, when Cook gave the Russians a telescope as a special 'token of their visit to those islands'.[20]

III

Rather as the Spaniards had originally seen their American empire as a source of funds for the struggle against the Turks, the tsars saw their assertion of sovereignty over the many peoples of eastern Siberia, and beyond that the Aleutian Islands and Alaska, as a way of funding their dreams of empire within Europe. There was a certain attraction in claiming to rule over parts of Europe, Asia and America, placing Russia notionally on a par with the multi-continental empires of Spain and Portugal. A memorandum by Counts Vorontosov and Bezborodko, of 1786, made the point explicitly: 'The north-west coast of America and the islands in the archipelagoes between there and Kamchatka, and from that peninsula to Japan, were discovered long ago by Russian seafarers ... According to a generally accepted rule, the first nation to discover an unknown land has the right to claim it.'[21] The great advantage the Russians possessed was that they were the pioneers in European penetration into the region; the great disadvantage was that overland trade was slow and cumbersome, and better suited to carrying tribute and tax receipts than vast amounts of goods, while maritime routes seemed impractical until the North-East Passage was brought into being – if it ever would be. Still, a 'United American Company' came into existence in 1797, and was transformed into the 'Russia–America Company' two years later.[22] It lay under 'imperial protection', with the full approval of Tsar Paul I, but the basic model was that of the many East India Companies that the Russians knew well from contact with their Baltic and North Sea neighbours. In view of the autocratic system of government in tsarist Russia, the freedom of action of the merchants taking part in this venture was counterbalanced by the supervision of a government department.

The merchant who did most to bring it into being, Grigory Ivanovich Shelikov, had already died by then, but he had been a fur-trader in the Pacific, living for some years on Kodiak Island, which is now part of Alaska. Of course, Alaska was not understood as the roughly square chunk of icy land that now forms a state within the Union; what interested the Russians was the opportunity to hunt sea otter along the coastline down to and beyond Sitka, a 600-mile strip of land that still acts as a barrier between Canada and the Pacific. Shelikov astutely described his plans to a colleague while Catherine the Great sat on Russia's throne:

> The main end of my enterprise has been to bring newly discovered waters, lands and islands into our empire before other powers occupy and claim

them, and to undertake new ventures to augment the glory of our empress
and bring profit both to her and our fellow-countrymen.[23]

Catherine, and then Paul, were far more occupied with relations with
western Europe than with the Pacific; but they were aware that what happened in the Pacific might have significant repercussions in the West: the
presence of the British and the Spaniards along the coast of California
made it certain that contact would be made with European ships and
trading stations as Russia consolidated its hold on the north and on supplies of high-quality fur for the Chinese and other markets. By 1800
traders from Great Britain and the United States were pumping vast numbers of skins along their maritime pipeline to Macau, while the Russians
were still trying to trade with the Chinese through stations along the Amur
River. But the cost of transport from Alaska to the Amur trading stations
proved prohibitive; it made more sense for fur merchants in northern
China to trek all the way down to Canton to obtain furs because the British, the Americans and the Spaniards were flooding Canton with sea otter
skins, with the result that prices were forced down. Moreover, the cost of
sending tea to Europe by sea was a small fraction of the cost of sending
it to St Petersburg overland.[24]

Much would depend on the quality of seamanship available out east;
yet the hopes that had brought Okhotsk and other settlements into being
were disappointed. One Russian admiral complained bitterly that the
sailors based at Okhotsk knew far too little about the character of the
difficult seas they were supposed to navigate, whose difficulties began at
Okhotsk itself, where shifting sands and shallow waters made entry into
the harbour a challenge. The quality of shipbuilding was also, he said,
well below the standard of the Baltic or the Black Sea. About fifty vessels
had been built at Okhotsk by the 1790s, and by then it was possible to
find iron nails to bolt the planking together, but these were not to the standards that Peter the Great had been trying to establish. By the start of the
nineteenth century the shipyards at Okhotsk contained rotting ships – a
Russian commentator likened Okhotsk to a naval museum.[25]

Creating a merchant navy out in the Sea of Okhotsk seemed beyond
Russian capabilities. Perhaps, then, the Russians would have to bite the
bullet and send ships all the way from the Baltic to the northern Pacific
by way of the Atlantic. Fortunately the Russian Admiralty identified a
man of unusual skill and experience to lead an expedition to the Far East.
Johann-Anton von Kruzenshtern was a Baltic German from Estonia who
had been seconded to the British Navy, fought the Revolutionary French
and sailed under the British flag to the Caribbean. But the more he heard

about the ocean world the more his attention turned to the Far East. He
wrote:

> During the time that I was serving with the English Navy in the revolution-
> ary war of 1793–9, my attention was particularly excited by the importance
> of the English trade with the East Indies and with China. It appeared to me
> by no means impossible for Russia to participate in the trade by sea with
> China and the Indies.[26]

Setting out on a British ship in 1797, Kruzenshtern called in at Calcutta
and Canton, reinforcing his sense that the Russians would never make a
success of their fur trade without access by sea to China's window on the
world. Once he was back in Russia, Kruzenshtern's voice was finally
heard, and he was commissioned to take a pair of ships all the way from
the Baltic to the Pacific. The first problem, though, was to find suitable
ships. Russia could offer nothing capable of such a long voyage. Even
Hamburg and Copenhagen had nothing available. Finally two suitable
vessels, the new *Leander* of 450 tons and the even newer *Thames*, of 370
tons, were found in England. They were renamed the *Nadezhda* and the
Neva and sent to the Baltic naval base at Kronstadt, to be prepared for a
voyage that, it was hoped, would reach as far as Japan, carrying on board
a certain Rezanov, gloriously appointed as Russia's ambassador to the
imperial court at Edo.[27]

Kruzenshtern's route took the ships along the coast of Brazil and round
Cape Horn, which proved quite manageable, although soon after that the
two ships were driven apart; the *Neva* found its way to Easter Island,
while the *Nadezhda* pressed on to the Marquesas. These were not, of
course, new discoveries, and Kruzenshtern had read Captain Cook with
close attention; but it was the first time Russian shipping had entered the
south Pacific. Kruzenshtern was determined that relations with the native
islanders should remain cordial, and his aim in calling in at the Marquesas
was to take on supplies. He permitted his men to barter for local goods,
so long as they did not do so on board the ship. This did not prevent naked
women from climbing on board who had, as a modern historian coyly
observed, 'more than fruit to sell the Russians'.[28] The two ships managed
to find one another in the Marquesas and made their way via Hawai'i into
the far north of the Pacific, bypassing Japan for lack of time – Kruzenshtern had promised to deliver a cargo of iron and other naval stores to
Petropavlovsk on the Kamchatka Peninsula, while the *Neva* sailed towards
Kodiak Island and the new Russian settlement at Sitka on the Alaskan
coast.

When they arrived, the Russians were horrified to discover that Sitka had been sacked by the Tlingits, the native population of the region. The Russia–America Company had made a fundamental error: by settling on the Alaskan coast and displacing the Tlingits, the Russians had created what a contemporary observer called 'an unalterable enmity against the Russians'. The Tlingits had been living off the resources of the coastline, including not just its fish but its sea otters, whose furs the Russians were now trying to monopolize. By contrast, the British and the Americans took care not to settle the area, but preferred to come on seasonal trading visits. The Tlingits were formidable warriors, who went into battle wearing armour made of leather and bone, capable of stopping a musket shot in its tracks; before long they acquired firearms of their own. The *Neva* therefore sailed straight into a battle zone, where the Russians and the Tlingits were literally at each other's throats. The Russians concluded that they would need to arm themselves well if they were going to gain control of the coastline and its furs.[29] For if they did not establish settlements, they left the door open to the British, the Americans and the Spaniards, who still had a significant presence in California and further north.

Another setback, this time for those aboard the larger ship, the *Nadezhda*, followed its arrival at long last in Japan, after setting out from Kamchatka in September 1804. The Russian ambassador, Rezanov, landed in Deshima, only to be berated by the Japanese for poaching on the territory, tiny though it was, that had been assigned to the Dutch; he was also criticized for arriving in a well-armed warship rather than a trading vessel. He hung around for three months before a curt message arrived from the shogun: 'it is our government's will not to open this place. Do not come again in vain. Sail home quickly.' To encourage him to go, the Japanese authorities sent a massive quantity of rice, salt and other foodstuffs, but Rezanov refused to accept the gift and made plain his anger at rejection, which the Japanese officials saw as a highly embarrassing breach of etiquette. They did explain that they would have to take the blame if he left the gifts behind, and would feel obliged to commit a mass act of *hara-kiri*. Rezanov had the good sense to take the gifts and leave, in April 1805.

Kruzenshtern had other plans, now that the embassy to Japan had failed so completely. After mapping the island of Sakhalin, to the north of Japan, he headed for Macau, which he knew from his earlier sojourn in Canton. There he was joined by the *Neva*, which had turned its back on the frightening Tlingits. But breaking into the Canton market was not straightforward. The other nations had their consulates and warehouses. Kruzenshtern was eventually able to convince an English merchant named Beale to negotiate on his behalf with a Hong merchant, Lucqua, and the cargo of the two ships was sold, apart from the best sea otter skins, which were known to fetch extortionate prices in Moscow. The ships loaded tea, nankeen cloth and porcelain. This time they would head westwards, through the East Indies and round the Cape of Good Hope, with one ship calling in at St Helena. The two ships were back in Kronstadt in August 1806, after a voyage lasting just over three years.[30] The profits were meagre, but there were grounds for rejoicing: Russian ships had circumnavigated the globe for the first time, and valuable information had been gathered about the Sea of Okhotsk and the coast of Alaska. It was understood that a pioneering expedition of this sort was bound to produce mixed results, but that any future successes would be built on the information gathered by these two ships.

The information these ships gathered is what historians tend to call the 'scientific' aspect of this and other voyages, such as those of Captain Cook and the Frenchman La Pérouse. However, it masks the more prosaic reality: even if the information about the daily life of the Tlingits in Alaska or the Ainu in Hokkaido aroused genuine interest, the prime purpose of these voyages was to uncover sources of wealth, and to reach them before rival European powers did so. This was especially important for the Russian tsars, who were constantly in need of sources of funds for ambitious campaigns around the Baltic and the Black Sea. The Russians failed to gain the lion's share of the Pacific fur trade, but the importance of their presence lies in the way that Russian pioneers penetrated ever deeper into unknown waters, building ships of questionable quality in unpromising locations very far from the Russian homeland, and setting out year after year into frozen islands.

IV

The Russians were the first to recognize the potential of the northern Pacific, even if their most important motive was to promote trade links with China. The period in which they were making these remarkable advances also saw closer contact between Europeans and the inhabitants of the Polynesian islands, particularly during the 1760s and 1770s. Here too there was a question mark. Did these islands have anything to offer? Coconuts were not going to draw in vast numbers of trading ships. The reputation of the islanders for cannibalism and human sacrifice was counterbalanced by the image that survived to and beyond the time of Gauguin, of islands where free love and a simple life without wants were to be had. This too was part of the Polynesian reality: European sailors were astonished and generally delighted by the readiness of local women to offer their bodies, as much for courtesy as for ecstasy. Tahiti became 'the island which encapsulated European images of the south Pacific, whether benign or malign'.[31] On the other hand, these islands lived largely from their own resources, and their subsistence economy found it hard to meet the demands of European sailors for food and other basic supplies, quite apart from the lack of luxury products on offer.

It is clearly a mistake to talk, as one otherwise illuminating book has done, of 'the discovery of Tahiti and Hawai'i' in this period.[32] What the Europeans discovered had been discovered centuries before by Polynesians. The arrival of the Europeans in the Polynesian islands led to vigorous exchanges of information, as each side began to see that they could learn from the other; in some areas, such as Hawai'i, this happened with startling rapidity, as the islanders adopted European clothes and even shipping. The Polynesians looked for similarities at least as much as they noticed differences; an extreme case was the experience of a Tahitian who travelled to the court of King George III in England, and who, while on board ship, had to be persuaded that the Christian rituals he witnessed on board would not culminate in human sacrifice – not that he was opposed to the practice, but he was afraid that he would be chosen as the victim. He was more comfortable with what he saw in Cambridge, where the sight of dons processing through the Senate House in their scarlet gowns brought to mind the processions of high priests back home.[33]

The best word to use to describe the first encounters in Tahiti is 'serendipity'. Captain Samuel Wallis, from Cornwall, in charge of the *Dolphin*, arrived there in June 1767 in the expectation that what was (relatively speaking) so large an island, with mountains looming out of fog in the distance, must be the long-sought Southern Continent for which he was seeking. The natives, who crowded around in hundreds of canoes, seemed friendly, 'particularly the women, who came down to the beach, and stripping themselves naked, endeavoured to allure them by many wanton gestures, the meaning of which could not possibly be mistaken'.[34] But it was unclear whether their attempts to attract sailors to land were a ploy to lure them into a trap and kill them. An attempt was made to conduct 'silent trade', with each side leaving goods on the beach, but the English sailors only took what they wanted (some pigs) and left behind the bark cloth they had been offered. For their part, the Tahitians ignored the axes and nails the English had left behind. The English realized that they had somehow offended the Tahitians, and on a second visit they collected the bark cloth and everything else the islanders had put out for them.

Even so, relations were at first difficult. Faced with an armada of boats, the *Dolphin* fired on the crowd that had gathered on the beach, which fled into the forests; after that, more than fifty canoes left on the shore were hacked to pieces by carpenters sent out from the ship under armed guard. The carpenters had good reason to be in a bad mood: women had in the end been allowed on board, but they had raided the boxes of nails they found lying around, and even pulled nails out of the ship's beams, which threatened to make her unsafe. Facing European violence, the Tahitians assumed that they were being treated to a display of the wrath of their gods, and the gift of a pig and a plantain leaf was intended to signify submission to a superhuman power. This was transformed into an acceptance that, even if the British, and later on the French, were made of the same flesh and blood as themselves, they still had to be appeased, since the alternative was that the newcomers would unleash destruction far worse than anything their own warring bands were capable of achieving.[35] In the end Captain Wallis struck up a friendship with the local queen, and they exchanged visits – he was impressed by the meeting house to which he was taken, which was about 100 metres long. Queen Obearea wept when the *Dolphin* set sail.[36]

Gradually, though, it was understood that this was not actually part of the Southern Continent, though surely it must be an island lying off its coast, rather like Hispaniola or Cuba in relation to the Americas? A year after Wallis arrived there, Louis de Bougainville, a high-born French captain, reached another part of Tahiti, knowing nothing of the arrival of the English. Bougainville was well read in classical literature, and, remembering the story of how Venus had been born in the sea and had been washed up on the island of Kythera, he called the island *Nouvelle Cythère*.[37] Bougainville titillated his male readers by describing how a Tahitian girl uncovered herself on deck and insisted that 'here Venus is the goddess of hospitality'. The nakedness of the Tahitians recalled the nakedness of ancient Greek athletes. For Bougainville what had been discovered was not just a paradise, but a classical paradise; he had, in effect, travelled back in time to experience 'the true youth of the world'. His experiences were much better than Wallis's: the Tahitians had learned that European firepower was irresistible, so they eagerly co-operated with the next lot of Europeans, probably unaware of any real difference between the British and the French. The peaceful nature of Bougainville's experiences in Tahiti led his readers, including Diderot, to enthuse about the grace and innocence of the islanders. As Matt Matsuda has observed, 'even theft seemed a sign of innocence in a world where all things were shared', not just objects but sexual relations. The impact of this voyage was all the greater, as Bougainville brought a Tahitian prince named Ahutoru back to Paris, where he became a favourite of Bougainville's backer, the powerful politician and courtier the Duc de Choiseul, and showed himself to be an opera lover.[38]

Choiseul had additional, less romantic, motives in supporting Bougainville's expedition. France could not permit itself to lag behind Britain. Both countries were keen to identify the resources of the Pacific islands, and both were still obsessed by the idea of the Southern Continent. Interest in unfamiliar plants was genuine: the late eighteenth-century French explorer La Pérouse had naturalists on board; Cook's companion Joseph Banks hungrily collected Pacific artefacts and kept filling up the South Sea Room which had been set up in the British Museum in 1775, forcing the museum authorities to enlarge the room within a mere six years.[39] Cook was not just looking for new lands, though: he was also checking reports of discoveries by the French, even if some of these discoveries, such as the aptly named 'Desolation Island', could be dismissed as of little interest.[40] The curiosity of the British took a more practical turn: rather than speculating about 'noble savages', Captain Cook and his men were requested to watch the expected transit of Venus across the sun from Tahiti, and to carry on the search for the Southern Continent. He was instructed to bear in mind 'the Honour of this Nation as a Maritime Power', which 'may tend greatly to the advancement of the Trade and Navigation thereof'.[41] One important feature of Cook's second and third voyages, of 1772 and 1776, was the testing of John Harrison's chronometer, a clock that was to prove accurate enough to make it possible to measure longitude; latitude was a much more straightforward problem, but dealing with the measurement of distance in the direction the earth turned was far more complicated. His use of Harrison's timepiece allowed him to chart the South Sea islands with impressive accuracy. It is said that at the moment Captain Cook was struck down and killed in Hawai'i the clock stopped.[42] But here again it is important to remember that science was being deployed in the service of trade and empire.

Cook, like Bougainville, appreciated the skills of Polynesian navigators. He persuaded Tupaia, a highly skilled navigator, priest and local nobleman, to come on board, and Tupaia accompanied Cook around the Polynesian islands, even drawing a famous map of large tracts of the Pacific from memory, sketching in such places as the Marquesas and the Cook Islands; Tupaia was just as helpful as Harrison's chronometer. Banks thought of Tupaia as another specimen, even if he was a highly intelligent one. Cook was less interested in playing that game, and was impressed by what Tupaia knew: 'we have no reason to doubt his veracity in this, by which it will appear that his Geographical knowlidge [sic] of those Seas is pretty extensive.' Tupaia knew the names of seventy-four islands, and his map covered a vast area of the Pacific roughly equal in size to Europe (including Russia-in-Europe). Most importantly, he explained the complex wind system of the Pacific, still poorly understood after several centuries of a European presence in this ocean.[43]

The adaptability of the Polynesians to European ways was striking. They were particularly adept at commercial deals. In the early nineteenth century, Pomare I, the ruler of Tahiti, traded with the British settlement in New South Wales and joined forces with the London Missionary Society (having converted to Christianity in 1812), sending a ship to Port Jackson, the bay that includes Sydney Harbour, in 1817; Pomare loaded pigs and sandalwood as the main cargo, and on later sailings by Pomare's merchant fleet pearls were gathered in other islands and forwarded to Sydney. The crews were largely Tahitian.[44] Both Ahutoru and Tupaia had already shown a willingness to work with people from a strange world and a fascination with European culture that was to develop in surprising ways once the Europeans (including the Russians) and the Americans developed an interest in Hawai'i.

V

Tupaia did not include the farthest-flung parts of the Polynesian world, Hawai'i, New Zealand and Easter Island, in his sailing directions.[45] His knowledge about the Pacific was an accumulation built up over many centuries and handed down by word of mouth, so that much of the detail was in place long before Hawai'i, Aotearoa and Rapa Nui were settled by Polynesian navigators. Just as it had taken these navigators a long while to cross the band of winds that separated the southern from the northern Pacific, so the arrival of the Europeans in the remote volcanic islands of Hawai'i took a long while, though the Manila galleons or other Spanish ships may well have passed through the archipelago when blown off course, or been attracted by plumes of smoke and fire from the still active volcanoes on Hawai'i Island. A handful of archaeological discoveries, including a piece of woven cloth found in a late sixteenth-century grave, suggest occasional outside contacts with Europeans.[46] In 1777 Cook's target was no longer the Southern Continent but that other persistent obsession of European governments keen to carve out fast and profitable trade routes: the North-West Passage. The British Parliament offered a prize of £20,000 to the crew that would find this route. Cook's trajectory northwards from Tahiti, across 3,000 miles of open ocean, took him to

O'ahu and Kaua'i, on the second of which he made landfall in January 1778. As in Tahiti, the obvious conclusion to be drawn from the arrival of the British was that these were not ordinary humans but the gods who lived far beyond the horizon.[47]

The story of the first encounter is a familiar one: women offered themselves to the sailors, fresh food was taken on board. Cook sailed off after a couple of weeks, returning to the islands from his icy and fruitless search for the North-West Passage in November of the same year. The king turned up to greet Cook on the main island, Hawai'i, and offered the captain feathered headdresses and a magnificent cloak, now preserved in the Te Papa National Museum in Wellington, New Zealand. This was a sign of exceptional respect: a royal cloak required 400,000 tiny red and yellow feathers, taken from 80,000 birds. One of the crew reported that 'we live now in the greatest Luxury, and as to the Choice & number of fine women there is hardly one among us that may not vie with the grand Turk himself'.[48] Yet the gifts of food placed a strain on the Hawai'ian economy, a subsistence economy that was not well suited to the extra demand generated by Cook's ships. After the British ships left the king placed a taboo on the land around the bay where Cook had anchored; this was normal practice when the land was exhausted and needed to revive, rather like the biblical sabbatical year. Forced back by bad weather, Cook re-entered the bay and found he was not welcome; the Hawai'ians began to steal from the British ships, and even sneaked away with the cutter attached to the *Discovery*, leaving Cook's main vessel without a lifeboat. Cook went on land, hoping to make peace with the increasingly fractious crowd of islanders, but guns and daggers were drawn and Cook was clubbed to death – not, however, at anyone's orders, for this was a fracas that had got badly out of control. The grief of the British crew was compounded by disgust when Cook's body was returned, in the form of de-boned hunks of flesh.[49]

The sudden and violent death of Captain Cook was his passport to eternal fame in Great Britain, one of those national heroes, like Lord Nelson, who did not live to see the results of his achievements. The islanders came to terms with the fact that the British were not after all divine by involving themselves in their trade from a very early date. In 1787 Captain John Meares came to the island of Kaua'i and agreed to take one islander, a prince named Kaiana, to China. Kaiana impressed the British by his build – he was six and a half feet tall – and was showered with presents by the English merchants in Canton, the most valuable in many ways being firearms. These he deployed to his advantage on his return to Hawai'i aboard another British ship; he learned that a coup had taken place on

Kaua'i, so he placed himself at the service of the king of the main island, Hawai'i. King Kamehameha I had grand ambitions of his own: he had brought Hawai'i Island under his single rule, and now he aimed to conquer all the lesser islands. Kaiana would be a powerful ally, but no less useful would be the British, with their massive ships armed with deadly cannon, which were also capable of carrying many more warriors than he could pack on to even the longest Polynesian craft.[50]

So began one of the most extraordinary moments in the history of Pacific navigation. The king needed more ships than could be obtained from reluctant British traders either by bargaining or – in some cases – by sending a squad of men on board to seize the ship. Kamehameha would therefore create his own fleet. In 1789, after a bloody confrontation with the crews of two American vessels in search of supplies, Kamehameha acquired the ship *Eleanor* and an accompanying schooner, and he appointed a couple of the officers to chiefdoms, which made sure that he kept hold of their nautical talent. Then, in 1792, his subjects built a vessel in the European style, under the guidance of an American ship's carpenter. By 1803 he was the proud owner of at least twenty ships, some of which had their keel sheathed in copper, the most modern defence against worms. As he became more involved in the sandalwood trade with China, he ordered more and more ships to be constructed. So to the British, French, American, Russian and Spanish fleets in the Pacific a European-style Hawai'ian fleet needs to be added. Three ships are known to have traversed the entire route from the American north-west to China regularly between 1800 and 1832, though most of the Hawai'ian ships set out for Vanuatu or other island groups, to pick up sandalwood, hogs and pearls that could be fed into the networks of not just Polynesia but the wider Pacific. However, the China voyages were financial disasters, because the Hawai'ians were dependent on unscrupulous agents in Canton who saw a good opportunity to exploit innocent newcomers.[51]

A new generation of Polynesian navigators familiarized themselves with European rather than Pacific shipping, and became an essential element in the crew of foreign ships as well as Hawai'ian ones. When American ships passed through the islands, they were often obliged to carry Hawai'ian supercargoes. The *New Hazard*, a 281-ton brig, carried a cargo of firearms, Indian cotton cloth, metal goods, tobacco and sugar, among other items, setting out from its home port of Boston in October 1810, rounding the Horn and reaching Hawai'i late in February of the next year. Most of this cargo was intended for the people living along the west coast of North America. However, sandalwood, potatoes, plantains and the inevitable willing young women were brought aboard in Hawai'i, and in due course it headed for Vancouver Island, in search of native American slaves as well as furs. Its job done, it returned to Hawai'i, where the reports wearily emphasize, once again: 'not much work done this afternoon being girls on board'. The culmination of its voyage was the crossing to Macau and Canton, anchoring at Whampoa, where the ship stood for four months, and where $300,000 worth of tea, nankeen cloth and porcelain was loaded. So, by way of repeated calls at Hawai'i, the routes linking the Atlantic seaboard of North America with the Pacific north-west of America, and China as well, were bound together.[52]

Kamehameha placed himself under the British Crown, for he saw that this would not weaken but rather strengthen his authority so far from London. At the start of the nineteenth century he decided that he could make a profitable deal with the Russians in Alaska, who were always short of supplies. The Hawai'ian king sent a letter to Alexander Baranov, who was running Russian operations in Alaska, suggesting that Kamehameha could solve his difficulties by sending a consignment each year from Hawai'i. Later, Kamehameha allowed the Russians to build a trading base on O'ahu.[53] Kamehameha was careful not to put all his eggs in one basket. As well as the British and the Russians, he had to deal with United States shipping. By 1800 the Americans, not the British, were the most frequent visitors to his islands. This reflected their involvement in the fur trade on the eastern and northern shores of the Pacific, and the tea and silk trade on its south-western shores, by way of Canton. He noted with interest the strength of the trade in Pacific sandalwood towards China, and he decided not just to create a royal monopoly but to encourage sandalwood production at the expense of food production. This resulted in occasional famines, while supplies of sandalwood in Hawai'i became so depleted that he had to issue orders that young trees were subject to taboo, until they had grown sufficiently. These measures were revolutionary: the subsistence economy of the islands was being transformed into a commercial economy, placing heavy demands on a native labour force that had traditionally lived easily off the natural produce of the land.[54] Further difficulties were created by Kamehameha's willingness to accept American imports on credit. Many of these imports were grandiose luxuries used to decorate the royal residences, such as Chinese porcelain, European crystal and American silverware, not to mention the fine Western-style clothing in which the king enjoyed being portrayed.

Difficulties accumulated after Kamehameha I died in 1819. His son, Kamehameha II, thought that the solution was to carry on expanding. His first new ship was a tempting and beautifully appointed yacht named *Cleopatra*; it was horribly expensive, was used for royal pleasure cruises around the islands, and was said to have been 'manned by a drunken, dissipated, irresponsible crew from the captain down to the cabin boy'. This crew managed to wreck the boat beyond repair in 1825.[55] Over the next few years the royal family attempted to restore its fortunes and those of Hawai'i (now denuded of sandalwood) by way of the sandalwood trade in Vanuatu, but that proved to be another disaster when the ship they had sent out disappeared without trace.[56] By the middle of the nineteenth century the Hawai'ian kings had given up trying to operate a fleet; but there had been a glory period under Kamehameha I during which Hawai'i had managed to assimilate European business practices with remarkable speed.

The most powerful economic force in the islands was fast becoming the United States, not Great Britain or Russia, even though the USA would only become master of these islands at the end of the nineteenth century. The success of the American traders partly reflected the fact that the shipping of the United States was unrestricted by Company rules, which stood in the way of English and Russian trade in the Pacific Ocean so long as the East India Company and the Russia–America Company insisted on licensing movement around the Pacific.[57] At least thirty-one American ships arrived in the Hawai'ian islands between 1778 and 1818, maybe as many as forty-three, while British numbers (including warships as well as trading vessels) stood at thirty-nine, and the Russians at eleven.[58] Hawai'i was well placed geographically to act as a supply station in the middle of the north Pacific; its role as middleman between the Asian and the American shores of the ocean provides a neat demonstration of how the entire Pacific was being drawn together into a complex network of maritime connections from the end of the eighteenth century onwards.

46

From the Lion's Gate
to the Fragrant Harbour

I

Competition for access to the markets of the Far East did not wane in the early nineteenth century, even though the nations that had created the first links to China and the East Indies no longer dominated the trade of the East. Having won Melaka from the Portuguese in 1641, after a series of attempts, the Dutch had to cede the city to Great Britain in 1795, and Britain took advantage of its war with Napoleon, and the incorporation of the Netherlands into the Bonaparte empire, to keep hold of the place for a while, without quite knowing what to do with it.[1] The Dutch had never based their government of the East Indies there, preferring Batavia (modern Jakarta), which lies on Java and was therefore closer to the Spice Islands. And yet the idea of creating a base on the Strait of Malacca made good sense for any European power keen to trade through the South China Sea: it was the best place to watch for the switching of the winds as one monsoon season gave way to another, and a safe route back west opened up to shipping.[2]

Melaka had been founded, at least according to legend, by a refugee prince from Temasek, or *Singapura*, generally translated as 'the Lion's Gate'. Fragments of sixteenth-century blue-and-white porcelain recovered from the Kallang River in Singapore reveal that the foundation of Melaka did not spell the end of Singapore; indeed, the sultan of Johor, the southernmost kingdom in Malaya, established a *shahbandar*, or overseer, of customs at Singapore, who was in his post by 1574. A few years later, in 1611, the Singapore settlement was burned to the ground; the entire region had become sucked into wars between the Portuguese and competing Malay and Indonesian rulers, into which the Dutch eventually inserted themselves as well. Probably there was not much to show on Singapore Island in 1703 when the sultan of Johor, who approved of the English, offered the site of the old settlement to a Scottish captain named Alexander

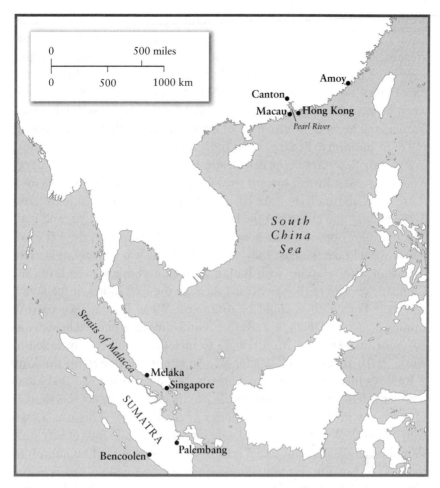

Hamilton. Even when it was offered for free, Singapore was beyond Hamilton's means, as he was expected to develop the site from his own limited resources. However, the East India Company began to recognize that Singapore lay in a perfect position overlooking the entrance to the main passageway between the Indian Ocean and the South China Sea; the islands opposite Singapore, which are now part of Indonesia, were the haunt of the Bugi pirates, who needed to be kept quiet – the surprise is that it took so long for Great Britain to create a base at Singapore.[3]

That Great Britain did so was the result of the vision and endeavours of two employees of the East India Company, Thomas Stamford Raffles and Major William Farquhar. Farquhar administered Melaka for a while before it was returned to the Dutch at the end of the Napoleonic Wars, and had a talent for winning the trust of local rulers, which was crucial in the foundation of British Singapore. Raffles, however, is much better documented; he is one of the most extraordinary figures in British imperial history, and is generally seen as a more attractive personality than the great majority of empire-builders.[4] He was born in 1781, and his origins were quite modest; he spent his early career in the gloomy offices of the East India Company on Leadenhall Street in London, joining as a clerk when he was only fourteen years old. But he was an exceedingly quick learner, and he won the attention of his superiors, so that he was sent off full of enthusiasm to Penang on the Indian Ocean coast of Malaya in 1805, as Assistant Secretary in the British administration of what, it was hoped, would become a British base to rival Calcutta and Bombay. Raffles took the trouble, unusually, to learn basic Malay; he also took a serious interest in the history and culture of the lands where he had been sent, and realized that new opportunities now existed for the British in the Far East, which would take the East India Company some way beyond its current obsession with relations with Indian princes, and might even bring the Company control of the spice trade through the East Indies, if the Dutch and their French allies could be dislodged. When Britain succeeded in gaining control of Dutch Java, Raffles found himself appointed lieutenant-governor, in 1811, but his attempts to introduce land reform failed to work, partly through lack of support. An important clue to his thinking is Raffles's insistence that 'Government should consider the inhabitants without reference to bare mercantile profits and to connect the sources of revenue with the general prosperity of the Colony.'[5] This was a man who deeply deplored slavery, and who insisted that 'all kinds of servitude should be abolished'. But social reform so far away was of no interest to the EIC in London. He was summoned back to London, and was disillusioned by the return of the East Indies to the Dutch in 1816, following the fall of Napoleon. Raffles redeemed his reputation back home – his scholarly interests were acknowledged when he became a Fellow of the Royal Society and received a knighthood, thanks to the support of Queen Charlotte. He used his time after his recall to London well, writing a *History of Java* in two volumes, which was as much a compendium of geography, natural history, ethnography and archaeology as a somewhat higgledy-piggledy history in the traditional sense. Dedicated, with his permission, to the Prince Regent, it was nonetheless an extraordinary work of scholarship, based on almost obsessive research and limitless curiosity.[6]

Still, there was work to be done out East, and Great Britain still retained a small and rather neglected post at Bencoolen in Sumatra, which the Dutch had tolerated for many years. Sent there in 1818, Sir Stamford Raffles, as he now liked to be known, was disappointed to find that the Dutch were vigorously rebuilding their network in the East Indies, while Great Britain had paltry resources east of India:

> The Dutch possess the only passes through which ships must sail into the Archipelago, the Straits of Sunda and Malacca; and the British have now not an inch of ground to stand upon between the Cape of Good Hope and China, nor a single friendly port at which they can water and obtain refreshment.[7]

To be sure, this was an overstatement (Penang was still in British hands), but Raffles managed to convince the governor-general of India, Lord Hastings, that some sort of base was needed close to the Malacca Strait. However, the only way to achieve this was by delicate negotiation with the Malay princes; and the view in Britain was that it was important not to offend the government of the Netherlands, which was now an ally, meaning that Raffles found himself treading on eggshells. The Dutch noted how Raffles was trying to extend British influence beyond Bencoolen to the other, more valuable, side of Sumatra – Raffles had Palembang, the old capital of Śri Vijaya in his sights; they complained to the EIC in Calcutta, and Raffles was warned off. Lord Hastings insisted that Raffles should only try to obtain a patch of land for a trading base, 'not the extension of any territorial influence'; should the Dutch have established themselves nearby, he was to go elsewhere.[8] In fact, the Dutch did establish themselves a very short distance away, in the Riau archipelago, but this did not deter Raffles and his close companion, Major Farquhar (who was to become governor of the new settlement). Fascinated by the evidence that Singapore had a distinguished history many centuries earlier, Raffles retained the traditional name of the site, when standard British practice was to choose a royal name or something recalling the past history of Great Britain.[9] This interest in the past only in part explains his choice of location. It was quite simply an ideal spot at which to park an EIC garrison; and the harbour, in the mouth of the Singapore River, was as good as or better than that of Melaka.

Farquhar was already on good terms with the sultan of Johor, Hussein, and in 1819 a first treaty allowed the British to create a base on a small piece of land they had leased at Singapore. The event was celebrated with great pomp and ceremony as the officers and soldiers of the EIC, with Sir Stamford Raffles in charge, received the sultan of Johor in a magnificently decorated tent, its floor covered with scarlet cloth. British observers were unimpressed by the sultan: he was half-naked, and his bulging stomach and sweaty face were sharply criticized, even though it is hard to imagine that there was anyone, Malay or British, who was not perspiring heavily in that humid environment. This agreement brought the sultan a hand-some rent of $5,000 a year, in Spanish coin; it was followed a few years later, in 1824, by another treaty, by which the sultan ceded the sovereignty of Singapore entirely to Great Britain. For the sultan's claim to rule was contested by his half-brother, and Hussein needed the British. Finally, the same year, the Dutch and the British agreed to divide and rule, with Britain taking Malaya (the 'Straits Settlements') and the Netherlands keeping the East Indies, though they had long been one world, culturally, economically and politically, and still use variants of the same Malay-Indonesian language.[10]

It was a challenge to make the new settlement flourish. While the Dutch enthusiastically quoted their compatriot Grotius to assert the freedom of the seas, that generally meant *their* freedom of the seas. Raffles saw that the future of Singapore would depend on its role as a free port: 'one free port in the seas must eventually destroy the spell of Dutch monopoly.' Having instructed Farquhar that 'it is not necessary at present to subject the trade of the port to any duties', Raffles sailed off to Bencoolen without any suggestion about how to make the new settlement pay its way. He would need to find the means to keep the Dutch away; they blockaded Singapore harbour. But none of this prevented a remarkable community from coming into being.[11] The trademark of Singapore has always been the mixture of peoples who live there, and by the time of the second treaty with Hussein the population had already reached around 5,000, many of whom had moved down from Melaka, thereby reversing the original migration over 400 years earlier that had brought people from medieval Singapore to newly founded Melaka.

Raffles came on a visit in 1822 and exclaimed: 'here all is life and activity; and it would be difficult to name a place on the face of the globe with brighter prospects or more pleasant satisfaction.' Taking charge of the town plan, he assigned quarters to the Chinese, Indians and other ethnic groups and mapped out where government buildings should be built. Raffles divided his town between a government area on the right side of the harbour, still the seat of power, that stretched towards Fort Canning Hill, on which his own villa was built; while on the left side the 'godowns', or warehouses, of the traders were put up, with a view to attracting Chinese, Indian and Malay traffic. He thus had a vision for the future of the city – an exaggerated one, for when he died in London in 1826 Singapore still had many difficulties to overcome.[12]

The colony continued to attract a great mix of people, but early on Singapore became a largely Chinese city, and by the 1830s it had already become the hub of the Chinese trade networks in the South China Sea and beyond, to the consternation of the Dutch in Batavia, which had been the main centre until then. In 1822, 1,776 ships visited Singapore, most of which were Asian.[13] Home to only 1,000 people in 1819, it grew massively from 1824 onwards and was home to over 97,000 people in 1871. In 1867, before the town had existed for half a century, it was already host to 55,000 Chinese, mainly from the south of China, and they accounted for 65 per cent of the population. To this must be added the Chinese in transit through Singapore, many of whom became coolies in other parts of south-east Asia, or in the case of women became domestic slaves or prostitutes – a human traffic that Raffles would not have wished to see develop.[14] At the other end of the social scale were the wealthy, multi-lingual 'Baba', or Peranakan, families, of mainly Chinese descent but long exposed to Malay culture – the term 'Peranakan' means 'local-born'. This placed them securely in the position of middlemen, often able to make a great fortune and to live in considerable style. Baba Tan Tock Seng was born in Melaka but arrived in Singapore with the stream of Melakan Chinese who had arrived during Farquhar's governorship. Originally a trader in chickens and greengrocery, he became the business partner of British traders, which brought him to the top of the ladder of wealth by the 1840s. Well-placed marriage alliances with mainland Chinese further enhanced his wealth and influence. He was as happy to spend money on worthy projects as to make it: in 1844 he founded the Tan Tock Seng Hospital, still in existence, at a cost of $7,000; he gave vigorous support to one of the main Chinese temples (helping to pay for the installation of a statue of the sea goddess Mazu after a lavish public ceremony); and he was appointed Justice of the Peace by the British authorities, the first Asian to hold this role not just in Singapore but in Malaya.[15] Tan and his peers, partly through their philanthropy and partly through their trade, did much to create the thriving city that Singapore gradually became.

The contribution of other ethnic groups was also very substantial. Malay sailors criss-crossed the waters around Singapore, linking the new colony to the islands on the other side of the Malacca Strait and to the Malayan mainland, and helped keep the city supplied with the necessities of life, because from its own resources it could offer little apart from fish.[16] One particular group of Malays, the piratical Bugis, based in the Riau islands just a short boat ride away from Singapore, upped sticks in 1820 after a quarrel with the Dutch masters of Riau, and 500 of them settled in British Singapore instead.[17] During the nineteenth century Singapore attracted Tamil Indians, Armenians (whose little church is a notable monument in the modern city), oriental Jews such as the Sassoon family of Bombay, and Arab settlers such as the Alkaff family, who arrived from southern Arabia in the middle of the century and owned a good number of the warehouses along the Singapore River. These Arab traders were already active in the waters off Melaka and Java, and the fact that some of them chose Singapore as their centre of operations is proof that the idea of creating a free-trade zone there was the key to success. By the 1880s there were already about 800 Arabs living in the city.[18] For Raffles understood that the prosperity of Singapore would depend on its role as an entrepôt through which goods flowed and where they were exchanged; and in the longer term, as steamships came into use, it became a resupply station, offering coal as well as food, for the early steamships were extremely voracious consumers of fuel. In the long term too Singapore would flourish as a centre for the redistribution beyond Malaya of Malay goods, most famously the rubber produced on the plantations introduced by British colonists.

II

The 'Lion's Gate' was indeed a gateway to the East, but it still lay a good distance from the source of the goods that Britain wanted to acquire out there. A base much closer to Canton was surely needed, so that Great Britain – or rather the East India Company – would be able to steal a lead over the old rivals, the Portuguese in Macau, the Dutch and the French. Moreover, British businessmen were looking for an easier way to pay for Chinese goods than the silver China craved and that the EIC was finding it increasingly difficult to supply. The EIC had reason to be worried about its future: it had lost its monopoly on the trade of the East in 1833, since Parliament decided that the key to Britain's prosperity lay in free trade; and in any case the EIC had become so embroiled in the internal affairs of India that it was no longer simply a great trading cartel.

With the cancellation of the EIC monopoly, the factory premises in Canton it had occupied were filled instead by private merchants. Several of the private merchants would later dominate the business affairs of Hong Kong: William Jardine, in conjunction with James Matheson; Thomas Dent; Framjee Cowasjee, a Parsee from India who dealt in opium. Jardine was a perfect example of the enterprising British businessman in search of opportunities. He was a Scot and a graduate in medicine from Edinburgh University, but when he took passage out East as surgeon's mate on an East Indiaman he began to realize how easy it would be to make his fortune out of the spice trade; he became active in the country trade between Bombay and Canton.[19] This enthusiasm for free trade had already spurred Raffles on to the refoundation of Singapore; and it was rooted in the thinking of the British pioneers of economics, the Scot Adam Smith and the Sephardic Jew David Ricardo. Among the readers of both these authors was James Matheson, who had their books sent to him in China and became an apostle for free trade, a philosophy that he and his colleague William Jardine took to an extreme. Jardine carried his Calvinist principles to the furthest limit, so that his office contained a single chair, and anyone who came to see him had to remain standing, which meant that business was conducted rapidly.[20]

Facing these difficulties, the EIC turned to the trade in opium. The source of opium was, to start off with, southern Arabia, but the poppy fields of Bengal were much closer and lay under the control of the East India Company, which was happy to send out the goods through Calcutta. Thus the 'country trade' that had enabled Europeans to maintain their commercial empires in the Indian Ocean reached a new level of intensity. While 5,000 chests of opium, containing up to forty balls of the drug, were exported in 1820, eleven years later the EIC was handling nearly four times as many. At that point, 5,000 chests were worth somewhere around $8,000,000. William Jardine believed that opium was far preferable to alcohol; but what had been treated at first as an exotic recreational drug spread down through society as prices fell (partly in response to competition from poppy fields in western India). The result was the creation of opium dens frequented by all sorts of Chinese. The image of the Chinese at this period as semi-conscious addicts living in a haze of opium smoke was a European image that was completely at variance with Chinese official policy; but it was an image that fitted the condescending attitude of the British to another, far older, imperial power. From a British perspective what really mattered was the access opium offered to all the products of an empire that had been (in their view) far too isolated from trade with the rest of the world. This led to the paradox with which the Dutch had lived quite comfortably for a couple of centuries: free trade was conducted most easily when one's nation possessed its own port and did not have to depend on the favours of local rulers or European rivals. This had become an especially acute problem in Canton, where customs officials interfered with merchants and their cargoes, though no doubt with good reason, in view of imperial displeasure at the opium traffic.[21]

This trade continued to boom despite the insistence of the Chinese authorities that they did not want it and that it had a potentially devastating effect on those who used it: 'its obnoxious odour ascends, irritating heaven and frightening the spirits.' These were the brave words of the Chinese imperial commissioner in Canton, Lin Zexu, who was stirred to send a complaint all the way to Queen Victoria, and who confiscated 20,000 cases of opium as well as imprisoning the foreign merchants in their factories. His actions, regarded in London as outrageously high-handed, set off a conflict with Great Britain, the First Opium War, which saw British troops capture port after port along the coast of China – Amoy, Ningbo, even Shanghai. British naval power proved unstoppable. This was a navy equipped with ironclad steamships, carrying thousands of troops, and determined to show that Great Britain would never ever suffer humiliation at the hands of a Chinese official. The short but sharp conflict was ended by the Treaty of Nanking in 1842, overwhelmingly favourable to Great Britain, in which perpetual British rule over a brand new settlement on Victoria Island was recognized.[22]

The British were convinced that they needed a permanent base at the mouth of the Pearl River where they would be entirely free from Chinese interference. Victoria Harbour was well sheltered; the island, with its steep mountain known as the Peak, offered little space for building compared to flat Singapore, but what was planned was a commercial station, not the teeming city that did emerge. Sir Henry Pottinger, who negotiated the Treaty of Nanking, declared that he 'had no predilection in raising a colony at Hong Kong', but simply wanted to gain 'an emporium for our trade and a place from which Her Majesty's subjects in China may alike be protected and controlled'.[23] British ships were already poking into the creeks and islands that lay on the opposite side of the estuary to Macau in 1829, when the EIC sent at least half a dozen vessels into what would become Victoria Harbour. The legal status of Macau had never been fixed; Hong Kong was to be different – a perpetual possession, with the advantage that its native population was small, maybe 7,500 people, mainly engaged in fishing, and with no sign of interest by the Chinese authorities.

Charles Elliot, the captain who planted the British flag there in January 1841, was another enthusiast for free trade. He had been entrusted with finding a suitable island or other perch along the coast of China, and, as a naval man, he was attracted primarily by the harbour, though back in London there were many doubts; Lord Palmerston was nonplussed, for it was 'a barren island with hardly a house on it', and 'it seems obvious that Hong Kong will not be a Mart of Trade', but simply a pleasure resort for British merchants who would still be tied to Canton. Queen Victoria was no more impressed, even though her name was attached to the territory. And yet had they seen Hong Kong they might have reacted differently: early visitors were also enthusiasts for the place itself, for – despite its humidity in summer – they were impressed by its lush natural beauty, its mountains and its waterways, which several writers compared to the

Scottish highlands.[24] In keeping with this, the name Hong Kong means 'fragrant harbour' in Cantonese, although the origin of the name is uncertain.

Just as at Singapore, land was earmarked for godowns, though strict conditions were attached to anyone who bought land: leases were limited to seventy-five years, and within six months the leaseholder had to spend £1,000 on construction, which guaranteed the mushroom growth of the new settlement. Sharp protests led to a change in policy: leases were extended to 999 years in 1847, but the only freehold property remains the Anglican cathedral. Jardine, Matheson & Co. were particularly active, building godowns for trade and houses for the settlers; they owned a godown 'so extensive, as to form almost a town'. The Chinese bazaar was said to be bigger than that of Macau within a year of the colony's foundation. Something of the tone of the colony can be gathered from the fact that one of the first buildings was that of the exclusive Hong Kong Club, at that time reserved for white British settlers, among whom Jardine and Matheson were the most prominent businessmen. Frederick Sassoon, who sat on the Legislative Council of the colony, was so worried that he would be excluded as a Jew that he did not apply for membership.[25]

From 1843 onwards Chinese settlers were also encouraged to come and live under the British flag, and there were at least 30,000 of them by the middle of the century, which was seventy-five times the number of Europeans, Indians and Americans. As in Singapore, the richest Chinese were often also the most generous philanthropists. All this resulted in a pleasing flow of trade: in 1844, only three years after the colony was established, it was visited by 538 recorded ships. Although the Treaty of Nanking had brought much-valued access to Shanghai and other 'Treaty Ports', Hong Kong rapidly seized the role of centre of operations, benefiting from its special status as a Crown Colony in which, unlike the concessionary areas of the Treaty Ports, Chinese officialdom had no influence at all. Moreover, having won the Opium War, Great Britain did not need to worry about its involvement in the opium trade, which completely dominated the trade of early Hong Kong, so much so that people used cakes of opium as currency and Macau lost its own opium business to Hong Kong. So firm was British ascendancy along the coast of China that the opium-traders had no difficulty in distributing the drug to buyers on the mainland.[26] This ascendancy was consolidated by the Second Opium War, which broke out in 1856 after Chinese troops mugged the captain of a British schooner out of Hong Kong. Canton was occupied (with French collaboration), Beijing was raided, and the Chinese were forced once again to make a humiliating peace. This gave the British access to yet more Treaty Ports, as well as the right to trade inland; and it brought part of Kowloon under British rule, the beginning of a gradual extension of British rule over the southern tip of the Chinese mainland.

Hong Kong and Singapore became essential links along the chain extending all the way from London and Liverpool to the Far East. The idealism of Raffles and Farquhar stands at some distance from the materialism and cynicism of those who promoted the opium trade through Hong Kong. Their continuing role as major international centres of trade and their transformation from cities marked by both extreme affluence and extreme poverty into two of the wealthiest cities in the world are excellent examples of the way in which maritime trade has fundamentally altered the world.

47

Muscateers and Mogadorians

Historians have rightly insisted that a strongly Eurocentric view of the world's history distorts reality; we are prisoners of our sources, but it is sometimes possible to break free and say something about less well-documented activities among non-European peoples. Even there, though, the shadow of Europe often hangs over what at first sight appear to be autonomous networks of maritime trade. An important example is provided by the history of the sultans of Oman, whose political and commercial power extended at its peak from points south and west of Zanzibar in east Africa, past their old capital at Muscat in Oman, and along the shores of what are now Pakistan and India, including the trading station at Gwadar, which the rulers of Oman only ceded to Pakistan in 1958, for a handsome fee of 5,500,000,000 rupees. The Omani 'empire' largely consisted of a string of pearls stretched across a vast expanse of the western Indian Ocean. By the middle of the nineteenth century the most valuable of these pearls was the small island of Zanzibar, previously a place of no great importance. This, then, was another of the newly successful trading towns of the era and, despite the involvement of the British and the French in its emergence, the real initiative came from the sultans themselves. Their success was based on three commodities: cloves, ivory and slaves, and their slave trade boomed just as the slave trade in other parts of the world was being vigorously suppressed by the British Navy.

Oman was already a lively centre of naval activity in the seventeenth century. By the middle of the century the Omanis had recovered Muscat from the Portuguese, and, once free from foreign shackles, the Omanis established a reputation for themselves as fearsome pirates. They raided the Portuguese bases along the coast of east Africa, as far south as Mozambique, beginning with an attack on Zanzibar in 1652, on Mombasa in 1661 and culminating in the capture of Mombasa in 1698. They also

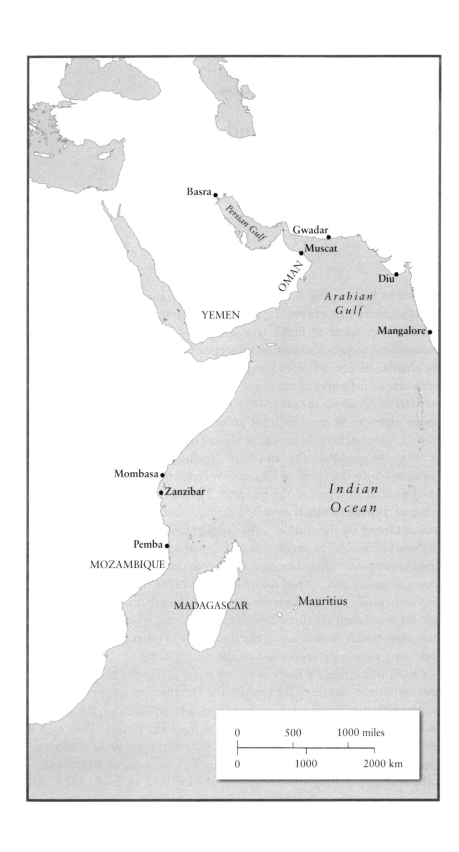

looked eastwards, sacking the Portuguese trading station at Diu in India in 1668.[1] The rise of Oman was not all plain sailing, though, as there were endless civil wars and contests for the throne; this left Mombasa for a long time under a different ruler, but the Omanis compensated by acquiring Zanzibar and its neighbour Pemba during the next century, thereafter extending their control over much of the Swahili coast and building commercial links through Arab merchants some way into the African interior. From there they acquired not just the ivory for which demand in western Europe was constantly growing but the slaves whom the French were using as a labour force in their sugar plantations on Mauritius and Réunion.[2]

Meanwhile Oman flourished as its ships inserted themselves successfully in the trade in coffee out of Yemen. By 1774, according to a British witness, most of the Mocca coffee carried up the Persian Gulf to Basra arrived on board Omani ships based in Muscat. The British were never far away: there was a British 'resident' in Basra who was entitled to a share of the import duties on coffee, by agreement with the Ottoman government of Iraq. The British praised 'the friendship which subsisted betwixt us and the Muscateers'. As their involvement with the European trade networks deepened around 1780, the 'Muscateers' penetrated markets in India as well, as far south as Mangalore, bringing the produce of Arabia – pearls, incense, dates, sold in exchange for sugar and spices which they bought from the Dutch, including products of the East Indies. As they became more involved with India, the Omanis attracted Indians, or 'Banyans', to their own shores, and communities of Indian merchants began to form in Muscat and, in due course, all the way down the coast of east Africa in the Omani-ruled ports. Around 1800 an Indian named Mowjee was customs farmer in Muscat: 'a fat cunning Man and the richest Subject in the Place', according to an English witness.[3] In 1762 the British in Bombay decided they needed plenty of slaves, who were to be sent to the new East India Company base that was being set up in Sumatra. The EIC turned to an Indian merchant in Muscat, and he provided a batch of African slaves for 10,000 rupees. Muscat began to acquire a reputation for its safety and its sheer convenience, particularly compared to ports within the Gulf that the Europeans had been using in the past; thieves suffered the Koranic penalty of losing their hand, so that 'merchandise lye constantly in the Streets, without the least fear of Pilferage'.[4]

The Omanis did not simply rely on traditional dhows, large and small, in all their variety. By the end of the eighteenth century the sultan was commissioning square-rigged ships of European design in India; in 1786 he is said to have possessed eight men-of-war, for alongside peaceful trade the sultan engaged in naval wars with his rebellious subjects, and the size of the fleet doubled in the last quarter of the eighteenth century, as did the volume of coffee handled by the Muscateers.[5] Before 1800, then, the Omanis had established themselves as valuable middlemen between the European colonies in India and Indonesia and lands ruled by the Ottomans, the Persians, African rulers and themselves. Their range extended as far as Calcutta, the new British base in India, even though this meant they had to sail their ships right round the subcontinent; but there they could mix with merchants and sailors from almost every maritime nation under the sun.[6] They could also take advantage of the steady reduction in importance of the Portuguese, in the Indian Ocean, both politically and commercially, and exploit the rivalry between other Europeans to insert themselves successfully into the maritime trade of the Indian Ocean.[7]

The rise of Muscat is only part of the remarkable story of the Omani maritime empire. Like the commercial empire of the ancient Phoenicians, it was built around ports, islands and trading counters; and like the Phoenician trading empire its centre of gravity shifted from its place of origin to a far-off base: Zanzibar was the new Carthage. Around 1800 Zanzibar was still 'composed of some few houses, and the rest are huts of straw mat', in the eyes of a British visitor. Yet it had already become the main meeting point in the western Indian Ocean for Europeans, Arabs, Indians and Africans, famous for its supplies of ivory.[8] By 1744 an Omani governor operated from Zanzibar, and by 1822, when the sultan signed a treaty with Captain Fairfax Moresby, representing Great Britain, in Muscat, the Omani ascendancy was clear. Under the terms of this agreement the Omanis promised to cease selling slaves to the western Europeans or in India, as part of the great British crusade against slave-trading across the world.[9]

This had the unexpected result of stimulating the Omani trade in east African slaves, as other sources of supply dried up, for there were still swathes of territory where slaves could be bought and sold, in their tens of thousands, including the islands of Zanzibar and Pemba. The worst form this already horrible trade took was the callous, indeed murderous, treatment of African boys in a Coptic monastery on Mount Jebel-Eter in Sudan that specialized in castration. Clamped to a table, the victims had their penis and scrotum removed in one quick swipe, leaving 'a large, gaping sore that does not heal kindly', all the more so since there was little attempt to staunch the flow of blood. The boys were then buried in packed sand to keep them immobile; 'it is estimated 35,000 little Africans are annually sacrificed to produce the Soudanese average quota of its 3,800 eunuchs.'[10] Even if the assumption that mortality approached 90 per cent is an exaggeration (and it is impossible to say), demand for eunuchs in princely courts around the Indian Ocean did not slacken.

The attractions of Zanzibar became more and more obvious to the sultans. One practical advantage was the quality of its well-protected deep-water harbours, and another was the excellent supply of fresh water, while the fact that it was a small island close to the African shore provided natural defences.[11] Sayyid Said bin Sultan made the decision to transfer his centre of government from Muscat to Zanzibar. He was a great traveller, visiting Zanzibar in 1802, aged only eleven, and again in 1828, while the Omanis were once again trying to conquer Mombasa. At this point he seems to have laid plans for the move, building a new palace and finally settling there in 1832; according to tradition he set sail on a ship owned by one of his favourite Banyan, or Indian, merchants. He lived another twenty-four years, so he had plenty of time to consolidate his interests in east Africa, as well as presiding over the growth of Zanzibar City. That became his preferred residence, but he continued to travel back and forth between his domains, dying while en route to Zanzibar on what would have been his ninth trip. Thus he took care not to neglect his ancestral lands just because his main base was now far away in east Africa.[12]

By now the Moresby Treaty was beginning to bite; but that did not prevent the sultan from devising a new way to make a fortune. The great transformation that now took place was the development of clove plantations in Zanzibar and Pemba, the most successful attempt so far to create a major source of this spice outside the Moluccas; it is said that he ordered his subjects to plant three clove trees for every one coconut palm on their land, subject to a penalty of confiscation of their farm if they failed to comply.[13] Transplanting cloves to soil closer to Europe had been the dream of colonists in Madagascar, Mauritius and elsewhere. In addition, vast numbers of elephants were slaughtered in the African hinterland to supply European demand for high-quality ivory; Arab and Swahili merchants penetrated deep into the interior, as far as Lake Nyasa, in their search for African goods. A very active market for ivory emerged in the United States, as elephants were sacrificed to manufacture piano keys, combs and billiard balls, while Zanzibaris hungered for American cotton cloths. In 1828, while Sayyid Said was in Zanzibar, he received an American merchant named Edmund Roberts and encouraged him to ask the US government to enter into a trade treaty. This was duly signed, and the benefits for the Omanis went beyond simple sales of raw materials: in 1840 an Omani ship, the *Sultanah*, sailed all the way to America, with the sultan's ambassador on board. Ivory prices continued to rise, and at the same time the cost of manufactured goods sent from Europe and America continued to fall. This placed Zanzibar in a very advantageous position. Indeed, Sultan Said was receiving more than 500,000 Maria Theresa silver dollars (MT$)

from customs dues and taxes levied in east Africa and Oman by the time of his death in 1856. By 1890 revenues from Muscat were in steep decline, but for Zanzibar this was only the beginning as revenues soared to reach MT$800,000.[14]

II

The patronage Sultan Said and his successors extended to Indian merchants, in many cases Hindu or Parsee, has intriguing parallels on the other side of Africa. Religious outsiders might suffer discrimination, but they could also build especially strong bonds to a ruler who cared for them. In the far north-west of the continent another dynasty of Muslim rulers anxious to make big profits out of trade extended its protection to Jewish merchants, and there too the result was the flowering of a new city.[15] Today Essaouira in south-western Morocco makes its money from tourism (the strong winds attract plenty of surfers) and from argan oil, of which it is the world's only source. However, before the First World War it was Morocco's window on the world, a place where merchants from England, France and Spain, along with Sephardic merchants from Morocco itself, and the sultan's watchful government, collaborated in a largely successful attempt to make it the richest port in Atlantic Morocco. Generally known, until Morocco recovered its independence in the 1950s, as Mogador, it will be called by that name in this chapter.

Like Hong Kong, Singapore and Zanzibar, Mogador was to all intents a new town, although the Phoenicians had traded from the rocky offshore island of Mogador, and the Portuguese and other foreign powers briefly occupied the site. Mogador's advantage was that there was a straight run across country to Marrakesh, which vied with Fez for the role of capital of Morocco, and which was the gateway through which much of the trans-Sahara caravan traffic passed. While it never rivalled in size Alexandria or Beirut, the intermediary role of Mogador gave it an importance out of all proportion to its physical size and population – up to 20,000 inhabitants towards the end of the nineteenth century, of whom at some points as many as half were Jews. The growth of this trading centre transformed the society and economy of the entire region, resulting in the creation of a 'capitalist' class of landowners and merchants, as well as increasing dependence on foreign rather than locally produced goods; and the ripples were felt as far away as sub-Saharan Africa, England and even China.[16]

Sidi Muhammad ibn Abdallah, the sultan of Morocco, founded Mogador in 1764 with the specific intention of making it into the prime centre

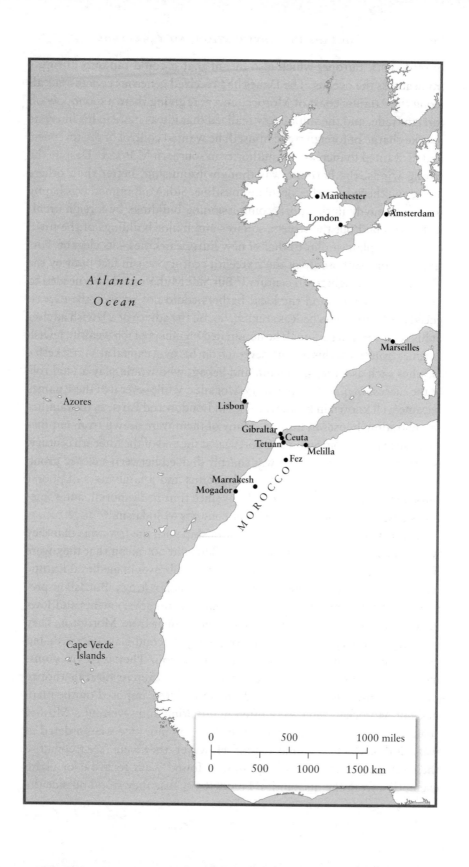

Atlantic
Ocean

Manchester
London
Amsterdam

Marseilles

Azores

Lisbon
Gibraltar
Tetuan Ceuta
Melilla
Fez
Marrakesh
Mogador

MOROCCO

Cape Verde
Islands

0	500	1000 miles
0	500	1000	1500 km

of trade with Europe, which also meant that it could tap into Europe's trade across the oceans. The Danes had received generous concessions all along the Atlantic coast of Morocco in 1751, giving them a monopoly on foreign trade, and the sultan now realized that it was more in his interests to take charge of foreign trade himself: he wanted control of the revenues, and he wanted to increase his authority in southern Morocco. Despite the strong winds, the harbour was thought promising, better than others along an otherwise rather desolate coastline. Sidi Muhammad was happy to invest heavily in this port, commissioning buildings by foreign architects, who laid out the streets, squares and major buildings of the town on a square plan similar to that of new European cities – its elegant 'Portuguese' fort supposedly of the sixteenth century was in fact built by the Genoese in the eighteenth century.[17] But Sidi Muhammad also needed to populate Mogador, and the local Berbers could not provide the experienced mercantile class he was seeking. So, on the advice of a Jewish adviser at his court, Samuel Sumbal, he nominated members of ten wealthy Jewish families from across his realms, several from his own capital at Marrakesh – families such as Corcos, Macnin and Sebag, who would play a vital role in the success of nineteenth-century Mogador, while several of these names became well known in business circles in London and Paris, as the families set up trading houses in Europe. Many of them were drawn from families that had arrived from Spain and Portugal at the end of the fifteenth century, for Moroccan Jewish society was sharply divided between a closed group of wealthy families claiming Spanish origins and a large mass of poorer Jews, living in their towns and villages since time immemorial, and sometimes descended from ancient Berber converts to Judaism.[18]

A crucial aspect of the sultan's relationship with the Jews was that they were, to use his own phrase, *his* Jews. This did not mean that they were his property, any more than the use of similar phrases in medieval Europe had meant that Jews were the slaves of Christian kings. But Islam prescribed a particular relationship between Muslim governments and Jews (or Christians – but native Christians were absent from Morocco). They were accepted as part of the fabric of society, 'second-class citizens – but citizens' in Bernard Lewis's concise formulation. They were *dhimmi*s, meaning 'protected persons', but they were not to exercise direct authority over Muslims. When fully applied, the restrictions imposed on the main mass of Moroccan Jews were often humiliating and severe: if a Muslim struck a Jew, the Jew had no right to reply in kind; they were ordered to wear dull black clothes; and so on.[19] However, they were free to practise their religion; and the leading families found ways to avoid or claim exemption from the disabilities. Precisely because they stood outside the political jungle of tribal and factional politics, rulers saw them as neutral but dependent and dependable agents, and nowhere more so than in the world of trade, where their knowledge of languages and family connections across wide spaces qualified them extremely well for the sultan's patronage.

So it was that families such as the Corcos, descended from Spanish refugees who had arrived in Marrakesh by way of Portugal and Fez, found themselves the intimates of the Moroccan sultans, advising the royal palace on political developments in the countryside, which their agents observed as they travelled between Mogador and their markets in the interior.[20] They and a few other leading families became the 'merchants of the sultan', *tujjār as-Sultān*; but this was more than a title, for they actually traded on the sultan's account, theoretically at least with his rather than their money; 'the sultan was in effect the pre-eminent merchant of the country.'[21] The underlying reality was that the sultan's own resources depended significantly on loans, taxes and gifts from the *tujjār*. All this was arranged carefully, since Islamic law forbids the direct payment of interest, with the result that the merchants paid a share of their profits to the sultan, rather than paying him interest on the sums that the government had entrusted to them for trade. When the father of Abraham Corcos died in 1853, the sultan sent letters to Corcos stating that 'your father was our friend and was one of us – his death has greatly distressed us'. A few years later, a letter arrived from the sultan's palace, reminding Abraham's brother Jacob that the sultan had ordered American linen cloth for his army, and asking for still more to be supplied to make covers for army horses. The supply of uniforms for his army depended heavily on the Corcos family's links to the outside world.[22]

With the sultan's blessing, then, the Jewish merchants dominated and looked outwards from Mogador. They were permitted to live in the fortified *casbah*, the royal quarter, while poorer Jews were ordered to live in the Jewish quarter, or *mellah*, established in Mogador in 1806.[23] At the end of the nineteenth century the right to live in the *casbah* was a special mercy, as immigration from the countryside by poor Jews led to severe overcrowding in the *mellah*, which became notorious for disease. The *casbah*, at the other end of town, contained handsome town houses built around shady courtyards in the traditional Moroccan style, several of which have now been converted into *riyad* hotels for tourists.[24] From the houses overlooking the royal square the sultan's merchants were able to look down on the harbour, barely five minutes' walk away, and see their goods being unloaded. Their own partnerships mirrored those of the Cairo Genizah a millennium earlier: they entered into written contracts where a sleeping partner put up funds and sent a travelling partner off on business, looking forward to a division of the profits on his return. These partnerships also took another form, as the leading business families married among themselves, or occasionally made marriage alliances with Sephardic families with whom they traded in London, Livorno or Lisbon, in Gibraltar, Marseilles or Amsterdam.[25] It was a tightly knit community and yet it was also a widespread one.

Foreign contacts took another form too. Abraham Corcos became vice-consul for the United States in Mogador in 1862. He extended US consular protection to his agents trading across Morocco; this unsettled the Moroccan authorities, because placing Jews under foreign protection undermined the claim of the sultan to be their protector. Corcos's initiative was followed by other honorary consuls in Mogador, as also happened in Alexandria, Salonika and Smyrna. It is not clear that Corcos's English was at all good, but what the foreign powers wanted was someone who could communicate on the ground. A photograph of him from 1880 shows an elderly bald figure in a frock coat, which increasingly became the uniform of the Mogador Jewish merchants.[26] This was part of a wider process of acculturation not to Moroccan but to European habits. Although the merchant houses were splendid examples of traditional Moroccan domestic architecture, the life lived within their walls took on an increasingly western European character, for the Mogador elite, like the Sephardic elite in Salonika or Alexandria, became fluent in French and English, and even established an English-speaking school.

The Sephardic diaspora, out of which early generations of Portuguese merchants trading in Italy, Turkey, the Atlantic islands, the Caribbean and even India had emerged, continued to hold together as Mogador came into existence. There were also some wealthy Muslim merchants in Mogador, with whom relations seem to have been perfectly cordial, but the significant business community other than the Jews consisted of the foreign merchants from England, Holland, Denmark, Spain and elsewhere. They were particularly important before 1800 – there was a Franciscan church to cater for the needs of the Spanish merchants. For more than forty years, from 1845 to 1886, a British consul, John Drummond Hay, exercised great influence in Mogador.[27] Great Britain was the biggest trade partner of Morocco by 1800. This meant that the Jews of Mogador and other Moroccan towns, who possessed close ties with the Spanish and Portuguese Synagogue in London, and who often had relatives in Gibraltar, were ideally placed to serve his needs.[28] A series of trade agreements between Morocco and Great Britain culminated in a treaty signed in 1856 that abolished or lowered many taxes and set a standard for future British trade agreements elsewhere in the world. The treaty acted as a spur to the vigorous development of trade through Mogador, in tea, sugar and Western manufactures.[29]

It has been seen that the sultan was keen to buy American cloth, but English cloth was in greater demand, woven in Manchester, where the Jewish families of Mogador often had agents, relatives and investments. Aaron Afriat set himself up in business in England in 1867, and specialized in tea and cloth. Indeed, *at-Tay Afriat*, 'Afriat Tea', was the Moroccan equivalent of Twinings or Tetley, available all over Morocco by way of Mogador, while Afriat's linen cloth was sold right across the Sahara.[30] Tea was the greatest contribution of the Mogador Jewish traders to Morocco – indeed to Moroccan civilization. Here was a product of India and China that had been carried from the Pacific, or at least the Indian Ocean, all the way to England, before being re-exported to north Africa. Although it was brewed and drunk in different ways to England (no milk but several sprigs of fresh mint), tea captured the markets of the Maghrib as successfully as it had already captured the markets of England, Sweden or the United States. Linked to the tea trade was the sugar trade out of the West Indies, since the Moroccans preferred their tea very sweet, generally placing a large lump of sugar in the mouth of the teapot, over which they poured hot water. The use of boiled water improved health across the north African population. As the tea craze gripped Morocco, demand for Chinese and Japanese porcelain grew in wealthy households, and it was brought in by way of London or Amsterdam.[31]

Morocco had much less to offer to the outside world. When Meir Macnin, who dubiously claimed to be the sultan's ambassador to the Court of St James, sailed to London in July 1799 aboard the *Aurora* there was nothing very exotic about its cargo of goatskins, calf hides, almonds and gum arabic. Morocco leather was the most famous product, and reached markets as far afield as Russia, by way of English or other intermediaries. Mules were sent to the West Indies. The sultan occasionally banned the export of potentially lucrative products such as olive oil and honey. There was, though, active demand for Moroccan cattle in Gibraltar, primarily to feed the British garrison, and the sultan had a consul there from 1796 or earlier. This trade, largely out of Tetuan rather than Mogador, netted the sultan a nice income.[32] However, the sultan's interest in Gibraltar was not simply economic: there were times when Sidi Muhammad imagined he could earn the trust of Great Britain and win support for his attempts to gain control of the Spanish *presidios* of Ceuta and Melilla. Moreover, the trade with Gibraltar had a military dimension: he obtained gunpowder and naval stores through the Rock.[33] Signs that Morocco might have more to offer were visible in 1784, just after the Great Siege of Gibraltar, when some merchants based on the Rock mentioned in a report that gold dust, ivory and ostrich feathers were now arriving. Later, by way of Mogador, the trade in ostrich feathers to England, France and elsewhere was to develop into a very lively business during the nineteenth and early twentieth centuries, driven by changing fashions in Europe. Yet what is also significant about these three products is that they were drawn from sub-Saharan Africa, carried on camel caravans all the way to the Atlantic coast for trans-shipment to western Europe. Just as Zanzibar was the gateway to the produce of south-eastern Africa, Mogador was the gateway to the produce of large tracts of west Africa.

III

Further proof that the Sephardic trading network had not lost its vitality within the Atlantic is provided by the way Moroccan Jews seized new trading opportunities across the Portuguese island world. Lisbon, already home to New Christians who practised their old religion out of sight, attracted settlers from Mogador and other Moroccan towns, and in 1816 the Portuguese government agreed to readmit those living openly as Jews.[34] Jews from Portugal and Morocco struck out across the Atlantic. Important economic initiatives were begun in the Portuguese Azores during the nineteenth century, thanks to the Bensaúde family, one of whom became a leading figure in Portuguese academic life (and an expert, among other things, on the voyages of discovery), while their company still dominates the economy of the archipelago. They arrived in 1818, and they exploited business contacts with England to tap into the shipping lines linking the Azores not just to Portugal, Great Britain and Morocco, but to Newfoundland and Brazil. One particularly prominent Jewish businessman was Elias Bensaúde, who possessed an enormous variety of interests, including a tobacco factory and inter-island trade. He had a penchant for oranges, which he sent in all directions, thanks to his close collaboration with partners in London, Manchester and beyond, from where he obtained ironmongery and other essentials that he sold in the islands. Although his family did much to transform the Azores from a sleepy outpost of Portugal into an Atlantic hub, the Bensaúdes were by no means alone, and there was a steady stream of Jewish immigrants from Morocco, so that in mid-century fifteen out of 167 members of the Commercial Chamber in Ponta Delgada, the capital of the Azores, were Jewish immigrants.[35]

Looking even deeper into the Atlantic, Moroccan Jews settled in the Cape Verde Islands, which had once been the haunt of New Christians. As Great Britain placed increasing pressure on its 'oldest ally', Portugal, to abolish its all-too-active slave trade, from 1818 onwards the Cape Verde Islands came under increasing scrutiny, as Portugal's main holding station for African slaves despatched to the West Indies. Looking for a source of income other than slaving, the Portuguese colonial regime installed coal depots in the islands, notably at Mindelo on São Vicente in 1838; the rise of the steamship created new opportunities for anyone prepared to maintain massive stocks of coal. But that meant importing coal; these are volcanic islands totally lacking in coal mines. In 1890, 156 ships are said to have unloaded more than 657,000,000 metric tons of coal, in a year when 2,264 ships visited Mindelo. It is hard to believe this figure, but even if it is exaggerated the fact remains that these ships carried nearly 344,000 people and that their cargo (other than coal) amounted to well over 4,000,000 tons.[36] Whatever the correct figures may have been, Mindelo attracted Jewish merchants from Tangier anxious to service this trade alongside coal merchants from England.[37]

The two examples of Zanzibar and Mogador are of special interest as success stories in which non-European rulers took important economic initiatives, making full use of the non-Muslim communities in and beyond their borders. That said, the European and American connections were vital to the success of these ports, and in both cases their rulers understood the importance of trade treaties with European powers. Similar stories of success can also be told about other marginal groups whose members took advantage of the expansion of commerce across the oceans to set up trading counters in improbable places: Armenians, Syrian Christians, Greeks (some of whom penetrated deep into central Africa), Indians (in South Africa). Sailors too came from many backgrounds. The Indian Ocean had provided manpower on board European ships since the sixteenth century; the 'Lascars' who helped sail European ships originated in lands as diverse as Somaliland, Yemen, India, Ceylon, Malaya and the Philippines, though in their case ill-treatment sometimes gave rise to mutiny against European captains. Still, without them it is hard to see how the routes across not just the Indian Ocean but all the oceans could have been maintained.[38] Another group of Jews, not Sephardim of Spanish and Portuguese descent but Mizrahi ('eastern') Jews from Baghdad, played a prominent role in the economic development of Hong Kong. In the age of the steamship the opportunities were endless and distances somehow seemed more manageable. Maybe, indeed, they could become more manageable still if ways through Suez and Panama could be created.

PART FIVE

The Oceans Contained,
AD 1850–2000

48

Continents Divided, Oceans Conjoined

I

The search for more direct routes from Europe to the Far East had continued without interruption since the days of Columbus and Cabot. The possibility of an Arctic route was still being mooted when Sir John Franklin led his disastrous and long-lamented expedition to the icy wastes north of Canada in 1845.[1] The increasing role in international trade of the east-coast ports of the United States also stimulated thinking about new routes to the riches of the Orient, since the voyage around Cape Horn and the voyage past the Cape of Good Hope were long and sometimes dangerous. In addition to the Pacific fur trade, the Americans were heavily involved in whaling, sending ships out from Nantucket and into the Pacific by way of the Indian Ocean. Ships suitable for whaling began to be constructed in Nantucket in 1694, and other New England towns followed suit: New Bedford had eighty large whalers by 1775. At first these ships hunted whales in cold northern waters or (when searching for sperm whales) in the warmer waters of the central Atlantic, but they began to penetrate the Pacific as well, by way of Cape Horn; in 1850 the whaler *Hannibal* sailed all the way to the still impenetrable north-west coast of Japan, three years before Commander Perry's famous attempt to break into Japanese trade.[2] Herman Melville enthused about the Pacific in his tale of American whalers, *Moby-Dick*:

> To any meditative Magian rover, this serene Pacific, once beheld, must ever after be the sea of his adoption. It rolls the midmost waters of the world, the Indian ocean and Atlantic being but its arms. The same waves wash the moles of the new-built California towns but yesterday planted by the recentest race of men, and lave the faded but still gorgeous skirts of Asiatic lands, older than Abraham; while all between float milky-ways of coral isles, and low-lying, endless, unknown Archipelagoes, and

impenetrable Japans. Thus this mysterious, divine Pacific zones the world's whole bulk about; makes all coasts one bay to it; seems the tide-beating heart of earth.[3]

After the United States acquired California from Mexico in 1848, American interest in the Pacific grew further; but a transcontinental railway was still a dream, and it was far easier to send Asian goods to New York by way of Mexico or the isthmus of Panama than across the Rocky Mountains and through the large expanses inhabited by native Americans. On the other hand, rumour had it that Japan was rich in coal, and naval strategists could see that it was vital to create coaling stations around the globe now that the steamship was coming into its own, as Great Britain had managed to do in Mindelo and elsewhere. Coal rather than silk brought the Americans to Japan. The Japanese were startled by Commander Perry's 'black ships', belching smoke, when the Americans reached Edo Bay in 1853, in an episode that is, rather exaggeratedly, seen as the moment Japan opened up to the wider world after centuries of near seclusion.

Like Ishmael in *Moby-Dick*, Perry had set out from the east coast of America, not from California. Perry travelled most of the way on a steam-powered paddleboat that took him around the bottom of Africa to Macau, Shanghai and the Ryukyu Islands, before he brazenly forced his way into Edo Bay (now known as Tokyo Bay), parading his ironclad steamboats and his firepower and flatly refusing to follow Japanese instructions: as far as the Japanese were concerned, there was a single place, Nagasaki, where foreigners could trade. Although he managed to secure a treaty on a second visit, in 1854, the agreement focused on consular representation for stranded sailors rather than trade, and powerful interests at court remained very hostile to the idea of opening up the imperial ports. In the short term, the main effect of Commander Perry's visit was that the Dutch argued for more generous terms of trade through their base at Deshima, and the Russians and the British obtained similar rights to the Americans.

It was not much; but the door to Japan was open a crack, and a commercial treaty was signed in 1858, permitting the Americans to trade through Yokohama, near Edo. From the American perspective the advantages of trading directly with Japan remained limited while the route to Japan was so arduous. From the Japanese perspective, trade with the outside world was at best a mixed blessing. The Americans might not yet account for much, but taken together foreign trade had a massive impact on the economy of Japan. Foreign goods began to compete with domestic products; powerful foreign demand for silk, tea and copper forced up prices for Japanese consumers; the low price of gold in relation to silver within Japan created strong foreign demand for its gold, which flowed out relentlessly and was replaced by foreign silver. These changes were not easy to absorb: they happened fast, and on an alarming scale; between 1854 and 1865 the price of raw silk trebled, and the price of tea doubled; even the price of the staple foodstuff, rice, shot up.[4] Not surprisingly, then, the arrival of the 'barbarians' opened up new controversies within Japan: should the intruders be welcomed, as one party more loyal to the shoguns insisted, or should they all be expelled, as the first stage in a return to traditional values, including proper reverence for the emperor rather than the shogun – to cite the much-read author Kamo Mabuchi (d. 1769), 'the Way of the gods is superior to the Ways of foreign lands'? The debate about the 'barbarians' and other arguments about the reform of government in Japan culminated in the abolition of the shogunate in 1868 and the creation of the emperor-centred Meiji regime, dedicated to modernization on Japanese terms. As Macpherson noted, 'Perry's black ships symbolize the challenge of possible western colonization. The response was not to withdraw further into an isolationist posture but to emulate and catch up with the West.' The encounter with Perry and with other foreign ships helped create a curious amalgam combining Japanese civilization with European technology. Vigorous and imaginative reforms attempted, with varying success, to adapt Japanese society to its new outward-facing existence, notably the creation of a Ministry of Commerce which made government loans available to producers.[5]

The foreigners were not expelled and the Americans became keen to capitalize on their new opportunities. Reaching Asia would become much less difficult if transit through the narrow neck of Central America could be made easier. Panama had long been a transfer point for goods brought from China and the Philippines. The name Panama meant 'the place where many fish are taken'. It was originally applied to a little town on the Pacific that was wrecked by Henry Morgan in 1671, whereupon a new settlement was created on the site of modern-day Panama City. Both gave access to a 'royal road' that was barely a mule track, across which goods were humped to Nombre de Dios, a very modest little port on the Caribbean, founded as far back as 1510. It failed to flourish since the larger town of Veracruz, in Mexico, was adopted instead as the main departure point for the ships carrying Asian goods, as well as Central American ones, towards Europe. But, in the eyes of nineteenth-century observers, the location looked just right for a railway linking the two oceans, or even – maybe an impossible dream – a canal cutting right through Central America.[6]

II

Although, after many frustrating decades, the Panama Canal was eventually built by the United States, the pioneers of this great project, the largest engineering project in human history, before the late twentieth century, were not American but French. Their enthusiasm for a canal through Central America was generated in part by their success in promoting what, on the surface, seemed a similar scheme, the Suez Canal.[7] Ambitious canal projects across large areas of land were in vogue in the middle of the nineteenth century: other examples of massive, and very successful, canal projects included the Erie Canal linking the Great Lakes in North America to the Hudson River and the sixty-mile Caledonian Canal across Scotland.[8] Actually, the digging of a canal between Africa and Asia was a lesser challenge than the building of the Panama Canal: the land was fairly flat; it was not crossed by powerful rivers; heavy rains did not interfere with the project; there were saltwater lakes through which a route could be dredged; there were traces of much older canals that proved such a route was possible; a labour supply was available among the Egyptian *fellahin*. There was, it is true, some anxiety about the lower level of the Mediterranean compared to the Indian Ocean; and, as at Panama, there were political and financial challenges that had to be met in addition to the technical problem of actually digging the canal.

The building of a canal through Suez excited romantic ideas of the 'conjoining of East and West' in ways that the building of a canal through Panama did not. In the 1830s Barthélemy-Prosper Enfantin became the self-appointed apostle of a new world order in which East and West would join in a single 'nuptial bed', consummating their marriage 'by the piercing of a canal through the isthmus of Suez'.[9] Enfantin was by any standards a colourful eccentric, with his sky-blue cloak and his exaggeratedly pseudo-oriental costume; but the Parisians took him to their heart, and his insistence (guided by the thinking of Saint-Simon) on the urgent need for both material and moral improvement appealed not just to the French but to the rulers of Egypt, beginning with the redoubtable Muhammad Ali. But Ali was less impressed by the argument for a canal than he was by the arguments for modernizing, even attempting to industrialize, Egypt: trade through Alexandria and other ports produced much-needed revenue for the treasury; and Ali was, nominally at least, only the viceroy of the Ottoman sultan in Constantinople, who was opposed to the plan, as, initially, were the British, who valued the existing link between Alexandria and England – a steam packet set out from Falmouth in Cornwall every month, bound for Malta and Alexandria. The last thing Great Britain wanted was France fishing in its own waters within the Indian Ocean, which would become much easier if a canal carried French shipping from Marseilles to India.[10]

Once Muhammad Ali had died, French attempts to convince the viceroy of the financial benefits Egypt, or rather the rulers of Egypt, could draw from a canal began to succeed. Its great proponent, Ferdinand de Lesseps, turned his charm on the new viceroy, Said, whose passion for macaroni had made him thoroughly obese; but he was a clever enough political operator, and he fell in with de Lesseps's attempts to sell shares in the scheme. This did not work out well for Said: when the shares offer was undersold, Said had to pick up the remaining shares, but at least the project was well under way by the time that Said died in 1863, and the viceroy received a special bonus: the new port at the northern end of the canal, where work had begun, was named Port Said in his honour. Said raised a labour force through a corvée imposed on Egyptian peasants, which was deeply unpopular with his subjects. His successor, Ismail, had never much liked the use of corvée labour, and its abolition left de Lesseps in a dilemma. The solution was to use machines rather than men, and a French machine-tool factory jumped at the opportunity to design a whole range of diggers and dredgers suitable for different soils, so that, by the time work was completed late in 1869, most of the hard work had been done by machine.

The financial situation was less satisfactory. Ismail spent 240,000,000 francs on the canal, and the political price was high: the Suez Canal Company assumed ever greater powers over the project and over the affairs of the Europeans living in the canal zone, to Ismail's consternation. The viceroys were promised 15 per cent of the profits, but by the time the canal was open Ismail had run out of money, and was paying hefty rates of interest on loans that de Lesseps had secured in Paris. Looking back, what is astonishing in the case of this canal and the Panama Canal is the willingness of investors to place money in projects which would, at best, produce returns far in the future, assuming the project proved viable. This reveals deep-rooted optimism about the desirability, even inevitability, of progress, and of man's mastery over nature. Traffic took time to pick up: although just under 500 ships passed through Suez in the first full year of operations, 1870, they accounted for less than 10 per cent of the cargo Ismail had expected to see; and the financial outlook was grim enough for the Suez Canal Company in Paris to declare no dividend.[11] Nor is this surprising: shipping companies had to adapt to the novelty of a route out East that was almost entirely different to the Cape route. Sadly, Ismail did

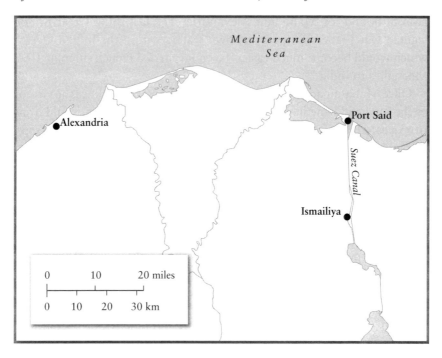

not reap the rewards he had been promised. Ever deeper in debt, spending more on servicing his debts (roughly £5,000,000 per annum) than he was receiving from the canal, the *khedive*, to give him the grand title conferred by the Ottoman sultan, made the reluctant decision to sell his shares, upon which Benjamin Disraeli stole a march on his French rivals and bought up 44 per cent of the canal for £4,000,000 in 1875. He understood perfectly the importance of the canal in assuring quick access to British India, and assured Queen Victoria that 'it is vital to Your Majesty's authority and power at this critical moment, that the Canal should belong to England'.[12] Ten years later the number of ships peaked, with, on average, ten a day passing through the waterway, and the tonnage easily exceeded the 5,000,000 Ismail had been told to expect.

The Suez Canal was, then, much more than a link between the Mediterranean and the Red Sea – it was a new and shorter route from the Atlantic to the Indian Ocean and Pacific. The route from Britain to the Far East became more than 3,000 miles shorter in distance and ten or twelve days shorter in time.[13] The principal beneficiary was Great Britain, not just politically but commercially: in 1889 more than 70 per cent of the goods sent through the canal were carried in British bottoms, while the French accounted for roughly 5 per cent. In London, the Board of Trade reported that 'the trade between Europe and the East flows more and more through the Canal, and the British flag covers an ever increasing proportion of this trade'.[14] Whether the cities around the Mediterranean benefited much from the canal is a moot point: Trieste, then under Austrian rule, did send ships through the canal, but the number was tiny by comparison with British numbers; and Alexandria lost its importance as a bridge between the Indian Ocean and the Mediterranean now that it could be bypassed through Port Said. Britain expanded its power and influence in the Mediterranean, but always with an eye on its route to India, along which its colonies of Gibraltar, Malta and eventually Cyprus became stepping stones. For British, German and other northern European ships, the Mediterranean became a passageway between two oceans, rather than a sea of interest in its own right.

III

The Panama Canal too was not created to service the needs of the local sea, the Caribbean, that lay on its Atlantic side, but to meet the interests of trading companies in Atlantic North America and Europe with ambitions in the Far East. Travelling by way of Cape Horn, the journey from New York to San Francisco would cover 13,000 miles, and it could take several months. By way of Panama, the journey covered only 5,000 miles.[15] However, war between Spain and Britain rendered Panama unsafe, even less safe than the Cape Horn route that Spanish treasure ships began to use from 1748 onwards, in the hope of avoiding British predators in the Caribbean. Meanwhile the French had been thinking that it might be possible to carve a waterway through Central America ever since 1735, when an astronomer was sent out in the hope that he could identify a suitable route. What he suggested, after five years of exploration, was a passage upriver through Nicaragua, then across Lake Nicaragua itself. This would have minimized the need to cut through difficult terrain, but it was a long way to go, assuming the river could carry ships all the way; and as the British built up their interests along the Mosquito Coast of Nicaragua, in competition with Spain, political sensitivities made this plan unworkable. A British alliance with the Indians who lived around the mouth of the river killed the project. The future Lord Nelson was given command of a small squadron whose task, he wrote, was 'to possess the Lake of Nicaragua which, for the present, may be looked upon as the inland Gibraltar of Spanish America'. Not for the first time, tropical diseases rather than a human enemy frustrated British attempts to hold on to Nicaragua.[16] Still, it was generally agreed that the best route across

Central America lay through Nicaragua, and this opinion was confirmed when, in 1811, the great German geographer Alexander von Humboldt declared that there was no suitable alternative. He was taken seriously because he knew South America so intimately, but the truth was that he had never visited either of the two sites.[17]

Political conditions proved to be crucial in solving the problem of where to place a route between the oceans. In the years around 1820 Spain lost control of its colonies in northern South America, resulting in the creation of 'Gran Colombia', known for a time as New Granada, which included the narrow neck of Panama as well as modern-day Colombia and several of its neighbours. Its inhabitants, and the government of New Granada, were keen to see a canal built through the isthmus. Licences to explore were put up for sale. Among the bidders were the Americans, encouraged by Andrew Jackson, the president, even though Jackson preferred them to bid for a Nicaragua route. And, while a canal would obviously take a good many years to plan and build, a railway across Central America could be constructed much more quickly.

Here the French, the British and the Americans jostled for position. The United States was keen to keep the British, the French and the Dutch out of Central America, and made a treaty with New Granada in 1848 that granted the Americans the right to send troops to Panama if other foreign forces began to interfere. The Americans avoided all foreign entanglements, and the decision, uniquely, to go ahead with the New Granadan treaty showed how greatly the United States valued the potential of Central America as a strategic route into the Pacific. Finally, in 1849, Lord Palmerston, as Foreign Secretary, accepted that tension with the United States had risen to a dangerous point and negotiated a deal with the USA under which neither side would try to gain exclusive rights over a canal across Central America. But the effect of this agreement was that neither side was really able to move ahead with its own project. That did not prevent an American businessman, William Aspinwall of New York, from buying the right to build a railway (and possibly a canal) between Panama City and the Caribbean. His plan was to meet the needs of passengers aboard his new shipping service from San Francisco to Panama, which would connect to shipping bound for New England.[18]

Events rushed ahead of Aspinwall. In 1848 news reached the eastern United States that gold had been discovered in California, which had only just been acquired from Mexico. By the end of the year a steamboat, the *Falcon*, was heading south by way of Louisiana, bound for the isthmus of Panama, where a couple of hundred passengers were to be transported across land in dreadful conditions that they had not stopped to consider

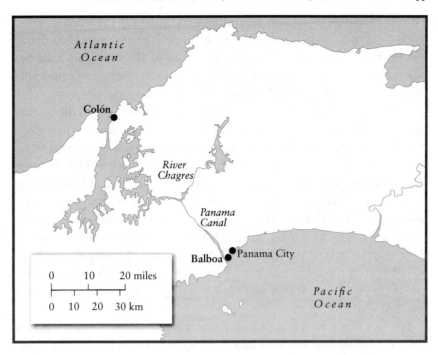

before sailing. This was only the first wave of a flood of people who imag-ined that they could enrich themselves at a stroke in the goldfields of California. Even the sailors who had manned the boats that took gullible Americans from Panama to San Francisco often abandoned ship when they reached California, which left a great many rotting ships in San Francisco Bay, and fewer and fewer ships ready for boarding in Panama. Meanwhile Panama City mushroomed much faster than its very limited infrastructure could manage. It became a shanty town of brothels and bars, with plenty of violence on the streets. One of its good-natured pioneers was the British widow Mary Seacole, partly of West Indian extraction, who set up the 'British Hotel' and tried to offer acceptable food while also ministering to victims of shootings and stabbings, not to mention the many victims of yellow fever and malaria.[19] Yet all this greed and gore showed ever more clearly that a manageable route across Central America was badly needed if the United States were to make full use of the opportunities created by the acquisition of a western seaboard.

So the railway did come into being, after a route was hacked through the jungle by thousands of navvies, very many of whom had arrived from Jamaica, where jobs were few and pay was low. Physical conditions in the isthmus were far worse than back home, but the West Indians had more natural immunity to yellow fever and were generally regarded as good workers, even though they were treated less well than whites. The railway was opened in February 1855. One historian of the Panama Canal has observed: 'Panama *was* the railway.' European governments, especially Great Britain, wondered if the United States had become too powerful in the isthmus, not just because of the heavy capital investment in the railway but because an American elite had installed itself there, and the new town of Colón, long to remain the principal American base there, was to all intents an American settlement, even if it had an extreme Wild West flavour. The cutting of the railway proved that Humboldt had been wrong: the mountains were not impassable, even if building a waterway was vastly more complicated than building a railway track that could handle reasonably steep gradients.[20] And, although the line had been laid mainly by sheer human muscle power, the railway, like the shipping routes from New England to Colón and from Panama City to San Francisco, made use of steam power, which was transforming communications in these decades.

The fact that a well-functioning railway now existed through Panama did not dent enthusiasm for a canal taking a completely different route. Nicaragua did seem to make good sense, and on the decision to go for Panama turns not just the future history of Central America but that of the United States as a world power. The wealthy American Cornelius Vanderbilt had it in mind to build a Nicaraguan canal in 1851, but he could not raise sufficient capital. A quarter of a century later the US government received a report that insisted Nicaragua was the only suitable route, and Nicaragua, not Panama, became the agreed way forward.[21] This left the Panama route available to interlopers, with the French at the head of the queue, inspired by de Lesseps's rhetoric and his sense that anything was possible – he even thought it should be possible to flood the Sahara by creating a channel through Tunisia.[22] With the Americans still talking of Nicaragua but not actually doing anything, the French were able to send their own explorers into Panama in 1876, led by the youthful Lucien Napoleon Bonaparte Wyse, a relative of the French emperors. Wyse's first discovery was how awful the conditions were in the isthmus jungle, where malaria was rampant and constant downpours meant that it was very hard to survey the land; much of his report was guesswork. Yet Wyse managed to win over the Colombian president, whose republic at this point still included the isthmus – not that it would if the French plan went ahead, as France was to be granted a 99-year lease on the canal, while Colombia would reap a 5 per cent profit on gross revenue from the canal. His clear preference was for a sea level canal, which would mean cutting right through the mountains, and one idea was to run the ships through a massive tunnel. Then there would be the literally overwhelming problem of the rush of water as the canal met the River Chagres, which flowed into the Caribbean close to Colón, and in full flood would sweep away anything that stood in its way.[23] But the superhuman nineteenth-century engineers of the generation of Brunel assumed they could achieve anything.

That is why the story of the French attempt to build a canal across the isthmus, mainly alongside the railway, is so tragic. No account was taken, even after Europeans had been poking around the area for several decades, of the threat of disease, particularly yellow fever, with its 50 per cent mortality. Enthusiasm for the scheme ensured that capital could be raised, reaching 700,000,000 francs by 1883, by which time 10,000 workers needed to be paid, a figure that doubled within fifteen months. Jamaicans still dominated the work force, attracted by good pay; ships reached Colón every four days carrying Jamaican labourers; back home in Kingston they fought to get a place on board.[24] Meanwhile the engineers faced a terrible fate as they saw their families die of yellow fever, like the wife, daughter, son and would-be son-in-law of the director-general of operations, Jules Dingler. Dingler expressed his despair by ordering the execution of his beloved horses.[25] French officials often brought their own coffin to Panama so that their remains could be repatriated if they caught one of the rampant diseases of Central America.[26] Observers increasingly wondered whether the plan for a canal was viable. In Paris, the mood was made darker still by the vicious anti-Semitic attacks launched by the publicist Drumont against Baron Jacques de Reinach, a wealthy Jewish banker who had been advising the Canal Company. As much as the Dreyfus Affair, the Panama Affair fuelled French anti-Semitism. Reinach died just as he was coming under investigation following accusations of bribery and corruption; he may well have committed suicide.[27] But by 1890 it was obvious that the project had failed, despite the considerable amount of investment and sheer physical work that had gone into it. The collapse of the Canal Company was the largest financial crash in the entire century.[28]

IV

The financial disaster in France brought the canal project to an end, even though channels had been dug, machinery had been sent to Panama and a great many labourers were now left without work or wages. An American journalist visited the remains of the canal in 1896 and described the all-but-abandoned machinery, which was still, oddly, oiled and main-tained in otherwise deserted yards.[29] Yet the disaster did not kill the idea of building a waterway between the oceans. The French had no appetite left for the project; but the Americans were keenly examining their own strategic interests in the Caribbean and the Pacific, and the argument for a direct link through Panama or Nicaragua now became overwhelmingly attractive. At the end of the nineteenth century American naval power grew prodigiously. The United States went to war with Spain in 1898 in defence of Cuban revolutionaries seeking independence. The *casus belli* was an explosion that destroyed the American battleship the USS *Maine* while it stood in Havana harbour. Nearly 300 sailors were killed, and, even though the reason for the explosion remains a mystery, this was enough to energize President McKinley. The outcome of the short conflict, which Spain was bound to lose, was that the United States occupied Cuba for several years and then imposed a treaty that seriously limited the new republic's sovereign powers. Another acquisition, one that remains in American hands, was Puerto Rico.[30]

Just as significant were gains in the Pacific. The United States occupied the Philippines following the defeat of the Spanish navy in Manila Bay in May 1898, during the same war. Hawai'i and Guam were also acquired. These, along with the Caribbean acquisitions, marked a significant change in American foreign policy, the beginning of a process of empire-building that would culminate in the acquisition of the Panama canal zone. Of course, the Americans denied that this was empire-building, but it is hard to see it as anything else. Theodore Roosevelt, a rising star, governor of New York, announced: 'I wish to see the United States the dominant power on the shores of the Pacific Ocean.' At the same time, he emphat-ically denied that his views smacked of imperialism. As one American historian has pithily explained: 'expansion was different; it was growth, it was progress, it was in the American grain.'[31] Roosevelt cannot be accused of ignorance about naval affairs: he was the author of a book on the war of 1812 between Great Britain and the United States, and a great admirer of the prophet of a new naval policy, Alfred Thayer Mahan.

Captain, later Admiral, Mahan's *The Influence of Sea-Power upon History, 1660–1783*, a work first published in Boston in 1890, had a powerful influence on strategic thinking in London, Berlin and Washing-ton on the eve of the First World War; it was required reading in naval academies both in the United States and in Europe. Mahan's aim was to reveal the importance for the United States of an active naval policy at a time when isolationism had long been the order of the day, and when even American merchant fleets were, he said, playing only a modest role in world trade. He pointed to the three maritime frontiers of the greatly expanded United States of his day: the Pacific, the Atlantic, and the vast area of the Gulf of Mexico and the Caribbean.[32] Yet one of his most revealing comments about the future direction of policy appears at first sight to concern the Mediterranean rather than the oceans:

> Circumstances have caused the Mediterranean Sea to play a greater part in the history of the world, both in a commercial and a military point of view, than any other sheet of water of the same size. Nation after nation has striven to control it, and the strife still goes on. Therefore a study of the conditions upon which preponderance in its waters has rested, and now rests, and of the relative military values of different points upon its coasts, will be more instructive than the amount of effort expended in another field. Furthermore, it has at the present time a very marked analogy in many respects to the Caribbean Sea, – an analogy which will be still closer if a Panama canal-route ever be completed.[33]

He had a good understanding of the strategic importance of the choke-points at the edges of the Mediterranean: the Strait of Gibraltar, the Dardanelles and now the Suez Canal as well. All this pointed to the obvious conclusion that America needed its own canal through Panama. Mahan's approach was founded upon a particular view of international relations as a great game in which nations competed for power and influence, expressing their power through control of the sea routes and using their power to promote trade. Rivalry was the fundamental concept. His book was a call to the United States administration to wake up to global realities, after a century of slumber.

Mahan's arguments were backed up by events. The USS *Oregon* had been sent from San Francisco to join the fray in the Atlantic when news arrived of the destruction of the *Maine* in Havana. The painfully slow voyage round Cape Horn to Palm Beach, Florida, took sixty-seven days. What more needed to be said in defence of a canal through Central America? On the other hand, Roosevelt, now Assistant Secretary of the Navy, wrote to Mahan in 1897 saying that he believed in the Nicaragua route. Congress was still enthusiastically discussing this option when Vice-President Roosevelt suddenly became president in 1901 following the assassination of McKinley. But new reports on the feasibility of different routes, along with the chance to buy out the property of the rump company in France that had taken over the now dormant Panama Canal project, led to a sudden change of policy in Washington. The Colombian government was also well disposed to the idea. The cost would be up to $40,000,000, but the big prize was to be the concession of permanent control over a canal zone either side of the waterway all the way across Panama.[34] Here was an opportunity to make real Mahan's insistence that the United States needed to assert its dominance within its maritime back-yard, the Caribbean, while creating an express route to its new possessions in the Pacific, and to markets in the Far East. And yet, while we may read this as proof of the will to create an American overseas empire, the canal project was not seen in those terms; rather it was proof that the United States, an inherently virtuous nation, was acting on behalf of all mankind, 'something bigger and better than empire', for how could the perfect republic be imperialist?[35]

This was the beginning, not the end, of over a decade of high drama, during which the USA gave its support to a revolutionary regime in Panama and the isthmus broke away from Colombia, still leaving the Americans with full authority over the canal zone, expressed before long in the despatch of American ships and the landing of American troops in order to secure the railway line across the isthmus. It was also a period of continued argument about the best route, as it became obvious that the French had made too many mistakes: the taming of the River Chagres was one of the most important and difficult issues, but it was managed by the building of a great dam and the creation of the Gatun Lake, spread across a large area of the canal zone, while a series of locks brought ships over the Panamanian ridges through which earlier excavators had somehow imagined they could slice their way. Meanwhile the US government con-structed the all-American towns of Balboa and Colón to service their needs in the canal zone. The zone required and was provided with schools, hospitals, post offices, churches, prisons, public restaurants, laundries, bakeries, street lamps, roads, bridges. Much of the female labour was employed within the newly built hospitals.[36]

The implantation of the Americans in Panama is sometimes seen as the crucial moment when the United States became committed to a world role, although there were earlier imperial acquisitions in both the Caribbean and the Pacific, and the acquisition of the canal zone was in many ways the consequence of these new responsibilities and ambitions. Roosevelt's view that the building of the canal was a dramatic step forward in the progress of humanity proved to be true in an important respect: hard work on the ground identified malaria and yellow fever as insect-borne diseases, and a massive effort to eradicate mosquitoes and other carriers of disease by thorough fumigation and by the removal of tainted water had impressive results; simple acts like removing ornamental trees that were growing in water-filled pots destroyed the breeding ground of the insects.[37] The build-ing of the canal was a key moment in the medical history of mankind.

Roosevelt saw the acquisition of the canal zone as the greatest achievement of his first administration, a decade before the canal itself was even completed. In November 1906 he became the first US president to leave the country while in office, when he sailed down to Panama aboard the grandest American battleship, the USS *Louisiana*. It was a remarkable visit for other reasons. He chose to come when conditions would be bad, during the rainy season, so he could witness the difficulties the engineers and labourers were facing. He visited the sick, unannounced. He was able to report optimistically to Congress, while greatly enjoying the positive publicity his visit had generated.[38] All this work was being carried out at the expense of the American government, at a cost of $352,000,000, four times the cost of the Suez Canal.[39] The American government invested hugely in massive new machinery able to run on newly constructed rails, as well as a vast labour force, in which this time not Jamaica but Barbados provided many of the best workers. The labour force was divided into 'gold' and 'silver' categories, American citizens counting as 'gold', although Americans of colour often found themselves demoted, at least unofficially, and the many Barbadians were relegated to 'silver'. 'Silver' was clearly a euphemism, but conditions did improve with time.[40] The fearful mortality of the days when the French were trying to build the link was a distant memory by the time the canal opened on the eve of the First World War. The outbreak of war limited its takings, with only four or five ships a day making the crossing, but after the war ended the boom began, catching up with Suez and eventually taking the annual figure to over 7,000 ships on the eve of the next world war.[41]

As with the Suez Canal, there had been last-minute blockages, and the new lake had to be filled with a massive Atlantic in-flow; but by April 1914 light cargo traffic was being towed through, beginning with a consignment of tinned pineapples from Hawai'i, another important if outwardly modest symbol of the new technology of the industrial era. The opening ceremony was quite muted, not nearly as grand as the opening of the Suez Canal, which had been attended by Empress Eugénie of France and Emperor Franz Joseph of Austria. Nonetheless, the ceremony featured not merely the president of the United States but the USS *Oregon*, which was recognized, justly enough, as the ship whose voyage from California to Florida by way of Cape Horn in 1898 had done most to demonstrate that a canal was urgently needed.[42] With the building of the two canals, Asia and Africa had been divided by a waterway, and North and South America were also physically divided; but the oceans were now joined together.

49

Steaming to Asia, Paddling to America

I

The building of first the Suez Canal and then the Panama Canal, along with the increasing use of steamships, did not bring to an end more traditional ways of crossing the oceans. Clippers and windjammers continued to sail vast distances carrying tea, grain and other basic goods. The wind was free, but coal had to be bought. Nonetheless, by the late nineteenth century massive changes in the use of ships had become visible. Passenger traffic across the Atlantic, increasingly carried on large ocean liners, grew prodigiously as migrants, fleeing famine in Ireland, poverty in Italy or persecution in Russia queued to be allowed past the newly dedicated Statue of Liberty into New York with its welcoming inscription by Emma Lazarus. The statue itself was cast in France, not America, and was carried in pieces to New York in 1885, aboard a French steamship. It goes without saying that the scale of this migration far exceeded the earlier trickle of Europeans across the Atlantic. Accompanying the stream of migrants, though generally in much more comfortable parts of the ship, could be found businessmen, along with more leisured visitors to the USA, willing to spend a week or so aboard a vessel that would adhere to a reasonably reliable timetable, and that would have a high standard of comfort and safety. Standards of safety proved less good than the public had been led to believe when the 'unsinkable' RMS *Titanic* foundered in 1912; but the inevitable response to the disaster was to look more closely at those standards, particularly lifeboat provision.

Early steamships ran risks: in 1840 Samuel Cunard was granted a contract for transatlantic shipping thanks to his insistence on 'safety first, profit second'; a shipping company lost two steamships because (so it seemed) their captains had tried to prove how fast they could cross the ocean.[1] In 1866 the steamship the *London* went down not far out of Plymouth, with the loss of 270 people, at the start of a long run to Melbourne

As well as sixty-nine crew, the ship carried 220 passengers who were looking forward to a new life in Australia. It also carried far too much heavy cargo, maybe as much as 1,200 tons of iron and 500 tons of coal, so that her deck stood only three and a half feet above the surface of the water – in calm conditions.[2] This was just one scandalous example of a much wider problem: one in six ships carrying passengers from Europe to America around this time eventually sank (which is not the same as saying that one in six voyages ended in shipwreck), and over 400 ships are said to have foundered off Great Britain in 1873–4.[3] As twenty-first-century migration across the Mediterranean shows, people are only too willing to entrust their life to unseaworthy vessels; and this applied just as much to the migrants of the late nineteenth and early twentieth century. The enormous growth of maritime traffic during the nineteenth century, particularly across the Atlantic, resulted in more and more maritime disasters; rapid industrialization brought both new benefits and new dangers. Critics insisted that unscrupulous shipowners were only too happy to claim on their insurance policy with Lloyd's: 'the wealthy merchant thrives, but what about the priceless freight of precious human lives?'[4]

Britain, set fair to become the greatest naval power on earth, mistress of an empire across the three great oceans, and heavily dependent on maritime trade, could not tolerate this state of affairs. It became obvious that Parliament needed to look closely at maritime safety, and the leader of the campaign was Samuel Plimsoll, who had started life as a coal merchant and had no naval background at all. He managed to win a seat in the House of Commons for the Liberal Party, and campaigned long and furiously for improvements in sailors' safety. He gained a huge popular following: a wool clipper had been named after him in 1873, and songs and poems were composed in his honour:

> A British Cheer for Plimsoll
> The sailor's honest friend
> In spite of opposition
> Their rights he dares defend
> Tho' wealth and pow'r united
> To put him down have sought
> His valour has defeated
> The forces 'gainst him brought.[5]

Benjamin Disraeli, accused of bending to the will of shipping magnates, was at first hostile to Plimsoll's demands for legislation, while Plimsoll's unrestrained and vigorous attacks on a shipowner named Bates, whose

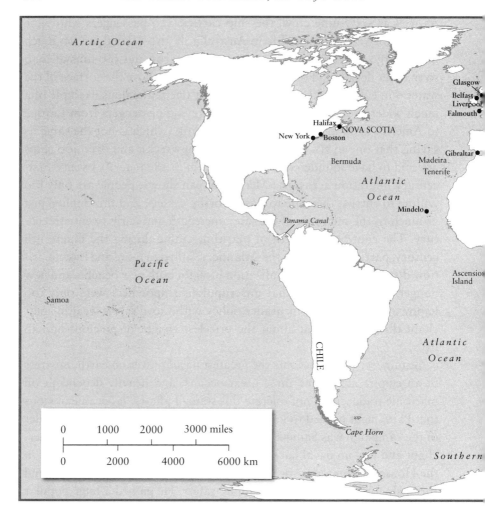

boats had a dismal safety record, almost landed him in court.[6] But of course Plimsoll was right. Finally, in 1876, the British government acknowledged the need for change, ten years after the wreck of the *London*. Clause 26 of the Merchant Shipping Act passed that year demanded that (with a few exemptions for small vessels and yachts):

> The owner of every British ship . . . shall, before entering his ship outwards from any port in the United Kingdom upon any voyage for which he is required to enter her, or, if that is not practicable, as soon after as may be, mark upon each of her sides amidships or as near thereto as is practicable, in white or yellow on a dark ground, or in black on a light ground, a circular disk twelve inches in diameter with a horizontal line drawn through its

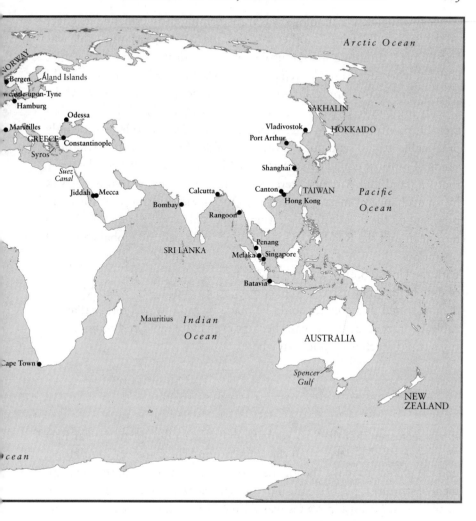

centre. The centre of this disk shall indicate the maximum load-line in salt water to which the owner intends to load the ship for that voyage.[7]

Even so, it was another thirty years before foreign shipping visiting British ports was obliged to follow suit, and the Plimsoll line, as it came to be known, was only adopted as an international standard in 1930. In the USA, Congress was hesitant, and the Plimsoll standard was applied only in 1929 for international shipping and in 1935 for domestic shipping – not a unique example of the United States going its own way for a good while. Plimsoll Days were long celebrated in a number of British towns, in gratitude for what Samuel Plimsoll achieved for British sailors.[8] He deserves to be remembered as a great national and indeed international hero.

Meanwhile, new technology was transforming the world, and its effect on the oceans was felt in another way too: the first transatlantic cable was laid in 1858, although it soon broke, and only in the 1860s were cables laid that worked reasonably well (using in part Isambard Kingdom Brunel's magnificent steamship the *Great Eastern*, which was twice the size of the already impressive *Great Britain* now preserved at Bristol). Even so, contact was painfully slow by later standards, since Morse code was the only practicable way to send pulses down the cable. The manufacture of thousands of miles of coiled cable was an achievement in itself, and the sense that England and America were now linked in a new way was marked by an exchange of messages between Queen Victoria and the American president on the first day of operation. Other cables were laid in the Mediterranean and the Red Sea, while London remained the global centre of operations: this was a means to communicate with the Empire, as well as with the United States, and the days when messages to viceroys were out of date before they arrived were coming to an end. Later, when Marconi demonstrated that contact could be made by radio waves rather than by cable, contact across the oceans became even more rapid and communications could reach just about anywhere.

II

It has been seen that the Suez route from northern Europe to the Far East was shorter and quicker than the route around the Cape of Good Hope, and the chance to make the journey even quicker arose with the development of sturdier types of steamship just as the Suez Canal opened. A pioneer of these new steamship routes was Alfred Holt, whose Ocean Steamship Company operated out of his native city, Liverpool. As he built up his fleet of trading ships he studied iron hulls, steam boilers and screw propellers, convinced that he could push down the cost of long-distance transport aboard steamships below that of sailing vessels. Perfecting the steamship had to be achieved by trial and error, sometimes at great cost – ships went down, taking goods and men with them. His idea that steam pressure could be raised to 60 lb per square inch took the technology of the time to its limits. His decision to build longer iron ships promised to increase cargo capacity, 'as it is the middle that carries and pays'.[9] Iron was certainly much stronger than wood, but making sure the rivets held the ship together was a problem. In the early days, iron steamships sometimes split in two. Holt therefore took the trouble to send the ship he had fitted with an experimental high-pressure engine as far as Brazil and Archangel.[10]

58. At midday on 7 June 1692 a huge earthquake and tsunami demolished the capital of English Jamaica, Port Royal, resulting in 4,000 deaths.

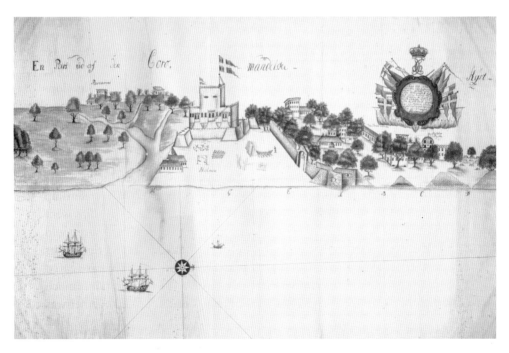

59. In the early seventeenth century the Danish East India Company acquired Fort Tranquebar from a south Indian ruler. Much of its business consisted of 'country trade' within the Indian Ocean and the South China Sea.

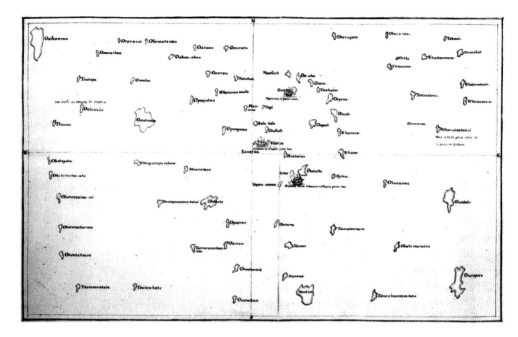

60. The Polynesian navigator Tupaia accompanied Captain Cook around the Pacific islands. His very detailed map was drawn from memory, but he had no knowledge of Hawai'i and New Zealand.

61. In 1791, King Kamehameha of Hawai'i, who had acquired a fleet of European-style ships, defeated his rivals at the Battle of the Red Mouthed Gun. Most Hawai'ians used traditional boats – note the similarity of the claw-shaped sails of Kamehameha's adversaries to that in Plate 1.

The Island of St HELEN.
belonging to the East India Company of England.

L'e Isle de St HELENE.
Appartenente a la Compagnie Anglese pour les Indes Orientales.

62. In 1658 Oliver Cromwell's son and momentary successor, Richard Cromwell, granted the English East India Company the right to settle St Helena, which became a resupply station for English operations across the oceans.

63. The warehouses of the European merchants trading in Canton proudly displayed their flags. In this image of c.1820 the flags of Britain, Sweden, the United States and other countries are visible.

64. Even if Commander Perry's visit to Japan in 1853 only opened the door to foreign traders by a crack, the sight of his ironclad steam paddleboat fascinated the Japanese.

65. The estuary of the Singapore River was lined with 'godowns', storage facilities for the goods that passed through the port between the Indian Ocean and the South China Sea.

66. The white houses on the right were home to the Jewish merchants of Mogador (Essaouira), who controlled the tea trade from England to Morocco. From their windows in the royal *casbah* they looked out over the wharves where their goods were unloaded.

67. The massive buildings erected in the port of Liverpool at the start of the twentieth century included the Royal Liver Building and the Cunard offices. This was the city's golden age.

68. In a similar style to the Liverpool waterfront, the bustling street along the river in Shanghai, known as the Bund, hosted banks and trading companies and included the vast Sassoon headquarters, far right.

69. Even after the triumph of the steamship, tea, grain and mail clippers raced to their loading stations in China and Australia and back to Europe. Here is the *Ocean Chief* in the 1850s on the Australia run.

70. The pride of the Cunard White Star fleet, the *Queen Mary*, arriving in New York on 8 August 1938. The interwar years were the great age of international liner voyages.

71. The largest cruise ship in the world at the time this book was being written, the *Allure of the Sea* has capacity for more than 7,000 passengers.

72. The largest container ship in the world at the time this book was being written, the *CSCL Globe* has capacity for more than 19,000 containers.

Holt's Liverpool was a city that had transformed itself from being a major base of the slave trade and sugar trade, in the eighteenth century, into the export hub of northern England, taking full advantage of the rapid industrialization taking place in Lancashire. Railways connected its wharves to Manchester, Chester and beyond. Its harbour was large and well situated. Its often infamous trade of earlier years had created a capital base for diversification into shipping business other than the trade in human beings. The links to slavery did not vanish after Parliament forbade the slave trade in 1807: the city continued to trade intensively with west Africa, and a mainstay of the city's business was the import of American cotton, produced on the slave plantations of the Deep South.[11] Like other port cities, Liverpool became home to a mixed population that included plenty of Irish, Welsh and Scots, but also Africans and Chinese, many of whom had arrived on the ships of Alfred Holt.[12] Liverpool did face local challenges: Manchester became a rival with the construction of the Manchester Ship Canal in 1894, but the main brokers dealing in imported cotton remained in Liverpool.[13] By the start of the twentieth century Liverpool businessmen were confident enough of the city's primacy to build the imposing Edwardian office buildings that are the city's great architectural glory.

In 1866 Alfred Holt announced the launch of his steamship company, with three sister ships, the *Agamemnon*, the *Ajax* and the *Achilles*, each over 2,000 tons. In April the *Agamemnon* set out for Shanghai, by way of the Cape, Mauritius, Penang in Malaya, Singapore and Hong Kong. Holt's first published timetable estimated the length of the outward voyage at seventy-seven days, with a slightly longer return schedule of ninety days, as the ships were to stop in south-eastern China to load the most important part of their cargo – tea. But this was still much better than the four months a sailing ship would require. Subtract from this the ten days or so that would be saved once the Suez Canal was in operation, and Holt's company seemed bound to succeed. On the other hand, Holt had to charge higher freight rates to cover his costs, for steamships cost more to build and to operate; and there were still doubts about their reliability, since they could be stopped in their tracks if coal supply stations were not created and maintained, though in the early days they did carry large amounts of sail, just in case.[14] But a long sea voyage by steamship was, at least before permanent coaling stations were created, complicated. When the rival Peninsular and Oriental Steam Navigation Company (P&O) sent the *Hindostan* to Calcutta in 1842, coal supply ships awaited her at Gibraltar, Mindelo in the Cape Verde Islands, Ascension Island, Cape Town, Mauritius and Sri Lanka.[15] In the eyes of many traders, the traditional sailing ship was familiar as well as beautiful. This became even clearer when the tea clippers, of which the *Cutty Sark*, still preserved at Greenwich, is the most famous, came into operation; by the 1850s sailing ships crept back into fashion. As early as 1828 the First Lord of the Admiralty had expressed himself decisively: 'the introduction of steam is calculated to strike a fatal blow at the supremacy of the Empire.' But the Royal Navy, unlike the Merchant Navy, was not interested in creating timetables and schedules for passengers and freight.[16]

The canal made all the difference, therefore, and it also opened up the route East to smaller ships that could not have coped with the Cape route. Holt charged ahead, smashing competition by building steamships at a furious rate. This paid off: by 1875 his managers insisted that they had run out of space for cargoes yet again, so that they needed three more ships; these cargoes were dominated by Lancashire cotton and woollen cloths (the cotton cloth being made largely out of imported Indian fibres, now re-exported as finished goods). Passengers were also carried: on the return leg, Muslim pilgrims were picked up and conveyed to Jiddah, from where they could reach Mecca for the haj, and this became big business for several British shipping companies; well over 13,000 Muslim pilgrims sailed on Blue Funnel ships in 1914, setting out from Singapore and Penang.[17] Journey times were slashed, falling as low as fifty-five, even forty-two, days out from England. The advantages of steam navigation became most obvious when Holt's ships joined the annual tea race, bringing the fresh crop as fast as possible to London. They not merely outpaced the tea clippers, which was to be expected, but they beat the steamships of rival companies. In 1869 his ships carried nearly 9,000,000 lb of tea to England, and, having beaten all competitors, Holt was able to take advantage of a seller's market and dispose of his tea at 2d per pound more than his late coming rivals.[18] In 1914 the Blue Funnel Line, as Holt's company came to be known, used more berths in Liverpool docks than any other cargo line and was the most frequent user of the Suez Canal, dominating the export of British textiles to east Asia.[19]

Holt's operations in China were boosted by his decision to work alongside a British merchant company based in China, Butterfield and Swire, which set up an office in Shanghai on 1 January 1867, and specialized not just in tea but in raw American cotton, which formed the bulk of the cargo of the *Achilles* when it left Shanghai a couple of weeks later.[20] The relationship with John Swire enabled the Blue Funnel line to draw goods from deeper inside China, as Swire's steamboats penetrated down the Yangtze River, bringing Chinese goods to Shanghai for trans-shipment. Swire was a great advocate of the Conference System, an agreement among competing shipping firms that they would set the same freight rate on outward cargoes, which left Holt uneasy, as there were pluses and minuses to this, especially after competition from faster ships than his own became a problem. After their pioneering start, the managers of the Blue Funnel Line sometimes displayed the conservatism that had delayed the introduction of steam power to other shipping companies: they were slow to follow the move over to steel from iron, and new types of engine were ignored.[21] Although the Blue Funnel Line is long gone, the Swire family remains a powerful force in the trade of China, Taiwan and Hong Kong to this day, though its best-known fleet now consists not of ships but of the aeroplanes of Cathay Pacific.

Holt was unnerved by competition from P&O. The company had come into being to serve routes towards Spain, Gibraltar and the eastern Mediterranean, and began to deploy its paddle-driven steamships either side of Suez even before the canal was built. This enabled the shipping line to gain the contract to run a mail service from Great Britain to India and Ceylon. A pride of the fleet was the *Hindostan* (mentioned above), which was sent out to the Indian Ocean in 1842 to service the route between Suez and British India. She even offered showers, hot or cold, for the passengers, which was a marvellous innovation. And she could cope with monsoon showers as well, blithely sailing from Calcutta to Suez through the thick of the monsoon in 1845, in just twenty-five days. The building of the Suez Canal should have made it still easier to send mail to and from India, but the mail contract insisted that letters had to be sent overland from the Mediterranean to the Red Sea: the mail was unloaded at Alexandria, sent overland to Suez, and reloaded there, or vice versa. Despite the objections of P&O, this bizarre comedy was maintained for several years until the bureaucrats realized how pointless it was.[22]

One major difference between P&O and Cunard was the quality of food. In January 1862 the menu aboard the P&O *Simla* bound from Suez to Ceylon included almost every variety of meat one can imagine – turkey, suckling pigs, mutton, geese, beef, chicken – all prepared, with the exception of curry, in a stalwart British fashion, but oddly no fish. Live animals were kept on board so that fresh meat could be served. The range of clarets brought a glow of pride to the cheeks of P&O officials.[23] P&O understood the need to diversify, in the face of competition. Ancillary short-distance routes were developed: the *Canton* ferried goods up and down the Pearl River between Hong Kong and Canton itself, though it was also put to good use in 1849 fighting Chinese pirates who attacked European ships from their junks – the waters around Hong Kong, and the new town on Victoria Island too, were notoriously unsafe at this period, and pirate raids on shipping slowed the growth of Hong Kong.[24]

Another side to P&O's activities that produced handsome revenue in its early days was cruising. The company's historians have claimed that P&O invented deep-sea cruising in 1844. These included trips from the Atlantic into the Mediterranean, as far as the coast of Ottoman Palestine, though this came to an end with the Crimean War. Then, towards the end of the century, a number of shipping lines took cruise passengers on trips as far away from England as the West Indies: the Orient Company advertised a Caribbean 'Pleasure Cruise', departing in January 1898, and spending sixty days afloat while the ship called in at Madeira, Tenerife and Bermuda; and it also ran cruises to the Norwegian fjords. Once again the use of steamers meant that one could keep, or try to keep, to a timetable, and this made cruises viable.[25]

The ironclad steamship transformed business in other parts of the Far East than China. Penang, under British encouragement, emerged as the new port of call in the approaches to the Malacca Strait. As it drew in ships that, in the days of sail, might have rounded Sumatra and entered the South China Sea through the Sunda Strait, business was diverted from the Dutch East Indies back to the traditional route past a now sleepy Melaka to the flourishing port of Singapore. In 1870 a ship reached Singapore from Marseilles by way of Suez in twenty-nine days. This is not simply a history of express voyages from Europe to the Far East, for within the Indian Ocean the British India Steam Navigation Company linked Singapore to Batavia in Java, and linked India to the Persian Gulf; steamships now ploughed their way along the route that 4,000 years earlier had tied Mesopotamia to the Indus cities.[26] To all this can be added the business that Holt conducted in Malaya, which was emerging as the great centre of rubber production, following the introduction of rubber trees by the British, as well as being a valuable source of tin.

III

Looking westwards, Liverpool was also the base of Samuel Cunard's British and North American Royal Mail Steam Packet Company, established in 1840, with four ships linking England to New York, Boston and Halifax. However, Cunard began in the days of wooden-hulled paddle boats, and tried to improve their performance, before finally accepting the inevitable and moving over to screw-driven ironclad steamships from 1852 onwards. Like Holt's, Cunard's company fell prey to a Conference System, designed to standardize transatlantic fares and freight rates. Here the issue was not so much cargo as passengers. Steerage fares were cheap, but they were good business, given the numbers wishing to set sail for New York. In the early days, Cunard ships were the Ryanair option for travel: the assumption was that passengers would always choose the cheapest fare, but facilities were basic, even for those travelling in cabin (or first) class. Food was provided, but in first class it was nothing special, and in steerage it was especially dire. But no modern airline could get away with Cunard's failure to implement Board of Trade standards that even the shareholders felt were being shamefully ignored. At the start of the new century an effort was at last made to improve the third-class accommodation, which became notorious for overcrowding and lack of hygiene. Cunard just about balanced the books on its voyages to America, while the cost of commissioning new ships was always a drain on company funds. In 1886 one of the faster ships, the *Etruria*, made a profit of over £7,000, but that was exceptional, and on some of the less prestigious ships only the profit from carrying freight kept the voyage financially above water.[27]

This issue became more and more significant as the volume of traffic increased at the end of the nineteenth century: Poles, Swedes, Russian Jews, Irish, Italians. The evil human traffic of past times had been replaced by a humane traffic of refugees escaping persecution and migrants looking for a better condition of life. With the rise in migration out of eastern Europe, speeded further by pogroms and economic misery, Cunard was faced with energetic rivals, the German shipping firms. In 1891 the Hamburg–Amerika Line carried nearly 76,000 steerage passengers across the Atlantic, 17 per cent of total numbers, and Cunard carried 6 per cent, over 27,000 people.[28] The scale of migration to North America dwarfed the scale of passenger traffic out of Europe in other directions, such as Australia and New Zealand, all the more so as it came by 1900 to embrace just about every European nationality. This formed part of a wider development, as passenger traffic became more important, whether migrants, businessmen or tourists, and freight (even if it made all the difference to the Cunard profits) was less often the motive for setting up a new route. In the age of the steamship, these routes were serviced by 'liners', a term that expressly meant that they followed a regular line according to a timetable; and in time this term would become attached to the big ocean-going steamships of the great international shipping lines.

In the British Isles, the boom in shipbuilding that followed the development of metal-hulled steamships transformed the economy of regions such as Clydeside, downriver from Glasgow, which became a major shipbuilding centre, as did Tyneside, in north-eastern England. But the most remarkable success story was Belfast, already established as the linen capital of the world and the only industrial boom town in Ireland. But one cannot construct ships out of linen, and old Belfast could only offer mediocre shipbuilding facilities until the 1840s. Its shipbuilders understood that their craft was turning into a major industry, as shipbuilders made more use of iron and steel and added steam engines to their vessels. This advanced thinking gave Belfast a lead, despite the lack of local supplies of either iron or coal, and despite the lack, at the start, of the skilled labour force that the new shipbuilding techniques required.[29] One company was dominant. Edward Harland had acquired his first Belfast shipyard in 1858, and three years later combined forces with his deputy, Gustav Wolff, who was of German Jewish origin. They established a company whose massive gantries have become the symbol of Belfast. The great trio of RMS *Titanic*, RMS *Olympic* and RMS *Britannic* were the largest ships ever built, and required brand new dockyards. Even when disaster struck the *Titanic*, this did not hamper business at Harland and Wolff, any more than the political troubles that were tearing Ireland apart, though the company did set up additional dockyards in Great Britain as Ireland became more unstable. The introduction of new safety standards meant that there was plenty of work to be done in Belfast bringing existing ships up to scratch, and the dockyard was busier than ever on the eve of the First World War, producing nearly 10 per cent of British merchant shipping, while commissions from the Royal Navy kept it very active during the next war as well – and made Belfast a target for German air attacks.[30]

IV

One of the interesting features of the history of shipping and maritime trade is that apparently small players sometimes prove to have been rather more important actors than is easily assumed. Lack of resources at home sent Norwegians and Greeks far from their homeland, and led to the creation of merchant fleets out of all proportion to the size and political or economic importance of their home nation. Population outstripped home resources, so labour costs were low, while both Norway and Greece had age-old connections with the sea, generated by the geography of their countries: the jagged, mountainous coasts of Norway and the scattered islands of Greece, which in each case made the inhabitants heavily dependent on travel by sea.[31] One way of measuring which are the largest maritime nations is to calculate deadweight tonnage (dwt) for every thousand inhabitants. In 2000 Norway and Greece were at the top of the scale, with a figure of over 12,000 dwt; the world average was a mere 121 dwt. But in

1890 Norway could already boast a figure of 1,100 dwt, twice the next largest figure, for the much more heavily populated United Kingdom, and seven times the figure for the country next door, which, at the end of the nineteenth century, was Norway's overlord, Sweden.

It has been seen how the Swedes became very active in the international tea trade by the nineteenth century. The Norwegian subjects of the kings of Sweden benefited especially from the presence of Swedish consuls out in Asian ports, and slowly and without ostentation built their own impressive network of shipping routes. Ancient links with Great Britain continued – the standard route followed by Scandinavian migrants to America brought them across the North Sea to Hull before being packed on to trains bound for Liverpool.[32] But the secret of Norway's success lay in the fact that it was a global operation. Following the opening of the Suez Canal, Norwegian ships began to appear in the Far East. By 1882 their ports of call included Java, Singapore and Rangoon; within twenty years their ships were appearing in the Philippines and Shanghai, as the axis shifted from Malaya and Indonesia towards China. The domestic market back home did not count for a great deal, so they inserted themselves in the carrying trade, ferrying rice from Vietnam to Hong Kong and along the coast of China. Their role in this trade has been described as nothing less than a 'stranglehold'; by 1902 this intra-Asian business accounted for more than 50 per cent of Norwegian trade in Asia.[33] Their ability to achieve this depended on their quick understanding of the radically new conditions under which maritime trade was now being conducted, following the opening of the Suez Canal and the introduction of long-distance steamer services.

By the end of the nineteenth century Norwegian ships were a familiar sight in the Indian Ocean and the Pacific, and the re-creation of the Norwegian kingdom in 1905 accelerated this development. The achievements of Amundsen and Nansen in polar exploration further strengthened the special reputation of the Norwegians. As profits grew, a new business elite back in Norway commissioned brand new boats and gained the confidence of the western Pacific powers, Russia, Japan and China, all jostling for position in the western Pacific, and all anxious to find different commercial partners to the traditional, and often menacing, European intruders led by Great Britain. Norway was neutral, but it was not exactly unimportant: by the start of the twentieth century it ranked third in the world in tonnage.[34] There was an enormous spike in business at the very start of the new century, stimulated by the brief Russian–Japanese War of 1904–5, which was a disaster for Russia. Instead of gaining a year-round port on the Pacific, as the Russians had intended at the start of the

campaign, the Russians lost much of their fleet, as well as control of Port
Arthur, and they even lost half the island of Sakhalin, to the north of
Hokkaido. Such conflicts provided the perfect conditions under which a
neutral body of traders could insert themselves into the region.[35]

One of those who took advantage of the new opportunities was Haakon
Wallem, a giant Norwegian born in Bergen who arrived in the Russian
port of Vladivostok in 1896, made his way to China, and then established
himself in Shanghai, buying his first ship, the *Oscar II*, in 1905. Wallem
hit the jackpot during the Russian–Japanese War, because freight rates shot
upwards, and also because the Japanese were so grateful for the unspecified
and mysterious help he had given them that they awarded him a prize of
¥100,000 or, if he preferred, a grand decoration; but, businessman that he
was, he took the money rather than the medal. He showed extraordinary
resilience, keeping his company afloat in what were increasingly difficult
times: he survived revolution in China and the loss of his first ship, becoming not just a prominent shipowner but a leading shipbroker, buying vessels
for clients, and managing to carry on business during the First World War,
during which Norway remained neutral.[36] His business career had many
ups and downs, but its main characteristic was his constant determination
to get back on his feet whenever there was a setback (notably during the
post-war depression). He was, as his biographer concisely states, 'a survivor', but so was the entire Norwegian shipping industry.[37]

Another remarkable example of vigorous participation in maritime
trade is provided by the Greeks. In the nineteenth century the term 'Greek'
is best used as an ethnic label, or rather as the ethnic descriptor of groups
of families from quite restricted areas within what would now be called
Greece, since some regions, such as the Ionian Islands, did not belong
to the emerging Greek state, and Greeks were active in ports far beyond
Greece itself, notably Odessa in the Black Sea. This is part of a longer
and very remarkable story: in 1894, 1 per cent of world shipping was
owned by Greeks, and by the end of the twentieth century that figure
had reached 16 per cent (3,251 ships), making the Greek-owned merchant
fleet the largest in the world, bearing in mind that the great majority of
ships sail under flags of convenience – Liberia, Panama, and so on – rather
than the Greek or Cypriot flag.[38]

In the early nineteenth century, as Greek merchant shipping grew in
scale, its focus was very much upon the Mediterranean, including Marseilles, Alexandria, Trieste and Livorno, and the leading families came
from Chios, whose position in the eastern Aegean helps explain why the
trade in Black Sea grain out of Odessa and other ports became a major
interest. London was certainly on their radar, and the Chiot trading

families had agents there, often bringing goods such as currants to Liverpool first of all, and taking Manchester cotton cloth out of the country for distribution across the world. But that is not to say that these goods travelled on Greek-owned ships; the most powerful Chiot business family, the Rallis, with agents in New York, Bombay and Calcutta, in Odessa, Trebizond and Constantinople, were dealers rather than shippers, and to move goods around they would often charter ships from outside their circle – indeed, they often took Austrian or French or British citizenship and played the role of consuls for various nations, just like the Jewish merchants of Mogador. Their business partners were as likely to be Odessan Jews or Lebanese Armenians as other Greeks.

The Rallis, who claimed descent from Raoul, an eleventh-century Norman knight in Byzantine service, operated out of Syros, a small and nowadays rather dull Aegean island whose modern claim to fame is its sticky nougat, but which once (as its opulent nineteenth-century town hall suggests) lay at the very heart of the Greek trading world. In the years after 1870 power and influence shifted to shipowners based in the Ionian Islands, and they looked further beyond the Mediterranean and the Black Sea. In the years up to the First World War the tonnage of Greek-owned ships overall grew quite gradually, but the number of steamships grew more rapidly – from just four back in 1864 to 191 in 1900 and 407 in 1914. Moreover, tonnage grew prodigiously in the first years of the twentieth century, from 327,000 tons in 1900 to 592,500 in 1914; in 1910 the Greek fleet was already the ninth largest in Europe, measured in tonnage, with Great Britain enjoying a massive lead – 45 per cent of world tonnage.[39] After recovery from the chaos of the First World War, in which Greece was only lightly involved, there was sufficient infrastructure and knowhow in place to enable the Greek shipowners to spread their wings, and become a global phenomenon, while other merchant fleets, such as the British one, had a much harder time trying to recover. This left a vacuum that Greek shipowners, along with the Norwegians and to some extent the Japanese, were very content to fill.[40] At the root of Greek success lay a willingness to act as a tramp fleet, picking up miscellaneous cargoes here and dropping them there, as they moved across the sea.

V

In some corners of Europe even more old-fashioned types of shipping than Cunard's paddle boats still flourished in the late nineteenth century and beyond. The best example of this is the Åland Islands, lying between

Sweden and Finland, and, since 1921, an autonomous territory under Finnish sovereignty. The capital of these islands, Mariehamn, was founded in 1861, while the territory lay under Russian rule – a quiet place for most of its history, but blessed with a deep port, and good supplies of wood for shipbuilding in the interior. Between 1850 and 1920 nearly 300 ships were built in the islands, and sixty more were bought from shipyards in Finland. The largest of these were tall sailing ships: in 1865 the Ålanders sent their first ship to America, and in 1882 an Åland ship circumnavigated the world, loading goods in Samoa. Meanwhile the islanders seized the opportunity to buy sailing ships cheaply on the international market, taking advantage of the shift away from wind power towards steam power, which meant that there were plenty of cheap sailing vessels (with modern iron or steel hulls) to be had at ship-breaker's prices, all the more so once the opening of the Suez Canal created a new and fast route from Europe to the Indies; these ships had been built in as varied places as Glasgow, Bremerhaven, Liverpool and Nova Scotia.[41] The result was the creation of a remarkable network of shipping routes managed by island-based companies, trading under the Finnish flag in timber, grain and other basic commodities as far afield as Chile, Canada, Australia and South Africa.

These companies were not created by big-time capitalists. By far the most successful was Gustaf Erikson. He was born in 1872, had started his career at the age of ten as a cabin boy, then cook, eventually bo'sun, second mate and master, and he shared ownership of the first ship he operated, the barque *Åland* – this sank after striking a coral reef in the Pacific, because the captain did not realize that a lighthouse nearby was not functioning. Erikson bounced back from this disaster, and never actually believed in insuring his ships: 'with so many ships it will be cheaper losing one a year than paying insurance premiums for all of them.'[42] During his career he owned twenty-nine ships, and was operating twenty of them around 1930. He knew his ships intimately and kept control of every aspect of the voyage from his office in the Åland Islands, specializing in grain shipments. He had no interest in being liked, paid the lowest wages he could, and was dedicated to making his business succeed; but for a couple of decades he was the respected head of a remarkable, worldwide, operation linking the Baltic to the Atlantic, the Indian Ocean, the Pacific and the Southern or Antarctic Ocean.

Shipping grain from the opposite side of the world on sailing vessels might not seem to be sound business, especially since many ships sailed out on ballast, for lack of goods to sell in Australia. But the prevailing winds enabled sailing ships to cover the distance to Australia at a comparable

speed to steamboats, wafted straight through the oceans without the need
to refuel that the steamships faced. These journeys are especially impressive because they were voyages right round the world with just one major
stop, in Australia: the normal route took the windjammers round the top
of Scotland and out across the Atlantic, past the Cape Verde Islands and
towards the coast of Brazil, from where, in classic mode, they sought out
the winds that would carry them past the Cape of Good Hope and across
the wide expanse of the southern Indian Ocean to Spencer Gulf in South
Australia. This stretch of water is separated from Adelaide Bay by a neck
of land, and port facilities were very basic, a far cry from the bustle of
Melbourne, Sydney or even Adelaide. On the other hand, Spencer Bay lay
much closer to the sources of grain, and using sailing vessels, which comfortably negotiated the winds and currents of the bay, avoided the nuisance
of having to hump the grain a hundred miles or so to Adelaide for collection by steamers. Loading their grain there, they then headed south of
New Zealand towards Cape Horn, which was generally much more
manageable when travelling eastwards out of the Pacific than in the other
direction: Eric Newby reported rain and snow as he rounded the cape
aboard Erikson's fast windjammer the *Moshulu* in 1939, but he also says
that 'the sea was not rough but there was a tremendous see-saw motion
of the water', and it was 'bitterly cold'. After that the windjammers wended
their way along a twisting route north through the Atlantic to Falmouth
in Cornwall or Cobh (Queenstown) in southern Ireland. These were the
'ports of orders', where the captain would receive instructions about who
had bought the grain (for it was sold in advance, and sometimes resold
and re-resold) and where he should take the ship for unloading. This could
be Bristol, Liverpool, Glasgow, Dublin or another British or Irish port.
On final arrival they unloaded their cargo of grain, which was a slow
process as the grain was loaded in bags – as many as 50,000 on one
windjammer.[43]

The Ålanders took great pride in these voyages: during the 1930s the
windjammers raced one another from Australia to the British Isles, the
record being eighty-three days in 1933, with the wooden spoon going to
another ship which took almost twice as long.[44] There was also a practical
side to these races: late arrival would mean that there was no time to return
to the Åland Islands and see one's family before the ship had to set out
yet again for Australia. Ships in Erikson's fleet were known for the relatively good quality of food aboard, and even attracted a small number of
passengers.[45] Although there were competitors, including German and
Swedish windjammers, the success of Erikson's trading fleet marks it out
as something special.

These operations came to an end with the outbreak of war in 1939, and only revived briefly after the war ended. Overall, what is impressive about the Ålander shipping network is the way the islanders were able to insert themselves in the grain trade of Britain and Ireland, coming in as complete outsiders with old-fashioned technology that proved its true worth. Little remains today: one impressive and lovingly preserved windjammer, the *Pommern*, forms part of the Åland Maritime Museum in Mariehamn, while the German-built *Passat*, acquired by Erikson in 1932 and kept in use until 1949, is now used as a training ship for young people, standing immobilized in the river mouth that leads from Travemünde to Lübeck.

50
War and Peace, and More War

I

Historians only began to write about 'globalization' from the 1990s onwards, and they by no means agree about its meaning and applicability. It is hard to dissent from those economic historians who see the concept as a red herring: if it can mean so many things, it is hardly likely that a debate about 'when did globalization begin?' will produce satisfactory results.[1] Was the Greco-Roman trade route that linked Egypt to south India and beyond a sign that some form of globalization could be found as early as the first century AD? It makes most sense to apply the term when one can see how the economy of regions very far apart physically became interdependent, as, for instance, when potters in central China went out of their way to meet the requests made by purchasers of their goods in Holland or Denmark for specific designs. Even then, some trades were more 'global' than others: the vast scale and reach of the Roman pepper trade, the Chinese porcelain trade, the sugar trade or the tea trade are good examples of how trading connections were all-encompassing, affecting not just elites but people of modest station, including artisans and slaves. This might be described, then, as a process of economic integration across large spaces. And yet, whatever claims are made for the centuries before the Industrial Revolution of the late eighteenth and nineteenth centuries, the global integration of the nineteenth and twentieth centuries is an altogether more complex phenomenon. Early in the twentieth century observers insisted that 'the railway, the steamship and the telegraph are rapidly mobilizing the peoples of the earth'.[2] The revolution in communications took place not just at sea, but in ways of reaching the seaports from which the steamships set out; and it was accompanied by other ways of communicating across the sea, beginning with the intercontinental cables that have already been mentioned.

For the economic historian Kevin O'Rourke, 'one indication that

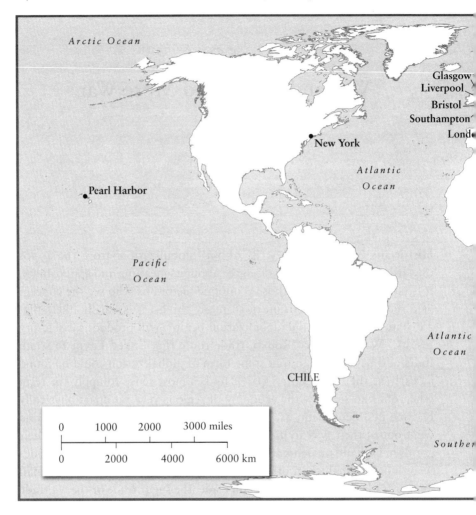

markets are integrated is when they have prices that are correlated with
each other.' Looking at the transatlantic wheat trade around 1900, and
analysing the gap in prices between wheat put on sale in Britain and wheat
put on sale in North America, he has concluded that a remarkable degree
of globalization can be observed at the start of the twentieth century.
Partly, this was the result of the use of steamships to transport goods, and
a fall in overall shipping costs. British demand for American wheat
'exploded' (he says) at the time of the First World War. The war, however,
marked the end of a period of worldwide economic convergence, and only
after the next world war did the process of integration resume successfully,
as controls on the movement of capital were relaxed under pressure from
markets. From the human perspective the late nineteenth century was a

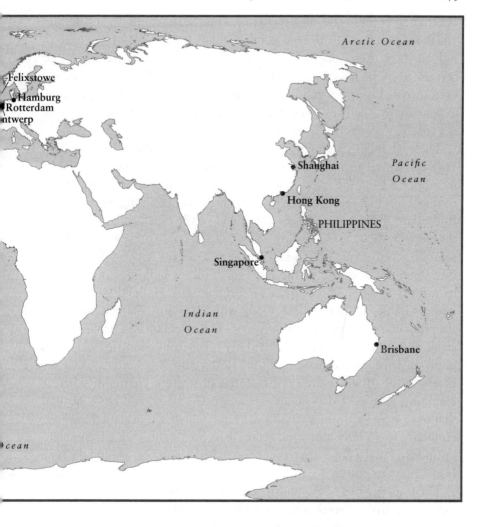

period of free movement, another possible indication of globalization, but early in the twentieth century this was challenged by restrictions imposed – not necessarily for economic reasons – by a number of governments, notably that of the United States, which forgot the words written on the Statue of Liberty.[3] These arguments, cogent as they are, do depend on a particular definition of globalization, and the new globalization of the years around 2000, based on the astonishing technological achievements of the computer age, undoubtedly has a different character to the globalization visible around 1900.

Yet the twentieth century saw a complete transformation in the character of ocean shipping, with the development of cruise lines at the start of the century, the loss of passenger services once jet traffic across the oceans had become safe, and, most importantly, the container revolution, which made it possible to send goods through ports without any need to unload them there, one consequence of which was the rise of new or revived ports such as Rotterdam and Felixstowe and the eclipse of old ones such as Liverpool and London. As the scale of maritime trade grew exponentially, the lives of people all around the world, mostly far from sea coasts, were decisively transformed.

These changes cannot be understood without taking into account railways as well as ports. The increasing ease with which goods could be transported from the interior, added to their position near the mouth of river systems that reached deep into Europe, gave Hamburg, Antwerp and Rotterdam distinct advantages at the end of the nineteenth century, all the more so when the Dutch built a new channel out to the sea. The Belgian solution was to create what is still the densest railway network in Europe.[4] Not for nothing is one of the most magnificent buildings in Antwerp its railway station. The benefits for Belgium and Holland were almost immeasurable, as they became, along with Hamburg, the exit points for the products of German heavy industry – as Rotterdam still remains. Two small and, by this time, not particularly prosperous countries were thus given an enormous economic fillip.[5] Rotterdam was better placed for access to the urban centres and factories of western Germany, whereas Hamburg was more dependent on eastern Germany, and lands beyond that were more lightly industrialized, or not industrialized at all. However, Hamburg was a busy industrial centre in its own right, with a busy smelting industry and a population that approached 2,000,000 around the time Hitler came to power.

The trading links of Hamburg reached as far as Chile, where the trading company of Vorwerk was already doing business in 1847, while there were also very intense links with Brazil and Argentina. In 1924 a substantial office block known as the *Chilehaus* was built in Hamburg in the avant-garde style known as Brick Expressionism.[6] Not to be outdone, the Dutch invested very heavily in Rotterdam, dredging new channels and constructing large basins where ships could moor and unload.[7] Intensely competitive, the three ports improved their facilities in leaps and bounds, determined to attract the largest volume of traffic possible; and ever greater port capacity stimulated companies such as Vorwerk as they worked hard to increase the volume of trade with South America, South Africa and the Far East.

Although New York was also a very successful port, handling a comparable quantity of goods, the northern European ports, taken together, dominated maritime traffic around the world. This becomes even clearer when the role of Great Britain is taken into account: over 8,500 steamships in 1914, 19,000,000 gross tonnage, two fifths of world tonnage. London retained its role as the largest port in Europe throughout the first half of the twentieth century, but the measuring stick is the physical extent of the port rather than the volume of goods it handled. Still, at the start of the century, especially when Liverpool is brought into the calculations, the dominance of Great Britain at sea was impossible to challenge. It had the largest and most effective navy; it had the largest and most successful merchant marine; it was home to extremely prestigious passenger lines, notwithstanding the growth of the Holland–Amerika Line and German firm HAPAG, which was larger than any other shipping company anywhere in the world on the eve of the First World War, boasting a million-ton fleet.[8] All this already disturbed the Germans in the decades before war broke out. Admiral von Tirpitz was determined to build a fleet that would outclass the British one, declaring in 1897 that 'for Germany at the moment the greatest enemy at sea is England' – *für Deutschland ist zur Zeit der gefährlichste Gegner zur See England.*[9] However, it might be argued that England only became an enemy because Tirpitz wished it so.

II

One can look at the maritime history of the two world wars from many perspectives, most obviously that of naval warfare. The perspective that will be adopted here is that of the shipping companies, particularly those based in Britain such as the Blue Funnel Line, Cunard and P&O. This enables one to see how war brought the shipping industry both disaster and profit; and a comparison with what came before and what came after conflict helps explain the survival, crises and regeneration of these firms. Although the First World War massively disrupted Britain's overseas trade, the attacks by U-boats on British shipping had less effect than the continuing command of the seas by British fleets, which left Germany struggling to obtain the goods it needed for its war effort; Germany was in effect subject to a maritime blockade; and Britain, a country whose ability to supply itself depended even more heavily on access to the sea, continued to rule the waves; Britain imported 79 per cent of its grain and 40 per cent of its meat in 1914, while some products such as sugar were still produced entirely overseas. The British government reserved the right to requisition merchant ships for military use, and gradually applied this rule more stringently, but it was obvious that the major role of merchant shipping would have to be the provisioning of Great Britain, including the carriage of large quantities of wheat from Canada and the United States. If anything, the shipping companies were accused of making excessive profits out of the war, partly through the increased freight charges they began to apply. Some companies, such as the Blue Funnel Line of Liverpool, saw their profits soar and suffered relatively minor losses; Cunard doubled the tonnage of its fleet between 1909 and 1919, and its assets soared towards £15,000,000. Even so, one third of Britain's tonnage disappeared under the waves, particularly after the Germans developed effective U-boats, the carriers of deadly torpedoes. 'Damned un-English' was the verdict of a British admiral on the use of boats that hid under the surface of the sea. They were not the only threat: enemy mines stood in the way of merchant shipping.[10]

Naval historians might argue about which side gained the upper hand in the Battle of Jutland at the end of May 1916, but the crucial consideration is the outcome: Germany proved unable to break British ascendancy at sea. It could neither gain a stranglehold on the British Isles nor open up Atlantic waters to its own imperial fleet and merchant navy. Where the Germans needed to think carefully was the threat they posed not just to British but to American shipping. Attacks on its ships would surely bring the United States into the conflict, however reluctant Woodrow Wilson was to commit his country to what might too easily be classed as a European war. The sinking of the *Lusitania* off Ireland in May 1915, with the loss of over 1,000 lives, many of them American, hardened opinion in the United States; the German counterargument was that the *Reich* had declared most of the open Atlantic a war zone and that it had warned American citizens that their safety could not be guaranteed. Even so, it took another two years for the USA to join the fray. And American fears were realized: merchant ships had never in human history been subjected to such relentless attacks. In February to May 1917, 2,500,000 tons of shipping were sent to the bottom of the sea, while P&O lost forty-four ships that year. The Atlantic was the most dangerous ocean, plagued by German U-boats, and British companies that operated in the Indian Ocean and Pacific waters stood to make respectable profits during the war.[11] Meanwhile the Germans suffered from the lack of vital metals such as tungsten and nickel, forcing them to leave machinery idle; and the food intake of ordinary Germans, though just about sufficient, was balanced more towards turnips and less towards *Wurst*, which, if nothing else, demoralized the population.

The First World War demonstrated that a global economy, of which Imperial Britain was the example par excellence, was also a fragile one in time of war. It demonstrated too that heavy steelclad battleships were still very vulnerable, once the art of building submarines had been mastered. And for Germany the maritime disaster was catastrophic. Having lost half its merchant navy during the war, it lost much of the rest under the draconian terms of the Treaty of Versailles. A few years after the war ended not even 1 per cent of the world fleet flew the flag of the Weimar Republic. Yet these figures also served as a reminder to Great Britain that its own losses had been devastating: 37 per cent of the merchant fleet, a gross tonnage of at least 7,000,000, maybe 9,000,000 units.[12] From this perspective, it is no surprise that economic historians have argued that the post-war period was less 'globalized' than the period leading right up to the outbreak of war. In 1920 the total volume of maritime trade around the world had fallen to a level one fifth below the pre-war level.[13]

III

The post-war picture is not all bleak. Slow recovery did take place, even though it was badly punctured by the Great Depression. One country that benefited was Japan: an ally of Great Britain during the war, it had even sent warships to the Mediterranean, but the importance of the First World War for Japan also lay in the experience it brought to the Meiji Empire: its fleet not just of warships but of merchant vessels continued to grow, rising from 1,700,000 tons on the eve of the war to almost 3,000,000 tons at war's end. Over the next twenty years the scale of the Japanese merchant marine grew exponentially; by 1939 Japan accounted for 13 per cent of world tonnage.[14] Others fared much less well: around a third of the German and Dutch merchant fleets was immobile in 1932. One or two places even boomed during the Depression: Hong Kong received ships totalling 20,000,000 tons when the Depression was at rock bottom, and Singapore also prospered, helped by the continued expansion of the Malay rubber industry. Those involved in the shipping industry, including governments as well as companies, strained every nerve to invest in new port structures and even, as will be seen, to stimulate the shipping industry by ordering and building new ships for cargoes and passengers.[15]

From the perspective of the British shipping companies, there were some significant changes. Shipping companies merged and the new enterprises operated gigantic fleets: Kylsant Royal Mail had more than 700 ships afloat in 1929, adding up to more than 2,500,000 tons – in the process the company had overextended itself. Kylsant Royal Mail collapsed the next year amid scandal: Lord Kylsant was accused of fixing the books to make the company appear a much better investment than it was, and after a sensational trial he became an involuntary guest of His Majesty the King in a British prison. He was as much the victim of the worldwide slump in business as a misguided chairman with exaggerated ambitions. For the storm clouds were gathering, and the enormous overcapacity of the world's merchant marine made the shipping industry particularly vulnerable. Problems were accentuated by the slump in business that heralded the Great Depression. In November 1931 Lord Inchcape, chairman of P&O, wrote: 'I have never known such a period of depression as that through which we have passed in the last 18 months. It has been heart-rending to see the steamers leaving London, week after week ... with thousands of tons of unoccupied space – so different from the old days.'[16]

One positive development concerned shipping technology. Oil-fired diesel engines were introduced, which used less fuel, even though the fuel was more expensive. Still, this reduced reliance on the scattered coal bunkers found all around the globe. There was no rush to oil: the Danish East India Company had introduced motor ships before the First World War, but the temptation to carry on using coal was particularly strong in Britain, given the ready availability of cheap Welsh coal. In 1926 the management of Cunard wondered whether it would have to convert some of the company's ships back to coal, if oil prices continued to rise. One way to reduce costs on oil-fired ships was to employ Chinese or other Far Eastern labour in the engine room, since one could pay these workers about half what European hands would be paid – a situation that still prevails aboard cruise liners.[17] Another possibility was to load oil in places where it was especially cheap, such as Aden.

Then there were sectors of the shipping industry that were hit by political changes in the post-war world. One of the most serious developments that Cunard faced was the increasing restrictiveness of United States policy towards immigrants. This nation whose very foundation lay in the fact that all its citizens (excluding the much-ignored native Americans) were of immigrant descent became mired in what can only be described as racist, and in their fullest form anti-Semitic, policies: in 1921 Congress decreed that immigration would be limited to 3 per cent of the number of each national group living in the USA at the time of the census of 1910. This had the effect of restricting immigration from parts of eastern Europe from which the flow to the tenements of the East Side, New York, had become increasingly strong. In 1923 Congress enacted a new law according to which the criteria would be set not by the census of 1910 but by that of 1890, which had the effect of further restricting numbers from eastern Europe. The result for the shipping companies was that passenger traffic, long dominated by the migrants in steerage, plummeted: in 1921

Cunard had the satisfaction of carrying nearly 50,000 passengers in third class from the British Isles to the United States; the next year there were not even 35,000 steerage passengers, and it was reported that 'third class space on many of our voyages went comparatively empty'. Needless to say, the shipping companies pressed the British government to argue in Washington for less restrictive measures, and in fact the reversion to the 1890 census meant that a slightly larger number of British and Irish immigrants could be admitted. Then, in 1929, Congress thought again; this time the 1920 census was to be the measuring rod, which greatly favoured migrants from the United Kingdom but slashed the numbers allowed to arrive from the newly constituted Irish Free State and from Germany. Still, Cunard had always carried not just migrants from the British Isles but a great many others who had arrived from continental Europe and Scandinavia in transit to America. The company therefore had to think of ways to diversify – as, indeed, did rival companies in other countries, notably German HAPAG, which developed a tourism department. Earnest German tourists could sail out to the USA, Cuba or Mexico on adventure and study tours, while the French company CGT began to invest in hotels in the vast swathe of the Maghrib that lay under French rule.[18]

Cunard looked over its shoulder and understood that its rivals had a clear advantage in another form of passenger traffic across the Atlantic: the express liner services that specialized more in first- and second-class accommodation and services. So the decision was made to start building, which also meant that there was an opportunity to adopt oil-fired engines in place of coal. This building programme was already well under way in 1922, and within three years the company was running ten routes, linking Southampton, Liverpool, London and Bristol to the United States, and even services from Hamburg and the Dutch ports to America. Old Cunard ships, including the former German *Imperator* (a great hulk now known as the *Berengaria*), had their first-class accommodation refitted, so that passengers could enjoy private baths and as much running hot water as they wanted; but competition on the Atlantic routes remained tough. Nor did the company neglect the less affluent passengers who traditionally had endured steerage class accommodation in dormitories deep in the hull of these liners. A new version of third class, 'tourist class', came into being, aimed in part at the increasing number of people visiting the United States for pleasure. This was intended to provide better accommodation, in cabins, than was offered in third class; the equivalent on a modern aeroplane would be premium economy.[19]

Cunard was still sailing in choppy waters after the Great Depression drew to an end. It was saved by what had seemed at first a potential disaster of the first magnitude, the building of the RMS *Queen Mary*, which began its career in 1936, though construction of what was then known as 'Hull no. 534' had begun at the end of 1930. The plan was to launch a ship unlike any other: it would be larger, faster, more luxurious and more powerful than any of its competitors, and it would, in conjunction with a sister ship, make possible a weekly service between Southampton, Cherbourg and New York (the second ship, the *Queen Elizabeth*, was still unfinished at the outbreak of the Second World War). Using one large ship rather than a couple of smaller ones could, in the long run, be economical, and the French shipping company CGT had the same idea when it launched its own mega-liner, the *Normandie*. Work on the *Queen Mary* was halted during the Great Depression, and it was only resumed thanks to a loan of up to £4,500,000 from the British government, which saw this as a prestige product that would enable Cunard to outclass its German and French rivals on the transatlantic passenger route. However, there was one important condition: Cunard was to merge with the White Star Line, its old rival, and operator of the doomed *Titanic*. White Star was in financial trouble, and work on its own rival to Hull no. 534 had also been suspended. The merger took place in 1934, the year that the *Queen Mary* was launched on the Clyde.[20] This degree of government intervention was not unique: Dutch and German shipping companies were also shored up by the state, and in Germany government interference went a stage further, as Jews were forced out of their positions in the HAPAG company: 'Jewish identity was purged from the collective memory of the firm, although the firm would have had no meaningful history without it.'[21]

Sir Percy Bates, chairman of Cunard White Star, looked back on the performance of the *Queen Mary* in 1941, when it and the *Queen Elizabeth* had been converted into troop ships, with proud nostalgia for its brief but brilliant pre-war career:

> I think the time has come for me to be more particular on the financial performance of *Queen Mary*. She is widely known as a masterpiece of British construction; it may not be equally appreciated that financially she has been very successful from the start, as the progress made in marine engineering has focused in *Queen Mary* a new economy in transportation across the Atlantic. Since 1922, when the full effect of the U.S. Immigration Quota Law first made itself felt, no steamer has ever made so much money in successive twelve months, as *Queen Mary* has done since being commissioned.[22]

It was not, though, simply a matter of profits. The *Queen Mary* displayed the prestige of the maritime nation that had built it and that sailed it. This too was what had prompted the British government to sink so much money into its construction – not to mention the stimulus that the building of the two *Queen*s gave to the economy of western Scotland. Not just in Great Britain but in France, Germany and elsewhere, sterling efforts were made to climb out of the pit of economic depression, and by the eve of the Second World War they were having some effect. Liverpool, it is true, was slowly losing its pre-eminence as a British port, but that meant business was being dispersed elsewhere around Great Britain, for instance to Southampton and Bristol.[23] How the outbreak of another world war, one that really did encompass almost the entire globe, would affect this now needs to be examined.

IV

The Second World War presents a paradox in maritime history, compared to the First. Even if the earlier conflict grew out of events deep within the Balkans, sea power had been a major concern of the Germans on the eve of the First World War, as Tirpitz's statement about the British threat makes plain. And yet the conflict at sea was largely limited to the Atlantic, despite the heavy losses of merchant marine. The Second World War originated in Germany's ambitions on land, in eastern Europe, and in 1939 British Appeasers were arguing that Great Britain should seize the opportunity to leave Hitler to his designs within Europe, in which case he would not interfere with British control of the seas. When war with Germany did break out, and when Japan joined the conflict on Germany's side, the conflict became a truly global one that embraced the three great oceans, and saw the fall of several of Britain's most precious bases in the Far East, notably Hong Kong (on Christmas Day 1941) and Singapore (on 15 February 1942). Whereas the trading networks of the British shipping companies that operated in the Far East had often prospered during the First World War, they were completely shattered during the Second World War, when even Australia came under Japanese attack. The Blue Funnel Line lost its Far Eastern bases, the longstanding sources of its success.[24]

The conflict at sea was also even more vicious than it had been in the days of the first U-boats: not merely had submarine technology advanced in leaps and bounds, but the addition of effective air power meant that attacks on ships were no longer being launched solely by other ships, above or below the waterline. The merchant marine not just of the Allied Powers but of neutral nations, including, until its belated entry into the war, the United States, was massively exposed to German and Japanese firepower. This also meant that the threat to Britain's supply of food and essential industrial goods was constant and serious, to a far higher degree than between 1914 and 1918. Some well-established supply routes were not accessible: sending troops to Egypt involved a massive circumnavigation of Africa.[25]

After the fall of France the Germans commandeered most of the French merchant navy. The fate of merchant navies in other lands conquered by the Germans was complicated. Much of the Norwegian merchant navy moved over to Britain after Hitler invaded Norway, as did many Dutch ships; after all, sailors had the advantage of mobility. To some extent, Allied losses at sea were compensated by the United States, first in helping to keep the supply lines to Britain open and then, after Pearl Harbor, in the loan of shipping which was being furiously constructed in American shipyards. This did not prevent the destruction of 21,000,000 tons of Allied merchant shipping during the Second World War, with about 15,000,000 tons the victim of U-boat attacks – nearly 4,800 ships. Showing exceptional bravery, merchant sailors were fully aware of the enormous risks as they zig-zagged around the oceans, trying to avoid German submarines.[26] In the Pacific, the struggle for control of the sea lanes took on a different character. Here the US fleet was determined to block Japanese trade within the forcibly created 'Greater East Asia Co-Prosperity Sphere' that, by the time of Pearl Harbor, included vast swathes of the coasts of China and south-east Asia under Meiji rule. The Americans, using submarines and air power, destroyed Japanese ships carrying iron, coal and oil from China to Japan, or rubber from occupied Malaya, and they also attacked long-distance shipping sent all the way to Japan from Germany loaded with machinery and chemicals.

The British shipping companies played an important role in the war, even if their ships were now under the operational control of the government, following orders issued on 26 August 1939, more than a week before war actually broke out, that permitted the Admiralty 'to adopt compulsory control of movements of merchant shipping', initially in the North Sea, Baltic, Mediterranean and Atlantic. The Germans were also prepared; they had already sent the pocket-battleships *Graf Spee* and *Deutschland* to the Atlantic, and had positioned thirty-nine U-Boats out of a submarine fleet of fifty-seven around the coasts of the United Kingdom. A lethal U-boat attack on a British liner on the very first day of the war made the British government realize that the Germans were not planning to abide by any rules of war protecting non-combatants. This led to the immediate organization of armed convoys, but Britain lacked sufficient resources to accompany ships deep into the Atlantic, a problem compounded by the abandonment of two British naval bases on the coast of the Irish Free State the year before, which meant that ships were sailing unprotected through a dangerous stretch of Irish waters. German mines, some of them magnetic ones that clamped themselves to the hulls of ships, were an even greater danger than the submarines; in 1939 alone seventy-eight ships were blown apart by German mines, adding up to more than 250,000 tons.

When the Luftwaffe began to attack British shipping in December 1939, the Admiralty stepped up its efforts to provide merchant shipping with anti-aircraft guns; and, again, there had been advance thinking – but the really useful guns had been ordered from Switzerland, and after the fall of France they were unobtainable. That meant Britain had to make its own, or buy them from the United States, but the situation was so bad that some ships were only supplied with fireworks, manufactured by the well-established firm of Brock's, in the not entirely vain hope that German planes, never very good at identifying what was floating on the sea, would take them more seriously than they deserved. A further problem was that the Royal Air Force did not seem to be keen to co-ordinate its activities with the Admiralty; traditional service rivalries came into play here. This meant that British planes were not available to provide cover for ships beyond Britain's shores. On the other hand, advance thinking about the Merchant Navy ensured that there were sufficient ships to ferry the British Expeditionary Force across the Channel to France from 9 September onwards. Moreover, Britain enjoyed some success in hunting down and destroying U-boats, even if they were being replaced over and over again, with almost Satanic fury, in German shipyards.[27] And then part of the Royal Navy had to be redeployed into the Mediterranean to face Mussolini, who had taken opportunistic advantage of the defeat of France to join Hitler.[28] That is just to mention the difficult conditions at the start of the war; the fortitude of the Merchant Navy in the face of what must often have seemed overwhelmingly strong opposition is a story of endurance without parallel in the maritime history of the world.

The experience of four shipping companies, three fully British and one of Norwegian origin, illustrates the difficulties shipping companies now faced. It has been seen that the British government requisitioned the two *Queen*s as troop carriers; in fact, the government had already requisitioned ten smaller Cunard ships before war even broke out; the problem with the *Queen Mary* was that she was stuck in New York, while the *Queen Elizabeth* was still in the builder's yard outside Glasgow, awaiting plenty of work on her cabins and public spaces. Her maiden voyage was an extraordinary event: she was sent to New York to be fitted out, and then on to Sydney, joining the *Queen Mary*. Both ships transported hundreds of thousands of troops, beginning with Australians bound for the

Middle East, and continuing, from 1942 onwards, with American GIs en route to Europe – what the historian of Cunard has called 'an achievement in transportation without parallel in the history of trooping'. By the time they were working the Atlantic crossing each ship had space for 15,000 men, half an infantry division, so it is no surprise that U-boat commanders competed to catch these mighty ships, and enemy agents plotted to sabotage them.[29]

P&O was also obliged to hand over shipping which was adorned with eight or so six-inch guns from the days before the Boer War – not much use against German submarines. By the end of the year one of the first P&O ships to be requisitioned, the *Rawalpindi*, had bravely attempted to sink the powerful German cruiser *Scharnhorst* in a hopeless encounter between Iceland and the Faroes – hopeless but not futile, as the Prime Minister rose in the House of Commons to praise the sailors on board as 'an inspiration to those who will come after them', of whom, alas, there were a great many from the P&O fleet alone. P&O troopships were heavily involved in the north African landings which took place in November 1942, 'Operation Torch'. But clearly the company's Far Eastern business had come to standstill.[30] This was even truer of those companies that operated from British bases in the Far East.

The Wallem shipping company, operating in Hong Kong and Shanghai, was forced to hand over six ships to the Japanese, although others escaped to India or Australia; its Norwegian origins, and its partly Norwegian staff, proved an advantage, as the Norwegians were at first left free to go about their business – but of course there was now much less business. The Wallem office in Hong Kong closed, and several of its staff were captured by the Japanese. The chief accountant, Kenneth Nelson, was a lucky survivor: he was placed on board a ship carrying more than 1,800 prisoners, but the Japanese had not painted Red Cross markings on the boat, and it was torpedoed by the Allies. Nelson broke out of the sinking ship through the gash left by the torpedo, swimming ashore only to find that he was in Japanese-occupied territory. He was sent back to Hong Kong, escaped from prison there, was shot by a Japanese patrol, but still managed to find his way to his favourite bar, where he ordered his favourite drink with the extra request: 'Make it a double!'[31]

Blue Funnel ships were scattered across the globe in Allied service; the fleet of eighty-seven ships managed by Alfred Holt & Co. of Liverpool in 1939 was whittled down to a fleet of thirty-six by war's end. Losses occurred in all three oceans – one ship was torpedoed off Brisbane, Australia, while German torpedoes finished off one Blue Funnel ship after another off west Africa or in the north Atlantic. For all the advantages of sailing in convoy, the first of Alfred Holt & Co.'s losses at sea occurred when a convoy broke up in strong winds in February 1940, leading to the sinking of the *Pyrrhus* by a U-boat lurking in high seas off Galicia.[32] However, as suspicions grew (more among the British than among the Americans) that Japan was about to attack Pearl Harbor, the company began to move its ships out of Hong Kong, presciently realizing that the threat was not just to the United States but to Germany's existing enemies. The speed at which the Japanese advanced across the Pacific left some Blue Funnel ships in the firing line. The *Tantalus*, which had been laid up in Hong Kong harbour for refitting, was spirited away, but its captain wrongly assumed that the Philippines, then under American rule, would offer a safe haven. The Japanese were in fact mercilessly bombarding Manila, and the ship was blasted to pieces, though fortunately the crew was by then on shore – however, the sailors were arrested by the conquering army and sent to a prison camp.[33]

The damage to shipping is only part of the story. Ports suffered immensely as well. Air raids on the Port of London and on Liverpool in autumn 1940 were directly aimed at the shipping industry, as were attacks on Bristol, Southampton and the great shipbuilding centres on the River Clyde: the Blitz was about much more than demoralization. Winston Churchill saw the attacks on the Mersey and the Clyde as the most significant moments of 1940. After London was knocked out, Great Britain became more dependent on Liverpool, so the fury unleashed against the city knew no bounds: the attacks in 1940 were only the beginning. Liverpool had lost 70 per cent of its port capacity by summer of the next year, by which time the German attacks ceased. The headquarters of Blue Funnel, which had only been in use for nine years, went up in smoke in May 1941. Once the docks were gone, it must have seemed an impossible task to keep the port open, but the Liverpudlians managed to do so; by the end of the war the tonnage passing through Liverpool had returned to the level of 1939. As the balance in the conflict shifted towards Britain, massive destruction occurred on the other side of the North Sea: Hamburg was bombed into near oblivion, while Rotterdam was wiped out following repeated attacks, first from invading Germans and then from the Allies. By the end of the war, HAPAG possessed one insignificant boat.[34]

The years that followed would, therefore, have to see massive reconstruction if maritime links across the globe were to be restored – ships had to be built, ports had to be repaired, finances had to be arranged. It was a moot point whether Britannia could continue to rule the waves in the new political and economic climate of the 1940s and 1950s.

I

By the end of the war, not just many ships but many ports had turned into wreckage – the Port of London, Liverpool, Rotterdam, Hamburg, but also Singapore, Hong Kong, Yokohama. Lifting world trade out of this trough was a challenge that was indeed met. As new tensions began to preoccupy the world, questions about the continuing supply of vital raw materials such as rubber acted as a stimulus to recovery. The Far East is a good place to look for evidence that the road to recovery was strewn with obstacles. British-owned firms were mapping out the sources of Malayan rubber within four months of the defeat of Japan. The board of the Sarawak Steamship Company, with no ships left out of its tiny pre-war fleet, began its meeting on 13 December 1945 by solemnly confirming the minutes of its session on 4 December 1941, as if all the misery in between had never occurred. P&O discovered that their Singapore office had been obliterated but their Hong Kong office had actually been smartened up by the Japanese.[1] The situation in the Far East was complicated by the withdrawal of the Dutch from Indonesia, a major evacuation involving tens of thousands of Europeans who had been stranded in Japanese-held territory for years; ships were summoned from all over the world, and somehow these survivors were transported up the Red Sea, where the Dutch government created a mock-up of a department store that even offered Dutch delicacies to the often emaciated migrants.[2] In the longer term, though, as the countries of south-east Asia gained their independence, the European producers tended to pull out. It was obvious that Malayan rubber would become a concern of the Malaysian government, which was not expected to be especially well disposed to the European companies.

The situation in China was a further serious complication, leaving Hong Kong in a parlous position, although both the People's Republic of China, founded in 1949, and the rival Republic of China, now based in

Taiwan, appreciated the value of the colony as a listening post in their conflict with one another. From the British perspective, Hong Kong was also a valuable bulwark against Communist Chinese expansion towards Malaya; the plain-speaking Foreign Secretary, Ernest Bevin, said he wanted the colony to serve as 'the Berlin of the Middle East', though (oddly for someone so involved in the affairs of Palestine) he seems to have confused the Middle East with the Far East. The recovery of Hong Kong was held back by two factors. One was the massive number of refugees flowing into the colony from revolutionary China. The authorities could not cope with the influx. The other factor was a downturn in trade through Hong Kong during and after the Korean War, partly led by the United States, which attempted to impose a total trade embargo on the People's Republic, while the United Nations banned the import into China of strategic goods. If anything, Hong Kong had stood to gain from the closing down of the European offices in Shanghai and other trading bases along the Chinese coast, so that trade out of China had been funnelled through Hong Kong. But this did not last in the new political conditions of the early 1950s. American embargo officers arrived in the colony. They went to work with unstoppable zeal. Shrimps found their way on to the list of banned goods, because it was not clear that they had originated in the colony; maybe they had lived their lives in the Chinese-controlled waters of the Pearl River.[3]

The other trading base of the British, Singapore, was not expected to stay under colonial rule for very long. There was plenty of sympathy in London for the independence movement in Malaya, but the emergence of guerrilla forces within Malaya, among whom were many ethnic Chinese who were also Communist, complicated the picture greatly. Moreover, the population of Singapore shot up, soon reaching a million (double the pre-war figure), for this colony, like Hong Kong, acted as a magnet to poverty-stricken mainlanders. As in Hong Kong, the result was that impoverished, disease-ravaged and crime-ridden shanty towns grew up around the handsome colonial core. Economic recovery was hindered by the lack of adequate port facilities: a great floating dock had been sunk. The colony pulled itself up by its bootstraps over the next few years, seizing the opportunity to become the world's biggest market for rubber, and drawing its rubber not just from Malay but from Indonesian trees. It was, then, well able to take advantage of its superb position between the Asian mainland and the former East Indies, and between the Indian Ocean and the Pacific, even if it took a much longer time to convert the squalor of post-war years into a prospering and peaceful powerhouse. When the Federation of Malaya came into existence, the rival Indonesian Republic tried to place an embargo on the export of rubber to Singapore, in the hope that this

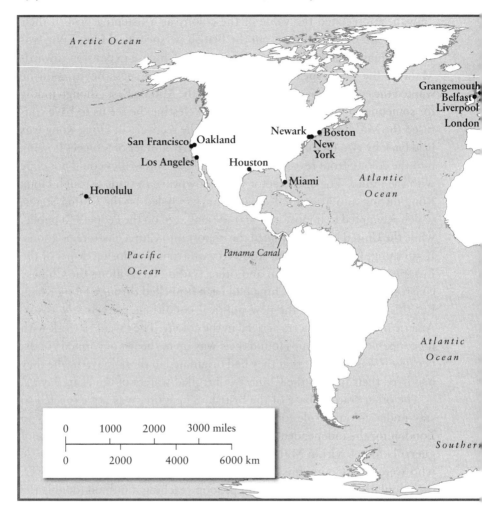

would strangle the trade of the city's still precarious economy; but exporters rapidly learned that all one needed to do was to set out from Indonesia
bound for Hong Kong, and then change direction once far enough out in
the South China Sea. Smuggling therefore became good business.[4]

Still, Singapore could not survive on what was in effect a pirate economy; real doubts were expressed about the possibility of making Singapore
work. In 1960 the United Nations, seriously worried about the future of
Singapore, sent a team to the island, led by a Dutch economist with plenty
of experience of the shipping world, Albert Winsemius. He was very
gloomy, expressing the view that 'Singapore was going down the drain'.
He was unimpressed by the port facilities. But he was just as much the
saviour of Singapore as its charismatic leader, Lee Kuan Yew: he saw that

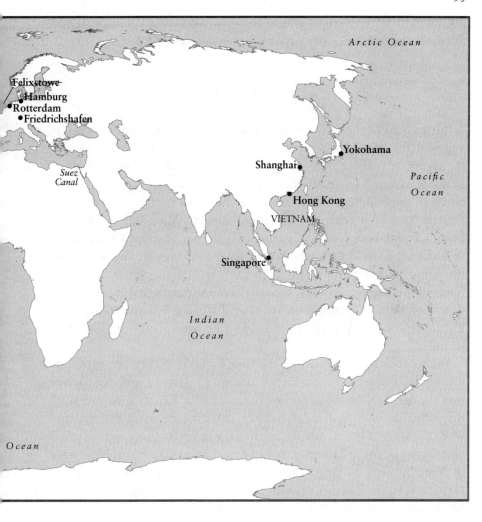

Singapore could seize the initiative if it learned to handle a new type of cargo, the container. Much more will need to be said about containers; but Winsemius was clearly a man of great vision. Another route to success was ship repair, taking advantage of the prime position of Singapore between the oceans; and this made it a favourite port of Japanese, Norwegian and Greek shipowners, who were exactly the sort of people the port needed to attract if it was to become a major centre of maritime trade.[5] Independence in 1965, following Singapore's expulsion from the Malaysian Federation (in which, as a Chinese-majority territory, it had not sat comfortably), created frightening new challenges. Attempts to develop local industries were now hampered by greater difficulty of access to raw materials on the mainland. The answer was to build on the ideas put forward by Winsemius and to turn the city into a commercial and financial middleman – one of Asia's greatest success stories.[6]

II

A full account of the recovery that took place in Europe would examine a great many factors, also present in the Far East, that sometimes slowed the recovery: massive damage to infrastructure, notably in the Port of London; external competition, as Japan in particular became a major centre of shipbuilding and re-created its merchant fleet on an ever larger scale; accompanying that, the decline of the shipbuilding industry in Great Britain. Poor labour relations, particularly the pay of seamen and the role of dockworkers in an increasingly mechanized world, were another factor, becoming more important as ports became less reliant on human labour (more of this shortly); in 1955, 1960 and 1966 seamen's strikes, each more damaging than its predecessor, seriously disrupted Britain's trade. P&O lost £1,250,000 as a result of the 1966 strike, which left five of its ships stranded.[7]

Events such as the closure of the Suez Canal in November 1956, following the disastrous Anglo-French attempt to restore European control over the canal following its nationalization by the Egyptian government, threw British shipping firms off balance; and the experience was repeated when the army of Israel roundly defeated the Egyptian army and occupied Sinai again in 1967.[8] However, not just the low-paid suffered. New ways of doing business no longer favoured the merchant middlemen who had played a key role in earlier decades. Middlemen in shipping agencies were being squeezed out as foreign clients tended increasingly to conduct business directly with producers within the United Kingdom; in part this refected the increasing technological sophistication of industrial goods (such as heavy machinery) that middlemen were not best placed to understand and explain.[9] British companies too might prefer to go straight to the tea estate, or wherever, from which they acquired their raw materials, making for proud boasts in the television advertisements of the 1950s and 1960s. Still, looked at globally, the post-war years saw a remarkable bounce back to prosperity. During the war P&O had lost just over half of its pre-war fleet of 371 ships, of 2,200,000 tons, but by 1949 it was already operating as many cargo ships as in 1939; as for passenger ships, it owned fewer, but they were larger. Moreover, P&O recognized that the future also lay in oil tankers, and in 1955 orders for this type of ship, which it had not operated before, were placed in British shipyards.[10]

Within twenty years London had restored its own maritime business to a level one and a half times that of 1939; the 1950s saw the Liverpool shipping companies recover reasonably well too, after a slow start, though these successes were punctuated by the seamen's strikes, and contraction gradually began; unemployment grew as container ships headed for other ports, much better adapted to their needs. This, as will be seen, was one of the truly great transformations of the late twentieth-century maritime world.[11]

The most impressive European success story was Rotterdam, whose almost total obliteration was the spur to ever more ambitious rebuilding and expansion. Rotterdam proper lies a good fifty kilometres inland and upriver, but the port, including the massive new 'Europoort', now extends as far as the North Sea – indeed, with typical Dutch enterprise, it includes the multiple basins of Maasvlakte, built well out into the sea, and capable of handling the vast oil tankers that have been part of Rotterdam's success story. As a container port it has achieved within Europe what Singapore has achieved within south-east Asia; another secret of success has been its pivotal role in the oil industry. In the 1960s its business was dominated by the oil that was delivered to and refined in Rotterdam and by the pipelines carrying oil deep into Europe, on behalf of Royal Dutch Shell and other companies.[12] The story is not so different from that of Singapore, in the sense that Rotterdam is able to play a vital role as a well-situated entrepôt: its port is perfectly situated at the mouth of the long and complex river system of the Rhine, the Meuse and the Scheldt that reaches deep into Germany, France and Switzerland. The Europoort is not just part of the largest port in Europe (and for a time of the world); it is also a truly European port, meeting the needs of European countries within and beyond what has become the European Union.

III

Rotterdam, like Singapore, had seen the future and adapted itself to it, as Liverpool did not. During the twentieth century every aspect of transoceanic travel was changing. It was no longer necessary to travel by boat to cross the oceans. In the 1930s Pan American Airways was just that, a pan-continental airline operating in North and South America and offering links between the United States and Panama, Lima, Santiago, Buenos Aires, Montevideo, Rio de Janeiro and the Caribbean. That is a list of ports; yet they could now be reached much more quickly by air. There was also a service from San Francisco to Hawai'i and on to Manila, both destinations being American colonies. On the other hand, the German transatlantic air service, provided by airships, often began from Fried-richshafen, on Lake Constance, deep in the heart of Europe, and some services crossed the United States, to reach Los Angeles. Here was a new way of linking the oceans and landmasses, though the project went up in flames with the crash of the Hindenburg in 1937; thereafter aeroplanes took charge of the skies.[13] In any case, the numbers able to travel on the airships were minute: the Hindenburg carried fifty passengers (later on, seventy-two), and that was a record figure; some early KLM flights were full when six passengers were on board.[14] Before the Second World War, few passengers travelled by air, and the journey from Europe to Asia with Imperial Airways or Deutsche Lufthansa would often involve stops over-night in hotels.

Some long-distance aircraft, such as the Empire Flying Boats jointly operated by Imperial Airways and QANTAS, were seaplanes, fitted out rather like a small ship, with bunks for passengers; these planes would settle down in the water off Mozambique or Crete, or even in the Nile at Cairo, en route to the Far East and Australia. Similar American planes, the Boeing 314 Clippers, could carry up to seventy-four passengers in some comfort; they were miniaturized luxury liners, with seats that converted into beds and a standard of service only perhaps captured in the best first-class cabins of the twenty-first century. Needless to say, this was also an exceptionally expensive way to travel: a return ticket from London to Hong Kong or Brisbane would have cost £288 in 1939, more than an entire year's salary for a great many people, and the airline made much of its limited profit from carrying the Royal Mail. Rather as with business class on modern aeroplanes, a high proportion of travellers were on expense accounts, for instance colonial civil servants of high or at least middling rank.[15] Ferrying such people to their destination much faster than could be done on a steamer made sense if the Empire was to be administered reasonably effectively.

By the early 1950s, with the formation of the British Overseas Airways Corporation, which specialized in flights beyond Europe, intercontinental travel by air was becoming more widely accepted, and that ate into the profits of the shipping companies. Air travel was also becoming much safer. The great breakthrough was the introduction of passenger jets. British technology produced the first Comet aircraft; they began flying in 1952, but they proved to have fatal design flaws, and were withdrawn, so it was only in 1958 that the Boeing 707, built in Seattle, began to provide regular transatlantic services for Pan-American Airways; it was soon followed by the Comet 4, operated by BOAC. These planes were not just fast but smooth, and the more comfortable travellers felt while in the air, the less they were inclined to use even the finest ships – the two British *Queen*s had a reputation for rolling in high seas, so that a voyage was not necessarily five days of bliss. As travellers shifted skywards, one option for shipping companies was to build close ties to the airlines. P&O began to buy airlines, including the somewhat bizarre Silver City Airways, which ferried holidaymakers and their cars across the English Channel in its bulbous little planes.[16] From 1962 Cunard jointly operated air services across the Atlantic with BOAC, and passengers had the option to fly out one way, travelling by ship the other way. Travelling by sea between European ports and New York was still seen as a perfectly sensible way to go, if there was no great hurry. But air travel became more common, and as it became more common it became cheaper, and as it became cheaper it rendered sea travel across the Atlantic less profitable by taking away customers. In 1966 the link between Cunard and BOAC came to an end.[17]

Cunard placed their hopes in another *Queen*, the *Queen Elizabeth* 2, which was built on the Clyde, went into service in 1969 and was only decommissioned in 2008; like the *Queen Mary* it was a statement of prestige as much as a sound economic proposition. When it entered service, Cunard was only operating three passenger ships, and the company had even sold its impressive old headquarters in Liverpool. The modern design of the *QE*2 did not convey the sense of late imperial luxury of the old *Queen Mary*, but it was used for passenger traffic to and from New York throughout its career – without, however, the possibility of a regular weekly service, since it had no sister ship. In fact, as Cunard realized, its main business was bound to lie elsewhere, in the cruise industry, and even before the *QE*2 first slid into the sea the two old *Queen*s were pottering around the Bahamas and the Mediterranean.[18] Similarly, the handsome SS *Canberra* was built at the Harland and Wolff shipyard in Belfast at a cost of £16,000,000. P&O originally planned to sail her on passenger routes linking Great Britain to Australia, but by 1974 the competition from air travel had begun to bite, and she became a cruise liner.[19] The world of passenger shipping had changed profoundly: cruises had long existed, but only towards the end of the twentieth century did they come to dominate all long-distance passenger movements by sea. Even then, they were often associated with air travel, as they might involve a flight from, say, London to Miami to board the ship.

The modern cruise industry has been traced back to Ted Arison, an Israeli chancer who, in 1966, seized the opportunity to acquire control of a Norwegian ship, which he moved across to Miami. He gradually built up his fleet under the name of Norwegian Caribbean Lines, though most of the ships were adapted ferry boats, and he deftly used the lower deck for a roll-on, roll-off cargo service between Miami and Jamaica. Arison had space on all his ships together for about 3,000 passengers, more space than Florida in those days was likely to fill; but the answer was to advertise across the United States, and to make Miami into the cruise capital of North America. His own success prompted others, notably the real Norwegians, to enter the market, making use of purpose-built ships, and further strengthening the role of Miami in the cruise business. One rival, Costa, decided to make Puerto Rico its main base, and began to fly passengers out there, including air tickets in the price of the cruise. The cruise was thus becoming an entire package. Even better than advertising was the effect of a television series, *The Love Boat*, that ran for nine years from 1977 onwards, was shown across the world, and cast the cruise industry in a rose-coloured romantic light.[20]

All this cast doubt on what cruises were really for. Is a tour of the Caribbean a chance to see the wonders of sixteenth-century Santo Domingo and to visit the Bridgetown Museum in Barbados, which, according to Wikitravel, one is likely to have all to oneself? That fact suggests that most of those who are daily decanted from cruise ships on to Caribbean shores will go shopping, or maybe try out the local cuisine. Specialist companies such as Swan Hellenic made their name as organizers of high-quality tours by sea, specializing in both human and natural history and expecting passengers to listen to what could be either exciting or boring lectures. That is feasible on a boat carrying 300 passengers or fewer; but the vast Leviathans that now prowl the oceans, bearing 3,000 passengers or more, are to all intents self-contained holiday centres, detached from the world around them, places to eat, sunbathe, sleep and enjoy light entertainment. The largest cruise ship afloat in 2017, the *Allure of the Seas*, operated by Royal Caribbean Lines, can house 7,148 passengers at peak capacity; it was launched in 2010, and with its two sister ships the total at sea rises to about 21,000 passengers. The company was founded by Norwegian rivals of Arison, and operates several other very large vessels, as does Norwegian Cruise Line. Norway's outstanding role in the cruise industry is not matched by Cunard, whose *Queen Mary 2* is a mere tiddler by comparison with the Norwegian giants, carrying at most 3,090 passengers. The damage these large ships inflict on the environment – a sore point in Venice – is matched by the inability of little towns or historic sites to cope when maybe 6,000 people arrive off cruise ships all at the same time. Setting aside the cruise ships, though, long-distance passenger travel by sea across and between the oceans has come to an end.

IV

The triumph of the aeroplane was not total. As cargo vessels, planes are expensive to use, even if they can deliver some fresh goods that ships cannot handle (such as flowers grown in Israel on sale within twenty-four hours in British marketplaces). In our own day, the vast majority of goods exported over long distances travel in container ships between continents and oceans. UNCTAD (the United Nations Conference on Trade and Development) estimates that 80 per cent of world trade by volume (nearly 10 billion tons) and 70 per cent by value is conducted by sea. The cost of bringing a can of beer from Asia to Europe on a container ship is roughly one US cent per can, five cents for a packet of biscuits and a mere ten cents for each television.

This came about through containerization. The history of the container reaches back into the 1920s, when American railroad companies experimented with steel containers that could be transferred back and forth between lorries and freight cars, using powerful forklift trucks. An obvious constraint on the use of containers to load ships was that the longshoremen were a powerful, unionized group of workers who understandably saw a threat to their own jobs in further mechanization. In the early 1950s this was not a major problem, since what containers there were had to be carefully fitted into the hold alongside loose cargo, which meant that the skills of the longshoremen were still in great demand. The cost of port-side labour might be as much as three times the cost of actually moving a cargo ship across the Atlantic, especially at the American end, since in the 1950s American dockworkers earned about five times what German ones could expect to be paid. Besides, the use of containers did not seem to be economical: containers were by and large not absolutely full, so that shippers who used them were packing empty space on board; by contrast, loose cargo could be slotted into every available nook in the hold.[21] This meant that the container could only become the standard form of transport when ships were built or adapted primarily to carry them rather than loose freight.

Traditionally, the creation of the container is linked to one inventive businessman, Malcolm McLean, who had long been frustrated by the cumbersome way that goods brought from the American hinterland had to be unloaded by longshoremen and then carefully replaced in the hold of a ship, a process that then had to be repeated back-to-front when the ship reached its destination. He is often credited with a sudden flash of genius that produced a prophetic vision of the container revolution, but his involvement in the creation of container traffic was more gradual, though it was certainly the product of successive insights. The basic idea of the container was not brand new, but the standardization that followed from his initiatives set in train a massive revolution in sea transport. He started on land: he owned a trucking company with over 600 trucks by 1954, and in the 1950s he worked hard to cut costs and to undercut his competitors. A constant innovator, he built an automated terminal in North Carolina, introduced diesel engines and redesigned his trucks so that they had crenellated sides, to reduce wind drag. His truck services along the east coast, often carrying prodigious amounts of tobacco, were, however, threatened by a different sort of competition. There were plenty of cheap cargo vessels on the market, left over from war service. Moving goods from the Deep South northwards by sea made sense, since the roads were often blocked, especially around the big New England cities – the long-distance highways had not yet been built.[22] Rather than attempting to fight a war against the cargo vessels, he would integrate them into his own system. In 1953 he mapped out plans for harbour terminals that would handle truck trailers, which could be driven straight on board, detached from the cab, carried to their destination (wheels and all), and then driven off again at the other end. The New York Port Authority was worried at the fall in domestic cargo and was keen to co-operate.

His fundamental insight was that shipping cargo was about moving goods, not moving ships. Indeed, part of the problem was that with old-fashioned loading ships did not move when they could and should: 'a ship earns money only when she's at sea. Where costs rise is in port,' McLean explained.[23] It made perfect sense to take goods trucked in from deep inside America, or brought to the coast by rail, and to send them to some other hinterland without having to unpack them. Still, the days when this would become an international operation were some way in the future. First, a uniform system had to be created. McLean devised an even more efficient way of conveying goods: instead of trailers, the ships should carry the detached bodies of the trailers. This meant that these large boxes could be taken to the side of the ship, lifted on board and – something impossible with wheeled trailers – stacked on top of one another and locked in place. His company analysed the cost of sending beer from Newark, New Jersey, to Miami. Traditional handling at both ends would cost $8 per ton, whereas container handling would cost 50c. It took time to acquire a suitable if ancient tanker and to obtain permission to send it to sea as a refitted and very special cargo ship. Only in 1956 was McLean able to launch his service under the flag of his Pan-Atlantic Steamship Company. Towards the end of April the *Ideal-X* was loaded with fifty-eight aluminium boxes taken off truck trailers and sent from Newark down to Houston, Texas. In order to do this McLean had had to order the boxes (he asked for 200, such was his confidence), and even had to redesign the cranes that would be able to lift the containers in one quick movement from shore to ship. They were so large and heavy that the rails along which they moved also had to be strengthened. This was not a simple operation, but a massive commitment that soon proved its worth: the cost of loading the *Ideal-X* was one thirty-seventh of the cost of traditional loading. With a sister ship, the *Ideal-X* provided a weekly service between New Jersey and Houston, which soon increased to a service every four days, as additional ships were acquired.[24]

Containers were, it was argued, preferable from the point of view of security. In high seas, cargo on traditional boats could shift around over much bigger spaces and suffer damage; besides, sealed boxes were much less likely to suffer from theft.[25] It was also possible to place refrigeration units in containers and to stack these containers along with all the others. McLean's own containers were thirty-five feet long; but, as it became more and more obvious that this was the way of the future, new standards were applied – from 1958 onwards (very soon, then, after the voyage of the *Ideal-X*) the American Standards Association pondered this question, and in due course international agreement emerged setting the length of containers at multiples of ten feet, the standard Trailer Equivalent Unit (TEU) being twenty feet.[26] The very fact that this name is used harks back to the origins of the container as the tail-end of a massive American truck. By 1960 other transport companies in the United States were beginning to eye McLean's operation enviously. The *Hawaiian Citizen*, with space for 356 containers, started to operate between San Francisco and Honolulu that year. It was not all plain sailing: longshoremen in Puerto Rico refused to unload McLean's containers, and McLean's company had to agree that large teams of dockworkers would be employed on tasks that, more realistically, could have been completed mechanically with far fewer men. This was only the beginning of a long saga: in New York and other mainland ports, the opposition to containerization within the unions was at times visceral. The threat to jobs was real, and along with the jobs traditional skills in handling loose goods disappeared. Eventually mediation by Kennedy, Johnson and government representatives achieved compromises that did something to protect jobs.[27]

McLean's company, renamed Sea–Land Service, extended its range to the Pacific and even Alaska. At first there was hesitation about crossing the Atlantic, if not the Pacific, and it took ten years from the sailing of the *Ideal-X* for a McLean ship to reach Rotterdam, with 226 boxes on board.

On its return it obligingly put in at the Scottish harbour of Grangemouth to load Scotch whisky, for the first time despatched by container. McLean believed that the sight of all this whisky reaching America by container convinced the world of shipping that the future lay with containers. At any rate, the transatlantic route was now open, and rapidly flourished, with European companies such as HAPAG soon taking part as well. HAPAG became a giant operator of container ships.[28] Meanwhile one special route did even more than the whisky bottles to convince the world of the usefulness of containers: during the Vietnam War. McLean became a regular supplier of the American army, arguing that containers were perfect for the delivery of vital supplies that otherwise were seeping from the ports of Vietnam into the hands of the Viet Cong. He also showed that the containers could be put to many uses, for example as offices and storage bunkers. In 1968 a fifth of the military supplies sent across the Pacific was sent in containers. It became obvious too that costs could be cut dramatically by making use of containers to supply the American troops in Vietnam, though the US High Command was slow to recognize the fact. Soon, though, the USA was sending half the military supplies it despatched to Europe in container ships. No doubt this made it even easier for American bases in Europe to supply the troops with half-and-half milk, American pizza, doughnuts American-style and other wonderments that astonish European visitors to these bases to this day – but it was also an important step towards global containerization.

By the 1980s McLean's operations spanned the world, including South as well as North America. What had begun as a medium-sized trucking company had become an international giant; more than that, its innovations decisively shaped the way in which international trade was conducted. The capacity of modern container ships was at last matched by the capacity of vast container ports such as Rotterdam, Singapore and Hong Kong. Among American beneficiaries of the shift to containers was Oakland, opposite San Francisco – 3,000,000 tons of movements in 1969, excluding what was being sent to American troops across the ocean. This was eight times the container traffic Oakland had handled four years earlier; the downside was that San Francisco saw its own maritime traffic shrink, as did Boston on the other side of the continent. Similarly, in Britain new ports displaced old ones; the London docks closed and only after years of desolation and decay were the Docklands regenerated, but as a financial centre, Olympic arena and even – a sign of how things have changed – an airport. Meanwhile, Felixstowe, previously a small and uninteresting coastal town, became the major British centre of container traffic, with an enormously long quayside and a deep port suitable for the largest cargo ships; by 1969 its annual tonnage was approaching 2,000,000. Its owner, Hutchison Ports, which traces its origins to the nineteenth-century Hong Kong and Whampoa Dock Company, also owns or has interests in a vast number of container ports across the world, including Hong Kong; its market share stands above 8 per cent and it was handling over 33,000,000 TEU (standard container units) in 2005. One beneficiary is Trinity College, Cambridge, which owns some of the land at Felixstowe and has increased its already enormous financial portfolio accordingly.[29] The largest container ship in the world in 2017, the *CSCL Globe*, owned in China, has put in at Felixstowe and can carry an astonishing 19,100 standard-size containers. Meanwhile, Maersk, the largest container shipping company in the world, which is a Danish enterprise, operates 600 ships; added together, its containers have a capacity well over 3,000,000 TEU. This is only the beginning: the future may well lie with a great power in the East which has a new vision of its place in the world. The era of Western dominance that began with Columbus and da Gama, and came to embrace North America as well, is coming to an end.

Conclusion

The heading 'Conclusion' is normally no more than a way of bringing a book to an end. But the word 'conclusion' has additional force when looking at the history of the oceans. Not just this book but ocean history is coming to an end, at least in its traditional form. In today's world, the nature of contact across the sea has been radically transformed, even allowing for the massive volume of maritime trade, beginning with the laying of telegraph cables, their partial and then total substitution by radio contact, and culminating in the triumph of air travel. Coasts are no longer the defining points in travel between Britain or Italy and the United States: the classic ports of past times have been displaced by container ports, many of which are not centres of trade inhabited by a colourful variety of people from many backgrounds, but processing plants in which machinery, not men, do the heavy work and no one sees the cargoes that have often been brought from far away and are sealed inside their big boxes. Felixstowe is, in effect, a great machine, not the humming hub of commercial give-and-take visible in early Aden or Melaka, or even Boston and Liverpool in more recent times. Cruise liners drop in on places but are not a way of travelling purposefully from place to place; ultimately those on board intend to return to their home after travelling around in a loop.

Most ships, though, carry cargo. The scale of trade through the container ports is now astonishing. Hong Kong sees a thousand ships pass through its nine container terminals each day; the harbour handles 20,000,000 containers each year, each weighing a maximum of twenty tons. Overall, 300,000,000 tons of goods pass through Hong Kong annually, mainly to and from the People's Republic of China. But Hong Kong is only one element in a much larger conurbation of 68,000,000 people: as well as Macau, which makes much of its money from gambling, there is the industrial city of Shenzhen, until 1980 a little town of small significance with 30,000 inhabitants and now a massive city of 13,000,000 people dedicated to hi-tech industries that presses right down on the border with the former

British colony. All the way to Guangzhou (Canton) industrial development has transformed the countryside. The Pearl River, long China's main window on the world, has become more important than ever not just to China but to the world economy. The People's Republic has begun to look out towards the sea with an enthusiasm not seen since the days of the Song Dynasty or Zheng He's voyages, and has staked its claims in the South China Sea in the face of opposition from the Philippines, Taiwan, Vietnam and other neighbours. The 'One Belt, One Road' project, re-creating the overland silk route by rail, as well as long-distance sea routes between China and Asia, Africa and Europe, will give China increasing control over the movement of the industrial goods it now produces in such vast quantities. This is not just a question of catching up with the West, and with nearby economies in Japan, South Korea and Taiwan; it is now a question of overtaking the West and China's neighbours.

Global warming is making journeys around the top of Canada and Russia feasible, linking the Pacific to the Atlantic in ways dreamed of in the days of Queen Elizabeth I. Not content with the historic silk routes, the State Council of the People's Republic announced in January 2018 that it would conduct trial voyages along a 'Polar Silk Route', corresponding to the North-East Passage, along which a Russian tanker had managed to sail all the way from Norway to South Korea in 2017. If receding ice permits regular traffic to flow along this route, the time taken to travel from the Far East to Europe could be reduced by 20 per cent. But this and the route over the top of Canada will be routes for container ships, or occasional cruise ships whose passengers prefer ice to heat. Meanwhile humans have inflicted severe environmental damage upon the oceans, threatening marine life by the dumping of plastics, some of which enter the fishy food chain, leading to depletion of fish stocks that are already threatened by overfishing – not to mention the massive decline in the numbers of several species of whale.[1] UNESCO rightly nominates World Heritage Sites in most of the countries of the globe. But there is one vast World Heritage Site that also needs to be nominated: the world-encompassing ocean sea, whose history is entering an entirely new phase. By the beginning of the twenty-first century, the ocean world of the last four millennia had ceased to exist.

Museums with Maritime Collections

A book ranging across the globe and across the millennia cannot be based on close reading of the millions of archival sources that exist. Instead, I have made extensive use of museum collections from many countries, whether in maritime museums, described as such, or more general museums with relevant material such as contemporary maps and documents, ceramic finds from shipwrecks, porcelain imported into Europe, and in some cases the physical remains of the ships themselves. This is a list of some of the museums that have provided me with the richest material and the most valuable insights. They are not all big or lavish. Sometimes a small hut containing a local collection has been as helpful as a vast repository.

CAPE VERDE ISLANDS

Praia, Santiago: Archaeological Museum; Ethnological Museum.

CHINA

Hong Kong SAR: Historical Museum; Maritime Museum. *Macau SAR:* Historical Museum. *Hangzhou:* City Museum.

DENMARK

Copenhagen: Nationalmuseet. *Helsingør:* National Maritime Museum. *Skagen:* By-og Egnsmuseum.

DOMINICAN REPUBLIC

Santo Domingo: Alcázar de Colón; Fundación García Arévalo, Pre-Hispanic Collection; Museo de la Casas Reales; Museo del Hombre Dominicano.

FINLAND

Mariehamn, Åland Islands: Maritime Museum.

GERMANY

Bremerhaven: Deutsches Schiffahrtsmuseum; Deutsches Auswanderer-haus. *Lübeck:* Hansemuseum.

ITALY

Genoa: Galata Maritime Museum.

JAPAN

Tokyo: National Museum.

MALAYSIA

Melaka: Cheng Ho Cultural Museum; Maritime Museum; Stadthuys Museum; Sultanate Palace Museum.

THE NETHERLANDS

Amsterdam: Rijksmuseum; Scheepvaart Museum.

NEW ZEALAND

Wellington: Te Papa National Museum; Wellington Museum.

NORWAY

Bergen: Bergen Museum; Hansa Museum. *Oslo:* Viking Ship Museum; National Museum.

PORTUGAL

Angra do Heroísmo, Terceira, Azores: Museum. *Faro:* Archaeological Museum. *Lisbon:* Museu Nacional de Arte Antiga; Gulbenkian Museum.

QATAR

Doha: Islamic Museum.

SINGAPORE

Asiatic Civilizations Museum; Historical Museum; Maritime Museum; Peranakan Museum.

SPAIN

Ceuta: Museum of the Instituto de Estudios Ceutíes. *La Rábida:* Convent and Museum.

SWEDEN

Gothenburg: Maritime Museum. *Stockholm:* Historiska Museet, Vasa Museum. *Visby, Gotland:* Museum.

TURKEY

Istanbul: Maritime Museum.

UNITED ARAB EMIRATES

Fujairah: Museum. *Sharjah:* Archaeological Museum; Maritime Museum; Islamic Museum.

UNITED KINGDOM

Belfast: Titanic Belfast. *Bristol:* M Shed; SS Great Britain. *Liverpool:* Maritime Museum. *London:* National Maritime Museum, Greenwich.

Further Reading

Chapter by chapter, the references indicate the large number of specific studies and primary sources on which I have relied. This bibliography presents books that deal more generally with the oceans. Some of the books deal with matters such as the ocean environment that have not been addressed closely in this book, but are certainly worth pursuing further. Most of the books cited appeared in the twenty-first century, quite a few even while this book was being written – this reflects the remarkable explosion in maritime history in the last couple of decades.

GLOBAL APPROACHES

A mass assault on maritime history is provided by C. Buchet general ed., *The Sea in History – La Mer dans l'histoire* (4 vols., Woodbridge, 2017), by an army of learned authors, but the end result is a miscellany of studies in French and English with an emphasis on Europe and the Mediterranean. As the saying goes, 'too many cooks spoil the broth', and the books lack a common approach, while coverage of some areas of the world is patchy, despite a claim that the book is 'comprehensive'. D. Armitage, A. Bashford and S. Sivasundaram, eds., *Oceanic Histories* (Cambridge, 2018), contains brief chapters by various hands on most of the world's major seas, including the Red Sea, the South China Sea and the Japan Sea, as well as about the oceans; however, the approach is resolutely historiographical, and occasionally mired in jargon; there are large bibliographies which are marked as much by surprising omissions, such as Beaujard's monumental study of the Indian Ocean, as by helpful inclusions. In most chapters, lack of attention to the ancient and medieval periods is a fault found in much of the existing literature.

L. Paine's readable *The Sea and Civilization: a Maritime History of the World* (New York, 2013; London, 2014) makes a clear and spirited case for the role of maritime connections in the development of human civilization. The book is excellent on nautical technology. A very brief but thoughtful thematic treatment of similar issues is P. de Souza, *Seafaring and Civilization: Maritime Perspectives on World History* (London, 2001). Michael North, an excellent economic historian based in Germany, has written a short but wide-ranging maritime history of the world: *Zwischen Hafen und Horizont: Weltgeschichte der Meere* (Munich, 2016); even briefer is R. Bohn, *Geschichte der Seefahrt* (Munich, 2011).

The archaeologist Brian Fagan has written a number of stimulating books showing how humans have interacted with the sea from the earliest times, including *Beyond the Blue Horizon: How the Earliest Mariners Unlocked the Secrets of the Oceans* (London, 2012), and *Fishing: How the Sea Fed Civilization* (New Haven, 2017), which deals with an aspect of maritime history largely left to one side in this book. J. Gillis, *The Human Shore: Seacoasts in History* (Chicago, 2012) is concise, lively and relevant. Maritime archaeology provides the basis for the enjoyable *A History of the World in Sixteen Shipwrecks* (Lebanon, NH, 2015), by S. Gordon. A fine survey of the oceans in the medieval and early modern period was provided by Geoffrey Scammell, *The World Encompassed: the First European Maritime Empires, c.800–1650* (London, 1981); Scammell also edited a series of four concise but valuable books on the seas and oceans that will be mentioned under the appropriate heading. Three classic accounts of seaborne empires cross the imagined boundaries between oceans: C. Boxer, *The Portuguese Seaborne Empire 1415–1825* (London, 1969); C. Boxer, *The Dutch Seaborne Empire 1600–1800* (London, 1965); J. H. Parry, *The Spanish Seaborne Empire* (London, 1966), all published in J. H. Plumb's pioneering series entitled *The History of Human Society*.

World trade, much of it maritime, and expanding demand for high-quality material goods, is the theme of B. Lemire's valuable *Global Trade and the Transformation of Consumer Cultures: the Material World Remade, c.1500–1820* (Cambridge, 2018). A superb account of the last century of maritime history, going far beyond Europe, is provided by M. Miller, *Europe and the Maritime World: a Twentieth-Century History* (Cambridge, 2012). The study of naval history and the study of the sort of maritime history portrayed in this book, with its emphasis on maritime trade, have diverged somewhat. R. Harding, *Modern Naval History: Debates and Prospects* (London, 2016), addresses problems such as the nature of sea power and the structure of national navies. The classic starting point is A. T. Mahan, *The Influence of Sea Power upon History, 1660–1783* (Boston, 1890), and subsequent works by the same author. Excellent examples of naval history are provided by N. A. M. Rodger in his multi-volume *A Naval History of Britain*: *The Safeguard of the Sea 660–1649* and *The Command of the Ocean 1649–1815* (London, 1997 and 2004).

Environmental histories of the oceans often look back to times before the coming of humans: D. Stow, *Vanished Ocean: How Tethys Reshaped the World* (Oxford, 2010); J. Zalasiewicz and M. Williams, *Ocean Worlds: the Story of Seas on Earth and Other Planets* (Oxford, 2014). But Callum Roberts has issued timely warnings about the way humans, and the climate changes they are generating, affect the seas, along with overfishing and other short-sighted policies: *Ocean of Life: How Our Seas are Changing* (London, 2012), and his earlier *The Unnatural History of the Sea: the Past and Future of Humanity and Fishing* (London, 2007). To these should be added a study of declining and extinct island populations (non-human): D. Quammen, *The Song of the Dodo: Island Biogeography in an Age of Extinction* (London, 1996).

In this book the Mediterranean, with less than 1 per cent of the earth's waters, is largely left offstage. The literature is vast but a few titles might help fill this gap. For the long view, see David Abulafia, *The Great Sea: a Human History of the Mediterranean* (London and New York, 2011), to which this book is a sister; also David Abulafia, ed., *The Mediterranean in History* (London and New York, 2003); for the earliest human presence, C. Broodbank, *The Making of the Middle Sea* (London, 2013); on ancient and early medieval 'connectivities', with relevance to other periods too, Peregrine Horden and Nicholas Purcell, *The Corrupting Sea* (Oxford, 2000) and more recently J. G. Manning, *The Open Sea* (Princeton, 2018), dealing with the economy of the ancient Mediterranean; on the sixteenth century but with much wider significance for the writing of all maritime history, Fernand Braudel's *The Mediterranean and the Mediterranean World in the Age of Philip II*, translated by Siân Reynolds (2 vols., London, 1972–3).

THE PACIFIC

This is the least studied of the three large oceans, though the literature is well aware of the need to look closely at the native population; for the long view, see M. Matsuda, *Pacific Worlds: a History of Seas, Peoples and Cultures* (Cambridge, 2012); D. Armitage and A. Bashford, eds., *Pacific Histories: Ocean, Land, People* (Basingstoke, 2014); and D. Freeman, *The Pacific* (Abingdon and New York, 2010), in the Scammell series. Narrower timescales are represented by A. Couper, *Sailors and Traders:*

a Maritime History of the Pacific Peoples (Honolulu, 2009), and D. Igler, *The Great Ocean: Pacific Worlds from Captain Cook to the Gold Rush* (Oxford and New York, 2013).

THE INDIAN OCEAN

Philippe Beaujard has been attempting to portray the Indian Ocean in its wider setting in his literally heavyweight *Les Mondes de l'Océan Indien* (2 vols., Paris, 2012). Inspired by Braudel, he sometimes wanders as deep into Asia as the Gobi Desert, so that it becomes less a maritime history than a rich and varied history of the continents touching the Indian Ocean. A readable survey is offered by R. Hall, *Empires of the Monsoon: a History of the Indian Ocean and Its Invaders* (London, 1996). Focusing on trade through the South China Sea and Indian Ocean, R. Ptak has written *Die maritime Seidenstrasse: Küstenräume, Seefahrt und Handel in vorkolonialer Zeit* (Munich, 2007). K. N. Chaudhuri's lively *Trade and Civilisation in the Indian Ocean: an Economic History from the Rise of Islam to 1750* (Cambridge, 1985) also lays an emphasis on trade, and like Beaujard he is heavily influenced by Braudel. M. Pearson, *The Indian Ocean* (Abingdon and New York, 2003), in Scammell's series, is by a master of Indian Ocean history.

THE ATLANTIC

The literature on the Atlantic is even more extensive than that on the Mediterranean. There are several handbooks that manage, more or less successfully, to draw together a great variety of topics, from life in the early colonies in North America to the slave trade. Where they generally collapse is their lack of attention to the Atlantic before 1492, apart from passing references to Norsemen in Vínland and the Portuguese in the Atlantic islands. They include: N. Canny and P. Morgan, eds., *The Oxford Handbook of the Atlantic World c.1450–c.1850* (Oxford, 2011); J. Greene and P. Morgan, eds., *Atlantic History: a Critical Appraisal* (New York, 2009); D. Coffman, A. Leonard and W. O'Reilly, eds., *The Atlantic World* (Abingdon and New York, 2015). The same reservation applies to single- or double-author books about the Atlantic: B. Bailyn, *Atlantic History: Concept and Contours* (Cambridge, Mass., 2005); C. Armstrong and L. Chmielewski, *The Atlantic Experience: Peoples, Places, Ideas* (Basingstoke and New York, 2013); F. Morelli, *Il mondo atlantico: una storia senza confini (secoli XV–XIX)* (Rome, 2013); but less so with C. Strobel, *The Global Atlantic 1400–1900* (Abingdon and New York, 2015), and with P. Butel, *The Atlantic* (London and New York, 1999), in the Scammell series. Bailyn's book has been particularly influential, but the Atlantic there conceived has a northern focus and comes into being with Columbus and Cabot.

The best route into the pre-Columbus eastern Atlantic is provided by Barry Cunliffe in *On the Ocean: the Mediterranean and the Atlantic from Prehistory to AD 1500* (Oxford, 2017), and his earlier *Facing the Ocean: the Atlantic and Its Peoples, 8000 BC to AD 1500* (Oxford, 2001). On the pre-Columbian Caribbean, the latest account, though rather densely written, is by W. Keegan and C. Hofman, *The Caribbean before Columbus* (Oxford and New York, 2017), and then for later centuries a book by the leading historian in the Dominican Republic, Frank Moya Pons, *History of the Caribbean: Plantations, Trade, and War in the Atlantic World* (Princeton, 2007), or another of the Caribbean histories mentioned in my references. For the Gulf of Mexico in modern times, see J. Davis, *The Gulf: the Making of an American Sea* (New York, 2017).

The Atlantic is understood in this book, and in Cunliffe's books, to embrace the North Sea, which itself cannot be understood without the Baltic. The most authoritative general history of the Baltic is that of Michael North, *The Baltic: a History* (Cambridge, Mass., 2015; original edition: *Geschichte der Ostsee*, Munich, 2011). D. Kirby and M.-L. Hinkkanen contributed a volume on *The Baltic and the North Seas* (London and New York, 2000) to the Scammell series, but its thematic organization does not always make it easy to identify long-term changes. M. Pye has written a lively history of the medieval North Sea: *The Edge of the World: How the North Sea Made Us Who We Are* (London, 2014), contentiously insisting that the North Sea was even more important in the development of European civilization than the Mediterranean. A general history of the English Channel is P. Unwin, *The Narrow Sea* (London, 2003). Finally, *The Routledge Handbook of Maritime Trade around Europe 1300–1600* (Abingdon and New York, 2017), edited by W. Blockmans, M. Krom and J. Wubs-Mrozewicz, has the virtue of physical breadth even if its chronological range is shorter than most of the works cited here.

THE ARCTIC OCEAN

Richard Vaughan, best known for his books on the Valois dukes of Burgundy, also wrote *The Arctic: a History* (Stroud, 1994), though he ranges beyond the borders of the Arctic Ocean, as does J. McCannon, *A History of the Arctic: Nature, Exploration and Exploitation* (London, 2012). The Arctic Ocean has a chapter in *Oceanic Histories*, mentioned earlier – as does the Southern or Antarctic Ocean (by S. Sörlin and A. Antonello respectively) on which see now J. McCann, *The Wild Sea: a History of the Southern Ocean* (Chicago, 2019).

References

Preface

1. On winds see F. Fernández-Armesto, 'The Indian Ocean in World History', in A. Disney and E. Booth, eds., *Vasco da Gama and the Linking of Europe and Asia* (New Delhi, 2000), pp. 14–16; A. Dudden, 'The Sea of Japan/Korea's East Sea', in D. Armitage, A. Bashford and S. Sivasundaram, eds., *Oceanic Histories* (Cambridge, 2018), pp. 189–90. 2. D. Armitage, A. Bashford and S. Sivasundaram, 'Writing World Oceanic Histories', in Armitage et al., *Oceanic Histories*, pp. 1, 8, 26. 3. D. Armitage, 'Three Concepts of Atlantic History', in D. Armitage and M. Braddick, eds., *The British Atlantic World* (London and New York, 2002), pp. 11–27; also now D. Armitage, 'Atlantic History', in Armitage et al., *Oceanic Histories*, pp. 85–110; R. Blakemore, 'The Changing Fortunes of Atlantic History', *English Historical Review*, vol. 131 (2016), pp. 851–68. 4. D. Quammen, *The Song of the Dodo: Island Biogeography in an Age of Extinction* (London, 1996). 5. E. Tagliacozzo, 'The South China Sea'; Dudden, 'Sea of Japan/Korea's East Sea'; J. Miran, 'The Red Sea': all in Armitage et al., *Oceanic Histories*, pp. 156–208. 6. S. Sörlin, 'The Arctic Ocean', and A. Antonello, 'The Southern Ocean', in Armitage et al., *Oceanic Histories*, pp. 269–318. 7. C. Roberts, *Ocean of Life: How Our Seas are Changing* (London, 2012), and his earlier *The Unnatural History of the Sea: the Past and Future of Humanity and Fishing* (London, 2007); for the origins of the oceans see D. Stow, *Vanished Ocean: How Tethys Reshaped the World* (Oxford, 2010); J. Zalasiewicz and M. Williams, *Ocean Worlds: the Story of Seas on Earth and Other Planets* (Oxford, 2014); H. Rozwadowski, *Vast Expanses: a History of the Oceans* (London, 2018). 8. A. Crosby, *Ecological Imperialism: the Biological Expansion of Europe, 900–1900* (Cambridge, 1986); A. Watson, *Agricultural Innovation in the Early Islamic World: the Diffusion of Crops and Farming Techniques, 700–1100* (Cambridge, 1983). 9. D. Abulafia, 'Mediterraneans', in W. Harris, *Rethinking the Mediterranean* (Oxford, 2005), pp. 64–93. 10. D. Abulafia, *The Discovery of Mankind: Atlantic Encounters in the Age of Columbus* (New Haven, 2008). 11. D. Abulafia, 'Asia, Africa and the Trade of Medieval Europe', in M. M. Postan, E. Miller and C. Postan, eds., *The Cambridge Economic History of Europe* (2nd edn, Cambridge, 1987), vol. 2, pp. 402–73.

PART ONE

THE OLDEST OCEAN: THE PACIFIC, 176,000 BC–AD 1350

1. The Oldest Ocean

1. Cited from Cook's journals by K. R. Howe, *The Quest for Origins: Who First Discovered and Settled the Pacific Islands?* (Auckland and Honolulu, 2003), p. 33. 2. P. V. Kirch, *On the Road of the Winds: an Archaeological History of the Pacific Islands before European Contact* (Berkeley and Los Angeles, 2000), p. 93; B. Finney, 'Ocean Sailing Canoes', in K. R.

Howe, ed., *Vaka Moana – Voyages of the Ancestors: the Discovery and Settlement of the Pacific* (Auckland, 2006), p. 109. See now C. Thompson, *Sea Peoples: In Search of the Ancient Navigators of the Pacific* (London, 2019) for rich new perspectives. **3.** Kirch, *Road of the Winds*, p. 91, citing the work of P. Bellwood. **4.** Kirch, *Road of the Winds*, pp. 44–50. **5.** G. Irwin, *The Prehistoric Exploration and Colonisation of the Pacific* (Cambridge, 1992), p. 19. **6.** G. Irwin, 'Voyaging and Settlement', in Howe, ed., *Vaka Moana*, p. 59; M. Morwood and P. van Osterzee, *A New Human: the Startling Discovery and Strange Story of the 'Hobbits' of Flores* (Washington DC, 2007). **7.** Howe, *Quest for Origins*, pp. 64–5. **8.** C. Clarkson and twenty-eight other authors, 'Human Occupation of Northern Australia by 65,000 Years Ago', *Nature*, vol. 547 (20 July 2017), pp. 306–26. **9.** S. O'Connor and P. Veth, 'The World's First Mariners: Savannah Dwellers in an Island Continent', in S. O'Connor and P. Veth, eds., *East of Wallace's Line: Studies of Past and Present Maritime Cultures of the Indo-Pacific Region* (Rotterdam, 2000), pp. 99–137; Kirch, *Road of the Winds*, pp. 67–8. **10.** Finney, 'Ocean Sailing Canoes', pp. 106–7. **11.** Irwin, *Prehistoric Exploration and Colonisation*, p. 27; B. Fagan, *Beyond the Blue Horizon: How the Earliest Mariners Unlocked the Secrets of the Oceans* (New York, 2012), pp. 17–30. **12.** O'Connor and Veth, 'World's First Mariners', pp. 100, 114, 130. **13.** N. Sharp, *Saltwater People: the Waves of Memory* (Toronto, 2002), p. 77; A. Barham, 'Late Holocene Maritime Societies in the Torres Strait Islands, Northern Australia – Cultural Arrival or Cultural Emergence?', in O'Connor and Veth, eds., *East of Wallace's Line*, pp. 223–314. **14.** Barham, 'Late Holocene Maritime Societies', pp. 230, 233. **15.** A. Clarke, 'The "Moorman's Trowsers": Macassan and Aboriginal Interactions and the Changing Fabric of Indigenous Social Life', in O'Connor and Veth, eds., *East of Wallace's Line*, pp. 315–35. **16.** Barham, 'Late Holocene Maritime Societies', pp. 228, 234; Sharp, *Saltwater People*, pp. 74–5, 78, 80. **17.** Barham, 'Late Holocene Maritime Societies', p. 248, fig. 5. **18.** Sharp, *Saltwater People*, p. 25. **19.** Fagan, *Beyond the Blue Horizon*, pp. 22–3; Sharp, *Saltwater People*, pp. 71, 78–9. **20.** Sharp, *Saltwater People*, p. 84. **21.** D. Roe, 'Maritime, Coastal and Inland Societies in Island Melanesia: the Bush–Saltwater Divide in Solomon Islands and Vanuatu', in O'Connor and Veth, eds., *East of Wallace's Line*, pp. 197–222. **22.** J. Allen, 'From Beach to Beach: the Development of Maritime Economies in Prehistoric Melanesia', in O'Connor and Veth, eds., *East of Wallace's Line*, pp. 139–76; Irwin, *Prehistoric Exploration and Colonisation*, p. 19. **23.** Irwin, *Prehistoric Exploration and Colonisation*, p. 29. **24.** Ibid., p. 53. **25.** Finney, 'Ocean Sailing Canoes', p. 133; A. A. Perminow et al., *Stjernestier over Stillehavet – Starpaths across the Pacific* (Oslo, 2008), pp. 54–6. **26.** Kirch, *Road of the Winds*, p. 111. **27.** A. Couper, *Sailors and Traders: a Maritime History of the Pacific Peoples* (Honolulu, 2009), p. 24; see also P. Rainbird, *The Archaeology of Micronesia* (Cambridge, 2004). **28.** Irwin, *Prehistoric Exploration and Colonisation*, p. 37. **29.** Howe, *Quest for Origins*, p. 79; Kirch, *Road of the Winds*, pp. 109–10. **30.** D. Lewis, *We, the Navigators: the Ancient Art of Landfinding in the Pacific*, 2nd edn (Honolulu, 1994), pp. 297–303; on whom see Thompson, *Sea Peoples*, pp. 262–73. **31.** Lewis, *We, the Navigators*, pp. 303–4. **32.** Kirch, *Road of the Winds*, p. 98. **33.** Ibid., pp. 97, 106–7, 111; Howe, *Quest for Origins*, p. 75. **34.** Kirch, *Road of the Winds*, pp. 101–6. **35.** B. Malinowski, *Argonauts of the Western Pacific* (London, 1922); M. K. Matsuda, *Pacific Worlds: a History of Seas, Peoples, and Cultures* (Cambridge, 2012), p. 16. **36.** Kirch, *Road of the Winds*, p. 113. **37.** Illustrations from across Oceania in Finney, 'Ocean Sailing Canoes', pp. 110–17, drawing on A. Haddon and J. Hornell, *Canoes of Oceania* (3 vols., Honolulu, 1936–9). **38.** B. Finney and S. Low, 'Navigation', in Howe, ed., *Vaka Moana*, p. 165; also Lewis, *We, the Navigators*, pp. 139–91. **39.** Irwin, 'Voyaging and Settlement', p. 73. **40.** Finney and Low, 'Navigation', pp. 170–71; J. Evans, *Polynesian Navigation and the Discovery of New Zealand* (Auckland, 2011; rev. edn of *The Discovery of Aotearoa*, Auckland, 1998), pp. 55–8. **41.** Lewis, *We, the Navigators*, pp. 102–11. **42.** D. Lewis, *The Voyaging Stars: Secrets of the Pacific Island Navigators* (Sydney, 1978), p. 19. **43.** Cited in Finney and Low, 'Navigation', p. 174. **44.** Finney and Low, 'Navigation', pp. 172, 178–9. **45.** Irwin, *Prehistoric Exploration and Colonisation*, pp. 46–7; Howe, *Quest for Origins*, pp. 104–5. **46.** Lewis, *We, the Navigators*, pp. 173–91; Finney and Low, 'Navigation', pp. 166–8; Howe, *Quest for Origins*, p. 103. **47.** A. Sharp, *Ancient Voyagers in the Pacific*

(Harmondsworth, 1956), on which see Thompson, *Sea Peoples*, pp. 250–61. **48.** Kirch, *Road of the Winds*, p. 96. **49.** Irwin, 'Voyaging and Settlement', p. 76.

2. Songs of the Navigators

1. G. Irwin, *The Prehistoric Exploration and Colonisation of the Pacific* (Cambridge, 1992), pp. 73–4, discussing the view that the interval is an illusion. **2.** P. V. Kirch, *On the Road of the Winds: an Archaeological History of the Pacific Islands before European Contact* (Berkeley and Los Angeles, 2000), p. 232. **3.** Irwin, *Prehistoric Exploration and Colonisation*, pp. 103–4. **4.** Cf. A. Sharp, *Ancient Voyagers in the Pacific* (Harmondsworth, 1956), p. 164. **5.** Kirch, *Road of the Winds*, pp. 283–4; A. A. Perminow, *Stjenestier over Stillehavet – Starpaths across the Pacific* (Oslo, 2008), p. 91. **6.** Perminow, *Stjenestier over Stillehavet*, pp. 83, 88–90; Kirch, *Road of the Winds*, p. 288; D. Lewis, *We, the Navigators: the Ancient Art of Landfinding in the Pacific* (2nd edn, Honolulu, 1994), p. 13. **7.** P. V. Kirch, *A Shark Going Inland is My Chief: the Island Civilization of Ancient Hawai'i* (Berkeley and Los Angeles, 2012), p. 17. **8.** P. V. Kirch, *How Chiefs Became Kings: Divine Kingship and the Rise of Archaic States in Ancient Hawai'i* (Berkeley and Los Angeles, 2010). **9.** Kirch, *Shark Going Inland*, pp. 108–9. **10.** Cited by Kirch, *Shark Going Inland*, p. 122. **11.** Kirch, *How Chiefs Became Kings*, pp. 84–6. **12.** Kirch, *Shark Going Inland*, pp. 126–30. **13.** Kirch, *Road of the Winds*, pp. 290–93. **14.** Ibid., pp. 289–300, drawing on M. Sahlins, *Islands of History* (Chicago, 1985), and P. Kirch and M. Sahlins, *Anabulu: the Anthropology of History in the Kingdom of Hawaii* (2 vols., Chicago, 1992). **15.** J. Flenley and P. Bahn, *The Enigmas of Easter Island* (2nd edn, Oxford, 2003), p. 35; C. Thompson, *Sea Peoples: In Search of the Ancient Navigators of the Pacific* (London, 2019). **16.** G. Irwin, 'Voyaging and Settlement', in K. R. Howe, ed., *Vaka Moana – Voyages of the Ancestors: the Discovery and Settlement of the Pacific* (Auckland, 2006), p. 83. **17.** L. Gamble, *The Chumash World at European Contact: Power, Trade, and Feasting among Complex Hunter-Gatherers* (Berkeley and Los Angeles, 2008); B. Miller, *Chumash: a Picture of Their World* (Los Osos, 1988). **18.** C. Lazcano Sahagún, *Pa-Tai: la Historia olvidada de Ensenada* (Ensenada, 2000), pp. 73–7. **19.** T. Heyerdahl and A. Skjølsvold, *Archeological Evidence of Pre-Spanish Visits to the Galápagos Islands* (Oslo, 1990; originally published in *American Antiquity*, vol. 22 (1956), no. 2, part 3). **20.** Flenley and Bahn, *Enigmas of Easter Island*, p. 34. **21.** Irwin, 'Voyaging and Settlement', p. 85. **22.** Flenley and Bahn, *Enigmas of Easter Island*, p. 40. **23.** Lewis, *We, the Navigators*, p. 353; Sharp, *Ancient Voyagers*, pp. 153–5. **24.** Flenley and Bahn, *Enigmas of Easter Island*, pp. 54–5, 75–7, 184–5. **25.** Ibid., p. 68. **26.** A. Di Piazza and E. Pearthree, 'A New Reading of Tupaia's Chart', *Journal of the Polynesian Society*, vol. 116 (2007), pp. 321–40; Thompson, *Sea Peoples*, pp. 88–98. **27.** Sharp, *Ancient Voyagers*, pp. 149, 156–7. **28.** D. R. Simmons, *The Great New Zealand Myth: a Study of the Discovery and Origin Traditions of the Maori* (Wellington, 1976), p. 57; Te Rangi Hiroa (Sir Peter Buck), *The Coming of the Maori* (Wellington, 1950), p. 5. **29.** J. C. Beaglehole, *The Discovery of New Zealand* (2nd edn, Wellington, 1961), pp. 1–8. **30.** R. Taonui, 'Polynesian Oral Traditions', in Howe, ed., *Vaka Moana*, pp. 35–6. **31.** Simmons, *Great New Zealand Myth*, pp. 7, 22. **32.** P. V. Kirch and R. C. Green, *Hawaiki, Ancestral Polynesia: an Essay in Historical Anthropology* (Cambridge, 2001). **33.** Taonui, 'Polynesian Oral Traditions', pp. 49, 52. **34.** Hiroa, *Coming of the Maori*, pp. 15, 29, 36–7. **35.** Ibid., p. 7. **36.** Simmons, *Great New Zealand Myth*, pp. 341–53; Hiroa, *Coming of the Maori*, pp. 5–6; J. Evans, *Polynesian Navigation and the Discovery of New Zealand* (Auckland, 2011; rev. edn of *The Discovery of Aotearoa*, Auckland, 1998), pp. 33–7. **37.** Hiroa, *Coming of the Maori*, pp. 10–11. **38.** Simmons, *Great New Zealand Myth*, pp. 23, 341–2. **39.** Text ibid., pp. 342–7; also pp. 71–3, 100. **40.** Hiroa, *Coming of the Maori*, p. 23. **41.** Irwin, 'Voyaging and Settlement', p. 91. **42.** Simmons, *Great New Zealand Myth*, pp. 344–5; Hiroa, *Coming of the Maori*, pp. 24–5. **43.** Hiroa, *Coming of the Maori*, pp. 33–4.

44. Simmons, *Great New Zealand Myth*, pp. 345–6; Hiroa, *Coming of the Maori*, pp. 26–7.   45. Hiroa, *Coming of the Maori*, p. 43.   46. Ibid., pp. 51, 64; Irwin, 'Voyaging and Settlement', pp. 89–90.   47. Simmons, *Great New Zealand Myth*, pp. 347–50.   48. Irwin, 'Voyaging and Settlement', p. 90.   49. D. Quammen, *The Song of the Dodo: Island Biogeography in an Age of Extinction* (London, 1996), pp. 193–4; Hiroa, *Coming of the Maori*, pp. 19–21.

PART TWO

THE MIDDLE OCEAN: THE INDIAN OCEAN

AND ITS NEIGHBOURS

3. The Waters of Paradise

1. J. Stanley-Baker, *Japanese Art* (London, 1984), pp. 47–9, and fig. 33.   2. M. Pearson, *The Indian Ocean* (London, 2003), p. 13; H. P. Ray, *The Archaeology of Seafaring in the Indian Ocean* (Cambridge, 2003), and other works by this prolific author.   3. P. Beaujard, *Les Mondes de l'Océan Indien*, vol. 1: *De la formation de l'État au premier système-monde afro-eurasien (4e millénaire av. J.-C.–6e siècle ap. J.-C.)* (Paris, 2012), p. 32; Pearson, *Indian Ocean*, p. 14.   4. Sultan Dr Muhammad bin Muhammad al-Qasimi, *The Gulf in Historic Maps 1478–1861* (Sharjah, UAE, 1999).   5. K. N. Chaudhuri, *Trade and Civilisation in the Indian Ocean: an Economic History from the Rise of Islam to 1750* (Cambridge, 1985), pp. 25, 27.   6. Beaujard, *Mondes*, vol. 1, pp. 32–5; Pearson, *Indian Ocean*, p. 21; Chaudhuri, *Trade and Civilisation*, pp. 22, 24, maps 2 and 3; Ray, *Archaeology of Seafaring*, pp. 20–22, figs. 1.1 and 1.2.   7. H. Crawford, *Dilmun and Its Gulf Neighbours* (Cambridge, 1998), p. 8.   8. D. T. Potts, *The Arabian Gulf in Antiquity*, vol. 1: *From Prehistory to the Fall of the Achaemenid Empire* (Oxford, 1990), p. 41; Crawford, *Dilmun*, p. 14.   9. Potts, *Arabian Gulf in Antiquity*, vol. 1, pp. 56, 59–61.   10. M. Roaf and J. Galbraith, 'Pottery and P-Values: "Seafaring Merchants of Ur" Re-Examined', *Antiquity*, vol. 68 (1994), no. 261, pp. 770–83; Crawford, *Dilmun*, pp. 24, 27.   11. D. K. Chakrabarti, *The External Trade of the Indus Civilization* (New Delhi, 1990), pp. 31–7, 141.   12. J. Connan, R. Carter, H. Crawford, et al., 'A Comparative Geochemical Study of Bituminous Boat Remains from H3, As-Sabiyah (Kuwait), and RJ-2, Ra's al-Jinz (Oman)', *Arabian Archaeology and Epigraphy*, vol. 16 (2005), pp. 21–66.   13. Beaujard, *Mondes*, vol. 1, pp. 67–8, 226.   14. Potts, *Arabian Gulf in Antiquity*, vol. 1, p. 44.   15. Crawford, *Dilmun*, pp. 21, 27, 30.   16. S. Lloyd, *Foundations in the Dust: a Story of Mesopotamian Exploration* (2nd edn, Harmondsworth, 1955), pp. 177–9.   17. A. George, *The Epic of Gilgamesh: the Babylonian Epic Poem and Other Texts in Akkadian and Sumerian* (London, 1999), pp. 198–9; S. N. Kramer, 'Dilmun: Quest for Paradise', *Antiquity*, vol. 37 (1963), no. 146, p. 111.   18. Beaujard, *Mondes*, vol. 1, pp. 127, 132–3.   19. Geoffrey Bibby, *Looking for Dilmun* (London and New York, 1970; new edns 1996, 2012), pp. 79–81.   20. Cf. M. Rice, *The Archaeology of the Arabian Gulf c. 5000–323 BC* (London, 1994), p. 135, understanding 'house of the quay' as a Dilmun temple.   21. Kramer, 'Dilmun', pp. 112–13.   22. W. F. Leemans, *Foreign Trade in the Old Babylonian Period as Revealed by Texts from Southern Mesopotamia* (Leiden, 1960), pp. 9–11; also cited by Rice in his often unreliable *Archaeology of the Arabian Gulf*, p. 108.   23. Slightly amended from the text cited by Potts, *Arabian Gulf in Antiquity*, vol. 1, p. 143.   24. Crawford, *Dilmun*, p. 104; Potts, *Arabian Gulf in Antiquity*, vol. 1, pp. 90, 113–25, especially fig. 15, p. 120.   25. Leemans, *Foreign Trade*, pp. 19–21; cf. Potts, *Arabian Gulf in Antiquity*, vol. 1, p. 183.   26. Crawford, *Dilmun*, pp. 104–24.   27. Leemans, *Foreign Trade*, pp. 26, 29, 31, 33.   28. Leemans, *Foreign Trade*, p. 36, doc. 14, with some alterations.   29. Cf. Bibby, *Looking for Dilmun*, taking the view he was of only moderate wealth.   30. Leemans, *Foreign Trade*, pp. 39–40, doc. 17, slightly amended; also pp. 51–2.   31. Rice,

Archaeology of the Arabian Gulf, pp. 276–80.   **32.** Crawford, *Dilmun*, p. 41.   **33.** My special thanks to the American University of Sharjah for facilitating my visit to this and other sites and museums.   **34.** Crawford, *Dilmun*, pp. 150–51; also Potts, *Arabian Gulf in Antiquity*, vol. 1, pp. 143, 149.   **35.** Chakrabarti, *External Trade*, pp. 145, 149; Potts, *Arabian Gulf in Antiquity*, vol. 1, p. 167.   **36.** Leemans, *Foreign Trade*, pp. 159–66; Chakrabarti, *External Trade*, pp. 145–50, citing at length various views.   **37.** G. Hourani, *Arab Seafaring in the Indian Ocean in Ancient and Early Medieval Times*, revised by J. Carswell (2nd edn, Princeton, 1995), pp. 129–30.   **38.** Rice, *Archaeology of the Arabian Gulf*, p. 271.   **39.** Excellent maps and an up-to-date survey in J. McIntosh, *The Ancient Indus Valley: New Perspectives* (Santa Barbara, 2008); Ray, *Archaeology of Seafaring*, p. 92, fig. 4.3; also S. Piggott, *Prehistoric India to 1000 BC* (2nd edn, Harmondsworth, 1952), p. 137, fig. 17.   **40.** L. N. Swamy, *Maritime Contacts of Ancient India with Special Reference to the West Coast* (New Delhi, 2000), pp. 21, 26; Ray, *Archaeology of Seafaring*, pp. 95–6; Leemans, *Foreign Trade*, p. 162, citing the views of Sir Mortimer Wheeler, excavator of the Indus sites.   **41.** Piggott, *Prehistoric India*, p. 138; also Beaujard, *Mondes*, vol. 1, p. 113.   **42.** Chakrabarti, *External Trade*, pp. 45–7; Piggott, *Prehistoric India*, pp. 208–9.   **43.** Chakrabarti, *External Trade*, pp. 47, 53–61, 139, 143; Swamy, *Maritime Contacts*, pp. 23–5.   **44.** Piggott, *Prehistoric India*, pp. 183–4.   **45.** Chakrabarti, *External Trade*, pp. 22–7, 29–30; Swamy, *Maritime Contacts*, p. 22.   **46.** Crawford, *Dilmun*, p. 150.   **47.** Bibby, *Looking for Dilmun*, p. 18.   **48.** Potts, *Arabian Gulf in Antiquity*, vol. 1, pp. 333–4; Ray, *Archaeology of Seafaring*, p. 105; Bibby, *Looking for Dilmun*, pp. 31, 45.   **49.** Crawford, *Dilmun*, p. 51; Bibby, *Looking for Dilmun*, p. 47; image of inscription: p. 49.   **50.** Potts, *Arabian Gulf in Antiquity*, vol. 1, pp. 88–9; cf. Kramer, 'Dilmun', pp. 111–15, recommending India.   **51.** Crawford, *Dilmun*, pp. 71–9; Potts, *Arabian Gulf in Antiquity*, vol. 1, pp. 168–72.   **52.** Crawford, *Dilmun*, pp. 15, 61; Potts, *Arabian Gulf in Antiquity*, vol. 1, p. 182.   **53.** Bibby, *Looking for Dilmun*, pp. 171–80.   **54.** Crawford, *Dilmun*, pp. 61–2, 87–94; Bibby, *Looking for Dilmun*, p. 253.   **55.** Potts, *Arabian Gulf in Antiquity*, vol. 1, pp. 186–8.   **56.** Crawford, *Dilmun*, pp. 95–6; Bibby, *Looking for Dilmun*, pp. 192–3, 354–5, 358–9.   **57.** Crawford, *Dilmun*, pp. 38, 41.   **58.** I. Finkel, *The Ark before Noah* (London, 2014).   **59.** Connan, Carter, Crawford et al., 'Comparative Geochemical Study', pp. 22–34.   **60.** Bibby, *Looking for Dilmun*, p. 193; Rice, *Archaeology of the Arabian Gulf*, pp. 148–9.   **61.** Connan, Carter, Crawford et al., 'Comparative Geochemical Study', pp. 34–54; Ray, *Archaeology of Seafaring*, pp. 57, 88–9.   **62.** J. Connan and T. Van de Velde, 'An Overview of the Bitumen Trade in the Near East from the Neolithic (c.8000 BC) to the Early Islamic Period', *Arabian Archaeology and Epigraphy*, vol. 21 (2010), pp. 1–19.   **63.** Crawford, *Dilmun*, pp. 38, 63.   **64.** Ray, *Archaeology of Seafaring*, pp. 59–61, 66–9; Beaujard, *Mondes*, vol. 1, p. 125.   **65.** Ray, *Archaeology of Seafaring*, p. 98; Beaujard, *Mondes*, vol. 1, p. 156.

4. The Journey to the Land of the God

1. David Abulafia, *The Great Sea: a Human History of the Mediterranean* (London, 2011), p. 38.   **2.** A. Gardiner, *The Egyptians: an Introduction* (2nd edn, London, 1999), pp. 387–8.   **3.** N. Groom, *Frankincense and Myrrh: a Study of the Arabian Incense Trade* (London, 1981), pp. 163–4.   **4.** Ibid., pp. 3, 12, 24–5; Herodotos, 2:86.   **5.** Pliny the Elder, *Natural History*, 12:32.58–62 and 65; Groom, *Frankincense and Myrrh*, pp. 136–7.   **6.** Groom, *Frankincense and Myrrh*, pp. 12–15, 17, 25.   **7.** R. J. Leprohon, *Texts from the Pyramid Age* (Leiden, 2005), p. 66; D. Fabre, *Seafaring in Ancient Egypt* (London, 2004), p. 89.   **8.** Illustrated in Fabre, *Seafaring in Ancient Egypt*, p. 90.   **9.** D. Abulafia, *The Discovery of Mankind: Atlantic Encounters in the Age of Columbus* (New Haven, 2008).   **10.** J. Baines, 'Interpreting the Story of the Shipwrecked Sailor', *Journal of Egyptian Archaeology*, vol. 76 (1990), pp. 55–72; Fabre, *Seafaring in Ancient Egypt*, p. 39; M. Cary and E. H. Warmington, *The Ancient Explorers* (2nd edn, Harmondsworth, 1963), pp. 75, 233–4.   **11.** I have used the English translation accompanying the transcription by M.-J. Nederhof, 'Shipwrecked Sailor', http://mjn.host.cs.st-andrews.ac.uk/egyptian/texts/corpus/pdf/Shipwrecked.pdf, as amended on 8 June 2009.   12. See the discussion in a later chapter based on M. D. Bukharin, P. de Geest, H. Dridi et al., *Foreign Sailors on Socotra: the Inscriptions and Drawings from the Cave Hoq* (Bremen, 2012); Z. Biedermann, *Soqotra: Geschichte einer christlichen Insel im Indischen Ozean bis zur frühen Neuzeit* (Wiesbaden, 2006).   13. Gardiner, *Egyptians*, pp. 176, 182.   14. Adapted from Cary and Warmington, *Ancient Explorers*, p. 75; and from Fabre, *Seafaring in Ancient Egypt*, p. 179.   15. Fabre, *Seafaring in Ancient Egypt*, pp. 158–60 for private traders.   16. Illustrated ibid., p. 180; Gardiner, *Egyptians*, p. 180.   17. Fabre, *Seafaring in Ancient Egypt*, p. 179.   18. Illustrated ibid., p. 144; cf. pp. 182–3 for the arrival of goods from Punt.   19. R. Fattovich, 'Egypt's Trade with Punt: New Discoveries on the Red Sea Coast', *British Museum Studies in Ancient Egypt and Sudan*, vol. 18 (2012), p. 4; see also K. Bard and R. Fattovich, eds., *Harbor of the Pharaohs to the Land of Punt: Archaeological Investigations at Marsa/Wadi Gawasis, Egypt, 2001–2005* (Naples, 2007).   20. Fattovich, 'Egypt's Trade with Punt', pp. 5, 9; Fabre, *Seafaring in Ancient Egypt*, pp. 80–83; E. H. Warmington, *The Commerce between the Roman Empire and India* (2nd edn, London, 1974), pp. 7–8.   21. Illustrated in Fattovich, 'Egypt's Trade with Punt', pp. 40, 46–7, 55, figs. 40, 46–8, 63.   22. Ibid., p. 14.   23. Abulafia, *Great Sea*, pp. 48–52.   24. Groom, *Frankincense and Myrrh*, pp. 198–204.   25. Ibid., pp. 32–3.   26. Babylonian Talmud, Treatise Kerithoth; see also Exodus 30:34–6.   27. I Kings 9:26–8; also I Chronicles 29:4; I. Finkelstein and N. A. Silberman, *David and Solomon* (New York, 2006), pp. 153, 170.   28. I Kings 10:11–22; also II Chronicles 8:18; II Chronicles 9.   29. For strong doubts about Phoenician identity see J. Quinn, *In Search of the Phoenicians* (Princeton, 2018); Abulafia, *Great Sea*, pp. 66–7.   30. S. Celestino and C. López-Ruiz, *Tartessos and the Phoenicians in Iberia* (Oxford, 2016), pp. 111–21.   31. Ezekiel 27; see also M. E. Aubet, *The Phoenicians and the West: Politics, Colonies and Trade* (2nd edn, Cambridge, 2001), pp. 364–71.   32. Ibid., p. 115.   33. G. Pratico, 'Nelson Glueck's 1938–1940 Excavations at Tell el-Kheleifeh: a Reappraisal', *Bulletin of the American Schools of Oriental Research*, no. 259 (1985), pp. 1–32.   34. B. Isserlin, *The Israelites* (London, 1998), p. 184.   35. Ibid., pp. 185, 226, also plate 44.   36. Matthew 2:11.   37. Groom, *Frankincense and Myrrh*, pp. 34–7.

5. Cautious Pioneers

1. Herodotos, 4:44; M. Cary and E. H. Warmington, *The Ancient Explorers* (2nd edn, Harmondsworth, 1963), pp. 78–9; D. T. Potts, *The Arabian Gulf in Antiquity*, vol. 2: *From Alexander the Great to the Coming of Islam* (Oxford, 1990), p. 2.   2. D. Fabre, *Seafaring in Ancient Egypt* (London, 2004), p. 78.   3. Cary and Warmington, *Ancient Explorers*, p. 79.   4. Herodotos, 4:42; Fabre, *Seafaring in Ancient Egypt*, p. 77; Cary and Warmington, *Ancient Explorers*, pp. 111–12.   5. Herodotos, 4:43.   6. Cary and Warmington, *Ancient Explorers*, pp. 114–17.   7. Arrian, *Anabasis*, 5:26.1–2.   8. Ibid., 7:20.9–10; Strabo, *Geography*, 16:1.11; Potts, *Arabian Gulf in Antiquity*, vol. 2, pp. 2–4.   9. David Abulafia, *The Great Sea: a Human History of the Mediterranean* (London, 2011), p. 180.   10. Arrian, *Anabasis*, 18:29–30; Cary and Warmington, *Ancient Explorers*, pp. 80–86.   11. Arrian, *Anabasis*, 18:31.   12. Polybios, 13:9; Potts, *Arabian Gulf in Antiquity*, vol. 2, pp. 11–13.   13. H. P. Ray, *The Archaeology of Seafaring in the Indian Ocean* (Cambridge, 2003), p. 173.   14. M. Rostovtzeff, *The Social and Economic History of the Hellenistic World* (3 vols., Oxford, 1940–41), vol. 1, pp. 457–8.   15. Potts, *Arabian Gulf in Antiquity*, vol. 2, pp. 85–97.   16. Polybios, 13:9.4–5.   17. Rostovtzeff, *Social and Economic History*, vol. 1, pp. 458–9; Potts, *Arabian Gulf in Antiquity*, vol. 2, p. 93.   18. Potts, *Arabian Gulf in Antiquity*, vol. 2, p. 34; and for Thaj generally, pp. 23–48.   19. Rostovtzeff, *Social and Economic History*, vol. 1, p. 461.   20. N. Groom, *Frankincense and Myrrh: a Study of the Arabian Incense Trade* (London, 1981), p. 194.   21. Potts, *Arabian Gulf in Antiquity*, vol. 2, p. 31.   22. Strabo, *Geography*, 16:3; Ray, *Archaeology of Seafaring*, p. 176.   23. P. Beaujard, *Les Mondes de l'Océan Indien*, vol. 1: *De la formation de l'État au premier*

système-monde afro-eurasien (4e millénaire av. J.-C.–6e siècle ap. J.-C.) (Paris, 2012), p. 361. **24.** Fabre, *Seafaring in Ancient Egypt*, pp. 78–9. **25.** Rostovtzeff, *Social and Economic History*, vol. 1, p. 384. **26.** Cary and Warmington, *Ancient Explorers*, pp. 87–8. **27.** Strabo, *Geography*, 2:5.12. **28.** Rostovtzeff, *Social and Economic History*, vol. 2, p. 925. **29.** Text copied by Photios, cited *in extenso* in Groom, *Frankincense and Myrrh*, pp. 68–72. **30.** Strabo, *Geography*, 2:98–102; Cary and Warmington, *Ancient Explorers*, pp. 90–91, 124–5. **31.** Rostovtzeff, *Social and Economic History*, vol. 2, p. 927; R. McLaughlin, *Rome and the Distant East: Trade Routes to the Ancient Lands of Arabia, India, and China* (London, 2010), p. 24.

6. Mastering the Monsoon

1. David Abulafia, *The Great Sea: a Human History of the Mediterranean* (London, 2011), pp. 164–5; M. Rostovtzeff, *The Social and Economic History of the Hellenistic World* (3 vols., Oxford, 1940–41), vol. 2, pp. 920–24. **2.** Cited in R. McLaughlin, *Rome and the Distant East: Trade Routes to the Ancient Lands of Arabia, India, and China* (London, 2010), p. 143. **3.** McLaughlin, *Rome and the Distant East*, p. 28. **4.** Lucian of Samosata, *Alexander the False Prophet*, c.44; R. Tomber, *Indo-Roman Trade: From Pots to Pepper* (Bristol and London, 2008), p. 66. **5.** E. H. Warmington, *The Commerce between the Roman Empire and India* (2nd edn, London, 1974), pp. 39–42; Tomber, *Indo-Roman Trade*, pp. 30–37. **6.** G. Hourani, *Arab Seafaring in the Indian Ocean in Ancient and Early Medieval Times*, revised by J. Carswell (2nd edn, Princeton, 1995), pp. 25–6. **7.** L. Casson, ed. and transl., *The Periplus Maris Erythraei* (Princeton, 1989), pp. 86–7; another translation by G. W. B. Huntingford, *The Periplus of the Erythraean Sea* (London, 1980), p. 52; most references are to the former, Casson's edition. I use the form *Periplous* because I cannot see any reason to latinize the title of a work written in Greek. Also, Warmington, *Commerce between the Roman Empire and India*, pp. 43–4. **8.** M. Cary and E. H. Warmington, *The Ancient Explorers* (2nd edn, Harmondsworth, 1963), pp. 95–6, 227. **9.** Casson, ed. and transl., *Periplus Maris Erythraei*, pp. 7–8. **10.** Casson in *Periplus Maris Erythraei*, p. 10; M. Wheeler, *Rome beyond the Imperial Frontiers* (2nd edn, Harmondsworth, 1955), p. 138. **11.** Casson in *Periplus Maris Erythraei*, p. 8; text, pp. 62–3; Wheeler, *Rome beyond the Imperial Frontiers*, p. 141. **12.** Casson in *Periplus Maris Erythraei*, pp. 5–7; cf. Huntingford in *Periplus of the Erythraean Sea*, pp. 8–12, dating it between 95 and 130. **13.** Casson in *Periplus Maris Erythraei*, pp. 50–51; S. Sidebotham, *Berenike and the Ancient Maritime Spice Route* (Berkeley and Los Angeles, 2011), p. 63. **14.** Cited from Huntingford's version in *Periplus of the Erythraean Sea*, p. 21. **15.** Casson, ed. and transl., *Periplus Maris Erythraei*, pp. 52–3, 113. **16.** Ibid., pp. 58–9, 133. **17.** Wheeler, *Rome beyond the Imperial Frontiers*, p. 138. **18.** Cary and Warmington, *Ancient Explorers*, p. 122; R. Darley, *Indo-Byzantine Exchange, 4th to 7th centuries: a Global History* (Birmingham University Ph.D. thesis, 2013). **19.** Tomber, *Indo-Roman Trade*, p. 98. **20.** Casson, ed. and transl., *Periplus Maris Erythraei*, pp. 60–61, 141–2. **21.** Ibid., pp. 62–3. **22.** Hourani, *Arab Seafaring*, pp. 32–3. **23.** L. N. Swamy, *Maritime Contacts of Ancient India with Special Reference to the West Coast* (New Delhi, 2000), p. 61. **24.** Casson, ed. and transl., *Periplus Maris Erythraei*, pp. 64–5, 158–9; also Huntingford in *Periplus of the Erythraean Sea*, pp. 9–10; Warmington, *Commerce between the Roman Empire and India*, p. 11. **25.** McLaughlin, *Rome and the Distant East*, pp. 3, 28. **26.** Casson, ed. and transl., *Periplus Maris Erythraei*, pp. 66–7. **27.** Ibid., pp. 70–71. **28.** P. Beaujard, *Les Mondes de l'Océan Indien*, vol. 1: *De la formation de l'État au premier système-monde afro-eurasien (4e millénaire av. J.-C.–6e siècle ap. J.-C.)* (Paris, 2012), p. 373. **29.** Hourani, *Arab Seafaring*, pp. 16–17. **30.** Casson, ed. and transl., *Periplus Maris Erythraei*, pp. 74–5, 190. **31.** Casson in *Periplus Maris Erythraei*, pp. 22, 26. **32.** Casson, ed. and transl., *Periplus Maris Erythraei*, pp. 74–7. **33.** Tomber, *Indo-Roman Trade*, pp. 125–6. **34.** Casson in *Periplus Maris Erythraei*, p. 210; Tomber, *Indo-Roman Trade*, p. 55. **35.** Pliny the Elder,

Natural History, 12:14; Wheeler, *Rome beyond the Imperial Frontiers*, p. 148.   **36.** Casson, ed. and transl., *Periplus Maris Erythraei*, pp. 80–81, 84–5.   **37.** Ibid., pp. 82–3; K. Hall, *Maritime Trade and State Development in Early Southeast Asia* (Honolulu, 1985), pp. 32–3.   **38.** Casson in *Periplus Maris Erythraei*, pp. 241–2.   **39.** Casson, ed. and transl., *Periplus Maris Erythraei*, pp. 86–7.   **40.** Map 14 ibid., p. 225.   **41.** Beaujard, *Mondes*, vol. 1, p. 379.   **42.** Sidebotham, *Berenike*, pp. 7, 9, 11.   **43.** Ibid., p. 12; also pp. 18–20.   **44.** Diodorus Siculus, 3:40.4–8; Sidebotham, *Berenike*, pp. 51–2, 195.   **45.** Sidebotham, *Berenike*, pp. 50–51.   **46.** Ibid., p. 196.   **47.** Abulafia, *Great Sea*, pp. 155–8.   **48.** Sidebotham, *Berenike*, pp. 68–81.   **49.** Tomber, *Indo-Roman Trade*, p. 62; Sidebotham, *Berenike*, pp. 81–5.   **50.** D. Peacock and L. Blue, eds., *Myos Hormos – Queser al-Qadim: Roman and Islamic Ports on the Red Sea*, vol. 1: *Survey and Excavations 1999–2003* (Oxford, 2006), and vol. 2: *Finds from the Excavations 1999–2003* (Oxford, 2011); L. Guo, *Commerce, Culture and Community in a Red Sea Port in the Thirteenth Century: the Arabic Documents from Queser* (Leiden, 2004); Strabo, *Geography*, 17:1.45; Tomber, *Indo-Roman Trade*, p. 57; McLaughlin, *Rome and the Distant East*, p. 28; Sidebotham, *Berenike*, pp. 184–6.   **51.** McLaughlin, *Rome and the Distant East*, p. 15.   **52.** Tomber, *Indo-Roman Trade*, p. 61.   **53.** McLaughlin, *Rome and the Distant East*, pp. 15–16, 159–60.   **54.** Ibid., p. 193 n. 298; Sidebotham, *Berenike*, pp. 223–4.   **55.** Sidebotham, *Berenike*, p. 225; Tomber, *Indo-Roman Trade*, pp. 26–7, 141; McLaughlin, *Rome and the Distant East*, p. 49; Wheeler, *Rome beyond the Imperial Frontiers*, p. 160.   **56.** Cited in H. P. Ray, *The Archaeology of Seafaring in the Indian Ocean* (Cambridge, 2003), p. 53; see also Beaujard, *Mondes*, vol. 1, p. 375.   **57.** McLaughlin, *Rome and the Distant East*, p. 144; Tomber, *Indo-Roman Trade*, p. 55.   **58.** Sidebotham, *Berenike*, pp. 226–7, and fig. 12.1; Tomber, *Indo-Roman Trade*, p. 76.   **59.** Cf. Sidebotham, *Berenike*, pp. 76, 228–30, 249–51.   **60.** McLaughlin, *Rome and the Distant East*, p. 63; Sidebotham, *Berenike*, pp. 175, 177.   **61.** Sidebotham, *Berenike*, pp. 231–2, 236–7.   **62.** McLaughlin, *Rome and the Distant East*, p. 19; Tomber, *Indo-Roman Trade*, p. 43.   **63.** Sidebotham, *Berenike*, pp. 232–4; Tomber, *Indo-Roman Trade*, pp. 81, 149.   **64.** McLaughlin, *Rome and the Distant East*, p. 159.   **65.** Pliny the Elder, *Natural History*, 12:41.84.   **66.** Tomber, *Indo-Roman Trade*, p. 31.   **67.** Warmington, *Commerce between the Roman Empire and India*, p. 68.   **68.** Cited by Tomber, *Indo-Roman Trade*, p. 67.   **69.** Tomber, *Indo-Roman Trade*, pp. 121–2; Beaujard, *Mondes*, vol. 1, pp. 401–39, on Buddhism and trade; Swamy, *Maritime Contacts*, pp. 58–60.   **70.** Tomber, *Indo-Roman Trade*, p. 145.   **71.** Warmington, *Commerce between the Roman Empire and India*, pp. 116–26.   **72.** Cited from McLaughlin, *Rome and the Distant East*, p. 56; also in Beaujard, *Mondes*, vol. 1, p. 371.   **73.** D. Keys, *Catastrophe: an Investigation into the Origins of the Modern World* (London, 1999).   **74.** Cf. V. Begley, 'Arikamedu Reconsidered', *American Journal of Archaeology*, vol. 87 (1983), pp. 461–81.   **75.** Warmington, *Commerce between the Roman Empire and India*, p. 68.   **76.** Begley, 'Arikamedu Reconsidered', p. 461.   **77.** Tomber, *Indo-Roman Trade*, pp. 133, 137; Begley, 'Arikamedu Reconsidered', p. 470.   **78.** Tomber, *Indo-Roman Trade*, p. 137; cf. the hyper-sceptical Darley, *Indo-Byzantine Exchange*, pp. 315–17.   **79.** Casson, ed. and transl., *Periplus Maris Erythraei*, pp. 88–9, 228–9; Wheeler, *Rome beyond the Imperial Frontiers*, pp. 173–9, and plates 19a and b; J. M. and G. Casal, *Fouilles de Virampatnam-Arikamedu: rapport de l'Inde et de l'Occident aux environs de l'Ère chrétienne* (Paris, 1949).   **80.** Hall, *Maritime Trade and State Development*, p. 35.   **81.** Strabo, *Geography*, 15:1.4; McLaughlin, *Rome and the Distant East*, p. 10.   **82.** McLaughlin, *Rome and the Distant East*, pp. 134–5.   **83.** Ibid., p. 58.   **84.** Sidebotham, *Berenike*, pp. 259–75.   **85.** Ibid., pp. 204–5.   **86.** Ibid., p. 200; McLaughlin, *Rome and the Distant East*, p. 36.   **87.** Sidebotham, *Berenike*, pp. 279–82; Darley, *Indo-Byzantine Exchange*, pp. 318–26.

7. Brahmins, Buddhists and Businessmen

1. P. Beaujard, *Les Mondes de l'Océan Indien*, vol. 1: *De la formation de l'État au premier système-monde afro-eurasien (4e millénaire av. J.-C.–6e siècle ap. J.-C.)* (Paris, 2012),

p. 381.   2. I. Strauch with M. D. Bukharin, P. de Geest, H. Dridi et al., *Foreign Sailors on Socotra: the Inscriptions and Drawings from the Cave Hoq* (Bremen, 2011), p. 13.   3. L. Casson, ed. and transl., *The Periplus Maris Erythraei* (Princeton, 1989), pp. 68–9, with minor alterations.   4. Casson in *Periplus Maris Erythraei*, pp. 167–70.   5. Strauch, *Foreign Sailors on Socotra*, p. 44.   6. K. Hall, *Maritime Trade and State Development in Early Southeast Asia* (Honolulu, 1985), p. 37; Strauch, *Foreign Sailors on Socotra*, p. 374.   7. Strauch, *Foreign Sailors on Socotra*, pp. 52–3, 309, 344–5; Casson, ed. and transl., *Periplus Maris Erythraei*, pp. 76–7.   8. Strauch, *Foreign Sailors on Socotra*, pp. 131–2, 141, 211; also p. 214; p. 181: 'the son of the captain Humiyaka'.   9. Ibid., pp. 227–8, 364–5, 377–9, and fig. 6.13.   10. M. Gorea ibid., pp. 448–83 (*šmmr*: pp. 455–6); also comments by Strauch, pp. 79, 338, 377–9.   11. Ibid., pp. 142, 183, 348, 497.   12. Ibid., pp. 375–6, 542.   13. Cited ibid., pp. 384–5.   14. S. Randrianja and S. Ellis, *Madagascar: a Short History* (London, 2009), pp. 24–6; K. McDonald, *Pirates, Merchants, Settlers, and Slaves: Colonial America and the Indo-Atlantic World* (Oakland, 2015), p. 62; R. Boothby, *A Briefe Discovery or Description of the Most Famous Island of Madagascar or St Laurence in Asia neare unto East-India; with relation of the healthfulnesse, pleasure, fertility and wealth of that country, also the condition of the natives: also the excellent meanes and accommodation to fit the planters there* (London, 1646).   15. Beaujard, *Mondes*, vol. 1, pp. 527–8, 538–43, 549–51, 553–8; Randrianja and Ellis, *Madagascar*, pp. 29, 35.   16. Beaujard, *Mondes*, vol. 1, p. 538; Randrianja and Ellis, *Madagascar*, p. 22.   17. A. Sherriff, *Dhow Cultures of the Indian Ocean: Cosmopolitanism, Commerce and Islam* (London and Zanzibar, 2010), pp. 197–9.   18. Beaujard, *Mondes*, vol. 1, pp. 525, 530.   19. Ibid., p. 553; Randrianja and Ellis, *Madagascar*, p. 20.   20. Sherriff, *Dhow Cultures*, p. 199.   21. Beaujard, *Mondes*, vol. 1, pp. 530–31.   22. Hall, *Maritime Trade and State Development*, p. 28.   23. C. C. Brown, ed., *Sějarah Mělayu, or 'Malay Annals'* (2nd edn, Kuala Lumpur and Singapore, 1970).   24. For example, Dionysios Periegetes, whose map is reconstructed in P. Wheatley, *The Golden Khersonese: Studies in the Historical Geography of the Malay Peninsula before AD 1500* (Kuala Lumpur, 1961), p. 131.   25. T. Suárez, *Early Mapping of Southeast Asia* (Hong Kong and Singapore, 1999), pp. 62–3.   26. For gold of Ophir see also D. C. West and A. Kling, eds., *The Libro de las profecías of Christopher Columbus* (Gainesville, 1991).   27. Wheatley, *Golden Khersonese*, pp. 136, 138–62; cf. O. W. Wolters, *Early Indonesian Commerce: a Study of the Origins of Śrīvijaya* (Ithaca, NY, 1967), p. 57.   28. Wang Gungwu, *The Nanhai Trade: Early Chinese Trade in the South China Sea* (new edn, Singapore, 2003; original edition: *Journal of the Malayan Branch of the Royal Asiatic Society*, vol. 31 (1958), part 2, pp. 1–135), p. 8.   29. Wang, *Nanhai Trade*, pp. xiii–xiv; D. Heng, *Sino-Malay Trade and Diplomacy from the Tenth through the Fourteenth Century* (Athens, Ohio, 2009), pp. 21–2.   30. Wang, *Nanhai Trade*, pp. xvii, 1–2, citing Ssu-Ma Ch'ien (1st c. BC).   31. See e.g. V. Hansen, *The Silk Road: a New History* (London, 2012); J. Millward, *The Silk Road: a Very Short Introduction* (Oxford, 2013); X. Liu, *The Silk Road in World History* (New York and Oxford, 2010); F. Wood, *The Silk Road* (London, 2002).   32. Wang, *Nanhai Trade*, p. xv.   33. Ibid., pp. 9, 15.   34. Ibid., p. 33.   35. K. Hall, *A History of Early Southeast Asia: Maritime Trade and Societal Development, 100–1500* (Lanham, 2011), pp. 41–4; Wheatley, *Golden Khersonese*, p. 14; Wolters, *Early Indonesian Commerce*, pp. 39–41.   36. Wheatley, *Golden Khersonese*, pp. 16–17, 26–30.   37. Ibid., p. 9, fig. 8.   38. Cited in Wolters, *Early Indonesian Commerce*, p. 44.   39. Wang, *Nanhai Trade*, pp. 35, 45, from the *Shih i Chi* cited in the *T'u Shu Chi Ch'eng*.   40. Ibid., pp. 50–51 (place names modified to Pinyin).   41. Ibid., pp. 24–5, 52.   42. Wheatley, *Golden Khersonese*, p. 12.   43. Text ibid., pp. 8–9, removing some square brackets; also in Wang, *Nanhai Trade*, p. 16; cf. Wolters, *Early Indonesian Commerce*, p. 61.   44. Wang, *Nanhai Trade*, p. 19.   45. Ibid., p. 37.   46. Wolters, *Early Indonesian Commerce*, pp. 77–8; Wang, *Nanhai Trade*, pp. 18, 59.   47. Wang, *Nanhai Trade*, p. 39.   48. J. Miksic, 'The Beginning of Trade in Ancient Southeast Asia: the Role of Oc Eo and the Lower Mekong River', in J. Khoo, ed., *Art and Archaeology of Fu Nan: Pre-Khmer Kingdom of the Lower Mekong Valley* (Bangkok, 2003), p. 22; Wang, *Nanhai Trade*, pp. 31–48.   49. K'ang Tai cited in Hall, *Maritime Trade and State Development*, p. 48 – also p. 272; Wheatley, *Golden Khersonese*, pp. 14–15,

285–7.   50. Miksic, 'Beginning of Trade', p. 13; K. Hall, 'Economic History of Early South-east Asia', in N. Tarling, ed., *The Cambridge History of Southeast Asia*, vol. 1: *From Early Times to c.1500* (Cambridge, 1992), p. 193.   51. Hall, *Maritime Trade and State Development*, pp. 49–51; J. C. van Leur, *Indonesian Trade and Society: Essays in Asian Social and Economic History* (The Hague, 1955).   52. Miksic, 'Beginning of Trade', p. 4.   53. Ibid., pp. 2–4, 18.   54. Vo Si Khai, 'The Kingdom of Fu Nan and the culture of Oc Eo', in Khoo, ed., *Art and Archaeology of Fu Nan*, p. 70.   55. Miksic, 'Beginning of Trade', p. 16; also Vo Si Khai, 'Kingdom of Fu Nan', p. 47 and map of waterways, p. 48.   56. K. Taylor, 'The Early Kingdoms', in Tarling, ed., *Cambridge History of Southeast Asia*, vol. 1, pp. 158–9.   57. Miksic, 'Beginning of Trade', pp. 14, 18–19; Vo Si Khai, 'Kingdom of Fu Nan', p. 70.   58. Miksic, 'Beginning of Trade', pp. 8–11; Wang, *Nanhai Trade*, p. 39.   59. Liang Shu in Miksic, 'Beginning of Trade', p. 22; Vo Si Khai, 'Kingdom of Fu Nan', p. 69.   60. E. H. Warmington, *The Commerce between the Roman Empire and India* (2nd edn, London, 1974), pp. 127–9; M. Cary and E. H. Warmington, *The Ancient Explorers* (2nd edn, Harmondsworth, 1963), p. 105; Suárez, *Early Mapping of Southeast Asia*, pp. 90–92.   61. My suggestion, with thanks to Dr Audrey Truschke for disentangling the Sanskrit, though other interpretations such as 'Strong City' exist; see Wheatley, *Golden Khersonese*, p. 205 for *Kathārsaritsāgara*.   62. K'ang Tai cited ibid., p. 16; also in Hall, *Maritime Trade and State Development*, pp. 64–5.   63. Text in Wheatley, *Golden Khersonese*, p. 17.   64. Text Ibid., pp. 37–9; Wolters, *Early Indonesian Commerce*, p. 65.   65. Text in Wheatley, *Golden Khersonese*, p. 38, with names converted to Pinyin spelling.   66. Wang, *Nanhai Trade*, pp. 41–2.   67. Text in Wheatley, *Golden Khersonese*, p. 39.   68. Hall, *Maritime Trade and State Development*, p. 37; also Hall, *History of Early Southeast Asia*, pp. 65–6.   69. Wang, *Nanhai Trade*, p. 56.   70. Miksic, 'Beginning of Trade', pp. 28–30; Vo Si Khai, 'Kingdom of Fu Nan', p. 84.   71. Wolters, *Early Indonesian Commerce*, pp. 81, 83–5, 129–63.

8. A Maritime Empire?

1. C. C. Brown, ed., *Sějarah Mělayu, or 'Malay Annals'* (2nd edn, Kuala Lumpur and Singapore, 1970), p. 15.   2. J. Miksic, *Singapore and the Silk Road of the Sea, 1300–1800* (Singapore, 2013), p. 55.   3. Michel Jacq-Hergoualc'h, transl. Victoria Hobson, *The Malay Peninsula* (Leiden, 2001), p. 233.   4. G. Ferrand, *L'Empire Sumatranais de Çrīvijaya* (Paris, 1922), pp. 5–6, 15–16; F. Hirth and W. W. Rockhill, eds., *Chau Ju-kua: His Work on the Chinese and Arab Trade in the Twelfth and Thirteenth Centuries, Entitled Chu-fan-chï* (St Petersburg, 1911), p. 114; also Wang Gungwu, *The Nanhai Trade: Early Chinese Trade in the South China Sea* (new edn, Singapore, 2003; original edition: *Journal of the Malayan Branch of the Royal Asiatic Society*, vol. 31 (1958), part 2, pp. 1–135), p. 96, for *Fo-chi*; D. Heng, *Sino-Malay Trade and Diplomacy from the Tenth through the Fourteenth Century* (Athens, Ohio, 2009), p. 27, for the mission in 683.   5. Hirth and Rockhill, eds., *Chau Ju-kua*, pp. 60, 114; Ferrand, *Empire Sumatranais*, pp. 1, 8; G. Coedès, *The Indianized States of Southeast Asia* (Honolulu, 1968).   6. Wang, *Nanhai Trade*, pp. 87, 91.   7. Cited ibid., p. 113.   8. Ferrand, *Empire Sumatranais*, pp. 7–8.   9. Miksic, *Singapore and the Silk Road*, pp. 37–8.   10. P. Wheatley, *The Golden Khersonese: Studies in the Historical Geography of the Malay Peninsula before AD 1500* (Kuala Lumpur, 1961), p. 45; Miksic, *Singapore and the Silk Road*, p. 67.   11. Hirth and Rockhill, eds., *Chau Ju-kua*, p. 61.   12. Ibid., p. 60.   13. Ibid., p. 61; Ferrand, *Empire Sumatranais*, pp. 8–13; slaves: Song historian, ibid., p. 16.   14. Ch'ên Ching, *Hsin tsuan hsiang p'u*, quoting the lost *Hsiang lu* of Yeh The'ing-kuei, cited in D. Abulafia, 'Asia, Africa and the Trade of Medieval Europe', in M. M. Postan, E. Miller and C. Postan, eds., *The Cambridge Economic History of Europe* (2nd edn, Cambridge, 1987), vol. 2, p. 445.   15. Ferrand, *Empire Sumatranais*, p. 18; Wang, *Nanhai Trade*, p. 117.   16. Heng, *Sino-Malay Trade*, p. 82.   17. Hirth and Rockhill, eds., *Chau Ju-kua*, p. 62; Ferrand, *Empire Sumatranais*, p. 2; Heng, *Sino-Malay Trade*, pp. 83–4.   18. Wang, *Nanhai Trade*, pp. 114–16; D. Twitchett, *Financial Administration under the Tang*

Dynasty (2nd edn, Cambridge, 1970). **19.** Hirth and Rockhill, eds., *Chau Ju-kua*, p. 62; Wheatley, *Golden Khersonese*, p. 63. **20.** Hirth and Rockhill, eds., *Chau Ju-kua*, p. 62; Ferrand, *Empire Sumatranais*, p. 13. **21.** Miksic, *Singapore and the Silk Road*. **22.** Abū Zayd al-Sīrāfi, 'Accounts of China and India', in T. Mackintosh-Smith and J. Montgomery, eds., *Two Arabic Travel Books* (New York, 2014), pp. 88–9; R. Hodges and D. Whitehouse, *Mohammed, Charlemagne and the Origins of Europe* (London, 1983), pp. 134–5. **23.** G. Ferrand, ed., *Voyage du Marchand Arabe Sulaymân en Inde et en Chine rédigé en 851 suivi de Remarques par Abû Zayd Ḥasan (vers 916)* (Paris, 1922), p. 95, also pp. 96–102, 142; Abū Zayd al-Sīrāfi, 'Accounts of China and India', pp. 32–3, 36–7, 88–91; Ferrand, *Empire Sumatranais*, pp. 53–4; Miksic, *Singapore and the Silk Road*, p. 80. **24.** Ibn al-Fakih al-Hamadhani (902), in Ferrand, *Empire Sumatranais*, pp. 54, 67. **25.** Abu Zayd Hasan in Ferrand, ed., *Voyage du Marchand Arabe*, pp. 96–7, 101; ibn Rosteh (c.903), in Ferrand, *Empire Sumatranais*, p. 55. **26.** Second Voyage of Sindbad, in *A Plain and Literal Translation of the Arabian Nights Entertainment now intituled The Book of the Thousand and One Nights*, transl. R. Burton, ed. P. H. Newby (London, 1950), p. 179. **27.** Abu Zayd Hasan (c.916) and al-Mas'udi (943), in Ferrand, *Empire Sumatranais*, pp. 56–9, 62–3; also Bakuwi (15th c.), ibid., p. 78. **28.** Al-Idrisi (1154), ibid., pp. 65–6. **29.** Ibid., p. 66. **30.** Ferrand, *Empire Sumatranais*, pp. 36, 38–41, 214, 218, 220–21; Jacq-Hergoualc'h, *Malay Peninsula*, pp. 239–48; Miksic, *Singapore and the Silk Road*, p. 77. **31.** Hirth and Rockhill, eds., *Chau Ju-kua*, p. 60; Ferrand, *Empire Sumatranais*, p. 9. **32.** Brown, ed., *Sějarah Mělayu*, pp. 77–8. **33.** Miksic, *Singapore and the Silk Road*, pp. 74–5, 77, 79; also fig. 2.09, p. 76. **34.** Jacq-Hergoualc'h, *Malay Peninsula*, pp. 234–7. **35.** Abulafia, 'Asia, Africa and the Trade of Medieval Europe', p. 447. **36.** Wang, *Nanhai Trade*, p. 95: embassies from Jambi (*Chan-pei*); Miksic, *Singapore and the Silk Road*, p. 72, for Jambi. **37.** Miksic, *Singapore and the Silk Road*, pp. 80–83. **38.** H. Kulke, 'Kadātuan–Śrivijaya: Empire or *Kraton* of Śrivijaya? A Reassessment of the Epigraphical Evidence', *Bulletin de l'École française d'Extrême Orient*, vol. 80 (1993), pp. 159–80; Jacq-Hergoualc'h, *Malay Peninsula*, pp. 248–55. **39.** J. Chaffee, *The Muslim Merchants of Pre-Modern China: the History of a Maritime Asian Trade Diaspora, 750–1400* (Cambridge, 2018), p. 24; O. W. Wolters, *Early Indonesian Commerce: a Study of the Origins of Śrivijaya* (Ithaca, NY, 1967), pp. 129–38. **40.** Wolters, *Early Indonesian Commerce*, p. 151. **41.** Jacq-Hergoualc'h, *Malay Peninsula*, p. 241. **42.** Wolters, *Early Indonesian Commerce*, pp. 154–8; Heng, *Sino-Malay Trade*, p. 28; Chaffee, *Muslim Merchants*, p. 29. **43.** Miksic, *Singapore and the Silk Road*, p. 91; Heng, *Sino-Malay Trade*, pp. 14–15. **44.** R. Krahl, J. Guy, J. K. Wilson and J. Raby, eds., *Shipwrecked: Tang Treasures and Monsoon Winds* (Singapore and Washington DC, 2010). **45.** J. Guy, 'Rare and Strange Goods: International Trade in Ninth-Century Asia', ibid., pp. 19, 30. **46.** J. K. Wilson and M. Flecker, 'Dating the Belitung Shipwreck', in Krahl et al., eds., *Shipwrecked*, p. 40. **47.** R. Krahl, 'Chinese Ceramics in the Late Tang Dynasty', in Krahl et al., eds., *Shipwrecked*, p. 52. **48.** Guy, 'Rare and Strange Goods', pp. 29–30. **49.** Krahl, 'Chinese Ceramics', p. 40. **50.** Guy, 'Rare and Strange Goods', pp. 23, 27. **51.** Liu Yang, 'Tang Dynasty Changsha Ceramics', in Krahl et al., eds., *Shipwrecked*, pp. 145–59; Krahl, 'Chinese Ceramics', p. 46. **52.** R. Krahl, 'Tang Blue-and-White', in Krahl et al., eds., *Shipwrecked*, pp. 209–11; Heng, *Sino-Malay Trade*, p. 33; also A. Kessler, *Song Blue and White Porcelain on the Silk Road* (Leiden, 2012). **53.** Krahl et al., eds., *Shipwrecked*, p. 22, fig. 14. **54.** Qi Dongfang, 'Gold and Silver Wares on the Belitung Shipwreck', ibid., pp. 221–7. **55.** Miksic, *Singapore and the Silk Road*, p. 71. **56.** J. Hallett, 'Pearl Cups like the Moon: the Abbasid Reception of Chinese Ceramics', in Krahl et al., eds., *Shipwrecked*, pp. 75–81. **57.** Krahl, 'Chinese Ceramics', p. 40; Miksic, *Singapore and the Silk Road*, p. 81. **58.** Miksic, *Singapore and the Silk Road*, pp. 86–91; Heng, *Sino-Malay Trade*, p. 29; Chaffee, *Muslim Merchants*, pp. 56–7. **59.** Li Qingxin, *Nanhai I and the Maritime Silk Road* (Beijing, 2009); Chaffee, *Muslim Merchants*, pp. 82–3; *China and the World: Shipwrecks and Export Porcelain on the Maritime Silk Road* (Beijing, 2017; text in Chinese with English and Chinese captions), pp. 190–201. **60.** Wang Gungwu, 'A Two-Ocean Mediterranean', in G. Wade and L. Tana, eds., *Anthony Reid and the Study of the Southeast Asian Past* (Singapore, 2012), pp. 68–84.

9. 'I am about to cross the Great Ocean'

1. T. Power, *The Red Sea from Byzantium to the Caliphate AD 500–1000* (Cairo, 2012); P. Crone, *Meccan Trade and the Rise of Islam* (Oxford, 1987).   2. Power, *Red Sea*, pp. 70–71, with telling criticisms of I. Shahid, 'Byzantium in South Arabia', *Dumbarton Oaks Papers*, vol. 33 (1979), pp. 27–94, especially p. 56; also G. Bowersock, *The Throne of Adulis: Red Sea Wars on the Eve of Islam* (Oxford, 2013), pp. 96–8.   3. Bowersock, *Throne of Adulis*, pp. 106–33.   4. David Abulafia, *The Great Sea: a Human History of the Mediterranean* (London, 2011), p. 221.   5. Power, *Red Sea*, pp. 103–9.   6. R. Hodges and D. Whitehouse, *Mohammed, Charlemagne and the Origins of Europe* (London, 1983), pp. 126–9.   7. Quintus Horatius Flaccus, *Epistles*, 2.1, ll.156–7.   8. Hodges and Whitehouse, *Mohammed, Charlemagne*, pp. 131–2.   9. Xinru Liu, *The Silk Road in World History* (Oxford and New York, 2010), pp. 96–101; F. Wood, *The Silk Road* (London, 2002); P. Frankopan, *The Silk Road: a New History of the World* (London, 2015).   10. Hodges and Whitehouse, *Mohammed, Charlemagne*, pp. 115–18.   11. Slightly modified from the passage cited by S. M. Stern, 'Ramisht of Siraf, a Merchant Millionaire of the Twelfth Century', *Journal of the Royal Asiatic Society*, n.s., vol. 99 (1967), pp. 10–14.   12. D. Abulafia, 'Asia, Africa and the Trade of Medieval Europe', in M. M. Postan, E. Miller and C. Postan, eds., *The Cambridge Economic History of Europe* (2nd edn, Cambridge, 1987), vol. 2, p. 451.   13. G. Ferrand, ed., *Voyage du Marchand Arabe Sulaymân en Inde et en Chine rédigé en 851 suivi de Remarques par Abû Zayd Ḥasan (vers 916)* (Paris, 1922), pp. 35–7; Abū Zayd al-Sīrāfī, 'Accounts of China and India', in T. Mackintosh-Smith and J. Montgomery, eds., *Two Arabic Travel Books* (New York, 2014), pp. 28–31 (pp. 5–6 for the problem of authorship; pp. 84–5, 88–9, 136 n. 28 for the 'China ships').   14. Ferrand, ed., *Voyage du Marchand Arabe*, pp. 75–7; Abū Zayd al-Sīrāfī, 'Accounts of China and India', pp. 66–71; D. Heng, *Sino-Malay Trade and Diplomacy from the Tenth through the Fourteenth Century* (Athens, Oh., 2009), pp. 29, 34–5, giving a date of 873; A. Schottenhammer, 'China's Emergence as a Maritime Power', in *The Cambridge History of China*, vol. 5, part 2: *Sung China 960–1279* (Cambridge, 2015), pp. 437–525.   15. Ferrand, ed., *Voyage du Marchand Arabe*, pp. 81, 84; Abū Zayd al-Sīrāfī, 'Accounts of China and India', pp. 72–9.   16. Hodges and Whitehouse, *Mohammed, Charlemagne*, pp. 133–41; D. Whitehouse, 'Sīrāf: a Medieval Port on the Persian Gulf', *World Archaeology*, vol. 2 (1970), pp. 141–58.   17. Abulafia, *Great Sea*, p. 389.   18. Ibid., pp. 258–67 for the Jewish merchants from Cairo; and, more generally, pp. 268–317.   19. Power, *Red Sea*, pp. 146, 148–9.   20. Ibid., pp. 155–7; G. T. Scanlon, 'Egypt and China: Trade and Imitation', in D. S. Richards, ed., *Islam and the Trade of Asia: a Colloquium* (Oxford, 1970), pp. 81–95.   21. S. D. Goitein and M. Friedman, *India Traders of the Middle Ages: Documents from the Cairo Geniza – 'India Book'* (Leiden, 2008), pp. 387–9; E. Lambourn, *Abraham's Luggage: a Social Life of Things in the Medieval Indian Ocean World* (Cambridge, 2018).   22. S. D. Goitein, *A Mediterranean Society: the Jewish Communities of the Arab World as Portrayed in the Cairo Geniza*, vol. 1: *Economic Foundations* (Berkeley and Los Angeles, 1967).   23. Cited in S. Reif, *A Jewish Archive from Old Cairo: the History of Cambridge University's Genizah Collection* (Richmond, Surrey, 2000), p. 173.   24. See e.g. Goitein and Friedman, *India Traders*, pp. 160–61, 527, 535.   25. Ibid., p. 159.   26. Li Guo, *Commerce, Culture, and Community in a Red Sea Port in the Thirteenth Century: the Arabic Documents from Quseir* (Leiden, 2004); A. Regourd, 'Arabic Language Documents on Paper', in D. Peacock and L. Blue, eds., *Myos Hormos – Quseir al-Qadim: Roman and Islamic Ports on the Red Sea*, vol. 2: *Finds from the Excavations 1999–2003* (Oxford, 2011), pp. 339–44.   27. Guo, *Commerce, Culture, and Community*, pp. 141, 143, 152, 159–60, 162, 235, texts 3, 4, 8, 11, 12, 43.   28. Ibid., p. 37.   29. Ibid., pp. 35–8.   30. Regourd, 'Arabic Language Documents', pp. 339–40.   31. Cited by Guo, *Commerce, Culture, and Community*, p. 29.   32. Goitein and Friedman, *India Traders*, p. 189: 'hiring two camels from Qus to Aydhab'.   33. D. Peacock, 'Regional Survey', in D. Peacock and L. Blue, eds., *Myos Hormos – Quseir al-Qadim: Roman and Islamic Ports on the Red Sea*, vol. 1: *Survey and Excavations 1999–2003* (Oxford, 2006), p. 12.   34. L. Blue, J. Whitewright and R. Thomas, 'Ships and Ships'

Fittings', in Peacock and Blue, eds., *Myos Hormos*, vol. 2, p. 184. **35.** Guo, *Commerce, Culture, and Community*, p. 137, text 1. **36.** M. van der Veen, A. Cox and J. Morales, 'Plant Remains', in Peacock and Blue, eds., *Myos Hormos*, vol. 2, pp. 228–31. **37.** F. Handley, 'Basketry, Matting and Cordage', in Peacock and Blue, eds., *Myos Hormos*, vol. 2, pp. 306–7. **38.** Guo, *Commerce, Culture, and Community*, pp. 38–9, 175, 181–2, 200, 203, 214–15, 219, 239, 257, 261, 280, texts 17, 20, 26, 27, 31, 32, 46, 58, 60, 67; Regourd, 'Arabic Language Documents', pp. 342–3. **39.** Guo, *Commerce, Culture, and Community*, pp. 225–6, text 36. **40.** Ibid., pp. 51–4. **41.** D. Agius, 'The Inscribed Ostrich Egg', in Peacock and Blue, eds., *Myos Hormos*, vol. 1, p. 159 (punctuation modified here). **42.** R. Bridgman, 'Celadon and Qingbai Sherds: Preliminary Thoughts on the Medieval Ceramics', in Peacock and Blue, eds., *Myos Hormos*, vol. 2, pp. 43–6. **43.** Guo, *Commerce, Culture, and Community*, pp. 63, 75–89, and plate 1, p. 79. **44.** R. Margariti, *Aden and the Indian Ocean Trade: 150 Years in the Life of a Medieval Arabian Port* (Chapel Hill, 2007), p. 71; Goitein and Friedman, *India Traders*, p. 295. **45.** Margariti, *Aden and the Indian Ocean Trade*, pp. 47–67. **46.** N. A. al-Shamrookh, *The Commerce and Trade of the Rasulids in the Yemen, 630–858/1231–1454* (Kuwait, 1996), pp. 101–29. **47.** Goitein and Friedman, *India Traders*, pp. 439–47. **48.** Alexandria: Abulafia, *Great Sea*, pp. 296–7, 309. **49.** Margariti, *Aden and the Indian Ocean Trade*, pp. 94–6, 101–2, 113, 115–19; for late medieval Yemen: al-Shamrookh, *Commerce and Trade of the Rasulids*, pp. 259–81, 315–36 (appendix 1). **50.** Goitein and Friedman, *India Traders*, pp. 508–9: 'no foreigner should be molested'; A. Hartman and D. Halkin, *Epistles of Maimonides: Crisis and Leadership* (Philadelphia, 1993). **51.** Margariti, *Aden and the Indian Ocean Trade*, pp. 120–21. **52.** Ibid., pp. 153–4. **53.** Goitein and Friedman, *India Traders*, p. 24. **54.** Ibid., p. 534. **55.** Ibid., pp. 147, 160–61. **56.** E. Lambourn, K. Veluthat and R. Tomber, eds., *The Kollam Plates in the World of the Ninth-Century Indian Ocean* (New Delhi, 2020). **57.** Ferrand, ed., *Voyage du Marchand Arabe*, pp. 18, 19, 40, 42; Abū Zayd al-Sīrāfī, 'Accounts of China and India', pp. 30–33; J. Chaffee, *The Muslim Merchants of Pre-Modern China: the History of a Maritime Asian Trade Diaspora, 750–1400* (Cambridge, 2018), pp. 21–3. **58.** S. Digby, 'The Maritime Trade of India', in T. Raychaudhuri and I. Habib, eds., *The Cambridge Economic History of India*, vol. 1: *c.1200–c.1750* (Cambridge, 1982), pp. 127, 146. **59.** Goitein and Friedman, *India Traders*, pp. 288–93, 373–6. **60.** Lambourn, *Abraham's Luggage.*, pp 00–0. **61.** F. Hirth and W. W. Rockhill, eds., *Chau Ju-kua: His Work on the Chinese and Arab Trade in the Twelfth and Thirteenth Centuries, Entitled Chu-fan-chï* (St Petersburg, 1911), pp. 88–9. **62.** Goitein and Friedman, *India Traders*, pp. 314–17, 332, 555. **63.** Digby, 'Maritime Trade of India', pp. 125–6; Goitein and Friedman, *India Traders*, pp. 346, 576. **64.** Goitein and Friedman, *India Traders*, pp. 54–68; also pp. 473, 476. **65.** Ibid., p. 71; Abulafia, *Great Sea*, pp. 319–20. **66.** Hirth and Rockhill, eds., *Chau Ju-kua*, p. 87. **67.** Goitein and Friedman, *India Traders*, pp. 35 n. 15, 210; Chaffee, *Muslim Merchants*, p. 31. **68.** Goitein and Friedman, *India Traders*, pp. 124–5. **69.** Ibid., pp. 387–9. **70.** Digby, 'Maritime Trade of India', p. 133. **71.** Abulafia, *Great Sea*, p. 296. **72.** Abulafia, 'Asia, Africa and the Trade of Medieval Europe', pp. 437–43; for Islamic maps of the Indian Ocean, Y. Rapoport and E. Savage-Smith, *Lost Maps of the Caliphs* (Oxford, 2018).

10. The Rising and the Setting Sun

1. I. Morris, *The World of the Shining Prince: Court Life in Ancient Japan* (Oxford, 1964), p. 87. **2.** See e.g. W. McCullough, 'The Heian Court, 794–1070', in *The Cambridge History of Japan*, vol. 2: *Heian Japan* (Cambridge, 1999), p. 83. **3.** C. von Verschuer, *Across the Perilous Sea: Japanese Trade with China and Korea from the Seventh to the Sixteenth Centuries* (Ithaca, NY, 2006), p. 3; B. Batten, *Gateway to Japan: Hakata in War and Peace, 500–1300* (Honolulu, 2006), pp. 61–2; also David C. Kang, *East Asia before the West: Five Centuries of Trade and Tribute* (New York, 2010), p. 60. **4.** Five embassies between 664 and 671: Batten, *Gateway to Japan*, p. 25. **5.** G. Sansom, *Japan: a Short Cultural History* (4th edn, Stanford, 1978), p. 35. **6.** Kim Pusik, *The Silla Annals of the Samguk Sagi* ['History of the Three Kingdoms'], ed. and transl. E. Shultz, H. Kang and D. Kane (Seongnam-si,

2012), p. 26.   7. I am very grateful to Professor Hiroshi Takayama of Tokyo University for showing me the Munakata Grand Shrine and its small but spectacular museum in 2000.   8. Von Verschuer, *Across the Perilous Sea*, p. 67; Batten, *Gateway to Japan*, p. 28; in fact Tsushima is a pair of islands very close together.   9. McCullough, 'Heian Court', p. 81.   10. Masao Yaku, *The Kojiki in the Life of Japan* (Tokyo, 1969).   11. Von Verschuer, *Across the Perilous Sea*, p. 2.   12. R. Bowring and P. Kornicki, eds., *Cambridge Encyclopaedia of Japan* (Cambridge, 1993), p. 47.   13. McCullough, 'Heian Court', p. 81; C. Eckert, K. Lee, Y. I. Lew et al., *Korea Old and New: a History* (Seoul and Cambridge, Mass., 1990), p. 42; Jung-Pang Lo, *China as a Sea Power, 1127–1368: a Preliminary Survey of the Maritime Expansion and Naval Exploits of the Chinese People during the Southern Song and Yuan Periods*, ed. B. Elleman (Singapore, 2012), pp. 52–4.   14. Batten, *Gateway to Japan*, pp. 52–3, 55, 57–8.   15. Kim Pusik, *Silla Annals*, p. 308; another T'aeryŏm served as ambassador to Tang China in 828 and brought back the seeds of tea-shrubs: p. 345; also p. 159 n. 42.   16. Ibid., p. 207.   17. Ibid., pp. 264, 267, 297; also p. 294 [742]: 'an envoy from Japan arrived, but he was not received.' Cf. pp. 329, 366, 371, 373.   18. R. Borgen, *Sugawara no Michizane and the Early Heian Court* (Cambridge, Mass., 1986), pp. 228–40.   19. Von Verschuer, *Across the Perilous Sea*, pp. 5–8, 11–13, 15; Batten, *Gateway to Japan*, p. 63, table 2.   20. Batten, *Gateway to Japan*, pp. 51–2; Kang, *East Asia before the West*, pp. 71–2.   21. Batten, *Gateway to Japan*, pp. 41–5; poem: pp. 41–2, cited from P. Doe, *A Warbler's Song in the Dusk: the Life and Work of Ōtomo Yakamochi (718–85)* (Berkeley, 1982), pp. 219–20.   22. Batten, *Gateway to Japan*, pp. 55, 59, 65.   23. Ibid., pp. 69–76, noting p. 72, table 3, and p. 74, fig. 10 (wooden toilet sticks).   24. Ibid., pp. 3–4, 55, 69–70; also p. 2, fig. 1.   25. Ibid., pp. 67–8.   26. Von Verschuer, *Across the Perilous Sea*, pp. 20–21; McCullough, 'Heian Court', p. 91.   27. Murasaki Shikibu, *The Tale of Genji*, transl. E. Siedensticker (London, 1992), p. 18.   28. Sansom, *Japan*, pp. 29–30.   29. C. von Verschuer, *Les Relations officielles du Japon avec la Chine aux VIIIᵉ et IXᵉ siècles* (Geneva, 1985), pp. 3, 55–60; Borgen, *Sugawara no Michizane*, p. 227.   30. J. Stanley-Baker, *Japanese Art* (London, 1984), pp. 100–101, fig. 67.   31. Von Verschuer, *Relations officielles*, p. 42.   32. Sansom, *Japan*, pp. 88–9.   33. Ibid., pp. 60–61.   34. G. Reeves, ed. and transl., *The Lotus Sutra* (Somerville, 2008); G. Tanabe, ed., *The Lotus Sutra in Japanese Culture* (Honolulu, 1989).   35. Von Verschuer, *Across the Perilous Sea*, p. 10.   36. Von Verschuer, *Relations officielles*, pp. 216–20; von Verschuer, *Across the Perilous Sea*, pp. 18–19.   37. Borgen, *Sugawara no Michizane*, pp. 242–3; McCullough, 'Heian Court', p. 85; see von Verschuer, *Relations officielles*, pp. 163–4, and her discussion, pp. 161–80.   38. Borgen, *Sugawara no Michizane*, pp. 227–53.   39. Von Verschuer, *Across the Perilous Sea*, pp. 14–16.   40. Stanley-Baker, *Japanese Art*, pp. 53–7; von Verschuer, *Across the Perilous Sea*, p. 18.   41. E. Reischauer, ed. and transl., *Ennin's Diary: the Record of a Pilgrimage to China* (New York, 1955); E. Reischauer, *Ennin's Travels in Tang China* (New York, 1955); the French edition, *Ennin: Journal d'un voyageur en Chine au IXe siècle* (Paris, 1961) is translated from Reischauer's English but has a useful introduction by R. Lévy. For Ken'in, see Reischauer, *Ennin's Travels*, p. 17, and *Ennin's Diary*, p. 410.   42. Reischauer, ed. and transl., *Ennin's Diary*, p. 5 n. 13.   43. Reischauer, *Ennin's Travels*, pp. 48–51.   44. Ibid., pp. 53–8.   45. Reischauer, ed. and transl., *Ennin's Diary*, pp. 100, 118.   46. Kim Pusik, *Silla Annals*, pp. 346–7.   47. Reischauer, *Ennin's Travels*, pp. 60, 63.   48. Ibid., p. 64.   49. Ibid., pp. 65–7.   50. Reischauer, ed. and transl., *Ennin's Diary*, p. 8.   51. Ibid., pp. 6–21; Reischauer, *Ennin's Travels*, pp. 70–71.   52. Reischauer, ed. and transl., *Ennin's Diary*, p. 34.   53. Ibid., pp. 97, 99–101.   54. Ibid., pp. 114–16.   55. Ibid., p. 98; also Reischauer, *Ennin's Travels*, p. 97.   56. Reischauer, *Ennin's Travels*, p. 83.   57. Ibid., pp. 81–6; Reischauer, ed. and transl., *Ennin's Diary*, pp. 95, 122–4; Lévy, *Ennin*, p. 17.   58. Reischauer, ed. and transl., *Ennin's Diary*, pp. 94–5; Reischauer, *Ennin's Travels*, pp. 84–5.   59. Von Verschuer, *Relations officielles*, p. 205.   60. Reischauer, ed. and transl., *Ennin's Diary*, pp. 102–3, 112.   61. Ibid., pp. 102–5; Lévy, *Ennin*, pp. 13–14.   62. Reischauer, ed. and transl., *Ennin's Diary*, pp. 105–7.   63. Ibid., p. 111.   64. Reischauer, *Ennin's Travels*, pp. 94–6.   65. Reischauer, ed. and transl., *Ennin's Diary*, p. 131; Reischauer, *Ennin's Travels*, pp. 289–90.   66. Reischauer, *Ennin's Travels*, pp. 100–113.   67. Ibid., p. 29; also pp. 217–71; Reischauer, ed. and transl., *Ennin's Diary*, pp. 342–89. **68.** Reischauer, ed. and transl., *Ennin's Diary*, pp. 390, 394. **69.** Ibid., pp. 398–404; Lévy, *Ennin*, pp. 32–3. **70.** Kim Pusik, *Silla Annals*, p. 344; Eckert, Lee, Lew et al., *Korea Old and New*, p. 59; von Verschuer, *Relations officielles*, p. 451 n. 488. **71.** Ilyon, *Samguk Yusa: Legends and History of the Three Kingdoms of Ancient Korea*, ed. and transl. Ha Tae-Hung and G. Mintz (Seoul, 2006), book ii, section 47. **72.** Von Verschuer, *Relations officielles*, p. 139; pp. 358–9, giving the text of a document of 842. **73.** Reischauer, ed. and transl., *Ennin's Diary*, pp. 100, 118; letters: pp. 167–9; Reischauer, *Ennin's Travels*, pp. 289–90. **74.** Kim Pusik, *Silla Annals*, p. 349. **75.** Ilyon, *Samguk Yusa*, book ii, section 47; cf. Reischauer, *Ennin's Travels*, pp. 287–94. **76.** Kim Pusik, *Silla Annals*, p. 356, where Wihūn is yet another name for Yomjang.

11. 'Now the world is the world's world'

1. K. Yamamura, 'The Growth of Commerce in Medieval Japan', in *The Cambridge History of Japan*, vol. 3: *Medieval Japan* (Cambridge, 1990), pp. 357, 364; E. Segal, *Coins, Trade, and the State: Economic Growth in Early Medieval Japan* (Cambridge, Mass., 2011), pp. 50–51. **2.** K. Shōji, 'Japan and East Asia', in *Cambridge History of Japan*, vol. 3, pp. 410–11. **3.** Yamamura, 'Growth of Commerce', pp. 347, 351–6; T. Toyoda, *History of pre-Meiji Commerce in Japan* (Tokyo, 1969), pp. 21–8. **4.** Segal, *Coins, Trade, and the State*, pp. 74–80. **5.** Ibid., p. 77, fig. 4. **6.** Yamamura, 'Growth of Commerce', pp. 359–60; Segal, *Coins, Trade, and the State*, pp. 46–7, 53. **7.** Segal, *Coins, Trade, and the State*, p. 93; S. Gay, *The Moneylenders of Late Medieval Kyoto* (Honolulu, 2001). **8.** P. F. Souyri, *The World Turned Upside Down: Medieval Japanese Society* (London, 2002), pp. 87–8, 92–5, 154–6; cf. David Abulafia, *The Great Sea: a Human History of the Mediterranean* (London, 2011), p. 400 and plate 51; Yamamura, 'Growth of Commerce', pp. 366–8. **9.** Segal, *Coins, Trade, and the State*, pp. 59, 84–5. **10.** C. von Verschuer, *Across the Perilous Sea: Japanese Trade with China and Korea from the Seventh to the Sixteenth Centuries* (Ithaca, NY, 2006), pp. 43, 45. **11.** W. McCullough, 'The Heian Court, 794–1070', in *The Cambridge History of Japan*, vol. 2: *Heian Japan* (Cambridge, 1999), pp. 87–8. **12.** Von Verschuer, *Across the Perilous Sea*, pp. 53–4, 61–2. **13.** Ibid., pp. 101–2. **14.** N. C. Rousmanière, *Vessels of Influence: China and the Birth of Porcelain in Medieval and Early Modern Japan* (London, 2012), pp. 78–82; C. von Verschuer, *Les Relations officielles du Japon avec la Chine aux VIIIe et IXe siècles* (Geneva, 1985), p. 251; von Verschuer, *Across the Perilous Sea*, pp. 63–8. **15.** Chinese thirteenth-century treatise quoted in von Verschuer, *Across the Perilous Sea*, p. 68. **16.** Von Verschuer, *Across the Perilous Sea*, pp. 71–3. **17.** Ibid., pp. 45–6, 60. **18.** Ibid., pp. 58–9. **19.** Ibid., p. 42. **20.** Ibid., p. 47. **21.** Souyri, *World Turned Upside Down*, pp. 1–2; for the Taira and Chinese trade, see Von Verschuer, *Across the Perilous Sea*, p. 46. **22.** Von Verschuer, *Across the Perilous Sea*, p. 79. **23.** Chung Yang Mo, 'The Kinds of Ceramic Articles Discovered in Sinan, and Problems about Them', in Tokyo kokuritsu kakabutsukan, *Shin'an kaitei hikiage bunbutsu: Sunken Treasures off the Sinan Coast* (Tokyo, Nagoya and Fukoaka, 1983), pp. 84–7; see also pp. 58–66 and colour plates 1–39 (celadons), pp. 69–70 and colour plates 53–6 (white porcelain). **24.** Segal, *Coins, Trade, and the State*, p. 53. **25.** Youn Moo-byong, 'Recovery of Seabed Relics at Sinan and Its Results from the Viewpoint of Underwater Archaeology', in *Shin'an kaitei hikiage bunbutsu*, pp. 81–3; von Verschuer, *Across the Perilous Sea*, pp. 95–7. **26.** Chung, 'Kinds of Ceramic Articles', p. 87. **27.** Von Verschuer, *Across the Perilous Sea*, p. 81; Shōji, 'Japan and East Asia', pp. 405–7. **28.** Souyri, *World Turned Upside Down*, pp. 158–60. **29.** Von Verschuer, *Across the Perilous Sea*, pp. 108–10; F. Gipouloux, *The Asian Mediterranean: Port Cities and Trading Networks in China, Japan and Southeast Asia, 13th–21st century* (Cheltenham, 2011), pp. 64–5; Toyoda, *History of pre-Meiji Commerce*, p. 30; Cs. Oláh, *Räuberische Chinesen und tückische Japaner: die diplomatischen Beziehungen zwischen China und Japan im 15. und 16. Jahrhundert* (Wiesbaden, 2009), pp. 141–5. **30.** Letters cited from Wang Yi-T'ung, *Official Relations between China and Japan 1368–1549* (Cambridge, Mass., 1953), pp. 18–19; Kanenaga: Toyoda, *History of pre-Meiji Commerce*,

p. 29.   **31.** Von Verschuer, *Across the Perilous Sea*, pp. 113–17; Gipouloux, *Asian Mediter-ranean*, pp. 65–6; Shōji, 'Japan and East Asia', pp. 428–32.   **32.** Von Verschuer, *Across the Perilous Sea*, p. 121.   **33.** T. Conlan, *In Little Need of Divine Intervention: Takezaki Suena-ga's Scrolls of the Mongol Invasions of Japan* (Ithaca, NY, 2001).   **34.** Shōji, 'Japan and East Asia', pp. 414–15; S. Turnbull, *The Mongol Invasions of Japan 1274 and 1281* (Botley, Oxford, 2010), pp. 8–10; J. Clements, *A Brief History of Khubilai Khan* (London, 2010); M. Rossabi, *Khubilai Khan: His Life and Times* (Berkeley and Los Angeles, 1988).   **35.** Slightly modernized from Henry Yule and Henri Cordier, transl. and eds., *The Travels of Marco Polo: the Complete Yule–Cordier Edition* (3 vols. bound as 2, New York, 1993), vol. 2, pp. 253–5; Shōji, 'Japan and East Asia', p. 419; cf. F. Wood, *Did Marco Polo Go to China?* (London, 1995).   **36.** Conlan, *In Little Need of Divine Intervention*, p. 201, doc. 1.   **37.** Turnbull, *Mongol Invasions*, p. 11.   **38.** J. Delgado, *Khubilai Khan's Lost Fleet: History's Greatest Naval Disaster* (London, 2009), pp. 89–90; Conlan, *In Little Need of Divine Inter-vention*, p. 256.   **39.** Shōji, 'Japan and East Asia', pp. 411–15; T. Brook, *The Troubled Empire: China in the Yuan and Ming Dynasties* (Cambridge, Mass., 2010), p. 26; Souyri, *World Turned Upside Down*, p. 79.   **40.** Turnbull, *Mongol Invasions*, p. 13.   **41.** Conlan, *In Little Need of Divine Intervention*, p. 205, doc. 5.   **42.** Brook, *Troubled Empire*, p. 26.   **43.** Conlan, *In Little Need of Divine Intervention*, p. 50.   **44.** Shōji, 'Japan and East Asia', p. 418; Turnbull, *Mongol Invasions*, pp. 32–50, especially pp. 49–50; Delgado, *Khu-bilai Khan's Lost Fleet*, pp. 92, 97.   **45.** Delgado, *Khubilai Khan's Lost Fleet*, pp. 73–4; Brook, *Troubled Empire*, p. 26.   **46.** Delgado, *Khubilai Khan's Lost Fleet*, p. 100.   **47.** B. Batten, *Gateway to Japan: Hakata in War and Peace, 500–1300* (Honolulu, 2006), pp. 48, 132–3, and p. 49, fig. 8; Conlan, *In Little Need of Divine Intervention*, pp. 235–6, doc. 41.   **48.** Turnbull, *Mongol Invasions*, pp. 56, 60–61, for maps.   **49.** For small boats, see illustrations from the war scrolls in Conlan, *In Little Need of Divine Intervention*, pp. 140–46, 151.   **50.** Turnbull, *Mongol Invasions*, pp. 63–4; Clements, *Brief History of Khu-bilai Khan*, p. 161.   **51.** Clements, *Brief History of Khubilai Khan*, p. 159.   **52.** Conlan, *In Little Need of Divine Intervention*, p. 154.   **53.** Kadenokōji Kanenanka (1243–1308), cited in Conlan, *In Little Need of Divine Intervention*, pp. 266–7; ibid., pp. 254, 259.   **54.** Del-gado, *Khubilai Khan's Lost Fleet*, pp. 106–8.   **55.** Yule and Cordier, transl. and eds., *Travels of Marco Polo*, vol. 2, p. 255; Delgado, *Khubilai Khan's Lost Fleet*, p. 111.   **56.** Yule and Cordier, transl. and eds., *Travels of Marco Polo*, pp. 255–60.   **57.** Clements, *Brief History of Khubilai Khan*, p. 163.   **58.** Delgado, *Khubilai Khan's Lost Fleet*, pp. 126–53.   **59.** Ibid., pp. 158–64 (Vietnam); pp. 164–7 (Java); Clements, *Brief History of Khubilai Khan*, pp. 192–206 (Vietnam), pp. 215–18 (Java); Yule and Cordier, transl. and eds., *Travels of Marco Polo*, vol. 2, pp. 272–5 (Java).   **60.** Conlan, *In Little Need of Divine Intervention*, pp. 246–53, docs. 57–65.   **61.** Souyri, *World Turned Upside Down*, p. 62.   **62.** A. Kobata and M. Matsuda, *Ryukyuan Relations with Korea and South Sea Countries: an Annotated Translation of Documents in the Rekidai Hōan* (Tokyo, 1969), p. 69.   **63.** R. Pearson, *Ancient Ryukyu: an Archaeological Study of Island Communities* (Honolulu, 2013), p. 196, and frontispiece.   **64.** Ibid., pp. 273–4, 290–91.   **65.** David C. Kang, *East Asia before the West: Five Centuries of Trade and Tribute* (New York, 2010), p. 72.   **66.** G. Kerr, *Okinawa: the History of an Island People* (2nd edn, Boston and Tokyo, 2000), pp. 22–3, 39–42, 45–50, 52.   **67.** Pearson, *Ancient Ryukyu*, pp. 202–4.   **68.** Kerr, *Okinawa*, pp. 55–6.   **69.** Ibid., pp. 62–71; Kobata and Matsuda, *Ryukyuan Relations*, pp. 1–2; Pearson, *Ancient Ryukyu*, p. 198.   **70.** Kobata and Matsuda, *Ryukyuan Relations*, p. 26.   **71.** Pearson, *Ancient Ryukyu*, pp. 207–11, 214–19.   **72.** Cited by Gipouloux, *Asian Mediterranean*, p. 66, and in part by Souyri, *World Turned Upside Down*, p. 152.   **73.** Cited by Gipouloux, *Asian Mediterranean*, p. 71; sapanwood: Wang, *Official Relations*, p. 97.   **74.** Gipouloux, *Asian Mediterranean*, p. 70; Pearson, *Ancient Ryukyu*, pp. 205–7.   **75.** Pearson, *Ancient Ryukyu*, pp. 224–5, table 8.2; also pp. 300–301, 315–18.   **76.** Gipouloux, *Asian Mediterranean*, p. 68.   **77.** G. Kerr, *Ryukyu Kingdom and Province before 1945* (Pacific Science Board, Wash-ington DC, 1953), p. 41 n. 36; Kobata and Matsuda, *Ryukyuan Relations*, p. 53.   **78.** Kobata and Matsuda, *Ryukyuan Relations*, plate section, p. 2.   **79.** Ibid., p. 19.   **80.** Ibid., pp. 55–6; Kerr, *Ryukyu*, p. 46.   **81.** Kobata and Matsuda, *Ryukyuan Relations*, pp. 86–7.   **82.** Ibid., pp. 93–6. 83. Kerr, *Okinawa*, p. 92. 84. Kobata and Matsuda, *Ryukyuan Relations*, pp. 104–5, 107. 85. Pearson, *Ancient Ryukyu*, pp. 309–14. 86. Kerr, *Okinawa*, pp. 93–5, 120; Kobata and Matsuda, *Ryukyuan Relations*, p. 24. 87. Kerr, *Ryukyu*, pp. 45–7 (and n. 38a); Kobata and Matsuda, *Ryukyuan Relations*, pp. 101–29 (Melaka), pp. 147–63 (Java), pp. 124–5 (licence of 1511); Souyri, *World Turned Upside Down*, p. 152. 88. Armando Cortesão, transl. and ed., *The Suma Oriental of Tomé Pires* (London, 1944), vol. 1, pp. 128–31; cf. Kobata and Matsuda, *Ryukyuan Relations*, pp. 126–9, citing the *Commentaries of the Great Afonso d'Albuquerque*. 89. Souyri, *World Turned Upside Down*, pp. 148–51.

12. The Dragon Goes to Sea

1. A. Schottenhammer, *Das Songzeitliche Quanzhou im Spannungsfeld zwischen Zentral-regierung und maritimem Handel: unerwartete Konsequenzen des Zentralstaatlichen Zug-riffs auf den Reichtum einer Küstenregion* (Stuttgart, 2002), pp. 5, 51, 176–7; Y. Shiba, *Commerce and Society in Sung China* (Ann Arbor, 1970), pp. 90–91. 2. B. Hayton, *The South China Sea: the Struggle for Power in Asia* (New Haven and London, 2014). 3. M. Pollak, *Mandarins, Jews, and Missionaries: the Jewish Experience in the Chinese Empire* (2nd edn, Philadelphia, 1983), pp. 266–7. 4. Jung-Pang Lo, *China as a Sea Power, 1127–1368: a Preliminary Survey of the Maritime Expansion and Naval Exploits of the Chinese People during the Southern Song and Yuan Periods*, ed. B. Elleman (Singapore, 2012), pp. 197–201; A. Schottenhammer, 'China's Emergence as a Maritime Power', in *The Cambridge History of China*, vol. 5, part 2: *Sung China 960–1279* (Cambridge, 2015), p. 492. 5. D. Heng, *Sino-Malay Trade and Diplomacy from the Tenth through the Fourteenth Century* (Athens, Ohio, 2009), pp. 133–4; Lo, *China as a Sea Power*, pp. 201–2. 6. H. Clark, *Community, Trade, and Networks: Southern Fujian Province from the Third to the Thirteenth Century* (Cambridge, 1991); W. Eichhorn, *Chinese Civilization: an Introduction* (London, 1969), pp. 262–7; Heng, *Sino-Malay Trade*, pp. 38–63; Schottenhammer, 'China's Emergence as a Maritime Power', pp. 437–525. 7. Schottenhammer, 'China's Emergence as a Maritime Power', p. 487, table 14. 8. Lo, *China as a Sea Power*, p. 204. 9. Ibid., pp. 56–7. 10. Heng, *Sino-Malay Trade*, pp. 40–44. 11. Ibid., p. 125. 12. Ibid., pp. 44–8, 59, 161–7; also Schottenhammer, 'China's Emergence as a Maritime Power', pp. 485–91. 13. Lo, *China as a Sea Power*, pp. 67–70. 14. Ibid., pp. 61–4. 15. Heng, *Sino-Malay Trade*, pp. 54–6, 59–62; Schottenhammer, 'China's Emergence as a Maritime Power', pp. 509–18. 16. Shiba, *Commerce and Society*, p. 46; Heng, *Sino-Malay Trade*, p. 58. 17. Heng, *Sino-Malay Trade*, pp. 149–90. 18. Lo, *China as a Sea Power*, p. 197. 19. Schottenhammer, 'China's Emergence as a Maritime Power', pp. 493–501. 20. J. Chaffee, 'The Impact of the Song Imperial Clan on the Overseas Trade of Quanzhou', in A. Schottenhammer, ed., *The Emporium of the World: Maritime Quanzhou, 1000–1400* (Leiden, 2001), pp. 34–5; J. Kuwabara, 'On P'u Shou-keng, a Man of the Western Regions, Who was Superintendent of the Trading Ships' Office in Ch'üan-ch'ou towards the End of the Sung Dynasty', *Memoirs of the Research Department of the Toyo Bunko*, vol. 2 (1928), pp. 1–79, and vol. 7 (1935), pp. 1–104. 21. Jung-Pang Lo, 'Maritime Commerce and Its Relation to the Sung Navy', *Journal of the Economic and Social History of the Orient*, vol. 12 (1969), p. 68; Lo, *China as a Sea Power*, pp. 121–85. 22. Zhu Yu (1111–17), cited in J. Needham and C. Ronan, *The Shorter Science and Civilization in China* (Cambridge, 1986), vol. 3 (largely devoted to navigation, and bringing together material from several parts of the complete work), pp. 28–9, and more extensively pp. 1–59; J. Needham, *Clerks and Craftsmen in China and the West* (Cambridge, 1970), pp. 243–4; also cited by A. Aczel, *The Riddle of the Compass: the Invention That Changed the World* (New York, 2001), p. 86; J. Huth, *The Lost Art of Finding Our Way* (Cambridge, Mass., 2013), p. 99. 23. Needham and Ronan, *Shorter Science and Civilization*, vol. 3, pp. 2, 9, 56, 59. 24. Lo, 'Maritime Commerce', p. 69; Schottenhammer, *Songzeitliche Quanzhou*, pp. 295–9; H. Clark, 'Overseas Trade and Social Change in Quanzhou through the Song', in Schottenhammer, ed., *Emporium of the World*, pp.

51–2. **25.** Schottenhammer, *Songzeitliche Quanzhou*, pp. 86–7. **26.** Clark, 'Overseas Trade and Social Change', p. 51; J. Guy, 'Tamil Merchant Guilds and the Quanzhou Trade', in Schottenhammer, ed., *Emporium of the World*, pp. 283–308; Schottenhammer, 'China's Emergence as a Maritime Power', p. 444. **27.** J. Stargardt, 'Behind the Shadows: Archaeological Data on Two-Way Sea-Trade between Quanzhou and Satingpra, South Thailand, 10th–14th century', in Schottenhammer, ed., *Emporium of the World*, pp. 308–93. **28.** K. Hall, *Maritime Trade and State Development in Early Southeast Asia* (Honolulu, 1985), p. 207. **29.** R. Pearson, Li Min and Li Guo, 'Port, City, and Hinterlands: Archaeological Perspectives on Quanzhou and Its Overseas Trade', in Schottenhammer, ed., *Emporium of the World*, pp. 194–201; G. Kerr, *Okinawa: the History of an Island People* (2nd edn, Boston and Tokyo, 2000), pp. 62–71. **30.** Lo, 'Maritime Commerce', pp. 70–77; Shiba, *Commerce and Society*, pp. 187–8. **31.** Hung Mai, cited in Shiba, *Commerce and Society*, pp. 192–3; Clark, 'Overseas Trade and Social Change', pp. 47–8; Champa: Hall, *Maritime Trade and State Development*, pp. 183, 187; J. Chaffee, *The Muslim Merchants of Pre-Modern China: the History of a Maritime Asian Trade Diaspora, 750–1400* (Cambridge, 2018), pp. 59–60. **32.** Yang Fang, cited in Shiba, *Commerce and Society*, p. 203. **33.** Shiba, *Commerce and Society*, pp. 204–6. **34.** Ibid., pp. 182–3; Clark, 'Overseas Trade and Social Change', pp. 53–4. **35.** David Abulafia, *The Great Sea: a Human History of the Mediterranean* (London, 2011), pp. 254–5, 270. **36.** Ho Chuimei, 'The Ceramic Boom in Minnan during Song and Yuan Times', in Schottenhammer, ed., *Emporium of the World*, pp. 237–81. **37.** Schottenhammer, *Songzeitliche Quanzhou*, pp. 197–215, 225–67; Shiba, *Commerce and Society*, pp. 6–10. **38.** Chaffee, 'Impact of the Song Imperial Clan', pp. 33–5. **39.** Schottenhammer, *Songzeitliche Quanzhou*, pp. 279–80 (diagram and photograph), 287–91; Needham and Ronan, *Shorter Science and Civilization*, vol. 3, pp. 87–9. **40.** Needham and Ronan, *Shorter Science and Civilization*, vol. 3, pp. 68–75. **41.** Henry Yule and Henri Cordier, transl. and eds., *The Travels of Marco Polo: the Complete Yule–Cordier Edition* (3 vols. bound as 2, New York, 1993), vol. 2, pp. 249–53; even more fanciful than the hungry whale is D. Selbourne, *The City of Light* (London, 1999), with its nonsensical claims that similarly grand ships owned by Spanish Jews regularly travelled back and forth from the Middle East to China in the thirteenth century; see D. Abulafia, 'Oriente ed Occidente: considerazioni sul commercio di Ancona nel Medioevo – East and West: Observations on the Commerce of Ancona in the Middle Ages', in *Atti e Memorie della Società Dalmata di Storia Patria*, vol. 26, M. P. Ghezzo, ed., *Città e sistema adriatico alla fine del Medioevo. Bilancio degli studi e prospettive di ricerca* (Venice, 1997), pp. 27–66. **42.** Yule and Cordier, transl. and eds., *Travels of Marco Polo*, vol. 2, pp. 234–6. **43.** Heng, *Sino-Malay Trade*, pp. 65–9. **44.** A. Schottenhammer, 'The Role of Metals and the Impact of the Introduction of Huizi Paper Notes in Quanzhou on the Development of Maritime Trade in the Song Period', in Schottenhammer, ed., *Emporium of the World*, pp. 125, 147, 149; Pearson, Min and Guo, 'Port, City, and Hinterlands', pp. 201–3. **45.** Schottenhammer, 'Role of Metals', p. 152.

13. Light over the Western Ocean

1. Wang Yi-T'ung, *Official Relations between China and Japan 1368–1549* (Cambridge, Mass., 1953), pp. 22–4; Shih-Shan Henry Tsai, *Perpetual Happiness: the Ming Emperor Yongle* (Seattle, 2001), pp. 193–6. **2.** E. Dreyer, *Zheng He: China and the Oceans in the Early Ming Dynasty, 1405–1433* (New York, 2007), p. 25. **3.** Ibid., p. 220; cf. L. Levathes, *When China Ruled the Seas: the Treasure Fleet of the Dragon Throne, 1405–33* (New York, 1994), p. 82; original text: Luo Maodeng, *San Bao tai jian xi yang ji* (Beijing, 1995) – I am grateful to Chang Na for supplying these details. **4.** Dreyer, *Zheng He*, p. 126. **5.** Ibid., pp. 99, 181; T. Brook, *The Troubled Empire: China in the Yuan and Ming Dynasties* (Cambridge, Mass., 2010), pp. 93–4; Zheng Kan-zhu, *Zheng He vs. Ge Lun-bu* (Hong Kong, 2005), with thanks again to Chang Na; and J. Needham, *Science and Civilization in China*, vol 1: *Introductory Orientations* (Cambridge, 1954); on Needham, there is an admiring but sensationalist biography by S. Winchester, *Bomb, Book and Compass: Joseph Needham and the Great Secrets of China* (London, 2008; US edition: *The Man Who Loved China*, New York, 2008). **6.** G. Menzies, *1421: the Year China Discovered the World* (London, 2004); G. Menzies, *1434: the Year a Magnificent Chinese Fleet Sailed to Italy and Ignited the Renaissance* (London, 2008); J. Needham and C. Ronan, *The Shorter Science and Civilization in China* (Cambridge, 1986), vol. 3, pp. 152-9. **7.** B. Olshin, *The Mysteries of the Marco Polo Maps* (Chicago, 2014). **8.** Wang Gungwu, 'The Opening of Relations between China and Malacca, 1403-05', in L. Suryadinata, *Admiral Zheng He and Southeast Asia* (Singapore, 2005); Tan Ta Sen, *Cheng Ho and Malacca* (Melaka and Singapore, 2005). **9.** Dreyer, *Zheng He*, p. 16. **10.** Tsai, *Perpetual Happiness*, pp. 178-86. **11.** Ibid., pp. 187-93. **12.** Ibid., p. 80. **13.** C. Clunas and J. Harrison-Hall, eds., *Ming: 50 Years That Changed China* (London, 2014). **14.** Tsai, *Perpetual Happiness*, p. 71; Hong-wu: Dreyer, *Zheng He*, pp. 17-20. **15.** Dreyer, *Zheng He*, p. 182. **16.** Ibid., pp. 147, 157-9, 162-3 (okapi), 182 (giraffe), 192 (giraffe); T. Filesi, *China and Africa in the Middle Ages* (London, 1972), pp. 29-30, 80 n. 99, and plate 6 (giraffe). **17.** Ma Huan, *Ying-Yai Sheng-Lan, 'The Overall Survey of the Ocean's Shores' [1433]*, transl. J. V. G. Mills (Cambridge, 1970); Fei Hsin, *Hsing-Ch'a Sheng-Lan: the Overall Survey of the Star Raft*, transl. J. V. G. Mills and R. Ptak (Wiesbaden, 1996). **18.** Ma Huan, *Ying-Yai Sheng-Lan*, pp. 34, 36; Fei Hsin, *Hsing-Ch'a Sheng-Lan*, pp. 81-97, including Cambodia, Taiwan, Ryukyu, etc. **19.** O. W. Wolters, *The Fall of Śrivijaya in Malay History* (London, 1970), p. 155. **20.** Cited from the Qing dynasty official history of the Ming by Dreyer, *Zheng He*, p. 180. **21.** Wolters, *Fall of Śrivijaya*, p. 156. **22.** Tan Ta Sen, *Cheng Ho and Islam in Southeast Asia* (Singapore, 2009); Dreyer, *Zheng He*, pp. 68-9. **23.** Dreyer, *Zheng He*, pp. 11-12; Levathes, *When China Ruled the Seas*, pp. 61-3. **24.** Dreyer, *Zheng He*, p. 50. **25.** Ibid., pp. 52, 148-9, and p. 191, doc. ii; Levathes, *When China Ruled the Seas*, pp. 89-92. **26.** Dreyer, *Zheng He*, pp. 18-19, 23. **27.** Fei Hsin, *Hsing-Ch'a Sheng-Lan*, p. 33: '27,000 government troops'; see the reconstruction of a ship's hold in the charming Cheng Ho Museum in Melaka; cf. Dreyer, *Zheng He*, p. 105. **28.** Henry Yule and Henri Cordier, transl. and eds., *The Travels of Marco Polo: the Complete Yule-Cordier Edition* (3 vols. bound as 2, New York, 1993), vol. 2, pp. 249-53; Dreyer, *Zheng He*, p. 109. **29.** Dreyer, *Zheng He*, pp. 102-3, 113, 116. **30.** Ibid., pp. 116-21. **31.** David Abulafia, *The Great Sea: a Human History of the Mediterranean* (London, 2011), p. 156; Dreyer, *Zheng He*, p. 112, table of dimensions. **32.** S. Church, 'Zheng He: an Investigation into the Plausibility of 450-ft Treasure Ships', *Monumenta Serica*, vol. 53 (2005), pp. 1-43. **33.** Levathes, *When China Ruled the Seas*, pp. 96-100, with quotation from the *Taizong Shilu* on p. 100. **34.** Ma Huan, *Ying-Yai Sheng-Lan*, pp. 137-40 (see p. 138 n. 9); Fei Hsin, *Hsing-Ch'a Sheng-Lan*, p. 67; Levathes, *When China Ruled the Seas*, pp. 100-101; on Ma Huan: J. L. L. Duyvendak, *Ma Huan Re-Examined* (Verhandelingen der Koninklijke akademie van wetenschappen te Amsterdam. Afdeeling letterkunde. Nieuwe reeks, deel XXXII, no. 2, Amsterdam, 1933); and Mills's introduction to Ma Huan, *Ying-Yai Sheng-Lan*, pp. 34-66. **35.** Wolters, *Fall of Śrivijaya*, p. 74. **36.** Fei Hsin, *Hsing-Ch'a Sheng-Lan*, p. 53; *Taizong Shilu*, cited in Dreyer, *Zheng He*, p. 55; Levathes, *When China Ruled the Seas*, p. 102; also Wolters, *Fall of Śrivijaya*, pp. 73-4. **37.** Liujiagang inscription of 1431, in Dreyer, *Zheng He*, Appendix ii, p. 192; also Changle inscription of 1431, ibid., Appendix iii, pp. 195-6; Levathes, *When China Ruled the Seas*, p. 103. **38.** Yule and Cordier, transl. and eds., *Travels of Marco Polo*, vol. 1, pp. 423-30. **39.** Melaka: Fei Hsin, *Hsing-Ch'a Sheng-Lan*, pp. 55. **40.** Dreyer, *Zheng He*, pp. 62-5. **41.** *Taizong Shilu* ibid., pp. 67-8; Fei Hsin, *Hsing-Ch'a Sheng-Lan*, pp. 64-5. **42.** Levathes, *When China Ruled the Seas*, p. 116. **43.** Ibid., pp. 116-17. **44.** Text in Levathes, *When China Ruled the Seas*, p. 113. **45.** Dreyer, *Zheng He*, pp. 68-9, 71. **46.** Text translated by Chu Hung-lam and J. Geiss in Levathes, *When China Ruled the Seas*, pp. 218-19 n. 108. **47.** Wolters, *Fall of Śrivijaya*, p. 157. **48.** Fei Hsin, *Hsing-Ch'a Sheng-Lan*, pp. 53-5. **49.** Tan, *Cheng Ho and Malacca*; Dreyer, *Zheng He*, pp. 77, 79-81. **50.** Maldives and Laccadives: Ma Huan, *Ying-Yai Sheng-Lan*, pp. 146-51; Hormuz (Hu-lu-mo-ssu): ibid., pp. 165-72. **51.** Dreyer, *Zheng He*, p. 78. **52.** Ma Huan, *Ying-Yai Sheng-Lan*, p. 168; also Fei Hsin, *Hsing-Ch'a Sheng-Lan*, pp. 70-72. **53.** Dreyer, *Zheng He*, pp. 84, 86. **54.** N. A.

al-Shamrookh, *The Commerce and Trade of the Rasulids in the Yemen, 630–858/1231–1454* (Kuwait, 1996); Dreyer, *Zheng He*, p. 87.   **55.** Ma Huan, *Ying-Yai Sheng-Lan*, pp. 154–9; also Fei Hsin, *Hsing-Ch'a Sheng-Lan*, pp. 98–9.   **56.** Dreyer, *Zheng He*, pp. 88–90; text of inscription in Filesi, *China and Africa*, pp. 60–61; Fei Hsin, *Hsing-Ch'a Sheng-Lan*, pp. 101–2.   **57.** Filesi, *China and Africa*, pp. 18–20.   **58.** G. T. Scanlon, 'Egypt and China: Trade and Imitation', in D. S. Richards, ed., *Islam and the Trade of Asia: a Colloquium* (Oxford, 1970), pp. 81–96; also N. Chittick, 'East African Trade with the Orient', ibid., pp. 97–104.   **59.** Filesi, *China and Africa*, p. 21.   **60.** Ibid., pp. 42–5; also plates 8–10 and 14.   **61.** Dreyer, *Zheng He*, pp. 91–7.   **62.** Ibid., p. 137.   **63.** Ibid., p. 144; Levathes, *When China Ruled the Seas*, pp. 162, 169.   **64.** Changle inscription of 1431, in Dreyer, *Zheng He*, Appendix iii, p. 197.   **65.** Liujiagang inscription of 1431, ibid., Appendix ii, p. 192.   **66.** Changle inscription of 1431, ibid., Appendix iii, p. 195; Levathes, *When China Ruled the Seas*, p. 170.   **67.** Ma Huan, *Ying-Yai Sheng-Lan*, pp. 159–65; Fei Hsin, *Hsing-Ch'a Sheng-Lan*, pp. 73–7; Dreyer, *Zheng He*, pp. 152–8; Dreyer implausibly considers that the 1431 description of storms at sea reflects experiences in 1432!   **68.** Ma Huan, *Ying-Yai Sheng-Lan*, pp. 173–8; cf. Fei Hsin, *Hsing-Ch'a Sheng-Lan*, pp. 104–5.   **69.** Cited from *Xuanzong Shilu* by Dreyer, *Zheng He*, pp. 162–3.   **70.** Levathes, *When China Ruled the Seas*, pp. 173–4.   **71.** Dreyer, *Zheng He*, p. 185; also Zheng, *Zheng He vs. Ge Lun-bu*.

14. Lions, Deer and Hunting Dogs

1. Henry Yule and Henri Cordier, transl. and eds., *The Travels of Marco Polo: the Complete Yule–Cordier Edition* (3 vols. bound as 2, New York, 1993), vol. 2, pp. 272–4.   **2.** K. Hall, *Maritime Trade and State Development in Early Southeast Asia* (Honolulu, 1985), pp. 176, 194; G. Spencer, *The Politics of Expansion: the Chola Conquest of Sri Lanka and Sri Vijaya* (Madras, 1983); D. Heng, *Sino-Malay Trade and Diplomacy from the Tenth through the Fourteenth Century* (Athens, Ohio, 2009), pp. 85, 87.   **3.** O. W. Wolters, *The Fall of Śrīvijaya in Malay History* (London, 1970), pp. 42–3, 48; Heng, *Sino-Malay Trade*, pp. 96–100, 117–18.   **4.** C. C. Brown, ed., *Sĕjarah Mĕlayu, or 'Malay Annals'* (2nd edn, Kuala Lumpur and Singapore, 1970), p. 36.   **5.** Hall, *Maritime Trade and State Development*, pp. 219–22.   **6.** D. Garnier, *Ayutthaya: Venice of the East* (Bangkok, 2004), p. 23.   **7.** Ibid., p. 39; C. Baker and P. Phongpaichit, *A History of Ayutthaya: Siam in the Early Modern World* (Cambridge, 2017), pp. 55–7; C. Kasetsiri, *The Rise of Ayudhya: a History of Siam in the Fourteenth and Fifteenth Centuries* (Kuala Lumpur, 1976), pp. 57–64; C. Kasetsiri, 'Origins of a Capital and Seaport: the Early Settlement of Ayutthaya and Its East Asian Trade', in K. Breazeale, ed., *From Japan to Arabia: Ayutthaya's Maritime Relations with Asia* (Bangkok, 1999), pp. 55–79.   **8.** Garnier, *Ayutthaya*, pp. 39, 41, 49.   **9.** Ibid., p. 18; K. Breazeale, 'Thai Maritime Trade and the Ministry Responsible', in Breazeale, ed., *From Japan to Arabia*, pp. 20–21.   **10.** Kasetsiri, 'Origins of a Capital', pp. 65, 68; Baker and Phongpaichit, *History of Ayutthaya*, pp. 51–5.   **11.** Garnier, *Ayutthaya*, pp. 13–18; Kasetsiri, 'Origins of a Capital', pp. 64–71; D. Wyatt, 'Ayutthaya, 1409–24: Internal Politics and International Relations', in Breazeale, ed., *From Japan to Arabia*, pp. 80–88.   **12.** Heng, *Sino-Malay Trade*, p. 106.   **13.** Ibid., pp. 107–9, 122.   **14.** Hall, *Maritime Trade and State Development*, p. 211; Wolters, *Fall of Śrīvijaya*, pp. 44–6.   **15.** Wolters, *Fall of Śrīvijaya*, p. 78; F. Hirth and W. W. Rockhill, eds., *Chau Ju-kua: His Work on the Chinese and Arab Trade in the Twelfth and Thirteenth Centuries, Entitled Chu-fan-chï* (St Petersburg, 1911), pp. 75–8, 82–5.   **16.** P. Rawson, *The Art of Southeast Asia* (London, 1967), pp. 254–72.   **17.** Hall, *Maritime Trade and State Development*, p. 234.   **18.** Ibid., pp. 235–7.   **19.** Ibid., pp. 238–41, 245–7.   **20.** Wolters, *Fall of Śrīvijaya*, p. 66.   **21.** E. Dreyer, *Zheng He: China and the Oceans in the Early Ming Dynasty, 1405–1433* (New York, 2007), p. 63.   **22.** Hall, *Maritime Trade and State Development*, pp. 253, 255.   **23.** V. Glendinning, *Raffles and the Golden Opportunity* (London, 2012), pp. 217–19; M. R. Frost and Yu-Mei Balasingamchow, *Singapore: a Biography* (Singapore and Hong Kong, 2009), pp. 40–45; J. Miksic, *Singapore and the Silk Road of the Sea, 1300–1800* (Singapore, 2013), pp. 154–5.   **24.** Brown, ed., *Sĕjarah Mĕlayu*, pp. x–xi; Miksic,

Singapore and the Silk Road, pp. 146–7; K. C. Guan, D. Heng and T. T. Yong, *Singapore: a 700-Year History* (National Archives, Singapore, 2009), pp. 11–15.   **25.** Brown, ed., *Sějarah Mělayu*, p. 2.   **26.** Ibid., p. 14; Miksic, *Singapore and the Silk Road*, pp. 147–8.   **27.** Wolters, *Fall of Śrīvijaya*, pp. 128–35.   **28.** Brown, ed., *Sějarah Mělayu*, p. 18.   **29.** Miksic, *Singapore and the Silk Road*, p. 150.   **30.** Brown, ed., *Sějarah Mělayu*, pp. 19–20; Miksic, *Singapore and the Silk Road*, pp. 150–51.   **31.** Frost and Balasingamchow, *Singapore*, p. 25; other interpretations of the name include 'stop-over place' and 'gateway'.   **32.** Brown, ed., *Sějarah Mělayu*, p. 21.   **33.** Ibid., pp. 22–3.   **34.** Ibid., p. 40; Frost and Balasingamchow, *Singapore*, p. 26; Miksic, *Singapore and the Silk Road*, pp. 152–3.   **35.** Brown, ed., *Sějarah Mělayu*, p. 41; Frost and Balasingamchow, *Singapore*, pp. 26, 28.   **36.** Wang Du-yuan in Miksic, *Singapore and the Silk Road*, pp. 174–5, 177–8; Guan, Heng and Yong, *Singapore*, pp. 27–8, 47.   **37.** Miksic, *Singapore and the Silk Road*, pp. 181–2, 185.   **38.** Dreyer, *Zheng He*, pp. 40–41.   **39.** Wolters, *Fall of Śrīvijaya*, pp. 113, 120–21; Dreyer, *Zheng He*, pp. 42–3.   **40.** Brown, ed., *Sějarah Mělayu*, pp. 20–21; Guan, Heng and Yong, *Singapore*, p. 10.   **41.** Guan, Heng and Yong, *Singapore*, pp. 28–9.   **42.** Ibid., p. 10, with illustration.   **43.** Brown, ed., *Sějarah Mělayu*, pp. 26–7; Miksic, *Singapore and the Silk Road*, pp. 12–16, fig. 0.17   **44.** Brown, ed., *Sějarah Mělayu*, p. 26.   **45.** Guan, Heng and Yong, *Singapore*, pp. 33–52.   **46.** Miksic, *Singapore and the Silk Road*, pp. 222–40.   **47.** Ibid., pp. 295–310.   **48.** Ibid., pp. 167–8; Wolters, *Fall of Śrīvijaya*, p. 131; Dreyer, *Zheng He*, p. 42.   **49.** Wolters, *Fall of Śrīvijaya*, pp. 77–153.   **50.** Armando Cortesão, transl. and ed., *The Suma Oriental of Tomé Pires* (London, 1944), vol. 2, p. 233; Miksic, *Singapore and the Silk Road*, pp. 156–62.   **51.** Brown, ed., *Sějarah Mělayu*, pp. 241–2; Wolters, *Fall of Śrīvijaya*, p. 108–9.   **52.** Cortesão, transl. and ed., *Suma Oriental of Tomé Pires*, vol. 2, p. 232.   **53.** Brown, ed., *Sějarah Mělayu*, p. 42; cf. Cortesão, transl. and ed., *Suma Oriental of Tomé Pires*, vol. 2, pp. 236–7.   **54.** Miksic, *Singapore and the Silk Road*, p. 400.   **55.** Brown, ed., *Sějarah Mělayu*, p. 127.   **56.** Ibid., pp. 43–4.   **57.** Wolters, *Fall of Śrīvijaya*, p. 240 n. 42; Cortesão, transl. and ed., *Suma Oriental of Tomé Pires*, vol. 2, p. 241.   **58.** Wolters, *Fall of Śrīvijaya*, pp. 160–63.   **59.** D. Freeman, *The Straits of Malacca: Gateway or Gauntlet?* (Montreal, 2003).   **60.** Dreyer, *Zheng He*, p. 42.   **61.** Brown, ed., *Sějarah Mělayu*, p. 80.   **62.** Ibid., p. 81.   **63.** Kamis bin Hj. Abbas, ed., *Melaka Dalam Dunia Maritim – Melaka in the Maritime World* (Melaka, 2004), p. 23; Brown, ed., *Sějarah Mělayu*, pp. 56, 58–9.   **64.** Brown, ed., *Sějarah Mělayu*, pp. 150–51.   **65.** Ibid., pp. 44–9.   **66.** F. Fernández-Armesto, *1492: the Year Our World Began* (London, 2010), pp. 226–7, 266, 268.   **67.** Brown, ed., *Sějarah Mělayu*, p. 151; Camoens, *The Lusiads*, transl. W. Atkinson (Harmondsworth, 1952), p. 242.

PART THREE

THE YOUNG OCEAN: THE ATLANTIC, 22,000 BC–AD 1500

15. Living on the Edge

1. B. Bailyn, *Atlantic History: Concept and Contours* (Cambridge, Mass., 2005).   **2.** B. Cunliffe, *Facing the Ocean: the Atlantic and Its Peoples 8000 BC–AD 1500* (Oxford, 2001); see also his *Europe between the Oceans, Themes and Variations: 9000 BC–AD 1000* (New Haven, 2008), *Britain Begins* (Oxford, 2012) and *On the Ocean: the Mediterranean and the Atlantic from Prehistory to AD 1500* (Oxford, 2017), and 'Atlantic Sea-Ways', *Revista de Guimarães*, special vol. 1 (Guimarães, 1999), pp. 93–105; E. G. Bowen, *Britain and the Western Seaways* (London, 1972).   **3.** J. Henderson, *The Atlantic Iron Age: Settlement and Identity in the First Millennium BC* (London, 2007), pp. 11–22, 27–34.   **4.** Ibid., p. 31, fig. 2.1.   **5.** Ibid., pp. 30–31.   **6.** Ibid., pp. 10–11; B. Quinn, *The Atlantean Irish: Ireland's Oriental and Maritime Heritage* (Dublin, 2005), which overstates its case.   **7.** Henderson, *Atlantic Iron Age*, p. 36.   **8.** V. Gaffney, K. Thomson and S. Fitch, *Mapping Doggerland:*

the Mesolithic Landscapes of the Southern North Sea (Oxford, 2007). **9.** Cunliffe, *Facing the Ocean*, p. 110. **10.** A. Saville, 'Orkney and Scotland before the Neolithic period', in A. Ritchie, ed., *Neolithic Orkney in Its European Context* (McDonald Institute Monographs, Cambridge, 2000), pp. 95–8. **11.** C. Finlayson, *The Humans Who Went Extinct: Why Neanderthals Died Out and We Survived* (Oxford, 2009); D. Papagianni and M. Morse, *The Neanderthals Rediscovered: How Modern Science is Rewriting Their Story* (London, 2013), pp. 174–7. **12.** Cunliffe, *Facing the Ocean*, pp. 109, 115. **13.** Henderson, *Atlantic Iron Age*, p. 52. **14.** P. Mellars et al., *Excavations on Oronsay: Prehistoric Human Ecology on a Small Island* (Edinburgh, 1987); Cunliffe, *Facing the Ocean*, pp. 124–5, and plate 4.11. **15.** G. Marchand, 'Le Mésolithique final en Bretagne: une combinaison des faits archéologiques', in S. J. de Laet, ed., *Acculturation and Continuity in Atlantic Europe Mainly during the Neolithic period and the Bronze Age: Papers Presented at the IV Atlantic Colloquium, Ghent, 1975* (Bruges, 1976), pp. 67–86; C. Dupont and Y. Gruet, 'Malacofaune et crustacés marins des amas coquilliers mésolithiques de Beg-an-Dorchenn (Plomeur, Finistère) et de Beg-er-Vil (Quiberon, Morbihan),' in de Laet, ed., *Acculturation and Continuity*, pp. 139–61; Cunliffe, *Facing the Ocean*, p. 417. **16.** Cunliffe, *Facing the Ocean*, pp. 120–22. **17.** M. Ruiz-Gálvez Priego, *La Europa atlántica en la Edad del Bronce* (Barcelona, 1998), pp. 126–7. **18.** C. Renfrew, 'Megaliths, Territories and Populations', in de Laet, ed., *Acculturation and Continuity*, pp. 200, 218. **19.** L. Laporte, 'Néolithisations de la façade atlantique du Centre-Ouest et de l'Ouest de la France', in de Laet, ed., *Acculturation and Continuity*, pp. 99–125. **20.** R. Schulting, 'Comme la mer qui se retire: les changements dans l'exploitation des ressources marines du Mésolithique au Néolithique en Bretagne', in de Laet, *Acculturation and Continuity*, pp. 163–88; Cunliffe, *Facing the Ocean*, p. 119. **21.** A. Sheridan, 'Les éléments d'origine bretonne autour de 4000 av. J.-C. en Écosse: témoignages d'alliance, d'influence, de déplacement, ou quoi d'autre?', in de Laet, ed., *Acculturation and Continuity*, pp. 25–37; N. Milner and P. Woodman, 'Combler les lacunes . . . L'événement le plus étudié, le mieux daté et le moins compris du Flandrien', in de Laet, ed., *Acculturation and Continuity*, pp. 39–46. **22.** Bowen, *Britain and the Western Seaways*, pp. 19–21. **23.** J. Briard, 'Acculturations néolithiques et campaniformes dans les tumulus armoricains', in de Laet, ed., *Acculturation and Continuity*, pp. 34–44. **24.** H. N. Savory, 'The Role of Iberian Communal Tombs in Mediterranean and Atlantic Prehistory', in V. Markotić, *Ancient Europe and the Mediterranean: Studies Presented in Honour of Hugh Hencken* (Warminster, 1977), pp. 161–80. **25.** A. A. Rodríguez Casal, 'An Introduction to the Atlantic Megalithic Complex', in A. A. Rodríguez Casal, ed., *Le Mégalithisme atlantique – the Atlantic Megaliths: Actes du XIVème Congrès UISPP, Université de Liège, Belgique, 2–8 septembre 2001* (BAR Interenational series, no. 1521, Oxford, 2006), p. 1. **26.** Renfrew, 'Megaliths, Territories and Populations', pp. 198–9; J. L'Helgouac'h, 'Les premiers monuments mégalithiques de l'Ouest de la France', in A. A. Rodríguez Casal, ed., *O Neolítico atlántico e as orixes do Megalitismo: actas do coloquio internacional (Santiago de Compostela, 1–6 de abril de 1996)* (Cursos e congresos da Universidade de Santiago de Compostela, no. 101, Santiago de Compostela, 1996), p. 199. **27.** Map in Bowen, *Britain and the Western Seaways*, p. 33; Rodríguez Casal, 'Introduction', p. 2. **28.** Renfrew, 'Megaliths, Territories and Populations', p. 199. **29.** Renfrew, 'Megaliths, Territories and Populations', p. 204; Rodríguez Casal, 'Introduction', p. 2. **30.** A. Ritchie, 'The First Settlers', in C. Renfrew, ed., *The Prehistory of Orkney BC 4000–1000 AD* (2nd edn, Edinburgh, 1990), pp. 36–9; A. Ritchie, *Prehistoric Orkney* (London, 1995), p. 21. **31.** D. V. Clarke and N. Sharples, 'Settlements and Subsistence in the Third Millennium BC', in Renfrew, ed., *Prehistory of Orkney*, p. 77. **32.** Ibid., pp. 58–68. **33.** Ritchie, 'First Settlers', pp. 41–50; Ritchie, *Prehistoric Orkney*, p. 22. **34.** H. Pálsson and P. Edwards, transl., *Orkneyinga Saga: the History of the Earls of Orkney* (Harmondsworth, 1981), p. 188, cap. 93. **35.** A. Henshall, 'The Chambered Cairns', in Renfrew, ed., *Prehistory of Orkney*, pp. 96–8. **36.** C. Renfrew, 'The Auld Hoose Spaeks: Society and Life in Stone Age Orkney', in A. Ritchie, ed., *Neolithic Orkney in Its European Context* (McDonald Institute Monographs, Cambridge, 2000), pp. 1–20; A. Shepherd, 'Skara Brae: Expressing Identity in a Neolithic Community', in Ritchie, ed., *Neolithic Orkney*, pp. 139–58. **37.** David Abulafia, *The Great Sea: a Human History of the Mediterranean* (London, 2011), pp. 10–12. **38.**

M. Fernández-Miranda, 'Aspects of Talayotic Culture', in M. Balmuth, A. Gilman and L. Prados-Torreira, eds., *Encounters and Transformations: the Archaeology of Iberia in Transition* (Sheffield, 1997), pp. 59–68.   **39.** G. Daniel, *The Megalith Builders of Western Europe* (2nd edn, Harmondsworth, 1963), pp. 26–8, 75–7, to cite just one work by this author; Savory, 'Role of Iberian Communal Tombs', pp. 169, 175; Rodríguez Casal, 'Introduction', pp. 4–5.   **40.** Savory, 'Role of Iberian Communal Tombs', p. 174; E. Shee Twohig, 'Megalithic Tombs and Megalithic Art in Atlantic Europe', in C. Scarre and F. Healy, eds., *Trade and Exchange in Prehistoric Europe: Proceedings of a Conference Held at the University of Bristol, April 1992* (Oxford, 1993), pp. 87–99; A. A. Rodríguez Casal, *O Megalitismo: a primeira arquitectura monumental de Galicia* (Santiago, 1990), pp. 135–41; also G. and V. Leisner, *Die Megalithgräber der Iberischen Halbinsel*, vol. I: *Der Süden* (2 vols., Berlin, 1943), and vol. II: *Der Westen* (3 vols., Berlin, 1965).   **41.** Renfrew, 'Megaliths, Territories and Populations', pp. 208, 218; and several articles and comments in Rodríguez Casal, ed., *O Neolítico atlántico*: E. Shee Twohig, 'Perspectives on the Megaliths of North West Europe', pp. 117–27; C.-T. Le Roux, 'Aspects non funéraires du mégalithisme armoricain', p. 234; C. Tavares da Silva, 'O Neolítico antigo e a origem do Megalitismo no Sul de Portugal', pp. 575–85; J. Soares, 'A transição para as formações sociais neolíticas na costa sudoeste portuguesa', pp. 587–608.

16. Swords and Ploughshares

1. A. Coffyn, *Le Bronze Final Atlantique dans la Péninsule Ibérique* (Paris, 1985), p. 113; also p. 112, fig. 53.   **2.** J. Henderson, *The Atlantic Iron Age: Settlement and Identity in the First Millennium BC* (London, 2007), p. 58; R. Harrison, *Spain at the Dawn of History* (London, 1988), p. 40; J. Briard, *The Bronze Age in Barbarian Europe: From the Megaliths to the Celts*, transl. M. Turton (London, 1979), p. 76.   **3.** M. Ruíz-Gálvez Priego, 'The West of Iberia: Meeting Point between the Mediterranean and the Atlantic at the End of the Bronze Age', in M. Balmuth, A. Gilman and L. Prados-Torreira, eds., *Encounters and Transformations: the Archaeology of Iberia in Transition* (Sheffield, 1997), pp. 95–120; Briard, *Bronze Age in Barbarian Europe*, pp. 95–7.   **4.** M. Ruiz-Gálvez Priego, *La Europa atlántica en la Edad del Bronce* (Barcelona, 1998), pp. 121–5.   **5.** M. C. Fernández Castro, *Iberia in Prehistory* (Oxford, 1995), p. 140; Briard, *Bronze Age in Barbarian Europe*, p. 200.   **6.** Briard, *Bronze Age in Barbarian Europe*, p. 76.   **7.** Coffyn, *Bronze Final Atlantique*, p. 17.   **8.** Henderson, *Atlantic Iron Age*, p. 59, fig. 3.1.   **9.** Ruiz-Gálvez, *Europa atlántica*, pp. 348–58.   **10.** Coffyn, *Bronze Final Atlantique*, pp. 140–41, map 22.   **11.** S. Bowman and S. Needham, 'The Dunaverney and Little Thetford Flesh-Hooks: History, Technology and Their Position within the Later Bronze Age Atlantic Zone Feasting Complex', *Antiquaries Journal*, vol. 87 (2007), pp. 53–108; Ruiz-Gálvez, *Europa atlántica*, pp. 281–2, figs. 89–90; Henderson, *Atlantic Iron Age*, pp. 63–8; map showing cauldrons, p. 64, fig. 3.5; swords: p. 66, fig. 3.7.   **12.** Coffyn, *Bronze Final Atlantique*, pp. 48, 82, 84; also pp. 106–7, figs. 48–9, and p. 135, map 18; quotation from p. 142.   **13.** C. Burgess and B. O'Connor, 'Iberia, the Atlantic Bronze Age and the Mediterranean', in S. Celestino, N. Rafel and X.-L. Armada, eds., *Contacto cultural entre el Mediterráneo y el Atlántico (siglos XII–VIII ANE): la precolonización a debate* (Rome and Madrid, 2008), pp. 41–58; Ruiz-Gálvez, *Europa atlántica*, p. 206; Coffyn, *Bronze Final Atlantique*, pp. 143, 181–2, 205–11; but cf. Ruiz-Gálvez, 'West of Iberia', p. 11 (arguing against a shipwreck).   **14.** H. Hencken, 'Carp's Tongue Swords in Spain, France and Italy', *Zephyrus*, vol. 7 (1956), pp. 125–78.   **15.** Henderson, *Atlantic Iron Age*, pp. 69–71; Briard, *Bronze Age in Barbarian Europe*, p. 202.   **16.** J. Briard, 'Relations between Brittany and Great Britain during the Bronze Age', in C. Scarre and F. Healy, eds., *Trade and Exchange in Prehistoric Europe: Proceedings of a Conference Held at the University of Bristol, April 1992* (Oxford, 1993), pp. 183–90.   **17.** K. Muckleroy, 'Middle Bronze Age Trade between Britain and Europe: a Maritime Perspective', *Proceedings of the Prehistoric Society*, vol. 47 (1981), pp. 275–97; Ruiz-Gálvez, *Europa atlántica*, p. 141.   **18.** Henderson, *Atlantic Iron Age*, pp. 80, 308 n. 11;

O. Crumlin-Pedersen, *Archaeology and the Sea in Scandinavia and Britain: a Personal Account* (Roskilde, 2010), pp. 56–7.   **19.** Briard, *Bronze Age in Barbarian Europe*, pp. 205–6.   **20.** Ibid., pp. 196–7.   **21.** Henderson, *Atlantic Iron Age*, pp. 93–5 and fig. 3.19; Ruiz-Gálvez, *Europa atlántica*, p. 207; Briard, *Bronze Age in Barbarian Europe*, pp. 206– 8.   **22.** Henderson, *Atlantic Iron Age*, pp. 86–8.   **23.** Ruiz-Gálvez, *Europa atlántica*, pp. 348–58; Henderson, *Atlantic Iron Age*, pp. 87, 99–116.   **24.** Ruiz-Gálvez, *Europa atlántica*, pp. 83–6, and fig. 17; Muckleroy, 'Middle Bronze Age Trade', pp. 279–80.   **25.** Coffyn, *Bronze Final Atlantique*, plate xiv.   **26.** S. McGrail, 'Prehistoric Seafaring in the Channel', in Scarre and Healy, eds., *Trade and Exchange in Prehistoric Europe*, pp. 199–210; Muckleroy, 'Middle Bronze Age Trade', p. 275; Briard, *Bronze Age in Barbarian Europe*, pp. 67–8.   **27.** Bercy boats: Ruiz-Gálvez, *Europa atlántica*, p. 91.   **28.** C. Renfrew, 'Trade beyond the Material', in Scarre and Healy, eds., *Trade and Exchange in Prehistoric Europe*, pp. 10–11.   **29.** Ruiz-Gálvez, 'West of Iberia', pp. 95, 99; S. Celestino and C. López-Ruiz, *Tartessos and the Phoenicians in Iberia* (Oxford, 2016), pp. 170–72; J. M. Gutiérrez López et al., 'La Cueva de Gorham (Gibraltar): un santuario fenicio en el confín occidental del Mediterráneo', in F. Prados, I. García and G. Bernard, eds., *Confines: el Extremo del Mundo durante la Antigüedad* (Alicante, 2012), pp. 303–81.   **30.** M. E. Aubet, *Phoenicians and the West: Politics, Colonies and Trade* (2nd edn, Cambridge, 2001), pp. 301–2.   **31.** A. Jodin, *Mogador: Comptoir phénicien du Maroc atlantique* (Tangier, 1966).   **32.** Burgess and O'Connor, 'Iberia, the Atlantic Bronze Age and the Mediterranean', p. 51.   **33.** Cf. G. Daniel, *The Megalith Builders of Western Europe* (2nd edn, Harmondsworth, 1963), pp. 89–91.

17. Tin Traders

1. J. Henderson, *The Atlantic Iron Age: Settlement and Identity in the First Millennium* BC (London, 2007), pp. 121–2.   **2.** Ibid., pp. 122, 136, 212.   **3.** A. Ritchie, *Prehistoric Orkney* (London, 1995), pp. 96–116.   **4.** Henderson, *Atlantic Iron Age*, p. 168.   **5.** Ibid., p. 276.   **6.** Julius Caesar, *Gallic Wars*, 3.12.   **7.** Henderson, *Atlantic Iron Age*, p. 129, fig. 4.13.   **8.** M. Costa et al., *Casa dos Nichos, núcleo de arqueologia* (Gabineto de Arqueologia, Viana do Castelo, s.d.).   **9.** J. Koch, *Tartessian: Celtic in the South-West at the Dawn of History* (2nd edn, Aberystwyth, 2013), p. 270.   **10.** Ibid., pp. 81 (J.14.1) and 223–4; cf. S. Celestino and C. López-Ruiz, *Tartessos and the Phoenicians in Iberia* (Oxford, 2016), pp. 289– 300.   **11.** Caesar, *Gallic Wars*, 3.13.   **12.** B. Cunliffe, *The Extraordinary Voyage of Pytheas the Greek* (2nd edn, London, 2002), pp. 104–5.   **13.** I. Finkel, *The Ark before Noah* (London, 2014).   **14.** Herodotos, 1.163–7; David Abulafia, *The Great Sea: a Human History of the Mediterranean* (London, 2011), pp. 123–5; Cunliffe, *Pytheas the Greek*, pp. 6–8.   **15.** Facsimile of *editio princeps* in Avienus, *Ora Maritima*, ed. J. P. Murphy (Chicago, 1977), pp. 101–39; see L. Antonelli, *Il Periplo nascosto: Lettura stratigrafica e Commento storico-archeologico dell'Ora Maritima di Avieno* (Padua, 1998) (with edition); F. J. González Ponce, *Avieno y el Periplo* (Ecija, 1995).   **16.** A. Jodin, *Mogador: Comptoir phénicien du Maroc atlantique* (Tangier, 1966), pp. 191–3.   **17.** Cunliffe, *Pytheas the Greek*, pp. 45–7.   **18.** Avienus, ll. 85, 267–74; Celestino and López-Ruiz, *Tartessos*, pp. 88–91.   **19.** Avienus, ll. 80–332, especially ll. 85, 113–16, 254, 308, 290–98.   **20.** Cunliffe, *Pytheas the Greek*, p. 46; Avienus, ll. 95–9, 154–7.   **21.** Avienus, ll. 98–109, modified from Murphy's translation.   **22.** Ibid., ll. 110–16.   **23.** Ibid., ll. 164–71.   **24.** Ibid., ll. 202–4.   **25.** Ibid., ll. 390–93.   **26.** Pytheas of Massalia, *On the Ocean*, ed. C. H. Roseman (Chicago, 1994).   **27.** M. Cary and E. H. Warmington, *The Ancient Explorers* (2nd edn, Harmondsworth, 1963), p. 47.   **28.** See the front cover of the Penguin edition of Cunliffe, *Pytheas the Greek*.   **29.** Strabo, *Geography*, 1:4.3, in Pytheas, *On the Ocean*, p. 25, and 3:2.11, p. 60, as also 1:4.5 and 2:3.5, pp. 38, 46.   **30.** Ibid., 2:4.2, pp. 48–9; the second quotation was cited by Strabo from the works of the cosmographer Eratosthenes.   **31.** Cf. Cary and Warmington, *Ancient Explorers*, p. 48.   **32.** Roseman in Pytheas, *On the Ocean*, pp. 152– 3.   **33.** Ibid., pp. 148–50.   **34.** Cf. Cary and Warmington, *Ancient Explorers*, p. 47.   **35.**

Cunliffe, *Pytheas the Greek*, pp. 56–8, 61; Roseman in Pytheas, *On the Ocean*, pp. 152–4. 36. Cunliffe, *Pytheas the Greek*, pp. 65–6. 37. Diodoros the Sicilian, 5.21; compare the imagery c.1500 in D. Abulafia, *The Discovery of Mankind: Atlantic Encounters in the Age of Columbus* (New Haven, 2008). 38. Roseman in Pytheas, *On the Ocean*, pp. 18–19; cf. Cunliffe, *Pytheas the Greek*, pp. 75–7; Cary and Warmington, *Ancient Explorers*, p. 49. 39. Diodoros the Sicilian, 5.1–4; Pliny the Elder, *Natural History*, 4.104; Cary and Warmington, *Ancient Explorers*, p. 47. 40. Strabo, *Geography*, 2:1.17. 41. Pliny the Elder, *Natural History*, 4.103, in Pytheas, *On the Ocean*, pp. 89–90; cf. Cunliffe, *Pytheas the Greek*, p. 100, assuming Pliny was definitely citing Pytheas. 42. Pliny the Elder, *Natural History*, 2.186–7 and 4.104, in Pytheas, *On the Ocean*, pp. 75, 91–2; Cunliffe, *Pytheas the Greek*, p. 127. 43. Cunliffe, *Pytheas the Greek*, p. 125. 44. J. Byock, *Viking Age Iceland* (London, 2001), p. 11. 45. Pliny the Elder, *Natural History*, 37.35–6; Cunliffe, *Pytheas the Greek*, p. 144. 46. Cunliffe, *Pytheas the Greek*, p. 140. 47. Ibid., p. 142.

18. North Sea Raiders

1. J. Jensen, *The Prehistory of Denmark from the Stone Age to the Vikings* (Copenhagen, 2013), pp. 74, 94, 99, 145, 159. 2. G. Graichen and A. Hesse, *Die Bernsteinstraße: Verborgene Handelswege zwischen Ostsee und Nil* (Hamburg, 2013); Jensen, *Prehistory of Denmark*, pp. 410–12, 503–6. 3. M. North, *The Baltic: a History* (Cambridge, Mass., 2015), pp. 25–6. 4. Jensen, *Prehistory of Denmark*, pp. 706, 753, 768. 5. Þ. Gylfason, ed., *Njál's Saga* (London, 1998), p. 10. 6. Jensen, *Prehistory of Denmark*, pp. 582–3. 7. Tacitus, *Germania*, ch. 44. 8. Jensen, *Prehistory of Denmark*, pp. 326–7, 812–15; J. Haywood, *Dark Age Naval Power: a Reassessment of Frankish and Anglo-Saxon Seafaring Activity* (London, 1991), pp. 63–5, with a diagram on p. 64; O. Crumlin-Pedersen, *Archaeology and the Sea in Scandinavia and Britain: a Personal Account* (Roskilde, 2010), pp. 65–7. 9. Haywood, *Dark Age Naval Power*, p. 66. 10. Ibid., pp. 17–18; R. Unger, *The Ship in the Medieval Economy 600–1600* (London, 1980), p. 60. 11. Tacitus, *Agricola*, ch. 28; Haywood, *Dark Age Naval Power*, pp. 5–6. 12. Haywood, *Dark Age Naval Power*, p. 9. 13. Tacitus, *Annals*, 11.19; E. Knoll and N. IJssennagger, 'Palaeogeography and People: Historical Frisians in an Archeological Light', in J. Hines and N. IJssennagger, *Frisians and Their North Sea Neighbours from the Fifth Century to the Viking Age* (Woodbridge, 2017), pp. 10–11. 14. Tacitus, *Histories*, 5.23. 15. C. Krebs, *A Most Dangerous Book: Tacitus's Germania from the Roman Empire to the Third Reich* (New York, 2011). 16. Haywood, *Dark Age Naval Power*, p. 12. 17. Ibid., pp. 24–34; L. P. Louwe Kooijmans, 'Archaeology and Coastal Change in the Netherlands', in F. H. Thompson, ed., *Archaeology and Coastal Change* (London, 1980), pp. 106–33. 18. Haywood, *Dark Age Naval Power*, pp. 37–41. 19. Ammianus Marcellinus, 26.4.5; 27.8.1. 20. J. N. L. Myres, *The Oxford History of England*, vol. 1b: *The English Settlements: English Political and Social Life from the Collapse of Roman Rule to the Emergence of Anglo-Saxon Kingdoms* (2nd edn, Oxford, 1989), pp. 74–103. 21. Ibid., pp. 55, 107–8. 22. Haywood, *Dark Age Naval Power*, pp. 78–85, 179 (with extracts from the sources); Gregory of Tours, *The History of the Franks*, transl. L. Thorpe (Harmondsworth, 1974), pp. 163–4. 23. *Beowulf*, l. 407 (in Seamus Heaney's translation, London, 2000); also ll. 812, 1202–14, 1820, 1830, 2354–68, 2497–2506. 24. R. Hodges and D. Whitehouse, *Mohammed, Charlemagne and the Origins of Europe* (London, 1983), p. 79. 25. B. Ward-Perkins, *The Fall of Rome and the End of Civilization* (Oxford, 2005). 26. Haywood, *Dark Age Naval Power*, pp. 66–73; Unger, *Ship in the Medieval Economy*, pp. 63–4; Crumlin-Pedersen, *Archaeology and the Sea*, pp. 96–7; G. Asaert, *Westeuropese Scheepvaart in de Middeleeuwen* (Bussum, 1974), pp. 14–15. 27. M. Alexander, transl., *The Earliest English Poems* (Harmondsworth, 1966), p. 70. 28. Ibid., p. 75. 29. *Beowulf*, ll. 32–40, 47–50, 240 (in Heaney's translation). 30. Ibid., ll. 216, 218–19. 31. Ibid., ll. 1905–13. 32. C. Loveluck, *Northwest Europe in the Early Middle Ages, c. AD 600–1150* (Cambridge, 2013), pp. 191–2; Knoll and IJssennagger, 'Paleogeography and People', pp. 6, 9–10. 33.

M. Pye, *The Edge of the World: How the North Sea Made Us Who We Are* (London, 2014), p. 35; R. Latouche, *The Birth of Western Economy: Economic Aspects of the Dark Ages* (London, 1961), pp. 122, 134–6.   **34.** Haywood, *Dark Age Naval Power*, pp. 88–9; S. Lebecq, *Marchands et navigateurs frisons du haut moyen âge* (2 vols., Lille, 1983), vol. 1, pp. 114, 123–7, and vol. 2, pp. 258–9, doc. 52.5.   **35.** Lebecq, *Marchands et navigateurs*, vol. 2, pp. 59, doc. 10.2, and p. 63, doc. 11.1; W. Levison, *England and the Continent in the Eighth Century* (Oxford, 1946), pp. 49–54; H. Mayr-Harting, *The Coming of Christianity to Anglo-Saxon England* (London, 1972), pp. 129–47; J. Hines, 'The Anglo-Frisian Question', and T. Pestell, 'The Kingdom of East Anglia, Frisia and Continental Connections, c. AD 600–900', both in Hines and IJssennagger, *Frisians*, pp. 25–42, 193–222.   **36.** Lebecq, *Marchands et navigateurs*, vol. 2, p. 232, doc. 46.5.   **37.** Loveluck, *Northwest Europe*, pp. 186, 194–7.   **38.** A. Verhulst, *The Rise of Cities in North-West Europe* (Cambridge, 1999), p. 20; D. Meier, *Seafarers, Merchants and Pirates in the Middle Ages* (Woodbridge, 2006), pp. 56–62.   **39.** Hodges and Whitehouse, *Mohammed, Charlemagne*, pp. 93–101; Lebecq, *Marchands et navigateurs*, vol. 1, pp. 78–83, 149–63; quotation from C. Wickham, *Framing the Early Middle Ages: Europe and the Mediterranean, 400–800* (Oxford, 2005), pp. 682–5, who gives a smaller area (sixty hectares).   **40.** Lebecq, *Marchands et navigateurs*, vol. 1, pp. 60–66; Verhulst, *Rise of Cities*, pp. 27–8; good illustrations in J. Rozemeyer, *De Ontdekking van Dorestad* (Breda, 2012), pp. 20–30 (ignoring the attempt to identify Dorestad as Utrecht), and also in Unger, *Ship in the Medieval Economy*, p. 79, fig. 5; Asaert, *Westeuropese Scheepvaart*, pp. 18–19.   **41.** Verhulst, *Rise of Cities*, pp. 45–6.   **42.** Lebecq, *Marchands et navigateurs*, vol. 1, pp. 169–76.   **43.** Ibid., vol. 1, pp. 190–95, 213–15, 258–61.   **44.** Pye, *Edge of the World*, p. 44.   **45.** Lebecq, *Marchands et navigateurs*, vol. 1, p. 260, and vol. 2, pp. 281–2; Alpertus van Metz, *Gebeurtenissen van deze tijd en Een fragment over bisschop Diederik I van Metz*, ed. H. van Rij and A. Sapir Abulafia (Amsterdam, 1980), pp. 18–19.

19. 'This iron-studded dragon'

1. From a poem by Þjóðólfr Arnórsson, cited by G. Williams, *The Viking Ship* (London, 2014), p. 8.   **2.** Out of a vast general literature see in particular J. Brøndsted, *The Vikings* (2nd edn, Harmondsworth, 1965); E. Oxenstierna, *The Norsemen* (London, 1966); G. Jones, *A History of the Vikings* (2nd edn, Oxford, 1984); E. Roesdahl, *The Vikings* (2nd edn, London, 1998); F. D. Logan, *The Vikings in History* (3rd edn, London, 2005); P. Parker, *The Norsemen's Fury: a History of the Viking World* (London, 2014).   **3.** *Anglo-Saxon Chronicle*, Cambridge MS (Parker Library, Corpus Christi College), s.a. 878.   **4.** Ibid., various versions, s.a. 789.   **5.** Ibid., Peterborough MS, s.a. 793, 794.   **6.** Ibid., Cambridge MS, s.a. 835, 837, 838, 855.   **7.** P. Sawyer, *The Age of the Vikings* (2nd edn, London, 1971), p. 202.   **8.** *Anglo-Saxon Chronicle*, Cambridge MS, s.a. 865.   **9.** Brøndsted, *Vikings*, p. 34.   **10.** *Anglo-Saxon Chronicle*, Cambridge MS, s.a. 882.   **11.** Ibid., s.a. 896.   **12.** J. Haywood, *Dark Age Naval Power: a Reassessment of Frankish and Anglo-Saxon Seafaring Activity* (London, 1991), pp. 75–6.   **13.** *Anglo-Saxon Chronicle*, Cambridge MS, s.a. 917.   **14.** M. Lawson, *Cnut: the Danes in England in the Early Eleventh Century* (Harlow, 1993), pp. 16–48.   **15.** M. Magnusson and H. Pálsson, eds. and transl., *King Harald's Saga: Harald Hardradi of Norway, from Snorri Sturluson's Heimskringla* (Harmondsworth, 1966), pp. 133–54.   **16.** Brøndsted, *Vikings*, pp. 36–9; J. Byock, *Viking Age Iceland* (London, 2001), pp. 12–13.   **17.** H. Ellis Davidson, *The Viking Road to Byzantium* (London, 1976); E. Christiansen, *The Northern Crusades* (2nd edn, London, 1997).   **18.** Brøndsted, *Vikings*, pp. 31–6.   **19.** Byock, *Viking Age Iceland*, pp. 82–4.   **20.** From the Old Norse poem *Hávamál*, transl. H. A. Bellows, *The Poetic Edda* (New York, 1923), p. 44, stanza 77; J. de Vries, *Heroic Song and Heroic Legend* (London and Oxford, 1963), pp. 184, 187.   **21.** H. Pálsson and P. Edwards, transl., *Orkneyinga Saga: the History of the Earls of Orkney* (Harmondsworth, 1981), pp. 214–16.   **22.** Sawyer, *Age of the Vikings*, p. 206.   **23.** Ibn Fadlān, 'The Book of Ahmad ibn Fadlān', in C. Stone and P. Lunde, ed. and transl., *Ibn*

Fadlān and the Land of Darkness: Arab Travellers in the Far North (London, 2012), pp. 45–55, and other extracts in the same volume. **24.** S. Kleingärtner and G. Williams, 'Contact and Exchange', in G. Williams, P. Pentz and M. Wemhoff, eds., *Vikings: Life and Legend* (London, 2014), p. 54. **25.** B. Magnus and I. Gustin, *Birka and Hovgården – a Story That Enriches Time* (Stockholm, 2012); D. Skre and F.-A. Stylegar, *Kaupang the Viking Town: the Kaupang Exhibition at UKM, Oslo, 2004–2005* (Oslo, 2004). **26.** R. Hodges and D. Whitehouse, *Mohammed, Charlemagne and the Origins of Europe* (London, 1983), p. 111; K. Struve, 'Haithabu and the Early Harbours of the Baltic Sea', in *The World of the Vikings: an Exhibition Mounted by the Statens Historiska Museum Stockholm in Co-operation with the National Maritime Museum, Greenwich, London* (London, 1973), pp. 27–8; D. Meier, *Seafarers, Merchants and Pirates in the Middle Ages* (Woodbridge, 2006), pp. 76–9. **27.** M. North, *The Baltic: a History* (Cambridge, Mass., 2015), pp. 14–15, for the Obodrites. **28.** Ibid., pp. 19–20. **29.** Meier, *Seafarers, Merchants and Pirates*, pp. 72–3, 80. **30.** J. Ahola, Frog and J. Lucenius, eds., *The Viking Age in Åland: Insights into Identity and Remnants of Culture* (Helsinki, 2014). **31.** Hodges and Whitehouse, *Mohammed, Charlemagne*, p. 116, fig. 46; generally, L. Thålin, 'Baltic Trade and the Varangians', in *World of the Vikings*, pp. 22–3. **32.** Hodges and Whitehouse, *Mohammed, Charlemagne*, p. 119, fig. 49. **33.** Ibid., p. 118. **34.** Ibid., pp. 114–15, 117, and fig. 47, p. 116. **35.** North, *Baltic*, p. 9, citing Adam of Bremen. **36.** R. Öhrman, *Gotlands Fornsal: Bildstenar* (2nd edn, Visby, 2000); E. Nylén and J. P. Lamm, *Stones, Ships and Symbols: the Picture Stones of Gotland from the Viking Age and Before* (Stockholm, 1988), pp. 62–3, 68–71, 109–35, 162–9; D. Rossi, ed., *Guta Saga: la Saga dei Gotlandesi* (Milan, 2010), pp. 26–7. **37.** Nylén and Lamm, *Stones, Ships and Symbols*, pp. 42, 166–7; R. Simek, *Die Schiffe der Wikinger* (Stuttgart, 2014), pp. 54–5. **38.** Williams, *Viking Ship*, pp. 34–9; Simek, *Schiffe der Wikinger*, pp. 79–82; D. Ellmers, 'The Ships of the Vikings', in *World of the Vikings*, pp. 13–14. **39.** J. Bill, 'The Oseberg Ship and Ritual Burial', in Williams et al., eds., *Vikings*, pp. 200–201. **40.** Williams, *Viking Ship*, pp. 26–7, 48–52; G. Asaert, *Westeuropese Scheepvaart in de Middeleeuwen* (Bussum, 1974), pp. 20–22; my special thanks go to Professor Jón Viðar Sigurðsson for guiding me around the Viking Ship Museum in Oslo. **41.** Williams, *Viking Ship*, pp. 52–5; R. Unger, *The Ship in the Medieval Economy 600–1600* (London, 1980), pp. 82–9. **42.** 'Zuhrī on Viking Ships c.1160', in Stone and Lunde, ed. and transl., *Ibn Fadlān and the Land of Darkness*, p. 110. **43.** A. Christys, *Vikings in the South: Voyages to Iberia and the Mediterranean* (London, 2015), pp. 19–25. **44.** 'Ibn Hayyān on the Viking Attack on Seville 844', in Stone and Lunde, ed. and transl., *Ibn Fadlān and the Land of Darkness*, pp. 105–9; E. Morales Romero, *Historia de los Vikingos en España: Ataques e Incursiones contra los Reinos Cristianos y Musulmanes de la Península Ibérica en los siglos IX–XI* (2nd edn, Madrid, 2006), pp. 127–47; Christys, *Vikings in the South*, pp. 29–45. **45.** Simek, *Schiffe der Wikinger*, pp. 64–5; F. Brandt, 'On the Navigation of the Vikings', in *World of the Vikings*, pp. 14–18. **46.** Williams, *Viking Ship*, p. 30; O. Crumlin-Pedersen, *Archaeology and the Sea in Scandinavia and Britain: a Personal Account* (Roskilde, 2010), pp. 82–8. **47.** The ship *Roskilde 6*, centrepiece of the British Museum Viking exhibition in 2014: J. Bill, 'Roskilde 6', in Williams et al., eds., *Vikings*, pp. 228–33; Williams, *Viking Ship*, pp. 67–73. **48.** Williams, *Viking Ship*, pp. 74–81; Unger, *Ship in the Medieval Economy*, p. 91; Crumlin-Pedersen, *Archaeology and the Sea*, pp. 109–13. **49.** M. Egeler, *Islands in the West: Classical Myth and the Medieval Norse and Irish Geographical Imagination* (Turnhout, 2017).

20. New Island Worlds

1. F. D. Logan, *The Vikings in History* (3rd edn, London, 2005), pp. 21–2, 26–8; A. Forte, R. Oram and F. Pedersen, *Viking Empires* (Cambridge, 2005), p. 265. **2.** H. Pálsson and P. Edwards, transl., *Orkneyinga Saga: the History of the Earls of Orkney* (Harmondsworth, 1981), p. 215. **3.** J. Jesch, *The Viking Diaspora* (London, 2015), pp. 32–3. **4.** Forte et al., *Viking Empires*, p. 268. **5.** Pálsson and Edwards, transl., *Orkneyinga Saga*, pp. 26–7. **6.** B. Crawford, *The Northern Earldoms: Orkney and Caithness from AD 870 to 1470*

(Edinburgh, 2013), pp. 36, 85–7.   7. Pálsson and Edwards, transl., *Orkneyinga Saga*, pp. 28–31.   8. Ibid., p. 34.   9. Ibid., pp. 36–8; Crawford, *Northern Earldoms*, pp. 125–8; Forte et al., *Viking Empires*, p. 270.   10. Pálsson and Edwards, transl., *Orkneyinga Saga*, pp. 50–53.   11. Ibid., p. 84.   12. Crawford, *Northern Earldoms*, pp. 68, 198–212; black-and-white plate 1.   13. Pálsson and Edwards, transl., *Orkneyinga Saga*, pp. 85–6.   14. Ibid., p. 85.   15. R. A. McDonald, 'The Manx Sea Kings and the Western Oceans: the Late Norse Isle of Man in Its North Atlantic Context, 1079–1265', in B. Hudson, ed., *Studies in the Medieval Atlantic* (New York, 2012), p. 150; P. Sawyer, *Kings and Vikings: Scandinavia and Europe AD 700–1100* (New York, 1994), p. 111; A. W. Moore, *A History of the Isle of Man* (London, 1900), vol. 1, p. 102.   16. Crawford, *Northern Earldoms*, pp. 166–7.   17. Sawyer, *Kings and Vikings*, p. 110; Logan, *Vikings in History*, pp. 27–8; M. Barnes, *The Norn Language of Orkney and Shetland* (Lerwick, 1998).   18. Logan, *Vikings in History*, p. 29.   19. Ibid., pp. 30, 32–5; D. Meier, *Seafarers, Merchants and Pirates in the Middle Ages* (Woodbridge, 2006), p. 108.   20. Logan, *Vikings in History*, pp. 38–40.   21. C. Sauer, *Northern Mists* (2nd edn, San Francisco, 1973), pp. 84–6; R. Painter, transl., *Faroe-Islander Saga* (Jefferson, NC, 2016).   22. Jesch, *Viking Diaspora*, pp. 48–9.   23. Ibid., p. 22; S. Auge, 'Vikings in the Faeroe Islands', in W. W. Fitzhugh and E. I. Ward, eds., *Vikings: the North Atlantic Saga* (Washington DC, 2000), pp. 154–63.   24. Jesch, *Viking Diaspora*, p. 30.   25. Cited from Logan, *Vikings in History*, p. 44 (with slight amendments); G. Turville-Petre, *The Heroic Age of Scandinavia* (London, 1951), pp. 95–6; G. J. Marcus, *The Conquest of the North Atlantic* (Woodbridge, 1980), pp. 22–3.   26. V. Szabo, 'Subsistence Whaling and the Norse Diaspora: Norsemen, Basques, and Whale Use in the Western North Atlantic, ca. AD 900–1640', in Hudson, ed., *Studies in the Medieval Atlantic*, p. 82.   27. Marcus, *Conquest of the North Atlantic*, pp. 16–17.   28. Irish *Life of St Brendan* in the *Book of Lismore*, in S. Webb, ed., *The Voyage of Saint Brendan* (2014), doc. 1.   29. *Navigatio Brendani*, in Webb, ed., *Voyage of Saint Brendan*, doc. 2.   30. Marcus, *Conquest of the North Atlantic*, pp. 19–20.   31. D. Abulafia, *The Discovery of Mankind: Atlantic Encounters in the Age of Columbus* (New Haven, 2008), p. 41; M. Egeler, *Islands in the West: Classical Myth and the Medieval Norse and Irish Geographical Imagination* (Turnhout, 2017).   32. Forte et al., *Viking Empires*, pp. 304–6; Logan, *Vikings in History*, pp. 43–5.   33. Logan, *Vikings in History*, p. 45; also Jesch, *Viking Diaspora*, p. 182.   34. Jesch, *Viking Diaspora*, pp. 194–8.   35. Citations from the twelfth-century *Landnámabók*, in Logan, *Vikings in History*, pp. 47–8; Turville-Petre, *Heroic Age of Scandinavia*, pp. 97–8; Sauer, *Northern Mists*, pp. 86–94.   36. J. Byock, *Viking Age Iceland* (London, 2001), pp. 48–51 (citing the *Saga of the Foster-Brothers*), and p. 56; Jesch, *Viking Diaspora*, p. 22; also Sauer, *Northern Mists*, pp. 94–6.   37. Jesch, *Viking Diaspora*, p. 40.   38. Byock, *Viking Age Iceland*, pp. 10–11.   39. Jesch, *Viking Diaspora*, pp. 34–5, 56–7.   40. Logan, *Vikings in History*, p. 51.   41. Jesch, *Viking Diaspora*, p. 39; Byock, *Viking Age Iceland*, pp. 57–62.   42. Logan, *Vikings in History*, pp. 45–7; Turville-Petre, *Heroic Age of Scandinavia*, pp. 100–101.   43. Marcus, *Conquest of the North Atlantic*, p. 26.   44. Byock, *Viking Age Iceland*, pp. 10–11, 82–4, 86.   45. Ibid., pp. 14, 174, 294; Logan, *Vikings in History*, p. 53.   46. Turville-Petre, *Heroic Age of Scandinavia*, pp. 101–2.   47. Byock, *Viking Age Iceland*, pp. 292–301; Logan, *Vikings in History*, p. 54; Turville-Petre, *Heroic Age of Scandinavia*, pp. 101, 107.   48. 'Egil's Saga', in *The Sagas of the Icelanders* (New York, 2000; edition based on *The Complete Sagas of Icelanders*, vols. 1–5, Reykjavík, 1997), ch. 27, pp. 46–7.   49. Ibid., ch. 33, p. 54.   50. Ibid., ch. 39, p. 61.   51. Ibid., ch. 46, pp. 71–4.   52. Ibid., ch. 63, p. 120; B. Gelsinger, *Icelandic Enterprise: Commerce and Economy in the Middle Ages* (Columbia, SC, 1981), p. 126.   53. Ibid., p. 31.   54. S. Bagge, *Cross and Scepter: the Rise of the Scandinavian Kingdoms from the Vikings to the Reformation* (Princeton, 2014), p. 137.   55. The major work on *vaðmal*, unfortunately only in Icelandic and with no summary, is: H. Þorláksson, *Vaðmal og Verðlag: Vaðmal í Utanlandsviðskiptum og Búskop Íslendinga á 13. og 14. Öld* ['*Vaðmal* and prices: *vaðmal* in the foreign shipping and farming of 13th and 14th-century Iceland'] (Reykjavik, 1991); but for its arguments see O. Vésteinsson, 'Commercial Shipping and the Political Economy of Medieval Iceland', in J. Barrett and D. Orton, eds., *Cod and Herring: the Archaeology and History of*

Medieval Sea Fishing (Oxford, 2016), pp. 71–9.   **56.** Gelsinger, *Icelandic Enterprise*, pp. 34–6, 46–7, 77–8.   **57.** Ibid., pp. 69–76.   **58.** E. Carus-Wilson, 'The Iceland Venture', in E. Carus-Wilson, *Medieval Merchant Venturers: Collected Studies* (2nd edn, London, 1967), pp. 98–142.   **59.** Gelsinger, *Icelandic Enterprise*, pp. 127, 154.   **60.** D. Abulafia, *Frederick II: a Medieval Emperor* (London, 1988), p. 268.   **61.** Gelsinger, *Icelandic Enterprise*, pp. 83, 151.

21. White Bears, Whales and Walruses

1. K. Seaver, *The Last Vikings: the Epic Story of the Great Norse Voyages* (2nd edn, London, 2015), fig. 2, p. xxiii, and p. 3; K. Seaver, *The Frozen Echo: Greenland and the Exploration of North America ca AD 1000–1500* (Stanford, 1996); also F. Gad, *The History of Greenland*, vol. 1: *Earliest Times to 1700* (London, 1970), pp. 1–7; and now the often acerbic A. Ned-kvitne, *Norse Greenland: Viking Peasants in the Arctic* (Abingdon, 2019).   **2.** H. Pálsson and M. Magnusson, ed. and transl., *The Vinland Sagas: the Norse Discovery of America* (Harmondsworth, 1965), pp. 15, 39; Seaver, *Last Vikings*, pp. 14–15.   **3.** Seaver, *Last Vikings*, p. 8; Nedkvitne, *Norse Greenland*, pp. 21–30.   **4.** Estimates from the 'Book of the Settlements' (*Landnámabók*), in G. Jones, *The Norse Atlantic Saga, being the Norse Voyages of Discovery and Settlement to Iceland, Greenland, and North America* (2nd edn, Oxford, 1986), p. 157; Pálsson and Magnusson, ed. and transl., *Vinland Sagas*, pp. 14–15.   **5.** Seaver, *Last Vikings*, p. 16; Gad, *History of Greenland*, vol. 1, p. 27.   **6.** Jones, *Norse Atlantic Saga*, pp. 73–7; Gad, *History of Greenland*, vol. 1, p. 29.   **7.** Gad, *History of Greenland*, vol. 1, pp. 103–4.   **8.** 'Greenlanders' Saga', in Jones, *Norse Atlantic Saga*, p. 187; Pálsson and Magnusson, ed. and transl., *Vinland Sagas*, p. 50.   **9.** Seaver, *Last Vikings*, pp. 15–16; Jones, *Norse Atlantic Saga*, p. 77.   **10.** Gad, *History of Greenland*, vol. 1, pp. 33–4, 42–5.   **11.** Objects in the Greenland room, Nationalmuseet, Copenhagen; Seaver, *Last Vikings*, p. 104; Gad, *History of Greenland*, vol. 1, p. 85; B. Star et al., 'Ancient DNA Reveals the Chron-ology of Walrus Ivory Trade in Norse Greenland', *Proceedings of the Royal Society B*, vol. 285 (2018), 2018.0978; Nedkvitne, *Norse Greenland*, pp. 170–72.   **12.** Seaver, *Last Vikings*, pp. 102–3; G. J. Marcus, *The Conquest of the North Atlantic* (Woodbridge, 1980), p. 92; D. Abulafia, *Frederick II: a Medieval Emperor* (London, 1988), p. 268.   **13.** Seaver, *Last Vikings*, p. 101; Marcus, *Conquest of the North Atlantic*, pp. 91, 96; J. Arneborg, 'Greenland and Europe', in W. W. Fitzhugh and E. I. Ward, eds., *Vikings: the North Atlantic Saga* (Washington DC, 2000), pp. 304–17.   **14.** Gad, *History of Greenland*, vol. 1, p. 172; G. Davies, *Vikings in America* (Edinburgh, 2009), pp. 130–38, discounting the arguments about metalworking.   **15.** Ari Frodi, *Íslendingabók*, cited in Gad, *History of Greenland*, vol. 1, p. 19.   **16.** Gad, *History of Greenland*, vol. 1, pp. 20–21.   **17.** Ibid., pp. 23–4, 91–3, 97–102; Jones, *Norse Atlantic Saga*, pp. 93–5; H. C. Gulløv, 'Natives and Norse in Greenland', in Fitzhugh and Ward, eds., *Vikings*, pp. 318–26; V. Szabo, 'Subsistence Whaling and the Norse Diaspora: Norsemen, Basques, and Whale Use in the Western North Atlantic, ca. AD 900–1640', in B. Hudson, ed., *Studies in the Medieval Atlantic* (New York, 2012), p. 83; Nedkvitne, *Norse Greenland*, p. 328.   **18.** Warp weight in the Greenland room, National-museet, Copenhagen; Jones, *Norse Atlantic Saga*, pp. 84–5; Seaver, *Last Vikings*, p. 35; Gad, *History of Greenland*, vol. 1, pp. 39, 84–5.   **19.** Seaver, *Last Vikings*, p. 23.   **20.** 'Eirík the Red's Saga', in Jones, *Norse Atlantic Saga*, pp. 216–17; Pálsson and Magnusson, ed. and transl., *Vinland Sagas*, pp. 85–6; Brattahlíð church: Gad, *History of Greenland*, vol. 1, pp. 41–2.   **21.** G. Turville-Petre, *The Heroic Age of Scandinavia* (London, 1951), p. 138; Seaver, *Last Vikings*, pp. 26–9.   **22.** 'Authun and the Bear', in G. Jones, ed. and transl., *Eirík the Red and Other Icelandic Sagas* (Oxford, 1961), pp. 163–70.   **23.** Gad, *History of Greenland*, vol. 1, pp. 57, 62–3; Marcus, *Conquest of the North Atlantic*, p. 92.   **24.** Seaver, *Last Vikings*, p. 114.   **25.** Ibid., pp. 111, 118–19.   **26.** Ívar Bárdason, cited by Marcus, *Conquest of the North Atlantic*, p. 98; also Jones, *Norse Atlantic Saga*, pp. 89–92.   **27.** Jones, *Norse Atlantic Saga*, p. 95; Nedkvitne, *Norse Greenland*, pp. 343–9.   **28.** J. Berglund, 'The Farm beneath the Sand', in Fitzhugh and Ward, eds., *Vikings*, pp. 295–303.   **29.** Objects in the Greenland room, Nationalmuseet, Copenhagen; Gad, *History of Greenland*, vol. 1, pp. 154–61; Jones, *Norse Atlantic Saga*, pp. 110–11; Seaver, *Last Vikings*, p. 112.   **30.** B. Fagan, *Fish on Friday: Feasting, Fasting, and the Discovery of the New World* (New York, 2007); Gad, *History of Greenland*, vol. 1, pp. 161–2, 181–2; Seaver, *Last Vikings*, p. 143.   **31.** T. McGovern, 'The Demise of Norse Greenland', in Fitzhugh and Ward, eds., *Vikings*, pp. 327–39.   **32.** Text in H. Ingstad, *Land under the Pole Star* (London, 1966), pp. 329–30; Gad, *History of Greenland*, vol. 1, pp. 158–9.   **33.** Gad, *History of Greenland*, vol. 1, p. 164; Jones, *Norse Atlantic Saga*, pp. 112–13.   **34.** 'Ungortok the Chief of Kakorttok', in Jones, *Norse Atlantic Saga*, Appendix iii, pp. 262–7.   **35.** McGovern, 'Demise of Norse Greenland', p. 338.   **36.** N. Lynnerup, 'Life and Death in Norse Greenland', in Fitzhugh and Ward, eds., *Vikings*, pp. 285–94.   **37.** Seaver, *Last Vikings*, pp. 159, 163.   **38.** Jones, *Norse Atlantic Saga*, p. 87.   **39.** Pálsson and Magnusson, ed. and transl., *Vinland Sagas*, pp. 29–35.   **40.** Rune-stone and carvings in the Greenland room, Nationalmuseet, Copenhagen; Pálsson and Magnusson, ed. and transl., *Vinland Sagas*, p. 21; Jones, *Norse Atlantic Saga*, p. 80; Seaver, *Last Vikings*, pp. 42, 112.   **41.** R. McGhee, 'Remarks on the Arctic Finds', in Jones, *Norse Atlantic Saga*, Appendix v, p. 283; P. Sutherland, 'The Norse and Native North Americans', in Fitzhugh and Ward, eds., *Vikings*, pp. 238–47.   **42.** P. Schledermann, 'Ellesmere: Vikings in the Far North', in Fitzhugh and Ward, eds., *Vikings*, pp. 248–56; Davies, *Vikings in America*, pp. 89–104.   **43.** Marcus, *Conquest of the North Atlantic*, p. 92; T. Haine, 'Greenland Norse Knowledge of the North Atlantic Environment', in Hudson, ed., *Studies in the Medieval Atlantic*, pp. 110–16.   **44.** Displayed in the Greenland room, Nationalmuseet, Copenhagen.   **45.** *Skálholtsannáll*, cited from Jones, *Norse Atlantic Saga*, p. 136; K. Seaver, 'Unanswered Questions', in Fitzhugh and Ward, eds., *Vikings*, p. 275; Seaver, *Last Vikings*, p. 59.   **46.** Cited in Pálsson and Magnusson, ed. and transl., *Vinland Sagas*, p. 15.   **47.** Jones, *Norse Atlantic Saga*, p. 285; M. Egeler, *Islands in the West: Classical Myth and the Medieval Norse and Irish Geographical Imagination* (Turnhout, 2017).   **48.** Among the justifiably incredulous: K. Seaver, *Maps, Myths, and Men: the Story of the Vínland Map* (Stanford, 2004); among the unjustifiably defensive: Davies, *Vikings in America*; among the supporters of the map: R. Skelton, T. Marston and G. Painter, *The Vinland Map and the Tartar Relation* (2nd edn, New Haven, 1995); see also S. Cox, 'A Norse Penny from Maine', in Fitzhugh and Ward, eds., *Vikings*, pp. 206–7.   **49.** Pálsson and Magnusson, ed. and transl., *Vinland Sagas*, pp. 53–4.   **50.** Jones, *Norse Atlantic Saga*, p. 117.   **51.** Pálsson and Magnusson, ed. and transl., *Vinland Sagas*, pp. 55–8.   **52.** E. Wahlgren, *The Vikings and America* (London, 1986), pp. 139–46, 158; cf. Davies, *Vikings in America*, pp. 74–5, and Jones, *Norse Atlantic Saga*, p. 124.   **53.** Sutherland, 'The Norse and Native North Americans', pp. 238–9.   **54.** Wahlgren, *Vikings and America*, pp. 74, 92–3.   **55.** Pálsson and Magnusson, ed. and transl., *Vinland Sagas*, pp. 64–5.   **56.** Ibid., pp. 66, 70–71.   **57.** Ibid., pp. 70–71.   **58.** Ibid., pp. 67–70, 100.   **59.** N. Brown, *The Far Traveler: Voyages of a Viking Woman* (New York, 2007); Pálsson and Magnusson, ed. and transl., *Vinland Sagas*, p. 71.   **60.** Pálsson and Magnusson, ed. and transl., *Vinland Sagas*, p. 63.   **61.** H. Ingstad, *Westward to Vinland: the Discovery of Pre-Columbian Norse House-Sites in North America* (London, 1969); B. Linderoth Wallace, 'The Viking Settlement at L'Anse aux Meadows', in Fitzhugh and Ward, eds., *Vikings*, pp. 208–16; B. Linderoth Wallace, 'The Anse aux Meadows site', in Jones, *Norse Atlantic Saga*, Appendix vii, pp. 285–304; Seaver, *Last Vikings*, pp. 50–52; Jones, *Norse Atlantic Saga*, pp. 129–30; Davies, *Vikings in America*, pp. 76–81; P. Bergþórsson, *The Wineland Millennium* (Reykjavik, 2000).

22. From Russia with Profit

1. P. Dollinger, *The German Hansa* (London, 1970), p. 3; H. Brand and E. Knol, eds., *Koggen, Kooplieden en Kantoren: de Hanze, een praktisch Netwerk* (Hilversum, 2011).   **2.** David Abulafia, *The Great Sea: a Human History of the Mediterranean* (London, 2011), pp. 287–369.   **3.** Dollinger, *German Hansa*, pp. xix–xx.   **4.** G. Graichen et al., *Die Deutsche Hanse: eine heimliche Supermacht* (Reinbek bei Hamburg, 2011), p. 115.   **5.** D. Abulafia, *Frederick II: a Medieval Emperor* (London, 1988), p. 229.   **6.** J. Schildhauer, K. Fritze and

W. Stark, *Die Hanse* (Berlin, DDR, 1982); J. Schildhauer, *The Hansa: History and Culture* (Leipzig, 1985). **7.** Graichen et al., *Deutsche Hanse*, p. 6. **8.** Dollinger, *German Hansa*, p. xx. **9.** See the EU-funded *Hansekarte: Map of the Hanseatic League* (Lübeck, 2014). **10.** J. Sarnowsky, 'Die Hanse und der Deutsche Orden – eine ertragreiche Beziehung', in Graichen et al., *Deutsche Hanse*, pp. 163–81. **11.** A. Kasekamp, *A History of the Baltic States* (Basingstoke, 2010), pp. 12–13. **12.** E. Christiansen, *The Northern Crusades* (2nd edn, London, 1997), pp. 94–5. **13.** Kasekamp, *History of the Baltic States*, p. 200 n. 37. **14.** Christiansen, *Northern Crusades*, pp. 79–82, 99–103. **15.** Kasekamp, *History of the Baltic States*, pp. 9, 11. **16.** Christiansen, *Northern Crusades*, pp. 54–5, 120. **17.** Dollinger, *German Hansa*, p. 4. **18.** Christiansen, *Northern Crusades*, pp. 29–31. **19.** Schildhauer, *The Hansa*, p. 20. **20.** Dollinger, *German Hansa*, doc. 1, p. 379. **21.** Ibid., p. 22. **22.** Ibid., doc. 1, p. 380; Schildhauer, *The Hansa*, p. 19. **23.** R. Hammel-Kiesow, 'Novgorod und Lübeck: Siedlungsgefüge zweier Handelsstädte im Vergleich', in N. Angermann and K. Friedland, eds., *Novgorod: Markt und Kontor der Hanse* (Cologne, 2002), p. 53. **24.** Dollinger, *German Hansa*, pp. 31–5; R. Bartlett, *The Making of Europe: Conquest, Colonization and Cultural Change 950–1300* (London, 1993). **25.** Abulafia, *Frederick II*, p. 229. **26.** G. Westholm, *Visby 1361 Invasionen* (Stockholm, 2007), and exhibits in the Gotland Museum, Visby, and Historiska Museet, Stockholm. **27.** Dollinger, *German Hansa*, pp. 70–71. **28.** Schildhauer, *The Hansa*, pp. 73–4. **29.** Hermen Rode's work is both in Sankt-Annen-Museum, Lübeck, and in Historiska Museet, Stockholm; M. North, *The Baltic: a History* (Cambridge, Mass., 2015), pp. 77–80. **30.** North, *Baltic*, pp. 80–82. **31.** D. Kattinger, *Die Gotländische Gesellschaft: der frühhansisch-gotländische Handel in Nord- und Westeuropa* (Cologne, 1999). **32.** Dollinger, *German Hansa*, pp. 7–8, 27; North, *Baltic*, pp. 43–6. **33.** M. W. Thompson, eds., *Novgorod the Great: Excavations at the Medieval City 1951–62 directed by A. V. Artikhovsky and B. A. Kolchin* (London, 1967), p. 12; Hammel-Kiesow, 'Novgorod und Lübeck', p. 60; E. A. Rybina, 'Früher Handel und westeuropäische Funde in Novgorod', in Angermann and Friedland, eds., *Novgorod*, pp. 121–32. **34.** Dating revised from 1189: A. Choroškevič, 'Der Ostsee Handel und der deutsch-russisch-gotländische Vertrag 1191/1192', in S. Jenks and M. North, eds., *Der Hansische Sonderweg? Beiträge zur Sozial- und Wirtschaftsgeschichte der Hanse* (Cologne, 1993), pp. 1–12; also B. Schubert, 'Die Russische Kaufmannschaft und ihre Beziehung zur Hanse', in Jenks and North, eds., *Hansische Sonderweg?*, pp. 13–22; B. Schubert, 'Hansische Kaufleute im Novgoroder Handelskontor', in Angermann and Friedland, eds., *Novgorod*, pp. 79–95; E. Harder-Gersdorff, 'Hansische Handelsgüter auf dem Großmarkt Novgorod (13.–17. Jh.): Grundstrukturen und Forschungsfragen', in Angermann and Friedland, eds., *Novgorod*, pp. 133–43. **35.** Dollinger, *German Hansa*, pp. 27–30. **36.** North, *Baltic*, pp. 40–43. **37.** G. Hoffmann and U. Schnall, eds., *Die Kogge: Sternstunde des deutschen Schiffsarchäologie* (Hamburg, 2003); also S. Rose, *The Medieval Sea* (London, 2007), pp. 16, 21–2. **38.** O. Crumlin-Pedersen, 'To be or not to be a cog: the Bremen Cog in Perspective', *International Journal of Nautical Archaeology*, vol. 29 (2000), pp. 230–46. **39.** B. Fagan, *Fish on Friday: Feasting, Fasting, and the Discovery of the New World* (New York, 2007), pp. 51–6. **40.** J. van Houtte, *An Economic History of the Low Countries 800–1800* (London, 1977), p. 90. **41.** Saxo Grammaticus (c.1150–c.1220), cited by J. Gade, *The Hanseatic Control of Norwegian Commerce during the Late Middle Ages* (Leiden, 1951), p. 17; P. Holm, 'Commercial Sea Fisheries in the Baltic Region c.AD 1000–1600', in J. Barrett and D. Orton, eds., *Cod and Herring: the Archaeology and History of Medieval Sea Fishing* (Oxford, 2016), pp. 13–22. **42.** Gade, *Hanseatic Control*, pp. 17–18. **43.** Schildhauer et al., *Die Hanse*, pp. 99–100. **44.** A. R. Bridbury, *England and the Salt Trade in the Later Middle Ages* (Oxford, 1955), pp. 94–8. **45.** A. de Oliveira Marques, *Hansa e Portugal na Idade Média* (Lisbon, 1993).

23. Stockfish and Spices

1. H. Spruyt, *The Sovereign State and Its Competitors: an Analysis of Systems Change* (Princeton, 1994), pp. 109–29; T. Brady, *Turning Swiss: Cities and Empire, 1450–1550*

(Cambridge, 1985). 2. P. Dollinger, *The German Hansa* (London, 1970), pp. 62–3. 3. Ibid., pp. 88–93. 4. Ibid., pp. ix–x. 5. Ibid., p. 91. 6. V. Etting, *Queen Margarete, 1353–1412, and the Founding of the Nordic Union* (Leiden, 2004). 7. M. Puhle, *Die Vitalienbrüder: Klaus Störtebeker und die Seeräuber der Hanse* (Frankfurt-am-Main, 1992). 8. Dollinger, *German Hansa*, p. 96. 9. W. Stieda, *Hildebrand Veckinchusen: Briefwechsel eines deutschen Kaufmanns im 15. Jahrhundert* (Leipzig, 1921); M. Lesnikov, *Die Handelsbücher des Hansischen Kaufmannes Veckinchusen* (Berlin, 1973); M. Lesnikov and W. Stark, *Die Handelsbücher des Hildebrand Veckinchusen* (Cologne, 2013); A. Lorenz-Ridderbecks, *Krisenhandel und Ruin des Hansekaufmanns Hildebrand Veckinchusen im späten Mittelalter: Untersuchung des Briefwechsels (1417–1428)* (Hamburg, 2014), pp. 13, 15, 27, 32–3; G. Graichen et al., *Die Deutsche Hanse: eine heimliche Supermacht* (Reinbek bei Hamburg, 2011), pp. 222, 233 (illustrating the chest full of pepper). 10. Graichen et al., *Die Deutsche Hanse*, p. 223. 11. Ibid., p. 227; Lorenz-Ridderbecks, *Krisenhandel und Ruin*, p. 25. 12. A. Vandewalle, *Hanze@M€dici: Bruges, Crossroads of European Cultures* (Oostkamp, 2002), pp. 48–9 and accompanying map. 13. J. van Houtte, *Bruges: essai d'histoire urbaine* (Brussels, 1967), p. 90. 14. Graichen et al., *Die Deutsche Hanse*, pp. 231–2. 15. Van Houtte, *Bruges*, pp. 41, 57–8; J. Murray, *Bruges, Cradle of Capitalism, 1280–1390* (Cambridge, 2005), pp. 244–5. 16. J. and F. Gies, *Merchants and Moneymen: the Commercial Revolution, 1000–1500* (London, 1972), pp. 199–202, 205. 17. Graichen et al., *Die Deutsche Hanse*, p. 229. 18. J. Martin, *Treasure in the Land of Darkness: the Fur Trade and Its Significance for Medieval Russia* (Cambridge, 1986). 19. Graichen et al., *Die Deutsche Hanse*, p. 234. 20. Gies, *Merchants and Moneymen*, p. 206. 21. P. Lantschner, *The Logic of Political Conflict in Medieval Cities: Italy and the Southern Low Countries, 1370–1440* (Oxford, 2015). 22. Gies, *Merchants and Moneymen*, pp. 206–8, 211. 23. Ibid., p. 209; Graichen et al., *Die Deutsche Hanse*, pp. 235–6; Lorenz-Ridderbecks, *Krisenhandel und Ruin*, pp. 33–40. 24. Dollinger, *German Hansa*, p. 216. 25. Gies, *Merchants and Moneymen*, pp. 210–11; Graichen et al., *Die Deutsche Hanse*, p. 239. 26. Gies, *Merchants and Moneymen*, p. 214; Graichen et al., *Die Deutsche Hanse*, pp. 240–42; Lorenz-Ridderbecks, *Krisenhandel und Ruin*, pp. 69–95. 27. In modern German: *Gott erbarme, daß es mit Dir so gekommen ist*: Lorenz-Ridderbecks, *Krisenhandel und Ruin*, p. 13. 28. Dollinger, *German Hansa*, pp. 165–6, 173–6; Gies, *Merchants and Moneymen*, pp. 209–14. 29. K. Helle, 'The Emergence of the Town of Bergen in the Light of the Latest Research Results', in A. Graßmann, ed., *Das Hansische Kontor zu Bergen und die Lübecker Bergenfahrer – International Workshop Lübeck 2003* (Lübeck, 2005), pp. 12–27; also A. Nedkvitne, *The German Hansa and Bergen 1100–1600* (Cologne, 2013). 30. A. Liestol, 'The Runes from Bergen: Voices from the Middle Ages', *Minnesota History*, vol. 40 (1966), part 2, pp. 49–58. 31. Cited from the *Sverre Saga*, ch. 104, in J. Gade, *The Hanseatic Control of Norwegian Commerce during the Late Middle Ages* (Leiden, 1951), pp. 30–31. 32. Text in Gade, *Hanseatic Control*, pp. 38–41. 33. Ibid., p. 30 n. 1. 34. Ibid., p. 55. 35. G. A. Ersland, 'Was the Kontor in Bergen a Topographically Closed Entity?', in Graßmann, ed., *Das Hansische Kontor zu Bergen*, pp. 41–57; Gade, *Hanseatic Control*, p. 51. 36. David Abulafia, *The Great Sea: a Human History of the Mediterranean* (London, 2011), pp. 298–9. 37. Ersland, 'Was the Kontor?', pp. 47, 53. 38. Gade, *Hanseatic Control*, pp. 74–7, 80–81.

24. The English Challenge

1. P. D. A. Harvey, 'The English Inflation of 1180–1220', *Past and Present*, no. 61 (1973), pp. 26–7. 2. T. H. Lloyd, *England and the German Hanse 1157–1611: a Study of Their Trade and Diplomacy* (Cambridge, 1991), p. 15; T. H. Lloyd, *Alien Merchants in England in the High Middle Ages* (Brighton, 1982), pp. 128–9. 3. P. Richards, 'The Hinterland and Overseas Trade of King's Lynn 1205–1537: an Introduction', in K. Friedland and P. Richards, eds., *Essays in Hanseatic History: the King's Lynn Symposium 1998* (Dereham, Norfolk, 2005), pp. 10–21. 4. Lloyd, *Alien Merchants*, pp. 130–31. 5. Lloyd, *England and the*

German Hanse, pp. 23–31. **6.** G. Cushway, *Edward III and the War at Sea, 1327–1377* (Woodbridge, 2011). **7.** Lloyd, *England and the German Hanse*, pp. 73, 89; S. Jenks, 'Lynn and the Hanse: Trade and Relations in the Middle Ages', in Friedland and Richards, eds., *Essays in Hanseatic History*, pp. 101–3. **8.** E. Carus-Wilson, 'Trends in the Export of English Woollens in the Fourteenth Century', in E. Carus-Wilson, *Medieval Merchant Venturers: Collected Studies* (2nd edn, London, 1967), pp. 239–64; J. Fudge, *Cargoes, Embargoes, and Emissaries: the Commercial and Political Interaction of England and the German Hanse 1450–1510* (Toronto, 1995), p. 5. **9.** Richards, 'Hinterland and Overseas Trade', p. 19; W. Stark, 'English Merchants in Danzig', in Friedland and Richards, eds., *Essays in Hanseatic History*, pp. 64–6; Fudge, *Cargoes, Embargoes*, p. 10. **10.** E. Christiansen, *The Northern Crusades* (2nd edn, London, 1997), pp. 156–7; Lloyd, *England and the German Hanse*, pp. 131–2; Fudge, *Cargoes, Embargoes*, pp. 7–9. **11.** M. Burleigh, *Prussian Society and the German Order: an Aristocratic Corporation in Crisis c.1410–1466* (Cambridge, 1984); Lloyd, *England and the German Hanse*, pp. 178–9; M. M. Postan, 'The Economic and Political Relations of England and the Hanse from 1400 to 1475', in M. M. Postan and E. Power, eds., *Studies in English Trade in the Fifteenth Century* (London, 1933), pp. 91–153; S. Jenks, *England, die Hanse und Preußen: Handel und Diplomatie 1377–1474* (3 vols., Cologne, 1992). **12.** Fudge, *Cargoes, Embargoes*, pp. 66–74. **13.** E. Carus-Wilson, 'The Overseas Trade of Bristol in the Fifteenth Century', in Carus-Wilson, *Medieval Merchant Venturers*, pp. 1–97; also Carus-Wilson, 'The Iceland Venture', ibid., pp. 98–142. **14.** Fudge, *Cargoes, Embargoes*, pp. 144–51. **15.** Cited in Jenks, 'Lynn and the Hanse', p. 103; Fudge, *Cargoes, Embargoes*, pp. 74, 109–10. **16.** D. Pifarré Torres, *El comerç internacional de Barcelona i el Mar del Nord (Bruges) a Finals del segle XIV* (Montserrat, 2002); J. Hinojosa Montalvo, *De Valencia a Flandes: la nave della frutta* (Valencia, 2007). **17.** A. Ruddock, *Italian Merchants and Shipping in Southampton, 1270–1600* (Southampton, 1951); D. Abulafia, 'Cittadino e denizen: mercanti mediterranei a Southampton e a Londra', in M. del Treppo, ed., *Sistema di rapporti ed élites economiche in Europa (secoli XII–XVII)* (Naples, 1994), pp. 273–91, repr. in D. Abulafia, *Mediterranean Encounters, Economic, Religious, Political, 1100–1550* (Aldershot, 2000), essay VII. **18.** C. Platt, *Medieval Southampton: the Port and the Trading Community, A.D. 1000–1600* (London, 1973), pp. 262–3. **19.** B. Kedar, *Merchants in Crisis: Genoese and Venetian Men of Affairs and the Fourteenth-Century Depression* (New Haven, 1976), pp. 31–7; P. Strohm, 'Trade, Treason and the Murder of Janus Imperial', *Journal of British Studies*, vol. 35 (1996), pp. 1–23. **20.** Abulafia, 'Cittadino e denizen', pp. 278–9; Platt, *Medieval Southampton*, pp. 229–30; Ruddock, *Italian Merchants*, pp. 183–5. **21.** Lloyd, *Alien Merchants*, p. 163. **22.** W. Childs, *Anglo-Castilian Trade in the Later Middle Ages* (Manchester, 1978); T. Ruiz, 'Castilian Merchants in England, 1248–1350', in W. C. Jordan, B. McNab and T. Ruiz, eds., *Order and Innovation in the Middle Ages: Essays in Honor of Joseph R. Strayer* (Princeton, 1976), pp. 173–85; Lloyd, *Alien Merchants*, pp. 164–5. **23.** E. Ferreira Priegue, *Galicia en el comercio marítimo medieval* (Santiago de Compostela, 1988). **24.** Childs, *Anglo-Castilian Trade*, pp. 227–30. **25.** G. Warner, ed., *The Libelle of Englyshe Polycye: a Poem on the Use of Sea-Power, 1436* (Oxford, 1926), p. 4. **26.** V. Kostić, *Dubrovnik i Engleska, 1300–1650* (Belgrade, 1975), pp. 113, 572, 576. **27.** M. Pratt, *Winchelsea: the Tale of a Medieval Town* (Bexhill-on-Sea, 2005), pp. 41–50. **28.** Ibid., p. 131. **29.** Ibid., pp. 95–8, 112. **30.** Ibid., p. 78. **31.** Carus-Wilson, *Medieval Merchant Venturers*, p. 2. **32.** T. O'Neill, *Merchants and Mariners in Medieval Ireland* (Dublin, 1987), pp. 29, 67–8, 108; Carus-Wilson, *Medieval Merchant Venturers*, pp. 13–28. **33.** Carus-Wilson, *Medieval Merchant Venturers*, pp. 5–11. **34.** A. Crawford, *Bristol and the Wine Trade* (Bristol, 1984); M. K. James, *Studies in the Medieval Wine Trade* (Oxford, 1971). **35.** J. Bernard, *Navires et gens de mer à Bordeaux (vers 1400–vers 1500)* (3 vols., Paris, 1968); Carus-Wilson, *Medieval Merchant Venturers*, pp. 32–6. **36.** Carus-Wilson, *Medieval Merchant Venturers*, p. 43. **37.** M. Barkham, 'The Offshore and Distant-Water Fisheries of the Spanish Basques, c.1500–1650', in D. Starkey, J. Þór and I. Heidbrink, eds., *A History of the North Atlantic Fisheries*, vol. 1: *From Early Times to the mid-Nineteenth Century* (Bremerhaven, 2009), pp. 229–49; J. Proulx, 'The Presence of Basques in Labrador in the 16th Century', in R. Grenier, M.-A.

Bernier and W. Stevens, eds., *The Underwater Archaeology of Red Bay: Basque Shipbuilding and Whaling in the 16th Century* (5 vols., Ottawa, 2007), vol. 1: *Archaeology Underwater: the Project*, pp. 25–42.   **38.** See the twelve first-class essays in E. Jones and R. Stone, eds., *The World of the Newport Medieval Ship: Trade, Politics and Shipping in the mid-Fifteenth Century* (Cardiff, 2018).   **39.** Carus-Wilson, *Medieval Merchant Venturers*, pp. 47–9, 53–4, 58–64; I. Sanderson, *A History of Whaling* (New York, 1993), pp. 136–41.   **40.** B. Little and J. Sansom, *The Story of Bristol from the Middle Ages to Today* (3rd edn, Wellington, Somerset, 2003), pp. 14–15; Carus-Wilson, *Medieval Merchant Venturers*, pp. 80–81.   **41.** S. Jenks, *Robert Sturmy's Commercial Expedition to the Mediterranean (1457/8)* (Bristol, 2006).   **42.** Carus-Wilson, *Medieval Merchant Venturers*, pp. 67–8.   **43.** D. H. Sacks, *The Widening Gate: Bristol and the Atlantic Economy, 1450–1700* (Berkeley and Los Angeles, 1991), p. 33; Carus-Wilson, *Medieval Merchant Venturers*, pp. 70–71.   **44.** B. Gelsinger, *Icelandic Enterprise: Commerce and Economy in the Middle Ages* (Columbia, SC, 1981), p. 190.   **45.** Cited in Carus-Wilson, *Medieval Merchant Venturers*, p. 111, and in Gelsinger, *Icelandic Enterprise*, p. 192.   **46.** Carus-Wilson, *Medieval Merchant Venturers*, pp. 101, 103–4, 110–13.   **47.** Ibid., pp. 113, 115, 118–20, 125, 131, 137.   **48.** Gelsinger, *Icelandic Enterprise*, p. 193; Carus-Wilson, *Medieval Merchant Venturers*, pp. 133–42.   **49.** Cited in D. Quinn, 'The Argument for the English Discovery of America between 1480 and 1494', *Geographical Journal*, vol. 127 (1961), p. 277; for the original text from Archivo General de Simancas, Estado de Castilla, leg. 2, f. 6r–v, see plates between p. 284 and p. 285; J. Williamson, ed., *The Cabot Voyages and Bristol Discovery under Henry VII* (Cambridge, 1962), pp. 30–31; E. Jones and M. Condon, *Cabot and Bristol's Age of Discovery: the Bristol Discovery Voyages 1480–1508* (Bristol, 2016), p. 18.   **50.** Williamson, ed., *Cabot Voyages*, pp. 19–32.   **51.** William of Worcester, *Itinerarium*, ibid., pp. 187–8 (doc. 6).   **52.** Williamson, ed., *Cabot Voyages*, pp. 19–20, 175 (doc. 1, ii).   **53.** Ibid., pp. 188–9 (doc. 7, i and ii); Jones and Condon, *Cabot and Bristol's Age of Discovery*, pp. 15–17.   **54.** Quinn, 'Argument for the English Discovery', pp. 278–9; Carus-Wilson, *Medieval Merchant Venturers*, p. 97 (conflating the two voyages); Williamson, ed., *Cabot Voyages*, pp. 23–4.   **55.** C. Verlinden, *The Beginnings of Modern Colonization* (Ithaca, NY, 1970), pp. 181–95.   **56.** Williamson, ed., *Cabot Voyages*, p. 176 (doc. 1, vi).   **57.** Ibid., pp. 15, 187 (doc. 5); J. Blake, *West Africa: Quest for God and Gold, 1454–1587* (London, 1977), pp. 60–62.

25. Portugal Rising

1. W. Childs, *Trade and Shipping in the Medieval West: Portugal, Castile and England* (Porto, 2013), p. 139.   **2.** A. Christys, *Vikings in the South: Voyages to Iberia and the Mediterranean* (London, 2015), pp. 49–50, 73, 87–8.   **3.** C. Picard, *L'Océan Atlantique musulman de la conquête arabe à l'époque almohade: Navigation et mise en valeur des côtes d'al-Andalus et du Maghreb occidental (Portugal–Espagne–Maroc)* (Paris, 1997), pp. 79–80, 112, 118; also his *Le Portugal musulman (VIIIe–XIIIe siècle): l'Occident d'al-Andalus sous domination islamique* (Paris, 2000).   **4.** Picard, *Océan Atlantique musulman*, pp. 112, 361–3, 375, 434–44, 518.   **5.** Ibid., pp. 39, 42–3, 132–4, 171.   **6.** C. W. David, ed., *De Expugnatione Lyxbonensi: the Conquest of Lisbon* (2nd edn, revised by J. Phillips, New York, 2001).   **7.** Picard, *Océan Atlantique musulman*, pp. 125, 174, 181, 353, 355–6; Picard, *Portugal musulman*, pp. 105, 110; S. Lay, *The Reconquest Kings of Portugal: Political and Cultural Reorientation on the Medieval Frontier* (Basingstoke, 2009), pp. 152–3.   **8.** B. Diffie, *Prelude to Empire: Portugal Overseas before Henry the Navigator* (Lincoln, Neb., 1960), pp. 30, 32–3.   **9.** F. Miranda, *Portugal and the Medieval Atlantic: Commercial Diplomacy, Merchants, and Trade, 1143–1488* (Porto, 2012), pp. 2, 72; T. Viula de Faria, *The Politics of Anglo-Portuguese Relations and Their Protagonists in the Later Middle Ages (c.1369–c.1449)* (D.Phil. thesis, University of Oxford, 2012); V. Shillington and A. Wallis Chapman, *The Commercial Relations of England and Portugal* (London, 1907), pp. 31, 41–5; Childs, *Trade and Shipping*, pp. 83, 109, 113–14.   **10.** Miranda, *Portugal and the Medieval Atlantic*, pp. 65, 161,

183. 11. Cited ibid., p. 64. 12. C. Verlinden, *The Beginnings of Modern Colonization* (Ithaca, NY, 1970), pp. 98–112. 13. F. Themudo Barata, *Navegação, comércio e relações políticas: os portugueses no Mediterrâneo Ocidental (1385–1466)* (Lisbon, 1998); J. Heers, 'L'Expansion maritime portugaise à la fin du Moyen-Âge: la Méditerranée', *Actas do III Colóquio internacional de estudios luso-brasileiros* (Lisbon, 1960), vol. 2, pp. 138–47, repr. in J. Heers, *Société et économie à Gênes (XIVe–XVe siècles)* (London, 1979), essay III; H. Ferhat, *Sabta des origines au XIVe siècle* (Rabat 1993; repr. with new pagination, Rabat, 2014). 14. E. Ferreira Priegue, *Galicia en el comercio marítimo medieval* (Santiago de Compostela, 1988); J. Heers, 'Le Commerce des Basques en Méditerranée au XVe siècle (d'après les archives de Gênes)', *Bulletin Hispanique*, vol. 57 (1955), pp. 292–324. 15. F. Fernández-Armesto, 'Atlantic Exploration before Columbus: the Evidence of Maps', *Renaissance and Modern Studies*, vol. 30 (1986), pp. 12–34, repr. in F. Fernández-Armesto, ed., *The European Opportunity: an Expanding World* (Aldershot, 1995), vol. 2, pp. 278–300. 16. D. Abulafia, *The Discovery of Mankind: Atlantic Encounters in the Age of Columbus* (New Haven, 2008), p. 34. 17. Dante Alighieri, *Divina Commedia*, 'Purgatorio', canto 26, verses 133–5; T. Cachey, *Le Isole Fortunate: appunti di storia letteraria italiana* (Rome, 1995), p. 18. 18. Abulafia, *Discovery of Mankind*, pp. 49–64. 19. Giovanni Boccaccio, *De Canaria*, in M. Pastore Stocchi, 'Il "De Canaria" boccaccesco e un locus deperditus nel "De Insulis" di Domenico Silvestri', *Rinascimento*, vol. 10 (1959), pp. 153–6. 20. Boccaccio, *De Canaria*, p. 155. 21. Abulafia, *Discovery of Mankind*, pp. 65–7; F. Fernández-Armesto, *Before Columbus: Exploration and Colonization from the Mediterranean to the Atlantic, 1229–1492* (London, 1987), pp. 153–9; A. Rumeu de Armas, *El obispado de Telde: misioneros mallorquines y catalanes en el Atlántico* (2nd edn, Madrid and Telde, 1986); J. Muldoon, *Popes, Lawyers and Infidels: the Church and the non-Christian world, 1250–1500* (Liverpool, 1979). 22. Abulafia, *Discovery of Mankind*, pp. 42–4. 23. M. Adhikari, 'Europe's First Settler Colonial Incursion into Africa: the Genocide of Aboriginal Canary Islanders', *African Historical Review*, vol. 49 (2017), pp. 1–26. 24. Fernández-Armesto, *Before Columbus*, pp. 158, 167. 25. Ferhat, *Sabta*, pp. 19–28 (old edn), pp. 17–25 (new edn); L. Miguel Duarte, *Ceuta 1415* (Lisbon, 2015), pp. 132–9; A. Unali, *Ceuta 1415* (Rome, 2000). 26. D. Abulafia, *The Two Italies: Economic Relations between the Norman Kingdom of Sicily and the Northern Communes* (Cambridge, 1977). 27. C. R. and W. D. Phillips, *Spain's Golden Fleece: Wool Production and the Wool Trade from the Middle Ages to the Nineteenth Century* (Baltimore, 1997). 28. F. Miranda, 'Os antecedentes económicos da conquista de Ceuta de 1415 reavaliados', *Congreso Internacional: Los orígines de la expansión europea: Ceuta 1415; VI Centenario de la Toma de Ceuta, Ceuta 1, 2 y 3 de octubre de 2015* (Ceuta, 2019); C. Gozalbes Cravioto, *Ceuta en los portulanos medievales, siglos XIII, XIV y XV* (Ceuta, 1997). 29. *Ceuta en el Medievo: la ciudad en el mundo árabe. II. Jornadas de historia de Ceuta* (Ceuta, 2002); M. Chérif, *Ceuta aux époques almohade et mérinide* (Paris, 1996). 30. D. Abulafia, *Frederick II: a Medieval Emperor* (London, 1988), p. 258. 31. Unali, *Ceuta 1415*, pp. 198–200. 32. Ibid., pp. 192–8. 33. Gomes Eanes de Zurara, *Crónica da Tomada de Ceuta* (Mem Martins, 1992), pp. 44–63. 34. King Duarte I, cited by P. Russell, *Prince Henry 'the Navigator': a Life* (New Haven and London, 2000), p. 40. 35. Ibid., p. 44. 36. Duarte, *Ceuta 1415*, pp. 88–90. 37. Russell, *Prince Henry*, pp. 49, 51–2. 38. P. Drumond Braga, *Uma lança em África: História da conquista de Ceuta* (Lisbon, 2015), p. 58. 39. Luis Vaz de Camões, *The Lusiads*, transl. L. White (Oxford, 1997), canto 4:49, p. 86. See also e.g. D. Nobre Santos, *Povoamento da ilha da Madeira e o sentido ecuménico da cultura lusíada* (Estudos Gerais Universitários de Angola, Sá da Bandeira, Angola, 1966). 40. B. Rogerson, *The Last Crusaders: the Hundred-Year Battle for the Centre of the World* (London, 2009), pp. 399–402. 41. Russell, *Prince Henry*, pp. 120, 291–2.

26. Virgin Islands

1. S. Halikowski Smith, 'The Mid-Atlantic Islands: a Theatre of Early Modern Ecocide?', *International Review of Social History*, vol. 55 (2010), Supplement, p. 52. 2. R. Carita,

História da Madeira (1420–1566): Povoamento e produção açucareira (Funchal, 1989), pp. 35–9; F. Fernández-Armesto, *Before Columbus: Exploration and Colonization from the Mediterranean to the Atlantic, 1229–1492* (London, 1987), pp. 195–6. 3. C. Verlinden, *The Beginnings of Modern Colonization* (Ithaca, NY, 1970), pp. 206–19. 4. P. Russell, *Prince Henry 'the Navigator': a Life* (New Haven and London, 2000), pp. 94, 98. 5. Ibid., p. 91; J. H. Parry, *The Discovery of the Sea* (2nd edn, Berkeley and Los Angeles, 1991), p. 97. 6. Halikowski Smith, 'Mid-Atlantic Islands', pp. 51–77. 7. A. da Cà da Mosto (Cadamosto), *The Voyages of Cadamosto and Other Documents on Western Africa in the Second Half of the Fifteenth Century*, ed. C. R. Crone (London, 1937), ch. 6, p. 9; Fernández-Armesto, *Before Columbus*, pp. 198–9. 8. D. Abulafia, 'Sugar in Spain', *European Review*, vol. 16 (2008), pp. 191–210. 9. V. Rau, 'The Madeiran Sugar Cane Plantations', in H. Johnson, ed., *From Reconquest to Empire: the Iberian Background to Latin American History* (New York, 1970), p. 75. 10. A. Vieira, 'Sugar Islands: the Sugar Economy of Madeira and the Canaries, 1450–1650', in S. Schwartz, ed., *Tropical Babylons: Sugar and the Making of the Atlantic World, 1450–1680* (Chapel Hill, 2004), pp. 42–84. 11. Carita, *História da Madeira*, p. 92. 12. Halikowski Smith, 'Mid-Atlantic Islands', p. 61. 13. Fernández-Armesto, *Before Columbus*, pp. 159–66. 14. R. Fuson, *Legendary Islands of the Ocean Sea* (Sarasota, 1995), pp. 44–55, 103–17; D. Johnson, *Phantom Islands of the Atlantic* (London, 1997), pp. 91–128. 15. Russell, *Prince Henry*, pp. 102–3. 16. Fernández-Armesto, *Before Columbus*, pp. 199–200; D. Birmingham, *Trade and Empire in the Atlantic, 1400–1600* (London, 2000), pp. 14–15. 17. Parry, *Discovery of the Sea*, p. 99; Halikowski Smith, 'Mid-Atlantic Islands', pp. 61–2. 18. Verlinden, *Beginnings of Modern Colonization*, pp. 220–27; A. Vieira, *O comércio inter-insular nos séculos XV e XVI: Madeira, Açores e Canárias* (Funchal, 1987). 19. *Angra, a Terceira e os Açores nas rotas da Índia e das Américas* (Angra do Heroísmo, 1999). 20. Verlinden, *Beginnings of Modern Colonization*, pp. 161–80; A. Peluffo, ed., *Antonio de Noli e l'inizio delle scoperte del Nuovo Mondo* (Noli, 2013; online English edition: M. Ferrado de Noli, ed., *Antonio de Noli and the Beginnings of the New World*), though some articles are tendentious. 21. A. Leão Silva, *Histórias de um Sahel Insular* (Praia, 1995); J. Blake, ed., *Europeans in West Africa (1450–1560): Documents to Illustrate the Nature and Scope of Portuguese Enterprise in West Africa* (2 vols., London, 1942); Halikowski Smith, 'Mid-Atlantic Islands', pp. 73–4. 22. T. Green, *The Rise of the Trans-Atlantic Slave Trade in Western Africa, 1300–1589* (Cambridge, 2012), pp. 95–115; T. Hall, ed. and transl., *Before Middle Passage: Translated Portuguese Manuscripts of Atlantic Slave Trading from West Africa to Iberian Territories, 1513–26* (Farnham, 2015). 23. Examples may be seen in the Ethnographic Museum in Praia, Santiago. 24. Green, *Rise of the Trans-Atlantic Slave Trade*, pp. 99–100; cotton: Hall, ed. and transl., *Before Middle Passage*, pp. 36, 149, 180, 213. 25. A. Carreira, *Cabo Verde: Formação e Extinção de uma Sociaedade escarvorata (1460–1878)* (3rd edn, Praia de Santiago, 2000). 26. C. Evans, M. L. Stig Sørensen and K. Richter, 'An Early Christian Church in the Tropics: Excavation of the N.ª S.ª de Conceição, Cidade Velha, Cape Verde', in T. Green, ed., *Brokers of Change: Atlantic Commerce and Cultures in Precolonial Western Africa* (*Proceedings of the British Academy*, vol. 178 (2012), pp. 173–92. 27. Hall, ed. and transl., *Before Middle Passage*, p. 15; T. Green, *Masters of Difference: Creolization and the Jewish Presence in Cabo Verde 1497–1672* (Ph.D. dissertation, University of Birmingham, 2007), p. 74; Green, *Rise of the Trans-Atlantic Slave Trade*, p. 98; Evans et al., 'An Early Christian Church in the Tropics', pp. 175–6; Catalans in the Atlantic: I. Armenteros Martínez, *Cataluña en la era de las navegaciones: la participación catalana en la primera economía atlántica (c.1470–1540)* (Barcelona, 2012). 28. T. Green, 'The Export of Rice and Millet from Upper Guinea into the Sixteenth-Century Atlantic Trade', in R. Law, S. Schwarz and S. Strickrodt, eds., *Commercial Agriculture, the Slave Trade and Slavery in Atlantic Africa* (Woodbridge, 2013), pp. 79–97; T. Hall, 'Portuguese Archival Documentation of Europe's First Colony in the Tropics: the Cape Verde Islands, 1460–1530', in L. McCrank, ed., *Discovery in the Archives of Spain and Portugal: Quincentenary Essays, 1492–1992* (New York, 1993), p. 389. 29. T. Hall, *The Role of Cape Verde Islanders in Organizing and Operating Maritime Trade between West Africa and Iberian Territories, 1441–1616* (Ph.D. dissertation, Johns Hopkins University, Baltimore, 1992, distributed by University Microfilms International, 1992),

p. 234; Hall, ed. and transl., *Before Middle Passage*, pp. 266, 275–6; Green, *Rise of the Trans-Atlantic Slave Trade*, p. 101.   **30.** I. Cabral, *A primeira elite colonial atlântica: dos 'homens honrados brancos' de Santiago à 'Nobreza da Terra', finais do séc. V–início do séc. XVII* (Praia, 2015); Z. Cohen, *Os filhos da folha (Cabo Verde – séculos XV–XVIII)* (Praia, 2007); Green, *Rise of the Trans-Atlantic Slave Trade*, pp. 103–7.   **31.** *História geral do Cabo Verde* (Lisbon and Praia de Santiago, 1991), vol. 1, pp. 264–7, 276–9; Hall, ed. and transl., *Before Middle Passage*, pp. 84–5.   **32.** *História geral do Cabo Verde, corpo documental* (Lisbon, 1988–90), vol. 2, pp. 234–8; Hall, ed. and transl., *Before Middle Passage*, pp. 185–91.   **33.** M. L. Stig Sørensen, C. Evans and K. Richter, 'A Place of History: Archaeology and Heritage at Cidade Velha, Cape Verde', in P. Lane and K. McDonald, eds., *Slavery in Africa: Archaeology and Memory (Proceedings of the British Academy*, vol. 168, 2011), pp. 421–42; 'A Place of Arrivals: Forging a Nation's Identity at Cidade Velha', *World Archaeology Magazine*, no. 75 (2016), pp. 32–6.   **34.** D. Blumenthal, *Enemies and Familiars: Slavery and Mastery in Fifteenth-Century Valencia* (Ithaca, NY, 2009).   **35.** J. Vogt, *Portuguese Rule on the Gold Coast 1469–1692* (Athens, Ga., 1979), pp. 19–92; P. E. H. Hair, *The Founding of the Castelo de São Jorge de Mina: an Analysis of the Sources* (Madison, 1994); C. DeCorse, *An Archaeology of Elmina: Africans and Europeans on the Gold Coast, 1400–1900* (Washington DC, 2006); A. Ryder, *Benin and the Europeans, 1485–1897* (London, 1969), pp. 42–5.   **36.** I. Batista de Sousa, *São Tomé et Príncipe de 1485 à 1755: une société coloniale, de Blanc à Noir* (Paris, 2008), p. 17; G. Seibert, 'São Tomé & Príncipe: the First Plantation Economy in the Tropics', in R. Law, S. Schwarz and S. Strickrodt, eds., *Commercial Agriculture, the Slave Trade and Slavery in Atlantic Africa* (Woodbridge, 2013), pp. 54–78.   **37.** R. Garfield, *A History of São Tomé Island, 1470–1655: the Key to Guinea* (San Francisco, 1992), p. 64.   **38.** Seibert, 'São Tomé & Príncipe', pp. 60–61.   **39.** Batista de Souza, *São Tomé*, pp. 21, 23; Garfield, *History of São Tomé*, pp. 31, 35–6.   **40.** I. Castro Henriques, *São Tomé e Príncipe: a invenção de uma sociedade* (Lisbon, 2000), p. 34.   **41.** F. Soyer, *The Persecution of the Jews and Muslims of Portugal: King Manuel I and the End of Religious Tolerance (1496–7)* (Leiden, 2007).   **42.** Blake, ed., *Europeans in West Africa*, vol. 1, doc. 9, pp. 86–7.   **43.** Seibert, 'São Tomé & Príncipe', p. 58.   **44.** Samuel Usque, *Consolation for the Tribulations of Israel*, transl. M. Cohen (Philadelphia, 1965), pp. 201–2; Isaac Abravanel, *Commentary to Exodus* (Jerusalem, 1984), p. 67, cited by D. E. Cohen, *The Biblical Exegesis of Don Isaac Abrabanel* (Ph.D. dissertation, School of Oriental and African Studies, University of London, 2015), pp. 120, 428.   **45.** Garfield, *History of São Tomé*, pp. 65, 71–2, 85; R. Garfield, 'Public Christians, Secret Jews: Religion and Political Conflict on São Tomé in the Sixteenth and Seventeenth Centuries', *The Sixteenth Century Journal*, vol. 21 (1990), pp. 645–54; Batista de Sousa, *São Tomé*, pp. 50–56; Henriques, *São Tomé e Príncipe*, pp. 63–92.   **46.** Garfield, *History of São Tomé*, p. 31.   **47.** Blake, ed., *Europeans in West Africa*, vol. 1, pp. 89–90.   **48.** Ryder, *Benin*, pp. 42–3 n. 4, 55.   **49.** Vogt, *Portuguese Rule*, pp. 38, 46–7, 57–8, 72–3.   **50.** D. Abulafia, *The Discovery of Mankind: Atlantic Encounters in the Age of Columbus* (New Haven, 2008), pp. 145–61; R. Kowner, *From White to Yellow: the Japanese in European Racial Thought, 1300–1735* (Montreal, 2014), pp. 50–51.   **51.** S. E. Morison, *Portuguese Voyages to America in the Fifteenth Century* (Cambridge, Mass., 1940).   **52.** Verlinden, *Beginnings of Modern Colonization*, pp. 181–95; Morison, *Portuguese Voyages to America*, pp. 44–50.

27. Guinea Gold and Guinea Slaves

1. Text from Zurara in M. Newitt, ed., *The Portuguese in West Africa, 1415–1670: a Documentary History* (Cambridge, 2010), doc. 35, pp. 149–50.   **2.** A. Saunders, *A Social History of Black Slaves and Freedmen in Portugal 1441–1555* (Cambridge, 1982), pp. 38–9.   **3.** D. Abulafia, *The Discovery of Mankind: Atlantic Encounters in the Age of Columbus* (New Haven, 2008), pp. 39, 43.   **4.** T. Hall, ed. and transl., *Before Middle Passage: Translated Portuguese Manuscripts of Atlantic Slave Trading From West Africa to Iberian Territories, 1513–26* (Farnham, 2015), p. 52, also pp. 43, 45, 65.   **5.** R. Collins and J. Burns, *A History of*

Sub-Saharan Africa (2nd edn, Cambridge, 2014), pp. 78–95; B. Davidson, *West Africa before the Colonial Era: a History to 1850* (Harlow, 1998); N. Levtzion, *Ancient Ghana and Mali* (London, 1973).   6. E. Bovill, *The Golden Trade of the Moors* (2nd edn, Oxford, 1970); Levtzion, *Ancient Ghana and Mali*, pp. 81–4; M. Gomez, *African Dominion: a New History of Empire in Early and Medieval West Africa* (Princeton, 2018).   7. J. Day, 'The Great Bullion Famine of the Fifteenth Century', *Past and Present*, no. 79 (1978), pp. 3–54.   8. S. Stantchev, *Spiritual Rationality: Papal Embargo as Cultural Practice* (Oxford, 2015).   9. J. H. Parry, *The Discovery of the Sea* (2nd edn, Berkeley and Los Angeles, 1991), pp. 99–100; J. Vogt, *Portuguese Rule on the Gold Coast 1469–1692* (Athens, Ga., 1979), p. 4.   10. Newitt, ed., *Portuguese in West Africa*, p. 47 n. 3.   11. J. Correia, *L'Implantation de la ville portugaise en Afrique du Nord de la prise de Ceuta jusqu'au milieu du XVIe siècle* (Porto, 2008; also published in a parallel Portuguese edition).   12. Newitt, ed., *Portuguese in West Africa*, pp. 148–50, doc. 35.   13. Vogt, *Portuguese Rule*, p. 7.   14. Hall, ed. and transl., *Before Middle Passage*, pp. 29–31.   15. A. da Cà da Mosto (Cadamosto), *The Voyages of Cadamosto and Other Documents on Western Africa in the Second Half of the Fifteenth Century*, ed. C. R. Crone (London, 1937), in Newitt, ed., *Portuguese in West Africa*, pp. 67–71, doc. 16.   16. Hall, ed. and transl., *Before Middle Passage*, p. 36.   17. Ibid., p. 39; T. Green, *Rise of the Trans-Atlantic Slave Trade in Western Africa, 1300–1589* (Cambridge, 2012), p. 248.   18. Hall, ed. and transl., *Before Middle Passage*, p. 227.   19. Ibid., pp. 5, 36, 222; C. Evans, M. L. Stig Sørensen and K. Richter, 'An Early Christian Church in the Tropics: Excavation of the N.ª S.ª de Conceição, Cidade Velha, Cape Verde', in T. Green, ed., *Brokers of Change: Atlantic Commerce and Cultures in Precolonial Western Africa* (*Proceedings of the British Academy*, vol. 178 (2012)), pp. 173–92.   20. J. Blake, *West Africa: Quest for God and Gold, 1454–1587* (London, 1977), pp. 32–4, 83.   21. I. Armenteros Martínez, *Cataluña en la era de las navegaciones: la participación catalana en la primera economía atlántica (c.1470–1540)* (Barcelona, 2012), pp. 72–80.   22. C. Verlinden, *The Beginnings of Modern Colonization* (Ithaca, NY, 1970), pp. 176–80.   23. Blake, *West Africa*, pp. 49–55.   24. Abulafia, *Discovery of Mankind*, p. 95; M. Á. Ladero Quesada, *Los últimos años de Fernando el Católico 1505–1517* (Madrid, 2016), p. 167 (1509 confirmation).   25. Vogt, *Portuguese Rule*, pp. 7–9.   26. A. Ryder, *Benin and the Europeans, 1485–1897* (London, 1969).   27. Vogt, *Portuguese Rule*, p. 9.   28. Armenteros Martínez, *Cataluña en la era de las navegaciones*, pp. 77–80.   29. Blake, *West Africa*, p. 37.   30. D. Escudier, ed., *Voyage d'Eustache Delafosse sur la côte de Guinée, au Portugal et en Espagne (1479–1481)* (Paris, 1992), pp. 12–15.   31. Ibid., pp. 16–17.   32. Ibid., pp. 24–5, 28–31.   33. Ibid., pp. 52–65.   34. Blake, *West Africa*, pp. 60–62.   35. P. E. H. Hair, *The Founding of the Castelo de São Jorge da Mina: an Analysis of the Sources* (Madison, 1994), p. 5.   36. C. Antero Ferreira, *Castelo da Mina: da fundação às representações iconográficas dos séculos XVI e XVII* (Lisbon, 2007), p. 10.   37. Hair, *Founding of the Castelo*, pp. 7, 10–11.   38. Vogt, *Portuguese Rule*, pp. 20–21; Hair, *Founding of the Castelo*, pp. 14–15.   39. Hair, *Founding of the Castelo*, pp. 15–17; Blake, *West Africa*, p. 99; Parry, *Discovery of the Sea*, p. 108.   40. Hair, *Founding of the Castelo*, pp. 20–31.   41. Pina and Barros in Hair, *Founding of the Castelo*, pp. 22–3, 100–101, 104–5; Pina in Newitt, ed., *Portuguese in West Africa*, pp. 93–4; Vogt, *Portuguese Rule*, p. 25.   42. Vogt, *Portuguese Rule*, pp. 26–31; C. DeCorse, *An Archeology of Elmina: Africans and Europeans on the Gold Coast, 1400–1900* (Washington DC, 2001), pp. 47–9; Blake, *West Africa*, p. 99.   43. DeCorse, *Archeology of Elmina*, pp. 49–51.   44. Vogt, *Portuguese Rule*, pp. 34–5, 38–9.   45. DeCorse, *Archeology of Elmina*, p. 51; Blake, *West Africa*, p. 100.   46. Letter of King João III of 1523 in Newitt, ed., *Portuguese in West Africa*, pp. 96–7, doc. 23.   47. H. Thomas, *The Slave Trade: a History of the Atlantic Slave Trade 1440–1870* (London, 1997), p. 73.   48. Vogt, *Portuguese Rule*, p. 57.   49. Ibid., p. 209.   50. Escudier, ed., *Voyage d'Eustache Delafosse*, pp. 30–31; E. Axelson, *Congo to Cape: Early Portuguese Explorers* (London, 1973), pp. 39, 41; D. Peres, *A History of the Portuguese Discoveries* (Lisbon, 1960), p. 59.   51. Cited by Axelson, *Congo to Cape*, p. 42.   52. C. Marinescu, *La Politique orientale d'Alfonse V d'Aragon roi de Naples (1416–1458)* (Barcelona, 1994), pp. 13–28.   53. Axelson, *Congo to Cape*, pp. 45–6, 50–51.   54. Ibid., p. 61; Peres, *History of the Portuguese Discoveries*, pp. 60–61.   55. J. Manuel Garcia, *Breve história dos descobrimentos e expansão de Portugal* (Lisbon, 1999), p. 50.   56. Axelson, *Congo to Cape*, pp. 63–4; Peres, *History of the*

Portuguese Discoveries, pp. 63–4.   57. Axelson, *Congo to Cape*, pp. 69–76.   58. Peres, *History of the Portuguese Discoveries*, p. 69.   59. Ibid., pp. 69–70.   60. Axelson, *Congo to Cape*, pp. 115–44, also plate vii opposite p. 113.   61. Ibid., p. 179.

PART FOUR

OCEANS IN CONVERSATION

28. The Great Acceleration

1. On Columbus: F. Fernández-Armesto, *Columbus* (Oxford, 1991); W. D. Phillips and C. Phillips, *The Worlds of Christopher Columbus* (Cambridge, 1992); E. Taviani, *Christopher Columbus* (London, 1985); S. E. Morison, *Admiral of the Ocean Sea* (new edn, New York, 1992); V. Flint, *The Imaginative Landscape of Christopher Columbus* (Princeton, 1992).   2. On Cabot: J. Williamson, ed., *The Cabot Voyages and Bristol Discovery under Henry VII* (Cambridge, 1962); J. Williamson, *The Voyages of John and Sebastian Cabot* (London, 1937); P. Pope, *The Many Landfalls of John Cabot* (Toronto, 1997); E. Jones, 'Alwyn Ruddock: "John Cabot and the Discovery of America" ', *Historical Research*, vol. 81 (2008), pp. 224–54; E. Jones and M. Condon, *Cabot and Bristol's Age of Discovery: the Bristol Discovery Voyages 1480–1508* (Bristol, 2016).   3. On Vespucci: L. Formisano, ed., *Letters from a New World: Amerigo Vespucci's Discovery of America* (New York, 1992); F. Fernández-Armesto, *Amerigo: the Man Who Gave His Name to America* (London, 2006).   4. *The World Encompassed by Sir Francis Drake, being his Next Voyage to that to Nombre de Dios formerly imprinted, Carefully collected out of the notes of Master Francis Fletcher* (London, 1628); this phrase is taken as the title of Geoffrey Scammell, *The World Encompassed: the First European Maritime Empires, c. 800–1650* (London, 1981); H. Kelsey, *Juan Rodriguez Cabrillo* (2nd edn, San Marino, Calif.,1998).   5. W. Keegan and C. Hofman, *The Caribbean before Columbus* (Oxford and New York, 2017), p. 23.   6. D. Abulafia, *The Discovery of Mankind: Atlantic Encounters in the Age of Columbus* (New Haven, 2008), pp. 115–30.   7. Keegan and Hofman, *Caribbean before Columbus*, pp. 11–15; P. Siegel, 'Caribbean Archaeology in Historical Perspective', pp. 21–46, and other articles in W. Keegan, C. Hofman and R. Rodríguez Ramos, *The Oxford Handbook of Caribbean Archaeology* (Oxford and New York, 2013); J. Granberry and G. Vescelius, *Languages of the pre-Columbian Antilles* (Tuscaloosa, 2004); F. Moya Pons and R. Flores Paz, eds, *Los Taínos en 1492: el debate demográfico* (Santo Domingo, 2013); I. Rouse, *The Tainos: Rise and Decline of the People Who Greeted Columbus* (New Haven, 1992).   8. S. Wilson, *The Archaeology of the Caribbean* (Cambridge, 2007), pp. 95–136.   9. Abulafia, *Discovery of Mankind*, p. 140; Ramon Pané, *An Account of the Antiquities of the Indians*, ed. J. J. Arrom and transl. S. Griswold (Durham, NC, 1999), ch. 10.   10. Abulafia, *Discovery of Mankind*, p. 181.   11. W. Keegan, *The People Who Discovered Columbus* (Gainesville, 1992), pp. 49–51; also Abulafia, *Discovery of Mankind*, p. 146.   12. Wilson, *Archaeology of the Caribbean*, pp. 137–54.   13. Abulafia, *Discovery of Mankind*, pp. 175–6.   14. Williamson, ed., *Cabot Voyages*, pp. 208–9, no. 23; Abulafia, *Discovery of Mankind*, p. 219.   15. Abulafia, *Discovery of Mankind*, p. 199.   16. D. C. West and A. Kling, eds., *The Libro de las profecías of Christopher Columbus* (Gainesville, 1991).   17. Abulafia, *Discovery of Mankind*, p. 13.   18. Fernández-Armesto, *Columbus*, pp. 17–20.   19. Flint, *Imaginative Landscape*, p. 40, plate 12.   20. Henry Yule and Henri Cordier, transl. and eds., *The Travels of Marco Polo: the Complete Yule–Cordier Edition* (3 vols. bound as 2, New York, 1993), vol. 2, p. 253.   21. Ibid., pp. 253–5.   22. *Focus Behaim-Globus* (2 vols., Nuremberg, 1992); Fernández-Armesto, *Columbus*, p. xxi; Phillips and Phillips, *Worlds of Christopher Columbus*, pp. 79–80.   23. Fernández-Armesto, *Columbus*, p. 1.   24. Jones and Condon, *Cabot and Bristol's Age of Discovery*, p. 21.   25. Fernández-Armesto, *Columbus*, p. 17.   26. C. Varela, *Colombo e i Fiorentini* (Florence, 1991), pp. 55–60.   27. F. Bruscoli, 'John Cabot and His Italian Financiers', *Historical Research*, vol. 85 (2012), pp. 372–93; and Jones and Condon, *Cabot and Bristol's Age of Discovery*, pp. 33–4, both published as part of a wider 'John Cabot Project' at the University

of Bristol. **28.** Varela, *Colombo e i Fiorentini*, pp. 44–100 (pp. 75–81 for Vespucci and Columbus). **29.** Abulafia, *Discovery of Mankind*, p. 28. **30.** Ibid., pp. 105–7. **31.** Fernández-Armesto, *Columbus*, p. 97. **32.** Ibid., pp. 72–94. **33.** Abulafia, *Discovery of Mankind*, p. 238. **34.** Fernández-Armesto, *Columbus*, pp. 102–14. **35.** Abulafia, *Discovery of Mankind*, pp. 216–17. **36.** Fernández-Armesto, *Columbus*, pp. 124–51. **37.** E. Mira Caballos, *La gran armada colonizadora de Nicolás de Ovando, 1501–1502* (Santo Domingo, 2014). **38.** C. Jant, ed., *The Four Voyages of Columbus* (2 vols., London, 1929–32), vol.2, pp. 90–93. **39.** Fernández-Armesto, *Columbus*, pp. 161–83. **40.** Abulafia, *Discovery of Mankind*, p. 112. **41.** C. Varela, *La caída de Cristóbal Colón: el juicio de Bobadilla* (Madrid, 2006); Pané, *Account of the Antiquities of the Indians*. **42.** C. Rogers, 'Christopher Who?', *History Today*, vol. 67 (August 2017), pp. 38–49; Keegan and Hofman, *Caribbean before Columbus*, pp. 8, 14. **43.** Abulafia, *Discovery of Mankind*, pp. 190–92. **44.** Ibid., pp. 13, 179. **45.** E. Jones, 'The *Matthew* of Bristol and the Financiers of John Cabot's 1497 Voyage to North America', *English Historical Review*, vol. 121 (2006), pp. 778–95; Williamson, ed., *Cabot Voyages*, p. 206, nos. 19–20; A. Williams, *John Cabot and Newfoundland* (St John's, Nfdl., 1996); J. Butman and S. Targett, *New World, Inc.: How England's Merchants Founded America and Launched the British Empire* (London, 2018), pp. 25–7. **46.** Jones, 'Alwyn Ruddock', pp. 230–31. **47.** Ibid., pp. 224–6, 253–4. **48.** N. Wey Gómez, *The Tropics of Empire: Why Columbus Sailed South to the Indies* (Cambridge, Mass., 2008). **49.** Williamson, ed., *Cabot Voyages*, p. 210, no. 24; Williamson, ibid., p. 41; Jones, 'Alwyn Ruddock', p. 230. **50.** Bruscoli, 'John Cabot and His Italian Financiers'; Jones, 'Alwyn Ruddock', pp. 231–2, 235–6. **51.** Williamson, ed., *Cabot Voyages*, pp. 204–5, no. 18. **52.** Jones and Condon, *Cabot and Bristol's Age of Discovery*, pp. 39–48. **53.** Williamson, ed., *Cabot Voyages*, pp. 208–9, no. 23; Jones and Condon, *Cabot and Bristol's Age of Discovery*, p. 18. **54.** Williamson, ed., *Cabot Voyages*, p. 213, no. 25. **55.** Jones and Condon, *Cabot and Bristol's Age of Discovery*, pp. 49–56. **56.** Williamson, ed., *Cabot Voyages*, p. 220, no. 31 (i); cf. Williamson, *Voyages of John and Sebastian Cabot*, p. 15. **57.** Williamson, ed., *Cabot Voyages*, p. 207, no. 21. **58.** Ibid., p. 233, no. 40; also Williamson, ibid., pp. 109–11; Jones, 'Alwyn Ruddock', pp. 244–5. **59.** Williamson, ed., *Cabot Voyages*, p. 202, no. 15; also Williamson, ibid., pp. 26–9. **60.** S. E. Morison, *Portuguese Voyages to America in the Fifteenth Century* (Cambridge, Mass., 1940), pp. 51–68. **61.** Ibid., pp. 68–72. **62.** Ibid., p. 52; cf. Williamson, *Voyages of John and Sebastian Cabot*, pp. 14–15; Williamson in *Cabot Voyages*, pp. 132–9. **63.** For dubious claims to Danish support, see S. Larsen, *Dinamarca e Portugal no século XV* (Lisbon, 1983).

29. Other Routes to the Indies

1. C. R. Boxer, *The Portuguese Seaborne Empire 1415–1825* (London, 1991), pp. 35–7. **2.** M. Kriegel and S. Subrahmanyam, 'The Unity of Opposites: Abraham Zacut, Vasco da Gama and the Chronicler Gaspar Correia', in A. Disney and E. Booth, eds., *Vasco da Gama and the Linking of Europe and Asia* (New Delhi, 2000), pp. 48–71. **3.** D. Abulafia, *The Discovery of Mankind: Atlantic Encounters in the Age of Columbus* (New Haven, 2008), pp. 24–30. **4.** C. Verlinden, *The Beginnings of Modern Colonization* (Ithaca, NY, 1970), pp. 181–95; S. E. Morison, *Portuguese Voyages to America in the Fifteenth Century* (Cambridge, Mass., 1940), pp. 44–50. **5.** S. Subrahmanyam, *The Career and Legend of Vasco da Gama* (Cambridge, 2007), pp. 54–7. **6.** Popular accounts: R. Watkins, *Unknown Seas: How Vasco da Gama Opened the East* (London, 2003); N. Cliff, *The Last Crusade: the Epic Voyages of Vasco da Gama* (London, 2012); best of all, R. Crowley, *Conquerors: How Portugal Seized the Indian Ocean and Forged the First Global Empire* (London, 2015). **7.** L. Adão da Fonseca, *Vasco da Gama: o Homem, a Viagem, a Época* (Lisbon, 1998), pp. 9–80; G. Ames, *Vasco da Gama: Renaissance Crusader* (New York, 2005), pp. 17–21. **8.** E. Ravenstein, ed., *A Journal of the First Voyage of Vasco da Gama 1497–1499* (new edn with introduction by J. M. Garcia, New Delhi and Madras, 1998), pp. 6–7. **9.** Ibid., pp. 11, 13. **10.** Ibid., pp. 17–20. **11.** Ibid., p. 23. **12.** Ibid., **13.** Ibid., p. 36. **14.** Fonseca, *Vasco da Gama*, pp. 149–52. **15.** Ravenstein, ed., *Journal of the First Voyage*, pp. 48, 53–5; Fonseca, *Vasco da Gama*, pp. 142–3.   **16.** Ravenstein, ed., *Journal of the First Voyage*, pp. 52 n. 3, 53 illustration, 53–4 n. 2, 54 n. 2.   **17.** Ibid., p. 36 n. 1.   **18.** 'Letter of Pedro Vaz de Caminha to King Manuel, 1 May 1500', in W. Greenlee, ed., *The Voyage of Pedro Álvares Cabral to Brazil and India from Contemporary Documents and Narratives* (London, 1938); Morison, *Portuguese Voyages to America*, pp. 119–42.   **19.** Greenlee, ed., *Voyage of Pedro Álvares Cabral*, pp. lxvii–lxix; Crowley, *Conquerors*, pp. 101–17.   **20.** 'Letter of Amerigo Vespucci to Lorenzo de' Medici', in Greenlee, ed., *Voyage of Pedro Álvares Cabral*, pp. 153–61.   **21.** Crowley, *Conquerors*, pp. 113–14; Subrahmanyam, *Career and Legend*, pp. 182–4; Ames, *Vasco da Gama*, pp. 84–5.   **22.** Subrahmanyam, *Career and Legend*, pp. 201–2, 206–10; Ames, *Vasco da Gama*, pp. 86, 89–90.   **23.** Ames, *Vasco da Gama*, pp. 93–4.   **24.** Subrahmanyam, *Career and Legend*, pp. 221–5; Ames, *Vasco da Gama*, pp. 93–100.   **25.** Subrahmanyam, *Career and Legend*, pp. 229–31.   **26.** D. Mearns, D. Parham and B. Frohlich, 'A Portuguese East Indiaman from the 1502–1503 Fleet of Vasco da Gama off Al Hallaniyah Island, Oman: an Interim Report', *International Journal of Nautical Archaeology*, vol. 45 (2016), pp. 331–51.   **27.** Girolamo Priuli cited by Crowley, *Conquerors*, p. 116.   **28.** 'The Diary of Girolamo Priuli', in Greenlee, ed., *Voyage of Pedro Álvares Cabral*, p. 136; also p. 134.   **29.** See also 'Letters sent by Bartolomeo Marchioni to Florence', in Greenlee, ed., *Voyage of Pedro Álvares Cabral*, p. 149.   **30.** K. O'Rourke and J. Williamson, *Did Vasco da Gama Matter for European Markets? Testing Frederick Lane's Hypothesis Fifty Years Later* (IIIS Discussion Paper no. 118, Dublin, 2006); E. Ashtor, 'La Découverte de la voie maritime aux Indes et le prix des épices', *Mélanges en l'honneur de Fernand Braudel*, vol. 1: *Histoire économique du monde Méditerranéen* (Toulouse, 1973), pp. 31–48; F. C. Lane, 'Pepper Prices before da Gama', *Journal of Economic History*, vol. 28 (1968), pp. 590–97.   **31.** 'Letters sent by Bartolomeo Marchioni to Florence', in Greenlee, ed., *Voyage of Pedro Álvares Cabral*, pp. 147–9; F. Guidi Bruscoli, *Bartolomeo Marchionni 'Homem de grossa fazenda' (ca. 1450–1530)* (Florence, 2014), pp. 135–86; K. Lowe, 'Understanding Cultural Exchange between Portugal and Italy in the Renaissance', in K. Lowe, ed., *Cultural Links between Portugal and Italy in the Renaissance* (Oxford, 2000), pp. 8–9; M. Spallanzani, *Mercanti fiorentini nell'Asia portoghese* (Florence, 1997), pp. 47–51.   **32.** Armando Cortesão, transl. and ed., *The Suma Oriental of Tomé Pires* (London, 1944), vol. 2, p. 268; M. Pearson, 'The East African Coast in 1498', in Disney and Booth, eds., *Vasco da Gama*, pp. 116–30; M. Pearson, *Port Cities and Intruders: the Swahili Coast, India, and Portugal in the Early Modern Era* (Baltimore, 1998), pp. 40–43.   **33.** Pearson, *Port Cities and Intruders*, pp. 131–4.   **34.** E. Axelson, *Portuguese in South-East Africa 1488–1600* (Cape Town, 1973), p. 35; E. Axelson, *South-East Africa 1488–1530* (London, 1940), p. 59.   **35.** S. Welch, *South Africa under King Manuel 1495–1521* (Cape Town and Johannesburg, 1946), p. 133.   **36.** Axelson, *South-East Africa*, p. 61.   **37.** Ibid., pp. 64–73; Welch, *South Africa under King Manuel*, pp. 138–41; Crowley, *Conquerors*, pp. 164–6.   **38.** Axelson, *South-East Africa*, pp. 73–8; quotation from Crowley, *Conquerors*, p. 170.   **39.** Axelson, *South-East Africa*, pp. 79–87, 110 n. 2, 112, 118–20; Axelson, *Portuguese in South-East Africa*, pp. 38–52.   **40.** Axelson, *South-East Africa*, pp. 98–107.

30. To the Antipodes

1. Thomas More, *Utopia*, ed. G. Logan and R. Adams (Cambridge, 1989), p. 10.   **2.** L. Formisano, ed., *Letters from a New World: Amerigo Vespucci's Discovery of America* (New York, 1992), app. E, p. 128.   **3.** F. Fernández-Armesto, *Amerigo: the Man Who Gave His Name to America* (London, 2006).   **4.** [Vespucci], *Letters from a New World*, app. E, p. 151.   **5.** Ibid., ep. VI, p. 67; *Lettera di Amerigo Vespucci delle isole nouamente trouate in quattro suoi viaggi* (Florence, 1505), f. 5v.   **6.** [Vespucci], *Letters from a New World*, ep. VI, p. 68; *Lettera di Amerigo Vespucci*, f. 5v.   **7.** [Vespucci], *Letters from a New World*, ep. VI, p. 69; *Lettera di Amerigo Vespucci*, f. 6r.   **8.** [Vespucci], *Letters from a New World*, ep. VI, p. 69; *Lettera di Amerigo Vespucci*, f. 6r.   **9.** [Vespucci], *Letters from a New World*, ep. VI, p. 71; *Lettera di Amerigo Vespucci*, f. 7r.   **10.** Cf. [Vespucci], *Letters from a New*

World, ep. I, p. 11. **11.** Ibid., ep. V, p. 47. **12.** Ibid., p. 45. **13.** D. Abulafia, *The Discovery of Mankind: Atlantic Encounters in the Age of Columbus* (New Haven, 2008), pp. 287–92; D. MacCulloch, *A History of Christianity* (London, 2009), p. 783. **14.** G. Eatough, ed., *Selections from Peter Martyr* (Turnhout, 1998), section 1:9:8. **15.** W. Phillips, ed., *Testimonies from the Columbian Lawsuits* (Turnhout, 2000), section 13:4. **16.** L. Vigneras, *The Discovery of South America and the Andalusian Voyages* (Chicago, 1976), p. 124. **17.** Ibid., pp. 103–4. **18.** R. Fuson, *Juan Ponce de León and the Spanish Discovery of Puerto Rico and Florida* (Blacksburg, Va., 2000); D. Peck, *Ponce de León and the Discovery of Florida: the Man, the Myth and the Truth* (Florida, 1995). **19.** J. Milanich, *Florida's Indians from Ancient Times to the Present* (Gainesville, 1998); J. Milanich, *Florida Indians and the Invasion from Europe* (Gainesville, 1995). **20.** D. Keith, J. Duff, S. James, et al., 'The Molasses Reef Wreck, Turks and Caicos Islands, B.W.I.: a Preliminary Report', *International Journal of Nautical Archaeology and Underwater Exploration*, vol. 13 (1984), pp. 45–63; D. Keith, 'The Molasses Reef Wreck', in *Heritage at Risk, Special Edition – Underwater Cultural Heritage at Risk: Managing Natural and Human Impacts*, ed. R. Grenier, D. Nutley and I. Cochran (International Council on Monuments and Sites, Paris, April 2006), pp. 82–4. **21.** P. Chaunu, *Séville et l'Amérique aux XVIe et XVIIe siècles* (Paris, 1977), pp. 75–6. **22.** T. Floyd, *The Columbus Dynasty in the Caribbean 1492–1526* (Albuquerque, 1973). **23.** A. Devereux, *Juan Ponce de León, King Ferdinand and the Fountain of Youth* (Spartanburg, 1993). **24.** T. Lester, *The Fourth Part of the World: the Epic Story of History's Greatest Map* (London, 2009). **25.** 'Mundus Novus', 'Terra Sanctae Crucis', 'Terra de Brazil', plus 'America Noviter Reperta': collection of the Jagiellonian University, Kraków; cf. the claims of S. Missinne, *The Da Vinci Globe* (Newcastle upon Tyne, 2018). **26.** J. Williamson, *The Voyages of John and Sebastian Cabot* (London, 1937), pp. 17–18. **27.** For highly sceptical views of the Gonneville narrative see J. L. de Pontharouart, *Paulmier de Gonneville: son voyage imaginaire* (Beauval-en-Caux, 2000), and the *Australian Journal of French Studies*, vol. 50 (2013), special issue edited by M. Sankey: M. Sankey, 'The Abbé Jean Paulmier and French Missions in the *Terres Australes*', pp. 3–15; J. Truchot, 'Dans le miroir d'un cacique normand', pp. 16–34; J. Leblond, 'L'Abbé Paulmier descendant d'un étranger des *Terres australes*?', pp. 35–49; J. Letrouit, 'Paulmier faussaire', pp. 50–74; W. Jennings, 'Gonneville's *Terra Australis*: Too Good to be True?', pp. 75–86; M. Sankey, 'L'Abbé Paulmier and the Rights of Man', pp. 87–99. **28.** Paulmier de Gonneville, *Relation authentique du voyage du Capitaine de Gonneville ès nouvelles terres des Indes*, ed. M. d'Avézac (Paris, 1869), pp. 88–91; other editions: L. Perrone-Moisés, ed., *Vinte Luas: viagem de Paulmier de Gonneville ao Brasil: 1503–1505* (São Paulo, 1992); *Le Voyage de Gonneville (1501–1505) et la découverte de la Normandie par les Indiens du Brésil* (Paris, 1995); I. Mendes dos Santos, *La Découverte du Brésil* (Paris, 2000), pp. 121–42. **29.** Gonneville, *Relation authentique*, p. 88. **30.** B. Diffie and G. Winius, *Europe and the World in an Age of Expansion*, vol. 1: *Foundations of the Portuguese Empire 1415–1580* (Minneapolis, 1977), p. 449. **31.** M. Mollat, *Le Commerce maritime normand à la fin du Moyen Âge: Étude d'histoire économique et sociale* (Paris, 1952). **32.** P. Whitfield, *The Charting of the Oceans: Ten Centuries of Maritime Maps* (London, 1996), pp. 54–8. **33.** Gonneville, *Relation authentique*, pp. 93, 95. **34.** Ibid., pp. 99–102. **35.** Ibid., pp. 105–6, 109. **36.** Dos Santos, *Découverte du Brésil*, p. 28. **37.** Ibid., pp. 147–8. **38.** Ibid., p. 29. **39.** Ibid., pp. 143–59. **40.** Mollat, *Commerce maritime normand*, pp. 120–21, 195, 215–21. **41.** H. Touchard, *Le Commerce maritime breton à la fin du Moyen Âge* (Paris, 1967), pp. 288–9; L. Wroth, *The Voyages of Giovanni da Verrazzano* (New Haven, 1970), pp. 8–9, 25–7. **42.** Mollat, *Commerce maritime normand*, pp. 498–507. **43.** Ibid., p. 501; Wroth, *Voyages of Giovanni da Verrazzano*, pp. 10–11, 57–64. **44.** Cited by G. Masini and I. Gori, *How Florence Invented America: Vespucci, Verrazzano, and Mazzei and Their Contribution to the Conception of the New World* (New York, 1998), p. 101. **45.** Wroth, *Voyages of Giovanni da Verrazzano*, pp. 14–16, 28–9. **46.** M. Mollat du Jourdin and J. Habert, *Giovanni et Girolamo Verrazano, navigateurs de François Ier: Dossiers de voyages* (Paris, 1982), pp. ix–x, 53, 66–7, 99. **47.** H. Murphy, *The Voyage of Verrazzano: a Chapter in the Early History of Maritime Discovery in America* (New York, 1875). **48.** Wroth, *Voyages of Giovanni da Verrazzano*, p. 228. **49.** Ibid., pp. 255–62; Mollat du Jourdin and Habert, *Giovanni et Girolamo Verrazano*, pp. 117, 122–3.

31. The Binding of the Oceans

1. John Keats, 'On First Looking into Chapman's Homer'. 2. D. Abulafia, *The Discovery of Mankind: Atlantic Encounters in the Age of Columbus* (New Haven, 2008), pp. 302–5. 3. G. Williams, ed., *The Quest for the Northwest Passage* (London, 2007); H. Dalton, *Merchants and Explorers: Roger Barlow, Sebastian Cabot, and Networks of Atlantic Exchange 1500–1560* (Oxford, 2016). 4. J. Evans, *Merchant Adventurers: the Voyage of Discovery That Transformed Tudor England* (London, 2013). 5. R. Silverberg, *The Longest Voyage: Circumnavigators in the Age of Discovery* (Athens, Oh., 1972), pp. 98–9; H. Kelsey, *The First Circumnavigators: Unsung Heroes of the Age of Discovery* (New Haven, 2016). 6. T. Joyner, *Magellan* (Camden, Me., 1992), pp. 38–49. 7. A. Pigafetta, *Magellan's Voyage: a Narrative Account of the First Circumnavigation*, ed. and transl. R. Skelton (2 vols., New Haven, 1994), vol. 1, p. 116; Joyner, *Magellan*, pp. 48–51; S. E. Morison, *The Great Explorers: the European Discovery of America* (New York, 1976), p. 553; M. Mitchell, *Elcano: the First Circumnavigator* (London, 1958), p. 69. 8. G. Badger, ed., and J. Winter Jones, transl., *The Travels of Ludovico di Varthema in Egypt, Syria, Arabia Deserta and Arabia Felix, in Persia, India, and Ethiopia, A.D. 1503 to 1508* (London, 1863), pp. lxxvii, xcii–iii, 245–6; Joyner, *Magellan*, pp. 311–12 n. 50. 9. M. Camino, *Exploring the Explorers: Spaniards in Oceania, 1519–1794* (Manchester, 2008), pp. 23–4. 10. M. Meilink-Roelofsz, *Asian Trade and European Influence in the Indonesian Archipelago between 1500 and about 1630* (The Hague, 1962), pp. 123–35. 11. Note the misleading title of L. Bergreen, *Over the Edge of the World: Magellan's Terrifying Circumnavigation of the Globe* (London, 2003). 12. Morison, *Great Explorers*, p. 553; Kelsey, *First Circumnavigators*, pp. 25–7. 13. Silverberg, *Longest Voyage*, pp. 97, 116–17; Mitchell, *Elcano*, pp. 41–2. 14. Mitchell, *Elcano*, p. 51. 15. A. Pigafetta, *The First Voyage around the World, 1519–1522: an Account of Magellan's Expedition*, ed. T. Cachey (Toronto, 2007); Pigafetta, *Magellan's Voyage*, vol. 1, based on the French version in the Beinecke Library, Yale University, reproduced in facsimile in vol. 2; Magellan's logbook, an account by Genoese pilot and other sources in *The First Voyage round the World by Magellan translated from the Account of Pigafetta and Other Contemporary Letters*, ed. Lord Stanley of Alderley (London, 1874). 16. Mitchell, *Elcano*, pp. 54–7. 17. Pigafetta, *Magellan's Voyage*, vol. 1, pp. 46–50. 18. Morison, *Great Explorers*, pp. 599–600, with drawing of Schöner's western hemisphere. 19. M. Estensen, *Discovery: The Quest for the Great South Land* (London, 1999), pp. 8–9; N. Crane, *Mercator: the Man Who Mapped the Planet* (London, 2002), pp. 97–100; A. Taylor, *The World of Gerard Mercator: the Mapmaker Who Revolutionized Geography* (New York, 2004), pp. 88–90. 20. Pigafetta, *Magellan's Voyage*, vol. 1, pp. 51–2, 57, 155. 21. Ibid., pp. 57, 60, 148. 22. Bergreen, *Over the Edge of the World*, pp. 211–14, 374–5, 381. 23. Pigafetta, *Magellan's Voyage*, vol. 1, pp. 60–62. 24. Ibid., pp. 67–9. 25. For example, ibid., pp. 95, 101, 103 (source of quotation). 26. Ibid., p. 75. 27. Ibid., pp. 79–84. 28. Ibid., pp. 87–9; Joyner, *Magellan*, pp. 191–6; Camino, *Exploring the Explorers*, p. 25. 29. Pigafetta, *Magellan's Voyage*, vol. 1, p. 100; Mitchell, *Elcano*, p. 65. 30. Pigafetta, *Magellan's Voyage*, vol. 1, pp. 113, 116. 31. Ibid., pp. 119–20, 169; Joyner, *Magellan*, pp. 214–15. 32. 'Genoese Pilot's Account', in Pigafetta, *First Voyage round the World*, pp. 26–9; Morison, *Great Explorers*, pp. 660–62; Camino, *Exploring the Explorers*, p. 27. 33. Letter of Elcano to Charles V, 6 September 1522, in Mitchell, *Elcano*, pp. 87–9; Pigafetta, *Magellan's Voyage*, vol. 1, pp. 146–7; Morison, *Great Explorers*, pp. 664–8. 34. Letter of Charles V, 31 October 1522, cited in Mitchell, *Elcano*, p. 106. 35. Mitchell, *Elcano*, p. 105. 36. Silverberg, *Longest Voyage*, pp. 229–30. 37. Mitchell, *Elcano*, p. 115. 38. A. Giráldez, *The Age of Trade: the Manila Galleons and the Dawn of the Global Economy* (Lanham, 2015), p. 49. 39. Ibid., pp. 49–50; D. Brand, 'Geographical Exploration by the Spaniards', in D. Flynn, A. Giráldez and J. Sobredo, eds., *The Pacific World: Lands, Peoples and History of the Pacific*, vol. 4: *European Entry into the Pacific* (Aldershot, 2001), p. 17 (original edition: H. Friis, ed., *The Pacific Basin: a History of Its Geographical Exploration* (New York, 1967), p. 121); Camino, *Exploring the Explorers*, pp. 28–9; M. Mitchell, *Friar Andrés de*

Urdaneta, O.S.A. (London, 1964). **40.** H. Kelsey, *Juan Rodríguez Cabrillo* (2nd edn, San Marino, Calif., 1998), pp. 65–78; *An Account of the Voyage of Juan Rodríguez Cabrillo* (San Diego, 1999), pp. 18–19. **41.** Brand, 'Geographical Exploration', p. 25 (original edition: p. 129); *Account of the Voyage of Juan Rodríguez Cabrillo*, pp. 23, 29, 32; Kelsey, *Juan Rodríguez Cabrillo*, pp. 125–6; N. Lemke, *Cabrillo: First European Explorer of the California Coast* (San Luis Obispo, 1991); L. Gamble, *The Chumash World at European Contact: Power, Trade, and Feasting among Complex Hunter-Gatherers* (Berkeley and Los Angeles, 2008), pp. 38–9.

32. A New Atlantic

1. D. Abulafia, *The Discovery of Mankind: Atlantic Encounters in the Age of Columbus* (New Haven, 2008), pp. 201–12; P. Chaunu, *Séville et l'Amérique aux XVIe et XVIIe siècles* (Paris, 1977), pp. 80–86. **2.** 'ADN dominicano: 49 per cent de origen africano', in the Dominican newspaper *Diario Libre*, 6 July 2016, p. 4, reporting research under the auspices of the Academia Dominicana de la Historia. **3.** R. Pike, 'Sevillian Society in the Sixteenth Century: Slaves and Freedmen', *Hispanic American Historical Review*, vol. 47 (1967), pp. 344–59, partly reprinted as 'Slavery in Seville at the Time of Columbus', in H. B. Johnson, ed., *From Reconquest to Empire: the Iberian Background to Latin American History* (New York, 1970), pp. 85–101. **4.** M. L. Stig Sørensen, C. Evans and K. Richter, 'A Place of History: Archaeology and Heritage at Cidade Velha, Cape Verde', in P. Lane and K. McDonald, eds., *Slavery in Africa: Archaeology and Memory* (*Proceedings of the British Academy*, vol. 168, 2011), pp. 422–5; A. Carreira, *Cabo Verde: Formação e Extinção de uma Sociaedade escarvorata (1460–1878)* (3rd edn, Praia de Santiago, 2000); T. Hall, ed. and transl., *Before Middle Passage: Translated Portuguese Manuscripts of Atlantic Slave Trading From West Africa to Iberian Territories, 1513–26* (Farnham, 2015). **5.** K. Deagan and J. M. Cruxent, *Archaeology at La Isabela: America's First European Town* (New Haven, 2002); K. Deagan and J. M. Cruxent, *Columbus's Outpost among the Taínos: Spain and America at La Isabela, 1493–1498* (New Haven, 2002); V. Flores Sasso and E. Prieto Vicioso, 'Aportes a la historia de La Isabela: Primera ciudad europea en el Nuevo Mundo', *Centro de Altos Estudios Humanísticos y del Idioma Español adscrito a la Universidad Nacional Pedro Henríquez Ureña, Anuario*, vol. 6 (2012–13), pp. 411–35. **6.** Deagan and Cruxent, *Columbus's Outpost*, pp. 53, 57, 96–7, 180–81; Abulafia, *Discovery of Mankind*, pp. 202–3. **7.** Deagan and Cruxent, *Columbus's Outpost*, pp. 146, 191–2. **8.** Ibid., pp. 194–8. **9.** T. Floyd, *The Columbus Dynasty in the Caribbean 1492–1526* (Albuquerque, 1973), p. 55. **10.** E. Mira Caballos, *La gran armada colonizadora de Nicolás de Ovando, 1501–1502* (Santo Domingo, 2014); E. Pérez Montás, E. Prieto Vicioso and J. Chez Checo, eds., *Basílica catedral de Santo Domingo* (Santo Domingo, 2011). **11.** Chaunu, *Séville et l'Amérique*, pp. 87–8. **12.** Abulafia, *Discovery of Mankind*, p. 156. **13.** R. Pike, *Enterprise and Adventure: the Genoese in Seville and the Opening of the New World* (Ithaca, NY, 1966), pp. 52–9; Floyd, *Columbus Dynasty*, pp. 67–8. **14.** G. Rodríguez Morel, 'The Sugar Economy of Española in the Sixteenth Century', in S. Schwartz, ed., *Tropical Babylons: Sugar and the Making of the Atlantic World, 1450–1680* (Chapel Hill, 2004), pp. 85–6; Pike, *Enterprise and Adventure*, pp. 128–33. **15.** M. Ratekin, 'The Early Sugar Industry in Española', *Hispanic American Historical Review*, vol. 34 (1954), pp. 3–7. **16.** Ibid., pp. 6, 9–11; Rodríguez Morel, 'Sugar Economy of Española', pp. 90–93, 105–6. **17.** Ratekin, 'Early Sugar Industry', p. 13; Rodríguez Morel, 'Sugar Economy of Española', pp. 103–4; Chaunu, *Séville et l'Amérique*, pp. 88–9. **18.** J. Friede, *Los Welser en la conquista de Venezuela* (Caracas and Madrid, 1961), p. 91. **19.** Friede, *Los Welser*, pp. 91, 580 n. 16. **20.** J. Denzer, 'Die Welser in Venezuela – das Scheiten ihrer wirtschaftlichen Ziele', in M. Häberlein and J. Burkhardt, *Die Welser: neue Forschungen zur Geschichte und Kultur des oberdeutschen Handelshauses* (Berlin, 2002), pp. 290, 308, 313. **21.** J. del Rio Moreno, *Los Inicios de la Agricultura europea en el Nuevo Mundo, 1492–1542* (2nd edn, Santo Domingo, 2012); J. del Rio Moreno, *Ganadería, plantaciones y comercio azucarero* *antillano: siglos XVI y XVII* (Santo Domingo, 2012); Pike, *Enterprise and Adventure*, p. 133. **22.** Chaunu, *Séville et l'Amérique*, pp. 90–91. **23.** Excellent maps displaying the volume of trade in Chaunu, *Séville et l'Amérique*, pp. 301–9. **24.** Cited by A. de la Fuente, *Havana and the Atlantic in the Sixteenth Century* (Chapel Hill, 2008), pp. 67–8. **25.** Chaunu, *Séville et l'Amérique*, p. 100. **26.** Abulafia, *Discovery of Mankind*, pp. 209–302; H. Thomas, *Rivers of Gold: the Rise of the Spanish Empire* (London, 2003), p. 282; A. de la Fuente, 'Sugar and Slavery', S. Schwartz, ed., in *Tropical Babylons: Sugar and the Making of the Atlantic World, 1450–1680* (Chapel Hill, 2004), pp. 117–19. **27.** Chaunu, *Séville et l'Amérique*, p. 99. **28.** De la Fuente, *Havana*, pp. 1–5; J. S. Dean, *Tropics Bound: Elizabeth's Seadogs on the Spanish Main* (Stroud, 2010). **29.** Table 2:2, showing imports and exports, 1587–1610, in de la Fuente, *Havana*, p. 15; Canary wine: ibid., pp. 22, 90–92; Chinese goods: ibid., pp. 44–5; shipbuilding: ibid., pp. 127–34. **30.** Ibid., pp. 94, 96, 98, 159, 186, 200, 223–4; Chaunu, *Séville et l'Amérique*, p. 102. **31.** D. Wheat, *Atlantic Africa and the Spanish Caribbean, 1570–1640* (Chapel Hill and Williamsburg, Va., 2016), pp. 29, 64, 77, 84, 121–3, 209–15.

33. The Struggle for the Indian Ocean

1. P. Brummett, *Ottoman Seapower and Levantine Diplomacy in the Age of Discovery* (Albany, NY, 1994); S. Özbaran, *Ottoman Expansion toward the Indian Ocean in the 16th Century* (Istanbul, 2009); G. Casale, *The Ottoman Age of Exploration* (New York, 2010). **2.** Brummett, *Ottoman Seapower*, pp. 32–3, 41, 143–70; K. Fleet, *European and Islamic Trade in the Early Ottoman State: the Merchants of Genoa and Turkey* (Cambridge, 1999). **3.** Brummett, *Ottoman Seapower*, p. 34; K. N. Chaudhuri, *Trade and Civilisation in the Indian Ocean: an Economic History from the Rise of Islam to 1750* (Cambridge, 1985), p. 67. **4.** Z. Biedermann, *Soqotra: Geschichte einer christlichen Insel im Indischen Ozean bis zur frühen Neuzeit* (Wiesbaden, 2006), pp. 68–76. **5.** Chaudhuri, *Trade and Civilisation*, p. 69. **6.** Özbaran, *Ottoman Expansion*, pp. 9, 40–41; W. Floor, *The Persian Gulf: a Political and Economic History of Five Port Cities* (Washington DC, 2006), pp. 7–24, 30–49, 89–106. **7.** Cited in C. R. Boxer, *The Portuguese Seaborne Empire 1415–1825* (London, 1991), p. 62; Floor, *Persian Gulf*, pp. 15–16. **8.** Floor, *Persian Gulf*, pp. 91–3; Manuel I of Portugal, *Gesta proxime per Portugalenses in India Ethiopia et alijs Orientalibus Terris* (1507; exemplar in John Carter Brown Library, Brown University). **9.** Brummett, *Ottoman Seapower*, pp. 45, 167; see also *Epistola Potentissimi Emanuelis Regis Portugalie et Algarbiorum etc. de Victorijs habitis in India et Malacha ad sancto in Christo Patrem et Dominum nostrum dominum Leonem decimum Pontificem maximum* (1513; exemplar in John Carter Brown Library, Brown University). **10.** Floor, *Persian Gulf*, pp. 101–6. **11.** Özbaran, *Ottoman Expansion*, pp. 53–4, 57. **12.** Chaudhuri, *Trade and Civilisation*, pp. 69, 71. **13.** Brummett, *Ottoman Seapower*, pp. 34–5, 42; R. Crowley, *Conquerors: How Portugal Seized the Indian Ocean and Forged the First Global Empire* (London, 2015), pp. 202–41. **14.** Brummett, *Ottoman Seapower*, pp. 42–3. **15.** Casale, *Ottoman Age of Exploration*, p. 33; Özbaran, *Ottoman Expansion*, pp. 47, 51–2, 70. **16.** 'A letter from Dom Aleixo de Meneses to King Manuel I; the Portuguese expedition to Jiddah in the Red Sea in 1527', in Özbaran, *Ottoman Expansion*, app. 1, pp. 325–9. **17.** Özbaran, *Ottoman Expansion*, pp. 49–50. **18.** Ibid., p. 51. **19.** Brummett, *Ottoman Seapower*, pp. 44–5; Crowley, *Conquerors*, pp. 324–38, citing quotation on p. 337. **20.** Özbaran, *Ottoman Expansion*, p. 61, engaging with F. Braudel, *The Mediterranean and the Mediterranean World in the Age of Philip II* (2 vols., London, 1972–3), vol. 1, p. 389; S. Özbaran, *The Ottoman Response to European Expansion: Studies on Ottoman–Portuguese Relations in the Indian Ocean and Ottoman Administration in the Arab Lands during the Sixteenth Century* (Istanbul, 1994), pp. 89–97. **21.** Casale, *Ottoman Age of Exploration*, pp. 25–6, 31. **22.** Özbaran, *Ottoman Expansion*, p. 9. **23.** Crowley, *Conquerors*, pp. 203–4, 227–39; Casale, *Ottoman Age of Exploration*, pp. 26–7. **24.** Letter cited by Casale, *Ottoman Age of Exploration*, p. 28. **25.** Casale, *Ottoman Age of Exploration*, pp. 29, 31. **26.** David Abulafia, *The Great Sea: a Human History of the Mediterranean* (London, 2011), pp. 418–23.   27. Casale, *Ottoman Age of Exploration*, pp. 40–41.   28. 'The report of Selman Reis written in 1525: the Ottoman guns and ships at the port of Jiddah, the description of the Red Sea and adjacent countries together with the Portuguese presence in the Indian Ocean', in Özbaran, *Ottoman Expansion*, app. 2, pp. 334–5; cited in Casale, *Ottoman Age of Exploration*, p. 43; Özbaran, *Ottoman Response*, pp. 99–109.   29. P. Risso, *Merchants and Faith: Muslim Commerce and Culture in the Indian Ocean* (Boulder, 1995), p. 58.   30. Casale, *Ottoman Age of Exploration*, pp. 41–7, 49; Özbaran, *Ottoman Expansion*, p. 8.   31. S. Soucek, *Studies in Ottoman Naval History and Maritime Geography* (Istanbul, 2008), pp. 79–82.   32. Casale, *Ottoman Age of Exploration*, p. 56.   33. Portuguese version of a letter to the Ottoman commander, cited in Casale, *Ottoman Age of Exploration*, pp. 57, 218 n. 17.   34. Özbaran, *Ottoman Expansion*, pp. 83–4; Casale, *Ottoman Age of Exploration*, pp. 59–63.   35. Chaudhuri, *Trade and Civilisation*, pp. 71–3; Özbaran, *Ottoman Expansion*, pp. 80–84; Casale, *Ottoman Age of Exploration*, p. 76.   36. Boxer, *Portuguese Seaborne Empire*, pp. 61–2.   37. Ibid., pp. 48–9.   38. M. Meilink-Roelofsz, *Asian Trade and European Influence in the Indonesian Archipelago between 1500 and about 1630* (The Hague, 1962), pp. 136–72; also L. F. Thomaz, *De Ceuta a Timor* (Algés, 1994), pp. 291–9, 513–65; also Armando Cortesão, transl. and ed., *The Suma Oriental of Tomé Pires* (London, 1944), vol. 2, pp. 229–89.   39. Casale, *Ottoman Age of Exploration*, pp. 133, 159.   40. 'Report of Selman Reis', in Özbaran, *Ottoman Expansion*, p. 333.   41. S. Soucek, *Piri Reis: Turkish Mapmaking after Columbus* (2nd edn, Istanbul, 2013); M. Özen, *Pîrî Reis and His Charts* (Istanbul, 2006).   42. Soucek, *Piri Reis*, pp. 47–63.   43. Ibid., pp. 102–11, 114–25, 128–31.   44. G. McIntosh, *The Piri Reis Map of 1513* (Athens, Ga., 2000), pp. 5–7; Özen, *Pîrî Reis*, pp. 3–10; Casale, *Ottoman Age of Exploration*, pp. 98–9; Soucek, *Studies in Ottoman Naval History*, pp. 57–65.   45. Özen, *Pîrî Reis*, pp. 20–22; Soucek, *Piri Reis*, p. 110.   46. Soucek, *Studies in Ottoman Naval History*, pp. 35–40, 45, 47.   47. Abulafia, *Great Sea*, pp. 486–7; Soucek, *Piri Reis*, p. 78.   48. Soucek, *Piri Reis*, pp. 30–41.   49. Soucek, *Studies in Ottoman Naval History*, p. 57; Soucek, *Piri Reis*, p. 79; McIntosh, *Piri Reis Map*, pp. 122–40.   50. Casale, *Ottoman Age of Exploration*, pp. 38–40, and fig. 2:1, p. 38 – not a map recording Magellan's route, as Casale supposes.   51. Cf. Soucek, *Piri Reis*, p. 65.   52. Plates in Özen, *Pîrî Reis*, pp. 69–70; 1528 map: Soucek, *Piri Reis*, pp. 96–7, 132; McIntosh, *Piri Reis Map*, pp. 52–68, makes bizarre claims about information handed down from a higher civilization and should be ignored.   53. Soucek, *Piri Reis*, pp. 68–9.   54. McIntosh, *Piri Reis Map*, pp. 45–6.   55. Text ibid., pp. 70–71; also in Soucek, *Piri Reis*, p. 75.   56. Piri Reis, *Kitab-i Bahriye* ['Book of Navigation'], cited by Soucek, *Studies in Ottoman Naval History*, p. 58.

34. The Great Galleons of Manila

1. M. Mitchell, *Friar Andrés de Urdaneta, O.S.A.* (London, 1964), pp. 75, 77.   2. Cited in Mitchell, *Friar Andrés de Urdaneta*, pp. 73–4.   3. M. Mitchell, *Elcano: the First Circumnavigator* (London, 1958), pp. 118, 124, 126–59; R. Silverberg, *The Longest Voyage: Circumnavigators in the Age of Discovery* (Athens, Oh., 1972), pp. 230–33.   4. R. Canosa, *Banchieri genovesi e sovrani spagnoli tra cinquecento e seicento* (Rome, 1998), pp. 12–13; R. Carande, *Carlos V y sus Banqueros*, vol. 3: *Los Caminos del Oro y de la Plata* (2nd edn, Barcelona, 1987).   5. M. Camino, *Exploring the Explorers: Spaniards in Oceania, 1519–1794* (Manchester, 2008), pp. 29–30; Mitchell, *Friar Andrés de Urdaneta*, p. 78.   6. W. Schurz, *The Manila Galleon* (New York, 1939), p. 21.   7. A. Giráldez, *The Age of Trade: the Manila Galleons and the Dawn of the Global Economy* (Lanham, 2015), pp. 51–2; Schurz, *Manila Galleon*, p. 23; Mitchell, *Friar Andrés de Urdaneta*, pp. 80–84; H. Kelsey, *The First Circumnavigators: Unsung Heroes of the Age of Discovery* (New Haven, 2016), pp. 59–100.   8. E. Hamilton, *American Treasure and the Price Revolution in Spain, 1501–1650* (Cambridge, Mass., 1934), pp. 232–3.   9. Mitchell, *Friar Andrés de Urdaneta*, pp. 99–105; Kelsey, *First Circumnavigators*, pp. 101–27.   10. S. Fish, *The Manila–Acapulco Galleons: the Treasure Ships of the Pacific* (Milton Keynes, 2011), pp. 60–61.   11. Mitchell, *Friar Andrés de Urdaneta*, pp. 117–18.   12. Giráldez, *Age of Trade*, p. 52; Mitchell, *Friar Andrés de Urdaneta*, pp. 142–4.   13. Giráldez,

Age of Trade, pp. 51–8; Schurz, *Manila Galleon*, p. 25; H. Thomas, *World Without End; the Global Empire of Philip II* (London, 2014), pp. 241–50. **14.** B. Legarda Jr, 'Two and a Half Centuries of the Galleon Trade', in D. Flynn, A. Giráldez and J. Sobredo, eds., *The Pacific World: Lands, Peoples and History of the Pacific*, vol. 4: *European Entry into the Pacific* (Aldershot, 2001), p. 37 (original edition: *Philippine Studies*, vol. 3 (1955), p. 345); Mitchell, *Friar Andrés de Urdaneta*, p. 135. **15.** 'Annotated List of the Transpacific Galleons 1565–1815', in Fish, *Manila–Acapulco Galleons*, pp. 492–523; also the figures and tables in P. Chaunu, *Les Philippines et le Pacifique des Ibériques, XVIe, XVIIe, XVIIIe siècles* (2 vols., Paris, 1960 and 1966), vols. 1 and 2. **16.** See now Giráldez, *Age of Trade*; also Schurz, *Manila Galleon*; Flynn, Giráldez and Sobredo, eds., *European Entry*; Chaunu, *Philippines*; P. Chaunu, 'Le Galion de Manille: Grandeur et décadence d'une route de la soie', in Flynn, Giráldez and Sobredo, eds., *European Entry*, pp. 187–202 (original edition: *Annales: Économies, Sociétés, Civilisations*, vol. 4 (1951), pp. 447–62); Fish, *Manila–Acapulco Galleons*. **17.** Han-sheng Chuan, 'The Chinese Silk Trade with Spanish-America from the Late Ming to to the mid-Ch'ing Period', in Flynn, Giráldez and Sobredo, eds., *European Entry*, pp. 241–59 (original edition: L. Thompson, ed., *Studia Asiatica: Essays in Asian Studies in Felicitation of the Seventy-Fifth Anniversary of Professor Ch'en Shou-yi* (San Francisco, 1975), pp. 99–117). **18.** R. von Glahn, *The Economic History of China from Antiquity to the Nineteenth Century* (Cambridge, 2016), p. 308; T. Brook, *The Confusions of Pleasure: Commerce and Culture in Ming China* (Berkeley and Los Angeles, 1998), pp. 204–5. **19.** Giráldez, *Age of Trade*, p. 57; Thomas, *World Without End*, p. 251. **20.** B. Laufer, 'The Relations of the Chinese to the Philippine Islands', in Flynn, Giráldez and Sobredo, eds., *European Entry*, pp. 65–6, 89–91 (original edition: *Smithsonian Institution, Miscellaneous Collections*, vol. 50, no. 13 (1907), pp. 258–9, 282–4). **21.** David Abulafia, *The Great Sea: a Human History of the Mediterranean* (London, 2011), p. 74. **22.** Schurz, *Manila Galleon*, pp. 23, 27–9, 34–42. **23.** F. Carletti, *My Voyage around the World*, ed. and transl. H. Weinstock (London, 1965), pp. 4–5. **24.** Ibid., pp. 69–70. **25.** Ibid., pp. 71, 74–6, 78. **26.** Ibid., pp. 79–80. **27.** Ibid., pp. 82, 89. **28.** Ibid., pp. 83–8. **29.** Ibid., pp. 96–7. **30.** Ibid., pp. 90–91, 100. **31.** Map in R. Bertrand, *Le Long Remords de la conquête: Manille–Mexico–Madrid, l'affaire Diego de Ávila (1577–1580)* (Paris, 2015), pp. 58–9; Giráldez, *Age of Trade*, p. 84; Fish, *Manila–Acapulco Galleons*, pp. 65–72. **32.** Thomas, *World Without End*, p. 252. **33.** Laufer, 'Relations of the Chinese', pp. 55–65 (pp. 248–58). **34.** Giráldez, *Age of Trade*, pp. 26–8; Fish, *Manila–Acapulco Galleons*, p. 111. **35.** Laufer, 'Relations of the Chinese', p. 85 (p. 278). **36.** Ibid., p. 75 n. 1 (p. 268 n. 1); Schurz, *Manila Galleon*, p. 63 n. 1. **37.** William Dampier's description, Canton, 1687, in Schurz, *Manila Galleon*, pp. 70–71; Giráldez, *Age of Trade*, p. 160; Schurz, *Manila Galleon*, pp. 74–8. **38.** Schurz, *Manila Galleon*, pp. 71–2; Giráldez, *Age of Trade*, p. 161; Fish, *Manila–Acapulco Galleons*, pp. 109–10. **39.** Cited in Schurz, *Manila Galleon*, pp. 73–4. **40.** Diego de Bobadilla, cited in Schurz, *Manila Galleon*, p. 74. **41.** C. Boxer, '*Plata es Sangre*: Sidelights on the Drain of Spanish-American Silver in the Far East, 1550–1700', in Flynn, Giráldez and Sobredo, eds., *European Entry*, p. 172 (original edition: *Philippine Studies*, vol. 18 (1970), p. 464); D. Flynn and A. Giráldez, 'Arbitrage, China, and World Trade in the Early Modern Period', in Flynn, Giráldez and Sobredo, eds., *European Entry*, pp. 261–80 (original edition: *Journal of the Economic and Social History of the Orient*, vol. 38 (1995), pp. 429–48). **42.** Laufer, 'Relations of the Chinese', p. 63 (p. 256). **43.** Flynn and Giráldez, 'Arbitrage, China, and World Trade', pp. 262–3 (pp. 431–2); von Glahn, *Economic History of China*, pp. 308–9. **44.** Giráldez, *Age of Trade*, pp. 31–2. **45.** Cited in von Glahn, *Economic History of China*, p. 308. **46.** Fish, *Manila–Acapulco Galleons*, p. 115. **47.** Schurz, *Manila Galleon*, pp. 79–81. **48.** Schurz, *Manila Galleon*, pp. 83–4; Laufer, 'Relations of the Chinese', pp. 68–9 (pp. 261–2); Fish, *Manila–Acapulco Galleons*, p. 126. **49.** Cavite: Fish, *Manila–Acapulco Galleons*, pp. 128–42, 156–86. **50.** Schurz, *Manila Galleon*, pp. 85–90. **51.** Extracts of Antonio de Morga and Ming Annals in Laufer, 'Relations of the Chinese', pp. 74–9 (pp. 267–72); Schurz, *Manila Galleon*, p. 91 and n. 6. **52.** Schurz, *Manila Galleon*, pp. 68–9; Thomas, *World Without End*, pp. 260–82; Laufer, 'Relations of the Chinese', p. 68 (p. 261). **53.** Thomas, *World Without End*, p. 282. **54.** J. L. Gasch-Tomás, *The Atlantic World and the Manila*

Galleons: Circulation, Market, and Consumption of Asian Goods in the Spanish Empire,
1565–1650 (Leiden, 2018).   **55.** A. Coates, *A Macao Narrative* (2nd edn, Hong Kong, 2009),
pp. 17–30; R. Neild, *The China Coast: Trade and the First Treaty Ports* (Hong Kong, 2010),
pp. 25–31, 94–5.   **56.** Schurz, *Manila Galleon*, pp. 66–7.   **57.** Chuan, 'Chinese Silk Trade',
p. 250 (p. 108).   **58.** Schurz, *Manila Galleon*, pp. 100–102.   **59.** R. Kowner, *From White
to Yellow: the Japanese in European Racial Thought, 1300–1735* (Montreal, 2014), pp. 152,
154; Schurz, *Manila Galleon*, pp. 116–18; Giráldez, *Age of Trade*, p. 106.   **60.** Kowner,
From White to Yellow, p. 177; Schurz, *Manila Galleon*, pp. 111–13.   **61.** Schurz, *Manila
Galleon*, pp. 108–12.   **62.** W. de Lange, *Pars Japonica: the First Dutch Expedition to Reach
the Shores of Japan* (Warren, Conn., 2006); G. Milton, *Samurai William: the Adventurer
Who Unlocked Japan* (London, 2002), pp. 65–87.   **63.** Giráldez, *Age of Trade*, pp. 107–8;
Milton, *Samurai William*, pp. 109, 122–4.   **64.** S. Endo, *The Samurai*, transl. Van C. Gessel
(New York, 1980).   **65.** Van C. Gessel, 'Postscript: Fact and Truth in *The Samurai*', in Endo,
Samurai, pp. 268–70.   **66.** Schurz, *Manila Galleon*, pp. 125–8; Giráldez, *Age of Trade*, pp.
107–9.   **67.** T. Toyoda, *History of pre-Meiji Commerce in Japan* (Tokyo, 1969), pp. 37–46,
59.   **68.** Milton, *Samurai William*, pp. 174–205.   **69.** Schurz, *Manila Galleon*, p. 120.   **70.**
Schurz, *Manila Galleon*, p. 115; Giráldez, *Age of Trade*, pp. 106, 189–90.

35. The Black Ships of Macau

1. D. Massarella, *A World Elsewhere: Europe's Encounter with Japan in the Sixteenth and
Seventeenth Centuries* (New Haven, 1990), p. 19.   **2.** C. R. Boxer, *Fidalgos in the Far East
1550–1770* (2nd edn, Hong Kong, 1968), p. 7.   **3.** J. Wills, 'Maritime Europe and the Ming',
in J. Wills, ed., *China and Maritime Europe, 1500–1800: Trade, Settlement, Diplomacy,
and Missions* (Cambridge, 2011), pp. 26–7, 29–31; A. Coates, *A Macao Narrative* (2nd edn,
Hong Kong, 2009), pp. 11–12.   **4.** Armando Cortesão, transl. and ed., *The Suma Oriental
of Tomé Pires* (London, 1944), vol. 1, pp. 128–131: *Lequíos* and *Jampon*; Massarella, *World
Elsewhere*, pp. 22–3; G. Kerr, *Okinawa: the History of an Island People* (2nd edn, Boston
and Tokyo, 2000), pp. 84, 88, 90–94; C. R. Boxer, *The Christian Century in Japan 1549–
1650* (2nd edn, Lisbon and Manchester, 1993), p. 14.   **5.** Cited by Boxer, *Christian Century*,
pp. 16–17; see also Wills, 'Maritime Europe and the Ming', pp. 26–8.   **6.** Boxer, *Christian
Century*, p. 27.   **7.** Coates, *Macao Narrative*, pp. 12–13.   **8.** Diogo de Couto (1597) in Boxer,
Christian Century, pp. 24–5; also Massarella, *World Elsewhere*, p. 24; Kowner, *From White
to Yellow*, p. 65.   **9.** Boxer, *Christian Century*, pp. 28, 30.   **10.** Japanese chronicle *Yaita-ki*,
quoted in Boxer, *Christian Century*, p. 29.   **11.** Wills, 'Maritime Europe and the Ming', pp.
32–4.   **12.** Coates, *Macao Narrative*, p. 50.   **13.** Wills, 'Maritime Europe and the Ming',
p. 37.   **14.** Boxer, *Christian Century*, p. 255.   **15.** Coates, *Macao Narrative*, pp. 25–30;
Boxer, *Fidalgos*, p. 3; Wills, 'Maritime Europe and the Ming', pp. 38, 41, 47–8; L. P. Barreto,
Macau: Poder e Saber, séculos XVI e XVII (Queluz de Baixo, 2006), pp. 215–16; cf.
F. Welsh, *A History of Hong Kong* (2nd edn, London, 1997), pp. 120–31.   **16.** Boxer,
Fidalgos, p. 4; Wills, 'Maritime Europe and the Ming', p. 35.   **17.** Wills, 'Maritime Europe
and the Ming', p. 37.   **18.** F. Carletti, *My Voyage around the World*, ed. and transl. H. Wein-
stock (London, 1965), p. 139.   **19.** Barreto, *Macau*, p. 116.   **20.** Wills, 'Maritime Europe
and the Ming', p. 47.   **21.** Ibid., p. 42.   **22.** Carletti, *My Voyage*, p. 140; Barreto, *Macau*,
pp. 138–41.   **23.** Barreto, *Macau*, p. 117.   **24.** Cited in Boxer, *Fidalgos*, p. 6; also in Boxer,
Christian Century, pp. 105–6.   **25.** C. R. Boxer, *The Great Ship from Amacon: Annals of
Macao and the Old Japan Trade, 1555–1640* (Lisbon, 1959), p. 17.   **26.** Boxer, *Christian
Century*, plate 14; N. Coolidge Rousmaniere, *Vessels of Influence: China and the Birth of
Porcelain in Medieval and Early Modern Japan* (Bristol and London, 2012), p. 109.   **27.**
Boxer, *Great Ship from Amacon*, pp. 13–14 and p. 13 n. 34.   **28.** For example, A. Jackson,
'Visual Responses: Depicting Europeans in East Asia', in A. Jackson and A. Jaffer, *Encoun-
ters: the Meeting of Asia and Europe 1500–1800* (London, 2004), pp. 202–3, plate 16.1;
Boxer, *Great Ship from Amacon*, plate opposite p. 20; Boxer, *Christian Century*, plates 13,

15. 29. For example, Boxer, *Great Ship from Amacon*, p. 35; also Boxer, *Christian Century*, p. 121. 30. Barreto, *Macau*, pp. 145, 160–61, 193, 220. 31. Boxer, *Great Ship from Amacon*, p. 47. 32. Ibid., pp. 34–5; Boxer, *Christian Century*, p. 100; Barreto, *Macau*, p. 143. 33. Barreto, *Macau*, p. 141. 34. M. Meilink-Roelofsz, *Asian Trade and European Influence in the Indonesian Archipelago between 1500 and about 1630* (The Hague, 1962), pp. 104–5, 134. 35. R. von Glahn, *The Economic History of China from Antiquity to the Nineteenth Century* (Cambridge, 2016), pp. 308–11. 36. *Prodotti e tecniche d'Oltremare nelle economie europee, secc. XIII–XVIII* (Florence, 1998); Barreto, *Macau*, p. 273. 37. Meilink-Roelofsz, *Asian Trade and European Influence*, pp. 123–4. 38. Boxer, *Great Ship from Amacon*, pp. 33–4, 317–18 (doc. E.ii, 1567–8). 39. Ibid., p. 115. 40. J. Moran, *The Japanese and the Jesuits: Alessandro Valignano in Sixteenth-Century Japan* (London, 1993), p. 67. 41. On Ricci: R. Po-chia Hsia, *A Jesuit in the Forbidden City: Matteo Ricci 1552–1610* (New York and Oxford, 2010); R. Po-chia Hsia, *Matteo Ricci and the Catholic Mission to China, 1583–1610: a Short History with Documents* (Indianapolis, 2016); M. Laven, *Mission to China: Matteo Ricci and the Jesuit Encounter with the East* (London, 2011); also C. R. Boxer, *The Church Militant and Iberian Expansion 1440–1770* (Baltimore, 1978), pp. 53–6. 42. Barreto, *Macau*, p. 141. 43. Boxer, *Christian Century*, p. 97. 44. Ibid., p. 120; Barreto, *Macau*, p. 141. 45. Cited in Boxer, *Christian Century*, p. 93. 46. Kowner, *From White to Yellow*, pp. 84, 128–35, 166–70; Barreto, *Macau*, p. 139: Luís de Almeida. 47. Boxer, *Christian Century*, pp. 139–49, 152–3; also Carletti, *My Voyage*, pp. 116–25. 48. Moran, *Japanese and Jesuits*, pp. 58–9, 62–3, 70, 89–90. 49. Carletti, *My Voyage*, p. 116. 50. Ibid., pp. 104–5. 51. Ibid., pp. 105–8, 121–4, 127–35. 52. Ibid., pp. 108–13; Barreto, *Macau*, p. 165. 53. Carletti, *My Voyage*, p. 132. 54. Coolidge Rousmaniere, *Vessels of Influence*, pp. 78, 81, 87–92, 101–3. 55. Ibid., pp. 64, 130–35, 161; T. Nagatake, *Classic Japanese Porcelain: Imari and Kaikemon* (Tokyo, 2003), pp. 49–50, 60–63. 56. Carletti, *My Voyage*, pp. 114–16. 57. S. Hawley, *The Imjin War: Japan's Sixteenth-Century Invasion of Korea and Attempt to Conquer China* (Seoul and Berkeley, 2005), pp. 301–48. 58. Cited in Hawley, *Imjin War*, p. 465. 59. Hawley, *Imjin War*, pp. 475–6. 60. Ibid., pp. 193, 195–9, and plate section, pp. vi–vii. 61. Ibid., pp. 482–90. 62. Ibid., p. 515. 63. Ibid., pp. 490, 554–5. 64. T. Toyoda, *History of pre-Meiji Commerce in Japan* (Tokyo, 1969), pp. 40–41, 49, 53–4. 65. Ibid., p. 43. 66. Letter cited in Hawley, *Imjin War*, p. 402; Boxer, *Christian Century*, p. 161; Moran, *Japanese and Jesuits*, p. 91. 67. Moran, *Japanese and Jesuits*, pp. 83–4. 68. Ibid., pp. 84–5, 89. 69. Barreto, *Macau*, p. 173. 70. Moran, *Japanese and Jesuits*, p. 86. 71. J. Clements, *Christ's Samurai: the True Story of the Shimabara Rebellion* (London, 2016). 72. Boxer, *Great Ship from Amacon*, pp. 158–61.

36. The Fourth Ocean

1. R. Vaughan, *The Arctic: a History* (Stroud, 1994), p. 36, plate 3. 2. Ibid., p. 37. 3. Cited in G. Connell-Smith, *Forerunners of Drake: a Study of English Trade with Spain in the Early Tudor Period* (London, 1954), p. 121 (dating from 1540); R. B. Wernham, *Before the Armada: the Growth of English Foreign Policy 1485–1588* (London, 1966). 4. T. S. Willan, *Studies in Elizabethan Foreign Trade* (Manchester, 1959), pp. 92–312. 5. H. Dalton, *Merchants and Explorers: Roger Barlow, Sebastian Cabot, and Networks of Atlantic Exchange 1500–1560* (Oxford, 2016), pp. 29–33, 49–62; 'Robert Thorne's Declaration', in Richard Hakluyt, *Voyages and Documents*, ed. J. Hampden (Oxford, 1958), pp. 17–19; G. Williams, *Arctic Labyrinth: The Quest for the Northwest Passage* (London, 2009), pp. 7–8; H. Wallis, 'England's Search for the Northern Passages in the Sixteenth and Early Seventeenth Centuries', *Arctic*, vol. 37 (1984), pp. 453–5; N. Crane, *Mercator: the Man Who Mapped the Planet* (London, 2002), colour plates, section 2, no. 4. 6. A. de Robilant, *Venetian Navigators: the Mystery of the Voyages of the Zen Brothers to the Far North* (London, 2011). 7. Wallis, 'England's Search', p. 457. 8. Hakluyt, *Voyages and Documents*, pp. 40, 44–5; Williams, *Arctic Labyrinth*, p. 8; J. Evans, *Merchant Adventurers: the Voyage of Discovery That Transformed Tudor England*

(London, 2013).   **9.** Williams, *Arctic Labyrinth*, p. 9; K. Mayers, *The First English Explorer: the Life of Anthony Jenkinson (1529–1611) and His Adventures en Route to the Orient* (Northam, Devon, 2015), p. 49.   **10.** Williams, *Arctic Labyrinth*, pp. 9–10; Vaughan, *Arctic*, p. 58; K. Mayers, *North-East Passage to Muscovy: Stephen Borough and the First Tudor Explorations* (Stroud, 2005); S. Alford, *London's Triumph: Merchant Adventurers and the Tudor City* (London, 2017), pp. 80–91, 130–41.   **11.** Mayers, *First English Explorer*, pp. 237–49; Alford, *London's Triumph*, pp. 132–41.   **12.** Mayers, *First English Explorer*, p. 244.   **13.** Vaughan, *Arctic*, p. 59.   **14.** A Plancius map is on display in the Real Colegio Seminario de Corpus Christi (Museo del Patriarca), Valencia; J. Tracy, *True Ocean Found: Paludanus's Letters on Dutch Voyages to the Kara Sea, 1595–1596* (Minneapolis, 1980), pp. 20–23.   **15.** J. de Hond and T. Mostert, *Novaya Zemlya* (Rijksmuseum, Amsterdam, n.d.); inventory of contents quoted in Vaughan, *Arctic*, pp. 62–3.   **16.** L. Hacquebord, *De Noordse Compagnie (1614–1642): Opkomst, bloei en ondergang* (Zutphen, 2014); I. Sanderson, *A History of Whaling* (New York, 1993), pp. 161, 164.   **17.** Vaughan, *Arctic*, p. 64.   **18.** Wallis, 'England's Search', pp. 457–60.   **19.** Williams, *Arctic Labyrinth*, pp. 13–15; P. Whitfield, *New Found Lands: Maps in the History of Exploration* (London, 1998), pp. 78–9 (with illustration of Humphrey Gilbert's world map).   **20.** J. McDermott, *Martin Frobisher: Elizabethan Privateer* (New Haven, 2001); Alford, *London's Triumph*, pp. 158–76.   **21.** Williams, *Arctic Labyrinth*, p. 16; G. Williams, ed., *The Quest for the Northwest Passage* (London, 2007), p. 7.   **22.** G. Best, *A True Discourse of the Late Voyage of Discovery for Finding a Passage to Cathaya* (London, 1578), in Williams, ed., *Quest for the Northwest Passage*, p. 8.   **23.** Christopher Hall, 'The First Voyage of Martin Frobisher', in Hakluyt, *Voyages and Documents*, p. 153.   **24.** D. Abulafia, *The Discovery of Mankind: Atlantic Encounters in the Age of Columbus* (New Haven, 2008), p. 245.   **25.** C. F. Hall reporting in 1865, cited by Vaughan, *Arctic*, p. 69; Williams, ed., *Quest for the Northwest Passage*, pp. 19, 30, 529–30.   **26.** Hall, 'First Voyage of Martin Frobisher', in Hakluyt, *Voyages and Documents*, pp. 153–4; 'The Second Voyage of Martin Frobisher', from Best's *True Discourse*, in Hakluyt, *Voyages and Documents*, pp. 175, 178; Best, *True Discourse*, in Williams, ed., *Quest for the Northwest Passage*, pp. 17, 18; Williams, *Arctic Labyrinth*, pp. 20, 22.   **27.** Wallis, 'England's Search', p. 461; Vaughan, *Arctic*, p. 67.   **28.** Williams, ed., *Quest for the Northwest Passage*, p. 20.   **29.** Williams, *Arctic Labyrinth*, p. 23.   **30.** Best, *True Discourse*, in Williams, ed., *Quest for the Northwest Passage*, pp. 23–31; J. McDermott, ed., *The Third Voyage of Martin Frobisher to Baffin Island 1578* (London, 2001); J. Butman and S. Targett, *New World, Inc.: How England's Merchants Founded America and Launched the British Empire* (London, 2018), pp. 127–35.   **31.** Williams, *Arctic Labyrinth*, pp. 25–9.   **32.** Documents and narratives in Hakluyt, *Voyages and Documents*, pp. 303–34; Williams, *Arctic Labyrinth*, pp. 32–8.   **33.** Vaughan, *Arctic*, pp. 65–7; Williams, *Arctic Labyrinth*, pp. 41–3; Whitfield, *New Found Lands*, p. 83 (Baffin's map of Hudson Bay).   **34.** Hakluyt, *Voyages and Documents*, pp. 192–224.   **35.** Ibid., p. 205.   **36.** Wallis, 'England's Search', p. 467.   **37.** 'Drake's Circumnavigation', in Hakluyt, *Voyages and Documents*, p. 210; D. Wilson, *The World Encompassed: Drake's Great Voyage 1577–1580* (London, 1977), p. 165.   **38.** Wallis, 'England's Search', p. 467.   **39.** 'The Expedition to Russia', in Hakluyt, *Voyages and Documents*, pp. 46–7.   **40.** Jens Munk in Williams, ed., *Quest for the Northwest Passage*, p. 75; T. Hansen, *North West to Hudson Bay: the Life and Times of Jens Munk* (London, 1970, abridged from Danish edition of 1965).   **41.** Vaughan, *Arctic*, pp. 72–4; Williams, ed., *Quest for the Northwest Passage*, pp. 65–7; Williams, *Arctic Labyrinth*, pp. 55–9.

37. The Rise of the Dutch

1. J. van Houtte, *An Economic History of the Low Countries 800–1800* (London, 1977), p. 175; P. Spufford, *From Antwerp to London: the Decline of Financial Centres in Europe* (Wassenaar, 2005), p. 15; H. van der Wee, *The Growth of the Antwerp Market* (3 vols., The Hague, 1963); J. Wegg, *Antwerp, 1477–1559* (London, 1916), pp. 48–56, 59.   **2.** W. Blokmans, *Metropolen aan de Noordzee: de geschiedenis van Nederland 1100–1560* (Amsterdam, 2010), pp. 580–81; Wegg, *Antwerp*, pp. 66–8.   **3.** Blokmans, *Metropolen aan* *de Noordzee*, pp. 575, 652.   **4.** Ibid., pp. 571, 575; Wegg, *Antwerp*, pp. 60–64.   **5.** O. Gelderblom, *Cities of Commerce: the Institutional Foundations of International Trade in the Low Countries, 1250–1650* (Princeton, 2013), pp. 29–30; Spufford, *From Antwerp to London*, pp. 13–14.   **6.** J. Guy, *Gresham's Law* (London, 2019). pp. 11–13.   **7.** J. N. Ball, *Merchants and Merchandise: the Expansion of Trade in Europe 1500–1630* (London, 1977), pp. 86–7.   **8.** Van Houtte, *Economic History of the Low Countries*, p. 176.   **9.** Spufford, *From Antwerp to London*, p. 16.   **10.** Cited in Spufford, *From Antwerp to London*, p. 17.   **11.** Ball, *Merchants and Merchandise*, pp. 87–8; Gelderblom, *Cities of Commerce*, pp. 55–6; Van Houtte, *Economic History of the Low Countries*, pp. 176, 187.   **12.** Spufford, *From Antwerp to London*, p. 18; Blokmans, *Metropolen aan de Noordzee*, pp. 616–17.   **13.** Gelderblom, *Cities of Commerce*, pp. 32–3; Van Houtte, *Economic History of the Low Countries*, pp. 188–9.   **14.** J. Israel, *The Dutch Republic: Its Rise, Greatness, and Fall 1477–1806* (Oxford, 1995), p. 307; also S. Schama, *The Embarrassment of Riches: an Interpretation of Dutch Culture in the Golden Age* (London, 1987).   **15.** J. Israel, *Dutch Primacy in World Trade* (Oxford, 1989), p. 13.   **16.** Ibid., pp. 22–4; Van Houtte, *Economic History of the Low Countries*, p. 106.   **17.** Israel, *Dutch Republic*, p. 316.   **18.** Ibid., pp. 18–21.   **19.** Van Houtte, *Economic History of the Low Countries*, pp. 66–7, 70, 147–8.   **20.** David Abulafia, *The Great Sea: a Human History of the Mediterranean* (London, 2011), pp. 460, 466, 468, 477.   **21.** Israel, *Dutch Primacy*, pp. 26–35.   **22.** Ibid., pp. 38–42.   **23.** Ball, *Merchants and Merchandise*, pp. 98–102.   **24.** J. Evans, *Merchant Adventurers: the Voyage of Discovery That Transformed Tudor England* (London, 2013), pp. 315–27.   **25.** Israel, *Dutch Primacy*, pp. 43–8.

38. Whose Seas?

1. P. Borschberg, ed., *Jacques de Coutre's Singapore and Johore 1594–c.1625* (Singapore, 2015), pp. 64, 66; P. Borschberg, *Hugo Grotius, the Portuguese and Free Trade in the East Indies* (Singapore, 2011); P. de Sousa Pinto, *The Portuguese and the Straits of Melaka 1575–1619: Power, Trade and Diplomacy* (Singapore and Kuala Lumpur, 2012), pp. 31–3, 107.   **2.** B. Hayton, *The South China Sea: the Struggle for Power in Asia* (New Haven and London, 2014).   **3.** Hugo Grotius, *Mare Liberum* (Leiden, 1609); quotations are from Richard Hakluyt's translation, which is reprinted in D. Armitage, ed., *The Free Sea* (Indianapolis, 2004), pp. 3–62.   **4.** Armitage, ed., *Free Sea*, p. 10.   **5.** Armitage in *Free Sea*, p. xi; W. Welwod, 'Of the Community and Propriety of the Seas', in Armitage, ed., *Free Sea*, pp. 65–74.   **6.** Armitage, ed., *Free Sea*, p. 12.   **7.** Ibid., p. 13.   **8.** Ibid., p. 26.   **9.** Ibid., p. 80, from Grotius's reply to Welwod.   **10.** Ibid., p. 32.   **11.** Armitage in *Free Sea*, p. xvi.   **12.** J. Israel, *Dutch Primacy in World Trade* (Oxford, 1989), pp. 53–6, and tables 3.3 and 3.4, p. 57.   **13.** Ibid., p. 61.   **14.** G. Seibert, 'São Tomé & Príncipe: the First Plantation Economy in the Tropics', in R. Law, S. Schwarz and S. Strickrodt, eds., *Commercial Agriculture, the Slave Trade and Slavery in Atlantic Africa* (Woodbridge, 2013), pp. 62, 68, 75.   **15.** Israel, *Dutch Primacy*, pp. 63–4; A. de la Fuente, *Havana and the Atlantic in the Sixteenth Century* (Chapel Hill, 2008), pp. 21, 49.   **16.** J. Boyajian, *Portuguese Trade in Asia under the Habsburgs, 1580–1640* (Baltimore, 1993), p. 93.   **17.** Israel, *Dutch Primacy*, pp. 67–73; C. R. Boxer, *The Dutch Seaborne Empire 1600–1800* (London, 1965), pp. 49–54, 105, 109; G. Winius and M. Vink, *The Merchant-Warrior Pacified: the VOC (Dutch East India Co.) and Its Changing Political Economy in India* (New Delhi and Oxford, 1991), pp. 9–12.   **18.** Israel, *Dutch Primacy*, p. 129, table 5.1, and pp. 140, 143, 146–9, with table 5.9 on p. 147.   **19.** Ibid., pp. 131–8.   **20.** Ibid., p. 143.   **21.** Israel, *Dutch Primacy*, pp. 160–64, and table 5.12, p. 163; C. R. Boxer, *The Portuguese Seaborne Empire 1415–1825* (London, 1991), pp. 113–14.   **22.** 'Lancaster's Voyage to the East Indies', in Richard Hakluyt, *Voyages and Documents*, ed. J. Hampden (Oxford, 1958), pp. 399–420; D. Wilson, *The World Encompassed: Drake's Great Voyage 1577–1580* (London, 1977), p. 100; Gastaldi's map (1546) and Sir Humphrey Gilbert's map (1576), in P. Whitfield, *New Found Lands: Maps in the History of Exploration* (London, 1998), pp. 76, 79.   **23.** 'Lancaster's Voyage to the East Indies', in Hakluyt, *Voyages and Documents*, p. 411;

G. Milton, *Nathaniel's Nutmeg: How One Man's Courage Changed the Course of History* (London, 1999), p. 50; J. Keay, *The Honourable Company: a History of the English East India Company* (London, 1991), pp. 10–23.   **24.** Milton, *Nathaniel's Nutmeg*, pp. 52, 65.   **25.** Keay, *Honourable Company*, pp. 14–15.   **26.** Cited in Keay, *Honourable Company*, p. 16.   **27.** Cited in Milton, *Nathaniel's Nutmeg*, pp. 86–7; Keay, *Honourable Company*, p. 17.   **28.** Milton, *Nathaniel's Nutmeg*, pp. 90, 92, 94.   **29.** Cited in Keay, *Honourable Company*, p. 40.   **30.** Keay, *Honourable Company*, pp. 45–6, 114; Milton, *Nathaniel's Nutmeg*, p. 302.   **31.** Quoted by Keay, *Honourable Company*, p. 43; also Milton, *Nathaniel's Nutmeg*, p. 273.   **32.** Milton, *Nathaniel's Nutmeg*, pp. 305–6.   **33.** Keay, *Honourable Company*, p. 31.   **34.** Ibid., pp. 48–50; Milton, *Nathaniel's Nutmeg*, pp. 321–42.   **35.** Keay, *Honourable Company*, pp. 21, 36, 38, 53, 58–9, 125–6.   **36.** P. Stern, *The Company-State: Corporate Sovereignty and the Early Modern Foundations of the British Empire in India* (New York and Oxford, 2011), p. 7.   **37.** P. Lawson, *The East India Company: a History* (Harlow, 1993), pp. 19–24.   **38.** G. Goodman, *Japan and the Dutch 1600–1853* (Richmond, Surrey, 2000), p. 9.   **39.** D. Mitchell, *The Thousand Autumns of Jacob de Zoet* (London, 2010).   **40.** Goodman, *Japan and the Dutch*, p. 8.   **41.** A. Clulow, *The Company She Keeps: the Dutch Encounter with Tokugawa Japan* (New York, 2014), pp. 39–40.   **42.** G. Milton, *Samurai William: the Adventurer Who Unlocked Japan* (London, 2002); W. de Lange, *Pars Japonica: the First Dutch Expedition to Reach the Shores of Japan* (Warren, Conn., 2006); also D. Massarella, *A World Elsewhere: Europe's Encounter with Japan in the Sixteenth and Seventeenth Centuries* (New Haven, 1990) (for England); Clulow, *The Company She Keeps*, pp. 10–11.   **43.** Clulow, *The Company She Keeps*, pp. 25, 33–9, 47–58.   **44.** Cited in Goodman, *Japan and the Dutch*, p. 13.   **45.** Boyajian, *Portuguese Trade in Asia*, pp. 78–80; Goodman, *Japan and the Dutch*, pp. 10–13.   **46.** Jonathan Swift, *Gulliver's Travels*, ch. 25; Clulow, *The Company She Keeps*, p. 17.   **47.** Goodman, *Japan and the Dutch*, pp. 14–15.   **48.** Cited in Goodman, *Japan and the Dutch*, p. 16.   **49.** Goodman, *Japan and the Dutch*, p. 19; Toyoda Takeshi, *A History of pre-Meiji Commerce* (Tokyo, 1969), p. 46.   **50.** Takeshi, *History of pre-Meiji Commerce*, p. 50.   **51.** Goodman, *Japan and the Dutch*, pp. 240–41; Takeshi, *History of pre-Meiji Commerce*, pp. 63–4.   **52.** Goodman, *Japan and the Dutch*, pp. 28–9; Clulow, *The Company She Keeps*, pp. 18, 95, 106–20.   **53.** Goodman, *Japan and the Dutch*, pp. 69–70.   **54.** Takeshi, *History of pre-Meiji Commerce*, p. 46.

39. Nations Afloat

1. D. Studnicki-Gizbert, '*La Nación* among the Nations: Portuguese and Other Maritime Trading Diasporas in the Atlantic, Sixteenth to Eighteenth Centuries', in R. Kagan and P. Morgan, eds., *Atlantic Diasporas: Jews, Conversos, and Crypto-Jews in the Age of Mercantilism, 1500–1800* (Baltimore, 2009), pp. 75–98.   **2.** D. Eltis and D. Richardson, *Atlas of the Transatlantic Slave Trade* (New Haven, 2010).   **3.** R. Smith, *The Spanish Guild Merchant: a History of the Consulado, 1250–1700* (Durham, NC, 1940), pp. 103–4.   **4.** Inquisition records in L. Wolf, ed., *The Jews in the Canary Islands* (new edn, Toronto, 2001).   **5.** Studnicki-Gizbert, '*La Nación* among the Nations', pp. 89–90.   **6.** D. Studnicki-Gizbert, *A Nation upon the Ocean Sea: Portugal's Atlantic Diaspora and the Crisis of the Spanish Empire, 1492–1640* (New York and Oxford, 2007), p. 11.   **7.** Cited by Studnicki-Gizbert, *A Nation upon the Ocean Sea*, p. 36.   **8.** Studnicki-Gizbert, *A Nation upon the Ocean Sea*, pp. 91–2.   **9.** R. Rowland, 'New Christian, Marrano, Jew', in P. Bernardini and N. Fiering, eds., *The Jews and the Expansion of Europe to the West 1450–1800* (New York, 2001), p. 135.   **10.** Studnicki-Gizbert, *A Nation upon the Ocean Sea*, p. 72.   **11.** H. Kellenbenz, *Sephardim an der unteren Elbe: ihre wirtschaftliche und politische Bedeutung vom Ende des 16. bis zum Beginn des 18. Jahrhunderts* (Wiesbaden, 1958), p. 489.   **12.** Y. Yovel, *The Other Within: the Marranos, Split Identity and Emerging Modernity* (Princeton, 2009).   **13.** Studnicki-Gizbert, *A Nation upon the Ocean Sea*, pp. 96–101; diagram of his connections, p. 99, fig. 4:1.   **14.** Hamburg: Kellenbenz, *Sephardim an der unteren Elbe*; Bayonne: G. Nahon, 'The Portuguese Jewish Nation of Saint-Esprit-lès-Bayonne: the American Dimension', in Bernardini and Fiering, eds., *Jews and the Expansion of Europe*, pp. 256–67.   **15.**

Studnicki-Gizbert, *A Nation upon the Ocean Sea*, p. 103, fig. 4:2; Kellenbenz, *Sephardim an der unteren Elbe*, end map no. 3; Morocco: pp. 146–9; Baltic: pp. 149–55.   16. P. Mark and J. da Silva Horta, 'Catholics, Jews, and Muslims in Early Seventeenth-Century Guiné', in Kagan and Morgan, eds., *Atlantic Diasporas*, pp. 170–94; P. Mark and J. da Silva Horta, *The Forgotten Diaspora: Jewish Communities in West Africa and the Making of the Atlantic World* (Cambridge, 2011).   17. T. Green, *The Rise of the Trans-Atlantic Slave Trade in Western Africa, 1300–1589* (Cambridge, 2012).   18. J. Boyajian, *Portuguese Trade in Asia under the Habsburgs, 1580–1640* (Baltimore, 1993).   19. Ibid., pp. 30–31, 42, 45–51, 239–40.   20. J. Boyajian, *Portuguese Bankers at the Court of Spain 1626–1650* (New Brunswick, 1983), p. 3.   21. C. Dauverd, *Imperial Ambition in the Early Modern Mediterranean: Genoese Merchants and the Spanish Crown* (Cambridge, 2014).   22. T. Kirk, *Genoa and the Sea: Policy and Power in an Early Modern Maritime Republic 1559–1684* (Baltimore, 2005), pp. 127–33.   23. Boyajian, *Portuguese Bankers*, pp. 21–2, 33, 106–7.   24. Ibid., pp. 108–16.   25. Ibid., pp. 154–80.   26. S. Aslanian, *From the Indian Ocean to the Mediterranean: the Global Trade Networks of Armenian Merchants from New Julfa* (Berkeley, 2011), p. xvii.   27. Ibid., pp. 24–36.   28. Ibid., pp. xvii, 226–7; I. Baghdiantz McCabe, 'Small Town Merchants, Global Ventures: the Maritime Trade of the New Julfan Armenians in the Seventeenth and Eighteenth Centuries', in M. Fusaro and A. Polónia, eds., *Maritime History as Global History* (St John's, Nfdl., 2010), pp. 125–57.   29. Aslanian, *From the Indian Ocean to the Mediterranean*, pp. 52–4.   30. Armando Cortesão, transl. and ed., *The Suma Oriental of Tomé Pires* (London, 1944), vol. 2, p. 269.   31. F. Trivellato, 'Sephardic Merchants in the Early Modern Atlantic and Beyond', in an and Morgan, eds., *Atlantic Diasporas*, p. 111.   32. Aslanian, *From the Indian Ocean to the Mediterranean*, pp. 48–51, 55–65, 78, 80.   33. Trivellato, 'Sephardic Merchants', p. 110.

40. The Nordic Indies

1. S. Diller, *Die Dänen in Indien, Südostasien und China (1620–1845)* (Wiesbaden, 1999), p. 133; O. Feldbæk, 'The Danish Asia Trade 1620–1807', *Scandinavian Economic History Review*, vol. 39 (1991), pp. 3–27.   2. H. Hodacs, *Silk and Tea in the North: Scandinavian Trade and the Market for Asian Goods in Eighteenth-Century Europe* (Basingstoke, 2016), pp. 1–20, 48–81.   3. Ibid., pp. 183, 187.   4. Diller, *Dänen in Indien*, pp. 11, 114, 267–99.   5. Ibid., p. 39.   6. K. Glamann, 'The Danish Asiatic Company, 1732–1772', *Scandinavian Economic History Review*, vol. 8 (1960), pp. 109–49; K. Glamann, 'The Danish East India Company', in M. Mollat, ed., *Sociétés et Compagnies de Commerce en Orient et dans l'Océan indien* (Paris, 1970), pp. 471–9; O. Feldbæk, 'The Danish Trading Companies of the Seventeenth and Eighteenth Centuries', *Scandinavian Economic History Review*, vol. 34 (1986), pp. 211–13; O. Feldbæk, *India Trade under the Danish Flag 1772–1808: European Enterprise and Anglo-Indian Remittance and Trade* (Odense, 1969).   7. E. Gøbel, 'Danish Trade to the West Indies and Guinea, 1671–1754', *Scandinavian Economic History Review*, vol. 31 (1983), pp. 21–49; G. Nørregård, *Danish Settlements in West Africa* (Boston, 1966); W. Westergaard, *The Danish West Indies under Company Rule (1671–1754)* (New York, 1917).   8. E. Gøbel, 'The Danish Asiatic Company's Voyages to China, 1732–1833', *Scandinavian Economic History Review*, vol. 27 (1979), p. 43.   9. A. Friis, 'La Valeur documentaire des Comptes du Péage du Sund: la période 1571–1618', in M. Mollat, ed., *Les Sources de l'histoire maritime en Europe, du Moyen Âge au XVIIIe siècle* (Paris, 1962), pp. 365–82.   10. Feldbæk, 'Danish Trading Companies', p. 204; S. Subrahmanyam, 'The Coromandel Trade of the Danish East India Company, 1618–1649', *Scandinavian Economic History Review*, vol. 37 (1989), p. 41; H. Furber, *Rival Empires of Trade in the Orient 1600–1800* (Minneapolis, 1976), reprinted in S. Subrahmanyam, ed., *Maritime India* (New Delhi, 2004), pp. 211, 216; Diller, *Dänen in Indien*, p. 23.   11. Subrahmanyam, 'Coromandel Trade', pp. 43–4.   12. Facsimile of treaty in Diller, *Dänen in Indien*, pp. 155–8, doc. 16a–d; Subrahmanyam, 'Coromandel Trade', p. 45.   13. Subrahmanyam, 'Coromandel Trade', p. 47.   14. Feldbæk, 'Danish Trading Companies', p. 207; Diller, *Dänen in Indien*,

p. 111.   15. Diller, *Dänen in Indien*, pp. 21, 25 (facsimiles), 34–5, 39, 61–2, 89, 92–3.   16. Feldbæk, 'Danish Asia Trade', p. 3.   17. Feldbæk, 'Danish Trading Companies', p. 206; Subrahmanyam, 'Coromandel Trade', p. 51.   18. Subrahmanyam, 'Coromandel Trade', pp. 52–3.   19. Diller, *Dänen in Indien*, pp. 81, 85, 87; T. Veschow, 'Voyages of the Danish Asiatic Company to India and China 1772–1792', *Scandinavian Economic History Review*, vol. 20 (1972), pp. 133–52.   20. D. McCall, 'Introduction', in Nørregård, *Danish Settlements*, pp. xi, xxii; Nørregård, *Danish Settlements*, pp. 142, 228.   21. Nørregård, *Danish Settlements*, p. 84.   22. Ibid., pp. 87–9.   23. H. Strömberg, *En guide till Göteborgs historia – An Historical Guide to Gothenburg* (Gothenburg, 2013), pp. 6, 9; Nørregård, *Danish Settlements*, pp. 9–10; C. Koninckx, *The First and Second Charters of the Swedish East India Company (1731–1766): a Contribution to the Maritime, Economic and Social History of North-Western Europe in Its Relationships with the Far East* (Kortrijk, 1980), pp. 33–4.   24. Koninckx, *First and Second Charters*, pp. 31–3; H. Lindqvist, *Våra kolonier: de vi hade och de som aldrig blev av* (Stockholm, 2015), pp. 11–13; Nørregård, *Danish Settlements*, pp. 7–8.   25. Lindqvist, *Våra kolonier*, pp. 90–99, 114, 117.   26. Nørregård, *Danish Settlements*, pp. 11–16.   27. Ibid., pp. 22–24, 29–34.   28. Ibid., pp. 33, 52–3, 57.   29. McCall, ibid., p. xix; H. Mattiesen, 'Jakob Kettler', *Neue deutsche Biographie*, vol. 10 (Berlin, 1974), p. 314.   30. Westergaard, *Danish West Indies*, pp. 256–62.   31. Ibid., pp. 31–8.   32. Ibid., pp. 41–2.   33. Gøbel, 'Danish Trade to the West Indies', pp. 24, 28–30.   34. Ibid., pp. 33–7.   35. Nørregård, *Danish Settlements*, pp. 143, 176.   36. Hodacs, *Silk and Tea in the North*, pp. 29–32; Furber, *Rival Empires of Trade*, pp. 217–21.   37. G. M. Young, ed., *Macaulay: Prose and Poetry* (London, 1952), pp. 213, 217.   38. G. Insh, *The Company of Scotland Trading to Africa and the Indies* (London and New York, 1932); Furber, *Rival Empires of Trade*, p. 217.   39. K. Söderpalm, 'SOIC – ett skotskt företag?', in K. Söderpalm et al., *Ostindiska Compagniet: Affärer och föremål* (Gothenburg, 2000), pp. 36–61, and English summary, pp. 281–2; R. Hermansson, *The Great East India Adventure: The Story of the Swedish East India Company* (Gothenburg, 2004), pp. 31–2.   40. Hodacs, *Silk and Tea in the North*, pp. 29, 31.   41. P. Forsberg, *Ostindiska Kompaniet: Några studier* (Gothenburg, 2015), pp. 90–94; Hermansson, *Great East India Adventure*, pp. 40–45.   42. Hermansson, *Great East India Adventure*, pp. 49–57.   43. Forsberg, *Ostindiska Kompaniet*, pp. 87–90.   44. Hodacs, *Silk and Tea in the North*, pp. 58–61, 64–6, 79–80.   45. K. Söderpalm, 'Beställningsporslin från Kina', in Söderpalm et al., *Ostindiska Compagniet*, pp. 168–83, 291–2.   46. Hermansson, *Great East India Adventure*, pp. 42–3.   47. Hodacs, *Silk and Tea in the North*, pp. 10–14.   48. Ibid., p. 153.   49. K. Söderpalm, 'Svenska Ostindiska Kompaniet 1731–1813: en översikt', in Söderpalm et al., *Ostindiska Compagniet*, pp. 9, 277; Hermansson, *Great East India Adventure*, pp. 11, 63, 67–71.

41. Austrialia or Australia?

1. M. Edmond, *Zone of the Marvellous: in Search of the Antipodes* (Auckland, 2009), p. 85; A. Stallard, *Antipodes: in Search of the Southern Continent* (Clayton, Vic., 2016).   2. M. Estensen, *Terra Australis Incognita: the Spanish Quest for the Mysterious Great South Land* (Crows Nest, NSW, 2006), pp. 8–12, 14 (whence the two quotations); N. Crane, *Mercator: the Man Who Mapped the Planet* (London, 2002), p. 97, fig. 12; M. Camino, *Exploring the Explorers: Spaniards in Oceania, 1519–1794* (Manchester, 2008), p. 83, fig. 2:3; Edmond, *Zone of the Marvellous*, pp. 32–4; H. Kelsey, *The First Circumnavigators: Unsung Heroes of the Age of Discovery* (New Haven, 2016), pp. 134–5; Stallard, *Antipodes*, pp. 86–111.   3. Camino, *Exploring the Explorers*, p. 36.   4. Ibid., p. 38; Stallard, *Antipodes*, pp. 120–24.   5. Mendaña's report, cited by Estensen, *Terra Australis Incognita*, p. 27; Camino, *Exploring the Explorers*, pp. 48–9.   6. D. Abulafia, *The Discovery of Mankind: Atlantic Encounters in the Age of Columbus* (New Haven, 2008), pp. 267–8.   7. Edmond, *Zone of the Marvellous*, p. 86.   8. Estensen, *Terra Australis Incognita*, pp. 19–56; Camino, *Exploring the Explorers*, pp. 39–61; Kelsey, *First Circumnavigators*, pp. 70–74.   9. Estensen,

Terra Australis Incognita, pp. 57–8. **10.** Camino, *Exploring the Explorers*, p. 19. **11.** Ibid., pp. 75–8, 80, 101; M. Estensen, *Discovery: The Quest for the Great South Land* (London, 1999), p. 101. **12.** Estensen, *Terra Australis Incognita*, pp. 129–33. **13.** Ibid., pp. 159–60; Camino, *Exploring the Explorers*, pp. 84, 95; Stallard, *Antipodes*, p. 130. **14.** Estensen, *Terra Australis Incognita*, pp. 182–3. **15.** Ibid., pp. 197–204. **16.** G. Seal, *The Savage Shore: Extraordinary Stories of Survival and Tragedy from the Early Voyages of Discovery* (New Haven, 2016), p. ix. **17.** Australian Electoral Commission, *History of the Indigenous Vote* (Canberra, 2006). **18.** P. Whitfield, *Charting of the Oceans: Ten Centuries of Maritime Maps* (London, 1996), pp. 55, 57–8. **19.** K. McIntyre, *The Secret Discovery of Australia: Portuguese Ventures 200 Years before Captain Cook* (Medindie and London, 1977); A. Sharp, *The Discovery of Australia* (Oxford, 1963), pp. 2, 4–15, and plate 3. **20.** Estensen, *Discovery*, pp. 53–8; Seal, *Savage Shore*, p. 15. **21.** Estensen, *Discovery*, pp. 56–8; Seal, *Savage Shore*, pp. 16–18. **22.** Seal, *Savage Shore*, p. 27. **23.** Ibid., pp. 22–5, 265 n. 8; Estensen, *Discovery*, pp. 119–22. **24.** Seal, *Savage Shore*, p. 28; Estensen, *Discovery*, pp. 128–9; Sharp, *Discovery of Australia*, p. 32. **25.** François Pelsaert, supercargo of the *Batavia*, cited by Estensen, *Discovery*, p. 158. **26.** Seal, *Savage Shore*, pp. 30–34; Estensen, *Discovery*, pp. 140–41; Sharp, *Discovery of Australia*, pp. 42–5. **27.** M. Dash, *Batavia's Graveyard* (London, 2002), pp. 53–7, 62–5. **28.** 'The Journals of Francisco Pelsaert', transl. E. Drok, in H. Drake-Brockman, *Voyage to Disaster: the Life of Francisco Pelsaert* (London, 1964), p. 122. **29.** Pelsaert's log, in Sharp, *Discovery of Australia*, p. 61; 'Journals of Francisco Pelsaert', p. 130. **30.** Text in Seal, *Savage Shore*, p. 65; also 'Journals of Francisco Pelsaert', p. 128. **31.** Seal, *Savage Shore*, p. 70; Dash, *Batavia's Graveyard*, pp. 30–35, 277–81; 'Journals of Francisco Pelsaert', pp. 158–77. **32.** Seal, *Savage Shore*, pp. 67–73; 'Journals of Francisco Pelsaert', pp. 142–4; Dash, *Batavia's Graveyard*, pp. 205–11. **33.** Seal, *Savage Shore*, pp. 78–80; Estensen, *Discovery*, pp. 160–61. **34.** Dash, *Batavia's Graveyard*, pp. 264–75, suggesting on p. 273 a slightly different scenario; Seal, *Savage Shore*, pp. 82–4. **35.** Seal, *Savage Shore*, p. 85; Estensen, *Discovery*, pp. 154–5; Sharp, *Discovery of Australia*, pp. 55–6. **36.** Estensen, *Discovery*, pp. 9, 87, 131, 148, 230; Sharp, *Discovery of Australia*, p. 39. **37.** Seal, *Savage Shore*, p. 97. **38.** Sharp, *Discovery of Australia*, pp. 70–79. **39.** A. Salmond, 'Two Worlds', in K. R. Howe, ed., *Vaka Moana – Voyages of the Ancestors: the Discovery and Settlement of the Pacific* (Auckland, 2006), pp. 251–2. **40.** Estensen, *Discovery*, pp. 179–81. **41.** Sharp, *Discovery of Australia*, pp. 87–8; Seal, *Savage Shore*, p. 96. **42.** P. Edwards, 'The First Voyage 1768–1771: Introduction', in James Cook, *The Journals* (2nd edn, London, 2003), p. 11.

42. Knots in the Network

1. C. Ebert, *Between Empires: Brazilian Sugar in the Early Atlantic Economy 1550–1630* (Leiden, 2008), pp. 140–41; G. Scammell, 'The English in the Atlantic Islands c.1450–1650', *Mariner's Mirror*, vol. 72 (1986), pp. 295–317. **2.** T. B. Duncan, *Atlantic Islands: Madeira, the Azores and the Cape Verdes in Seventeenth-Century Commerce and Navigation* (Chicago, 1972), p. 5. **3.** Ebert, *Between Empires*, pp. 104–5; F. Mauro, *Le Portugal, le Brésil et l'Atlantique au XVIIe siècle (1570–1670)* (Paris and Lisbon, 1983; revised edition of *Le Portugal et l'Atlantique au XVIIe siècle: Étude Économique* (Paris, 1960)), pp. 209–12. **4.** A. Simon, ed., *The Bolton Letters: the Letters of an English Merchant in Madeira 1695–1714*, vol. 1: *1695–1700* (London, 1928), pp. 17–19, and p. 56, letter 16; Duncan, *Atlantic Islands*, pp. 38–9. **5.** Simon, ed., *Bolton Letters*, p. 20; Duncan, *Atlantic Islands*, p. 42; Mauro, *Le Portugal, le Brésil*, pp. 411–21. **6.** Duncan, *Atlantic Islands*, pp. 38–9, 46, 52, 54–60. **7.** Simon, ed., *Bolton Letters*, p. 14. **8.** Biographies ibid., pp. 6–7, footnote. **9.** East Indies: Simon, ed., *Bolton Letters*, p. 132, letter 62. **10.** Ibid., p. 8; Azorean wheat: ibid., p. 29, letter 4, p. 76, letter 27, p. 87, letter 34, p. 119, letter 55; Dutch wheat: ibid., p. 49, letter 12; Scottish beef, butter and herrings: ibid., p. 65, letter 21; sugar unloaded in Madeira: ibid., p. 82, letter 31; Mauro, *Le Portugal, le Brésil*, p. 352; A. Vieira, *O comércio inter-insular nos séculos XV e XVI: Madeira, Açores e Canárias* (Funchal, 1987). **11.** Simon, ed., *Bolton Letters*, pp. 24–5, letter 2.   **12.** Ibid., pp. 41–4, letter 10.   **13.** Ibid., p. 172, letter 88, p. 174, letter 90.   **14.** Ibid., p. 124, letter 58.   **15.** Duncan, *Atlantic Islands*, pp. 88–9, 108–10, tables 16–18.   **16.** Ibid., pp. 111, 124, 140, 147, 151–3, 156.   **17.** Ibid., pp. 125–7.   **18.** Ibid., pp. 135–6; *Angra, a Terceira e os Açores nas Rotas da Índia e das Américas* (Angra do Heroísmo, 1999).   **19.** Duncan, *Atlantic Islands*, pp. 168–71.   **20.** A. Crosby, *Ecological Imperialism: the Biological Expansion of Europe, 900–1900* (Cambridge, 1986).   **21.** Duncan, *Atlantic Islands*, pp. 167, 176, 188.   **22.** A. J. d'Oliveira Bouças, *Apelo em pró das ruínas da antiga cidade da Ribeira Grande em Santiago – C. Verde 1533–1933* (Praia, 1933; new edn as *Cidade velha: Ribeira Grande de Santiago*, Praia, 2013).   **23.** T. Green, *The Rise of the Trans-Atlantic Slave Trade in Western Africa, 1300–1589* (Cambridge, 2012); A. Carreira, *Cabo Verde: Formação e Extinção de uma Sociedade escravocrata (1460–1878)* (3rd edn, Praia de Santiago, 2000).   **24.** Mauro, *Le Portugal, le Brésil*, pp. 188–9; Duncan, *Atlantic Islands*, pp. 199–200; M. L. Stig Sørensen, C. Evans and K. Richter, 'A Place of History: Archaeology and Heritage at Cidade Velha, Cape Verde', in P. Lane and K. McDonald, eds., *Slavery in Africa: Archaeology and Memory* (Proceedings of the British Academy, vol. 168, 2011), pp. 421–42.   **25.** Duncan, *Atlantic Islands*, pp. 230–31; baptism: Carreira, *Cabo Verde*, pp. 259–80.   **26.** P. Mark and J. da Silva Horta, *The Forgotten Diaspora Jewish Communities in West Africa and the Making of the Atlantic World* (Cambridge, 2011); Green, *Rise of the Trans-Atlantic Slave Trade*; Carreira, *Cabo Verde*, pp. 55–78, 146.   **27.** Duncan, *Atlantic Islands*, p. 215.   **28.** Ibid., pp. 219–24.   **29.** Ibid., pp. 207, 210.   **30.** S. Royle, *The Company's Island: St Helena, Company Colonies and the Colonial Endeavour* (London, 2007), pp. 9, 11 (whence the seventeenth-century quotation).   **31.** A. R. Azzam, *The Other Exile: the Remarkable Story of Fernão Lopes, the Island of Saint Helena, and a Paradise Lost* (London, 2017); Royle, *Company's Island*, p. 12; chapel: ibid., p. 19, fig. 2:7.   **32.** Royle, *Company's Island*, p. 14, fig. 2:3.   **33.** 'Prosperous voyage of the worshipful Thomas Candish', in J. Beeching, ed., *Hakluyt: Voyages and Discoveries* (Harmondsworth, 1972) pp. 276–97.   **34.** Royle, *Company's Island*, pp. 11–19; P. Stern, *The Company-State: Corporate Sovereignty and the Early Modern Foundations of the British Empire in India* (New York and Oxford, 2011), p. 21; J. McAleer, *Britain's Maritime Empire: Southern Africa, the South Atlantic and the Indian Ocean, 1763–1820* (Cambridge, 2017), p. 74.   **35.** McAleer, *Britain's Maritime Empire*, pp. 73–7.   **36.** Ibid., pp. 34–5; Royle, *Company's Island*, pp. 85–7.   **37.** Royle, *Company's Island*, pp. 23–4, 27–8, 46, 51 (fig. 3:1), 175–7 (tables 3:2, 3:3, 3:4 – adjusting Royle's figures to accommodate 'free blacks' as non-slaves).   **38.** Ibid., pp. 39–41.   **39.** Ibid., pp. 101–2.   **40.** McAleer, *Britain's Maritime Empire*, pp. 78–9; Royle, *The Company's Island*, pp. 53–4.   **41.** McAleer, *Britain's Maritime Empire*, pp. 78–80.   **42.** Ibid., pp. 2, 9–10, 17, 24–7.   **43.** W. Hamond, *Madagascar, the Richest and most Fruitfull Island in the world* (London, 1643; title-page reproduced in K. McDonald, *Pirates, Merchants, Settlers, and Slaves: Colonial America and the Indo-Atlantic World* (Oakland, 2015), p. 73, fig. 8); W. Hamond, *A Paradox Prooving that the Inhabitants of the Isle called Madagascar or St Laurence (in Temporall things) are the happiest People in the World* (London, 1640).   **44.** S. Randrianja and S. Ellis, *Madagascar: a Short History* (London, 2009), pp. 54–66.   **45.** Ibid., pp. 110–11.   **46.** Ibid., pp. 4, 102, 226.   **47.** R. Allen, *European Slave Trading in the Indian Ocean, 1500–1850* (Athens, Oh., 2014), p. 59; D. Eltis and D. Richardson, *Atlas of the Transatlantic Slave Trade* (New Haven, 2010), pp. 4–5, map 1; pp. 18–19, map 11; pp. 154–5, maps 107–9.   **48.** Allen, *European Slave Trading*, pp. 37, 49.   **49.** McDonald, *Pirates, Merchants*, pp. 82–3.   **50.** Ibid., pp. 84–92; Allen, *European Slave Trading*, pp. 72–8.   **51.** Allen, *European Slave Trading*, pp. 36, 48; also p. 58, table 8..   **52.** McDonald, *Pirates, Merchants*, pp. 116–21; Randrianja and Ellis, *Madagascar*, p. 106.   **53.** Allen, *European Slave Trading*, pp. 47–56, and p. 54, table 7.   **54.** Ibid., pp. 50, 75–6; and p. 75, table 10, calculating average cargoes out of Madagascar, 1718–1809.

43. The Wickedest Place on Earth

1. N. Zahedieh, '"A Frugal, Prudential and Hopeful Trade": Privateering in Jamaica, 1655–89', *Journal of Imperial and Commonwealth History*, vol. 18 (1990), p. 149.   **2.** S. Talty,

Empire of Blue Water: Henry Morgan and the Pirates Who Ruled the Caribbean Waves (London, 2007), pp. 39–40; David Abulafia, *The Great Sea: a Human History of the Mediterranean* (London, 2011), pp. 415–20; cattle in Hispaniola: J. del Rio Moreno, *Ganadería, plantaciones y comercio azucarero antillano, siglos XVI y XVII* (Santo Domingo, 2012). **3.** Talty, *Empire of Blue Water*, pp. 131–2. **4.** P. Neher, 'The Pure Theory of the Muggery', *American Economic Review*, vol. 68 (1978), pp. 437–45; I owe my knowledge of this work and my awareness of its use in discussing piracy to Peter Earle. See also Zahedieh, '"Frugal, Prudential and Hopeful Trade"', p. 145. **5.** J. Rogoziński, *A Brief History of the Caribbean from the Arawak and the Carib to the Present Day* (New York, 1992), pp. 101–2. **6.** K. O. Kuperman, *Roanoke, the Abandoned Colony* (2nd edn, Lanham, 2007). **7.** K. O. Kupperman, *The Jamestown Project* (Cambridge, Mass., 2007); J. Evans, *Emigrants: Why the English Sailed to the New World* (London, 2017), p. 4; J. Butman and S. Targett, *New World, Inc.: How England' Merchants Founded America and Launched the British Empire* (London, 2018), pp. 260–74. **8.** M. Jarvis, *In the Eye of All Trade: Bermuda, Bermudians, and the Maritime Atlantic World, 1680–1783* (Chapel Hill and Williamsburg, Va., 2010), pp. 11–18, 26–32, 37–50, 105, 111, 113, and table 3, p. 114. **9.** Evans, *Emigrants*, pp. 5–6. **10.** R. Fraser, *The Mayflower Generation: the Winslow Family and the Fight for the New World* (London, 2017). **11.** Evans, *Emigrants*, pp. 84–91. **12.** S. White, *A Cold Welcome: the Little Ice Age and Europe's Encounter with North America* (Cambridge, Mass., 2017); G. Parker, *Global Crisis: War, Climate Change and Catastrophe in the Seventeenth Century* (New Haven, 2013); Evans, *Emigrants*, pp. 246–58, 268. **13.** H. Beckles, *A History of Barbados from Amerindian Settlement to Caribbean Single Market* (Cambridge, 2006), pp. 8–9; P. Drewett, ed., *Prehistoric Barbados* (Bridgetown and London, 1991). **14.** Rogoziński, *Brief History of the Caribbean*, p. 67. **15.** Cited by T. Hunt, *Ten Cities That Made an Empire* (London, 2014), p. 72. **16.** Beckles, *History of Barbados*, pp. 18–20, 31, 36–8, 50–51, 53–8. **17.** B. Higman, *A. Concise History of the Caribbean* (Cambridge, 2011), pp. 87–8, 169–70. **18.** Rogoziński, *Brief History of the Caribbean*, p. 69; Higman, *Concise History of the Caribbean*, pp. 98–109; P. Jones, *Satan's Kingdom: Bristol and the Transatlantic Slave Trade* (Bristol, 2007), pp. 12–13. **19.** C. G. Pestana, *The English Conquest of Jamaica: Oliver Cromwell's Bid for Empire* (Cambridge, Mass., 2017); L. H. Roper, *Advancing Empire: English Interests and Overseas Expansion, 1613–1688* (Cambridge, 2017), pp. 154–6. **20.** F. Morales Padrón, *Spanish Jamaica* (Kingston, Jamaica, 2003), p. 183; E. Kritzler, *Jewish Pirates of the Caribbean* (New York, 2008), pp. 183–5; cf. L. Wolf, *Jews in the Canary Islands, being a Calendar of Jewish Cases Extracted from the Records of the Canariote Inquisition in the Collection of the Marquess of Bute* (London, 1926; new edn, Toronto, 2001), pp. xxxviii–xl. **21.** B. Vega, *La derrota de los Ingleses en Santo Domingo, 1655* (Aranjuez, 2013), pp. 24, 27–9, 94–6; Pestana, *English Conquest of Jamaica*, pp. 66–92; passage about English position cited from Kritzler, *Jewish Pirates*, p. 191; see also M. Hanna, *Pirate Nests and the Rise of the British Empire, 1570–1740* (Chapel Hill, 2015), pp. 98–101. **22.** Vega, *Derrota de los Ingleses*, pp. 37–102; Morales Padrón, *Spanish Jamaica*, p. 184. **23.** Roper, *Advancing Empire*, pp. 156–7. **24.** Pestana, *English Conquest of Jamaica*, pp. 98–105. **25.** Cited by Kritzler, *Jewish Pirates*, p. 189. **26.** Morales Padrón, *Spanish Jamaica*, pp. 51–121, 172; P. Hoffman, *The Spanish Crown and the Defense of the Caribbean, 1535–1585: Precedent, Patrimonialism, and Royal Parsimony* (Baton Rouge, 1980), p. 121. **27.** N. Zahedieh, 'Trade, Plunder and Economic Development in Early English Jamaica, 1655–89', *Economic History Review*, ser. 2, vol. 39 (1986), pp. 205–22. **28.** Pestana, *English Conquest of Jamaica*, p. 119. **29.** Ibid., pp. 119–21. **30.** Vega, *Derrota de los Ingleses*, p. 107; Pestana, *English Conquest of Jamaica*, p. 138; Kritzler, *Jewish Pirates*, p. 192. **31.** Roper, *Advancing Empire*, p. 159. **32.** W. Westergaard, *The Danish West Indies under Company Rule (1671–1754)* (New York, 1917), pp. 31–42; Higman, *Concise History of the Caribbean*, pp. 91–4; Rogoziński, *Brief History of the Caribbean*, pp. 57–82. **33.** Kritzler, *Jewish Pirates*, p. 194; S. Fortune, *Merchants and Jews: the Struggle for British West Indian Commerce, 1650–1750* (Gainesville, 1984). **34.** Kritzler, *Jewish Pirates*, pp. 216–19, 233–4, 257–63; N. Zahedieh, 'The Merchants of Port Royal, Jamaica, and the Spanish Contraband Trade, 1655–1692', *William and Mary Quarterly*, vol. 43 (1986), pp. 579–80; treasure chest: R. Marx, *Pirate Port: the Story of the*

Sunken City of Port Royal (London, 1968), pp. 177–80; Hanna, *Pirate Nests*, pp. 109–10.   **35.** Zahedieh, 'Merchants of Port Royal', pp. 574–5; Zahedieh, '"Frugal, Prudential and Hopeful Trade"', p. 146.   **36.** Pestana, *English Conquest of Jamaica*, p. 255; C. Pestana, 'Early English Jamaica without Pirates', *William and Mary Quarterly*, vol. 71 (2014), pp. 321–60.   **37.** D. Pope, *Harry Morgan's Way: the Biography of Sir Henry Morgan 1635–1684* (London, 1977), pp. 76–81.   **38.** Talty, *Empire of Blue Water*, pp. 41–5; Pope, *Harry Morgan's Way*, pp. 90–99.   **39.** J. Beeching, 'Introduction', in A. Exquemeling, *The Buccaneers of America*, transl. A. Brown (Harmondsworth, 1969), pp. 14–15; cf. Hanna, *Pirate Nests*, p. 104.   **40.** Pope, *Harry Morgan's Way*, pp. 67, 73.   **41.** Talty, *Empire of Blue Water*, pp. 101–21; Zahedieh, 'Trade, Plunder and Economic Development', p. 216: about £60 per head, three times the annual plantation wage.   **42.** P. Earle, *The Sack of Panamá* (London, 1981); Pope, *Harry Morgan's Way*, pp. 212–47.   **43.** G. Thomas, *The Buccaneer King: the Story of Captain Henry Morgan* (London, 2014), pp. ix, 7; Hanna, *Pirate Nests*, pp. 103–4.   **44.** Zahedieh, '"Frugal, Prudential and Hopeful Trade"', p. 152.   **45.** Pope, *Harry Morgan's Way*, pp. 333–5; Hanna, *Pirate Nests*, pp. 138–40.   **46.** Hanna, *Pirate Nests*, pp. 106–7.   **47.** Zahedieh, '"Frugal, Prudential and Hopeful Trade"', pp. 155–6.   **48.** Zahedieh, 'Merchants of Port Royal', pp. 570–71; Zahedieh, '"Frugal, Prudential and Hopeful Trade"', pp. 158, 161.   **49.** Zahedieh, '"Frugal, Prudential and Hopeful Trade"', p. 148.   **50.** M. Pawson and D. Buisseret, *Port Royal Jamaica* (2nd edn, Kingston, Jamaica, 2000), p. 94.   **51.** Marx, *Pirate Port*, p. 175.   **52.** Pawson and Buisseret, *Port Royal Jamaica*, p. 87.   **53.** Ibid., p. 89.   **54.** Zahedieh, 'Merchants of Port Royal', pp. 583–4, 589–92; Pawson and Buisseret, *Port Royal Jamaica*, p. 92.   **55.** Zahedieh, 'Trade, Plunder and Economic Development', p. 220; Marx, *Pirate Port*, pp. 158–9.   **56.** Marx, *Pirate Port*, pp. 122, 134, 153, etc.   **57.** Pawson and Buisseret, *Port Royal Jamaica*, pp. 158–61; cf. Talty, *Empire of Blue Water*, pp. 130, 132–5.   **58.** Pawson and Buisseret, *Port Royal Jamaica*, pp. 135–6.   **59.** Ibid., pp. 109–11, 120–21.   **60.** Ibid., pp. 165–8.

44. A Long Way to China

1. K. McDonald, *Pirates, Merchants, Settlers, and Slaves: Colonial America and the Indo-Atlantic World* (Oakland, 2015); R. Allen, *European Slave Trading in the Indian Ocean, 1500–1850* (Athens, Oh., 2014).   **2.** J. Goldstein, *Philadelphians and the China Trade 1682–1846: Commercial, Cultural, and Attitudinal Effects* (University Park, Pa., 1978), p. 17; M. Christman, *Adventurous Pursuits: Americans and the China Trade 1784–1844* (Washington DC, 1984).   **3.** C. Matson, *Merchants and Empire: Trading in Colonial New York* (Baltimore, 1998), pp. 142–3, 146–8; source of quotation: p. 183; C. Frank, *Objectifying China: Chinese Commodities in Early America* (Chicago, 2011), p. 56, table 1:2; Goldstein, *Philadelphians and the China Trade*, pp. 17–20.   **4.** Frank, *Objectifying China*, pp. 5, 1, 12.   **5.** Ibid., pp. 13–22, 92; examples from the 1790s of E PLURIBUS UNUM in Rhode Island School of Design Museum, Providence, RI.   **6.** Christman, *Adventurous Pursuits*, p. 22.   **7.** J. Fichter, *So Great a Proffit: How the East Indies Trade Transformed Anglo-American Capitalism* (Cambridge, Mass., 2010), pp. 93–4, 209.   **8.** Frank, *Objectifying China*, pp. 31, 34–7.   **9.** Ibid., pp. 31, 34–7; Goldstein, *Philadelphians and the China Trade*, pp. 18, 20.   **10.** He Sibing, *Macao in the Making of Sino-American Relations, 1784–1844* (Macau, 2015), p. 42.   **11.** E. Dolin, *When America First Met China: an Exotic History of Tea, Drugs, and Money in the Age of Sail* (New York, 2012), pp. 65–71.   **12.** Cited by Frank, *Objectifying China*, p. 203.   **13.** Dolin, *When America First Met China*, pp. 4–6.   **14.** James Cook, *The Journals* (2nd edn, London, 2003), p. 559.   **15.** Dolin, *When America First Met China*, pp. 9–11; J. Kirker, *Adventures to China: Americans in the Southern Oceans 1792–1812* (New York, 1970), pp. 8, 13–19.   **16.** Dolin, *When America First Met China*, pp. 12–13; He, *Macao in the Making of Early Sino-American Relations*, p. 43.   **17.** Dolin, *When America First Met China*, pp. 20–21.   **18.** Text in Goldstein, *Philadelphians and the China Trade*, p. 32.   **19.** Cited by Dolin, *When America First Met China*, p. 22.   **20.** Cited by Dolin, *When America First Met China*, p. 74; on Shaw: He, *Macao in* *the Making of Sino-American Relations*, p. 44. **21.** Dolin, *When America First Met China*, pp. 80–84. **22.** Ibid., p. 78; text of sea letter in He, *Macao in the Making of Sino-American Relations*, p. 43; 'New People': p. 45. **23.** Cited by He, *Macao in the Making of Sino-American Relations*, p. 45. **24.** J. Downs, *The Golden Ghetto: the American Commercial Community at Canton and the Shaping of American China Policy, 1784–1844* (Bethlehem, Pa., and Cranbury, NJ, 1997), pp. 26–9. **25.** R. Nield, *The China Coast: Trade and the First Treaty Ports* (Hong Kong, 2010), pp. 48–55, 124–6; Downs, *Golden Ghetto*, pp. 29, 37, 45, 48, 65–6. **26.** W. E. Cheong, *The Hong Merchants of Canton: Chinese Merchants in Sino-Western Trade* (Richmond, Surrey, 1997), pp. 193–213; Downs, *Golden Ghetto*, pp. 73–4. **27.** P. Van Dyke, *The Canton Trade: Life and Enterprise on the China Coast, 1700–1845* (Hong Kong and Macau, 2005), pp. 19–33; Christman, *Adventurous Pursuits*, p. 23; P. Van Dyke, *Merchants of Canton and Macao*, vol. 1: *Politics and Strategies in Eighteenth-Century Chinese Trade* (Hong Kong, 2011), pp. 49–66, and vol. 2: *Success and Failure in Chinese Trade* (Hong Kong, 2016); Downs, *Golden Ghetto*, p. 77. **28.** Downs, *Golden Ghetto*, pp. 81–5, 151–4; Nield, *China Coast*, pp. 48–50; Dolin, *When America First Met China*, pp. 173–6; Christman, *Adventurous Pursuits*, pp. 85–91. **29.** He, *Macao in the Making of Sino-American Relations*, pp. 46–7. **30.** Fichter, *So Great a Proffit*, pp. 31–5. **31.** Kirker, *Adventures to China*, pp. 13–23, 35–47; J. Harrison, *Forgotten Footprints: Lost Stories in the Discovery of Antactica* (Cardigan, 2012). **32.** R. Dana Jr, *Two Years before the Mast: a Personal Narrative of Life at Sea* (New York, 1840, and later editions), ch. 5. **33.** Fichter, *So Great a Proffit*, pp. 49–5; Christman, *Adventurous Pursuits*, p. 35; S. Ridley, *Morning of Fire: John Kendrick's Daring American Odyssey in the Pacific* (New York, 2010), p. 23. **34.** Ridley, *Morning of Fire*, pp. 30–34. **35.** Ibid., p. 33. **36.** Ibid., pp. 61–3. **37.** Ibid., pp. 67–8. **38.** Fichter, *So Great a Proffit*, pp. 51–2. **39.** D. Pethick, *The Nootka Connection: Europe and the Northwest Coast 1790–1795* (Vancouver, 1980), p. 5. **40.** Christman, *Adventurous Pursuits*, pp. 34–5. **41.** Pethick, *Nootka Connection*, pp. 56–61. **42.** Kirker, *Adventures to China*, pp. 35–6. **43.** Ibid., pp. 19–21, 50–64. **44.** Fichter, *So Great a Proffit*, pp. 272–7.

45. Fur and Fire

1. R. Makarova, *Russians on the Pacific 1743–1799* (Kingston, Ont., 1975), ed. and transl. R. Pierce and A. Donnelly from the original edition (Moscow, 1968), pp. 78–84 – an interesting example of Soviet-era historical interpretation. **2.** See Muller's account of Dezhnev's voyage in F. Golder, *Russian Expansion on the Pacific 1641–1850* (2nd edn, New York, 1971), pp. 268–81, followed by Dezhnev's own report, pp. 282–8. **3.** Makarova, *Russians on the Pacific*, pp. 31–2. **4.** Ibid., p. 107; J. Gibson, *Feeding the Russian Fur Trade: Provisionment of the Okhotsk Seaboard and the Kamchatka Peninsula 1639–1856* (Madison, 1969), p. 131. **5.** Golder, *Russian Expansion on the Pacific*, pp. 71–95, 98–9; Makarova, *Russians on the Pacific*, p. 32. **6.** Golder, *Russian Expansion on the Pacific*, p. 33. **7.** Ibid., pp. 40–55. **8.** B. Dmytryshyn, E. Crownhart-Vaughan and T. Vaughan, eds., *To Siberia and Russian America: Three Centuries of Russian Eastward Expansion*, vol. 2: *Russian Penetration of the North Pacific Ocean 1700–1797: a Documentary Record* (Portland, Ore., 1988), doc. 12, pp. 59–63, standardizing spelling in the quotation. **9.** G. Barratt, *Russia in Pacific Waters, 1715–1825: a Survey of the Origins of Russia's Naval Presence in the North and South Pacific* (Vancouver, 1981), pp. 7–9. **10.** Instructions of 23 December 1724, signed on 26 January 1725, in Golder, *Russian Expansion on the Pacific*, p. 134; Dmytryshyn et al., eds., *Russian Penetration of the North Pacific Ocean*, doc. 15, pp. 66–7; also Barratt, *Russia in Pacific Waters*, pp. 13–14. **11.** M. North, *The Baltic: a History* (Cambridge, Mass., 2015), pp. 146, 180. **12.** Barratt, *Russia in Pacific Waters*, pp. 18–19. **13.** Dmytryshyn et al., eds., *Russian Penetration of the North Pacific Ocean*, p. xxxvii, and doc. 22, pp. 96–100. **14.** Ibid., doc. 22, p. 99. **15.** Golder, *Russian Expansion on the Pacific*, pp. 220–26. **16.** Makarova, *Russians on the Pacific*, p. 69: Egor Peloponisov. **17.** Makarova, *Russians on the Pacific*, pp. 45–6. **18.** Ibid., pp. 66, 96–7. **19.** Ibid., pp. 67–9. **20.** Ibid., pp. 71–2. **21.** Dmytryshyn et al., eds., *Russian Penetration of the North Pacific Ocean*, doc. 50, p. 321.   **22.** Ibid., doc. 86, pp. 510–15.   **23.** Shelikov cited by Barratt, *Russia in Pacific Waters*, pp. 100–101; Makarova, *Russians on the Pacific*, p. 4.   **24.** J. Gibson, *Otter Skins, Boston Ships, and China Goods: the Maritime Fur Trade of the Northwest Coast, 1785–1841* (Seattle and Montreal, 1992), p. 16; Barratt, *Russia in Pacific Waters*, p. 110.   **25.** Barratt, *Russia in Pacific Waters*, pp. 102, 110.   **26.** Cited ibid., p. 109.   **27.** Barratt, *Russia in Pacific Waters*, pp. 114–15.   **28.** Ibid., pp. 119–20.   **29.** Ibid., pp. 123–9; Gibson, *Otter Skins*, pp. 14–16.   **30.** Barratt, *Russia in Pacific Waters*, pp. 131–8.   **31.** J. Gascoigne, *Encountering the Pacific in the Age of Enlightenment* (Cambridge, 2014), pp. 133, 408.   **32.** T. Lummis, *Pacific Paradises: the Discovery of Tahiti and Hawaii* (Stroud, 2005).   **33.** Gascoigne, *Encountering the Pacific*, p. 195; N. Thomas, *Islanders: the Pacific in the Age of Empire* (New Haven, 2010).   **34.** Cited in Lummis, *Pacific Paradises*, p. 5; M. K. Matsuda, *Pacific Worlds: a History of Seas, Peoples, and Cultures* (Cambridge, 2012), pp. 133–4; A. Couper, *Sailors and Traders: a Maritime History of the Pacific Peoples* (Honolulu, 2009), pp. 64–5; Gascoigne, *Encountering the Pacific*, pp. 134–7.   **35.** Gascoigne, *Encountering the Pacific*, pp. 134–7.   **36.** Lummis, *Pacific Paradises*, pp. 7–10.   **37.** A. Salmond, *Aphrodite's Island: the European Discovery of Tahiti* (Berkeley and Los Angeles, 2009), pp. 20–21.   **38.** Lummis, *Pacific Paradises*, pp. 13–14; Matsuda, *Pacific Worlds*, pp. 134–6; Gascoigne, *Encountering the Pacific*, pp. 146–8, 203–4; D. Igler, *The Great Ocean: Pacific Worlds from Captain Cook to the Gold Rush* (Oxford and New York, 2013), pp. 49–51.   **39.** Gascoigne, *Encountering the Pacific*, p. 233.   **40.** Ibid., pp. 141, 265.   **41.** Ibid., pp. 110, 137.   **42.** D. Sobel, *Longitude: the True Story of a Lone Genius Who Solved the Greatest Scientific Problem of His Time* (London, 1995), pp. 138–51.   **43.** Matsuda, *Pacific Worlds*, pp. 136–7; Gascoigne, *Encountering the Pacific*, pp. 138–9; Salmond, *Aphrodite's Island*, pp. 36–8, 174–7, 203–35; Thomas, *Islanders*, pp. 17–19 (Tupaia's map: fig. 4, p. 18); Couper, *Sailors and Traders*, pp. 1–2, 67–8.   **44.** Couper, *Sailors and Traders*, pp. 1–2.   **45.** Ibid., pp. 36–7.   **46.** Lummis, *Pacific Paradises*, pp. 77–8.   **47.** Ibid., pp. 64–5.   **48.** Cited in Lummis, *Pacific Paradises*, p. 70; feather cloaks: ibid., p. 78.   **49.** Ibid., pp. 71–6.   **50.** Couper, *Sailors and Traders*, pp. 83–4.   **51.** Ibid., pp. 83–5, 88.   **52.** S. Reynolds, *The Voyage of the New Hazard to the Northwest Coast, Hawaii and China, 1810–1813*, ed. F. Howay (2nd edn, Fairfield, Wash., 1970); Couper, *Sailors and Traders*, pp. 86–8.   **53.** Lummis, *Pacific Paradises*, pp. 80–86, 95–7.   **54.** Ibid., pp. 87–91.   **55.** Cited by Couper, *Sailors and Traders*, p. 88.   **56.** Matsuda, *Pacific Worlds*, p. 189.   **57.** Couper, *Sailors and Traders*, p. 83.   **58.** Lummis, *Pacific Paradises*, pp. 94–101.

46. From the Lion's Gate to the Fragrant Harbour

1. M. R. Frost and Yu-Mei Balasingamchow, *Singapore: a Biography* (Singapore and Hong Kong, 2009), pp. 34–5; J. C. Perry, *Singapore: Unlikely Power* (New York, 2017), pp. 29, 34.   **2.** Perry, *Singapore*, p. 5.   **3.** K. C. Guan, D. Heng and T. T. Yong, *Singapore: a 700-Year History* (Singapore, 2009), pp. 53–82; Frost and Balasingamchow, *Singapore*, pp. 34–7; Perry, *Singapore*, p. 27.   **4.** Cf., however, the darker view of N. Wright, *William Farquhar and Singapore: Stepping Out from Raffles' Shadow* (Penang, 2017).   **5.** Cited by V. Glendinning, *Raffles and the Golden Opportunity* (London, 2012), p. 111.   **6.** Glendinning, *Raffles*, pp. 176–9; Perry, *Singapore*, p. 34; Sir Stamford Raffles, *The History of Java* (2 vols., 2nd edn, London, 1830); cf. Wright, *William Farquhar*, pp. 7–13.   **7.** Cited by Guan et al., *Singapore*, p. 85, and in Frost and Balasingamchow, *Singapore*, p. 47.   **8.** Frost and Balasingamchow, *Singapore*, pp. 54–5.   **9.** Perry, *Singapore*, p. 39; also K. C. Guan, 'Singapura as a Central Place in Malay History and Identity', and C. Skott, 'Imagined Centrality: Sir Stamford Raffles and the Birth of Modern Singapore', both in K. Hack, J.-L. Margolin and K. Delaye, eds., *Singapore from Temasek to the 21st Century: Reinventing the Global City* (Singapore, 2010), pp. 133–54, 155–84.   **10.** Frost and Balasingamchow, *Singapore*, pp. 41–6, 73–5; Perry, *Singapore*, pp. 37, 41.   **11.** Perry, *Singapore*, p. 40.   **12.** Frost and Balasingamchow, *Singapore*, pp. 63, 65–9.   **13.** Guan et al., *Singapore*, p. 111; Wright, *William*

Farquhar, p. 119.   **14.** Guan et al., *Singapore*, p. 113; C. Paix, 'Singapore as a Central Place between the West, Asia and China: From the 19th to the 21st Centuries', in Hack et al., *Singapore from Temasek to the 21st Century*, p. 212.   **15.** Peranakans are also known as 'Straits Chinese' – see the exhibits in the Peranakan Museum, Singapore; Frost and Balasingamchow, *Singapore*, pp. 93–8.   **16.** Perry, *Singapore*, pp. 13–14, 35   **17.** Guan et al., *Singapore*, pp. 108–9; Wright, *William Farquhar*, p. 108.   **18.** Guan et al., *Singapore*, pp. 116–20.   **19.** F. Welsh, *A History of Hong Kong* (2nd edn, London, 1997), pp. 52–5; R. Nield, *The China Coast: Trade and the First Treaty Ports* (Hong Kong, 2010), pp. 127–8; T. Hunt, *Ten Cities That Made an Empire* (London, 2014), pp. 233–4.   **20.** Hunt, *Ten The Cities*, pp. 232, 234   **21.** Welsh, *History of Hong Kong*, pp. 43, 79; R. Nield, *China Coast*, p. 129.   **22.** Lin Zexu's letter to Queen Victoria cited by Hunt, *Ten Cities*, p. 235; J. Lovell, *The Opium War: Drugs, Dreams and the Making of China* (London, 2011).   **23.** Quoted by Hunt, *Ten Cities*, p. 238.   **24.** Welsh, *History of Hong Kong*, pp. 106–12 (Palmerston on p. 108); Hunt, *Ten Cities*, p. 240.   **25.** Nield, *China Coast*, pp. 175–8, 181; Hunt, *Ten Cities*, pp. 239, 242, 245, 255–6.   **26.** Nield, *China Coast*, pp. 179–80, 184.

47. Muscateers and Mogadorians

1. M. Pearson, *Port Cities and Intruders: the Swahili Coast, India, and Portugal in the Early Modern Era* (Baltimore, 1998), p. 159; N. Bennett, *A History of the Arab State of Zanzibar* (London, 1978), pp. 11–12.   **2.** Pearson, *Port Cities and Intruders*, p. 162.   **3.** Cited by P. Risso, *Oman and Muscat: an Early Modern History* (London, 1986), p. 192; M. R. Bhacker, *Trade and Empire in Muscat and Zanzibar: Roots of British Domination* (London, 1992), pp. 12, 67–74.   **4.** Risso, *Oman and Muscat*, pp. 78–85; Bennett, *History of the Arab State*, pp. 14–15.   **5.** Risso, *Oman and Muscat*, pp. 101, 106, 170–72; Bhacker, *Trade and Empire*, p. 26.   **6.** T. Hunt, *Ten Cities That Made an Empire* (London, 2014), p. 202.   **7.** Risso, *Oman and Muscat*, pp. 198–9.   **8.** Cited by Bennett, *History of the Arab State*, p. 14.   **9.** Bennett, *History of the Arab State*, pp. 19–21.   **10.** Cited from a nineteenth-century French source by W. Phillips, *Oman: a Short History* (London, 1967), p. 127.   **11.** A. al-Maamiry, *Omani Sultans in Zanzibar (1832–1964)* (New Delhi, 1988), pp. 3–4.   **12.** J. Jones and N. Ridout, *A History of Modern Oman* (Cambridge, 2015), pp. 53–4; Bennett, *History of the Arab State*, pp. 57–8; Bhacker, *Trade and Empire*, pp. 71, 92–3; UNESCO, *World's Heritage* (4th edn, Paris and Glasgow, 2015), p. 612.   **13.** A. Sheriff, *Slaves, Spices and Ivory in Zanzibar: Integration of an East African Commercial Empire into the World Economy, 1770–1873* (London, Nairobi and Dar-es-Salaam, 1987), pp. 49, 62–5; al-Maamiry, *Omani Sultans in Zanzibar*, p. 6.   **14.** Jones and Ridout, *History of Modern Oman*, pp. 61–2; Sheriff, *Slaves, Spices and Ivory*, pp. 77, 91–9; al-Maamiry, *Omani Sultans in Zanzibar*, p. 5; Bennett, *History of the Arab State*, p. 43; Bhacker, *Trade and Empire*, pp. 77–8 (graph and table showing revenues from Muscat and Zanzibar), also pp. 108–10, 121.   **15.** D. Cesarani and G. Romain, eds., *Jews and Port Cities 1590–1990: Commerce, Community and Cosmopolitanism* (London, 2006).   **16.** D. Schroeter, *Merchants of Essaouira: Urban Society and Imperialism in Southwestern Morocco, 1844–1886* (Cambridge, 1988), pp. 1, 219–21.   **17.** Ibid., pp. 7–12, and map 3, pp. 16–17.   **18.** D. Schroeter, *The Sultan's Jew: Morocco and the Sephardi World* (Stanford, 2002), pp. 44–5.   **19.** P. Fenton and D. Littman, *Exile in the Maghreb: Jews under Islam, Sources and Documents, 997–1912* (Madison, 2016).   **20.** Schroeter, *Merchants of Essaouira*, pp. 34–42.   **21.** Quoted from Schroeter, *Sultan's Jew*, p. 86; see also J. A. O. C. Brown, *Crossing the Strait: Morocco, Gibraltar and Great Britain in the 18th and 19th Centuries* (Leiden, 2012), p. 45.   **22.** M. Abitbol, *Les Commerçants du roi – Tujjār al-Sulṭān: une élite économique judéo-marocaine au XIXe siècle* (Paris, 1998), letters 5–6, pp. 30–31, and letter 11, p. 37; M. Abitbol, *Témoins et acteurs: les Corcos et l'histoire du Maroc contemporain – Mishpahat Qorqos: ve-ha-Historiya shel Maroqo bizemanenu* (Jerusalem, 1977); Schroeter, *Merchants of Essaouira*, pp. 21, 23.   **23.** D. Corcos, 'Les Juifs du Maroc et leurs mellahs', in D. Corcos, *Studies in the History of the Jews of*

Morocco (Jerusalem, 1976), pp. 64–130; cf. S. Deshen, *The Mellah Society: Jewish Community Life in Sherifian Morocco* (Chicago, 1989). **24.** Schroeter, *Sultan's Jew*, p. 110, fig. 14. **25.** For example, Schroeter, *Merchants of Essaouira*, p. 49. **26.** Ibid., pp. 40–41; Schroeter, *Sultan's Jew*, p. 19. **27.** Schroeter, *Merchants of Essaouira*, pp. 19, 79, 95–120. **28.** Brown, *Crossing the Strait*, pp. 125–7. **29.** Schroeter, *Merchants of Essaouira*, pp. 125–8. **30.** Ibid., p. 50. **31.** Brown, *Crossing the Strait*, p. 129. **32.** Ibid., pp. 94–120, 127, 129–30. **33.** Schroeter, *Sultan's Jew*, pp. 46, 78; Brown, *Crossing the Strait*, pp. 17, 49–51. **34.** Schroeter, *Sultan's Jew*, pp. 44–5. **35.** F. Sequeira Dias, 'Os empresários micaelenses no séclo XIX: o exemplo de sucesso de Elias Bensaúde (1807–1868)', *Análise Social*, vol. 31 (1996), pp. 437–64, drawing on her doctoral thesis, *Uma estratégia de sucesso numa economia periférica: a Casa Bensaúde e os Açores, 1800–1873* (Ponta Delgada, 1993). **36.** Figures from T. B. Duncan, *Atlantic Islands: Madeira, the Azores and the Cape Verdes in Seventeenth-Century Commerce and Navigation* (Chicago, 1972), pp. 1–4, 22, 162–3; A. Prata, 'Porto Grande of S. Vicente: the Coal Business on an Atlantic Island', in M. Suárez Bosa, ed., *Atlantic Ports and the First Globalisation c.1850–1930* (Basingstoke, 2014), pp. 49–69. **37.** M. Serels, *The Jews of Cape Verde: a Brief History* (Brooklyn, 1997), pp. 21–4, 38. **38.** A. Jaffer, *Lascars and Indian Ocean Seafaring, 1780–1860: Shipboard Life, Unrest and Mutiny* (Martlesham, 2015).

PART FIVE

THE OCEANS CONTAINED

48. Continents Divided, Oceans Conjoined

1. G. Williams, ed., *The Quest for the Northwest Passage* (London, 2007), pp. 433–58. **2.** I. Sanderson, *A History of Whaling* (New York, 1993), pp. 213–17; A. Dudden, 'The Sea of Japan/Korea's East Sea', in D. Armitage, A. Bashford and S. Sivasundaram, eds., *Oceanic Histories* (Cambridge, 2018), pp. 197–8. **3.** H. Melville, *Moby-Dick; or, The Whale* (New York, 1851), ch. 111. **4.** T. Toyoda, *History of pre-Meiji Commerce in Japan* (Tokyo, 1969), pp. 92–4. **5.** W. Beasley, *The Japanese Experience: a Short History of Japan* (London, 1999), pp. 191–3; B. Walker, *A Concise History of Japan* (Cambridge, 2015), pp. 145–6; W. J. Macpherson, *The Economic Development of Japan 1868–1941* (2nd edn, Cambridge, 1995), p. 70, and also pp. 23–4; Toyoda, *History of pre-Meiji Commerce*, pp. 95–100. **6.** D. McCullough, *The Path between the Seas: the Creation of the Panama Canal 1870–1914* (New York, 1977), p. 112. **7.** What follows is based on my *Great Sea*, pp. 545–55, where the creation of the Suez Canal is discussed at greater length. **8.** M. Parker, *Hell's Gorge: the Battle to Build the Panama Canal* (2nd edn of *Panama Fever* (London, 2007), London, 2008), p. 15. **9.** Z. Karabell, *Parting the Desert: the Creation of the Suez Canal* (London, 2003), pp. 28–37; J. Marlowe, *The Making of the Suez Canal* (London, 1964), pp. 44–5. **10.** Karabell, *Parting the Desert*, pp. 131–2; Lord Kinross, *Between Two Seas: the Creation of the Suez Canal* (London, 1968), pp. 98–9. **11.** Karabell, *Parting the Desert*, p. 260; Kinross, *Between Two Seas*, p. 287. **12.** Marlowe, *Making of the Suez Canal*, pp. 255–75; Karabell, *Parting the Desert*, pp. 262–5; R. Blake, *Disraeli* (London, 1966), pp. 581–70. **13.** F. Hyde, *Blue Funnel: a History of Alfred Holt and Company of Liverpool from 1865 to 1914* (Liverpool, 1956), pp. 20, 24. **14.** G. Lo Giudice, *L'Austria, Trieste ed il Canale di Suez* (Catania, 1981), pp. 180–81; Marlowe, *Making of the Suez Canal*, p. 260. **15.** McCullough, *Path between the Seas*, p. 34. **16.** *Index to the Reports of the Chief of Engineers, U.S. Army (including the Reports of the Isthmian Canal Commission, 1899–1914), 1866–1912*, vol. 2: *Fortifications, Bridges, Panama Canal, etc., February 16 1914* (63rd Congress, 2nd Session, House of Representatives, Document no. 740, Washington DC, 1916), p. 2551; Parker, *Hell's Gorge*, pp. 11–12. **17.** McCullough, *Path between the Seas*, pp. 28–30. **18.** Parker, *Hell's Gorge*, pp. 18–19. **19.** McCullough, *Path between the Seas*, p. 33; Parker, *Hell's Gorge*, pp. 20–24. **20.** Quotation from Parker, *Hell's Gorge*, p. 32, and more generally see pp. 27–33.

21. Parker, *Hell's Gorge*, pp. 38–9.   22. McCullough, *Path between the Seas*, pp. 61–7; Parker, *Hell's Gorge*, p. 46.   23. Parker, *Hell's Gorge*, pp. 55–6.   24. Ibid., pp. 107, 109–10.   25. McCullough, *Path between the Seas*, pp. 160–61; Parker, *Hell's Gorge*, pp. 119–23.   26. J. Greene, *The Canal Builders: Making America's Empire at the Panama Canal* (New York, 2009), p. 42.   27. McCullough, *Path between the Seas*, pp. 205–12; Parker, *Hell's Gorge*, pp. 160–62.   28. Parker, *Hell's Gorge*, p. 159.   29. McCullough, *Path between the Seas*, pp. 240–41.   30. Ibid., p. 254.   31. Ibid., p. 255, whence also the quotation from Roosevelt.   32. J. Davis, *The Gulf: the Making of an American Sea* (New York, 2017).   33. A. T. Mahan, *The Influence of Sea-Power upon History, 1660–1783* (Boston, 1890), p. 33.   34. McCullough, *Path between the Seas*, pp. 253, 254–5, 259, 262–3, 268–9; Parker, *Hell's Gorge*, p. 173.   35. Greene, *Canal Builders*, pp. 10, 19–20.   36. Greene, *Canal Builders*, pp. 46–7, 111–16.   37. McCullough, *Path between the Seas*, pp. 409–21; Parker, *Hell's Gorge*, pp. 238–48.   38. McCullough, *Path between the Seas*, pp. 492–50, 428–9 (illustrations); Parker, *Hell's Gorge*, pp. 211, 306–9; Greene, *Canal Builders*, pp. 15–18.   39. McCullough, *Path between the Seas*, p. 610.   40. Greene, *Canal Builders*, pp. 51, 95–107, 123–58.   41. McCullough, *Path between the Seas*, pp. 611–12.   42. Parker, *Hell's Gorge*, pp. 368–70.

49. Steaming to Asia, Paddling to America

1. N. Jones, *The Plimsoll Sensation: the Great Campaign to Save Lives at Sea* (London, 2006), p. 10.   2. Jones, *Plimsoll Sensation*, pp. 1–3.   3. I take this to be the meaning of the comment by L. Paine, *The Sea and Civilization: a Maritime History of the World* (London, 2014), pp. 531–2.   4. Jones, *Plimsoll Sensation*, 'Appendix: Songs and Poems', p. 314.   5. Quoted in Jones, *Plimsoll Sensation*, 'Appendix: Songs and Poems', p. 315, from 1875.   6. Jones, *Plimsoll Sensation*, pp. 201–10.   7. Cited in Jones, *Plimsoll Sensation*, p. 236.   8. Jones, *Plimsoll Sensation*, pp. 283–5.   9. F. Hyde, *Blue Funnel: A History of Alfred Holt and Company of Liverpool From 1865 to 1914* (Liverpool, 1956), pp. 13–16; F. Hyde, *Liverpool and the Mersey: an Economic History of a Port 1700–1970* (Newton Abbot, 1971), pp. 54–5 – much of the literature on Liverpool shipping was written by this one scholar.   10. Hyde, *Blue Funnel*, p. 19; M. Falkus, *The Blue Funnel Legend: A History of the Ocean Steamship Company* (Basingstoke, 1990), pp. 92–8.   11. G. Milne, 'North of England Shipowners and Their Business Connections', in L. Fischer and E. Lange, eds., *International Merchant Shipping in the Nineteenth and Twentieth Centuries: the Comparative Dimension* (St John's, Nfdl., 2008), pp. 154–7.   12. T. Hunt, *Ten Cities That Made an Empire* (London, 2014), pp. 387–94; Hyde, *Liverpool and the Mersey*, pp. 31–4; F. Hyde, *Cunard and the North Atlantic 1840–1973: a History of Shipping and Financial Management* (London, 1975), pp. 129–30.   13. Milne, 'North of England Shipowners', pp. 153, 159–64.   14. Falkus, *Blue Funnel Legend*, p. 102, fig. 10, steamship *Nestor I*; A. Prata, 'Porto Grande of S. Vicente: the Coal Business on an Atlantic Island', in M. Suárez Bosa, ed., *Atlantic Ports and the First Gobalisation c. 1850–1930* (Basingstoke, 2014)', pp. 49–53.   15. D. Howarth and S. Howarth, *The Story of P&O: the Peninsular and Oriental Steam Navigation Company* (2nd edn, London, 1994), pp. 33–4.   16. Hyde, *Liverpool and the Mersey*, pp. 51–2; Howarth and Howarth, *Story of P&O*, pp. 15, 94.   17. Falkus, *Blue Funnel Legend*, pp. 37–9.   18. F. Hyde, *Far Eastern Trade 1860–1914* (London, 1973), p. 22; Hyde, *Blue Funnel*, pp. 37–9; also Howarth and Howarth, *Story of P&O*, pp. 94–5.   19. Falkus, *Blue Funnel Legend*, p. 4.   20. Hyde, *Blue Funnel*, pp. 24–5, 32–3, 182 (table of ships in fleet); Hyde, *Liverpool and the Mersey*, pp. 57, 59–61; Hyde, *Far Eastern Trade*, pp. 25–7; Falkus, *Blue Funnel Legend*, pp. 60–66.   21. Falkus, *Blue Funnel Legend*, pp. 105–7, 111; Hyde, *Blue Funnel*, pp. 56–70; Hyde, *Far Eastern Trade*, pp. 23, 28–32.   22. Howarth and Howarth, *Story of P&O*, pp. 30–35, 101.   23. Ibid., pp. 60–62.   24. Ibid., p. 80; F. Welsh, *A History of Hong Kong* (2nd edn, London, 1997), p. 162.   25. Ibid., pp. 54–5.   26. Hyde, *Far Eastern Trade*, pp. 17–19.   27. Hyde, *Cunard and the North Atlantic*, pp. 75, 84–6.   28. Ibid., pp. 15–16, 28–9, 77, 94–101.   29. R. Gillespie, *Early Belfast: the Origins and Growth of an Ulster Town to*

1750 (Belfast, 2007); S. Royle, *Portrait of an Industrial City: Changing Belfast 1750–1914* (Belfast, 2011); J. P. Lynch, *An Unlikely Success Story: the Belfast Shipping Industry 1880–1935* (Belfast, 2001), pp. 2–9, 67.   **30.** M. Moss and J. Hume, *Shipbuilders to the World: 125 Years of Harland and Wolff, Belfast, 1861–1986* (Belfast, 1986), pp. 12–14, 144, 146; Lynch, *Unlikely Success Story*, p. 61.   **31.** S. Tenold, 'Norwegian Shipping in the Twentieth Century', in Fischer and Lange, eds., *International Merchant Shipping*, p. 57.   **32.** Hyde, *Cunard and the North Atlantic*, pp. 61–2.   **33.** C. Brautaset and S. Tenold, 'Lost in Calculation? Norwegian Merchant Shipping in Asia, 1870–1914', in M. Fusaro and A. Polónia, eds., *Maritime History as Global History* (St John's, Nfdl., 2010), pp. 206, 217, 219–20.   **34.** Tenold, 'Norwegian Shipping', pp. 59–60.   **35.** Brautaset and Tenold, 'Lost in Calculation?', p. 207.   **36.** A. Hardy, *Typhoon Wallem: a Personalised Chronicle of the Wallem Group Limited* (Cambridge, 2003), pp. 1–2, 21–3, 25, 37–8.   **37.** Ibid., p. 45.   **38.** G. Harlaftis, *A History of Greek-Owned Shipping: the Making of an International Tramp Fleet, 1830 to the Present Day* (London, 1996), p. xx; G. Harlaftis, 'The Greek Shipping Sector, c.1850–2000', in Fischer and Lange, eds., *International Merchant Shipping*, p. 79.   **39.** Harlaftis, *History of Greek-Owned Shipping*, pp. 52–4, 108–9, table 4; Harlaftis, 'The Greek Shipping Sector', p. 80, and table 2, p. 81.   **40.** Harlaftis, 'The Greek Shipping Sector', pp. 82–4.   **41.** Åland Maritime Museum, *The Last Windjammers: Grain Races round Cape Horn* (Mariehamn, 1998), pp. 10–11, 15; E. Newby, *The Last Grain Race* (3rd edn, London, 2014), p. xx.   **42.** Åland Maritime Museum, *Last Windjammers*, p. 14; Newby, *Last Grain Race*, pp. xx–xxi; H. Thesleff, *Farewell Windjammer: an Account of the Last Circumnavigation of the Globe by a Sailing Ship and the Last Grain Race from Australia to England* (London, 1951), pp. 2–3.   **43.** Thesleff, *Farewell Windjammer*, pp. 3, 134; Newby, *Last Grain Race*, pp. 201–3; Åland Maritime Museum, *Last Windjammers*, pp. 22–6, 30.   **44.** Newby, *Last Grain Race*; Thesleff, *Farewell Windjammer*, pp. 4–5.   **45.** Thesleff, *Farewell Windjammer*, p. 9; Åland Maritime Museum, *Last Windjammers*, pp. 22, 41–2.

50. War and Peace, and More War

1. K. O'Rourke, 'The Economist and Global History', in J. Belich, J. Darwin, M. Frenz and C. Wickham, *The Prospect of Global History* (Oxford, 2016), p. 47, especially n. 11.   **2.** Cited by S. Conrad, *What is Global History?* (Princeton, 2016), pp. 93–4.   **3.** O'Rourke, 'Economist and Global History', pp. 48–9, 55 (and n. 30); also K. O'Rourke and J. Williamson, *Globalization and History: the Evolution of a Nineteenth-Century Atlantic Economy* (Cambridge, Mass., 1999).   **4.** M. Miller, *Europe and the Maritime World: a Twentieth-Century History* (Cambridge, 2012), pp. 25–9, 35–49, and map 2, p. 42.   **5.** Ibid., pp. 56–9.   **6.** Ibid., pp. 39–40, 107 fig. 2 (*Chilehaus*).   **7.** Ibid., p. 45.   **8.** Ibid., pp. 49–55, 75–9.   **9.** Cited in J. Steinberg, *Yesterday's Deterrent: Tirpitz and the Birth of the German Battle Fleet* (London, 1965), p. 208.   **10.** Miller, *Europe and the Maritime World*, pp. 213, 217–18; M. Falkus, *The Blue Funnel Legend: A History of the Ocean Steamship Company* (Basingstoke, 1990), pp. 157–61; F. Hyde, *Cunard and the North Atlantic 1840–1973: A History of Shipping and Financial Management* (London, 1975), p. 169; D. Howarth and S. Howarth, *The Story of P&O: The Peninsular and Oriental Steam Navigation Company* (2nd edn, London, 1994), p. 117.   **11.** Miller, *Europe and the Maritime World*, pp. 217, 231; Falkus, *Blue Funnel Legend*, p. 173; Howarth, *Story of P&O*, p. 124; F. Hyde, *Liverpool and the Mersey: an Economic History of a Port 1700–1970* (Newton Abbott, 1971), p. 147.   **12.** Miller, *Europe and the Maritime World*, pp. 235–7.   **13.** O'Rourke, 'Economist and Global History', p. 55; Falkus, *Blue Funnel Legend*, p. 203.   **14.** Howarth and Howarth, *Story of P&O*, p. 125; W. J. Macpherson, *The Economic Development of Japan 1868–1941* (2nd edn, Cambridge, 1995), p. 31.   **15.** Miller, *Europe and the Maritime World*, pp. 247, 269.   **16.** Cited in Howarth, *Story of P&O*, p. 129; Falkus, *Blue Funnel Legend*, p. 229; Hyde, *Liverpool and the Mersey*, p. 149.   **17.** Falkus, *Blue Funnel Legend*, pp. 175, 190–92; Hyde, *Cunard and the North Atlantic*, p. 181.   **18.** Hyde, *Cunard and the North Atlantic*, pp. 171–3, 180; Miller, *Europe and the Maritime World*, pp. 254–5.   **19.** Hyde, *Cunard and the North Atlantic*, pp. 173–6, 180, 227–34.   **20.** Ibid., pp. 191–218; loan figures: pp. 214–15; Miller, *Europe and the Maritime World*, pp. 253–4.   21. Miller, *Europe and the Maritime World*, p. 248.   22. Quoted by Hyde, *Cunard and the North Atlantic*, p. 255; also pp. 264–7, 280.   23. Hyde, *Liverpool and the Mersey*, pp. 160–77.   24. Falkus, *Blue Funnel Legend*, pp. 240, 245.   25. Miller, *Europe and the Maritime World*, pp. 277–8; Falkus, *Blue Funnel Legend*, p. 236.   26. Miller, *Europe and the Maritime World*, pp. 282–3.   27. S. Roskill, *A Merchant Fleet in War: Alfred Holt & Co., 1939–1945* (London, 1962), pp. 19, 23–8.   28. Ibid., p. 47.   29. Hyde, *Cunard and the North Atlantic*, pp. 260–67.   30. Howarth, *Story of P&O*, pp. 138–40, 145–6.   31. A. Hardy, *Typhoon Wallem a Personalised Chronicle of the Wallem Group Limited* (Cambridge, 2003), pp. 64–6; F. Welsh, *A History of Hong Kong* (2nd den, London, 1977), pp. 412–23.   32. Roskill, *Merchant Fleet in War*, map of ships sunk in the war, on front endpaper; 87 ships: p. 11; *Pyrrhus*: pp. 29–33; Falkus, *Blue Funnel Legend*, p. 237 gives 77.   33. Falkus, *Blue Funnel Legend*, pp. 237–40, 245.   34. Hyde, *Liverpool and the Mersey*, pp. 178–80; Miller, *Europe and the Maritime World*, pp. 281, 284, 304–6; Falkus, *Blue Funnel Legend*, pp. 247–8 (Churchill).

51. The Oceans in a Box

1. D. Howarth and S. Howarth, *The Story of P&O: the Peninsular and Oriental Steam Navigation Company* (2nd edn, London, 1994), p. 151.   2. M. Miller, *Europe and the Maritime World: a Twentieth-Century History* (Cambridge, 2012), pp. 290–93.   3. F. Welsh, *A History of Hong Kong* (2nd edn, London, 1997), pp. 442, 444, 451–2.   4. Miller, *Europe and the Maritime World*, pp. 299–300.   5. J. C. Perry, *Singapore: Unlikely Power* (New York, 2017), pp. 165–8, 171.   6. M. R. Frost and Yu-Mei Balasingamchow, *Singapore: a Biography* (Singapore and Hong Kong, 2009), pp. 322–35; Perry, *Singapore*, pp. 148–9, 163; Miller, *Europe and the Maritime World*, pp. 67–8.   7. F. Hyde, *Liverpool and the Mersey: an Economic History of a Port 1700–1970* (Newton Abbot, 1971), p. 191; Howarth and Howarth, *Story of P&O*, p. 173; on shipyard workers: A. Reid, *The Tide of Democracy: Shipyard Workers and Social Relations in Britain, 1870–1950* (Manchester, 2010).   8. Howarth and Howarth, *Story of P&O*, pp. 165–6, 174.   9. Hyde, *Liverpool and the Mersey*, p. 187.   10. Howarth and Howarth, *Story of P&O*, pp. 151, 156–7.   11. Miller, *Europe and the Maritime World*, p. 306; Hyde, *Liverpool and the Mersey*, pp. 192–3, 197.   12. Miller, *Europe and the Maritime World*, pp. 311–13; p. 312: map of Rotterdam port.   13. K. Hudson and J. Pettifer, *Diamonds in the Sky: a Social History of Air Travel* (London, 1979), pp. 58, 61.   14. Ibid., p. 67.   15. Ibid., pp. 69, 79, 81, 84–7.   16. Howarth and Howarth, *Story of P&O*, p. 163.   17. F. Hyde, *Cunard and the North Atlantic 1840–1973: a History of Shipping and Financial Management* (London, 1975), pp. 296–302.   18. Ibid., pp. 309, 313.   19. Howarth and Howarth, *Story of P&O*, pp. 160–61.   20. B. Dickinson and A. Vladimir, *$elling the Sea: an Inside Look at the Cruise Industry* (2nd edn, Hoboken, 2008), pp. 21–2.   21. M. Levinson, *The Box: How the Shipping Container Made the World Smaller and the World Economy Bigger* (2nd edn, Princeton, 2008), pp. 29–30, 34.   22. Ibid., pp. xi, 36–49, 53; B. Cudahy, *Box Boats: How Container Ships Changed the World* (New York, 2006), pp. 20–25.   23. Levinson, *The Box*, pp. xi, 53; quotation cited by Cudahy, *Box Boats*, p. 35.   24. Ibid., pp. 50–53, 57; Cudahy, *Box Boats*, pp. 26–32.   25. Levinson, *The Box*, p. xiii.   26. Ibid., pp. 55–7; Cudahy, *Box Boats*, pp. 35–6, 40–41.   27. Levinson, *The Box*, pp. 58, 101–26.   28. Cudahy, *Box Boats*, pp. 69, 75, 84–9 (the observant will note that the ship loaded whisky, not whiskey as Cudahy opines), 100–106.   29. Levinson, *The Box*, pp. 171–88, 196, 201, 204–5; Cudahy, *Box Boats*, pp. 106–8, 153.

Conclusion

1. A. Antonello, 'The Southern Ocean', in D. Armitage, A. Bashford and S. Sivasundaram, eds., *Oceanic Histories* (Cambridge, 2018), pp. 301–8.

Index

Entries starting with the Old Norse letter thorn (Þ) are filed after Z.